Corporate Finance

The McGraw-Hill/Irwin Series in Finance, Insurance, and Real Estate

Stephen A. Ross
Franco Modigliani Professor of Finance and Economics
Sloan School of Management
Massachusetts Institute of Technology
Consulting Editor

Financial Management

Adair
Excel Applications for Corporate Finance
First Edition

Benninga and Sarig
Corporate Finance: A Valuation Approach

Block and Hirt
Foundations of Financial Management
Eleventh Edition

Brealey and Myers
Principles of Corporate Finance
Seventh Edition

Brealey, Myers, and Marcus
Fundamentals of Corporate Finance
Fourth Edition

Brooks
FinGame Online 4.0

Bruner
Case Studies in Finance: Managing for Corporate Value Creation
Fourth Edition

Chew
The New Corporate Finance: Where Theory Meets Practice
Third Edition

Chew and Gillan
Corporate Governance at the Crossroads: A Book of Readings
First Edition

DeMello
Cases in Finance

Grinblatt and Titman
Financial Markets and Corporate Strategy
Second Edition

Helfert
Techniques of Financial Analysis: A Guide to Value Creation
Eleventh Edition

Higgins
Analysis for Financial Management
Seventh Edition

Kester, Ruback, and Tufano
Case Problems in Finance
Twelfth Edition

Ross, Westerfield, and Jaffe
Corporate Finance
Seventh Edition

Ross, Westerfield, and Jordan
Essentials of Corporate Finance
Fourth Edition

Ross, Westerfield and Jordan
Fundamentals of Corporate Finance
Sixth Edition

Smith
The Modern Theory of Corporate Finance
Second Edition

White
Financial Analysis with an Electronic Calculator
Fifth Edition

Investments

Bodie, Kane, and Marcus
Essentials of Investments
Fifth Edition

Bodie, Kane, and Marcus
Investments
Sixth Edition

Cohen, Zinbarg, and Zeikel
Investment Analysis and Portfolio Management
Fifth Edition

Corrado and Jordan
Fundamentals of Investments: Valuation and Management
Third Edition

Farrell
Portfolio Management: Theory and Applications
Second Edition

Hirt and Block
Fundamentals of Investment Management
Seventh Edition

Financial Institutions and Markets

Cornett and Saunders
Fundamentals of Financial Institutions Management

Rose and Hudgins
Commercial Bank Management
Sixth Edition

Rose
Money and Capital Markets: Financial Institutions and Instruments in a Global Marketplace
Eighth Edition

Santomero and Babbel
Financial Markets, Instruments, and Institutions
Second Edition

Saunders and Cornett
Financial Institutions Management: A Risk Management Approach
Fourth Edition

Saunders and Cornett
Financial Markets and Institutions: A Modern Perspective
Second Edition

International Finance

Beim and Calomiris
Emerging Financial Markets

Eun and Resnick
International Financial Management
Third Edition

Levich
International Financial Markets: Prices and Policies
Second Edition

Real Estate

Brueggeman and Fisher
Real Estate Finance and Investments
Twelfth Edition

Corgel, Ling, and Smith
Real Estate Perspectives: An Introduction to Real Estate
Fourth Edition

Ling and Archer
Real Estate Principles: A Value Approach
First Edition

Financial Planning and Insurance

Allen, Melone, Rosenbloom and Mahoney
Pension Planning: Pension, Profit-Sharing, and Other Deferred Compensation Plans
Ninth Edition

Crawford
Life and Health Insurance Law
Eighth Edition (LOMA)

Harrington and Niehaus
Risk Management and Insurance
Second Edition

Hirsch
Casualty Claim Practice
Sixth Edition

Kapoor, Dlabay, and Hughes
Personal Finance
Seventh Edition

Williams, Smith, and Young
Risk Management and Insurance
Eighth Edition

Seventh Edition

Corporate Finance

Stephen A. Ross

Sloan School of Management
Massachusetts Institute of Technology

Randolph W. Westerfield

Marshall School of Business
University of Southern California

Jeffrey Jaffe

Wharton School of Business
University of Pennsylvania

Boston Burr Ridge, IL Dubuque, IA Madison, WI New York
San Francisco St. Louis Bangkok Bogotá Caracas Kuala Lumpur
Lisbon London Madrid Mexico City Milan Montreal New Delhi
Santiago Seoul Singapore Sydney Taipei Toronto

The **McGraw·Hill** Companies

CORPORATE FINANCE
International Edition 2005

Published by McGraw-Hill/Irwin, a business unit of The McGraw-Hill Companies, Inc., 1221 Avenue of the Americas, New York, NY 10020.

10 09 08 07 06 05 04 03 02 01
20 09 08 07 06 05 04
CTF   MPM

Library of Congress Cataloging-in-Publication Data

Ross, Stephen A.
    Corporate finance / Stephen A. Ross, Randolph W. Westerfield, Jeffrey Jaffe.—7th ed.
        p.   cm. –(The McGraw-Hill/Irwin series in finance, insurance, and real estate)
    Includes bibliographical references and index.
    ISBN 007-282920-6
    1.   Corporations—Finance. I. Westerfield, Randolph. II. Jaffe, Jaffrey F., 1946—III. Title.
IV. Series.
    HG4026.R675 2005
    658.15—dc22   2003065973

ISBN 007-123844-1 (Powerweb and S&P Card)

When ordering this title, use ISBN 007-123937-5 (Powerweb Card)

Printed in Singapore

www.mhhe.com

To our family and friends with love and gratitude.

About the Authors

STEPHEN A. ROSS *Sloan School of Management, Massachusetts Institute of Technology* Stephen Ross is presently the Franco Modigliani Professor of Financial Economics at the Sloan School of Management, Massachusetts Institute of Technology. One of the most widely published authors in finance and economics, Professor Ross is recognized for his work in developing the Arbitrage Pricing Theory, as well as for having made substantial contributions to the discipline through his research in signaling, agency theory, option pricing, and the theory of the term structure of interest rates, among other topics. A past president of the American Finance Association, he currently serves as an associate editor of several academic and practitioner journals. He is a trustee of CalTech, and a director of the College Retirement Equity Fund (CREF), Freddie Mac, and Algorithmics, Inc. He is also the cochairman of Roll and Ross Asset Management Corporation.

RANDOLPH W. WESTERFIELD *Marshall School of Business, University of Southern California* Randolph W. Westerfield is Dean of the University of Southern California's Marshall School of Business and holder of the Robert R. Dockson Dean's Chair of Business Administration.

He came to USC from the Wharton School, University of Pennsylvania, where he was the chairman of the finance department and member of the finance faculty for 20 years. He is a member of several public company boards of directors including Health Management Associates, Inc., William Lyon Homes, and the Nicholas Applegate growth fund. His areas of expertise include corporate financial policy, investment management, and stock market price behavior.

JEFFREY F. JAFFE *Wharton School of Business, University of Pennsylvania* Jeffrey F. Jaffe has been a frequent contributor to finance and economic literature in such journals as the *Quarterly Economic Journal, The Journal of Finance, The Journal of Financial and Quantitative Analysis, The Journal of Financial Economics,* and *The Financial Analysts Journal.* His best known work concerns insider trading, where he showed both that corporate insiders earn abnormal profits from their trades and that regulation has little effect on these profits. He has also made contributions concerning initial public offerings, regulation of utilities, the behavior of marketmakers, the fluctuation of gold prices, the theoretical effect of inflation on the interest rate, the empirical effect of inflation on capital asset prices, the relationship between small capitalization stocks and the January effect, and the capital structure decision.

Preface

The teaching and the practicing of corporate finance are more challenging and exciting than ever before. The last decade has seen fundamental changes in financial markets and financial instruments. In the early years of the 21st century, we still see announcements in the financial press about such matters as takeovers, junk bonds, financial restructuring, initial public offerings, bankruptcy, and derivatives. In addition, there is the new recognition of "real" options (Chapters 20 and 21), private equity and venture capital (Chapter 18), and the disappearing dividend (Chapter 17). The world's financial markets are more integrated than ever before. Both the theory and practice of corporate finance have been moving ahead with uncommon speed, and our teaching must keep pace.

These developments place new burdens on the teaching of corporate finance. On one hand, the changing world of finance makes it more difficult to keep materials up to date. On the other hand, the teacher must distinguish the permanent from the temporary and avoid the temptation to follow fads. Our solution to this problem is to emphasize the modern fundamentals of the theory of finance and make the theory come to life with contemporary examples. Increasingly, many of these examples are outside the United States. All too often, the beginning student views corporate finance as a collection of unrelated topics that are unified largely because they are bound together between the covers of one book. As in the previous editions, our aim is to present corporate finance as the working of a small number of integrated and powerful institutions.

The Intended Audience of This Book

This book has been written for the introductory courses in corporate finance at the MBA level, and for the intermediate courses in many undergraduate programs. Some instructors will find our text appropriate for the introductory course at the undergraduate level as well.

We assume that most students either will have taken, or will be concurrently enrolled in, courses in accounting, statistics, and economics. This exposure will help students understand some of the more difficult material. However, the book is self-contained, and a prior knowledge of these areas is not essential. The only mathematics prerequisite is basic algebra.

New to the Seventh Edition

Following are key revisions and updates to this edition:

- Significant reorganization and expanded content of **financial accounting, cash flows, and growth.** Material on corporate financial models and long-term planning is now included with the early chapters to provide earlier, more foundational coverage of **cash flow** (*Chapter 2*) and **sustainable growth** (*Chapter 3*) to bridge accounting and valuation concepts.

- New material on **alternatives to NPV** such as modified Internal Rate of Return (IRR) and better treatment of the profitability index is presented in *Chapter 6*. There is also new material on **capital budgeting "best practices,"** where the authors relate what companies actually do to theoretical models, showcasing the latest research and scholarship.

- **New material on risk analysis and real options** (*Chapter 8*) is reflected in the new chapter title, Risk Analysis, Real Options, and Capital Budgeting. This reinforces the capital budgeting material from the previous chapter. New coverage of real options is now earlier in the book, as is coverage of Monte Carlo simulation techniques.

- *Chapter 13* includes new material on **efficient markets behavioral finance.** This content covers a new way of thinking about financial markets and behavioral users versus efficient markets theory.

- Incorporates the latest theoretical developments in **capital budgeting, capital structure, and dividends** throughout *Chapters 7, 15, 16, and 18*. The recent **tax code** is also included, which covers the new marginal individual tax rates and the lower taxes on dividends and capital gains.

- **New problems** added in most chapters.

For a complete look at the new and updated seventh edition features, please see pages (xviii)–(xxi).

Supplements for Instructors

Instructor's Resource CD-ROM   007287189X

The Instructor's Resource CD-ROM contains the following assets:

Instructor's Manual, *prepared by John Stansfield, University of Missouri—Columbia*

Thoroughly revised and updated, each chapter includes a list of PowerPoint slides, a brief chapter outline and introduction, and an annotated outline. The annotated outline contains references to the PowerPoint slides, additional explanations and examples, and teaching tips.

Test Bank, *prepared by Patricia Ryan, Colorado State University*

This Test Bank, in Microsoft Word, provides a variety of question formats (multiple-choice questions and problems and essay questions) and levels of difficulty to meet any instructor's testing needs.

Computerized Test Bank

Available in Windows format, this software provides you with the Test Bank in electronic form. The keyword search option lets you browse through the question bank for problems containing a specific word or phrase. Password protection is available for saved tests or for the entire database. Questions can be added, modified, or deleted.

PowerPoint Presentation, *prepared by John Stansfield, University of Missouri—Columbia*

This presentation system was developed in conjunction with the Instructor's Manual by the same author, allowing for a complete and integrated teaching package. These slides contain useful outlines, summaries, and exhibits from the text. If you have PowerPoint installed on your PC, you have the ability to edit, print, or rearrange the complete transparency presentation to meet your specific needs.

Solutions Manual   007287192X

Overseen by the authors, contains many new worked-out solutions for all of the problems in the end-of-chapter material. It has also been thoroughly revised and reviewed for accuracy by multiple sources. The Solutions Manual is also available to be purchased for your students.

Videos   0072871938

McGraw-Hill/Irwin's finance videos are 10-minute case studies on topics such as Financial Markets, Careers, Rightsizing, Capital Budgeting, EVA (Economic Value Added), Mergers, and Foreign Exchange. Questions to accompany these videos can be found on the book's Online Learning Center (OLC) at www.mhhe.com/rwj.

Supplements for Students

New!—Student CD-ROM

The Student CD-ROM is packaged free with each new book purchased and contains the following assets:

Self-Study Questions, *prepared by Robert Hanson, Eastern Michigan University*

10 questions per chapter to quiz students on core concepts of each chapter.

Links to:

- The book's Online Learning Center (OLC, please see details under Online Resources)
- Excel Templates
- Corporate Finance Online
- Finance Around the World
- Select videoclips on key corporate finance topics

Student Problem Manual, *prepared by Robert Hanson, Eastern Michigan University*
0072871911

The Student Problem Manual is a direct companion to the text. It is uniquely designed to involve the student in the learning process. Each chapter contains a Mission Statement, and average of 20 fill-in-the-blank Concept Test questions and answers, and an average of 15 problems and worked-out solutions. This product can be purchased separately, or can be packaged with this text.

Online Resources

Online Learning Center (OLC) with PowerWeb
www.mhhe.com/rwj

This website follows the text chapter-by-chapter with digital supplementary content specific to this book. The Instructor's Manual and PowerPoint Presentation are available to the Instructor in the password-protected Instructor's Center. As students read the book, they can go online to the Student Center to take self-grading quizzes, review material, and work through interactive exercises. Included with new copies of this book is an insert card that includes a password for access for PowerWeb for Ethics in Finance. Students will have quicker access to real-world news and essays that pertain to the discipline they are studying. OLCs can be delivered in multiple ways—through the textbook website, through PageOut, or within a course management system (i.e., Blackboard, WebCT, TopClass and eCollege).

Corporate Finance Online

As part of this OLC, instructors and students will also have access to Corporate Finance Online, found on the opening page of the textbook website. Corporate Finance Online is an exclusive Web tool from McGraw-Hill/Irwin. This site provides over 54 exercises for 27 key corporate finance topics, allowing students to complete challenging exercises and discussion questions that draw on recent articles, company reports, government data, and other Web-based resources. For Instructors, there are also password protected teaching notes to assist with classroom integration of the material.

Standard & Poor's Educational Version of Market Insight

McGraw-Hill/Irwin and the Institutional Market Services division of Standard & Poor's is pleased to announce an exclusive partnership that offers instructors and students FREE access to the educational version of Standard & Poor's Market Insight with each new textbook. The Educational Version of Market Insight is a rich online resource that provides six years of fundamental financial data for over 650 companies in the database. S&P-specific problems can be found at the end of almost all chapters in this text. For more details, please see the bound-in card inside the front cover of this text, or visit www.mhhe.com/edumarketinsight.

Acknowledgments

The plan for developing this edition began with a number of our colleagues who had an interest in the book and regularly teach the MBA introductory course. We integrated their comments and recommendations throughout the Seventh Edition. Contributors to this edition include:

Mike Barry
Boston College

Mark Copper
Wayne State University

Raymond Cox
Central Michigan University

Demissew Ejara
University of Massachusetts—Boston

Raymond Jackson
University of Massachusetts—Dartmouth

Naval Modani
University of Central Florida

Gary Patterson
University of South Florida

Stuart Rosenstein
University of Colorado—Denver

Over the years, many others have contributed their time and expertise to the development and writing of this text. We extend our thanks once again for their assistance and countless insights:

R. Aggarwal
John Carroll University

Christopher Anderson
University of Missouri–Columbia

James J. Angel
Georgetown University

Nasser Arshadi
University of Missouri–St. Louis

Kevin Bahr
University of Wisconsin–Milwaukee

Robert Balik
Western Michigan University

John W. Ballantine
Babson College

Thomas Bankston
Angelo State University

Brad Barber
University of California–Davis

Michael Barry
Boston College

Swati Bhatt
Rutgers University

Roger Bolton
Williams College

Gordon Bonner
University of Delaware

Oswald Bowlin
Texas Technical University

Ronald Braswell
Florida State University

William O. Brown
Claremont McKenna College

Kirt Butler
Michigan State University

Bill Callahan
Southern Methodist University

Steven Carvell
Cornell University

Indudeep S. Chhachhi
Western Kentucky University

Andreas Christofi
Monmouth University

Jeffrey L. Coles
Arizona State University

James Cotter
University of Iowa

Jay Coughenour
University of Massachusetts–Boston

Arnold Cowan
Iowa State University

Raymond Cox
Central Michigan University

John Crockett
George Mason University

Mark Cross
Louisiana Technical University

Ron Crowe
Jacksonville University

William Damon
Vanderbilt University

Sudip Datta
Bentley College

Anand Desai
University of Florida

Miranda Lam Detzler
University of Massachusetts–Boston

David Distad
University of California–Berkeley

Dennis Draper
University of Southern California

Jean-Francois Dreyfus
New York University

Gene Drzycimski
University of Wisconsin–Oshkosh

Robert Duvic
The University of Texas at Austin

Robert Eldridge
Fairfield University

Gary Emery
University of Oklahoma

Theodore Eytan
City University of New York–Baruch College

Don Fehrs
University of Notre Dame

Steven Ferraro
Pepperdine University

Andrew Fields
University of Delaware

Paige Fields
Texas A&M

Adlai Fisher
New York University

Michael Fishman
Northwestern University

Yee-Tien Fu
Stanford University

Bruno Gerard
University of Southern California

Frank Ghannadian
Mercer University–Atlanta

Michael Goldstein
University of Colorado

Indra Guertler
Babson College

James Haltiner
College of William and Mary

Delvin Hawley
University of Mississippi

Hal Heaton
Brigham Young University

John A. Helmuth
University of Michigan–Dearborn

John Helmuth
Rochester Institute of Technology

Michael Hemler
University of Notre Dame

Stephen Heston
Washington University

Andrea Heuson
University of Miami

Edith Hotchkiss
Boston College

Charles Hu
Claremont McKenna College

Hugh Hunter
Eastern Washington University

James Jackson
Oklahoma State University

Raymond Jackson
University of Massachusetts–Dartmouth

Prem Jain
Tulane University

Narayanan Jayaraman
Georgia Institute of Technology

Brad Jordan
University of Kentucky

Jarl Kallberg
New York University

Jonathan Karpoff
University of Washington

Paul Keat
American Graduate School of International Management

Dolly King
University of Wisconsin–Milwaukee

Brian Kluger
University of Cincinnati

Narayana Kocherlakota
University of Iowa

Ronald Kudla
The University of Akron

Youngsik Kwak
Delaware State University

Nelson Lacey
University of Massachusetts

Gene Lai
University of Rhode Island

Josef Lakonishok
University of Illinois

Dennis Lasser
SUNY–Binghamton

Paul Laux
Case Western Reserve University

Bong-Su Lee
University of Minnesota

Youngho Lee
Howard University

James T. Lindley
University of Southern Mississippi

Dennis Logue
Dartmouth College

Michael Long
Rutgers University

Yulong Ma
Cal State–Long Beach

Ileen Malitz
Fairleigh Dickinson University

Terry Maness
Baylor University

Surendra Mansinghka
San Francisco State University

Michael Mazzco
Michigan State University

Robert I. McDonald
Northwestern University

Hugh McLaughlin
Bentley College

Larry Merville
University of Texas–Richardson

Joe Messina
San Francisco State University

Roger Mesznik
City College of New York–Baruch College

Rick Meyer
University of South Florida

Richard Miller
Wesleyan University

Naval Modani
University of Central Florida

Richard Mull
New Mexico State University

Jim Musumeci
Southern Illinois University–Carbondale

Robert Nachtmann
University of Pittsburgh

Edward Nelling
Georgia Tech

Gregory Niehaus
University of South Carolina

Peder Nielsen
Oregon State University

Ingmar Nyman
Hunter College

Dennis Officer
University of Kentucky

Joseph Ogden
State University of New York

Venky Panchapagesan
Washington University–St. Louis

Bulent Parker
University of Wisconsin–Madison

Ajay Patel
University of Missouri–Columbia

Dilip Kumar Patro
Rutgers University

Glenn N. Pettengill
Emporia State University

Pegaret Pichler
University of Maryland

Christo Pirinsky
Ohio State University

Jeffrey Pontiff
University of Washington

Franklin Potts
Baylor University

Annette Poulsen
University of Georgia

N. Prabhala
Yale University

Mao Qiu
University of Utah–Salt Lake City

Latha Ramchand
University of Houston

Gabriel Ramirez
Virginia Commonwealth University

Narendar Rao
Northeastern Illinois University

Steven Raymar
Indiana University

Stuart Rosenstein
Southern Illinois University

Stuart Rosenstein
University of Colorado at Denver

Bruce Rubin
Old Dominion University

Patricia Ryan
Drake University

Jaime Sabal
New York University

Anthony Sanders
Ohio State University

Andy Saporoschenko
University of Akron

William Sartoris
Indiana University

James Schallheim
University of Utah

Mary Jean Scheuer
California State University at Northridge

Faruk Selcuk
University of Bridgeport

Timothy Thompson
Northwestern University

Lemma Senbet
University of Maryland

Karin Thorburn
Dartmouth College

Kuldeep Shastri
University of Pittsburgh

Satish Thosar
University of Massachusetts–Dorchester

Sudhir Singh
Frostburg State University

Charles Trzcinka
State University of New York–Buffalo

Scott Smart
Indiana University

Haluk Unal
University of Maryland–College Park

Jackie So
Southern Illinois University

Oscar Varela
University of New Orleans

John Stansfield
Columbia College

Steven Venti
Dartmouth College

John S. Strong
College of William and Mary

Avinash Verma
Washington University

A. Charlene Sullivan
Purdue University

Lankford Walker
Eastern Illinois University

Michael Sullivan
University of Nevada–Las Vegas

Ralph Walkling
Ohio State University

Timothy Sullivan
Bentley College

F. Katherine Warne
Southern Bell College

R. Bruce Swensen
Adelphi University

Susan White
University of Texas–Austin

Ernest Swift
Georgia State University

Robert Whitelaw
New York University

Alex Tang
Morgan State University

Berry Wilson
Georgetown University

Richard Taylor
Arkansas State University

Thomas Zorn
University of Nebraska–Lincoln

Andrew C. Thompson
Virginia Polytechnic Institute

Kent Zumwalt
Colorado State University

For their help on the Seventh Edition, we would like to thank Linda De Angelo, Dennis Draper, Kim Dietrich, Harry De Angelo, Aris Protopapadakis, and Suh-Pyng Ku, all of the Marshall School of Business at the University of Southern California; Stephen Harris and Matthew Pascale, both of the Wharton School of Business at the University of Pennsylvania; Mark Westerfield, MIT; Jordan Strauss Esq.; Joe Walker, University of Alabama–Birmingham; Russell Gregory-Allen, SUNY-Albany; John Stansfield, University of Missouri–Columbia, for his work on the Instructor's Manual and PowerPoint; Patricia Ryan, Colorado State University, for her work on the Test Bank; Robert Hanson, Eastern Michigan University, for his work on the Student Problem Manual; Joe Smolira, Belmont University, for his work on the S & P Problems; and Michael Griffin, University of Massachusetts–Dartmouth, for his contributions to this edition. We also owe a debt of gratitude to Edward I. Altman, of New York University; Robert S. Hansen, of Virginia Tech; and Jay Ritter, of the University of Florida, who have provided several thoughtful comments and immeasurable help.

Over the past three years, readers have provided assistance by detecting and reporting errors. Our goal is to offer the best textbook available on the subject, so this information was invaluable as we prepared the Seventh Edition. We want to ensure that all future editions are error-free and therefore we will offer $10 per arithmetic error to the first individual reporting it. Any arithmetic error resulting in subsequent errors will be counted double. All errors should be reported using the Feedback Form on the Corporate Finance Online Learning Center at *www.mhhe.com/rwj*.

In addition, Gohar Palanjian and Wendy Wat have given significant assistance in preparing the manuscript.

Many talented professionals at McGraw-Hill/Irwin have contributed to the development of Corporate Finance, Seventh Edition. We would like to especially thank Michele Janicek, Jennifer Rizzi, Rhonda Seelinger, Christine Vaughan, Keith McPherson, Rose Hepburn, and Carol Loreth.

Finally, we wish to thank our families and friends, Carol, Kate, Jon, Jan, Mark, and Lynne for their forbearance and help.

Stephen A. Ross
Randolph W. Westerfield
Jeffrey F. Jaffe

Pedagogy

NEW AND ENHANCED PEDAGOGY

In this edition of *Corporate Finance,* we have updated and improved our features to present material in a way that makes it coherent and easy to understand. In addition, *Corporate Finance* is rich in valuable learning tools and support, to help students succeed in learning the fundamentals of financial management.

Part II

Value and Capital Budgeting

Firms and individuals invest in a large variety of assets. Some are real assets such as machinery and land, and some are financial assets such as stocks and bonds. The object of an investment is to maximize the value of the investment. In the simplest terms, this means to find assets that have more value to the firm than they cost. To do this we need a theory of value. We develop a theory of value in Part II.

Finance is the study of markets and instruments that deal with cash flows over time. In Chapter 4 we extend the concept of net present value to more than one time period. The mathematics of compounding and discounting are presented. In Chapter 5 we apply net present value to bonds and stocks. This is a very important chapter because net present value can be used to determine the value of a wide variety of financial instruments.

Although we have made a strong case for using the NPV rule in Chapters 4 and 6 presents four other rules: the payback rule, the accounting-rate-of-return rule, the internal rate of return (IRR), and the profitability index. Each of these alternatives has some redeeming features, but these qualities aren't sufficient to let any of the alternatives replace the NPV rule.

In Chapter 7 we analyze how to estimate the cash flows required for capital budgeting. We start the chapter with a discussion of the concept of incremental cash flows—the difference between the cash flows for the firm with and without the project. Chapter 8 focuses on assessing the reliability and reasonableness of estimates of NPV. The chapter introduces techniques for dealing with uncertain incremental cash flows in capital budgeting, including break-even analysis, decision trees, sensitivity analysis, and real options.

4 Net Present Value

5 How to Value Bonds and Stocks

6 Some Alternative Investment Rules

7 Net Present Value and Capital Budgeting

8 Risk Analysis, Real Options, and Capital Budgeting

59

◄ **Part Introductions**
Updated part introductions explain what is found in the chapters that follow, and the links between the different concepts.

Chapter 3

Financial Planning and Growth

EXECUTIVE SUMMARY

Financial planning establishes guidelines for change in the firm. These guidelines should include (1) an identification of the firm's financial goals, (2) an analysis of the differences between these goals and the current financial status of the firm, and (3) a statement of the actions needed for the firm to achieve its financial goals. In other words, as one member of GM's board was heard to say, "Planning is a process that at best helps the firm avoid stumbling into the future backwards."

The basic elements of financial planning comprise (1) the investment opportunities the firm elects to take advantage of, (2) the amount of debt the firm chooses to employ, and (3) the amount of cash the firm thinks is necessary and appropriate to pay shareholders. These are the financial policies that the firm must decide upon for its growth and profitability.

Almost all firms identify a companywide growth rate as a major component of their financial planning.[1] In one famous case Inter-

national Business Machines' stated growth goal was simple but typical: to match the growth of the computer industry, which was projected to be 15 percent per year through the end of the 1990s. Though we may have had some doubts about IBM's ability to sustain a 15-percent growth rate, we are certain there are important financial implications of the strategies that IBM will adopt to achieve that rate. There are direct connections between the growth that a company can achieve and its financial policy. One purpose of this chapter is to look at the financial aspects of how fast a firm can grow.

The chapter first describes what is usually meant by financial planning. This enables us to make an important point: Investment and financing decisions frequently interact. The different interactions of investment and financing decisions can be analyzed in the financial statements. We show how financial statements can be used to better understand how growth is achieved.

[1] We think that a firm's growth should be a consequence of its trying to achieve maximum shareholder value.

Executive Summaries ►
Each chapter begins with a "roadmap" that describes the objectives of the chapter and how it connects with concepts already learned in previous chapters. Real company examples that will be discussed are highlighted in this section.

FIGURE 4.11

Annual, Semiannual, and Continuous Compounding

Annual compounding | Semiannual compounding | Continuous compounding

EXAMPLE

The Michigan state lottery is going to pay you $1,000 at the end of four years. If the annual continuously compounded rate of interest is 8 percent, what is the present value of this payment?

$$\$1,000 \times \frac{1}{e^{0.08 \times 4}} = \$1,000 \times \frac{1}{1.3771} = \$726.16$$

Concept Questions

1. What is a stated annual interest rate?
2. What is an effective annual interest rate?
3. What is the relationship between the stated annual interest rate and the effective annual interest rate?
4. Define continuous compounding.

4.4 Simplifications

The first part of this chapter has examined the concepts of future value and present value. Although these concepts allow one to answer a host of problems concerning the time value of money, the human effort involved can frequently be excessive. For example, consider a bank calculating the present value on a 20-year monthly mortgage. Because this mortgage has 240 (20 × 12) payments, a lot of time is needed to perform a conceptually simple task.

Because many basic finance problems are potentially so time-consuming, we search out simplifications in this section. We provide simplifying formulas for four classes of cash flow streams:

◄ Figures and Tables

This text makes extensive use of real data and presents them in various figures and tables. Explanations in the narrative, examples, and end-of-chapter problems will refer to many of these exhibits.

◄ Examples

Separate called-out examples are integrated throughout the chapters. Each example illustrates an intuitive or mathematical application in a step-by-step format. There is enough detail in the explanations so the student doesn't have to look elsewhere for additional information.

"In Their Own Words" Boxes ►

Located throughout the chapters, this unique series consists of articles written by distinguished scholars or practitioners on key topics in the text. Boxes include essays by Edward I. Altman, Anthony Bourdain, Robert S. Hansen, Robert C. Higgins, Michael C. Jensen, Richard M. Levich, Merton Miller, and Jay R. Ritter.

In Their Own Words

Robert C. Higgins on Sustainable Growth

Most financial officers know intuitively that it takes money to make money. Rapid sales growth requires increased assets in the form of accounts receivable, inventory, and fixed plant, which, in turn, require money to pay for assets. They also know that if their company does not have the money when needed, it can literally "grow broke." The sustainable growth equation states these intuitive truths explicitly.

Sustainable growth is often used by bankers and other external analysts to assess a company's creditworthiness. They are aided in this exercise by several sophisticated computer software packages that provide detailed analyses of the company's past financial performance, including its annual sustainable growth rate.

Bankers use this information in several ways. Quick comparison of a company's actual growth rate to its sustainable rate tells the banker what issues will be at the top of management's financial agenda. If actual growth consistently exceeds sustainable growth, management's problem will be where to get the cash to finance growth. The banker thus can anticipate interest in loan products. Conversely, if sustainable growth consistently exceeds actual, the banker had best be prepared to talk about

investment products, because management's problem will be what to do with all the cash that keeps piling up in the till.

Bankers also find the sustainable growth equation useful for explaining to financially inexperienced small business owners and overly optimistic entrepreneurs that, for the long-run viability of their business, it is necessary to keep growth and profitability in proper balance.

Finally, comparison of actual to sustainable growth rates helps a banker understand why a loan applicant needs money and for how long the need might continue. In one instance, a loan applicant requested $100,000 to pay off several insistent suppliers and promised to repay in a few months when he collected some accounts receivable that were coming due. A sustainable growth analysis revealed that the firm had been growing at four to six times its sustainable growth rate and that this pattern was likely to continue in the foreseeable future. This alerted the banker that impatient suppliers were only a symptom of the much more fundamental disease of overly rapid growth, and that a $100,000 loan would likely prove to be only the down payment on a much larger, multiyear commitment.

Robert C. Higgins is Professor of Finance at the University of Washington. He pioneered the use of sustainable growth as a tool for financial analysis.

Concept Questions

1. What is the difference between independent projects and mutually exclusive projects?
2. What are two problems with the IRR approach that apply to both independent and mutually exclusive projects?
3. What is MIRR?
4. What are two additional problems applying only to mutually exclusive projects?

◄ Concept Questions

Included after each major section in a chapter, Concept Questions point to essential material and allow students to test their recall and comprehension before moving forward.

top management serve as corporate officers and manage the operation of the corporation in the best interest of the shareholders. In closely held corporations with few shareholders, there may be a large overlap among the shareholders, the directors, and the top management. However, in larger corporations the shareholders, directors, and the top management are likely to be distinct groups.

The potential separation of ownership from management gives the corporation several advantages over proprietorships and partnerships:

1. Because ownership in a corporation is represented by shares of stock, ownership can be readily transferred to new owners. Because the corporation exists independently of those who own its shares, there is no limit to the transferability of shares as there is in partnerships.

2. The corporation has unlimited life. Because the corporation is separate from its owners, the death or withdrawal of an owner does not affect its legal existence. The corporation can continue on after the original owners have withdrawn.

3. The shareholders' liability is limited to the amount invested in the ownership shares. For example, if a shareholder purchased $1,000 in shares of a corporation, the potential loss would be $1,000. In a partnership, a general partner with a $1,000 contribution could lose the $1,000 plus any other indebtedness of the partnership.

Limited liability, ease of ownership transfer, and perpetual succession are the major advantages of the corporation form of business organization. These give the corporation an enhanced ability to raise cash.

There is, however, one great disadvantage to incorporation. The federal government taxes corporate income. This tax is in addition to the personal income tax that shareholders pay on dividend income they receive. This is double taxation for shareholders when compared to taxation on proprietorships and partnerships.

Case Study ➤

There are 10 case studies that are highlighted in the Seventh Edition that present situations with real companies and how they rationalized decisions they made to solve various problems. They provide extended examples of the material covered in the chapter. The cases are highlighted in the detailed Table of Contents.

CASE STUDY

Making the Decision to Become a Corporation: The Case of PLM International, Inc.*

In 1972, several entrepreneurs agreed to start a company they called PLM (Professional Lease Management, Inc.). Their idea was to sponsor, syndicate, and manage public and private limited partnerships with the purpose of acquiring and leasing transportation equipment. They created an operating subsidiary called FSI (Financial Services, Inc.) to be the general partner of each of the partnerships. PLM had limited success in its early years, but during the period 1981 to 1986 more than

*The S–4 Registration Statement, PLM International, Inc., filed with the Securities and Exchange Commission, Washington, D.C., August 1987, gives further details.

1.4 Goals of the Corporate Firm

What is the primary goal of the corporation? The traditional answer is that managers in a corporation make decisions for the stockholders because the stockholders own and control the corporation. If so, the goal of the corporation is to add value for the stockholders. This goal is a little vague and so we will try to come up with a precise formulation. It is also impossible to give a definitive answer to this important question because the corporation is an artificial being, not a natural person. It exists in the "contemplation of the law."[3]

It is necessary to precisely identify who controls the corporation. We shall consider the set-of-contracts viewpoint. This viewpoint suggests the corporate firm will attempt to maximize the shareholders' wealth by taking actions that increase the current value per share of existing stock of the firm.

◄ Key Terms

Students will note that important words are highlighted in boldface type the first time they appear. They are also listed at the end of each chapter, along with the page number on which they first appear, as well as in the glossary at the end of the book.

48   Part I   Value and Capital Budgeting

The Income Statement

We start out with the most recent income statement for the Rosengarten Corporation, as shown in Table 3.1. Notice we have still simplified things by including costs, depreciation, and interest in a single cost figure. We separate these out in a later section.

Rosengarten has projected a 10 percent increase in sales for the coming year, so we are anticipating sales of $20 million × 1.1 = $22 million. To generate a pro forma income statement, we assume that total costs will continue to run at $16.9697 million/$20 million = 84.85% of sales. With this assumption, Rosengarten's pro forma income statement is as shown in Table 3.2. The effect here of assuming that costs are a constant percentage of sales is to assume that the profit margin is constant. To check this, notice that the profit margin was $2 million/$20 million = 10%. In our pro forma, the profit margin is $2.2 million/$22 million = 10%; so it is unchanged.

Next, we need to project the dividend payment. This amount is up to Rosengarten's management. We will assume Rosengarten has a policy of paying out a constant fraction of net income in the form of a cash dividend. For the most recent year, the dividend payout ratio was:

$$\text{Dividend payout ratio} = \text{Cash dividends/Net income}$$

$$= \$1 \text{ million}/\$2 \text{ million} = 50\% \qquad (3.1)$$

We can also calculate the ratio of the addition to retained earnings to net income as:

$$\text{Addition to retained earnings/Net income} = \$1 \text{ million}/\$2 \text{ million} = 50\%$$

This ratio is called the retention ratio or plowback ratio, and it is equal to 1 minus the dividend payout ratio because everything not paid out is retained. Assuming that the payout ratio is constant, the projected dividends and addition to retained earnings will be:

$$\text{Projected dividends paid to shareholders} = \$1.1 \text{ million} \times \tfrac{1}{2} = \$ \ 550 \text{ thousand}$$

$$\text{Projected addition to retained earnings} = \$1.1 \text{ million} \times \tfrac{1}{2} = \underline{\ 550 \text{ thousand}}$$
$$\underline{\$1,100 \text{ thousand}}$$

◄ Numbered Equations

Key equations are numbered and listed on the back end sheets for easy reference.

END-OF-CHAPTER MATERIAL

The end-of-chapter material reflects and builds upon the concepts learned from the chapter and study features.

<table>
<tr><td>

Chapter 3 Financial Planning and Growth

55

3.6 SUMMARY AND CONCLUSIONS

Financial planning forces the firm to think about and forecast the future. It involves the following:

1. Building a corporate financial model.
2. Describing different scenarios of future development from worst to best cases.
3. Using the models to construct pro forma financial statements.
4. Running the model under different scenarios (conducting sensitivity analysis).
5. Examining the financial implications of ultimate strategic plans.

Corporate financial planning should not become a purely mechanical activity. If it does, it will probably focus on the wrong things. In particular, plans are formulated all too often in terms of a growth target with an explicit linkage to creation of value. We talk about a particular financial planning model called sustainable growth. It is a very simple model. Nonetheless, the alternative to financial planning is stumbling into the future.

KEY TERMS

aggregation, 45	plug, 46
asset requirements, 46	pro forma statements, 46
dividend payout ratio, 48	retention ratio (plowback ratio), 48
economic assumptions, 46	sales forecast, 45
financial requirements, 46	sustainable growth rate, 52
percentage of sales approach, 47	

SUGGESTED READINGS

Some aspects of economic growth and stock market returns are covered in:

Ritter, Jay. "Economic Growth—Equity Returns." Unpublished working paper. University of Florida, March 1, 2003.

We also recommend:

Campbell, John K., and Robert Shiller. "Valuation Ratios and the Long Run Stock Market Outlook: An Update." Cowles Foundation Discussion Paper, no. 1295.

Jorion, Phillippe, and William Coetzmann. "Global Stock Markets in the Twentieth Century." Journal of Finance (1995).

Owen, Lamont. "Earnings and Expect Returns." Journal of Finance, 53 (1998).

QUESTIONS & PROBLEMS

FINANCIAL-PLANNING MODELS: THE INGREDIENTS

3.1 After examining patterns from recent years, management found the following regression-estimated relationships between some company balance sheets and income statement accounts and sales.

$$CA = 0.5 \text{ million} + 0.25S$$
$$FA = 1.0 \text{ million} + 0.50S$$
$$CL = 0.1 \text{ million} + 0.10S$$
$$NP = 0.0 \text{ million} + 0.02S$$

where

CA = Current assets
FA = Fixed assets
CL = Current liabilities
NP = Net profit after taxes
S = Sales

Visit us at www.mhhe.com/rwj
</td></tr>
</table>

◀ **Summary and Conclusions**

The numbered summary provides a quick review of key concepts in the chapter.

◀ **List of Key Terms**

A list of the boldfaced key terms in the text with page numbers is included for easy reference.

◀ **Suggested Readings**

Each chapter is followed by a short, annotated list of books, articles, and websites to which interested students can refer for additional information on key topics.

◀ **Questions and Problems**

Because solving problems is so critical to a student's learning, new questions and problems have been added, and existing questions and problems have been revised. All problems have also been thoroughly reviewed and accuracy-checked.

Problems have been grouped according to the concepts they test on, with the concept headings listed in the margin.

Additionally, we have tried to make the problems in the critical "concept" chapters, such as those on value, risk, and capital structure, especially challenging and interesting.

We provide answers to selected problems in Appendix B at the end of the book.

S&P Problems ▶

New! Now included in the end-of-chapter material are problems directly incorporating the Educational Version of Market Insight, a service based on Standard & Poor's renowned Compustat database. These problems provide you with an easy method of including current real-world data into your course.

S & P PROBLEM

STANDARD &POOR'S

4.55 Under the "Excel Analytics" link find the "Mthly. Adj. Price" for Elizabeth Arden (RDEN) stock. What was your annual return over the last four years assuming you purchased the stock at the close price four years ago? (Assume no dividends were paid.) Using this same return, what price will Elizabeth Arden stock sell for five years from now? Ten years from now? What if the stock prices increases at 11 percent per year?

Excel Problems ▶

Indicated by the Excel icon in the margin, these problems can be found at the end of almost all chapters. Located on the book's website (see Online Resources), Excel templates have been created for each of these problems, where students can use the data in the problem to work out the solution using Excel skills.

4.36 You are saving for the college education of your two children. They are two years apart in age; one will begin college 15 years from today and the other will begin 17 years from today. You estimate your children's college expenses to be $21,000 per year per child, payable at the end of each school year. The annual interest rate is 15 percent. How much money must you deposit in an account each year to fund your children's education? Your deposits begin one year from today. You will make your last deposit when your oldest child enters college.

4.37 A well-known insurance company offers a policy known as the "Estate Creator Six Pay." Typically, a parent or grandparent buys a policy for a child at the child's birth. The details of the policy are as follows. The purchaser (say, the parent) makes the following six payments to the insurance company.

First birthday	$750	Fourth birthday	$800
Second birthday	$750	Fifth birthday	$800
Third birthday	$750	Sixth birthday	$800

No more payments are made after the child's sixth birthday. When the child reaches the age of 65, he or she receives $250,000. If the relevant interest rate is 6 percent for the first six years and 7 percent for all subsequent years, is the policy worth buying?

Minicase ▶

This end-of-chapter feature, located in Chapters 12 and 29, parallels the Case Study feature found in various chapters. These Minicases apply what is learned in a number of chapters to a real-world type of scenario. After presenting the facts, the student is given guidance in rationalizing a sound business decision.

MINICASE AlliedProducts

AlliedProducts, Inc., has recently won approval from the Federal Aviation Administration (FAA) for its Enhanced Ground Proximity Warning System (GPWS). This system is designed to give airplane pilots additional warning of approaching ground danger and thus help prevent crashes. AlliedProducts has spent $10 million in research and development the past four years developing GPWS. The GPWS will be put on the market beginning this year and AlliedProducts expects it to stay on the market for a total of five years.

As a financial analyst specializing in the aerospace industry for USC Pension & Investment, Inc., you are asked by your managing partner, Mr. Adam Smith, to evaluate the potential of this new GPWS project.

Initially, AlliedProducts will need to acquire $42 million in production equipment to make the GPWS. The equipment is expected to have a seven-year useful life. This equipment can be sold for $12 million at the end of five years. AlliedProducts intends to sell

Brief Contents

Contents

Chapter 5

How to Value Bonds and Stocks   106

Chapter 6

Some Alternative Investment Rules   144

Chapter 7

Net Present Value and Capital Budgeting   178

Chapter 8

Risk Analysis, Real Options, and Capital Budgeting 211

Part III

Risk 233

Chapter 9

Capital Market Theory: *An Overview* 234

Chapter 10

Return and Risk: *The Capital-Asset-Pricing Model (CAPM)* 255

Chapter 11

An Alternative View of Risk and Return: *The Arbitrage Pricing Theory* 297

Chapter 31

International Corporate Finance 847

Part I

Overview

To engage in business the financial managers of a firm must find answers to three kinds of important questions. First, what long-term investments should the firm take on? This is the capital budgeting decision. Second, how can cash be raised for the required investments? We call this the financing decision. Third, how will the firm manage its day-to-day cash and financial affairs? These decisions involve short-term finance and concern net working capital.

In Chapter 1 we discuss these important questions, briefly introducing the basic ideas of this book and describing the nature of the modern corporation and why it has emerged as the leading form of the business firm. Using the set-of-contracts perspective, the chapter discusses the goals of the modern corporation. Though the goals of shareholders and managers may not always be the same, conflicts usually will be resolved in favor of the shareholders. Finally, the chapter reviews some of the salient features of modern financial markets. This preliminary material will be familiar to students who have some background in accounting, finance, and economics.

Chapter 2 examines the basic accounting statements. It is review material for students with an accounting background. We describe the balance sheet and the income statement. The point of the chapter is to show the ways of converting data from accounting statements into cash flow. Understanding how to identify cash flow from accounting statements is especially important for later chapters on capital budgeting.

Chapter 3 examines the basic elements of financial planning and introduces the concept of sustainable growth. Sustainable growth is a useful organizing framework when working with financial statements.

Introduction to Corporate Finance

EXECUTIVE SUMMARY

The Video Product Company designs and manufactures very popular software for video game consoles. The company was started in 2002, and soon thereafter its game "Gadfly" appeared on the cover of *Billboard* magazine. Company sales in 2003 were over $20 million. Video Product's initial financing of $2 million came from Seed Ltd., a venture-capital firm, in exchange for a 15-percent equity stake in the company. Now the financial management of Video Product realizes that its initial financing was too small. In the long run Video Product would like to expand its design activity to the education and business areas. It would also like to significantly enhance its website for future Internet sales. However, at present the company has a short-run cash flow problem and cannot even buy $200,000 of materials to fill its holiday orders.

Video Product's experience illustrates the basic concerns of corporate finance:

1. What long-term investment strategy should a company take on?
2. How can cash be raised for the required investments?
3. How much short-term cash flow does a company need to pay its bills?

These are not the only questions of corporate finance. They are, however, among the most important questions, and taken in order, they provide a rough outline of our book.

One way that companies raise cash to finance their investment activities is by selling or "issuing" securities. The securities, sometimes called *financial instruments* or *claims,* may be roughly classified as *equity* or *debt,* loosely called *stocks* or *bonds.* The difference between equity and debt is a basic distinction in the modern theory of finance. All securities of a firm are claims that depend on or are contingent on the value of the firm.[1] In Section 1.2 we show how debt and equity securities depend on the firm's value, and we describe them as different contingent claims.

In Section 1.3 we discuss different organizational forms and the pros and cons of the decision to become a corporation.

In Section 1.4 we take a close look at the goals of the corporation and discuss why maximizing shareholder wealth is likely to be the primary goal of the corporation. Throughout the rest of the book, we assume that the firm's performance depends on the value it creates for its shareholders. Shareholders are better off when the value of their shares is increased by the firm's decisions.

A company raises cash by issuing securities to the financial markets. The market value of outstanding long-term corporate debt and equity securities traded in the U.S. financial markets is in excess of $25 trillion. In Section 1.5 we describe some of the basic features of the financial markets. Roughly speaking, there are two basic types of financial markets: the money markets and the capital markets. The last section of the chapter provides an outline of the rest of the book.

---

[1]We tend to use the words *firm, company,* and *business* interchangeably. However, there is a difference between a firm and a corporation. We discuss this difference in Section 1.3.

1.1 What Is Corporate Finance?

Suppose you decide to start a firm to make tennis balls. To do this, you hire managers to buy raw materials, and you assemble a workforce that will produce and sell finished tennis balls. In the language of finance, you make an investment in assets such as inventory, machinery, land, and labor. The amount of cash you invest in assets must be matched by an equal amount of cash raised by financing. When you begin to sell tennis balls, your firm will generate cash. This is the basis of value creation. The purpose of the firm is to create value for you, the owner. The firm must generate more cash flow than it uses. The value is reflected in the framework of the simple balance-sheet model of the firm.

The Balance-Sheet Model of the Firm

Suppose we take a financial snapshot of the firm and its activities at a single point in time. Figure 1.1 shows a graphic conceptualization of the balance sheet, and it will help introduce you to corporate finance.

The assets of the firm are on the left-hand side of the balance sheet. These assets can be thought of as current and fixed. *Fixed assets* are those that will last a long time, such as buildings. Some fixed assets are tangible, such as machinery and equipment. Other fixed assets are intangible, such as patents, trademarks, and the quality of management. The other category of assets, *current assets,* comprises those that have short lives, such as inventory. The tennis balls that your firm has made but has not yet sold are part of its inventory. Unless you have overproduced, they will leave the firm shortly.

Before a company can invest in an asset, it must obtain financing, which means that it must raise the money to pay for the investment. The forms of financing are represented on the right-hand side of the balance sheet. A firm will issue (sell) pieces of paper called *debt* (loan agreements) or *equity shares* (stock certificates). Just as assets are classified as

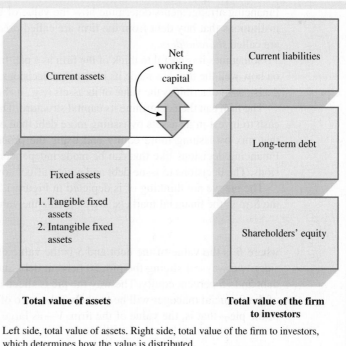

FIGURE 1.1

The Balance-Sheet Model of the Firm

Left side, total value of assets. Right side, total value of the firm to investors, which determines how the value is distributed.

long-lived or short-lived, so too are liabilities. A short-term debt is called a *current liability.* Short-term debt represents loans and other obligations that must be repaid within one year. Long-term debt is debt that does not have to be repaid within one year. Shareholders' equity represents the difference between the value of the assets and the debt of the firm. In this sense it is a residual claim on the firm's assets.

From the balance-sheet model of the firm it is easy to see why finance can be thought of as the study of the following three questions:

1. In what long-lived assets should the firm invest? This question concerns the left-hand side of the balance sheet. Of course, the type and proportions of assets the firm needs tend to be set by the nature of the business. We use the terms **capital budgeting** and *capital expenditures* to describe the process of making and managing expenditures on long-lived assets.

2. How can the firm raise cash for required capital expenditures? This question concerns the right-hand side of the balance sheet. The answer to this involves the firm's **capital structure,** which represents the proportions of the firm's financing from current and long-term debt and equity.

3. How should short-term operating cash flows be managed? This question concerns the upper portion of the balance sheet. There is often a mismatch between the timing of cash inflows and cash outflows during operating activities. Furthermore, the amount and timing of operating cash flows are not known with certainty. The financial managers must attempt to manage the gaps in cash flow. From a balance-sheet perspective, short-term management of cash flow is associated with a firm's **net working capital.** Net working capital is defined as current assets minus current liabilities. From a financial perspective, the short-term cash flow problem comes from the mismatching of cash inflows and outflows. It is the subject of short-term finance.

Capital Structure

Financing arrangements determine how the value of the firm is sliced up. The persons or institutions that buy debt from the firm are called *creditors.*[2] The holders of equity shares are called *shareholders.*

Sometimes it is useful to think of the firm as a pie. Initially, the size of the pie will depend on how well the firm has made its investment decisions. After a firm has made its investment decisions, it determines the value of its assets (e.g., its buildings, land, and inventories).

The firm can then determine its capital structure. The firm might initially have raised the cash to invest in its assets by issuing more debt than equity; now it can consider changing that mix by issuing more equity and using the proceeds to buy back some of its debt. Financing decisions like this can be made independently of the original investment decisions. The decisions to issue debt and equity affect how the pie is sliced.

The pie we are thinking of is depicted in Figure 1.2. The size of the pie is the value of the firm in the financial markets. We can write the value of the firm, V, as

$$V = B + S$$

where B is the value of the debt and S is the value of the equity. The pie diagrams consider two ways of slicing the pie: 50 percent debt and 50 percent equity, and 25 percent debt and 75 percent equity. The way the pie is sliced could affect its value. If so, the goal of the financial manager will be to choose the ratio of debt to equity that makes the value of the pie—that is, the value of the firm, V—as large as it can be.

---

[2]We tend to use the words *creditors, debtholders,* and *bondholders* interchangeably. In later chapters we examine the differences among the kinds of creditors. In algebraic notation, we will usually refer to the firm's debt with the letter B (for bondholders).

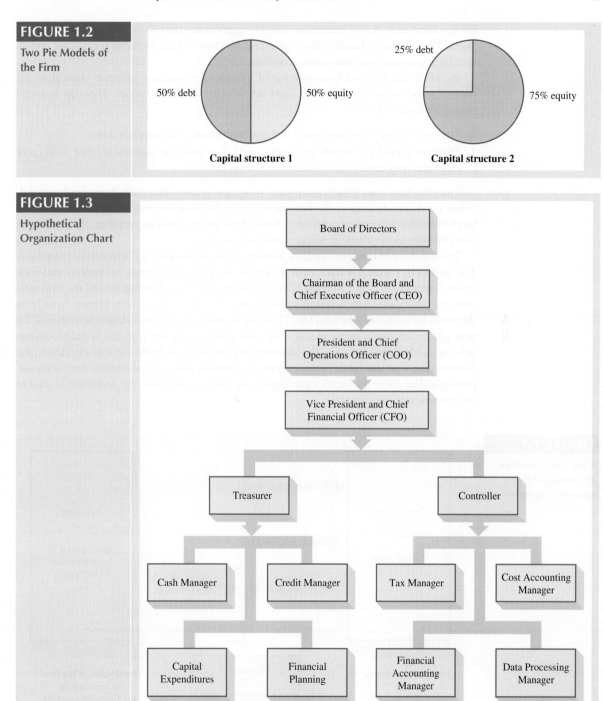

FIGURE 1.2

Two Pie Models of the Firm

50% debt   50% equity

Capital structure 1

25% debt   75% equity

Capital structure 2

FIGURE 1.3

Hypothetical Organization Chart

Board of Directors

Chairman of the Board and Chief Executive Officer (CEO)

President and Chief Operations Officer (COO)

Vice President and Chief Financial Officer (CFO)

Treasurer

Controller

Cash Manager

Credit Manager

Tax Manager

Cost Accounting Manager

Capital Expenditures

Financial Planning

Financial Accounting Manager

Data Processing Manager

The Financial Manager

In large firms the finance activity is usually associated with a top officer of the firm, such as the vice president and chief financial officer, and some lesser officers. Figure 1.3 depicts a general organizational structure emphasizing the finance activity within the firm. Reporting to the chief financial officer are the treasurer and the controller. The treasurer is responsible for handling cash flows, managing capital-expenditures decisions, and making financial plans. The controller handles the accounting function, which includes taxes, cost and financial accounting, and information systems.

We think that the most important job of a financial manager is to create value from the firm's capital budgeting, financing, and net working-capital activities. How do financial managers create value?

1. The firm should try to buy assets that generate more cash than they cost.
2. The firm should sell bonds and stocks and other financial instruments that raise more cash than they cost.

Thus the firm must create more cash flow than it uses. The cash flows paid to bondholders and stockholders of the firm should be higher than the cash flows put into the firm by the bondholders and stockholders. To see how this is done, we can trace the cash flows from the firm to the financial markets and back again.

The interplay of the firm's finance with the financial markets is illustrated in Figure 1.4. The arrows in Figure 1.4 trace cash flow from the firm to the financial markets and back again. Suppose we begin with the firm's financing activities. To raise money the firm sells debt and equity shares to investors in the financial markets. This results in cash flows from the financial markets to the firm (A). This cash is invested in the investment activities of the firm (B) by the firm's management. The cash generated by the firm (C) is paid to shareholders and bondholders (F). The shareholders receive cash in the form of dividends; the bondholders who lent funds to the firm receive interest and, when the initial loan is repaid, principal. Not all of the firm's cash is paid out. Some is retained (E), and some is paid to the government as taxes (D).

FIGURE 1.4

Cash Flows between the Firm and the Financial Markets

(A) Firm issues securities to raise cash (the financing decision).
(B) Firm invests in assets (capital budgeting).
(C) Firm's operations generate cash flow.
(D) Cash is paid to government as taxes.
(E) Retained cash flows are reinvested in firm.
(F) Cash is paid out to investors in the form of interest and dividends.

Over time, if the cash paid to shareholders and bondholders (F) is greater than the cash raised in the financial markets (A), value will be created.

Identification of Cash Flows Unfortunately, it is not all that easy to observe cash flows directly. Much of the information we obtain is in the form of accounting statements, and much of the work of financial analysis is to extract cash flow information from accounting statements. The following example illustrates how this is done.

EXAMPLE

The Midland Company refines and trades gold. At the end of the year it sold 2,500 ounces of gold for $1 million. The company had acquired the gold for $900,000 at the beginning of the year. The company paid cash for the gold when it was purchased. Unfortunately, it has yet to collect from the customer to whom the gold was sold. The following is a standard accounting of Midland's financial circumstances at year-end:

THE MIDLAND COMPANY
Accounting View
Income Statement
Year Ended December 31

Sales	$1,000,000
−Costs	−900,000
Profit	$ 100,000

By generally accepted accounting principles (GAAP), the sale is recorded even though the customer has yet to pay. It is assumed that the customer will pay soon. From the accounting perspective, Midland seems to be profitable. However, the perspective of corporate finance is different. It focuses on cash flows:

THE MIDLAND COMPANY
Corporate Finance View
Income Statement
Year Ended December 31

Cash inflow	$ 0
Cash outflow	−900,000
	−$900,000

The perspective of corporate finance is interested in whether cash flows are being created by the gold-trading operations of Midland. Value creation depends on cash flows. For Midland, value creation depends on whether and when it actually receives $1 million.

Timing of Cash Flows The value of an investment made by the firm depends on the timing of cash flows. One of the most important assumptions of finance is that individuals prefer to receive cash flows earlier rather than later. One dollar received today is worth more than one dollar received next year. This time preference plays a role in stock and bond prices.

EXAMPLE

The Midland Company is attempting to choose between two proposals for new products. Both proposals will provide additional cash flows over a four-year period and will initially cost $10,000. The cash flows from the proposals are as follows:

Year	New Product A	New Product B
1	$ 0	$ 4,000
2	0	4,000
3	0	4,000
4	20,000	4,000
Total	$20,000	$16,000

At first it appears that new product A would be best. However, the cash flows from proposal B come earlier than those of A. Without more information we cannot decide which set of cash flows would create the most value to the bondholders and shareholders. It depends on whether the value of getting cash from B up front outweighs the extra total cash from A. Bond and stock prices reflect this preference for earlier cash, and we will see how to use them to decide between A and B.

Risk of Cash Flows The firm must consider risk. The amount and timing of cash flows are not usually known with certainty. Most investors have an aversion to risk.

EXAMPLE

The Midland Company is considering expanding operations overseas. It is evaluating Europe and Japan as possible sites. Europe is considered to be relatively safe, whereas operating in Japan is seen as very risky. In both cases the company would close down operations after one year.

After doing a complete financial analysis, Midland has come up with the following cash flows of the alternative plans for expansion under three equally likely scenarios—pessimistic, most likely, and optimistic:

	Pessimistic	Most Likely	Optimistic
Europe	$75,000	$100,000	$125,000
Japan	0	150,000	200,000

If we ignore the pessimistic scenario, perhaps Japan is the best alternative. When we take the pessimistic scenario into account, the choice is unclear. Japan appears to be riskier, but it also offers a higher expected level of cash flow. What is risk and how can it be defined? We must try to answer this important question. Corporate finance cannot avoid coping with risky alternatives, and much of our book is devoted to developing methods for evaluating risky opportunities.

Concept Questions

1. What are three basic questions of corporate finance?
2. Describe capital structure.
3. How is value created?
4. List the three reasons why value creation is difficult.

1.2 Corporate Securities as Contingent Claims on Total Firm Value

What is the essential difference between debt and equity? The answer can be found by thinking about what happens to the payoffs to debt and equity when the value of the firm changes.

The basic feature of a debt is that it is a promise by the borrowing firm to repay a fixed dollar amount by a certain date.

EXAMPLE

The Officer Corporation promises to pay $100 to the Brigham Insurance Company at the end of one year. This is a debt of the Officer Corporation. Holders of the debt will receive $100 if the value of the Officer Corporation's assets is equal to or more than $100 at the end of the year.

Formally, the debtholders have been promised an amount F at the end of the year. If the value of the firm, X, is equal to or greater than F at year-end, debtholders will get F. Of course, if the firm does not have enough to pay off the promised amount, the firm will be "broke." It may be forced to liquidate its assets for whatever they are worth, and the bondholders will receive X. Mathematically this means that the debtholders have a claim to X or F, whichever is smaller. Figure 1.5 illustrates the general nature of the payoff structure to debtholders.

Suppose at year-end the Officer Corporation's value is equal to $100. The firm has promised to pay the Brigham Insurance Company $100, so the debtholders will get $100.

Now suppose the Officer Corporation's value is $200 at year-end and the debtholders are promised $100. How much will the debtholders receive? It should be clear that they will receive the same amount as when the Officer Corporation was worth $100.

Suppose the firm's value is $75 at year-end and debtholders are promised $100. How much will the debtholders receive? In this case the debtholders will get $75.

FIGURE 1.5

Debt and Equity as Contingent Claims

F is the promised payoff to debtholders. $X - F$ is the payoff to equity shareholders if $X - F > 0$. Otherwise the payoff is 0.

The stockholders' claim on firm value at the end of the period is the amount that remains after the debtholders are paid. Of course, stockholders get nothing if the firm's value is equal to or less than the amount promised to the debtholders.

EXAMPLE

The Officer Corporation will sell its assets for $200 at year-end. The firm has promised to pay the Brigham Insurance Company $100 at that time. The stockholders will get the residual value of $100.

Algebraically, the stockholders' claim is $X - F$ if $X > F$ and zero if $X \leq F$. This is depicted in Figure 1.5. The sum of the debtholders' claim and the stockholders' claim is always the value of the firm at the end of the period.

The debt and equity securities issued by a firm derive their value from the total value of the firm. In the words of finance theory, debt and equity securities are **contingent claims** on the total firm value.

When the value of the firm exceeds the amount promised to the debtholders, the shareholders obtain the residual of the firm's value over the amount promised the debtholders, and the debtholders obtain the amount promised. When the value of the firm is less than the amount promised the debtholders, the shareholders receive nothing and the debtholders get the value of the firm.

Concept Questions

1. What is a contingent claim?
2. Describe equity and debt as contingent claims.

1.3 The Corporate Firm

The firm is a way of organizing the economic activity of many individuals, and there are many reasons why so much economic activity is carried out by firms and not by individuals. The theory of firms, however, does not tell us much about why most large firms are corporations rather than any of the other legal forms that firms can assume.

A basic problem of the firm is how to raise cash. The corporate form of business, that is, organizing the firm as a corporation, is the standard method for solving problems encountered in raising large amounts of cash. However, businesses can take other forms. In this section we consider the three basic legal forms of organizing firms, and we see how firms go about the task of raising large amounts of money under each form.

The Sole Proprietorship

A **sole proprietorship** is a business owned by one person. Suppose you decide to start a business to produce mousetraps. Going into business is simple: You announce to all who will listen, "Today I am going to build a better mousetrap."

Most large cities require that you obtain a business license. Afterward you can begin to hire as many people as you need and borrow whatever money you need. At year-end all the profits and the losses will be yours.

Here are some factors that are important in considering a sole proprietorship:

1. The sole proprietorship is the cheapest business to form. No formal charter is required, and few government regulations must be satisfied for most industries.
2. A sole proprietorship pays no corporate income taxes. All profits of the business are taxed as individual income.
3. The sole proprietorship has unlimited liability for business debts and obligations. No distinction is made between personal and business assets.
4. The life of the sole proprietorship is limited by the life of the sole proprietor.
5. Because the only money invested in the firm is the proprietor's, the equity money that can be raised by the sole proprietor is limited to the proprietor's personal wealth.

The Partnership

Any two or more persons can get together and form a **partnership.** Partnerships fall into two categories: (1) general partnerships and (2) limited partnerships.

In a *general partnership* all partners agree to provide some fraction of the work and cash and to share the profits and losses. Each partner is liable for the debts of the partnership. A partnership agreement specifies the nature of the arrangement. The partnership agreement may be an oral agreement or a formal document setting forth the understanding.

Limited partnerships permit the liability of some of the partners to be limited to the amount of cash each has contributed to the partnership. Limited partnerships usually require that (1) at least one partner be a general partner and (2) the limited partners do not participate in managing the business. Here are some things that are important when considering a partnership:

1. Partnerships are usually inexpensive and easy to form. Written documents are required in complicated arrangements, including general and limited partnerships. Business licenses and filing fees may be necessary.
2. General partners have unlimited liability for all debts. The liability of limited partners is usually limited to the contribution each has made to the partnership. If one general partner is unable to meet his or her commitment, the shortfall must be made up by the other general partners.
3. The general partnership is terminated when a general partner dies or withdraws (but this is not so for a limited partner). It is difficult for a partnership to transfer ownership without dissolving. Usually, all general partners must agree. However, limited partners may sell their interest in a business.
4. It is difficult for a partnership to raise large amounts of cash. Equity contributions are usually limited to a partner's ability and desire to contribute to the partnership. Many companies, such as Apple Computer, start life as a proprietorship or partnership, but at some point they choose to convert to corporate form.
5. Income from a partnership is taxed as personal income to the partners.
6. Management control resides with the general partners. Usually a majority vote is required on important matters, such as the amount of profit to be retained in the business.

It is very difficult for large business organizations to exist as sole proprietorships or partnerships. The main advantage to a sole proprietorship or partnership is the cost of getting started. Afterward, the disadvantages, which may become severe, are (1) unlimited liability, (2) limited life of the enterprise, and (3) difficulty of transferring ownership. These three disadvantages lead to (4) the difficulty of raising cash.

The Corporation

Of the many forms of business enterprises, the **corporation** is by far the most important. It is a distinct legal entity. As such, a corporation can have a name and enjoy many of the legal powers of natural persons. For example, corporations can acquire and exchange property. Corporations can enter into contracts and may sue and be sued. For jurisdictional purposes, the corporation is a citizen of its state of incorporation. (It cannot vote, however.)

Starting a corporation is more complicated than starting a proprietorship or partnership. The incorporators must prepare articles of incorporation and a set of bylaws. The articles of incorporation must include the following:

1. Name of the corporation.
2. Intended life of the corporation (it may be forever).
3. Business purpose.
4. Number of shares of stock that the corporation is authorized to issue, with a statement of limitations and rights of different classes of shares.

5. Nature of the rights granted to shareholders.

6. Number of members of the initial board of directors.

The bylaws are the rules to be used by the corporation to regulate its own existence, and they concern its shareholders, directors, and officers. Bylaws range from the briefest possible statement of rules for the corporation's management to hundreds of pages of text.

In its simplest form, the corporation comprises three sets of distinct interests: the shareholders (the owners), the directors, and the corporation officers (the top management). Traditionally, the shareholders control the corporation's direction, policies, and activities. The shareholders elect a board of directors, who in turn selects top management. Members of top management serve as corporate officers and manage the operation of the corporation in the best interest of the shareholders. In closely held corporations with few shareholders, there may be a large overlap among the shareholders, the directors, and the top management. However, in larger corporations the shareholders, directors, and the top management are likely to be distinct groups.

The potential separation of ownership from management gives the corporation several advantages over proprietorships and partnerships:

1. Because ownership in a corporation is represented by shares of stock, ownership can be readily transferred to new owners. Because the corporation exists independently of those who own its shares, there is no limit to the transferability of shares as there is in partnerships.

2. The corporation has unlimited life. Because the corporation is separate from its owners, the death or withdrawal of an owner does not affect its legal existence. The corporation can continue on after the original owners have withdrawn.

3. The shareholders' liability is limited to the amount invested in the ownership shares. For example, if a shareholder purchased $1,000 in shares of a corporation, the potential loss would be $1,000. In a partnership, a general partner with a $1,000 contribution could lose the $1,000 plus any other indebtedness of the partnership.

Limited liability, ease of ownership transfer, and perpetual succession are the major advantages of the corporation form of business organization. These give the corporation an enhanced ability to raise cash.

There is, however, one great disadvantage to incorporation. The federal government taxes corporate income. This tax is in addition to the personal income tax that shareholders pay on dividend income they receive. This is double taxation for shareholders when compared to taxation on proprietorships and partnerships.

CASE STUDY

Making the Decision to Become a Corporation: The Case of PLM International, Inc.*

In 1972, several entrepreneurs agreed to start a company they called PLM (Professional Lease Management, Inc.). Their idea was to sponsor, syndicate, and manage public and private limited partnerships with the purpose of acquiring and leasing transportation equipment. They created an operating subsidiary called FSI (Financial Services, Inc.) to be the general partner of each of the partnerships. PLM had limited success in its early years, but during the period 1981 to 1986 more than

*The S—4 Registration Statement, PLM International, Inc., filed with the Securities and Exchange Commission, Washington, D.C., August 1987, gives further details.

27 public partnerships were formed. Each partnership was set up to acquire and lease transportation equipment, such as aircraft, tractors and trailers, cargo containers, and railcars, to transportation companies.

Until the Tax Reform Act of 1986, PLM enjoyed considerable success with its partnerships. It became one of the largest equipment-leasing firms in the United States. The partnerships appealed to high-tax-bracket individuals because unlike corporations, partnerships are not taxed. The partnerships were set up to be self-liquidating (i.e., all excess cash flow was to be distributed to the partners), and no reinvestment could take place. No ready market for the partnership units existed, and each partnership invested in a narrow class of transportation equipment. PLM's success depended on creating tax-sheltered cash flow from accelerated depreciation and investment tax credits. However, the 1986 Tax Reform Act had a devastating impact on tax-sheltered limited partnerships. The act substantially flattened personal tax rates, eliminated the investment tax credit, shortened depreciation schedules, and established an alternative minimum tax rate. The act caused PLM to think about different types of equipment-leasing organizational forms. What was needed was an organization form that could take advantage of potential growth and diversification opportunities and that wasn't based entirely upon tax sheltering.

In 1987 PLM, with the advice and assistance of the now-bankrupt Drexel Burnham Lambert investment banking firm, terminated its partnerships and converted consenting partnerships to a new umbrella corporation called PLM International. After much legal maneuvering, PLM International publicly announced that a majority of the partnerships had consented to the consolidation and incorporation. (A majority vote was needed for voluntary termination and some partnerships decided not to incorporate.) On February 2, 1988, PLM International's common stock began trading

A Comparison of Partnership and Corporations

	Corporation	Partnership
Liquidity and marketability	Shares can be exchanged without termination of the corporation. Common stock can be listed on stock exchange.	Units are subject to substantial restrictions on transferability. There is usually no established trading market for partnership units.
Voting rights	Usually each share of common stock entitles the holder to one vote per share on matters requiring a vote and on the election of the directors. Directors determine top management.	Some voting rights by limited partners. However, general partner has exclusive control and management of operations.
Taxation	Corporations have double taxation: Corporate income is taxable, and dividends to shareholders are also taxable.	Partnerships are not taxable. Partners pay taxes on distributed shares of partnership.
Reinvestment and dividend payout	Corporations have broad latitude on dividend payout decisions.	Partnerships are generally prohibited from reinvesting partnership cash flow. All net cash flow is distributed to partners.
Liability	Shareholders are not personally liable for obligations of the corporation.	Limited partners are not liable for obligations of partnerships. General partners may have unlimited liability.
Continuity of existence	Corporations have perpetual life.	Partnerships have limited life.

on the American Stock Exchange (AMEX) at about $8 per share. On February 6, 2002, MILPI Acquisition Corp. acquired PLM International for a price of 3.46 per share of stock. PLM International ceased to be a publicly traded corporation.

The decision to become a corporation is complicated, and there are several pros and cons. PLM International cited several basic reasons to support the consolidation and incorporation of its transportation-equipment–leasing activities.

- Enhanced access to equity and debt capital for future growth.
- The possibility of reinvestment for future profit opportunities.
- Better liquidity for investors through common stock listing on AMEX.

These are all good reasons for incorporating, and they provided potential benefits to the new shareholders of PLM International that may have outweighed the disadvantages of double taxation that came from incorporating. However, not all the PLM partnerships wanted to convert to the corporation. Sometimes it is not easy to determine whether a partnership or a corporation is the best organizational form. Corporate income is taxable at the personal and corporation levels. Because of this double taxation, firms having the most to gain from incorporation share the following characteristics:

- Low taxable income.
- Low marginal corporate tax rates.
- Low marginal personal tax rates among potential shareholders.

In addition, firms with high rates of reinvestment relative to current income are good candidates for the corporate form because corporations can more easily retain profits for reinvestment than partnerships. Also, it is easier for corporations to sell shares of stock on public stock markets to finance possible investment opportunities.

Concept Questions	1. **Define a proprietorship, a partnership, and a corporation.**
	2. **What are the advantages of the corporate form of business organization?**

1.4 Goals of the Corporate Firm

What is the primary goal of the corporation? The traditional answer is that managers in a corporation make decisions for the stockholders because the stockholders own and control the corporation. If so, the goal of the corporation is to add value for the stockholders. This goal is a little vague and so we will try to come up with a precise formulation. It is also impossible to give a definitive answer to this important question because the corporation is an artificial being, not a natural person. It exists in the "contemplation of the law."[3]

It is necessary to precisely identify who controls the corporation. We shall consider the **set-of-contracts viewpoint.** This viewpoint suggests the corporate firm will attempt to maximize the shareholders' wealth by taking actions that increase the current value per share of existing stock of the firm.

Agency Costs and the Set-of-Contracts Perspective

The set-of-contracts theory of the firm states that the firm can be viewed as a set of contracts.[4] One of the contract claims is a residual claim (equity) on the firm's assets and cash

---

[3]These are the words of Chief Justice John Marshall from *The Trustees of Dartmouth College* v. *Woodward,* 4, Wheaton 636 (1819).

[4]M. C. Jensen and W. Meckling, "Theory of the Firm: Managerial Behavior, Agency Costs and Ownership Structure," *Journal of Financial Economics* 3 (1976).

flows. The equity contract can be defined as a principal-agent relationship. The members of the management team are the agents, and the equity investors (shareholders) are the principals. It is assumed that the managers and the shareholders, if left alone, will each attempt to act in his or her own self-interest.

The shareholders, however, can discourage the managers from diverging from the shareholders' interests by devising appropriate incentives for managers and then monitoring their behavior. Doing so, unfortunately, is complicated and costly. The cost of resolving the conflicts of interest between managers and shareholders are special types of costs called *agency costs*. These costs are defined as the sum of (1) the monitoring costs of the shareholders and (2) the costs of implementing control devices. It can be expected that contracts will be devised that will provide the managers with appropriate incentives to maximize the shareholders' wealth. Thus, the set-of-contracts theory suggests that managers in the corporate firm will usually act in the best interest of shareholders. However, agency problems can never be perfectly solved and, as a consequence, shareholders may experience residual losses. *Residual losses* are the lost wealth of the shareholders due to divergent behavior of the managers.

Managerial Goals

Managerial goals may be different from those of shareholders. What goals will managers maximize if they are left to pursue their own rather than shareholders' goals?

Williamson proposes the notion of *expense preference*.[5] He argues that managers obtain value from certain kinds of expenses. In particular, company cars, office furniture, office location, and funds for discretionary investment have value to managers beyond that which comes from their productivity.

Donaldson conducted a series of interviews with the chief executives of several large companies.[6] He concluded that managers are influenced by two basic motivations:

1. *Survival.* Organizational survival means that management will always try to command sufficient resources to avoid the firm's going out of business.

2. *Independence and self-sufficiency.* This is the freedom to make decisions without encountering external parties or depending on outside financial markets. The Donaldson interviews suggested that managers do not like to issue new shares of stock. Instead, they like to be able to rely on internally generated cash flow.

These motivations lead to what Donaldson concludes is the basic financial objective of managers: the maximization of corporate wealth. Corporate wealth is that wealth over which management has effective control; it is closely associated with corporate growth and corporate size. Corporate wealth is not necessarily shareholder wealth. Corporate wealth tends to lead to increased growth by providing funds for growth and limiting the extent to which new equity is raised. Increased growth and size are not necessarily the same thing as increased shareholder wealth.

Separation of Ownership and Control

Some people argue that shareholders do not completely control the corporation. They argue that shareholder ownership is too diffuse and fragmented for effective control of management.[7] A striking feature of the modern large corporation is the diffusion of ownership

---

[5] O. Williamson, "Managerial Discretion and Business Behavior," *American Economic Review* 53 (1963).

[6] G. Donaldson, *Managing Corporate Wealth: The Operations of a Comprehensive Financial Goals System* (New York: Praeger Publishers, 1984).

[7] Work by Gerald T. Garvey and Peter L. Swan, "The Economics of Corporate Governance: Beyond the Marshallian Firm," *Journal of Corporate Finance* 1 (1994), surveys literature on the stated assumption of shareholder maximization.

TABLE 1.1	Company	Market Value* (in $ billions)	Shares Outstanding (in millions)	Number of Shareholders
Some of the World's Largest Industrial Corporations, 2003	Microsoft	$266.0	10715	92,130
	General Electric	255.6	3714	534,000
	Pfizer	179.4	4138	105,000
	IBM	136.4	1875	616,000
	Merck	114.1	2968	269,600
	Intel	112.4	3555	203,000
	Coca-Cola	98.9	3464	366,000
	Toyota	80.4	1802	100,000

*Market price multiplied by shares outstanding.

SOURCES: *Value Line, Business Week,* and *Standard & Poor's Security Owners Stock Guide.*

among thousands of investors. For example, Table 1.1 shows that approximately 616,000 persons and institutions own shares of IBM stock.

One of the most important advantages of the corporate form of business organization is that it allows ownership of shares to be transferred. The resulting diffuse ownership, however, brings with it the separation of ownership and control of the large corporation. The possible separation of ownership and control raises an important question: Who controls the firm?

Do Shareholders Control Managerial Behavior?

The claim that managers can ignore the interests of shareholders is deduced from the fact that ownership in large corporations is widely dispersed. As a consequence, it is often claimed that individual shareholders cannot control management. There is some merit in this argument, but it is too simplistic.

When a conflict of interest exists between management and shareholders, who wins? Does management or the shareholders control the firm? There is no doubt that ownership in large corporations is diffuse when compared to the closely held corporation. However, several control devices used by shareholders bond management to the self-interest of shareholders:

1. Shareholders determine the membership of the board of directors by voting. Thus, shareholders control the directors, who in turn select the management team.

2. Contracts with management and arrangements for compensation, such as stock option plans, can be made so that management has an incentive to pursue the goal of the shareholders. Another device is called *performance shares.* These are shares of stock given to managers on the basis of performance as measured by earnings per share and similar criteria.

3. If the price of a firm's stock drops too low because of poor management, the firm may be acquired by another group of shareholders, by another firm, or by an individual. This is called a *takeover.* In a takeover, the top management of the acquired firm may find themselves out of a job. This puts pressure on the management to make decisions in the stockholders' interests. Fear of a takeover gives managers an incentive to take actions that will maximize stock prices.

4. Competition in the managerial labor market may force managers to perform in the best interest of stockholders. Otherwise they will be replaced. Firms willing to pay the most will lure good managers. These are likely to be firms that compensate managers based on the value they create.

The available evidence and theory are consistent with the ideas of shareholder control and shareholder value maximization. Indeed, our emphasis will be on how the corporate firm can maximize shareholder value. However, there can be no doubt that at times corporations pursue managerial goals at the expense of shareholders. There is also evidence that the diverse claims of customers, vendors, and employees must frequently be considered in the goals of the corporation.

Concept
Questions

1. What are the two types of agency costs?
2. How are managers bonded to shareholders?
3. Can you recall some managerial goals?
4. What is the set-of-contracts perspective?

1.5 Financial Markets

As indicated in Section 1.1, firms offer two basic types of securities to investors. *Debt securities* are contractual obligations to repay corporate borrowing. *Equity securities* are shares of common stock and preferred stock that represent noncontractual claims to the residual cash flow of the firm. Issues of debt and stock that are publicly sold by the firm are then traded on the financial markets.

The financial markets are composed of the **money markets** and the **capital markets.** Money markets are the markets for debt securities that will pay off in the short term (usually less than one year). Capital markets are the markets for long-term debt (with a maturity at over one year) and for equity shares.

The term *money market* applies to a group of loosely connected markets. They are dealer markets. Dealers are firms that make continuous quotations of prices for which they stand ready to buy and sell money-market instruments for their own inventory and at their own risk. Thus, the dealer is a principal in most transactions. This is different from a stockbroker acting as an agent for a customer in buying or selling common stock on most stock exchanges; an agent does not actually acquire the securities.

At the core of the money markets are the money-market banks (these are large banks mostly in New York), more than 30 government securities dealers (some of which are the large banks), a dozen or so commercial-paper dealers, and a large number of money brokers. Money brokers specialize in finding short-term money for borrowers and placing money for lenders. The financial markets can be classified further as the *primary market* and the *secondary markets.*

The Primary Market: New Issues

The primary market is used when governments and corporations initially sell securities. Corporations engage in two types of primary-market sales of debt and equity: public offerings and private placements.

Most publicly offered corporate debt and equity come to the market underwritten by a syndicate of investment banking firms. The *underwriting* syndicate buys the new securities from the firm for the syndicate's own account and resells them at a higher price. Publicly issued debt and equity must be registered with the Securities and Exchange Commission. *Registration* requires the corporation to disclose all of the material information in a registration statement.

The legal, accounting, and other costs of preparing the registration statement are not negligible. In part to avoid these costs, privately placed debt and equity are sold on the basis of private negotiations to large financial institutions, such as insurance companies and mutual funds. Private placements are not registered with the Securities and Exchange Commission.

Secondary Markets

After debt and equity securities are originally sold, they are traded in the secondary markets. There are two kinds of secondary markets: the *auction markets* and the *dealer markets*.

The equity securities of most large U.S. firms trade in organized auction markets, such as the New York Stock Exchange, the American Stock Exchange, and regional exchanges, such as the Midwest Stock Exchange. The New York Stock Exchange (NYSE) is the most important auction exchange. It usually accounts for more than 85 percent of all shares traded in U.S. auction exchanges. Bond trading on auction exchanges is inconsequential.

Most debt securities are traded in dealer markets. The many bond dealers communicate with one another by telecommunications equipment—wires, computers, and telephones. Investors get in touch with dealers when they want to buy or sell, and can negotiate a deal. Some stocks are traded in the dealer markets. When they are, it is referred to as the *over-the-counter (OTC) market*.

In February 1971, the National Association of Securities Dealers made available to dealers and brokers in the OTC market an automated quotation system called the National Association of Securities Dealers Automated Quotation (NASDAQ) system. The market value of shares of OTC stocks in the NASDAQ system at the end of 1998 was about 25 percent of the market value of the shares on the NYSE.

Exchange Trading of Listed Stocks

Auction markets are different from dealer markets in two ways. First, trading in a given auction exchange takes place at a single site on the floor of the exchange. Second, transaction prices of shares traded on auction exchanges are communicated almost immediately to the public by computer and other devices.

The NYSE is one of the preeminent securities exchanges in the world. All transactions in stocks listed on the NYSE occur at a particular place on the floor of the exchange called a *post*. At the heart of the market is the specialist. Specialists are members of the NYSE who *make a market* in designated stocks. Specialists have an obligation to offer to buy and sell shares of their assigned NYSE stocks. It is believed that this makes the market liquid because the specialist assumes the role of a buyer for investors if they wish to sell and a seller if they wish to buy.

Listing

Firms that want their equity shares to be traded on the NYSE must apply for listing. To be listed initially on the NYSE a company is expected to satisfy certain minimum requirements. Some of these for U.S. companies are as follows:

1. Demonstrated earning power of either $2.5 million before taxes for the most recent year and $2 million before taxes for each of the preceding two years, *or* an aggregate for the last three years of $6.5 million together with a minimum in the most recent year of $4.5 million (all years must be profitable).
2. Net tangible assets equal to at least $40 million.
3. A market value for publicly held shares of $40 million.
4. A total of at least 1.1 million publicly held shares.
5. A total of at least 2,000 holders of 100 shares of stock or more.

The listing requirements for non–U.S. companies are somewhat more stringent. Table 1.2 gives the market value of NYSE-listed stocks and bonds.

TABLE 1.2	End-of-Year	Number of Companies	Market Value ($ millions)
Market Value of NYSE-Listed Securities	NYSE-listed stocks*		
	2001	2798	11,713,707
	2000	2862	12,372,304
	1999	3025	12,296,057
	1998	3114	10,864,472
	NYSE-listed bonds†		
	2001	369	1,653,549
	2000	392	2,124,789
	1999	416	2,401,605
	1998	474	2,554,122

*Includes preferred stock and common stock.

†Includes government issues.

SOURCE: Data from the *New York Stock Exchange Fact Book 2001*, published by the New York Stock Exchange. In the case of bonds, in some instances we report the face value.

Concept Questions

1. **Distinguish between money markets and capital markets.**
2. **What is listing?**
3. **What is the difference between a primary market and a secondary market?**

1.6 OUTLINE OF THE TEXT

Now that we've taken the quick tour through all of corporate finance, we can take a closer look at this book. The book is divided into eight parts. The long-term investment decision is covered first. Financing decisions and working capital are covered next. Finally a series of special topics are covered. Here are the eight parts:

Part I	Overview
Part II	Value and Capital Budgeting
Part III	Risk
Part IV	Capital Structure and Dividend Policy
Part V	Long-Term Financing
Part VI	Options, Futures, and Corporate Finance
Part VII	Short-Term Finance
Part VIII	Special Topics

Part II describes how investment opportunities are valued in financial markets. This part contains basic theory. Because finance is a subject that builds understanding from the ground up, the material is very important. The most important concept in Part II is *net present value*. We develop the net present value rule into a tool for valuing investment alternatives. We discuss general formulas and apply them to a variety of different financial instruments.

Part III introduces basic measures of risk. The capital-asset pricing model (CAPM) and the arbitrage pricing theory (APT) are used to devise methods for incorporating risk in valuation. As part of this discussion, we describe the famous beta coefficient. Finally, we use the above pricing models to handle capital budgeting under risk.

Part IV examines two interrelated topics: capital structure and dividend policy. Capital structure is the extent to which the firm relies on debt. It cannot be separated from the amount of cash dividends the firm decides to pay out to its equity shareholders.

Part V concerns long-term financing. We describe the securities that corporations issue to raise cash, as well as the mechanics of offering securities for a public sale. Here we discuss call provisions, warrants, convertibles, and leasing.

Part VI discusses special contractual arrangements called Options.

Part VII is devoted to financial planning and short-term finance. The first chapter describes financial planning. Next we focus on managing the firm's current assets and current liabilities. We describe aspects of the firm's short-term financial management. Separate chapters on cash management and on credit management are included.

Part VIII covers two important special topics: mergers and international corporate finance.

KEY TERMS

capital budgeting, *4*	money markets, *17*
capital markets, *17*	net working capital, *4*
capital structure, *4*	partnership, *10*
contingent claims, *10*	set-of-contracts viewpoint, *14*
corporation, *11*	sole proprietorship, *10*

SUGGESTED READINGS

Evidence is provided on the tax factor in choosing to incorporate in:

Mackie-Mason, J. K., and R. H. Gordon. "How Much Do Taxes Discourage Incorporation?" *Journal of Finance* (June 1997).

Do American managers pay too little attention to shareholders? This is the question posed in:

Miller, M. "Is American Corporate Governance Fatally Flawed?" *Journal of Applied Corporate Finance* (Winter 1994).

What are the patterns of corporate ownership around the world? This is the question posed by:

La Porta, R., F. Lopez-De-Silanes, and A. Shleifer. "Corporate Ownership Around the World." *Journal of Finance* 54 (1999).

A recent survey of international corporate governance can be found in:

Denis, D. K., and J. S. McConnel. "International Corporate Governance." *Journal of Financial Quantitative Analysis* 38 (March 2003).

Barca, F., and M. Becht. *The Corporate Control of Europe.* Oxford University Press, 2002.

S & P PROBLEM

1.1   On the Market Insight Home Page, follow the "Industry" link. From the pull down menu you can select various industries. Answer the following questions for these industries: Aerospace & Defense, Application Software, Diversified Capital Markets, Homebuilding, Personal Products, Restaurants, and Precious Metals & Minerals.

   a. How many companies are in each industry?

   b. What are the total sales of each industry?

   c. Does the industry with the largest total sales have the largest number of competitors? What does this tell you about the competition in each industry?

Accounting Statements and Cash Flow

EXECUTIVE SUMMARY

Chapter 2 describes the basic accounting statements used for reporting corporate activity. The focus of the chapter is the practical details of cash flow. It will become obvious to you in the next several chapters that knowing how to determine cash flow helps the financial manager make better decisions. Students who have had accounting courses will not find the material new and can think of it as a review with an emphasis on finance. We will discuss cash flow further in later chapters.

2.1 The Balance Sheet

The **balance sheet** is an accountant's snapshot of the firm's accounting value on a particular date, as though the firm stood momentarily still. The balance sheet has two sides: On the left are the *assets* and on the right are the *liabilities* and *stockholders' equity*. The balance sheet states what the firm owns and how it is financed. The accounting definition that underlies the balance sheet and describes the balance is

$$\text{Assets} \equiv \text{Liabilities} + \text{Stockholders' equity}$$

We have put a three-line equality in the balance equation to indicate that it must always hold, by definition. In fact, the stockholders' equity is *defined* to be the difference between the assets and the liabilities of the firm. In principle, equity is what the stockholders would have remaining after the firm discharged its obligations.

Table 2.1 gives the 20X2 and 20X1 balance sheet for the fictitious U.S. Composite Corporation. The assets in the balance sheet are listed in order by the length of time it normally would take an ongoing firm to convert them to cash. The asset side depends on the nature of the business and how management chooses to conduct it. Management must make decisions about cash versus marketable securities, credit versus cash sales, whether to make or buy commodities, whether to lease or purchase items, the types of business in which to engage, and so on. The liabilities and the stockholders' equity are listed in the order in which they must be paid.

The liabilities and stockholders' equity side reflects the types and proportions of financing, which depend on management's choice of capital structure, as between debt and equity and between current debt and long-term debt.

TABLE 2.1	The Balance Sheet of the U.S. Composite Corporation

U.S. COMPOSITE CORPORATION
Balance Sheet
20X2 and 20X1
(in $ millions)

Assets	20X2	20X1	Liabilities (Debt) and Stockholders' Equity	20X2	20X1
Current assets:			Current liabilities:		
Cash and equivalents	$ 140	$ 107	Accounts payable	$ 213	$ 197
Accounts receivable	294	270	Notes payable	50	53
Inventories	269	280	Accrued expenses	223	205
Other	58	50	Total current liabilities	$ 486	$ 455
Total current assets	$ 761	$ 707			
			Long-term liabilities:		
Fixed assets:			Deferred taxes	$ 117	$ 104
Property, plant, and equipment	$1,423	$1,274	Long-term debt[1]	471	458
Less accumulated depreciation	(550)	(460)	Total long-term liabilities	$ 588	$ 562
Net property, plant, and equipment	873	814	Stockholders' equity:		
Intangible assets and others	245	221	Preferred stock	$ 39	$ 39
Total fixed assets	$1,118	$1,035	Common stock ($1 par value)	55	32
			Capital surplus	347	327
			Accumulated retained earnings	390	347
			Less treasury stock[2]	(26)	(20)
			Total equity	$ 805	$ 725
			Total liabilities and		
Total assets	$1,879	$1,742	stockholders' equity[3]	$1,879	$1,742

[1]Long-term debt rose by $471 million − $458 million = $13 million. This is the difference between $86 million new debt and $73 million in retirement of old debt.

[2]Treasury stock rose by $6 million. This reflects the repurchase of $6 million of U.S. Composite's company stock.

[3]U.S. Composite reports $43 million in new equity. The company issued 23 million shares at a price of $1.87. The par value of common stock increased by $23 million, and capital surplus increased by $20 million.

When analyzing a balance sheet, the financial manager should be aware of three concerns: accounting liquidity, debt versus equity, and value versus cost.

Accounting Liquidity

Accounting liquidity refers to the ease and quickness with which assets can be converted to cash. *Current assets* are the most liquid and include cash and those assets that will be turned into cash within a year from the date of the balance sheet. *Accounts receivable* are amounts not yet collected from customers for goods or services sold to them (after adjustment for potential bad debts). *Inventory* is composed of raw materials to be used in production, work in process, and finished goods. *Fixed assets* are the least liquid kind of assets. Tangible fixed assets include property, plant, and equipment. These assets do not convert to cash from normal business activity, and they are not usually used to pay expenses, such as payroll.

Some fixed assets are not tangible. Intangible assets have no physical existence but can be very valuable. Examples of intangible assets are the value of a trademark or the value of a patent. The more liquid a firm's assets, the less likely the firm is to experience problems meeting short-term obligations. Thus, the probability that a firm will avoid financial distress can be linked to the firm's liquidity. Unfortunately, liquid assets frequently have lower rates of return than fixed assets; for example, cash generates no investment income. To the extent a firm invests in liquid assets, it sacrifices an opportunity to invest in more profitable investment vehicles.

Debt versus Equity

Liabilities are obligations of the firm that require a payout of cash within a stipulated time period. Many liabilities involve contractual obligations to repay a stated amount and interest over a period. Thus, liabilities are debts and are frequently associated with nominally fixed cash burdens, called *debt service,* that put the firm in default of a contract if they are not paid. *Stockholders' equity* is a claim against the firm's assets that is residual and not fixed. In general terms, when the firm borrows, it gives the bondholders first claim on the firm's cash flow.[1] Bondholders can sue the firm if the firm defaults on its bond contracts. This may lead the firm to declare itself bankrupt. Stockholders' equity is the residual difference between assets and liabilities:

$$\text{Assets} - \text{Liabilities} \equiv \text{Stockholders' equity}$$

This is the stockholders' share in the firm stated in accounting terms. The accounting value of stockholders' equity increases when retained earnings are added. This occurs when the firm retains part of its earnings instead of paying them out as dividends.

Value versus Cost

The accounting value of a firm's assets is frequently referred to as the *carrying value* or the *book value* of the assets.[2] Under **generally accepted accounting principles (GAAP)**, audited financial statements of firms in the United States carry the assets at cost.[3] Thus the terms *carrying value* and *book value* are unfortunate. They specifically say "value," when in fact the accounting numbers are based on cost. This misleads many readers of financial statements to think that the firm's assets are recorded at true market values. *Market value* is the price at which willing buyers and sellers trade the assets. It would be only a coincidence if accounting value and market value were the same. In fact, management's job is to create a value for the firm that is higher than its cost.

Many people use the balance sheet although the information each may wish to extract is not the same. A banker may look at a balance sheet for evidence of accounting liquidity and working capital. A supplier may also note the size of accounts payable and therefore the general promptness of payments. Many users of financial statements, including managers and investors, want to know the value of the firm, not its cost. This is not found on the balance sheet. In fact, many of the true resources of the firm do not appear on the balance sheet: good management, proprietary assets, favorable economic conditions, and so on.

---

[1]Bondholders are investors in the firm's debt. They are creditors of the firm. In this discussion, the term *bondholder* means the same thing as *creditor.*

[2]Confusion often arises because many financial accounting terms have the same meaning. This presents a problem with jargon for the reader of financial statements. For example, the following terms usually refer to the same thing: assets minus liabilities, net worth, stockholders' equity, owner's equity, and equity capitalization.

[3]Generally, GAAP requires assets to be carried at the lower of cost or market value. In most instances cost is lower than market value. However, in some cases when a fair market value can be readily determined, the assets have their value adjusted to the fair market value.

1. **What is the balance-sheet equation?**
2. **What three things should be kept in mind when looking at a balance sheet?**

2.2 The Income Statement

The **income statement** measures performance over a specific period of time, say, a year. The accounting definition of income is

$$\text{Revenue} - \text{Expenses} \equiv \text{Income}$$

If the balance sheet is like a snapshot, the income statement is like a video recording of what the people did between two snapshots. Table 2.2 gives the income statement for the U.S. Composite Corporation for 20X2.

The income statement usually includes several sections. The operations section reports the firm's revenues and expenses from principal operations. One number of particular importance is earnings before interest and taxes (EBIT), which summarizes earnings before taxes and financing costs. Among other things, the nonoperating section of the income

TABLE 2.2	U.S. COMPOSITE CORPORATION	
The Income Statement of the U.S. Composite Corporation	Income Statement 20X2 (in $ millions)	
Total operating revenues		$2,262
Cost of goods sold		(1,655)
Selling, general, and administrative expenses		(327)
Depreciation		(90)
Operating income		$ 190
Other income		29
Earnings before interest and taxes (EBIT)		$ 219
Interest expense		(49)
Pretax income		$ 170
Taxes		(84)
Current: $ 71		
Deferred: $ 13		
Net income		$ 86
Retained earnings:		$ 43
Dividends:		$ 43

NOTE:
There are 29 million shares outstanding. Earnings per share and dividends per share can be calculated as follows:

$$\text{Earnings per share} = \frac{\text{Net income}}{\text{Total shares outstanding}}$$

$$= \frac{\$86}{29}$$

$$= \$2.97 \text{ per share}$$

$$\text{Dividends per share} = \frac{\text{Dividends}}{\text{Total shares outstanding}}$$

$$= \frac{\$43}{29}$$

$$= \$1.48 \text{ per share}$$

statement includes all financing costs, such as interest expense. Usually a second section reports as a separate item the amount of taxes levied on income. The last item on the income statement is the bottom line, or net income. Net income is frequently expressed per share of common stock, that is, earnings per share.

When analyzing an income statement, the financial manager should keep in mind GAAP, noncash items, time, and costs.

Generally Accepted Accounting Principles

Revenue is recognized on an income statement when the earnings process is virtually completed and an exchange of goods or services has occurred. Therefore, the unrealized appreciation in owning property will not be recognized as income. This provides a device for smoothing income by selling appreciated property at convenient times. For example, if the firm owns a tree farm that has doubled in value, then, in a year when its earnings from other businesses are down, it can raise overall earnings by selling some trees. The matching principle of GAAP dictates that revenues be matched with expenses. Thus, income is reported when it is earned, or accrued, even though no cash flow has necessarily occurred (for example, when goods are sold for credit, sales and profits are reported).

Noncash Items

The economic value of assets is intimately connected to their future incremental cash flows. However, cash flow does not appear on an income statement. There are several **noncash items** that are expenses against revenues, but that do not affect cash flow. The most important of these is *depreciation*. Depreciation reflects the accountant's estimate of the cost of equipment used up in the production process. For example, suppose an asset with a five-year life and no resale value is purchased for $1,000. According to accountants, the $1,000 cost must be expensed over the useful life of the asset. If straight-line depreciation is used, there will be five equal installments and $200 of depreciation expense will be incurred each year. From a finance perspective, the cost of the asset is the actual negative cash flow incurred when the asset is acquired (that is, $1,000, *not* the accountant's smoothed $200-per-year depreciation expense).

Another noncash expense is *deferred taxes*. Deferred taxes result from differences between accounting income and true taxable income.[4] Notice that the accounting tax shown on the income statement for the U.S. Composite Corporation is $84 million. It can be broken down as current taxes and deferred taxes. The current tax portion is actually sent to the tax authorities (for example, the Internal Revenue Service). The deferred tax portion is not. However, the theory is that if taxable income is less than accounting income in the current year, it will be more than accounting income later on. Consequently, the taxes that are not paid today will have to be paid in the future, and they represent a liability of the firm. This shows up on the balance sheet as deferred tax liability. From the cash flow perspective, though, deferred tax is not a cash outflow.

Time and Costs

It is often useful to think of all of future time as having two distinct parts, the *short run* and the *long run*. The short run is that period of time in which certain equipment, resources, and commitments of the firm are fixed; but the time is long enough for the firm to vary its

---

[4]One situation in which taxable income may be lower than accounting income is when the firm uses accelerated depreciation expense procedures for the IRS but uses straight-line procedures allowed by GAAP for reporting purposes.

output by using more labor and raw materials. The short run is not a precise period of time that will be the same for all industries. However, all firms making decisions in the short run have some fixed costs, that is, costs that will not change because of fixed commitments. In real business activity, examples of fixed costs are bond interest, overhead, and property taxes. Costs that are not fixed are variable. Variable costs change as the output of the firm changes; some examples are raw materials and wages for laborers on the production line.

In the long run, all costs are variable.[5] Financial accountants do not distinguish between variable costs and fixed costs. Instead, accounting costs usually fit into a classification that distinguishes product costs from period costs. Product costs are the total production costs incurred during a period—raw materials, direct labor, and manufacturing overhead—and are reported on the income statement as cost of goods sold. Both variable and fixed costs are included in product costs. Period costs are costs that are allocated to a time period; they are called *selling, general, and administrative expenses.* One period cost would be the company president's salary.

Concept Questions

1. What is the income statement equation?
2. What are three things to keep in mind when looking at an income statement?
3. What are noncash expenses?

2.3 Net Working Capital

Net working capital is current assets minus current liabilities. Net working capital is positive when current assets are greater than current liabilities. This means the cash that will become available over the next 12 months will be greater than the cash that must be paid out. The net working capital of the U.S. Composite Corporation is $275 million in 20X2 and $252 million in 20X1:

	Current assets ($ millions)	−	Current liabilities ($ millions)	=	Net working capital ($ millions)
20X2	$761	−	$486	=	$275
20X1	707	−	455	=	252

In addition to investing in fixed assets (i.e., capital spending), a firm can invest in net working capital. This is called the *change in net working capital.* The **change in net working capital** in 20X2 is the difference between the net working capital in 20X2 and 20X1; that is, $275 million − $252 million = $23 million. The change in net working capital is usually positive in a growing firm.

Concept Questions

1. What is net working capital?
2. What is the change in net working capital?

2.4 Financial Cash Flow

Perhaps the most important item that can be extracted from financial statements is the actual **cash flow** of the firm. There is an official accounting statement called the *statement of cash flows.* This statement helps to explain the change in accounting cash and equivalents,

---

[5]When one famous economist was asked about the difference between the long run and the short run, he said, "In the long run we are all dead."

TABLE 2.3	**U.S. COMPOSITE CORPORATION** **Financial Cash Flow** **20X2** **(in $ millions)**	
Financial Cash Flow of the U.S. Composite Corporation	*Cash Flow of the Firm*	
	Operating cash flow	$238
	(Earnings before interest and taxes	
	plus depreciation minus taxes)	
	Capital spending	(173)
	(Acquisitions of fixed assets	
	minus sales of fixed assets)	
	Additions to net working capital	(23)
	Total	$ 42
	Cash Flow to Investors in the Firm	
	Debt	$ 36
	(Interest plus retirement of debt	
	minus long-term debt financing)	
	Equity	6
	(Dividends plus repurchase of	
	equity minus new equity financing)	
	Total	$ 42

which for U.S. Composite is $33 million in 20X2. (See Section 2.5.) Notice in Table 2.1 that cash and equivalents increase from $107 million in 20X1 to $140 million in 20X2. However, we will look at cash flow from a different perspective, the perspective of finance. In finance the value of the firm is its ability to generate financial cash flow. (We will talk more about financial cash flow in Chapter 7.)

The first point we should mention is that cash flow is not the same as net working capital. For example, increasing inventory requires using cash. Because both inventories and cash are current assets, this does not affect net working capital. In this case, an increase in a particular net working capital account, such as inventory, is associated with decreasing cash flow.

Just as we established that the value of a firm's assets is always equal to the value of the liabilities and the value of the equity, the cash flows received from the firm's assets (that is, its operating activities), CF(*A*), must equal the cash flows to the firm's creditors, CF(*B*), and equity investors, CF(*S*):

$$CF(A) \equiv CF(B) + CF(S)$$

The first step in determining cash flows of the firm is to figure out the *cash flow from operations*. As can be seen in Table 2.3, operating cash flow is the cash flow generated by business activities, including sales of goods and services. Operating cash flow reflects tax payments, but not financing, capital spending, or changes in net working capital.

	In $ Millions
Earnings before interest and taxes	$219
Depreciation	90
Current taxes	(71)
Operating cash flow	$238

Another important component of cash flow involves *changes in fixed assets*. For example, when U.S. Composite sold its power systems subsidiary in 20X2 it generated $25 in cash flow. The net change in fixed assets equals sales of fixed assets minus the acquisition of fixed assets. The result is the cash flow used for capital spending:

Acquisition of fixed assets	$198	
Sales of fixed assets	(25)	
Capital spending	$173	($149 + $24 = Increase in property, plant, and equipment + Increase in intangible assets)

Cash flows are also used for making investments in net working capital. In U.S. Composite Corporation in 20X2, *additions to net working capital* are:

Additions to net working capital	$23

Total cash flows generated by the firm's assets are the sum of:

Operating cash flow	$238
Capital spending	(173)
Additions to net working capital	(23)
Total cash flow of the firm	$ 42

The total outgoing cash flow of the firm can be separated into cash flow paid to creditors and cash flow paid to stockholders. The cash flow paid to creditors represents a regrouping of the data in Table 2.3 and an explicit recording of interest expense. Creditors are paid an amount generally referred to as *debt service*. Debt service is interest payments plus repayments of principal (that is, retirement of debt).

An important source of cash flow is from selling new debt. U.S. Composite's long-term debt increased by $13 million (the difference between $86 million in new debt and $73 million in retirement of old debt).[6] Thus, an increase in long-term debt is the net effect of new borrowing and repayment of maturing obligations plus interest expense.

Cash Flow Paid to Creditors (in $ millions)	
Interest	$49
Retirement of debt	73
Debt service	122
Proceeds from long-term debt sales	(86)
Total	$36

Cash flow of the firm also is paid to the stockholders. It is the net effect of paying dividends plus repurchasing outstanding shares of stock and issuing new shares of stock.

---

[6]New debt and the retirement of old debt are usually found in the "notes" to the balance sheet.

Cash Flow to Stockholders (in $ millions)	
Dividends	$43
Repurchase of stock	6
Cash to stockholders	49
Proceeds from new stock issue	(43)
Total	$ 6

Some important observations can be drawn from our discussion of cash flow:

1. Several types of cash flow are relevant to understanding the financial situation of the firm. **Operating cash flow,** defined as earnings before interest and depreciation minus taxes, measures the cash generated from operations not counting capital spending or working capital requirements. It should usually be positive; a firm is in trouble if operating cash flow is negative for a long time because the firm is not generating enough cash to pay operating costs. **Total cash flow of the firm** includes adjustments for capital spending and additions to net working capital. It will frequently be negative. When a firm is growing at a rapid rate, the spending on inventory and fixed assets can be higher than cash flow from sales.[7]

2. Net income is not cash flow. The net income of the U.S. Composite Corporation in 20X2 was $86 million, whereas cash flow was $42 million. The two numbers are not usually the same. In determining the economic and financial condition of a firm, cash flow is more revealing.

Concept
Questions

1. **How is cash flow different from changes in net working capital?**
2. **What is the difference between operating cash flow and total cash flow of the firm?**

2.5 The Accounting Statement of Cash Flows

As previously mentioned, there is an official accounting statement called the statement of cash flows. This statement helps explain the change in accounting cash, which for U.S. Composite is $33 million in 20X2. It is very useful in understanding financial cash flow.

The first step in determining the change in cash is to figure out cash flow from operating activities. This is the cash flow that results from the firm's normal activities producing and selling goods and services. The second step is to make an adjustment for cash flow from investing activities. The final step is to make an adjustment for cash flow from financing activities. Financing activities are the net payments to creditors and owners (excluding interest expense) made during the year.

The three components of the statement of cash flows are determined below.

Cash Flow from Operating Activities

To calculate cash flow from operating activities we start with net income. Net income can be found on the income statement and is equal to $86 million. We now need to add back noncash expenses and adjust for changes in current assets and liabilities (other than cash). The result is cash flow from operating activities.

---

[7]Sometimes financial analysts refer to a firm's **free cash flow.** Free cash flow is the cash flow in excess of that required to fund profitable capital projects. We call free cash flow the *total cash flow* of the firm.

U.S. COMPOSITE CORPORATION
Cash Flow from Operating Activities
20X2
(in $ millions)

Net income	$ 86
Depreciation	90
Deferred taxes	13
Change in assets and liabilities	
Accounts receivable	(24)
Inventories	11
Accounts payable	16
Accrued expense	18
Notes payable	(3)
Other	(8)
Cash flow from operating activities	**$199**

Cash Flow from Investing Activities

Cash flow from investing activities involves changes in capital assets: acquisition of fixed assets and sales of fixed assets (i.e., net capital expenditures). The result for U.S. Composite is below.

U.S. COMPOSITE CORPORATION
Cash Flow from Investing Activities
20X2
(in $ millions)

Acquisition of fixed assets	$(198)
Sales of fixed assets	25
Cash flow from investing activities	**$(173)**

Cash Flow from Financing Activities

Cash flows to and from creditors and owners include changes in equity and debt.

U.S. COMPOSITE CORPORATION
Cash Flow from Financing Activities
20X2
(in $ millions)

Retirement of debt (includes notes)	$(73)
Proceeds from long-term debt sales	86
Dividends	(43)
Repurchase of stock	(6)
Proceeds from new stock issue	43
Cash flow from financing activities	**$ 7**

The statement of cash flows is the addition of cash flows from operations, cash flows from investing activities, and cash flows from financing activities, and is produced in Table 2.4. When we add all the cash flows together, we get the change in cash on the balance sheet of $33 million.

There is a close relationship between the official accounting statement called the statement of cash flows and the total cash flow of the firm used in finance. Going back to the previous section, you should note a slight conceptual problem here. Interest paid should

TABLE 2.4	U.S. COMPOSITE CORPORATION

U.S. COMPOSITE CORPORATION
Statement of Cash Flows
20X2
(in $ millions)

Operations	
Net income	$ 86
Depreciation	90
Deferred taxes	13
Changes in assets and liabilities	
Accounts receivable	(24)
Inventories	11
Accounts payable	16
Accrued expenses	18
Notes payable	(3)
Other	(8)
Total cash flow from operations	**$ 199**
Investing activities	
Acquisition of fixed assets	$(198)
Sales of fixed assets	25
Total cash flow from investing activities	**$(173)**
Financing activities	
Retirement of debt (including notes)	$ (73)
Proceeds of long-term debt	86
Dividends	(43)
Repurchase of stock	(6)
Proceeds from new stock issues	43
Total cash flow from financing activities	**$ 7**
Change in cash (on the balance sheet)	**$ 33**

Statement of
Consolidated Cash
Flows of the
U.S. Composite
Corporation

really go under financing activities, but unfortunately that is not how the accounting is handled. The reason is that interest is deducted as an expense when net income is computed. As a consequence the primary difference between the accounting cash flow and the financial cash flow of the firm (see Table 2.3) is interest expense.

Concept Question

1. How is the statement of cash flows in Table 2.4 different from cash flow of the firm in Table 2.3?

2.6 SUMMARY AND CONCLUSIONS

Besides introducing you to corporate accounting, the purpose of this chapter has been to teach you how to determine cash flow from the accounting statements of a typical company.

1. Cash flow is generated by the firm and paid to creditors and shareholders. It can be classified as:
   a. Cash flow from operations.
   b. Cash flow from changes in fixed assets.
   c. Cash flow from changes in working capital.

2. Calculations of cash flow are not difficult, but they require care and particular attention to detail in properly accounting for noncash expenses such as depreciation and deferred taxes. It is especially important that you do not confuse cash flow with changes in net working capital and net income.

Visit us at www.mhhe.com/rwj

KEY TERMS

balance sheet, *21*
cash flow, *26*
change in net working capital, *26*
free cash flow, *29*
generally accepted accounting
    principles (GAAP), *23*

income statement, *24*
noncash items, *25*
operating cash flow, *29*
total cash flow of the firm, *29*

SUGGESTED READING

There are many excellent textbooks on accounting. The one that we have found helpful is:

Kieso, D. E., J. J. Weygandt, and T. O. Warfield. *Intermediate Accounting,* 10th ed. New York: John Wiley. 2001.

QUESTIONS & PROBLEMS

THE BALANCE SHEET

2.1   Prepare a December 31 balance sheet using the following data:

Cash	$ 4,000
Patents	82,000
Accounts payable	6,000
Accounts receivable	8,000
Taxes payable	2,000
Machinery	34,000
Bonds payable	7,000
Accumulated retained earnings	6,000
Capital surplus	19,000

The par value of the firm's common stock is $100.

2.2   The following table presents the long-term liabilities and stockholders' equity of Information Control Corp. of one year ago.

Long-term debt	$50,000,000
Preferred stock	30,000,000
Common stock	100,000,000
Retained earnings	20,000,000

During the past year, Information Control issued $10 million of new common stock. The firm generated $5 million of net income and paid $3 million of dividends. Construct today's balance sheet reflecting the changes that occurred at Information Control Corp. during the year.

THE INCOME STATEMENT

2.3   Prepare an income statement using the following data.

Sales	$500,000
Cost of goods sold	200,000
Administrative expenses	100,000
Interest expense	50,000

The firm's tax rate is 34 percent.

2.4   The Flying Lion Corporation reported the following data on the income statement of one of its divisions. Flying Lion Corporation has other profitable divisions.

	20X2	20X1
Net sales	$800,000	$500,000
Cost of goods sold	560,000	320,000
Operating expenses	75,000	56,000
Depreciation	300,000	200,000
Tax rate (%)	30	30

a. Prepare an income statement for each year.

b. Determine the operating cash flow during each year.

FINANCIAL CASH FLOW

2.5   What are the differences between accounting profit and cash flow?

2.6   During 1998, the Senbet Discount Tire Company had gross sales of $1 million. The firm's cost of goods sold and selling expenses were $300,000 and $200,000, respectively. These figures do not include depreciation. Senbet also had notes payable of $1 million. These notes carried an interest rate of 10 percent. Depreciation was $100,000. Senbet's tax rate in 1998 was 35 percent.

a. What was Senbet's net operating income?

b. What were the firm's earnings before taxes?

c. What was Senbet's net income?

d. What was Senbet's operating cash flow?

2.7   The Stancil Corporation provided the following current information:

Proceeds from short-term borrowing	$ 6,000
Proceeds from long-term borrowing	20,000
Proceeds from the sale of common stock	1,000
Purchases of fixed assets	1,000
Purchases of inventories	4,000
Payment of dividends	22,000

Determine the cash flow of the Stancil Corporation.

2.8   Ritter Corporation's accountants prepared the following financial statements for year-end 20X2.

RITTER CORPORATION
Income Statement
20X2

Revenue	$400
Expenses	250
Depreciation	50
Net income	$100
Dividends	$ 50

RITTER CORPORATION
Balance Sheets
December 31

	20X2	20X1
Assets		
Cash	$ 25	$ 5
Other current assets	125	95
Net fixed assets	200	100
Total assets	$350	$200
Liabilities and Equity		
Current liabilities	$ 75	$ 50
Long-term debt	75	0
Stockholders' equity	200	150
Total liabilities and equity	$350	$200

a. Explain the change in cash during the year 20X2.

b. Determine the change in net working capital in 20X2.

c. Determine the cash flow of the firm during the year 20X2.

S & P PROBLEMS

STANDARD
&POOR'S

2.9 Enter the ticker symbol "MMM" for 3M (Minnesota Mining and Manufacturing) and follow the "Excel Analytics" link. You will find the annual balance sheets for MMM for each of the past five years. Calculate the change in net working capital for each year. How has net working capital for MMM changed over this entire period?

2.10 Under the "Excel Analytics" link for Amgen, download the annual income statements and balance sheets for Amgen (AMGN). Calculate the operating cash flow, cash flow to creditors, and cash flow to stockholders for the most recent year. After you have completed your calculations, download the annual cash flow report and compare the numbers given to your calculations.

Appendix 2A

Financial Statement Analysis

The objective of this appendix is to show how to rearrange information from financial statements into financial ratios that provide information about five areas of financial performance:

1. *Short-term solvency*—the ability of the firm to meet its short-run obligations.
2. *Activity*—the ability of the firm to control its investment in assets.
3. *Financial leverage*—the extent to which a firm relies on debt financing.
4. *Profitability*—the extent to which a firm is profitable.
5. *Value*—the value of the firm.

Financial statements cannot provide the answers to the preceding five measures of performance. However, management must constantly evaluate how well the firm is doing, and financial statements provide useful information. The financial statements of the U.S. Composite Corporation, which appear in Tables 2.1, 2.2, and 2.3, provide the information for the examples that follow. (Monetary values are given in $ millions.)

Short-Term Solvency

Ratios of short-term solvency measure the ability of the firm to meet recurring financial obligations (that is, to pay its bills). To the extent a firm has sufficient cash flow, it will be able to avoid defaulting on its financial obligations and, thus, avoid experiencing financial distress. Accounting liquidity measures short-term solvency and is often associated with net working capital, the difference between current assets and current liabilities. Recall that current liabilities are debts that are due within one year from the date of the balance sheet. The basic source from which to pay these debts is current assets.

The most widely used measures of accounting liquidity are the current ratio and the quick ratio.

Current Ratio   To find the current ratio, divide current assets by current liabilities. For the U.S. Composite Corporation, the figure for 20X2 is

$$\text{Current ratio} = \frac{\text{Total current assets}}{\text{Total current liabilities}} = \frac{761}{486} = 1.57$$

If a firm is having financial difficulty, it may not be able to pay its bills (accounts payable) on time or it may need to extend its bank credit (notes payable). As a consequence, current liabilities may rise faster than current assets and the current ratio may fall. This may be the first sign of financial trouble. Of course, a firm's current ratio should be calculated over several years for historical perspective, and it should be compared to the current ratios of other firms with similar operating activities.

Quick Ratio   The quick ratio is computed by subtracting inventories from current assets and dividing the difference (called *quick assets*) by current liabilities:

$$\text{Quick ratio} = \frac{\text{Quick assets}}{\text{Total current liabilities}} = \frac{492}{486} = 1.01$$

Quick assets are those current assets that are quickly convertible into cash. Inventories are the least liquid current assets. Many financial analysts believe it is important to determine a firm's ability to pay off current liabilities without relying on the sale of inventories.

Activity

Ratios of activity are constructed to measure how effectively the firm's assets are being managed. The level of a firm's investment in assets depends on many factors. For example, Toys 'Я Us might have a large stock of toys at the peak of the Christmas season; yet that same inventory in January would be undesirable. How can the appropriate level of investment in assets be measured? One logical starting point is to compare assets with sales for the year to arrive at turnover. The idea is to find out how effectively assets are used to generate sales.

Total Asset Turnover   The total asset turnover ratio is determined by dividing total operating revenues for the accounting period by the average of total assets. The total asset turnover ratio for the U.S. Composite Corporation for 20X2 is

$$\text{Total asset turnover}^8 = \frac{\text{Total operating revenues}}{\text{Total assets (average)}} = \frac{2{,}262}{1{,}810.5} = 1.25$$

$$\text{Average total assets} = \frac{1{,}879 + 1{,}742}{2} = 1{,}810.5$$

This ratio is intended to indicate how effectively a firm is using all of its assets. If the asset turnover ratio is high, the firm is presumably using its assets effectively in generating sales. If the ratio is low, the firm is not using its assets to their capacity and must either increase sales or dispose of some of the assets. One problem in interpreting this ratio is that it is maximized by using older assets because their accounting value is lower than newer assets. Also, firms with relatively small investments in fixed assets, such as retail and wholesale trade firms, tend to have high ratios of total asset turnover when compared with firms that require a large investment in fixed assets, such as manufacturing firms.

Receivables Turnover   The ratio of receivables turnover is calculated by dividing sales by average receivables during the accounting period. If the number of days in the year (365) is divided by the receivables turnover ratio, the average collection period can be determined. Net receivables are used for these calculations.[9] The receivables turnover ratio

---

[8]Notice that we use an average of total assets in our calculation of total asset turnover. Many financial analysts use the end of period total asset amount for simplicity. On the other hand it might be more theoretically correct to use (for reasons that will be more apparent in the next few chapters) the end of the previous period total asset amount.

[9]Net receivables are determined after an allowance for potential bad debts.

Visit us at www.mhhe.com/rwj

and average collection period for the U.S. Composite Corporation are

$$\text{Receivables turnover} = \frac{\text{Total operating revenues}}{\text{Receivables (average)}} = \frac{2{,}262}{282} = 8.02$$

$$\text{Average receivables} = \frac{294 + 270}{2} = 282$$

$$\text{Average collection period} = \frac{\text{Days in period}}{\text{Receivables turnover}} = \frac{365}{8.02} = 45.5 \text{ days}$$

The receivables turnover ratio and the average collection period provide some information on the success of the firm in managing its investment in accounts receivable. The actual value of these ratios reflects the firm's credit policy. If a firm has a liberal credit policy, the amount of its receivables will be higher than would otherwise be the case. One common rule of thumb that financial analysts use is that the average collection period of a firm should not exceed the time allowed for payment in the credit terms by more than 10 days.

Inventory Turnover   The ratio of inventory turnover is calculated by dividing the cost of goods sold by average inventory. Because inventory is always stated in terms of historical cost, it must be divided by cost of goods sold instead of sales (sales include a margin for profit and are not commensurate with inventory). The number of days in the year divided by the ratio of inventory turnover yields the ratio of days in inventory. The ratio of days in inventory is the number of days it takes to get goods produced and sold; it is called *shelf life* for retail and wholesale trade firms. The inventory ratios for the U.S. Composite Corporation are

$$\text{Inventory turnover} = \frac{\text{Cost of goods sold}}{\text{Inventory (average)}} = \frac{1{,}655}{274.5} = 6.03$$

$$\text{Average inventory} = \frac{269 + 280}{2} = 274.5$$

$$\text{Days in inventory} = \frac{\text{Days in period}}{\text{Inventory turnover}} = \frac{365}{6.03} = 60.5 \text{ days}$$

The inventory ratios measure how quickly inventory is produced and sold. They are significantly affected by the production technology of goods being manufactured. It takes longer to produce a gas turbine engine than a loaf of bread. The ratios also are affected by the perishability of the finished goods. A large increase in the ratio of days in inventory could suggest an ominously high inventory of unsold finished goods or a change in the firm's product mix to goods with longer production periods.

The method of inventory valuation can materially affect the computed inventory ratios. Thus, financial analysts should be aware of the different inventory valuation methods and how they might affect the ratios.

Financial Leverage

Financial leverage is related to the extent to which a firm relies on debt financing rather than equity. Measures of financial leverage are tools in determining the probability that the firm will default on its debt contracts. The more debt a firm has, the more likely it is that the firm will become unable to fulfill its contractual obligations. In other words, too much debt can lead to a higher probability of insolvency and financial distress.

On the positive side, debt is an important form of financing, and provides a significant tax advantage because interest payments are tax deductible. If a firm uses debt, creditors and equity investors may have conflicts of interest. Creditors may want the firm to invest in less risky ventures than those the equity investors prefer.

Debt Ratio   The debt ratio is calculated by dividing total debt by total assets. We can also use several other ways to express the extent to which a firm uses debt, such as the debt-to-equity ratio and the equity multiplier (that is, total assets divided by equity). The debt ratios for the U.S. Composite Corporation for 20X2 are

$$\text{Debt ratio} = \frac{\text{Total debt}}{\text{Total assets}} = \frac{1,074}{1,879} = 0.57$$

$$\text{Debt-to-equity ratio} = \frac{\text{Total debt}}{\text{Total equity}} = \frac{1,074}{805} = 1.33$$

$$\text{Equity multiplier} = \frac{\text{Total assets}}{\text{Total equity}} = \frac{1,879}{805} = 2.33$$

Debt ratios provide information about protection of creditors from insolvency and the ability of firms to obtain additional financing for potentially attractive investment opportunities. However, debt is carried on the balance sheet simply as the unpaid balance. Consequently, no adjustment is made for the current level of interest rates (which may be higher or lower than when the debt was originally issued) or risk. Thus, the accounting value of debt may differ substantially from its market value. Some forms of debt may not appear on the balance sheet at all, such as pension liabilities or lease obligations.

Interest Coverage   The ratio of interest coverage is calculated by dividing earnings (before interest and taxes) by interest. This ratio emphasizes the ability of the firm to generate enough income to cover interest expense. This ratio for the U.S. Composite Corporation is

$$\text{Interest coverage} = \frac{\text{Earnings before interest and taxes}}{\text{Interest expense}} = \frac{219}{49} = 4.5$$

Interest expense is an obstacle that a firm must surmount if it is to avoid default. The ratio of interest coverage is directly connected to the ability of the firm to pay interest. However, it would probably make sense to add depreciation to income in computing this ratio and to include other financing expenses, such as payments of principal and lease payments.

A large debt burden is a problem only if the firm's cash flow is insufficient to make the required debt service payments. This is related to the uncertainty of future cash flows. Firms with predictable cash flows are frequently said to have more *debt capacity* than firms with high, uncertain cash flows. Therefore, it makes sense to compute the variability of the firm's cash flows. One possible way to do this is to calculate the standard deviation of cash flows relative to the average cash flow.

Profitability

One of the most difficult attributes of a firm to conceptualize and to measure is profitability. In a general sense, accounting profits are the difference between revenues and costs. Unfortunately, there is no completely unambiguous way to know when a firm is profitable. At best, a financial analyst can measure current or past accounting profitability. Many business opportunities, however, involve sacrificing current profits for future profits. For example, all new products require large start-up costs and, as a consequence, produce low initial profits. Thus, current profits can be a poor reflection of true future profitability. Another problem with accounting-based measures of profitability is that they ignore risk. It would be false to conclude that two firms with identical current profits were equally profitable if the risk of one was greater than the other.

The most important conceptual problem with accounting measures of profitability is they do not give us a benchmark for making comparisons. In general, a firm is profitable in the economic sense only if its profitability is greater than investors can achieve on their own in the capital markets.

Profit Margin   Profit margins are computed by dividing profits by total operating revenue and thus they express profits as a percentage of total operating revenue. The most important margin is the net profit margin. The net profit margin for the U.S. Composite Corporation is

$$\text{Net profit margin} = \frac{\text{Net income}}{\text{Total operating revenue}} = \frac{86}{2,262} = 0.038 \ (3.8\%)$$

$$\text{Gross profit margin} = \frac{\text{Earnings before interest and taxes}}{\text{Total operating revenues}} = \frac{219}{2,262} = 0.097 \ (9.7\%)$$

In general, profit margins reflect the firm's ability to produce a product or service at a low cost or a high price. Profit margins are not direct measures of profitability because they are based on total operating revenue, not on the investment made in assets by the firm or the equity investors. Trade firms tend to have low margins and service firms tend to have high margins.

Return on Assets   One common measure of managerial performance is the ratio of income to average total assets, both before tax and after tax. These ratios for the U.S. Composite Corporation for 20X2 are

$$\text{Net return on assets} = \frac{\text{Net income}}{\text{Average total assets}} = \frac{86}{1,810.5} = 0.0475 \ (4.75\%)$$

$$\text{Gross return on assets} = \frac{\text{Earnings before interest and taxes}}{\text{Average total assets}} = \frac{219}{1,810.5} = 0.121 \ (12.1\%)$$

One of the most interesting aspects of return on assets (ROA) is how some financial ratios can be linked together to compute ROA. One implication of this is usually referred to as the *DuPont system of financial control*. This system highlights the fact that ROA can be expressed in terms of the profit margin and asset turnover. The basic components of the system are as follows:

$$\text{ROA} = \text{Profit margin} \times \text{Asset turnover}$$

$$\text{ROA (net)} = \frac{\text{Net income}}{\text{Total operating revenue}} \times \frac{\text{Total operating revenue}}{\text{Average total assets}}$$

$$0.0475 = 0.038 \times 1.25$$

$$\text{ROA (gross)} = \frac{\text{Earnings before interest and taxes}}{\text{Total operating revenue}} \times \frac{\text{Total operating revenue}}{\text{Average total assets}}$$

$$0.121 = 0.097 \times 1.25$$

Firms can increase ROA by increasing profit margins or asset turnover. Of course, competition limits their ability to do so simultaneously. Thus, firms tend to face a trade-off between turnover and margin. In retail trade, for example, mail-order outfits such as L. L. Bean have low margins and high turnover, whereas high-quality jewelry stores such as Tiffany & Co. have high margins and low turnover.

It is often useful to describe financial strategies in terms of margins and turnover. Suppose a firm selling pneumatic equipment is thinking about providing customers with more liberal credit terms. This will probably decrease asset turnover (because receivables would increase more than sales). Thus, the margins will have to go up to keep ROA from falling.

Return on Equity This ratio (ROE) is defined as net income (after interest and taxes) divided by average common stockholders' equity, which for the U.S. Composite Corporation is[10]

$$\text{ROE} = \frac{\text{Net income}}{\text{Average stockholders' equity}} = \frac{86}{765} = 0.112 \ (11.2\%)$$

$$\text{Average stockholders' equity} = \frac{805 + 725}{2} = 765$$

The most important difference between ROA and ROE is due to financial leverage. To see this, consider the following breakdown of ROE:

$$\text{ROE} = \text{Profit margin} \times \text{Asset turnover} \times \text{Equity multiplier}$$

$$= \frac{\text{Net income}}{\text{Total operating revenue}} \times \frac{\text{Total operating revenue}}{\text{Average total assets}} \times \frac{\text{Average total assets}}{\text{Average stockholders' equity}}$$

$$0.112 = 0.038 \times 1.25 \times 2.36$$

From the preceding numbers, it would appear that financial leverage always magnifies ROE. Actually, this occurs only when ROA (gross) is greater than the interest rate on debt.

Payout Ratio The payout ratio is the proportion of net income paid out in cash dividends. For the U.S. Composite Corporation

$$\text{Payout ratio} = \frac{\text{Cash dividends}}{\text{Net income}} = \frac{43}{86} = 0.5$$

The *retention ratio* for the U.S. Composite Corporation is

$$\text{Retention ratio} = \frac{\text{Retained earnings}}{\text{Net income}} = \frac{43}{86} = 0.5$$

$$\text{Retained earnings} = \text{Net income} - \text{Dividends}$$

Market Value Ratios

We can learn many things from a close examination of balance sheets and income statements. However, one very important characteristic of a firm that cannot be found on an accounting statement is its market value.

---

[10]You will notice that as before we are calculating ROE (and ROA) using average stockholders' equity. Some texts use end-of-period stockholders' equity, or $86/805 = .1068$ (10.68%). On the other hand, some financial experts argue it might be more appropriate to use the beginning of the period stockholders' equity in computing ROE, or $86/725 = .1186$ (11.86%).

Visit us at www.mhhe.com/rwj

Market Price   The market price of a share of common stock is the price that buyers and sellers establish when they trade the stock. The market value of the common equity of a firm is the market price of a share of common stock multiplied by the number of shares outstanding.

Sometimes the words "fair market value" are used to describe market prices. *Fair market value* is the amount at which common stock would change hands between a willing buyer and a willing seller, both having knowledge of the relevant facts. Thus, market prices give guesses about the true worth of the assets of a firm. In an efficient stock market, market prices reflect all relevant facts about firms, and thus market prices reveal the true value of the firm's underlying assets.

The market value of IBM is many times greater than that of Apple Computer. This may suggest nothing more than the fact that IBM is a bigger firm than Apple (hardly a surprising revelation). Financial analysts construct ratios to extract information that is independent of a firm's size.

Price-to-Earnings (P/E) Ratio   One way to calculate the P/E ratio is to divide the current market price by the earnings per share of common stock for the latest year. The P/E ratios of some of the largest firms in the United States and Japan are as follows:

P/E Ratios 2002			
United States		**Japan**	
Microsoft	25	Nippon Telegraph & Telephone	—
General Motors	8	Toyota Motor	11
Hewlett Packard	14	Sony	17

As can be seen, some firms have high P/E ratios (Microsoft, for example) and some firms have low ones (General Motors). And some don't have any (Nippon Telegraph & Telephone).[11]

Dividend Yield   The dividend yield is calculated by annualizing the last observed dividend payment of a firm and dividing by the current market price:

$$\text{Dividend yield} = \frac{\text{Dividend per share}}{\text{Market price per share}}$$

The dividend yields for several large firms in the United States and Japan are:

Dividend Yield (%) 2002			
United States		**Japan**	
Microsoft	1.2	Nippon Telegraph & Telephone	1.2
General Motors	5.6	Toyota Motor	1.1
Hewlett Packard	1.9	Sony	0.8

Dividend yields are related to the market's perception of future growth prospects for firms. Firms with high growth prospects will generally have lower dividend yields.

---

[11]Firms will not have a P/E ratio if earnings are negative.

Market-to-Book (M/B) Value and the *Q* Ratio   The market-to-book value ratio is calculated by dividing the market price per share by the book value per share.

The market-to-book ratios of several of the largest firms in the United States and Japan are:

Market-to-Book Ratios 2002			
United States		**Japan**	
Microsoft	4.8	Nippon Telegraph & Telephone	1.2
General Motors	2.1	Toyota Motor	1.3
Hewlett Packard	1.4	Sony	1.2

There is another ratio, called *Tobin's Q*, that is very much like the M/B ratio.[12] Tobin's *Q* ratio divides the market value of all of the firm's debt plus equity by the replacement value of the firm's assets. The *Q* ratios for several firms are:

		Q Ratio[13]
High Qs	Coca-Cola	4.2
	IBM	4.2
Low Qs	National Steel	0.53
	U.S. Steel	0.61

The *Q* ratio differs from the M/B ratio in that the *Q* ratio uses market value of the debt plus equity. It also uses the replacement value of all assets and not the historical cost value.

It should be obvious that if a firm has a *Q* ratio above 1 it has an incentive to invest that is probably greater than a firm with a *Q* ratio below 1. Firms with high *Q* ratios tend to be those firms with attractive investment opportunities or a significant competitive advantage.

SUMMARY AND CONCLUSIONS

Much research indicates that accounting statements provide important information about the value of the firm. Financial analysts and managers learn how to rearrange financial statements to squeeze out the maximum amount of information. In particular, analysts and managers use financial ratios to summarize the firm's liquidity, activity, financial leverage, and profitability. When possible, they also use market values. This appendix describes the most popular financial ratios. You should keep in mind the following points when trying to interpret financial statements:

1. Measures of profitability such as return on equity suffer from several potential deficiencies as indicators of performance. They do not take into account the risk or timing of cash flows.

2. Financial ratios are linked to one another. For example, return on equity is determined from the profit margins, the asset turnover ratio, and the financial leverage.

---

[12]Kee H. Chung and Stephen W. Pruitt, "A Simple Approximation of Tobin's *Q*," *Financial Management* Vol. 23, No. 3 (Autumn 1994).

[13]E. B. Lindberg and S. Ross, "Tobin's *Q* and Industrial Organization," *Journal of Business* 54 (January 1981).

Appendix 2B

U.S. Federal Tax Rates

As of the printing date of this text, the following United States federal tax rules apply.

1. The top marginal rate for corporations is 39 percent (see Table 2B.1). The highest marginal rate for individuals is 35 percent (see Table 2B.2).

2. Short-term realized capital gains and ordinary income are taxed at the corporation's or individual's marginal rate.

3. For individuals, long-term capital gains (in excess of long-term and short-term capital losses) are taxed at a preferential rate. Generally, the top rate for long-term capital gains is 15 percent for capital assets held more than 12 months. For taxpayers in the 10 percent or 15 percent bracket, the rate is 5 percent for capital assets held more than 12 months.

4. Dividends received by a U.S. corporation are 100 percent exempt from taxation if the dividend-paying corporation is fully owned by the other corporation. The exemption is 80 percent if the receiving corporation owns between 20 and 80 percent of the paying corporation. In all other cases, the exemption is 70 percent. Individual taxpayers are taxed at a rate of 15 percent (or 5 percent for taxpayers in the 10 percent or 15 percent tax bracket).

Alternative Minimum Tax (AMT)

Corporations and individuals must pay either their regularly calculated tax or an alternative minimum tax, whichever is higher. The alternative minimum tax is calculated with lower rates (either 26 or 28 percent for individuals or 20 percent for corporations) applied to a

TABLE 2B.1

Corporation Income Tax Rates for 2003

Taxable Income		Tax Rate
Over	Not Over	
$ 0	$ 50,000	15%
50,000	75,000	25
75,000	100,000	34
100,000	335,000	39
335,000	10,000,000	34
10,000,000	15,000,000	35
15,000,000	18,333,333	38
18,333,333	—	35

TABLE 2B.2

Tax Rates for Married Individuals Filing Jointly—2003

Taxable Income	Tax Rate
$0 – 14,000	10%
14,000	15
56,800	25
114,650	28
174,700	33
311,950	35

broader base of income. The broader base is determined by taking taxable income and adding back certain tax preference items, e.g., accelerated depreciation, which reduce regular taxable income.

Tax Operating Loss Carrybacks and Carryforwards

The federal tax law permits corporations to carry back net operating losses two years and to carry forward net operating losses for 20 years.

Financial Planning and Growth

EXECUTIVE SUMMARY

Financial planning establishes guidelines for change in the firm. These guidelines should include (1) an identification of the firm's financial goals, (2) an analysis of the differences between these goals and the current financial status of the firm, and (3) a statement of the actions needed for the firm to achieve its financial goals. In other words, as one member of GM's board was heard to say, "Planning is a process that at best helps the firm avoid stumbling into the future backwards."

The basic elements of financial planning comprise (1) the investment opportunities the firm elects to take advantage of, (2) the amount of debt the firm chooses to employ, and (3) the amount of cash the firm thinks is necessary and appropriate to pay shareholders. These are the financial policies that the firm must decide upon for its growth and profitability.

Almost all firms identify a companywide growth rate as a major component of their financial planning.[1] In one famous case International Business Machines' stated growth goal was simple but typical: to match the growth of the computer industry, which was projected to be 15 percent per year through the end of the 1990s. Though we may have had some doubts about IBM's ability to sustain a 15-percent growth rate, we are certain there are important financial implications of the strategies that IBM will adopt to achieve that rate. There are direct connections between the growth that a company can achieve and its financial policy. One purpose of this chapter is to look at the financial aspects of how fast a firm can grow.

The chapter first describes what is usually meant by financial planning. This enables us to make an important point: Investment and financing decisions frequently interact. The different interactions of investment and financing decisions can be analyzed in the financial statements. We show how financial statements can be used to better understand how growth is achieved.

---

[1] We think that a firm's growth should be a consequence of its trying to achieve maximum shareholder value.

3.1 What Is Financial Planning?

Financial planning formulates the method by which financial goals are to be achieved. It has two dimensions: a time frame and a level of aggregation.

A financial plan is a statement of what is to be done in a future time. The GM board member was right on target when he explained the virtues of financial planning. Most decisions have long lead times, which means they take a long time to implement. In an uncertain world, this requires that decisions be made far in advance of their implementation. If a firm wants to build a factory in 2006, it may need to line up contractors in 2004. It is sometimes useful to think of the future as having a short run and a long run. The short run, in practice, is usually the coming 12 months. Initially, we focus our attention on financial planning over the long run, which is usually taken to be a two-year to five-year period of time.

Financial plans are compiled from the capital-budgeting analyses of each of a firm's projects. In effect, the smaller investment proposals of each operational unit are added up and treated as a big project. This process is called **aggregation.**

Financial plans always entail alternative sets of assumptions. For example, suppose a company has two separate divisions: one for consumer products and one for gas turbine engines. The financial-planning process might require each division to prepare three alternative business plans for the next three years.

1. *A Worst Case.* This plan would require making the worst possible assumptions about the company's products and the state of the economy. It could mean divestiture and liquidation.

2. *A Normal Case.* This plan would require making the most likely assumptions about the company and the economy.

3. *A Best Case.* Each division would be required to work out a case based on the most optimistic assumptions. It could involve new products and expansion.

Because the company is likely to spend a lot of time preparing proposals on different scenarios that will become the basis for the company's financial plan, it seems reasonable to ask what the planning process will accomplish.

1. *Interactions.* The financial plan must make the linkages between investment proposals for the different operating activities of the firm and the financing choices available to the firm explicit. IBM's 15-percent growth target goes hand in hand with its financing program.

2. *Options.* The financial plan provides the opportunity for the firm to work through various investment and financing options. The firm addresses questions of what financing arrangements are optimal and evaluates options of closing plants or marketing new products.

3. *Feasibility.* The different plans must fit into the overall corporate objective of maximizing shareholder wealth.

4. *Avoiding Surprises.* Financial planning should identify what may happen in the future if certain events take place. Thus, one of the purposes of financial planning is to avoid surprises.

Concept
Questions

1. What are the two dimensions of the financial planning process?
2. Why should firms draw up financial plans?

3.2 A Financial-Planning Model: The Ingredients

Just as companies differ in size and products, financial plans are not the same for all companies. However, there are some common elements:

1. **Sales forecast.** All financial plans require a sales forecast. Perfectly accurate sales forecasts are not possible, because sales depend on the uncertain future state of the economy. Firms can get help from businesses specializing in macroeconomic and industry projections. A good sales forecast should be the consequence of having identified all valuable investment opportunities.

2. **Pro forma statements.** The financial plan will have a forecast balance sheet, an income statement, and a sources-and-uses statement. These are called *pro forma statements,* or *pro formas.*

3. **Asset requirements.** The plan will describe projected capital spending. In addition, it will discuss the proposed uses of net working capital.

4. **Financial requirements.** The plan will include a section on financing arrangements. This part of the plan should discuss dividend policy and debt policy. Sometimes firms will expect to raise equity by selling new shares of stock. In this case the plan must consider what kinds of securities must be sold and what methods of issuance are most appropriate.

5. **Plug.** Suppose a financial planner assumes that sales, costs, and net income will rise at a particular rate, g_1. Further suppose that the planner wants assets and liabilities to grow at a different rate, g_2. These two different growth rates may be incompatible unless a third variable is also adjusted. For example, compatibility may only be reached if outstanding stock grows at a different rate, g_3. In this example, we treat the growth in outstanding stock as the *plug* variable. That is, the growth rate in outstanding stock is chosen to make the growth rate in income-statement items consistent with the growth rate in balance-sheet items. Surprisingly, even if the income-statement items grow at the *same* rate as the balance-sheet items, consistency might be achieved only if outstanding stock grows at a different rate.

    Of course, the growth rate in outstanding stock need not be the plug variable. One could have income-statement items grow at g_1, and assets, long-term debt, and outstanding stock grow at g_2. In this case, compatibility between g_1 and g_2 might be achieved by letting short-term debt grow at a rate of g_3.

6. **Economic assumptions.** The plan must explicitly state the economic environment in which the firm expects to reside over the life of the plan. Among the economic assumptions that must be made is the level of interest rates.

EXAMPLE

The Computerfield Corporation's 20X1 financial statements are as follows:

Income Statement 20X1				Balance Sheet Year-End 20X1		
Sales	$1,000		Assets	$500	Debt	$250
Costs	800				Equity	250
Net income	$ 200		Total	$500	Total	$500

In 20X1, Computerfield's profit margin is 20 percent, and it has never paid a dividend. Its debt-equity ratio is 1. This is also the firm's *target* debt-equity ratio. Unless otherwise stated, the financial planners at Computerfield assume that all variables are tied directly to sales and that current relationships are optimal.

Suppose that sales increase by 20 percent from 20X1 to 20X2. Because the planners would then also forecast a 20-percent increase in costs, the pro forma income statement would be

Income Statement 20X2	
Sales	$1,200
Costs	960
Net income	$ 240

The assumption that all variables will grow by 20 percent will enable us to construct the pro forma balance sheet as well:

Balance Sheet Year-End 20X2			
Assets	$600	Debt	$300
		Equity	300
Total	$600	Total	$600

Now we must reconcile these two pro formas. How, for example, can net income be equal to $240 and equity increase by only $50? The answer is that Computerfield must have paid a dividend or repurchased stock equal to $190. In this case dividends are the plug variable.

Suppose Computerfield does not pay a dividend and does not repurchase its own stock. With these assumptions, Computerfield's equity will grow to $490, and debt must be retired to keep total assets equal to $600. In this case the debt-to-equity ratio is the plug variable with $600 in total assets and $490 in equity, debt will have to be $600 − $490, or $110. Since we started with $250 in debt, Computerfield will have to retire $250 − $110, or $140 of debt. The resulting balance sheet would look like this:

Balance Sheet Year-End 20X2			
Asset	$600	Debt	$110
		Equity	490
Total	$600	Total	$600

The thing to notice in our simple example is the way the change in liabilities and equity depends on the firm's financing policy and the firm's dividend policy. The firm ensures growth in assets by having a plan in place to finance such growth.

This example shows the interaction of sales growth and financial policy. The next section focuses on the need for external funds. It identifies a six-step procedure for constructing the pro forma balance sheet.

3.3 The Percentage Sales Method

In the previous section, we described a simple planning model in which every item increased at the same rate as sales. This may be a reasonable assumption for some elements. For others, such as long-term borrowing, it probably is not, because the amount of long-term borrowing is something set by management, and it does not necessarily relate directly to the level of sales.

In this section, we describe an extended version of our simple model. The basic idea is to separate the income statement and balance sheet accounts into two groups, those that do vary directly with sales and those that do not. Given a sales forecast, we will then be able to calculate how much financing the firm will need to support the predicted sales level.

The financial planning model we describe next is based on the **percentage of sales approach.** Our goal here is to develop a quick and practical way of generating pro forma statements. We defer discussion of some "bells and whistles" to a later section.

The Income Statement

We start out with the most recent income statement for the Rosengarten Corporation, as shown in Table 3.1. Notice we have still simplified things by including costs, depreciation, and interest in a single cost figure. We separate these out in a later section.

Rosengarten has projected a 10 percent increase in sales for the coming year, so we are anticipating sales of $20 million × 1.1 = $22 million. To generate a pro forma income statement, we assume that total costs will continue to run at $16.9697 million/$20 million = 84.85% of sales. With this assumption, Rosengarten's pro forma income statement is as shown in Table 3.2. The effect here of assuming that costs are a constant percentage of sales is to assume that the profit margin is constant. To check this, notice that the profit margin was $2 million/$20 million = 10%. In our pro forma, the profit margin is $2.2 million/$22 million = 10%; so it is unchanged.

Next, we need to project the dividend payment. This amount is up to Rosengarten's management. We will assume Rosengarten has a policy of paying out a constant fraction of net income in the form of a cash dividend. For the most recent year, the **dividend payout ratio** was:

$$\text{Dividend payout ratio} = \text{Cash dividends/Net income}$$
$$= \$1 \text{ million}/\$2 \text{ million} = 50\% \qquad (3.1)$$

We can also calculate the ratio of the addition to retained earnings to net income as:

$$\text{Addition to retained earnings/Net income} = \$1 \text{ million}/\$2 \text{ million} = 50\%$$

This ratio is called the **retention ratio** or **plowback ratio,** and it is equal to 1 minus the dividend payout ratio because everything not paid out is retained. Assuming that the payout ratio is constant, the projected dividends and addition to retained earnings will be:

$$\text{Projected dividends paid to shareholders} = \$1.1 \text{ million} \times \tfrac{1}{2} = \$\ \ 550 \text{ thousand}$$

$$\text{Projected addition to retained earnings} = \$1.1 \text{ million} \times \tfrac{1}{2} = \underline{\ \ \ 550} \text{ thousand}$$
$$\underline{\$1,100} \text{ thousand}$$

TABLE 3.1	**ROSENGARTEN CORPORATION** **Income Statement** **($ in thousands)**	
	Sales	$20,000
	Costs	16,969.848
	Taxable income	$ 3,030.3
	Taxes (34%)	1,030.3
	Net income	$ 2,000
	Dividends	$1,000
	Addition to retained earnings	1,000

TABLE 3.2	**ROSENGARTEN CORPORATION** **Pro Forma Income Statement** **($ in thousands)**	
	Sales (projected)	$22,000
	Costs (84.85% of sales)	18,666
	Taxable income	$ 3,334
	Taxes (34%)	1,134
	Net income	$ 2,200

The Balance Sheet

To generate a pro forma balance sheet, we start with the most recent statement, as shown in the table below.

On our balance sheet, we assume that most of the items vary directly with sales. Only common stock does not. For those items that do vary with sales, we express each as a percentage of sales for the year just completed. When an item does not vary directly with sales, we write "constant."

For example, on the asset side, fixed assets are equal to 120 percent of sales ($24 million/$20 million) for the year just ended. We assume this percentage applies to the coming year, so for each $1 increase in sales, fixed assets will rise by $1.20.

Current Balance Sheet ($ in thousands)		Pro Forma Balance Sheet ($ in thousands)	
			Explanation
Current assets	$ 6,000	$ 6,600	30% of sales
Fixed assets	24,000	26,400	120% of sales
Total assets	$30,000	$33,000	150% of sales
Short-term debt	$10,000	$11,000	50% of sales
Long-term debt	6,000	6,600	30% of sales
Common stock	4,000	4,000	Constant
Retained earnings	10,000	11,100	Net income
Total financing	$30,000	$32,700	
		$ 300	Funds needed (the difference between total assets and total financing)

From this information we can determine the pro forma balance sheet, which is on the right-hand side. The change in retained earnings will be

$$\text{Net income} \quad - \quad \text{Dividends} \quad = \text{Change in retained earnings}$$
$$(0.10 \times \$22 \text{ million}) - (0.5 \times 0.10 \times \$22 \text{ million}) = \$1.1 \text{ million}$$

In this example the plug variable is new shares of stock. The company must issue $300,000 of new stock. The equation that can be used to determine if external funds are needed is

External Funds Needed (EFN):

$$\left(\frac{\text{Assets}}{\text{Sales}}\right) \times \Delta\text{Sales} - \frac{\text{Debt}}{\text{Sales}} \times \Delta\text{Sales} - (p \times \text{Projected sales}) \times (1 - d)$$
$$= (1.5 \times \$2 \text{ million}) - (0.80 \times \$2 \text{ million}) - (0.10 \times \$22 \text{ million} \times 0.5)$$
$$= \$1.4 \text{ million} \qquad\qquad\qquad - \$1.1 \text{ million}$$
$$= \$0.3 \text{ million}$$

where

$$\frac{\text{Assets}}{\text{Sales}} = 1.5$$

$$\frac{\text{Debt}}{\text{Sales}} = 0.8$$

$$p = \text{Net profit margin} = 0.10$$
$$d = \text{Dividend payout ratio} = 0.5$$
$$\Delta\text{Sales} = \text{Projected change in sales}$$

The steps in the estimation of the pro forma sheet for the Rosengarten Corporation and the external funds needed (EFN) are as follows:

1. Express balance-sheet items that vary with sales as a percentage of sales.
2. Multiply the percentages determined in step (1) by projected sales to obtain the amount for the future period.
3. Where no percentage applies, simply insert the previous balance-sheet figure in the future period.
4. Compute projected retained earnings as follows:

$$\text{Projected retained earnings} = \text{Present retained earnings}$$
$$+ \text{ Projected net income} - \text{Cash dividends}$$

5. Add the asset accounts to determine projected assets. Next, add the liabilities and equity accounts to determine the total financing; any difference is the *shortfall*. This equals external funds needed (EFN).
6. Use the plug to fill EFN.

Table 3.3 computes EFN for several different growth rates. For low growth rates, Rosengarten will run a surplus, and for high growth rates, it will run a deficit. The "break-even" growth rate is 7.7 percent. Figure 3.1 illustrates the relation between projected sales

TABLE 3.3	Projected Sales Growth	Increase in Assets Required	Addition to Retained Earnings	External Financing Needed (EFN)	Projected Debt-to-Equity Ratio
Projected Sales Growth and EFN for the Rosengarten Corporation	0 %	$ 0	$1,000,000	−$1,000,000	83.6%
	5	1,500,000	1,050,000	−350,000	86.8
	7.7	2,310,000	1,077,000	—	89.2
	10	3,000,000	1,100,000	300,000	91.2
	20	6,000,000	1,200,000	1,600,000	100.0

FIGURE 3.1

Growth and EFN for the Rosengarten Corporation

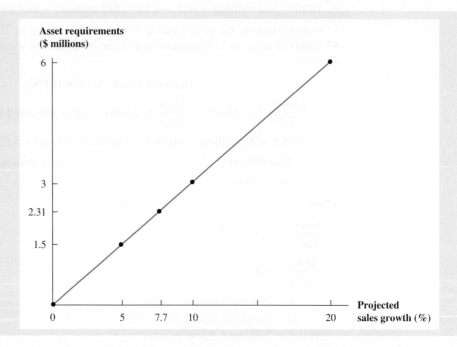

growth and EFN. As can be seen, the need for new assets from projected sales growth grows much faster than the additions to retained earnings plus new debt. Eventually, a deficit is created and a need for external financing becomes evident.

3.4 What Determines Growth?

This section furthers our discussion of a firm's growth and its accounting statements. Firms frequently make growth forecasts an explicit part of financial planning. Donaldson reports on the pervasiveness of stating corporate goals in terms of growth rates.[2] This may seem puzzling in the light of our previous emphasis on maximizing the shareholder's value as the central goal of management. One way to reconcile the difference is to think of growth as an intermediate goal that leads to higher value. Rappaport correctly points out that, in applying the shareholder value approach, growth should not be a goal but must be a consequence of decisions that maximize shareholder value.[3] In fact, if the firm is willing to accept any project just to grow in size, growth will probably make the stockholders worse off.

Donaldson also concludes that most major industrial companies are very reluctant to use external equity as a regular part of their financial planning. To illustrate the linkages between the ability of a firm to grow and its accounting statements when the firm does not issue equity, we can make some planning assumptions.

1. The firm's assets will grow in proportion to its sales.
2. Net income is a constant proportion of its sales.
3. The firm has a given dividend-payout policy and a given debt-equity ratio.
4. The firm will not change the number of outstanding shares of stock.

There is only one growth rate that is consistent with the preceding assumptions. In effect, with these assumptions, growth has been made a plug variable. To see this, recall that a change in assets must always be equal to a change in debt plus a change in equity:

$$
\boxed{\text{Change in assets}} \;=\; \boxed{\text{Change in debt} + \text{Change in equity}}
$$

Now we can write the conditions that ensure this equality and solve for the growth rate that will give it to us.

The variables used in this demonstration are the following:

T = The ratio of total assets to sales

p = The net profit margin on sales

d = The dividend-payout ratio

L = The debt-equity ratio

S_0 = Sales this year

ΔS = The change in sales ($S_1 - S_0 = \Delta S$)

----

[2]G. Donaldson, *Managing Corporation Wealth: The Operations of a Comprehensive Financial Goals System* (New York: Praeger, 1984).

[3]A. Rappaport, *Creating Shareholder Value: The New Standard for Business Performance* (New York: Free Press, 1986).

S_1 = Next year's projected sales

RE = Retained earnings = Net income × Retention ratio = $S_1 \times p \times (1 - d)$

NI = Net income = $S_1 \times p$

If the firm is to increase sales by ΔS during the year, it must increase assets by $T\Delta S$. The firm is assumed not to be able to change the number of shares of stock outstanding, so the equity financing must come from retained earnings. Retained earnings will depend on next year's sales, the payout ratio, and the profit margin. The amount of borrowing will depend on the amount of retained earnings and the debt-equity ratio.

New equity: $S_1 \times p \times (1 - d)$
plus
Borrowing: $[S_1 \times p \times (1 - d)] \times L$
equals
Capital spending: $T\Delta S$

Moving things around a little gives the following:

$$T\Delta S = [S_1 \times p \times (1 - d)] + [S_1 \times p \times (1 - d) \times L]$$

and

$$\frac{\Delta S}{S_0} = \frac{p \times (1 - d) \times (1 + L)}{T - [p \times (1 - d) \times (1 + L)]} = \text{Growth rate in sales} \qquad (3.2)$$

This is the growth-rate equation. Given the profit margin (p), the payout ratio (d), the debt-equity ratio (L), and the asset-requirement ratio (T), the growth rate can be determined. It is the only growth possible with the preset values for the four variables. Higgins has referred to this growth rate as the firm's **sustainable growth rate**.[4]

EXAMPLE

Table 3.4 shows the current income statement, the sources-and-uses-of-funds statement, and the balance sheet for the Hoffman Corporation. Net income for the corporation was 16.5 percent ($1,650/$10,000) of sales revenue. The company paid out 72.4 percent ($1,195/$1,650) of its net income in dividends. The interest rate on debt was 10 percent, and the long-term debt was 50 percent ($5,000/$10,000) of assets. (Notice that, for simplicity, we use the single term *net working capital*, in Table 3.4, instead of separating current assets from current liabilities.) Hoffman's assets grew at the rate of 10 percent ($910/$9,090). In addition, sales grew at 10 percent, though this increase is not shown in Table 3.4.

The cash flow generated by Hoffman was enough not only to pay a dividend but also to increase net working capital and fixed assets by $455 each. The company did not issue any shares of stock during the year. Its debt-equity ratio and dividend-payout ratio remained constant throughout the year.

The sustainable growth rate for the Hoffman Corporation is 10 percent, or[5]

$$\frac{0.165 \times 0.276 \times 2}{1 - (0.165 \times 0.276 \times 2)} = 0.1$$

However, suppose its desired growth rate was to be 20 percent. It is possible for Hoffman's desired growth to exceed its sustainable growth because Hoffman is able to issue new shares of stock. A

---

[4] R. C. Higgins, "Sustainable Growth under Inflation," *Financial Management* (Autumn 1981). The definition of sustainable growth was popularized by the Boston Consulting Group and others.

[5] This expression is exactly equal to the rate of return on equity (ROE) multiplied by the retention rate (RR): ROE × RR if by ROE we mean net income this year divided by equity *last year*, i.e., $1,650/$4,545 = 36.3%. In this case ROE × RR = 36.3% × 27.6% = 10% = sustainable growth in sales. On the other hand, if by ROE we mean net income this year divided by equity *this year*, i.e., $1,650/$5,000 = 33%, the sustainable growth rate in sales = ROE × RR/1 − (ROE × RR).

TABLE 3.4	THE HOFFMAN CORPORATION

Current Financial Statements: The Hoffman Corporation (in thousands)

THE HOFFMAN CORPORATION
Income Statement

	This Year
Net sales (S)	$10,000
Cost of sales	7,000
Earnings before taxes and interest	3,000
Interest expense	500
Earnings before taxes	2,500
Taxes	850
Net income (NI)	$ 1,650

Sources and Uses of Cash

	This Year
Sources:	
Net income (NI)	$ 1,650
Depreciation	500
Operating cash flow	2,150
Borrowing	455
New stock issue	0
Total sources	$ 2,605
Uses:	
Increase in net working capital	455
Capital spending	955
Dividends	1,195
Total uses	$ 2,605

Balance Sheet

	This Year	Last Year	Change
Assets			
Net working capital	$ 5,000	$4,545	$455
Fixed assets	5,000	4,545	455
Total assets	$10,000	$9,090	$910
Liabilities and Stockholders' Equity			
Debt	$ 5,000	$4,545	$455
Equity	5,000	4,545	455
Total liabilities and stockholders' equity	$10,000	$9,090	$910

firm can do several things to increase its sustainable growth rate as seen from the Hoffman example:

1. Sell new shares of stock.
2. Increase its reliance on debt.
3. Reduce its dividend-payout ratio.
4. Increase profit margins.
5. Decrease its asset-requirement ratio.

Now we can see the use of a financial-planning model to test the feasibility of the planned growth rate. If sales are to grow at a rate higher than the sustainable growth rate, the firm must improve operating performance, increase financial leverage, decrease dividends, or sell new shares. Of course, the planned rates of growth should be the result of a complete maximization of shareholder value-based planning process.

Robert C. Higgins on Sustainable Growth

Most financial officers know intuitively that it takes money to make money. Rapid sales growth requires increased assets in the form of accounts receivable, inventory, and fixed plant, which, in turn, require money to pay for assets. They also know that if their company does not have the money when needed, it can literally "grow broke." The sustainable growth equation states these intuitive truths explicitly.

Sustainable growth is often used by bankers and other external analysts to assess a company's creditworthiness. They are aided in this exercise by several sophisticated computer software packages that provide detailed analyses of the company's past financial performance, including its annual sustainable growth rate.

Bankers use this information in several ways. Quick comparison of a company's actual growth rate to its sustainable rate tells the banker what issues will be at the top of management's financial agenda. If actual growth consistently exceeds sustainable growth, management's problem will be where to get the cash to finance growth. The banker thus can anticipate interest in loan products. Conversely, if sustainable growth consistently exceeds actual, the banker had best be prepared to talk about

investment products, because management's problem will be what to do with all the cash that keeps piling up in the till.

Bankers also find the sustainable growth equation useful for explaining to financially inexperienced small business owners and overly optimistic entrepreneurs that, for the long-run viability of their business, it is necessary to keep growth and profitability in proper balance.

Finally, comparison of actual to sustainable growth rates helps a banker understand why a loan applicant needs money and for how long the need might continue. In one instance, a loan applicant requested $100,000 to pay off several insistent suppliers and promised to repay in a few months when he collected some accounts receivable that were coming due. A sustainable growth analysis revealed that the firm had been growing at four to six times its sustainable growth rate and that this pattern was likely to continue in the foreseeable future. This alerted the banker that impatient suppliers were only a symptom of the much more fundamental disease of overly rapid growth, and that a $100,000 loan would likely prove to be only the down payment on a much larger, multiyear commitment.

Robert C. Higgins is Professor of Finance at the University of Washington. He pioneered the use of sustainable growth as a tool for financial analysis.

Concept Questions

1. When might the goals of growth and value maximization be in conflict, and when would they be aligned?
2. What are the determinants of growth?

3.5 Some Caveats of Financial-Planning Models

Financial-planning models such as sustainable growth suffer from a great deal of criticism. We present two commonly voiced attacks below.

First, financial-planning models do not indicate which financial policies are the best. For example, our model could not tell us whether Hoffman's decision to issue new equity to achieve a higher growth rate raises the shareholder value of the firm.

Second, financial-planning models are too simple. In reality, costs are not always proportional to sales, assets need not be a fixed percentage of sales, and capital-budgeting involves a sequence of decisions over time. These assumptions are generally not incorporated into financial plans.

Financial-planning models are necessary to assist in planning the future investment and financial decisions of the firm. Without some sort of long-term financial plan, the firm may find itself adrift in a sea of change without a rudder for guidance. But, because of the assumptions and the abstractions from reality necessary in the construction of the financial plan, we also think that they should carry the label: Let the user beware!

3.6 SUMMARY AND CONCLUSIONS

Financial planning forces the firm to think about and forecast the future. It involves the following:

1. Building a corporate financial model.
2. Describing different scenarios of future development from worst to best cases.
3. Using the models to construct pro forma financial statements.
4. Running the model under different scenarios (conducting sensitivity analysis).
5. Examining the financial implications of ultimate strategic plans.

Corporate financial planning should not become a purely mechanical activity. If it does, it will probably focus on the wrong things. In particular, plans are formulated all too often in terms of a growth target with an explicit linkage to creation of value. We talk about a particular financial planning model called sustainable growth. It is a very simple model. Nonetheless, the alternative to financial planning is stumbling into the future.

KEY TERMS

aggregation, 45
asset requirements, 46
dividend payout ratio, 48
economic assumptions, 46
financial requirements, 46
percentage of sales approach, 47

plug, 46
pro forma statements, 46
retention ratio (plowback ratio), 48
sales forecast, 45
sustainable growth rate, 52

SUGGESTED READINGS

Some aspects of economic growth and stock market returns are covered in:

Ritter, Jay. "Economic Growth—Equity Returns." Unpublished working paper. University of Florida, March 1, 2003.

We also recommend:

Campbell, John K., and Robert Shiller. "Valuation Ratios and the Long Run Stock Market Outlook: An Update." Cowles Foundation Discussion Paper, no. 1295.

Jorion, Phillippe, and William Coetzmann. "Global Stock Markets in the Twentieth Century." *Journal of Finance* (1995).

Owen, Lamont. "Earnings and Expect Returns." *Journal of Finance* 53 (1998).

QUESTIONS & PROBLEMS

FINANCIAL-PLANNING MODELS: THE INGREDIENTS

3.1 After examining patterns from recent years, management found the following regression-estimated relationships between some company balance sheets and income statement accounts and sales.

$$CA = 0.5 \text{ million} + 0.25S$$
$$FA = 1.0 \text{ million} + 0.50S$$
$$CL = 0.1 \text{ million} + 0.10S$$
$$NP = 0.0 \text{ million} + 0.02S$$

where

CA = Current assets
FA = Fixed assets
CL = Current liabilities
NP = Net profit after taxes
S = Sales

Visit us at www.mhhe.com/rwj

The company's sales for last year were $10 million. The year-end balance sheet is reproduced below.

Current assets	$3,000,000	Current liabilities	$1,100,000
Fixed assets	6,000,000	Bonds	2,500,000
		Common stock	2,000,000
		Retained earnings	3,400,000
Total	$9,000,000	Total	$9,000,000

Management further found that the company's sales bear a relationship to GNP. That relationship is

$$S = 0.00001 \times GNP$$

The forecast of GNP for next year is $2.05 trillion. The firm pays out 34 percent of net profits after taxes in dividends.

Create a pro forma balance sheet for this firm.

3.2 Cheryl Colby, the CFO of Charming Florist Ltd., has created the firm's pro forma balance sheet for the next fiscal year. Sales are projected to grow at 10 percent to the level of $330 million. Current assets, fixed assets, short-term debt, and long-term debt are 25 percent, 150 percent, 40 percent, and 45 percent of the total sales, respectively. Charming Florist pays out 40 percent of net income. The value of common stock is constant at $50 million. The profit margin on sales is 12 percent.
   a. Based on Ms. Colby's forecast, how much external fund does Charming Florist need?
   b. Reconstruct the current balance sheet based on the projected figures.
   c. Lay out the firm's pro forma balance sheet for the next fiscal year.

WHAT DETERMINES GROWTH?

3.3 The Stieben Company has determined that the following will be true next year:

   T = Ratio of total assets to sales = 1
   P = Net profit margin on sales = 5%
   d = Dividend-payout ratio = 50%
   L = Debt-equity ratio = 1

   a. What is Stieben's sustainable growth rate in sales?
   b. Can Stieben's actual growth rate in sales be different from its sustainable growth rate? Why or why not?
   c. How can Stieben change its sustainable growth?

3.4 The Optimal Scam Company would like to see its sales grow at 20 percent for the foreseeable future. Its financial statements for the current year are presented below.

Income Statement ($ millions)		Balance Sheet ($ millions)	
Sales	32.00	Current assets	16
Costs	28.97	Fixed assets	16
Gross profit	3.03	Total assets	32
Taxes	1.03		
Net income	2.00	Current debt	10
		Long-term debt	4
Dividends	1.40	Total debt	14
Retained earnings	0.60	Common stock	14
		Ret. earnings	4
		Total liabilities and equity	32

The current financial policy of the Optimal Scam Company includes

Dividend-payout ratio (d) = 70%
Debt-to-equity ratio (L) = 77.78%
Net profit margin (P) = 6.25%
Assets-sales ratio (T) = 1

a. Determine Optimal Scam's need for external funds next year.
b. Construct a pro forma balance sheet for Optimal Scam.
c. Calculate the sustainable growth rate for the Optimal Scam Company.
d. How can Optimal Scam change its financial policy to achieve its growth objective?

3.5 The MBI Company does not want to grow. The company's financial management believes it has no positive NPV projects. The company's operating financial characteristics are

Profit margin = 10%
Assets-sales ratio = 150%
Debt-equity ratio = 100%
Dividend-payout ratio = 50%

a. Calculate the sustainable growth rate for the MBI Company.
b. How can the MBI Company achieve its stated growth goal?

3.6 Throughout this text, you have learned that financial managers should select positive shareholder value projects. How does this project-selection criterion relate to financial-planning models?

3.7 Your firm recently hired a new MBA. She insists that your firm is incorrectly computing its sustainable growth rate. Your firm computes the sustainable growth rate using the following formula:

$$\frac{P \times (1 - d) \times (1 + L)}{T - P \times (1 - d) \times (1 - L)}$$

P = Net profit margin on sales
d = Dividend-payout ratio
L = Debt-equity ratio
T = Ratio of total assets to sales

Your new employee claims that the correct formula is ROE $\times$ (1 − d) where ROE is net profit divided by net worth and d is dividends divided by net profit. Is your new employee correct?

3.8 Atlantic Transportation Co. has a payout ratio of 60 percent, debt-equity ratio of 50 percent, return on equity of 16 percent, and an assets-sales ratio of 175 percent.
a. What is its sustainable growth rate?
b. What must its profit margin be in order to achieve its sustainable growth rate?

SOME CAVEATS OF FINANCIAL-PLANNING MODELS

3.9 What are the shortcomings of financial-planning models that we should be aware of?

S & P PROBLEMS

3.10 Use the annual income statements and balance sheets under the "Excel Analytics" link to calculate the sustainable growth rate for Coca-Cola (KO) each year for the past four years. Is the sustainable growth rate the same every year? What are possible reasons the sustainable growth rate may vary from year to year?

3.11 Extended Stay America (ESA) operates over 450 hotels in the United States. Under the "Financial Highlights" link you can find a five-year growth rate for sales. Using this growth rate and the most recent income statement and balance sheet, compute the external funds needed for ESA next year.

Visit us at www.mhhe.com/rwj

Value and Capital Budgeting

Firms and individuals invest in a large variety of assets. Some are real assets such as machinery and land, and some are financial assets such as stocks and bonds. The object of an investment is to maximize the value of the investment. In the simplest terms, this means to find assets that have more value to the firm than they cost. To do this we need a theory of value. We develop a theory of value in Part II.

Finance is the study of markets and instruments that deal with cash flows over time. In Chapter 4 we extend the concept of net present value to more than one time period. The mathematics of compounding and discounting are presented. In Chapter 5 we apply net present value to bonds and stocks. This is a very important chapter because net present value can be used to determine the value of a wide variety of financial instruments.

Although we have made a strong case for using the NPV rule in Chapter 4, Chapter 6 presents four other rules: the payback rule, the accounting-rate-of-return rule, the internal rate of return (IRR), and the profitability index. Each of these alternatives has some redeeming features, but these qualities aren't sufficient to let any of the alternatives replace the NPV rule.

In Chapter 7 we analyze how to estimate the cash flows required for capital budgeting. We start the chapter with a discussion of the concept of incremental cash flows—the difference between the cash flows for the firm with and without the project. Chapter 8 focuses on assessing the reliability and reasonableness of estimates of NPV. The chapter introduces techniques for dealing with uncertain incremental cash flows in capital budgeting, including break-even analysis, decision trees, sensitivity analysis, and real options.

Net Present Value

EXECUTIVE SUMMARY

We now examine one of the most important concepts in all of corporate finance, the relationship between $1 today and $1 in the future. Consider the following example: A firm is contemplating investing $1 million in a project that is expected to pay out $200,000 per year for nine years. Should the firm accept the project? One might say yes at first glance, since total inflows of $1.8 million (= $200,000 × 9) are greater than $1 million outflow. However, the $1 million is paid out *immediately,* whereas the $200,000 per year will be received in the future. Also, the immediate payment is known with certainty, whereas the later inflows can only be estimated. Thus, we need to know the relationship between a dollar today and a (possibly uncertain) dollar in the future before deciding on the project.

This relationship is called the *time-value-of-money concept.* It is important in such areas as capital budgeting, lease versus buy decisions, accounts receivable analysis, financing arrangements, mergers, and pension funding.

The basics are presented in this chapter. We begin by discussing two fundamental concepts, future value and present value. Next, we treat simplifying formulas such as perpetuities and annuities.

4.1 The One-Period Case

EXAMPLE

Keith Vaughn is trying to sell a piece of raw land in Alaska. Yesterday, he was offered $10,000 for the property. He was about ready to accept the offer when another individual offered him $11,424. However, the second offer was to be paid a year from now. Keith has satisfied himself that both buyers are honest and financially solvent, so he has no fear that the offer he selects will fall through. These two offers are pictured as cash flows in Figure 4.1. Which offer should Mr. Vaughn choose?

Mike Tuttle, Keith's financial advisor, points out that if Keith takes the first offer, he could invest the $10,000 in the bank at an insured rate of 12 percent. At the end of one year, he would have

$$\underbrace{\$10{,}000}_{\substack{\text{Return of} \\ \text{principal}}} + \underbrace{(0.12 \times \$10{,}000)}_{\text{Interest}} = \$10{,}000 \times 1.12 = \$11{,}200$$

Because this is less than the $11,424 Keith could receive from the second offer, Mr. Tuttle recommends that he take the latter. This analysis uses the concept of **future value** or **compound value,** which is the value of a sum after investing over one or more periods. The compound or future value of $10,000 is $11,200.

FIGURE 4.1

Cash Flow for
Mr. Vaughn's Sale

An alternative method employs the concept of **present value.** One can determine present value by asking the following question: How much money must Keith put in the bank today so that he will have $11,424 next year? We can write this algebraically as

$$PV \times 1.12 = \$11,424 \tag{4.1}$$

We want to solve for present value (PV), the amount of money that yields $11,424 if invested at 12 percent today. Solving for PV, we have

$$PV = \frac{\$11,424}{1.12} = \$10,200$$

The formula for PV can be written as

Present Value of Investment:

$$PV = \frac{C_1}{1 + r}$$

where C_1 is cash flow at date 1 and r is the appropriate interest rate. r is the rate of return that Keith Vaughn requires on his land sale. It is sometimes referred to as the *discount rate.*

Present value analysis tells us that a payment of $11,424 to be received next year has a present value of $10,200 today. In other words, at a 12-percent interest rate, Mr. Vaughn could not care less whether you gave him $10,200 today or $11,424 next year. If you gave him $10,200 today, he could put it in the bank and receive $11,424 next year.

Because the second offer has a present value of $10,200, whereas the first offer is for only $10,000, present value analysis also indicates that Mr. Vaughn should take the second offer. In other words, both future value analysis and present value analysis lead to the same decision. As it turns out, present value analysis and future value analysis must always lead to the same decision.

As simple as this example is, it contains the basic principles that we will be working with over the next few chapters. We now use another example to develop the concept of net present value.

EXAMPLE

Lida Jennings, a financial analyst at Kaufman & Broad, a leading real estate firm, is thinking about recommending that Kaufman & Broad invest in a piece of land that costs $85,000. She is certain that next year the land will be worth $91,000, a sure $6,000 gain. Given that the guaranteed interest rate in the bank is 10 percent, should Kaufman & Broad undertake the investment in land? Ms. Jennings' choice is described in Figure 4.2 with the cash flow time chart.

A moment's thought should be all it takes to convince her that this is not an attractive business deal. By investing $85,000 in the land, she will have $91,000 available next year. Suppose, instead, that Kaufman & Broad puts the same $85,000 into the bank. At the interest rate of 10 percent, this $85,000 would grow to

$$(1 + 0.10) \times \$85,000 = \$93,500$$

next year.

FIGURE 4.2

Cash Flows for Land
Investment

It would be foolish to buy the land when investing the same $85,000 in the financial market would produce an extra $2,500 (that is, $93,500 from the bank minus $91,000 from the land investment). This is a future-value calculation.

Alternatively, she could calculate the present value of the sale price next year as

$$\text{Present value} = \frac{\$91,000}{1.10} = \$82,727.27$$

Because the present value of next year's sales price is less than this year's purchase price of $85,000, present-value analysis also indicates that she should not recommend purchasing the property.

Frequently, businesspeople want to determine the exact *cost* or *benefit* of a decision. The decision to buy this year and sell next year can be evaluated as

Net Present Value of Investment:

$$-\$2,273 \;=\; \underset{\substack{\text{Cost of land} \\ \text{today}}}{-\$85,000} \;+\; \underset{\substack{\text{Present value of} \\ \text{next year's sales price}}}{\frac{\$91,000}{1.10}} \tag{4.2}$$

The formula for NPV can be written as

$$\text{NPV} = -\text{Cost} + \text{PV}$$

Equation (4.2) says that the value of the investment is −$2,273, after stating all the benefits and all the costs as of date 0. We say that −$2,273 is the **net present value** (NPV) of the investment. That is, NPV is the present value of future cash flows minus the present value of the cost of the investment. Because the net present value is negative, Lida Jennings should not recommend purchasing the land.

Both the Vaughn and the Jennings examples deal with perfect certainty. That is, Keith Vaughn knows with perfect certainty that he could sell his land for $11,424 next year. Similarly, Lida Jennings knows with perfect certainty that Kaufman & Broad could receive $91,000 for selling its land. Unfortunately, businesspeople frequently do not know future cash flows. This uncertainty is treated in the next example.

EXAMPLE

Professional Artworks, Inc., is a firm that speculates in modern paintings. The manager is thinking of buying an original Picasso for $400,000 with the intention of selling it at the end of one year. The manager *expects* that the painting will be worth $480,000 in one year. The relevant cash flows are depicted in Figure 4.3.

Of course, this is only an expectation—the painting could be worth more or less than $480,000. Suppose the guaranteed interest rate granted by banks is 10 percent. Should the firm purchase the piece of art?

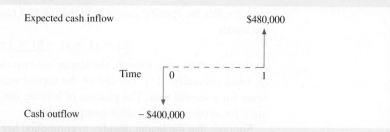

FIGURE 4.3

Cash Flows for
Investment in
Painting

Our first thought might be to discount at the interest rate, yielding

$$\frac{\$480,000}{1.10} = \$436,364$$

Because \$436,364 is greater than \$400,000, it looks at first glance as if the painting should be purchased. However, 10 percent is the return one can earn on a riskless investment. Because the painting is quite risky, a higher *discount rate* is called for. The manager chooses a rate of 25 percent to reflect this risk. In other words, he argues that a 25-percent expected return is fair compensation for an investment as risky as this painting.

The present value of the painting becomes

$$\frac{\$480,000}{1.25} = \$384,000$$

Thus, the manager believes that the painting is currently overpriced at \$400,000 and does not make the purchase.

The preceding analysis is typical of decision making in today's corporations, though real-world examples are, of course, much more complex. Unfortunately, any example with risk poses a problem not faced by a riskless example. In an example with riskless cash flows, the appropriate interest rate can be determined by simply checking with a few banks.[1] The selection of the discount rate for a risky investment is quite a difficult task. We simply don't know at this point whether the discount rate on the painting should be 11 percent, 25 percent, 52 percent, or some other percentage.

Because the choice of a discount rate is so difficult, we merely wanted to broach the subject here. The rest of the chapter will revert to examples under perfect certainty. We must wait until the specific material on risk and return is covered in later chapters before a risk-adjusted analysis can be presented.

Concept
Questions

1. Define future value and present value.
2. How does one use net present value when making an investment decision?

4.2 The Multiperiod Case

The previous section presented the calculation of future value and present value for one period only. We will now perform the calculations for the multiperiod case.

Future Value and Compounding

Suppose an individual were to make a loan of \$1. At the end of the first year, the borrower would owe the lender the principal amount of \$1 plus the interest on the loan at the interest

---

[1]In Chapter 9, we discuss estimation of the riskless rate in more detail.

rate of r. For the specific case where the interest rate is, say, 9 percent, the borrower owes the lender

$$\$1 \times (1 + r) = \$1 \times 1.09 = \$1.09$$

At the end of the year, though, the lender has two choices. She can either take the $1.09— or, more generally, $(1 + r)$—out of the capital market, or she can leave it in and lend it again for a second year. The process of leaving the money in the capital market and lending it for another year is called **compounding.**

Suppose that the lender decides to compound her loan for another year. She does this by taking the proceeds from her first one-year loan, $1.09, and lending this amount for the next year. At the end of next year, then, the borrower will owe her

$$\$1 \times (1 + r) \times (1 + r) = \$1 \times (1 + r)^2 = 1 + 2r + r^2$$

$$\$1 \times (1.09) \times (1.09) = \$1 \times (1.09)^2 = \$1 + \$0.18 + \$0.0081 = \$1.1881$$

This is the total she will receive two years from now by compounding the loan.

In other words, the capital market enables the investor, by providing a ready opportunity for lending, to transform $1 today into $1.1881 at the end of two years. At the end of three years, the cash will be $\$1 \times (1.09)^3 = \$1.2950$.

The most important point to notice is that the total amount that the lender receives is not just the $1 that she lent out plus two years' worth of interest on $1:

$$2 \times r = 2 \times \$0.09 = \$0.18$$

The lender also gets back an amount r^2, which is the interest in the second year on the interest that was earned in the first year. The term, $2 \times r$, represents **simple interest** over the two years, and the term, r^2, is referred to as the *interest on interest.* In our example this latter amount is exactly

$$r^2 = (\$0.09)^2 = \$0.0081$$

When cash is invested at **compound interest,** each interest payment is reinvested. With simple interest, the interest is not reinvested. Benjamin Franklin's statement, "Money makes money and the money that money makes makes more money," is a colorful way of explaining compound interest. The difference between compound interest and simple interest is illustrated in Figure 4.4. In this example the difference does not amount to much because the

FIGURE 4.4

Simple and Compound Interest

The dark-shaded area indicates the difference between compound and simple interest. The difference is substantial over a period of many years or decades.

loan is for $1. If the loan were for $1 million, the lender would receive $1,188,100 in two years' time. Of this amount, $8,100 is interest on interest. The lesson is that those small numbers beyond the decimal point can add up to big dollar amounts when the transactions are for big amounts. In addition, the longer-lasting the loan, the more important interest on interest becomes.

The general formula for an investment over many periods can be written as

Future Value of an Investment:

$$FV = C_0 \times (1 + r)^T$$

where C_0 is the cash to be invested at date 0, r is the interest rate, and T is the number of periods over which the cash is invested.

EXAMPLE

Suh-Pyng Ku has put $500 in a savings account at the First National Bank of Kent. The account earns 7 percent, compounded annually. How much will Ms. Ku have at the end of three years?

$$\$500 \times 1.07 \times 1.07 \times 1.07 = \$500 \times (1.07)^3 = \$612.52$$

Figure 4.5 illustrates the growth of Ms. Ku's account.

FIGURE 4.5

Suh-Pyng Ku's
Savings Account

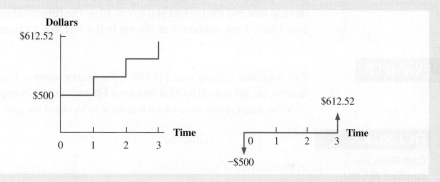

EXAMPLE

Jay Ritter invested $1,000 in the stock of the SDH Company. The company pays a current dividend of $2, which is expected to grow by 20 percent per year for the next two years. What will the dividend of the SDH Company be after two years?

$$\$2 \times (1.20)^2 = \$2.88$$

Figure 4.6 illustrates the increasing value of SDH's dividends.

FIGURE 4.6

The Growth of the
SDH Dividends

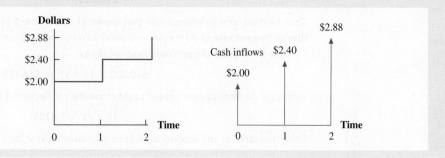

The two previous examples can be calculated in any one of three ways. The computations could be done by hand, by calculator, or with the help of a table. The appropriate table is Table A.3, which appears in the back of the text. This table presents *Future values of $1 at the end of t periods.* The table is used by locating the appropriate interest rate on the horizontal and the appropriate number of periods on the vertical.

For example, Suh-Pyng Ku would look at the following portion of Table A.3:

	Interest Rate		
Period	**6%**	**7%**	**8%**
1	1.0600	1.0700	1.0800
2	1.1236	1.1449	1.1664
3	1.1910	1.2250	1.2597
4	1.2625	1.3108	1.3605

She could calculate the future value of her $500 as

$$\underset{\substack{\text{Initial} \\ \text{investment}}}{\$500} \quad \times \quad \underset{\substack{\text{Future value} \\ \text{of }\$1}}{1.2250} \quad = \quad \$612.50$$

In the example concerning Suh-Pyng Ku, we gave you both the initial investment and the interest rate and then asked you to calculate the future value. Alternatively, the interest rate could have been unknown, as shown in the following example.

EXAMPLE

Carl Voigt, who recently won $10,000 in the lottery, wants to buy a car in five years. Carl estimates that the car will cost $16,105 at that time. His cash flows are displayed in Figure 4.7.

What interest rate must he earn to be able to afford the car?

FIGURE 4.7

Cash Flows for
Purchase of Carl
Voigt's Car

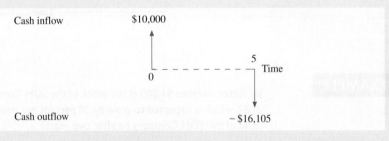

The ratio of purchase price to initial cash is

$$\frac{\$16,105}{\$10,000} = 1.6105$$

Thus, he must earn an interest rate that allows $1 to become $1.6105 in five years. Table A.3 tells us that an interest rate of 10 percent will allow him to purchase the car.

One can express the problem algebraically as

$$\$10,000 \times (1 + r)^5 = \$16,105$$

where *r* is the interest rate needed to purchase the car. Because $16,105/$10,000 = 1.6105, we have

$$(1 + r)^5 = 1.6105$$

Either the table or any sophisticated hand calculator solves[2] for *r*.

---

[2]Conceptually, we are taking the fifth roots of both sides of the equation. That is,

$$r = \sqrt[5]{1.6105} - 1$$

The Power of Compounding: A Digression

Most people who have had any experience with compounding are impressed with its power over long periods of time. Take the stock market, for example. Ibbotson and Sinquefield have calculated what the stock market returned as a whole from 1926 through 2001.[3] They find that one dollar placed in these stocks at the beginning of 1926 would have been worth $2,279.13 at the end of 2001. This is 10.71 percent compounded annually for 76 years, i.e., $(1.1071)^{76} = \$2,279.13$. (*Note:* We are rounding 10.7086% to 10.71%.)

The example illustrates the great difference between compound and simple interest. At 10.71 percent, simple interest on $1 is 10.71 cents a year. Simple interest over 76 years is $8.14 (76 × $0.1071). That is, an individual withdrawing 10.71 cents every year would have withdrawn $8.14 (76 × $0.1071) over 76 years. This is quite a bit below the $2,279.13 that was obtained by reinvestment of all principal and interest.

The results are more impressive over even longer periods of time. A person with no experience in compounding might think that the value of $1 at the end of 152 years would be twice the value of $1 at the end of 76 years, if the yearly rate of return stayed the same. Actually the value of $1 at the end of 152 years would be the *square* of the value of $1 at the end of 76 years. That is, if the annual rate of return remained the same, a $1 investment in common stocks should be worth $5,194,443.36 [$1 × (2,279.13 × 2,279.13)].

A few years ago an archaeologist unearthed a relic stating that Julius Caesar lent the Roman equivalent of one penny to someone. Since there was no record of the penny ever being repaid, the archaeologist wondered what the interest and principal would be if a descendant of Caesar tried to collect from a descendant of the borrower in the 20th century. The archaeologist felt that a rate of 6 percent might be appropriate. To his surprise, the principal and interest due after more than 2,000 years was far greater than the entire wealth on earth.

The power of compounding can explain why the parents of well-to-do families frequently bequeath wealth to their grandchildren rather than to their children. That is, they skip a generation. The parents would rather make the grandchildren very rich than make the children moderately rich. We have found that in these families the grandchildren have a more positive view of the power of compounding than do the children.

EXAMPLE

Some people have said that it was the best real estate deal in history. Peter Minuit, director–general of New Netherlands, the Dutch West India Company's Colony in North America, in 1626 allegedly bought Manhattan Island for 60 guilders' worth of trinkets from native Americans. By 1667 the Dutch were forced to exchange it for Suriname with the British (perhaps the worst real estate deal ever). This sounds cheap but did the Dutch really get the better end of the deal? It is reported that 60 guilders was worth about $24 at the prevailing exchange rate. If the native Americans had sold the trinkets at a fair market value and invested the $24 at 5 percent (tax free), it would now, 377 years later, be worth more than $2.0 billion. Today, Manhattan is undoubtedly worth more than $2 billion, and so at a 5 percent rate of return, the native Americans got the worst of the deal. However, if invested at 10 percent, the amount of money they received would be worth about

$$\$24(1 + r)^T = 1.1^{377} \cong \$97 \text{ quadrillion}$$

This is a lot of money. In fact, $97 quadrillion is more than all the real estate in the world is worth today. No one in the history of the world has ever been able to find an investment yielding 10 percent every year for 377 years.

---

[3]*Stocks, Bonds, Bills and Inflation* [SBBI]. 2002 Yearbook. Ibbotson Associates, Chicago, 2003.

Present Value and Discounting

We now know that an annual interest rate of 9 percent enables the investor to transform $1 today into $1.1881 two years from now. In addition, we would like to know:

> How much would an investor need to lend today so that she could receive $1 two years from today?

Algebraically, we can write this as

$$PV \times (1.09)^2 = \$1$$

In the preceding equation, PV stands for present value, the amount of money we must lend today in order to receive $1 in two years' time.

Solving for PV in this equation, we have

$$PV = \frac{\$1}{1.1881} = \$0.84$$

This process of calculating the present value of a future cash flow is called **discounting**. It is the opposite of compounding. The difference between compounding and discounting is illustrated in Figure 4.8.

To be certain that $0.84 is in fact the present value of $1 to be received in two years, we must check whether or not, if we loaned out $0.84 and rolled over the loan for two years, we would get exactly $1 back. If this were the case, the capital markets would be saying that $1 received in two years' time is equivalent to having $0.84 today. Checking the exact numbers, we get

$$\$0.84168 \times 1.09 \times 1.09 = \$1$$

In other words, when we have capital markets with a sure interest rate of 9 percent, we are indifferent between receiving $0.84 today or $1 in two years. We have no reason to treat these two choices differently from each other, because if we had $0.84 today and loaned it out for two years, it would return $1 to us at the end of that time. The value 0.84 [$1/(1.09)^2$] is called the **present value factor**. It is the factor used to calculate the present value of a future cash flow.

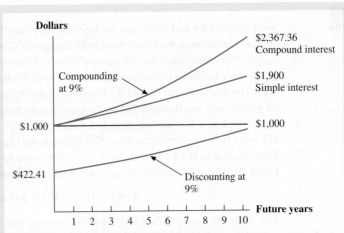

FIGURE 4.8

Compounding and Discounting

The top line shows the growth of $1,000 at compound interest with the funds invested at 9 percent: $1,000 \times (1.09)^{10} = \$2,367.36$. Simple interest is shown on the next line. It is $1,000 + [10 \times (\$1,000 \times 0.09)] = \$1,900$. The bottom line shows the discounted value of $1,000 if the interest rate is 9 percent.

In the multiperiod case, the formula for PV can be written as

Present Value of Investment

$$PV = \frac{C_T}{(1 + r)^T}$$ (4.3)

where C_T is cash flow at date T and r is the appropriate interest rate.

EXAMPLE

Bernard Dumas will receive $10,000 three years from now. Bernard can earn 8 percent on his investments, and so the **appropriate discount rate** is 8 percent. What is the present value of his future cash flow?

$$PV = \$10,000 \times \left(\frac{1}{1.08}\right)^3$$

$$= \$10,000 \times 0.7938$$

$$= \$7,938$$

Figure 4.9 illustrates the application of the present value factor to Bernard's investment.

FIGURE 4.9

Discounting Bernard Dumas' Opportunity

When his investments grow at an 8 percent rate of interest, Bernard Dumas is equally inclined toward receiving $7,938 now and receiving $10,000 in three years' time. After all, he could convert the $7,938 he receives today into $10,000 in three years by lending it at an interest rate of 8 percent.

Bernard Dumas could have reached his present value calculation in one of three ways. The computation could have been done by hand, by calculator, or with the help of Table A.1, which appears in the back of the text. This table presents *present value of $1 to be received after t periods.* The table is used by locating the appropriate interest rate on the horizontal and the appropriate number of periods on the vertical. For example, Bernard Dumas would look at the following portion of Table A.1:

	Interest Rate		
Period	**7%**	**8%**	**9%**
1	0.9346	0.9259	0.9174
2	0.8734	0.8573	0.8417
3	0.8163	0.7938	0.7722
4	0.7629	0.7350	0.7084

The appropriate present value factor is 0.7938.

In the preceding example, we gave both the interest rate and the future cash flow. Alternatively, the interest rate could have been unknown.

EXAMPLE

A customer of the Chaffkin Corp. wants to buy a tugboat today. Rather than paying immediately, he will pay $50,000 in three years. It will cost the Chaffkin Corp. $38,610 to build the tugboat immediately. The relevant cash flows to Chaffkin Corp. are displayed in Figure 4.10. By charging what interest rate would the Chaffkin Corp. neither gain nor lose on the sale?

FIGURE 4.10

Cash Flows for Tugboat

The ratio of construction cost to sale price is

$$\frac{\$38,610}{\$50,000} = 0.7722$$

We must determine the interest rate that allows $1 to be received in three years to have a present value of $0.7722. Table A.1 tells us that 9 percent is that interest rate.[4]

Frequently, an investor or a business will receive more than one cash flow. The present value of the set of cash flows is simply the sum of the present values of the individual cash flows. This is illustrated in the following example.

EXAMPLE

Dennis Draper has won the Kentucky state lottery and will receive the following set of cash flows over the next two years:

Year	Cash Flow
1	$2,000
2	$5,000

Mr. Draper can currently earn 6 percent in his passbook savings account, and so, the appropriate discount rate is 6 percent. The present value of the cash flows is

Year	Cash Flow × Present Value Factor		= Present Value
1	$2,000 × $\dfrac{1}{1.06}$	= 0.943	$1,887
2	$5,000 × $\left(\dfrac{1}{1.06}\right)^2$	= 0.890	$4,450
		Total	$6,337

In other words, Mr. Draper is equally inclined toward receiving $6,337 today and receiving $2,000 and $5,000 over the next two years.

---

[4]Algebraically, we are solving for r in the equation

$$\frac{\$50,000}{(1 + r)^3} = \$38,610$$

or, equivalently,

$$\frac{\$1}{(1 + r)^3} = \$0.7722$$

EXAMPLE

Finance.com has an opportunity to invest in a new high-speed computer that costs $50,000. The computer will generate cash flows (from cost savings) of $25,000 one year from now, $20,000 two years from now, and $15,000 three years from now. The computer will be worthless after three years, and no additional cash flows will occur. Finance.com has determined that the appropriate discount rate is 7 percent for this investment. Should Finance.com make this investment in a new high-speed computer? What is the present value of the investment?

The cash flows and present value factors of the proposed computer are as follows.

	Cash Flows	Present Value Factor
Year 0	−$50,000	$1 = 1$
1	$25,000	$\frac{1}{1.07} = 0.9346$
2	$20,000	$\left(\frac{1}{1.07}\right)^2 = 0.8734$
3	$15,000	$\left(\frac{1}{1.07}\right)^3 = 0.8163$

The present values of the cash flows are:

Cash flows $\times$ Present value factor = Present value

Year 0	−$50,000 × 1	= −$50,000
1	$25,000 × 0.9346	= $23,365
2	$20,000 × 0.8734	= $17,468
3	$15,000 × 0.8163	= $12,244.5
	Total:	$3,077.5

Finance.com should invest in a new high-speed computer because the present value of its future cash flows is greater than its cost. The NPV is $3,077.5.

The Algebraic Formula

To derive an algebraic formula for net present value of a cash flow, recall that the PV of receiving a cash flow one year from now is

$$PV = C_1/(1 + r)$$

and the PV of receiving a cash flow two years from now is

$$PV = C_2/(1 + r)^2$$

We can write the NPV of a T-period project as

$$NPV = -C_0 \frac{C_1}{1 + r} + \frac{C_2}{(1 + r)^2} + \cdots + \frac{C_T}{(1 + r)^T} = -C_0 + \sum_{i=1}^{T}\frac{C_i}{(1 + r)^i}$$

The initial flow, $-C_0$, is assumed to be negative because it represents an investment. The Σ is shorthand for the sum of the series.

Concept Questions

1. **What is the difference between simple interest and compound interest?**
2. **What is the formula for the net present value of a project?**

4.3 Compounding Periods

So far we have assumed that compounding and discounting occur yearly. Sometimes compounding may occur more frequently than just once a year. For example, imagine that a bank pays a 10-percent interest rate "compounded semiannually." This means that a $1,000 deposit in the bank would be worth $1,000 × 1.05 = $1,050 after six months, and $1,050 × 1.05 = $1,102.50 at the end of the year.

The end-of-the-year wealth can be written as[5]

$$\$1,000\left(1 + \frac{0.10}{2}\right)^2 = \$1,000 \times (1.05)^2 = \$1,102.50$$

Of course, a $1,000 deposit would be worth $1,100 ($1,000 × 1.10) with yearly compounding. Note that the future value at the end of one year is greater with semiannual compounding than with yearly compounding. With yearly compounding, the original $1,000 remains the investment base for the full year. The original $1,000 is the investment base only for the first six months with semiannual compounding. The base over the second six months is $1,050. Hence, one gets *interest on interest* with semiannual compounding.

Because $1,000 × 1.1025 = $1,102.50, 10 percent compounded semiannually is the same as 10.25 percent compounded annually. In other words, a rational investor could not care less whether she is quoted a rate of 10 percent compounded semiannually, or a rate of 10.25 percent compounded annually.

Quarterly compounding at 10 percent yields wealth at the end of one year of

$$\$1,000\left(1 + \frac{0.10}{4}\right)^4 = \$1,103.81$$

More generally, compounding an investment m times a year provides end-of-year wealth of

$$C_0\left(1 + \frac{r}{m}\right)^m \tag{4.4}$$

where C_0 is one's initial investment and r is the **stated annual interest rate.** The stated annual interest rate is the annual interest rate without consideration of compounding. Banks and other financial institutions may use other names for the stated annual interest rate. **Annual percentage rate** is perhaps the most common synonym.

EXAMPLE

What is the end-of-year wealth if Jane Christine receives a stated annual interest rate of 24 percent compounded monthly on a $1 investment?

Using (4.4), her wealth is

$$\$1\left(1 + \frac{0.24}{12}\right)^{12} = \$1 \times (1.02)^{12}$$
$$= \$1.2682$$

The annual rate of return is 26.82 percent. This annual rate of return is either called the **effective annual interest rate** or the **effective annual yield.** Due to compounding, the effective annual interest rate is greater than the stated annual interest rate of 24 percent. Algebraically, we can rewrite the effective annual interest rate as

Effective Annual Interest Rate:

$$\left(1 + \frac{r}{m}\right)^m - 1 \tag{4.5}$$

---

[5]In addition to using a calculator, one can still use Table A.3 when the compounding period is less than a year. Here, one sets the interest rate at 5 percent and the number of periods at two.

Students are often bothered by the subtraction of 1 in (4.5). Note that end-of-year wealth is composed of both the interest earned over the year and the original principal. We remove the original principal by subtracting one in (4.5).

If the stated annual rate of interest, 8 percent, is compounded quarterly, what is the effective annual rate of interest?

Using (4.5), we have

$$\left(1 + \frac{r}{m}\right)^m - 1 = \left(1 + \frac{0.08}{4}\right)^4 - 1 = 0.0824 = 8.24\%$$

Referring back to our original example where $C_0 = \$1,000$ and $r = 10\%$, we can generate the following table:

C_0	Compounding Frequency (m)	C_1	Effective Annual Interest Rate = $\left(1 + \frac{r}{m}\right)^m - 1$
$1,000	Yearly ($m = 1$)	$1,100.00	0.10
1,000	Semiannually ($m = 2$)	1,102.50	0.1025
1,000	Quarterly ($m = 4$)	1,103.81	0.10381
1,000	Daily ($m = 365$)	1,105.16	0.10516

Distinction between Stated Annual Interest Rate and Effective Annual Interest Rate

The distinction between the stated annual interest rate (SAIR) and the effective annual interest rate (EAIR) is frequently quite troubling to students. One can reduce the confusion by noting that the SAIR becomes meaningful only if the compounding interval is given. For example, for an SAIR of 10 percent, the future value at the end of one year with semiannual compounding is $[1 + (.10/2)]^2 = 1.1025$. The future value with quarterly compounding is $[1 + (.10/4)]^4 = 1.1038$. If the SAIR is 10 percent but no compounding interval is given, one cannot calculate future value. In other words, one does not know whether to compound semiannually, quarterly, or over some other interval.

By contrast, the EAIR is meaningful *without* a compounding interval. For example, an EAIR of 10.25 percent means that a $1 investment will be worth $1.1025 in one year. One can think of this as an SAIR of 10 percent with semiannual compounding or an SAIR of 10.25 percent with annual compounding, or some other possibility.

Compounding over Many Years

Formula (4.4) applies for an investment over one year. For an investment over one or more (T) years, the formula becomes

Future Value with Compounding:

$$\text{FV} = C_0\left(1 + \frac{r}{m}\right)^{mT} \tag{4.6}$$

Harry DeAngelo is investing $5,000 at a stated annual interest rate of 12 percent per year, compounded quarterly, for five years. What is his wealth at the end of five years?

Using formula (4.6), his wealth is

$$\$5,000 \times \left(1 + \frac{0.12}{4}\right)^{4 \times 5} = \$5,000 \times (1.03)^{20} = \$5,000 \times 1.8061 = \$9,030.50$$

Continuous Compounding (Advanced)

The previous discussion shows that one can compound much more frequently than once a year. One could compound semiannually, quarterly, monthly, daily, hourly, each minute, or even more often. The limiting case would be to compound every infinitesimal instant, which is commonly called **continuous compounding.** Surprisingly, banks and other financial institutions frequently quote continuously compounded rates, which is why we study them.

Though the idea of compounding this rapidly may boggle the mind, a simple formula is involved. With continuous compounding, the value at the end of T years is expressed as

$$C_0 \times e^{rT} \tag{4.7}$$

where C_0 is the initial investment, r is the stated annual interest rate, and T is the number of years over which the investment runs. The number e is a constant and is approximately equal to 2.718. It is not an unknown like C_0, r, and T.

EXAMPLE

Linda DeFond invested $1,000 at a continuously compounded rate of 10 percent for one year. What is the value of her wealth at the end of one year?

From formula (4.7) we have

$$\$1,000 \times e^{0.10} = \$1,000 \times 1.1052 = \$1,105.20$$

This number can easily be read from our Table A.5. One merely sets r, the value on the horizontal dimension, to 10% and T, the value on the vertical dimension, to 1. For this problem, the relevant portion of the table is

Period	Continuously Compounded Rate (r)		
(T)	9%	10%	11%
1	1.0942	1.1052	1.1163
2	1.1972	1.2214	1.2461
3	1.3100	1.3499	1.3910

Note that a continuously compounded rate of 10 percent is equivalent to an annually compounded rate of 10.52 percent. In other words, Linda DeFond could not care less whether her bank quoted a continuously compounded rate of 10 percent or a 10.52-percent rate, compounded annually.

EXAMPLE

Linda DeFond's brother, Mark, invested $1,000 at a continuously compounded rate of 10 percent for two years.

The appropriate formula here is

$$\$1,000 \times e^{0.10 \times 2} = \$1,000 \times e^{0.20} = \$1,221.40$$

Using the portion of the table of continuously compounded rates reproduced above, we find the value to be 1.2214.

Figure 4.11 illustrates the relationship among annual, semiannual, and continuous compounding. Semiannual compounding gives rise to both a smoother curve and a higher ending value than does annual compounding. Continuous compounding has both the smoothest curve and the highest ending value of all.

FIGURE 4.11

Annual, Semiannual, and Continuous Compounding

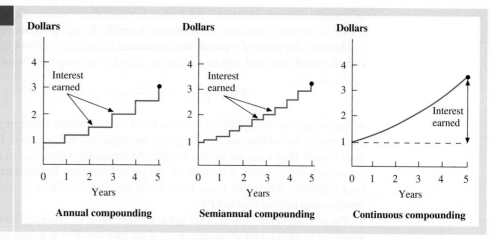

EXAMPLE

The Michigan state lottery is going to pay you $1,000 at the end of four years. If the annual continuously compounded rate of interest is 8 percent, what is the present value of this payment?

$$\$1,000 \times \frac{1}{e^{0.08 \times 4}} = \$1,000 \times \frac{1}{1.3771} = \$726.16$$

Concept Questions

1. **What is a stated annual interest rate?**
2. **What is an effective annual interest rate?**
3. **What is the relationship between the stated annual interest rate and the effective annual interest rate?**
4. **Define continuous compounding.**

4.4 Simplifications

The first part of this chapter has examined the concepts of future value and present value. Although these concepts allow one to answer a host of problems concerning the time value of money, the human effort involved can frequently be excessive. For example, consider a bank calculating the present value on a 20-year monthly mortgage. Because this mortgage has 240 (20 × 12) payments, a lot of time is needed to perform a conceptually simple task.

Because many basic finance problems are potentially so time-consuming, we search out simplifications in this section. We provide simplifying formulas for four classes of cash flow streams:

- Perpetuity
- Growing perpetuity
- Annuity
- Growing annuity

Perpetuity

A **perpetuity** is a constant stream of cash flows without end. If you are thinking that perpetuities have no relevance to reality, it will surprise you that there is a well-known case of an unending cash flow stream: the British bonds called *consols*. An investor purchasing a consol is entitled to receive yearly interest from the British government forever.

How can the price of a consol be determined? Consider a consol that pays a coupon of C dollars each year and will do so forever. Simply applying the PV formula gives us

$$PV = \frac{C}{1 + r} + \frac{C}{(1 + r)^2} + \frac{C}{(1 + r)^3} + \cdots$$

where the dots at the end of the formula stand for the infinite string of terms that continues the formula. Series like the preceding one are called *geometric series*. It is well known that even though they have an infinite number of terms, the whole series has a finite sum because each term is only a fraction of the preceding term. Before turning to our calculus books, though, it is worth going back to our original principles to see if a bit of financial intuition can help us find the PV.

The present value of the consol is the present value of all of its future coupons. In other words, it is an amount of money that, if an investor had it today, would enable him to achieve the same pattern of expenditures that the consol and its coupons would. Suppose that an investor wanted to spend exactly C dollars each year. If he had the consol, he could do this. How much money must he have today to spend the same amount? Clearly he would need exactly enough so that the interest on the money would be C dollars per year. If he had any more, he could spend more than C dollars each year. If he had any less, he would eventually run out of money spending C dollars per year.

The amount that will give the investor C dollars each year, and therefore the present value of the consol, is simply

$$PV = \frac{C}{r} \tag{4.8}$$

To confirm that this is the right answer, notice that if we lend the amount C/r, the interest it earns each year will be

$$\text{Interest} = \frac{C}{r} \times r = C$$

which is exactly the consol payment.[6] To sum up, we have shown that for a consol

Formula for Present Value of Perpetuity:

$$PV = \frac{C}{1 + r} + \frac{C}{(1 + r)^2} + \frac{C}{(1 + r)^3} + \cdots$$

$$= \frac{C}{r}$$

It is comforting to know how easily we can use a bit of financial intuition to solve this mathematical problem.

---

[6]We can prove this by looking at the PV equation:

$$PV = C/(1 + r) + C/(1 + r)^2 + \cdots$$

Let $C/(1 + r) = a$ and $1/(1 + r) = x$. We now have

$$PV = a(1 + x + x^2 + \cdots) \tag{1}$$

Next we can multiply by x:

$$xPV = ax + ax^2 + \cdots \tag{2}$$

Subtracting (2) from (1) gives

$$PV(1 - x) = a$$

Now we substitute for a and x and rearrange:

$$PV = C/r$$

EXAMPLE

Consider a perpetuity paying $100 a year. If the relevant interest rate is 8 percent, what is the value of the consol?

Using formula (4.8), we have

$$PV = \frac{\$100}{0.08} = \$1,250$$

Now suppose that interest rates fall to 6 percent. Using (4.8), the value of the perpetuity is

$$PV = \frac{\$100}{0.06} = \$1,666.67$$

Note that the value of the perpetuity rises with a drop in the interest rate. Conversely, the value of the perpetuity falls with a rise in the interest rate.

Growing Perpetuity

Imagine an apartment building where cash flows to the landlord after expenses will be $100,000 next year. These cash flows are expected to rise at 5 percent per year. If one assumes that this rise will continue indefinitely, the cash flow stream is termed a **growing perpetuity.** The relevant interest rate is 11 percent. Therefore, the appropriate discount rate is 11 percent and the present value of the cash flows can be represented as

$$PV = \frac{\$100,000}{1.11} + \frac{\$100,000(1.05)}{(1.11)^2} + \frac{\$100,000(1.05)^2}{(1.11)^3} + \cdots + \frac{\$100,000(1.05)^{N-1}}{(1.11)^N} + \cdots$$

Algebraically, we can write the formula as

$$PV = \frac{C}{1+r} + \frac{C \times (1+g)}{(1+r)^2} + \frac{C \times (1+g)^2}{(1+r)^3} + \cdots + \frac{C \times (1+g)^{N-1}}{(1+r)^N} + \cdots \quad (4.9)$$

where C is the cash flow to be received one period hence, g is the rate of growth per period, expressed as a percentage, and r is the appropriate discount rate.

Fortunately, formula (4.9) reduces to the following simplification:[7]

Formula for Present Value of Growing Perpetuity:

$$PV = \frac{C}{r-g} \quad (4.10)$$

From formula (4.10), the present value of the cash flows from the apartment building is

$$\frac{\$100,000}{0.11 - 0.05} = \$1,666,667$$

---

[7]PV is the sum of an infinite geometric series:

$$PV = a(1 + x + x^2 + \cdots)$$

where $a = C/(1+r)$ and $x = (1+g)/(1+r)$. Previously we showed that the sum of an infinite geometric series is $a/(1-x)$. Using this result and substituting for a and x, we find

$$PV = C/(r-g)$$

Note that this geometric series converges to a finite sum only when x is less than 1. This implies that the growth rate, g, must be less than the interest rate, r.

There are three important points concerning the growing perpetuity formula:

1. *The Numerator.* The numerator in (4.10) is the cash flow one period hence, not at date 0. Consider the following example:

EXAMPLE

Rothstein Corporation is *just about* to pay a dividend of $3.00 per share. Investors anticipate that the annual dividend will rise by 6 percent a year forever. The applicable interest rate is 11 percent. What is the price of the stock today?

The numerator in formula (4.10) is the cash flow to be received next period. Since the growth rate is 6 percent, the dividend next year is $3.18 ($3.00 × 1.06). The price of the stock today is

$$\$66.60 \quad = \quad \underset{\substack{\text{Imminent} \\ \text{dividend}}}{\$3.00} \quad + \quad \underset{\substack{\text{Present value of all} \\ \text{dividends beginning} \\ \text{a year from now}}}{\dfrac{\$3.18}{0.11 - 0.06}}$$

The price of $66.60 includes both the dividend to be received immediately and the present value of all dividends beginning a year from now. Formula (4.10) only makes it possible to calculate the present value of all dividends beginning a year from now. Be sure you understand this example; test questions on this subject always seem to trip up a few of our students.

2. *The Interest Rate and the Growth Rate.* The interest rate r must be greater than the growth rate g for the growing perpetuity formula to work. Consider the case in which the growth rate approaches the interest rate in magnitude. Then the denominator in the growing perpetuity formula gets infinitesimally small and the present value grows infinitely large. The present value is in fact undefined when r is less than g.

3. *The Timing Assumption.* Cash generally flows into and out of real-world firms both randomly and nearly continuously. However, formula (4.10) assumes that cash flows are received and disbursed at regular and discrete points in time. In the example of the apartment, we assumed that the net cash flows of $100,000 only occurred once a year. In reality, rent checks are commonly received every month. Payments for maintenance and other expenses may occur anytime within the year.

The growing perpetuity formula of (4.10) can be applied only by assuming a regular and discrete pattern of cash flow. Although this assumption is sensible because the formula saves so much time, the user should never forget that it is an *assumption*. This point will be mentioned again in the chapters ahead.

A few words should be said about terminology. Authors of financial textbooks generally use one of two conventions to refer to time. A minority of financial writers treat cash flows as being received on exact *dates*, for example date 0, date 1, and so forth. Under this convention, date 0 represents the present time. However, because a year is an interval, not a specific moment in time, the great majority of authors refer to cash flows that occur at the end of a year (or alternatively, the end of a *period*). Under this *end-of-the-year* convention, the end of year 0 is the present, the end of year 1 occurs one period hence, and so on. (The beginning of year 0 has already passed and is not generally referred to.)[8]

---

[8]Sometimes financial writers merely speak of a cash flow in year *x*. Although this terminology is ambiguous, such writers generally mean the *end of year x*.

The interchangeability of the two conventions can be seen from the following chart:

We strongly believe that the *dates convention* reduces ambiguity. However, we use both conventions because you are likely to see the *end-of-year convention* in later courses. In fact, both conventions may appear in the same example for the sake of practice.

Annuity

An **annuity** is a level stream of regular payments that lasts for a fixed number of periods. Not surprisingly, annuities are among the most common kinds of financial instruments. The pensions that people receive when they retire are often in the form of an annuity. Leases and mortgages are also often annuities.

To figure out the present value of an annuity we need to evaluate the following equation:

$$\frac{C}{1 + r} + \frac{C}{(1 + r)^2} + \frac{C}{(1 + r)^3} + \cdots + \frac{C}{(1 + r)^T}$$

The present value of only receiving the coupons for T periods must be less than the present value of a consol, but how much less? To answer this we have to look at consols a bit more closely.

Consider the following time chart:

Consol 1 is a normal consol with its first payment at date 1. The first payment of consol 2 occurs at date $T + 1$.

The present value of having a cash flow of C at each of T dates is equal to the present value of consol 1 minus the present value of consol 2. The present value of consol 1 is given by

$$\text{PV} = \frac{C}{r} \tag{4.11}$$

Consol 2 is just a consol with its first payment at date $T + 1$. From the perpetuity formula, this consol will be worth C/r at date T.[9] However, we do not want the value at date T. We want the value now; in other words, the present value at date 0. We must discount C/r back by T periods. Therefore, the present value of consol 2 is

$$\text{PV} = \frac{C}{r}\left[\frac{1}{(1 + r)^T}\right] \tag{4.12}$$

---

[9]Students frequently think that C/r is the present value at date $T + 1$ because the consol's first payment is at date $T + 1$. However, the formula values the annuity as of one period prior to the first payment.

The present value of having cash flows for T years is the present value of a consol with its first payment at date 1 minus the present value of a consol with its first payment at date $T + 1$. Thus, the present value of an annuity is formula (4.11) minus formula (4.12). This can be written as

$$\frac{C}{r} - \frac{C}{r}\left[\frac{1}{(1 + r)^T}\right]$$

This simplifies to

Formula for Present Value of Annuity:[10, 11]

$$\text{PV} = C\left[\frac{1}{r} - \frac{1}{r(1 + r)^T}\right] \qquad (4.13)$$

EXAMPLE

Mark Young has just won the state lottery, paying $50,000 a year for 20 years. He is to receive his first payment a year from now. The state advertises this as the Million Dollar Lottery because $1,000,000 = $50,000 × 20. If the interest rate is 8 percent, what is the true value of the lottery? Formula (4.13) yields

$$\begin{array}{c}\text{Present value of}\\\text{Million Dollar Lottery}\end{array} = \$50,000 \times \left[\frac{1}{0.08} - \frac{1}{0.08(1.08)^{20}}\right]$$

$$\begin{array}{ccc}\text{Periodic payment} & & \text{Annuity factor}\\ = \$50,000 & \times & 9.8181\end{array}$$

$$= \$490,905$$

Rather than being overjoyed at winning, Mr. Young sues the state for misrepresentation and fraud. His legal brief states that he was promised $1 million but received only $490,905.[12]

The term we use to compute the value of the stream of level payments, C, for T years is called an **annuity factor.** The annuity factor in the current example is 9.8181. Because the annuity factor is used so often in PV calculations, we have included it in Table A.2 in the back of this book. The table gives the values of these factors for a range of interest rates, r, and maturity dates, T.

The annuity factor as expressed in the brackets of (4.13) is a complex formula. For simplification, we may from time to time refer to the annuity factor as

$$A_r^T \qquad (4.14)$$

That is, expression (4.14) stands for the present value of $1 a year for T years at an interest rate of r.

---

[10]This can also be written as

$$C[1 - 1/(1 + r)^T]/r$$

[11]We can also provide a formula for the future value of an annuity.

$$\text{FV} = C\left[\frac{(1 + r)^T}{r} - \frac{1}{r}\right]$$

[12]To solve this problem on a common type HP19B II financial calculator, you should do the following:

  a. Press "FIN" and "TVM."
  b. Enter the payment 50,000 and press "PMT."
  c. Enter the interest rate 8 and press "I % YR."
  d. Enter the number of periods 20 and press "N."
  e. Finally, press "PV" to solve.

Notice your answer is $490,907.370372. The calculator uses 11 digits for the annuity factor and the answer, whereas the example uses only 4 digits in the annuity factor and rounds the final answer to the nearest dollar. That is why the answer in the text example differs from the one using the calculator. In practice, the answer using the calculator is the best because it is more precise.

Our experience is that annuity formulas are not hard, but tricky, for the beginning student. We present four tricks below.

Trick 1: A Delayed Annuity   One of the tricks in working with annuities or perpetuities is getting the timing exactly right. This is particularly true when an annuity or perpetuity begins at a date many periods in the future. We have found that even the brightest beginning student can make errors here. Consider the following example.

EXAMPLE

Danielle Caravello will receive a four-year annuity of $500 per year, beginning at date 6. If the interest rate is 10 percent, what is the present value of her annuity? This situation can be graphed as:

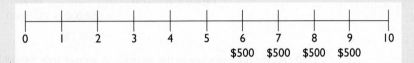

The analysis involves two steps:

1. Calculate the present value of the annuity using (4.13). This is

Present Value of Annuity at Date 5:

$$\$500\left[\frac{1}{0.10} - \frac{1}{0.10(1.10)^4}\right] = \$500 \times A_{0.10}^4$$

$$= \$500 \times 3.1699$$

$$= \$1,584.95$$

Note that $1,584.95 represents the present value at *date 5*.

Students frequently think that $1,584.95 is the present value at date 6, because the annuity begins at date 6. However, our formula values the annuity as of one period prior to the first payment. This can be seen in the most typical case where the first payment occurs at date 1. The formula values the annuity as of date 0 here.

2. Discount the present value of the annuity back to date 0. That is

Present Value at Date 0:

$$\frac{\$1,584.95}{(1.10)^5} = \$984.13$$

Again, it is worthwhile mentioning that, because the annuity formula brings Danielle's annuity back to date 5, the second calculation must discount over the remaining 5 periods. The two-step procedure is graphed in Figure 4.12.

FIGURE 4.12

Discounting Danielle Caravello's Annuity

Step one: Discount the four payments back to date 5 by using the annuity formula.
Step two: Discount the present value at date 5 ($1,584.95) back to present value at date 0.

Trick 2: Annuity in Advance The annuity formula of (4.13) assumes that the first annuity payment begins a full period hence. This type of annuity is frequently called an *annuity in arrears*. What happens if the annuity begins today, in other words, at date 0?

EXAMPLE

In a previous example, Mark Young received $50,000 a year for 20 years from the state lottery. In that example, he was to receive the first payment a year from the winning date. Let us now assume that the first payment occurs immediately. The total number of payments remains 20.

Under this new assumption, we have a 19-date annuity with the first payment occurring at date 1—plus an extra payment at date 0. The present value is

$$\underset{\text{Payment at date 0}}{\$50,000} \quad + \quad \underset{\text{19-year annuity}}{\$50,000 \times A_{0.08}^{19}}$$

$$= \$50,000 + (\$50,000 \times 9.6036)$$

$$= \$530,180$$

$530,180, the present value in this example, is greater than $490,905, the present value in the earlier lottery example. This is to be expected because the annuity of the current example begins earlier. An annuity with an immediate initial payment is called an *annuity in advance*. Always remember that formula (4.13), as well as Table A.2, in this book refers to an *annuity in arrears*.

Trick 3: The Infrequent Annuity The following example treats an annuity with payments occurring less frequently than once a year.

EXAMPLE

Ms. Ann Chen receives an annuity of $450, payable once every two years. The annuity stretches out over 20 years. The first payment occurs at date 2, that is, two years from today. The annual interest rate is 6 percent.

The trick is to determine the interest rate over a two-year period. The interest rate over two years is

$$(1.06 \times 1.06) - 1 = 12.36\%$$

That is, $100 invested over two years will yield $112.36.

What we want is the present value of a $450 annuity over 10 periods, with an interest rate of 12.36 percent per period. This is

$$\$450 \left[\frac{1}{0.1236} - \frac{1}{0.1236 \times (1.1236)^{10}} \right] = \$450 \times A_{0.1236}^{10} = \$2,505.57$$

Trick 4: Equating Present Value of Two Annuities The following example equates the present value of inflows with the present value of outflows.

EXAMPLE

Harold and Helen Nash are saving for the college education of their newborn daughter, Susan. The Nashes estimate that college expenses will run $30,000 per year when their daughter reaches college in 18 years. The annual interest rate over the next few decades will be 14 percent. How much money must they deposit in the bank each year so that their daughter will be completely supported through four years of college?

To simplify the calculations, we assume that Susan is born today. Her parents will make the first of her four annual tuition payments on her 18th birthday. They will make equal bank deposits on each of her first 17 birthdays, but no deposit at date 0. This is illustrated as

Mr. and Ms. Nash will be making deposits to the bank over the next 17 years. They will be withdrawing $30,000 per year over the following four years. We can be sure they will be able to withdraw fully $30,000 per year if the present value of the deposits is equal to the present value of the four $30,000 withdrawals.

This calculation requires three steps. The first two determine the present value of the withdrawals. The final step determines yearly deposits that will have a present value equal to that of the withdrawals.

1. We calculate the present value of the four years at college using the annuity formula.

$$\$30{,}000 \times \left[\frac{1}{0.14} - \frac{1}{0.14 \times (1.14)^4} \right] = \$30{,}000 \times A_{0.14}^4$$

$$= \$30{,}000 \times 2.9137 = \$87{,}411$$

We assume that Susan enters college on her 18th birthday. Given our discussion in Trick 1 $87,411 represents the present value at date 17.

2. We calculate the present value of the college education at date 0 as

$$\frac{\$87{,}411}{(1.14)^{17}} = \$9{,}422.91$$

3. Assuming that Helen and Harold Nash make deposits to the bank at the end of each of the 17 years, we calculate the annual deposit that will yield a present value of all deposits of $9,422.91. This is calculated as

$$C \times A_{0.14}^{17} = \$9{,}422.91$$

Because $A_{0.14}^{17} = 6.3729$,

$$C = \frac{\$9{,}422.91}{6.3729} = \$1{,}478.59$$

Thus, deposits of $1,478.59 made at the end of each of the first 17 years and invested at 14 percent will provide enough money to make tuition payments of $30,000 over the following four years.

An alternative method would be to (1) calculate the present value of the tuition payments at Susan's 18th birthday and (2) calculate annual deposits such that the future value of the deposits at her 18th birthday equals the present value of the tuition payments at that date. Although this technique can also provide the right answer, we have found that it is more likely to lead to errors. Therefore, we only equate present values in our presentation.

Growing Annuity

Cash flows in business are very likely to grow over time, due either to real growth or to inflation. The growing perpetuity, which assumes an infinite number of cash flows, provides one formula to handle this growth. We now consider a **growing annuity,** which is a *finite* number of growing cash flows. Because perpetuities of any kind are rare, a formula for a growing annuity would be useful indeed. The formula is[13]

Formula for Present Value of Growing Annuity:

$$PV = C\left[\frac{1}{r-g} - \frac{1}{r-g} \times \left(\frac{1+g}{1+r}\right)^{T}\right] \tag{4.15}$$

where, as before, C is the payment to occur at the end of the first period, r is the interest rate, g is the rate of growth per period, expressed as a percentage, and T is the number of periods for the annuity.

EXAMPLE

Stuart Gabriel, a second-year MBA student, has just been offered a job at $80,000 a year. He anticipates his salary increasing by 9 percent a year until his retirement in 40 years. Given an interest rate of 20 percent, what is the present value of his lifetime salary?

We simplify by assuming he will be paid his $80,000 salary exactly one year from now, and that his salary will continue to be paid in annual installments. The appropriate discount rate is 20 percent. From (4.15), the calculation is

$$\begin{array}{l} \text{Present value} \\ \text{of Stuart's} \\ \text{lifetime salary} \end{array} = \$80,000 \times \left[\frac{1}{0.20 - 0.09} - \frac{1}{0.20 - 0.09}\left(\frac{1.09}{1.20}\right)^{40}\right] = \$711,731$$

Though the growing annuity is quite useful, it is more tedious than the other simplifying formulas. Whereas most sophisticated calculators have special programs for perpetuity, growing perpetuity, and annuity, there is no special program for growing annuity. Hence, one must calculate all the terms in formula (4.15) directly.

EXAMPLE

In a previous example, Harold and Helen Nash planned to make 17 identical payments in order to fund the college education of their daughter, Susan. Alternatively, imagine that they planned to increase their payments at 4 percent per year. What would their first payment be?

The first two steps of the previous Nash family example showed that the present value of the college costs was $9,422.91. These two steps would be the same here. However, the third step must be altered. Now we must ask, How much should their first payment be so that, if payments increase by 4 percent per year, the present value of all payments will be $9,422.91?

---

[13]This can be proved as follows. A growing annuity can be viewed as the difference between two growing perpetuities. Consider a growing perpetuity A, where the first payment of C occurs at date 1. Next, consider growing perpetuity B, where the first payment of $C(1 + g)^{T}$ is made at date $T + 1$. Both perpetuities grow at rate g. The growing annuity over T periods is the difference between annuity A and annuity B. This can be represented as:

Date	0	1	2	3	$\cdots$	T	$T+1$	$T+2$	$T+3$
Perpetuity A	C	$C \times (1+g)$	$C \times (1+g)^2$	$\cdots$ $C \times (1+g)^{T-1}$		$C \times (1+g)^T$	$C \times (1+g)^{T+1}$	$C \times (1+g)^{T+2}\cdots$
Perpetuity B							$C \times (1+g)^T$	$C \times (1+g)^{T+1}$	$C \times (1+g)^{T+2}\cdots$
Annuity	C	$C \times (1+g)$	$C \times (1+g)^2$	$\cdots$ $C \times (1+g)^{T-1}$				

The value of perpetuity A is

$$\frac{C}{r-g}$$

The value of perpetuity B is

$$\frac{C \times (1+g)^T}{r-g} \times \frac{1}{(1+r)^T}$$

The difference between the two perpetuities is given by (4.15).

We set the growing-annuity formula equal to \$9,422.91 and solve for C.

$$C\left[\frac{1}{r-g} - \frac{1}{r-g}\left(\frac{1+g}{1+r}\right)^T\right] = C\left[\frac{1}{0.14-0.04} - \frac{1}{0.14-0.04}\left(\frac{1.04}{1.14}\right)^{17}\right]$$

$$= \$9,422.91$$

Here, $C = \$1,192.78$. Thus, the deposit on their daughter's first birthday is \$1,192.78, the deposit on the second birthday is \$1,240.49 ($1.04 \times \$1,192.78$), and so on.

<table>
<tr><td>Concept
Questions</td><td>1. What are the formulas for perpetuity, growing perpetuity, annuity, and growing annuity?
2. What are three important points concerning the growing-perpetuity formula?
3. What are four tricks concerning annuities?</td></tr>
</table>

Making the Decision to Convert Lottery Prize Winnings: The Case of the Singer Asset Finance Company

CASE STUDY

In 1987, Rosalind Setchfield won more than \$1.3 million in the Arizona state lottery. The winnings were to be paid in 20 yearly installments of \$65,276.79. Six years later, in 1995, Mrs. Setchfield received a phone call from a salesman for the Singer Asset Finance Company of West Palm Beach, Florida. The Singer company offered to give her \$140,000 immediately for one-half of the next nine lottery checks (i.e., \$140,000 now for \$32,638.39 × 9 = \$293,745.51 over nine years). Singer is a prize broker with many employees whose main job is to track down million-dollar-lottery prize-winners like Mrs. Setchfield. Singer knows that many people are eager to trade all or part of their promised winnings for a discounted lump sum immediately. Singer is part of a growing \$700 million prize-broker business. Singer and Woodbridge Sterling Capital currently account for about 80 percent of the market for lottery prize conversions. Prize brokers like Singer resell their rights to receive future payouts (called structured payouts) to institutional investors such as SunAmerica, Inc., or the John Hancock Mutual Life Insurance Co. In the case of Mrs. Setchfield, the investor was the Enhance Financial Service Group, a New York municipal bond reinsurer. Singer had arranged to sell its stake in Mrs. Setchfield's lottery prize to Enhance for \$196,000 and would make a quick \$56,000 profit if she accepted the offer. Mrs. Setchfield accepted Singer's offer and the deal was made.

How was Singer able to structure a deal that resulted in a \$56,000 profit? The answer is that individuals and institutions have different intertemporal consumption preferences. Mrs. Setchfield's family had experienced some financial difficulties and was in need of some immediate cash. She didn't want to wait nine years for her prize winnings. On the other hand, the Enhance Group had some excess cash and was very willing to make a \$196,000 investment in order to receive the rights to obtain half of Mrs. Setchfield's prize winnings, or \$32,638.39 a year for nine years. The discount rate the Enhance Group applied to the future payouts was about 8.96 percent (i.e., the discount rate that equates the present value of \$196,000 with Singer's right to receive their equal payments of \$32,638.39).

The discount rate that Mrs. Setchfield used was 18.1 percent, reflecting her aversion to deferred cash flows.

SOURCE: Vanessa Williams, "How Major Players Turn Lottery Jackpots into Guaranteed Bet," *The Wall Street Journal,* September 23, 1997.

4.5 What Is a Firm Worth?

Suppose you are in the business of trying to determine the value of small companies. (You are a business appraiser.) How can you determine what a firm is worth? One way to think about the question of how much a firm is worth is to calculate the present value of its future cash flows.

Let us consider the example of a firm that is expected to generate net cash flows (cash inflows minus cash outflows) of $5,000 in the first year and $2,000 for each of the next five years. The firm can be sold for $10,000 seven years from now. The owners of the firm would like to be able to make 10 percent on their investment in the firm.

The value of the firm is found by multiplying the net cash flows by the appropriate present-value factor. The value of the firm is simply the sum of the present values of the individual net cash flows.

The present value of the net cash flows is given next.

End of Year	Net Cash Flow of the Firm	Present Value Factor (10%)	Present Value of Net Cash Flows
1	$ 5,000	.90909	$ 4,545.45
2	2,000	.82645	1,652.90
3	2,000	.75131	1,502.62
4	2,000	.68301	1,366.02
5	2,000	.62092	1,241.84
6	2,000	.56447	1,128.94
7	10,000	.51315	5,131.58
		Present value of firm	$16,569.35

The Present Value of the Firm

We can also use the simplifying formula for an annuity to give us

$$\frac{\$5,000}{1.1} + \frac{(2,000 \times A^5_{0.10})}{1.1} + \frac{10,000}{(1.1)^7} = \$16,569.35$$

Suppose you have the opportunity to acquire the firm for $12,000. Should you acquire the firm? The answer is yes because the NPV is positive.

$$NPV = PV - Cost$$
$$\$4,569.35 = \$16,569.35 - \$12,000$$

The incremental value (NPV) of acquiring the firm is $4,569.35.

EXAMPLE

The Trojan Pizza Company is contemplating investing $1 million in four new outlets in Los Angeles. Andrew Lo, the firm's Chief Financial Officer (CFO), has estimated that the investments will pay out cash flows of $200,000 per year for nine years and nothing thereafter. (The cash flows will occur at the end of each year and there will be no cash flow after year 9.) Mr. Lo has determined that the relevant discount rate for this investment is 15 percent. This is the rate of return that the firm can earn at comparable projects. Should the Trojan Pizza Company make the investments in the new outlets?

The decision can be evaluated as:

$$NPV = -\$1,000,000 + \frac{\$200,000}{1.15} + \frac{\$200,000}{(1.15)^2} + \cdots + \frac{\$200,000}{(1.15)^9}$$

$$= -\$1,000,000 + \$200,000 \times A^9_{0.15}$$

$$= -\$1,000,000 + \$954,316.78$$

$$= -\$45,683.22$$

The present value of the four new outlets is only \$954,316.78. The outlets are worth less than they cost. The Trojan Pizza Company should not make the investment because the NPV is −\$45,683.22. If the Trojan Pizza Company requires a 15 percent rate of return, the new outlets are not a good investment.

4.6 SUMMARY AND CONCLUSIONS

1. Two basic concepts, *future value* and *present value*, were introduced in the beginning of this chapter. With a 10-percent interest rate, an investor with \$1 today can generate a future value of \$1.10 in a year, \$1.21 [\$1 × (1.10)^2] in two years, and so on. Conversely, present-value analysis places a current value on a later cash flow. With the same 10-percent interest rate, a dollar to be received in one year has a present value of \$0.909 (\$1/1.10) in year 0. A dollar to be received in two years has a present value of \$0.826 [\$1/(1.10)^2].

2. One commonly expresses the interest rate as, say, 12 percent per year. However, one can speak of the interest rate as 3 percent per quarter. Although the stated annual interest rate remains 12 percent (3 percent × 4), the effective annual interest rate is 12.55 percent [(1.03)^4 − 1]. In other words, the compounding process increases the future value of an investment. The limiting case is continuous compounding, where funds are assumed to be reinvested every infinitesimal instant.

3. A basic quantitative technique for financial decision making is net present value analysis. The net present value formula for an investment that generates cash flows (C_i) in future periods is

$$NPV = -C_0 + \frac{C_1}{(1+r)} + \frac{C_2}{(1+r)^2} + \cdots + \frac{C_N}{(1+r)^N} = -C_0 + \sum_{i=1}^{N} \frac{C_i}{(1+r)^i}$$

The formula assumes that the cash flow at date 0 is the initial investment (a cash outflow).

4. Frequently, the actual calculation of present value is long and tedious. The computation of the present value of a long-term mortgage with monthly payments is a good example of this. We presented four simplifying formulas:

$$\text{Perpetuity: } PV = \frac{C}{r}$$

$$\text{Growing perpetuity: } PV = \frac{C}{r - g}$$

$$\text{Annuity: } PV = C \left[\frac{1}{r} - \frac{1}{r \times (1+r)^T} \right]$$

$$\text{Growing annuity: } PV = C \left[\frac{1}{r - g} - \frac{1}{r - g} \times \left(\frac{1+g}{1+r} \right)^T \right]$$

5. We stressed a few practical considerations in the application of these formulas:
   a. The numerator in each of the formulas, *C*, is the cash flow to be received *one full period hence*.

b. Cash flows are generally irregular in practice. To avoid unwieldy problems, assumptions to create more regular cash flows are made both in this textbook and in the real world.

c. A number of present value problems involve annuities (or perpetuities) beginning a few periods hence. Students should practice combining the annuity (or perpetuity) formula with the discounting formula to solve these problems.

d. Annuities and perpetuities may have periods of every two or every *n* years, rather than once a year. The annuity and perpetuity formulas can easily handle such circumstances.

e. One frequently encounters problems where the present value of one annuity must be equated with the present value of another annuity.

KEY TERMS

annual percentage rate, 72	effective annual yield, 72
annuity, 79	future value, 60
annuity factor, 80	growing annuity, 84
appropriate discount rate, 69	growing perpetuity, 77
compounding, 64	net present value, 62
compound interest, 64	perpetuity, 75
compound value, 60	present value, 61
continuous compounding, 74	present value factor, 68
discounting, 68	simple interest, 64
effective annual interest rate, 72	stated annual interest rate, 72

SUGGESTED READINGS

To learn how to perform the mathematics of present value, we encourage you to see the handbooks that come with the Hewlett-Packard HP 19BII calculator.

We also recommend:

White, M. *Financial Analysis with a Calculator.* 5th ed. Burr Ridge, Ill.: McGraw-Hill/Irwin, 2004.

QUESTIONS & PROBLEMS[14]

ANNUAL COMPOUNDING

4.1 Compute the future value of $1,000 compounded annually for
  a. 10 years at 5 percent
  b. 10 years at 7 percent
  c. 20 years at 5 percent
  d. Why is the interest earned in part (*c*) not twice the amount earned in part (*a*)?

4.2 Calculate the present value of the following cash flows discounted at 10 percent.
  a. $1,000 received seven years from today.
  b. $2,000 received one year from today.
  c. $500 received eight years from today.

4.3 Would you rather receive $1,000 today or $2,000 in 10 years? Assume a discount rate of 8 percent.

4.4 The government has issued a bond that will pay $1,000 in 25 years. The bond will pay no interim coupon payments. What is the present value of the bond if the discount rate is 10 percent?

4.5 A firm has an estimated pension liability of $1.5 million due 27 years from today. If the firm can invest in a risk-free security with an interest rate of 8 percent, how much must the firm invest today to be able to make the $1.5 million payment?

---

[14]The following conventions are used in the questions and problems for this chapter.

  If more frequent compounding than once a year is indicated, the problem will either state: (1) both a stated annual interest rate and a compounding period, or (2) an effective annual interest rate.

  If annual compounding is indicated, the problem will provide an annual interest rate. Since the stated annual interest rate and the effective annual interest rate are the same here, we use the simpler annual interest rate.

4.6 You have won the Florida state lottery. Lottery officials offer you the choice of the following alternative payouts:

Alternative 1: $10,000,000 one year from now.
Alternative 2: $20,000,000 five years from now.

Which alternative should you choose if the discount rate is:
a. 0 percent?
b. 10 percent?
c. 20 percent?
d. What discount rate makes the two alternatives equally attractive to you?

4.7 You are selling your house. The Smiths have offered you $115,000. They will pay you immediately. The Joneses have offered you $150,000, but they cannot pay you until three years from today. The interest rate is 10 percent. Which offer should you choose?

4.8 Suppose you bought a bond that will pay $1,000 in 20 years. No intermediate coupon payments will be made. If the appropriate interest rate is 8 percent,
a. what is the current price of the bond?
b. what will the price be 10 years from today?
c. what will the price be 15 years from today?
Assume the interest rate does not change over the life of the bond.

4.9 Ann Woodhouse wants to invest in raw land. She expects to own the property for 10 years and to sell it at the end of the 10th year for $5 million. There are no other cash flows. What is the most she would be willing to pay for the property if the appropriate discount rate is 12 percent?

4.10 You have the opportunity to make an investment of $900,000. If you make this investment now, you will receive $120,000, $250,000 and $800,000 one, two, and three years from today, respectively. The appropriate discount rate for this investment is 12 percent.
a. Should you make the investment?
b. What is the net present value (NPV) of this opportunity?
c. If the discount rate is 11 percent, should you invest? Compute the NPV to support your answer.

4.11 You have the opportunity to invest in a machine that costs $340,000. The machine generates revenues of $100,000 at the end of each year and requires maintenance costs of $10,000 at the beginning of each year. The machine incurs a maintenance cost today because of start-up expenses. If the economic life of the machine is five years and the relevant discount rate is 10 percent, should you buy the machine? What if the relevant discount rate is 9 percent?

4.12 Today a firm signed a contract to sell a capital asset for $90,000. The firm will receive the payment five years from today. The asset costs $60,000 to produce, payable immediately.
a. If the appropriate discount rate is 10 percent, what is the NPV of the contract?
b. At what discount rate will the firm break even on the sale of the asset?

4.13 Your aunt owns an auto dealership. She promised to pay you $3,000 for your car when you graduate one year from now. However, your roommate offered you $3,500 for the car now. The prevailing interest rate is 12 percent. If the future value of the benefit from owning the car for one additional year is $1,000, should you accept your aunt's offer? You are not planning to buy another car and will not need the car after you graduate.

4.14 You wish to purchase a new convertible 12 years from today. At that time, the car will cost $80,000. You currently have $10,000 to invest. What rate of interest must your investment earn so that you can pay for the car?

4.15 Suppose you deposit $1,000 in an account at the end of each of the next four years. If the account earns 12 percent annually, how much will be in the account at the end of seven years?

COMPOUNDING PERIODS

4.16 What is the future value three years hence of $1,000 invested in an account with a stated annual interest rate of 8 percent,
  a. compounded annually?
  b. compounded semiannually?
  c. compounded monthly?
  d. compounded continuously?
  e. Why does the future value increase as the compounding period shortens?

4.17 Compute the future value of $1,000 continuously compounded for
  a. five years at a stated annual interest rate of 12 percent.
  b. three years at a stated annual interest rate of 10 percent.
  c. 10 years at a stated annual interest rate of 5 percent.
  d. eight years at a stated annual interest rate of 7 percent.

4.18 Calculate the present value of $5,000 received 12 years from today. Assume a stated annual interest rate of 10 percent, compounded quarterly.

4.19 Bank America offers a stated annual interest rate of 4.1 percent, compounded quarterly, while Bank USA offers a stated annual interest rate of 4.05 percent, compounded monthly. In which bank should you deposit your money?

PERPETUITIES AND GROWING PERPETUITIES

4.20 An investor purchasing a British consol is entitled to receive annual payments from the British government forever. What is the price of a consol that pays $120 annually if the next payment occurs one year from today? The market interest rate is 15 percent.

ANNUAL COMPOUNDING

4.21 Assuming an interest rate of 10 percent, calculate the present value of the following streams of yearly payments:
  a. $1,000 per year, forever, with the first payment one year from today.
  b. $500 per year, forever, with the first payment two years from today.
  c. $2,420 per year, forever, with the first payment three years from today.

4.22 Given an interest rate of 10 percent per year, what is the value at the end of year 5 of a perpetual stream of $120 annual payments starting at the end of year 9?

4.23 Harris, Inc., paid a $3 dividend yesterday. If the firm raises its dividend 5 percent every year and the appropriate discount rate is 12 percent, what is the price of Harris stock?

4.24 In its most recent corporate report, Williams, Inc., apologized to its stockholders for not paying a dividend. The report states that management will pay a $1 dividend next year. That dividend will grow at four percent every year thereafter. If the discount rate is 10 percent, how much are you willing to pay for a share of Williams, Inc.?

4.25 Mark Weinstein has been working on an advanced technology in laser eye surgery. His technology will be available in the near term. He anticipates his first annual cash flow from the technology to be $200,000, received two years from today. Subsequent annual cash flows will grow at 5 percent, in perpetuity. What is the present value of the technology if the discount rate is 10 percent?

4.26 Barrett Pharmaceuticals is considering a drug project that costs $100,000 today and is expected to generate end-of-year annual cash flow of $50,000, forever. At what discount rate would Barrett be indifferent between accepting or rejecting the project?

COMPOUNDING PERIODS

4.27 A prestigious investment bank designed a new security that pays a quarterly dividend of $10 in perpetuity. The first dividend occurs one quarter from today. What is the price of the security if the stated annual interest rate is 12 percent, compounded quarterly?

4.28 World Transportation, Inc., is expected to initiate its quarterly dividend of $1 five years from today and the dividend is expected to remain constant, forever. What is the price of World Transportation stock if the stated annual interest rate is 15 percent, compounded quarterly?

ANNUITIES AND GROWING ANNUITIES

ANNUAL COMPOUNDING

4.29 Should you buy an asset that will generate income of $1,200 at the end of each year for eight years? The price of the asset is $6,200 and the annual interest rate is 10 percent.

4.30 What is the present value of an annuity of $2,000 per year, with the first cash flow received three years from today and the last one received 22 years from today? Use a discount rate of 8 percent.

4.31 What is the value today of a 15-year annuity that pays $500 a year? The annuity's first payment occurs at the end of year 6. The annual interest rate is 12 percent for years 1 through 5, and 15 percent thereafter.

4.32 You are offered the opportunity to buy a note for $12,800. The note will pay $2,000 at the end of each of the next 10 years. If you buy the note, what rate of interest will you receive?

4.33 You need $25,000 to buy a car five years from now.
  a. In order to buy the car, you plan to make equal payments at the end of every year into an account yielding 7 percent per year. What are these annual payments?
  b. Your rich uncle died and left you $20,000. How much of it must you put into the same account as a lump sum today to meet your goal if you do not want to make any of the annual payments calculated in part (*a*)?

4.34 Nancy Ferris bought a building for $120,000. She paid 15 percent down and agreed to pay the balance in 20 equal, end-of-year, installments. What are the equal installments if the annual interest rate is 10 percent?

4.35 You have recently won the super jackpot in the Washington state lottery. On reading the fine print, you discover that you have the following two options:
  a. You receive 31 annual payments of $160,000, with the first payment being delivered today. The income will be taxed at a rate of 28 percent. Taxes are withheld when the checks are issued.
  b. You receive $446,000 now, and you will not have to pay taxes on this amount. In addition, beginning one year from today, you will receive $101,055 each year for 30 years. The cash flows from this annuity will be taxed at 28 percent.
  Using a discount rate of 10 percent, which option should you select?

4.36 You are saving for the college education of your two children. They are two years apart in age; one will begin college 15 years from today and the other will begin 17 years from today. You estimate your children's college expenses to be $21,000 per year per child, payable at the end of each school year. The annual interest rate is 15 percent. How much money must you deposit in an account each year to fund your children's education? Your deposits begin one year from today. You will make your last deposit when your oldest child enters college.

4.37 A well-known insurance company offers a policy known as the "Estate Creator Six Pay." Typically, a parent or grandparent buys a policy for a child at the child's birth. The details of the policy are as follows. The purchaser (say, the parent) makes the following six payments to the insurance company.

First birthday	$750	Fourth birthday	$800
Second birthday	$750	Fifth birthday	$800
Third birthday	$750	Sixth birthday	$800

No more payments are made after the child's sixth birthday. When the child reaches the age of 65, he or she receives $250,000. If the relevant interest rate is 6 percent for the first six years and 7 percent for all subsequent years, is the policy worth buying?

4.38 Your company is considering either buying or leasing a $120,000 piece of equipment for the next 10 years. The company plans to use the equipment indefinitely. The annual lease payments of $15,000 begin today. The lease includes an option for your company to buy the equipment for $25,000 at the end of the leasing period (i.e., 10 years). Assume that, if the company decides to lease, the company will exercise the option to buy the equipment at the end of the 10-year lease. Should your company accept the lease offer if the appropriate discount rate is 8 percent per year?

4.39 Your job pays you only once a year, for all the work you did over the previous 12 months. Today, December 31, you just received your salary of $50,000 and you plan to spend all of it. However, you want to start saving for retirement beginning next year. You have decided that one year from today you will begin depositing 2 percent of your annual salary in an account that will earn 8 percent per year. Your salary will increase at 4 percent per year throughout your career. How much money will you have on the date of your retirement 40 years from today?

4.40 You must decide whether or not to purchase new capital equipment. The cost of the machine is $5,000. It will produce the following cash flows.

Year	Cash Flow
1	$ 700
2	900
3	1,000
4	1,000
5	1,000
6	1,000
7	1,250
8	1,375

The appropriate discount rate is 10 percent. Should you purchase the equipment?

4.41 Your younger brother has come to you for advice. He is about to enter college and has two options open to him. His first option is to study engineering. If he does this, his undergraduate degree would cost him $12,000 a year for four years. Having obtained his undergraduate degree, he would need to gain two years of practical experience. He would earn $20,000 in the first year and he would earn $25,000 in the second year. He would then need to obtain his master's degree, which will cost $15,000 a year for two years. After completion of his master's degree, he will be fully qualified as an engineer and can earn $40,000 per year for 25 years.

His other alternative is to study accounting. If he does this, he would pay $13,000 a year for four years and then he would earn $31,000 per year for 30 years.

The effort involved in the two careers is the same, so he is only interested in the earnings that the jobs provide. All earnings and costs are paid at the end of the year.
   a. What advice would you give him if the market interest rate is 5 percent?
   b. A day later he comes back and says that he took your advice, but in fact, the market interest rate was 6 percent. Has your brother made the right choice?

4.42 Tom Adams has received a job offer from a large investment bank as a clerk to an associate banker. His base salary will be $35,000. He will receive his first annual salary payment one year from the day he begins to work. In addition, he will get an immediate $10,000 bonus for joining the company. His salary will grow at 4 percent each year. Each year he will receive a bonus equal to 10 percent of his salary. Mr. Adams is expected to work for 25 years. What is the present value of the offer if the discount rate is 12 percent?

4.43 Southern California Publishing Company is trying to decide whether or not to revise its popular textbook, *Financial Psychoanalysis Made Simple*. They have estimated that the revision will cost $40,000. Cash flows from increased sales will be $10,000 the first year. These cash flows will increase by 7 percent per year. The book will go out of print five years from now. Assume that the initial cost is paid now and revenues are received at the end of each year. If the company requires a 10 percent return for such an investment, should it undertake the revision?

4.44 Ian Krassner wants to save money to meet two objectives. First, he wants to retire 31 years from today with a retirement income of $300,000 per year for 20 years. The first retirement payment will occur 31 years from today. Second, he would like to purchase a cabin in the mountains 10 years from today at an estimated cost of $350,000. He can afford to save only $40,000 at the end of each year for the first 10 years. He expects to earn 7 percent per year on his savings. Assuming he saves the same amount each year, what must Ian save annually at the end of year 11 through year 30 to meet his objectives?

COMPOUNDING
PERIODS

4.45 On January 1, Jack Ferguson signed a three-year contract to work for a computer software company. He will be paid $5,000 at the end of each month and will receive a bonus of $10,000 at each year-end. What is the present value of the contract if the stated annual interest rate, compounded monthly, is 12 percent?

4.46 Sarah Buchwalter bought a $15,000 Honda Civic with 20 percent down and financed the rest with a four-year loan at an 8 percent stated annual interest rate, compounded monthly. What is her monthly payment if she makes the first payment one month after the purchase?

4.47 On September 1, 2000, Susan Chao bought a motorcycle for $10,000. She paid $1,000 down and financed the balance with a five-year loan at a stated annual interest rate of 9.6 percent, compounded monthly. She started the monthly payments exactly one month after the purchase, i.e., October 1, 2000. Two years later, at the end of October, 2002, Susan got a new job and decided to pay off the loan. If the bank charges her a 1 percent prepayment penalty based on the loan balance, how much must she pay the bank on November 1, 2002?

4.48 When Marilyn Monroe died, ex-husband Joe DiMaggio vowed to place fresh flowers on her grave every Sunday as long as he lived. The week after she died in 1962, a bunch of fresh flowers that the former baseball player thought appropriate for the star cost about $5. Based on actuarial tables, "Joltin' Joe" could expect to live for 30 years after the actress died. Assume that the stated annual interest rate, compounded weekly, is 10.4 percent. Also, assume that the price of the flowers will increase at 3.9 percent per year, when expressed as a stated annual growth rate, compounded weekly. Assuming that each year has exactly 52 weeks, what is the present value of this commitment? Joe began purchasing flowers the week after Marilyn died.

4.49 In January 1984, Richard "Goose" Gossage signed a contract to play for the San Diego Padres that guaranteed him a minimum of $9,955,000 (undiscounted). The guaranteed payments were $875,000 in 1984, $650,000 in 1985, $800,000 in 1986, $1 million in 1987, $1 million in 1988, and $300,000 in 1989. In addition, the contract called for $5,330,000 (undiscounted) in deferred money payable at the rate of $240,000 per year from 1990 through 2006 and then $125,000 a year from 2007 through 2016. If the annual interest rate is 9 percent and all payments are made on July 1 of each year, what would the present value of these guaranteed payments be on January 1, 1984? Assume an interest rate of 4.4 percent per six months. If he were to receive an equal annual salary at the end of each of the five years from 1984 through 1988, what would his equivalent annual salary be? Ignore taxes throughout this problem.

4.50 Mike Bayles has just arranged to purchase a $400,000 vacation home in the Bahamas with a 20 percent down payment. The mortgage has an 8 percent stated annual interest rate, compounded monthly, and calls for equal monthly payments over the next 30 years. His first payment will be due one month from now. However, the mortgage has an eight-year balloon payment, meaning that the balance of the loan must be paid off at the end of year 8. There were no other transaction costs or finance charges. How much will Mike's balloon payment be in eight years?

4.51 You want to lease a set of golf clubs from Pings Ltd. The lease contract is in the form of 24 equal monthly payments at a 12 percent stated annual interest rate, compounded monthly. Since the clubs cost $4,000 retail, Pings wants the PV of the lease payments to equal $4,000. Suppose that your first payment is due immediately. What will your monthly lease payments be?

4.52 A 10-year annuity pays $900 per year. The first $900 will be paid five years from now. If the stated interest rate is 8 percent, compounded quarterly, what is the present value of this annuity?

4.53 Larry Harris, CFO of MakeMyDecision, is evaluating the financial viability of a new production line for graphite electrodes. His research team has provided him with the following information:

Investment required to set up the production line: $1.8 million

Cash flow projections:
  First year of production (production begins 3 years after initial investment): $60,000
  Cash flow grows at 4% annually for first 5 years and then at a constant rate forever
Required rate of return: 10%

For Larry to accept the project, what should the growth rate be after first 5 years of operation?

4.54 Paul Adams owns a health club in downtown Los Angeles. He charges his customers an annual fee of $400 and has an existing customer base of 500. Paul plans to raise the annual fee by 10 percent every year and expects the club membership to grow at a constant rate of 3 percent for the next five years. The overall expenses of running the health club are $80,000 a year and are expected to grow at the inflation rate of 2 percent annually. After five years, Paul plans to buy a luxury boat for $500,000, close the health club, and travel the world in his boat for the rest of his life. What is the annual amount that Paul can spend while on his world tour if he will have no money left in the bank when he dies? Assume Paul has a remaining life of 15 years and earns 8 percent on his savings.

S & P PROBLEM

STANDARD &POOR'S

4.55 Under the "Excel Analytics" link find the "Mthly. Adj. Price" for Elizabeth Arden (RDEN) stock. What was your annual return over the last four years assuming you purchased the stock at the close price four years ago? (Assume no dividends were paid.) Using this same return, what price will Elizabeth Arden stock sell for five years from now? Ten years from now? What if the stock prices increases at 11 percent per year?

Appendix 4A

Net Present Value: First Principles of Finance

In this appendix, we show the theoretical underpinnings of the net present value rule. We first show how individuals make intertemporal consumption choices, and then we explain the net present value (NPV) rule. The appendix should appeal to students who like a theoretical model. Those of you who can accept the NPV analysis contained in Chapter 4 can skip to Chapter 5.

4A.1 Making Consumption Choices over Time

Figure 4A.1 illustrates the situation faced by a representative individual in the financial market. This person is assumed to have an income of $50,000 this year and an income of $60,000 next year. The market allows him not only to consume $50,000 worth of goods this year and $60,000 next year, but also to borrow and lend at the equilibrium interest rate.

The line AB in Figure 4A.1 shows all of the consumption possibilities open to the person through borrowing or lending, and the shaded area contains all of the feasible choices. Let's look at this figure more closely to see exactly why points in the shaded area are available.

We will use the letter r to denote the interest rate—the equilibrium rate—in this market. The rate is risk-free because we assume that no default can take place. Look at point A on the vertical axis of Figure 4A.1. Point A is a height of

$$A = \$60,000 + [\$50,000 \times (1 + r)]$$

For example, if the rate of interest is 10 percent, then point A would be

$$A = \$60,000 + [\$50,000 \times (1 + 0.1)]$$
$$= \$60,000 + \$55,000$$
$$= \$115,000$$

FIGURE 4A.1

Intertemporal
Consumption
Opportunities

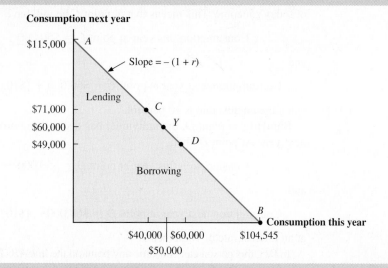

Point A is the maximum amount of wealth that this person can spend in the second year. He gets to point A by lending the full income that is available this year, $50,000, and consuming none of it. In the second year, then, he will have the second year's income of $60,000 plus the proceeds from the loan that he made in the first year, $55,000, for a total of $115,000.

Now let's take a look at point B. Point B is a distance of

$$B = \$50,000 + [\$60,000/(1 + r)]$$

along the horizontal axis. If the interest rate is 10 percent, point B will be

$$B = \$50,000 + [\$60,000/(1 + 0.1)]$$
$$= \$50,000 + \$54,545$$
$$= \$104,545$$

(We have rounded off to the nearest dollar.)

Why do we divide next year's income of $60,000 by $(1 + r)$, or 1.1 in the preceding computation? Point B represents the maximum amount available for this person to consume this year. To achieve that maximum he would borrow as much as possible and repay the loan from the income, $60,000, that he was going to receive next year. Because $60,000 will be available to repay the loan next year, we are asking how much he could borrow this year at an interest rate of r and still be able to repay the loan. The answer is

$$\$60,000/(1 + r)$$

because if he borrows this amount, he must repay it next year with interest. Thus, next year he must repay

$$[\$60,000/(1 + r)] \times (1 + r) = \$60,000$$

no matter what the interest rate, r, is. In our example we found that he could borrow $54,545 and, sure enough,

$$\$54,545 \times 1.1 = \$60,000$$

(after rounding off to the nearest dollar).

Furthermore, by borrowing and lending different amounts the person can achieve any point on the line AB. For example, point C is a point where he has chosen to lend $10,000

Visit us at www.mhhe.com/rwj

of today's income. This means that at point C he will have

Consumption this year at point $C = \$50,000 - \$10,000 = \$40,000$

and

Consumption next year at point $C = \$60,000 + [\$10,000 \times (1 + r)] = \$71,000$

when the interest rate is 10 percent.

Similarly, at point D, the individual has decided to borrow $10,000 and repay the loan next year. At point D, then,

Consumption this year at point $D = \$50,000 + \$10,000 = \$60,000$

and

Consumption next year at point $D = \$60,000 - [\$10,000 \times (1 + r)] = \$49,000$

at an interest rate of 10 percent.

In fact, this person can consume any point on the line AB. This line has a slope of $-(1 + r)$, which means that for each dollar that is added to the x coordinate along the line, $(1 + r)$ dollars are subtracted from the y coordinate. Moving along the line from point A, the initial point of $50,000 this year and $60,000 next year, toward point B gives the person more consumption today and less next year. In other words, moving toward point B is borrowing. Similarly, moving up toward point A, he is consuming less today and more next year and is lending. The line is a straight line because the individual has no effect on the interest rate. This is one of the assumptions of perfectly competitive financial markets.

Where will the person actually be? The answer to that question depends on the individual's tastes and personal situation, just as it did before there was a market. If the person is impatient, he might wish to borrow money at a point such as D, and if he is patient, he might wish to lend some of this year's income and enjoy more consumption next year at, for example, a point such as C.[15]

Notice that whether we think of someone as patient or impatient depends on the interest rate he or she faces in the market. Suppose that our individual was impatient and chose to borrow $10,000 and move to point D. Now suppose that we raise the interest rate to 20 percent or even 50 percent. Suddenly our impatient person may become very patient and might prefer to lend some of this year's income to take advantage of the very high interest rate. The general result is depicted in Figure 4A.2. We can see that lending at point C' yields much greater future income and consumption possibilities than before.[16]

Concept
Questions

1. **How does an individual change his consumption across periods through borrowing and lending?**
2. **How do interest rate changes affect one's degree of impatience?**

---

[15]In this section we are assuming a certain kind of financial market. In the language of economics, individuals who respond to rates and prices by acting as though they have no influence on them are called *price takers*, and this assumption is sometimes called the *price-taking assumption*. It is the condition of perfectly competitive financial markets (or, more simply, *perfect markets*). The following conditions are likely to lead to this:

1. Trading is costless. Access to the financial markets is free.
2. Information about borrowing and lending opportunities is available.
3. There are many traders, and no single trader can have a significant impact on market prices.

[16]Those familiar with consumer theory might be aware of the surprising case where raising the interest rate actually makes people borrow more or lowering the rate makes them lend more. The latter case might occur, for example, if the decline in the interest rate made the lenders have so little consumption next year that they have no choice but to lend out even more than they were lending before just to subsist. Nothing we do depends on excluding such cases, but it is much easier to ignore them, and the resulting analysis fits the real markets more closely.

FIGURE 4A.2

The Effect of Different Interest Rates on Consumption Opportunities

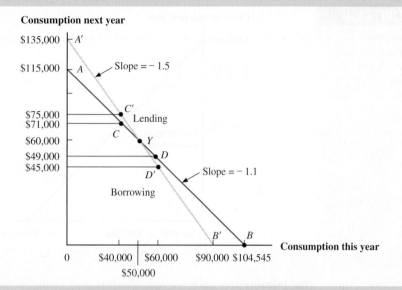

4A.2 Making Investment Choices

A Lending Example   Consider a person who is concerned only about this year and the next. She has an income of $100,000 this year and expects to make the same amount next year. The interest rate is 10 percent. This individual is thinking about investing in a piece of land that costs $70,000. She is certain that next year the land will be worth $75,000, a sure $5,000 gain. Should she undertake the investment? This situation is described in Figure 4A.3 with the cash flow time chart.

A moment's thought should be all it takes to convince her that this is not an attractive business deal. By investing $70,000 in the land, she will have $75,000 available next year. Suppose, instead, that she puts the same $70,000 into a loan in the financial market. At the 10-percent rate of interest this $70,000 would grow to

$$(1 + 0.1) \times \$70,000 = \$77,000$$

next year.

It would be foolish to buy the land when the same $70,000 investment in the financial market would beat it by $2,000 (that is, $77,000 from the loan minus $75,000 from the land investment).

Figure 4A.4 illustrates this situation. Notice that the $70,000 loan gives no less income today and $2,000 more next year. This example illustrates some amazing features of the financial markets. It is remarkable to consider all of the information that we did *not* use when arriving at the decision not to invest in the land. We did not need to know how much income the person has this year or next year. We also did not need to know whether the person preferred more income this year or next.

We did not need to know any of these other facts, and more important, the person making the decision did not need to know them either. She only needed to be able to compare

FIGURE 4A.3

Cash Flows for Investment in Land

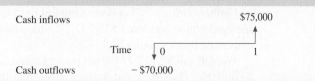

FIGURE 4A.4

Consumption
Opportunities with
Borrowing and
Lending

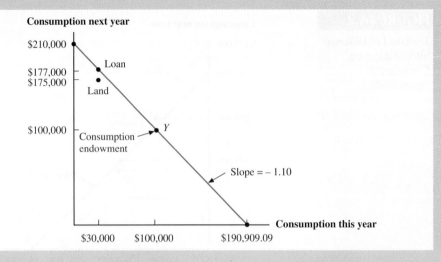

the investment with a relevant alternative available in the financial market. When this investment fell short of that standard—by $2,000 in the previous example—regardless of what the individual wanted to do, she knew that she should not buy the land.

A Borrowing Example   Let us sweeten the deal a bit. Suppose that instead of being worth $75,000 next year, the land would be worth $80,000. What should our investor do now? This case is a bit more difficult. After all, even if the land seems like a good deal, this person's income this year is $100,000. Does she really want to make a $70,000 investment this year? Won't that leave only $30,000 for consumption?

The answers to these questions are yes, the individual should buy the land; yes, she does want to make a $70,000 investment this year; and, most surprising of all, even though her income is $100,000, making the $70,000 investment will not leave her with $30,000 to consume this year! Now let us see how finance lets us get around the basic laws of arithmetic.

The financial markets are the key to solving our problem. First, the financial markets can be used as a standard of comparison against which any investment project must be measured. Second, they can be used as a tool to actually help the individual undertake investments. These twin features of the financial markets enable us to make the right investment decision.

Suppose that the person borrows the $70,000 initial investment that is needed to purchase the land. Next year she must repay this loan. Because the interest rate is 10 percent, she will owe the financial market $77,000 next year. This is depicted in Figure 4A.5. Because the land will be worth $80,000 next year, she can sell it, pay off her debt of $77,000, and have $3,000 extra cash.

If she wishes, this person can now consume an extra $3,000 worth of goods and services next year. This possibility is illustrated in Figure 4A.6. In fact, even if she wants to do all of her consuming this year, she is still better off taking the investment. All she must do is take out a loan this year and repay it from the proceeds of the land next year and profit by $3,000.

Furthermore, instead of borrowing just the $70,000 that she needed to purchase the land, she could have borrowed $72,727.27. She could have used $70,000 to buy the land and consumed the remaining $2,727.27.

We will call $2,727.27 the net present value of the transaction. Notice that it is equal to $3,000 × 1/1.1. How did we figure out that this was the exact amount that she could

FIGURE 4A.5

Cash Flows of
Borrowing to Purchase
the Land

Cash flows of borrowing

Cash inflows $70,000

                                                          1
Time   0

Cash outflows   − $77,000

Cash flows of investing in land

Cash inflows $80,000

Time   0   1

Cash outflows   − $70,000

Cash flows of borrowing and investing in land

Cash inflows $3,000

Time   0   1

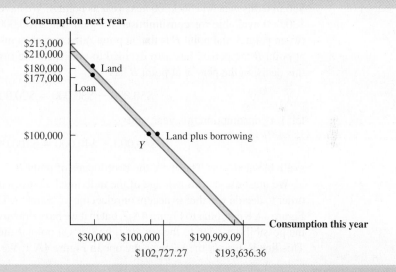

FIGURE 4A.6

Consumption
Opportunities
with Investment
Opportunity and
Borrowing and
Lending

Consumption next year

$213,000
$210,000
$180,000 • Land
$177,000
                Loan

$100,000 • Land plus borrowing
                        Y

                                Consumption this year

$30,000 $100,000 $190,909.09
        $102,727.27 $193,636.36

borrow? It was easy: If $72,727.27 is the amount that she borrows, then, because the interest rate is 10 percent, she must repay

$$\$72{,}727.27 \times (1 + 0.1) = \$80{,}000$$

next year, and that is exactly what the land will be worth. The line through the investment position in Figure 4A.6 illustrates this borrowing possibility.

The amazing thing about both of these cases, one where the land is worth $75,000 next year and the other where it is worth $80,000 next year, is that we needed only to compare the investment with the financial markets to decide whether it was worth undertaking or not. This is one of the more important points in all of finance. It is true regardless of the consumption preferences of the individual. This is one of a number of **separation theorems** in finance. It states that the value of an investment to an individual is not dependent on consumption preferences. In our examples we showed that the person's decision to invest in land was not affected by consumption preferences. However, these preferences dictated whether she borrowed or lent.

Concept
Questions

1. Describe how the financial markets can be used to evaluate investment alternatives.
2. What is the separation theorem? Why is it important?

4A.3 Illustrating the Investment Decision

Figure 4A.1 describes the possibilities open to a person who has an income of $50,000 this year and $60,000 next year and faces a financial market in which the interest rate is 10 percent. But, at that moment, the person has no investment possibilities beyond the 10-percent borrowing and lending that is available in the financial market.

Suppose that we give this person the chance to undertake an investment project that will require a $30,000 outlay of cash this year and that will return $40,000 to the investor next year. Refer to Figure 4A.1 and determine how you could include this new possibility in that figure and how you could use the figure to help you decide whether to undertake the investment.

Now look at Figure 4A.7. In Figure 4A.7 we have labeled the original point with $50,000 this year and $60,000 next year as point A. We have also added a new point B, with $20,000 available for consumption this year and $100,000 next year. The difference between point A and point B is that at point A the person is just where we started him off, and at point B the person has also decided to undertake the investment project. As a result of this decision the person at point B has

$$\$50,000 - \$30,000 = \$20,000$$

left for consumption this year, and

$$\$60,000 + \$40,000 = \$100,000$$

available next year. These are the coordinates of point B.

We must use our knowledge of the individual's borrowing and lending opportunities in order to decide whether to accept or reject the investment. This is illustrated in Figure 4A.8. Figure 4A.8 is similar to Figure 4A.7, but in it we have drawn a line through point A that shows the possibilities open to the person if he stays at point A and does not take the investment. This line is exactly the same as the one in Figure 4A.1. We have also drawn a parallel line

FIGURE 4A.7

Consumption Choices
with Investment but
No Financial Markets

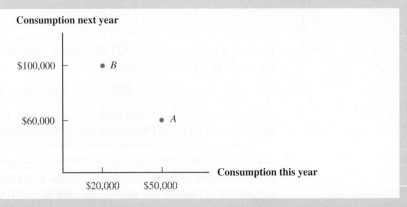

FIGURE 4A.8

Consumption Choices
with Investment
Opportunities and
Financial Markets

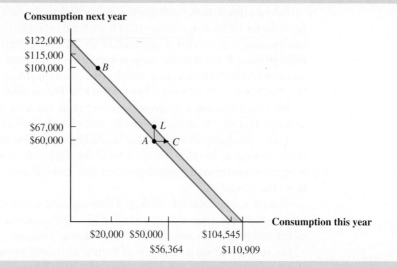

through point B that shows the new possibilities that are available to the person if he undertakes the investment. The two lines are parallel because the slope of each is determined by the same interest rate, 10 percent. It does not matter whether the person takes the investment and goes to point B or does not and stays at point A; in the financial market, each dollar of lending is a dollar less available for consumption this year and moves him to the left by a dollar along the x-axis. Because the interest rate is 10 percent, the $1 loan repays $1.10 and it moves him up by $1.10 along the y-axis.

It is easy to see from Figure 4A.8 that the investment has made the person better off. The line through point B is higher than the line through point A. Thus, no matter what pattern of consumption this person wanted this year and next, he could have more in each year if he undertook the investment.

For example, suppose that our individual wanted to consume everything this year. If he did not take the investment, the point where the line through point A intersected the x-axis would give the maximum amount of consumption he could enjoy this year. This point has $104,545 available this year. To recall how we found this figure, review the analysis of Figure 4A.1. But in Figure 4A.8 the line that goes through point B hits the x-axis at a higher point than the line that goes through point A. Along this line the person can have the $20,000 that is left after investing $30,000, plus all that he can borrow and repay with both next year's income and the proceeds from the investment. The total amount available to consume today is therefore

$$= \$50,000 - \$30,000 + (\$60,000 + \$40,000)/(1 + 0.1)$$
$$= \$20,000 + (\$100,000/1.1)$$
$$= \$110,909$$

The additional consumption available this year from undertaking the investment and using the financial market is the difference on the x-axis between the points where these two lines intersect:

$$\$110,909 - \$104,545 = \$6,364$$

This difference is an important measure of what the investment is worth to the person. It answers a variety of questions. For example, it is the answer to the question: How much money would we need to give the investor this year to make him just as well off as he is with the investment?

Visit us at www.mhhe.com/rwj

Because the line through point B is parallel to the line through point A but has been moved over by $6,364, we know that if we were to add this amount to the investor's current income this year at point A and take away the investment, he would wind up on the line through point B and with the same possibilities. If we do this, the person will have $56,364 this year and $60,000 next year, which is the situation of the point on the line through point B that lies to the right of point A in Figure 4A.8. This is point C.

We could also ask a different question: How much money would we need to give the investor next year to make him just as well off as he is with the investment?

This is the same as asking how much higher the line through point B is than the line through point A. In other words, what is the difference in Figure 4A.8 between the point where the line through A intercepts the y-axis and the point where the line through B intercepts the y-axis?

The point where the line through A intercepts the y-axis shows the maximum amount the person could consume next year if all of his current income were lent out and the proceeds of the loan were consumed along with next year's income.

As we showed in our analysis of Figure 4A.1, this amount is $115,000. How does this compare with what the person can have next year if he takes the investment? By taking the investment we saw that he would be at point B where he has $20,000 left this year and would have $100,000 next year. By lending the $20,000 that is left this year and adding the proceeds of this loan to the $100,000, we find the line through B intercepts the y-axis at:

$$(\$20,000 \times 1.1) + \$100,000 = \$122,000$$

The difference between this amount and $115,000 is

$$\$122,000 - \$115,000 = \$7,000$$

which is the answer to the question of how much we would need to give the person next year to make him as well off as he is with the investment.

There is a simple relationship between these two numbers. If we multiply $6,364 by 1.1 we get $7,000! Consider why this must be so. The $6,364 is the amount of extra cash we must give the person this year to substitute for having the investment. In a financial market with a 10-percent rate of interest, however, $1 this year is worth exactly the same as $1.10 next year. Thus, $6,364 this year is the same as $6,364 \times 1.1$ next year. In other words, the person does not care whether he has the investment, $6,364, this year or $6,364 \times 1.1$ next year. But we already showed that the investor is equally willing to have the investment and to have $7,000 next year. This must mean that

$$\$6,364 \times 1.1 = \$7,000$$

You can also verify this relationship between these two variables by using Figure 4A.8. Because the lines through A and B each have the same slope of -1.1, the difference of $7,000 between where they intersect on the x-axis must be in the ratio of 1.1 to 1.

Now we can show you how to evaluate the investment opportunity on a stand-alone basis. Here are the relevant facts: The individual must give up $30,000 this year to get $40,000 next year. These cash flows are illustrated in Figure 4A.9.

FIGURE 4A.9

Cash Flows for the Investment Project

The investment rule that follows from the previous analysis is the net present value (NPV) rule. Here we convert all consumption values to the present and add them up:

$$\text{Net present value} = -\$30,000 + \$40,000 \times (1/1.1)$$
$$= -\$30,000 + \$36,364$$
$$= \$6,364$$

The future amount, $40,000, is called the *future value* (FV).

The net present value of an investment is a simple criterion for deciding whether or not to undertake an investment. NPV answers the question of how much cash an investor would need to have today as a substitute for making the investment. If the net present value is positive, the investment is worth taking on because doing so is essentially the same as receiving a cash payment equal to the net present value. If the net present value is negative, taking on the investment today is equivalent to giving up some cash today, and the investment should be rejected.

We use the term *net present value* to emphasize that we are already including the current cost of the investment in determining its value and not simply what it will return. For example, if the interest rate is 10 percent and an investment of $30,000 today will produce a total cash return of $40,000 in one year's time, the *present value* of the $40,000 by itself is

$$\$40,000/1.1 = \$36,364$$

but the *net present value* of the investment is $36,364 minus the original investment:

$$\text{Net present value} = \$36,364 - \$30,000 = \$6,364$$

The present value of a future cash flow is the value of that cash flow after considering the appropriate market interest rate. The net present value of an investment is the present value of the investment's future cash flows, minus the initial cost of the investment. We have just decided that our investment is a good opportunity. It has a positive net present value because it is worth more than it costs.

In general, the above can be stated in terms of the **net present value rule:**

An investment is worth making if it has a positive NPV. If an investment's NPV is negative, it should be rejected.

Concept Questions

1. Give the definitions of net present value, future value, and present value.
2. **What information does a person need to compute an investment's net present value?**

4A.4 SUMMARY AND CONCLUSIONS

Finance is a subject that builds understanding from the ground up. Whenever you come up against a new problem or issue in finance, you can always return to the basic principles of this chapter for guidance.

1. Financial markets exist because people want to adjust their consumption over time. They do this by borrowing and lending.

2. Financial markets provide the key test for investment decision making. Whether a particular investment decision should or should not be taken depends only on this test: If there is a superior alternative in the financial markets, the investment should be rejected; if not, the investment is worth taking. The most important thing about this principle is that the investor need not use his

preferences to decide whether the investment should be taken. Regardless of the individual's preference for consumption this year versus the next, regardless of how patient or impatient the individual is, making the proper investment decision depends only on comparing it with the alternatives in the financial markets.

3. The net present value of an investment helps us make the comparison between the investment and the financial market. If the NPV is positive, our rule tells us to undertake the investment. This illustrates the second major feature of the financial markets and investment. Not only does the NPV rule tell us which investments to accept and which to reject, the financial markets also provide us with the tools for actually acquiring the funds to make the investments. In short, we use the financial markets to decide both what to do and how to do it.

4. The NPV rule can be applied to corporations as well as to individuals. The separation theorem developed in this appendix conveys that all of the owners of the firm would agree that the firm should use the NPV rule even though each might differ in personal tastes for consumption and savings.

QUESTIONS & PROBLEMS

MAKING CONSUMPTION CHOICES

THE COMPETITIVE FINANCE MARKET

ILLUSTRATING THE INVESTMENT DECISION

4A.1 Currently, Jim Morris makes $100,000. Next year his income will be $120,000. Jim is a big spender and he wants to consume $150,000 this year. The equilibrium interest rate is 10 percent. What will be Jim's consumption potential next year if he consumes $150,000 this year?

4A.2 Rich Pettit is a miser. His current income is $50,000; next year he will earn $40,000. He plans to consume only $20,000 this year. The current interest rate is 12 percent. What will Rich's consumption potential be next year?

4A.3 What is the basic reason that financial markets develop?

4A.4 The following figure depicts the financial situation of Ms. J. Fawn. In period 0 her labor income and current consumption is $40; later, in period 1, her labor income and consumption will be $22. She has an opportunity to make the investment represented by point D. By borrowing and lending, she will be able to reach any point along the line FDE.

a. What is the market rate of interest? (Hint: The new market interest rate line EF is parallel to AH.)
b. What is the NPV of point D?
c. If Ms. Fawn wishes to consume the same quantity in each period, how much should she consume in period 0?

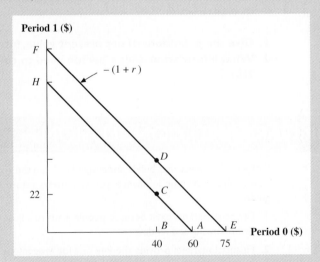

4A.5 Harry Hernandez has $60,000 this year. He faces the investment opportunities represented by point B in the following figure. He wants to consume $20,000 this year and $67,500 next year. This pattern of consumption is represented by point F.

a. What is the market interest rate?
b. How much must Harry invest in financial assets and productive assets today if he follows an optimum strategy?
c. What is the NPV of his investment in nonfinancial assets?

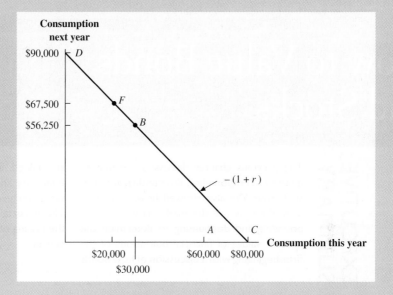

How to Value Bonds and Stocks

EXECUTIVE SUMMARY

The previous chapter discussed the mathematics of compounding, discounting, and present value. We also showed how to value a firm. We now use the mathematics of compounding and discounting to determine the present values of financial obligations of the firm, beginning with a discussion of how bonds are valued. Since the future cash flows of bonds are known, application of net-present-value techniques is fairly straightforward. The uncertainty of future cash flows makes the pricing of stocks according to NPV more difficult.

5.1 Definition and Example of a Bond

A *bond* is a certificate showing that a borrower owes a specified sum. In order to repay the money, the borrower has agreed to make interest and principal payments on designated dates. For example, imagine that Kreuger Enterprises just issued 100,000 bonds for $1,000 each, where the bonds have a coupon rate of 5 percent and a maturity of two years. Interest on the bonds is to be paid yearly. This means that:

1. $100 million (100,000 × $1,000) has been borrowed by the firm.
2. The firm must pay interest of $5 million (5% × $100 million) at the end of one year.
3. The firm must pay both $5 million of interest and $100 million of principal at the end of two years.

We now consider how to value a few different types of bonds.

5.2 How to Value Bonds

Pure Discount Bonds

The **pure discount bond** is perhaps the simplest kind of bond. It promises a single payment, say $1, at a fixed future date. If the payment is one year from now, it is called a *one-year discount bond;* if it is two years from now, it is called a *two-year discount bond,* and so on. The date when the issuer of the bond makes the last payment is called the **maturity date** of the bond, or just its *maturity* for short. The bond is said to mature or *expire* on the date of its final payment. The payment at maturity ($1 in this example) is termed the bond's **face value.**

FIGURE 5.1

Different Types of
Bonds: *C*, Coupon
Paid Every 6 Months;
F, Face Value at
Year 4 (maturity for
pure discount and
coupon bonds)

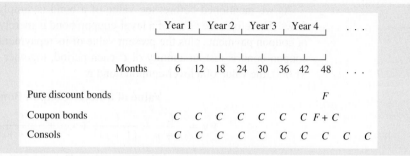

Pure discount bonds are often called *zero-coupon bonds* or zeros to emphasize the fact that the holder receives no cash payments until maturity. We will use the terms *zero, bullet,* and *discount* interchangeably to refer to bonds that pay no coupons.

The first row of Figure 5.1 shows the pattern of cash flows from a four-year pure discount bond. Note that the face value, *F*, is paid when the bond expires in the 48th month. There are no payments of either interest or principal prior to this date.

In the previous chapter, we indicated that one discounts a future cash flow to determine its present value. The present value of a pure discount bond can easily be determined by the techniques of the previous chapter. For short, we sometimes speak of the *value* of a bond instead of its present value.

Consider a pure discount bond that pays a face value of *F* in *T* years, where the interest rate is *r* in each of the *T* years. (We also refer to this rate as the *market interest rate*.) Because the face value is the only cash flow that the bond pays, the present value of this face amount is

Value of a Pure Discount Bond:

$$PV = \frac{F}{(1 + r)^T}$$

The present value formula can produce some surprising results. Suppose that the interest rate is 10 percent. Consider a bond with a face value of $1 million that matures in 20 years. Applying the formula to this bond, its PV is given by

$$PV = \frac{\$1 \text{ million}}{(1.1)^{20}}$$

$$= \$148,644$$

or only about 15 percent of the face value.

Level-Coupon Bonds

Many bonds, however, are not of the simple, pure discount variety. Typical bonds issued by either governments or corporations offer cash payments not just at maturity, but also at regular times in between. For example, payments on U.S. government issues and American corporate bonds are made every six months until the bond matures. These payments are called the **coupons** of the bond. The middle row of Figure 5.1 illustrates the case of a four-year, *level-coupon bond:* The coupon, *C*, is paid every six months and is the same throughout the life of the bond.

Note that the face value of the bond, *F*, is paid at maturity (end of year 4). *F* is sometimes called the *principal* or the *denomination*. Bonds issued in the United States typically have face values of $1,000, though this can vary with the type of bond.

As we mentioned before, the value of a bond is simply the present value of its cash flows. Therefore, the value of a level-coupon bond is merely the present value of its stream of coupon payments plus the present value of its repayment of principal. Because a level-coupon bond is just an annuity of C each period, together with a payment at maturity of $1,000, the value of a level-coupon bond is

Value of a Level-Coupon Bond:

$$PV = \frac{C}{1+r} + \frac{C}{(1+r)^2} + \cdots + \frac{C}{(1+r)^T} + \frac{\$1,000}{(1+r)^T}$$

where C is the coupon and the face value, F, is $1,000. The value of the bond can be rewritten as

Value of a Level-Coupon Bond:

$$PV = C \times A_r^T + \frac{\$1,000}{(1+r)^T}$$

As mentioned in the previous chapter, A_r^T is the present value of an annuity of $1 per period for T periods at an interest rate per period of r.

EXAMPLE

Suppose it is November 2003 and we are considering a government bond. We see in *The Wall Street Journal* some *13s* of November 2007. This is jargon that means the annual coupon rate is 13 percent.[1] The face value is $1,000, implying that the yearly coupon is $130 (13% × $1,000). Interest is paid each May and November, implying that the coupon every six months is $65 ($130/2). The face value will be paid out in November 2007, four years from now. By this we mean that the purchaser obtains claims to the following cash flows:

5/04	11/04	5/05	11/05	5/06	11/06	5/07	11/07
$65	$65	$65	$65	$65	$65	$65	$65 + $1,000

If the stated annual interest rate in the market is 10 percent per year, what is the present value of the bond?

Our work on compounding in the previous chapter showed that the interest rate over any six-month interval is one half of the stated annual interest rate. In the current example, this semiannual rate is 5 percent (10%/2). Since the coupon payment in each six-month period is $65, and there are eight of these six-month periods from November 2003 to November 2007, the present value of the bond is

$$PV = \frac{\$65}{(1.05)} + \frac{\$65}{(1.05)^2} + \cdots + \frac{\$65}{(1.05)^8} + \frac{\$1,000}{(1.05)^8}$$

$$= \$65 \times A_{0.05}^8 + \$1,000/(1.05)^8$$

$$= (\$65 \times 6.463) + (\$1,000 \times 0.677)$$

$$= \$420.095 + \$677$$

$$= \$1,097.095$$

Traders will generally quote the bond as 109.7095,[2] indicating that it is selling at 109.7095 percent of the face value of $1,000.

---

[1]The coupon rate is specific to the bond. The coupon rate indicates what cash flow should appear in the numerator of the NPV equation. The coupon rate does *not* appear in the denominator of the NPV equation.

[2]Bond prices are actually quoted in 32nds of a dollar, so a quote this precise would not be given.

At this point, it is worthwhile to relate the above example of bond-pricing to the discussion of compounding in the previous chapter. At that time we distinguished between the stated annual interest rate and the effective annual interest rate. In particular, we pointed out that the effective annual interest rate is

$$(1 + r/m)^m - 1$$

where r is the stated annual interest rate and m is the number of compounding intervals. Since $r = 10\%$ and $m = 2$ (because the bond makes semiannual payments), the effective annual interest rate is

$$[1 + (0.10/2)]^2 - 1 = (1.05)^2 - 1 = 10.25\%$$

In other words, because the bond is paying interest twice a year, the bondholder earns a 10.25-percent return when compounding is considered.[3]

One final note concerning level-coupon bonds: Although the preceding example concerns government bonds, corporate bonds are identical in form. For example, DuPont Corporation has an 8½-percent bond maturing in 2006. This means that DuPont will make semiannual payments of $42.50 (8½%/2 × $1,000) between now and 2006 for each face value of $1,000.

Consols

Not all bonds have a final maturity date. As we mentioned in the previous chapter, consols are bonds that never stop paying a coupon, have no final maturity date, and therefore never mature. Thus, a consol is a perpetuity. In the 18th century the Bank of England issued such bonds, called "English consols." These were bonds that the Bank of England guaranteed would pay the holder a cash flow forever! Through wars and depressions, the Bank of England continued to honor this commitment, and you can still buy such bonds in London today. The U.S. government also once sold consols to raise money to build the Panama Canal. Even though these U.S. bonds were supposed to last forever and to pay their coupons forever, don't go looking for any. There is a special clause in the bond contract that gives the government the right to buy them back from the holders, and that is what the government has done. Clauses like that are *call provisions*, and we study them later.

An important example of a consol, though, is called *preferred stock*. Preferred stock is stock that is issued by corporations and that provides the holder a fixed dividend in perpetuity. If there were never any question that the firm would actually pay the dividend on the preferred stock, such stock would in fact be a consol.

These instruments can be valued by the perpetuity formula of the previous chapter. For example, if the marketwide interest rate is 10 percent, a consol with a yearly interest payment of $50 is valued at

$$\frac{\$50}{0.10} = \$500$$

[3]For an excellent discussion of how to value semiannual payments, see J. T. Lindley, B. P. Helms, and M. Haddad, "A Measurement of the Errors in Intra-Period Compounding and Bond Valuation," *The Financial Review* 22 (February 1987). We benefited from several conversations with the authors of this article.

Concept
Questions

1. **Define pure discount bonds, level-coupon bonds, and consols.**
2. **Contrast the stated interest rate and the effective annual interest rate for bonds paying semiannual interest.**

5.3 Bond Concepts

We complete our discussion on bonds by considering two concepts concerning them. First, we examine the relationship between interest rates and bond prices. Second, we define the concept of yield to maturity.

Interest Rates and Bond Prices

The above discussion on level-coupon bonds allows us to relate bond prices to interest rates. Consider the following example.

EXAMPLE

The interest rate is 10 percent. A two-year bond with a 10-percent coupon pays interest of $100 ($1,000 × 10%). For simplicity, we assume that the interest is paid annually. The bond is priced at its face value of $1,000:

$$\$1,000 = \frac{\$100}{1.10} + \frac{\$1,000 + \$100}{(1.10)^2}$$

If the interest rate unexpectedly rises to 12 percent, the bond sells at

$$\$966.20 = \frac{\$100}{1.12} + \frac{\$1,000 + \$100}{(1.12)^2}$$

Because $966.20 is below $1,000, the bond is said to sell at a **discount**. This is a sensible result. Now that the interest rate is 12 percent, a newly issued bond with a 12-percent coupon rate will sell at $1,000. This newly issued bond will have coupon payments of $120 (0.12 × $1,000). Because our bond has interest payments of only $100, investors will pay less than $1,000 for it.

If interest rates fell to 8 percent, the bond would sell at

$$\$1,035.67 = \frac{\$100}{1.08} + \frac{\$1,000 + \$100}{(1.08)^2}$$

Because $1,035.67 is above $1,000, the bond is said to sell at a **premium.**

Thus, we find that bond prices fall with a rise in interest rates and rise with a fall in interest rates. Furthermore, the general principle is that a level-coupon bond sells in the following ways.

1. At the face value of $1,000 if the coupon rate is equal to the marketwide interest rate.
2. At a discount if the coupon rate is below the marketwide interest rate.
3. At a premium if the coupon rate is above the marketwide interest rate.

Yield to Maturity

Let's now consider the previous example *in reverse.* If our bond is selling at $1,035.67, what return is a bondholder receiving? This can be answered by considering the following equation:

$$\$1,035.67 = \frac{\$100}{1 + y} + \frac{\$1,000 + \$100}{(1 + y)^2}$$

The unknown, y, is the discount rate that equates the price of the bond with the discounted value of the coupons and face value. Our earlier work implies that $y = 8\%$. Thus, traders

The Present Value Formulas for Bonds

Pure Discount Bonds

$$PV = \frac{F}{(1 + r)^T}$$

Level-Coupon Bonds

$$PV = C\left[\frac{1}{r} - \frac{1}{r \times (1 + r)^T}\right] + \frac{F}{(1 + r)^T} = C \times A_r^T + \frac{F}{(1 + r)^T}$$

where F is typically $1,000 for a level-coupon bond.

Consols

$$PV = \frac{C}{r}$$

state that the bond is yielding an 8-percent return. Bond traders also state that the bond has a **yield to maturity** of 8 percent. The yield to maturity is frequently called the bond's yield for short. So we would say the bond with its 10-percent coupon is priced to yield 8 percent at $1,035.67.

Bond Market Reporting

Almost all corporate bonds are traded by institutional investors and are traded on the over-the-counter market (OTC for short). There is a corporate bond market associated with the New York Stock Exchange. This bond market is mostly a retail market for individual investors for smaller trades. It represents a very small fraction of total corporate bond trading.

Table 5.1 reproduces some bond data that can be found in *The Wall Street Journal* on any particular day. At the bottom of the list you will find AT&T and an entry AT&T 8⅛/22. This entry represents AT&T bonds that mature in the year 2022 and have a coupon rate of 8⅛. The coupon rate means 8⅛ percent of the par value (or face value) of $1,000. Therefore, the annual coupon for AT&T bonds is $81.25.

TABLE 5.1	Bonds	Cur. Yld.	Vol.	Close		Net Chg.
Bond Market	AMF 10⅞ 06	25.3	10	43		. . .
Reporting	AMR 9s16	8.8	25	102	−	.38
	ATT 5⅛ 01	5.2	30	98.50	+	.13
	ATT 7⅛ 02	7.1	55	100.13	−	.13
	ATT 6½ 02	6.6	50	99	+	.88
	ATT 6¾ 04	6.9	52	97.75	+	.38
	ATT 5⅝ 04	6.0	138	94.38		. . .
	ATT 7½ 06	7.4	60	100.75	−	.50
	ATT 7¾ 07	7.6	83	101.50	+	.50
	ATT 6s09	6.7	40	89	+	.63
	ATT 8⅛ 22	8.1	97	100	+	.38

Under the heading "Close," you will find the last price for the AT&T bonds at the close of this particular day. The price is quoted as a percentage of the par value. So the last price for the AT&T bonds on this particular day was 100 percent of $1,000 or $1,000.00. This bond is trading at a price less than its par value, and so it is trading at a "discount." The last column is "Net Chg." AT&T bonds traded up from the day before by .38 of 1 percent (a rounded .375, or ⅜). The AT&T bonds have a current yield of 8.1 percent. The current yield is simply the current coupon divided by the current price, or 81.25 divided by 1,000, equal to 8.1 percent (rounded to one decimal place).

You should know from our discussion of bond yields that the current yield is not the same thing as the bonds' yield to maturity. The yield to maturity is not usually reported on a daily basis by the financial press. The "Vol" column is the daily volume of 97. This is the number of bonds that were traded on the New York Stock Exchange on this particular day.

Concept Questions	1. **What is the relationship between interest rates and bond prices?** 2. **How does one calculate the yield to maturity on a bond?**

5.4 The Present Value of Common Stocks

Dividends versus Capital Gains

Our goal in this section is to value common stocks. We learned in the previous chapter that an asset's value is determined by the present value of its future cash flows. A stock provides two kinds of cash flows. First, most stocks pay dividends on a regular basis. Second, the stockholder receives the sale price when she sells the stock. Thus, in order to value common stocks, we need to answer an interesting question: Is the value of a stock equal to

1. The discounted present value of the sum of next period's dividend plus next period's stock price, or
2. The discounted present value of all future dividends?

This is the kind of question that students would love to see on a multiple-choice exam, because both (1) and (2) are right.

To see that (1) and (2) are the same, let's start with an individual who will buy the stock and hold it for one year. In other words, she has a one-year *holding period*. In addition, she is willing to pay P_0 for the stock today. That is, she calculates

$$P_0 = \frac{\text{Div}_1}{1 + r} + \frac{P_1}{1 + r} \tag{5.1}$$

Div_1 is the dividend paid at year's end and P_1 is the price at year's end. P_0 is the PV of the common-stock investment. The term in the denominator, r, is the discount rate of the stock. It will be equal to the interest rate in the case where the stock is riskless. It is likely to be greater than the interest rate in the case where the stock is risky.

That seems easy enough, but where does P_1 come from? P_1 is not pulled out of thin air. Rather, there must be a buyer at the end of year 1 who is willing to purchase the stock for P_1. This buyer determines price by

$$P_1 = \frac{\text{Div}_2}{1 + r} + \frac{P_2}{1 + r} \tag{5.2}$$

Substituting the value of P_1 from (5.2) into equation (5.1) yields

$$P_0 = \frac{1}{1+r}\left[\mathrm{Div}_1 + \left(\frac{\mathrm{Div}_2 + P_2}{1+r}\right)\right]$$

$$= \frac{\mathrm{Div}_1}{1+r} + \frac{\mathrm{Div}_2}{(1+r)^2} + \frac{P_2}{(1+r)^2} \tag{5.3}$$

We can ask a similar question for formula (5.3): Where does P_2 come from? An investor at the end of year 2 is willing to pay P_2 because of the dividend and stock price at year 3. This process can be repeated *ad nauseam*.[4] At the end, we are left with

$$P_0 = \frac{\mathrm{Div}_1}{1+r} + \frac{\mathrm{Div}_2}{(1+r)^2} + \frac{\mathrm{Div}_3}{(1+r)^3} + \cdots = \sum_{t=1}^{\infty}\frac{\mathrm{Div}_t}{(1+r)^t} \tag{5.4}$$

Thus the value of a firm's common stock to the investor is equal to the present value of all of the expected future dividends.

This is a very useful result. A common objection to applying present value analysis to stocks is that investors are too shortsighted to care about the long-run stream of dividends. These critics argue that an investor will generally not look past his or her time horizon. Thus, prices in a market dominated by short-term investors will reflect only near-term dividends. However, our discussion shows that a long-run dividend-discount model holds even when investors have short-term time horizons. Although an investor may want to cash out early, she must find another investor who is willing to buy. The price this second investor pays is dependent on dividends *after* his date of purchase.

Valuation of Different Types of Stocks

The above discussion shows that the value of the firm is the present value of its future dividends. How do we apply this idea in practice? Equation (5.4) represents a very general model and is applicable regardless of whether the level of expected dividends is growing, fluctuating, or constant. The general model can be simplified if the firm's dividends are expected to follow some basic patterns: (1) zero growth, (2) constant growth, and (3) differential growth. These cases are illustrated in Figure 5.2.

Case 1 (Zero Growth)   The value of a stock with a constant dividend is given by

$$P_0 = \frac{\mathrm{Div}_1}{1+r} + \frac{\mathrm{Div}_2}{(1+r)^2} + \cdots = \frac{\mathrm{Div}}{r}$$

Here it is assumed that $\mathrm{Div}_1 = \mathrm{Div}_2 = \cdots = \mathrm{Div}$. This is just an application of the perpetuity formula of the previous chapter.

Case 2 (Constant Growth)   Dividends grow at rate g, as follows:

End of Year	1	2	3	4	...
Dividend	Div	Div(1 + g)	Div(1 + g)²	Div(1 + g)³	

Note that Div is the dividend at the end of the *first* period.

---

[4]This procedure reminds us of the physicist lecturing on the origins of the universe. He was approached by an elderly gentleman in the audience who disagreed with the lecture. The attendee said that the universe rests on the back of a huge turtle. When the physicist asked what the turtle rested on, the gentleman said another turtle. Anticipating the physicist's objections, the attendee said, "Don't tire yourself out, young fellow. It's turtles all the way down."

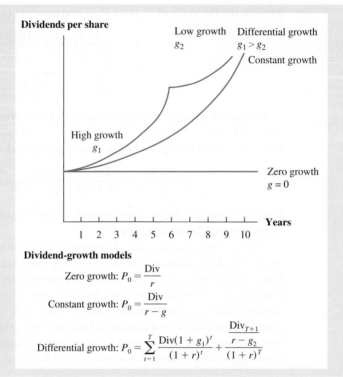

Dividend-growth models

Zero growth: $P_0 = \dfrac{\text{Div}}{r}$

Constant growth: $P_0 = \dfrac{\text{Div}}{r - g}$

Differential growth: $P_0 = \displaystyle\sum_{t=1}^{T} \dfrac{\text{Div}(1 + g_1)^t}{(1 + r)^t} + \dfrac{\dfrac{\text{Div}_{T+1}}{r - g_2}}{(1 + r)^T}$

EXAMPLE

Hampshire Products will pay a dividend of $4 per share a year from now. Financial analysts believe that dividends will rise at 6 percent per year for the foreseeable future. What is the dividend per share at the end of each of the first five years?

End of Year	1	2	3	4	5
Dividend	$4.00	$4 × (1.06) = $4.24	$4 × (1.06)² = $4.4944	$4 × (1.06)³ = $4.7641	$4 × (1.06)⁴ = $5.0499

The value of a common stock with dividends growing at a constant rate is

$$P_0 = \frac{\text{Div}}{1 + r} + \frac{\text{Div}(1 + g)}{(1 + r)^2} + \frac{\text{Div}(1 + g)^2}{(1 + r)^3} + \frac{\text{Div}(1 + g)^3}{(1 + r)^4} + \cdots$$

$$= \frac{\text{Div}}{r - g}$$

where g is the growth rate. Div is the dividend on the stock at the end of the first period. This is the formula for the present value of a growing perpetuity, which we derived in the previous chapter.

EXAMPLE

Suppose an investor is considering the purchase of a share of the Utah Mining Company. The stock will pay a $3 dividend a year from today. This dividend is expected to grow at 10 percent per year ($g = 10\%$) for the foreseeable future. The investor thinks that the required return (r) on this stock is 15 percent, given her assessment of Utah Mining's risk. (We also refer to r as the discount rate of the stock.) What is the value of a share of Utah Mining Company's stock?

Using the constant growth formula of case 2, we assess the value to be $60:

$$\$60 = \frac{\$3}{0.15 - 0.10}$$

P_0 is quite dependent on the value of g. If g had been estimated to be 12½ percent, the value of the share would have been

$$\$120 = \frac{\$3}{0.15 - 0.125}$$

The stock price doubles (from $60 to $120) when g only increases 25 percent (from 10 percent to 12.5 percent). Because of P_0's dependency on g, one must maintain a healthy sense of skepticism when using this constant growth of dividends model.

Furthermore, note that P_0 is equal to infinity when the growth rate, g, equals the discount rate, r. Because stock prices do not grow infinitely, an estimate of g greater than r implies an error in estimation. More will be said of this point later.

Case 3 (Differential Growth)   In this case, an algebraic formula would be too unwieldy. Instead, we present examples.

EXAMPLE

Consider the stock of Elixir Drug Company, which has a new back-rub ointment and is enjoying rapid growth. The dividend for a share of stock a year from today will be $1.15. During the next four years, the dividend will grow at 15 percent per year (g_1 = 15%). After that, growth (g_2) will be equal to 10 percent per year. Can you calculate the present value of the stock if the required return (r) is 15 percent?

Figure 5.3 displays the growth in the dividends. We need to apply a two-step process to discount these dividends. We first calculate the net present value of the dividends growing at 15 percent per annum. That is, we first calculate the present value of the dividends at the end of each of the first five years. Second, we calculate the present value of the dividends beginning at the end of year 6.

FIGURE 5.3

Growth in Dividends
for Elixir Drug
Company

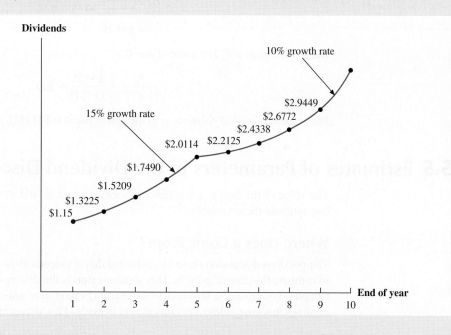

Calculate Present Value of First Five Dividends   The present value of dividend payments in years 1 through 5 is as follows:

Future Year	Growth Rate (g_1)	Expected Dividend	Present Value
1	0.15	$1.15	$1
2	0.15	1.3225	1
3	0.15	1.5209	1
4	0.15	1.7490	1
5	0.15	2.0114	1
Years 1–5		The present value of dividends = $5	

The growing-annuity formula of the previous chapter could normally be used in this step. However, note that dividends grow at 15 percent, which is also the discount rate. Since $g = r$, the growing-annuity formula cannot be used in this example.

Calculate Present Value of Dividends Beginning at End of Year 6   This is the procedure for deferred perpetuities and deferred annuities that we mentioned in the previous chapter. The dividends beginning at the end of year 6 are

End of Year	6	7	8	9
Dividend	$Div_5 \times (1 + g_2)$ 2.0114×1.10 = $2.2125	$Div_5 \times (1 + g_2)^2$ $2.0114 \times (1.10)^2$ = $2.4338	$Div_5 \times (1 + g_2)^3$ $2.0114 \times (1.10)^3$ = $2.6772	$Div_5 \times (1 + g_2)^4$ $2.0114 \times (1.10)^4$ = $2.9449

As stated in the previous chapter, the growing-perpetuity formula calculates present value as of one year prior to the first payment. Because the payment begins at the end of year 6, the present value formula calculates present value as of the end of year 5.

The price at the end of year 5 is given by

$$P_5 = \frac{Div_6}{r - g_2} = \frac{\$2.2125}{0.15 - 0.10}$$
$$= \$44.25$$

The present value of P_5 at the end of year 0 is

$$\frac{P_5}{(1 + r)^5} = \frac{\$44.25}{(1.15)^5} = \$22$$

The present value of *all* dividends as of the end of year 0 is $27 ($22 + $5).

5.5 Estimates of Parameters in the Dividend-Discount Model

The value of the firm is a function of its growth rate, g, and its discount rate, r. How does one estimate these variables?

Where Does g Come From?

The previous discussion on stocks assumed that dividends grow at the rate g. We now want to estimate this rate of growth. This section extends the discussion of growth contained in Chapter 3. Consider a business whose earnings next year are expected to be the same as earnings this year unless a *net investment* is made. This situation is likely to occur, because net investment is equal to gross, or total, investment less depreciation. A net investment of zero occurs when *total investment* equals depreciation. If total investment is equal to depreciation, the firm's physical plant is maintained, consistent with no growth in earnings.

Net investment will be positive only if some earnings are not paid out as dividends, that is, only if some earnings are retained.[5] This leads to the following equation:

$$
\begin{matrix}
\text{Earnings} & & \text{Earnings} & & \text{Retained} & & \text{Return on} \\
\text{next} & = & \text{this} & + & \text{earnings} & \times & \text{retained} \\
\text{year} & & \text{year} & & \text{this year} & & \text{earnings}
\end{matrix}
\qquad (5.5)
$$
$$
\underbrace{\phantom{\text{Retained earnings this year} \times \text{Return on retained earnings}}}_{\text{Increase in earnings}}
$$

The increase in earnings is a function of both the *retained earnings* and the *return on the retained earnings.*

We now divide both sides of (5.5) by earnings this year, yielding

$$
\frac{\text{Earnings next year}}{\text{Earnings this year}} = \frac{\text{Earnings this year}}{\text{Earnings this year}} + \left(\frac{\text{Retained earnings this year}}{\text{Earnings this year}} \right)
$$
$$
\times \text{Return on retained earnings} \qquad (5.6)
$$

The left-hand side of (5.6) is simply one plus the growth rate in earnings, which we write as $1 + g$.[6] The ratio of retained earnings to earnings is called the **retention ratio.** Thus, we can write

$$
1 + g = 1 + \text{Retention ratio} \times \text{Return on retained earnings} \qquad (5.7)
$$

It is difficult for a financial analyst to determine the return to be expected on currently retained earnings, because the details on forthcoming projects are not generally public information. However, it is frequently assumed that the projects selected in the current year have an anticipated return equal to returns from projects in other years. Here, we can estimate the anticipated return on current retained earnings by the historical **return on equity,** or ROE. After all, ROE is simply the return on the firm's entire equity, which is the return on the cumulation of all the firm's past projects.[7]

From (5.7), we have a simple way to estimate growth:

Formula for Firm's Growth Rate:
$$
g = \text{Retention ratio} \times \text{Return on retained earnings} \qquad (5.8)
$$

EXAMPLE

Pagemaster Enterprises just reported earnings of $2 million. It plans to retain 40 percent of its earnings. The historical return on equity (ROE) has been 0.16, a figure that is expected to continue into the future. How much will earnings grow over the coming year?

We first perform the calculation without reference to equation (5.8). Then we use (5.8) as a check.

---

[5]We ignore the possibility of the issuance of stocks or bonds in order to raise capital. These possibilities are considered in later chapters.

[6]Previously *g* referred to growth in dividends. However, the growth in earnings is equal to the growth rate in dividends in this context, because as we will presently see, the ratio of dividends to earnings is held constant. In fact, you have probably figured out that *g* is the sustainable growth rate introduced in Chapter 3.

[7]Students frequently wonder whether return on equity (ROE) or return on assets (ROA) should be used here. ROA and ROE are identical in our model because debt financing is ignored. However, most real-world firms have debt. Because debt is treated in later chapters, we are not yet able to treat this issue in depth now. Suffice it to say that ROE is the appropriate rate, because both ROE for the firm as a whole and the return to equityholders from a future project are calculated after interest has been deducted.

Calculation without Reference to Equation (5.8)　The firm will retain $800,000 (40% × $2 million). Assuming that historical ROE is an appropriate estimate for future returns, the anticipated increase in earnings is

$$\$800,000 \times 0.16 = \$128,000$$

The percentage growth in earnings is

$$\frac{\text{Change in earnings}}{\text{Total earnings}} = \frac{\$128,000}{\$2 \text{ million}} = 0.064$$

This implies that earnings in one year will be $2,128,000 ($2,000,000 × 1.064).

Check Using Equation (5.8)　We use g = Retention ratio × ROE. We have

$$g = 0.4 \times 0.16 = 0.064$$

Where Does r Come From?

In this section, we want to estimate r, the rate used to discount the cash flows of a particular stock. There are two methods developed by academics. We present one method below but must defer the second until we give it extensive treatment in later chapters.

The first method begins with the concept that the value of a growing perpetuity is

$$P_0 = \frac{\text{Div}}{r - g}$$

Solving for r, we have

$$r = \frac{\text{Div}}{P_0} + g \tag{5.9}$$

As stated earlier, Div refers to the dividend to be received one year hence.

Thus, the discount rate can be broken into two parts. The ratio, Div/P_0, places the dividend return on a percentage basis, frequently called the *dividend yield*. The second term, g, is the growth rate of dividends.

Because information on both dividends and stock price is publicly available, the first term on the right-hand side of equation (5.9) can be easily calculated. The second term on the right-hand side, g, can be estimated from (5.8).

EXAMPLE

Pagemaster Enterprises, the company examined in the previous example, has 1,000,000 shares of stock outstanding. The stock is selling at $10. What is the required return on the stock?

Because the retention ratio is 40 percent, the **payout ratio** is 60 percent (1 − Retention ratio). The payout ratio is the ratio of dividends/earnings. Because earnings a year from now will be $2,128,000 ($2,000,000 × 1.064), dividends will be $1,276,800 (0.60 × $2,128,000). Dividends per share will be $1.28 ($1,276,800/1,000,000). Given our previous result that g = 0.064, we calculate r from (5.9) as follows:

$$0.192 = \frac{\$1.28}{\$10.00} + 0.064$$

A Healthy Sense of Skepticism

It is important to emphasize that our approach merely *estimates* g; our approach does not *determine* g precisely. We mentioned earlier that our estimate of g is based on a number of assumptions. For example, we assume that the return on reinvestment of future retained earnings is equal to the firm's past ROE. We assume that the future retention ratio is equal to the past retention ratio. Our estimate for g will be off if these assumptions prove to be wrong.

Unfortunately, the determination of r is highly dependent on g. For example, if g is estimated to be 0, r equals 12.8 percent ($\$1.28/\$10.00$). If g is estimated to be 12 percent, r equals 24.8 percent ($\$1.28/\$10.00 + 12\%$). Thus, one should view estimates of r with a healthy sense of skepticism.

Because of the preceding, some financial economists generally argue that the estimation error for r or a single security is too large to be practical. Therefore, they suggest calculating the average r for an entire industry. This r would then be used to discount the dividends of a particular stock in the same industry.

One should be particularly skeptical of two polar cases when estimating r for individual securities. First, consider a firm currently paying no dividend. The stock price will be above zero because investors believe that the firm may initiate a dividend at some point or the firm may be acquired at some point. However, when a firm goes from no dividends to a positive number of dividends, the implied growth rate is *infinite*. Thus, equation (5.9) must be used with extreme caution here, if at all—a point we emphasize later in this chapter.

Second, we mentioned earlier that the value of the firm is infinite when g is equal to r. Because prices for stocks do not grow infinitely, an analyst whose estimate of g for a particular firm is equal to or above r must have made a mistake. Most likely, the analyst's high estimate for g is correct for the next few years. However, firms simply cannot maintain an abnormally high growth rate *forever*. The analyst's error was to use a short-run estimate of g in a model requiring a perpetual growth rate.

5.6 Growth Opportunities

We previously spoke of the growth rate of dividends. We now want to address the related concept of growth opportunities. Imagine a company with a level stream of earnings per share in perpetuity. The company pays all of these earnings out to stockholders as dividends. Hence,

$$EPS = Div$$

where EPS is *earnings per share* and Div is dividends per share. A company of this type is frequently called a *cash cow*.

From the perpetuity formula of the previous chapter, the value of a share of stock is:

Value of a Share of Stock When Firm Acts as a Cash Cow:

$$\frac{EPS}{r} = \frac{Div}{r}$$

where r is the discount rate on the firm's stock.

This policy of paying out all earnings as dividends may not be the optimal one. Many firms have *growth* opportunities, that is, opportunities to invest in profitable projects. Because these projects can represent a significant fraction of the firm's value, it would be foolish to forgo them in order to pay out all earnings as dividends.

Although firms frequently think in terms of a *set* of growth opportunities, let's focus on only one opportunity, that is, the opportunity to invest in a single project. Suppose the firm retains the entire dividend at date 1 in order to invest in a particular capital budgeting project. The net present value *per share* of the project as of date 0 is *NPVGO,* which stands for the *net present value (per share) of the growth opportunity.*

What is the price of a share of stock at date 0 if the firm decides to take on the project at date 1? Because the per share value of the project is added to the original stock price, the stock price must now be:

Stock Price after Firm Commits to New Project:

$$\frac{EPS}{r} + NPVGO \qquad (5.10)$$

Thus, equation (5.10) indicates that the price of a share of stock can be viewed as the sum of two different items. The first term (EPS/r) is the value of the firm if it rested on its laurels, that is, if it simply distributed all earnings to the stockholders. The second term is the *additional* value if the firm retains earnings in order to fund new projects.

EXAMPLE

Sarro Shipping, Inc., expects to earn $1 million per year in perpetuity if it undertakes no new investment opportunities. There are 100,000 shares of stock outstanding, so earnings per share equal $10 ($1,000,000/100,000). The firm will have an opportunity at date 1 to spend $1,000,000 in a new marketing campaign. The new campaign will increase earnings in every subsequent period by $210,000 (or $2.10 per share). This is a 21-percent return per year on the project. The firm's discount rate is 10 percent. What is the value per share before and after deciding to accept the marketing campaign?

The value of a share of Sarro Shipping before the campaign is

Value of a Share of Sarro When Firm Acts as a Cash Cow:

$$\frac{EPS}{r} = \frac{\$10}{0.1} = \$100$$

The value of the marketing campaign as of date 1 is:

Value of Marketing Campaign at Date 1:

$$-\$1,000,000 + \frac{\$210,000}{0.1} = \$1,100,000 \qquad (5.11)$$

Because the investment is made at date 1 and the first cash inflow occurs at date 2, equation (5.11) represents the value of the marketing campaign as of date 1. We determine the value at date 0 by discounting back one period as follows:

Value of Marketing Campaign at Date 0:

$$\frac{\$1,100,000}{1.1} = \$1,000,000$$

Thus, NPVGO per share is $10 ($1,000,000/100,000).

The price per share is

$$EPS/r + NPVGO = \$100 + \$10 = \$110$$

The calculation can also be made on a straight net-present-value basis. Because all the earnings at date 1 are spent on the marketing effort, no dividends are paid to stockholders at that date. Dividends in all subsequent periods are $1,210,000 ($1,000,000 + $210,000). In this case, $1,000,000 is the annual dividend when Sarro is a cash cow. The additional contribution to the dividend from the marketing effort is $210,000. Dividends per share are $12.10 ($1,210,000/100,000). Because these dividends start at date 2, the price per share at date 1 is $121 ($12.10/0.1). The price per share at date 0 is $110 ($121/1.1).

Note that value is created in this example because the project earned a 21-percent rate of return when the discount rate was only 10 percent. No value would have been created had the project earned a 10-percent rate of return. The NPVGO would have been zero, and value would have been negative had the project earned a percentage return below 10 percent. The NPVGO would be negative in that case.

Two conditions must be met in order to increase value.

1. Earnings must be retained so that projects can be funded.[8]
2. The projects must have positive net present value.

Surprisingly, a number of companies seem to invest in projects known to have *negative* net present values. For example, Jensen has pointed out that, in the late 1970s, oil companies and tobacco companies were flush with cash.[9] Due to declining markets in both industries, high dividends and low investment would have been the rational action. Unfortunately, a number of companies in both industries reinvested heavily in what were widely perceived to be negative-NPVGO projects. A study by McConnell and Muscarella documents this perception.[10] They find that, during the 1970s, the stock prices of oil companies generally decreased on the days that announcements of increases in exploration and development were made.

Given that NPV analysis (such as that presented in the previous chapter) is common knowledge in business, why would managers choose projects with negative NPVs? One conjecture is that some managers enjoy controlling a large company. Because paying dividends in lieu of reinvesting earnings reduces the size of the firm, some managers find it emotionally difficult to pay high dividends.

Growth in Earnings and Dividends versus Growth Opportunities

As mentioned earlier, a firm's value increases when it invests in growth opportunities with positive NPVGOs. A firm's value falls when it selects opportunities with negative NPVGOs. However, dividends grow whether projects with positive NPVs or negative NPVs are selected. This surprising result can be explained by the following example.

EXAMPLE

Lane Supermarkets, a new firm, will earn $100,000 a year in perpetuity if it pays out all its earnings as dividends. However, the firm plans to invest 20 percent of its earnings in projects that earn 10 percent per year. The discount rate is 18 percent. An earlier formula tells us that the growth rate of dividends is

$$g = \text{Retention ratio} \times \text{Return on retained earnings} = 0.2 \times 0.10 = 2\%$$

For example, in this first year of the new policy, dividends are $80,000 [$(1 - 0.2) \times \$100,000$]. Dividends next year are $81,600 ($80,000 × 1.02). Dividends the following year are $83,232 [$80,000 × $(1.02)^2$] and so on. Because dividends represent a fixed percentage of earnings, earnings must grow at 2 percent a year as well.

---

[8]Later in the text we speak of issuing stock or debt in order to fund projects.

[9]M. C. Jensen, "Agency Costs of Free Cash Flows, Corporate Finance and Takeovers," *American Economic Review* (May 1986).

[10]J. J. McConnell and C. J. Muscarella, "Corporate Capital Expenditure Decisions and the Market Value of the Firm," *Journal of Financial Economics* 14 (1985).

However, note that the policy reduces value because the rate of return on the projects of 10 percent is less than the discount rate of 18 percent. That is, the firm would have had a higher value at date 0 if it had a policy of paying all its earnings out as dividends. Thus, a policy of investing in projects with negative NPVs rather than paying out earnings as dividends will lead to growth in dividends and earnings, but will reduce value.

Dividends or Earnings: Which to Discount?

As mentioned earlier, this chapter applied the growing-perpetuity formula to the valuation of stocks. In our application, we discounted dividends, not earnings. This is sensible since investors select a stock for what they can get out of it. They only get two things out of a stock: dividends and the ultimate sales price, which is determined by what future investors expect to receive in dividends.

The calculated stock price would be too high were earnings to be discounted instead of dividends. As we saw in our estimation of a firm's growth rate, only a portion of earnings goes to the stockholders as dividends. The remainder is retained to generate future dividends. In our model, retained earnings are equal to the firm's investment. To discount earnings instead of dividends would be to ignore the investment that a firm must make today in order to generate future returns.

The No-Dividend Firm

Students frequently ask the following questions: If the dividend-discount model is correct, why aren't no-dividend stocks selling at zero? This is a good question and gets at the goals of the firm. A firm with many growth opportunities is faced with a dilemma. The firm can pay out dividends now, or it can forgo dividends now so that it can make investments that will generate even greater dividends in the future.[11] This is often a painful choice, because a strategy of dividend deferment may be optimal yet unpopular among certain stockholders.

Many firms choose to pay no dividends—and these firms sell at positive prices.[12] Rational shareholders believe that they will either receive dividends at some point or they will receive something just as good. That is, the firm will be acquired in a merger, with the stockholders receiving either cash or shares of stock at that time.

Of course, the actual application of the dividend-discount model is difficult for firms of this type. Clearly, the model for constant growth of dividends does not apply. Though the differential growth model can work in theory, the difficulties of estimating the date of first dividend, the growth rate of dividends after that date, and the ultimate merger price make application of the model quite difficult in reality.

Empirical evidence suggests that firms with high growth rates are likely to pay lower dividends, a result consistent with the above analysis. For example, consider McDonald's Corporation. The company started in the 1950s and grew rapidly for many years. It paid its first dividend in 1975, though it was a billion-dollar company (in both sales and market value of stockholder's equity) prior to that date. Why did it wait so long to pay a dividend? It waited because it had so many positive growth opportunities, that is, additional locations for new hamburger outlets, to take advantage of.

Utilities are an interesting contrast because, as a group, they have few growth opportunities. Because of this, they pay out a large fraction of their earnings in dividends. For example, Consolidated Edison, Sempra Energy, and Kansas City Power and Light have had payout ratios of over 70 percent in many recent years.

---

[11] A third alternative is to issue stock so that the firm has enough cash both to pay dividends and to invest. This possibility is explored in a later chapter.

[12] For example, most Internet firms, such as Amazon.com, Earthlink, Inc., and Ebay, Inc., pay no dividends.

5.7 The Dividend-Growth Model and the NPVGO Model (Advanced)

This chapter has revealed that the price of a share of stock is the sum of its price as a cash cow plus the per-share value of its growth opportunities. The Sarro Shipping example illustrated this formula using only one growth opportunity. We also used the growing-perpetuity formula to price a stock with a steady growth in dividends. When the formula is applied to stocks, it is typically called the *dividend-growth model*. A steady growth in dividends results from a continual investment in growth opportunities, not just investment in a single opportunity. Therefore, it is worthwhile to compare the dividend-growth model with the *NPVGO model* when growth occurs through continual investing.

EXAMPLE

Cumberland Book Publishers has EPS of $10 at the end of the first year, a dividend-payout ratio of 40 percent, a discount rate of 16 percent, and a return on its retained earnings of 20 percent. Because the firm retains some of its earnings each year, it is selecting growth opportunities each year. This is different from Sarro Shipping, which had a growth opportunity in only one year. We wish to calculate the price per share using both the dividend-growth model and the NPVGO model.

The Dividend-Growth Model

The dividends at date 1 are $0.40 \times \$10 = \$4$ per share. The retention ratio is 0.60 $(1 - 0.40)$, implying a growth rate in dividends of 0.12 (0.60×0.20).

From the dividend-growth model, the price of a share of stock is

$$\frac{\text{Div}}{r - g} = \frac{\$4}{0.16 - 0.12} = \$100$$

The NPVGO Model

Using the NPVGO model, it is more difficult to value a firm with growth opportunities each year (like Cumberland) than a firm with growth opportunities in only one year (like Sarro). In order to value according to the NPVGO model, we need to calculate on a per-share basis (1) the net present value of a single growth opportunity, (2) the net present value of all growth opportunities, and (3) the stock price if the firm acts as a cash cow, that is, the value of the firm without these growth opportunities. The value of the firm is the sum of (2) + (3).

1. *Value per Share of a Single Growth Opportunity* Out of the earnings per share of $10 at date 1, the firm retains $6 $(0.6 \times \$10)$ at that date. The firm earns $1.20 $(\$6 \times 0.20)$ per year in perpetuity on that $6 investment. The NPV from the investment is

Per-Share NPV Generated from Investment at Date 1:

$$-\$6 + \frac{\$1.20}{0.16} = \$1.50 \tag{5.12}$$

That is, the firm invests $6 in order to reap $1.20 per year on the investment. The earnings are discounted at 0.16, implying a value per share from the project of $1.50. Because the investment occurs at date 1 and the first cash flow occurs at date 2, $1.50 is the value of the investment at *date 1*. In other words, the NPV from the date 1 investment has *not* yet been brought back to date 0.

2. *Value per Share of All Opportunities*   As pointed out earlier, the growth rate of earnings and dividends is 12 percent. Because retained earnings are a fixed percentage of total earnings, retained earnings must also grow at 12 percent a year. That is, retained earnings at date 2 are $6.72 ($6 × 1.12), retained earnings at date 3 are $7.5264 [$6 × $(1.12)^2$], and so on.

Let's analyze the retained earnings at date 2 in more detail. Because projects will always earn 20 percent per year, the firm earns $1.344 ($6.72 × 0.20) in each future year on the $6.72 investment at date 2.

The NPV from the investment is

NPV per Share Generated from Investment at Date 2:

$$-\$6.72 + \frac{\$1.344}{0.16} = \$1.68 \tag{5.13}$$

$1.68 is the NPV as of date 2 of the investment made at date 2. The NPV from the date 2 investment has *not* yet been brought back to date 0.

Now consider the retained earnings at date 3 in more detail. The firm earns $1.5053 ($7.5264 × 0.20) per year on the investment of $7.5264 at date 3.

The NPV from the investment is

NPV per Share Generated from Investment at Date 3:

$$-\$7.5264 + \frac{\$1.5053}{0.16} = \$1.882 \tag{5.14}$$

From equations (5.12), (5.13), and (5.14), the NPV per share of all of the growth opportunities, discounted back to date 0, is

$$\frac{\$1.50}{1.16} + \frac{\$1.68}{(1.16)^2} + \frac{\$1.882}{(1.16)^3} + \cdots \tag{5.15}$$

Because it has an infinite number of terms, this expression looks quite difficult to compute. However, there is an easy simplification. Note that retained earnings are growing at 12 percent per year. Because all projects earn the same rate of return per year, the NPVs in (5.12), (5.13), and (5.14) are also growing at 12 percent per year. Hence, we can write equation (5.15) as

$$\frac{\$1.50}{1.16} + \frac{\$1.50 \times 1.12}{(1.16)^2} + \frac{\$1.50 \times (1.12)^2}{(1.16)^3} + \cdots$$

This is a growth perpetuity whose value is

$$\text{NPVGO} = \$\frac{1.50}{0.16 - 0.12} = \$37.50$$

Because the first NPV of $1.50 occurs at date 1, the NPVGO is $37.50 as of date 0. In other words, the firm's policy of investing in new projects from retained earnings has an NPV of $37.50.

3. *Value per Share if Firm Is a Cash Cow*   We now assume that the firm pays out all of its earnings as dividends. The dividends would be $10 per year in this case. Since there would be no growth, the value per share would be evaluated by the perpetuity formula:

$$\frac{\text{Div}}{r} = \frac{\$10}{0.16} = \$62.50$$

Summation

Formula (5.10) states that value per share is the value of a cash cow plus the value of the growth opportunities. This is

$$\$100 = \$62.50 + \$37.50$$

Hence, value is the same whether calculated by a discounted-dividend approach or a growth-opportunities approach. The share prices from the two approaches must be equal, because the approaches are different yet equivalent methods of applying concepts of present value.

5.8 Price-Earnings Ratio

We argued earlier that one should not discount earnings in order to determine price per share. Nevertheless, financial analysts frequently relate earnings and price per share, as made evident by their heavy reliance on the price-earnings (or P/E) ratio.

Our previous discussion stated that

$$\text{Price per share} = \frac{\text{EPS}}{r} + \text{NPVGO}$$

Dividing by EPS yields

$$\frac{\text{Price per share}}{\text{EPS}} = \frac{1}{r} + \frac{\text{NPVGO}}{\text{EPS}}$$

The left-hand side is the formula for the price-earnings ratio. The equation shows that the P/E ratio is related to the net present value of growth opportunities. As an example, consider two firms, each having just reported earnings per share of $1. However, one firm has many valuable growth opportunities while the other firm has no growth opportunities at all. The firm with growth opportunities should sell at a higher price, because an investor is buying both current income of $1 and growth opportunities. Suppose that the firm with growth opportunities sells for $16 and the other firm sells for $8. The $1 earnings per share number appears in the denominator of the P/E ratio for both firms. Thus, the P/E ratio is 16 for the firm with growth opportunities, but only 8 for the firm without the opportunities.

This explanation seems to hold fairly well in the real world. Electronic and other high-tech stocks generally sell at very high P/E ratios (or *multiples,* as they are often called) because they are perceived to have high growth rates. In fact, some technology stocks sell at high prices even though the companies have never earned a profit. The P/E ratios of these companies are infinite. Conversely, railroads, utilities, and steel companies sell at lower multiples because of the prospects of lower growth.

Of course, the market is merely pricing *perceptions* of the future, not the future itself. We will argue later in the text that the stock market generally has realistic perceptions of a firm's prospects. However, this is not always true. In the late 1960s, many electronics firms were selling at multiples of 200 times earnings. The high perceived growth rates did not materialize, causing great declines in stock prices during the early 1970s. In earlier decades, fortunes were made in stocks like IBM and Xerox because the high growth rates were not anticipated by investors. Most recently we have experienced the dot-com collapse when many Internet stocks were trading at multiples of thousands of times annual earnings. In fact, most Internet stocks had no earnings.

One of the most puzzling phenomena to American investors has been the high P/E ratios in the Japanese stock market. The average P/E ratio for the Tokyo Stock Exchange has varied between 40 and 100 in recent years, while the average American stock had a multiple of around 25 during this time. Our formula indicates that Japanese companies have been

TABLE 5.2	Country Composite	1994	1997	2000
International P/E	United States	24	21	30
Ratios	Japan	101	44	38
	Germany	35	31	31
	Britain	18	18	20
	France	29	25	27
	Canada	45	25	21
	Sweden	52	17	20
	Italy	29	22	28

SOURCE: Abstracted from "The Global 1000," *Business Week*, July 11, 1994, July 7, 1997, and *Forbes*, July 24, 2000.

perceived to have great growth opportunities. However, American commentators have frequently suggested that investors in the Japanese markets have been overestimating these growth prospects.[13] This enigma (at least to American investors) can only be resolved with the passage of time. Some selected country average P/E ratios appear in Table 5.2. You can see Japan's P/E ratio has trended down, and today is about the same as for U.S. stocks.

There are two additional factors explaining the P/E ratio. The first is the discount rate, r. The above formula shows that the P/E ratio is *negatively* related to the firm's discount rate. We have already suggested that the discount rate is positively related to the stock's risk or variability. Thus, the P/E ratio is negatively related to the stock's risk. To see that this is a sensible result, consider two firms, A and B, behaving as cash cows. The stock market *expects* both firms to have annual earnings of $1 per share forever. However, the earnings of firm A are known with certainty while the earnings of firm B are quite variable. A rational stockholder is likely to pay more for a share of firm A because of the absence of risk. If a share of firm A sells at a higher price and both firms have the same EPS, the P/E ratio of firm A must be higher.

The second additional factor concerns the firm's choice of accounting methods. Under current accounting rules, companies are given a fair amount of leeway. For example, consider inventory accounting where either FIFO or LIFO may be used. In an inflationary environment, *FIFO (first in–first out)* accounting understates the true cost of inventory and hence inflates reported earnings. Inventory is valued according to more recent costs under *LIFO (last in–first out)*, implying that reported earnings are lower here than they would be under FIFO. Thus, LIFO inventory accounting is a more *conservative* method than FIFO. Similar accounting leeway exists for construction costs (*completed-contracts* versus *percentage-of-completion methods*) and depreciation (*accelerated depreciation* versus *straight-line depreciation*).

As an example, consider two identical firms, C and D. Firm C uses LIFO and reports earnings of $2 per share. Firm D uses the less conservative accounting assumptions of FIFO and reports earnings of $3 per share. The market knows that both firms are identical and prices both at $18 per share. This price-earnings ratio is 9 ($18/$2) for firm C and 6 ($18/$3) for firm D. Thus, the firm with the more conservative principles has the higher P/E ratio.

This last example depends on the assumption that the market sees through differences in accounting treatments. A significant portion of the academic community believes that the market sees through virtually all accounting differences. These academics are adherents of the hypothesis of *efficient capital markets,* a theory that we explore in great detail later in the text. Though many financial people might be more moderate in their beliefs regarding this issue, the consensus view is certainly that many of the accounting differences are seen through. Thus, the proposition that firms with conservative accountants have high P/E ratios is widely accepted.

---

[13]It has been suggested that Japanese companies use more conservative accounting practices, thereby creating higher P/E ratios. This point, which will be examined shortly for firms in general, appears to explain only a small part of Japan's high multiples.

This discussion argued that the P/E ratio is a function of three different factors. A company's ratio or multiple is likely to be high if (1) it has many growth opportunities, (2) it has low risk, and (3) it is accounted for in a conservative manner. While each of the three factors is important, it is our opinion that the first factor is much more so. Thus, our discussion of growth is quite relevant in understanding price-earnings multiples.

Concept
Question

1. **What are the three factors determining a firm's P/E ratio?**

5.9 Stock Market Reporting

The Wall Street Journal, the *New York Times,* or your own local newspaper provides useful information on a large number of stocks in several stock exchanges. Table 5.3 reproduces what has been reported on a particular day for several stocks listed on the New York Stock Exchange. In Table 5.3, you can easily find the line for General Electric (i.e., "GenElec"). Reading left to right, the first two numbers are the high and low share prices over the last 52 weeks. For example, the highest price that General Electric traded for at the end of any particular day over the last 52 weeks was 60^{50}. This is read as 60 and the decimal .50. The stock symbol for General Electric is GE. Its annual dividend is $0.55. Most dividend-paying companies such as General Electric pay dividends on a quarterly basis. So the annual dividend is actually the last quarterly dividend of .138 multiplied by 4 (i.e., .138 × 4 = $0.55).

Some firms like GenenTech do not pay dividends. The Div column for GenenTech is blank. The "Yld" column stands for dividend yield. General Electric's dividend yield is the current annual dividend, $0.55, divided by the current closing daily price, which is 56^{63} (you can find the closing price for this particular day in the next to last column). Note that $0.55/56^{63} \cong 1.0$ percent. The next column is labeled PE, which is the symbol for the price-earnings ratio. The price-earnings ratio is the closing price divided by the current earnings per share (based upon the latest quarterly earnings per share multiplied by 4). General Electric's price-earnings ratio is 51. If we were financial analysts or investment bankers, we would say General Electric "sells for 51 times earnings." The next column is the volume of shares traded on this particular day (in hundreds). For General Electric, 18,305,100 shares traded. This was a heavy trading day for General Electric. The last columns are the High, the Low, and the Last (Close) share prices on this day. The "Net Chg" tells us that the General Electric closing price of 56^{63} was lower than its closing price on the previous day by 1^{44}. In other words, the price of General Electric dropped from 58^{07} to 56^{63}, in one day.

TABLE 5.3		Stock Market Reporting of NYSE-Listed Securities										
52 Weeks					**Yld**		**Vol**					**Net**
Hi	**Lo**	**Stock**	**Sym**	**Div**	**%**	**PE**	**100s**	**Hi**	**Lo**	**Close**		**Chg**
53^{75}	19^{06}	Gap Inc	GPS	.09	.5	15	65172	20^{50}	19	19^{25}	−	1^{75}
22^{25}	9^{56}	GartnerGp	IT		...	22	2331	10^{94}	10^{31}	10^{94}		...
84	43	Gateway	GTW		...	31	23354	47^{40}	42^{15}	44^{62}	−	1^{29}
245	66^{88}	Genentech	DNA		...	dd	21468	159	147	149	−	4^{31}
15^{44}	2^{50}	GenDatacm	GDC		...	dd	456	4^{25}	4	4^{06}	−	0^{25}
64^{94}	36^{25}	GenDynam	GD	1.04	1.6	17	23318	64^{81}	63^{44}	64^{56}	+	1
60^{50}	38^{21}	GenElec	GE	.55	1.0	51	183051	57^{69}	55^{31}	56^{63}	−	1^{44}
43^{94}	29^{38}	GenMills	GIS	1.10	2.9	18	5054	37^{94}	37^{31}	37^{69}	+	0^{13}
94^{63}	56^{94}	GenMotor	GM	2.00	3.4	7	22653	61^{13}	58^{38}	58^{63}	−	1^{06}

Concept
Questions

From Table 5.3:

1. **What is the closing price of Gateway, Inc.?**
2. **What is the PE of Gateway, Inc.?**
3. **What is the annual dividend of General Motors?**

5.10 SUMMARY AND CONCLUSIONS

In this chapter we use general present-value formulas from the previous chapter to price bonds and stock.

1. Pure discount bonds and perpetuities can be viewed as the polar cases of bonds. The value of a pure discount bond (also called a zero-coupon bond, or simply a zero) is

$$PV = \frac{F}{(1 + r)^T}$$

The value of a perpetuity (also called a *consol*) is

$$PV = \frac{C}{r}$$

2. Level-payment bonds can be viewed as an intermediate case. The coupon payments form an annuity and the principal repayment is a lump sum. The value of this type of bond is simply the sum of the values of its two parts.

3. The yield to maturity on a bond is that single rate that discounts the payments on the bond to its purchase price.

4. A stock can be valued by discounting its dividends. We mention three types of situations:
   a. The case of zero growth of dividends.
   b. The case of constant growth of dividends.
   c. The case of differential growth.

5. An estimate of the growth rate of a stock is needed for formulas (4b) or (4c) above. A useful estimate of the growth rate is

$$g = \text{Retention ratio} \times \text{Return on retained earnings}$$

6. It is worthwhile to view a share of stock as the sum of its worth, if the company behaves like a cash cow (the company does no investing), and the value per share of its growth opportunities. We write the value of a share as

$$\frac{EPS}{r} + NPVGO$$

We show that, in theory, share price must be the same whether the dividend-growth model or the above formula is used.

7. From accounting, we know that earnings are divided into two parts: dividends and retained earnings. Most firms continually retain earnings in order to create future dividends. One should not discount earnings to obtain price per share since part of earnings must be reinvested. Only dividends reach the stockholders and only they should be discounted to obtain share price.

8. We suggest that a firm's price-earnings ratio is a function of three factors:
   a. The per-share amount of the firm's valuable growth opportunities.
   b. The risk of the stock.
   c. The type of accounting method used by the firm.

KEY TERMS

coupons, 107
discount, 110
face value, 106
maturity date, 106
payout ratio, 118

premium, 110
pure discount bond, 106
retention ratio, 117
return on equity, 117
yield to maturity, 111

SUGGESTED READING

The best place to look for additional information is in investment textbooks. A good one is:

Bodie, Z., A. Kane, and A. Marcus. *Investments.* 5th ed. Burr Ridge, Ill.: Irwin/McGraw-Hill, 2002.

QUESTIONS & PROBLEMS

HOW TO VALUE BONDS

5.1 What is the present value of a 10-year, pure discount bond paying $1,000 at maturity if the appropriate interest rate is:
   a. 5 percent
   b. 10 percent
   c. 15 percent

5.2 Microhard has issued a bond with the following characteristics:
   Principal: $1,000
   Time to maturity: 20 years
   Coupon rate: 8 percent, compounded semiannually
   Semiannual payments
   Calculate the price of this bond if the stated annual interest rate, compounded semiannually, is:
   a. 8 percent
   b. 10 percent
   c. 6 percent

5.3 Consider a bond with a face value of $1,000. The coupon payment is made semiannually and the yield on the bond is 12 percent (effective annual yield). How much would you pay for the bond if:
   a. The coupon rate is 8 percent and the remaining time to maturity is 20 years?
   b. The coupon rate is 10 percent and the remaining time to maturity is 15 years?

5.4 Jay's Trucking, Inc., has issued an 8 percent, 20-year bond paying interest semiannually. The bond has a face value of $1,000. If the yield on the bond is 10 percent (effective annual yield), what is the price of the bond?

5.5 A bond is sold at $923.14 (below its par value of $1,000). The bond matures in 15 years and has a 10-percent yield, expressed as a stated annual interest rate, compounded semiannually. What is the coupon rate on the bond if the coupon is paid semiannually? The next payment occurs six months from today.

5.6 You have just purchased a newly issued $1,000 five-year Vanguard Company bond at par. This five-year bond pays $60 in interest semiannually. You are also considering the purchase of another Vanguard Company bond that pays $30 in semiannual interest payments and has six years remaining before maturity. This bond has a face value of $1,000.
   a. What is the yield on the five-year bond (expressed as an effective annual yield)?
   b. Assume that the five-year bond and the six-year bond have the same yield. What should you be willing to pay for the six-year bond?
   c. How will your answer in part (*b*) change if the five-year bond pays $40 in semiannual interest instead of $60? Assume that the five-year bond paying $40 semiannually is purchased at par.

BOND CONCEPTS

5.7 Consider two bonds, *A* and *B*. The coupon rates are 10 percent and the face values are $1,000 for both bonds. Both bonds have annual coupons. Bond *A* has 20 years to maturity while bond *B* has 10 years to maturity.
   a. What are the prices of the two bonds if the relevant market interest rate for both bonds is 10 percent?
   b. If the market interest rate increases to 12 percent, what will be the prices of the two bonds?
   c. If the market interest rate decreases to 8 percent, what will be the prices of the two bonds?

5.8 **a.** If the market interest rate unexpectedly increases, what would be the effect on the prices of long-term bonds? Why?
b. How would a rise in the interest rate affect the general level of stock prices? Why?

5.9 Consider a bond paying an annual coupon of $80 with a face value of $1,000. Calculate the yield to maturity if the bond has:
a. 20 years remaining to maturity and is priced at $1,200.
b. 10 years remaining to maturity and is priced at $950.

5.10 HexCorp Inc. has two different bonds currently outstanding. Bond A has a face value of $40,000 and matures in 20 years. The bond makes no payments for the first six years, pays $2,000 semiannually for the subsequent eight years, and finally pays $2,500 semiannually for the last six years. Bond B also has a face value of $40,000 and matures in 20 years. However, it makes no coupon payments over the life of the bond. If the stated annual interest rate is 12 percent, compounded semiannually,
a. What is the current price of Bond A?
b. What is the current price of Bond B?

5.11 Use the following February 11, 2002, *Wall Street Journal* quotation for AT&T Corp. Which of the following statement are false?
a. The closing price of the bond with the shortest time to maturity is $1,000.
b. The annual coupon for the bond maturing in 2018 is $90.
c. The price on the day before this quotation (February 9) for the AT&T bond maturing in 2024 is $1,075 per bond contract.
d. The current yield on the AT&T bond maturing in 2004 is 7.125 percent.
e. The AT&T bond maturing in 2004 has a yield to maturity of less than 7.125 percent.

Bonds	Current Yield	Volume	Close	Net Change
ATT 9s 18	?	10	117	+.25
ATT 5$^1/_8$ 03	?	5	100	+.75
ATT 7$^1/_8$ 04	?	193	104.125	+.25
ATT 8$^1/_8$ 24	?	39	107.375	−.13 ($^1/_8$)

5.12 The following are selected quotations from *The Wall Street Journal* on Friday, April 23, 2002. Which of the following statements about Wilson's bond are false?
a. The bond maturing in 2003 has a yield to maturity greater than 6$^3/_8$ percent.
b. The closing price of the bond with the shortest time to maturity on the day before the quotation is $1,003.25.
c. The annual coupon payment for the bond maturing in 2016 is $75.
d. The current yield on the Wilson's bond with the longest time to maturity is 7.29 percent.
e. None of the above.

Bonds	Current Yield	Volume	Close	Net Change
WILSON 6$^3/_8$ 02	?	76	100.375	−.13 ($^1/_8$)
WILSON 6$^3/_8$ 03	?	9	98	+.5
WILSON 7$^1/_4$ 05	?	39	103.625	+.13 ($^1/_8$)
WILSON 7$^1/_2$ 16	?	225	102.825	−.13 ($^1/_8$)

THE PRESENT VALUE OF COMMON STOCKS

5.13 A common stock just paid an annual dividend of $2 yesterday. The dividend is expected to grow at 8 percent annually for the next three years, after which it will grow at 4 percent in perpetuity. The appropriate discount rate is 12 percent. What is the price of the stock?

5.14 Use the following February 12, 2002, *Wall Street Journal* quotation for Merck & Co. to answer the next question.

52 Weeks		Stock	Sym	Div	Yield %	PE	Vol. 100s	Hi	Low	Close	Net Change
Hi	Low										
120	80.19	Merck	MRK	1.80	?	30	195111	115.9	114.5	115	−1.25

Which of the following statements are false?
a. The dividend yield is approximately 1.6 percent.
b. The closing price per share on February 10, 2002, was $113.75.
c. The closing price per share on February 11, 2002, was $115.
d. The earnings per share were about $3.83.

5.15 Examine the following stock quote for Citigroup:

52 Weeks		Stock	Sym	Div	Yield %	PE	Vol. 100s	Hi	Low	Close	Net Change
Hi	Low										
126.25	72.50	Citigroup	CCI	1.30	1.32	16	20925	98.4	97.8	98.13	−.13

The expected growth rate of Citigroup's dividends is 7 percent per year. According to the constant-growth dividend model, what is the stock's required return? Assume that the annual dividend of $1.30 was paid yesterday.

5.16 You own $100,000 worth of Smart Money stock. One year from now, you will receive a dividend of $2 per share. You will receive a $4 dividend two years from now. You will sell the stock for $50 per share three years from now. Dividends are taxed at the rate of 28 percent. Assume there is no capital gains tax. The required rate of return is 15 percent. How many shares of stock do you own?

5.17 Consider the stock of Davidson Company, which will pay an annual dividend of $2 one year from today. The dividend will grow at a constant annual rate of 5 percent, forever. The market requires a 12-percent return on the company's stock.
a. What is the current price of a share of the stock?
b. What will the stock price be 10 years from today?

5.18 Scubaland, Inc., is experiencing a period of rapid growth. Earnings and dividends per share are expected to grow at a rate of 18 percent during the next two years, 15 percent in the third year, and 6 percent thereafter. Yesterday, Scubaland paid a dividend of $1.15. If the required rate of return on the stock is 12 percent, what is the price of a share of the stock today?

5.19 Calamity Mining Company's iron ore reserves are being depleted, and its costs of recovering a declining quantity of ore are rising each year. As a result, the company's earnings are declining at a rate of 10 percent per year. If the dividend per share to be paid tomorrow is $5 and the required rate of return is 14 percent, what is the value of the firm's stock? Assume that the dividend payments are based on a fixed percentage of the firm's earnings.

5.20 Pasqually Mineral Water, Inc., will pay a quarterly dividend per share of $1 at the end of each of the next 12 quarters. Thereafter, the dividend will grow at a quarterly rate of 0.5 percent, forever. The appropriate rate of return on the stock is 10 percent, compounded quarterly. What is the current stock price?

5.21 Suppose Amsterdam Foods, Inc., has just paid a dividend of $1.40 per share. Its dividend is expected to grow at 5 percent per year in perpetuity. If the required return is 10 percent, what is the value of a share of Amsterdam Foods?

5.22 In order to buy back its own shares, Pennzoil Co. has decided to suspend its dividends for the next two years. It will resume its annual cash dividend of $2.00 in year 3 and year 4. Thereafter, its dividend payments will grow at an annual growth rate of 6 percent, forever. The required rate of return on Pennzoil's stock is 16 percent. According to the discounted-dividend model, what should Pennzoil's current share price be?

Visit us at www.mhhe.com/rwj

5.23 The Webster Co. has just paid a dividend of $5.25 per share. The company will increase its dividend by 14 percent next year. The company will then reduce its dividend growth rate by 3 percent each year until the dividend reaches the industry average of 5 percent growth. The company will maintain that dividend growth rate, forever. The required rate of return for the Webster Co. is 14 percent. What is the price of the stock?

ESTIMATES OF PARAMETERS IN THE DIVIDEND-DISCOUNT MODEL

5.24 Allen, Inc., is expected to pay equal dividends at the end of each of the next two years. Thereafter, the dividend will grow at a constant annual rate of 4 percent, forever. The current stock price is $30. What is next year's dividend payment if the required rate of return is 12 percent?

5.25 The newspaper reported last week that Bradley Enterprises earned $20 million this year. The report also stated that the firm's return on equity is 14 percent. Bradley retains 60 percent of its earnings.
  a. What is the firm's earnings growth rate?
  b. What will next year's earnings be?

5.26 Juggernaut Satellite Corporation earned $10 million for the fiscal year ending yesterday. The firm also paid out 25 percent of its earnings as dividends yesterday. The firm will continue to pay out 25 percent of its earnings as annual, end-of-year dividends. The remaining 75 percent of earnings is retained by the company for use in projects. The company has 1.25 million shares of common stock outstanding. The current stock price is $30. The historical return on equity (ROE) of 12 percent is expected to continue in the future. What is the required rate of return on the stock?

5.27 Four years ago, Bling Diamond, Inc., paid a dividend of $.80 per share. Bling paid a dividend of $1.66 per share yesterday. Dividends will grow over the next five years at the same rate they grew over the last four years. Thereafter, dividends will grow at 8 percent per year. The required return on the stock is 18 percent. What will Bling Diamond's cash dividend be in seven years?

GROWTH OPPORTUNITIES

5.28 Rite Bite Enterprises sells toothpicks. Gross revenues last year were $3 million, and total costs were $1.5 million. Rite Bite has 1 million shares of common stock outstanding. Gross revenues and costs are expected to grow at 5 percent per year. Rite Bite pays no income taxes. All earnings are paid out as dividends.
  a. If the appropriate discount rate is 15 percent and all cash flows are received at year's end, what is the price per share of Rite Bite stock?
  b. Rite Bite has decided to produce toothbrushes. The project requires an immediate outlay of $15 million. In one year, another outlay of $5 million will be needed. The year after that, net cash inflows will be $6 million. That profit level will be maintained in perpetuity. What effect will undertaking this project have on the price per share of the stock?

5.29 California Real Estate, Inc., expects to earn $100 million per year in perpetuity if it does not undertake any new projects. The firm has an opportunity to invest $15 million today and $5 million in one year in real estate. The new investment will generate annual earnings of $10 million in perpetuity, beginning two years from today. The firm has 20 million shares of common stock outstanding, and the required rate of return on the stock is 15 percent. Land investments are not depreciable. Ignore taxes.
  a. What is the price of a share of stock if the firm does not undertake the new investment?
  b. What is the value of the investment?
  c. What is the per-share stock price if the firm undertakes the investment?

5.30 The annual earnings of Avalanche Skis Inc. will be $4 per share in perpetuity if the firm makes no new investments. Under such a situation, the firm would pay out all of its earnings as dividends. Assume the first dividend will be received exactly one year from now.
    Alternatively, assume that three years from now, and in every subsequent year in perpetuity, the company can invest 25 percent of its earnings in new projects. Each project will earn 40 percent at year-end, in perpetuity. The firm's discount rate is 14 percent.

a. What is the price per share of Avalanche Skis Inc. stock today without the company making the new investment?
b. If Avalanche announces that the new investment will be made, what will the per-share stock price be today?

PRICE-EARNINGS RATIO

5.31 Consider Pacific Energy Company and U.S. Bluechips, Inc., both of which reported cash flows of $800,000 and have 500,000 shares of common stock outstanding. Without new projects, both firms will continue to generate cash flows of $800,000 in perpetuity. Assume that the cash flows are equal to earnings. Assume both firms require a 15 percent rate of return.
a. Pacific Energy Company has a new project that will generate additional cash flows of $100,000 each year in perpetuity. Calculate the P/E ratio of the company.
b. U.S. Bluechips has a new project that will increase cash flows by $200,000 in perpetuity. Calculate the P/E ratio of the firm.

5.32 (Challenge Question) Lewin Skis Inc. (today) expects to earn $4 per share for each of the future operating periods (beginning at time 1) if the firm makes no new investments (and returns the earnings as dividends to the shareholders). However, Clint Williams, president and CEO, has discovered an opportunity to retain (and invest) 25 percent of the earnings beginning three years from today (starting at time 3). This opportunity to invest will continue (for each period) indefinitely. He expects to earn 40 percent (per year) on this new equity investment (ROE of 40), the return beginning one year after each investment is made. The firm's equity discount rate is 14 percent throughout.
a. What is the price per share (now at time 0) of Lewin Skis Inc. stock *without* making the new investment?
b. If the new investment is expected to be made, per the preceding information, what would the value of the stock (per share) be now (at time 0)?
c. What is the expected capital gain yield for the second period, assuming the proposed investment is made? What is the expected capital gain yield for the second period if the proposed investment is *not* made?
d. What is the expected dividend yield for the second period if the new investment is made? What is the expected dividend yield for the second period if the new investment is *not* made?

VALUATION OF STOCKS

5.33 ABC Inc. has a P/E ratio of 12 and maintains a dividend payout ratio of 40 percent. The stock price of ABC Inc. on January 1 is $32. What would the value of stock be if the dividend payout ratio was 60 percent?

5.34 XYZ Inc. has earnings of $10 million and is projected to grow at a constant rate of 5 percent forever because of the benefits gained from the learning curve. Currently all earnings are paid out as dividends. The company plans to launch a new project two years from now which would be completely internally funded and require 20 percent of the earnings that year. The project would start generating revenues one year after the launch of the project and the earnings from the new project in any year are estimated to be constant at $0.5 million. The company has 10 million shares of stock outstanding. Estimate the value of XYZ stock. The discount rate is 10 percent.

S & P PROBLEMS

STANDARD &POOR'S

5.35 Enter the ticker symbol "WMT" for Wal-Mart. Using the most recent balance sheet and income statement under the "Excel Analytics" link, calculate the sustainable growth rate for Wal-Mart. Now download the "Mthly. Adj. Price" and find the closing stock price for the same month as the balance sheet and income statement you used. What is the implied required return on Wal-Mart according to the dividend growth model? Does this number make sense? Why or why not?

5.36 Assume that investors require an 11 percent return on Harley-Davidson (HDI) stock. Under the "Excel Analytics" link find the "Mthly. Adj. Price" and find the closing price for the month of the most recent fiscal year-end for HDI. Using this stock price and the EPS for the most recent year, calculate the NPVGO for Harley-Davidson. What is the appropriate P/E ratio for Harley-Davidson using these calculations?

Appendix 5A

The Term Structure of Interest Rates, Spot Rates, and Yield to Maturity

In the main body of this chapter, we have assumed that the interest rate is constant over all future periods. In reality, interest rates vary through time. This occurs primarily because inflation rates are expected to differ through time.

To illustrate, we consider two zero-coupon bonds. Bond A is a one-year bond and bond B is a two-year bond. Both have face values of $1,000. The one-year interest rate, r_1, is 8 percent. The two-year interest rate, r_2, is 10 percent. These two rates of interest are examples of *spot rates*. Perhaps this inequality in interest rates occurs because inflation is expected to be higher over the second year than over the first year. The two bonds are depicted in the following time chart.

We can easily calculate the present value for bond A and bond B as

$$PV_A = \$925.93 = \frac{\$1,000}{1.08}$$

$$PV_B = \$826.45 = \frac{\$1,000}{(1.10)^2}$$

Of course, if PV_A and PV_B were observable and the spot rates were not, we could determine the spot rates using the PV formula, because

$$PV_A = \$925.93 = \frac{\$1,000}{(1 + r_1)} \rightarrow r_1 = 8\%$$

and

$$PV_B = \$826.45 = \frac{\$1,000}{(1 + r_2)^2} \rightarrow r_2 = 10\%$$

Now we can see how the prices of more complicated bonds are determined. Try to do the next example. It illustrates the difference between spot rates and yields to maturity.

EXAMPLE

Given the spot rates, r_1 equals 8 percent and r_2 equals 10 percent, what should a 5-percent coupon, two-year bond cost? The cash flows C_1 and C_2 are illustrated in the following time chart.

The bond can be viewed as a portfolio of zero-coupon bonds with one- and two-year maturities. Therefore,

$$PV = \frac{\$50}{1 + 0.08} + \frac{\$1,050}{(1 + 0.10)^2} = \$914.06 \qquad \text{(A.1)}$$

We now want to calculate a single rate for the bond. We do this by solving for y in the following equation:

$$\$914.06 = \frac{\$50}{1+y} + \frac{\$1,050}{(1+y)^2} \qquad (A.2)$$

In (A.2), y equals 9.95 percent. As mentioned in the chapter, we call y the *yield to maturity* on the bond. Solving for y for a multiyear bond is generally done by means of trial and error.[14] While this can take much time with paper and pencil, it is virtually instantaneous on a hand-held calculator.

It is worthwhile to contrast equation (A.1) and equation (A.2). In (A.1), we use the marketwide spot rates to determine the price of the bond. Once we get the bond price, we use (A.2) to calculate its yield to maturity. Because equation (A.1) employs two spot rates whereas only one appears in (A.2), we can think of yield to maturity as some sort of average of the two spot rates.[15]

Using the above spot rates, the yield to maturity of a two-year coupon bond whose coupon rate is 12 percent and PV equals $1,036.73 can be determined by

$$\$1,036.73 = \frac{\$120}{1+r} + \frac{\$1,120}{(1+r)^2} \rightarrow r = 9.89\%$$

As these calculations show, two bonds with the same maturity will usually have different yields to maturity if the coupons differ.

Graphing the Term Structure   The *term structure* describes the relationship of spot rates with different maturities. Figure 5A.1 graphs a particular term structure. In Figure 5A.1 the spot rates are increasing with longer maturities, that is, $r_3 > r_2 > r_1$. Graphing the term structure is easy if we can observe spot rates. Unfortunately, this can be done only if there are enough zero-coupon government bonds.

A given term structure, such as that in Figure 5A.1, exists for only a moment in time, say, 10:00 A.M., July 30, 1990. Interest rates are likely to change in the next minute, so that a different (though quite similar) term structure would exist at 10:01 A.M.

Concept Question

1. What is the difference between a spot interest rate and the yield to maturity?

FIGURE 5A.1

The Term Structure of Interest Rates

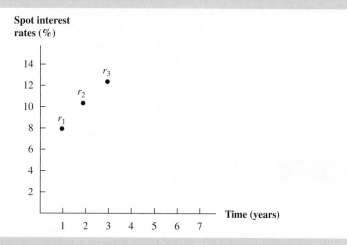

---

[14]The quadratic formula may be used to solve for y for a two-year bond. However, formulas generally do not apply for longer-term bonds.

[15]Yield to maturity is not a simple average of r_1 and r_2. Rather, financial economists speak of it as a time-weighted average of r_1 and r_2.

FIGURE 5A.2

Breakdown of a Two-Year Spot Rate into a One-Year Spot Rate and Forward Rate over the Second Year

With a two-year spot rate of 10 percent, investor in two-year bond receives $1.21 at date 2.

This is the same return *as if* investor received the spot rate of 8 percent over the first year and 12.04-percent return over the second year.

$1 ———— 8% ———— $1.08 ——12.04%——$1 × 1.08 × 1.1204 = $1.21

Because both the one-year spot rate and the two-year spot rate are known at date 0, the forward rate over the second year can be calculated at date 0.

Explanations of the Term Structure

Figure 5A.1 showed one of many possible relationships between the spot rate and maturity. We now want to explore the relationship in more detail. We begin by defining a new term, the forward rate. Next, we relate this forward rate to future interest rates. Finally, we consider alternative theories of the term structure.

Definition of Forward Rate   Earlier in this appendix, we developed a two-year example where the spot rate over the first year is 8 percent and the spot rate over the two years is 10 percent. Here, an individual investing $1 in a two-year zero-coupon bond would have $1 × (1.10)^2$ in two years.

In order to pursue our discussion, it is worthwhile to rewrite[16]

$$\$1 \times (1.10)^2 = \$1 \times 1.08 \times 1.1204 \tag{A.3}$$

Equation (A.3) tells us something important about the relationship between one- and two-year rates. When an individual invests in a two-year zero-coupon bond yielding 10 percent, his wealth at the end of two years is the same as if he received an 8-percent return over the first year and a 12.04-percent return over the second year. This hypothetical rate over the second year, 12.04 percent, is called the *forward rate*. Thus, we can think of an investor with a two-year zero-coupon bond as getting the one-year spot rate of 8 percent and *locking in* 12.04 percent over the second year. This relationship is presented in Figure 5A.2.

More generally, if we are given spot rates, r_1 and r_2, we can always determine the forward rate, f_2, such that:

$$(1 + r_2)^2 = (1 + r_1) \times (1 + f_2) \tag{A.4}$$

We solve for f_2, yielding:

$$f_2 = \frac{(1 + r_2)^2}{1 + r_1} - 1 \tag{A.5}$$

EXAMPLE

If the one-year spot rate is 7 percent and the two-year spot rate is 12 percent, what is f_2?
    We plug in equation (A.5), yielding

$$f_2 = \frac{(1.12)^2}{1.07} - 1 = 17.23\%$$

---

[16]12.04 percent is equal to

$$\frac{(1.10)^2}{1.08} - 1$$

when rounding is performed after four digits.

Consider an individual investing in a two-year zero-coupon bond yielding 12 percent. We say it is as if he receives 7 percent over the first year and simultaneously locks in 17.23 percent over the second year. Note that both the one-year spot rate and the two-year spot rate are known at date 0. Because the forward rate is calculated from the one-year and two-year spot rates, it can be calculated at date 0 as well.

Forward rates can be calculated over later years as well. The general formula is

$$f_n = \frac{(1 + r_n)^n}{(1 + r_{n-1})^{n-1}} - 1 \tag{A.6}$$

where f_n is the forward rate over the nth year, r_n is the n-year spot rate, and r_{n-1} is the spot rate for $n - 1$ years.

EXAMPLE

Assume the following set of rates:

Year	Spot Rate
1	5%
2	6
3	7
4	6

What are the forward rates over each of the four years?

The forward rate over the first year is, *by definition,* equal to the one-year spot rate. Thus, we do not generally speak of the forward rate over the first year. The forward rates over the later years are

$$f_2 = \frac{(1.06)^2}{1.05} - 1 = 7.01\%$$

$$f_3 = \frac{(1.07)^3}{(1.06)^2} - 1 = 9.03\%$$

$$f_4 = \frac{(1.06)^4}{(1.07)^3} - 1 = 3.06\%$$

An individual investing $1 in the two-year zero-coupon bond receives $1.1236 [$1 $\times$ (1.06)^2] at date 2. He can be viewed as receiving the one-year spot rate of 5 percent over the first year and receiving the forward rate of 7.01 percent over the second year. An individual investing $1 in a three-year zero-coupon bond receives $1.2250 [$1 $\times$ (1.07)^3] at date 3. She can be viewed as receiving the two-year spot rate of 6 percent over the first two years and receiving the forward rate of 9.03 percent over the third year. An individual investing $1 in a four-year zero-coupon bond receives $1.2625 [$1 $\times$ (1.06)^4] at date 4. He can be viewed as receiving the three-year spot rate of 7 percent over the first three years and receiving the forward rate of 3.06 percent over the fourth year.

Note that all of the four spot rates in this problem are known at date 0. Because the forward rates are calculated from the spot rates, they can be determined at date 0 as well.

The material in this appendix is likely to be difficult for a student exposed to term structure for the first time. It helps to state what the student should know at this point. Given equations (A.5) and (A.6), a student should be able to calculate a set of forward rates given a set of spot rates. This can simply be viewed as a mechanical computation. In addition to the calculations, a student should understand the intuition of Figure 5A.2.

We now turn to the relationship between the forward rate and the expected spot rates in the future.

Estimating the Price of a Bond at a Future Date   In the example from the body of this chapter, we considered zero-coupon bonds paying $1,000 at maturity and selling at a discount prior to maturity. We now wish to change the example slightly. Now, each bond initially sells at par so that payment at maturity is above $1,000.[17] Keeping the spot rates at 8 percent and 10 percent, we have

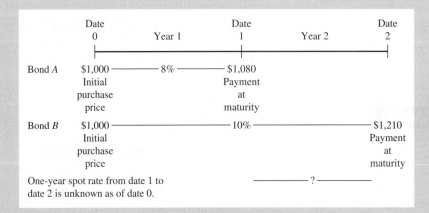

The payments at maturity are $1,080 and $1,210 for the one- and two-year zero-coupon bonds, respectively. The initial purchase price of $1,000 for each bond is determined as

$$\$1,000 = \frac{\$1,080}{1.08}$$

$$\$1,000 = \frac{\$1,210}{(1.10)^2}$$

We refer to the one-year bond as bond A and the two-year bond as bond B.

There will be a different one-year spot rate when date 1 arrives. This will be the spot rate from date 1 to date 2. We can also call it the spot rate over year 2. This spot rate is not known as of date 0. For example, should the rate of inflation rise between date 0 and date 1, the spot rate over year 2 would likely be high. Should the rate of inflation fall between date 0 and date 1, the spot rate over year 2 would likely be low.

Now that we have determined the price of each bond at date 0, we want to determine what the price of each bond will be at date 1. The price of the one-year bond (bond A) must be $1,080 at date 1, because the payment at maturity is made then. The hard part is determining what the price of the two-year bond (bond B) will be at that time.

Suppose we find that, on date 1, the one-year spot rate from date 1 to date 2 is 6 percent. We state that this is the one-year spot rate *over* year 2. This means that I can invest $1,000 at date 1 and receive $1,060 ($1,000 × 1.06) at date 2. Because one year has already passed for bond B, the bond has only one year left. Because bond B pays $1,210 at date 2, its value at date 1 is

$$\$1,141.51 = \frac{\$1,210}{1.06} \tag{A.7}$$

Note that no one *knew* ahead of time the price that bond B would sell for on date 1, because no one knew that the one-year spot rate over year 2 would be 6 percent.

---

[17]This change in assumptions simplifies our presentation but does not alter any of our conclusions.

TABLE 5A.1	**Price of Bond *B* at Date 1**	**Spot Rate over Year 2**
Price of Bond *B* at Date 1 as a Function of Spot Rate over Year 2	$\$1{,}141.51 = \dfrac{\$1{,}210}{1.06}$	6%
	$\$1{,}130.84 = \dfrac{\$1{,}210}{1.07}$	7%
	$\$1{,}061.40 = \dfrac{\$1{,}210}{1.14}$	14%

Suppose the one-year spot rate beginning at date 1 turned out not to be 6 percent, but to be 7 percent instead. This means that I can invest $1,000 at date 1 and receive $1,070 ($1,000 × 1.07) at date 2. In this case, the value of bond *B* at date 1 would be

$$\$1{,}130.84 = \frac{\$1{,}210}{1.07} \qquad (A.8)$$

Finally, suppose that the one-year spot rate at date 1 turned out to be neither 6 percent nor 7 percent, but 14 percent instead. This means that I can invest $1,000 at date 1 and receive $1,140 ($1,000 × 1.14) at date 2. In this case, the value of bond *B* at date 1 would be

$$\$1{,}061.40 = \frac{\$1{,}210}{1.14}$$

The above possible bond prices are represented in Table 5A.1. The price that bond *B* will sell for on date 1 is not known before date 1 since the one-year spot rate prevailing over year 2 is not known until date 1.

It is important to reemphasize that, although the forward rate is known at date 0, the one-year spot rate beginning at date 1 is *unknown* ahead of time. Thus, the price of bond *B* at date 1 is unknown ahead of time. Prior to date 1, we can speak only of the amount that bond *B* is *expected* to sell for on date 1. We write this as[18]

The Amount That Bond *B* Is Expected to Sell for on Date 1:

$$\frac{\$1{,}210}{1 + \text{Spot rate expected over year 2}} \qquad (A.9)$$

It is worthwhile making two points now. First, because each individual is different, the expected value of bond *B* differs across individuals. Later we will speak of a consensus expected value across investors. Second, equation (A.9) represents one's forecast of the price that the bond will be selling for on date 1. The forecast is made ahead of time, that is, on date 0.

The Relationship between Forward Rate over Second Year and Spot Rate Expected over Second Year

Given a forecast of bond *B*'s price, an investor can choose one of two strategies at date 0:

I. Buy a one-year bond. Proceeds at date 1 would be

$$\$1{,}080 = \$1{,}000 \times 1.08 \qquad (A.10)$$

---

[18]Technically, equation (A.9) is only an approximation due to *Jensen's inequality*. That is, expected values of

$$\frac{\$1{,}210}{1 + \text{Spot rate}} > \frac{\$1{,}210}{1 + \text{Spot rate expected over year 2}}$$

However, we ignore this very minor issue in the rest of the analysis.

II. Buy a two-year bond but sell at date 1. *Expected* proceeds would be

$$\frac{\$1,000 \times (1.10)^2}{1 + \text{Spot rate expected over year 2}} \tag{A.11}$$

Given our discussion of forward rates, we can rewrite (A.11) as

$$\frac{\$1,000 \times 1.08 \times 1.1204}{1 + \text{Spot rate expected over year 2}} \tag{A.12}$$

(Remember that 12.04 percent was the forward rate over year 2; i.e., $f_2 = 12.04\%$.)

Under what condition will the return from strategy I equal the expected return from strategy II? In other words, under what condition will formula (A.10) equal formula (A.12)? The two strategies will yield the same expected return only when

$$12.04\% = \text{Spot rate expected over year 2} \tag{A.13}$$

In other words, if the forward rate equals the expected spot rate, one would expect to earn the same return over the first year whether one

1. invested in a one-year bond, or
2. invested in a two-year bond but sold after one year.

The Expectations Hypothesis

Equation (A.13) seems fairly reasonable. That is, it is reasonable that investors would set interest rates in such a way that the forward rate would equal the spot rate expected by the marketplace a year from now.[19] For example, imagine that individuals in the marketplace do not concern themselves with risk. If the forward rate, f_2, is less than the spot rate expected over year 2, individuals desiring to invest for one year would always buy a one-year bond. That is, our work above shows that an individual investing in a two-year bond but planning to sell at the end of one year would expect to earn less than if he simply bought a one-year bond.

Equation (A.13) was stated for the specific case where the forward rate was 12.04 percent. We can generalize this to:

Expectations Hypothesis:
$$f_2 = \text{Spot rate expected over year 2} \tag{A.14}$$

Equation (A.14) says that the forward rate over the second year is set to the spot rate that people expect to prevail over the second year. This is called the *expectations hypothesis*. It states that investors will set interest rates such that the forward rate over the second year is equal to the one-year spot rate expected over the second year.

Liquidity-Preference Hypothesis

At this point, many students think that equation (A.14) *must* hold. However, note that we developed (A.14) by assuming that investors were risk-neutral. Suppose, alternatively, that investors are averse to risk.

---

[19]Of course, each individual will have different expectations, so (A.13) cannot hold for all individuals. However, financial economists generally speak of a *consensus* expectation. This is the expectation of the market as a whole.

Which strategy would appear more risky for an individual who wants to invest for one year?

I. Invest in a one-year bond.

II. Invest in a two-year bond but sell at the end of one year.

Strategy (I) has no risk because the investor knows that the rate of return must be r_1. Conversely, strategy (II) has much risk; the final return is dependent on what happens to interest rates.

Because strategy (II) has more risk than strategy (I), no risk-averse investor will choose strategy (II) if both strategies have the same expected return. Risk-averse investors can have no preference for one strategy over the other only when the expected return on strategy (II) is *above* the return on strategy (I). Because the two strategies have the same expected return when f_2 equals the spot rate expected over year 2, strategy (II) can only have a higher rate of return when

Liquidity-Preference Hypothesis:

$$f_2 > \text{Spot rate expected over year 2} \tag{A.15}$$

That is, in order to induce investors to hold the riskier two-year bonds, the market sets the forward rate over the second year to be above the spot rate expected over the second year. Equation (A.15) is called the *liquidity-preference* hypothesis.

We developed the entire discussion by assuming that individuals are planning to invest over one year. We pointed out that for these types of individuals, a two-year bond has extra risk because it must be sold prematurely. What about those individuals who want to invest for two years? (We call these people investors with a two-year *time horizon.*)

They could choose one of the following strategies:

III. Buy a two-year zero-coupon bond.

IV. Buy a one-year bond. When the bond matures, immediately buy another one-year bond.

Strategy (III) has no risk for an investor with a two-year time horizon, because the proceeds to be received at date 2 are known as of date 0. However, strategy (IV) has risk since the spot rate over year 2 is unknown at date 0. It can be shown that risk-averse investors will prefer neither strategy (III) nor strategy (IV) over the other when

$$f_2 < \text{Spot rate expected over year 2} \tag{A.16}$$

Note that the assumption of risk aversion gives contrary predictions. Relationship (A.15) holds for a market dominated by investors with a one-year time horizon. Relationship (A.16) holds for a market dominated by investors with a two-year time horizon. Financial economists have generally argued that the time horizon of the typical investor is generally much shorter than the maturity of typical bonds in the marketplace. Thus, economists view (A.15) as the best depiction of equilibrium in the bond market with *risk-averse* investors.

However, do we have a market of risk-neutral or risk-averse investors? In other words, can the expectations hypothesis of equation (A.14) or the liquidity-preference hypothesis of equation (A.15) be expected to hold? As we will learn later in this book, economists view investors as being risk-averse for the most part. Yet economists are never satisfied with a casual examination of a theory's assumptions. To them, empirical evidence of a theory's predictions must be the final arbiter.

There has been a great deal of empirical evidence on the term structure of interest rates. Unfortunately (perhaps fortunately for some students), we will not be able to present the evidence in any detail. Suffice it to say that, in our opinion, the evidence supports the liquidity-preference hypothesis over the expectations hypothesis. One simple result might give students the flavor of this research. Consider an individual choosing between one of the following two strategies:

I. Invest in a 1-year bond.

II'. Invest in a 20-year bond but sell at the end of 1 year.

[Strategy (II') is identical to strategy (II), except that a 20-year bond is substituted for a 2-year bond.]

The expectations hypothesis states that the expected returns on both strategies are identical. The liquidity-preference hypothesis states that the expected return on strategy (II') should be above the expected return on strategy (I). Though no one knows what returns are actually expected over a particular time period, actual returns from the past may allow us to infer expectations. The results from January 1926 to December 1999 are illuminating. The average yearly return on strategy (I) is 3.8 percent and 5.5 percent on strategy (II') over this time period.[20,21] This evidence is generally considered to be consistent with the liquidity-preference hypothesis and inconsistent with the expectations hypothesis.

Concept
Questions

1. Define the forward rate.
2. What is the relationship between the one-year spot rate, the two-year spot rate, and the forward rate over the second year?
3. What is the expectations hypothesis?
4. What is the liquidity-preference hypothesis?

QUESTIONS & PROBLEMS

5A.1 The one-year spot rate is 10 percent and the two-year spot rate is 11 percent.
   a. What is the price of a two-year bond that pays an annual coupon of 6 percent?
   b. What is the yield to maturity of this bond?

5A.2 The one-year spot rate is 10 percent and the two-year spot rate is 8 percent. What is the price of a two-year bond that pays an annual coupon of 5 percent?

5A.3 If the one-year spot rate is 9 percent and the two-year spot rate is 10 percent, what is the one-year forward rate over the second year?

5A.4 Assume the following spot rates:

Year	Spot Rate (%)
1	5
2	7
3	10

   a. Calculate the one-year forward rate over the second year.
   b. Calculate the one-year forward rate over the third year.

---

[20]Taken from *Stocks, Bonds, Bills and Inflation 2000 Yearbook* (Chicago: Ibbotson Associates, Inc.). Ibbotson Associates annually updates work by Roger G. Ibbotson and Rex A. Sinquefield.

[21]It is important to note that strategy (II') does not involve buying a 20-year bond and holding it to maturity. Rather, it consists of buying a 20-year bond and selling it 1 year later, that is, when it has become a 19-year bond. This round-trip transaction occurs 74 times in the 74-year sample from January 1926 to December 1999.

TERM STRUCTURE

5A.5 Assume the following forward rates

Maturity	Forward Rates
1	5%
2	12%

Compute the spot rate for years 1 and 2.

5A.6 Given the following two scenarios, for what range of spot rate expected over year 2 would you be better off adopting strategy I? Explain.

Strategy I: Buy a two-year bond and then sell it in year 1.
Strategy II: Buy a one-year bond.

Some Alternative Investment Rules

EXECUTIVE SUMMARY

Chapter 4 examined the relationship between $1 today and $1 in the future. For example, a corporate project can be valued by discounting its cash flows, an approach called the *net-present-value* (NPV) method. While we believe that this method is the place to start for eval-uating capital budgeting projects, our treatment would be incomplete if we ignored alternatives. This chapter first considers the NPV approach as a benchmark. Next we examine three alternatives—payback, accounting rates of return, and internal rate of return.

6.1 Why Use Net Present Value?

This chapter, as well as the next two, focuses on *capital budgeting,* the decision-making process for accepting or rejecting projects. This chapter develops the basic capital budgeting methods, leaving much of the practical application to Chapters 7 and 8. But we don't have to develop these methods from scratch. In Chapter 4, we pointed out that a dollar received in the future is worth less than a dollar received today. The reason, of course, is that today's dollar can be reinvested, yielding a greater amount in the future. And we showed in Chapter 4 that the exact worth of a dollar to be received in the future is its present value. Furthermore, Section 4.1 suggested calculating the *net present value* of any project. That is, the section suggested calculating the difference between the sum of the present values of the project's future cash flows and the initial cost of the project.

The net present value (NPV) method is the first one to be considered in this chapter. We begin by reviewing the approach with a simple example. Next we ask why the method leads to good decisions.

EXAMPLE

The Alpha Corporation is considering investing in a riskless project costing $100. The project receives $107 in one year and has no other cash flows. The interest rate is 6 percent.

The NPV of the project can easily be calculated as:

$$\$0.94 = -\$100 + \frac{\$107}{1.06} \tag{6.1}$$

From Chapter 4, we know that the project should be accepted since its NPV is positive. Had the NPV of the project been negative, as would have been the case with an interest rate greater than 7 percent, the project should be rejected.

The basic investment rule can be generalized to:

Accept a project if the NPV is greater than zero.
Reject a project if NPV is less than zero.

We refer to this as the **NPV rule.**

Now why does the NPV rule lead to good decisions? Consider the following two strategies available to the managers of Alpha Corporation:

1. Use $100 of corporate cash to invest in the project. The $107 will be paid as a dividend in one year.
2. Forgo the project and pay the $100 of corporate cash as a dividend today.

If strategy 2 is employed, the stockholder might deposit the dividend in his bank for one year. With an interest rate of 6 percent, strategy 2 would produce cash of $106 ($100 × 1.06) at the end of the year. The stockholder would prefer strategy 1, since strategy 2 produces less than $107 at the end of the year.

Thus, our basic point is:

Accepting positive NPV projects benefits the stockholders.

How do we interpret the exact NPV of $0.94? This is the increase in the value of the firm from the project. For example, imagine that the firm today has productive assets worth $V and has $100 of cash. If the firm foregoes the project, the value of the firm today would simply be:

$$\$V + \$100 \tag{6.2}$$

If the firm accepts the project, the firm will receive $107 in one year but will have no cash today. Thus, the firm's value today would be:

$$\$V + \frac{\$107}{1.06} \tag{6.3}$$

The difference between equation (6.2) and equation (6.3) is just $0.94, the present value of equation (6.1). Thus:

The value of the firm rises by the NPV of the project.

Note that the value of the firm is merely the sum of the values of the different projects, divisions, or other entities within the firm. This property, called **value-additivity,** is quite important. It implies that the contribution of any project to a firm's value is simply the NPV of the project. As we will see later, alternative methods discussed in this chapter do not generally have this nice property.

One detail remains. We assumed that the project was riskless, a rather implausible assumption. Future cash flows of real-world projects are invariably risky. In other words, cash flows can only be estimated, rather than known. Imagine that the managers of Alpha *expect* the cash flow of the project to be $107 next year. That is, the cash flow could be higher, say $117, or lower, say $97. With this slight change, the project is risky. Suppose the project is about as risky as the stock market as a whole, where the expected return this year is, say 10 percent. Well, 10 percent becomes the discount rate, implying that the NPV of the project would be:

$$-\$2.73 = -\$100 + \frac{\$107}{1.10}$$

Since the NPV is negative, the project should be rejected. This makes sense since a stockholder of Alpha receiving a $100 dividend today could invest it in the stock market, expecting a 10 percent return. Why accept a project with the same risk as the market but with an expected return of only 7 percent?

Conceptually, the discount rate on a risky project is the return that one can expect to earn on a financial asset of comparable risk. This discount rate is often referred to as an *opportunity cost,* since corporate investment in the project takes away the stockholder's opportunity to invest the dividend in a financial asset. If the actual calculation of the discount rate strikes you as extremely difficult in the real world, you are probably right. While you can call a bank to find out the interest rate, whom do you call to find the expected return on the market this year? And, if the risk of the project differs from that of the market, how do you make the adjustment? However, the calculation is by no means impossible. While we forgo the calculation in this chapter, we present it in later chapters of the text.

Having shown that NPV is a sensible approach, how can we tell whether alternative methods are as good as NPV? The key to NPV is its three attributes:

1. *NPV Uses Cash Flows.* Cash flows from a project can be used for other corporate purposes (e.g., dividend payments, other capital-budgeting projects, or payments of corporate interest). By contrast, earnings are an artificial construct. While earnings are useful to accountants, they should not be used in capital budgeting because they do not represent cash.

2. *NPV Uses All the Cash Flows of the Project.* Other approaches ignore cash flows beyond a particular date; beware of these approaches.

3. *NPV Discounts the Cash Flows Properly.* Other approaches may ignore the time value of money when handling cash flows. Beware of these approaches as well.

Concept
Questions

1. **What is the NPV rule?**
2. **Why does this rule lead to good investment decisions?**

6.2 The Payback Period Method

Defining the Rule

One of the most popular alternatives to NPV is **payback.** Here is how payback works.

Consider a project with an initial investment of −$50,000. Cash flows are $30,000, $20,000, and $10,000 in the first three years, respectively. These flows are illustrated in Figure 6.1. A useful way of writing down investments like the preceding is with the notation:

$$(-\$50,000, \$30,000, \$20,000, \$10,000)$$

FIGURE 6.1

Cash Flows of an
Investment Project

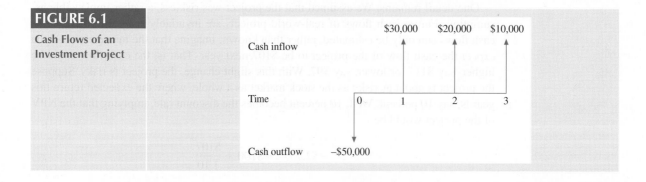

The minus sign in front of the $50,000 reminds us that this is a cash outflow for the investor, and the commas between the different numbers indicate that they are received—or if they are cash outflows, that they are paid out—at different times. In this example we are assuming that the cash flows occur one year apart, with the first one occurring the moment we decide to take on the investment.

The firm receives cash flows of $30,000 and $20,000 in the first two years, which add up to the $50,000 original investment. This means that the firm has recovered its investment within two years. In this case two years is the *payback period* of the investment.

The **payback period rule** for making investment decisions is simple. A particular cutoff date, say two years, is selected. All investment projects that have payback periods of two years or less are accepted and all of those that pay off in more than two years—if at all—are rejected.

Problems with the Payback Method

There are at least three problems with payback. To illustrate the first two problems, we consider the three projects in Table 6.1. All three projects have the same three-year payback period, so they should all be equally attractive—right?

Actually, they are not equally attractive, as can be seen by a comparison of different *pairs* of projects.

Problem 1: Timing of Cash Flows within the Payback Period   Let us compare project A with project B. In years 1 through 3, the cash flows of project A rise from $20 to $50 while the cash flows of project B fall from $50 to $20. Because the large cash flow of $50 comes earlier with project B, its net present value must be higher. Nevertheless, we saw above that the payback periods of the two projects are identical. Thus, a problem with the payback method is that it does not consider the timing of the cash flows within the payback period. This example shows that the payback method is inferior to NPV because, as we pointed out earlier, the NPV method *discounts the cash flows properly.*

Problem 2: Payments after the Payback Period   Now consider projects B and C, which have identical cash flows within the payback period. However, project C is clearly preferred because it has a cash flow of $60,000 in the fourth year. Thus, another problem with the payback method is that it ignores all cash flows occurring after the payback period. Because of the short-term orientation of the payback method, some valuable long-term projects are likely to be rejected. The NPV method does not have this flaw since, as we pointed out earlier, this method *uses all the cash flows of the project.*

Problem 3: Arbitrary Standard for Payback Period   We do not need to refer to Table 6.1 when considering a third problem with the payback method. Capital markets help us estimate the discount rate used in the NPV method. The riskless rate, perhaps proxied by the yield on a Treasury instrument, would be the appropriate rate for a riskless investment.

TABLE 6.1	Year	A	B	C
Expected Cash Flows for Projects A through C ($)	0	−100	−100	−100
	1	20	50	50
	2	30	30	30
	3	50	20	20
	4	60	60	60,000
	Payback period (years)	3	3	3

Later chapters of this textbook show how to use historical returns in the capital markets in order to estimate the discount rate for a risky project. However, there is no comparable guide for choosing the payback cutoff date, so the choice is somewhat arbitrary.

Managerial Perspective

The payback method is often used by large, sophisticated companies when making relatively small decisions. The decision to build a small warehouse, for example, or to pay for a tune-up for a truck is the sort of decision that is often made by lower-level management. Typically a manager might reason that a tune-up would cost, say, $200, and if it saved $120 each year in reduced fuel costs, it would pay for itself in less than two years. On such a basis the decision would be made.

Although the treasurer of the company might not have made the decision in the same way, the company endorses such decision making. Why would upper management condone or even encourage such retrograde activity in its employees? One answer would be that it is easy to make decisions using payback. Multiply the tune-up decision into 50 such decisions a month, and the appeal of this simple method becomes clearer.

The payback method also has some desirable features for managerial control. Just as important as the investment decision itself is the company's ability to evaluate the manager's decision-making ability. Under the NPV method, a long time may pass before one decides whether or not a decision was correct. With the payback method we know in two years whether the manager's assessment of the cash flows was correct.

It has also been suggested that firms with good investment opportunities but no available cash may justifiably use payback. For example, the payback method could be used by small, privately held firms with good growth prospects but limited access to the capital markets. Quick cash recovery enhances the reinvestment possibilities for such firms.

Finally, practitioners often argue that standard academic criticisms of payback overstate any real-world problems with the method. For example, textbooks typically make fun of payback by positing a project with low cash inflows in the early years but a huge cash inflow right after the payback cutoff date. This project is likely to be rejected under the payback method, though its acceptance would, in truth, benefit the firm. Project *C* in our Table 6.1 is an example of such a project. Practitioners point out that the pattern of cash flows in these textbook examples is much too stylized to mirror the real world. In fact, a number of executives have told us that, for the overwhelming majority of real-world projects, both payback and NPV lead to the same decision. In addition, these executives indicate that, if an investment like project *C* were encountered in the real world, decision makers would almost certainly make *ad hoc* adjustments to the payback rule so that the project would be accepted.

Notwithstanding all of the preceding rationale, it is not surprising to discover that as the decision grows in importance, which is to say when firms look at bigger projects, NPV becomes the order of the day. When questions of controlling and evaluating the manager become less important than making the right investment decision, payback is used less frequently. For big-ticket decisions, such as whether or not to buy a machine, build a factory, or acquire a company, the payback method is seldom used.

Summary of Payback

The payback method differs from NPV and is therefore conceptually wrong. With its arbitrary cutoff date and its blindness to cash flows after that date, it can lead to some flagrantly foolish decisions if it is used too literally. Nevertheless, because of its simplicity, as well as its other advantages mentioned above, companies often use it as a screen for making the myriad of minor investment decisions they continually face.

Although this means that you should be wary of trying to change approaches such as the payback method when you encounter them in companies, you should probably be careful not to accept the sloppy financial thinking they represent. After this course, you would do your company a disservice if you used payback instead of NPV when you had a choice.

| **Concept** Questions | 1. **List the problems of the payback method.** |
| | 2. **What are some advantages?** |

6.3 The Discounted Payback Period Method

Aware of the pitfalls of payback, some decision makers use a variant called the **discounted payback period method.** Under this approach, we first discount the cash flows. Then we ask how long it takes for the discounted cash flows to equal the initial investment.

For example, suppose that the discount rate is 10 percent and the cash flows on a project are given by

$$(-\$100, \$50, \$50, \$20)$$

This investment has a payback period of two years, because the investment is paid back in that time.

To compute the project's discounted payback period, we first discount each of the cash flows at the 10-percent rate. These discounted cash flows are

$$[-\$100, \$50/1.1, \$50/(1.1)^2, \$20/(1.1)^3] = (-\$100, \$45.45, \$41.32, \$15.03)$$

The discounted payback period of the original investment is simply the payback period for these discounted cash flows. The payback period for the discounted cash flows is slightly less than three years since the discounted cash flows over the three years are $101.80 ($45.45 + $41.32 + $15.03). As long as the cash flows are positive, the discounted payback period will never be smaller than the payback period, because discounting reduces the value of the cash flows.

At first glance discounted payback may seem like an attractive alternative, but on closer inspection we see that it has some of the same major flaws as payback. Like payback, discounted payback first requires us to make a somewhat magical choice of an arbitrary cutoff period, and then it ignores all of the cash flows after that date.

If we have already gone to the trouble of discounting the cash flows, any small appeal to simplicity or to managerial control that payback may have, has been lost. We might just as well add up all the discounted cash flows and use NPV to make the decision. Although discounted payback looks a bit like NPV, it is just a poor compromise between the payback method and NPV.

6.4 The Average Accounting Return Method

Defining the Rule

Another attractive, but fatally flawed, approach to financial decision-making is the **average accounting return.** The average accounting return is the average project earnings after taxes and depreciation, divided by the average book value of the investment during its life. In spite of its flaws, the average accounting return method is worth examining because it is used frequently in the real world.

EXAMPLE

Consider a company that is evaluating whether to buy a store in a new mall. The purchase price is $500,000. We will assume that the store has an estimated life of five years and will need to be completely scrapped or rebuilt at the end of that time. The projected yearly sales and expense figures are shown in Table 6.2.

TABLE 6.2		Year 1	Year 2	Year 3	Year 4	Year 5
Projected Yearly	Revenue	$433,333	$450,000	$266,667	$200,000	$133,333
Revenue and Costs	Expenses	200,000	150,000	100,000	100,000	100,000
for Average	Before-tax cash flow	233,333	300,000	166,667	100,000	33,333
Accounting Return	Depreciation	100,000	100,000	100,000	100,000	100,000
	Earnings before taxes	133,333	200,000	66,667	0	−66,667
	Taxes ($T_c = 0.25$)*	33,333	50,000	16,667	0	−16,667
	Net income	$100,000	$150,000	$ 50,000	$ 0	−$ 50,000

$$\text{Average net income} = \frac{(\$100,000 + 150,000 + 50,000 + 0 - 50,000)}{5} = \$50,000$$

$$\text{Average investment} = \frac{\$500,000 + 0}{2} = \$250,000$$

$$\text{AAR} = \frac{\$50,000}{\$250,000} = 20\%$$

*Corporate tax rate = T_c. The tax rebate in year 5 of −$16,667 occurs if the rest of the firm is profitable. Here, the loss in the project reduces taxes of entire firm.

It is worth examining this table carefully. In fact, the first step in any project assessment is a careful look at projected cash flows. First-year sales for the store are estimated to be $433,333. Before-tax cash flow will be $233,333. Sales are expected to rise and expenses are expected to fall in the second year, resulting in a before-tax cash flow of $300,000. Competition from other stores and the loss in novelty will reduce before-tax cash flow to $166,667, $100,000, and $33,333, respectively, in the next three years.

To compute the average accounting return (AAR) on the project, we divide the average net income by the average amount invested. This can be done in three steps.

Step One: Determining Average Net Income   Net income in any year is net cash flow minus depreciation and taxes. Depreciation is *not* a cash outflow.[1] Rather, it is a charge reflecting the fact that the investment in the store becomes less valuable every year.

We assume the project has a useful life of five years, at which time it will be worthless. Because the initial investment is $500,000 and because it will be worthless in five years, we assume that it loses value at the rate of $100,000 each year. This steady loss in value of $100,000 is called *straight-line depreciation*. We subtract both depreciation and taxes from before-tax cash flow to derive net income, as shown in Table 6.2. Net income is $100,000 in the first year, $150,000 in year 2, $50,000 in year 3, zero in year 4, and −$50,000 in the last year. The average net income over the life of the project is therefore

Average Net Income:

$$[\$100,000 + \$150,000 + \$50,000 + \$0 + (-\$50,000)]/5 = \$50,000$$

---

[1]Depreciation will be treated in more detail in the next chapter.

Step Two: Determining Average Investment   We stated earlier that, due to depreciation, the investment in the store becomes less valuable every year. Because depreciation is $100,000 per year, the value at the end of year zero is $500,000, the value at the end of year 1 is $400,000 and so on. What is the average value of the investment over the life of the investment?

The mechanical calculation is

Average Investment:

$$(\$500,000 + \$400,000 + \$300,000 + \$200,000 + \$100,000 + \$0)/6 = \$250,000 \quad (6.4)$$

We divide by 6 and not 5, because $500,000 is what the investment is worth at the beginning of the five years and $0 is what it is worth at the beginning of the sixth year. In other words, there are six terms in the parentheses of equation (6.4).

Step Three: Determining AAR   The average return is simply

$$\text{AAR} = \frac{\$50,000}{\$250,000} = 20\%$$

If the firm had a targeted accounting rate of return greater than 20 percent, the project would be rejected, and if its targeted return were less than 20 percent, it would be accepted.

Analyzing the Average Accounting Return Method

By now you should be able to see what is wrong with the AAR method.

The most important flaw with AAR is that it does not work with the right raw materials. It uses net income and book value of the investment, both of which come from the accounting books. Accounting numbers are somewhat arbitrary. For example, certain cash outflows, such as the cost of a building, are depreciated under current accounting rules. Other flows, such as maintenance, are expensed. In real-world situations, the decision to depreciate or expense an item involves judgment. Thus, the basic inputs of the AAR method, income and average investment, are affected by the accountant's judgment. Conversely, the NPV method *uses cash flows*. Accounting judgments do not affect cash flow.

Second, AAR takes no account of timing. In the previous example, the AAR would have been the same if the $100,000 net income in the first year had occurred in the last year. However, delaying an inflow for five years would have lowered the NPV of the investment. As mentioned earlier in this chapter, the NPV approach *discounts properly*.

Third, just as payback requires an arbitrary choice of the cutoff date, the AAR method offers no guidance on what the right targeted rate of return should be. It could be the discount rate in the market. But then again, because the AAR method is not the same as the present value method, it is not obvious that this would be the right choice.

Given these problems, is the AAR method employed in practice? Like the payback method, the AAR (and variations of it) is frequently used as a "backup" to discounted cash flow methods. Perhaps this is so because it is easy to calculate and uses accounting numbers readily available from the firm's accounting system. In addition, both stockholders and the media pay a lot of attention to the overall profitability of a firm. Thus, some managers may feel pressured to select projects that are profitable in the near term, even if the projects come up short in terms of NPV. These managers may focus on the AAR of individual projects more than they should.

Concept
Questions

1. **What are the three steps in calculating AAR?**
2. **What are some flaws with the AAR method?**

6.5 The Internal Rate of Return

Now we come to the most important alternative to the NPV method, the internal rate of return, universally known as the IRR. The IRR is about as close as you can get to the NPV without actually being the NPV. The basic rationale behind the IRR method is that it provides a single number summarizing the merits of a project. That number does not depend on the interest rate prevailing in the capital market. That is why it is called the internal rate of return; the number is internal or intrinsic to the project and does not depend on anything except the cash flows of the project.

For example, consider the simple project (−$100, $110) in Figure 6.2. For a given rate, the net present value of this project can be described as

$$\text{NPV} = -\$100 + \frac{\$110}{1 + r} \tag{6.5}$$

where r is the discount rate.

What must the discount rate be to make the NPV of the project equal to zero?

We begin by using an arbitrary discount rate of 0.08, which yields

$$\$1.85 = -\$100 + \frac{\$110}{1.08} \tag{6.6}$$

Since the NPV in equation (6.6) is positive, we now try a higher discount rate, say, 0.12. This yields

$$-\$1.79 = -\$100 + \frac{\$110}{1.12} \tag{6.7}$$

Since the NPV in equation (6.7) is negative, we lower the discount rate to, say, 0.10. This yields

$$0 = -\$100 + \frac{\$110}{1.10} \tag{6.8}$$

This trial-and-error procedure tells us that the NPV of the project is zero when r equals 10 percent.[2] Thus, we say that 10 percent is the project's **internal rate of return** (IRR). In general, the IRR is the rate that causes the NPV of the project to be zero. The implication of this exercise is very simple. The firm should be equally willing to accept or reject the project if the discount rate is 10 percent. The firm should accept the project if the discount rate is below 10 percent. The firm should reject the project if the discount rate is above 10 percent.

The general investment rule is clear:

Accept the project if IRR is greater than the discount rate. Reject the project if IRR is less than the discount rate.

We refer to this as the **basic IRR rule.** Now we can try the more complicated example (−$200, $100, $100, $100) in Figure 6.3.

As we did in equations (6.6) to (6.8), let's use trial and error to calculate the internal rate of return. We try 20 percent and 30 percent, yielding

Discount Rate	NPV
20%	$10.65
30	−18.39

---

[2]Of course, we could have directly solved for r in equation (6.5) after setting NPV equal to zero. However, with a long series of cash flows, one cannot generally directly solve for r. Instead, one is forced to use a trial-and-error method similar to that in (6.6), (6.7), and (6.8).

FIGURE 6.2

Cash Flows for a Simple Project

FIGURE 6.3

Cash Flows for a More Complex Project

After much more trial and error, we find that the NPV of the project is zero when the discount rate is 23.37 percent. Thus, the IRR is 23.37 percent. With a 20-percent discount rate the NPV is positive and we would accept it. However, if the discount rate were 30 percent, we would reject it.

Algebraically, IRR is the unknown in the following equation:[3]

$$0 = -\$200 + \frac{\$100}{1 + IRR} + \frac{\$100}{(1 + IRR)^2} + \frac{\$100}{(1 + IRR)^3}$$

Figure 6.4 illustrates what the IRR of a project means. The figure plots the NPV as a function of the discount rate. The curve crosses the horizontal axis at the IRR of 23.37 percent because this is where the NPV equals zero.

It should also be clear that the NPV is positive for discount rates below the IRR and negative for discount rates above the IRR. This means that if we accept projects like this one when the discount rate is less than the IRR, we will be accepting positive NPV projects. Thus, the IRR rule coincides exactly with the NPV rule.

If this were all there were to it, the IRR rule would always coincide with the NPV rule. This would be a wonderful discovery because it would mean that just by computing the IRR for a project we would be able to tell where it ranks among all of the projects we are considering. For example, if the IRR rule really works, a project with an IRR of 20 percent will always be at least as good as one with an IRR of 15 percent.

But the world of finance is not so kind. Unfortunately, the IRR rule and the NPV rule are the same only for examples like the ones above. Several problems with the IRR approach occur in more complicated situations.

Concept Question

1. How does one calculate the IRR of a project?

----

[3]One can derive the IRR directly for a problem with an initial outflow and either one or two subsequent inflows. In the case of two subsequent inflows, the quadratic formula is needed. In general, however, only trial and error will work for an outflow and three or more subsequent inflows. Hand calculators calculate IRR by trial and error, though at lightning speed.

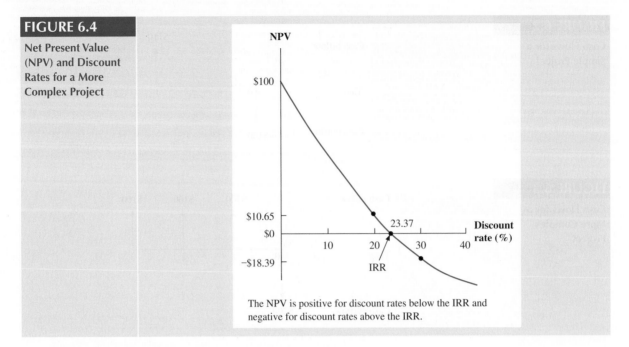

The NPV is positive for discount rates below the IRR and
negative for discount rates above the IRR.

6.6 Problems with the IRR Approach

Definition of Independent and Mutually Exclusive Projects

An **independent project** is one whose acceptance or rejection is independent of the acceptance or rejection of other projects. For example, imagine that McDonald's is considering putting a hamburger outlet on a remote island. Acceptance or rejection of this unit is likely to be unrelated to the acceptance or rejection of any other restaurant in their system. The remoteness of the outlet in question ensures that it will not pull sales away from other outlets.

Now consider the other extreme, **mutually exclusive investments.** What does it mean for two projects, A and B, to be mutually exclusive? You can accept A or you can accept B or you can reject both of them, but you cannot accept both of them. For example, A might be a decision to build an apartment house on a corner lot that you own, and B might be a decision to build a movie theater on the same lot.

We now present two general problems with the IRR approach that affect both independent and mutually exclusive projects. Next, we deal with two problems affecting mutually exclusive projects only.

Two General Problems Affecting Both Independent and Mutually Exclusive Projects

We begin our discussion with project A, which has the following cash flows:

$$(-\$100, \$130)$$

The IRR for project A is 30 percent. Table 6.3 provides other relevant information on the project. The relationship between NPV and the discount rate is shown for this project in Figure 6.5. As you can see, the NPV declines as the discount rate rises.

Problem 1: Investing or Financing?   Now consider project B, with cash flows of

$$(\$100, -\$130)$$

TABLE 6.3	The Internal Rate of Return and Net Present Value								
	Project A			**Project B**			**Project C**		
Dates:	**0**	**1**	**2**	**0**	**1**	**2**	**0**	**1**	**2**
Cash flows	−$100	$130		$100	−$130		−$100	$230	−$132
IRR		30%			30%		10%	and	20%
NPV @10%		$18.2			−$18.2			0	
Accept if market rate		<30%			>30%		>10%	but	<20%
Financing or investing		Investing			Financing			Mixture	

FIGURE 6.5	Net Present Value and Discount Rates for Projects A, B, and C

Project A has a cash outflow at date 0 followed by a cash inflow at date 1. Its NPV is negatively related to the discount rate.
Project B has a cash inflow at date 0 followed by a cash outflow at date 1. Its NPV is positively related to the discount rate.
Project C has two changes of sign in its cash flows. It has an outflow at date 0, an inflow at date 1, and an outflow at date 2.
Projects with more than one change of sign can have multiple rates of return.

These cash flows are exactly the reverse of the flows for project A. In project B, the firm receives funds first and then pays out funds later. While unusual, projects of this type do exist. For example, consider a corporation conducting a seminar where the participants pay in advance. Because large expenses are frequently incurred at the seminar date, cash inflows precede cash outflows.

Consider our trial-and-error method to calculate IRR:

$$-\$4 = +\$100 - \frac{\$130}{1.25}$$

$$\$0 = +\$100 - \frac{\$130}{1.30}$$

$$\$3.70 = +\$100 - \frac{\$130}{1.35}$$

As with project A, the internal rate of return is 30 percent. However, notice that the net present value is *negative* when the discount rate is *below* 30 percent. Conversely, the net present value is positive when the discount rate is above 30 percent. The decision rule is exactly the opposite of our previous result. For this type of a project, the rule is

Accept the project when IRR is less than the discount rate. Reject the project when IRR is greater than the discount rate.

This unusual decision rule follows from the graph of project B in Figure 6.5. The curve is upward sloping, implying that NPV is *positively* related to the discount rate.

The graph makes intuitive sense. Suppose that the firm wants to obtain $100 immediately. It can either (1) accept project B or (2) borrow $100 from a bank. Thus, the project is actually a substitute for borrowing. In fact, because the IRR is 30 percent, taking on project B is tantamount to borrowing at 30 percent. If the firm can borrow from a bank at, say, only 25 percent, it should reject the project. However, if a firm can only borrow from a bank at, say, 35 percent, it should accept the project. Thus, project B will be accepted if and only if the discount rate is *above* the IRR.[4]

This should be contrasted with project A. If the firm has $100 of cash to invest, it can either (1) accept project A or (2) lend $100 to the bank. The project is actually a substitute for lending. In fact, because the IRR is 30 percent, taking on project A is tantamount to lending at 30 percent. The firm should accept project A if the lending rate is below 30 percent. Conversely, the firm should reject project A if the lending rate is above 30 percent.

Because the firm initially pays out money with project A but initially receives money with project B, we refer to project A as an *investing-type project* and project B as a *financing-type project*. Investing-type projects are the norm. Since the IRR rule is reversed for financing-type projects, be careful when using it with this type of project.

Problem 2: Multiple Rates of Return Suppose the cash flows from a project are

$$(-\$100, \$230, -\$132)$$

Because this project has a negative cash flow, a positive cash flow, and another negative cash flow, we say that the project's cash flows exhibit two changes of signs, or "flip-flops." While this pattern of cash flows might look a bit strange at first, many projects require outflows of cash after receiving some inflows. An example would be a strip-mining project. The first stage in such a project is the initial investment in excavating the mine. Profits from operating the mine are received in the second stage. The third stage involves a further investment to reclaim the land and satisfy the requirements of environmental-protection legislation. Cash flows are negative at this stage.

Projects financed by lease arrangements may produce a similar pattern of cash flows. Leases often provide substantial tax subsidies, generating cash inflows after an initial investment. However, these subsidies decline over time, frequently leading to negative cash flows in later years. (The details of leasing will be discussed in a later chapter.)

It is easy to verify that this project has not one but two IRRs, 10 percent and 20 percent.[5] In a case like this, the IRR does not make any sense. What IRR are we to use, 10 percent or 20 percent? Because there is no good reason to use one over the other, IRR simply cannot be used here.

---

[4]This paragraph implicitly assumes that the cash flows of the project are risk-free. In this way, we can treat the borrowing rate as the discount rate for a firm needing $100. With risky cash flows, another discount rate would be chosen. However, the intuition behind the decision to accept when IRR is less than the discount rate would still apply.

[5]The calculations are

$$-\$100 + \frac{\$230}{1.1} - \frac{\$132}{(1.1)^2}$$

$$0 = -\$100 + \$209.09 - \$109.09$$

and

$$-\$100 + \frac{\$230}{1.2} - \frac{\$132}{(1.2)^2}$$

$$0 = -\$100 + \$191.67 - \$91.67$$

Thus, we have multiple rates of return.

Why does this project have multiple rates of return? Project *C* generates multiple internal rates of return because both an inflow and an outflow occur after the initial investment. In general, these flip-flops or changes in sign produce multiple IRRs. In theory, a cash flow stream with *K* changes in sign can have up to *K* sensible internal rates of return (IRRs above −100%).[6] Therefore, since project *C* has two changes in sign, it can have as many as two IRRs. As we pointed out, projects whose cash flows change sign repeatedly can occur in the real world.

NPV Rule   Of course, we should not be too worried about multiple rates of return. After all, we can always fall back on the NPV rule. Figure 6.5 plots the NPV of project *C* (−$100, $230, −$132) as a function of the discount rate. As the figure shows, the NPV is zero at both 10 percent and 20 percent and negative outside the range. Thus, the NPV rule tells us to accept the project if the appropriate discount rate is between 10 percent and 20 percent. The project should be rejected if the discount rate lies outside of this range.

Modified IRR   As an alternative to NPV, we now introduce the **modified IRR (MIRR)** method, which handles the multiple-IRR problem by combining cash flows until only one change in sign remains. To see how it works, consider project *C* again. With a discount rate of, say, 14 percent, the value of the last cash flow, −$132, is:

$$-\$132/1.14 = -\$115.79$$

as of date 1. Since $230 is already received at that time, the "adjusted" cash flow at date 1 is $114.21 (230 − 115.79). Thus, the MIRR approach produces the following two cash flows for the project:

$$(-\$100, \$114.21)$$

Note that, by discounting and then combining cash flows, we are left with only one change in sign. The IRR rule can now be applied. The IRR of these two cash flows is 14.21 percent, implying that the project should be accepted given our assumed discount rate of 14 percent.

Of course, project *C* is relatively simple to begin with, since it has only three cash flows and two changes in sign. However, the same procedure can easily be applied to more complex projects; that is, just keep discounting and combining the later cash flows until only one change of sign remains.

---

[6]Those of you who are steeped in algebra might have recognized that finding the IRR is like finding the root of a polynomial equation. For a project with cash flows of $(C_0, \ldots, C_T)$, the formula for computing the IRR requires us to find the interest rate, *r*, that makes

$$\text{NPV} = C_0 + C_1/(1 + r) + \cdots + C_T/(1 + r)^T = 0$$

If we let the symbol *x* stand for the discount factor,

$$x = 1/(1 + r)$$

then the formula for the IRR becomes

$$\text{NPV} = C_0 + C_1 x + C_2 x^2 + \cdots + C_T x^T = 0$$

Finding the IRR, then, is the same as finding the roots of this polynomial equation. If a particular value x^* is a root of the equation, then, because

$$x = 1/(1 + r)$$

it follows that there is an associated IRR:

$$r^* = (1/x^*) - 1$$

From the theory of polynomials, it is well known that an *n*th-order polynomial has *n* roots. Generally, an IRR above −100% is considered sensible. Since each root that is positive generates an IRR above −100%, any positive root can have a sensible IRR associated with it. Applying Descartes' rule of signs gives the result that a stream of *n* cash flows can have up to *K* IRRs above −100%, where *K* is the number of changes in sign for the cash flows.

While this adjustment does correct for multiple IRRs, it appears, at least to us, to violate the "spirit" of the IRR approach. As stated earlier, the basic rationale behind the IRR method is that it provides a single number summarizing the merits of a project. That number does not depend on the discount rate. In fact, that is why it is called the internal rate of return; the number is *internal,* or intrinsic, to the project and does not depend on anything except the cash flows of the project. By contrast, MIRR is clearly a function of the discount rate. However, this point is not meant to be a criticism of MIRR. A firm using this adjustment will avoid the multiple-IRR problem, just as a firm using the NPV rule will avoid it.

The Guarantee against Multiple IRRs If the first cash flow of a project is negative—because it is the initial investment—and if all of the remaining flows are positive, there can be only a single, unique IRR, no matter how many periods the project lasts. This is easy to understand by using the concept of the time value of money. For example, it is simple to verify that project *A* in Table 6.3 has an IRR of 30 percent, because using a 30-percent discount rate gives

$$NPV = -\$100 + \$130/(1.3)$$
$$= 0$$

How do we know that this is the only IRR? Suppose that we were to try a discount rate greater than 30 percent. In computing the NPV, changing the discount rate does not change the value of the initial cash flow of −$100 because that cash flow is not discounted. But raising the discount rate can only lower the present value of the future cash flows. In other words, because the NPV is zero at 30 percent, any increase in the rate will push the NPV into the negative range. Similarly, if we try a discount rate of less than 30 percent, the overall NPV of the project will be positive. Though this example has only one positive flow, the above reasoning still implies a single, unique IRR if there are many inflows (but no outflows) after the initial investment.

If the initial cash flow is positive—and if all of the remaining flows are negative—there can only be a single, unique IRR. This result follows from reasoning similar to that above. Both these cases have only one change of sign or flip-flop in the cash flows. Thus, we are safe from multiple IRRs whenever there is only one sign change in the cash flows.

General Rules The following chart summarizes our rules:[7]

Flows	Number of IRRs	IRR Criterion	NPV Criterion
First cash flow is negative and all remaining cash flows are positive.	1	Accept if IRR > r Reject if IRR < r	Accept if NPV > 0 Reject if NPV < 0
First cash flow is positive and all remaining cash flows are negative.	1	Accept if IRR < r Reject if IRR > r	Accept if NPV > 0 Reject if NPV < 0
Some cash flows after first are positive and some cash flows after first are negative.	May be more than 1	No valid IRR	Accept if NPV > 0 Reject if NPV < 0

---

[7]IRR stands for internal rate of return, NPV stands for net present value, and *r* stands for discount rate.

Note that the NPV criterion is the same for each of the three cases. In other words, NPV analysis is always appropriate. Conversely, the IRR can be used only in certain cases. When it comes to NPV, the preacher's words, "You just can't lose with the stuff I use," clearly apply.

Problems Specific to Mutually Exclusive Projects

As mentioned earlier, two or more projects are mutually exclusive if the firm can, at most, accept only one of them. We now present two problems dealing with the application of the IRR approach to mutually exclusive projects. These two problems are quite similar, though logically distinct.

The Scale Problem   A professor we know motivates class discussions on this topic with the statement: "Students, I am prepared to let one of you choose between two mutually exclusive 'business' propositions. Opportunity 1—You give me $1 now and I'll give you $1.50 back at the end of the class period. Opportunity 2—You give me $10 and I'll give you $11 back at the end of the class period. You can only choose one of the two opportunities. And you cannot choose either opportunity more than once. I'll pick the first volunteer."

Which would you choose? The correct answer is opportunity 2.[8] To see this, look at the following chart:

	Cash Flow at Beginning of Class	Cash Flow at End of Class (90 minutes later)	NPV[9]	IRR
Opportunity 1	−$1	+$1.50	$0.50	50%
Opportunity 2	−10	+11.00	1.00	10

As we have stressed earlier in the text, one should choose the opportunity with the highest NPV. This is opportunity 2 in the example. Or, as one of the professor's students explained it: "I'm bigger than the professor, so I know I'll get my money back. And I have $10 in my pocket right now so I can choose either opportunity. At the end of the class, I'll be able to play two rounds of my favorite electronic game with opportunity 2 and still have my original investment, safe and sound.[10] The profit on opportunity 1 buys only one round."

This business proposition illustrates a defect with the internal rate of return criterion. The basic IRR rule indicates the selection of opportunity 1, because the IRR is 50 percent. The IRR is only 10 percent for opportunity 2.

Where does IRR go wrong? The problem with IRR is that it ignores issues of *scale*. While opportunity 1 has a greater IRR, the investment is much smaller. In other words, the high percentage return on opportunity 1 is more than offset by the ability to earn at least a decent return[11] on a much bigger investment under opportunity 2.

Since IRR seems to be misguided here, can we adjust or correct it? We illustrate how in the next example.

---

[8]The professor uses real money here. Though many students have done poorly on the professor's exams over the years, no student ever chose opportunity 1. The professor claims that his students are "money players."

[9]We assume a zero rate of interest because his class lasted only 90 minutes. It just seemed like a lot longer.

[10]At press time for this text, electronic games cost $0.50 apiece.

[11]A 10-percent return is more than decent over a 90-minute interval!

Stanley Jaffe and Sherry Lansing have just purchased the rights to *Corporate Finance:The Motion Picture*. They will produce this major motion picture on either a small budget or a big budget. The estimated cash flows are

	Cash Flow at Date 0	Cash Flow at Date 1	NPV @25%	IRR
Small budget	−$10 million	$40 million	$22 million	300%
Large budget	−25 million	65 million	27 million	160

Because of high risk, a 25-percent discount rate is considered appropriate. Sherry wants to adopt the large budget because the NPV is higher. Stanley wants to adopt the small budget because the IRR is higher. Who is right?

For the reasons espoused in the classroom example above, NPV is correct. Hence, Sherry is right. However, Stanley is very stubborn where IRR is concerned. How can Sherry justify the large budget to Stanley using the IRR approach?

This is where *incremental IRR* comes in. Sherry calculates the incremental cash flows from choosing the large budget instead of the small budget as

	Cash Flow at Date 0 (in $ millions)	Cash Flow at Date 1 (in $ millions)
Incremental cash flows from choosing large budget instead of small budget	−25 − (−10) = −15	65 − 40 = 25

This chart shows that the incremental cash flows are −$15 million at date 0 and $25 million at date 1. Sherry calculates incremental IRR as

Formula for Calculating the Incremental IRR:

$$0 = -\$15 \text{ million} + \frac{\$25 \text{ million}}{1 + \text{IRR}}$$

IRR equals 66.67 percent in this equation implying that the **incremental IRR** is 66.67 percent. Incremental IRR is the IRR on the incremental investment from choosing the large project instead of the small project.

In addition, we can calculate the NPV of the incremental cash flows:

NPV of Incremental Cash Flows:

$$-\$15 \text{ million} + \frac{\$25 \text{ million}}{1.25} = \$5 \text{ million}$$

We know the small-budget picture would be acceptable as an independent project since its NPV is positive. We want to know whether it is beneficial to invest an additional $15 million in order to make the large-budget picture instead of the small-budget picture. In other words, is it beneficial to invest an additional $15 million in order to receive an additional $25 million next year? First, the above calculations show the NPV on the incremental investment to be positive. Second, the incremental IRR of 66.67 percent is higher than the discount rate of 25 percent. For both reasons, the incremental investment can be justified. Hence, the large-budget movie should be made. The second reason is what Stanley needed to hear to be convinced.

In review, we can handle this example (or any mutually exclusive example) in one of three ways:

1. *Compare the NPVs of the two choices.* The NPV of the large-budget picture is greater than the NPV of the small-budget picture. That is, $27 million is greater than $22 million.
2. *Calculate the incremental NPV from making the large-budget picture instead of the small-budget picture.* Because the incremental NPV equals $5 million, we choose the large-budget picture.
3. *Compare the incremental IRR to the discount rate.* Because the incremental IRR is 66.67 percent and the discount rate is 25 percent, we take the large-budget picture.

All three approaches always give the same decision. However, we must *not* compare the IRRs of the two pictures. If we did, we would make the wrong choice. That is, we would accept the small-budget picture.

While students frequently think that problems of scale are relatively unimportant, the truth is just the opposite. A well-known chef on TV often says, "I don't know about your flour, but the flour I buy don't come seasoned." The same thing applies to capital budgeting. No real-world project comes in one clear-cut size. Rather, the firm has to *determine* the best size for the project. The movie budget of $25 million is not fixed in stone. Perhaps an extra $1 million to hire a bigger star or to film at a better location will increase the movie's gross. Similarly, an industrial firm must decide whether it wants a warehouse of, say, 500,000 square feet or 600,000 square feet. And, earlier in the chapter we imagined McDonald's opening an outlet on a desert island. If it does this, it must decide how big the outlet should be. For almost any project, someone in the firm has to decide on its size, implying that problems of scale abound in the real world.

One final note here. Students often ask which project should be subtracted from the other in calculating incremental flows. Notice that we are subtracting the smaller project's cash flows from the bigger project's cash flows. This leaves an *outflow* at date 0. We then use the basic IRR rule on the incremental flows.[12]

The Timing Problem   Next we illustrate another, but quite similar, problem with the IRR approach when evaluating mutually exclusive projects.

EXAMPLE

Suppose that the Kaufold Corporation has two alternative uses for a warehouse. It can store toxic waste containers (investment A) or electronic equipment (investment B). The cash flows are as follows:

	Cash Flow at Year				NPV			
Year:	0	1	2	3	@0%	@10%	@15%	IRR
Investment A	−$10,000	$10,000	$1,000	$ 1,000	$2,000	$669	$ 109	16.04%
Investment B	−10,000	1,000	1,000	12,000	4,000	751	−484	12.94

---

[12]Alternatively, we could have subtracted the larger project's cash flows from the smaller project's cash flows. This would have left an *inflow* at date 0, making it necessary to use the IRR rule for financing situations. This would work but we find it more confusing.

We find that the NPV of investment B is higher with low discount rates, and the NPV of investment A is higher with high discount rates. This is not surprising if you look closely at the cash flow patterns. The cash flows of A occur early, whereas the cash flows of B occur later. If we assume a high discount rate, we favor investment A because we are implicitly assuming that the early cash flow (for example, $10,000 in year 1) can be reinvested at that rate. Because most of investment B's cash flows occur in year 3, B's value is relatively high with low discount rates.

The patterns of cash flow for both projects appear in Figure 6.6. Project A has an NPV of $2,000 at a discount rate of zero. This is calculated by simply adding up the cash flows without discounting them. Project B has an NPV of $4,000 at the zero rate. However, the NPV of project B declines more rapidly as the discount rate increases than does the NPV of project A. As we mentioned above, this occurs because the cash flows of B occur later. Both projects have the same NPV at a discount rate of 10.55 percent. The IRR for a project is the rate at which the NPV equals zero. Because the NPV of B declines more rapidly, B actually has a lower IRR.

As with the movie example presented above, we can select the better project with one of three different methods:

1. *Compare NPVs of the Two Projects.* Figure 6.6 aids our decision. If the discount rate is below 10.55 percent, one should choose project B because B has a higher NPV. If the rate is above 10.55 percent, one should choose project A because A has a higher NPV.

2. *Compare Incremental IRR to Discount Rate.* The above method employed NPV. Another way of determining that B is a better project is to subtract the cash flows of A from the cash flows of B and then to calculate the IRR. This is the incremental IRR approach we spoke of earlier.

The incremental cash flows are

| | | | | | | NPV of Incremental Cash Flows | | |
| | | | | | | | | |
Year:	0	1	2	3	Incremental IRR	@0%	@10%	@15%
B − A	0	−$9,000	0	$11,000	10.55%	$2,000	$83	−$593

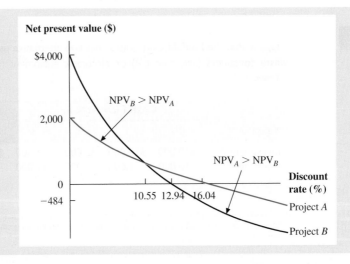

FIGURE 6.6

Net Present Value and the Internal Rate of Return for Mutually Exclusive Projects

This chart shows that the incremental IRR is 10.55 percent. In other words, the NPV on the incremental investment is zero when the discount rate is 10.55 percent. Thus, if the relevant discount rate is below 10.55 percent, project *B* is preferred to project *A*. If the relevant discount rate is above 10.55 percent, project *A* is preferred to project *B*.[13]

3. *Calculate NPV on Incremental Cash Flows.* Finally, one could calculate the NPV on the incremental cash flows. The chart that appears with the previous method displays these NPVs. We find that the incremental NPV is positive when the discount rate is either 0 percent or 10 percent. The incremental NPV is negative if the discount rate is 15 percent. If the NPV is positive on the incremental flows, one should choose *B*. If the NPV is negative, one should choose *A*.

In summary, the same decision is reached whether one (*a*) compares the NPVs of the two projects, (*b*) compares the incremental IRR to the relevant discount rate, or (*c*) examines the NPV of the incremental cash flows. However, as mentioned earlier, one should *not* compare the IRR of project *A* with the IRR of project *B*.

We suggested earlier that one should subtract the cash flows of the smaller project from the cash flows of the bigger project. What do we do here since the two projects have the same initial investment? Our suggestion in this case is to perform the subtraction so that the *first* nonzero cash flow is negative. In the Kaufold Corporation example, we achieved this by subtracting *A* from *B*. In this way, we can still use the basic IRR rule for evaluating cash flows.

The preceding examples illustrate problems with the IRR approach in evaluating mutually exclusive projects. Both the professor-student example and the motion-picture example illustrate the problem that arises when mutually exclusive projects have different initial investments. The Kaufold Corp. example illustrates the problem that arises when mutually exclusive projects have different cash flow timing. When working with mutually exclusive projects, it is not necessary to determine whether it is the scale problem or the timing problem that exists. Very likely both occur in any real-world situation. Instead, the practitioner should simply use either an incremental IRR or an NPV approach.

Redeeming Qualities of IRR

IRR probably survives because it fills a need that NPV does not. People seem to want a rule that summarizes the information about a project in a single rate of return. This single rate provides people with a simple way of discussing projects. For example, one manager in a firm might say to another, "Remodeling the north wing has a 20-percent IRR."

To their credit, however, companies that employ the IRR approach seem to understand its deficiencies. For example, companies frequently restrict managerial projections of cash flows to be negative at the beginning and strictly positive later. Perhaps, then, the ability of the IRR approach to capture a complex investment project in a single number and the ease of communicating that number explain the survival of the IRR.

A Test

To test your knowledge, consider the following two statements:

1. You must know the discount rate to compute the NPV of a project but you compute the IRR without referring to the discount rate.

2. Hence, the IRR rule is easier to apply than the NPV rule because you don't use the discount rate when applying IRR.

---

[13]In this example, we first showed that the NPVs of the two projects are equal when the discount rate is 10.55 percent. We next showed that the incremental IRR is also 10.55 percent. This is not a coincidence; this equality must *always* hold. The incremental IRR is the rate that causes the incremental cash flows to have zero NPV. The incremental cash flows have zero NPV when the two projects have the same NPV.

The first statement is true. The discount rate is needed to *compute* NPV. The IRR is *computed* by solving for the rate where the NPV is zero. No mention is made of the discount rate in the mere computation. However, the second statement is false. In order to *apply* IRR, you must compare the internal rate of return with the discount rate. Thus, the discount rate is needed for making a decision under either the NPV or IRR approach.

Concept Questions

1. **What is the difference between independent projects and mutually exclusive projects?**
2. **What are two problems with the IRR approach that apply to both independent and mutually exclusive projects?**
3. **What is MIRR?**
4. **What are two additional problems applying only to mutually exclusive projects?**

6.7 The Profitability Index

Another method that is used to evaluate projects is called the **profitability index.** It is the ratio of the present value of the future expected cash flows *after* initial investment divided by the amount of the initial investment. The profitability index can be represented as

$$\text{Profitability index (PI)} = \frac{\text{PV of cash flows } subsequent \text{ to initial investment}}{\text{Initial investment}}$$

EXAMPLE

Hiram Finnegan, Inc. (HFI), applies a 12-percent discount rate to two investment opportunities.

Project	Cash Flows ($000,000)			PV @12% of Cash Flows Subsequent to Initial Investment ($000,000)	Profit- ability Index	NPV @12% ($000,000)
	C_0	C_1	C_2			
1	−20	70	10	70.5	3.53	50.5
2	−10	15	40	45.3	4.53	35.3

Calculation of Profitability Index

The profitability index is calculated for project 1 as follows. The present value of the cash flows *after* the initial investment is:

$$\$70.5 = \frac{\$70}{1.12} + \frac{\$10}{(1.12)^2} \qquad (6.9)$$

The profitability index is obtained by dividing the result of equation (6.9) by the initial investment of $20. This yields

$$3.53 = \frac{\$70.5}{\$20}$$

Application of the Profitability Index   How do we use the profitability index? We consider three situations:

1. *Independent Projects.* Assume that HFI's two projects are independent. According to the NPV rule, both projects should be accepted since NPV is positive in each case. The

profitability index (PI) is greater than one whenever the NPV is positive. Thus, the PI *decision rule* is

Accept an independent project if PI > 1.
Reject if PI < 1.

2. *Mutually Exclusive Projects.* Let us now assume that HFI can only accept one of its two projects. NPV analysis says accept project 1 because this project has the bigger NPV. Since project 2 has the higher PI, the profitability index leads to the wrong selection.

The problem with the profitability index for mutually exclusive projects is the same as the scale problem with the IRR that we mentioned earlier. Project 2 is smaller than project 1. Because the PI is a ratio, this index misses the fact that project 1 has a larger investment than project 2 has. Thus, like IRR, PI ignores differences of scale for mutually exclusive projects.

However, like IRR, the flaw with the PI approach can be corrected using incremental analysis. We write the incremental cash flows after subtracting project 2 from project 1 as follows:

Project	Cash Flows ($000,000)			PV @12% of Cash Flows Subsequent to Initial Investment ($000,000)	Profit-ability Index	NPV @12% ($000,000)
	C_0	C_1	C_2			
1 − 2	−10	55	−30	25.2	2.52	15.2

Because the profitability index on the incremental cash flows is greater than 1.0, we should choose the bigger project, that is, project 1. This is the same decision we get with the NPV approach.

3. *Capital Rationing.* The two cases above implicitly assumed that HFI could always attract enough capital to make any profitable investments. Now consider the case when the firm does not have enough capital to fund all positive NPV projects. This is the case of **capital rationing.**

Imagine that the firm has a third project, as well as the first two. Project 3 has the following cash flows:

Project	Cash Flows ($000,000)			PV @12% of Cash Flows Subsequent to Initial Investment ($000,000)	Profit-ability Index	NPV @12% ($000,000)
	C_0	C_1	C_2			
3	−10	−5	60	43.4	4.34	33.4

Further, imagine that (*a*) the projects of Hiram Finnegan, Inc., are independent, but (*b*) the firm has only $20 million to invest. Because project 1 has an initial investment of $20 million, the firm cannot select both this project and another one. Conversely, because projects 2 and 3 have initial investments of $10 million each, both these projects can be chosen. In other words, the cash constraint forces the firm to choose either project 1 or projects 2 and 3.

What should the firm do? Individually, projects 2 and 3 have lower NPVs than project 1 has. However, when the NPVs of projects 2 and 3 are added together, the sum is higher than the NPV of project 1. Thus, common sense dictates that projects 2 and 3 shall be accepted.

What does our conclusion have to say about the NPV rule or the PI rule? In the case of limited funds, we cannot rank projects according to their NPVs. Instead, we should rank them according to the ratio of present value to initial investment. This is the PI rule. Both project 2 and project 3 have higher PI ratios than does project 1. Thus, they should be ranked ahead of project 1 when capital is rationed.

The usefulness of the profitability index under capital rationing can be explained in military terms. The Pentagon speaks highly of a weapon with a lot of "bang for the buck." In capital budgeting, the profitability index measures the bang (the dollar return) for the buck invested. Hence, it is useful for capital rationing.

It should be noted that the profitability index does not work if funds are also limited beyond the initial time period. For example, if heavy cash outflows elsewhere in the firm were to occur at date 1, project 3, which also has a cash outflow at date 1, might need to be rejected. In other words, the profitability index cannot handle capital rationing over multiple time periods.

In addition, what economists term *indivisibilities* may reduce the effectiveness of the PI rule. Imagine that HFI has $30 million available for capital investment, not just $20 million. The firm now has enough cash for projects 1 and 2. Since the sum of the NPVs of these two projects is greater than the sum of the NPVs of projects 2 and 3, the firm would be better served by accepting projects 1 and 2. Since projects 2 and 3 still have the highest profitability indexes, the PI rule now leads to the wrong decision. Why does the PI rule lead us astray here? The key is that projects 1 and 2 use up all of the $30 million, while projects 2 and 3 have a combined initial investment of only $20 million (10 + 10). If projects 2 and 3 are accepted, the remaining $10 million must be left in the bank.

The above situation points out that care should be exercised when using the profitability index in the real world. Nevertheless, while not perfect, the profitability index goes a long way towards handling capital rationing.

Concept Questions
1. **How does one calculate a project's profitability index?**
2. **How is the profitability index applied to independent projects, mutually exclusive projects, and situations of capital rationing?**

6.8 The Practice of Capital Budgeting

So far, this chapter has asked the question: Which capital budgeting methods should companies be using? An equally important question is: Which methods *are* companies using? Table 6.4 goes a long way towards answering this question. As can be seen from the table, approximately three-quarters of U.S. and Canadian companies use the IRR and NPV methods. This is not surprising, given the theoretical advantages of these approaches. Over

TABLE 6.4 Percent of CFOs Who Always or Almost Always Use a Given Technique		% Always or Almost Always
	Internal rate of return (IRR)	75.6%
	Net present value (NPV)	74.9
	Payback method	56.7
	Discounted payback	29.5
	Accounting rate of return	30.3
	Profitability index	11.9

SOURCE: Figure 2 from John R. Graham and Campbell R. Harvey, "The Theory and Practice of Corporate Finance: Evidence from the Field," *Journal of Financial Economics* 60 (2001). Based on a survey of 392 CFOs.

Kitchen Confidential: Adventures in the Culinary Underbelly by Anthony Bourdain (Bloomsbury Press, 2000)

To want to own a restaurant can be a strange and terrible affliction. What causes such a destructive urge in so many otherwise sensible people? Why would anyone who has worked hard, saved money, often been successful in other fields, want to pump their hard-earned cash down a hole that statistically, at least, will almost surely prove dry? Why venture into an industry with enormous fixed expenses (rent, electricity, gas, water, linen, maintenance, insurance, license fees, trash removal, etc.), with a notoriously transient and unstable workforce and highly perishable inventory of assets? The chances of ever seeing a return on your investment are about one in five. What insidious spongi-form bacteria so riddles the brains of men and women that they stand there on the tracks, watching the lights of the oncoming locomotive, knowing full well it will eventually run them over? After all these years in the business, I still don't know.

Anthony Bourdain is also the author of the novels *Bone in the Throat* and *Bone Bamboo*. He is the executive chef at Brasserie Les Halles in New York.

one-half of these companies use the payback method, a rather surprising result given the conceptual problems with this approach. And while discounted payback represents a theoretical improvement over regular payback, the usage here is far less. Perhaps companies are attracted to the user-friendly nature of payback. In addition, the flaws of this approach, as mentioned in the current chapter, may be relatively easy to correct. For example, while the payback method ignores all cash flows after the payback period, an alert manager can make ad hoc adjustments for a project with back-loaded cash flows.

One might expect the capital budgeting methods of large firms to be more sophisticated than the methods of small firms. After all, large firms have the financial resources to hire more sophisticated employees. Table 6.5 provides some support for this idea. Here, firms indicate frequency of use of the various capital budgeting methods on a scale of 0 (never) to 4 (always). Both the IRR and NPV methods are used more frequently, and payback less frequently, in large firms than in small firms. Conversely, large and small firms employ the last three approaches about equally.

Noncash flow factors such as ego may occasionally play a role in capital budgeting decisions. The classic example is the retired dentist who was always told he threw a great dinner party. "You should open a restaurant," his friends tell him. And our dentist believes them. He wants to get in the business—not to make money, but to swan about the dining room signing dinner checks, like Rick in *Casablanca*. (See our In Their Own Words box.)

The use of quantitative techniques in capital budgeting varies with the industry. As one would imagine, firms that are better able to estimate cash flows are more likely to use NPV. For example, estimation of cash flow in certain aspects of the oil business is quite feasible. Because of this, energy-related firms were among the first to use NPV analysis.

TABLE 6.5		Large Firms	Small Firms
Frequency of Use of Various Capital Budgeting Methods	Internal rate of return (IRR)	3.41	2.87
	Net present value (NPV)	3.42	2.83
	Payback method	2.25	2.72
	Discounted payback	1.55	1.58
	Accounting rate of return	1.25	1.41
	Profitability index	0.75	0.78

Firms indicate frequency of use on a scale from 0 (never) to 4 (always). Numbers in table are averages across respondents.

SOURCE: Table 2 from Graham and Harvey (2001), op. cit.

Conversely, the cash flows in the motion-picture business are very hard to project. The grosses of the great hits like *Titanic, Harry Potter,* and *Star Wars* were far, far greater than anyone imagined. The big failures like *Heaven's Gate* and *Waterworld* were unexpected as well. Because of this, NPV analysis is frowned upon in the movie business.

How does Hollywood perform capital budgeting? The information that a studio uses to accept or reject a movie idea comes from the *pitch.* An independent movie producer schedules an extremely brief meeting with a studio to pitch his or her idea for a movie. Consider the following four paragraphs of quotes concerning the pitch from the thoroughly delightful book *Reel Power.*[14]

> "They [studio executives] don't want to know too much," says Ron Simpson. "They want to know concept . . . . They want to know what the three-liner is, because they want it to suggest the ad campaign. They want a title . . . . They don't want to hear any esoterica. And if the meeting lasts more than five minutes, they're probably not going to do the project."
>
> "A guy comes in and says this is my idea: '*Jaws* on a spaceship,'" says writer Clay Frohman (*Under Fire*). "And they say, 'Brilliant, fantastic.' Becomes *Alien.* That is *Jaws* on a spaceship, ultimately . . . . And that's it. That's all they want to hear. Their attitude is 'Don't confuse us with the details of the story.'"
>
> ". . . Some high-concept stories are more appealing to the studios than others. The ideas liked best are sufficiently original that the audience will not feel it has already seen the movie, yet similar enough to past hits to reassure executives wary of anything too far-out. Thus, the frequently used shorthand: It's *Flashdance* in the country (*Footloose*) or *High Noon* in outer space (*Outland*)."
>
> ". . . One gambit not to use during a pitch," says executive Barbara Boyle, "is to talk about big box-office grosses your story is sure to make. Executives know as well as anyone that it's impossible to predict how much money a movie will make, and declarations to the contrary are considered pure malarkey."

6.9 SUMMARY AND CONCLUSIONS

1. In this chapter we cover different investment decision rules. We evaluate the most popular alternatives to the NPV: the payback period, the accounting rate of return, the internal rate of return, and the profitability index. In doing so, we learn more about the NPV.

2. While we find that the alternatives have some redeeming qualities, when all is said and done, they are not the NPV rule; for those of us in finance, that makes them decidedly second-rate.

3. Of the competitors to NPV, IRR must be ranked above either payback or accounting rate of return. In fact, IRR always reaches the same decision as NPV in the normal case where the initial outflows of an independent investment project are only followed by a series of inflows.

4. We classified the flaws of IRR into two types. First, we considered the general case applying to both independent and mutually exclusive projects. There appeared to be two problems here:
   a. Some projects have cash inflows followed by one or more outflows. The IRR rule is inverted here: One should accept when the IRR is *below* the discount rate.
   b. Some projects have a number of changes of sign in their cash flows. Here, there are likely to be multiple internal rates of return. The practitioner must use either NPV or modified internal rate of return here.

5. Next, we considered the specific problems with the NPV for mutually exclusive projects. We showed that, either due to differences in size or in timing, the project with the highest IRR need not have the highest NPV. Hence, the IRR rule should not be applied. (Of course, NPV can still be applied.)

---

[14]Mark Litwak, *Reel Power: The Struggle for Influence and Success in the New Hollywood* (New York: William Morrow and Company, Inc., 1986), pp. 73, 74, and 77.

However, we then calculated incremental cash flows. For ease of calculation, we suggested subtracting the cash flows of the smaller project from the cash flows of the larger project. In that way, the incremental initial cash flow is negative. One can always reach a correct decision by accepting the larger project if the incremental IRR is greater than the discount rate.

6. We describe capital rationing as the case where funds are limited to a fixed dollar amount. With capital rationing the profitability index is a useful method of adjusting the NPV.

KEY TERMS

average accounting return, *149*
basic IRR rule, *152*
capital rationing, *165*
discounted payback period method, *149*
incremental IRR, *160*
independent project, *154*
internal rate of return, *152*

modified IRR (MIRR), *157*
mutually exclusive investments, *154*
NPV rule, *145*
payback, *146*
payback period rule, *147*
profitability index, *164*
value-additivity, *145*

SUGGESTED READINGS

For a discussion of real-world capital budgeting techniques, see:

Graham, John R., and Campbell R. Harvey. "The Theory and Practice of Corporate Finance: Evidence from the Field." *Journal of Financial Economics* 60 (2001).

For an in-depth look at the capital budgeting procedures of 12 firms in the process industry:

Ross, Marc. "Capital Budgeting Practices of Twelve Large Manufacturers." *Financial Management* (Winter 1986).

QUESTIONS & PROBLEMS

THE PAYBACK PERIOD RULE

6.1   Fuji Software, Inc., has the following mutually exclusive projects.

Year	Project A	Project B
0	−$7,500	−$5,000
1	4,000	2,500
2	3,500	1,200
3	1,500	3,000

a. Suppose Fuji's payback period cutoff is two years. Which of these two projects should be chosen?

b. Suppose Fuji uses the NPV rule to rank these two projects. Which project should be chosen if the appropriate discount rate is 15 percent?

6.2   Suppose Peach Paving, Inc., invests $1 million today on a new construction project. The project will generate annual cash flows of $150,000 in perpetuity. The appropriate annual discount rate for the project is 10 percent.

a. What is the payback period for the project? If Peach Paving, Inc.'s, cutoff is 10 years, should the project be accepted?

b. What is the discounted payback period for the project?

c. What is the NPV of the project?

THE AVERAGE ACCOUNTING RETURN

6.3   Your firm is considering purchasing a machine with the following annual, end-of-year, book-investment accounts.

	Purchase Date	Year 1	Year 2	Year 3	Year 4
Gross investment	$16,000	$16,000	$16,000	$16,000	$16,000
Less: Accumulated depreciation	0	4,000	8,000	12,000	16,000
Net investment	$16,000	$12,000	$ 8,000	$ 4,000	$ 0

The machine generates, on average, $4,500 per year in additional net income.

a. What is the average accounting return for this machine?

b. What three flaws are inherent in this decision rule?

6.4 Western Printing Co. has an opportunity to purchase a $2 million printing machine. The machine has an economic life of five years and will be worthless after that time. It will generate net income of $100,000 one year from today and the income stream will grow at 7 percent per year thereafter. The company uses straight-line depreciation (i.e., equal depreciation each year). What is the average accounting return of the investment? Should the machine be purchased if Western Printing's average accounting return cutoff is 20 percent?

6.5 The Bluerock Group has invested $8,000 in a high-tech project lasting three years. Depreciation is $4,000, $2,500, and $1,500 in years 1, 2, and 3, respectively. The project generates pretax income of $2,000 each year. The pretax income already includes the depreciation expense. If the tax rate is 25 percent, what is the project's average accounting return (AAR)?

THE INTERNAL
RATE OF RETURN

6.6 Compute the internal rate of return on projects with the following cash flows.

Cash Flows ($)

Year	Project A	Project B
0	−3,000	−6,000
1	2,500	5,000
2	1,000	2,000

6.7 Teddy Bear Planet, Inc., has a project with the following cash flows.

Year	Cash Flows ($)
0	−8,000
1	4,000
2	3,000
3	2,000

a. Compute the internal rate of return on the project.

b. Suppose the appropriate discount rate is 8 percent. Should the project be accepted?

6.8 Compute the internal rate of return for the cash flows of the following two projects.

Cash Flows ($)

Year	Project A	Project B
0	−2,000	−1,500
1	2,000	500
2	8,000	1,000
3	8,000	1,500

6.9 Suppose you are offered $5,000 today but must make the following payments.

Year	Cash Flows ($)
0	5,000
1	−2,500
2	−2,000
3	−1,000
4	−1,000

a. What is the IRR of this offer?
b. If the appropriate discount rate is 10 percent, should you accept this offer?
c. If the appropriate discount rate is 20 percent, should you accept this offer?
d. What is the NPV of the offer if the appropriate discount rate is 10 percent? 20 percent?
e. Are the decisions under the NPV rule in part (d) consistent with those of the IRR rule?

6.10 As the chief financial officer of the Orient Express, you are offered the following two mutually exclusive projects.

| Year | Cash Flows ($) | |
	Project A	Project B
0	−5,000	−100,000
1	3,500	65,000
2	3,500	65,000

a. What are the IRRs of these two projects?
b. If you are told only the IRRs of the projects, which would you choose?
c. What did you ignore when you made your decision in part (b)?
d. How can the problem be remedied? Perform the appropriate calculation.
e. Based on your answer to part (d), which project should you choose? The appropriate discount rate is 15 percent.
f. According to the NPV rule, which of these two projects should be pursued? Again, assume a 15 percent discount rate.

6.11 Consider two streams of cash flows, A and B. Stream A's first cash flow is $5,000 and is received three years from today. Future cash flows in stream A grow by 4 percent in perpetuity. Stream B's first cash flow is −$6,000 and is received two years from today and will continue in perpetuity. Assume that the appropriate discount rate is 12 percent.
a. What is the present value of each stream?
b. Suppose that the two streams are combined into one project, called C. What is the IRR of project C?
c. What is the correct IRR rule for project C?

6.12 The investment in project A is $1 million, and the investment in project B is $2 million. Both projects have a unique internal rate of return of 20 percent. Is the following statement true or false?

For any discount rate from zero percent to 20 percent, project B has an NPV twice as great as that of project A.

Explain your answer.

THE PROFITABILITY INDEX

6.13 Suppose the following two independent investment opportunities are available to Greenplain, Inc. The appropriate discount rate is 10 percent.

Year	Project Alpha	Project Beta
0	−$500	−$2,000
1	300	300
2	700	1,800
3	600	1,700

a. Compute the profitability indices for each of the two projects.
b. Which project(s) should Greenplain accept based on the profitability index rule?

6.14 Consider the following two mutually exclusive projects available to Global Investments, Inc.

	C_0	C_1	C_2	Profitability Index	NPV
A	−$1,000	$1,000	$500	1.32	$322
B	−500	500	400	1.57	285

The appropriate discount rate for the projects is 10 percent. Global Investments chose to undertake project A. At a luncheon for shareholders, the manager of a pension fund that owns a substantial amount of the firm's stock asks you why the firm chose project A instead of project B when project B has a higher profitability index.

How would you, the CFO, justify your firm's action? Are there any circumstances under which Global Investments should choose project B?

6.15 The treasurer of Amaro Canned Fruits, Inc., has projected the cash flows of projects A, B, and C as follows.

Year	Project A	Project B	Project C
0	−$100,000	−$200,000	−$100,000
1	70,000	130,000	75,000
2	70,000	130,000	60,000

Suppose the relevant discount rate is 12 percent a year.
a. Compute the profitability indices for each of the three projects.
b. Compute the NPV for each of the three projects.
c. Suppose these three projects are independent. Which project(s) should Amaro accept based on the profitability index rule?
d. Suppose these three projects are mutually exclusive. Which project(s) should Amaro accept based on the profitability index rule?
e. Suppose Amaro's budget for these projects is $300,000. The projects are not divisible. Which project(s) should Amaro accept?

6.16 Bill plans to open a self-serve grooming center in a storefront. The grooming equipment will cost $160,000, paid immediately. Bill expects after-tax cash inflows of $40,000 annually for seven years, after which he plans to scrap the equipment and retire to the beaches of Nevis. The first cash inflow occurs at the end of the first year. Assume the required return is 15 percent. What is the project's PI? Should it be accepted?

COMPARISON OF INVESTMENT RULES

6.17 Define each of the following investment rules. In your definition, state the criterion for accepting or rejecting independent projects under each rule.
a. Payback period
b. Average accounting return
c. Internal rate of return
d. Profitability index
e. Net present value

6.18 Consider the following after-tax cash flows of two mutually exclusive projects for the *China Daily News.*

Year	New Sunday Early Edition	New Saturday Late Edition
0	−$1,200	−$2,100
1	600	1,000
2	550	900
3	450	800

a. Based on the payback period rule, which project should be chosen?

b. Which project has the greater IRR?

c. Based on the incremental IRR rule, which project should be chosen? The appropriate discount rate is 12 percent.

d. Now imagine that for the same cash flows, the annual earnings for the New Sunday Early Edition are $400, $350, and $300. The annual earnings for the New Saturday Late Edition are $800, $700, and $600. Suppose there is no corporate tax and the earnings represent income after depreciation. The firm uses straight-line depreciation (i.e., equal amounts of depreciation in each year). What is the average accounting return for each of these two projects?

6.19 Consider the following cash flows on two mutually exclusive projects for the Bahamas Recreation Corporation (BRC). Both projects require an annual return of 15 percent.

Year	Deepwater Fishing	New Submarine Ride
0	−$600,000	−$1,800,000
1	270,000	1,000,000
2	350,000	700,000
3	300,000	900,000

As a financial analyst for BRC, you are asked the following questions.

a. Based on the discounted payback period rule, which project should be chosen?

b. If your decision rule is to accept the project with the greater IRR, which project should you choose?

c. Since you are fully aware of the IRR rule's scale problem, you calculate the incremental IRR for the cash flows. Based on your computation, which project should you choose?

d. To be prudent, you compute the NPV for both projects. Which project should you choose? Is it consistent with the incremental IRR rule?

6.20 The Utah Mining Corporation is set to open a gold mine near Provo, Utah. According to the treasurer, Monty Goldstein, "This is a golden opportunity." The mine will cost $600,000 to open and will have an economic life of 11 years. It will generate a cash inflow of $100,000 at the end of the first year and the cash inflows are projected to grow at 8 percent per year for the next 10 years. After 11 years, the mine will be abandoned. Abandonment costs will be $50,000 at the end of year 11.

a. What is the IRR for the gold mine?

b. The Utah Mining Corporation requires a 10 percent return on such undertakings. Should the mine be opened?

6.21 An investment under consideration has a payback of five years, a cost of $250,000, and the required rate of return is 12 percent.

a. What is the worst case NPV? Explain.

b. What is the best case NPV? Explain.

6.22 Consider the following cash flows of two mutually exclusive projects for Totally Electric Inc. Assume the discount rate for Totally Electric is 10 percent and the minimum acceptable IRR is 20 percent.

Year	Project A	Project B
0	−$150,000	−$80,000
1	15,000	60,000
2	35,000	40,000
3	50,000	20,000
4	200,000	13,000

a. Based on the payback period rule, which project would you choose? Why?

b. Based on the average accounting return, which project would you choose? Why? (Assume there is no corporate tax, the cash flow above are income before depreciation. The firm uses a straight-line depreciation method.)

c. Based on the NPV, which project would you choose? Why?

d. Based on the IRR, which project would you choose? Why?

6.23 Pinnacle electronics, a TV manufacturer, needs to decide the future of its company. They can either invest their R&D in standard HDTV technology, or in the new plasma technology, but not both. Consider the following cash flows of the two mutually exclusive projects for Pinnacle. Assume the discount rate for Pinnacle is 10 percent and the minimum acceptable IRR is 25 percent.

Year	HDTV	Plasma
0	− $1,000	− $2,200
1	1,000	700
2	600	1,100
3	300	2,200

a. Based on the profitability index decision rule, which project should the firm invest in?

b. Based on the NPV, which project should the firm invest in?

c. Based on your findings in (*a*) and (*b*), what would you recommend to the CEO of Pinnacle and why?

6.24 Mario Brothers, a game manufacturer, has a new idea for an adventure game. They can either market the game as a traditional board game or as an interactive CD-ROM, but not both. Consider the following cash flows of the two mutually exclusive projects for Mario Brothers. Assume the discount rate for Mario Brothers is 10 percent and the minimum acceptable IRR is 20 percent.

Year	Board Game	CD-ROM
0	− $300	− $1,500
1	400	1,100
2	100	800
3	100	400

a. Based on the payback period rule, which project should be chosen?

b. Based on the NPV, which project should be chosen?

c. Based on the IRR, which project should be chosen?

d. Based on the incremental IRR, which project should be chosen?

6.25 Hanmi Group, a consumer electronics conglomerate, is reviewing its annual budget in wireless technology. They are considering investments in three different technologies to develop wireless communication devices. Consider the following cash flows of the three independent projects for Hanmi. Assume the discount rate for Hanmi is 10 percent. Further, Hanmi Group only has $30 million to invest in new projects this year.

Cash Flows (in millions)

Year	CDMA	G4	Wi-Fi
0	− $10	− $20	− $ 30
1	25	20	20
2	15	50	40
3	5	40	100

a. Based on the profitability index decision rule, rank these investments.
b. Based on the NPV, rank these investments.
c. Based on your findings in (a) and (b), what would you recommend to the CEO of Hanmi Group and why?

6.26 Consider the following cash flows of two mutually exclusive projects for AZ-Motorcars. Assume the discount rate for AZ-Motorcars is 10 percent and the minimum acceptable IRR is 30 percent.

Year	AZM Mini-SUV	AZF Full-SUV
0	−$200,000	−$500,000
1	200,000	200,000
2	150,000	300,000
3	150,000	300,000
SUM	$300,000	$300,000

a. Based on the payback period, which project should be taken?
b. Based on the NPV, which project should be taken?
c. Based on the IRR, which project should be taken?
d. Based on the above analysis, is incremental IRR analysis necessary? If yes, please conduct the analysis.

6.27 Consider the following cash flows of two mutually exclusive projects for Tokyo Rubber Company. Assume the discount rate for Tokyo Rubber Company is 10 percent and the minimum acceptable IRR is 30 percent.

Year	Dry Prepreg	Solvent Prepreg
0	−$1,000,000	−$500,000
1	600,000	500,000
2	400,000	300,000
3	1,000,000	100,000
SUM	$1,000,000	$400,000

a. Based on the payback period, which project should be taken?
b. Based on the NPV, which project should be taken?
c. Based on the IRR, which project should be taken?
d. Based on the above analysis, is incremental IRR analysis necessary? If yes, please conduct the analysis.

6.28 Consider two mutually exclusive new product launch projects that Nagano Golf is considering. Assume the discount rate for Nagano Golf is 15 percent and the minimum acceptable IRR is 40 percent.

Project A: Nagano NP-30
            Professional clubs that will take an initial investment of $100,000 at time 0.
            Next five years (years 1–5) of sales will generate a consistent cash profit of $40,000 per year.
            Introduction of new product at year 6 terminates further cash flows from this project.

Project B: Nagano NX-20
            High-end amateur clubs that will take an initial investment of $30,000 at time 0.
            Cash profit at year 1 is $20,000. In each subsequent year cash profit will grow at 15 percent per year.
            Introduction of new product at year 6 terminates further cash flows from this project.

Year	NP-30	NX-20
0	− $100,000	− $ 30,000
1	40,000	20,000
2	40,000	23,000
3	40,000	26,450
4	40,000	30,418
5	40,000	34,980
SUM	$100,000	$104,848

Please fill in the following table:

	NP-30	NX-20	Implications
NPV			
IRR			
Incremental IRR			
PI			

6.29 Consider two mutually exclusive R&D projects that ADM is considering: Assume the discount rate for ADM is 15 percent and the minimum acceptable IRR is 25 percent.

Project A: Server CPU 0.13 micron processing project
By shrinking the die size to 0.13 micron, ADM will be able to offer server CPU chips with lower power consumption and heat generation, meaning faster CPUs.

Project B: New telecom chip project
Entry into this industry will require introduction of a new chip for cellphones. The know-how will require large upfront capital, but success of the project will lead to large cash flows later on.

Year	A	B
0	− $100,000	− $200,000
1	50,000	60,000
2	50,000	60,000
3	40,000	60,000
4	30,000	100,000
5	20,000	200,000
SUM	$ 90,000	$280,000

Please fill in the following table:

	A	B	Implications
NPV			
IRR			
Incremental IRR			
PI			

6.30 You are a senior manager at Poeing Aircrafts and have been authorized to spend up to $200,000 for projects. The three projects that you are considering have the following characteristics:

Project A: Initial investment of $150,000. Cash flow of $50,000 at year 1 and
              $100,000 at year 2.
              This is a plant expansion project, where the required rate of return is
              10 percent.

Project B: Initial investment of $200,000. Cash flow of $200,000 at year 1 and
              $100,000 at year 2.
              This is a new product development project, where the required rate of
              return is 20 percent.

Project C: Initial investment of $100,000. Cash flow of $100,000 at year 1 and
              $100,000 at year 2.
              This is a market expansion project, where the required rate of return is
              20 percent.

Assume the corporate discount rate is 10 percent.

Please offer your recommendations, backed by your analysis.

Year	B	C
0	−$200,000	−$100,000
1	200,000	100,000
2	111,000	100,000
SUM	$111,000	$100,000

	B	C	Implications
NPV			
IRR			
Incremental IRR			
PI			
Payback			

SOME ALTERNATIVE INVESTMENT RULES

6.31 Darin Clay, the CFO of MakeMoney.com, has to decide between the following two projects:

Year	Project Million	Project Billion
0	−1,500	−I_o
1	$I_o + 200$	$I_o + 500$
2	1,200	1,500
3	1,500	2,000

The expected rate of return for either of the two projects is 12 percent. What is the range of initial investment (I_o) for which Project Billion is more financially attractive than Project Million?

6.32 Projects A and B have the following cash flows:

Year	Project A	Project B
0	−1,000	−2,000
1	C1A	C1B
2	C2A	C2B
3	C3A	C3B

a. Which of the two projects would have a higher IRR? Why?
b. A student claims $IRR_A = 2IRR_B$. Is it true or false? Why?
c. If $C1B = 2C1A$, $C2B = 2C2A$, and $C3B = 2C3A$, then is $IRR_A = IRR_B$?

Net Present Value and Capital Budgeting

EXECUTIVE SUMMARY

In late 1990, the Boeing Company announced its intention to build the Boeing 777, a commercial airplane that could carry up to 390 passengers and fly 7,600 miles. This was expected to be an enormous undertaking. Analysts believed the up-front investment and research and development expenditures necessary to manufacture the Boeing 777 would be as much as $8 billion. Delivery of the planes was expected to begin in 1995 and to continue for at least 35 years. Was the 777 a good project for Boeing? This chapter shows you how to answer this important question.

The previous chapter discussed the basics of capital budgeting. We now move beyond these basics into real-world application. We show you how to use the net present value (NPV) method and the internal rate of return (IRR) method for real-world capital budgeting decisions.

In this chapter, we identify the relevant cash flows of a project, including initial investment outlays, requirements for working capital, and operating cash flows. We look at the effects of depreciation and taxes. We examine the impact of inflation on interest rates and on a project's discount rate, and we show why inflation must be handled consistently in NPV analysis.

7.1 Incremental Cash Flows

Cash Flows—Not Accounting Income

You may not have thought about it, but there is a big difference between corporate finance courses and financial accounting courses. Techniques in corporate finance generally use cash flows, whereas financial accounting generally stresses income or earnings numbers. Certainly, our text has followed this tradition since our net present value techniques discounted cash flows, not earnings. When considering a single project, we discounted the cash flows that the firm receives from the project. When valuing the firm as a whole, we discounted dividends—not earnings—because dividends are the cash flows that an investor receives.

EXAMPLE

The Weber-Decker Co. just paid $1 million in cash for a building, as part of a new capital budgeting project. This entire $1 million is an immediate cash outflow. However, assuming straight-line depreciation over 20 years, only $50,000 ($1 million/20) is considered an accounting expense in the current year. Current earnings are thereby reduced by only $50,000. The remaining $950,000 is expensed over the following 19 years. For capital budgeting purposes, the relevant cash outflow at date 0 is the full $1 million, not the reduction in earnings of only $50,000.

Always discount cash flows, not earnings, when performing a capital budgeting calculation. Earnings do not represent real money. You can't spend out of earnings, you can't eat out of earnings, and you can't pay dividends out of earnings. You can only do these things out of cash flow.

In addition, it is not enough to use cash flows. In calculating the NPV of a project, only cash flows that are *incremental* to the project should be used. These cash flows are the changes in the firm's cash flows that occur as a direct consequence of accepting the project. That is, we are interested in the difference between the cash flows of the firm with the project and the cash flows of the firm without the project.

The use of incremental cash flows sounds easy enough, but pitfalls abound in the real world. We describe below how to avoid some of the pitfalls of determining incremental cash flows.

Sunk Costs

A **sunk cost** is a cost that has already occurred. Because sunk costs are in the past, they cannot be changed by the decision to accept or reject the project. Just as we "let bygones be bygones," we should ignore such costs. Sunk costs are not incremental cash outflows.

EXAMPLE

The General Milk Company is currently evaluating the NPV of establishing a line of chocolate milk. As part of the evaluation the company had paid a consulting firm $100,000 to perform a test-marketing analysis. This expenditure was made last year. Is this cost relevant for the capital budgeting decision now confronting the management of General Milk Company?

The answer is no. The $100,000 is not recoverable, so the $100,000 expenditure is a sunk cost, or spilled milk. Of course, the decision to spend $100,000 for a marketing analysis was a capital budgeting decision itself and was perfectly relevant *before* it was sunk. Our point is that once the company incurred the expense, the cost became irrelevant for any future decision.

Opportunity Costs

Your firm may have an asset that it is considering selling, leasing, or employing elsewhere in the business. If the asset is used in a new project, potential revenues from alternative uses are lost. These lost revenues can meaningfully be viewed as costs. They are called **opportunity costs** because, by taking the project, the firm forgoes other opportunities for using the assets.

EXAMPLE

Suppose the Weinstein Trading Company has an empty warehouse in Philadelphia that can be used to store a new line of electronic pinball machines. The company hopes to sell these machines to affluent northeastern consumers. Should the warehouse be considered a cost in the decision to sell the machines?

The answer is yes. The company could sell the warehouse, if the firm decides not to market the pinball machines. Thus, the sales price of the warehouse is an opportunity cost in the pinball machine decision.

Side Effects

Another difficulty in determining incremental cash flows comes from the side effects of the proposed project on other parts of the firm. A side effect is classified as either **erosion** or **synergy.** Erosion occurs when a new product reduces the sales and, hence, the cash flows, of existing products. Synergy occurs when a new project increases the cash flows of existing projects.

EXAMPLE

Suppose the Innovative Motors Corporation (IMC) is determining the NPV of a new convertible sports car. Some of the customers who would purchase the car are owners of IMC's compact sedan. Are all sales and profits from the new convertible sports car incremental?

The answer is no because some of the cash flow represents transfers from other elements of IMC's product line. This is erosion, which must be included in the NPV calculation. Without taking erosion into account, IMC might erroneously calculate the NPV of the sports car to be, say, $100 million. If half the customers are transfers from the sedan and lost sedan sales have an NPV of −$150 million, the true NPV is −$50 million ($100 million − $150 million).

IMC is also contemplating the formation of a racing team. The team is forecasted to lose money for the foreseeable future, with perhaps the best projection showing an NPV of −$35 million for the operation. However, IMC's managers are aware that the team will likely generate great publicity for all of IMC's products. A consultant estimates that the increase in cash flows elsewhere in the firm has a present value of $65 million. Assuming that the consultant's estimates of synergy are trustworthy, the net present value of the team is $30 million ($65 million − $35 million). The managers should form the team.

Allocated Costs

Frequently a particular expenditure benefits a number of projects. Accountants allocate this cost across the different projects when determining income. However, for capital budgeting purposes, this **allocated cost** should be viewed as a cash outflow of a project only if it is an incremental cost of the project.

EXAMPLE

The Voetmann Consulting Corp. devotes one wing of its suite of offices to a library requiring a cash outflow of $100,000 a year in upkeep. A proposed capital budgeting project is expected to generate revenue equal to 5 percent of the overall firm's sales. An executive at the firm, H. Sears, argues that $5,000 (5% × 100,000) should be viewed as the proposed project's share of the library's costs. Is this appropriate for capital budgeting?

The answer is no. One must ask the question: What is the difference between the cash flows of the entire firm with the project and the cash flows of the entire firm without the project? The firm will spend $100,000 on library upkeep whether or not the proposed project is accepted. Since acceptance of the proposed project does not affect this cash flow, the cash flow should be ignored when calculating the NPV of the project.

Concept Questions

1. What are the four difficulties in determining incremental cash flows?
2. Define sunk costs, opportunity costs, side effects, and allocated costs.

7.2 The Baldwin Company: An Example

We next consider the example of a proposed investment in machinery and related items. Our example involves the Baldwin Company and colored bowling balls.

The Baldwin Company, originally established in 1965 to make footballs, is now a leading producer of tennis balls, baseballs, footballs, and golf balls. In 1973 the company introduced "High Flite," its first line of high-performance golf balls. The Baldwin management has sought opportunities in whatever businesses seem to have some potential for cash flow. In 2002 W. C. Meadows, vice president of the Baldwin Company, identified another segment of the sports ball market that looked promising and that he felt was not adequately served by larger manufacturers. That market was for brightly colored bowling balls, and he believed a large number of bowlers valued appearance and style above performance. He also believed that it would be difficult for competitors to take advantage of the opportunity because of both Baldwin's cost advantages and its highly developed marketing skills.

As a result, in late 2003 the Baldwin Company investigated the marketing potential of brightly colored bowling balls. Baldwin sent a questionnaire to consumers in three markets: Philadelphia, Los Angeles, and New Haven. The results of the three questionnaires were much better than expected and supported the conclusion that the brightly colored bowling ball could achieve a 10- to 15-percent share of the market. Of course, some people at Baldwin complained about the cost of the test marketing, which was $250,000. (As we shall see later, this is a sunk cost and should not be included in project evaluation.)

In any case, the Baldwin Company is now considering investing in a machine to produce bowling balls. The bowling balls would be manufactured in a building owned by the firm and located near Los Angeles. This building, which is vacant, and the land can be sold for $150,000 after taxes.

Working with his staff, Meadows is preparing an analysis of the proposed new product. He summarizes his assumptions as follows: The cost of the bowling ball machine is $100,000. The machine has an estimated market value at the end of five years of $30,000. Production by year during the five-year life of the machine is expected to be as follows: 5,000 units, 8,000 units, 12,000 units, 10,000 units, and 6,000 units. The price of bowling balls in the first year will be $20. The bowling ball market is highly competitive, so Meadows believes that the price of bowling balls will increase at only 2 percent per year, as compared to the anticipated general inflation rate of 5 percent. Conversely, the plastic used to produce bowling balls is rapidly becoming more expensive. Because of this, production cash outflows are expected to grow at 10 percent per year. First-year production costs will be $10 per unit. Meadows has determined, based upon Baldwin's taxable income, that the appropriate incremental corporate tax rate in the bowling ball project is 34 percent.

Net working capital is defined as the difference between current assets and current liabilities. Like any other manufacturing firm, Baldwin finds that it must maintain an investment in working capital. It will purchase raw materials before production and sale, giving rise to an investment in inventory. It will maintain cash as a buffer against unforeseen expenditures. And, its credit sales will generate accounts receivable. Management determines that an immediate (year 0) investment in the different items of working capital of $10,000 is required. Working capital is forecasted to rise in the early years of the project but to fall to $0 by the project's end. In other words, the investment in working capital is completely recovered by the end of the project's life.

Projections based on these assumptions and Meadows's analysis appear in Tables 7.1 through 7.4. In these tables all cash flows are assumed to occur at the *end* of the year. Because of the large amount of information in these tables, it is important to see how the tables are related. Table 7.1 shows the basic data for both investment and income. Supplementary schedules on operations and depreciation, as presented in Tables 7.2 and 7.3, help explain where the numbers in Table 7.1 come from. Our goal is to obtain projections of cash flow. The data in Table 7.1 are all that are needed to calculate the relevant cash flows, as shown in Table 7.4.

TABLE 7.1	The Worksheet for Cash Flows of the Baldwin Company (in $ thousands) (All cash flows occur at the *end* of the year.)					

	Year 0	Year 1	Year 2	Year 3	Year 4	Year 5
Investments:						
(1) Bowling ball machine	−$100.00					$21.76*
(2) Accumulated depreciation		$20.00	$52.00	$71.20	$82.72	94.24
(3) Adjusted basis of machine after depreciation (end-of-year)		80.00	48.00	28.80	17.28	5.76
(4) Opportunity cost (warehouse)	−150.00					150.00
(5) Net working capital (end-of-year)	10.00	10.00	16.32	24.97	21.22	0
(6) Change in net working capital	−10.00		−6.32	−8.65	3.75	21.22
(7) Total cash flow of investment [(1) + (4) + (6)]	−260.00		−6.32	−8.65	3.75	192.98
Income:						
(8) Sales revenues		$100.00	$163.20	$249.72	$212.20	$129.90
(9) Operating costs		−50.00	−88.00	−145.20	−133.10	−87.84
(10) Depreciation		−20.00	−32.00	−19.20	−11.52	−11.52
(11) Income before taxes [(8) − (9) − (10)]		−30.00	−43.20	−85.32	−67.58	−30.54
(12) Tax at 34 percent		−10.20	−14.69	−29.01	−22.98	−10.38
(13) Net income		19.80	28.51	56.31	44.60	20.16

*We assume that the ending market value of the capital investment at year 5 is $30 (in thousands). Capital gain is the difference between the ending market value and the adjusted basis of the machine. The adjusted basis is the original purchase price of the machine less depreciation. The capital gain is $24.24 ($30 − $5.76). Capital gains for corporations are taxed at the ordinary income rate (34% in this example), so the capital gains tax here is $8.24 [0.34 × ($30 − $5.76)]. The after-tax capital gain is $30 − [0.34 × ($30 − $5.76)] = $21.76.

TABLE 7.2	(1) Year	(2) Production	(3) Price	(4) Sales Revenues	(5) Cost per Unit	(6) Operating Costs
Operating Revenues and Costs of the Baldwin Company	1	5,000	$20.00	$100,000	$10.00	$ 50,000
	2	8,000	20.40	163,200	11.00	88,000
	3	12,000	20.81	249,720	12.10	145,200
	4	10,000	21.22	212,200	13.31	133,100
	5	6,000	21.65	129,900	14.64	87,840

Prices rise at 2% a year.
Unit costs rise at 10% a year.

An Analysis of the Project

Investments   The investment outlays for the project are summarized in the top segment of Table 7.1. They consist of three parts:

1. *The Bowling Ball Machine.* The purchase requires an immediate (year 0) cash outflow of $100,000. The firm realizes a cash inflow when the machine is sold in year 5. These cash flows are shown in line 1 of Table 7.1. As indicated in the footnote to the table, taxes are incurred when the asset is sold.

2. *The Opportunity Cost of Not Selling the Warehouse.* If Baldwin accepts the bowling-ball project, it will use a warehouse and land that could otherwise be sold. The estimated sales price of the warehouse and land is therefore included as an *opportunity cost* in year 0, as presented in line 4. Opportunity costs are treated as cash outflows for purposes of capital budgeting. However, note that if the project is accepted, management assumes that the warehouse will be sold for $150,000 (after taxes) in year 5.

TABLE 7.3		Recovery Period Class					
Depreciation (in percent) under Modified Accelerated Cost Recovery System (MACRS)	**Year**	**3 Years**	**5 Years**	**7 Years**	**10 Years**	**15 Years**	**20 Years**
	1	0.333	0.200	0.143	0.100	0.050	0.038
	2	0.444	0.320	0.245	0.180	0.095	0.072
	3	0.148	0.192	0.175	0.144	0.086	0.067
	4	0.074	0.115	0.125	0.115	0.077	0.062
	5		0.115	0.089	0.092	0.069	0.057
	6		0.058	0.089	0.074	0.062	0.053
	7			0.089	0.066	0.059	0.049
	8			0.045	0.066	0.059	0.045
	9				0.066	0.059	0.045
	10				0.066	0.059	0.045
	11				0.033	0.059	0.045
	12–15					0.059	0.045
	16					0.030	0.045
	17–20						0.045
	21						0.022

Depreciation is expressed as a percent of the asset's cost. These schedules are based on the IRS publication *Depreciation*. Details on depreciation are presented in the appendix. Three-year depreciation actually carries over four years because the IRS assumes purchase is made in midyear.

TABLE 7.4	Incremental Cash Flows for the Baldwin Company (in $ thousands)					
	Year 0	**Year 1**	**Year 2**	**Year 3**	**Year 4**	**Year 5**
(1) Sales revenue [line 8, Table 7.1]		$100.00	$163.20	$249.72	$212.20	$129.90
(2) Operating costs [line 9, Table 7.1]		−50.00	−88.00	−145.20	−133.10	−87.84
(3) Taxes [line 12, Table 7.1]		−10.20	−14.69	−29.01	−22.98	−10.38
(4) Cash flow from operations [(1) − (2) − (3)]		39.80	60.51	75.51	56.12	31.68
(5) Total cash flow of investment [line 7, Table 7.1]	−$260.00		−6.32	−8.65	3.75	192.98
(6) Total cash flow of project [(4) + (5)]	−260.00	39.80	54.19	66.86	59.87	224.66
NPV @ 4%	123.641					
10%	51.588					
15%	5.472					
15.67%	0					
20%	−31.351					

The test marketing cost of $250,000 is not included. The tests occurred in the past and should be viewed as a *sunk cost*.

3. *The Investment in Working Capital.* Required working capital appears in line 5. Working capital rises over the early years of the project as expansion occurs. However, all working capital is assumed to be recovered at the end, a common assumption in capital budgeting. In other words, all inventory is sold by the end, the cash balance maintained as a buffer is liquidated, and all accounts receivable are collected. Increases in working capital in the early years must be funded by cash generated elsewhere in the firm. Hence, these increases are viewed as cash *outflows*. To reiterate, it is the *increase* in working capital over a year that leads to a cash outflow in that year. Even if working capital is at a high level, there will be no cash outflow over a year if working capital stays constant over that year. Conversely, decreases in working capital in the later years are viewed as cash inflows. All

of these cash flows are presented in line 6. A more complete discussion of working capital is provided later in this section.

To recap, there are three investments in this example: the bowling ball machine (line 1 in Table 7.1), the opportunity cost of the warehouse (line 4), and the changes in working capital (line 6). The total cash flow from the above three investments is shown in line 7.

Income and Taxes   Next, the determination of income is presented in the bottom segment of Table 7.1. While we are ultimately interested in cash flow—not income—we need the income calculation in order to determine taxes. Lines 8 and 9 of Table 7.1 show sales revenues and operating costs, respectively. The projections in these lines are based on the sales revenues and operating costs computed in columns 4 and 6 of Table 7.2. The estimates of revenues and costs follow from assumptions made by the corporate planning staff at Baldwin. In other words, the estimates critically depend on the fact that product prices are projected to increase at 2 percent per year and costs per unit are projected to increase at 10 percent per year.

Depreciation of the $100,000 capital investment is shown in line 10 of Table 7.1. Where do these numbers come from? Depreciation for tax purposes for U.S. companies is based on the Modified Accelerated Cost Recovery System (MACRS).[1] Each asset is assigned a useful life under MACRS, with an accompanying depreciation schedule as shown in Table 7.3.[2] The IRS ruled that Baldwin is to depreciate its capital investment over five years, so the second column of the table applies in this case. Since depreciation in the table is expressed as a percentage of the asset's cost, multiply the percentages in this column by $100,000 to arrive at depreciation in dollars.

Income before taxes is calculated in line 11 of Table 7.1. Taxes are provided in line 12 of this table, and net income is calculated in line 13.

Cash Flow   Cash flow is finally determined in Table 7.4. We begin by reproducing lines 8, 9, and 12 in Table 7.1 as lines 1, 2, and 3 in Table 7.4. Cash flow from operations, which is sales minus both operating costs and taxes, is provided in line 4 of Table 7.4. Total investment cash flow, taken from line 7 of Table 7.1, appears as line 5 of Table 7.4. Cash flow from operations plus total cash flow of the investment equals total cash flow of the project, which is displayed as line 6 of Table 7.4.

Net Present Value   The NPV of the Baldwin bowling ball project can be calculated from the cash flows in line 6. As can be seen at the bottom of Table 7.4, the NPV is $51,588 if 10 percent is the appropriate discount rate and −$31,351 if 20 percent is the appropriate discount rate. If the discount rate is 15.67 percent, the project will have a zero NPV. In other words, the project's internal rate of return is 15.67 percent. If the discount rate of the Baldwin bowling ball project is above 15.67 percent, it should not be accepted because its NPV would be negative.

Which Set of Books?

It should be noted that the firm's management generally keeps two sets of books, one for the IRS (called the *tax books*) and another for its annual report (called the *stockholders' books*). The tax books follow the rules of the IRS. The stockholders' books follow the rules

---

[1]Depreciation rules are discussed in detail in the appendix to this chapter.

[2]Under current IRS rules, 30 percent of the value of the asset may be depreciated in the first year. This is referred to as *bonus depreciation.* The depreciation percentages in the table then apply to the 70 percent of the asset that remains. Bonus depreciation does not apply to real estate. We have not included bonus depreciation in the Baldwin example since, at the time this textbook went to press, the relevant rule was scheduled to expire on January 1, 2005.

of the *Financial Accounting Standards Board* (FASB), the governing body in accounting. The two sets of rules differ widely in certain areas. For example, income on municipal bonds is ignored for tax purposes while being treated as income by the FASB. The differences almost always benefit the firm, because the rules permit income on the stockholders' books to be higher than income on the tax books. That is, management can look profitable to the stockholders without needing to pay taxes on all of the reported profit. In fact, there are plenty of large companies that consistently report positive earnings to the stockholders while reporting losses to the IRS.

We present a synopsis of the IRS rules on depreciation in the appendix. The rules on depreciation for the stockholders' books differ, as they do in many other accounting areas. Which of the two sets of rules on depreciation do we use to create the previous tables for Baldwin? Clearly, we are interested in the IRS rules. Our purpose is to calculate net cash flow, and tax payments are cash outflows. The FASB regulations determine accounting income, not cash flow.

A Note on Net Working Capital

The investment in net working capital is an important part of any capital budgeting analysis. While we explicitly considered net working capital in lines 5 and 6 of Table 7.1, students may be wondering where the numbers in these lines came from. An investment in net working capital arises whenever (1) inventory is purchased, (2) cash is kept in the project as a buffer against unexpected expenditures, and (3) credit sales are made, generating accounts receivable rather than cash. (The investment in net working capital is reduced by credit purchases, which generate accounts payables.) This investment in net working capital represents a cash outflow, because cash generated elsewhere in the firm is tied up in the project.

To see how the investment in net working capital is built from its component parts, we focus on year 1. We see in Table 7.1 that Baldwin's managers predict sales in year 1 to be $100,000 and operating costs to be $50,000. If both the sales and costs were cash transactions, the firm would receive $50,000 ($100,000 − $50,000). As stated earlier, this cash flow would occur at the *end* of year 1.

Now let's give you more information. The managers:

1. Forecast that $9,000 of the sales will be on credit, implying that cash receipts at the end of year 1 will be only $91,000 ($100,000 − $9,000). The accounts receivable of $9,000 will be collected at the end of year 2.

2. Believe that they can defer payment on $3,000 of the $50,000 of costs, implying that cash disbursements at the end of year 1 will be only $47,000 ($50,000 − $3,000). Baldwin will pay off the $3,000 of accounts payable at the end of year 2.

3. Decide that inventory of $2,500 should be left on hand at the end of year 1 to avoid *stockouts* (that is, running out of inventory).

4. Decide that cash of $1,500 should be earmarked for the project at the end of year 1 to avoid running out of cash.

Thus, net working capital at the end of year 1 is

$9,000	−	$3,000	+	$2,500	+	$1,500	=	$10,000
Accounts receivable		Accounts payable		Inventory		Cash		Net working capital

Because $10,000 of cash generated elsewhere in the firm must be used to offset this requirement for net working capital, Baldwin's managers correctly view the investment in net working capital as a cash outflow of the project. As the project grows over time, needs for net working capital increase. *Changes* in net working capital from year to year represent further cash flows, as indicated by the negative numbers for the first few years of line 6 of Table 7.1. However, in the declining years of the project, net working capital is reduced—ultimately to zero. That is, accounts receivable are finally collected, the project's cash buffer is returned to the rest of the corporation, and all remaining inventory is sold off. This frees up cash in the later years, as indicated by positive numbers in years 4 and 5 on line 6.

Typically, corporate worksheets (such as Table 7.1) treat net working capital as a whole. The individual components of working capital (receivables, inventory, etc.) do not generally appear in the worksheets. However, the reader should remember that the working capital numbers in the worksheets are not pulled out of thin air. Rather, they result from a meticulous forecast of the components, just as we illustrated for year 1.

Interest Expense

It may have bothered you that interest expense was ignored in the Baldwin example. After all, many projects are at least partially financed with debt, particularly a bowling ball machine that is likely to increase the debt capacity of the firm. As it turns out, our approach of assuming no debt financing is rather standard in the real world. Firms typically calculate a project's cash flows under the assumption that the project is financed only with equity. Any adjustments for debt financing are reflected in the discount rate, not the cash flows. The treatment of debt in capital budgeting will be covered in depth later in the text. Suffice it to say at this time that the full ramifications of debt financing are well beyond our current discussion.

Concept Questions

1. What are the items leading to cash flow in any year?
2. Why did we determine income when NPV analysis discounts cash flows, not income?
3. Why is working capital viewed as a cash outflow?

7.3 The Boeing 777: A Real-World Example

Will the principles discussed in the previous sections of this chapter allow us to perform capital budgeting in the real world? Let's see by examining the Boeing 777 project, which we mentioned in the executive summary of this chapter. As stated there, the Boeing Company announced in late 1990 its intention to build the 777. The company anticipated selling several thousand of these planes over a 35-year period, beginning in 1995.

The relevant projected information is presented in Table 7.5, with the determination of annual net cash flow being the ultimate goal of the table. Net cash flow can be determined in three steps:

1. *Taxes.* In order to determine taxes each year, we begin with taxable income, which can be expressed as:

$$\text{Taxable income} = \text{Sales revenue} - \text{Operating costs} - \text{Depreciation}$$

Choosing a representative year, say, 2005, we have:

$$\text{Taxable income} = \$19,468.56 - \$17,911.07 - \$116.83 = \$1440.66$$

Boeing forecasts a tax rate of 34 percent, implying taxes in 2005 of:

$$0.34 \times \$1440.66 = \$489.82$$

2. *Investment.* Investment is the sum of the *change* in net working capital and the *amount* of capital expenditures, which is $450.88 ($431.41 + $19.47) for 2005.

TABLE 7.5 Incremental Cash Flows: Boeing 777

Year	Number of Planes Delivered	Sales Revenue	Operating Costs	Depreciation	Income before Taxes	Taxes	Change in Net Working Capital	Capital Expenditures	Investment	Net Cash Flow
1991			$ 865.00	$ 40.00	$ (905.00)	$ (307.70)		$400.00	$ 400.00	$ (957.30)
1992			1,340.00	96.00	(1,436.00)	(488.24)		600.00	600.00	(1,451.76)
1993			1,240.00	116.40	(1,356.40)	(461.18)		300.00	300.00	(1,078.82)
1994			840.00	124.76	(964.76)	(328.02)		200.00	200.00	(711.98)
1995	14	$ 1,847.55	1,976.69	112.28	(241.42)	(82.08)	$ 181.06	1.85	182.91	(229.97)
1996	145	19,418.96	17,865.45	101.06	1,452.45	493.83	1,722.00	19.42	1,741.42	681.74
1997	140	19,244.23	16,550.04	90.95	2,603.24	885.10	(17.12)	19.42	2.30	1,806.79
1998	111	15,737.95	13,377.26	82.72	2,277.97	774.51	(343.62)	15.74	(327.88)	1,914.06
1999	107	16,257.35	13,656.17	77.75	2,523.43	857.97	50.90	16.26	67.16	1,676.05
2000	102	15,333.42	12,726.74	75.63	2,531.05	860.56	90.54	15.33	105.87	1,640.25
2001	92	14,289.29	11,860.11	75.00	2,354.18	800.42	(102.33)	14.29	(88.04)	1,716.80
2002	92	14,717.97	12,068.74	75.00	2,574.23	875.24	42.01	14.72	56.73	1,717.26
2003	105	17,233.97	14,131.85	99.46	3,002.66	1,020.90	246.57	244.64	491.21	1,590.01
2004	89	15,066.42	12,354.47	121.48	2,590.47	880.76	(212.42)	244.64	32.22	1,798.97
2005	111	19,468.56	17,911.07	116.83	1,440.66	489.82	431.41	19.47	450.88	616.79
2006	130	23,307.53	20,510.63	112.65	2,684.25	912.65	376.22	23.31	399.53	1,484.73
2007	118	21,911.40	18,843.81	100.20	2,967.39	1,008.91	(136.82)	21.91	(114.91)	2,173.59
2008	94	17,944.00	15,252.40	129.20	2,562.40	871.22	(388.81)	567.22	178.41	1,641.97
2009	123	24,103.23	22,174.98	96.99	1,831.26	622.63	603.60	24.10	627.70	677.92
2010	125	25,316.97	22,278.94	76.84	2,961.19	1,006.80	118.95	25.32	144.27	1,886.96
2011	125	26,076.48	22,425.77	65.81	3,584.90	1,218.87	74.43	26.08	100.51	2,331.33
2012	98	21,133.07	17,963.10	61.68	3,108.29	1,056.82	(484.45)	21.13	(463.32)	2,576.47
2013	84	18,550.25	15,582.21	57.96	2,910.08	989.43	(253.12)	18.55	(234.57)	2,213.18
2014	89	20,321.64	16,866.97	54.61	3,400.06	1,156.02	173.60	20.32	193.92	2,104.73
2015	89	20,931.29	17,372.97	52.83	3,505.49	1,191.87	59.75	20.93	80.68	2,285.77
2016	89	21,559.23	17,894.16	52.83	3,612.24	1,228.16	61.54	21.56	83.10	2,353.81
2017	89	22,206.00	18,430.98	52.83	3,722.19	1,265.54	63.38	22.21	85.59	2,423.89
2018	89	22,872.18	18,983.92	52.83	3,835.43	1,304.05	65.29	22.87	88.16	2,496.05
2019	89	23,558.35	19,553.43	47.52	3,957.40	1,345.52	67.24	23.56	90.80	2,568.60
2020	89	24,265.10	20,140.03	35.28	4,089.79	1,390.53	69.26	24.27	93.53	2,641.01
2021	89	24,993.05	20,744.23	28.36	4,220.46	1,434.96	71.34	24.99	96.33	2,717.53
2022	89	25,742.85	21,366.56	28.36	4,347.93	1,478.30	73.48	25.74	99.22	2,798.77
2023	89	26,515.13	22,007.56	28.36	4,479.21	1,522.93	75.68	26.52	102.20	2,882.44
2024	89	$27,310.58	$22,667.78	$ 16.05	$4,626.75	$1,573.10	$ 77.95	$ 27.31	$ 105.26	$ 2,964.45

NOTES:
Tax rate is 34 percent.
Net Cash Flow for a given year can be determined by adding across the columns. Recall that Net Cash Flow is equal to Sales Revenue − Operating Costs − Taxes − Investment.

SOURCE: Robert Bruner, Case Studies in Finance, 4th edition (Burr Ridge, Ill.: McGraw-Hill/Irwin, 2003).

3. *Final calculation.* We calculate net cash flow as:

Sales revenue − Operating costs − Taxes − Investment

which for 2005 is

$19,468.56 − $17,911.07 − $489.82 − $450.88 = $616.79

The last column in Table 7.5 provides net cash flow for each of the 35 years.

In addition to the items in the table, Boeing invested several hundred million dollars in research and development prior to late 1990. Since these outflows were incurred prior to the decision to build the plane, they are sunk costs and should properly be excluded from the table.

The net present value (NPV) of the Boeing 777 project is calculated by discounting the net cash flows in the last column of the table. Of course, the NPV of any project is dependent on the discount rate. Figure 7.1 graphs NPV as a function of the discount rate. NPV must be negatively related to this rate, since there is only one change in the signs of the cash flows. The net present value of the project is 0 for a discount rate of 21 percent. Hence, the internal rate of return (IRR) of the project is 21 percent. Boeing should accept the project if their discount rate is less than 21 percent but should reject the project if their discount rate is above 21 percent.

It should be mentioned that the analysis in Table 7.5, as well as the analysis for any project, is entirely based on forecasts. The subsequent reality may be much different, as was the case with the 777. Though the table shows delivery of 711 planes by the end of 1999, only 282 planes had actually been delivered through May 2000.

FIGURE 7.1   **NPV of the Boeing 777 Project as a Function of the Discount Rate**

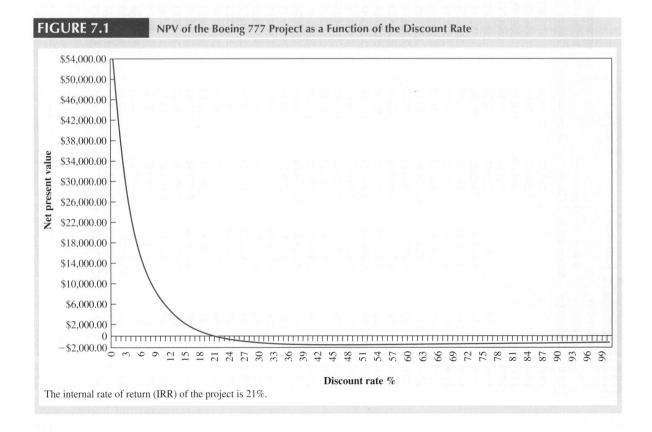

The internal rate of return (IRR) of the project is 21%.

7.4 Inflation and Capital Budgeting

Inflation is an important fact of economic life, and it must be considered in capital budgeting. We begin our examination of inflation by considering the relationship between interest rates and inflation.

Interest Rates and Inflation

Suppose that a bank offers a one-year interest rate of 10 percent. This means that an individual who deposits $1,000 will receive $1,100 ($1,000 × 1.10) in one year. While 10 percent may seem like a handsome return, one can only put it in perspective after examining the rate of inflation.

Imagine that the rate of inflation is 6 percent over the year and it affects all goods equally. For example, a restaurant that charges $1.00 for a hamburger today will charge $1.06 for the same hamburger at the end of the year. You can use your $1,000 to buy 1,000 hamburgers today (date 0). Alternatively, if you put your money in the bank, you can buy 1,038 ($1,100/$1.06) hamburgers at date 1. Thus, lending increases your hamburger consumption by only 3.8 percent.

Since the prices of all goods rise at this 6-percent rate, lending lets you increase your consumption of any single good or any combination of goods by only 3.8 percent. Thus, 3.8 percent is what you are *really* earning through your savings account, after adjusting for inflation. Economists refer to the 3.8-percent number as the **real interest rate.** Economists refer to the 10-percent rate as the **nominal interest rate** or simply the *interest rate*. This discussion is illustrated in Figure 7.2.

We have used an example with a specific nominal interest rate and a specific inflation rate. In general, the formula between real and nominal interest rates can be written as

$$1 + \text{Nominal interest rate} = (1 + \text{Real interest rate}) \times (1 + \text{Inflation rate})$$

Rearranging terms, we have

$$\text{Real interest rate} = \frac{1 + \text{Nominal interest rate}}{1 + \text{Inflation rate}} - 1 \qquad (7.1)$$

The formula indicates that the real interest rate in our example is 3.8 percent (1.10/1.06 − 1).

The above formula determines the real interest rate precisely. The following formula is an approximation:

$$\text{Real interest rate} \cong \text{Nominal interest rate} - \text{Inflation rate} \qquad (7.2)$$

The symbol $\cong$ indicates that the equation is approximately true. This latter formula calculates the real rate in our example as:

$$4\% = 10\% - 6\%$$

FIGURE 7.2

Calculation of Real Rate of Interest

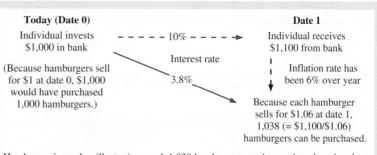

Hamburger is used as illustrative good. 1,038 hamburgers can be purchased on date 1 instead of 1,000 hamburgers at date 0. Real interest rate = 1,038/1,000 − 1 = 3.8%.

The student should be aware that, while equation (7.2) may seem more intuitive than equation (7.1), (7.2) is only an approximation.

This approximation is reasonably accurate for low rates of interest and inflation. In our example, the difference between the approximate calculation and the exact one is only 0.2 percent (4 percent − 3.8 percent). Unfortunately, the approximation becomes poor when rates are higher.

EXAMPLE

The little-known monarchy of Gerberovia recently had a nominal interest rate of 300 percent and an inflation rate of 280 percent. According to equation (7.2), the real interest rate is:

$$300\% - 280\% = 20\% \qquad \text{(Approximate formula)}$$

However, according to equation (7.1), this rate is:

$$\frac{1 + 300\%}{1 + 280\%} - 1 = 5.26\% \qquad \text{(Exact formula)}$$

How do we know that the second formula is indeed the exact one? Let's think in terms of hamburgers again. Had you deposited $1,000 in a Gerberovian bank a year ago, the account would be worth $4,000 [$1,000 × (1 + 300%)] today. However, while a hamburger cost $1 a year ago, it costs $3.80 (1 + 280%) today. Therefore, you would now be able to buy 1052.6 (4,000/3.80) hamburgers, implying a real interest rate of 5.26 percent.

The recent real and nominal interest rates for the United States are presented in Figure 7.3. The figure suggests that the nominal rate of interest exhibits more variability from year to year than does the real rate, a finding that seems to hold over most time periods.

FIGURE 7.3   Nominal and Real Interest Rates and Inflation for the United States

Nominal interest rates are based on three-month Treasury bills (or equivalent). The measure of inflation used is the Consumer Price Index. Real rates are calculated according to equation (7.1).

Cash Flow and Inflation

The above analysis defines two types of interest rates, nominal rates and real rates, and relates them through equation (7.1). Capital budgeting requires data on cash flows as well as on interest rates. Like interest rates, cash flows can be expressed in either nominal or real terms.

A **nominal cash flow** refers to the actual dollars to be received (or paid out). A **real cash flow** refers to the cash flow's purchasing power. Like most definitions, these definitions are best explained by examples.

EXAMPLE

Burrows Publishing has just purchased the rights to the next book of famed romantic novelist Barbara Musk. Still unwritten, the book should be available to the public in four years. Currently, romantic novels sell for $10.00 in softcover. The publishers believe that inflation will be 6 percent a year over the next four years. Since romantic novels are so popular, the publishers anticipate that their prices will rise about 2 percent per year more than the inflation rate over the next four years. Burrows Publishing plans to sell the novel at $13.60 [$(1.08)^4 \times \$10.00$] four years from now, anticipating sales of 100,000 copies.

The expected cash flow in the fourth year of $1.36 million ($13.60 × 100,000) is a *nominal cash flow*. That is, the firm expects to receive $1.36 million at that time. In other words, a nominal cash flow refers to the actual dollars to be received in the future.

The purchasing power of $1.36 million in four years is

$$\$1.08 \text{ million} = \frac{\$1.36 \text{ million}}{(1.06)^4}$$

The figure, $1.08 million, is a *real cash flow* since it is expressed in terms of purchasing power. Extending our hamburger example, the $1.36 million to be received in four years will only buy 1.08 million hamburgers because the price of a hamburger will rise from $1 to $1.26 [$\$1 \times (1.06)^4$] over the period.

EXAMPLE

EOBII Publishers, a competitor of Burrows, recently bought a printing press for $2,000,000 to be depreciated by the straight-line method over five years. This implies yearly depreciation of $400,000 ($2,000,000/5). Is this $400,000 figure a real or a nominal quantity?

Depreciation is a *nominal* quantity because $400,000 is the actual tax deduction over each of the next four years. Depreciation becomes a real quantity if it is adjusted for purchasing power. Hence, $316,837 [$\$400,000/(1.06)^4$] is depreciation in the fourth year, expressed as a real quantity.

Discounting: Nominal or Real?

Our previous discussion showed that interest rates can be expressed in either nominal or real terms. Similarly, cash flows can be expressed in either nominal or real terms. Given these choices, how should one express interest rates and cash flows when performing capital budgeting?

Financial practitioners correctly stress the need to maintain *consistency* between cash flows and discount rates. That is,

Nominal cash flows must be discounted at the *nominal* rate.

Real cash flows must be discounted at the *real* rate.

As long as one is consistent, either approach is correct. In order to minimize computational error, it is generally advisable in practice to choose the approach that is easiest. This idea is illustrated in the following two examples.

EXAMPLE

Shields Electric forecasts the following nominal cash flows on a particular project:

Date	0	1	2
Cash flow	−$1,000	$600	$650

The nominal interest rate is 14 percent, and the inflation rate is forecast to be 5 percent. What is the value of the project?

Using Nominal Quantities   The NPV can be calculated as

$$\$26.47 = -\$1,000 + \frac{\$600}{1.14} + \frac{\$650}{(1.14)^2}$$

The project should be accepted.

Using Real Quantities   The real cash flows are

Date	0	1	2
Cash flow	−$1,000	$571.43 $\left(\dfrac{\$600}{1.05}\right)$	$589.57 $\left(\dfrac{\$650}{(1.05)^2}\right)$

The real interest rate is 8.57143 percent ($1.14/1.05 − 1$).
    The NPV can be calculated as

$$\$26.47 = -\$1,000 + \frac{\$571.43}{1.0857143} + \frac{\$589.57}{(1.0857143)^2}$$

The NPV is the same whether cash flows are expressed in nominal or in real quantities. It must always be the case that the NPV is the same under the two different approaches.

Because both approaches always yield the same result, which one should be used? As mentioned above, use the approach that is simpler, since the simpler approach generally leads to fewer computational errors. Because the Shields Electric example begins with nominal cash flows, nominal quantities produce a simpler calculation here.

EXAMPLE

Altshuler, Inc., generated the following forecast for a capital budgeting project:

	Year		
	0	1	2
Capital expenditure	$1,210		
Revenues (in real terms)		$1,900	$2,000
Cash expenses (in real terms)		950	1,000
Depreciation (straight line)		605	605

The president, David Altshuler, estimates inflation to be 10 percent per year over the next two years. In addition, he believes that the cash flows of the project should be discounted at the nominal rate of 15.5 percent. His firm's tax rate is 40 percent.

Mr. Altshuler forecasts all cash flows in *nominal* terms, leading to the following spreadsheet:

	Year		
	0	**1**	**2**
Capital expenditure	−$1,210		
Revenues		$2,090 (= 1,900 × 1.10)	$2,420 [= 2,000 × (1.10)^2]
− Expenses		−1,045 (= 950 × 1.10)	−1,210 [= 1,000 × (1.10)^2]
− Depreciation		−605 (= 1,210/2)	−605
Taxable income		440	605
− Taxes (40%)		−176	−242
Income after taxes		264	363
+ Depreciation		+605	+605
Cash flow		$ 869	$ 968

$$NPV = -\$1,210 + \frac{\$869}{1.155} + \frac{\$968}{(1.155)^2} = \$268$$

Mr. Altshuler's sidekick, Stuart Weiss, prefers working in real terms. He first calculates the real rate to be 5 percent (=1.155/1.10 − 1). Next, he generates the following spreadsheet in *real* quantities:

	Year		
	0	**1**	**2**
Capital expenditure	−$1,210		
Revenues		$1,900	$2,000
− Expenses		−950	−1,000
− Depreciation		−550 (= 605/1.1)	−500 [= 605/(1.1)^2]
Taxable income		400	500
− Taxes (40%)		−160	−200
Income after taxes		240	300
+ Depreciation		+550	+500
Cash flow		$ 790	$ 800

$$NPV = -\$1,210 + \frac{\$790}{1.05} + \frac{\$800}{(1.05)^2} = \$268$$

In explaining his calculations to Mr. Altshuler, Mr. Weiss points out:

1. Since the capital expenditure occurs at date 0 (today), its nominal value and its real value are equal.

2. Because yearly depreciation of $605 is a nominal quantity, one converts it to a real quantity by discounting at the inflation rate of 10 percent.

3. It is no coincidence that both Mr. Altshuler and Mr. Weiss arrive at the same NPV number. Both methods must always generate the same NPV.

Concept Questions

1. **What is the difference between the nominal and the real interest rate?**
2. **What is the difference between nominal and real cash flows?**

7.5 Investments of Unequal Lives: The Equivalent Annual Cost Method

Suppose a firm must choose between two machines of unequal lives. Both machines can do the same job, but they have different operating costs and will last for different time periods. A simple application of the NPV rule suggests taking the machine whose costs have the lower present value. This choice might be a mistake, however, because the lower-cost machine may need to be replaced before the other one.

EXAMPLE

The Downtown Athletic Club must choose between two mechanical tennis ball throwers. Machine A costs less than machine B but will not last as long. The cash outflows from the two machines are:

Machine	Date				
	0	**1**	**2**	**3**	**4**
A	$500	$120	$120	$120	
B	$600	$100	$100	$100	$100

Machine A costs $500 and lasts three years. There will be maintenance expenses of $120 to be paid at the end of each of the three years. Machine B costs $600 and lasts four years. There will be maintenance expenses of $100 to be paid at the end of each of the four years. We place all costs in *real* terms, an assumption greatly simplifying the analysis. Revenues per year are assumed to be the same, regardless of machine, so they are ignored in the analysis. Note that all numbers in the above chart are *outflows*.

To get a handle on the decision, let's take the present value of the costs of each of the two machines. Assuming a discount rate of 10 percent, we have:

$$\text{Machine } A: \$798.42 = \$500 + \frac{\$120}{1.1} + \frac{\$120}{(1.1)^2} + \frac{\$120}{(1.1)^3} \tag{7.3}$$

$$\text{Machine } B: \$916.99 = \$600 + \frac{\$100}{1.1} + \frac{\$100}{(1.1)^2} + \frac{\$100}{(1.1)^3} + \frac{\$100}{(1.1)^4}$$

Machine B has a higher present value of outflows. A naive approach would be to select machine A because of its lower present value. However, machine B has a longer life so perhaps its cost per year is actually lower.

How might one properly adjust for the difference in useful life when comparing the two machines? Perhaps the easiest approach involves calculating something called the *equivalent annual cost* of each machine. This approach puts costs on a per-year basis.

Equation (7.3) showed that payments of ($500, $120, $120, $120) are equivalent to a single payment of $798.42 at date 0. We now wish to equate the single payment of $798.42 at date 0 with a three-year annuity. Using techniques of previous chapters, we have

$$\$798.42 = C \times A_{0.10}^3$$

$A_{0.10}^3$ is an annuity of $1 a year for three years, discounted at 10 percent. C is the unknown—the annuity payment per year such that the present value of all payments equals $798.42. Because $A_{0.10}^3$ equals 2.4869, C equals $321.05 ($798.42/2.4869). Thus, a payment stream of ($500, $120, $120, $120) is equivalent to annuity payments of $321.05 made at the *end* of each year for three years. We refer to $321.05 as the *equivalent annual cost* of machine A.

This idea is summarized in the little chart below:

	Date			
	0	**1**	**2**	**3**
Cash outflows of Machine A	$500	$120	$120	$120
Equivalent annual cost of Machine A		$321.05	$321.05	$321.05

The Downtown Athletic Club should be indifferent between cash outflows of ($500, $120, $120, $120) and cash outflows of ($0, $321.05, $321.05, $321.05). Alternatively, one can say that the purchase of the machine is financially equivalent to a rental agreement calling for annual lease payments of $321.05.

Now let's turn to machine B. We calculate its equivalent annual cost from

$$\$916.99 = C \times A^4_{0.10}$$

Because $A^4_{0.10}$ equals 3.1699, C equals $916.99/3.1699, or $289.28.

As we did above for machine A, the following chart can be created for machine B:

	Date				
	0	1	2	3	4
Cash outflows of Machine B	$600	$100	$100	$100	$100
Equivalent annual cost of Machine B		$289.28	$289.28	$289.28	$289.28

The decision is easy once the charts of the two machines are compared. Would you rather make annual lease payments of $321.05 or $289.28? Put this way, the problem becomes a no-brainer. Clearly, a rational person would rather pay the lower amount. Thus, machine B is the preferred choice.

Two final remarks are in order. First, it is no accident that we specified the costs of the tennis ball machines in real terms. While B would still have been the preferred machine had the costs been stated in nominal terms, the actual solution would have been much more difficult. As a general rule, always convert cash flows to real terms when working through problems of this type.

Second, the above analysis applies only if one anticipates that both machines can be replaced. The analysis would differ if no replacement were possible. For example, imagine that the only company that manufactured tennis ball throwers just went out of business and no new producers are expected to enter the field. In this case, machine B would generate revenues in the fourth year whereas machine A would not. Here, simple net present value analysis for mutually exclusive projects including both revenues and costs would be appropriate.

The General Decision to Replace (Advanced)

The previous analysis concerned the choice between machine A and machine B, both of which were new acquisitions. More typically, firms must decide when to replace an existing machine with a new one. This decision is actually quite straightforward. One should replace if the annual cost of the new machine is less than the annual cost of the old machine. As with much else in finance, an example clarifies this approach better than further explanation.

EXAMPLE

Consider the situation of BIKE, which must decide whether to replace an existing machine. BIKE currently pays no taxes. The replacement machine costs $9,000 now and requires maintenance of $1,000 at the end of every year for eight years. At the end of eight years the machine would be sold for $2,000.

The existing machine requires increasing amounts of maintenance each year, and its salvage value falls each year, as shown:

Year	Maintenance	Salvage
Present	$ 0	$4,000
1	1,000	2,500
2	2,000	1,500
3	3,000	1,000
4	4,000	0

This chart tells us that the existing machine can be sold for $4,000 now. If it is sold one year from now, the resale price will be $2,500, and $1,000 must be spent on maintenance during the year to keep it running. For ease of calculation, we assume that this maintenance fee is paid at the end of the year. The machine will last for four more years before it falls apart. In other words, salvage value will be zero at the end of year 4. If BIKE faces an opportunity cost of capital of 15 percent, when should it replace the machine?

As we said above, our approach is to compare the annual cost of the replacement machine with the annual cost of the old machine. The annual cost of the replacement machine is simply its *equivalent annual cost* (EAC). Let's calculate that first.

Equivalent Annual Cost of New Machine   The present value of the cost of the new replacement machine is as follows:

$$PV_{costs} = \$9,000 + \$1,000 \times A_{0.15}^{8} - \frac{\$2,000}{(1.15)^{8}}$$

$$= \$9,000 + \$1,000 \times (4.4873) - \$2,000 \times (0.3269)$$

$$= \$12,833$$

Notice that the $2,000 salvage value is an inflow. It is treated as a *negative* number in the above equation because it *offsets* the cost of the machine.

The EAC of a new replacement machine equals

$$PV/\text{8-year annuity factor at } 15\% = \frac{PV}{A_{0.15}^{8}} = \frac{\$12,833}{4.4873} = \$2,860$$

This calculation implies that buying a replacement machine is financially equivalent to renting this machine for $2,860 per year.

Cost of Old Machine   This calculation is a little trickier. If BIKE keeps the old machine for one year, the firm must pay maintenance costs of $1,000 a year from now. But this is not BIKE's only cost from keeping the machine for one year. BIKE will receive $2,500 at date 1 if the old machine is kept for one year but would receive $4,000 today if the old machine were sold immediately. This reduction in sales proceeds is clearly a cost as well.

Thus, the PV of the costs of keeping the machine one more year before selling it equals

$$\$4,000 + \frac{\$1,000}{1.15} - \frac{\$2,500}{1.15} = \$2,696$$

That is, if BIKE holds the old machine for one year, BIKE does *not* receive the $4,000 today. This $4,000 can be thought of as an opportunity cost. In addition, the firm must pay $1,000 a year from now. Finally, BIKE does receive $2,500 a year from now. This last item is treated as a negative number because it offsets the other two costs.

While we normally express cash flows in terms of present value, the analysis to come is made easier if we express the cash flow in terms of its future value one year from now. This future value is

$$\$2,696 \times 1.15 = \$3,100$$

In other words, the cost of keeping the machine for one year is equivalent to paying $3,100 at the end of the year.

Making the Comparison   Now let's review the cash flows. If we replace the machine immediately, we can view our annual expense as $2,860, beginning at the end of the year. This annual expense occurs forever, if we replace the new machine every eight years. This cash flow stream can be written as

	Year 1	Year 2	Year 3	Year 4	. . .
Expenses from replacing machine immediately	$2,860	$2,860	$2,860	$2,860	. . .

If we replace the old machine in one year, our expense from using the old machine for that final year can be viewed as $3,100, payable at the end of the year. After replacement, our annual expense is $2,860, beginning at the end of two years. This annual expense occurs forever, if we replace the new machine every eight years. This cash flow stream can be written as

	Year 1	Year 2	Year 3	Year 4	. . .
Expenses from using old machine for one year and then replacing it	$3,100	$2,860	$2,860	$2,860	. . .

Put this way, the choice is a no-brainer. Anyone would rather pay $2,860 at the end of the year than $3,100 at the end of the year. Thus, BIKE should replace[3] the old machine immediately in order to minimize the expense at year 1.

Two final points should be made on the decision to replace. First, we have examined a situation where both the old machine and the replacement machine generate the same revenues. Because revenues are unaffected by the choice of machine, revenues do not enter our analysis. This situation is common in business. For example, the decision to replace either the heating system or the air conditioning system in one's home office will likely not affect firm revenues. However, sometimes revenues will be greater with a new machine. The above approach can easily be amended to handle differential revenues.

Second, we want to stress the importance of the above approach. Applications of the above approach are pervasive in business, since *every* machine must be replaced at some point.

Concept Question	**1. What is the equivalent annual cost method of capital budgeting?**

7.6 SUMMARY AND CONCLUSIONS

This chapter discusses a number of practical applications of capital budgeting.

1. Capital budgeting must be placed on an incremental basis. This means that sunk costs must be ignored, while both opportunity costs and side effects must be considered.

2. In the Baldwin case, we computed NPV using the following two steps:
   a. Calculate the net cash flow from all sources for each period.
   b. Calculate the NPV using the cash flows calculated above.

---

[3]One caveat is in order. Perhaps the old machine's maintenance is high in the first year but drops after that. A decision to replace immediately might be premature in that case. Therefore, we need to check the cost of the old machine in future years.

The cost of keeping the existing machine a second year is

$$\text{PV of costs at time 1} = \$2,500 + \frac{\$2,000}{1.15} - \frac{\$1,500}{1.15} = \$2,935$$

which has future value of $3,375 ($2,935 × 1.15).

The costs of keeping the existing machine for years 3 and 4 are also greater than the EAC of buying a new machine. Thus, BIKE's decision to replace the old machine immediately is still valid.

3. Inflation must be handled consistently. One approach is to express both cash flows and the discount rate in nominal terms. The other approach is to express both cash flow and the discount rate in real terms. Because either approach yields the same NPV calculation, the simpler method should be used. The simpler method will generally depend on the type of capital budgeting problem.

4. A firm should use the equivalent annual cost approach when choosing between two machines of unequal lives.

KEY TERMS

allocated cost, 180
erosion, 179
net working capital, 181
nominal cash flow, 191
nominal interest rate, 189

opportunity cost, 179
real cash flow, 191
real interest rate, 189
sunk cost, 179
synergy, 179

SUGGESTED READING

An excellent in-depth examination of the capital budgeting decision is contained in:

Copeland, T., T. Koller, and J. Murrin. *Valuation: Measuring and Managing the Value of Companies,* 3rd ed. The McKinsey Company, 1996.

QUESTIONS & PROBLEMS

NPV AND CAPITAL BUDGETING

7.1 Which of the following should be treated as incremental cash flows when computing the NPV of an investment?
  a. A reduction in the sales of a company's other products caused by the investment.
  b. An expenditure on plant and equipment that has not yet been made and will be made only if the project is accepted.
  c. Costs of research and development undertaken in connection with the product during the past three years.
  d. Annual depreciation expense from the investment.
  e. Dividend payments by the firm.
  f. The resale value of plant and equipment at the end of the project's life.
  g. Salary and medical costs for production personnel who will be employed only if the project is accepted.

7.2 Your company currently produces and sells steel-shaft golf clubs. The board of directors wants you to consider the introduction of a new line of titanium bubble woods with graphite shafts. Which of the following costs are *not* relevant?
  I. Land you already own that will be used for the project, but otherwise will be sold for $700,000, its market value.
  II. A $300,000 drop in your sales of steel-shaft clubs if the titanium woods with graphite shafts are introduced.
  III. $200,000 spent on research and development last year on graphite shafts.
    a. I only
    b. II only
    c. III only
    d. I and III only
    e. II and III only

7.3 The Best Manufacturing Company is considering a new investment. Financial projections for the investment are tabulated below. Cash flows are in $ thousands, and the corporate tax rate is 34 percent. Assume all sales revenue is received in cash, all operating costs and income taxes are paid in cash, and all cash flows occur at the end of the year.

	Year 0	Year 1	Year 2	Year 3	Year 4
Investment	$10,000	—	—	—	—
Sales revenue	—	$7,000	$7,000	$7,000	$7,000
Operating costs	—	2,000	2,000	2,000	2,000
Depreciation	—	2,500	2,500	2,500	2,500
Net working capital (end of year)	200	250	300	200	—

a. Compute the incremental net income of the investment for each year.

b. Compute the incremental cash flows of the investment for each year.

c. Suppose the appropriate discount rate is 12 percent. What is the NPV of the project?

7.4   According to the February 7, 2002, issue of *The Sports Universe,* the Seattle Mariner's designated runner, Andy Schneider, signed a three-year contract in January 2002 with the following provisions:

a. $1,400,000 signing bonus

b. $2,500,000 salary per year for three years

c. 10 years of deferred payments of $1,250,000 per year (these payments begin in year 4)

d. Several bonus provisions that total as much as $750,000 per year for the three years of the contract

Assume that Schneider has a 60-percent probability of receiving the bonuses each year, and that he signed the contract on January 1, 2002. Use the expected value of the bonuses as incremental cash flows. Assume that expected cash flows are discounted at 12.36 percent. Ignore taxes. Schneider's signing bonus was paid on January 1, 2002. Schneider's salary and bonuses other than the signing bonus are paid at the end of the year. What was the present value of this contract in January when Schneider signed it?

7.5   Benson Enterprises is evaluating alternative uses for a three-story manufacturing and warehousing building that it has purchased for $225,000. The company can continue to rent the building to the present occupants for $12,000 per year. The present occupants have indicated an interest in staying in the building for at least another 15 years. Alternatively, the company could modify the existing structure to use for its own manufacturing and warehousing needs. Benson's production engineer feels the building could be adapted to handle one of two new product lines. The cost and revenue data for the two product alternatives are as follows:

	Product A	Product B
Initial cash outlay for building modifications	$ 36,000	$ 54,000
Initial cash outlay for equipment	144,000	162,000
Annual pretax cash revenues (generated for 15 years)	105,000	127,500
Annual pretax expenditures (generated for 15 years)	60,000	75,000

The building will be used for only 15 years for either Product A or Product B. After 15 years, the building will be too small for efficient production of either product line. At that time, Benson plans to rent the building to firms similar to the current occupants. To rent the building again, Benson will need to restore the building to its present layout. The estimated cash cost of restoring the building if Product A has been undertaken is $3,750. If Product B has been manufactured, the cash cost will be $28,125. These cash costs can be deducted for tax purposes in the year the expenditures occur.

Benson will depreciate the original building shell (purchased for $225,000) over a 30-year life to zero, regardless of which alternative it chooses. The building modifications and equipment purchases for either product are estimated to have a 15-year life. They will be depreciated by the straight-line method. The firm's tax rate is 34 percent, and its required rate of return on such investments is 12 percent.

For simplicity, assume all cash flows occur at the end of the year. The initial outlays for modifications and equipment will occur today (year 0), and the restoration outlays will occur at the end of year 15. Benson has other profitable ongoing operations that are sufficient to cover any losses. Which use of the building would you recommend to management?

7.6   Dickinson Brothers, Inc., is considering investing in a machine to produce computer keyboards. The price of the machine will be $400,000 and its economic life is five years. The machine will be fully depreciated by the straight-line method. The machine will produce 10,000 keyboards each year. The price of each keyboard will be $40 in the first year and will increase by 5 percent per year. The production cost per keyboard will be $20 in the first year and will increase by 10 percent per year. The corporate tax rate for the company is 34 percent. If the appropriate discount rate is 15 percent, what is the NPV of the investment?

7.7   Scott Investors, Inc., is considering the purchase of a $500,000 computer with an economic life of five years. The computer will be fully depreciated over five years using the straight-line method. The market value of the computer will be $100,000 in five years. The computer will replace five office employees whose combined annual salaries are $120,000. The machine will also immediately lower the firm's required net working capital by $100,000. This amount of net working capital will need to be replaced once the machine is sold. The corporate tax rate is 34 percent. Is it worthwhile to buy the computer if the appropriate discount rate is 12 percent?

7.8   The Gap is considering buying cash register software from Microsoft so that it can more effectively deal with its retail sales. The software package costs $750,000 and will be depreciated down to zero using the straight-line method over its five-year economic life. The marketing department predicts that sales will be $600,000 per year for the next three years, after which the market will cease to exist. Cost of goods sold and operating expenses are predicted to be 25 percent of sales. After three years the software can be sold for $40,000. The Gap also needs to add net working capital of $25,000 immediately. The additional net working capital will be recovered in full at the end of the project life. The corporate tax rate for the Gap is 35 percent and the required rate of return relevant to the project is 17 percent. What is the NPV of the new software?

7.9   Commercial Real Estate, Inc., is considering the purchase of a $4 million building. The company will enter into a long-term lease to commercial tenants, with payments made annually. The building will be fully depreciated over 20 years via the straight-line method. In addition, the market value of the building will be zero at that time. The annual lease payments will increase at 3 percent per year. The appropriate discount rate for all cash flows is 12 percent. The corporate tax rate is 34 percent. What is the least amount of money that Commercial Real Estate should ask for the first-year lease payment? Assume that the first lease payment is made immediately after the signing of the contract.

7.10 Royal Dutch Petroleum is considering a new project that complements its existing business. The machine required for the project costs $2 million. The marketing department predicts that sales related to the project will be $1.2 million per year for the next four years, after which the market will cease to exist. The machine will be depreciated down to zero over its five-year economic life using the straight-line method. Cost of goods sold and operating expenses related to the project are predicted to be 25 percent of sales. After four years the machine can be sold for $150,000. Royal Dutch also needs to add net working capital of $100,000 immediately. The additional net working capital will be recovered in full at the end of the project's life. The corporate tax rate is 35 percent. The required rate of return for Royal Dutch Petroleum is 16.55 percent. Should Royal Dutch proceed with the project?

7.11 Majestic Mining Corporation (MMC) is negotiating the purchase of a new piece of equipment for its current operations. MMC wants to know the maximum price that it should be willing to pay for the equipment. You are given the following facts:
  a. The new equipment would replace existing equipment with a current market value of $20,000.
  b. The new equipment would not affect revenues, but before-tax operating costs would be reduced by $10,000 per year for eight years. These savings in cost occur at year-end.
  c. The old equipment is now five years old. It is expected to last for another eight years, and will have no resale value at that time. It was purchased for $40,000 and is being depreciated to zero by the straight-line method over 10 years.
  d. The new equipment will be depreciated to zero by the straight-line method over five years. MMC expects to sell the equipment for $5,000 at the end of eight years. The proceeds from this sale will be subject to taxes at the ordinary corporate income tax rate of 34 percent.
  e. MMC has profitable ongoing operations.
  f. The appropriate discount rate is 8 percent.

7.12 A firm is considering an investment of $28 million (purchase price) in new equipment to replace old equipment with a book value of $12 million and a market value of $20 million. If the firm replaces the old equipment with the new equipment, it expects to save $17.5 million in operating costs the first year. The amount of these savings will grow at a rate of 12 percent per year for each of the following three years. The old equipment has a remaining life of four years. It is being depreciated by the straight-line method. 33.3 percent of the original book value of the new equipment will be depreciated in the first year, 39.9 percent will be depreciated in the second year, 14.8 percent will be depreciated in the third year, and 12.0 percent will be depreciated in the final year. The salvage value of both the old equipment and the new equipment at the end of four years is 0. In addition, replacement of the old equipment with the new equipment requires an immediate increase in net working capital of $5 million, which will not be recovered until the end of the four-year investment. Assume that the purchase and sale of equipment occurs today and all other cash flows occur at the end of their respective years. If the firm's cost of capital is 14 percent and is subject to a 40 percent tax rate, find:

a. The net investment.

b. The after-tax incremental cash flow at the end of each year.

c. The internal rate of return on the investment.

d. The net present value of the investment.

7.13 Shoe-tek, Inc., is a leading manufacturer of running shoes. With the baby boomers getting older, they realized the potential market in shoes specifically designed for walking rather than running. Market research suggests that the walking shoe market will be $100 million and Shoe-tek could capture 20 percent of this market because of its strong brand. However, it is estimated that 10 percent of Shoe-tek's current sales of running shoes are already being used by baby boomers for walking. If Shoe-tek introduces a walking shoe, half of these consumers would switch from Shoe-tek's running shoe to walking shoes. Shoe-tek has already spent $10 million on R&D for its running shoes and could leverage this and produce a totally new walking shoe for an additional $1 million in R&D. Shoe-tek would also need to construct an extension to their warehouse to accommodate the additional materials and inventory. This extension would cost $1 million. If annual revenues for Shoe-tek are $80 million, what is the amount to use as the annual sales figure when evaluating this project? Why?

7.14 Carson Palmer, the 2002 Heisman Trophy winner, was the #1 draft pick in the NFL. His agent was asking for a five-year contract with the following provisions:

- $5 million signing bonus
- $2 million a year salary
- Several bonus provisions that total as much as $2 million a year, for each of the five years

Assume that Carson has a 50 percent probability of receiving the entire bonus each year and that he signs the contract on January 1. Also, assume an effective annual interest rate of 12 percent and ignore taxes. Carson's salary and bonus are paid at the end of the year. What is the present value of Carson's contract in January?

7.15 With the growing popularity of casual surf print clothing, two recent MBA graduates decided to broaden this casual surf concept to encompass a "surf lifestyle for the home." With limited capital, they decided to focus on surf print table and floor lamps to accent people's homes. They projected unit sales of these lamps to be 5,000 in the first year, with growth of 15 percent each year, for the next five years. Production of these lamps will require $28,000 in net working capital to start, and additional net working capital investments each year equal to 40 percent of the projected sales increase for that year. Total fixed costs are $75,000 per year, variable production costs are $20 per unit, and the units are priced at $45 each. The equipment needed to begin production will cost $60,000. The equipment will be depreciated using a straight-line method over a five-year life and is not expected to have a salvage value. The effective tax rate is 34 percent and the required rate of return is 25 percent. What is the NPV of this project?

7.16 The Big Burrito is planning to purchase a touch screen order system for its drive-thru window that would allow customers to select their order as soon as they arrive. This would reduce customer wait time and increase order accuracy. The touch screen and software would cost the Big Burrito $150,000 and would last five years. There would also be an annual maintenance cost of $5,000. In addition to improved customer service, the Big Burrito would gain two benefits. First, they could totally eliminate the full-time worker who used to accept and enter these orders. His annual salary plus benefits total $30,000 per year. Second, they expect drive-thru sales to increase by $15,000 a year due to improved customer perception and increased through-put. Cost of goods sold is 25 percent of the incremental sales. Net working capital (NWC) is expected to increase by $5,000 in the first year and be recovered at the end of five years. If the appropriate discount rate is 15 percent and you ignore taxes, should the Big Burrito go ahead with this investment?

7.17 A new basketball star, Jun, is coming from Seoul, Korea! The following are the provisions of his four-year deal with the San Francisco Golden Gates!

> $500,000 signing bonus
>
> $800,000 salary per year for four years.
>
> 8 years of deferred payments of $100,000 per year beginning year 5.
>
> Several bonus provisions that total about $150,000 per year for the four years of the contract.

Assuming that Jun has a 55 percent chance of receiving the bonus each year, and that he signed the contract on January 1, what is the present value of his contract at signing? Jun's salary and bonus are paid at the end of each year. The effective annual interest rate is at 10.5 percent. Please ignore taxes.

7.18 Maruta is considering the purchase of a $1.5 million automation machine for its popular Kamury sedan line. The automation machine will have a useful life of five years and will depreciate based on the system enacted by the Tax Reform Act of 1986. (See Table 7.3 for the depreciation schedules.) The market value of the automation machine will be $0.4 million in five years. On the benefit side, the automation machine will replace 20 factory workers, whose annual salaries are $0.3 million. In addition, the use of the machine will lower net working capital requirements by $0.5 million, although that requirement will return to normal after the five years. The corporate tax rate is 34 percent.

Is it worthwhile to purchase the automation machine if the discount rate is 15 percent?

7.19 Raphael Restaurant is considering the purchase of a $10,000 souffle maker. The souffle maker has an economic life of five years and will be fully depreciated by the straight-line method. The machine will produce 2,000 souffles per year, with each costing $2 to make and priced at $5. As for additional cost, the increase in net working capital requirements is $1,000, which will be fully recovered at the end of year 5. Assume that the discount rate is 17 percent and the tax rate is 34 percent.

Is it worthwhile for Raphael to make the purchase?

7.20 Galweiser Glass is considering adding a machine that will make 2.0 liter glass bottles. The machine will cost $1 million and will produce 2 million bottles per year with each bottle costing $0.10. The useful economic life of the machine is five years, which will be depreciated straight-line with no salvage value. The increase in net working capital requirements is $10,000, which will be fully recovered at the end of year 5. Assume that the discount rate is 13 percent and the tax rate is 34 percent.

a. At what price per bottle will the NPV of the machine be 0?

b. If the market value per bottle is $0.25, is it worthwhile for Galweiser to make the investment?

CAPITAL BUDGETING WITH INFLATION

7.21 Consider the following cash flows on two mutually exclusive projects.

Year	Project A	Project B
0	−$40,000	−$50,000
1	20,000	10,000
2	15,000	20,000
3	15,000	40,000

The cash flows of Project A are expressed in real terms while those of Project B are expressed in nominal terms. The appropriate nominal discount rate is 15 percent and the inflation rate is 4 percent. Which project should you choose?

7.22 Etonic Inc. is considering an investment of $250,000 in an asset with an economic life of five years. The firm estimates that the nominal annual cash revenues and expenses at the end of the first year will be $200,000 and $50,000, respectively. Both revenues and expenses will grow thereafter at the annual inflation rate of 3 percent. Etonic will use the straight-line method to depreciate its asset to zero over five years. The salvage value of the asset is estimated to be $30,000 in nominal terms at that time. The one-time net working capital investment of $10,000 is required immediately and will be recovered at the end of the project. The nominal discount rate for all cash flows is 15 percent. All corporate cash flows are subject to a 34 percent tax rate. What is the project's total nominal cash flow from assets in year 5?

7.23 Sanders Enterprises, Inc. has been considering the purchase of a new manufacturing facility for $120,000. The facility is to be fully depreciated on a straight-line basis over seven years. It is expected to have no resale value after the seven years. Operating revenues from the facility are expected to be $50,000, in nominal terms, at the end of the first year. The revenues are expected to increase at the inflation rate of 5 percent. Production costs at the end of the first year will be $20,000, in nominal terms, and they are expected to increase at 7 percent per year. The real discount rate is 14 percent. The corporate tax rate is 34 percent. Sanders has other ongoing, profitable operations. Should the company accept the project?

7.24 Phillips Industries runs a small manufacturing operation. For this fiscal year, it expects real net cash flows of $120,000. Phillips is an ongoing operation, but it expects competitive pressures to erode its real net cash flows at 6 percent per year in perpetuity. The appropriate real discount rate for Phillips is 11 percent. All net cash flows are received at year-end. What is the present value of the net cash flows from Phillips's operations?

7.25 The Biological Insect Control Corporation (BICC) has hired you as a consultant to evaluate the NPV of their proposed toad ranch. BICC plans to breed toads and sell them as ecologically desirable insect-control mechanisms. They anticipate that the business will continue into perpetuity. Following the negligible start-up costs, BICC expects the following nominal cash flows at the end of the year.

Revenues	$150,000
Labor costs	80,000
Other costs	40,000

The company will lease machinery for $20,000 per year. The lease payments start at the end of year 1 and are expressed in nominal terms. Revenues will increase by 5 percent per year in real terms. Labor costs will increase by 3 percent per year in real terms. Other costs will decrease by 1 percent per year in real terms. The rate of inflation is expected to be 6 percent per year. BICC's required rate of return is 10 percent in real terms. There are no taxes. All cash flows occur at year-end. What is the NPV of BICC's proposed toad ranch today?

7.26 Sony International has an investment opportunity to produce a new stereo color TV. The required investment on January 1 of this year is $32 million. The firm will depreciate the investment to zero using the straight-line method over four years. The investment has no resale value after completion of the project. The firm is in the 34 percent tax bracket. The price of the product will be $400 per unit, in real terms, and will not change over the life of the project. Labor costs for Year 1 will be $15.30 per hour, in real terms, and will increase at 2 percent per year in real terms. Energy costs for Year 1 will be $5.15 per physical unit, in real terms, and will increase at 3 percent per year in real terms. The inflation rate is 5 percent per year. Revenues are received and costs are paid at year-end. Refer to the table below for the production schedule.

	Year 1	Year 2	Year 3	Year 4
Physical production, in units	100,000	200,000	200,000	150,000
Labor input, in hours	2,000,000	2,000,000	2,000,000	2,000,000
Energy input, physical units	200,000	200,000	200,000	200,000

The real discount rate for Sony is 8 percent. Calculate the NPV of this project.

Visit us at www.mhhe.com/rwj

7.27 Sparkling Water, Inc., expects to sell 2 million bottles of drinking water each year in perpetuity. This year, each bottle will sell for $2.50 in real terms and will cost $0.70 in real terms. Sales income and costs occur at year-end. Revenues will rise at a real rate of 7 percent annually, while real costs will rise at a real rate of 5 percent annually. The real discount rate is 10 percent. The corporate tax rate is 34 percent. What is Sparkling worth today?

7.28 International Buckeyes is building a factory that can make 1 million buckeyes a year for five years, after which the market will cease to exist. The factory costs $6 million, paid immediately. In year 1, each buckeye will sell for $3.15 in nominal terms. The price will increase 5 percent each year in real terms. Variable costs will be $0.2625 per buckeye in nominal terms in year 1 and will rise by 2 percent each subsequent year in real terms. International Buckeyes will fully depreciate the factory over five years by the straight-line method. The firm will be able to sell the factory for $638,140.78 in nominal terms at the end of year 5. The nominal discount rate for cash flows is 20 percent. The rate of inflation is 5 percent. Cash flows, except for the initial investment, occur at the end of each year. The corporate tax rate is 34 percent. What is the NPV of the project?

7.29 After extensive medical and marketing research, Pill, Inc. believes it can penetrate the pain reliever market. It is considering two alternative products. The first is to produce a medication for headache pain. The second is a pill for headache and arthritis pain. Both products would be introduced at a price of $4 per package in real terms. The headache-only medication is projected to sell 5 million packages a year, while the headache and arthritis remedy would sell 10 million packages a year. Cash costs of production in the first year are expected to be $1.50 per package in real terms for the headache-only brand. Production costs are expected to be $1.70 in real terms for the headache and arthritis pill. All prices and costs are expected to rise at the general inflation rate of 5 percent.

Either product requires further investment. The headache-only pill could be produced using equipment costing $10.2 million. That equipment would last three years and have no resale value. The machinery required to produce the broader remedy would cost $12 million and last three years. The firm expects that equipment to have a $1 million resale value (in real terms) at the end of year 3.

Pill, Inc., uses straight-line depreciation. The firm faces a corporate tax rate of 34 percent and believes that the appropriate real discount rate is 13 percent. Which pain reliever should the firm produce?

EQUIVALENT ANNUAL COST AND REPLACEMENT WITH UNEQUAL LIVES

7.30 A machine with a four-year life is purchased for $12,000. The annual year-end operating cost is $6,000. At the end of four years, the machine is sold for $2,000. The cash outflows each year can be represented as follows:

C_0	C_1	C_2	C_3	C_4
$12,000	$6,000	$6,000	$6,000	$4,000

The cost of capital is 6 percent. Ignore taxes. What is the present value of the cost of operating a series of such machines in perpetuity?

7.31 A machine costs $60,000 and requires $5,000 maintenance for each year of its three-year life. The maintenance costs are paid at the end of each year. After three years, the machine will be replaced. Assume a tax rate of 34 percent and a discount rate of 14 percent. If the machine is depreciated over three years using the straight-line method, with no salvage value, what is the equivalent annual cost (EAC)?

7.32 United Healthcare, Inc., needs a new admitting system. The system costs $60,000, requires $2,000 in maintenance for each year of its five-year economic life, and has no salvage value. The maintenance costs are paid at the end of each year. The system will be fully depreciated using the straight-line method over five years. Assume a tax rate of 35 percent and an annual discount rate of 18 percent. What is the equivalent annual cost of this admitting system?

7.33   Bridgton Golf Academy is evaluating different golf practice equipment. The "Dimple-Max" equipment costs $45,000, has a three-year life, and costs $5,000 per year to operate. The relevant discount rate is 12 percent. Assume that the straight-line depreciation method is used and that the equipment is fully depreciated to zero. Furthermore, assume the equipment has a salvage value of $10,000 at the end of the project's life. The relevant tax rate for income and capital gains is 34 percent. All cash flows occur at the end of the year. What is the equivalent annual cost (EAC) of this equipment?

7.34   Office Automation, Inc., must choose between two copiers, the XX40 or the RH45. The XX40 costs less than the RH45, but its economic life is shorter. The costs and maintenance expenses of these two copiers, expressed in real terms, are given as follows:

Copier	Year 0	Year 1	Year 2	Year 3	Year 4	Year 5
XX40	$700	$100	$100	$100	—	—
RH45	$900	$110	$110	$110	$110	$110

All cash flows occur at year-end. The inflation rate is 5 percent, and the nominal discount rate is 14 percent. Assume that revenues are the same regardless of the copier, and assume that whichever copier the company chooses, it will continue to buy that model forever. Which copier should the company choose? Ignore taxes and depreciation.

7.35   Plexi Glasses, Inc., must choose between two facilities. Facility 1 costs $2.1 million and has an economic life of seven years. The maintenance costs for Facility 1 are $60,000 per year. Facility 2 costs $2.8 million and has an economic life of 10 years. The annual maintenance costs for Facility 2 are $100,000 per year. Both facilities will be fully depreciated to zero by the straight-line method. The facilities will have no resale values at the end of their economic lives. The corporate tax rate is 34 percent. Revenues from the facilities are the same. The company is assumed to earn sufficient revenues to generate tax shields from depreciation. Assume all cash flows besides the initial investment occur at the end of the year. If the appropriate discount rate is 10 percent, which facility should Plexi Glasses, Inc., choose?

7.36   Pilot Plus Pens is deciding when to replace its old machine. The old machine's current salvage value is $2 million. Its current book value is $1 million. If not sold, the old machine will require maintenance costs of $400,000 at the end of the year for the next five years. Depreciation on the old machine is $200,000 per year. At the end of five years, the old machine will have a salvage value of $200,000 and a book value of $0. A replacement machine costs $3 million now and requires maintenance costs of $500,000 at the end of each year during its economic life of five years. At the end of the five years, the new machine will have a salvage value of $500,000. It will be fully depreciated by the straight-line method. In five years, a replacement machine will cost $3,500,000. Pilot will need to purchase this machine regardless of what choice it makes today. The corporate tax rate is 34 percent and the appropriate discount rate is 12 percent. The company is assumed to earn sufficient revenues to generate tax shields from depreciation. Should Pilot Plus Pens replace the old machine now or at the end of five years?

7.37   Gold Star Industries is contemplating a purchase of computers. The firm has narrowed its choices to the SAL 5000 and the DET 1000. Gold Star would need 10 SALs, where each SAL costs $3,750 and requires $500 of maintenance each year. At the end of the computer's eight-year life, Gold Star expects to sell each one for $500. Alternatively, Gold Star could buy eight DETs. Each DET costs $5,250 and requires $700 of maintenance every year. Each DET lasts for six years and has a resale value of $600 at the end of its economic life. Gold Star will continue to purchase the model that it chooses today into perpetuity. Ignore tax effects and assume that the maintenance costs occur at year-end. Which model should Gold Star buy if the appropriate discount rate is 11 percent?

7.38   Harwell University must purchase word processors for its typing lab. The university can buy 10 EVF word processors that cost $8,000 each and have annual, year-end maintenance costs of $2,000 per machine. The EVF word processors will be replaced at the end of year 4 and have no value at that time. Alternatively, Harwell can buy 11 AEH word processors to accomplish the same work. The AEH word processors will be replaced after three years. They each cost $5,000, and have annual, year-end maintenance costs of $2,500 per machine. Each AEH word processor will have a resale value of $500 at the end of three years. The university's opportunity cost of funds for this type of investment is 14 percent. Because the university is a nonprofit institution, it does not pay taxes. It is anticipated that whichever manufacturer is chosen now will be the supplier of future machines. Would you recommend purchasing 10 EVF word processors or 11 AEH machines?

7.39   DJ Party, Inc., is considering the replacement of its old, fully depreciated sound mixer. Two new models are available. Mixer X costs $400,000, has a five-year economic life, and yields cash flow savings of $120,000 per year. Mixer Y costs $600,000, has an eight-year economic life, and yields cash flow savings of $130,000 per year. No new technological developments are expected. Ignore taxes. The cost of capital is 11 percent. Should DJ Party, Inc., replace the old mixer with X or Y?

7.40   KZD Construction must choose between two pieces of equipment. Tamper A costs $600,000 and lasts five years. This tamper requires $110,000 of maintenance each year. Tamper B costs $750,000, but lasts 7 years. Maintenance costs for Tamper B are $90,000 per year. All maintenance costs occur at the end of the year. The appropriate discount rate for KZD Construction is 12 percent. Ignore taxes. Which machine should KZD purchase?

7.41   Klious Pharmaceuticals must decide when to replace its autoclave. Klious's current autoclave will require increasing amounts of maintenance at the end of each year. The resale value of the equipment falls every year. For example, if the firm replaces the old machine today, it will incur no maintenance costs related to the old machine and will be able to sell it immediately for $900. If the firm replaces the old machine at the end of the first year, it will incur maintenance costs of $200 and be able to sell the machine for $850. Refer to the following table for complete data:

Year	Maintenance Costs	Resale Value
0 (Today)	$ 0	$900
1	200	850
2	275	775
3	325	700
4	450	600
5	500	500

In any year, Klious can purchase a new autoclave for $3,000. The equipment has an economic life of five years. At the end of each year, the equipment requires $20 of maintenance. Klious expects to sell the machine for $1,200 at the end of five years. Klious pays no taxes and employs a discount rate of 10 percent. Maintenance costs and the realization of the resale value occur at the end of each year. (Note: the forgone resale value occurs at the beginning of each year.) When should Klious replace its current machine?

MINICASES   Goodweek Tires, Inc.

After extensive research and development, Goodweek Tires, Inc., has recently developed a new tire, the SuperTread, and must decide whether to make the investment necessary to produce and market the SuperTread. The tire would be ideal for drivers doing a large amount of wet weather and off-road driving in addition to its normal freeway usage. The research and development costs so far total about $10 million. The SuperTread would be put on the market beginning this year and Goodweek expects it to stay on the market for a total of four years. Test marketing costing $5 million shows that there is a significant market for a SuperTread-type tire.

As a financial analyst at Goodweek Tires, you are asked by your CFO, Mr. Adam Smith, to evaluate the SuperTread project and provide a recommendation on whether to go ahead with the investment. You are informed that all previous investments in the SuperTread are sunk costs and only future cash flows should be considered. Except for the initial investment which will occur immediately, assume all cash flows will occur at year-end.

Goodweek must initially invest $120 million in production equipment to make the SuperTread. The equipment is expected to have a seven-year useful life. This equipment can be sold for $51,428,571 at the end of four years. Goodweek intends to sell the SuperTread to two distinct markets:

1. *The Original Equipment Manufacturer (OEM) Market* The OEM market consists primarily of the large automobile companies (e.g., General Motors) who buy tires for new cars. In the OEM market, the SuperTread is expected to sell for $36 per tire. The variable cost to produce each tire is $18.

2. *The Replacement Market* The replacement market consists of all tires purchased after the automobile has left the factory. This market allows higher margins and Goodweek expects to sell the SuperTread for $59 per tire there. Variable costs are the same as in the OEM market.

Goodweek Tires intends to raise prices at 1 percent *above* the inflation rate. Variable costs will also increase 1 percent *above* the inflation rate. In addition, the SuperTread project will incur $25 million in marketing and general administration costs the first year (this figure is expected to increase at the inflation rate in the subsequent years).

Goodweek's corporate tax rate is 40 percent. Annual inflation is expected to remain constant at 3.25 percent. The company uses a 15.9 percent discount rate to evaluate new product decisions.

The Tire Market

Automotive industry analysts expect automobile manufacturers to produce 2 million new cars this year and production to grow at 2.5 percent per year thereafter. Each new car needs four tires (the spare tires are undersized and are in a different category). Goodweek Tires expects the SuperTread to capture 11 percent of the OEM market.

Industry analysts estimate that the replacement tire market size will be 14 million tires this year and that it will grow at 2 percent annually. Goodweek expects the SuperTread to capture an 8 percent market share.

You decide to use the MACRS depreciation schedule (seven-year property class). You also decide to consider net working capital (NWC) requirements in this scenario. The immediate initial working capital requirement is $11 million, and thereafter the net working capital requirements will be 15 percent of sales. What will be the NPV, payback period, discounted payback period, AAR, IRR, and PI on this project?

I.Q., Inc.

In order to maintain its leadership position in the computer peripherals industry, particularly inkjet printers and accessories, I.Q. has begun to develop a new ink for its 8xx line of inkjet printers. As a marketing manager of the 8xx line of inkjet printers and accessories, you are in the position to make a decision whether or not to continue the development. The project is codenamed IQ8Ink.

Research efforts for the IQ8Ink has cost I.Q., Inc., $1 million so far, in addition to a positive test marketing effort costing $0.5 million. However, these are sunk costs and will not impact your decision making. What should be considered are the new investment and future cash inflows. From your observation, you know that you can invest immediately and start production now. You also know that the economic life of this effort is only four years, meaning potentially four years of production.

I.Q.'s CEO K. Fione is very pleased with the progress of the 8xx line so far and wishes to congratulate you on a job well done. So, the decision on the development of IQ8Ink is critical. From engineering, you know that you will need to invest another $1 million in production equipment to make this new ink. The equipment will have a useful life of five years and will depreciate by the straight-line method. At year 4, you expect to sell the equipment for $0.3 million. Furthermore, the net working capital requirement will increase by $1 million immediately and will be recaptured at year 4.

As for the potential customers, there are two distinct segments:

1. New 8xx printers—For every new 8xx printer, one unit of this new ink will be used. (Assume complete retirement of old ink models with no costs associated.) Internal transfer price is at $2 now. The variable cost to produce per unit is $0.50.
2. Existing 8xx printers—While competitors exist, offering generic ink, IQ8Ink is superior and will take a large percentage of market share. Wholesale price is at $10 now. The variable cost to produce per unit is the same as above.

Note that on average, ink price and cost rise at 2 percent above the inflation rate. In addition, marketing and administration efforts will cost $0.5 million the first year and increase at inflation each subsequent year.

From economic data, inflation is expected to remain constant at 3 percent. I.Q.'s corporate tax rate is 34 percent and the division has a discount rate of 15 percent.

Last, you know that production of new 8xx printers will be 300,000 units in the first year and will increase by 10 percent per year. Additionally, the demand for ink from existing 8xx printers is 1 million units in the first year and increases by 10 percent per year. Out of the demand for ink from existing 8xx printers, I.Q. expects to capture 80 percent.

Jimmy's Hot Dog Stands

Jimmy Levitin owns a popular hot dog stand on a trendy section of Melrose Boulevard. Following the success of his first hot dog stand, "Jimmy's," which has been in operations for five years, Jimmy is now considering opening a second hot dog stand in another trendy location, on Sunset Boulevard in the Silver Lake area. Jimmy's market research shows that the clientele in both areas is similar: young professionals, typically without children, who like the traditional aspect of eating hot dogs, but also relish his gourmet, specially manufactured low-fat dogs and the healthy side dishes his stand also sells. Jimmy's overall plan is to get the second stand up and running for five years, and then sell both stands off to a new owner and retire to Santa Barbara.

Jimmy estimates that the cost of starting up a second stand will be as follows:

Purchase of real estate (retail food outlet)	$400,000
Installation of specialized kitchen equipment	40,000
Furniture and fittings	25,000

Jimmy estimates that net working capital will increase by $20,000 for the first year for the new outlet. He also estimates that yearly operating costs of the new location would be almost identical to those of his current stand:

Labor costs, inclusive of all overhead costs:	
Kitchen and service staff (4 persons)	$ 96,000
Raw materials:	
Hot dogs: 200 per day × 7 days × 52 weeks	54,600
Drinks	18,400
Other food supplies	72,800
Nonfood supplies	22,200
Total raw materials	$168,000
The revenues at his current location are as follows:	
Sales of hot dogs and other food items	$418,000
Drinks	92,000
Total revenues	$510,000

In addition to contributing profits, Jimmy expects that opening a second stand will decrease the cost of purchasing gourmet hot dogs from 75 cents to 60 cents in both locations. This is due to economies of scale, since the new outlet would double output over the current level of demand. Jimmy also expects that he will be able to manage both locations himself, avoiding hiring a second manager for the new location.

Assume that:

- The marginal tax rate is 34 percent.
- The required rate of return is 10 percent.
- Depreciate over five years using the straight-line method.

What is the NPV of this investment?

Appendix 7A

Depreciation

The Baldwin case made some assumptions about depreciation. Where did these assumptions come from? Assets are currently depreciated for tax purposes according to the provisions of the 1986 Tax Reform Act. There are seven classes of depreciable property.

- The three-year class includes certain specialized short-lived property. Tractor units and racehorses over two years old are among the very few items fitting into this class.
- The five-year class includes (a) cars and trucks; (b) computers and peripheral equipment, as well as calculators, copiers, and typewriters; and (c) specific items used for research purposes.
- The seven-year class includes office furniture, equipment, books, and single-purpose agricultural structures. It is also a catch-all category, because any asset not designated to be in another class is included here.
- The 10-year class includes vessels, barges, tugs, and similar equipment related to water transportation.
- The 15-year class encompasses a variety of specialized items. Included are equipment of telephone distribution plants and similar equipment used for voice and data communications, and sewage treatment plants.
- The 20-year class includes farm buildings, sewer pipe, and other very long-lived equipment.

Visit us at www.mhhe.com/rwj

- Real property that is depreciable is separated into two classes: residential and nonresidential. The cost of residential property is recovered over 27½ years and non-residential property over 31½ years.

Items in the three-, five-, and seven-year classes are depreciated using the 200-percent declining-balance method, with a switch to straight-line depreciation at a point specified in the Tax Reform Act. Items in the 15- and 20-year classes are depreciated using the 150-percent declining-balance method, with a switch to straight-line depreciation at a specified point. All real estate is depreciated on a straight-line basis.

All calculations of depreciation include a half-year convention, which treats all property as if it were placed in service at midyear. To be consistent, the IRS allows half a year of depreciation for the year in which property is disposed of or retired. The effect of this is to spread the deductions for property over one year more than the name of its class, for example, six tax years for five-year property.

Risk Analysis, Real Options, and Capital Budgeting

EXECUTIVE SUMMARY

Chapters 6 and 7 covered the basic principles of capital budgeting, with particular emphasis on the net present value (NPV) approach. However, this is not the end of the story. Real-world practitioners often wonder how much confidence they should place in NPV calculations. This chapter examines sensitivity analysis, scenario analysis, break-even analysis, and Monte Carlo simulations, all of which help the practitioner determine the degree of confidence to be placed in a capital budgeting calculation.

Information is uncovered as a project unfolds, allowing a manager to make sequential decisions over the life of the project. This chapter covers decision trees and real options, capital budgeting techniques that specifically take the sequential nature of decision-making into account.

8.1 Decision Trees

There is usually a sequence of decisions in NPV project analysis. This section introduces the device of **decision trees** for identifying these sequential decisions.

Imagine you are the treasurer of the Solar Electronics Corporation (SEC), and the engineering group has recently developed the technology for solar-powered jet engines. The jet engine is to be used with 150-passenger commercial airplanes. The marketing staff has proposed that SEC develop some prototypes and conduct test marketing of the engine. A corporate planning group, including representatives from production, marketing, and engineering, estimates that this preliminary phase will take a year and will cost $100 million. Furthermore, the group believes there is a 75-percent chance that the marketing tests will prove successful.

If the initial marketing tests are *successful*, SEC can go ahead with full-scale production. This investment phase will cost $1,500 million. Production and sales will occur over the next five years. The preliminary cash flow projection appears in Table 8.1. Should SEC go ahead with investment and production on the jet engine, the NPV at a discount rate of 15 percent (in millions) is

$$
\begin{aligned}
\text{NPV} &= -\$1,500 + \sum_{t=1}^{5} \frac{\$900}{(1.15)^t} \\
&= -\$1,500 + \$900 \times A_{0.15}^5 \\
&= \$1,517
\end{aligned}
$$

TABLE 8.1	Investment	Year 1	Years 2–6
Cash Flow Forecasts for Solar Electronics Corporation's Jet Engine Base Case (millions)*	Revenues		$6,000
	Variable costs		(3,000)
	Fixed costs		(1,791)
	Depreciation		(300)
	Pretax profit		909
	Tax ($T_c = 0.34$)		(309)
	Net profit		$ 600
	Cash flow		$ 900
	Initial investment costs	−$1,500	

*Assumptions: (1) Investment is depreciated in years 2 through 6 using the straight-line method; (2) tax rate is 34 percent; (3) the company receives no tax benefits on initial development costs.

FIGURE 8.1	
Decision Tree ($ millions) for SEC	

Squares represent decision points. Circle represents receipt of information.
SEC must make 2 decisions:
  1. Whether to develop and test engine
  2. Whether to invest for full-scale production

Note that the NPV is calculated as of date 1, the date at which the investment of $1,500 million is made. Later we bring this number back to date 0.

If the initial marketing tests are *unsuccessful,* SEC's $1,500 million investment has an NPV of −$3,611 million. This figure is also calculated as of date 1. (To save space, we will not provide the raw numbers leading to this calculation.)

Figure 8.1 displays the problem concerning the jet engine as a decision tree. If SEC decides to conduct test marketing, there is a 75-percent probability that the test marketing will be successful. If the tests are successful, the firm faces a second decision: whether to invest

$1,500 million in a project that yields $1,517 million NPV or to stop. If the tests are unsuccessful, the firm faces a different decision: whether to invest $1,500 million in a project that yields −$3,611 million NPV or to stop.

To review, SEC has the following two decisions to make:

1. Whether to develop and test the solar-powered jet engine.
2. Whether to invest for full-scale production following the results of the test.

One makes decisions in reverse order with decision trees. Thus we analyze the second-stage investment of $1,500 million first. If the tests are successful, should SEC make the second-stage investment? The answer is obviously yes, since $1,517 million is greater than zero. If the tests are unsuccessful, should the second-stage investment be made? Just as obviously, the answer is no, since −$3,611 million is below zero.

Now we move back to the first stage, where the decision boils down to the question: Should SEC invest $100 million now to obtain a 75-percent chance of $1,517 million one year later? The expected payoff evaluated at date 1 (in millions) is

$$\text{Expected payoff} = \begin{pmatrix} \text{Probability} \\ \text{of} \\ \text{success} \end{pmatrix} \times \begin{pmatrix} \text{Payoff} \\ \text{if} \\ \text{successful} \end{pmatrix} + \begin{pmatrix} \text{Probability} \\ \text{of} \\ \text{failure} \end{pmatrix} \times \begin{pmatrix} \text{Payoff} \\ \text{if} \\ \text{failure} \end{pmatrix}$$

$$= (0.75 \times \$1,517) + (0.25 \times \$0)$$
$$= \$1,138$$

The NPV of testing computed at date 0 (in millions) is

$$\text{NPV} = -\$100 + \frac{\$1,138}{1.15}$$
$$= \$890$$

Since the NPV is a positive number, the firm should test the market for solar-powered jet engines.

Warning   We have used a discount rate of 15 percent for both the testing and the investment decisions. Perhaps a higher discount rate should have been used for the initial test-marketing decision, which is likely to be riskier than the investment decision.

Concept Questions
1. What is a decision tree?
2. How do decision trees handle sequential decisions?

8.2 Sensitivity Analysis, Scenario Analysis, and Break-Even Analysis

One thrust of this book is that NPV analysis is a superior capital budgeting technique. In fact, because the NPV approach uses cash flows rather than profits, uses all the cash flows, and discounts the cash flows properly, it is hard to find any theoretical fault with it. However, in our conversations with practical businesspeople, we hear the phrase "a false sense of security" frequently. These people point out that the documentation for capital budgeting proposals is often quite impressive. Cash flows are projected down to the last thousand dollars (or even the last dollar) for each year (or even each month). Opportunity costs and side effects are handled quite properly. Sunk costs are ignored—also quite properly. When a high net present value appears at the bottom, one's temptation is to say yes immediately. Nevertheless, the projected cash flow often goes unmet in practice, and the firm ends up with a money loser.

Sensitivity Analysis and Scenario Analysis

How can the firm get the net-present-value technique to live up to its potential? One approach is **sensitivity analysis** (a.k.a. *what-if analysis* and *bop* analysis[1]), which examines how sensitive a particular NPV calculation is to changes in underlying assumptions. We illustrate the technique with Solar Electronics' solar-powered jet engine from the previous section. As pointed out earlier, the cash flow forecasts for this project appear in Table 8.1. We begin by considering the assumptions underlying revenues, costs, and after-tax cash flows shown in the table.

Revenues   Sales projections for the proposed jet engine have been estimated by the marketing department as

$$\begin{array}{ccccc} \text{Number of jet} & = & \text{Market Share} & \times & \text{Size of jet} \\ \text{engines sold} & & & & \text{engine market} \\ 3{,}000 & = & 0.30 & \times & 10{,}000 \end{array}$$

$$\begin{array}{ccccc} \text{Sales revenues} & = & \text{Number of jet} & \times & \text{Price per} \\ & & \text{engines sold} & & \text{engine} \\ \$6{,}000 \text{ million} & = & 3{,}000 & \times & \$2 \text{ million} \end{array}$$

Thus, it turns out that the revenue estimates depend on three assumptions.

1. Market share.
2. Size of jet engine market.
3. Price per engine.

Costs   Financial analysts frequently divide costs into two types: variable costs and fixed costs. **Variable costs** change as the output changes, and they are zero when production is zero. Costs of direct labor and raw materials are usually variable. It is common to assume that a variable cost is constant per unit of output, implying that total variable costs are proportional to the level of production. For example, if direct labor is variable and one unit of final output requires $10 of direct labor, then 100 units of final output should require $1,000 of direct labor.

Fixed costs are not dependent on the amount of goods or services produced during the period. Fixed costs are usually measured as costs per unit of time, such as rent per month or salaries per year. Naturally, fixed costs are not fixed forever. They are only fixed over a predetermined time period.

The engineering department has estimated variable costs to be $1 million per engine. Fixed costs are $1,791 million per year. The cost breakdowns are

$$\begin{array}{ccccc} \text{Variable} & = & \text{Variable cost} & \times & \text{Number of jet} \\ \text{cost} & & \text{per unit} & & \text{engines sold} \\ \$3{,}000 \text{ million} & = & \$1 \text{ million} & \times & 3{,}000 \end{array}$$

$$\begin{array}{ccccc} \text{Total cost before taxes} & = & \text{Variable cost} & + & \text{Fixed cost} \\ \$4{,}791 \text{ million} & = & \$3{,}000 \text{ million} & + & \$1{,}791 \text{ million} \end{array}$$

---

[1]Bop stands for best, optimistic, pessimistic.

TABLE 8.2	Variable	Pessimistic	Expected or Best	Optimistic
Different Estimates for Solar Electronics' Solar Plane	Market size (per year)	5,000	10,000	20,000
	Market share	20%	30%	50%
	Price	$1.9 million	$2 million	$2.2 million
	Variable cost (per plane)	$1.2 million	$1 million	$0.8 million
	Fixed cost (per year)	$1,891 million	$1,791 million	$1,741 million
	Investment	$1,900 million	$1,500 million	$1,000 million

TABLE 8.3		Pessimistic	Expected or Best	Optimistic
NPV Calculations as of Date 1	Market size	−$1,802*	$1,517	$8,154
(in $ millions) for the	Market share	−696*	1,517	5,942
Solar Plane Using	Price	853	1,517	2,844
Sensitivity Analysis	Variable cost	189	1,517	2,844
	Fixed cost	1,295	1,517	1,628
	Investment	1,208	1,517	1,903

Under sensitivity analysis, one input is varied while all other inputs are assumed to meet their expectation. For example, an NPV of −$1,802 occurs when the pessimistic forecast of 5,000 is used for market size. However, the expected forecasts from Table 8.2 are used for all other variables when −$1,802 is generated.

*We assume that the other divisions of the firm are profitable, implying that a loss on this project can offset income elsewhere in the firm, thereby reducing the overall taxes of the firm.

The above estimates for market size, market share, price, variable cost, and fixed cost, as well as the estimate of initial investment, are presented in the middle column of Table 8.2. These figures represent the firm's expectations or best estimates of the different parameters. For purposes of comparison, the firm's analysts prepared both optimistic and pessimistic forecasts for the different variables. These are also provided in the table.

Standard sensitivity analysis calls for an NPV calculation for all three possibilities of a single variable, along with the expected forecast for all other variables. This procedure is illustrated in Table 8.3. For example, consider the NPV calculation of $8,154 million provided in the upper right-hand corner of this table. This occurs when the optimistic forecast of 20,000 units per year is used for market size. However, the expected forecasts from Table 8.2 are employed for all other variables when the $8,154 million figure is generated. Note that the same number of $1,517 million appears in each row of the middle column of Table 8.3. This occurs because the expected forecast is used for the variable that was singled out, as well as for all other variables.

Table 8.3 can be used for a number of purposes. First, taken as a whole, the table can indicate whether NPV analysis should be trusted. In other words, it reduces the false sense of security we spoke of earlier. Suppose that NPV is positive when the expected forecast for each variable is used. However, further suppose that every number in the pessimistic column is highly negative and every number in the optimistic column is highly positive. Even a single error in this forecast greatly alters the estimate, making one leery of the net present value approach. A conservative manager might well scrap the entire NPV analysis in this situation. Fortunately, this does not seem to be the case in Table 8.3, because all but two of the numbers are positive. Managers viewing the table will likely consider NPV analysis to be useful for the solar-powered jet engine.

Second, sensitivity analysis shows where more information is needed. For example, error in the estimate of investment appears to be relatively unimportant because, even under the pessimistic scenario, the NPV of $1,208 million is still highly positive. By contrast, the pessimistic forecast for market share leads to a negative NPV of −$696 million, and a pessimistic forecast for market size leads to a substantially negative NPV of −$1,802 million. Since the effect of incorrect estimates on revenues is so much greater than the effect of incorrect estimates on costs, more information on the factors determining revenues might be needed.

Because of these advantages, sensitivity analysis is widely used in practice. Graham and Harvey[2] report that slightly over 50 percent of the 392 firms in their sample subject their capital budgeting calculations to sensitivity analysis. This number is particularly large when one considers that only about 75 percent of the firms in their sample use NPV analysis.

Unfortunately, sensitivity analysis also suffers from some drawbacks. For example, sensitivity analysis may unwittingly *increase* the false sense of security among managers. Suppose all pessimistic forecasts yield positive NPVs. A manager might feel that there is no way the project can lose money. Of course, the forecasters may simply have an optimistic view of a pessimistic forecast. To combat this, some companies do not treat optimistic and pessimistic forecasts subjectively. Rather, their pessimistic forecasts are always, say, 20 percent less than expected. Unfortunately, the cure in this case may be worse than the disease, because a deviation of a fixed percentage ignores the fact that some variables are easier to forecast than others.

In addition, sensitivity analysis treats each variable in isolation when, in reality, the different variables are likely to be related. For example, if ineffective management allows costs to get out of control, it is likely that variable costs, fixed costs, and investment will all rise above expectation at the same time. If the market is not receptive to a solar plane, both market share and price should decline together.

Managers frequently perform **scenario analysis,** a variant of sensitivity analysis, to minimize this problem. Simply put, this approach examines a number of different likely scenarios, where each scenario involves a confluence of factors. As a simple example, consider the effect of a few airline crashes. These crashes are likely to reduce flying in total, thereby limiting the demand for any new engines. Furthermore, even if the crashes did not involve solar-powered aircraft, the public could become more averse to any innovative and controversial technologies. Hence, SEC's market share might fall as well. Perhaps the cash flow calculations would look like those in Table 8.4 under the scenario of a plane crash. Given the calculations in the table, the NPV (in millions) would be

$$-\$2,023 = -\$1,500 - \$156 \times A_{0.15}^5$$

A series of scenarios like this might illuminate issues concerning the project better than the standard application of sensitivity analysis would.

Break-Even Analysis

Our discussion of sensitivity analysis and scenario analysis suggests that there are many ways to examine variability in forecasts. We now present another approach, **break-even analysis.** As its name implies, this approach determines the sales needed to break even. The approach is a useful complement to sensitivity analysis, because it also sheds light on the severity of incorrect forecasts. We calculate the break-even point in terms of both accounting profit and present value.

[2]See Figure 2 of John Graham and Campbell Harvey, "The Theory and Practice of Corporate Finance: Evidence from the Field," *Journal of Financial Economics* (May/June 2001).

TABLE 8.4		Year I	Years 2–6
Cash Flow Forecast (in $ millions) under the Scenario of a Plane Crash*	Revenues		$2,800
	Variable costs		−1,400
	Fixed costs		−1,791
	Depreciation		−300
	Pretax profit		−691
	Tax ($T_c = 0.34$)[†]		235
	Net profit		−456
	Cash flow		−156
	Initial investment cost	−$1,500	

*Assumptions are

    Market size   7,000 (70 percent of expectation)
    Market share   20% (2/3 of expectation)

Forecasts for all other variables are the expected forecasts as given in Table 8.2.

[†]Tax loss offsets income elsewhere in firm.

TABLE 8.5		Revenues and Costs of Project under Different Sales Assumptions (in $ millions, except unit sales)							
Year I			**Years 2–6**						
Initial Invest- ment	**Annual Unit Sales**	**Revenues**	**Variable Costs**	**Fixed Costs**	**Depreci- ation**	**Taxes* ($T_c = 0.34$)**	**Net Profit**	**Operating Cash Flows**	**NPV (evaluated date 1)**
$1,500	0	$ 0	$ 0	−$1,791	−$300	$ 711	−$1,380	−$1,080	−$5,120
1,500	1,000	2,000	−1,000	−1,791	−300	371	−720	−420	−2,908
1,500	3,000	6,000	−3,000	−1,791	−300	−309	600	900	1,517
1,500	10,000	20,000	−10,000	−1,791	−300	−2,689	5,220	5,520	17,004

*Loss is incurred in the first two rows. For tax purposes, this loss offsets income elsewhere in the firm.

Accounting Profit   Net profit under four different sales forecasts is

Unit Sales	Net Profit (in $ millions)
0	−$1,380
1,000	−720
3,000	600
10,000	5,220

A more complete presentation of costs and revenues appears in Table 8.5.

We plot the revenues, costs, and profits under the different assumptions about sales in Figure 8.2. The revenue and cost curves cross at 2,091 jet engines. This is the break-even point, i.e., the point where the project generates no profits or losses. As long as sales are above 2,091 jet engines, the project will make a profit.

This break-even point can be calculated very easily. Because the sales price is $2 million per engine and the variable cost is $1 million per engine,[3] the after-tax difference per engine is

$$\text{(Sales price} - \text{Variable cost)} \times (1 - T_c) = (\$2 \text{ million} - \$1 \text{ million}) \times (1 - 0.34)$$
$$= \$0.66 \text{ million}$$

---

[3]Though the previous section considered both optimistic and pessimistic forecasts for sales price and variable cost, break-even analysis uses just the expected or best estimates of these variables.

FIGURE 8.2

Break-Even Point
Using Accounting
Numbers

where T_c is the corporate tax rate of 34 percent. This after-tax difference is called the **contribution margin** because each additional engine contributes this amount to after-tax profit.

Fixed costs are $1,791 million and depreciation is $300 million, implying that the after-tax sum of these costs is

$$(\text{Fixed costs} + \text{Depreciation}) \times (1 - T_c) = (\$1,791 \text{ million} + \$300 \text{ million})$$
$$\times (1 - 0.34) = \$1,380 \text{ million}$$

That is, the firm incurs costs of $1,380 million, regardless of the number of sales. Because each engine contributes $0.66 million, sales must reach the following level to offset the above costs:

Accounting Profit Break-Even Point:

$$\frac{(\text{Fixed costs} + \text{Depreciation}) \times (1 - T_c)}{(\text{Sales price} - \text{Variable costs}) \times (1 - T_c)} = \frac{\$1,380 \text{ million}}{\$0.66 \text{ million}} = 2,091$$

Thus, 2,091 engines is the break-even point required for an accounting profit.

Present Value As we stated many times in the text, we are more interested in present value than we are in net profits. Therefore, we must calculate the present value of the cash flows. Given a discount rate of 15 percent, we have

Unit Sales	NPV ($ millions)
0	−5,120
1,000	−2,908
3,000	1,517
10,000	17,004

These NPV calculations are reproduced in the last column of Table 8.5. We can see that the NPV is negative if SEC produces 1,000 jet engines and positive if it produces 3,000 jet engines. Obviously, the zero NPV point occurs between 1,000 and 3,000 jet engines.

The present value break-even point can be calculated very easily. The firm originally invested $1,500 million. This initial investment can be expressed as a five-year equivalent annual cost (EAC), determined by dividing the initial investment by the appropriate five-year annuity factor:

$$\text{EAC} = \frac{\text{Initial investment}}{\text{5-year annuity factor at 15\%}} = \frac{\text{Initial investment}}{A^5_{0.15}}$$
$$= \frac{\$1,500 \text{ million}}{3.3522} = \$447.5 \text{ million}$$

Note that the EAC of $447.5 million is greater than the yearly depreciation of $300 million. This must occur since the calculation of EAC implicitly assumes that the $1,500 million investment could have been invested at 15 percent.

After-tax costs, regardless of output, can be viewed as

$$\frac{\$1,528}{\text{million}} = \frac{\$447.5}{\text{million}} + \frac{\$1,791}{\text{million}} \times 0.66 - \frac{\$300}{\text{million}} \times 0.34$$

$$= \text{EAC} + \frac{\text{Fixed}}{\text{costs}} \times (1 - T_c) - \frac{\text{Depreci-}}{\text{ation}} \times T_c$$

That is, in addition to the initial investment's equivalent annual cost of $447.5 million, the firm pays fixed costs each year and receives a depreciation tax shield each year. The depreciation tax shield is written as a negative number since it offsets the costs in the equation. Because each plane contributes $0.66 million to after-tax profit, it will take the following sales to offset the above costs:

Present Value Break-Even Point:

$$\frac{\text{EAC} + \text{Fixed costs} \times (1 - T_c) - \text{Depreciation} \times T_c}{(\text{Sales price} - \text{Variable costs}) \times (1 - T_c)} = \frac{\$1,528 \text{ million}}{\$0.66 \text{ million}} = 2,315$$

Thus, 2,315 planes is the break-even point from the perspective of present value.

Why is the accounting break-even point different from the financial break-even point? When we use accounting profit as the basis for the break-even calculation, we subtract depreciation. Depreciation for the solar-jet-engines project is $300 million. If 2,091 solar jet engines are sold, SEC will generate sufficient revenues to cover the $300 million depreciation expense plus other costs. Unfortunately, at this level of sales SEC will not cover the economic opportunity costs of the $1,500 million laid out for the investment. If we take into account that the $1,500 million could have been invested at 15 percent, the true annual cost of the investment is $447.5 million and not $300 million. Depreciation understates the true costs of recovering the initial investment. Thus, companies that break even on an accounting basis are really losing money. They are losing the opportunity cost of the initial investment.

Concept
Questions

1. **What is a sensitivity analysis?**
2. **Why is it important to perform a sensitivity analysis?**
3. **What is a break-even analysis?**
4. **Describe how sensitivity analysis interacts with break-even analysis.**

8.3 Monte Carlo Simulation

Both sensitivity analysis and scenario analysis attempt to answer the question, "What if?" However, while both analyses are frequently used in the real world, each has its own limitations. Sensitivity analysis allows only one variable to change at a time. By contrast, many variables are likely to move at the same time in the real world. Scenario analysis follows specific scenarios, such as changes in inflation, government regulation, or the number of competitors. While this methodology is often quite helpful, it cannot cover all sources of variability. In fact, projects are likely to exhibit a lot of variability under just one economic scenario.

Monte Carlo simulation is a further attempt to model real-world uncertainty. This approach takes its name from the famous European casino, because it analyzes projects the way one might analyze gambling strategies. Imagine a serious blackjack player who wonders if he should take a third card whenever his first two cards total 16. Most likely, a formal mathematical model would be too complex to be practical here. However, he could play thousands of hands in a casino, sometimes drawing a third card when his first two cards add to 16 and sometimes not drawing that third card. He could compare his winnings (or losings) under the two strategies in order to determine which was better. Of course, since he would probably lose a lot of money performing this test in a real casino, simulating the results from the two strategies on a computer might be cheaper. Monte Carlo simulation of capital budgeting projects is in this spirit.

Imagine that Backyard Barbeques, Inc. (BBI), a manufacturer of both charcoal and gas grills, has the blueprint for a new grill that cooks with compressed hydrogen. The CFO, Edward H. Comiskey, being dissatisfied with simpler capital budgeting techniques, wants a Monte Carlo simulation for this new grill. A consultant specializing in the Monte Carlo approach, Lester Mauney, takes him through the five basic steps of the method.

Step 1: Specify the Basic Model
Les Mauney breaks up cash flow into three components: annual revenue, annual costs, and initial investment. The revenue in any year is viewed as:

$$\begin{pmatrix} \text{Number of grills sold} \\ \text{by entire industry} \end{pmatrix} \times \begin{pmatrix} \text{Market share of BBI's} \\ \text{hydrogen grill (in percent)} \end{pmatrix} \times \begin{pmatrix} \text{Price per} \\ \text{hydrogen grill} \end{pmatrix} \quad (8.1)$$

The cost in any year is viewed as:

$$\text{Fixed manufacturing costs} + \text{Variable manufacturing costs} + \text{Marketing costs} + \text{Selling costs}$$

Initial investment is viewed as:

$$\text{Cost of patent} + \text{Test-marketing costs} + \text{Cost of production facility}$$

Step 2: Specify a Distribution for Each Variable in the Model
Here comes the hard part. Let's start with revenue, which has three components in (8.1). The consultant first models overall market size, that is, the number of grills sold by the entire industry. The trade publication, *Outdoor Food (OF)*, reported that 10 million grills of all types were sold in the continental United States last year and it forecasts sales of 10.5 million next year. Mr. Mauney, using *OF*'s forecast and his own intuition, creates the following distribution for next year's sales of grills by the entire industry:

Probability	20%	60%	20%
Next year's industrywide unit sales	10 million	10.5 million	11 million

The tight distribution here reflects the slow but steady historical growth in the grill market.

Lester Mauney realizes that estimating the market share of BBI's hydrogen grill is more difficult. Nevertheless, after a great deal of analysis, he determines the distribution of next year's market share to be:

Probability	10%	20%	30%	25%	10%	5%
Market share of BBI's hydrogen grill next year	1%	2%	3%	4%	5%	8%

While the consultant assumed a symmetrical distribution for industrywide unit sales, he believes a skewed distribution makes more sense for the project's market share. In his mind, there is always the small possibility that sales of the hydrogen grill will really take off.

The above forecasts assume that unit sales for the overall industry are unrelated to the project's market share. In other words, the two variables are *independent* of each other. Mr. Mauney reasons that, while an economic boom might increase industrywide grill sales and a recession might decrease them, the project's market share is unlikely to be related to economic conditions.

Now Mr. Mauney must determine the distribution of price per grill. Mr. Comiskey, the CFO, informs him that the price will be in the area of $200 per grill, given what other competitors are charging. However, the consultant believes that the price per hydrogen grill will almost certainly depend on the size of the overall market for grills. As in any business, you can usually charge more if demand is high.

After rejecting a number of complex models for price, Mr. Mauney settles on the following specification:

$$\frac{\text{Next year's price}}{\text{per hydrogen grill}} = \$190 + \$1 \times \text{Industrywide unit sales (in millions)} +/- \$3 \quad (8.2)$$

The grill price in (8.2) is dependent on the unit sales of the industry. In addition, random variation is modeled via the term "$+/- \$3$," where a drawing of $+\$3$ and a drawing of $-\$3$ each occur 50 percent of the time. For example, if industrywide unit sales are 11 million, the price per share would be either:

$$\$190 + \$11 + \$3 = \$203 \qquad (50\% \text{ probability})$$
$$\$190 + \$11 - \$3 = \$197 \qquad (50\% \text{ probability})$$

The consultant now has distributions for each of the three components of next year's revenue. However, he needs distributions for future years as well. Using forecasts from *Outdoor Food* and other publications, Mr. Mauney forecasts the distribution of growth rates for the entire industry over the second year to be:

Probability	20%	60%	20%
Growth rate of industrywide unit sales in second year	1%	3%	5%

Given both the distribution of next year's industrywide unit sales and the distribution of growth rates for this variable over the second year, we can generate the distribution of industrywide unit sales for the second year. A similar extension should give Mr. Mauney a distribution for later years as well, though we won't go into the details here. And, just as the consultant extended the first component of revenue (industrywide unit sales) to later years, he would want to do the same thing for market share and unit price.

The above discussion shows how the three components of revenue can be modeled. Step 2 would be complete once the components of cost and of investment are modeled in a similar way. Special attention must be paid to the interactions between variables here, since ineffective management will likely allow the different cost components to rise together. However, since you are probably getting the idea now, we will skip the rest of this step.

Step 3: The Computer Draws One Outcome
As we said above, next year's revenue in our model is the product of three components. Imagine that the computer randomly picks industrywide unit sales of 10 million, a market share for BBI's hydrogen grill of 2 percent and a $+\$3$ random price variation. Given these drawings, next year's price per hydrogen grill will be:

$$\$190 + \$10 + \$3 = \$203$$

and next year's revenue for BBI's hydrogen grill will be:

$$10 \text{ million} \times 0.02 \times \$203 = \$40.6 \text{ million}$$

Of course, we are not done with the entire outcome yet. We would have to perform drawings for revenue in each future year. In addition, we would perform drawings for costs in each future year. Finally, a drawing for initial investment would have to be made as well. In this way, a single outcome would generate a cash flow from the project in each future year.

How likely is it that the specific outcome above would be drawn? We can answer this because we know the probability of each component. Since industry sales of $10 million has a 20 percent probability, a market share of 2 percent also has a 20 percent probability, and a random price variation of +$3 has a 50 percent probability, the probability of these three drawings together in the same outcome is:

$$0.02 = 0.20 \times 0.20 \times 0.50 \qquad (8.3)$$

Of course, the probability would get even smaller once drawings for future revenues, future costs, and the initial investment are included in the outcome.

This step generates the cash flow for each year from a single outcome. What we are ultimately interested in is the *distribution* of cash flow each year across many outcomes. We ask the computer to randomly draw over and over again to give us this distribution, which is just what is done in the next step.

Step 4: Repeat the Procedure

While the above three steps generate one outcome, the essence of Monte Carlo simulation is repeated outcomes. Depending on the situation, the computer may be called on to generate thousands or even millions of outcomes. The result of all these drawings is a distribution of cash flow for each future year. This distribution is the basic output of Monte Carlo simulation.

Consider Figure 8.3. Here, repeated drawings have produced the simulated distribution of the third year's cash flow. There would be, of course, a distribution like the one in this figure for each future year. This leaves us with just one more step.

Step 5: Calculate NPV

Given the distribution of cash flow for the third year in Figure 8.3, one can determine the expected cash flow for this year. In a similar manner, one can also determine the expected

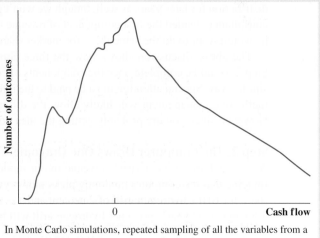

FIGURE 8.3

Simulated
Distribution of the
Third Year's Cash
Flow for BBI's New
Hydrogen Grill

In Monte Carlo simulations, repeated sampling of all the variables from a specific model generates a statistical distribution cash flow for each future year and can then calculate the net present value of the project by discounting these expected cash flows at an appropriate rate.

Monte Carlo simulation is often viewed as a step beyond either sensitivity analysis or scenario analysis. Interactions between the variables are explicitly specified in Monte Carlo so, at least in theory, this methodology provides a more complete analysis. And, as a by-product, having to build a precise model deepens the forecaster's understanding of the project.

Since Monte Carlo simulations have been around for at least 35 years, you might think that most firms would be performing them by now. Surprisingly, this does not seem to be the case. In our experience, executives are frequently skeptical of all the complexity. It is difficult to model either the distributions of each variable or the interactions between variables. In addition, the computer output is often devoid of economic intuition. Thus, while Monte Carlo simulations are used in certain real-world situations,[4] the approach is not likely to be "the wave of the future." In fact, Graham and Harvey[5] report that only about 15 percent of the firms in their sample use capital budgeting simulations.

8.4 Real Options

In Chapter 6, we stressed the superiority of net present value (NPV) analysis over other approaches when valuing capital budgeting projects. However, both scholars and practitioners have pointed out problems with NPV. The basic idea here is that NPV analysis, as well as all the other approaches in Chapter 6, ignores the adjustments that a firm can make after a project is accepted. These adjustments are called **real options.** In this respect, NPV underestimates the true value of a project. NPV's conservatism here is best explained through a series of examples.

The Option to Expand

Conrad Willig, an entrepreneur, recently learned of a chemical treatment causing water to freeze at 100 degrees Fahrenheit, rather than 32 degrees. Of all the many practical applications for this treatment, Mr. Willig liked the idea of hotels made of ice more than anything else. Conrad estimated the annual cash flows from a single ice hotel to be $2 million, based on an initial investment of $12 million. He felt that 20 percent was an appropriate discount rate, given the risk of this new venture. Assuming that the cash flows were perpetual, Mr. Willig determined the NPV of the project to be:

$$-\$12,000,000 + \$2,000,000/0.20 = -\$2 \text{ million}$$

Most entrepreneurs would have rejected this venture, given its negative NPV. But Conrad was not your typical entrepreneur. He reasoned that NPV analysis missed a hidden source of value. While he was pretty sure that the initial investment would cost $12 million, there was some uncertainty concerning annual cash flows. His cash flow estimate of $2 million per year actually reflected his belief that there was a 50 percent probability that annual cash flows will be $3 million and a 50 percent probability that annual cash flows will be $1 million.

The NPV calculations for the two forecasts are:

Optimistic forecast: $-\$12$ million $+ \$3$ million$/0.20 = \$3$ million

Pessimistic forecast: $-\$12$ million $+ \$1$ million$/0.20 = -\$7$ million

---

[4]More than perhaps any other, the pharmaceutical industry has pioneered applications of this methodology. For example, see, Nancy A. Nichols, "Scientific Management at Merck: An Interview with CFO Judy Lewent," *Harvard Business Review* (January/February 1994).

[5]See Figure 2 of Graham and Harvey, *op. cit.*

FIGURE 8.4

Decision Tree for Ice
Hotel

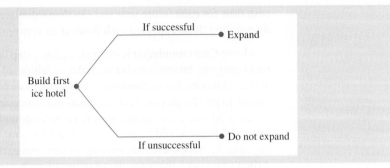

On the surface, this new calculation doesn't seem to help Mr. Willig very much since an average of the two forecasts yields an NPV for the project of:

$$50\% \times \$3 \text{ million} + 50\% \times (-\$7 \text{ million}) = -\$2 \text{ million}$$

just the value he calculated in the first place.

However, if the optimistic forecast turns out to be correct, Mr. Willig would want to *expand*. If he believes that there are, say, 10 locations in the country that can support an ice hotel, the true NPV of the venture would be:

$$50\% \times 10 \times \$3 \text{ million} + 50\% \times (-\$7 \text{ million}) = \$11.5 \text{ million}$$

The idea here, which is represented in Figure 8.4, is both basic and universal. The entrepreneur has the option to expand if the pilot location is successful. For example, think of all the people that start restaurants, most of them ultimately failing. These individuals are not necessarily overly optimistic. They may realize the likelihood of failure but go ahead anyway because of the small chance of starting the next McDonald's or Burger King.

The Option to Abandon

Managers also have the option to abandon existing projects. While abandonment may seem cowardly, it can often save companies a great deal of money. Because of this, the option to abandon increases the value of any potential project.

The above example on ice hotels, which illustrated the option to expand, can also illustrate the option to abandon. To see this, imagine that Mr. Willig now believes that there is a 50 percent probability that annual cash flows will be $6 million and a 50 percent probability that annual cash flows will be −$2 million. The NPV calculations under the two forecasts become:

Optimistic forecast: $-\$12 \text{ million} + \$6 \text{ million}/0.2 = \$18 \text{ million}$

Pessimistic forecast: $-\$12 \text{ million} - \$2 \text{ million}/0.2 = -\$22 \text{ million}$

yielding an NPV for the project of:

$$50\% \times \$18 \text{ million} + 50\% \times (-\$22 \text{ million}) = -\$2 \text{ million} \qquad (8.4)$$

Furthermore, now imagine that Mr. Willig wants to own, at most, just one ice hotel, implying that there is no option to expand. Since the NPV in (8.4) is negative, it looks as if he will not build the hotel.

But things change when we consider the abandonment option. As of date 1, the entrepreneur will know which forecast has come true. If cash flows equal those under the optimistic forecast, Conrad will keep the project alive. If, however, cash flows equal those under the

FIGURE 8.5

The Abandonment Option in the Movie Industry

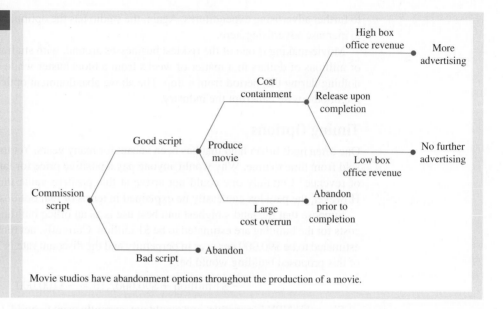

Movie studios have abandonment options throughout the production of a movie.

pessimistic forecast, he will abandon the hotel. Knowing these possibilities ahead of time, the NPV of the project becomes:

$$50\% \times \$18 \text{ million} + 50\% \times (-\$12 \text{ million} - \$2 \text{ million}/1.20) = \$2.17 \text{ million}$$

Since Mr. Willig abandons after experiencing the cash flow of −$2 million at date 1, he does not have to endure this outflow in any of the later years. Because the NPV is now positive, Conrad will accept the project.

The example here is clearly a stylized one. While many years may pass before a project is abandoned in the real world, our ice hotel was abandoned after just one year. And, while salvage values generally accompany abandonment, we assumed no salvage value for the ice hotel. Nevertheless, abandonment options are pervasive in the real world.

For example, consider the movie-making industry. As shown in Figure 8.5, movies begin with either the purchase or development of a script. A completed script might cost a movie studio a few million dollars and potentially lead to actual production. However, the great majority of scripts (perhaps well in excess of 80 percent) are abandoned. Why would studios abandon scripts that they had commissioned in the first place? While the studios know ahead of time that only a few scripts will be promising, they don't know which ones. Thus, they cast a wide net, commissioning many scripts to get a few good ones. And, the studios must be ruthless with the bad scripts, since the expenditure here pales in comparison to the huge losses from producing a bad movie.

The few lucky scripts will then move into production, where costs might be budgeted in the tens of millions of dollars, if not much more. At this stage, the dreaded phrase is that on-location production gets "bogged down," creating cost overruns. But the studios are equally ruthless here. Should these overruns become excessive, production is likely to be abandoned in midstream. Interestingly, abandonment almost always occurs due to high costs, not due to the fear that the movie won't be able to find an audience. Little information on that score will be obtained until the movie is actually released.

Release of the movie is accompanied by significant advertising expenditures, perhaps in the range of $10 to $20 million. Box office success in the first few weeks is likely to lead to further advertising expenditures. Again, the studio has the option, but not the obligation, to increase advertising here.

Movie-making is one of the riskiest businesses around, with studios receiving hundreds of millions of dollars in a matter of weeks from a blockbuster while receiving practically nothing during this period from a flop. The above abandonment options contain costs that might otherwise bankrupt the industry.

Timing Options

One often finds urban land that has been vacant for many years. Yet this land is bought and sold from time to time. Why would anyone pay a positive price for land that has no source of revenue? Certainly one could not arrive at this positive value through NPV analysis. However, the paradox can easily be explained in terms of real options.

Suppose that the land's highest and best use is as an office building. Total construction costs for the building are estimated to be $1 million. Currently, net rents (after all costs) are estimated to be $90,000 per year in perpetuity and the discount rate is 10 percent. The NPV of this proposed building would be:

$$-\$1 \text{ million} + \$90,000/.10 = -\$100,000$$

Since this NPV is negative, one would not currently want to build. In addition, it appears as if the land is worthless. However, suppose that the federal government is planning various urban revitalization programs for the city. Office rents will likely increase if the programs succeed. In this case, the property's owner might want to erect the office building after all. Conversely, office rents will remain the same, or even fall, if the programs fail. The owner will not build in this case.

We say that the property owner has a *timing option*. While he does not currently want to build, he will want to build in the future should rents in the area rise substantially. This timing option explains why vacant land often has value. While there are costs, such as taxes, from holding raw land, the value of an office building after a substantial rise in rents may more than offset these holding costs. Of course, the exact value of the vacant land depends on both the probability of success in the revitalization program and the extent of the rent increase. Figure 8.6 illustrates this timing option.

Mining operations almost always provide timing options as well. Suppose you own a copper mine where the cost of mining each ton of copper exceeds the sales revenue. It's a no-brainer to say that you would not want to mine the copper currently. And since there are costs of ownership such as property taxes, insurance, and security, you might actually want to pay someone to take the mine off your hands. However, we would caution you not to do

---

FIGURE 8.6

Decision Tree for Vacant Land

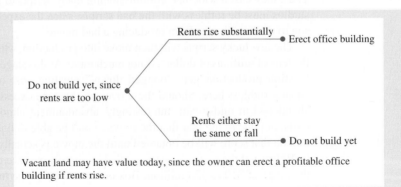

Vacant land may have value today, since the owner can erect a profitable office building if rents rise.

so hastily. Copper prices in the future might very well increase enough so that production is profitable. Given that possibility, you could likely find someone to pay a positive price for the property today.

Concept Questions	1. What are the different types of real options?
	2. Why does traditional NPV analysis tend to underestimate the true value of a capital project?

8.5 SUMMARY AND CONCLUSIONS

This chapter discusses a number of practical applications of capital budgeting.

1. Though NPV is the best capital budgeting approach conceptually, it has been criticized in practice for providing managers with a false sense of security. Sensitivity analysis shows NPV under varying assumptions, giving managers a better feel for the project's risks. Unfortunately, sensitivity analysis modifies only one variable at a time, while many variables are likely to vary together in the real world. Scenario analysis examines a project's performance under different scenarios (e.g., war breaking out or oil prices skyrocketing). Finally, managers want to know how bad forecasts must be before a project loses money. Break-even analysis calculates the sales figure at which the project breaks even. Though break-even analysis is frequently performed on an accounting profit basis, we suggest that a net present value basis is more appropriate.

2. Monte Carlo simulation begins with a model of the firm's cash flows, based on both the interactions between different variables and the movement of each individual variable over time. Random sampling generates a distribution of these cash flows for each period, leading to a net present value calculation.

3. We analyze the hidden options in capital budgeting, such as the option to expand, the option to abandon, and timing options.

KEY TERMS

break-even analysis, *216*
contribution margin, *218*
decision trees, *211*
fixed costs, *214*
Monte Carlo simulation, *219*

real options, *223*
scenario analysis, *216*
sensitivity analysis, *214*
variable costs, *214*

SUGGESTED READINGS

The classic article on break-even analysis is:

Reinhart, U. E. "Breakeven Analysis for Lockheed's Tristar: An Application of Financial Theory." *Journal of Finance* (September 1977).

An excellent book on real options is:

Amram, Martha, and Nalin Kulatilaka. *Real Options: Managing Strategic Investment in an Uncertain World.* Boston: Harvard Business School Press (1999).

A fascinating discussion of real options in the movie business can be found in:

Martin, Laura, "Film Studio Reel Options." Unpublished manuscript, Credit Suisse First Boston (CSFB) (May 11, 2001). Obtainable at www.valuesweep.com

QUESTIONS & PROBLEMS

DECISION TREES

8.1 Sony Electronics, Inc., has developed a new VCR. If the VCR is successful, the present value of the payoff (at the time the product is brought to market) is $20 million. If the VCR fails, the present value of the payoff is $5 million. If the product goes directly to market, there is a 50 percent chance of success. Alternatively, Sony can delay the launch by one year and spend $2 million to test market the VCR. Test marketing allows the firm to improve the product and increase the probability of success to 75 percent. The appropriate discount rate is 15 percent. Should the firm conduct test marketing?

8.2   The manager for a growing firm is considering the launch of a new product. If the product goes directly to market, there is a 50 percent chance of success. For $120,000, the manager can conduct a focus group that will increase the product's chance of success to 70 percent. Alternatively, the manager has the option to pay a consulting firm $400,000 to research the market and refine the product. The consulting firm successfully launches new products 90 percent of the time. If the firm successfully launches the product, the payoff will be $1.2 million. If the product is a failure, the firm will receive $0. Which action will result in the highest expected payoff to the firm?

8.3   The sales of Tandem Bicycles, Inc., are decreasing because of foreign competition. The firm's chief financial officer (CFO) is considering the following mutually exclusive options to maintain market share this year:

- Price the products more aggressively. With this option, there is a 55 percent chance that Tandem will only lose $1.3 million in cash flow due to the decreased revenue. However, there is a 45 percent probability that Tandem's pricing strategy will fail, and the firm will lose a total of $1,850,000 in cash flow.
- Pay $800,000 for a lobbyist to convince the regulators to impose tariffs on overseas bicycle manufacturers. With the lobbyists, there is a 75 percent chance that Tandem will lose no cash flow to the foreign competition. If the lobbyists do not succeed, Tandem Bicycles will lose $2 million in cash flow.

Assume all cash flows occur today, and that Tandem Bicycles will cease operations after this year. As the assistant to the CFO, which strategy would you recommend to maximize expected cash flow?

8.4   B&B has a new baby powder ready to market. If the firm goes directly to the market with the product, there is only 55 percent chance of success. However, the firm can conduct customer segment research, which will take a year and cost $1 million. By going through research, B&B will be able to better target potential customers and will increase the probability of success to 70 percent. If successful, the baby powder will bring a present value profit (at time of initial selling) of $30 million. If unsuccessful, the present value payoff is only $3 million. Should the firm conduct customer segment research or go directly to market? The appropriate discount rate is 15 percent.

8.5   Young screenwriter Carl Draper has just finished his first script. It has action, drama, humor, and he thinks it will be a blockbuster. He takes the script to every motion picture studio in town and tries to sell it but to no avail. Finally, ACME studios offers to buy the script, for either a) $5,000 or b) 1 percent of the movie's profits. There are two decisions that will take place for the studio. First is if the script is good or bad, and second if the movie is good or bad. First, there is a 90 percent chance that the script is bad. If it is bad, the studio does nothing more and throws the script out. If the script is good, they will shoot the movie. After the movie is shot, the studio will review it and there is a 70 percent chance that the movie is bad. If the movie is bad, the movie will not be promoted and will not turn a profit. If the movie is good, the studio will promote heavily and the average profit is $10 million. Carl rejects the $5,000 and says he wants the 1 percent of profits. Was this a good decision by Carl?

ACCOUNTING BREAK-EVEN ANALYSIS

8.6   Samuelson, Inc., has just purchased a $600,000 machine to produce calculators. The machine will be fully depreciated by the straight-line method over its economic life of five years and will produce 20,000 calculators each year. The variable production cost per calculator is $15 and total fixed costs are $900,000 per year. The corporate tax rate for the company is 30 percent. For the firm to break even (in terms of accounting profit), how much should the firm charge per calculator?

8.7   Consider the following information for a big-screen television distributor:

Sales price per TV	= $1,500
Variable costs per TV	= $1,100
Fixed costs per year	= $120,000
Depreciation per year	= $20,000
Tax rate	= 35%

How many units must the distributor sell in a given year to break even (in terms of accounting profit)?

8.8 You are considering investing in a company that cultivates abalone for sale to local restaurants. Use the following information:

Sales price per abalone	= $2.00
Variable costs per abalone	= $0.72
Fixed costs per year	= $340,000
Depreciation per year	= $20,000
Tax rate	= 35%

a. How many abalone must be harvested and sold per year for you to receive any profit (accounting break-even point)?

b. How much profit will you receive if he sells 300,000 abalone per year?

8.9 What is the minimum number of times that a video arcade must be played in a given period to break even?

Game price	= $0.50
Variable cost	= $0.02
Fixed costs	= $1,000
Depreciation	= $50
Tax rate	= 34%

8.10 Your buddy comes to you with a sure fire way to make some quick money and help pay off your student loans. His idea is to sell T-shirts with the words "I get" on them. "You get it?" He says, "You see all those bumper stickers and T-shirts that say, 'got milk' or 'got surf.' So this says, 'I get.' It's funny! All we have to do is buy a used silk screen press for $2,000 and we are in business!" Assume there are no fixed costs, and you depreciate the $2,000 in the first period. Further, taxes are 30 percent.

a. How many shirts would you need to sell to break even if each shirt costs $8 to make, and you can sell them for $10 a piece?

Now assume one year has passed and you have sold 5,000 shirts! You find out that the Dairy Farmers of America have copyrighted the "got milk" slogan and are requiring you to pay $10,000 to continue operations. You expect this craze will last for another three years and that your discount rate is 12 percent.

b. What is the present value break-even point for you enterprise now?

PRESENT VALUE BREAK-EVEN ANALYSIS

8.11 Using the information in Problem 8.8, calculate the present value break-even point if the discount rate is 15 percent, the initial investment is $140,000, and the project's economic life is seven years. Assume the initial investment is fully depreciated by the straight-line method over its economic life.

8.12 L.J.'s Toys Inc. just purchased a $200,000 machine to produce toy cars. The machine will be fully depreciated by the straight-line method over its five-year economic life. Each toy sells for $25. The variable cost per toy is $5, and the firm incurs fixed costs of $350,000 each year. The corporate tax rate for the company is 25 percent. The appropriate discount rate is 12 percent. What is the present value break-even point for the project?

8.13 The Cornchopper Company is considering the purchase of a new harvester. Cornchopper has hired you to determine the break-even purchase price (in terms of present value) of the harvester. This break-even purchase price is the price at which the project's NPV is zero. Base your analysis on the following facts:

- The new harvester is not expected to affect revenues, but pretax operating expenses will be reduced by $10,000 per year for 10 years.

- The old harvester is now 5 years old, with 10 years of its scheduled life remaining. It was originally purchased for $45,000 and has been depreciated by the straight-line method.
- The old harvester can be sold for $20,000 today.
- The new harvester will be depreciated by the straight-line method over its 10-year life.
- The corporate tax rate is 34 percent.
- The firm's required rate of return is 15 percent.
- The initial investment, the proceeds from selling the old harvester, and any resulting tax effects occur immediately. Capital gains and losses are taxed at the corporate rate of 34 percent when they are realized.
- All other cash flows occur at year-end.
- The market value of each harvester at the end of its economic life is zero.

8.14 Niko has purchased a brand new machine to produce its High Flight line of shoes. The machine has an economic life of five years. The depreciation schedule for the machine is straight-line with no salvage value. The machine costs $300,000.

  The sales price per pair of shoes is $60, while the variable cost is $8. $100,000 of fixed cost per year is attributed to the machine.

  Assume that the corporate tax rate is 34 percent and the appropriate discount rate is 8 percent. What is the present value break-even point?

SCENARIO
ANALYSIS

8.15 The CFO of Mercer, Inc., is considering an investment of $420,000 in a machine that will be depreciated by the straight-line method over its seven-year economic life. The appropriate discount rate is 13 percent, and the corporate tax rate for the company is 35 percent. Assume all revenues and expenses, which are presented below, are received and paid in cash.

	Pessimistic	Expected	Optimistic
Unit sales	23,000	25,000	27,000
Price	$ 38	$ 40	$ 42
Variable costs per unit	$ 21	$ 20	$ 19
Fixed costs per year	$320,000	$300,000	$280,000

a. Calculate the NPV of the project in each of the above scenarios.
b. If each scenario is equally likely, is the machine a worthwhile investment?

8.16 You are the financial analyst for a tennis racket manufacturer. The company is considering a project using a graphite-like material in its rackets. Given the following information about the market for a racket with the new material, will you recommend the project?

	Pessimistic	Expected	Optimistic
Market size	110,000	120,000	130,000
Market share	22%	25%	27%
Selling price	$ 115	$ 120	$ 125
Variable costs per year	$ 72	$ 70	$ 68
Fixed costs per year	$ 850,000	$ 800,000	$ 750,000
Initial investment	$1,500,000	$1,500,000	$1,500,000

Assume the appropriate discount rate is 13 percent. The corporate tax rate is 40 percent. The firm will fully depreciate the initial investment over the next five years by the straight-line method. Each of the three scenarios is equally likely. Assume all revenues and expenses are received and paid in cash.

8.17 Xrco Petroleum has identified a new type of fuel additive and is considering launching this new product. As a marketing manager, you have come up with the following scenarios for the launch. From finance, you know that the tax rate for the company is 34 percent and the effective discount rate is 10 percent. You also know that the depreciation is $100,000 per year and that production will occur over the next five years only. Will you undertake the project?

	Pessimistic	Expected	Optimistic	
Market size	100,000	150,000	200,000	* Per year
Market share	20%	25%	30%	
Price	$ 100	120	140	
Variable cost	$ 80	75	70	
Fixed cost	$ 300,000	250,000	200,000	* Per year
Investment	$1,000,000	1,000,000	1,000,000	

8.18 The Big Burrito is planning to purchase a touch screen order system for its drive-thru window that would allow customers to select their order as soon as they arrive. This would reduce customer wait time and increase order accuracy. The touch screen and software would cost the Big Burrito $150,000 and would last five years. There would also be an annual maintenance cost of $5,000. In addition to improved customer service, the Big Burrito would gain two benefits. First, it could totally eliminate the full-time worker who used to accept and enter these orders. His annual salary plus benefits total $30,000 per year. Second, it expects drive-thru sales to increase but it doesn't know how much. The estimates are:

	Pessimistic	Expected	Optimistic
Revenue increase (decrease)	$(5,000)	$15,000	$20,000
COGS, 25% of rev increase	(1,250)	3,750	5,000

Net working capital (NWC) is expected to increase by $5,000 in the first year and be recovered at the end of year 5. If the appropriate discount rate is 15 percent and you ignore taxes, should the Big Burrito go ahead with this investment?

Pessimistic

	Year 0	Year 1	Year 2	Year 3	Year 4	Year 5	NPV
Investments:							
Touch screen system	$(150,000)						
Annual maintenance		$ (5,000)	$ (5,000)	$ (5,000)	$ (5,000)	$ (5,000)	
Change in NWC		(5,000)				5,000	
Wages saved		30,000	30,000	30,000	30,000	30,000	
Total cash flow from investments	$(150,000)	$20,000	$25,000	$25,000	$25,000	$30,000	
Income:							
Revenue		$ (5,000)	$ (5,000)	$ (5,000)	$ (5,000)	$ (5,000)	
COGS		1,250	1,250	1,250	1,250	1,250	
Cash flow from operations		$ (3,750)	$ (3,750)	$ (3,750)	$ (3,750)	$ (3,750)	
Total cash flow from project	$(150,000)	$16,250	$21,250	$21,250	$21,250	$26,250	
PV 15% (CF)	=CF	=CF/1.15	=CF/(1.15)^2	=CF/(1.15)^3	=CF/(1.15)^4	=CF/(1.15)^5	
	(150,000)	14,130	16,068	13,972	12,150	13,051	($80,629)

THE OPTION TO ABANDON

8.19 M.V.P. Games, Inc., has hired you to perform a feasibility study of a new video game that requires a $4 million initial investment. M.V.P. expects total annual operating cash flow of $750,000 for the next 10 years. The relevant discount rate is 10 percent. Ignore depreciation and taxes. Cash flows occur at year-end.
  a. What is the NPV of the new video game?
  b. After one year, the estimate of remaining annual cash flows will either be revised upward to $1.5 million or revised downward to $0. Each revision has an equal probability of occurring. At that time, the video game project can be sold for $200,000. What is the revised NPV, given that the firm can abandon the project after one year?
  c. What is the option value of abandonment?

8.20 Allied Products, Inc., is considering a new product launch. The firm expects to have annual operating cash flow of $200 million for the next ten years. Allied Products uses a discount rate of 20 percent for new product launches. The initial investment is $100 million. Ignore taxes and assume that the project has no salvage value at the end of its economic life.
  a. What is the NPV of the new product?
  b. After the first year, the project can be dismantled and sold for $50 million. If the estimate of remaining cash flows can be revised based on the first year's experience, at what level of expected cash flows does it make sense to abandon the project?

8.21 Applied Nanotech is thinking about introducing a new surface cleaning machine. The marketing department has come up with the estimate that Applied Nanotech can sell 10 units per year at $0.3 million net cash flow per unit for the next five years. The engineering department has come up with the estimate that developing the machine will take $10 million initial investment. The finance department has estimated that 25 percent discount rate should be used.
  a. What is the base case NPV?
  b. If unsuccessful, after the first year the project can be dismantled and sold for scrap for $5 million. Also, after the first year, expected cash flows will be revised up to 20 units per year or to 0 units, with equal probability. If so, what is the option value of abandonment? What is the revised NPV?

8.22 Snapple is planning to enter the bottled water market. They expect to sell 5 million bottles per year at a net cash flow of $.50 a piece for the next five years but they are unsure about the market. At the end of the first year, they will learn if the product is a success or failure. If it is a success, they can revise their forecast to 8 million bottles per year. If it is a failure, unit sales will be 1 million. Success and failure are equally likely. The relevant discount rate is 15 percent and the initial investment required is $3 million. If they abandon the project after year 1, they can recover $1.5 million of the initial investment.
  a. What is the base case NPV?
  b. What is the value of the option to abandon?

Part III

Risk

This part of the book examines the relationship between expected return and risk for portfolios and individual assets. When capital markets are in equilibrium, they determine a trade-off between expected return and risk. The returns that shareholders can expect to obtain in the capital markets are the ones they will require from firms when the firms evaluate risky investment projects. The shareholders' required return is the firm's cost of equity capital.

Chapter 9 examines the modern history of the U.S. capital markets. A central fact emerges: The return on risky assets has been higher on average than the return on risk-free assets. This fact supports the perspective for our examination of risk and return. In Chapter 9 we introduce several key intuitions of modern finance and show how they can be useful in determining a firm's cost of capital.

Chapters 10 and 11 contain more advanced discussions of risk and expected return. The chapters are self-contained and build on the material in Chapter 9.

Chapter 10 shows what determines the relationship between return and risk for portfolios. The model of risk and expected return used in the chapter is called the *capital-asset-pricing model* (CAPM).

Chapter 11 examines risk and return from another perspective: the arbitrage pricing theory (APT). This approach yields insights that one cannot get from the CAPM. The key concept is that the total risk of individual stocks can be divided into two parts: systematic and unsystematic. The fundamental principle of diversification is that, for highly diversified portfolios, unsystematic risk disappears; only systematic risk survives.

The section on risk finishes with a discussion in Chapter 12 on estimating a firm's cost of equity capital and some of the problems that are encountered in doing so.

233

Capital Market Theory: *An Overview*

We learned in Chapter 4 that riskless cash flows should be discounted at the riskless rate of interest. Because most capital-budgeting projects involve risky flows, a different discount rate must be used. The next four chapters are devoted to determining the discount rate for risky projects.

Past experience indicates that students find the upcoming material among the most difficult in the entire textbook. Because of this, we always teach the material by presenting the results and conclusions first. By seeing where we are going ahead of time, it is easier to absorb the material when we get there. A synopsis of the four chapters follows:

1. Because our ultimate goal is to discount risky cash flows, we must first find a way to measure risk. In the current chapter we measure the variability of an asset by the variance or standard deviation of its returns. If an individual holds only *one* asset, its variance or standard deviation would be the appropriate measure of risk.

2. While Chapter 9 considers one type of asset in isolation, Chapter 10 examines a portfolio of many assets. In this case, we are interested in the *contribution* of the security to the risk of the entire portfolio. Because much of an individual security's variance is dispersed in a large diversified portfolio, neither the security's variance nor its standard deviation can be viewed as the security's contribution to the risk of a large portfolio. Rather, this contribution is best measured by the security's beta (β). As an example,

consider a stock whose returns are high when the returns on a large, diversified portfolio are low—and vice versa. This stock has a negative beta. In other words, it acts as a hedge, implying that the stock actually tends to reduce the risk of the portfolio. However, the stock could have a high variance, implying high risk for an investor holding only this security.

3. Investors will only hold a risky security if its expected return is high enough to compensate for its risk. Given the above, the expected return on a security should be positively related to the security's beta. In fact, the relationship between risk and expected return can be expressed more precisely by the following equation:

$$\begin{array}{l}\text{Expected return} \\ \text{on a security}\end{array} = \begin{array}{l}\text{Risk-free} \\ \text{rate}\end{array} + \text{Beta}$$
$$\times \left(\begin{array}{l}\text{Expected return on} \\ \text{market portfolio}\end{array} - \begin{array}{l}\text{Risk-free} \\ \text{rate}\end{array} \right).$$

Because the term in parentheses on the right-hand side is positive, this equation says that the expected return on a security is a positive function of its beta. This equation is frequently referred to as the *capital-asset-pricing model* (CAPM).

4. We derive the relationship between risk and return in a different manner in Chapter 11. However, many of the conclusions are quite similar. This chapter is based on the *arbitrage pricing theory* (APT).

5. The theoretical ideas in Chapters 9, 10, and 11 are intellectually challenging. Fortunately, Chapter 12, which applies

the above theory to the selection of discount rates, is much simpler. In a world where (a) a project has the same risk as the firm, and (b) the firm has no debt, the expected return on the stock should serve as the project's discount rate. This expected return is taken from the capital-asset-pricing model, as presented above.

Because we have a long road ahead of us, the maxim that any journey begins with a single step applies here. We start with the perhaps mundane calculation of a security's return.

9.1 Returns

Dollar Returns

Suppose the Video Concept Company has several thousand shares of stock outstanding and you are a shareholder. Further suppose that you purchased some of the shares of stock in the company at the beginning of the year; it is now year-end and you want to figure out how well you have done on your investment. The return you get on an investment in stocks, like that in bonds or any other investment, comes in two forms.

First, over the year most companies pay dividends to shareholders. As the owner of stock in the Video Concept Company, you are a part owner of the company. If the company is profitable, it generally will distribute some of its profits to the shareholders. Therefore, as the owner of shares of stock, you will receive some cash, called a *dividend,* during the year.[1] This cash is the *income component* of your return. In addition to the dividends, the other part of your return is the *capital gain*—or, if it is negative, the *capital loss* (negative capital gain)—on the investment.

For example, suppose we are considering the cash flows of the investment in Figure 9.1 and you purchased 100 shares of stock at the beginning of the year at a price of $37 per share. Your total investment, then, would be

$$C_0 = \$37 \times 100 = \$3,700$$

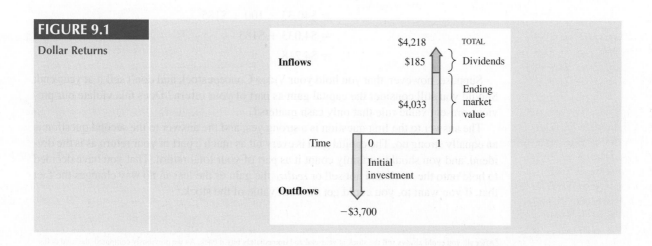

FIGURE 9.1

Dollar Returns

---

[1]In fact, companies often continue to pay dividends even when they have lost money during the year.

Suppose that over the year the stock paid a dividend of $1.85 per share. During the year, then, you would have received income of

$$Div = \$1.85 \times 100 = \$185$$

Suppose, lastly, that at the end of the year the market price of the stock is $40.33 per share. Because the stock increased in price, you have a capital gain of

$$Gain = (\$40.33 - \$37) \times 100 = \$333$$

The capital gain, like the dividend, is part of the return that shareholders require to maintain their investment in the Video Concept Company. Of course, if the price of Video Concept stock had dropped in value to, say, $34.78, you would have recorded a capital loss of

$$Loss = (\$34.78 - \$37) \times 100 = -\$222$$

The *total dollar return* on your investment is the sum of the dividend income and the capital gain or loss on the investment:

$$Total\ dollar\ return = Dividend\ income + Capital\ gain\ (or\ loss)$$

(From now on we will refer to *capital losses* as *negative capital gains* and not distinguish them.) In our first example, then, the total dollar return is given by

$$Total\ dollar\ return = \$185 + \$333 = \$518$$

Notice that if you sold the stock at the end of the year, your total amount of cash would be the initial investment plus the total dollar return. In the preceding example, then, you would have

$$Total\ cash\ if\ stock\ is\ sold = Initial\ investment + Total\ dollar\ return$$
$$= \$3,700 + \$518$$
$$= \$4,218$$

As a check, notice that this is the same as the proceeds from the sale of stock plus the dividends:

$$Proceeds\ from\ stock\ sale + Dividends$$
$$= \$40.33 \times 100 + \$185$$
$$= \$4,033 + \$185$$
$$= \$4,218$$

Suppose, however, that you hold your Video Concept stock and don't sell it at year-end. Should you still consider the capital gain as part of your return? Does this violate our previous present value rule that only cash matters?

The answer to the first question is a strong yes, and the answer to the second question is an equally strong no. The capital gain is every bit as much a part of your return as is the dividend, and you should certainly count it as part of your total return. That you have decided to hold onto the stock and not sell or *realize* the gain or the loss in no way changes the fact that, if you want to, you could get the cash value of the stock.[2]

---

[2]After all, you could always sell the stock at year-end and immediately buy it back. As we previously computed, the total dollar return on the investment would be $518 before you bought the stock back. The total amount of cash you would have at year-end would be this $518 plus your initial investment of $3,700. You would not lose this return when you bought back 100 shares of stock. In fact, you would be in exactly the same position as if you had not sold the stock (assuming, of course, that there are no tax consequences and no brokerage commissions from selling the stock).

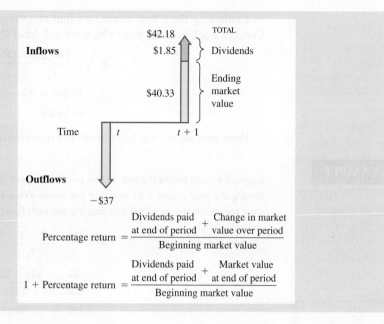

Percentage Returns

It is more convenient to summarize the information about returns in percentage terms than in dollars, because the percentages apply to any amount invested. The question we want to answer is: How much return do we get for each dollar invested? To find this out, let t stand for the year we are looking at, let P_t be the price of the stock at the beginning of the year, and let Div_{t+1} be the dividend paid on the stock during the year. Consider the cash flows in Figure 9.2.

In our example, the price at the beginning of the year was $37 per share and the dividend paid during the year on each share was $1.85. Hence the percentage of income return,[3] sometimes called the *dividend yield,* is

$$\text{Dividend yield} = \text{Div}_{t+1}/P_t$$
$$= \$1.85/\$37$$
$$= 0.05$$
$$= 5\%$$

Capital gain is the change in the price of the stock divided by the initial price. Letting P_{t+1} be the price of the stock at year-end, the capital gain can be computed

$$\text{Capital gain} = (P_{t+1} - P_t)/P_t$$
$$= (\$40.33 - \$37)/\$37$$
$$= \$3.33/\$37$$
$$= 0.09$$
$$= 9\%$$

---

[3]We will use 0.05 and 5 percent interchangeably. Keep in mind that, although $(0.05)^2 = 0.0025$, $(5^2)\% = 25\%$. Thus, it is important to keep track of parentheses so that decimal points land where they belong.

Combining these two results, we find that the *total return* on the investment in Video Concept stock over the year, which we will label R_{t+1}, was

$$R_{t+1} = \frac{\text{Div}_{t+1}}{P_t} + \frac{(P_{t+1} - P_t)}{P_t}$$

$$= 5\% + 9\%$$

$$= \$14\%$$

From now on we will refer to returns in percentage terms.

EXAMPLE

Suppose a stock begins the year with a price of $25 per share and ends with a price of $35 per share. During the year it paid a $2 dividend per share. What are its dividend yield, its capital gain, and its total return for the year? We can imagine the cash flows in Figure 9.3.

$$R_1 = \frac{\text{Div}_1}{P_0} + \frac{P_1 - P_0}{P_0}$$

$$= \frac{\$2}{\$25} + \frac{\$35 - \$25}{\$25} = \frac{\$12}{\$25}$$

$$= 8\% \ + \quad 40\% \quad = 48\%$$

Thus, the stock's dividend yield, its capital gain yield, and its total return are 8 percent, 40 percent, and 48 percent, respectively.

Suppose you had $5,000 invested. The total dollar return you would have received on an investment in the stock is $5,000 × 0.48 = $2,400. If you know the total dollar return on the stock, you do not need to know how many shares you would have had to purchase to figure out how much money you would have made on the $5,000 investment. You just use the total dollar return.[4]

FIGURE 9.3

Cash Flow—An Investment Example

---

[4]Consider the stock in the previous example. We have ignored the question of when during the year you receive the dividend. Does it make a difference? To explore this question, suppose first that the dividend is paid at the very beginning of the year, and you receive it the moment after you have purchased the stock. Suppose, too, that interest rates are 10 percent, and that immediately after receiving the dividend you loan it out. What will be your total return, including the loan proceeds, at the end of the year?

Alternatively, instead of loaning out the dividend you could have reinvested it and purchased more of the stock. If that is what you do with the dividend, what will your total return be? (Warning: This does not go on forever, and when you buy more stock with the cash from the dividend on your first purchase, you are too late to get yet another dividend on the new stock.)

Finally, suppose the dividend is paid at year-end. What answer would you get for the total return?

As you can see, by ignoring the question of when the dividend is paid when we calculate the return, we are implicitly assuming that it is received at the end of the year and cannot be reinvested during the year. The right way to figure out the return on a stock is to determine exactly when the dividend is received and to include the return that comes from reinvesting the dividend in the stock. This gives a pure stock return without confounding the issue by requiring knowledge of the interest rate during the year.

Concept Questions	1. **What are the two parts of total return?**
	2. **Why are unrealized capital gains or losses included in the calculation of returns?**
	3. **What is the difference between a dollar return and a percentage return?**

9.2 Holding-Period Returns

A famous set of studies dealing with rates of return on common stocks, bonds, and Treasury bills was conducted by Roger Ibbotson and Rex Sinquefield.[5] They present year-by-year historical rates of return for the following five important types of financial instruments in the United States:

1. *Large-Company Common Stocks.* The common-stock portfolio is based on the Standard & Poor's (S&P) composite index. At present, the S&P composite includes 500 of the largest (in terms of market value) stocks in the United States.

2. *Small-Company Common Stocks.* This is a portfolio composed of the bottom fifth of stocks traded on the New York Stock Exchange in which stocks are ranked by market value (i.e., the price of the stock multiplied by the number of shares outstanding).

3. *Long-Term Corporate Bonds.* This is a portfolio of high-quality corporate bonds with a 20-year maturity.

4. *Long-Term U.S. Government Bonds.* This is a portfolio of U.S. government bonds with a maturity of 20 years.

5. *U.S. Treasury Bills.* This is a portfolio of Treasury bills of three-month maturity.

None of the returns are adjusted for taxes or transactions costs. In addition to the year-by-year returns on financial instruments, the year-to-year change in the consumer price index is computed. This is a basic measure of inflation. Year-by-year real returns can be calculated by subtracting annual inflation.

Before looking closely at the different portfolio returns, we graphically present the returns and risks available from U.S. capital markets in the 77-year period from 1926 to 2002. Figure 9.4 shows the growth of $1 invested at the beginning of 1926. Notice that the vertical axis is logarithmic, so that equal distances measure the same number of percentage changes. The figure shows that if $1 were invested in large company common stocks and all dividends were reinvested, the dollar would have grown to $1,775.34 by the end of 2002. The biggest growth was in the small-stock portfolio. If $1 were invested in small stocks in 1926, the investment would have grown to $6,816.41. However, when you look carefully at Figure 9.4, you can see great variability in the returns on small stocks, especially in the earlier part of the period. A dollar in long-term government bonds was very stable as compared with a dollar in common stocks. Figures 9.5 to 9.8 plot each year-to-year percentage return as a vertical bar drawn from the horizontal axis for large-company common stocks, for small-company stocks, for long-term bonds and Treasury bills, and for inflation, respectively.

Figure 9.4 gives the growth of a dollar investment in the stock market from 1926 through 2002. In other words, it shows what the worth of the investment would have been if the dollar had been left in the stock market and if each year the dividends from the previous year had been reinvested in more stock. If R_t is the return in year t (expressed in

---

[5]The most recent update of this work is *Stocks, Bonds, Bills and Inflation: 2003 Yearbook*™ (Chicago: Ibbotson Associates). All rights reserved.

FIGURE 9.4	
Wealth Indices of Investments in the U.S. Capital Markets (Year-End 1925 = $1.00)	

from 1925 to 2002

Redrawn from *Stocks, Bonds, Bills and Inflation: 2003 Yearbook,*™ annual updates work by Roger G. Ibbotson and Rex A. Sinquefield (Chicago: Ibbotson Associates). All rights reserved.

FIGURE 9.5	
Year-by-Year Total Returns on Large-Company Common Stocks	

Redrawn from *Stocks, Bonds, Bills and Inflation: 2003 Yearbook,*™ annual updates work by Roger G. Ibbotson and Rex A. Sinquefield (Chicago: Ibbotson Associates). All rights reserved.

FIGURE 9.6

Year-by-Year Total
Returns on Small-
Company Stocks

FIGURE 9.7

Year-by-Year Total
Returns on Bonds
and Bills

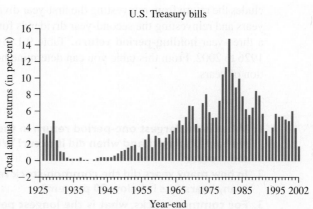

FIGURE 9.8

Year-by-Year Inflation

decimals), the value you would have at the end of year T is the product of 1 plus the return in each of the years:

$$(1 + R_1) \times (1 + R_2) \times \cdots \times (1 + R_t) \times \cdots \times (1 + R_T)$$

For example, if the returns were 11 percent, −5 percent, and 9 percent in a three-year period, an investment of $1 at the beginning of the period would be worth

$$\begin{aligned}(1 + R_1) \times (1 + R_2) \times (1 + R_3) &= (\$1 + 0.11) \times (\$1 - 0.05) \times (\$1 + 0.09) \\ &= \$1.11 \times \$0.95 \times \$1.09 \\ &= \$1.15\end{aligned}$$

at the end of the three years. Notice that 0.15 or 15 percent is the total return and that it includes the return from reinvesting the first-year dividends in the stock market for two more years and reinvesting the second-year dividends for the final year. The 15 percent is called a three-year **holding-period return**. Table 9.1 gives the annual returns each year from 1926 to 2002. From this table you can determine holding-period returns for any combination of years.

Concept
Questions

1. **What is the largest one-period return in the 77-year history of common stocks we have displayed, and when did it occur? What is the smallest return, and when did it occur?**
2. **In how many years did the common-stock return exceed 30 percent, and in how many years was it below 20 percent?**
3. **For common stocks, what is the longest period of time without a single losing year? What is the longest streak of losing years?**
4. **What is the longest period of time such that if you had invested at the beginning of the period, you would still not have had a positive return on your common-stock investment by the end?**

TABLE 9.1	Year-by-Year Total Returns, 1926–2002			
Year	Large-Company Stocks	Long-Term Government Bonds	Long-Term Corporate Bonds	U.S. Treasury Bills	Inflation
1926	13.70%	6.40%	7.00%	4.40%	−1.10%
1927	35.80%	4.51%	6.54%	4.21%	−2.33%
1928	45.14%	0.18%	3.42%	4.87%	−1.14%
1929	−8.88%	5.66%	4.33%	6.05%	0.63%
1930	−25.22%	4.16%	6.34%	3.72%	−6.45%
1931	−43.75%	0.41%	−2.45%	2.63%	−9.23%
1932	−8.38%	5.61%	12.23%	2.95%	−10.29%
1933	53.11%	5.92%	5.24%	1.66%	0.68%
1934	−2.41%	5.95%	9.75%	1.04%	1.63%
1935	46.94%	3.22%	6.89%	0.29%	2.94%
1936	32.35%	1.73%	6.22%	0.15%	1.43%
1937	−35.68%	4.63%	2.50%	0.44%	2.81%
1938	32.29%	4.74%	4.36%	0.07%	−2.74%
1939	−1.54%	2.26%	4.28%	0.00%	0.00%
1940	−10.54%	4.25%	4.49%	0.00%	0.77%
1941	−12.14%	1.56%	1.78%	0.07%	9.90%
1942	20.98%	1.82%	3.14%	0.36%	9.01%
1943	25.52%	2.00%	3.35%	0.36%	2.97%
1944	19.46%	2.28%	3.12%	0.36%	2.26%
1945	36.35%	5.23%	3.51%	0.36%	2.31%
1946	−8.48%	0.54%	2.52%	0.43%	18.09%
1947	4.96%	−0.93%	0.46%	0.57%	8.83%
1948	4.95%	2.62%	3.72%	0.99%	2.98%
1949	17.74%	4.53%	4.32%	1.12%	−2.08%
1950	30.04%	−0.92%	1.91%	1.25%	5.99%
1951	23.88%	−0.14%	−0.24%	1.51%	5.94%
1952	18.44%	2.42%	3.45%	1.76%	0.81%
1953	−1.11%	2.32%	2.05%	1.93%	0.74%
1954	52.44%	3.07%	4.65%	0.98%	−0.73%
1955	31.65%	−0.69%	1.07%	1.68%	0.34%
1956	6.90%	−1.61%	−1.78%	2.66%	3.01%
1957	−10.53%	6.75%	4.48%	3.34%	2.92%
1958	43.73%	−1.61%	0.85%	1.79%	1.76%
1959	12.02%	−1.89%	0.15%	3.35%	1.67%
1960	0.45%	11.04%	6.71%	3.13%	1.40%
1961	26.90%	2.24%	3.69%	2.32%	0.66%
1962	−8.79%	6.03%	6.20%	2.80%	1.31%
1963	22.72%	1.42%	3.17%	3.20%	1.65%
1964	16.43%	3.89%	3.97%	3.56%	0.98%
1965	12.37%	1.05%	2.10%	4.02%	1.95%
1966	−10.10%	4.81%	−0.26%	4.90%	3.43%
1967	24.04%	−2.36%	−1.17%	4.49%	3.05%
1968	11.03%	1.66%	4.17%	5.42%	4.70%
1969	−8.47%	−4.82%	−2.46%	6.81%	6.20%
1970	4.00%	18.15%	11.18%	6.68%	5.56%
1971	14.35%	11.39%	9.70%	4.51%	3.28%
1972	19.00%	2.51%	8.32%	4.04%	3.40%
1973	−14.85%	3.50%	2.99%	6.98%	8.72%

(continued)

TABLE 9.1	Year-by-Year Total Returns, 1926–2002 *(concluded)*			
Year	Large-Company Stocks	Long-Term Government Bonds	Long-Term Corporate Bonds	U.S. Treasury Bills	Inflation
1974	−26.58%	3.82%	0.22%	8.09%	16.20%
1975	37.42%	5.63%	11.04%	6.04%	3.40%
1976	23.76%	15.20%	14.57%	5.16%	4.84%
1977	−7.38%	0.55%	5.50%	5.26%	6.71%
1978	6.54%	−0.99%	1.84%	7.23%	9.02%
1979	18.59%	0.50%	−1.55%	10.32%	13.30%
1980	32.61%	−0.63%	−4.99%	12.04%	12.51%
1981	−4.97%	2.62%	8.98%	15.21%	8.92%
1982	21.67%	43.98%	34.90%	11.28%	3.85%
1983	22.57%	2.03%	7.30%	8.89%	3.78%
1984	6.19%	15.96%	17.10%	10.04%	3.96%
1985	31.85%	30.34%	29.37%	7.70%	3.79%
1986	18.68%	22.86%	21.26%	6.18%	1.10%
1987	5.22%	−3.24%	−1.82%	5.87%	4.44%
1988	16.58%	6.86%	13.78%	6.73%	4.42%
1989	31.75%	18.64%	15.30%	8.48%	4.65%
1990	−3.13%	7.26%	8.60%	7.85%	6.10%
1991	30.53%	18.52%	15.63%	5.71%	3.06%
1992	7.62%	8.52%	10.88%	3.57%	2.89%
1993	10.07%	13.45%	14.68%	3.08%	2.75%
1994	1.27%	−7.31%	−2.42%	4.15%	2.68%
1995	37.80%	24.86%	22.03%	5.64%	2.53%
1996	22.74%	1.63%	3.87%	5.12%	3.32%
1997	33.43%	10.89%	11.11%	5.22%	1.70%
1998	28.13%	13.44%	11.44%	5.06%	1.61%
1999	21.03%	−7.12%	−2.30%	4.85%	2.69%
2000	−9.10%	17.22%	11.69%	5.98%	3.39%
2001	−11.89%	5.51%	11.46%	3.33%	1.55%
2002	−22.10%	15.15%	11.18%	1.61%	2.38%

Global Financial Data (www.globalfindata.com) copyright 2003.

9.3 Return Statistics

The history of capital-market returns is too complicated to be handled in its undigested form. To use the history we must first find some manageable ways of describing it, dramatically condensing the detailed data into a few simple statements.

This is where two important numbers summarizing the history come in. The first and most natural number is some single measure that best describes the past annual returns on the stock market. In other words, what is our best estimate of the return that an investor could have realized in a particular year over the 1926-to-2002 period? This is the *average return*.

Figure 9.9 plots the histogram of the yearly stock market returns given in Table 9.1. This plot is the **frequency distribution** of the numbers. The height of the graph gives the number of sample observations in the range on the horizontal axis.

Given a frequency distribution like that in Figure 9.9, we can calculate the **average** or **mean** of the distribution. To compute the arithmetic average of the distribution, we add up all of the values and divide by the total (T) number (77 in our case because we have 77 years of data). The bar over the R is used to represent the mean, and the formula is the

FIGURE 9.9	Histogram of Returns on Common Stocks, 1926–2002

Large-company stocks

```
                                    2000        1988        1997
                                    1990        1986  1999  1995
                                    1981  1994  1979  1998  1991
                                    1977  1993  1972  1996  1989
                                    1969  1992  1971  1983  1985
                                    1962  1987  1968  1982  1980
                                    1953  1984  1965  1976  1975
                                    1946  1978  1964  1967  1955
                              2001  1940  1970  1959  1963  1950
                              1973  1939  1960  1952  1961  1945
                        2002  1966  1934  1956  1949  1951  1938  1958
                        1974  1957  1932  1948  1944  1943  1936  1935  1954
            1931  1937  1930  1941  1929  1947  1926  1942  1927  1928  1933
```

−80 −70 −60 −50 −40 −30 −20 −10   0   10   20   30   40   50   60   70   80   90

Percent

Small-company stocks

```
                                          2001
                                          1999
                                          1997
                                          1993
                              2000        1992
                              1998        1988
                              1987  1994  1985
                              1984  1986  1982  1995
                              1966  1972  1978  1983
                        2002  1960  1956  1996  1977  1980
                        1974  1953  1952  1989  1964  1968  1991
                        1970  1948  1951  1981  1963  1961  1979
                        1962  1941  1947  1971  1955  1950  1965  1976  1958
            1937  1973  1990  1957  1940  1939  1959  1934  1938  1942  1975  1954              1967
            1929  1931  1930  1969  1946  1932  1926  1949  1927  1928  1935  1944  1936  1945  1943        1933
```

−80 −70 −60 −50 −40 −30 −20 −10   0   10   20   30   40   50   60   70   80   90   140   150

Percent

Redrawn from *Stocks, Bonds, Bills and Inflation: 2003 Yearbook*,™ annual updates work by Roger G. Ibbotson and Rex A. Sinquefield (Chicago: Ibbotson Associates). All rights reserved.

ordinary formula for the average:

$$\text{Mean} = \bar{R} = \frac{(R_1 + \cdots + R_T)}{T}$$

The arithmetic mean of the 77 annual returns from 1926 to 2002 is 12.2 percent.[6]

EXAMPLE

The returns on common stock from 1926 to 1929 are 0.1370, 0.3580, 0.4514, and −0.0888, respectively. (These numbers are taken from Table 9.1.) The average, or mean, return over these four years is

$$\bar{R} = \frac{0.1370 + 0.3580 + 0.4514 - 0.0888}{4} = 0.2144 \ (21.44\%)$$

---

[6]We can also calculate the geometric mean for the 77-year sample of annual returns. It is equal to $\sqrt[77]{1,775.34} - 1 = 10.2\%$ for large-company stocks.

9.4 Average Stock Returns and Risk-Free Returns

Now that we have computed the average return on the stock market, it seems sensible to compare it with the returns on other securities. The most obvious comparison is with the low-variability returns in the government-bond market. These are free of most of the volatility we see in the stock market.

The government borrows money by issuing bonds, which the investing public holds. As we discussed in an earlier chapter, these bonds come in many forms, and the ones we will look at here are called *Treasury bills,* or *T-bills.* Once a week the government sells some bills at an auction. A typical bill is a pure discount bond that will mature in a year or less. Because the government can raise taxes to pay for the debt it incurs—a trick that many of us would like to be able to perform—this debt is virtually free of the risk of default. Thus we will call this the *risk-free return* over a short time (one year or less).[7]

An interesting comparison, then, is between the virtually risk-free return on T-bills and the very risky return on common stocks. This difference between risky returns and risk-free returns is often called the *excess return on the risky asset.* It is called *excess* because it is the additional return resulting from the riskiness of common stocks and is interpreted as an equity **risk premium.**

Table 9.2 shows the average stock return, bond return, T-bill return, and inflation rate for the period from 1926 through 2002. From this we can derive excess returns. The average excess return from large-company common stocks for the entire period was 8.4 percent (12.2% − 3.8%).

One of the most significant observations of stock market data is this long-run excess of the stock return over the risk-free return.[8] An investor for this period was rewarded for investment in the stock market with an extra or excess return over what would have been achieved by simply investing in T-bills.

Why was there such a reward? Does it mean that it never pays to invest in T-bills and that someone who invested in them instead of in the stock market needs a course in finance? A complete answer to these questions lies at the heart of modern finance, and Chapter 10 is devoted entirely to this. However, part of the answer can be found in the variability of the various types of investments. We see in Table 9.1 many years when an investment in T-bills achieved higher returns than an investment in common stocks. Also, we note that the returns from an investment in common stocks are frequently negative whereas an investment in T-bills never produces a negative return. So, we now turn our attention to measuring the variability of returns and an introductory discussion of risk.

Now we look more closely at Table 9.2. We see that the standard deviation of T-bills is substantially less than that of common stocks. This suggests that the risk of T-bills is less than that of common stocks. Because the answer turns on the riskiness of investments in common stock, we now turn our attention to measuring this risk.

Concept Questions

1. **What is the major observation about capital markets that we will seek to explain?**
2. **What does the observation tell us about investors for the period from 1926 through 2002?**

---

[7] A Treasury bill with a 90-day maturity is risk-free only during that particular time period.

[8] The notion of a risk-free rate depends upon the time period over which returns are being measured. The 90-day Treasury bill is risk free for 90 days but not for 10 years. On the other hand, the 10-year Treasury bond is risk free for 10 years but not for 90 days. Many equity risk premium computations start with a long-term Treasury bond instead of a 90-day Treasury bill. If so, the historical equity risk premium for large company stocks for the past 77 years has been 6.4% (12.2% − 5.8%). This viewpoint reflects the idea that most investments have long time horizons and a longer-term risk-free rate is appropriate. There is a debate in the academic world over which is the better way to measure historical equity risk premiums—a short-term horizon or a longer-term horizon.

TABLE 9.2	Series	Arithmetic Mean	Risk Premium (relative to U.S. Treasury bills)	Standard Deviation	Distribution
Total Annual Returns, 1926–2002					
	Large-company stocks	12.2%	8.4%	20.5%	
	Small-company stocks	16.9	13.1	33.2	*
	Long-term corporate bonds	6.2	2.4	8.7	
	Long-term government	5.8	2.0	9.4	
	U.S. Treasury bills	3.8		3.2	
	Inflation	3.1		4.4	
					−90% 0% 90%

*The 1933 small-company stock total return was 142.9 percent.

Modified from *Stocks, Bonds, Bills and Inflation: 2003 Yearbook,*™ annual updates work by Roger G. Ibbotson and Rex A. Sinquefield (Chicago: Ibbotson Associates). All rights reserved.

9.5 Risk Statistics

The second number that we use to characterize the distribution of returns is a measure of the risk in returns. There is no universally agreed-upon definition of risk. One way to think about the risk of returns on common stock is in terms of how spread out the frequency distribution in Figure 9.9 is.[9] The spread, or dispersion, of a distribution is a measure of how much a particular return can deviate from the mean return. If the distribution is very spread out, the returns that will occur are very uncertain. By contrast, a distribution whose returns are all within a few percentage points of each other is tight, and the returns are less uncertain. The measures of risk we will discuss are variance and standard deviation.

Variance

The **variance** and its square root, the **standard deviation,** are the most common measures of variability or dispersion. We will use Var and σ^2 to denote the variance and SD and σ to represent the standard deviation. σ is, of course, the Greek letter sigma.

EXAMPLE

The returns on common stocks from 1926 to 1929 are (in decimals) 0.1370, 0.3580, 0.4514, and −0.0888, respectively. The variance of this sample is computed as

$$\text{Var} = \frac{1}{T-1}\left[(R_1 - \bar{R})^2 + (R_2 - \bar{R})^2 + (R_3 - \bar{R})^2 + (R_4 - \bar{R})^2\right]$$

$$0.0582 = \tfrac{1}{3}[(0.1370 - 0.2144)^2 + (0.3580 - 0.2144)^2$$
$$+ (0.4514 - 0.2144)^2 + (-0.0888 - 0.2144)^2]$$

$$\text{SD} = \sqrt{0.0582} = 0.2413 \quad (\text{i.e., } 24.13\%)$$

---

[9]Several condensed frequency distributions are also in the extreme right column of Table 9.2.

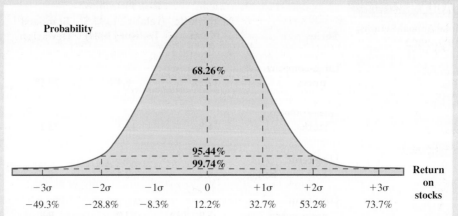

FIGURE 9.10

The Normal
Distribution

In the case of a normal distribution, there is a 68.26-percent probability that a return will be within one standard deviation of the mean. In this example, there is a 68.26-percent probability that a yearly return will be between −8.3 percent and 32.7 percent.

There is a 95.44-percent probability that a return will be within two standard deviations of the mean. In this example, there is a 95.44-percent probability that a yearly return will be between −28.8 percent and 53.2 percent.

Finally, there is a 99.74-percent probability that a return will be within three standard deviations of the mean. In this example, there is a 99.74-percent probability that a yearly return will be between −49.3 percent and 73.7 percent.

This formula tells us just what to do: Take the T individual returns ($R_1, R_2, \ldots$) and subtract the average return $\bar{R}$, square the result, and add them up. Finally, this total must be divided by the number of returns less one ($T − 1$). The standard deviation is always just the square root of the variance.

Using the actual stock returns in Table 9.1 for the 77-year period from 1926 through 2002 in the above formula, the resulting standard deviation of stock returns is 20.5 percent. The standard deviation is the standard statistical measure of the spread of a sample, and it will be the measure we use most of the time. Its interpretation is facilitated by a discussion of the normal distribution.

Normal Distribution and Its Implications for Standard Deviation

A large enough sample drawn from a **normal distribution** looks like the bell-shaped curve drawn in Figure 9.10. As you can see, this distribution is *symmetric* about its mean, not *skewed,* and it has a much cleaner shape than the actual distribution of yearly returns drawn in Figure 9.9.[10] Of course, if we had been able to observe stock market returns for 1,000 years, we might have filled in a lot of the jumps and jerks in Figure 9.9 and had a smoother curve.

In classical statistics the normal distribution plays a central role, and the standard deviation is the usual way to represent the spread of a normal distribution. For the normal distribution, the probability of having a return that is above or below the mean by a certain amount depends only on the standard deviation. For example, the probability of having a return that is within one standard deviation of the mean of the distribution is approximately

---

[10]Some people define risk as the possibility of obtaining a return below the average. Some measures of risk, such as *semivariance,* use only the negative deviations from the average return. However, for symmetric distributions, such as the normal distribution, this method of measuring downside risk is equivalent to measuring risk with deviations from the mean on both sides.

0.68 or 2/3, and the probability of having a return that is within two standard deviations of the mean is approximately 0.95.

The 20.5-percent standard deviation we found for stock returns from 1926 through 2002 can now be interpreted in the following way: If stock returns are roughly normally distributed, the probability that a yearly return will fall within 20.5 percent of the mean of 12.2 percent will be approximately 2/3. That is, about 2/3 of the yearly returns will be between −8.3 percent and 32.7 percent. (Note that −8.3% = 12.2% − 20.5% and 32.7% = 12.2% + 20.5%.) The probability that the return in any year will fall within two standard deviations is about 0.95. That is, about 95 percent of yearly returns will be between −28.8 percent and 53.2 percent.

The distribution in Figure 9.10 is a theoretical distribution, sometimes called the *population distribution* or *true distribution*. There is no assurance that the actual distribution of observations in a given sample will produce a histogram that looks exactly like the theoretical distribution. We can see how messy the actual frequency function of historical observations is by observing Figure 9.9. If we were to keep on generating observations for a long enough period of time, however, the aberrations in the sample would disappear, and the actual historical distribution would start to look like the underlying theoretical distribution.

This points out that sampling error exists in any individual sample. In other words, the distribution of the sample only approximates the true distribution: We always measure the truth with some error. For example, we do not know what the true expected return was for common stocks in the 77-year history. However, we are sure that our 12.2 percent realized return is close to it.

Concept Questions	1. **What is the definition of sample estimates of variance and standard deviation?** 2. **How does the normal distribution help us interpret standard deviation?**

9.6 SUMMARY AND CONCLUSIONS

1. This chapter presents returns for a number of different asset classes. The general conclusion is that stocks have outperformed bonds over most of the 20th century, though stocks have also exhibited more risk.

2. The statistical measures in this chapter are necessary building blocks for the material of the next three chapters. In particular, standard deviation and variance measure the variability of the return on an individual security and on portfolios of securities. In the next chapter, we will argue that standard deviation and variance are appropriate measures of the risk of an individual security if an investor's portfolio is composed of that security only.

KEY TERMS

average (mean), *244*	normal distribution, *248*
capital gain, *237*	risk premium, *246*
frequency distribution, *244*	standard deviation, *247*
holding-period return, *242*	variance, *247*

SUGGESTED READINGS

An important record of the performance of financial instruments in the U.S. capital markets can be found in:

Ibbotson, Roger G., and Rex A. Sinquefield. *Stocks, Bonds, Bills and Inflation: 2003 Yearbook.*™ Chicago: Ibbotson Associates.

What is the equity risk premium? This is the question addressed by:

Cornell, Bradford. *The Equity Risk Premium: The Long Term Future of the Stock Market.* New York: John Wiley, 1999 and Shiller, Robert S. *Irrational Exuberance.* Princeton, N.J.: Princeton University Press, 2000.

Visit us at www.mhhe.com/rwj

For a look at market risk premiums worldwide, see:

Jorion, P., and W. N. Goetzmann, "Global Stock Markets in the Twentieth Century." *Journal of Finance* 54 (1999).

QUESTIONS & PROBLEMS

RETURNS

9.1 One year ago, you bought 500 shares of Webster, Inc., stock at $37 per share. You just received a dividend of $1,000 and Webster stock now sells for $38.
   a. How much did you earn in capital gains?
   b. What was your total dollar return?
   c. What was your percentage return?
   d. Must you sell the stock to include the capital gain in your return?

9.2 One year ago, Mr. Seth Cohen invested $10,400 in 200 shares of First Industries, Inc., stock and just received a dividend of $600. Today, he sold the 200 shares at $54.25 per share.
   a. What was his capital gain?
   b. What was his total dollar return?
   c. What was his percentage return?
   d. What was the stock's dividend yield?

9.3 You purchased a stock one year ago at $42 per share. The stock just paid a dividend of $2.40 per share. Today, you sold the stock at $31 per share. What is the percentage return on this stock?

9.4 Lydian Stock currently trades at $52 per share. You intend to buy the stock today and hold it for two years. Two years from today, you expect to sell the stock at $54.75 per share. What is the expected holding period return on the stock?

9.5 Calculate the average real annual returns for each of the following asset classes using the information below:

Series	Mean of Annual Total Return (1926–2002)
Large-company stocks	12.2%
Long-term corporate bonds	6.2
Long-term government bonds	5.8
U.S. Treasury bills	3.8
Inflation	3.1

   a. Large-company stocks
   b. Long-term corporate bonds
   c. Long-term government bonds
   d. U.S. Treasury bills

9.6 Suppose the current interest rate on U.S. Treasury bills is 2 percent. The average return on Treasury bills from 1926 through 2002 was 3.8 percent. The average return on common stocks during the same period was 12.2 percent. Given this information, what is the current expected return on common stocks?

9.7 Two years ago, General Materials and Standard Fixtures' stock prices were the same. Over the first year, General Materials' stock price increased by 10 percent while Standard Fixtures' stock price decreased by 10 percent. Over the second year, General Materials' stock price decreased by 10 percent and Standard Fixtures' stock price increased by 10 percent. Do these two stocks have the same prices today? Explain.

9.8 Using the returns for the period 1981 to 1985 listed below, calculate the five-year holding-period return on the S&P 500 index.

	1981	1982	1983	1984	1985
S&P 500 index return (%)	−4.97	21.67	22.57	6.19	31.85

9.9   *The Wall Street Journal* announced yesterday that the current rate for one-year Treasury bills is 2 percent, while the historical average annual return on Treasury bills for the period from 1926 through 2002 was 3.8 percent. During the same period, the average return on long-term corporate bonds was 6.2 percent. What is the historical risk premium of the long-term corporate bonds? What is the expected return on long-term corporate bonds?

AVERAGE RETURNS, EXPECTED RETURNS, AND VARIANCE

9.10   The returns on both a portfolio of common stocks and a portfolio of Treasury bills are contingent on the state of the economy, as shown below.

Economic Condition	Probability	Market Return	Treasury Bills
Recession	0.25	−8.2%	3.5%
Normal	0.50	12.3	3.5
Boom	0.25	25.8	3.5

a. Calculate the expected returns on the Treasury bills and on the market.
b. Calculate the expected risk premium.

9.11   Suppose during the past seven years, the annual returns on a portfolio of long-term corporate bonds were:

Year	Long-Term Corporate Bonds
−7	−2.6%
−6	−1.0
−5	43.8
−4	4.7
−3	16.4
−2	30.1
Last	19.9

a. Calculate the average return for long-term corporate bonds over this period.
b. Calculate the variance and the standard deviation of the returns for long-term corporate bonds during this period.

9.12   Below are the hypothetical returns during the past seven years on a market portfolio of common stocks and a portfolio of Treasury bills.

Year	Common Stocks	Treasury Bills
−7	32.4%	11.2%
−6	−4.9	14.7
−5	21.4	10.5
−4	22.5	8.8
−3	6.3	9.9
−2	32.2	7.7
Last	18.5	6.2

The realized risk premium is the return on common stocks less the return on Treasury bills.
a. Calculate the realized risk premium of common stocks over Treasury bills in each year.
b. Calculate the average risk premium of common stocks over Treasury bills during the seven-year period.
c. Is it possible for the observed risk premium to be negative? Explain.

Visit us at www.mhhe.com/rwj

9.13 The probability that the economy will contract is 0.2. The probability of moderate growth is 0.6, and the probability of a rapid expansion is 0.2. If the economy contracts, you can expect a return on your portfolio of 5 percent. With moderate growth, your return will be 8 percent. If there is a rapid expansion, your portfolio will return 15 percent.

    a. What is your expected return?

    b. What is the standard deviation of the return?

9.14 Below are the probabilities for the economy's five possible states next year, with the corresponding returns on the market and on Trebli, Inc., stock.

Economic Condition	Probability	Market Return	Trebli Return
Rapid expansion	0.12	0.23	0.12
Moderate expansion	0.40	0.18	0.09
No growth	0.25	0.15	0.05
Moderate contraction	0.15	0.09	0.01
Serious contraction	0.08	0.03	−0.02

    a. What is the expected return on the market?

    b. What is the expected return on Trebli stock?

 9.15 Four equally likely states of the economy may occur next year. Below are the returns on the stocks of Belinkie Enterprises and Overlake Company under each of the possible states.

State	Belinkie Enterprises	Overlake Company
1	0.04	0.05
2	0.06	0.07
3	0.09	0.10
4	0.04	0.14

    a. What is the expected return on each stock?

    b. What is the variance of the returns on each stock?

9.16 Tabulated below are the returns from 1935 through 1939 on small-company stocks and on the large-company common stocks.

Year	Small-Company Stocks (%)	Large-Company Common Stocks (%)
1935	47.7	46.9
1936	33.9	32.4
1937	−35.0	−35.7
1938	31.0	32.3
1939	−0.5	−1.5

    a. Calculate the average return for the small-company stocks and for the large-company common stocks.

    b. Calculate the variance and standard deviation of the small-company returns and the large-company returns.

 9.17 Annual returns for a seven-year period on large-company common stocks, small-company stocks, long-term corporate bonds, long-term U.S. government bonds, and U.S. Treasury bills are presented below:

Year	Large Common Stock	Small Stocks	Long-Term Corporate Bonds	Long-Term Government Bonds	U.S. Treasury Bills
1	0.3242	0.3988	−0.0262	−0.0395	0.1124
2	−0.0491	0.1388	−0.0096	0.0185	0.1471
3	0.2141	0.2801	0.4379	0.4035	0.1054
4	0.2251	0.3967	0.0470	0.0068	0.0880
5	0.0627	−0.0667	0.1639	0.1543	0.0985
6	0.3216	0.2466	0.3090	0.3097	0.0772
7	0.1847	0.0685	0.1985	0.2444	0.0616

Calculate the average return and variance for each type of security.

9.18 Annual returns from 1986 to 1991 on small-company stocks and U.S. Treasury bills are presented below:

Year	Small-Company Stocks	U.S. Treasury Bills
1986	6.85%	6.18%
1987	−9.30	5.87
1988	22.87	6.73
1989	10.18	8.48
1990	−21.56	7.85
1991	44.63	5.71

a. Calculate the average returns on small-company stocks and U.S. Treasury bills.
b. Calculate the variances and standard deviations of the returns on small-company stocks and U.S. Treasury bills.
c. Compare the returns and risks of the two assets.

9.19 Suppose International Trading Company's stock returns follow a normal distribution with a mean of 17.5 percent and a standard deviation of 8.5 percent. What is the range in which roughly 95 percent of the returns fall?

S & P PROBLEMS

9.20 Go to the "Excel Analytics" link for Exxon-Mobil (XOM) and download the monthly adjusted stock prices. Assuming you invested $1,000 in Exxon-Mobil at the close 12 months ago, what is your ending investment value? What was the average monthly geometric return over this period? What was the average monthly arithmetic return?

9.21 Go to the "Excel Analytics" link for General Mills (GIS) and download the monthly adjusted stock prices. What was the average monthly return for General Mills over the past year? What was the monthly variance of returns? The monthly standard deviation?

Appendix 9A

The Historical Market Risk Premium: The Very Long Run

The data in Chapter 9 indicate that the returns on common stock have historically been much higher than the returns on short-term government securities. This phenomenon has bothered economists, since it is difficult to justify why large numbers of rational investors purchase the lower yielding bills and bonds.

Visit us at www.mhhe.com/rwj

TABLE 9A.1	1802–1870	1871–1925	1926–2002	Overall 1802–2002
Common stock	8.1	8.4	12.2	9.7
Treasury bills	5.2	3.8	3.8	4.3
Risk premium	2.9	4.6	8.4	5.4

In 1985 Mehra and Prescott published a very influential paper that showed that the historical returns for common stocks are far too high when compared to the rates of return on short-term government securities.[11] They point out that the difference in returns (frequently called the *equity premium*) implies a very high degree of risk aversion on the part of investors. Since the publication of the Mehra and Prescott research, financial economists have tried to explain the so-called equity risk premium puzzle. The high historical equity risk premium is especially intriguing compared to the very low historical rate of return on Treasury securities. This seems to imply behavior that has not actually happened. For example, if people have been very risk-averse and historical borrowing rates have been low, it suggests that persons should have been willing to borrow in periods of economic uncertainty and downturn to avoid the possibility of a reduced standard of living. However, we do not observe increased borrowing during recessions.

The equity risk premium puzzle of Mehra and Prescott has been generally viewed as an unexplained paradox. However, recently, Jeremy Seigel has shown that the historical risk premium may be substantially lower than previously realized (see Table 9A.1). He shows that, while the risk premium averaged 8.4 percent from 1926 to 2002, it averaged only 2.9 percent from 1802 to 1870, and 4.6 percent from 1871 to 1925.[12] It is puzzling that the trend has been rising over the last 200 years. It has been especially high since 1926. However, the key point is that historically the risk premium has been lower than in more recent times and we should be somewhat cautious about assumptions we make concerning the current risk premium.

[11]Rajnish Mehra and Edward C. Prescott, "The Equity Premium: A Puzzle," *Journal of Monetary Economics* 15 (1985), pp. 145–61.

[12]Jeremy J. Seigel, *Stocks for the Long Run,* 3rd ed. (New York: McGraw-Hill, 2002).

Return and Risk: *The Capital-Asset-Pricing Model (CAPM)*

EXECUTIVE SUMMARY

The previous chapter achieved two purposes. First, we acquainted you with the history of U.S. capital markets. Second, we presented statistics such as expected return, variance, and standard deviation. Our ultimate goal in the next three chapters is to determine the appropriate discount rate for capital budgeting projects. Because the discount rate on a project is a function of its risk, the discussion in the previous chapter on standard deviation is a necessary first step. However, we shall see that standard deviation is not the final word on risk.

Our next step is to investigate the relationship between the risk and the return of individual securities when these securities are part of a large portfolio. This task is taken up in Chapter 10. The actual treatment of the appropriate discount rate for capital budgeting is reserved for Chapter 12.

The crux of the current chapter can be summarized as follows: An individual who holds one security should use expected return as the measure of the security's return. Standard deviation or variance is the proper measure of the security's risk. An individual who holds a diversified portfolio cares about the *contribution* of each security to the expected return and the risk of the portfolio. It turns out that a security's expected return is the appropriate measure of the security's contribution to the expected return on the portfolio. However, neither the security's variance nor the security's standard deviation is an appropriate measure of a security's contribution to the risk of a portfolio. The contribution of a security to the risk of a portfolio is best measured by beta.

10.1 Individual Securities

In the first part of Chapter 10 we will examine the characteristics of individual securities. In particular, we will discuss:

1. *Expected Return.* This is the return that an individual expects a stock to earn over the next period. Of course, because this is only an expectation, the actual return may be either higher or lower. An individual's expectation may simply be the average return per period a security has earned in the past. Alternatively, it may be based on a detailed analysis of a firm's prospects, on some computer-based model, or on special (or inside) information.

2. *Variance and Standard Deviation.* There are many ways to assess the volatility of a security's return. One of the most common is variance, which is a measure of the squared deviations of a security's return from its expected return. Standard deviation is the square root of the variance.

3. *Covariance and Correlation.* Returns on individual securities are related to one another. Covariance is a statistic measuring the interrelationship between two securities. Alternatively,

this relationship can be restated in terms of the correlation between the two securities. Covariance and correlation are building blocks to an understanding of the beta coefficient.

10.2 Expected Return, Variance, and Covariance

Expected Return and Variance

Suppose financial analysts believe that there are four equally likely states of the economy: depression, recession, normal, and boom times. The returns on the Supertech Company are expected to follow the economy closely, while the returns on the Slowpoke Company are not. The return predictions are as follows:

	Supertech Returns R_{At}	Slowpoke Returns R_{Bt}
Depression	−20%	5%
Recession	10	20
Normal	30	−12
Boom	50	9

Variance can be calculated in four steps. An additional step is needed to calculate standard deviation. (The calculations are presented in Table 10.1.) The steps are:

1. Calculate the expected return:

Supertech

$$\frac{-0.20 + 0.10 + 0.30 + 0.50}{4} = 0.175 = 17.5\% = \overline{R}_A$$

Slowpoke

$$\frac{0.05 + 0.20 - 0.12 + 0.09}{4} = 0.055 = 5.5\% = \overline{R}_B$$

2. For each company, calculate the deviation of each possible return from the company's expected return given previously. This is presented in the third column of Table 10.1.

3. The deviations we have calculated are indications of the dispersion of returns. However, because some are positive and some are negative, it is difficult to work with them in this form. For example, if we were to simply add up all the deviations for a single company, we would get zero as the sum.

   To make the deviations more meaningful, we multiply each one by itself. Now all the numbers are positive, implying that their sum must be positive as well. The squared deviations are presented in the last column of Table 10.1.

4. For each company, calculate the average squared deviation, which is the variance:[1]

Supertech

$$\frac{0.140625 + 0.005625 + 0.015625 + 0.105625}{4} = 0.066875$$

---

[1]In this example, the four states give rise to four *possible* outcomes for each stock. Had we used past data, the outcomes would have actually occurred. In that case, statisticians argue that the correct divisor is $N - 1$, where N is the number of observations. Thus the denominator would be 3 (= (4 − 1)) in the case of past data, not 4. Note that the example in Section 9.5 involved past data and we used a divisor of $N - 1$. While this difference causes grief to both students and textbook writers, it is a minor point in practice. In the real world, samples are generally so large that using N or $N - 1$ in the denominator has virtually no effect on the calculation of variance.

TABLE 10.1	**(1)** **State of Economy**	**(2)** **Rate of Return**	**(3)** **Deviation from Expected Return**	**(4)** **Squared Value of Deviation**
Calculating Variance and Standard Deviation		**Supertech*** R_{At}	**(Expected return = 0.175)** $(R_{At} - \bar{R}_A)$	$(R_{At} - \bar{R}_A)^2$
	Depression	−0.20	−0.375 $(= -0.20 - 0.175)$	0.140625 $[= (-0.375)^2]$
	Recession	0.10	−0.075	0.005625
	Normal	0.30	0.125	0.015625
	Boom	0.50	0.325	0.105625
				0.267500
		Slowpoke† R_{Bt}	**(Expected return = 0.055)** $(R_{Bt} - \bar{R}_B)$	$(R_{Bt} - \bar{R}_B)^2$
	Depression	0.05	−0.005 $(= 0.05 - 0.055)$	0.000025 $[= (-0.005)^2]$
	Recession	0.20	0.145	0.021025
	Normal	−0.12	−0.175	0.030625
	Boom	0.09	0.035	0.001225
				0.052900

$$* \bar{R}_A = \frac{-0.20 + 0.10 + 0.30 + 0.50}{4} = 0.175 = 17.5\%$$

$$\text{Var}(R_A) = \sigma_A^2 = \frac{0.2675}{4} = 0.066875$$

$$\text{SD}(R_A) = \sigma_A = \sqrt{0.066875} = 0.2586 = 25.86\%$$

$$\dagger \bar{R}_B = \frac{0.05 + 0.20 - 0.12 + 0.09}{4} = 0.055 = 5.5\%$$

$$\text{Var}(R_B) = \sigma_B^2 = \frac{0.0529}{4} = 0.013225$$

$$\text{SD}(R_B) = \sigma_B = \sqrt{0.013225} = 0.1150 = 11.50\%$$

Slowpoke
$$\frac{0.000025 + 0.021025 + 0.030625 + 0.001225}{4} = 0.013225$$

Thus, the variance of Supertech is 0.066875, and the variance of Slowpoke is 0.013225.

5. Calculate standard deviation by taking the square root of the variance:

Supertech
$$\sqrt{0.066875} = 0.2586 = 25.86\%$$

Slowpoke
$$\sqrt{0.013225} = 0.1150 = 11.50\%$$

Algebraically, the formula for variance can be expressed as

$$\text{Var}(R) = \text{Expected value of } (R - \bar{R})^2$$

where $\bar{R}$ is the security's expected return and R is the actual return.

A look at the four-step calculation for variance makes it clear why it is a measure of the spread of the sample of returns. For each observation, one squares the difference between the actual return and the expected return. One then takes an average of these squared differences.

Squaring the differences makes them all positive. If we used the differences between each return and the expected return and then averaged these differences, we would get zero because the returns that were above the mean would cancel the ones below.

However, because the variance is still expressed in squared terms, it is difficult to interpret. Standard deviation has a much simpler interpretation, which was provided in Section 9.5. Standard deviation is simply the square root of the variance. The general formula for the standard deviation is

$$SD(R) = \sqrt{Var(R)}$$

Covariance and Correlation

Variance and standard deviation measure the variability of individual stocks. We now wish to measure the relationship between the return on one stock and the return on another. Enter **covariance** and **correlation.**

Covariance and correlation measure how two random variables are related. We explain these terms by extending the Supertech and Slowpoke example presented earlier in this chapter.

EXAMPLE

We have already determined the expected returns and standard deviations for both Supertech and Slowpoke. (The expected returns are 0.175 and 0.055 for Supertech and Slowpoke, respectively. The standard deviations are 0.2586 and 0.1150, respectively.) In addition, we calculated the deviation of each possible return from the expected return for each firm. Using these data, covariance can be calculated in two steps. An extra step is needed to calculate correlation.

1. For each state of the economy, multiply Supertech's deviation from its expected return and Slowpoke's deviation from its expected return together. For example, Supertech's rate of return in a depression is -0.20, which is -0.375 $(-0.20 - 0.175)$ from its expected return. Slowpoke's rate of return in a depression is 0.05, which is -0.005 $(0.05 - 0.055)$ from its expected return. Multiplying the two deviations together yields 0.001875 $[(-0.375) \times (-0.005)]$. The actual calculations are given in the last column of Table 10.2. This procedure can be written algebraically as

$$(R_{At} - \bar{R}_A) \times (R_{Bt} - \bar{R}_B) \tag{10.1}$$

   where R_{At} and R_{Bt} are the returns on Supertech and Slowpoke in state t. $\bar{R}_A$ and $\bar{R}_B$ are the expected returns on the two securities.

2. Calculate the average value of the four states in the last column. This average is the covariance. That is,[2]

$$\sigma_{AB} = Cov(R_A, R_B) = \frac{-0.0195}{4} = -0.004875$$

Note that we represent the covariance between Supertech and Slowpoke as either $Cov(R_A, R_B)$ or σ_{AB}. Equation (10.1) illustrates the intuition of covariance. Suppose Supertech's return is generally above its average when Slowpoke's return is above its average, and Supertech's return is generally below its average when Slowpoke's return is below its average. This is indicative of a positive dependency or a positive relationship between the two returns. Note that the term in equation (10.1) will be *positive* in any state where both returns are *above* their averages. In addition, (10.1) will still be *positive* in any state where both terms are *below* their averages. Thus, a positive relationship between the two returns will give rise to a positive value for covariance.

---

[2]As with variance, we divided by N (4 in this example) because the four states give rise to four *possible* outcomes. However, had we used past data, the correct divisor would be $N - 1$ (3 in this example).

TABLE 10.2					Calculating Covariance and Correlation
State of Economy	Rate of Return of Supertech R_{At}	Deviation from Expected Return $(R_{At} - \bar{R}_A)$	Rate of Return of Slowpoke R_{Bt}	Deviation from Expected Return $(R_{Bt} - \bar{R}_B)$	Product of Deviations $(R_{At} - \bar{R}_A) \times (R_{Bt} - \bar{R}_B)$
		(Expected return = 0.175)		(Expected return = 0.055)	
Depression	−0.20	−0.375 (= −0.20 − 0.175)	0.05	−0.005 (= 0.05 − 0.055)	0.001875 (= −0.375 × −0.005)
Recession	0.10	−0.075	0.20	0.145	−0.010875 (= −0.075 × 0.145)
Normal	0.30	0.125	−0.12	−0.175	−0.021875 (= 0.125 × −0.175)
Boom	0.50	0.325	0.09	0.035	0.011375 (= 0.325 × 0.035)
	0.70		0.22		−0.0195

$$\sigma_{AB} = \text{Cov}(R_A, R_B) = \frac{-0.0195}{4} = -0.004875$$

$$\rho_{AB} = \text{Corr}(R_A, R_B) = \frac{\text{Cov}(R_A, R_B)}{\text{SD}(R_A) \times \text{SD}(R_B)} = \frac{-0.004875}{0.2586 \times 0.1150} = -0.1639$$

Conversely, suppose Supertech's return is generally above its average when Slowpoke's return is below its average, and Supertech's return is generally below its average when Slowpoke's return is above its average. This is indicative of a negative dependency or a negative relationship between the two returns. Note that the term in equation (10.1) will be *negative* in any state where one return is above its average and the other return is below its average. Thus, a negative relationship between the two returns will give rise to a negative value for covariance.

Finally, suppose there is no relation between the two returns. In this case, knowing whether the return on Supertech is above or below its expected return tells us nothing about the return on Slowpoke. In the covariance formula, then, there will be no tendency for the deviations to be positive or negative together. On average, they will tend to offset each other and cancel out, making the covariance zero.

Of course, even if the two returns are unrelated to each other, the covariance formula will not equal zero exactly in any actual history. This is due to sampling error; randomness alone will make the calculation positive or negative. But for a historical sample that is long enough, if the two returns are not related to each other, we should expect the covariance to come close to zero.

The covariance formula seems to capture what we are looking for. If the two returns are positively related to each other, they will have a positive covariance, and if they are negatively related to each other, the covariance will be negative. Last, and very important, if they are unrelated, the covariance should be zero.

The formula for covariance can be written algebraically as

$$\sigma_{AB} = \text{Cov}(R_A, R_B) = \text{Expected value of } [(R_A - \bar{R}_A) \times (R_B - \bar{R}_B)]$$

where $\bar{R}_A$ and $\bar{R}_B$ are the expected returns for the two securities, and R_A and R_B are the actual returns. The ordering of the two variables is unimportant. That is, the covariance of A with B is equal to the covariance of B with A. This can be stated more formally as $\text{Cov}(R_A, R_B) = \text{Cov}(R_B, R_A)$ or $\sigma_{AB} = \sigma_{BA}$.

The covariance we calculated is −0.004875. A negative number like this implies that the return on one stock is likely to be above its average when the return on the other stock is below its average, and vice versa. However, the size of the number is difficult to interpret. Like the variance figure, the covariance is in squared deviation units. Until we can put it in perspective, we don't know what to make of it.

We solve the problem by computing the correlation:

3. To calculate the correlation, divide the covariance by the standard deviations of both of the two securities. For our example, we have:

$$\rho_{AB} = \text{Corr}(R_A, R_B) = \frac{\text{Cov}(R_A, R_B)}{\sigma_A \times \sigma_B} = \frac{-0.004875}{0.2586 \times 0.1150} = -0.1639 \qquad (10.2)$$

where σ_A and σ_B are the standard deviations of Supertech and Slowpoke, respectively. Note that we represent the correlation between Supertech and Slowpoke either as $\text{Corr}(R_A, R_B)$ or ρ_{AB}. As with covariance, the ordering of the two variables is unimportant. That is, the correlation of A with B is equal to the correlation of B with A. More formally, $\text{Corr}(R_A, R_B) = \text{Corr}(R_B, R_A)$ or $\rho_{AB} = \rho_{BA}$.

Because the standard deviation is always positive, the sign of the correlation between two variables must be the same as that of the covariance between the two variables. If the correlation is positive, we say that the variables are *positively correlated;* if it is negative, we say that they are *negatively*

FIGURE 10.1

Examples of Different Correlation Coefficients—the Graphs in the Figure Plot the Separate Returns on the Two Securities through Time

Perfect positive correlation
$\text{Corr}(R_A, R_B) = 1$

Both the return on security A and the return on security B are higher than average at the same time. Both the return on security A and the return on security B are lower than average at the same time.

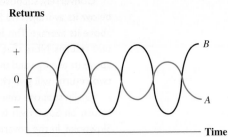

Perfect negative correlation
$\text{Corr}(R_A, R_B) = -1$

Security A has a higher-than-average return when security B has a lower-than-average return, and vice versa.

Zero correlation
$\text{Corr}(R_A, R_B) = 0$

The return on security A is completely unrelated to the return on security B.

correlated; and if it is zero, we say that they are *uncorrelated.* Furthermore, it can be proved that the correlation is always between $+1$ and -1. This is due to the standardizing procedure of dividing by the two standard deviations.

We can compare the correlation between different *pairs* of securities. For example, it turns out that the correlation between General Motors and Ford is much higher than the correlation between General Motors and IBM. Hence, we can state that the first pair of securities is more interrelated than the second pair.

Figure 10.1 shows the three benchmark cases for two assets, A and B. The figure shows two assets with return correlations of $+1$, -1, and 0. This implies perfect positive correlation, perfect negative correlation, and no correlation, respectively. The graphs in the figure plot the separate returns on the two securities through time.

10.3 The Return and Risk for Portfolios

Suppose that an investor has estimates of the expected returns and standard deviations on individual securities and the correlations between securities. How then does the investor choose the best combination or **portfolio** of securities to hold? Obviously, the investor would like a portfolio with a high expected return and a low standard deviation of return. It is therefore worthwhile to consider:

1. The relationship between the expected return on individual securities and the expected return on a portfolio made up of these securities.
2. The relationship between the standard deviations of individual securities, the correlations between these securities, and the standard deviation of a portfolio made up of these securities.

The Example of Supertech and Slowpoke

In order to analyze the above two relationships, we will use the same example of Supertech and Slowpoke that was presented previously. The relevant calculations are as follows.

The Expected Return on a Portfolio

The formula for expected return on a portfolio is very simple:

> The expected return on a portfolio is simply a weighted average of the expected returns on the individual securities.

Relevant Data from Example of Supertech and Slowpoke

Item	Symbol	Value
Expected return on Supertech	$\overline{R}_{Super}$	0.175 = 17.5%
Expected return on Slowpoke	$\overline{R}_{Slow}$	0.055 = 5.5%
Variance of Supertech	σ^2_{Super}	0.066875
Variance of Slowpoke	σ^2_{Slow}	0.013225
Standard deviation of Supertech	σ_{Super}	0.2586 = 25.86%
Standard deviation of Slowpoke	σ_{Slow}	0.1150 = 11.50%
Covariance between Supertech and Slowpoke	$\sigma_{Super, Slow}$	−0.004875
Correlation between Supertech and Slowpoke	$\rho_{Super, Slow}$	−0.1639

Consider Supertech and Slowpoke. From the preceding box, we find that the expected returns on these two securities are 17.5 percent and 5.5 percent, respectively.

The expected return on a portfolio of these two securities alone can be written as

$$\text{Expected return on portfolio} = X_{\text{Super}}(17.5\%) + X_{\text{Slow}}(5.5\%) = \bar{R}_P$$

where X_{Super} is the percentage of the portfolio in Supertech and X_{Slow} is the percentage of the portfolio in Slowpoke. If the investor with \$100 invests \$60 in Supertech and \$40 in Slowpoke, the expected return on the portfolio can be written as

$$\text{Expected return on portfolio} = 0.6 \times 17.5\% + 0.4 \times 5.5\% = 12.7\%$$

Algebraically, we can write

$$\text{Expected return on portfolio} = X_A \bar{R}_A + X_B \bar{R}_B = \bar{R}_P \qquad (10.3)$$

where X_A and X_B are the proportions of the total portfolio in the assets A and B, respectively. (Because our investor can only invest in two securities, $X_A + X_B$ must equal 1 or 100 percent.) $\bar{R}_A$ and $\bar{R}_B$ are the expected returns on the two securities.

Now consider two stocks, each with an expected return of 10 percent. The expected return on a portfolio composed of these two stocks must be 10 percent, regardless of the proportions of the two stocks held. This result may seem obvious at this point, but it will become important later. The result implies that you do not reduce or *dissipate* your expected return by investing in a number of securities. Rather, the expected return on your portfolio is simply a weighted average of the expected returns on the individual assets in the portfolio.

Variance and Standard Deviation of a Portfolio

The Variance   The formula for the variance of a portfolio composed of two securities, A and B, is

The Variance of the Portfolio

$$\text{Var(portfolio)} = X_A^2 \sigma_A^2 + 2X_A X_B \sigma_{A,B} + X_B^2 \sigma_B^2$$

Note that there are three terms on the right-hand side of the equation. The first term involves the variance of $A(\sigma_A^2)$, the second term involves the covariance between the two securities ($\sigma_{A,B}$), and the third term involves the variance of $B(\sigma_B^2)$. (As stated earlier in this chapter, $\sigma_{A,B} = \sigma_{B,A}$. That is, the ordering of the variables is not relevant when expressing the covariance between two securities.)

The formula indicates an important point. The variance of a portfolio depends on both the variances of the individual securities and the covariance between the two securities. The variance of a security measures the variability of an individual security's return. Covariance measures the relationship between the two securities. For given variances of the individual securities, a positive relationship or covariance between the two securities increases the variance of the entire portfolio. A negative relationship or covariance between the two securities decreases the variance of the entire portfolio. This important result seems to square with common sense. If one of your securities tends to go up when the other goes down, or vice versa, your two securities are offsetting each other. You are achieving what we call a *hedge* in finance, and the risk of your entire portfolio will be low. However, if both your securities rise and fall together, you are not hedging at all. Hence, the risk of your entire portfolio will be higher.

The variance formula for our two securities, Super and Slow, is

$$\text{Var(portfolio)} = X_{\text{Super}}^2 \sigma_{\text{Super}}^2 + 2X_{\text{Super}}X_{\text{Slow}}\sigma_{\text{Super, Slow}} + X_{\text{Slow}}^2 \sigma_{\text{Slow}}^2 \qquad (10.4)$$

Given our earlier assumption that an individual with $100 invests $60 in Supertech and $40 in Slowpoke, $X_{\text{Super}} = 0.6$ and $X_{\text{Slow}} = 0.4$. Using this assumption and the relevant data from the previous box, the variance of the portfolio is

$$0.023851 = 0.36 \times 0.066875 + 2 \times [0.6 \times 0.4 \times (-0.004875)] + 0.16 \times 0.013225 \qquad (10.4')$$

The Matrix Approach   Alternatively, equation (10.4) can be expressed in the following matrix format:

	Supertech	*Slowpoke*
Supertech	$X_{\text{Super}}^2 \sigma_{\text{Super}}^2$ $0.024075 = 0.36 \times 0.066875$	$X_{\text{Super}}X_{\text{Slow}}\sigma_{\text{Super, Slow}}$ $-0.00117 = 0.6 \times 0.4 \times (-0.004875)$
Slowpoke	$X_{\text{Super}}X_{\text{Slow}}\sigma_{\text{Super, Slow}}$ $-0.00117 = 0.6 \times 0.4 \times (-0.004875)$	$X_{\text{Slow}}^2 \sigma_{\text{Slow}}^2$ $0.002116 = 0.16 \times 0.013225$

There are four boxes in the matrix. We can add the terms in the boxes to obtain equation (10.4), the variance of a portfolio composed of the two securities. The term in the upper left-hand corner involves the variance of Supertech. The term in the lower right-hand corner involves the variance of Slowpoke. The other two boxes contain the term involving the covariance. These two boxes are identical, indicating why the covariance term is multiplied by 2 in equation (10.4).

At this point, students often find the box approach to be more confusing than equation (10.4). However, the box approach is easily generalized to more than two securities, a task we perform later in this chapter.

Standard Deviation of a Portfolio   Given (10.4'), we can now determine the standard deviation of the portfolio's return. This is

$$\sigma_P = \text{SD(portfolio)} = \sqrt{\text{Var(portfolio)}} = \sqrt{0.023851} \qquad (10.5)$$
$$= 0.1544 = 15.44\%$$

The interpretation of the standard deviation of the portfolio is the same as the interpretation of the standard deviation of an individual security. The expected return on our portfolio is 12.7 percent. A return of -2.74 percent ($12.7\% - 15.44\%$) is one standard deviation below the mean and a return of 28.14 percent ($12.7\% + 15.44\%$) is one standard deviation above the mean. If the return on the portfolio is normally distributed, a return between -2.74 percent and $+28.14$ percent occurs about 68 percent of the time.[3]

The Diversification Effect   It is instructive to compare the standard deviation of the portfolio with the standard deviation of the individual securities. The weighted average of the standard deviations of the individual securities is

$$\text{Weighted average of standard deviations} = X_{\text{Super}}\sigma_{\text{Super}} + X_{\text{Slow}}\sigma_{\text{Slow}} \qquad (10.6)$$
$$0.2012 = 0.6 \times 0.2586 + 0.4 \times 0.115$$

---

[3]There are only four equally probable returns for Supertech and Slowpoke, so neither security possesses a normal distribution. Thus, probabilities would be slightly different in our example.

One of the most important results in this chapter concerns the difference between equations (10.5) and (10.6). In our example, the standard deviation of the portfolio is *less* than a weighted average of the standard deviations of the individual securities.

We pointed out earlier that the expected return on the portfolio is a weighted average of the expected returns on the individual securities. Thus, we get a different type of result for the standard deviation of a portfolio than we do for the expected return on a portfolio.

It is generally argued that our result for the standard deviation of a portfolio is due to diversification. For example, Supertech and Slowpoke are slightly negatively correlated ($\rho = -0.1639$). Supertech's return is likely to be a little below average if Slowpoke's return is above average. Similarly, Supertech's return is likely to be a little above average if Slowpoke's return is below average. Thus, the standard deviation of a portfolio composed of the two securities is less than a weighted average of the standard deviations of the two securities.

The above example has negative correlation. Clearly, there will be less benefit from diversification if the two securities exhibit positive correlation. How high must the positive correlation be before all diversification benefits vanish?

To answer this question, let us rewrite (10.4) in terms of correlation rather than covariance. The covariance can be rewritten as[4]

$$\sigma_{\text{Super, Slow}} = \rho_{\text{Super, Slow}} \sigma_{\text{Super}} \sigma_{\text{Slow}} \qquad (10.7)$$

The formula states that the covariance between any two securities is simply the correlation between the two securities multiplied by the standard deviations of each. In other words, covariance incorporates both (1) the correlation between the two assets and (2) the variability of each of the two securities as measured by standard deviation.

From our calculations earlier in this chapter we know that the correlation between the two securities is -0.1639. Given the variances used in equation (10.4'), the standard deviations are 0.2586 and 0.115 for Supertech and Slowpoke, respectively. Thus, the variance of a portfolio can be expressed as

Variance of the Portfolio's Return

$$= X_{\text{Super}}^2 \sigma_{\text{Super}}^2 + 2 X_{\text{Super}} X_{\text{Slow}} \rho_{\text{Super, Slow}} \sigma_{\text{Super}} \sigma_{\text{Slow}} + X_{\text{Slow}}^2 \sigma_{\text{Slow}}^2 \qquad (10.8)$$

$$0.023851 = 0.36 \times 0.066875 + 2 \times 0.6 \times 0.4 \times (-0.1639)$$
$$\times 0.2586 \times 0.115 + 0.16 \times 0.013225$$

The middle term on the right-hand side is now written in terms of correlation, ρ, not covariance.

Suppose $\rho_{\text{Super, Slow}} = 1$, the highest possible value for correlation. Assume all the other parameters in the example are the same. The variance of the portfolio is

Variance of the portfolio's return $= 0.040466 = 0.36 \times 0.066875 + 2 \times (0.6 \times 0.4 \times 1 \times 0.2586 \times 0.115) + 0.16 \times 0.013225$

The standard deviation is

Standard variation of portfolio's return $= \sqrt{0.040466} = 0.2012 = 20.12\%$ (10.9)

Note that equations (10.9) and (10.6) are equal. That is, the standard deviation of a portfolio's return is equal to the weighted average of the standard deviations of the individual returns when $\rho = 1$. Inspection of (10.8) indicates that the variance and hence the standard

---

[4]As with covariance, the ordering of the two securities is not relevant when expressing the correlation between the two securities. That is, $\rho_{\text{Super,Slow}} = \rho_{\text{Slow,Super}}$.

TABLE 10.3	Asset	Standard Deviation
Standard Deviations for Standard & Poor's 500 Index and for Selected Stocks in the Index	S&P 500 Index	13.33%
	Bell Atlantic	28.60
	Ford Motor Co.	31.39
	Walt Disney Co.	41.05
	General Electric	29.54
	IBM	32.18
	McDonald's Corp.	32.38
	Sears, Roebuck & Co.	29.76
	Toys "R" Us Inc.	32.23
	Amazon.com	59.21

As long as the correlations between pairs of securities are less than 1, the standard deviation of an index is less than the weighted average of the standard deviations of the individual securities within the index.

deviation of the portfolio must fall as the correlation drops below 1. This leads to:

> As long as $\rho < 1$, the standard deviation of a portfolio of two securities is *less* than the weighted average of the standard deviations of the individual securities.

In other words, the diversification effect applies as long as there is less than perfect correlation (as long as $\rho < 1$). Thus, our Supertech-Slowpoke example is a case of overkill. We illustrated diversification by an example with negative correlation. We could have illustrated diversification by an example with positive correlation—as long as it was not *perfect* positive correlation.

An Extension to Many Assets   The preceding insight can be extended to the case of many assets. That is, as long as correlations between pairs of securities are less than 1, the standard deviation of a portfolio of many assets is less than the weighted average of the standard deviations of the individual securities.

Now consider Table 10.3, which shows the standard deviation of the Standard & Poor's 500 Index and the standard deviations of some of the individual securities listed in the index over a recent 10-year period. Note that all of the individual securities in the table have higher standard deviations than that of the index. In general, the standard deviations of most of the individual securities in an index will be above the standard deviation of the index itself, though a few of the securities could have lower standard deviations than that of the index.

Concept
Questions

1. What are the formulas for the expected return, variance, and standard deviation of a portfolio of two assets?
2. What is the diversification effect?
3. What are the highest and lowest possible values for the correlation coefficient?

10.4 The Efficient Set for Two Assets

Our results on expected returns and standard deviations are graphed in Figure 10.2. In the figure, there is a dot labeled Slowpoke and a dot labeled Supertech. Each dot represents both the expected return and the standard deviation for an individual security. As can be seen, Supertech has both a higher expected return and a higher standard deviation.

The box or "□" in the graph represents a portfolio with 60 percent invested in Supertech and 40 percent invested in Slowpoke. You will recall that we have previously calculated both the expected return and the standard deviation for this portfolio.

FIGURE 10.2

Expected Returns and Standard Deviations for Supertech, Slowpoke, and a Portfolio Composed of 60 Percent in Supertech and 40 Percent in Slowpoke

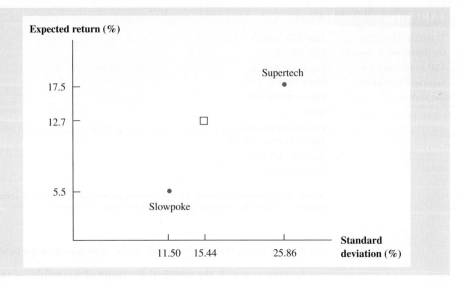

The choice of 60 percent in Supertech and 40 percent in Slowpoke is just one of an infinite number of portfolios that can be created. The set of portfolios is sketched by the curved line in Figure 10.3.

Consider portfolio *1*. This is a portfolio composed of 90 percent Slowpoke and 10 percent Supertech. Because it is weighted so heavily toward Slowpoke, it appears close to the Slowpoke point on the graph. Portfolio *2* is higher on the curve because it is composed of 50 percent Slowpoke and 50 percent Supertech. Portfolio *3* is close to the Supertech point on the graph because it is composed of 90 percent Supertech and 10 percent Slowpoke.

There are a few important points concerning this graph.

1. We argued that the diversification effect occurs whenever the correlation between the two securities is below 1. The correlation between Supertech and Slowpoke is −0.1639. The diversification effect can be illustrated by comparison with the straight line between the Supertech point and the Slowpoke point. The straight line represents points that would have been generated had the correlation coefficient between the two securities been 1. The diversification effect is illustrated in the figure since the curved line is always to the left of the straight line. Consider point *1′*. This represents a portfolio composed of 90 percent in Slowpoke and 10 percent in Supertech *if* the correlation between the two were exactly 1. We argue that there is no diversification effect if $\rho = 1$. However, the diversification effect applies to the curved line, because point *1* has the same expected return as point *1′* but has a lower standard deviation. (Points *2′* and *3′* are omitted to reduce the clutter of Figure 10.3.)

Though the straight line and the curved line are both represented in Figure 10.3, they do not simultaneously exist in the same world. *Either* $\rho = -0.1639$ and the curve exists *or* $\rho = 1$ and the straight line exists. In other words, though an investor can choose between different points on the curve if $\rho = -0.1639$, she cannot choose between points on the curve and points on the straight line.

2. The point MV represents the minimum variance portfolio. This is the portfolio with the lowest possible variance. By definition, this portfolio must also have the lowest possible standard deviation. (The term *minimum variance portfolio* is standard in the literature, and we will use that term. Perhaps minimum standard deviation would actually be better, because standard deviation, not variance, is measured on the horizontal axis of Figure 10.3.)

FIGURE 10.3

Set of Portfolios Composed of Holdings in Supertech and Slowpoke (correlation between the two securities is −0.1639)

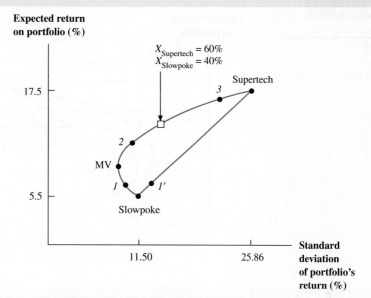

Portfolio *1* is composed of 90 percent Slowpoke and 10 percent Supertech ($\rho = -0.1639$).
Portfolio *2* is composed of 50 percent Slowpoke and 50 percent Supertech ($\rho = -0.1639$).
Portfolio *3* is composed of 10 percent Slowpoke and 90 percent Supertech ($\rho = -0.1639$).
Portfolio *1'* is composed of 90 percent Slowpoke and 10 percent Supertech ($\rho = 1$).
Point MV denotes the minimum variance portfolio. This is the portfolio with the lowest possible variance. By definition, the same portfolio must also have the lowest possible standard deviation.

3. An individual contemplating an investment in a portfolio of Slowpoke and Supertech faces an **opportunity set** or **feasible set** represented by the curved line in Figure 10.3. That is, he can achieve any point on the curve by selecting the appropriate mix between the two securities. He cannot achieve any point above the curve because he cannot increase the return on the individual securities, decrease the standard deviations of the securities, or decrease the correlation between the two securities. Neither can he achieve points below the curve because he cannot lower the returns on the individual securities, increase the standard deviations of the securities, or increase the correlation. (Of course, he would not want to achieve points below the curve, even if he were able to do so.)

Were he relatively tolerant of risk, he might choose portfolio *3*. (In fact, he could even choose the end point by investing all his money in Supertech.) An investor with less tolerance for risk might choose portfolio *2*. An investor wanting as little risk as possible would choose MV, the portfolio with minimum variance or minimum standard deviation.

4. Note that the curve is backward bending between the Slowpoke point and MV. This indicates that, for a portion of the feasible set, standard deviation actually decreases as one increases expected return. Students frequently ask, "How can an increase in the proportion of the risky security, Supertech, lead to a reduction in the risk of the portfolio?"

This surprising finding is due to the diversification effect. The returns on the two securities are negatively correlated with each other. One security tends to go up when the other goes down and vice versa. Thus, an addition of a small amount of Supertech acts as a hedge to a portfolio composed only of Slowpoke. The risk of the portfolio is reduced, implying backward bending. Actually, backward bending always occurs if $\rho \leq 0$. It may or may not occur when $\rho > 0$. Of course, the curve bends backward only for a portion of its length. As

FIGURE 10.4

Opportunity Sets
Composed of
Holdings in
Supertech and
Slowpoke

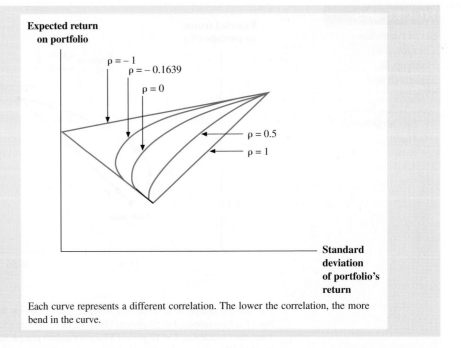

Each curve represents a different correlation. The lower the correlation, the more bend in the curve.

one continues to increase the percentage of Supertech in the portfolio, the high standard deviation of this security eventually causes the standard deviation of the entire portfolio to rise.

5. No investor would want to hold a portfolio with an expected return below that of the minimum variance portfolio. For example, no investor would choose portfolio *1*. This portfolio has less expected return but more standard deviation than the minimum variance portfolio has. We say that portfolios such as portfolio *1* are *dominated* by the minimum variance portfolio. Though the entire curve from Slowpoke to Supertech is called the *feasible set*, investors only consider the curve from MV to Supertech. Hence, the curve from MV to Supertech is called the **efficient set** or the **efficient frontier.**

Figure 10.3 represents the opportunity set where ρ = −0.1639. It is worthwhile to examine Figure 10.4, which shows different curves for different correlations. As can be seen, the lower the correlation, the more bend there is in the curve. This indicates that the diversification effect rises as ρ declines. The greatest bend occurs in the limiting case where ρ = −1. This is perfect negative correlation. While this extreme case where ρ = −1 seems to fascinate students, it has little practical importance. Most pairs of securities exhibit positive correlation. Strong negative correlation, let alone perfect negative correlation, are unlikely occurrences indeed.[5]

Note that there is only one correlation between a pair of securities. We stated earlier that the correlation between Slowpoke and Supertech is −0.1639. Thus, the curve in Figure 10.4 representing this correlation is the correct one, and the other curves should be viewed as merely hypothetical.

The graphs we examined are not mere intellectual curiosities. Rather, efficient sets can easily be calculated in the real world. As mentioned earlier, data on returns, standard deviations, and correlations are generally taken from past observations, though subjective notions can be used to determine the values of these parameters as well. Once the parameters have

---

[5]A major exception occurs with derivative securities. For example, the correlation between a stock and a put on the stock is generally strongly negative. Puts will be treated later in the text.

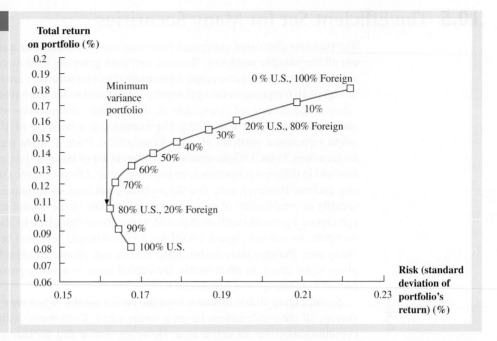

FIGURE 10.5

Return/Risk Trade-off for World Stocks: Portfolio of U.S. and Foreign Stocks

been determined, any one of a whole host of software packages can be purchased to generate an efficient set. However, the choice of the preferred portfolio within the efficient set is up to you. As with other important decisions like what job to choose, what house or car to buy, and how much time to allocate to this course, there is no computer program to choose the preferred portfolio.

An efficient set can be generated where the two individual assets are portfolios themselves. For example, the two assets in Figure 10.5 are a diversified portfolio of American stocks and a diversified portfolio of foreign stocks. Expected returns, standard deviations, and the correlation coefficient were calculated over the recent past. No subjectivity entered the analysis. The U.S. stock portfolio with a standard deviation of about 0.173 is less risky than the foreign stock portfolio, which has a standard deviation of about 0.222. However, combining a small percentage of the foreign stock portfolio with the U.S. portfolio actually reduces risk, as can be seen by the backward-bending nature of the curve. In other words, the diversification benefits from combining two different portfolios more than offset the introduction of a riskier set of stocks into one's holdings. The minimum variance portfolio occurs with about 80 percent of one's funds in American stocks and about 20 percent in foreign stocks. Addition of foreign securities beyond this point increases the risk of one's entire portfolio.

The backward-bending curve in Figure 10.5 is important information that has not bypassed American money managers. In recent years, pension-fund and mutual-fund managers in the United States have sought out investment opportunities overseas. Another point worth pondering concerns the potential pitfalls of using only past data to estimate future returns. The stock markets of many foreign countries have had phenomenal growth in the past 25 years. Thus, a graph like Figure 10.5 makes a large investment in these foreign markets seem attractive. However, because abnormally high returns cannot be sustained forever, some subjectivity must be used when forecasting future expected returns.

Concept
Question

1. **What is the relationship between the shape of the efficient set for two assets and the correlation between the two assets?**

10.5 The Efficient Set for Many Securities

The previous discussion concerned two securities. We found that a simple curve sketched out all the possible portfolios. Because investors generally hold more than two securities, we should look at the same graph when more than two securities are held. The shaded area in Figure 10.6 represents the opportunity set or feasible set when many securities are considered. The shaded area represents all the possible combinations of expected return and standard deviation for a portfolio. For example, in a universe of 100 securities, point 1 might represent a portfolio of, say, 40 securities. Point 2 might represent a portfolio of 80 securities. Point 3 might represent a different set of 80 securities, or the same 80 securities held in different proportions, or something else. Obviously, the combinations are virtually endless. However, note that all possible combinations fit into a confined region. No security or combination of securities can fall outside of the shaded region. That is, no one can choose a portfolio with an expected return above that given by the shaded region. Furthermore, no one can choose a portfolio with a standard deviation below that given in the shady area. Perhaps more surprisingly, no one can choose an expected return below that given in the curve. In other words, the capital markets actually prevent a self-destructive person from taking on a guaranteed loss.[6]

So far, Figure 10.6 is different from the earlier graphs. When only two securities are involved, all the combinations lie on a single curve. Conversely, with many securities the combinations cover an entire area. However, notice that an individual will want to be somewhere on the upper edge between MV and X. The upper edge, which we indicate in Figure 10.6 by a thick curve, is called the *efficient set*. Any point below the efficient set would receive less expected return and the same standard deviation as a point on the efficient set. For example, consider R on the efficient set and W directly below it. If W contains the risk you desire, you should choose R instead in order to receive a higher expected return.

FIGURE 10.6

The Feasible Set of Portfolios Constructed from Many Securities

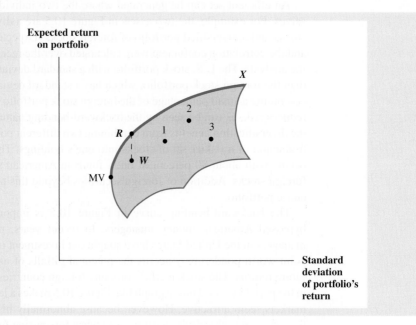

---

[6]Of course, someone dead set on parting with his money can do so. For example, he can trade frequently without purpose, so that commissions more than offset the positive expected returns on the portfolio.

TABLE 10.4	Stock	1	2	3	...	N
Matrix Used to Calculate the Variance of a Portfolio	1	$X_1^2\sigma_1^2$	$X_1X_2\text{Cov}(R_1,R_2)$	$X_1X_3\text{Cov}(R_1,R_3)$		$X_1X_N\text{Cov}(R_1,R_N)$
	2	$X_2X_1\text{Cov}(R_2,R_1)$	$X_2^2\sigma_2^2$	$X_2X_3\text{Cov}(R_2,R_3)$		$X_2X_N\text{Cov}(R_2,R_N)$
	3	$X_3X_1\text{Cov}(R_3,R_1)$	$X_3X_2\text{Cov}(R_3,R_2)$	$X_3^2\sigma_3^2$		$X_3X_N\text{Cov}(R_3,R_N)$
	.					
	.					
	.					
	N	$X_NX_1\text{Cov}(R_N,R_1)$	$X_NX_2\text{Cov}(R_N,R_2)$	$X_NX_3\text{Cov}(R_N,R_3)$		$X_N^2\sigma_N^2$

The variance of the portfolio is the sum of the terms in all the boxes.
σ_i is the standard deviation of stock i.
$\text{Cov}(R_i, R_j)$ is the covariance between stock i and stock j.
Terms involving the standard deviation of a single security appear on the diagonal. Terms involving covariance between two securities appear off the diagonal.

In the final analysis, Figure 10.6 is quite similar to Figure 10.3. The efficient set in Figure 10.3 runs from MV to Supertech. It contains various combinations of the securities Supertech and Slowpoke. The efficient set in Figure 10.6 runs from MV to X. It contains various combinations of many securities. The fact that a whole shaded area appears in Figure 10.6 but not in Figure 10.3 is just not an important difference; no investor would choose any point below the efficient set in Figure 10.6 anyway.

We mentioned before that an efficient set for two securities can be traced out easily in the real world. The task becomes more difficult when additional securities are included because the number of observations grows. For example, using subjective analysis to estimate expected returns and standard deviations for, say, 100 or 500 securities may very well become overwhelming, and the difficulties with correlations may be greater still. There are almost 5,000 correlations between pairs of securities from a universe of 100 securities.

Though much of the mathematics of efficient-set computation had been derived in the 1950s,[7] the high cost of computer time restricted application of the principles. In recent years, the cost has been drastically reduced. A number of software packages allow the calculation of an efficient set for portfolios of moderate size. By all accounts these packages sell quite briskly, so that our discussion above would appear to be important in practice.

Variance and Standard Deviation in a Portfolio of Many Assets

We earlier calculated the formulas for variance and standard deviation in the two-asset case. Because we considered a portfolio of many assets in Figure 10.6, it is worthwhile to calculate the formulas for variance and standard deviation in the many-asset case. The formula for the variance of a portfolio of many assets can be viewed as an extension of the formula for the variance of two assets.

To develop the formula, we employ the same type of matrix that we used in the two-asset case. This matrix is displayed in Table 10.4. Assuming that there are N assets, we write the numbers 1 through N on the horizontal axis and 1 through N on the vertical axis. This creates a matrix of $N \times N = N^2$ boxes. The variance of the portfolio is the sum of the terms in all the boxes.

---

[7]The classic treatise is Harry Markowitz, *Portfolio Selection* (New York: John Wiley & Sons, 1959). Markowitz won the Nobel Prize in economics in 1990 for his work on modern portfolio theory.

TABLE 10.5	Number of Stocks in Portfolio	Total Number of Terms	Number of Variance Terms (number of terms on diagonal)	Number of Covariance Terms (number of terms off diagonal)
Number of Variance and Covariance Terms as a Function of the Number of Stocks in the Portfolio	1	1	1	0
	2	4	2	2
	3	9	3	6
	10	100	10	90
	100	10,000	100	9,900
	·	·	·	·
	·	·	·	·
	·	·	·	·
	N	N^2	N	$N^2 - N$

In a large portfolio, the number of terms involving covariance between two securities is much greater than the number of terms involving variance of a single security.

Consider, for example, the box in the second row and the third column. The term in the box is $X_2 X_3 \, \text{Cov}(R_2, R_3)$. X_2 and X_3 are the percentages of the entire portfolio that are invested in the second asset and the third asset, respectively. For example, if an individual with a portfolio of \$1,000 invests \$100 in the second asset, $X_2 = 10\%$ (\$100/\$1,000). $\text{Cov}(R_3, R_2)$ is the covariance between the returns on the third asset and the returns on the second asset. Next, note the box in the third row and the second column. The term in this box is $X_3 X_2 \, \text{Cov}(R_3, R_2)$. Because $\text{Cov}(R_3, R_2) = \text{Cov}(R_2, R_3)$, both boxes have the same value. The second security and the third security make up one pair of stocks. In fact, every pair of stocks appears twice in the table, once in the lower left-hand side and once in the upper right-hand side.

Now consider boxes on the diagonal. For example, the term in the first box on the diagonal is $X_1^2 \sigma_1^2$. Here, σ_1^2 is the variance of the return on the first security.

Thus, the diagonal terms in the matrix contain the variances of the different stocks. The off-diagonal terms contain the covariances. Table 10.5 relates the numbers of diagonal and off-diagonal elements to the size of the matrix. The number of diagonal terms (number of variance terms) is always the same as the number of stocks in the portfolio. The number of off-diagonal terms (number of covariance terms) rises much faster than the number of diagonal terms. For example, a portfolio of 100 stocks has 9,900 covariance terms. Since the variance of a portfolio's returns is the sum of all the boxes, we have:

> The variance of the return on a portfolio with many securities is more dependent on the covariances between the individual securities than on the variances of the individual securities.

Concept Questions

1. What is the formula for the variance of a portfolio for many assets?
2. How can the formula be expressed in terms of a box or matrix?

10.6 Diversification: An Example

The preceding point can be illustrated by altering the matrix in Table 10.4 slightly. Suppose that we make the following three assumptions:

1. All securities possess the same variance, which we write as $\overline{\text{var}}$. In other words, $\sigma_i^2 = \overline{\text{var}}$ for every security.

TABLE 10.6	Stock	*1*	*2*	*3*	...	*N*
Matrix Used to Calculate the Variance of a Portfolio When (a) All Securities Possess the Same Variance, Which We Represent as $\overline{var}$; (b) All Pairs of Securities Possess the Same Covariance, Which We Represent as $\overline{cov}$; (c) All Securities Are Held in the Same Proportion, Which Is $1/N$	*1*	$(1/N^2)\overline{var}$	$(1/N^2)\overline{cov}$	$(1/N^2)\overline{cov}$		$(1/N^2)\overline{cov}$
	2	$(1/N^2)\overline{cov}$	$(1/N^2)\overline{var}$	$(1/N^2)\overline{cov}$		$(1/N^2)\overline{cov}$
	3	$(1/N^2)\overline{cov}$	$(1/N^2)\overline{cov}$	$(1/N^2)\overline{var}$		$(1/N^2)\overline{cov}$
	.					
	.					
	.					
	N	$(1/N^2)\overline{cov}$	$(1/N^2)\overline{cov}$	$(1/N^2)\overline{cov}$		$(1/N^2)\overline{var}$

2. All covariances in Table 10.4 are the same. We represent this uniform covariance as $\overline{cov}$. In other words, $\text{Cov}(R_i, R_j) = \overline{cov}$ for every pair of securities. It can easily be shown that $\overline{var} > \overline{cov}$.

3. All securities are equally weighted in the portfolio. Because there are N assets, the weight of each asset in the portfolio is $1/N$. In other words, $X_i = 1/N$ for each security i.

Table 10.6 is the matrix of variances and covariances under these three simplifying assumptions. Note that all of the diagonal terms are identical. Similarly, all of the off-diagonal terms are identical. As with Table 10.4, the variance of the portfolio is the sum of the terms in the boxes in Table 10.6. We know that there are N diagonal terms involving variance. Similarly, there are $N \times (N - 1)$ off-diagonal terms involving covariance. Summing across all the boxes in Table 10.6 we can express the variances of the portfolio as

$$\text{Variance of portfolio} = \underset{\substack{\text{Number of} \\ \text{diagonal} \\ \text{terms}}}{N} \times \underset{\substack{\text{Each} \\ \text{diagonal} \\ \text{term}}}{\left(\frac{1}{N^2}\right)\overline{var}} + \underset{\substack{\text{Number of} \\ \text{off-diagonal} \\ \text{terms}}}{N(N-1)} \times \underset{\substack{\text{Each} \\ \text{off-diagonal} \\ \text{term}}}{\left(\frac{1}{N^2}\right)\overline{cov}} \qquad (10.10)$$

$$= \left(\frac{1}{N}\right)\overline{var} + \left(\frac{N^2 - N}{N^2}\right)\overline{cov}$$

$$= \left(\frac{1}{N}\right)\overline{var} + \left(1 - \frac{1}{N}\right)\overline{cov}$$

Equation (10.10) expresses the variance of our special portfolio as a weighted sum of the average security variance and the average covariance.[8]

Now, let's increase the number of securities in the portfolio without limit. The variance of the portfolio becomes

$$\text{Variance of portfolio (when } N \to \infty) = \overline{cov} \qquad (10.11)$$

This occurs because (1) the weight on the variance term, $1/N$, goes to 0 as N goes to infinity, and (2) the weight on the covariance term, $1 - 1/N$, goes to 1 as N goes to infinity.

---

[8]Equation (10.10) is actually a weighted *average* of the variance and covariance terms because the weights, $1/N$ and $1 - 1/N$, sum to 1.

FIGURE 10.7

Relationship between the Variance of a Portfolio's Return and the Number of Securities in the Portfolio*

*This graph assumes
   a. All securities have constant variance, var.
   b. All securities have constant covariance, cov.
   c. All securities are equally weighted in portfolio.
The variance of a portfolio drops as more securities are added to the portfolio. However, it does not drop to zero. Rather, $\overline{cov}$ serves as the floor.

Formula (10.11) provides an interesting and important result. In our special portfolio, the variances of the individual securities completely vanish as the number of securities becomes large. However, the covariance terms remain. In fact, the variance of the portfolio becomes the average covariance, $\overline{cov}$. One often hears that one should diversify. In other words, you should not put all your eggs in one basket. The effect of diversification on the risk of a portfolio can be illustrated in this example. The variances of the individual securities are diversified away, but the covariance terms cannot be diversified away.

The fact that part, but not all, of one's risk can be diversified away should be explored. Consider Mr. Smith, who brings $1,000 to the roulette table at a casino. It would be very risky if he put all his money on one spin of the wheel. For example, imagine that he put the full $1,000 on red at the table. If the wheel showed red, he would get $2,000, but if the wheel showed black, he would lose everything. Suppose, instead, he divided his money over 1,000 different spins by betting $1 at a time on red. Probability theory tells us that he could count on winning about 50 percent of the time. This means that he could count on pretty nearly getting all his original $1,000 back.[9] In other words, risk is essentially eliminated with 1,000 different spins.

Now, let's contrast this with our stock market example, which we illustrate in Figure 10.7. The variance of the portfolio with only one security is, of course, $\overline{var}$ because the variance of a portfolio with one security is the variance of the security. The variance of the portfolio drops as more securities are added, which is evidence of the diversification effect. However, unlike Mr. Smith's roulette example, the portfolio's variance can never

---

[9]This example ignores the casino's cut.

drop to zero. Rather it reaches a floor of $\overline{\text{cov}}$, which is the covariance of each pair of securities.[10]

Because the variance of the portfolio asymptotically approaches $\overline{\text{cov}}$, each additional security continues to reduce risk. Thus, if there were neither commissions nor other transactions costs, it could be argued that one can never achieve too much diversification. However, there is a cost to diversification in the real world. Commissions per dollar invested fall as one makes larger purchases in a single stock. Unfortunately, one must buy fewer shares of each security when buying more and more different securities. Comparing the costs and benefits of diversification, Meir Statman argues that a portfolio of about 30 stocks is needed to achieve optimal diversification.[11]

We mentioned earlier that $\overline{\text{var}}$ must be greater than $\overline{\text{cov}}$. Thus, the variance of a security's return can be broken down in the following way:

$$
\begin{array}{ccc}
\text{Total risk of} & & \text{Unsystematic or} \\
\text{individual security} = \text{Portfolio risk} + \text{diversifiable risk} \\
(\overline{\text{var}}) & (\overline{\text{cov}}) & (\overline{\text{var}} - \overline{\text{cov}})
\end{array}
$$

Total risk, which is $\overline{\text{var}}$ in our example, is the risk that one bears by holding onto one security only. *Portfolio risk* is the risk that one still bears after achieving full diversification, which is $\overline{\text{cov}}$ in our example. Portfolio risk is often called **systematic** or **market risk** as well. **Diversifiable, unique,** or **unsystematic risk** is that risk that can be diversified away in a large portfolio, which must be $(\overline{\text{var}} - \overline{\text{cov}})$ by definition.

To an individual who selects a diversified portfolio, the total risk of an individual security is not important. When considering adding a security to a diversified portfolio, the individual cares about only that portion of the risk of a security that cannot be diversified away. This risk can alternatively be viewed as the *contribution* of a security to the risk of an entire portfolio. We will talk later about the case where securities make different contributions to the risk of the entire portfolio.

Risk and the Sensible Investor

Having gone to all this trouble to show that unsystematic risk disappears in a well-diversified portfolio, how do we know that investors even want such portfolios? Suppose they like risk and don't want it to disappear?

We must admit that, theoretically at least, this is possible, but we will argue that it does not describe what we think of as the typical investor. Our typical investor is **risk averse.** Risk-averse behavior can be defined in many ways, but we prefer the following example: A fair gamble is one with zero expected return; a risk-averse investor would prefer to avoid fair gambles.

Why do investors choose well-diversified portfolios? Our answer is that they are risk averse, and risk-averse people avoid unnecessary risk, such as the unsystematic risk on a stock. If you do not think this is much of an answer, consider whether you would take on such a risk. For example, suppose you had worked all summer and had saved $5,000, which you intended to use for your college expenses. Now, suppose someone came up to you and offered to flip a coin for the money: heads, you would double your money, and tails, you would lose it all.

---

[10]Though it is harder to show, this risk reduction effect also applies to the general case where variances and covariances are *not* equal.

[11]Meir Statman, "How Many Stocks Make a Diversified Portfolio?" *Journal of Financial and Quantitative Analysis* (September 1987).

Would you take such a bet? Perhaps you would, but most people would not. Leaving aside any moral question that might surround gambling and recognizing that some people would take such a bet, it's our view that the average investor would not.

To induce the typical risk-averse investor to take a fair gamble, you must sweeten the pot. For example, you might need to raise the odds of winning from 50–50 to 70–30 or higher. The risk-averse investor can be induced to take fair gambles only if they are sweetened so that they become unfair to the investor's advantage.

Concept Questions

1. **What are the two components of the total risk of a security?**
2. **Why doesn't diversification eliminate all risk?**

10.7   Riskless Borrowing and Lending

Figure 10.6 assumes that all the securities on the efficient set are risky. Alternatively, an investor could combine a risky investment with an investment in a riskless or *risk-free* security, such as an investment in United States Treasury bills. This is illustrated in the following example.

EXAMPLE

Ms. Bagwell is considering investing in the common stock of Merville Enterprises. In addition, Ms. Bagwell will either borrow or lend at the risk-free rate. The relevant parameters are

	Common Stock of Merville	Risk-Free Asset
Expected return	14%	10%
Standard deviation	0.20	0

Suppose Ms. Bagwell chooses to invest a total of $1,000, $350 of which is to be invested in Merville Enterprises and $650 placed in the risk-free asset. The expected return on her total investment is simply a weighted average of the two returns:

$$\text{Expected return on portfolio composed of one riskless and one risky asset} = 0.114 = (0.35 \times 0.14) + (0.65 \times 0.10) \qquad (10.12)$$

Because the expected return on the portfolio is a weighted average of the expected return on the risky asset (Merville Enterprises) and the risk-free return, the calculation is analogous to the way we treated two risky assets. In other words, equation (10.3) applies here.

Using equation (10.4), the formula for the variance of the portfolio can be written as

$$X^2_{\text{Merville}}\sigma^2_{\text{Merville}} + 2X_{\text{Merville}}X_{\text{Risk-free}}\sigma_{\text{Merville, Risk-free}} + X^2_{\text{Risk-free}}\sigma^2_{\text{Risk-free}}$$

However, by definition, the risk-free asset has no variability. Thus, both $\sigma_{\text{Merville, Risk-free}}$ and $\sigma^2_{\text{Risk-free}}$ are equal to zero, reducing the above expression to

$$\text{Variance of portfolio composed of one riskless and one risky asset} = X^2_{\text{Merville}}\sigma^2_{\text{Merville}} \qquad (10.13)$$

$$= (0.35)^2 \times (0.20)^2$$

$$= 0.0049$$

FIGURE 10.8

Relationship between Expected Return and Risk for a Portfolio of One Risky Asset and One Riskless Asset

The standard deviation of the portfolio is

$$\begin{array}{l}\text{Standard deviation of portfolio composed} \\ \text{of one riskless and one risky asset}\end{array} = X_{\text{Merville}}\sigma_{\text{Merville}} \qquad (10.14)$$
$$= 0.35 \times 0.20$$
$$= 0.07$$

The relationship between risk and expected return for one risky and one riskless asset can be seen in Figure 10.8. Ms. Bagwell's split of 35–65 percent between the two assets is represented on a *straight* line between the risk-free rate and a pure investment in Merville Enterprises. Note that, unlike the case of two risky assets, the opportunity set is straight, not curved.

Suppose that, alternatively, Ms. Bagwell borrows $200 at the risk-free rate. Combining this with her original sum of $1,000, she invests a total of $1,200 in Merville. Her expected return would be

$$\begin{array}{l}\text{Expected return on portfolio} \\ \text{formed by borrowing} \\ \text{to invest in risky asset}\end{array} = 14.8\% = 1.20 \times 0.14 + (-0.2 \times 0.10)$$

Here, she invests 120 percent of her original investment of $1,000 by borrowing 20 percent of her original investment. Note that the return of 14.8 percent is greater than the 14-percent expected return on Merville Enterprises. This occurs because she is borrowing at 10 percent to invest in a security with an expected return greater than 10 percent.

The standard deviation is

$$\begin{array}{l}\text{Standard deviation of portfolio formed} \\ \text{by borrowing to invest in risky asset}\end{array} = 0.24 = 1.20 \times 0.2$$

The standard deviation of 0.24 is greater than 0.20, the standard deviation of the Merville investment, because borrowing increases the variability of the investment. This investment also appears in Figure 10.8.

So far, we have assumed that Ms. Bagwell is able to borrow at the same rate at which she can lend.[12] Now let us consider the case where the borrowing rate is above the lending rate. The dotted line in Figure 10.8 illustrates the opportunity set for borrowing opportunities in this case. The dotted line is below the solid line because a higher borrowing rate lowers the expected return on the investment.

The Optimal Portfolio

The previous section concerned a portfolio formed between one riskless asset and one risky asset. In reality, an investor is likely to combine an investment in the riskless asset with a *portfolio* of risky assets. This is illustrated in Figure 10.9.

Consider point Q, representing a portfolio of securities. Point Q is in the interior of the feasible set of risky securities. Let us assume the point represents a portfolio of 30 percent in AT&T, 45 percent in General Motors (GM), and 25 percent in IBM. Individuals combining investments in Q with investments in the riskless asset would achieve points along the straight line from R_F to Q. We refer to this as line I. For example, point I on the line represents a portfolio of 70 percent in the riskless asset and 30 percent in stocks represented by Q. An investor with $100 choosing point I as his portfolio would put $70 in the risk-free asset and $30 in Q. This can be restated as $70 in the riskless asset, $9 ($0.3 \times 30) in AT&T, $13.50 ($0.45 \times 30) in GM, and $7.50 ($0.25 \times 30) in IBM. Point 2 also represents a portfolio of the risk-free asset and Q, with more (65%) being invested in Q.

Point 3 is obtained by borrowing to invest in Q. For example, an investor with $100 of his own would borrow $40 from the bank or broker in order to invest $140 in Q. This can

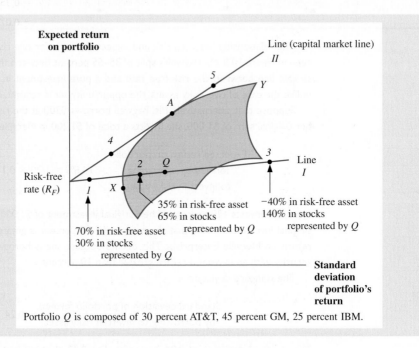

FIGURE 10.9

Relationship between Expected Return and Standard Deviation for an Investment in a Combination of Risky Securities and the Riskless Asset

Portfolio Q is composed of 30 percent AT&T, 45 percent GM, 25 percent IBM.

---

[12]Surprisingly, this appears to be a decent approximation because a large number of investors are able to borrow from a stockbroker (called *going on margin*) when purchasing stocks. The borrowing rate here is very near the riskless rate of interest, particularly for large investors. More will be said about this in a later chapter.

be stated as borrowing $40 and contributing $100 of one's money in order to invest $42 (0.3 × $140) in AT&T, $63 (0.45 × $140) in GM, and $35 (0.25 × $140) in IBM.

The above investments can be summarized as:

	Point Q	Point I (lending $70)	Point 3 (borrowing $40)
AT&T	$ 30	$ 9	$ 42
GM	45	13.50	63
IBM	25	7.50	35
Risk-free	0	70.00	−40
Total investment	$100	$100	$100

Though any investor can obtain any point on line I, no point on the line is optimal. To see this, consider line II, a line running from R_F through A. Point A represents a portfolio of risky securities. Line II represents portfolios formed by combinations of the risk-free asset and the securities in A. Points between R_F and A are portfolios in which some money is invested in the riskless asset and the rest is placed in A. Points past A are achieved by borrowing at the riskless rate to buy more of A than one could with one's original funds alone.

As drawn, line II is tangent to the efficient set of risky securities. Whatever point an individual can obtain on line I, he can obtain a point with the same standard deviation and a higher expected return on line II. In fact, because line II is tangent to the efficient set of risky assets, it provides the investor with the best possible opportunities. In other words, line II can be viewed as the efficient set of *all* assets, both risky and riskless. An investor with a fair degree of risk aversion might choose a point between R_F and A, perhaps point *4*. An individual with less risk aversion might choose a point closer to A or even beyond A. For example, point *5* corresponds to an individual borrowing money to increase his investment in A.

The graph illustrates an important point. With riskless borrowing and lending, the portfolio of *risky* assets held by any investor would always be point A. Regardless of the investor's tolerance for risk, he would never choose any other point on the efficient set of risky assets (represented by curve XAY) nor any point in the interior of the feasible region. Rather, he would combine the securities of A with the riskless assets if he had high aversion to risk. He would borrow the riskless asset to invest more funds in A had he low aversion to risk.

This result establishes what financial economists call the **separation principle.** That is, the investor's investment decision consists of two separate steps:

1. After estimating (*a*) the expected returns and variances of individual securities, and (*b*) the covariances between pairs of securities, the investor calculates the efficient set of risky assets, represented by curve XAY in Figure 10.9. He then determines point A, the tangency between the risk-free rate and the efficient set of risky assets (curve XAY). Point A represents the portfolio of risky assets that the investor will hold. This point is determined solely from his estimates of returns, variances, and covariances. No personal characteristics, such as degree of risk aversion, are needed in this step.

2. The investor must now determine how he will combine point A, his portfolio of risky assets, with the riskless asset. He might invest some of his funds in the riskless asset and some in portfolio A. He would end up at a point on the line between R_F and A in this case. Alternatively, he might borrow at the risk-free rate and contribute some of his own funds

as well, investing the sum in portfolio *A*. He would end up at a point on line *II* beyond *A*. His position in the riskless asset, that is, his choice of where on the line he wants to be, is determined by his internal characteristics, such as his ability to tolerate risk.

1. **What is the formula for the standard deviation of a portfolio composed of one riskless and one risky asset?**
2. **How does one determine the optimal portfolio among the efficient set of risky assets?**

10.8 Market Equilibrium

Definition of the Market-Equilibrium Portfolio

The above analysis concerns one investor. His estimates of the expected returns and variances for individual securities and the covariances between pairs of securities are his and his alone. Other investors would obviously have different estimates of the above variables. However, the estimates might not vary much because all investors would be forming expectations from the same data on past price movements and other publicly available information.

Financial economists often imagine a world where all investors possess the *same* estimates on expected returns, variances, and covariances. Though this can never be literally true, it can be thought of as a useful simplifying assumption in a world where investors have access to similar sources of information. This assumption is called **homogeneous expectations**.[13]

If all investors had homogeneous expectations, Figure 10.9 would be the same for all individuals. That is, all investors would sketch out the same efficient set of risky assets because they would be working with the same inputs. This efficient set of risky assets is represented by the curve *XAY*. Because the same risk-free rate would apply to everyone, all investors would view point *A* as the portfolio of risky assets to be held.

This point *A* takes on great importance because all investors would purchase the risky securities that it represents. Those investors with a high degree of risk aversion might combine *A* with an investment in the riskless asset, achieving point *4*, for example. Others with low aversion to risk might borrow to achieve, say, point *5*. Because this is a very important conclusion, we restate it:

> In a world with homogeneous expectations, all investors would hold the portfolio of risky assets represented by point A.

If all investors choose the same portfolio of risky assets, it is possible to determine what that portfolio is. Common sense tells us that it is a market-value-weighted portfolio of all existing securities. It is the **market portfolio.**

In practice, financial economists use a broad-based index such as the Standard & Poor's (S&P) 500 as a proxy for the market portfolio. Of course all investors do not hold the same portfolio in practice. However, we know that a large number of investors hold diversified portfolios, particularly when mutual funds or pension funds are included. A broad-based index is a good proxy for the highly diversified portfolios of many investors.

---

[13]The assumption of homogeneous expectations states that all investors have the same beliefs concerning returns, variances, and covariances. It does not say that all investors have the same aversion to risk.

Definition of Risk When Investors Hold the Market Portfolio

The previous section states that many investors hold diversified portfolios similar to broad-based indices. This result allows us to be more precise about the risk of a security in the context of a diversified portfolio.

Researchers have shown that the best measure of the risk of a security in a large portfolio is the *beta* of the security. We illustrate beta by an example.

EXAMPLE

Consider the following possible returns on both the stock of Jelco, Inc., and on the market:

State	Type of Economy	Return on Market (percent)	Return on Jelco, Inc. (percent)
I	Bull	15	25
II	Bull	15	15
III	Bear	−5	−5
IV	Bear	−5	−15

Though the return on the market has only two possible outcomes (15% and −5%), the return on Jelco has four possible outcomes. It is helpful to consider the expected return on a security for a given return on the market. Assuming each state is equally likely, we have

Type of Economy	Return on Market (percent)	Expected Return on Jelco, Inc. (percent)
Bull	15%	$20\% = 25\% \times \frac{1}{2} + 15\% \times \frac{1}{2}$
Bear	−5%	$-10\% = -5\% \times \frac{1}{2} + (-15\%) \times \frac{1}{2}$

Jelco, Inc., responds to market movements because its expected return is greater in bullish states than in bearish states. We now calculate exactly how responsive the security is to market movements. The market's return in a bullish economy is 20 percent [15% − (−5%)] greater than the market's return in a bearish economy. However, the expected return on Jelco in a bullish economy is 30 percent [20% − (−10%)] greater than its expected return in a bearish state. Thus, Jelco, Inc., has a responsiveness coefficient of 1.5 (30%/20%).

This relationship appears in Figure 10.10. The returns for both Jelco and the market in each state are plotted as four points. In addition, we plot the expected return on the security for each of the two possible returns on the market. These two points, each of which we designate by an X, are joined by a line called the **characteristic line** of the security. The slope of the line is 1.5, the number calculated in the previous paragraph. This responsiveness coefficient of 1.5 is the **beta** of Jelco.

The interpretation of beta from Figure 10.10 is intuitive. The graph tells us that the returns of Jelco are magnified 1.5 times over those of the market. When the market does well, Jelco's stock is expected to do even better. When the market does poorly, Jelco's stock is expected to do even worse. Now imagine an individual with a portfolio near that of the market who is considering the addition of Jelco to his portfolio. Because of Jelco's *magnification factor* of 1.5, he will view this stock as contributing much to the risk of the portfolio. (We will show shortly that the beta of the average security in the market is 1.) Jelco contributes more to the risk of a large, diversified portfolio than does an average security because Jelco is more responsive to movements in the market.

FIGURE 10.10

Performance of Jelco, Inc., and the Market Portfolio

The two points marked X represent the expected return on Jelco for each possible outcome of the market portfolio. The expected return on Jelco is positively related to the return on the market. Because the slope is 1.5, we say that Jelco's beta is 1.5. Beta measures the responsiveness of the security's return to movement in the market.

*(15%, 20%) refers to the point where the return on the market is 15 percent and the return on the security is 20 percent.

TABLE 10.7	Stock	Beta
Estimates of Beta for Selected Individual Stocks	High-beta stocks	
	Oracle, Inc.	1.63
	Inprise Corporation	1.58
	Citicorp	2.29
	Average-beta stocks	
	Du Pont	1.08
	Kimberly-Clark Corp.	0.80
	Ford Motor Co.	0.96
	Low-beta stocks	
	Green Mountain Power	0.26
	Homestake Mining	0.22
	Bell Atlantic	0.37

The beta is defined as $Cov(R_i, R_M)/Var(R_M)$, where $Cov(R_i, R_M)$ is the covariance of the return on an individual stock, R_i, and the return on the market, R_M. $Var(R_M)$ is the variance of the return on the market, R_M.

Further insight can be gleaned by examining securities with negative betas. One should view these securities as either hedges or insurance policies. The security is expected to do well when the market does poorly and vice versa. Because of this, adding a negative-beta security to a large, diversified portfolio actually reduces the risk of the portfolio.[14]

Table 10.7 presents empirical estimates of betas for individual securities. As can be seen, some securities are more responsive to the market than others. For example, Oracle has a beta of 1.63. This means that, for every 1 percent movement in the market,[15] Oracle

---

[14]Unfortunately, empirical evidence shows that virtually no stocks have negative betas.

[15]In Table 10.7, we use the Standard & Poor's 500 Index as the proxy for the market portfolio.

is expected to move 1.63 percent in the same direction. Conversely, Green Mountain Power has a beta of only 0.26. This means that, for every 1 percent movement in the market, Green Mountain is expected to move 0.26 percent in the same direction.

We can summarize our discussion of beta by saying:

Beta measures the responsiveness of a security to movements in the market portfolio.

The Formula for Beta

Our discussion so far has stressed the intuition behind beta. The actual definition of beta is

$$\beta_i = \frac{\text{Cov}(R_i, R_M)}{\sigma^2(R_M)} \tag{10.15}$$

where $\text{Cov}(R_i, R_M)$ is the covariance between the return on asset i and the return on the market portfolio and $\sigma^2(R_M)$ is the variance of the market.

One useful property is that the average beta across all securities, when weighted by the proportion of each security's market value to that of the market portfolio, is 1. That is,

$$\sum_{i=1}^{N} X_i \beta_i = 1 \tag{10.16}$$

where X_i is the proportion of security i's market value to that of the entire market and N is the number of securities in the market.

Equation (10.16) is intuitive, once you think about it. If you weight all securities by their market values, the resulting portfolio is the market. By definition, the beta of the market portfolio is 1. That is, for every 1 percent movement in the market, the market must move 1 percent—*by definition.*

A Test

We have put these questions on past corporate finance examinations:

1. What sort of investor rationally views the variance (or standard deviation) of an individual security's return as the security's proper measure of risk?
2. What sort of investor rationally views the beta of a security as the security's proper measure of risk?

A good answer might be something like the following:

> A rational, risk-averse investor views the variance (or standard deviation) of her portfolio's return as the proper measure of the risk of her portfolio. If for some reason or another the investor can hold only one security, the variance of that security's return becomes the variance of the portfolio's return. Hence, the variance of the security's return is the security's proper measure of risk.
>
> If an individual holds a diversified portfolio, she still views the variance (or standard deviation) of her portfolio's return as the proper measure of the risk of her portfolio. However, she is no longer interested in the variance of each individual security's return. Rather, she is interested in the contribution of an individual security to the variance of the portfolio.

Under the assumption of homogeneous expectations, all individuals hold the market portfolio. Thus, we measure risk as the contribution of an individual security to the variance of the market portfolio. This contribution, when standardized properly, is the beta of the security. While very few investors hold the market portfolio exactly, many hold reasonably diversified portfolios. These portfolios are close enough to the market portfolio so that the beta of a security is likely to be a reasonable measure of its risk.

1. **If all investors have homogeneous expectations, what portfolio of risky assets do they hold?**
2. **What is the formula for beta?**
3. **Why is beta the appropriate measure of risk for a single security in a large portfolio?**

10.9 Relationship between Risk and Expected Return (CAPM)

It is commonplace to argue that the expected return on an asset should be positively related to its risk. That is, individuals will hold a risky asset only if its expected return compensates for its risk. In this section, we first estimate the expected return on the stock market as a whole. Next, we estimate expected returns on individual securities.

Expected Return on Market

Financial economists frequently argue that the expected return on the market can be represented as:

$$\overline{R}_M = R_F + \text{Risk premium}$$

In words, the expected return on the market is the sum of the risk-free rate plus some compensation for the risk inherent in the market portfolio. Note that the equation refers to the *expected* return on the market, not the actual return in a particular month or year. Because stocks have risk, the actual return on the market over a particular period can, of course, be below R_F, or can even be negative.

Since investors want compensation for risk, the risk premium is presumably positive. But exactly how positive is it? It is generally argued that the place to start looking for the risk premium in the future is the average risk premium in the past. As reported in Chapter 9, Ibbotson and Sinquefield found that the average return on large-company common stocks was 12.2 percent over 1926–2002. The average risk-free rate over the same time interval was 3.8 percent. Thus, the average difference between the two was 8.4 percent (12.2% − 3.8%). Financial economists find this to be a useful estimate of the difference to occur in the future.[16]

For example, if the risk-free rate, estimated by the current yield on a one-year Treasury bill, is 1 percent, the expected return on the market is

$$9.4\% = 1\% + 8.4\%$$

Of course, the future equity risk premium could be higher or lower than the historical equity risk premium. This could be true if future risk is higher or lower than past risk or if individual risk aversions are higher or lower than those of the past.

Expected Return on Individual Security

Now that we have estimated the expected return on the market as a whole, what is the expected return on an individual security? We have argued that the beta of a security is the appropriate measure of risk in a large, diversified portfolio. Since most investors are diversified, the expected return on a security should be positively related to its beta. This is illustrated in Figure 10.11.

---

[16]This is not the only way to estimate the market-risk premium. In fact, there are several useful ways to estimate the market-risk premium. For example, refer to Table 9.2 and note the average return on common stocks (12.2%) and long-term government bonds (5.8%). As noted in footnote 9 in Chapter 9, one could argue that the long-term government bond return is the best measure of the long-term historical risk-free rate. If so, a good estimate of the historical market risk premium would be 12.2% − 5.8% = 7.4%. With this empirical version of the CAPM, one would use the current long-term government bond return to estimate the current risk-free rate.

FIGURE 10.11

Relationship between
Expected Return
on an Individual
Security and Beta
of the Security

The Security Market Line (SML) is the graphical depiction of the capital-asset-pricing model (CAPM).
The expected return on a stock with a beta of 0 is equal to the risk-free rate.
The expected return on a stock with a beta of 1 is equal to the expected return on the market.

Actually, financial economists can be more precise about the relationship between expected return and beta. They posit that, under plausible conditions, the relationship between expected return and beta can be represented by the following equation.[17]

Capital-Asset-Pricing Model

$$\overline{R} \quad = \quad R_F \quad + \quad \beta \quad \times \quad (\overline{R}_M - R_F) \qquad (10.17)$$

| Expected return on a security | = | Risk-free rate | + | Beta of the security | × | Difference between expected return on market and risk-free rate |

This formula, which is called the **capital-asset-pricing model** (or CAPM for short), implies that the expected return on a security is linearly related to its beta. Since the average return on the market has been higher than the average risk-free rate over long periods of time, $\overline{R}_M - R_F$ is presumably positive. Thus, the formula implies that the expected return on a security is *positively* related to its beta. The formula can be illustrated by assuming a few special cases:

• *Assume that* $\beta = 0$. Here $\overline{R} = R_F$, that is, the expected return on the security is equal to the risk-free rate. Because a security with zero beta has no relevant risk, its expected return should equal the risk-free rate.

• *Assume that* $\beta = 1$. Equation (10.17) reduces to $\overline{R} = \overline{R}_M$. That is, the expected return on the security is equal to the expected return on the market. This makes sense since the beta of the market portfolio is also 1.

Formula (10.17) can be represented graphically by the upward-sloping line in Figure 10.11. Note that the line begins at R_F and rises to $\overline{R}_M$ when beta is 1. This line is frequently called the **security market line** (SML).

---

[17]This relationship was first proposed independently by John Lintner and William F. Sharpe.

As with any line, the SML has both a slope and an intercept. R_F, the risk-free rate, is the intercept. Because the beta of a security is the horizontal axis, $R_M - R_F$ is the slope. The line will be upward-sloping as long as the expected return on the market is greater than the risk-free rate. Because the market portfolio is a risky asset, theory suggests that its expected return is above the risk-free rate. As mentioned, the empirical evidence of the previous chapter showed that the average return per year on the market portfolio (e.g., large-company stocks) over the past 77 years was 8.4 percent above the risk-free rate.

EXAMPLE

The stock of Aardvark Enterprises has a beta of 1.5 and that of Zebra Enterprises has a beta of 0.7. The risk-free rate is assumed to be 3 percent, and the difference between the expected return on the market and the risk-free rate is assumed to be 8.0 percent. The expected returns on the two securities are:

Expected Return for Aardvark

$$15.0\% = 3\% + 1.5 \times 8.0\% \tag{10.18}$$

Expected Return for Zebra

$$8.6\% = 3\% + 0.7 \times 8.0\%$$

Three additional points concerning the CAPM should be mentioned:

1. *Linearity.* The intuition behind an upwardly sloping curve is clear. Because beta is the appropriate measure of risk, high-beta securities should have an expected return above that of low-beta securities. However, both Figure 10.11 and equation (10.17) show something more than an upwardly sloping curve; the relationship between expected return and beta corresponds to a *straight* line.

It is easy to show that the line of Figure 10.11 is straight. To see this, consider security S with, say, a beta of 0.8. This security is represented by a point below the security market line in the figure. Any investor could duplicate the beta of security S by buying a portfolio with 20 percent in the risk-free asset and 80 percent in a security with a beta of 1. However, the homemade portfolio would itself lie on the SML. In other words, the portfolio dominates security S because the portfolio has a higher expected return and the same beta.

Now consider security T with, say, a beta greater than 1. This security is also below the SML in Figure 10.11. Any investor could duplicate the beta of security T by borrowing to invest in a security with a beta of 1. This portfolio must also lie on the SML, thereby dominating security T.

Because no one would hold either S or T, their stock prices would drop. This price adjustment would raise the expected returns on the two securities. The price adjustment would continue until the two securities lay on the security market line. The preceding example considered two overpriced stocks and a straight SML. Securities lying above the SML are *underpriced.* Their prices must rise until their expected returns lie on the line. If the SML is itself curved, many stocks would be mispriced. In equilibrium, all securities would be held only when prices changed so that the SML became straight. In other words, linearity would be achieved.

2. *Portfolios as well as securities.* Our discussion of the CAPM considered individual securities. Does the relationship in Figure 10.11 and equation (10.17) hold for portfolios as well?

Yes. To see this, consider a portfolio formed by investing equally in our two securities, Aardvark and Zebra. The expected return on the portfolio is

Expected Return on Portfolio

$$11.8\% = 0.5 \times 15.0\% + 0.5 \times 8.6\% \tag{10.19}$$

The beta of the portfolio is simply a weighted average of the betas of the two securities. Thus we have

Beta of Portfolio

$$1.1 = 0.5 \times 1.5 + 0.5 \times 0.7$$

Under the CAPM, the expected return on the portfolio is

$$11.8\% = 3\% + 1.1 \times 8.0\% \qquad (10.20)$$

Because the expected return in (10.19) is the same as the expected return in (10.20), the example shows that the CAPM holds for portfolios as well as for individual securities.

3. *A potential confusion.* Students often confuse the SML in Figure 10.11 with line *II* in Figure 10.9. Actually, the lines are quite different. Line *II* traces the efficient set of portfolios formed from both risky assets and the riskless asset. Each point on the line represents an entire portfolio. Point *A* is a portfolio composed entirely of risky assets. Every other point on the line represents a portfolio of the securities in *A* combined with the riskless asset. The axes on Figure 10.9 are the expected return on a *portfolio* and the standard deviation of a *portfolio*. Individual securities do not lie along line *II*.

The SML in Figure 10.11 relates expected return to beta. Figure 10.11 differs from Figure 10.9 in at least two ways. First, beta appears in the horizontal axis of Figure 10.11, but standard deviation appears in the horizontal axis of Figure 10.9. Second, the SML in Figure 10.11 holds both for all individual securities and for all possible portfolios, whereas line *II* in Figure 10.9 holds only for efficient portfolios.

We stated earlier that, under homogeneous expectations, point *A* in Figure 10.9 becomes the market portfolio. In this situation, line *II* is referred to as the **capital market line (CML)**.

<table>
<tr><td>

Concept
Questions

</td><td>

1. **Why is the SML a straight line?**
2. **What is the capital-asset-pricing model?**
3. **What are the differences between the capital market line and the security market line?**

</td></tr>
</table>

10.10 SUMMARY AND CONCLUSIONS

This chapter sets forth the fundamentals of modern portfolio theory. Our basic points are these:

1. This chapter shows us how to calculate the expected return and variance for individual securities, and the covariance and correlation for pairs of securities. Given these statistics, the expected return and variance for a portfolio of two securities *A* and *B* can be written as

$$\text{Expected return on portfolio} = X_A \bar{R}_A + X_B \bar{R}_B$$
$$\text{Var(portfolio)} = X_A^2 \sigma_A^2 + 2X_A X_B \sigma_{AB} + X_B^2 \sigma_B^2$$

2. In our notation, *X* stands for the proportion of a security in one's portfolio. By varying *X*, one can trace out the efficient set of portfolios. We graphed the efficient set for the two-asset case as a curve, pointing out that the degree of curvature or bend in the graph reflects the diversification effect: The lower the correlation between the two securities, the greater the bend. The same general shape of the efficient set holds in a world of many assets.

3. Just as the formula for variance in the two-asset case is computed from a 2×2 matrix, the variance formula is computed from an $N \times N$ matrix in the N-asset case. We show that, with a large number of assets, there are many more covariance terms than variance terms in the matrix. In fact, the variance terms are effectively diversified away in a large portfolio but the covariance terms are not. Thus, a diversified portfolio can only eliminate some, but not all, of the risk of the individual securities.

4. The efficient set of risky assets can be combined with riskless borrowing and lending. In this case, a rational investor will always choose to hold the portfolio of risky securities represented by point A in Figure 10.9. Then he can either borrow or lend at the riskless rate to achieve any desired point on line II in the figure.

5. The contribution of a security to the risk of a large, well-diversified portfolio is proportional to the covariance of the security's return with the market's return. This contribution, when standardized, is called the beta. The beta of a security can also be interpreted as the responsiveness of a security's return to that of the market.

6. The CAPM states that

$$\overline{R} = R_F + \beta(\overline{R}_M - R_F)$$

In other words, the expected return on a security is positively (and linearly) related to the security's beta.

KEY TERMS

beta, 281
capital-asset-pricing model, 285
capital market line, 287
characteristic line, 281
correlation, 258
covariance, 258
diversifiable (unique)
   (unsystematic) risk, 275
efficient set (efficient frontier), 268

homogeneous expectations, 280
market portfolio, 280
opportunity (feasible) set, 267
portfolio, 261
risk averse, 275
security market line, 285
separation principle, 279
systematic (market) risk, 275

SUGGESTED READINGS

The capital-asset-pricing model was originally published in these two classic articles:

Lintner, J. "Security Prices, Risk and Maximal Gains from Diversification." *Journal of Finance* (December 1965).

Sharpe, W. F. "Capital Asset Prices: A Theory of Market Equilibrium under Conditions of Risk." *Journal of Finance* (September 1964). (William F. Sharpe won the Nobel Prize in Economics in 1990 for his development of CAPM.)

The seminal influence of Harry Markowitz is described in:

Markowitz, H. "Travels along the Efficient Frontier." *Dow Jones Asset Management* (May/June 1997).

QUESTIONS & PROBLEMS

EXPECTED RETURN, VARIANCE, AND COVARIANCE

10.1   Ms. Sharp thinks that the distribution of rates of return on Q-mart stock is as follows:

State of Economy	Probability of State Occurring	Q-Mart Stock Return (%)
Depression	0.1	−4.5
Recession	0.2	4.4
Normal	0.5	12.0
Boom	0.2	20.7

a. What is the expected return on the stock?
b. What is the standard deviation of returns on the stock?

10.2 Suppose you have invested only in two stocks, A and B. The returns on the two stocks depend on the following three states of the economy, which are equally likely to happen:

State of Economy	Return on Stock A (%)	Return on Stock B (%)
Bear	6.30	−3.70
Normal	10.50	6.40
Bull	15.60	25.30

   a. Calculate the expected return on each stock.
   b. Calculate the standard deviation of returns on each stock.
   c. Calculate the covariance and correlation between the returns on the two stocks.

10.3 Mr. Henry can invest in Highbull stock and Slowbear stock. His projection of the returns on these two stocks is as follows:

State of Economy	Probability of State Occurring	Return on Highbull Stock (%)	Return on Slowbear Stock (%)
Recession	0.25	−2.00	5.00
Normal	0.60	9.20	6.20
Boom	0.15	15.40	7.40

   a. Calculate the expected return on each stock.
   b. Calculate the standard deviation of returns on each stock.
   c. Calculate the covariance and correlation between the returns on the two stocks.

PORTFOLIOS

10.4 A portfolio consists of 120 shares of Atlas stock, which sell for $50 per share, and 150 shares of Babcock stock, which sell for $20 per share. What are the weights of the two stocks in this portfolio?

10.5 Security F has an expected return of 12 percent and a standard deviation of 9 percent per year. Security G has an expected return of 18 percent and a standard deviation of 25 percent per year.
   a. What is the expected return on a portfolio composed of 30 percent of security F and 70 percent of security G?
   b. If the correlation between the returns of security F and security G is 0.2, what is the standard deviation of the portfolio described in part (a)?

10.6 Suppose the expected returns and standard deviations of stocks A and B are $E(R_A) = 0.15$, $E(R_B) = 0.25$, $\sigma_A = 0.1$, and $\sigma_B = 0.2$, respectively.
   a. Calculate the expected return and standard deviation of a portfolio that is composed of 40 percent A and 60 percent B when the correlation between the returns on A and B is 0.5.
   b. Calculate the standard deviation of a portfolio that is composed of 40 percent A and 60 percent B when the correlation coefficient between the returns on A and B is −0.5.
   c. How does the correlation between the returns on A and B affect the standard deviation of the portfolio?

10.7 Suppose Janet Smith holds 100 shares of Macrosoft stock and 300 shares of Intelligence stock. Macrosoft's stock currently sells at $80 per share, while Intelligence's stock sells at $40 per share. The expected return on Macrosoft's stock is 15 percent, while the expected return on Intelligence's stock is 20 percent. The correlation between the returns on the two stocks is 0.38.
   a. Calculate the expected return and standard deviation of her portfolio.
   b. Today she sold 200 shares of Intelligence stock in order to pay her tuition. Calculate the expected return and standard deviation of her new portfolio.

10.8   Consider the possible rates of return on stocks A and B over the next year:

State of Economy	Probability of State Occurring	Stock A Return If State Occurs (%)	Stock B Return If State Occurs (%)
Recession	0.2	7	−5
Normal	0.5	7	10
Boom	0.3	7	25

    a. Determine the expected returns, variances, and standard deviations for stock A and stock B.

    b. Determine the covariance and correlation between the returns of stock A and stock B.

    c. Determine the expected return and standard deviation of an equally weighted portfolio of stock A and stock B.

10.9   Suppose there are only two stocks in the world: stock A and stock B. The expected returns on these two stocks are 10 percent and 20 percent, while the standard deviations of the stocks are 5 percent and 15 percent, respectively. The correlation between the returns on the two stocks is 0.

    a. Calculate the expected return and standard deviation of a portfolio that is composed of 30 percent A and 70 percent B.

    b. Calculate the expected return and standard deviation of a portfolio that is composed of 90 percent A and 10 percent B.

    c. Suppose you are risk averse. Would you hold 100 percent in stock A? How about 100 percent stock B? Explain.

10.10   If a portfolio has a positive weight for each asset, can the expected return on the portfolio be greater than the expected return on the asset in the portfolio with the highest expected return? Can the expected return on the portfolio be less than the expected return on the asset in the portfolio with the lowest expected return? Explain.

10.11   Miss Maple is considering two securities, A and B, with the relevant information given below:

State of Economy	Probability	Return on Security A (%)	Return on Security B (%)
Bear	0.4	3.0	6.5
Bull	0.6	15.0	6.5

    a. Calculate the expected return and standard deviation of each of the two securities.

    b. Suppose Miss Maple invested $2,500 in security A and $3,500 in security B. Calculate the expected return and standard deviation of her portfolio.

10.12   A broker has advised you not to invest in oil industry stocks because they have high standard deviations. Is the broker's advice sound for a risk-averse investor like yourself? Why or why not?

 10.13   There are three securities in the market. The following chart shows their possible payoffs.

State	Probability of Outcome	Return on Security 1 (%)	Return on Security 2 (%)	Return on Security 3 (%)
1	0.1	0.25	0.25	0.10
2	0.4	0.20	0.15	0.15
3	0.4	0.15	0.20	0.20
4	0.1	0.10	0.10	0.25

a. What is the expected return and standard deviation of each security?

b. What are the covariances and correlations between the pairs of securities?

c. What is the expected return and standard deviation of a portfolio with half of its funds invested in security *1* and half in security *2*?

d. What is the expected return and standard deviation of a portfolio with half of its funds invested in security *1* and half in security *3*?

e. What is the expected return and standard deviation of a portfolio with half of its funds invested in security *2* and half in security *3*?

f. What do your answers in parts (*a*), (*c*), (*d*), and (*e*) imply about diversification?

10.14 The return on Stock *A* is uncorrelated with the return on stock *B*. Stock *A* has a 40 percent chance of having a return of 15 percent and a 60 percent chance of a return of 10 percent. Stock *B* has a one-half chance of a 35 percent return and a one-half chance of a −5 percent return.

a. Write a list of all of the possible outcomes and their probabilities.

b. What is the expected return on a portfolio with 50 percent invested in stock *A* and 50 percent invested in stock *B*?

10.15 Assume there are *N* securities in the market. The expected return on every security is 10 percent. All securities also have the same variance of 0.0144. The covariance between any pair of securities is 0.0064.

a. What is the expected return and variance of an equally weighted portfolio containing all *N* securities? Note: the weight of each security in the portfolio is 1/*N*.

b. What will happen to the variance of the portfolio as *N* approaches infinity?

c. What characteristics of a security are most important in the determination of the variance of a well-diversified portfolio?

10.16 Is the following statement true or false? Explain.

> The most important characteristic in determining the variance of a well-diversified portfolio is the variance of each of the individual stocks.

10.17 Briefly explain why the covariance of a security with the rest of a well-diversified portfolio is a more appropriate measure of the risk of the security than the security's variance.

10.18 Consider the following quotation from a leading investment manager:

> The shares of Southern Co. have traded close to $12 for most of the past three years. Since Southern's stock has demonstrated very little price movement, the stock has a low beta. Texas Instruments, on the other hand, has traded as high as $150 and as low as its current $75. Since TI's stock has demonstrated a large amount of price movement, the stock has a very high beta.

Do you agree with this analysis? Explain.

10.19 The market portfolio has an expected return of 12 percent and a standard deviation of 10 percent. The risk-free rate is 5 percent.

a. What is the expected return on a well-diversified portfolio with a standard deviation of 7 percent?

b. What is the standard deviation of a well-diversified portfolio with an expected return of 20 percent?

10.20 Consider the following information on the returns on the market and Fuji stock.

Type of Economy	Return on Market (%)	Expected Return on Fuji (%)
Bear	2.50	3.40
Bull	16.3	12.8

Calculate the beta of Fuji.

10.21 William Shakespeare's character Polonius in *Hamlet* says, "Neither a borrower nor a lender be." Under the assumptions of the capital-asset-pricing model, what would be the composition of Polonius's portfolio?

10.22 Securities *A*, *B*, and *C* have the following characteristics:

Security	Expected Return (%)	Beta
A	10	0.7
B	14	1.2
C	20	1.8

a. What is the expected return on a portfolio with equal weights?
b. What is the beta of a portfolio with equal weights?
c. Are the three securities priced correctly according to the capital-asset-pricing model?

10.23 Holup, Inc., makes pneumatic equipment. The beta of Holup's stock is 1.2. The expected market risk premium is 8.5 percent, and the current risk-free rate is 6 percent. Assume the capital-asset-pricing model holds. What is the expected return on Holup's stock?

10.24 The beta of stock *A* is 0.80. The risk-free rate is 6 percent, and the market risk premium is 8.5 percent. Assume the capital-asset-pricing model holds. What is the expected return on stock *A*?

10.25 The risk-free rate is 8 percent. The beta of stock *B* is 1.5, and the expected return on the market portfolio is 15 percent. Assume the capital-asset-pricing model holds. What is the expected return on stock *B*?

10.26 Suppose the expected market risk premium is 7.5 percent and the risk-free rate is 3.7 percent. The expected return on TriStar's stock is 14.2 percent. Assume the capital-asset-pricing model holds. What is the beta of TriStar's stock?

10.27 Consider the following two stocks:

	Beta	Expected Return
Murck Pharmaceutical	1.4	25%
Pizer Drug Corp	0.7	14%

Assume the capital-asset-pricing model holds. Based on the CAPM, what is the risk-free rate? What is the expected return on the market portfolio?

10.28 Suppose you observe the following situation:

		Return If State Occurs	
State of Economy	Probability of State	Stock A	Stock B
Bust	0.25	−0.1	−0.3
Normal	0.5	0.1	0.05
Boom	0.25	0.2	0.4

a. Calculate the expected return on each stock.
b. Assuming the capital-asset-pricing model holds and stock *A*'s beta is greater than stock *B*'s beta by 0.25, what is the expected market risk premium?

10.29 Assume the capital-asset-pricing model holds.
a. Draw the security market line for the case where the expected market risk premium is 5 percent and the risk-free rate is 7 percent.
b. Suppose that an asset has a beta of 0.8 and an expected return of 9 percent. Does the expected return of this asset lie above or below the security market line that you drew in part (*a*)? Is the security properly priced? If not, explain what will happen in this market.

c. Suppose that an asset has a beta of 3 and an expected return of 25 percent. Does the expected return of this asset lie above or below the security market line that you drew in part (*a*)? Is the security properly priced? If not, explain what will happen in this market.

10.30 A stock has a beta of 1.8. A security analyst who specializes in studying this stock expects its return to be 18 percent. Suppose the risk-free rate is 5 percent and the expected market risk premium is 8 percent. Is the analyst pessimistic or optimistic about this stock relative to the market's expectations?

10.31 Suppose the expected return on the market portfolio is 13.8 percent and the risk-free rate is 6.4 percent. Solomon Inc. stock has a beta of 1.2. Assume the capital-asset-pricing model holds.
a. What is the expected return on Solomon's stock?
b. If the risk-free rate decreases to 3.5 percent, what is the expected return on Solomon's stock?

10.32 A portfolio that combines the risk-free asset and the market portfolio has an expected return of 25 percent and a standard deviation of 4 percent. The risk-free rate is 5 percent, and the expected return on the market portfolio is 20 percent. Assume the capital-asset-pricing model holds. What expected rate of return would a security earn if it had a 0.5 correlation with the market portfolio and a standard deviation of 2 percent?

10.33 The risk-free rate is 7.6 percent. Potpourri Inc. stock has a beta of 1.7 and an expected return of 16.7 percent. Assume the capital-asset-pricing model holds.
a. What is the expected market risk premium?
b. Magnolia Industries stock has a beta of 0.8. What is the expected return on the Magnolia stock?
c. Suppose you have invested $10,000 in a combination of Potpourri and Magnolia stock. The beta of the portfolio is 1.07. How much did you invest in each stock? What is the expected return of the portfolio?

10.34 Suppose the risk-free rate is 6.3 percent and the market portfolio has an expected return of 14.8 percent. The market portfolio has a variance of 0.0121. Portfolio Z has a correlation coefficient with the market of 0.45 and a variance of 0.0169. According to the capital-asset-pricing model, what is the expected return on portfolio Z?

10.35 You have access to the following data concerning the Durham Company and the market portfolio:

> Variance of returns on the market portfolio = 0.04326
> Covariance between the returns on Durham and the market portfolio = 0.0635

The expected market risk premium is 9.4 percent and the expected return on Treasury bills is 4.9 percent.
a. Write the equation of the security market line.
b. What is the required return on Durham Company's stock?

10.36 Johnson Paint stock has an expected return of 19 percent and a beta of 1.7, while Williamson Tire stock has an expected return of 14 percent and a beta of 1.2. Assume the capital-asset-pricing model holds. What is the expected return on the market? What is the risk-free rate?

10.37 Is the following statement true or false? Explain.

> A risky security cannot have an expected return that is less than the risk-free rate because no risk-averse investor would be willing to hold this asset in equilibrium.

10.38 Suppose you have invested $30,000 in the following four stocks:

Security	Amount Invested	Beta
Stock A	$ 5,000	0.75
Stock B	10,000	1.1
Stock C	8,000	1.36
Stock D	7,000	1.88

Visit us at www.mhhe.com/rwj

The risk-free rate is 4 percent and the expected return on the market portfolio is 15 percent. Based on the capital-asset-pricing model, what is the expected return on the above portfolio?

10.39 You have been provided the following data on the securities of three firms, the market portfolio, and the risk-free asset:

Security	Expected Return	Standard Deviation	Correlation*	Beta
Firm A	0.13	0.12	(i)	0.9
Firm B	0.16	(ii)	0.4	1.1
Firm C	0.25	0.24	0.75	(iii)
The market portfolio	0.15	0.1	(iv)	(v)
The risk-free asset	0.05	(vi)	(vii)	(viii)

*With the market portfolio.

    a. Fill in the missing values in the table.

    b. Is the stock of Firm A correctly priced according to the capital-asset-pricing model (CAPM)? What about the stock of Firm B? Firm C? If these securities are not correctly priced, what is your investment recommendation for someone with a well-diversified portfolio?

10.40 There are two stocks in the market, stock A and stock B. The price of stock A today is $50. The price of stock A next year will be $40 if the economy is in a recession, $55 if the economy is normal, and $60 if the economy is expanding. The probabilities of recession, normal times, and expansion are 0.1, 0.8, and 0.1, respectively. Stock A pays no dividends and has a correlation of 0.8 with the market portfolio. Stock B has an expected return of 9 percent, a standard deviation of 12 percent, a correlation with the market portfolio of 0.2, and a correlation with stock A of 0.6. The market portfolio has a standard deviation of 10 percent. Assume the CAPM holds.

    a. If you are a typical, risk-averse investor with a well-diversified portfolio, which stock would you prefer? Why?

    b. What are the expected return and standard deviation of a portfolio consisting of 70 percent of stock A and 30 percent of stock B?

    c. What is the beta of the portfolio in part (b)?

**ADVANCED
(REQUIRES
CALCULUS)**

10.41 Assume stocks A and B have the following characteristics:

Stock	Expected Return (%)	Standard Deviation %
A	5	10
B	10	20

The covariance between the returns on the two stocks is 0.001.

    a. Suppose an investor holds a portfolio consisting of only stock A and stock B. Find the portfolio weights, X_A and X_B, such that the variance of his portfolio is minimized. (Hint: Remember that the sum of the two weights must equal 1.)

    b. What is the expected return on the minimum variance portfolio?

    c. If the covariance between the returns on the two stocks is −0.02, what are the minimum variance weights?

    d. What is the variance of the portfolio in part (c)?

NOTE: While these problems can be calculated manually, it is recommended that a spreadsheet program such as Excel® be used for calculations.

10.42 Go to the "Excel Analytics" link for Johnson and Johnson (JNJ) and Southwest Airlines (LUV) and download the monthly adjusted stock prices. Copy the monthly returns for each stock into a new spreadsheet. Calculate the covariance and correlation between the two stock returns. Would you expect a higher or lower correlation if you had chosen Procter & Gamble instead of Southwest Airlines? What is the standard deviation of a portfolio 75 percent invested in JNJ and 25 percent in LUV? What about a portfolio equally invested in the two stocks? What about a portfolio 25 percent in JNJ and 75 percent in LUV?

10.43 Go to the "Excel Analytics" link for Amazon.com (AMZN) and download the monthly adjusted stock prices. Copy the monthly returns for Amazon.com and the monthly S&P 500 returns in a new spreadsheet. Calculate the beta of Amazon.com for the entire period of data available. Now download the monthly stock prices for Duke Energy (DUK) and calculate the beta for this company. Are the betas similar? Would you have expected the beta for Amazon to be higher or lower than the beta for Duke Energy? Why?

Appendix 10A

Is Beta Dead?

The capital-asset-pricing model represents one of the most important advances in financial economics. It is clearly useful for investment purposes, since it shows how the expected return on an asset is related to its beta. In addition, we will show in Chapter 12 that it is useful in corporate finance, since the discount rate on a project is a function of the project's beta. However, one must never forget that, as with any other model, the CAPM is not revealed truth but, rather, a construct to be empirically tested.

The first empirical tests of the CAPM occurred over 20 years ago and were quite supportive. Using data from the 1930s to the 1960s, researchers showed that the average return on a portfolio of stocks was positively related to the beta of the portfolio,[18] a finding consistent with the CAPM. Though some evidence in these studies was less consistent with the CAPM,[19] financial economists were quick to embrace the CAPM following these empirical papers.

While a large body of empirical work developed in the following decades, often with varying results, the CAPM was not seriously called into question until the 1990s. Two papers by Fama and French[20] (yes, the same Fama whose joint paper in 1973 with James MacBeth supported the CAPM) present evidence inconsistent with the model. Their work has received a great deal of attention, both in academic circles and in the popular press, with newspaper articles displaying headlines such as "Beta Is Dead!" These papers make two related points. First, they conclude that the relationship between average return and beta is weak over the period from 1941 to 1990 and virtually nonexistent from 1963 to 1990. Second, they argue that the average return on a security is negatively related to both the firm's price-to-earnings (P/E) ratio and the firm's market value-to-book value (M/B) ratio. These contentions, if confirmed by other research, would be quite damaging to the CAPM. After all, the CAPM states that the expected returns on stocks should be related *only* to beta, and not to other factors such as P/E and M/B.

However, a number of researchers have criticized the Fama-French papers. While we avoid an in-depth discussion of the fine points of the debate, we mention a few issues. First, although Fama and French cannot reject the hypothesis that average returns are unrelated to beta, one can also not reject the hypothesis that average returns are related to beta exactly

---

[18]Perhaps the two most well-known papers were Fischer Black, Michael C. Jensen, and Myron S. Scholes, "The Capital Asset Pricing Model: Some Empirical Tests," in M. Jensen, ed., *Studies in the Theory of Capital Markets* (New York: Praeger, 1972), and Eugene F. Fama and James MacBeth, "Risk, Return and Equilibrium: Some Empirical Tests," *Journal of Political Economy* 8 (1973), pp. 607–36.

[19]For example, the studies suggest that the average return on a zero-beta portfolio is above the risk-free rate, a finding inconsistent with the CAPM.

[20]Eugene F. Fama and Kenneth R. French, "The Cross-Section of Expected Stock Returns," *Journal of Finance* 47 (1992), pp. 427–66, and E. F. Fama and K. R. French, "Common Risk Factors in the Returns on Stocks and Bonds," *Journal of Financial Economics* 17 (1993), pp. 3–56.

Visit us at www.mhhe.com/rwj

as specified by the CAPM. In other words, while 50 years of data seem like a lot, they may simply not be enough to test the CAPM properly. Second, the result with P/E and M/B may be due to a statistical fallacy called a hindsight bias.[21] Third, P/E and M/B are merely two of an infinite number of possible factors. Thus, the relationship between average return and both P/E and M/B may be spurious, being nothing more than the result of data mining. Fourth, average returns are positively related to beta over the period from 1927 to the present. There appears to be no compelling reason for emphasizing a shorter period than this one. Fifth, average returns are actually positively related to beta over shorter periods when annual data, rather than monthly data, are used to estimate beta.[22] There appears to be no compelling reason for preferring either monthly data over annual data or vice versa. Thus, we believe that, while the results of Fama and French are quite intriguing, they cannot be viewed as the final word.

---

[21]For example, see William J. Breen and Robert A. Koraczyk, "On Selection Biases in Book-to-Market Based Tests of Asset Pricing Models," unpublished paper. Northwestern University, November 1993; and S. P. Kothari, Jay Shanken, and Richard G. Sloan, "Another Look at the Cross-Section of Expected Stock Returns," *Journal of Finance* (March 1995).

[22]Points 4 and 5 are addressed in the Kothari, Shanken, and Sloan paper.

An Alternative View of Risk and Return: *The Arbitrage Pricing Theory*

EXECUTIVE SUMMARY

The previous two chapters mentioned the obvious fact that returns on securities are variable. This variability is measured by variance and by standard deviation. Next, we mentioned the somewhat less obvious fact that the returns on securities are interdependent. We measured the degree of interdependence between a pair of securities by covariance and by correlation. This interdependence led to a number of interesting results. First, we showed that diversification in stocks can eliminate some, but not all, risk. By contrast, we showed that diversification in a casino can eliminate all risk. Second, the interdependence of returns led to the capital-asset-pricing model (CAPM). This model posits a positive (and linear) relationship between the beta of a security and its expected return.

The CAPM was developed in the early 1960s.[1] An alternative to the CAPM, called the *arbitrage pricing theory* (APT), has been developed more recently.[2] For our purposes, the differences between the two models stem from the APT's treatment of interrelationship among the returns on securities.[3] The APT assumes that returns on securities are generated by a number of industrywide and marketwide factors. Correlation between a pair of securities occurs when these two securities are affected by the same factor or factors. By contrast, though the CAPM allows correlation among securities, it does not specify the underlying factors causing the correlation.

Both the APT and the CAPM imply a positive relationship between expected return and risk. In our (perhaps biased) opinion, the APT allows this relationship to be developed in a particularly intuitive manner. In addition, the APT views risk more generally than just the standardized covariance or beta of a security with the market portfolio. Therefore, we offer this approach as an alternative to the CAPM.

---

[1]In particular, see Jack Treynor, "Toward a Theory of the Market Value of Risky Assets," unpublished manuscript (1961); William F. Sharpe, "Capital Asset Prices: A Theory of Market Equilibrium under Conditions of Risk," *Journal of Finance* (September 1964); and John Lintner, "The Valuation of Risky Assets and the Selection of Risky Investments in Stock Portfolios and Capital Budgets," *Review of Economics and Statistics* (February 1965).

[2]See Stephen A. Ross, "The Arbitrage Theory of Capital Asset Pricing," *Journal of Economic Theory* (December 1976).

[3]This is by no means the only difference in the assumptions of the two models. For example, the CAPM usually assumes either that the returns on assets are normally distributed or that investors have quadratic utility functions. The APT does not require either assumption. While this and other differences are quite important in research, they are not relevant to the material presented in our text.

11.1 Factor Models: Announcements, Surprises, and Expected Returns

We learned in the previous chapter how to construct portfolios and how to evaluate their returns. We now step back and examine the returns on individual securities more closely. By doing this we will find that the portfolios inherit and alter the properties of the securities they comprise.

To be concrete, let us consider the return on the stock of a company called Flyers. What will determine this stock's return in, say, the coming month?

The return on any stock traded in a financial market consists of two parts. First, the *normal* or *expected return* from the stock is the part of the return that shareholders in the market predict or expect. It depends on all of the information shareholders have that bears on the stock, and it uses all of our understanding of what will influence the stock in the next month.

The second part is the *uncertain* or *risky return* on the stock. This is the portion that comes from information that will be revealed within the month. The list of such information is endless, but here are some examples:

- News about Flyers' research.
- Government figures released on the gross national product (GNP).
- Results of the latest arms-control talks.
- Discovery that a rival's product has been tampered with.
- News that Flyers' sales figures are higher than expected.
- A sudden drop in interest rates.
- The unexpected retirement of Flyers' founder and president.

A way to write the return on Flyers' stock in the coming month, then, is

$$R = \bar{R} + U$$

where R is the actual total return in the month, $\bar{R}$ is the expected part of the return, and U stands for the unexpected part of the return.

Some care must be exercised in studying the effect of these or other news items on the return. For example, the government might give us GNP or unemployment figures for this month, but how much of that is new information for shareholders? Surely at the beginning of the month shareholders will have some idea or forecast of what the monthly GNP will be. To the extent to which the shareholders had forecast the government's announcement, that forecast should be factored into the expected part of the return as of the beginning of the month, $\bar{R}$. On the other hand, insofar as the announcement by the government is a surprise and to the extent to which it influences the return on the stock, it will be part of U, the unanticipated part of the return.

As an example, suppose shareholders in the market had forecast that the GNP increase this month would be 0.5 percent. If GNP influences our company's stock, this forecast will be part of the information shareholders use to form the expectation, $\bar{R}$, of the monthly return. If the actual announcement this month is exactly 0.5 percent, the same as the forecast, then the shareholders learned nothing new, and the announcement is not news. It is like hearing a rumor about a friend when you knew it all along. Another way of saying this is that shareholders had already discounted the announcement. This use of the word *discount* is different from that in computing present value, but the spirit is similar. When we discount a dollar in the future, we say that it is worth less to us because of the time value of money. When we discount an announcement or a news item in the future, we mean that it has less impact on the market because the market already knew much of it.

On the other hand, suppose the government announced that the actual GNP increase during the year was 1.5 percent. Now shareholders have learned something—that the increase is one percentage point higher than they had forecast. This difference between the actual result and the forecast, one percentage point in this example, is sometimes called the *innovation* or *surprise.*

Any announcement can be broken into two parts, the anticipated or expected part and the surprise or innovation:

$$\text{Announcement} = \text{Expected part} + \text{Surprise}$$

The expected part of any announcement is part of the information the market uses to form the expectation, $\overline{R}$, of the return on the stock. The surprise is the news that influences the unanticipated return on the stock, U.

To give another example, if shareholders knew in January that the president of a firm was going to resign, the official announcement in February will be fully expected and will be discounted by the market. Because the announcement was expected before February, its influence on the stock will have taken place before February. The announcement itself in February will contain no surprise and the stock's price should not change at all at the announcement in February.

When we speak of news, then, we refer to the surprise part of any announcement and not the portion that the market has expected and therefore has already discounted.

Concept Questions

1. **What are the two basic parts of a return?**
2. **Under what conditions will some news have no effect on common stock prices?**

11.2 Risk: Systematic and Unsystematic

The unanticipated part of the return—that portion resulting from surprises—is the true risk of any investment. After all, if we got what we had expected, there would be no risk and no uncertainty.

There are important differences, though, among various sources of risk. Look at our previous list of news stories. Some of these stories are directed specifically at Flyers, and some are more general. Which of the news items are of specific importance to Flyers?

Announcements about interest rates or GNP are clearly important for nearly all companies, whereas the news about Flyers' president, its research, its sales, or the affairs of a rival company are of specific interest to Flyers. We will divide these two types of announcements and the resulting risk, then, into two components: a systematic portion, called *systematic risk,* and the remainder, which we call *specific* or *unsystematic risk.* The following definitions describe the difference:

- A *systematic risk* is any risk that affects a large number of assets, each to a greater or lesser degree.
- An *unsystematic risk* is a risk that specifically affects a single asset or a small group of assets.[4]

Uncertainty about general economic conditions, such as GNP, interest rates, or inflation, is an example of systematic risk. These conditions affect nearly all stocks to some degree.

---

[4]In the previous chapter, we briefly mentioned that unsystematic risk is risk that can be diversified away in a large portfolio. This result will also follow from the present analysis.

An unanticipated or surprise increase in inflation affects wages and the costs of the supplies that companies buy, the value of the assets that companies own, and the prices at which companies sell their products. These forces to which all companies are susceptible are the essence of systematic risk.

In contrast, the announcement of a small oil strike by a company may very well affect that company alone or a few other companies. Certainly, it is unlikely to have an effect on the world oil market. To stress that such information is unsystematic and affects only some specific companies, we sometimes call it an *idiosyncratic risk*.

The distinction between a systematic risk and an unsystematic risk is never as exact as we make it out to be. Even the most narrow and peculiar bit of news about a company ripples through the economy. It reminds us of the tale of the war that was lost because one horse lost a shoe; even a minor event may have an impact on the world. But this degree of hair-splitting should not trouble us much. To paraphrase a Supreme Court Justice's comment when speaking of pornography, we may not be able to define a systematic risk and an unsystematic risk exactly, but we know them when we see them.

This permits us to break down the risk of Flyers' stock into its two components: the systematic and the unsystematic. As is traditional, we will use the Greek epsilon, ϵ, to represent the unsystematic risk and write

$$R = \bar{R} + U$$
$$= \bar{R} + m + \epsilon$$

where we have used the letter m to stand for the systematic risk. Sometimes systematic risk is referred to as *market risk*. This emphasizes the fact that m influences all assets in the market to some extent.

The important point about the way we have broken the total risk, U, into its two components, m and ϵ, is that ϵ, because it is specific to the company, is unrelated to the specific risk of most other companies. For example, the unsystematic risk on Flyers' stock, ϵ_F, is unrelated to the unsystematic risk of Xerox's stock, ϵ_X. The risk that Flyers' stock will go up or down because of a discovery by its research team—or its failure to discover something—probably is unrelated to any of the specific uncertainties that affect Xerox stock.

Using the terms of the previous chapter, this means that the unsystematic risk of Flyers' stock and Xerox's stock are unrelated to each other, or uncorrelated. In the symbols of statistics,

$$\text{Corr}(\epsilon_F, \epsilon_X) = 0$$

Concept
Questions

1. **Describe the difference between systematic risk and unsystematic risk.**
2. **Why is unsystematic risk sometimes referred to as *idiosyncratic risk*?**

11.3 Systematic Risk and Betas

The fact that the unsystematic parts of the returns on two companies are unrelated to each other does not mean that the systematic portions are unrelated. On the contrary, because both companies are influenced by the same systematic risks, individual companies' systematic risks and therefore their total returns will be related.

For example, a surprise about inflation will influence almost all companies to some extent. How sensitive is Flyers' stock return to unanticipated changes in inflation? If Flyers' stock tends to go up on news that inflation is exceeding expectations, we would say that it is positively related to inflation. If the stock goes down when inflation exceeds expectations and up when inflation falls short of expectations, it is negatively related. In the unusual case where a stock's return is uncorrelated with inflation surprises, inflation has no effect on it.

We capture the influence of a systematic risk like inflation on a stock by using the **beta coefficient.** The beta coefficient, β, tells us the response of the stock's return to a systematic risk. In the previous chapter, beta measured the responsiveness of a security's return to a specific risk factor, the return on the market portfolio. We used this type of responsiveness to develop the capital-asset-pricing model. Because we now consider many types of systematic risks, our current work can be viewed as a generalization of our work in the previous chapter.

If a company's stock is positively related to the risk of inflation, that stock has a positive inflation beta. If it is negatively related to inflation, its inflation beta is negative, and if it is uncorrelated with inflation, its inflation beta is zero.

It's not hard to imagine some stocks with positive inflation betas and other stocks with negative inflation betas. The stock of a company owning gold mines will probably have a positive inflation beta because an unanticipated rise in inflation is usually associated with an increase in gold prices. On the other hand, an automobile company facing stiff foreign competition might find that an increase in inflation means that the wages it pays are higher, but that it cannot raise its prices to cover the increase. This profit squeeze, as the company's expenses rise faster than its revenues, would give its stock a negative inflation beta.

Some companies that have few assets and that act as brokers—buying items in competitive markets and reselling them in other markets—might be relatively unaffected by inflation, because their costs and their revenues would rise and fall together. Their stock would have an inflation beta of zero.

Some structure is useful at this point. Suppose we have identified three systematic risks on which we want to focus. We may believe that these three are sufficient to describe the systematic risks that influence stock returns. Three likely candidates are inflation, GNP, and interest rates. Thus, every stock will have a beta associated with each of these systematic risks: an inflation beta, a GNP beta, and an interest-rate beta. We can write the return on the stock, then, in the following form:

$$R = \bar{R} + U$$
$$= \bar{R} + m + \epsilon$$
$$= \bar{R} + \beta_I F_I + \beta_{GNP} F_{GNP} + \beta_r F_r + \epsilon$$

where we have used the symbol β_I to denote the stock's inflation beta, β_{GNP} for its GNP beta, and β_r to stand for its interest-rate beta. In the equation, F stands for a surprise, whether it be in inflation, GNP, or interest rates.

Let us go through an example to see how the surprises and the expected return add up to produce the total return, R, on a given stock. To make it more familiar, suppose that the return is over a horizon of a year and not just a month. Suppose that at the beginning of the year, inflation is forecast to be 5 percent for the year, GNP is forecast to increase by 2 percent, and interest rates are expected not to change. Suppose the stock we are looking at has the following betas:

$$\beta_I = 2$$
$$\beta_{GNP} = 1$$
$$\beta_r = -1.8$$

The magnitude of the beta describes how great an impact a systematic risk has on a stock's returns. A beta of +1 indicates that the stock's return rises and falls one for one with the systematic factor. This means, in our example, that because the stock has a GNP beta of 1, it experiences a 1-percent increase in return for every 1-percent surprise increase in GNP. If its GNP beta were -2, it would fall by 2 percent when there was an unanticipated increase of 1 percent in GNP, and it would rise by 2 percent if GNP experienced a surprise 1-percent decline.

Finally, let us suppose that during the year the following occurs: Inflation rises by 7 percent, GNP rises by only 1 percent, and interest rates fall by 2 percent. Last, suppose we learn some good news about the company, perhaps that it is succeeding quickly with some new business strategy, and that this unanticipated development contributes 5 percent to its return. In other words,

$$\epsilon = 5\%$$

Let us assemble all of this information to find what return the stock had during the year.

First, we must determine what news or surprises took place in the systematic factors. From our information we know that

$$\text{Expected inflation} = 5\%$$
$$\text{Expected GNP change} = 2\%$$

and

$$\text{Expected change in interest rates} = 0\%$$

This means that the market had discounted these changes, and the surprises will be the difference between what actually takes place and these expectations:

$$\begin{aligned} F_I &= \text{Surprise in inflation} \\ &= \text{Actual inflation} - \text{Expected inflation} \\ &= 7\% - 5\% \\ &= 2\% \end{aligned}$$

Similarly,

$$\begin{aligned} F_{\text{GNP}} &= \text{Surprise in GNP} \\ &= \text{Actual GNP} - \text{Expected GNP} \\ &= 1\% - 2\% \\ &= -1\% \end{aligned}$$

and

$$\begin{aligned} F_r &= \text{Surprise in change in interest rates} \\ &= \text{Actual change} - \text{Expected change} \\ &= -2\% - 0\% \\ &= -2\% \end{aligned}$$

The total effect of the systematic risks on the stock return, then, is

$$\begin{aligned} m &= \text{Systematic risk portion of return} \\ &= \beta_I F_I + \beta_{\text{GNP}} F_{\text{GNP}} + \beta_r F_r \\ &= [2 \times 2\%] + [1 \times (-1\%)] + [(-1.8) \times (-2\%)] \\ &= 6.6\% \end{aligned}$$

Combining this with the unsystematic risk portion, the total risky portion of the return on the stock is

$$m + \epsilon = 6.6\% + 5\% = 11.6\%$$

Last, if the expected return on the stock for the year was, say, 4 percent, the total return from all three components will be

$$R = \bar{R} + m + \epsilon$$
$$= 4\% + 6.6\% + 5\%$$
$$= 15.6\%$$

The model we have been looking at is called a **factor model,** and the systematic sources of risk, designated F, are called the *factors*. To be perfectly formal, a *k-factor model* is a model where each stock's return is generated by

$$R = \bar{R} + \beta_1 F_1 + \beta_2 F_2 + \cdots + \beta_k F_k + \epsilon$$

where ϵ is specific to a particular stock and uncorrelated with the ϵ term for other stocks. In our preceding example we had a three-factor model. We used inflation, GNP, and the change in interest rates as examples of systematic sources of risk, or factors. Researchers have not settled on what is the correct set of factors. Like so many other questions, this might be one of those matters that is never laid to rest.

In practice, researchers frequently use a one-factor model for returns. They do not use all of the sorts of economic factors we used previously as examples; instead, they use an index of stock market returns—like the S&P 500, or even a more broadly based index with more stocks in it—as the single factor. Using the single-factor model we can write returns as

$$R = \bar{R} + \beta(R_{\text{S\&P500}} - \bar{R}_{\text{S\&P500}}) + \epsilon$$

Where there is only one factor (the returns on the S&P 500–portfolio index), we do not need to put a subscript on the beta. In this form (with minor modifications) the factor model is called a **market model.** This term is employed because the index that is used for the factor is an index of returns on the whole (stock) market. The market model is written as

$$R = \bar{R} + \beta(R_M - \bar{R}_M) + \epsilon$$

where R_M is the return on the market portfolio.[5] The single β is called the *beta coefficient*.

Concept Questions

1. **What is an inflation beta? A GNP beta? An interest-rate beta?**
2. **What is the difference between a *k*-factor model and the market model?**
3. **Define the beta coefficient.**

11.4 Portfolios and Factor Models

Now let us see what happens to portfolios of stocks when each of the stocks follows a one-factor model. For purposes of discussion, we will take the coming one-month period and examine returns. We could have used a day or a year or any other time period. If the period represents the time between decisions, however, we would rather it be short than long, and a month is a reasonable time frame to use.

We will create portfolios from a list of N stocks, and we will use a one-factor model to capture the systematic risk. The ith stock in the list will therefore have returns

$$R_i = \bar{R}_i + \beta_i F + \epsilon_i \tag{11.1}$$

---

[5]Alternatively, the market model could be written as

$$R = \alpha + \beta R_M + \epsilon$$

Here alpha (α) is an intercept term equal $\bar{R} - \beta\bar{R}_M$.

where we have subscripted the variables to indicate that they relate to the ith stock. Notice that the factor F is not subscripted. The factor that represents systematic risk could be a surprise in GNP, or we could use the market model and let the difference between the S&P 500 return and what we expect that return to be, $R_{S\&P500} - \overline{R}_{S\&P500}$, be the factor. In either case, the factor applies to all of the stocks.

The β_i is subscripted because it represents the unique way the factor influences the ith stock. To recapitulate our discussion of factor models, if β_i is zero, the returns on the ith stock are

$$R_i = \overline{R}_i + \epsilon_i$$

In words, the ith stock's returns are unaffected by the factor, F, if β_i is zero. If β_i is positive, positive changes in the factor raise the ith stock's returns, and declines lower them. Conversely, if β_i is negative, its returns and the factor move in opposite directions.

Figure 11.1 illustrates the relationship between a stock's excess returns, $R_i - \overline{R}_i$, and the factor F for different betas, where $\beta_i > 0$. The lines in Figure 11.1 plot equation (11.1) on the assumption that there has been no unsystematic risk. That is, $\epsilon_i = 0$. Because we are assuming positive betas, the lines slope upward, indicating that the return on the stock rises with F. Notice that if the factor is zero ($F = 0$), the line passes through zero on the y-axis.

Now let us see what happens when we create stock portfolios where each stock follows a one-factor model. Let X_i be the proportion of security i in the portfolio. That is, if an individual with a portfolio of $100 wants $20 in General Motors, we say $X_{GM} = 20\%$. Because the Xs represent the proportions of wealth we are investing in each of the stocks, we know that they must add up to 100 percent or 1. That is,

$$X_1 + X_2 + X_3 + \cdots + X_N = 1$$

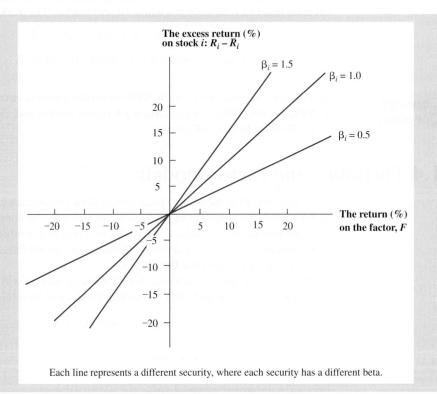

FIGURE 11.1

The One-Factor Model

The excess return (%) on stock i: $R_i - \overline{R}_i$

$\beta_i = 1.5$

$\beta_i = 1.0$

$\beta_i = 0.5$

The return (%) on the factor, F

Each line represents a different security, where each security has a different beta.

We know that the portfolio return is the weighted average of the returns on the individual assets in the portfolio. Algebraically, this can be written as:

$$R_P = X_1 R_1 + X_2 R_2 + X_3 R_3 + \cdots + X_N R_N \tag{11.2}$$

We saw from equation (11.1) that each asset, in turn, is determined by both the factor F and the unsystematic risk of ϵ_i. Thus, by substituting equation (11.1) for each R_i in equation (11.2), we have

$$R_P = \underset{\text{(Return on stock } 1)}{X_1(\bar{R}_1 + \beta_1 F + \epsilon_1)} \qquad \underset{\text{(Return on stock } 2)}{+ X_2(\bar{R}_2 + \beta_2 F + \epsilon_2)} \tag{11.3}$$

$$\underset{\text{(Return on stock } 3)}{+ X_3(\bar{R}_3 + \beta_3 F + \epsilon_3)} + \cdots \underset{\text{(Return on stock } N)}{+ X_N(\bar{R}_N + \beta_N F + \epsilon_N)}$$

Equation (11.3) shows us that the return on a portfolio is determined by three sets of parameters:

1. The expected return on each individual security, $\bar{R}_i$.
2. The beta of each security multiplied by the factor F.
3. The unsystematic risk of each individual security, ϵ_i.

We express equation (11.3) in terms of these three sets of parameters as

Weighted Average of Expected Returns:
$$R_P = X_1\bar{R}_1 + X_2\bar{R}_2 + X_3\bar{R}_3 + \cdots + X_N\bar{R}_N \tag{11.4}$$

(Weighted Average of Betas)F:
$$+ (X_1\beta_1 + X_2\beta_2 + X_3\beta_3 + \cdots + X_N\beta_N)F$$

Weighted Average of Unsystematic Risks:
$$+ X_1\epsilon_1 + X_2\epsilon_2 + X_3\epsilon_3 + \cdots + X_N\epsilon_N$$

This rather imposing equation is actually straightforward. The first row is the weighted average of each security's expected return. The items in the parentheses of the second row represent the weighted average of each security's beta. This weighted average is, in turn, multiplied by the factor F. The third row represents a weighted average of the unsystematic risks of the individual securities.

Where does uncertainty appear in equation (11.4)? There is no uncertainty in the first row because only the expected value of each security's return appears there. Uncertainty in the second row is reflected by only one item, F. That is, while we know that the expected value of F is zero, we do not know what its value will be over a particular time period. Uncertainty in the third row is reflected by each unsystematic risk, ϵ_i.

Portfolios and Diversification

In the previous sections of this chapter, we expressed the return on a single security in terms of our factor model. Portfolios were treated next. Because investors generally hold diversified portfolios, we now want to know what equation (11.4) looks like in a *large* or diversified portfolio.[6]

As it turns out, something unusual occurs to equation (11.4); the third row actually *disappears* in a large portfolio. To see this, consider a gambler who divides $1,000 by betting on

---

[6]Technically, we can think of a large portfolio as one where an investor keeps increasing the number of securities without limit. In practice, *effective* diversification would occur if at least a few dozen securities were held.

red over many spins of the roulette wheel. For example, he may participate in 1,000 spins, betting $1 at a time. Though we do not know ahead of time whether a particular spin will yield red or black, we can be confident that red will win about 50 percent of the time. Ignoring the house take, the investor can be expected to end up with just about his original $1,000.

Though we are concerned with stocks, not roulette wheels, the same principle applies. Each security has its own unsystematic risk, where the surprise for one stock is unrelated to the surprise of another stock. By investing a small amount in each security, the weighted average of the unsystematic risks will be very close to zero in a large portfolio.[7]

Although the third row completely vanishes in a large portfolio, nothing unusual occurs in either row 1 or row 2. Row 1 remains a weighted average of the expected returns on the individual securities as securities are added to the portfolio. Because there is no uncertainty at all in the first row, there is no way for diversification to cause this row to vanish. The terms inside the parentheses of the second row remain a weighted average of the betas. They do not vanish, either, when securities are added. Because the factor F is unaffected when securities are added to the portfolios, the second row does not vanish.

Why does the third row vanish while the second row does not, though both rows reflect uncertainty? The key is that there are many unsystematic risks in row 3. Because these risks are independent of each other, the effect of diversification becomes stronger as we add more assets to the portfolio. The resulting portfolio becomes less and less risky, and the return becomes more certain. However, the systematic risk, F, affects all securities because it is outside the parentheses in row 2. Since one cannot avoid this factor by investing in many securities, diversification does not occur in this row.

EXAMPLE

The preceding material can be further explained by the following example. We keep our one-factor model here but make three specific assumptions:

1. All securities have the same expected return of 10 percent. This assumption implies that the first row of equation (11.4) must also equal 10 percent because this row is a weighted average of the expected returns of the individual securities.

2. All securities have a beta of 1. The sum of the terms inside the parentheses in the second row of (11.4) must equal 1 because these terms are a weighted average of the individual betas. Since the terms inside the parentheses are multiplied by F, the value of the second row is $1 \times F = F$.

3. In this example, we focus on the behavior of one individual, Walter V. Bagehot. Mr. Bagehot decides to hold an equally weighted portfolio. That is, the proportion of each security in his portfolio is $1/N$.

We can express the return on Mr. Bagehot's portfolio as

Return on Walter V. Bagehot's Portfolio:

$$R_P = 10\% + F + \left(\frac{1}{N}\epsilon_1 + \frac{1}{N}\epsilon_2 + \frac{1}{N}\epsilon_3 + \cdots + \frac{1}{N}\epsilon_N \right) \qquad (11.4')$$

From row 1 of (11.4)   From row 2 of (11.4)   From row 3 of (11.4)

---

[7]More precisely, we say that the weighted average of the unsystematic risk approaches zero as the number of equally weighted securities in a portfolio approaches infinity.

FIGURE 11.2

Diversification and the Portfolio Risk for an Equally Weighted Portfolio

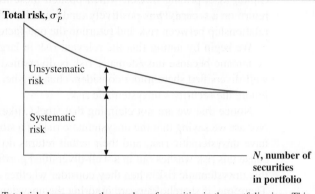

Total risk decreases as the number of securities in the portfolio rises. This drop occurs only in the unsystematic-risk component. Systematic risk is unaffected by diversification.

We mentioned before that, as N increases without limit, row 3 of (11.4) becomes equal to zero.[8] Thus, the return to Walter Bagehot's portfolio when the number of securities is very large is

$$R_P = 10\% + F \tag{11.4''}$$

The key to diversification is exhibited in (11.4″). The unsystematic risk of row 3 vanishes, while the systematic risk of row 2 remains.

This is illustrated in Figure 11.2. Systematic risk, captured by variation in the factor F, is not reduced through diversification. Conversely, unsystematic risk diminishes as securities are added, vanishing as the number of securities becomes infinite. Our result is analogous to the diversification example of the previous chapter. In that chapter, we said that undiversifiable or systematic risk arises from positive covariances between securities. In this chapter, we say that systematic risk arises from a common factor F. Because a common factor causes positive covariances, the arguments of the two chapters are parallel.

Concept Questions

1. **How can the return on a portfolio be expressed in terms of a factor model?**
2. **What risk is diversified away in a large portfolio?**

11.5 Betas and Expected Returns

The Linear Relationship

We have argued many times that the expected return on a security compensates for its risk. In the previous chapter we showed that market beta (the standardized covariance of the security's returns with those of the market) was the appropriate measure of risk under the assumptions of homogeneous expectations and riskless borrowing and lending. The

---

[8]Our presentation on this point has been nonrigorous. The student interested in more rigor should note that the variance of row 3 is

$$\frac{1}{N^2}\sigma_\epsilon^2 + \frac{1}{N^2}\sigma_\epsilon^2 + \frac{1}{N^2}\sigma_\epsilon^2 + \cdots + \frac{1}{N^2}\sigma_\epsilon^2 = \frac{1}{N^2}N\sigma_\epsilon^2$$

where σ_ϵ^2 is the variance of each ϵ. This can be rewritten as σ_ϵ^2/N, which tends to 0 as N goes to infinity.

capital-asset-pricing model, which posited these assumptions, implied that the expected return on a security was positively (and linearly) related to its beta. We will find a similar relationship between risk and return in the one-factor model of this chapter.

We begin by noting that the relevant risk in large and well-diversified portfolios is all systematic because unsystematic risk is diversified away. An implication is that, when a well-diversified shareholder considers changing her holdings of a particular stock, she can ignore the security's unsystematic risk.

Notice that we are not claiming that stocks, like portfolios, have no unsystematic risk. Nor are we saying that the unsystematic risk of a stock will not affect its returns. Stocks do have unsystematic risk, and their actual returns do depend on the unsystematic risk. Because this risk washes out in a well-diversified portfolio, however, shareholders can ignore this unsystematic risk when they consider whether or not to add a stock to their portfolio. Therefore, if shareholders are ignoring the unsystematic risk, only the systematic risk of a stock can be related to its *expected* return.

This relationship is illustrated in the security market line of Figure 11.3. Points *P, C, A,* and *L* all lie on the line emanating from the risk-free rate of 10 percent. The points representing each of these four assets can be created by combinations of the risk-free rate and any of the other three assets. For example, since *A* has a beta of 2.0 and *P* has a beta of 1.0, a portfolio of 50 percent in asset *A* and 50 percent in the riskless rate has the same beta as asset *P*. The risk-free rate is 10 percent and the expected return on security *A* is 35 percent, implying that the combination's return of 22.5 percent [(10% + 35%)/2] is identical to security *P*'s expected return. Because security *P* has both the same beta and the same expected return as a combination of the riskless asset and security *A*, an individual is equally inclined to add a small amount of security *P* and to add a small amount of this combination to her portfolio. However, the unsystematic risk of security *P* need not be equal to the unsystematic risk of the combination of security *A* and the risk-free rate because unsystematic risk is diversified away in a large portfolio.

Of course, the potential combinations of points on the security market line are endless. One can duplicate *P* by combinations of the risk-free rate and either *C* or *L* (or both of them). One can duplicate *C* (or *A* or *L*) by borrowing at the risk-free rate to invest in *P*. The infinite number of points on the security market line that are not labeled can be used as well.

Now consider security *B*. Because its expected return is below the line, no investor would hold it. Instead, the investor would prefer security *P*, a combination of security *A* and the

FIGURE 11.3

A Graph of Beta and Expected Return for Individual Stocks under the One-Factor Model riskless asset, or some other combination. Thus, security B's price is too high. Its price will fall in a competitive market, forcing its expected return back up to the line in equilibrium.

The preceding discussion allows us to provide an equation for the security market line of Figure 11.3. We know that a line can be described algebraically from two points. It is perhaps easiest to focus on the risk-free rate and asset P, since the risk-free rate has a beta of 0 and P has a beta of 1.

Because we know that the return on any zero-beta asset is R_F and the expected return on asset P is $\overline{R}_P$, it can easily be shown that

$$\overline{R} = R_F + \beta(\overline{R}_P - R_F) \tag{11.5}$$

In equation (11.5), $\overline{R}$ can be thought of as the expected return on any security or portfolio lying on the security market line. β is the beta of that security or portfolio.

The Market Portfolio and the Single Factor

In the CAPM, the beta of a security measures the security's responsiveness to movements in the market portfolio. In the one-factor model of the APT, the beta of a security measures its responsiveness to the factor. We now relate the market portfolio to the single factor.

A large, diversified portfolio has no unsystematic risk because the unsystematic risks of the individual securities are diversified away. Assuming enough securities so that the market portfolio is fully diversified and assuming that no security has a disproportionate market share, this portfolio is fully diversified and contains no unsystematic risk.[9] In other words, the market portfolio is perfectly correlated with the single factor, implying that the market portfolio is really a scaled-up or scaled-down version of the factor. After scaling properly, we can treat the market portfolio as the factor itself.

The market portfolio, like every security or portfolio, lies on the security market line. When the market portfolio is the factor, the beta of the market portfolio is 1 by definition. This is shown in Figure 11.4. (We deleted the securities and the specific expected returns from Figure 11.3 for clarity: The two graphs are otherwise identical.) With the market

---

FIGURE 11.4

A Graph of Beta and Expected Return for Individual Stocks under the One-Factor Model

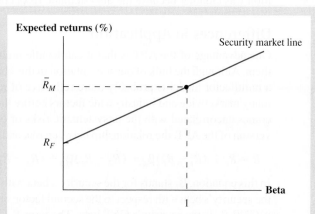

The factor is scaled so that it is identical to the market portfolio. The beta of the market portfolio is 1.

---

[9]This assumption is plausible in the real world. For example, even the market value of General Electric is only 3 percent to 4 percent of the market value of the S&P 500 Index.

portfolio as the factor, equation (11.5) becomes

$$\bar{R} = R_F + \beta(\bar{R}_M - R_F)$$

where $\bar{R}_M$ is the expected return on the market. This equation shows that the expected return on any asset, $\bar{R}$, is linearly related to the security's beta. The equation is identical to that of the CAPM, which we developed in the previous chapter.

**Concept
Question**

1. **What is the relationship between the one-factor model and the CAPM?**

11.6 The Capital-Asset-Pricing Model and the Arbitrage Pricing Theory

The CAPM and the APT are alternative models of risk and return. It is worthwhile to consider the differences between the two models, both in terms of pedagogy and in terms of application.

Differences in Pedagogy

We feel that the CAPM has at least one strong advantage from the student's point of view. The derivation of the CAPM necessarily brings the reader through a discussion of efficient sets. This treatment—beginning with the case of two risky assets, moving to the case of many risky assets, and finishing when a riskless asset is added to the many risky ones—is of great intuitive value. This sort of presentation is not as easily accomplished with the APT.

However, the APT has an offsetting advantage. The model adds factors until the unsystematic risk of any security is uncorrelated with the unsystematic risk of every other security. Under this formulation, it is easily shown that (1) unsystematic risk steadily falls (and ultimately vanishes) as the number of securities in the portfolio increases but (2) the systematic risks do not decrease. This result was also shown in the CAPM, though the intuition was cloudier because the unsystematic risks could be correlated across securities.

Differences in Application

One advantage of the APT is that it can handle multiple factors while the CAPM ignores them. Although the bulk of our presentation in this chapter focused on the one-factor model, a multifactor model is probably more reflective of reality. That is, one must abstract from many marketwide and industrywide factors before the unsystematic risk of one security becomes uncorrelated with the unsystematic risks of other securities. Under this multifactor version of the APT, the relationship between risk and return can be expressed as:

$$\bar{R} = R_F + (\bar{R}_1 - R_F)\beta_1 + (\bar{R}_2 - R_F)\beta_2 + (\bar{R}_3 - R_F)\beta_3 + \cdots + (\bar{R}_K - R_F)\beta_K \quad (11.6)$$

In this equation, β_1 stands for the security's beta with respect to the first factor, β_2 stands for the security's beta with respect to the second factor, and so on. For example, if the first factor is GNP, β_1 is the security's GNP beta. The term $\bar{R}_1$ is the expected return on a security (or portfolio) whose beta with respect to the first factor is 1 and whose beta with respect to all other factors is zero. Because the market compensates for risk, $(\bar{R}_1 - R_F)$ will be positive in the normal case.[10] (An analogous interpretation can be given to $\bar{R}_2$, $\bar{R}_3$, and so on.)

---

[10]Actually, $(\bar{R}_i - R_F)$ could be negative in the case where factor i is perceived as a hedge of some sort.

The equation states that the security's expected return is related to the security's factor betas. The intuition in equation (11.6) is straightforward. Each factor represents risk that cannot be diversified away. The higher a security's beta with regard to a particular factor is, the higher is the risk that the security bears. In a rational world, the expected return on the security should compensate for this risk. The above equation states that the expected return is a summation of the risk-free rate plus the compensation for each type of risk that the security bears.

As an example, consider a study where the factors were monthly growth in industrial production (IP), change in expected inflation (ΔEI), unanticipated inflation (UI), unanticipated change in the risk premium between risky bonds and default-free bonds (URP), and unanticipated change in the difference between the return on long-term government bonds and the return on short-term government bonds (UBR).[11] Using the period 1958–1984, the empirical results of the study indicated that the expected monthly return on any stock, $\overline{R}_S$, can be described as

$$\overline{R}_S = 0.0041 + 0.0136\beta_{IP} - 0.0001\beta_{\Delta EI} - 0.0006\beta_{UI} + 0.0072\beta_{URP} - 0.0052\beta_{UBR}$$

Suppose a particular stock had the following betas: $\beta_{IP} = 1.1$, $\beta_{\Delta EI} = 2$, $\beta_{UI} = 3$, $\beta_{URP} = 0.1$, $\beta_{UBR} = 1.6$. The expected monthly return on that security would be

$$\overline{R}_S = 0.0041 + 0.0136 \times 1.1 - 0.0001 \times 2 - 0.0006 \times 3 + 0.0072 \times 0.1 - 0.0052 \times 1.6$$
$$= 0.0095$$

Assuming that a firm is unlevered and that one of the firm's projects has risk equivalent to that of the firm, this value of 0.0095 (i.e., .95%) can be used as the monthly discount rate for the project. (Because annual data are often supplied for capital budgeting purposes, the annual rate of 0.120 [$(1.0095)^{12} - 1$] might be used instead.)

Because many factors appear on the right-hand side of equation (11.5), the APT formulation has the potential to measure expected returns more accurately than does the CAPM. However, as we mentioned earlier, one cannot easily determine which are the appropriate factors. The factors in the above study were included for reasons of both common sense and convenience. They were not derived from theory.

By contrast, the use of the market index in the CAPM formulation is implied by the theory of the previous chapter. We suggested in earlier chapters that the S&P 500 Index mirrors stock market movements quite well. Using the Ibbotson-Sinquefield results showing that the yearly return on the S&P 500 Index was, on average, 8.4 percent greater than the risk-free rate, the last chapter easily calculated expected returns on different securities from the CAPM.[12]

11.7 Empirical Approaches to Asset Pricing

Empirical Models

The CAPM and the APT by no means exhaust the models and techniques used in practice to measure the expected return on risky assets. Both the CAPM and the APT are *risk-based models*. They each measure the risk of a security by its beta(s) on some systematic factor(s), and they each argue that the expected excess return must be proportional to the

---

[11]N. Chen, R. Roll, and S. Ross, "Economic Forces and the Stock Market," *Journal of Business* (July 1986).

[12]Though many researchers assume that surrogates for the market portfolio are easily found, Richard Roll, "A Critique of the Asset Pricing Theory's Tests," *Journal of Financial Economics* (March 1977), argues that the absence of a universally acceptable proxy for the market portfolio seriously impairs application of the theory. After all, the market must include real estate, racehorses, and other assets that are not in the stock market.

beta(s). While we have seen that this is intuitively appealing and has a strong basis in theory, there are alternative approaches.

Most of these alternatives can be lumped under the broad heading of parametric or **empirical models.** The word *empirical* refers to the fact that these approaches are based less on some theory of how financial markets work and more on simply looking for regularities and relations in the history of market data. In these approaches the researcher specifies some parameters or attributes associated with the securities in question and then examines the data directly for a relation between these attributes and expected returns. For example, an extensive amount of research has been done on whether the expected return on a firm is related to its size. Is it true that small firms have higher average returns than large firms? Researchers have also examined a variety of accounting measures such as the ratio of the price of a stock to the accounting earnings, the P/E ratio, and the closely related ratio of the market value of the stock to the book value of the company, the M/B ratio. Here it might be argued that companies with low P/E's or low M/B's are "undervalued" and can be expected to have higher returns in the future.

To use the empirical approach to determine the expected return, we would estimate the following equation:

$$\bar{R}_i = R_F + k_{\text{P/E}}(\text{P/E})_i + k_{\text{M/B}}(\text{M/B})_i + k_{\text{size}}(\text{size})_P$$

where $\bar{R}_i$ is the expected return of firm i, and where the k's are coefficients that we estimate from stock market data. Notice that this is the same form as equation (11.6) with the firm's attributes in place of betas and with the k's in place of the excess factor portfolio returns.

When tested with data, these parametric approaches seem to do quite well. In fact, when comparisons are made between using parameters and using betas to predict stock returns, the parameters, such as P/E and M/B, seem to work better. There are a variety of possible explanations for these results, and the issues have certainly not been settled. Critics of the empirical approach are skeptical of what they call *data mining*. The particular parameters that researchers work with are often chosen because they have been shown to be related to returns. For instance, suppose that you were asked to explain the change in SAT test scores over the past 40 years in some particular state. Suppose that to do this you searched through all of the data series you could find. After much searching, you might discover, for example, that the change in the scores was directly related to the jackrabbit population in Arizona. We know that any such relation is purely accidental but if you search long enough and have enough choices, you will find something even if it is not really there. It's a bit like staring at clouds. After a while you will see clouds that look like anything you want, clowns, bears, or whatever, but all you are really doing is data mining.

Needless to say, the researchers on these matters defend their work by arguing that they have not mined the data and have been very careful to avoid such traps by not snooping at the data to see what will work.

Of course, as a matter of pure theory, since anyone in the market can easily look up the P/E ratio of a firm, one would certainly not expect to find that firms with low P/E's did better than firms with high P/E's simply because they were undervalued. In an efficient market, such public measures of undervaluation would be quickly exploited and would not expect to last.

Perhaps a better explanation for the success of empirical approaches lies in a synthesis of the risk-based approaches and the empirical methods. In an efficient market, risk and return are related, hence perhaps the parameters or attributes which appear to be related to returns are also better measures of risk. For example, if we were to find that low P/E firms outperformed high P/E firms and that this was true even for firms that had the same beta(s), then we have at least two possible explanations. First, we could simply discard the risk-based theories as incorrect. Furthermore, we could argue that markets are inefficient and that buying low P/E stocks provides us with an opportunity to make higher than predicted returns. Second, we could argue that *both* views of the world are correct and that the P/E is really just a better way to measure systematic risk, i.e., beta(s), than directly estimating beta from the data.

Style Portfolios

In addition to their use as a platform for estimating expected returns, stock attributes are also widely used as a way of characterizing money management styles. For example, a portfolio that has a P/E ratio much in excess of the market average might be characterized as a high P/E or a **growth stock portfolio.** Similarly, a portfolio made up of stocks with an average P/E less than that for a market index might be characterized as a low P/E or a **value portfolio.**

To evaluate how well a portfolio manager is doing, often their performance is compared with the performance of some basic indexes. For example, the portfolio returns of a manager who purchases large U.S. stocks might be compared to the performance of the S&P 500 Index. In such a case the S&P 500 is said to be the **benchmark** against which their performance is measured. Similarly, an international manager might be compared against some common index of international stocks. In choosing an appropriate benchmark, care should be taken to identify a benchmark that contains only those types of stocks that the manager targets as representative of his or her style and that are also available to be purchased. A manager who was told not to purchase any stocks in the S&P 500 Index would not consider it legitimate to be compared against the S&P 500.

Increasingly, too, managers are compared not only against an index, but also against a peer group of similar managers. The performance of a fund that advertises itself as a growth fund might be measured against the performance of a large sample of similar funds. For instance, the performance over some period commonly is assigned to quartiles. The top 25 percent of the funds are said to be in the first quartile, the next 25 percent in the second quartile, the next 25 percent in the third quartile, and the worst performing 25 percent of the funds in the last quartile. If the fund we are examining happens to have a performance that falls in the second quartile, then we speak of it as a second quartile manager.

Similarly, we call a fund that purchases low M/B stocks a value fund and would measure its performance against a sample of similar value funds. These approaches to measuring performance are relatively new, and they are part of an active and exciting effort to refine our ability to identify and use investment skills.

Concept
Questions

1. Empirical models are sometimes called factor models. What is the difference between a factor as we have used it previously in this chapter and an attribute as we use it in this section?
2. What is data mining and why might it overstate the relation between some stock attribute and returns?
3. What is wrong with measuring the performance of a U.S. growth stock manager against a benchmark composed of English stocks?

11.8 SUMMARY AND CONCLUSIONS

The previous chapter developed the capital-asset-pricing model (CAPM). As an alternative, this chapter develops the arbitrage pricing theory (APT).

1. The APT assumes that stock returns are generated according to factor models. For example, we might describe a stock's return as

$$R = \bar{R} + \beta_I F_I + \beta_{GNP} F_{GNP} + \beta_r F_r = \epsilon$$

where I, GNP, and r stand for inflation, gross national product, and the interest rate, respectively. The three factors F_I, F_{GNP}, and F_r represent systematic risk because these factors affect many securities. The term ϵ is considered unsystematic risk because it is unique to each individual security.

2. For convenience, we frequently describe a security's return according to a one-factor model:

$$R = \bar{R} + \beta F + \epsilon$$

3. As securities are added to a portfolio, the unsystematic risks of the individual securities offset each other. A fully diversified portfolio has no unsystematic risk but still has systematic risk. This result indicates that diversification can eliminate some, but not all, of the risk of individual securities.

4. Because of this, the expected return on a stock is positively related to its systematic risk. In a one-factor model, the systematic risk of a security is simply the beta of the CAPM. Thus, the implications of the CAPM and the one-factor APT are identical. However, each security has many risks in a multifactor model. The expected return on a security is positively related to the beta of the security with each factor.

5. Empirical or parametric models that capture the relations between returns and stock attributes such as P/E or M/B ratios can be estimated directly from the data without any appeal to theory. These ratios are also used to measure the style of a portfolio manager and to construct benchmarks and samples against which they are measured.

KEY TERMS

benchmark, *313*
beta coefficient, *301*
empirical model, *312*
factor model, *303*

growth stock portfolios, *313*
market model, *303*
value portfolios, *313*

SUGGESTED READINGS

Complete treatments of the APT can be found in both of the following articles:

Ross, S. A. "Return, Risk and Arbitrage." In Friend and Bicksler, eds., *Risk and Return in Finance.* New York: Heath Lexington, 1974.

Ross, S. A. "The Arbitrage Theory of Asset Pricing." *Journal of Economic Theory* (December 1976).

Two less technical discussions of APT are:

Bower, D. H., R. S. Bower, and D. Logue. "A Primer on Arbitrage Pricing Theory." *Midland Corporate Finance Journal* (Fall 1984).

Roll, R., and S. Ross. "The Arbitrage Pricing Theory Approach to Strategic Portfolio Planning." *Financial Analysts Journal* (May/June 1984).

The following article describes the idea of style portfolios:

Roll, R. "Style Return Differentials: Illusions, Risk Premia, or Investment Opportunities." In Fabozzi (ed.), *Handbook of Equity Style Management.* New Hope, PA: Frank Fabozzi Associates, 1995.

QUESTIONS & PROBLEMS

FACTOR MODELS AND RISK

11.1 You own stock in the Lewis-Striden Drug Company. Suppose you had expected the following events to occur last month.

    a. The government would announce that real GNP would have grown 1.2 percent during the previous quarter. The returns of Lewis-Striden are positively related to real GNP.

    b. The government would announce that inflation over the previous quarter was 3.7 percent. The returns of Lewis-Striden are negatively related to inflation.

    c. Interest rates would rise 2.5 percentage points. The returns of Lewis-Striden are negatively related to interest rates.

    d. The president of the firm would announce his retirement. The retirement would be effective six months from the announcement day. The president is well liked: In general he is considered an asset to the firm.

    e. Research data would conclusively prove the efficacy of an experimental drug. Completion of the efficacy testing means the drug will be on the market soon.

Suppose the following events actually occurred.

    a. The government announced that real GNP grew 2.3 percent during the previous quarter.

    b. The government announced that inflation over the previous quarter was 3.7 percent.

    c. Interest rates rose 2.1 percentage points.

    d. The president of the firm died suddenly of a heart attack.

    e. Research results in the efficacy testing were not as strong as expected. The drug must be tested another six months and the efficacy results must be resubmitted to the FDA.

    f. Lab researchers had a breakthrough with another drug.

    g. A competitor announced that it will begin distribution and sale of a medicine that will compete directly with one of Lewis-Striden's top-selling products.

        i. Discuss how each of the actual occurrences affects the returns on your Lewis-Striden stock.

        ii. Which events represent systematic risk?

        iii. Which events represent unsystematic risk?

11.2 Suppose a three-factor model is appropriate to describe the returns of a stock. Information about those three factors is presented in the following chart. Suppose this is the only information you have concerning the factors.

Factor	Beta of Factor	Expected Value	Actual Value
GNP	0.0042	$4,416	$4,480
Inflation	−1.40	3.1%	4.3%
Interest rate	−0.67	9.5%	11.8%

    a. What is the systematic risk of the stock return?

    b. Suppose unexpected bad news about the firm was announced that dampens the returns by 2.6 percentage points. What is the unsystematic risk of the stock return?

    c. Suppose the expected return of the stock is 9.5 percent. What is the total return on this stock?

 11.3 Suppose a factor model is appropriate to describe the returns on a stock. Information about those factors is presented in the following chart.

Factor	Beta of Factor	Expected Value (%)	Actual Value (%)
Growth in GNP	2.04	3.5%	4.8%
Interest rates	−1.90	14.0	15.2
Stock return		10.0	

    a. What is the systematic risk of the stock return?

    b. The firm announced that its market share had unexpectedly increased from 23 percent to 27 percent. Investors know from their past experience that the stock return will increase by 0.36 percent per an increase of 1 percent in its market share. What is the unsystematic risk of the stock?

    c. What is the total return on this stock?

11.4 The following three stocks are available in the market.

	Expected Return (%)	Beta
Stock A	10.5%	1.20
Stock B	13.0	0.98
Stock C	15.7	1.37
Market	14.2	1.00

Assume the market model is valid.
  a. Write the market-model equation for each stock.
  b. What is the return on a portfolio that is 30-percent stock A, 45-percent stock B, and 25-percent stock C?
  c. Suppose the return on the market is 15 percent and there are no unsystematic surprises in the returns.
    i. What is the return on each stock?
    ii. What is the return on the portfolio?

11.5 You are forming an equally weighted portfolio of stocks. There are many stocks that all have the same beta of 0.84 for factor 1 and the same beta of 1.69 for factor 2. All stocks also have the same expected return of 11 percent. Assume a two-factor model describes the returns on each of these stocks.
  a. Write the equation of the returns on your portfolio if you place only five stocks in it.
  b. Write the equation of the returns on your portfolio if you place in it a very large number of stocks that all have the same expected returns and the same betas.

THE APT

11.6 There are two stock markets, each driven by the same common force F with an expected value of zero and standard deviation of 10 percent. There are a large number of securities in each market; thus, you can invest in as many stocks as you wish. Due to restrictions, however, you can invest in only one of the two markets. The expected return on every security in both markets is 10 percent.

The returns for each security i in the first market are generated by the relationship

$$R_{1i} = 0.10 + 1.5F + \epsilon_{1i}$$

where ϵ_{1i} is the term that measures the surprises in the returns of stock i in market 1. These surprises are normally distributed; their mean is zero. The returns for security j in the second market are generated by the relationship

$$R_{2j} = 0.10 + 0.5F + \epsilon_{2j}$$

where ϵ_{2j} is the term that measures the surprises in the returns of stock j in market 2. These surprises are normally distributed; their mean is zero. The standard deviation of ϵ_{1i} and ϵ_{2j} for any two stocks, i and j, is 20 percent.
  a. If the correlation between the surprises in the returns of any two stocks in the first market is zero, and if the correlation between the surprises in the returns of any two stocks in the second market is zero, in which market would a risk-averse person prefer to invest? (Note: The correlation between ϵ_{1i} and ϵ_{1j} for any i and j is zero, and the correlation between ϵ_{2i} and ϵ_{2j} for any i and j is zero.)
  b. If the correlation between ϵ_{1i} and ϵ_{1j} in the first market is 0.9 and the correlation between ϵ_{2i} and ϵ_{2j} in the second market is zero, in which market would a risk-averse person prefer to invest?
  c. If the correlation between ϵ_{1i} and ϵ_{1j} in the first market is zero and the correlation between ϵ_{2i} and ϵ_{2j} in the second market is 0.5, in which market would a risk-averse person prefer to invest?
  d. In general, what is the relationship between the correlations of the disturbances in the two markets that would make a risk-averse person equally willing to invest in either of the two markets?

11.7 Assume that the following market model adequately describes the return-generating behavior of risky assets.

$$R_{it} = \alpha_i + \beta_i R_{Mt} + \epsilon_{it}$$

where
$$R_{it} = \text{The return for the } i\text{th asset at time } t$$
and
$$R_{Mt} = \text{The return on a portfolio containing all risky}$$
$$\text{assets in some proportion, at time } t$$

R_{Mt} and ϵ_{it} are statistically independent.

Suppose the following data are true.

Asset	β_i	$E(R_i)$	$Var(\epsilon_i)$
A	0.7	8.41%	1.00%
B	1.2	12.06	1.44
C	1.5	13.95	2.25
$Var(R_{Mt}) = 1.21\%$			

a. Calculate the standard deviation of returns for each asset.
b. Assume short selling is allowed.
  i. Calculate the variance of return of three portfolios containing an infinite number of asset types A, B, or C, respectively.
  ii. Assume: $R_F = 3.3\%$ and $\bar{R}_M = 10.6\%$. Which asset will not be held by rational investors?
  iii. What equilibrium state will emerge such that no arbitrage opportunities exist? Why?

11.8 Assume that the returns of individual securities are generated by the following two-factor model:

$$R_{it} = E(R_{it}) + \beta_{i1}F_{1t} + \beta_{i2}F_{2t}$$

R_{it} is the return for security i at time t. F_{1t} and F_{2t} are market factors with zero expectation and zero covariance. In addition, assume that there is a capital market for four securities, where each one has the following characteristics:

Security	β_1	β_2	$E(R_{it})$
1	1.0	1.5	20%
2	0.5	2.0	20
3	1.0	0.5	10
4	1.5	0.75	10

The capital market for these four assets is perfect in the sense that there are no transactions costs and short sales can take place.

a. Construct a portfolio containing (long or short) securities *1* and *2*, with a return that does not depend on the market factor, F_{1t}, in any way. (Hint: Such a portfolio will have $\beta_1 = 0$.) Compute the expected return and β_2 coefficient for this portfolio.
b. Following the procedure in (*a*), construct a portfolio containing securities *3* and *4* with a return that does not depend on the market factor, F_{1t}. Compute the expected return and β_2 coefficient for this portfolio.
c. Consider a risk-free asset with expected return equal to 5 percent, $\beta_1 = 0$, and $\beta_2 = 0$. Describe a possible arbitrage opportunity in such detail that an investor could implement it.
d. What effect would the existence of these kinds of arbitrage opportunities have on the capital markets for these securities in the short and long run? Graph your analysis.

Risk, Cost of Capital, and Capital Budgeting

EXECUTIVE SUMMARY

Our text has devoted a number of chapters to net present value (NPV) analysis. We pointed out that a dollar to be received in the future is worth less than a dollar received today for two reasons. First, there is the simple time-value-of-money argument in a riskless world. If you have a dollar today, you can invest it in the bank and receive more than a dollar by some future date. Second, a risky dollar is worth less than a riskless dollar. Consider a firm expecting a $1 cash flow. If actuality exceeds expectations (revenues are especially high or expenses are especially low), perhaps $1.10 or $1.20 will be received. If actuality falls short of expectations, perhaps only $0.80 or $0.90 will be received. This risk is unattractive to the typical firm.

Our work on NPV allowed us to value riskless cash flows precisely. That is, we discounted by the riskless interest rate. However, because most real-world cash flows in the future are risky, business demands a procedure for discounting risky cash flows. This chapter applies the concept of net present value to risky cash flows.

Let us review what previous work in the text has to say about NPV. In earlier chapters we learned that the basic NPV formula for an investment that generates cash flows (C_t) in future periods is

$$NPV = C_0 + \sum_{t=1}^{T} \frac{C_t}{(1+r)^t}$$

For risky projects, expected incremental cash flows $\overline{C_t}$ are placed in the numerator, and the NPV formula becomes

$$NPV = C_0 + \sum_{t=1}^{T} \frac{\overline{C_t}}{(1+r)^t}$$

In this chapter, we will learn that the discount rate used to determine the NPV of a risky project can be computed from the CAPM (or APT). For example, if an all-equity firm is seeking to value a risky project, such as renovating a warehouse, the firm will determine the required return, r_S, on the project by using the SML. We call r_S the firm's **cost of equity capital.**

When firms finance with both debt and equity, the discount rate to use is the project's overall cost of capital. The overall cost of capital is a weighted average of the cost of debt and the cost of equity.

12.1 The Cost of Equity Capital

Whenever a firm has extra cash, it can take one of two actions. On the one hand, it can pay out the cash immediately as a dividend. On the other hand, the firm can invest extra cash in a project, paying out the future cash flows of the project as dividends. Which procedure would the stockholders prefer? If a stockholder can reinvest the dividend in a financial asset (a stock or bond) with the same risk as that of the project, the stockholders would desire the

FIGURE 12.1

Choices of a Firm
with Extra Cash

Corporation receives cash.
It can either

Pay dividend

Invest cash in project

Shareholder invests
dividend in financial asset

Stockholders want the firm to invest in a project only if the
expected return on the project is at least as great as that of a
financial asset of comparable risk.

alternative with the highest expected return. In other words, the project should be undertaken only if its expected return is greater than that of a financial asset of comparable risk. This is illustrated in Figure 12.1. This discussion implies a very simple capital-budgeting rule:

> The discount rate of a project should be the expected return on a financial asset of comparable risk.

From the firm's perspective, the expected return is the cost of equity capital. Under the CAPM, the expected return on the stock is

$$\overline{R} = R_F + \beta \times (\overline{R}_M - R_F) \tag{12.1}$$

where R_F is the risk-free rate and $\overline{R}_M - R_F$ is the difference between the expected return on the market portfolio and the riskless rate. This difference is often called the expected *excess* market return.[1]

We now have the tools to estimate a firm's cost of equity capital. To do this, we need to know three things:

- The risk-free rate, R_F
- The market-risk premium, $\overline{R}_M - R_F$
- The company beta, β_i

EXAMPLE

Suppose the stock of the Quatram Company, a publisher of college textbooks, has a beta (β) of 1.3. The firm is 100-percent equity financed; that is, it has no debt. Quatram is considering a number of capital-budgeting projects that will double its size. Because these new projects are similar to the firm's existing ones, the average beta on the new projects is assumed to be equal to Quatram's existing beta. The risk-free rate is 5 percent. What is the appropriate discount rate for these new projects, assuming a market-risk premium of 8.4 percent?

---

[1]Of course, we can use the *k*-factor APT model (Chapter 11) and estimate several beta coefficients. However, for our purposes it is sufficient to estimate a single beta.

We estimate the cost of equity r_S for Quatram as

$$r_S = 5\% + (8.4\% \times 1.3)$$
$$= 5\% + 10.92\%$$
$$= 15.92\%$$

Two key assumptions were made in this example: (1) The beta risk of the new projects is the same as the risk of the firm, and (2) The firm is all-equity financed. Given these assumptions, it follows that the cash flows of the new projects should be discounted at the 19.35-percent rate.

EXAMPLE

Suppose Alpha Air Freight is an all-equity firm with a beta of 1.21. Further suppose the market-risk premium is 9.5 percent, and the risk-free rate is 5 percent. We can determine the expected return on the common stock of Alpha Air Freight by using the SML of equation (12.1). We find that the expected return is

$$5\% + (1.21 \times 9.5\%) = 16.495\%$$

Because this is the return that shareholders can expect in the financial markets on a stock with a β of 1.21, it is the return they expect on Alpha Air Freight's stock.

Further suppose Alpha is evaluating the following non-mutually exclusive projects:

Project	Project's Beta (β)	Project's Expected Cash Flows Next Year	Project's Internal Rate of Return	Project's NPV When Cash Flows Are Discounted at 16.495%	Accept or Reject
A	1.21	$140	40%	$20.2	Accept
B	1.21	120	20	3.0	Accept
C	1.21	110	10	−5.6	Reject

Each project initially costs $100. All projects are assumed to have the same risk as the firm as a whole. Because the cost of equity capital is 16.495 percent, projects in an all-equity firm are discounted at this rate. Projects A and B have positive NPVs, and C has a negative NPV. Thus, only A and B will be accepted.[2] This is illustrated in Figure 12.2.

---

[2]In addition to the SML, the dividend-valuation model presented earlier in the text can be used to represent the firm's cost of equity capital. Using this model, the present value (P) of the firm's expected dividend payments can be expressed as

$$P = \frac{\text{Div}_1}{(1 + r_S)} + \frac{\text{Div}_2}{(1 + r_S)^2} + \cdots + \frac{\text{Div}_N}{(1 + r_S)^N} + \cdots \qquad (a)$$

where r_S is the required return of shareholders and the firm's cost of equity capital. If the dividends are expected to grow at a constant rate, g, equation (a) reduces to

$$P = \frac{\text{Div}_1}{r_S - g} \qquad (b)$$

Equation (b) can be reformulated as

$$r_S = \frac{\text{Div}_1}{P} + g \qquad (c)$$

We can use equation (c) to estimate r_S. Div_1/P is the dividend yield expected over the next year. An estimate of the cost of equity capital is determined from an estimate of Div_1/P and g.

The dividend-valuation model is generally considered more difficult to apply practically than the SML. In addition, J. R. Graham and C. R. Harvey, "The Theory and Practice of Corporate Finance: Evidence from the Field," *Journal of Financial Economics* 60 (2001) present evidence that only about 15 percent of real-world companies use the dividend-valuation model, a far smaller percentage than use the SML approach. Hence, examples in this chapter calculate cost of equity capital using the SML approach.

FIGURE 12.2

Using the Security-
Market Line to
Estimate the Risk-
Adjusted Discount
Rate for Risky
Projects

The diagonal line represents the relationship between the cost of equity capital and the firm's beta. An all-equity firm should accept a project whose internal rate of return is greater than the cost of equity capital, and should reject a project whose internal rate of return is less than the cost of equity capital. (The above graph assumes that all projects are as risky as the firm.)

12.2 Estimation of Beta

In the previous section we assumed that the beta of the company was known. Of course, beta must be estimated in the real world. We pointed out earlier that the beta of a security is the standardized covariance of a security's return with the return on the market portfolio. The formula for security i, first given in Chapter 10, is

$$\text{Beta of security } i = \frac{\text{Cov}(R_i, R_M)}{\text{Var}(R_M)} = \frac{\sigma_{i,M}}{\sigma_M^2}$$

In words, the beta is the covariance of a security with the market, divided by the variance of the market. Because we calculated both covariance and variance in earlier chapters, calculating beta involves no new material.

EXAMPLE (ADVANCED)

Suppose we sample the returns on the stock of the General Tool Company and the returns on the S&P 500 Index for four years. They are tabulated as follows:

Year	General Tool Company R_G	S&P 500 Index R_M
1	−10%	−40%
2	3	−30
3	20	10
4	15	20

TABLE 12.1		Calculating Beta				
(1)	**(2)**	**(3)**	**(4)**	**(5)**	**(6)**	**(7)**
Year	Rate of Return on General Tool (R_G)	General Tool's Deviation from Average Return* $(R_G - \bar{R}_G)$	Rate of Return on Market Portfolio	Market Portfolio's Deviation from Average Return† $(R_M - \bar{R}_M)$	Deviation of General Tool Multiplied by Deviation of Market Portfolio	Squared Deviation of Market Portfolio
1	−0.10	−0.17 (−0.10 − 0.07)	−0.40	−0.30	0.051 [(−0.17) × (−0.30)]	0.090 [(−0.30) × (−0.30)]
2	0.03	−0.04	−0.30	−0.20	0.008	0.040
3	0.20	0.13	0.10	0.20	0.026	0.040
4	0.15	0.08	0.20	0.30	0.024	0.090
	Avg = 0.07		Avg = −0.10		Sum: 0.109	Sum: 0.260

Beta of General Tool: $0.419 = \dfrac{0.109}{0.260}$.

*Average return for General Tool is 0.07.

†Average return for market is −0.10.

We can calculate beta in six steps.

1. Calculate average return on each asset:

Average Return on General Tool:

$$\frac{-0.10 + 0.03 + 0.20 + 0.15}{4} = 0.07 \ (7\%)$$

Average Return on Market Portfolio:

$$\frac{-0.40 - 0.30 + 0.10 + 0.20}{4} = -0.10 \ (-10\%)$$

2. For each asset, calculate the deviation of each return from the asset's average return determined above. This is presented in columns 3 and 5 of Table 12.1.

3. Multiply the deviation of General Tool's return by the deviation of the market's return. This is presented in column 6. This procedure is analogous to our calculation of covariance in an earlier chapter. The procedure will be used in the numerator of the beta calculation.

4. Calculate the squared deviation of the market's return. This is presented in column 7. This procedure is analogous to our calculation of variance in Chapter 9. This procedure will be used in the denominator of the beta calculation.

5. Take the sum of column 6 and the sum of column 7. They are

Sum of Deviation of General Tool Multiplied by Deviation of Market Portfolio:

$$0.051 + 0.008 + 0.026 + 0.024 = 0.109$$

Sum of Squared Deviation of Market Portfolio:

$$0.090 + 0.040 + 0.040 + 0.090 = 0.260$$

6. The beta is the sum of column 6 divided by the sum of column 7. This is

Beta of General Tool:

$$0.419 = \frac{0.109}{0.260}$$

Measuring Company Betas

The basic method of measuring company betas is to estimate:

$$\frac{\text{Cov}(R_{it}, R_{Mt})}{\text{Var}(R_{Mt})}$$

using $t = 1, 2, \ldots, T$ observations

Problems

1. Betas may vary over time.
2. The sample size may be inadequate.
3. Betas are influenced by changing financial leverage and business risk.

Solutions

1. Problems 1 and 2 (above) can be moderated by more sophisticated statistical techniques.
2. Problem 3 can be lessened by adjusting for changes in business and financial risk.
3. Look at average beta estimates of several comparable firms in the industry.

Real-World Betas

The General Tool Company discussed in the previous example is fictional. It is instructive to see how betas are determined for actual real-world companies. Figure 12.3 plots monthly returns for four large firms against monthly returns on the Standard & Poor's (S&P) 500 Index. As mentioned in Chapter 10, each firm has its own characteristic line. The slope of the characteristic line is beta, as estimated using the technique of Table 12.1. This technique is called *regression*. Though we have not shown it in the table, one can also determine the intercept (commonly called alpha) of the characteristic line by regression. Since a line can be created from its intercept and slope, the regression allows one to estimate the characteristic line of a firm.

We use five years of monthly data for each plot. While this choice is arbitrary, it is in line with calculations performed in the real world. Practitioners know that the accuracy of the beta coefficient is suspect when too few observations are used. Conversely, since firms may change their industry over time, observations from the distant past are out-of-date.

We stated in Chapter 10 that the average beta across all stocks in an index is 1. Of course, this need not be true for a subset of the index. For example, of the four securities in our figure, three have betas above 1 and one has a beta below 1. Since beta is a measure of the risk of a single security for someone holding a large, diversified portfolio, our results indicate that Coca-Cola has relatively low risk and Philip Morris has relatively high risk. A more detailed discussion of the determinants of beta is presented in Section 12.3.

Stability of Beta

We stated above that the beta of a firm is likely to change if the firm changes its industry. It is also interesting to ask the reverse question: Does the beta of a firm stay the same if its industry stays the same?

Take the case of General Electric, a large, diversified firm that for the most part has stayed in the same industries for many decades. Figure 12.4 plots the returns on General Electric and the returns on the S&P 500 for four successive five-year periods. As can be seen from the figure, GE's beta has increased slightly from the first to the third subperiod

FIGURE 12.3   Plots of Five Years of Monthly Returns on Four Individual Securities against Five Years
of Monthly Returns on the Standard & Poor's (S&P) 500 Index

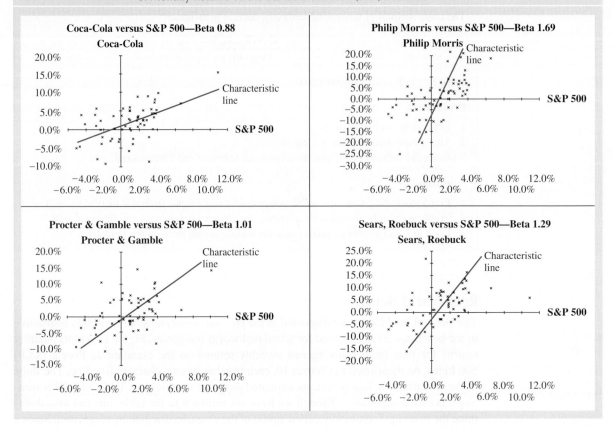

while falling in the last subperiod. However, this movement in beta is probably nothing
more than random variation.[3] Thus, for practical purposes, GE's beta has been approximately constant over the two decades covered in the figure. While GE is just one company,
most analysts argue that betas are generally stable for firms remaining in the same industry.

However, this is not to say that, as long as a firm stays in the same industry, its beta will
never change. Changes in product line, changes in technology, or changes in the market
may affect a firm's beta. For example, the deregulation of the airline industry has increased
the betas of airline firms. Furthermore, as we will show in a later section, an increase in
the leverage of a firm (i.e., the amount of debt in its capital structure) will increase the firm's
beta.

Using an Industry Beta

Our approach of estimating the beta of a company from its own past data may seem com-
monsensical to you. However, it is frequently argued that one can better estimate a firm's
beta by involving the whole industry. Consider Table 12.2, which shows the betas of some
of the more prominent firms in the software industry. The average beta across all of the firms
in the table is 1.65. Imagine a financial executive at Oracle Corp. trying to estimate the firm's
beta. Because beta-estimation is subject to large random variation in this volatile industry,

---

[3]More precisely, one can say that the beta coefficients over the four periods are not statistically different from each other.

FIGURE 12.4	Plots of Monthly Returns on General Electric and on the Standard & Poor's 500 Index for Four Five-Year Periods

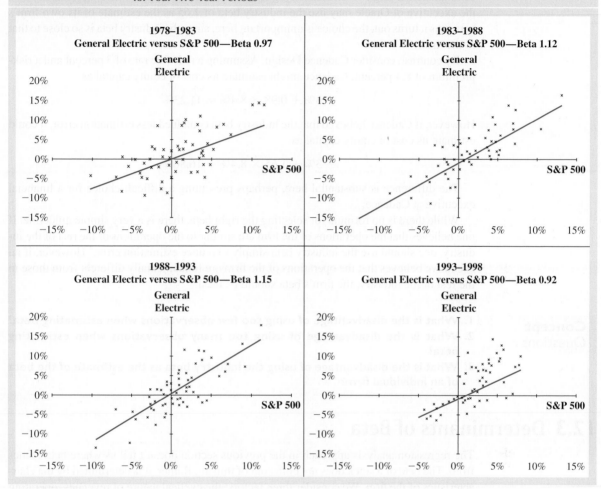

TABLE 12.2	**Company**	**Beta**
Betas for Firms in the Software Industry	Adobe Systems Inc.	1.51
	BMC Software Inc.	0.96
	Cadence Design	0.98
	Cerner Corp.	1.87
	Citrix Systems Inc.	1.29
	Comshare Inc.	1.22
	Informix Corp.	2.09
	Int. Lottery & Totalizator Sys. Inc.	3.34
	Microsoft Corp.	1.11
	Oracle Corp.	1.63
	Symantec Corp.	1.82
	Veritas Software	1.94
	Equally weighted portfolio	1.65

the executive may be uncomfortable with the estimate of 1.63. However, the error in beta-estimation on a single stock is much higher than the error for a portfolio of securities. Thus, the executive of Oracle may use the industry beta of 1.65 as the estimate of its own firm's beta. (As it turns out, the choice is unimportant here, since the industry beta is so close to that of the firm.)

By contrast, consider Cadence Design. Assuming a risk-free rate of 3 percent and a risk-premium of 8.4 percent, Cadence might estimate its cost of equity capital as:

$$3\% + 0.98 \times 8.4\% = 11.23\%$$

However, if Cadence believed that the industry beta contained less estimation error, it could estimate its cost of equity capital as:

$$3\% + 1.65 \times 8.4\% = 16.86\%$$

The difference is substantial here, perhaps presenting a difficult choice for a financial executive at Cadence.

While there is no formula for selecting the right beta, there is a very simple guideline. If one believes that the operations of the firm are similar to the operations of the rest of the industry, one should use the industry beta simply to reduce estimation error.[4] However, if an executive believes that the operations of the firm are fundamentally different from those in the rest of the industry, the firm's beta should be used.

Concept
Questions

1. **What is the disadvantage of using too few observations when estimating beta?**
2. **What is the disadvantage of using too many observations when estimating beta?**
3. **What is the disadvantage of using the industry beta as the estimate of the beta of an individual firm?**

12.3 Determinants of Beta

The regression analysis approach in the previous section doesn't tell us where beta comes from. The beta of a stock does not come out of thin air. Rather, it is determined by the characteristics of the firm. We consider three factors: the cyclical nature of revenues, operating leverage, and financial leverage.

Cyclicality of Revenues

The revenues of some firms are quite cyclical. That is, these firms do well in the expansion phase of the business cycle and do poorly in the contraction phase. Empirical evidence suggests high-tech firms, retailers, and automotive firms fluctuate with the business cycle. Firms in industries such as utilities, railroads, food, and airlines are less dependent upon the cycle. Because beta is the standardized covariability of a stock's return with the market's return, it is not surprising that highly cyclical stocks have high betas. For example, Sears's beta, as shown in Figure 12.3, is high because its sales are dependent on the market cycle.

It is worthwhile to point out that cyclicality is not the same as variability. For example, a movie-making firm has highly variable revenues because hits and flops are not easily predicted. However, because the revenues of a studio are more dependent on the quality of its releases than upon the phase of the business cycle, motion-picture companies are not

---

[4]As we will see later, an adjustment must be made when the debt level in the industry is different from that of the firm. However, we ignore this adjustment here, since firms in the software industry generally have little debt.

particularly cyclical. In other words, stocks with high standard deviations need not have high betas, a point we have stressed before.

Operating Leverage

We distinguished fixed costs from variable costs earlier in the text. At that time, we mentioned that fixed costs do not change as quantity changes. Conversely, variable costs increase as the quantity of output rises. This difference between variable and fixed costs allows us to define operating leverage.

EXAMPLE

Consider a firm that can choose either technology A or technology B when making a particular product. The relevant differences between the two technologies are displayed below:

Technology A	Technology B
Fixed cost: $1,000/year	Fixed cost: $2,000/year
Variable cost: $8/unit	Variable cost: $6/unit
Price: $10/unit	Price: $10/unit
Contribution margin: $2 ($10 − $8)	Contribution margin: $4 ($10 − $6)

Technology A has lower fixed costs and higher variable costs than does technology B. Perhaps technology A involves less mechanization than does B. Or, the equipment in A may be leased whereas the equipment in B must be purchased. Alternatively, perhaps technology A involves few employees but many subcontractors, whereas B involves only highly skilled employees who must be retained in bad times. Because technology B has both lower variable costs and higher fixed costs, we say that it has higher **operating leverage**.[5]

Figure 12.5 graphs the costs under both technologies. The slope of each total-cost line represents variable costs under a single technology. The slope of A's line is steeper, indicating greater variable costs.

FIGURE 12.5

Illustration of Two Different Technologies

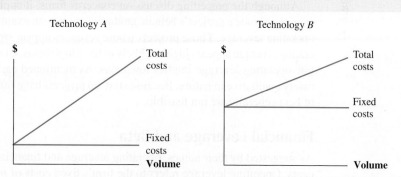

Technology A has higher variable costs and lower fixed costs than does technology B. Technology B has higher operating leverage.

[5]The actual definition of operating leverage is

$$\frac{\text{Change in EBIT}}{\text{EBIT}} \times \frac{\text{Sales}}{\text{Change in sales}}$$

where EBIT is the earnings before interest and taxes. That is, operating leverage measures the percentage change in EBIT for a given percentage change in sales or revenues. It can be shown that operating leverage increases as fixed costs rise and as variable costs fall.

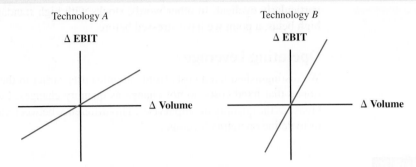

Technology B has lower variable costs than A, implying a higher contribution margin. The profits of the firm are more responsive to changes in volume under technology B than under A.

Because the two technologies are used to produce the same products, a unit price of $10 applies for both cases. We mentioned in an earlier chapter that contribution margin is the difference between price and variable cost. It measures the incremental profit from one additional unit. Because the contribution margin in B is greater, its technology is riskier. An unexpected sale increases profit by $2 under A but increases profit by $4 under B. Similarly, an unexpected sale cancellation reduces profit by $2 under A but reduces profit by $4 under B. This is illustrated in Figure 12.6. This figure shows the change in earnings before interest and taxes for a given change in volume. The slope of the right-hand graph is greater, indicating that technology B is riskier.

The cyclicality of a firm's revenues is a determinant of the firm's beta. Operating leverage magnifies the effect of cyclicality on beta. As mentioned earlier, business risk is generally defined as the risk of the firm without financial leverage. Business risk depends both on the responsiveness of the firm's revenues to the business cycle and on the firm's operating leverage.

Although the preceding discussion concerns firms, it applies to projects as well. If one cannot estimate a project's beta in another way, one can examine the project's revenues and operating leverage. Those projects whose revenues appear strongly cyclical and whose operating leverage appears high are likely to have high betas. Conversely, weak cyclicality and low operating leverage implies low betas. As mentioned earlier, this approach is unfortunately qualitative in nature. Because start-up projects have little data, quantitative estimates of beta generally are not feasible.

Financial Leverage and Beta

As suggested by their names, operating leverage and financial leverage are analogous concepts. Operating leverage refers to the firm's fixed costs of *production*. Financial leverage is the extent to which a firm relies on debt and a levered firm is a firm with some debt in its capital structure. Because a *levered* firm must make interest payments regardless of the firm's sales, financial leverage refers to the firm's fixed costs of *finance*.

Consider our discussion in Section 10.8 concerning the beta of Jelco, Inc. In that example, we estimated beta from the returns on Jelco *stock*. Similarly, we estimated General Tool's beta in Section 12.1 from stock returns. Furthermore, the betas in Figures 12.3 and 12.4 from real-world firms were estimated from returns on stock. Thus, in each case, we estimated the firm's stock or **equity beta.** The beta of the assets of a levered firm is different from the beta of its equity. As the name suggests, the **asset beta** is the beta of the assets of the firm. The asset beta could also be thought of as the beta of the common stock had the firm been financed only with equity.

Imagine an individual who owns all the firm's debt and all its equity. In other words, this individual owns the entire firm. What is the beta of her portfolio of the firm's debt and equity?

As with any portfolio, the beta of this portfolio is a weighted average of the betas of the individual items in the portfolio. Hence, we have

$$\beta_{\text{Asset}} = \frac{\text{Debt}}{\text{Debt} + \text{Equity}} \times \beta_{\text{Debt}} + \frac{\text{Equity}}{\text{Debt} + \text{Equity}} \times \beta_{\text{Equity}} \qquad (12.2)$$

where β_{Equity} is the beta of the stock of the *levered* firm. Notice that the beta of debt is multiplied by debt/(debt + equity), the percentage of debt in the capital structure. Similarly, the beta of equity is multiplied by the percentage of equity in the capital structure. Because the portfolio contains both the debt of the firm and the equity of the firm, the beta of the portfolio is the *asset beta*. As we said above, the asset beta can also be viewed as the beta of the common stock had the firm been all equity.

The beta of debt is very low in practice. If we make the commonplace assumption that the beta of debt is zero, we have

$$\beta_{\text{Asset}} = \frac{\text{Equity}}{\text{Debt} + \text{Equity}} \times \beta_{\text{Equity}} \qquad (12.3)$$

Because equity/(debt + equity) must be below 1 for a levered firm, it follows that $\beta_{\text{Asset}} < \beta_{\text{Equity}}$. Rearranging this equation, we have

$$\beta_{\text{Equity}} = \beta_{\text{Asset}} \left(1 + \frac{\text{Debt}}{\text{Equity}} \right)$$

The equity beta will always be greater than the asset beta with financial leverage.[6]

EXAMPLE

Consider a tree-growing company, Rapid Cedars, Inc., which is currently all equity and has a beta of 0.8. The firm has decided to move to a capital structure of one part debt to two parts equity. Because the firm is staying in the same industry, its asset beta should remain at 0.8. However, assuming a zero beta for its debt, its equity beta would become

$$\beta_{\text{Equity}} = \beta_{\text{Asset}} \left(1 + \frac{\text{Debt}}{\text{Equity}} \right)$$

$$1.2 = 0.8 \left(1 + \frac{1}{2} \right)$$

If the firm had one part debt to one part equity in its capital structure, its equity beta would be

$$1.6 = 0.8(1 + 1)$$

However, as long as it stayed in the same industry, its asset beta would remain at 0.8. The effect of leverage, then, is to increase the equity beta.

---

[6]It can be shown that the relationship between a firm's asset beta and its equity beta with corporate taxes is

$$\beta_{\text{Equity}} = \beta_{\text{Asset}} \left[1 + (1 - T_C) \frac{\text{Debt}}{\text{Equity}} \right]$$

See Chapter 17 for more details.

Concept
Questions

1. **What are determinants of equity betas?**
2. **What is the difference between an asset beta and an equity beta?**

12.4 Extensions of the Basic Model

The Firm versus the Project: Vive la Différence

We now assume that the risk of a project differs from that of the firm, while going back to the all-equity assumption. We began the chapter by pointing out that each project should be paired with a financial asset of comparable risk. If a project's beta differs from that of the firm, the project should be discounted at the rate commensurate with its own beta. This is a very important point because firms frequently speak of a *corporate discount rate*. (*Hurdle rate, cutoff rate, benchmark,* and *cost of capital* are frequently used synonymously.) Unless all projects in the corporation are of the same risk, choosing the same discount rate for all projects is incorrect.

EXAMPLE

D. D. Ronnelley Co., a publishing firm, may accept a project in computer software. Noting that computer software companies have high betas, the publishing firm views the software venture as more risky than the rest of its business. It should discount the project at a rate commensurate with the risk of software companies. For example, it might use the average beta of a portfolio of publicly traded software firms. Instead, if all projects in D. D. Ronnelley Co. were discounted at the same rate, a bias would result. The firm would accept too many high-risk projects (software ventures) and reject too many low-risk projects (books and magazines). This point is illustrated in Figure 12.7.

FIGURE 12.7

Relationship between the Firm's Cost of Capital and the Security Market Line

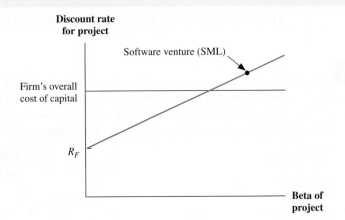

Use of a firm's cost of capital in calculations may lead to incorrect capital-budgeting decisions. Projects with high risk, such as the software venture for D. D. Ronnelley Co., should be discounted at a high rate. By using the firm's cost of equity, the firm is likely to accept too many high-risk projects.

   Projects with low risk should be discounted at a low rate. By using the firm's cost of capital, the firm is likely to reject too many low-risk projects.

The D. D. Ronnelley example assumes that the proposed project has identical risk to that of the software industry, allowing the industry beta to be used. However, the beta of a new project may be greater than the beta of existing firms in the same industry because the very newness of the project likely increases its responsiveness to economywide movements. For example, a start-up computer venture may fail in a recession while IBM, Compaq, or Hewlett-Packard will still be around. Conversely, in an economywide expansion, the venture may grow much faster than the old-line computer firms.

Fortunately, a slight adjustment is all that is needed here. The new venture should be assigned a somewhat higher beta than that of the industry to reflect added risk. The adjustment is necessarily ad hoc, so no formula can be given. Our experience indicates that this approach is widespread in practice today.

However, a problem does arise for the rare project constituting its own industry. For example, consider the firms providing consumer shopping by television. Today, one can obtain a reasonable estimate for the beta of this industry, since a few of the firms have publicly traded stock. However, when the ventures began in the 1980s, any beta estimate was suspect. At that time, no one knew whether shopping by TV belonged in the television industry, the retail industry, or in an entirely new industry.

What beta should be used in the rare case when an industrywide beta is not appropriate? One approach, which considers the determinants of the project's beta, was treated earlier in this chapter. Unfortunately, that approach is only qualitative in nature.

The Cost of Capital with Debt

Section 12.1 showed how to choose the discount rate when a project is all-equity financed. In this section, we discuss an adjustment when the project is financed with both debt and equity.

Suppose a firm uses both debt and equity to finance its investments. If the firm pays r_B for its debt financing and r_S for its equity, what is the overall or average cost of its capital? The cost of equity is r_S, as discussed in earlier sections. The cost of debt is the firm's borrowing rate, r_B. If a firm uses both debt and equity, the cost of capital is a weighted average of each. This works out to be

$$\frac{S}{S + B} \times r_S + \frac{B}{S + B} \times r_B$$

The weights in the formula are, respectively, the proportion of total value represented by the equity

$$\left(\frac{S}{S + B}\right)$$

and the proportion of total value represented by debt

$$\left(\frac{B}{S + B}\right)$$

This is only natural. If the firm had issued no debt and was therefore an all-equity firm, its average cost of capital would equal its cost of equity, r_S. At the other extreme, if the firm had issued so much debt that its equity was valueless, it would be an all-debt firm, and its average cost of capital would be its cost of debt, r_B.

Of course, interest is tax deductible at the corporate level, a point to be treated in more detail in Chapter 15. The after-tax cost of debt is

$$\text{Cost of debt (after corporate tax)} = r_B \times (1 - T_C)$$

where T_C is the corporation's tax rate.

Assembling these results, we get the average cost of capital (after tax) for the firm:

$$\text{Average cost of capital} = \left(\frac{S}{S+B}\right) \times r_S + \left(\frac{B}{S+B}\right) \times r_B \times (1 - T_C) \quad (12.4)$$

Because the average cost of capital is a weighting of its cost of equity and its cost of debt, it is usually referred to as the **weighted average cost of capital, r_{WACC}**, and from now on we will use this term.

EXAMPLE

Consider a firm whose debt has a market value of $40 million and whose stock has a market value of $60 million (3 million outstanding shares of stock, each selling for $20 per share). The firm pays a 15-percent rate of interest on its new debt and has a beta of 1.41. The corporate tax rate is 34 percent. [Assume that the SML holds, that the risk premium on the market is 9.5 percent (slightly higher than the historical equity risk premium), and that the current Treasury bill rate is 11 percent (very much higher than the current Treasury bill rate).] What is this firm's r_{WACC}?

To compute the r_{WACC} using equation (12.4), we must know (1) the after-tax cost of debt, $r_B \times (1 - T_C)$, (2) the cost of equity, r_S, and (3) the proportions of debt and equity used by the firm. These three values are computed below.

1. The pretax cost of debt is 15 percent, implying an after-tax cost of 9.9 percent [15% × (1 − 0.34)].
2. The cost of equity capital is computed by using the SML:

$$r_S = R_F + \beta \times [\bar{R}_M - R_F]$$
$$= 11\% + 1.41 \times 9.5\%$$
$$= 24.40\%$$

3. The proportions of debt and equity are computed from the market values of debt and equity. Because the market value of the firm is $100 million ($40 million + $60 million), the proportions of debt and equity are 40 and 60 percent, respectively.

The cost of equity, r_S, is 24.40 percent, and the after-tax cost of debt, $r_B \times (1 - T_C)$, is 9.9 percent. B is $40 million and S is $60 million. Therefore,

$$r_{WACC} = \frac{B}{B+S} \times r_B \times (1 - T_C) + \frac{S}{B+S} \times r_S$$
$$= \left(\frac{40}{100} \times 9.9\%\right) + \left(\frac{60}{100} \times 24.40\%\right) = 18.60\%$$

This procedure is presented in chart form next:

(1) Financing Components	(2) Market Values	(3) Weight	(4) Cost of Capital (after corporate tax)	(5) Weighted Cost of Capital
Debt	$ 40,000,000	0.40	15% × (1 − 0.34) = 9.9%	3.96%
Equity	60,000,000	0.60	11% + 1.41 × 9.5% = 24.40%	14.64
	$100,000,000	1.00		18.60%

The weights we used in the previous example were market-value weights. Market-value weights are more appropriate than book-value weights because the market values of the securities are closer to the actual dollars that would be received from their sale. Actually it is usually useful to think in terms of "target" market weights. These are the market weights expected to prevail over the life of the firm or project.

EXAMPLE

Suppose that a firm has both a current and a target debt-equity ratio of 0.6, a cost of debt of 15.15 percent, and a cost of equity of 20 percent. The corporate tax rate is 34 percent.

Our first step calls for transforming the debt-to-equity (B/S) ratio to a debt-to-value ratio. A B/S ratio of 0.6 implies 6 parts debt for 10 parts equity. Since value is equal to the sum of the debt plus the equity, the debt-to-value ratio is $6/(6 + 10) = 0.375$. Similarly, the equity-to-value ratio is $10/(6 + 10) = 0.625$. The r_{WACC} will then be

$$r_{WACC} = \left(\frac{S}{S + B}\right) \times r_S + \left(\frac{B}{S + B}\right) \times r_B \times (1 - T_C)$$

$$= .625 \times 20\% + .375 \times 15.15\% \times (.66) = 16.25\%$$

Suppose the firm is considering taking on a warehouse renovation costing $50 million that is expected to yield cost savings of $12 million a year for six years. Using the NPV equation and discounting the six years of expected cash flows from the renovation at the r_{WACC}, we have[7]

$$NPV = -\$50 + \frac{\$12}{(1 + r_{WACC})} + \cdots + \frac{\$12}{(1 + r_{WACC})^6}$$

$$= -\$50 + \$12 \times A^6_{.1625}$$

$$= -\$50 + (12 \times 3.66)$$

$$= -\$6.07$$

Should the firm take on the warehouse renovation? The project has a negative NPV using the firm's r_{WACC}. This means that the financial markets offer superior projects in the same risk class (namely, the firm's risk class). The answer is clear: The firm should reject the project.

12.5 Estimating International Paper's Cost of Capital

In the previous section, we calculated the cost of capital in two examples. Now, we will do the same thing for a real-world company. Table 12.3 lists nine large and well-known firms in the paper and pulp mills industry. We will calculate the cost of capital for one of them, International Paper (IP).

From the previous section, we know that there are two steps in the calculation of the cost of capital. First, we estimate the cost of equity and cost of debt. Second, we determine the weighted average cost of capital by weighting these two costs appropriately.

Cost of Equity and Debt

We will tackle the cost of equity first. We need a beta estimate to determine International Paper's cost of equity and Table 12.3 shows the betas of the nine firms in the industry. The table tells us that IP's beta is 0.83 and the industry's average beta is 0.82. Which number should we use? We argued earlier in the chapter that there is less measurement error with the industry beta. Therefore, we will work with 0.82, though IP's beta is so close to the average of the industry that either number would have been fine.

As discussed in Chapter 9, 8.4 percent is a good estimate of the market's risk premium (but not the only plausible estimate). If the risk-free rate is 3 percent, a good estimate of

---

[7]This discussion of r_{WACC} has been implicitly based on perpetual cash flows. However, an important paper by J. Miles and R. Ezzel, "The Weighted Average Cost of Capital, Perfect Capital Markets and Project Life: A Clarification," *Journal of Financial and Quantitative Analysis* (September 1980), shows that the r_{WACC} is appropriate even when cash flows are not perpetual.

TABLE 12.3	Company	Beta
Betas for Firms in the Pulp and Paper Mills Industry	Abitibi-Price Inc.	0.74
	American Israeli Paper Mills, Ltd.	0.41
	Boise Cascade Corp.	0.97
	Glatfelter, P. H., Co.	0.57
	International Paper Co.	0.83
	Kimberly-Clark Corp.	0.90
	Mead Corp.	1.14
	Union Camp Corp.	0.85
	Westvaco Corp.	0.97
	Equally weighted portfolio	0.82

International Paper's cost of equity capital is:

$$R_F + \beta \times [\bar{R}_M - R_F]$$
$$= 3\% + 0.82 \times 8.4\%$$
$$= 9.89\%$$

The yield on the company's debt is about 8 percent, which we will use as the (pretax) cost of debt capital, r_B.

Determining r_{WACC}

Now that we have estimates of both r_S, the cost of equity, and r_B, the cost of debt, we are ready to determine the weighted average cost of capital. However, we still need the percentages of debt and equity in IP's capital structure and the tax rate. We find that the ratio of debt-to-value is 32 percent and the ratio of equity-to-value is 68 percent. The tax rate is 37 percent.[8] These inputs allow us to calculate the weighted average cost of capital:

$$r_{WACC} = \left(\frac{S}{S+B}\right) \times r_S + \left(\frac{B}{S+B}\right) \times r_B \times (1 - T_C)$$
$$= 0.68 \times 9.89\% + 0.32 \times 8\% \times (1 - .37)$$
$$= 8.34\%$$

Thus, 8.34 percent is International Paper's cost of capital. It should be used to discount any project where one believes that the project's risk is equal to the risk of the firm as a whole, and the project has the same leverage as the firm as a whole.

12.6 Reducing the Cost of Capital

Chapters 9–12 develop the idea that both the expected return on a stock and the cost of capital of the firm are positively related to risk. Recently, a number of academics have argued that expected return and cost of capital are negatively related to liquidity as well.[9] In addition, these scholars make the interesting point that, although it is quite difficult to lower the

---

[8]These numbers were taken from *Value Line Investment Survey*. The tax rate includes both federal and local taxes.

[9]For example, see Y. Amihud and H. Mendelson, "The Liquidity Route to a Lower Cost of Capital," *Journal of Applied Corporate Finance* (Winter 2000) and M. J. Brennan and C. Tamarowski, "Investor Relations, Liquidity, and Stock Prices," *Journal of Applied Corporate Finance* (Winter 2000).

335

risk of a firm, it is much easier to increase the liquidity of the firm's stock. Therefore, they suggest that a firm can actually lower its cost of capital through liquidity enhancement. We develop this idea next.

What Is Liquidity?

Anyone who owns his or her own home probably thinks of liquidity in terms of the time it takes to buy or sell the home. For example, condominiums in large metropolitan areas are generally quite liquid. Particularly in good times, a condominium may sell within days of being placed on the market. By contrast, single-family homes in suburban areas may take weeks or months to sell. Special properties such as multimillion dollar mansions may take longer still.

The concept of liquidity is similar, but not identical, in stocks. Here, we speak of the *cost* of buying and selling instead. That is, those stocks that are expensive to trade are considered less liquid than those that trade cheaply. What do we mean by the cost to trade? We generally think of three costs here: brokerage fees, the bid-ask spread, and market-impact costs.

Brokerage fees are the easiest to understand, because you must pay a broker to execute a trade. More difficult is the bid-ask spread. Consider the New York Stock Exchange (NYSE), where all trades on a particular stock must go through the stock's specialist, who is physically on the floor of the exchange. If you want to trade 100 shares of XYZ Co., your broker must get the *quote* from XYZ's specialist. Suppose the specialist provides a quote of $100–100\frac{1}{8}$. This means that you can buy from the specialist at $100\frac{1}{8}$ per share and sell to the specialist at $100 per share. Note that the specialist makes money here, since she buys from you at $100 and sells to you (or to someone else) at $100\frac{1}{8}$. The gain to the specialist is a cost to you, because you are losing $\frac{1}{8}$ dollar per share over a round-trip transaction (over a purchase and a subsequent sale).

Finally, we have *market-impact costs.* Suppose that a trader wants to sell 10,000 shares instead of just 100 shares. Here, the specialist has to take on extra risk when buying. First, she has to pay out $100,000 (10,000 × $100), cash which may not be easily available to her. Second, the trader may be selling this large amount because she has special information that the stock will fall imminently. The specialist bears the risk of losing a lot of money on that trade. Consequently, to compensate for these risks, the specialist may not buy at $100/share but at a lower price. Similarly, the specialist may be willing to sell a large block of stock only at a price above $100\frac{1}{8}$. The price drop associated with a large sale and the price rise associated with a large purchase are the market-impact costs.

Liquidity, Expected Returns, and the Cost of Capital

The cost of trading a nonliquid stock reduces the total return that an investor receives. That is, if one buys a stock for $100 and sells it later for $105, the gain before trading costs is $5. If one must pay a dollar of commission when buying and another dollar when selling, the gain after trading costs is only $3. Both the bid-ask spread and market-impact costs would reduce this gain still further.

As we will see later, trading costs vary across securities. In the last four chapters, we have stressed that investors demand a high expected return as compensation when investing in high risk, e.g., high-beta, stocks. Because the expected return to the investor is the cost of capital to the firm, the cost of capital is positively related to beta. Now, we are saying the same thing for trading costs. Investors demand a high expected return when investing in stocks with high trading costs, i.e., low liquidity. And, this high expected return implies a high cost of capital to the firm. This idea is illustrated in Figure 12.8.

FIGURE 12.8

Liquidity and the
Cost of Capital

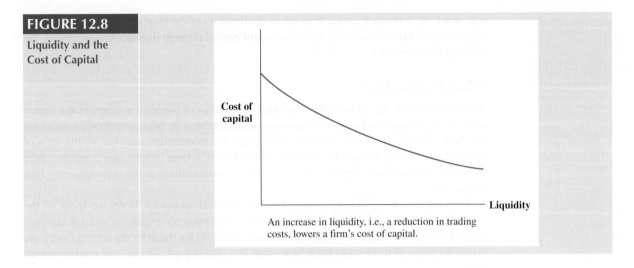

An increase in liquidity, i.e., a reduction in trading
costs, lowers a firm's cost of capital.

Liquidity and Adverse Selection

Liquidity varies across stocks, because the factors determining liquidity vary across stocks. Although there are a number of factors, we focus on just one, *adverse selection*. As mentioned before, the specialist will lose money on a trade if the trader has information that the specialist does not have. If you have special information that the stock is worth $110 in the preceding example, you will want to buy shares at $100\frac{1}{8}$. The specialist is obligated to sell to you at this price, which is considerably below the true price of $110. Conversely, if you know that the stock is worth only $90 and you currently own 100 shares, you will be happy to sell these shares to the specialist at $100. Again, the specialist loses, since he pays $100/share for a stock worth only $90. In either of these cases, we say that the specialist has been *picked off,* or has been subject to adverse selection.

The specialist must protect himself in some way here. Of course, he cannot forbid informed individuals from trading, because he does not know ahead of time who these investors are. His next best alternative is to widen the bid-ask spread, thereby increasing the costs of trading to *all* traders—both informed and uninformed. That is, if the spread is widened to, say $99\frac{7}{8}$–$100\frac{1}{4}$, each trader pays a round-trip cost of $\$\frac{3}{8}$ per share.

The key here is that the spread should be positively related to the ratio of informed to uninformed traders. That is, informed traders will pick off the specialist and uninformed traders will not. Thus, informed traders in a stock raise the required return on equity, thereby increasing the cost of capital.

What the Corporation Can Do

The corporation has an incentive to lower trading costs because—given the preceding discussion—a lower cost of capital should result. Amihud and Mendelson identify two general strategies for corporations. First, they argue that firms should try to bring in more uninformed investors. Stock splits may be a useful tool here. Imagine that a company has 1 million shares outstanding with a price per share of $100. Because investors generally buy in round lots of 100 shares, these investors would need $10,000 ($100 × 100 shares) for a purchase. A number of small investors might be "priced out" of the stock, although large investors would not be. Thus, the ratio of large investors to small investors would be high. Because large investors are generally more likely than small investors to be informed, the ratio of informed investors to uninformed investors will likely be high.

A 2:1 stock split would give two shares of stock for every one that the investor previously held. Because every investor would still hold the same proportional interest in the firm, each investor would be no better off than before. Thus, it is likely that the price per share will fall to $50 from $100. Here, an individual with 100 shares worth $10,000 ($100 × 100 shares) finds herself still worth $10,000 (= $50 × 200 shares) after the split.

However, a round lot becomes more affordable, thereby bringing more small and uninformed investors into the firm. Consequently, the adverse selection costs are reduced, allowing the specialist to lower the bid-ask spread. In turn, it is hoped that the expected return on the stock, and the cost of equity capital, will fall as well. If this happens, the stock might actually trade at a price slightly above $50.

This idea is a new one and empirical evidence is not yet in. Amihud and Mendelson themselves point out the possibility that this strategy might backfire, because brokerage commissions are often higher on lower-priced securities. We must await confirmation of this intriguing suggestion.

Companies can also attract small investors by facilitating stock purchases through the Internet. Direct stock purchase plans and dividend reinvestment programs handled online allow small investors the opportunity to buy securities cheaply. In addition, Amihud and Mendelson state, "And when these plans are administered over the Internet using web sites like Stockpower.com, moneypaper.com and Netstockdirect.com, the process is fast and efficient for both the company and the investor."[10]

Secondly, companies can disclose more information. This narrows the gap between uninformed and informed investors, thereby lowering the cost of capital. Suggestions include providing greater financial data on corporate segments and more management forecasts. An interesting study by Coller and Yohn[11] concludes that the bid-ask spread is reduced after the release of these forecasts.

This section would not be complete without a discussion of security analysts. These analysts are employed by brokerage houses to follow the companies in individual industries. For example, an analyst for a particular brokerage house might follow all the firms in, say, the auto industry. This analyst distributes reports and other information to the clients of the brokerage house. Virtually all brokerage houses have analysts following the major industries. Again, through dissemination of the information, these analysts narrow the gap between the informed and the uninformed investors, thereby tending to reduce the bid-ask spread.

Although all major industries are covered, the smaller firms in these industries are often ignored, implying a higher bid-ask spread and a higher cost of capital for these firms. Analysts frequently state that they avoid following companies that release little information, pointing out that these companies are more trouble than they are worth. Thus, it behooves companies that are not followed to release as much information as possible to security analysts in the hopes of attracting their interest. Friendliness toward security analysts would be very helpful as well. The argument here is not to get the analysts to make buy recommendations. Rather, it is simply to interest the analysts in following the company, thereby reducing the information asymmetry between informed and uninformed investors.

Concept
Questions

1. **What is liquidity?**
2. **What is the relation between liquidity and expected returns?**
3. **What is adverse selection?**
4. **What can a corporation do to lower its cost of capital?**

---

[10]Ibid., p. 19.

[11]M. Coller and T. Yohn, "Management Forecasts and Information Asymmetry: An Examination of Bid-Ask Spreads," *Journal of Accounting Research* (Fall 1997).

12.7 SUMMARY AND CONCLUSIONS

Earlier chapters on capital budgeting assumed that projects generate riskless cash flows. The appropriate discount rate in that case is the riskless interest rate. Of course, most cash flows from real-world capital-budgeting projects are risky. This chapter discusses the discount rate when cash flows are risky.

1. A firm with excess cash can either pay a dividend or make a capital expenditure. Because stockholders can reinvest the dividend in risky financial assets, the expected return on a capital-budgeting project should be at least as great as the expected return on a financial asset of comparable risk.

2. The expected return on any asset is dependent upon its beta. Thus, we showed how to estimate the beta of a stock. The appropriate procedure employs regression analysis on historical returns.

3. We considered the case of a project whose beta risk was equal to that of the firm. If the firm is unlevered, the discount rate on the project is equal to

$$R_F + \beta \times (\bar{R}_M - R_F)$$

where $\bar{R}_M$ is the expected return on the market portfolio and R_F is the risk-free rate. In words, the discount rate on the project is equal to the CAPM's estimate of the expected return on the security.

4. If the project's beta differs from that of the firm, the discount rate should be based on the project's beta. The project's beta can generally be estimated by determining the average beta of the project's industry.

5. The beta of a company is a function of a number of factors. Perhaps the three most important are
   - Cyclicality of revenues
   - Operating leverage
   - Financial leverage

6. Sometimes one cannot use the average beta of the project's industry as an estimate of the beta of the project. For example, a new project may not fall neatly into any existing industry. In this case, one can estimate the project's beta by considering the project's cyclicality of revenues and its operating leverage. This approach is qualitative in nature.

7. If a firm uses debt, the discount rate to use is the r_{WACC}. In order to calculate r_{WACC}, the cost of equity and the cost of debt applicable to a project must be estimated. If the project is similar to the firm, the cost of equity can be estimated using the SML for the firm's equity. Conceptually, a dividend-growth model could be used as well, though it is likely to be far less accurate in practice.

8. A number of academics have argued that expected returns are negatively related to liquidity, where high liquidity is equivalent to low costs of trading. These scholars have further suggested that firms can reduce their cost of capital by lowering these trading costs. Practical suggestions include stock splits, more complete dissemination of information, and more effective assistance to security analysts.

KEY TERMS

asset beta, *328*
cost of equity capital, *318*
equity beta, *328*

operating leverage, *327*
weighted average cost of capital (r_{WACC}), *332*

SUGGESTED READINGS

The following article contains a superb discussion of some of the subtleties of using WACC for project evaluation:

Miles, J., and R. Ezzel. "The Weighted Average Cost of Capital, Perfect Capital Markets and Project Life: A Clarification." *Journal of Financial and Quantitative Analysis* 15 (September 1980).

The following article provides a comprehensive survey of capital budgeting in practice, including the determination of the cost of capital:

Graham, J. R., and C. R. Harvey, "The Theory and Practice of Corporate Finance: Evidence from the Field." *Journal of Financial Economics* 60 (2001).

Estimates of the cost of capital under both the capital asset pricing model and the arbitrage pricing theory are contained in:

Fama, E. F., and K. R. French. "Industry Cost of Capital." *Journal of Financial Economics* (February 1997).

One of the best "how-to" guides is:

Copeland, T., T. Koller, and J. Murrin. *Valuation: Measuring and Managing the Value of Companies.* 2nd ed. New York: John Wiley & Sons, 1995.

QUESTIONS & PROBLEMS

BETA AND THE COST OF EQUITY

12.1   Furniture Depot, Inc., is an all-equity firm with a beta of 0.95. The market risk premium is 9 percent and the risk-free rate is 5 percent. The company is considering a project that will generate annual after-tax cash flows of $340,000 at year-end for five years. The project requires an immediate investment of $1.2 million. If the project has the same risk as the firm as a whole, should Furniture Depot undertake the project?

12.2   The returns for the past five years on Douglas stock and the New York Stock Exchange Composite Index (NYSE) are listed below:

Douglas	NYSE
−0.05	−0.12
0.05	0.01
0.08	0.06
0.15	0.10
0.10	0.05

   a. What are the average returns on Douglas stock and on the market?
   b. Compute the beta of Douglas stock.

12.3   The correlation between the returns on Ceramics Craftsman, Inc., and the returns on the S&P 500 is 0.675. The variance of the returns on Ceramics Craftsman, Inc., is 0.004225, and the variance of the returns on the S&P 500 is 0.001467. What is the beta of Ceramics Craftsman stock?

12.4   The returns from the past 13 quarters on Mercantile Bank Corporation and the market are listed below.

Mercantile	Market
−0.009	0.023
0.051	0.058
−0.001	−0.020
−0.045	−0.050
0.085	0.071
0.000	0.012
−0.080	−0.075
0.020	0.050
0.125	0.120
0.110	0.049
−0.100	−0.030
0.040	0.028

Visit us at www.mhhe.com/rwj

The covariance of Mercantile Bank Corporation's return with the market's return is 0.038711. The market variance is 0.038588. The expected returns on Mercantile and the market are 0.016333 and 0.019667, respectively.

a. What is the beta of Mercantile Bank Corporation stock?

b. Is Mercantile's beta higher or lower than the beta of the average stock?

12.5 The following table lists possible rates of return on two risky assets, L and J. The table also lists their joint probabilities, that is, the probabilities that the two observations will occur simultaneously.

R_L	R_J	Prob(R_L, R_J)
0.16	0.16	0.10
0.16	0.18	0.06
0.16	0.22	0.04
0.18	0.18	0.12
0.18	0.20	0.36
0.18	0.22	0.12
0.20	0.18	0.02
0.20	0.20	0.04
0.20	0.22	0.04
0.20	0.24	0.10

a. List the possible values for R_L and the probabilities that correspond to those values.

b. Compute the following items for R_L.

   1. Expected value

   2. Variance

   3. Standard deviation

c. List the possible values for R_J and the probabilities that correspond to those values.

d. Compute the following items for R_J.

   1. Expected value

   2. Variance

   3. Standard deviation

e. Calculate the covariance and correlation coefficient of R_L and R_J.

f. Assume L is the market portfolio. Calculate the beta coefficient for security J.

12.6 If you use the stock beta and the security market line to compute the discount rate for a project, what assumptions are you implicitly making?

12.7 Jang Cosmetics is evaluating a project to produce a perfume line. Jang currently produces no body-scent products and is an all-equity firm.

a. Should Jang Cosmetics use its stock beta to evaluate the project?

b. How should Jang Cosmetics compute the appropriate beta to evaluate the project?

 12.8 The following table lists possible rates of return on Compton Technology's stock and debt and on the market portfolio. The probability of each state is also listed.

State	Probability	Return on Stock (%)	Return on Debt (%)	Return on the Market (%)
1	0.1	3%	8%	5%
2	0.3	8	8	10
3	0.4	20	10	15
4	0.2	15	10	20

a. What is the beta of Compton Technology debt?

b. What is the beta of Compton Technology stock?

c. If the debt-to-equity ratio of Compton Technology is 0.5, what is the asset beta of Compton Technology? Assume no taxes.

12.9   Consider a levered firm's projects that have similar risks to the firm as a whole. Is the discount rate for the projects higher or lower than the rate computed using the security market line? Why?

12.10   What factors determine the beta of a stock? Define and describe each.

WEIGHTED-
AVERAGE COST
OF CAPITAL

12.11   Lizpaz Inc. is a levered firm with a debt-to-equity ratio of 0.25. The beta of the common stock is 1.15, while the beta of the debt is 0.3. The market-risk premium is 10 percent and the risk-free rate is 6 percent. The corporate tax rate is 35 percent.
    a.   What is the firm's cost of equity capital?
    b.   If a new company project has the same risk as the overall firm, what is the weighted average cost of capital for the project?

12.12   Adobe Online Inc. has an equity beta of 1.29 and a debt-to-equity ratio of 1.0. The expected return on the market is 13 percent and the risk-free rate is seven percent. The before-tax cost of debt capital is 7 percent. The corporate tax rate is 35 percent.
    a.   What is Adobe Online's cost of equity?
    b.   What is Adobe Online's weighted average cost of capital?

12.13   Calculate the weighted average cost of capital for the Luxury Porcelain Company. The book value of Luxury's outstanding debt is $60 million. Currently, the debt is trading at 120 percent of book value and is priced to yield 12 percent. The 5 million outstanding shares of Luxury stock are trading at $20 per share. The required return on Luxury stock is 18 percent. The tax rate is 25 percent.

12.14   First Data Co. has 20 million shares of common stock outstanding that are currently trading at $25 per share. The firm's debt is publicly trading at 95 percent of its $180 million face value. The before-tax cost of debt is 10 percent and the cost of equity is 20 percent. What is the weighted average cost of capital for the firm? Assume a corporate tax rate of 40 percent.

12.15   Lavan Industries, Inc., is considering a new project with a $25 million initial outlay. The project will generate after-tax (year-end) cash flows of $7 million for five years. The firm has a debt-to-equity ratio of 0.75. The cost of equity is 15 percent and the before-tax cost of debt is 9 percent. The corporate tax rate is 35 percent. The project has the same risk as the overall firm. Should Lavan accept the project?

12.16   Suppose Garageband.com has a 28 percent cost of equity capital and a 10 percent before-tax cost of debt capital. The firm's debt-to-equity ratio is 1.0. Garageband.com is interested in investing in a guitar factory that will cost $1,000,000 and will provide $600,000 pretax annual cash flows for five years. The project risk is similar to the overall risk of the firm. What is the net present value of this project if Garageband.com's tax rate is 35 percent?

Visit us at www.mhhe.com/rwj

MINICASE   AlliedProducts

AlliedProducts, Inc., has recently won approval from the Federal Aviation Administration (FAA) for its Enhanced Ground Proximity Warning System (GPWS). This system is designed to give airplane pilots additional warning of approaching ground danger and thus help prevent crashes. AlliedProducts has spent $10 million in research and development the past four years developing GPWS. The GPWS will be put on the market beginning this year and AlliedProducts expects it to stay on the market for a total of five years.

As a financial analyst specializing in the aerospace industry for USC Pension & Investment, Inc., you are asked by your managing partner, Mr. Adam Smith, to evaluate the potential of this new GPWS project.

Initially, AlliedProducts will need to acquire $42 million in production equipment to make the GPWS. The equipment is expected to have a seven-year useful life. This equipment can be sold for $12 million at the end of five years. AlliedProducts intends to sell two different versions of the GPWS:

1. *New GPWS*—intended for installation in new aircraft. The selling price is $70,000 per system and the variable cost of production is $50,000 per system. (Assume cash flows occur at year-end.)

2. *Upgrade GPWS*—intended for installation on existing aircraft with an older version ground proximity radar in place. The selling price of the Upgrade system is $35,000 per system and the variable cost to produce it is $22,000 per system.

AlliedProducts intends to raise prices at the same rate as inflation. Variable costs will also increase with inflation. In addition, the GPWS project will also incur $3 million in marketing and general administration costs the first year (expected to increase at the same rate as inflation).

AlliedProducts' corporate tax rate is 40 percent. Assume that the equity beta listed in *Value Line Investment Survey* (the latest edition) is the best estimate of AlliedProducts' beta. A five-year U.S. Treasury Bond has a rate of 6.20 percent and the S&P 500 recent years' historical average excess return (i.e., the market return less the Treasury bond rate) is 8.3 percent. Annual inflation is expected to remain constant at 3 percent. Further, suppose AlliedProducts' cost of debt is 6.2 percent and (although somewhat unrealistic) its debt-to-equity ratio is 50 percent and will remain at 50 percent for at least five years.

Commercial Aircraft Market

The state of the economy has a major impact on the airplane manufacturing industry. Airline industry analysts have the following production expectations, depending on the annual state of the economy for the next five years:

TABLE 12.4	State of Economy	Probability of State	New Aircraft (year 1)	Annual Growth
	Strong growth	.15	350	.15
	Moderate growth	.45	250	.10
	Mild recession	.30	150	.06
	Severe recession	.10	50	.03

While probabilities of each state of the economy will not change during the next five years, airplane production for each category will increase, as shown in Table 12.4, each year after year 1. The FAA requires that these planes have new ground proximity warning systems, of which there are a number of manufacturers besides AlliedProducts.

AlliedProducts estimates that there are approximately 12,500 existing aircraft that comprise the market for its GPWS Upgrade package. Due to FAA regulations, all existing aircraft will be required to get an upgraded ground proximity warning system within the next five years, again, not necessarily from AlliedProducts. AlliedProducts believes the upgrades of the existing aircraft fleet will be spread evenly over the five years (the time value of money would suggest manufacturers defer purchasing upgrades until the fifth year; however, consumer demand for the additional safety will induce earlier upgrades).

AlliedProducts uses the MACRS depreciation schedule (seven-year property class). The immediate initial working capital requirement is $2 million and thereafter the net working capital requirements will be 5 percent of sales.

AlliedProducts has a number of competitors both in the new GPWS and upgrade GPWS markets but expects to dominate the market with a 45 percent share.

Assignment

First, use the CAPM to determine the appropriate discount rate for this product. Then, use computer spreadsheets such as Excel or Lotus 1-2-3 to analyze the project.

Will the GPWS project improve the wealth of AlliedProducts' shareholders, such as your firm—USC Pension & Investment, Inc.?

Appendix 12A

Economic Value Added and the Measurement of Financial Performance

Chapter 12 shows how to calculate the appropriate discount rate for capital budgeting and other valuation problems. We now consider the measurement of financial performance. We introduce the concept of economic value added, which uses the same discount rate developed for capital budgeting. We begin with a simple example.

Many years ago, Henry Bodenheimer started Bodie's Blimps, one of the largest high-speed blimp manufacturers. Because growth was so rapid, Henry put most of his effort into capital budgeting. His approach to capital budgeting paralleled that of Chapter 12. He forecasted cash flows for various projects and discounted them at the cost of capital appropriate to the beta of the blimp business. However, these projects have grown rapidly, in some cases becoming whole divisions. He now needs to evaluate the performance of these divisions in order to reward his division managers. How does he perform the appropriate analysis?

Henry is aware that capital budgeting and performance measurement are essentially mirror images of each other. Capital budgeting is forward-looking by nature because one must estimate future cash flows to value a project. By contrast, performance measurement is backward-looking. As Henry stated to a group of his executives, "Capital budgeting is like looking through the windshield while driving a car. You need to know what lies further down the road to calculate a net present value. Performance measurement is like looking into the rearview mirror. You find out where you have been."

Henry first measured the performance of his various divisions by return on assets (ROA), an approach that we treated in the appendix to Chapter 2. For example, if a division had earnings after tax of $1,000 and had assets of $10,000, the ROA would be[12]

$$\frac{\$1,000}{\$10,000} = 10\%$$

He calculated the ROA ratio for each of his divisions, paying a bonus to each of his division managers based on the size of that division's ROA. However, while ROA was generally effective in motivating his managers, there were a number of situations where it appeared that ROA was counterproductive.

For example, Henry always believed that Sharon Smith, head of the supersonic division, was his best manager. The ROA of Smith's division was generally in the high double digits, but the best estimate of the weighted average cost of capital for the division was only 20 percent. Furthermore, the division had been growing rapidly. However, as soon as Henry paid bonuses based on ROA, the division stopped growing. At that time, Smith's division had after tax earnings of $2,000,000 on an asset base of $2,000,000, for an ROA of 100 percent ($2 million/$2 million).

---

[12]Earnings after tax is EBIT $(1 - T_c)$ where EBIT is earnings before interest and taxes and T_c is the tax rate.

Visit us at www.mhhe.com/rwj

Henry found out why the growth stopped when he suggested a project to Smith that would earn $1,000,000 per year on an investment of $2,000,000. This was clearly an attractive project with an ROA of 50 percent ($1 million/$2 million). He thought that Smith would jump at the chance to place his project into her division, because the ROA of the project was much higher than the cost of capital of 20 percent. However, Smith did everything she could to kill the project. And, as Henry later figured out, Smith was rational to do so. Smith must have realized that if the project were accepted, the division's ROA would become

$$\frac{\$2,000,000 + \$1,000,000}{\$2,000,000 + \$2,000,000} = 75\%$$

Thus, the ROA of Smith's division would fall from 100 percent to 75 percent if the project were accepted, with Smith's bonus falling in tandem.

Henry was later exposed to the economic-value-added (EVA) approach,[13] which seems to obviate this particular problem. The formula for EVA is

$$[\text{ROA} - \text{Weighted average cost of capital}] \times \text{Total capital}$$

Without the new project, the EVA of Smith's division would be:

$$[100\% - 20\%] \times \$2,000,000 = \$1,600,000$$

This is an annual number. That is, the division would bring in $1.6 million above and beyond the cost of capital to the firm each year.

With the new project included, the EVA jumps to

$$[75\% - 20\%] \times \$4,000,000 = \$2,200,000$$

If Sharon Smith knew that her bonus was based on EVA, she would now have an incentive to accept, not reject, the project. Although ROA appears in the EVA formula, EVA differs substantially from ROA. The big difference is that ROA is a percentage number and EVA is a dollar value. In the preceding example, EVA increased when the new project was added even though the ROA actually decreased. In this situation, EVA correctly incorporates the fact that a high return on a large division may be better than a very high return on a smaller division. The situation here is quite similar to the scale problem in capital budgeting that we discussed in Section 6.6.

Further understanding of EVA can be achieved by rewriting the EVA formula. Because ROA × total capital is equal to earnings after tax, we can write the EVA formula as:

$$\text{Earnings after tax} - \text{Weighted average cost of capital} \times \text{Total capital}$$

Thus, EVA can simply be viewed as earnings after capital costs. Although accountants subtract many costs (including depreciation) to get the earnings number shown in financial reports, they do not subtract out capital costs. One can see the logic of accountants, because the cost of capital is very subjective. By contrast, costs such as COGS (cost of goods sold), SGA (sales, general and administration), and even depreciation can be measured more objectively. However, even if the cost of capital is difficult to estimate, it is hard to justify ignoring it completely. After all, this textbook argues that the cost of capital is a necessary input to capital budgeting. Shouldn't it also be a necessary input to performance measurement?

This example argues that EVA can increase investment for those firms that are currently underinvesting. However, there are many firms in the reverse situation; the managers are so focused on increasing earnings that they take on projects for which the profits do not justify the capital outlays. These managers either are unaware of capital costs or, knowing these

---

[13]Stern Stewart & Company have a copyright on the terms economic value added and EVA. Details on the Stern Stewart & Company EVA can be found in J. M. Stern, G. B. Stewart, and D. A. Chew, "The EVA Financial Management System," *Journal of Applied Corporate Finance* (Summer 1999).

costs, choose to ignore them. Because the cost of capital is right in the middle of the EVA formula, managers will not easily ignore these costs when evaluated on an EVA system.

One other advantage of EVA is that it is so stark; the number is either positive or it is negative. Plenty of divisions have negative EVAs for a number of years. Because these divisions are destroying more value than they are creating, a strong point can be made for liquidating these divisions. Although managers are generally emotionally opposed to this type of action, EVA analysis makes liquidation harder to ignore.

The preceding discussion puts EVA in a very positive light. However, one can certainly find much to criticize with EVA as well. We now focus on two well-known problems with EVA. First, the preceding example uses EVA for performance measurement, where we believe it properly belongs. To us, EVA seems a clear improvement over ROA and other financial ratios. However, EVA has little to offer for capital budgeting because EVA focuses only on current earnings. By contrast, net-present-value analysis uses projections of all future cash flows, where the cash flows will generally differ from year to year. Thus, as far as capital budgeting is concerned, NPV analysis has a richness that EVA does not have. Although supporters may argue that EVA correctly incorporates the weighted average cost of capital, one must remember that the discount rate in NPV analysis is the same weighted average cost of capital. That is, both approaches take the cost of equity capital based on beta and combine it with the cost of debt to get an estimate of this weighted average.

A second problem with EVA is that it may increase the shortsightedness of managers. Under EVA, a manager will be well rewarded today if earnings are high today. Future losses may not harm the manager, because there is a good chance that she will be promoted or have left the firm by then. Thus, the manager has an incentive to run a division with more regard for short-term than long-term value. By raising prices or cutting quality, the manager may increase current profits (and, therefore, current EVA). However, to the extent that customer satisfaction is reduced, future profits (and therefore future EVA) are likely to fall. However, one should not be too harsh with EVA here, because the same problem occurs with ROA. A manager who raises prices or cuts quality will increase current ROA at the expense of future ROA. The problem, then, is not EVA per se but with the use of accounting numbers in general. Because stockholders want the discounted present value of all cash flows to be maximized, managers with bonuses based on some function of current profits or current cash flows are likely to behave in a shortsighted way.

EXAMPLE

Assume the following figures for the International Trade Corporation

$$EBIT = \$2.5 \text{ billion}$$
$$T_c = .4$$
$$r_{WACC} = 11\%$$
$$\text{Total capital contributed} = \text{Total debt} + \text{Equity}$$
$$= \$10 \text{ billion} + \$10 \text{ billion}$$
$$= \$20 \text{ billion}$$

Now we can calculate International Trade's EVA:

$$EVA = EBIT\,(1 - T_c) - r_{WACC} \times \text{Total capital}$$
$$= (\$2.5 \text{ billion} \times .6) - (.11 \times \$20 \text{ billion})$$
$$= \$1.5 \text{ billion} - \$2.2 \text{ billion}$$
$$= -\$700 \text{ million}$$

Visit us at www.mhhe.com/rwj

Capital Structure and Dividend Policy

Part II discussed the capital budgeting decisions of the firm. We argued that the objective of the firm should be to create value from its capital budgeting decisions. To do this the firm must find investments with a positive net present value. In Part IV we concentrate on financing decisions. As with capital budgeting decisions, the firm seeks to create value with its financing decisions. To do this the firm must find positive NPV financing arrangements. However, financial markets do not provide as many opportunities for positive NPV transactions as do nonfinancial markets. We show that the sources of NPV in financing are taxes, bankruptcy costs, and agency costs.

Chapter 13 introduces the concept of efficient markets, where current market prices reflect available information. We describe several forms of efficiency: the weak form, the semistrong form, and the strong form. The chapter offers a number of important lessons for the corporate financial manager in understanding the logic behind efficient financial markets.

In Chapter 14 we describe the basic types of long-term financing: common stock, preferred stock, and bonds. We then briefly analyze the major trends and patterns of long-term financing.

We consider the firm's overall capital-structure decision in Chapters 15 and 16. In general, a firm can choose any capital structure it desires: common stocks, bonds, preferred stocks, and so on. How should a firm choose its capital structure? Changing the capital structure of the firm changes the way the firm pays out its cash flows. Firms that borrow pay lower taxes than firms that do not. Because of corporate taxes, the value of a firm that borrows may be higher than the value of one that does not. However, with costly bankruptcy, a firm that borrows may have lower value. The combined effects of taxes and bankruptcy costs can produce an optimal capital structure.

Chapter 17 discusses capital budgeting for firms with some debt in their capital structures. It extends some of the material of Chapter 12. This chapter presents three alternative valuation methods: the weighted-average-cost-of-capital approach, the flows-to-equity approach, and the adjusted-present-value approach.

We discuss dividend policy in Chapter 18. It seems surprising that much empirical evidence and logic suggest that dividend policy does not matter. There are some good reasons for firms to pay low levels of dividends: lower taxes and costs of issuing new equity. However, there are also some good reasons to pay high levels of dividends: to reduce agency costs and to satisfy low-tax, high-income clienteles.

Corporate-Financing Decisions and Efficient Capital Markets

EXECUTIVE SUMMARY

The section on value concentrated on the firm's capital budgeting decisions—the left-hand side of the balance sheet of the firm. This chapter begins our analysis of corporate-financing decisions—the right-hand side of the balance sheet. We take the firm's capital budgeting decision as fixed in this section of the text.

The point of this chapter is to introduce the concept of *efficient capital markets* and its implications for corporate finance. Efficient capital markets are those in which market prices reflect available information. This means that market prices reflect the underlying present value of securities, and there is no way to make unusual or excess profits by using the available information.

This concept has profound implications for financial managers, because market efficiency eliminates many value-enhancing strategies of firms. In particular, we show that in an efficient market

1. Stock price should not be affected by a firm's choice of accounting method.
2. Financial managers cannot time issues of bonds and stocks.
3. Firms cannot expect to gain through speculation in currency and bond markets.
4. Financial managers should pay attention to the information in market prices.

However, the evidence on market efficiency is not one-sided. A very influential school of thought, known as *behavioral finance,* argues that markets are simply not efficient. Ultimately, whether or not capital markets are efficient is an empirical question. We will describe several studies examining efficient markets.

13.1 Can Financing Decisions Create Value?

Earlier parts of the book show how to evaluate projects according to the net present value criterion. The real world is a competitive one where projects with positive net present value are not always easy to come by. However, through hard work or through good fortune, a firm can identify winning projects. For example, to create value from capital budgeting decisions, the firm is likely to

1. Locate an unsatisfied demand for a particular product or service.
2. Create a barrier to make it more difficult for other firms to compete.
3. Produce products or services at lower cost than the competition.
4. Be the first to develop a new product.

The next five chapters concern *financing* decisions. Typical financing decisions include how much debt and equity to sell, what types of debt and equity to sell, and when to sell them. Just as the net present value criterion was used to evaluate capital budgeting projects, we now want to use the same criterion to evaluate financing decisions.

Though the procedure for evaluating financing decisions is identical to the procedure for evaluating projects, the results are different. It turns out that the typical firm has many more capital-expenditure opportunities with positive net present values than financing opportunities with positive net present values. In fact, we later show that some plausible financial models imply that no valuable financial opportunities exist at all.

Though this dearth of profitable financing opportunities will be examined in detail later, a few remarks are in order now. We maintain that there are basically three ways to create valuable financing opportunities:

1. *Fool Investors.* Assume that a firm can raise capital either by issuing stock or by issuing a more complex security, say, a combination of stock and warrants. Suppose that, in truth, 100 shares of stock are worth the same as 50 units of our complex security. If investors have a misguided, overly optimistic view of the complex security, perhaps the 50 units can be sold for more than the 100 shares of stock can be. Clearly this complex security provides a valuable financing opportunity because the firm is getting more than fair value for it.

Financial managers try to package securities to receive the greatest value. A cynic might view this as attempting to fool investors.

However, the theory of efficient capital markets implies that investors cannot easily be fooled. It says that securities are appropriately priced at all times, implying that the market as a whole is very shrewd indeed. In our example, 50 units of the complex security would sell for the same price as 100 shares of stock. Thus, corporate managers cannot attempt to create value by fooling investors. Instead, managers must create value in other ways.

2. *Reduce Costs or Increase Subsidies.* We show later in the book that certain forms of financing have greater tax advantages than other forms. Clearly, a firm packaging securities to minimize taxes can increase firm value. In addition, any financing technique involves other costs. For example, investment bankers, lawyers, and accountants must be paid. A firm packaging securities to minimize these costs can also increase its value.

EXAMPLE

Suppose Vermont Electronics Company is thinking about relocating its plant to Mexico where labor costs are lower. In the hope that it can stay in Vermont, the company has submitted an application to the State of Vermont to issue $2 million in five-year, tax-exempt industrial bonds. The coupon rate on industrial revenue bonds in Vermont is currently 5 percent. This is an attractive rate because the normal cost of debt capital for Vermont Electronics Company is 10 percent. What is the NPV of this potential financing transaction?

If the application is accepted and the industrial revenue bonds are issued by the Vermont Electronics Company, the NPV (ignoring corporate taxes) is

$$NPV = \$2,000,000 - \left[\frac{\$100,000}{1.1} + \frac{\$100,000}{(1.1)^2} + \frac{\$100,000}{(1.1)^3} + \frac{\$100,000}{(1.1)^4} + \frac{\$2,100,000}{(1.1)^5} \right]$$

$$= \$2,000,000 - \$1,620,921$$

$$= \$379,079$$

This transaction has a positive NPV. The Vermont Electronics Company obtains subsidized financing where the value of the subsidy is $379,079.

3. *Create a New Security.* There has been a surge in financial innovation in recent years. For example, in a speech on financial innovation, Nobel laureate Merton Miller asked the rhetorical question, "Can any twenty-year period in recorded history have witnessed even

a tenth as much new development? Where corporations once issued only straight debt and straight common stock, they now issue zero-coupon bonds, adjustable-rate notes, floating-rate notes, putable bonds, credit-enhanced debt securities, receivable-backed securities, adjusted-rate preferred stock, convertible adjustable preferred stock, auction-rate preferred stock, single-point adjustable-rate stock, convertible exchangeable preferred stock, adjustable-rate convertible debt, zero-coupon convertible debt, debt with mandatory common-stock-purchase contracts—to name just a few!"[1] And, financial innovation has occurred even more rapidly in the years following Miller's speech.

Though the advantage of each instrument is different, one general theme is that these new securities cannot easily be duplicated by combinations of existing securities. Thus, a previously unsatisfied clientele may pay extra for a specialized security catering to its needs. For example, putable bonds let the purchaser sell the bond at a fixed price back to the firm. This innovation creates a price floor, allowing the investor to reduce his or her downside risk. Perhaps risk-averse investors or investors with little knowledge of the bond market would find this feature particularly attractive.

Corporations gain by issuing these unique securities at high prices. However, the value captured by the innovator may well be small in the long run because the innovator usually cannot patent or copyright his idea. Soon many firms are issuing securities of the same kind, forcing prices down as a result.

This brief introduction sets the stage for the next five chapters of the book. The rest of this chapter examines the efficient-capital-markets hypothesis. We show that if capital markets are efficient, corporate managers cannot create value by fooling investors. This is quite important, because managers must create value in other, perhaps more difficult, ways. The following four chapters concern the costs and subsidies of various forms of financing. A discussion of new financing instruments is postponed until later chapters of the text.

Concept Question	I. List three ways financing decisions can create value.

13.2 A Description of Efficient Capital Markets

An efficient capital market is one in which stock prices fully reflect available information. To illustrate how an efficient market works, suppose the F-stop Camera Corporation (FCC) is attempting to develop a camera that will double the speed of the auto-focusing system now available. FCC believes this research has positive NPV.

Now consider a share of stock in FCC. What determines the willingness of investors to hold shares of FCC at a particular price? One important factor is the probability that FCC will be the first company to develop the new auto-focusing system. In an efficient market we would expect the price of the shares of FCC to increase if this probability increases.

Suppose FCC hires a well-known engineer to develop the new auto-focusing system. In an efficient market, what will happen to FCC's share price when this is announced? If the well-known scientist is paid a salary that fully reflects his or her contribution to the firm, the price of the stock will not necessarily change. Suppose, instead, that hiring the scientist is a positive NPV transaction. In this case, the price of shares in FCC will increase because the firm can pay the scientist a salary below his or her true value to the company.

---

[1]M. Miller, "Financial Innovation: The Last Twenty Years and the Next," *Journal of Financial and Quantitative Analysis* (December 1986). However, Peter Tufano, "Securities Innovations: A Historical and Functional Perspective," *Journal of Applied Corporate Finance* (Winter 1995), shows that many securities commonly believed to have been invented in the 1970s and 1980s can be traced as far back as the 1830s.

When will the increase in the price of FCC's shares take place? Assume that the hiring announcement is made in a press release on Wednesday morning. In an efficient market, the price of shares in FCC will *immediately* adjust to this new information. Investors should not be able to buy the stock on Wednesday afternoon and make a profit on Thursday. This would imply that it took the stock market a day to realize the implication of the FCC press release. The efficient-market hypothesis predicts that the price of shares of FCC stock on Wednesday afternoon will already reflect the information contained in the Wednesday morning press release.

The **efficient-market hypothesis** (EMH) has implications for investors and for firms.

- Because information is reflected in prices immediately, investors should only expect to obtain a normal rate of return. Awareness of information when it is released does an investor no good. The price adjusts before the investor has time to trade on it.

- Firms should expect to receive fair value for securities that they sell. *Fair* means that the price they receive for the securities they issue is the present value. Thus, valuable financing opportunities that arise from fooling investors are unavailable in efficient capital markets.

EXAMPLE

Suppose IBM announces it has invented a microprocessor that will make its computer 30 times faster than existing computers. The price of a share of IBM should increase immediately to a new equilibrium level.

Figure 13.1 presents several possible adjustments in stock prices. The solid line represents the path taken by the stock in an efficient market. In this case the price adjusts immediately to the new information with no further price changes. The dotted line depicts a delayed reaction. Here it takes the market 30 days to fully absorb the information. Finally, the broken line illustrates an overreaction and subsequent correction back to the true price. The broken line and the dotted line show the paths that the stock price might take in an inefficient market. If the price of the stock takes several days to adjust, trading profits would be available to investors who bought at the date of the announcement and sold once the price settled back to the equilibrium.[2]

Foundations of Market Efficiency

Figure 13.1 shows the consequences of market efficiency. But what are the conditions that *cause* market efficiency? Andrei Shleifer argues that there are three conditions, any one of which will lead to efficiency:[3] (1) rationality, (2) independent deviations from rationality, and (3) arbitrage. A discussion of these conditions follows.

Rationality   Imagine that all investors are rational. When new information is released in the marketplace, all investors will adjust their estimates of stock prices in a rational way. In our example, investors will use the information in FCC's press release, in conjunction with

---

[2]Now you should understand the following short story. A student was walking down the hall with his finance professor when they both saw a $20 bill on the ground. As the student bent down to pick it up, the professor shook his head slowly and, with a look of disappointment on his face, said patiently to the student, "Don't bother. If it was really there, someone else would have already picked it up."

The moral of the story reflects the logic of the efficient-market hypothesis: If you think you have found a pattern in stock prices or a simple device for picking winners, you probably have not. If there were such a simple way to make money, someone else would have found it before. Furthermore, if people tried to exploit the information, their efforts would become self-defeating and the pattern would disappear.

[3]Shleifer, Andrei, *Inefficient Markets: An Introduction to Behavioral Finance,* Oxford University Press, Oxford, United Kingdom (2000).

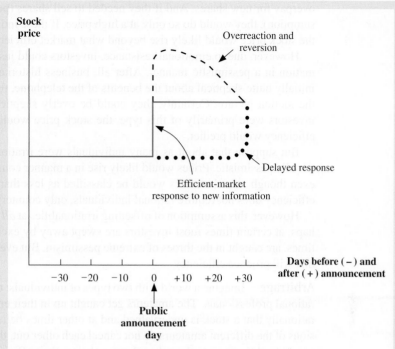

FIGURE 13.1

Reaction of Stock
Price to New
Information in
Efficient and
Inefficient Markets

Efficient-market response: The price instantaneously adjusts to and fully reflects new information; there is no tendency for subsequent increases and decreases.

Delayed response: The price adjusts slowly to the new information; 30 days elapse before the price completely reflects the new information.

Overreaction: The price overadjusts to the new information; there is a bubble in the price sequence.

existing information on the firm, to determine the NPV of FCC's new venture. If the information in the press release implies that the NPV of the venture is $10 million and there are 2 million shares, investors will calculate that the NPV is $5 per share. While FCC's old price might be, say, $40, no one would now transact at that price. Anyone interested in selling would only sell at a price of at least $45 (40 + 5). And anyone interested in buying would now be willing to pay up to $45. In other words, the price would rise by $5. And the price would rise immediately, since rational investors would see no reason to wait before trading at the new price.

Of course, we all know times when family members, friends, and yes, even ourselves seem to behave less than perfectly rationally. Thus, perhaps it is too much to ask that *all* investors behave rationally. But the market will still be efficient if the following scenario holds.

Independent Deviations from Rationality   Suppose that FCC's press release is not all that clear. How many new cameras are likely to be sold? At what price? What is the likely cost per camera? Will other camera companies be able to develop competing products? How long will this likely take? If these, and other, questions cannot be answered easily, it will be difficult to estimate NPV.

Now imagine that, with so many questions going unanswered, many investors do not think clearly. Some investors might get caught up in the romance of a new product, hoping, and ultimately believing, in sales projections well above what is rational. They would overpay for new shares. And if they needed to sell shares (perhaps to finance current consumption), they would do so only at a high price. If these individuals dominate the market, the stock price would likely rise beyond what market efficiency would predict.

However, due to emotional resistance, investors could just as easily react to new information in a pessimistic manner. After all, business historians tell us that investors were initially quite skeptical about the benefits of the telephone, the copier, the automobile, and the motion picture. Certainly, they could be overly skeptical about this new camera. If investors were primarily of this type, the stock price would likely rise less than market efficiency would predict.

But suppose that about as many individuals were irrationally optimistic as were irrationally pessimistic. Prices would likely rise in a manner consistent with market efficiency, even though most investors would be classified as less than fully rational. Thus, market efficiency does not require rational individuals, only countervailing irrationalities.

However, this assumption of offsetting irrationalities at *all* times may be unrealistic. Perhaps, at certain times most investors are swept away by excessive optimism and, at other times, are caught in the throes of extreme pessimism. But even here, there is an assumption that will produce efficiency.

Arbitrage   Imagine a world with two types of individuals: the irrational amateurs and the rational professionals. The amateurs get caught up in their emotions, at times believing irrationally that a stock is undervalued and at other times believing the opposite. If the passions of the different amateurs do not cancel each other out, these amateurs, by themselves, would tend to carry stocks either above or below their efficient prices.

Now let's bring in the professionals. Suppose professionals go about their business methodically and rationally. They study companies thoroughly, they evaluate the evidence objectively, they estimate stock prices coldly and clearly, and they act accordingly. If a stock is underpriced, they would buy it. If overpriced, they would sell it (or even sell it short).[4] And their confidence would likely be greater than that of the amateurs. While an amateur might risk only a small sum, these professionals might risk large ones, *knowing* as they do that the stock is mispriced. Furthermore, they would be willing to rearrange their entire portfolio in search of a profit. If they find that General Motors is underpriced, they might sell the Ford stock they own (or even sell Ford short) in order to buy GM. *Arbitrage* is the word that comes to mind here, since arbitrage generates profit from the simultaneous purchase and sale of different, but substitute, securities. If the arbitrage of professionals dominates the speculation of amateurs, markets would still be efficient.

Concept
Questions

1. Can you define an efficient market?
2. Name the three foundations of market efficiency.

13.3 The Different Types of Efficiency

In our previous discussion, we assumed that the market responds immediately to all available information. In actuality, certain information may affect stock prices more quickly than other information. To handle differential response rates, researchers separate information into different types. The most common classification system identifies three types: information on past prices, publicly available information, and all information. The effect of these three information sets on prices is examined next.

---

[4]When an investor short-sells a stock, his position is such that he gains from a fall in the stock and loses from a rise in the stock. Thus, short-selling a stock can be viewed as the opposite of buying a stock.

The Weak Form

Imagine a trading strategy that recommends buying a stock after it has gone up three days in a row and recommends selling a stock after it has gone down three days in a row. This strategy uses information based only on past prices. It does not use any other information, such as earnings, forecasts, merger announcements, or money-supply figures. A capital market is said to be *weakly efficient* or to satisfy **weak-form efficiency** if it fully incorporates the information in past stock prices. Thus, the above strategy would not be able to generate profits if weak-form efficiency holds.

Often weak-form efficiency is represented mathematically as

$$P_t = P_{t-1} + \text{Expected return} + \text{Random error}_t \tag{13.1}$$

Equation (13.1) states that the price today is equal to the sum of the last observed price plus the expected return on the stock plus a random component occurring over the interval. The last observed price could have occurred yesterday, last week, or last month, depending on one's sampling interval. The expected return is a function of a security's risk and would be based on the models of risk and return in previous chapters. The random component is due to new information on the stock. It could be either positive or negative and has an expectation of zero. The random component in any one period is unrelated to the random component in any past period. Hence, this component is not predictable from past prices. If stock prices follow equation (13.1), they are said to follow a **random walk**.[5]

Weak-form efficiency is about the weakest type of efficiency that we would expect a financial market to display because historical price information is the easiest kind of information about a stock to acquire. If it were possible to make extraordinary profits simply by finding patterns in stock price movements, everyone would do it, and any profits would disappear in the scramble.

This effect of competition can be seen in Figure 13.2. Suppose the price of a stock displays a cyclical pattern, as indicated by the wavy curve. Shrewd investors would buy at the low points, forcing those prices up. Conversely, they would sell at the high points, forcing

FIGURE 13.2

Investor Behavior Tends to Eliminate Cyclical Patterns

If a stock's price follows a cyclical pattern, the pattern will be quickly eliminated in an efficient market. A random pattern will emerge as investors buy at the trough and sell at the peak of a cycle.

---

[5]For purposes of this text, the random walk can be considered synonymous with weak-form efficiency. Technically, the random walk is a slightly more restrictive hypothesis because it assumes that stock returns are identically distributed through time.

prices down. Via competition, cyclical regularities would be eliminated, leaving only random fluctuations.

The Semistrong and Strong Forms

If weak-form efficiency is controversial, even more contentious are the two stronger types of efficiency, **semistrong-form efficiency** and **strong-form efficiency.** A market is semistrong-form efficient if prices reflect (incorporate) all publicly available information, including information such as published accounting statements for the firm as well as historical price information. A market is strong-form efficient if prices reflect all information, public or private.

The information set of past prices is a subset of the information set of publicly available information, which in turn is a subset of all information. This is shown in Figure 13.3. Thus, strong-form efficiency implies semistrong-form efficiency, and semistrong-form efficiency implies weak-form efficiency. The distinction between semistrong-form efficiency and weak-form efficiency is that semistrong-form efficiency requires not only that the market be efficient with respect to historical price information, but that *all* of the information available to the public be reflected in price.

To illustrate the different forms of efficiency, imagine an investor who always sold a particular stock after its price had risen. A market that was only weak-form efficient and not semistrong-form efficient would still prevent such a strategy from generating positive profits. According to weak-form efficiency, a recent price rise does not imply that the stock is overvalued.

Now consider a firm reporting increased earnings. An individual might consider investing in the stock after hearing of the news release giving this information. However, if the

---

FIGURE 13.3

Relationship among
Three Different
Information Sets

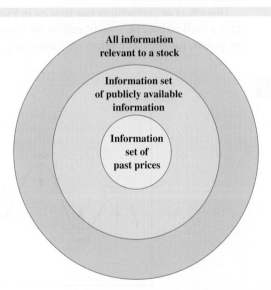

The information set of past prices is a subset of the set of all publicly available information, which in turn is a subset of all information. If today's price reflects only information on past prices, the market is weak-form efficient. If today's price reflects all publicly available information, the market is semistrong-form efficient. If today's price reflects all information, both public and private, the market is strong-form efficient.

Semistrong-form efficiency implies weak-form efficiency and strong-form efficiency implies semistrong-form efficiency.

market is semistrong efficient, the price should rise immediately upon the news release. Thus, the investor would end up paying the higher price, eliminating all chance for profit.

At the furthest end of the spectrum is strong-form efficiency. This form says that anything that is pertinent to the value of the stock and that is known to at least one investor is, in fact, fully incorporated into the stock price. A strict believer in strong-form efficiency would deny that an insider who knew whether a company mining operation had struck gold could profit from that information. Such a devotee of the strong-form efficient-market hypothesis might argue that as soon as the insider tried to trade on his or her information, the market would recognize what was happening, and the price would shoot up before he or she could buy any of the stock. Alternatively, believers in strong-form efficiency argue that there are no secrets, and as soon as the gold is discovered, the secret gets out.

One reason to expect that markets are weak-form efficient is that it is so cheap and easy to find patterns in stock prices. Anyone who can program a computer and knows a little bit of statistics can search for such patterns. It stands to reason that if there were such patterns, people would find and exploit them, in the process causing them to disappear.

Semistrong-form efficiency, though, implies more sophisticated investors than does weak-form efficiency. An investor must be skilled at economics and statistics, and steeped in the idiosyncrasies of individual industries and companies. Furthermore, to acquire and use such skills requires talent, ability, and time. In the jargon of the economist, such an effort is costly and the ability to be successful at it is probably in scarce supply.

As for strong-form efficiency, this is just farther down the road than semistrong-form efficiency. It is difficult to believe that the market is so efficient that someone with valuable inside information cannot prosper from it. And empirical evidence tends to be unfavorable to this form of market efficiency.

Some Common Misconceptions about the Efficient-Market Hypothesis

No idea in finance has attracted as much attention as that of efficient markets, and not all of the attention has been flattering. To a certain extent this is because much of the criticism has been based on a misunderstanding of what the hypothesis does and does not say. We illustrate three misconceptions below.

The Efficacy of Dart Throwing   When the notion of market efficiency was first publicized and debated in the popular financial press, it was often characterized by the following quote: ". . . throwing darts at the financial page will produce a portfolio that can be expected to do as well as any managed by professional security analysts."[6, 7] This is almost, but not quite, true.

All the efficient-market hypothesis really says is that, on average, the manager will not be able to achieve an abnormal or excess return. The excess return is defined with respect to some benchmark expected return, such as that from the security market line of Chapter 10 (SML). The investor must still decide how risky a portfolio he or she wants. In addition, a random dart thrower might wind up with all of the darts sticking into one or two high-risk stocks that deal in genetic engineering. Would you really want all of your stock investments in two such stocks?

The failure to understand this has often led to a confusion about market efficiency. For example, sometimes it is wrongly argued that market efficiency means that it does not matter

---

[6]B. G. Malkiel, *A Random Walk Down Wall Street,* 7th ed. (New York: Norton, 1999).

[7]Older articles often referred to the benchmark of "dart-throwing monkeys." As government involvement in the securities industry grew, the benchmark was oftentimes restated as "dart-throwing congressmen."

what you do because the efficiency of the market will protect the unwary. However, someone once remarked, "The efficient market protects the sheep from the wolves, but nothing can protect the sheep from themselves."

What efficiency does say is that the price that a firm obtains when it sells a share of its stock is a fair price in the sense that it reflects the value of that stock given the information that is available about it. Shareholders need not worry that they are paying too much for a stock with a low dividend or some other characteristic, because the market has already incorporated it into the price. However, investors still have to worry about such things as their level of risk exposure and their degree of diversification.

Price Fluctuations   Much of the public is skeptical of efficiency because stock prices fluctuate from day to day. However, daily price movement is in no way inconsistent with efficiency; a stock in an efficient market adjusts to new information by changing price. A great deal of new information comes into the stock market each day. In fact, the *absence* of daily price movements in a changing world might suggest an inefficiency.

Stockholder Disinterest   Many laypersons are skeptical that the market price can be efficient if only a fraction of the outstanding shares changes hands on any given day. However, the number of traders in a stock on a given day is generally far less than the number of people following the stock. This is true because an individual will trade only when his appraisal of the value of the stock differs enough from the market price to justify incurring brokerage commissions and other transaction costs. Furthermore, even if the number of traders following a stock is small relative to the number of outstanding shareholders, the stock can be expected to be efficiently priced as long as a number of interested traders use the publicly available information. That is, the stock price can reflect the available information even if many stockholders never follow the stock and are not considering trading in the near future.

Concept
Questions

1. **Can you describe the three forms of the efficient-market hypothesis?**
2. **Does market efficiency mean you can throw darts at** *The Wall Street Journal* **listing of New York Stock Exchange stocks to pick a portfolio?**
3. **What does it mean to say the price you pay for a stock is fair?**

13.4   The Evidence

The evidence on the efficient-market hypothesis is extensive, with studies covering the broad categories of weak form, semistrong form, and strong-form efficiency. In the first category we investigate whether stock price changes are random. We review both *event studies* and studies of the performance of mutual funds in the second category. In the third category, we look at the performance of corporate insiders.

The Weak Form

The random-walk hypothesis, as expressed in equation (13.1), implies that a stock's price movement in the past is unrelated to its price movement in the future. The work of Chapter 10 allows us to test this implication. In that chapter, we discussed the concept of correlation between the returns on two different stocks. For example, the correlation between the return on General Motors and the return on Ford is likely to be high because both stocks are in the same industry. Conversely, the correlation between the return on General Motors and the return on the stock of, say, a European fast-food chain is likely to be low.

Financial economists frequently speak of **serial correlation,** which involves only one security. This is the correlation between the current return on a security and the return on

TABLE 13.1	Company	Serial Correlation Coefficient
Serial Correlation Coefficients for 8 Large U.S. Companies	Boeing Co.	0.038
	Bristol-Myers Squibb Co.	0.064
	Coca-Cola Co.	0.041
	IBM Corporation	−0.004
	Philip Morris Companies Inc.	0.075
	Procter & Gamble Co.	0.030
	Sears, Roebuck & Co.	0.046
	Texaco Inc.	0.005

Boeing's coefficient of 0.038 is slightly positive, implying that a positive return today makes a positive return tomorrow slightly more likely. IBM's coefficient is negative, implying that a negative return today makes a positive return tomorrow slightly more likely. However, the coefficients are so small relative to estimation error and transaction costs that the results are generally considered to be consistent with efficient capital markets.

the same security over a later period. A positive coefficient of serial correlation for a particular stock indicates a tendency toward *continuation*. That is, a higher-than-average return today is likely to be followed by higher-than-average returns in the future. Similarly, a lower-than-average return today is likely to be followed by lower-than-average returns in the future.

A negative coefficient of serial correlation for a particular stock indicates a tendency toward *reversal*. A higher-than-average return today is likely to be followed by lower-than-average returns in the future. Similarly, a lower-than-average return today is likely to be followed by higher-than-average returns in the future. Both significantly positive and significantly negative serial-correlation coefficients are indications of market inefficiencies; in either case, returns today can be used to predict future returns.

Serial correlation coefficients for stock returns near zero would be consistent with the random-walk hypothesis. Thus, a current stock return that is higher than average is as likely to be followed by lower-than-average returns as by higher-than-average returns. Similarly, a current stock return that is lower than average is as likely to be followed by higher-than-average returns as by lower-than-average returns.

Table 13.1 shows the serial correlation for daily stock-price changes for eight large U.S. companies. These coefficients indicate whether or not there are relationships between yesterday's return and today's return. As can be seen, the correlation coefficients are predominantly positive, implying that a higher-than-average return today makes a higher-than-average return tomorrow slightly more likely. Conversely, IBM's coefficient is slightly negative, implying that a lower-than-average return today makes a higher-than-average return tomorrow slightly more likely.

However, because correlation coefficients can, in principle, vary between −1 and 1, the reported coefficients are quite small. In fact, the coefficients are so small relative to both estimation errors and to transactions costs that the results are generally considered to be consistent with weak-form efficiency.

The weak form of the efficient-market hypothesis has been tested in many other ways as well. Our view of the literature is that the evidence, taken as a whole, is consistent with weak-form efficiency.

This finding raises an interesting thought: If price changes are truly random, why do so many believe that prices follow patterns? The work of both psychologists and statisticians suggests that most people simply do not know what randomness looks like. For example, consider Figure 13.4. The top graph was generated by a computer using random numbers and equation (13.1). Because of this it must follow a random walk. Yet, we have found that

FIGURE 13.4

Simulated and
Actual Stock-Price
Movements

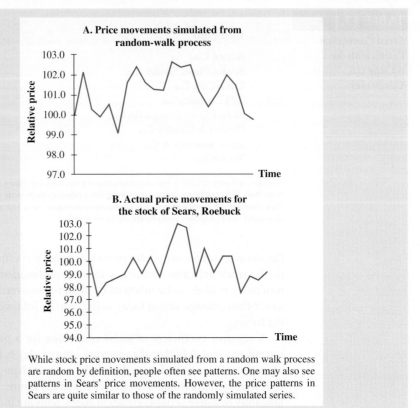

A. Price movements simulated from random-walk process

B. Actual price movements for the stock of Sears, Roebuck

While stock price movements simulated from a random walk process are random by definition, people often see patterns. One may also see patterns in Sears' price movements. However, the price patterns in Sears are quite similar to those of the randomly simulated series.

people examining the chart generally see patterns. Different people see different patterns and forecast different future price movements. However, in our experience, viewers are all quite confident of the patterns they see.

Next, consider the bottom graph, which tracks actual movements in Sears, Roebuck's stock price. This graph may look quite nonrandom to some, suggesting weak-form inefficiency. However, it also bears a close visual resemblance to the simulated series above, and statistical tests indicate that it indeed behaves like a purely random series. Thus, in our opinion, people claiming to see patterns in stock-price data are probably seeing optical illusions.

The Semistrong Form

The semistrong form of the efficient-market hypothesis implies that prices should reflect all publicly available information. We present two types of tests of this form.

Event Studies   The *abnormal return* (AR) on a given stock for a particular day can be calculated by subtracting the market's return on the same day (R_m)—as measured by a broad-based index such as the S&P composite index—from the actual return (R) on the stock for that day.[8] We write this algebraically as:

$$AR = R - R_m$$

---

[8]The abnormal return can also be measured by using the market model. In this case the abnormal return is

$$AR = R - (\alpha + \beta R_m)$$

The following system will help us understand tests of the semistrong form:

Information released at time $t - 1 \rightarrow AR_{t-1}$

Information released at time $t \rightarrow AR_t$

Information released at time $t + 1 \rightarrow AR_{t+1}$

The arrows indicate that the return in any time period is related only to the information released during that period.

According to the efficient-market hypothesis, a stock's abnormal return at time t, AR_t, should reflect the release of information at the same time, t. Any information released before then should have no effect on abnormal returns in this period, because all of its influence should have been felt before. In other words, an efficient market would already have incorporated previous information into prices. Because a stock's return today cannot depend on what the market does not yet know, information that will be known only in the future cannot influence the stock's return either. Hence the arrows point in the direction that is shown, with information in any one time period affecting only that period's abnormal return. *Event studies* are statistical studies that examine whether the arrows are as shown or whether the release of information influences returns on other days.

These studies also speak of *cumulative abnormal returns (CARs),* as well as abnormal returns (ARs). As an example, consider a firm with ARs of 1%, −3%, and 6% for dates −1, 0, and 1 relative to a corporate announcement. The CARs for dates −1, 0, and 1 would be 1%, −2% [1% + (−3%)], and 4% [1% + (−3%) + 6%], respectively.

As an example, consider the study by Szewczyk, Tsetsekos, and Zantout[9] on dividend omissions. Figure 13.5 shows the plot of CARs for a sample of companies announcing dividend omissions. Since dividend omissions are generally considered to be bad events, we would expect abnormal returns to be negative around the time of the announcements. They are, as evidenced by a drop in the CAR on both the day before the announcement (day −1) and the day of the announcement (day 0).[10] However, note that there is virtually no movement in the CARs in the days following the announcement. This implies that the bad news is fully incorporated into the stock price by the announcement day, a result consistent with market efficiency.

Over the years this type of methodology has been applied to a large number of events. Announcements of dividends, earnings, mergers, capital expenditures, and new issues of stock are a few examples of the vast literature in the area. The early event-study tests generally supported the view that the market is semistrong-form (and therefore also weak-form) efficient. However, a number of more recent studies present evidence that the market does not impound all relevant information immediately. Some conclude from this that the market is not efficient. Others argue that this conclusion is unwarranted, given statistical and methodological problems in the studies. This issue will be addressed in more detail later in the chapter.

---

[9]Samuel H. Szewczyk, George P. Tsetsekos, and Zaher Z. Zantout, "Do Dividend Omissions Signal Future Earnings or Past Earnings?" *Journal of Investing* (Spring 1997).

[10]An astute reader may wonder why the abnormal return is negative on day −1, as well as on day 0. To see why, first note that the announcement date is generally taken in academic studies to be the publication date of the story in *The Wall Street Journal (WSJ).* Then consider a company announcing a dividend omission via a press release at noon on Tuesday. The stock should fall on Tuesday. The announcement will be reported in the *WSJ* on Wednesday, because the Tuesday edition of the *WSJ* has already been printed. For this firm, the stock price falls on the day *before* the announcement in the *WSJ.*

Alternatively, imagine another firm announcing a dividend omission via a press release on Tuesday at 8 P.M. Since the stock market is closed at that late hour, the stock price will fall on Wednesday. Because the *WSJ* will report the announcement on Wednesday, the stock price falls on the day of the announcement in the *WSJ.*

Since firms may either make announcements during trading hours or after trading hours, stocks should fall on both day −1 and day 0 relative to publication in the *WSJ.*

FIGURE 13.5   Cumulative Abnormal Returns for Companies Announcing Dividend Omissions

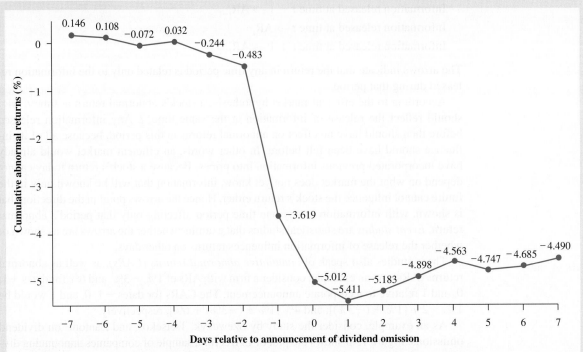

Cumulative abnormal returns (CARs) fall on both the day before the announcement and the day of the announcement of dividend omissions. CARs have very little movement after the announcement date. This pattern is consistent with market efficiency.

From Exhibit 2 in S. H. Szewczyk, George P. Tsetsekos, and Zaher Zantout, "Do Dividend Omissions Signal Future Earnings or Past Earnings?" *Journal of Investing* (Spring 1997).

Tests of market efficiency can be found in the oddest places. The price of frozen orange juice depends to a large extent on the weather in Orlando, Florida, where many of the oranges that are frozen for juice are grown. One researcher found that he could actually use frozen-orange-juice prices to improve the U.S. Weather Bureau's forecast of the temperature for the following night.[11] Clearly the market knows something that the weather forecasters do not.

Another group of researchers found that, as expected, stock prices generally fall on the date when the *sudden* death of a chief executive is announced.[12] However, the stock price generally rises for the sudden death of a company's founder if he was still heading up the firm prior to his death. The implication is that many of these individuals have outlived their usefulness to their firms.

The Record of Mutual Funds

If the market is efficient in the semistrong form, then no matter what publicly available information mutual-fund managers rely on to pick stocks, their average returns should be the same as those of the average investor in the market as a whole. We can test efficiency, then, by comparing the performance of these professionals with that of a market index.

---

[11]These findings are reported in R. Roll, "Orange Juice and Weather," *American Economic Review* (December 1984).

[12]W. B. Johnson, R. P. Magee, N. J. Nagarajan, and H. A. Newman, "An Analysis of the Stock Price Reaction to Sudden Executive Deaths: Implications for the Managerial Labor Market," *Journal of Accounting and Economics* (April 1985).

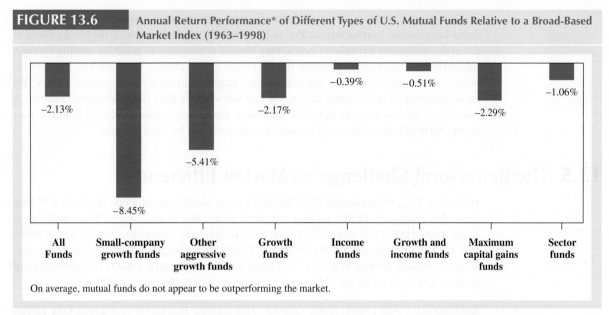

FIGURE 13.6   Annual Return Performance* of Different Types of U.S. Mutual Funds Relative to a Broad-Based Market Index (1963–1998)

On average, mutual funds do not appear to be outperforming the market.

SOURCE: Taken from Table 2 of Lubos Pastor and Robert F. Stambaugh, "Mutual Fund Performance and Seemingly Unrelated Assets," *Journal of Financial Economics,* 63 (2002).

*Performance is relative to the market-model.

Consider Figure 13.6, which presents the performance of various types of mutual funds relative to the stock market as a whole. The far left of the figure shows that the universe of all funds covered in the study underperforms the market by 2.13 percent per year, after an appropriate adjustment for risk.[13] Thus, rather than outperforming the market, the evidence shows underperformance. This underperformance holds for a number of types of funds as well. Returns in this study are net of fees, expenses, and commissions, so fund returns would be higher if these costs were added back. However, the study shows no evidence that funds, as a whole, are *beating* the market.

Perhaps nothing rankles successful stock market investors more than to have some professor tell them that they are not necessarily smart, just lucky. However, while Figure 13.6 represents only one study, there have been many papers on mutual funds. The overwhelming evidence here is that mutual funds, on average, do not beat broad-based indices.

By and large, mutual-fund managers rely on publicly available information. Thus the finding that they do not outperform market indices is consistent with semistrong-form and weak-form efficiency.

However, this evidence does not imply that mutual funds are bad investments for individuals. Though these funds fail to achieve better returns than some indices of the market, they do permit the investor to buy a portfolio that has a large number of stocks in it (the phrase "a well-diversified portfolio" is often used). They might also be very good at providing a variety of services such as keeping custody and records of all the stocks.

The Strong Form

Even the strongest adherents to the efficient-market hypothesis would not be surprised to find that markets are inefficient in the strong form. After all, if an individual has information that no one else has, it is likely that he can profit from it.

---

[13]This finding is similar to those reported by R. Wermers, "Mutual Fund Performance: An Empirical Decomposition into Stock-Picking, Talent, Style, Transactions Costs, and Expenses," *Journal of Finance* (August 2000).

One group of studies of strong-form efficiency investigates insider trading. Insiders in firms have access to information that is not generally available. But if the strong form of the efficient-market hypothesis holds, they should not be able to profit by trading on their information. A government agency, the Securities and Exchange Commission, requires insiders in companies to reveal any trading they might do in their own company's stock. By examining the record of such trades, we can see whether they made abnormal returns. A number of studies support the view that these trades were abnormally profitable. Thus, strong-form efficiency does not seem to be substantiated by the evidence.[14]

13.5 The Behavioral Challenge to Market Efficiency

In Section 13.2, we presented Prof. Shleifer's three conditions, any one of which will lead to market efficiency. In that section, we made a case that at least one of the conditions is likely to hold in the real world. However, there is definitely disagreement here. Many members of the academic community (including Prof. Shleifer) argue that none of the three conditions are likely to hold in reality. This point of view is based on what is called *behavioral finance.* Let us examine the behavioral view on each of these three conditions.

Rationality   Are people really rational? Not always. Just travel to Atlantic City or Las Vegas to see people gambling, sometimes with large sums of money. The casino's take implies a negative expected return for the gambler. Since gambling is risky and has a negative expected return, it can never be on the efficient frontier of our Chapter 10. In addition, gamblers will often bet on black at a roulette table after black has occurred a number of consecutive times, thinking that the run will continue. This strategy is faulty, since roulette tables have no memory.

But, of course, gambling is only a side-show as far as finance is concerned. Do we see irrationality in financial markets as well? The answer may very well be yes. Many investors do not achieve the degree of diversification that they should. Others trade frequently, generating both commissions and taxes. In fact, taxes can be handled optimally by selling losers and holding on to winners. While some individuals invest with tax minimization in mind, plenty of them do just the opposite. Many are more likely to sell their winners than their losers, a strategy leading to high tax payments. The behavioral view is not that *all* investors are irrational. Rather, it is that some, perhaps many, investors are.

Independent Deviations from Rationality   Are deviations from rationality generally random, thereby likely to cancel out in a whole population of investors? To the contrary, psychologists have long argued that people deviate from rationality in accordance with a number of basic principles. While not all of these principles have an application to finance and market efficiency, at least two seem to do so.

The first principle, called *representativeness,* can be explained with the gambling example used above. The gambler believing a run of black will continue is in error since, in reality, the probability of a black spin is still only 50 percent. Gamblers behaving in this way exhibit the psychological trait of representativeness. That is, they draw conclusions from too little data. In other words, the gambler believes the small sample he observed is more representative of the population than it really is.

How is this related to finance? Perhaps a market dominated by representativeness leads to bubbles. People see a sector of the market, for example, Internet stocks, having a short

---

[14]H. N. Seyhun, *Investor Intelligence from Insider Trading,* MIT Press: Cambridge, Mass., 1998.

history of high revenue growth and extrapolate that it will continue forever. When the growth inevitably stalls, prices have nowhere to go but down.

The second principle is *conservatism,* which means that people are too slow in adjusting their beliefs to new information. Suppose that your goal since childhood was to become a dentist. Perhaps you came from a family of dentists, perhaps you liked the security and relatively high income that comes with that profession, or perhaps teeth always fascinated you. As things stand now, you could probably look forward to a long and productive career in that occupation. However, suppose that a new drug was developed that would prevent tooth decay. That drug would clearly reduce, or even eliminate, the demand for dentists. How quickly would you realize the implications as stated here? If you were emotionally attached to dentistry, you might adjust your beliefs very slowly. Family and friends could tell you to switch out of predental courses in college but you just might not be psychologically ready to do that. Instead you might cling to your rosy view of dentistry's future.

Perhaps there is a relationship to finance here. Prices seem to adjust slowly to the information contained in earnings announcements.[15] Could it be that, because of conservatism, investors are slow in adjusting their beliefs to new information? More will be said on this in the next section.

Arbitrage   In Section 13.2, we suggested that professional investors, knowing that securities are mispriced, could buy the underpriced ones while selling correctly priced (or even overpriced) substitutes. This might well undo any mispricing caused by emotional amateurs.

However, trading of this sort is likely to be more risky than it appears at first glance. Suppose professionals generally believed that McDonalds stock was underpriced. They would buy it, while selling their holdings in, say, Burger King and Wendy's. However, if amateurs were taking opposite positions, prices would adjust to correct levels only if the positions of amateurs were small relative to those of the professionals. In a world of many amateurs, a few professionals would have to take big positions to bring prices into line, perhaps even engaging heavily in short selling. Buying large amounts of one stock and short selling large amounts of other stocks is quite risky, even if the two stocks are in the same industry. Here, unanticipated bad news about McDonalds and unanticipated good news about the other two stocks would cause the professionals to register large losses.

In addition, if amateurs mispriced McDonalds today, what is to prevent McDonalds from being even *more* mispriced tomorrow? This risk of further mispricing, even in the presence of no new information, may also cause professionals to cut back their arbitrage positions. As an example, imagine a shrewd professional who believed Internet stocks were overpriced in 1998. Had he short sold at that time, he would have lost in the near term, since prices rose through March of 2000. Yes, he would have eventually made money, since prices later fell. However, near-term risk may reduce the size of arbitrage strategies.

In conclusion, the arguments presented here suggest that the theoretical underpinnings of the efficient capital markets hypothesis, presented in Section 13.2, might not hold in reality. That is, investors may be irrational, irrationality may be related across investors rather than canceling out across investors, and arbitrage strategies may involve too much risk to eliminate market efficiencies.

Concept Questions

1. **What do representativeness and conservatism mean?**
2. **What are the risks involved in arbitrage?**

---

[15]See, for example, Bernard, V. and J. Thomas, "Evidence That Stock Prices Do Not Fully Reflect the Implications of Current Earnings for Future Earnings," *Journal of Accounting and Economics* 13 (1990).

13.6 Empirical Challenges to Market Efficiency

Section 13.4 presented empirical evidence supportive of market efficiency. We now present evidence challenging this hypothesis. (Adherents of market efficiency generally refer to results of this type as *anomalies*.)

1. *Limits to arbitrage.* Royal Dutch Petroleum and Shell Transport merged their interests in 1907, with all subsequent cash flows being split on a 60 percent–40 percent basis between the two companies. However, both companies continued to be publicly traded. One might imagine that the market value of Royal Dutch would always be 1.5 (60/40) times that of Shell. That is, if Royal Dutch ever became overpriced, rational investors would buy Shell instead of Royal Dutch. If Royal Dutch were underpriced, investors would buy Royal Dutch. In addition, arbitrageurs would go further by buying the underpriced security and selling the overpriced security short.

However, Figure 13.7 shows that Royal Dutch traded below the parity ratio of 1.5 from 1980 to 1984 and above the ratio for much of the next 10 years. Why would these deviations occur? As stated in the previous section, behavioral finance suggests that there are limits to arbitrage. That is, an investor buying the overpriced asset and selling the underpriced asset does not have a sure thing. Deviations from parity could actually *increase* in the short run, implying losses for the arbitrageur. The well-known statement, "Markets can stay irrational longer than you can stay solvent," attributed to John Maynard Keynes, applies here. Thus, risk considerations may force arbitrageurs to take positions that are too small to move prices back to parity.

Academics have documented a number of these deviations from parity. Froot and Dabora show similar results for both the twin companies of Unilever N.V. and Unilever PLC and for two classes of SmithKline Beecham stock.[16] Lamont and Thaler present similar findings for 3Com and its subsidiary Palm Inc.[17] Other researchers find price behavior in closed-end mutual funds suggestive of parity deviations.

2. *Earnings surprises.* Common sense suggests that prices should rise when earnings are reported to be higher than expected and prices should fall when the reverse occurs. However, market efficiency implies that prices will adjust immediately to the announcement, while behavioral finance would predict another pattern. Chan, Jegadeesh, and Lakonishok rank companies by the extent of their *earnings surprise,* that is, the difference between current quarterly earnings and quarterly earnings four quarters ago, divided by the standard deviation of quarterly earnings.[18] They form a portfolio of companies with the most extreme positive surprises and another portfolio of companies with the most extreme negative surprises. Figure 13.8 shows returns from buying the two portfolios. As can be seen, prices adjust slowly to the earnings announcements, with the portfolio with the positive surprises outperforming the portfolio with the negative surprises over both the next six months and the next year. Many other researchers obtain similar results.

Why do prices adjust slowly? Behavioral finance suggests that investors exhibit conservatism here, as they are slow to adjust to the information contained in the announcements.

3. *Size.* In 1981, two important papers presented evidence that, in the United States, the returns on stocks with small **market capitalizations**[19] were greater than the returns on

---

[16]Froot, Kenneth A. and Emil M. Dabora, "How are Stock Prices Affected by the Location of Trade?" *Journal of Financial Economics* 53 (August 1999).

[17]Lamont, Owen and Richard Thaler, "Can the Market Add and Subtract? Mispricing in Tech Stock Carve-Outs," forthcoming in *Journal of Political Economy.*

[18]Chan, Louis K.C., Narasimhan Jegadeesh, and Josef Lakonishok, "Momentum Strategies," *Journal of Finance* (December 1996).

[19]Market capitalization is the price per share of stock multiplied by the number of shares outstanding.

FIGURE 13.7

Deviations of the Ratio of the Market Value of Royal Dutch to the Market Value of Shell from the Theoretical Value of 1.5

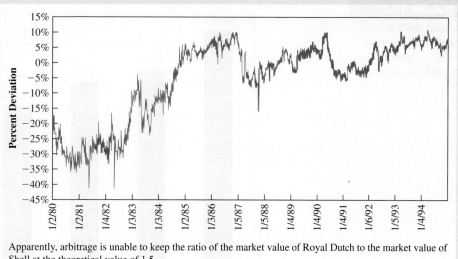

Apparently, arbitrage is unable to keep the ratio of the market value of Royal Dutch to the market value of Shell at the theoretical value of 1.5.

SOURCE: Figure I of Froot and Dabora, "How Are Stock Prices Affected by the Location of Trade?" *Journal of Financial Economics* 53 (August 1999).

FIGURE 13.8

Returns to Two Investment Strategies Based on Earnings Surprise

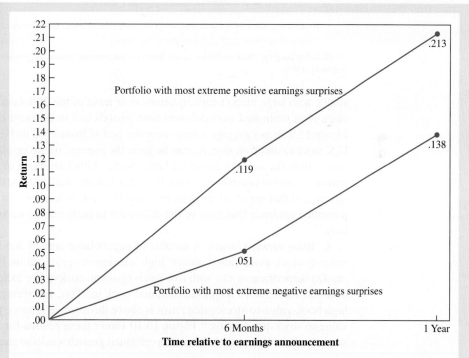

This figure shows returns to a strategy of buying stocks with extremely high positive earnings surprise (the difference between current quarterly earnings and quarterly earnings four quarters ago, divided by the standard deviation of quarterly earnings) and to a strategy of buying stocks with extremely high negative earnings surprise. The graph shows a slow adjustment to the information in the earnings announcement.

SOURCE: Adapted from Table III of L. C. Chan, N. Jegadeesh, and J. Lakonishok, "Momentum Strategies," *Journal of Finance* (December 1996).

FIGURE 13.9

Annual Stock Returns
on Portfolios Sorted
by Size (Market
Capitalization)

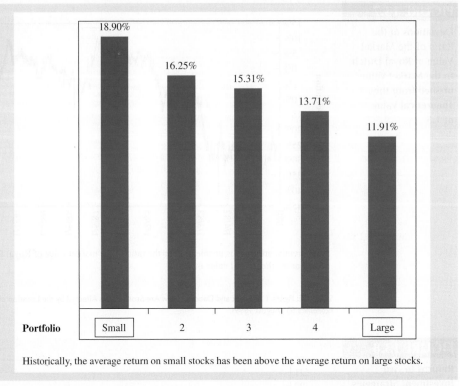

Historically, the average return on small stocks has been above the average return on large stocks.

SOURCE: Tim Loughran, "Book-to-Market across Firm Size, Exchange and Seasonality," *Journal of Financial and Quantitative Analysis* 32 (1997).

stocks with large market capitalizations over most of the 20th century.[20] The studies have since been replicated over different time periods and in different countries. For example, Figure 13.9 shows average returns over the period from 1963 to 1995 for five portfolios of U.S. stocks ranked on size. As can be seen, the average return on small stocks is quite a bit higher than the average return on large stocks. Although much of the differential performance is merely compensation for the extra risk of small stocks, researchers have generally argued that not all of it can be explained by risk differences. In addition, Donald Keim presented evidence that most of the difference in performance occurs in the month of January.[21]

4. *Value versus Growth.* A number of papers have argued that stocks with high book-value-to-stock-price ratios and/or high earnings-to-price ratios (generally called *value stocks*) outperform stocks with low ratios (growth stocks). For example, Fama and French find that, for 12 of 13 major international stock markets, the average return on stocks with high book-value-to-stock-price ratios is above the average return on stocks with low book-value-to-stock-price ratios.[22] Figure 13.10 shows these returns for the world's five largest stock markets. Value stocks have outperformed growth stocks in each of these five markets.

---

[20]See R. W. Banz, "The Relationship between Return and Market Value of Common Stocks," *Journal of Financial Economics* (March 1981), and M. R. Reinganum, "Misspecification of Capital Asset Pricing: Empirical Anomalies Based on Earnings Yields and Market Values," *Journal of Financial Economics* (March 1981).

[21]D. B. Keim, "Size-Related Anomalies and Stock Return Seasonality: Further Empirical Evidence," *Journal of Financial Economics* (June 1983).

[22]Taken from Table III of Eugene F. Fama and Kenneth R. French, "Value versus Growth: The International Evidence," *Journal of Finance* 53 (December, 1998).

FIGURE 13.10

Annual U.S. Dollar Returns* (in percent) on Low Book-to-Price Firms and High Book-to-Price Firms in Selected Countries

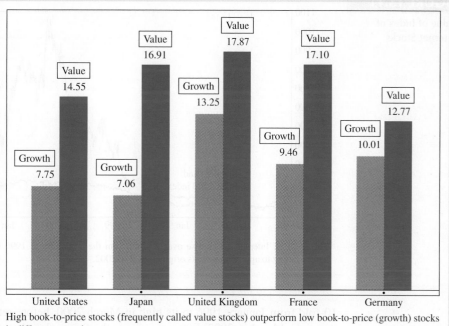

High book-to-price stocks (frequently called value stocks) outperform low book-to-price (growth) stocks in different countries.

SOURCE: Eugene F. Fama and Kenneth R. French, "Value versus Growth: The International Evidence," *Journal of Finance* (December 1998).

*Returns are expressed as the excess over the return on U.S. Treasury bills.

Because the return difference is so large and because the above ratios can be obtained so easily for individual stocks, the results may constitute strong evidence against market efficiency. However, a number of papers suggest that the unusual returns are due to biases in the commercial databases or to differences in risk, not to a true inefficiency.[23] Since the debate revolves around arcane statistical issues, we will not pursue the issue further. However, it is safe to say that no conclusion is warranted at this time. As with so many other topics in finance and economics, further research is needed.

5. *Crashes and Bubbles.* The stock market crash of October 19, 1987, is extremely puzzling. The market dropped between 20 percent and 25 percent on a Monday following a weekend during which little surprising news was released. A drop of this magnitude for no apparent reason is not consistent with market efficiency. Because the crash of 1929 is still an enigma, it is doubtful that the more recent debacle will be explained anytime soon. The recent comments of an eminent historian are apt here: When asked what, in his opinion, the effect of the French Revolution of 1789 was, he replied that it was too early to tell.

Perhaps the two stock market crashes are evidence consistent with the **bubble theory** of speculative markets. That is, security prices sometimes move wildly above their true values. Eventually prices fall back to their original level, causing great losses for investors. Consider, for example, the behavior of Internet stocks of the late 1990s. Figure 13.11 shows values of an index of Internet stocks from 1996 through 2002. The index rose over

[23]For example, see S. P. Kothari, J. Shanken, and R. G. Sloan, "Another Look at the Cross Section of Expected Stock Returns," *Journal of Finance* (March 1995), and E. F. Fama and K. R. French, "Multifactor Explanations of Asset Pricing Anomalies," *Journal of Finance* 51 (March 1996).

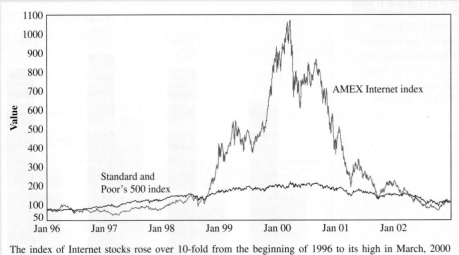

FIGURE 13.11

Value of Index of
Internet Stocks

The index of Internet stocks rose over 10-fold from the beginning of 1996 to its high in March, 2000 before falling to approximately its original level in 2002.

10-fold from January 1996 to its high in March 2000, before retreating to approximately its original level in 2002. For comparison, the figure also shows price movement for the Standard and Poor 500 Index. While this index rose and fell over the same period, the price movement was quite muted, relative to that of Internet stocks.

Many commentators describe the rise and fall of Internet stocks as a *bubble.* Is it correct to do so? Unfortunately, there is no precise definition of the term. Some academics argue that the price movement in the figure is consistent with rationality. Prices rose initially, they say, because it appeared that the Internet would soon capture a large chunk of international commerce. Prices fell when later evidence suggested this would not occur quite so quickly. However, others argue that the initial rosy scenario was never supported by the facts. Rather, prices rose due to nothing more than "irrational exuberance." Perhaps Prof. Burton Malkiel, author of *A Random Walk Down Wall Street,* said it most colorfully: "We have just lived through the biggest bubble of all time." Malkiel now calls himself a "random walker with a crutch."[24]

Concept
Question

1. **Name five empirical challenges to market efficiency.**

13.7 Reviewing the Differences

It is fair to say that the controversy over efficient capital markets has not yet been resolved. Rather, academic financial economists have sorted themselves into three camps, with some adhering to market efficiency, some believing in behavioral finance, and others (perhaps the majority) not yet convinced that either side has won the argument. This state of affairs is certainly different from, say, 20 years ago, when market efficiency went unchallenged. In addition, the controversy here is perhaps the most contentious of any area of financial economics. Only in this area do grown-up finance professors come close to fisticuffs over an idea.

---

[24]Justin Fox, "Is the Market Rational?" *Fortune* (December 9, 2002), p. 124.

Because of the controversy, it does not appear that our textbook, or any textbook, can easily resolve the differing points of view. However, we can illustrate the differences between the two camps by relating the two psychological principles mentioned earlier, representativeness and conservatism, to stock returns.

Representativeness

This principle implies overweighting the results of small samples, as with the gambler who thinks a few consecutive spins of black on the roulette wheel makes black a more likely outcome than red on the next spin. Financial economists have argued that representativeness leads to *overreaction* in stock returns. We mentioned earlier that financial bubbles are likely overreactions to news. Internet companies showed great revenue growth for a short time in the late 1990s, causing many to believe that this growth would continue indefinitely. Stock prices rose (too much) at this point. When, at last, investors realized that this growth could not be sustained, prices plummeted.

Conservatism

This principle states that individuals adjust their beliefs too slowly to new information. A market composed of this type of investor would likely lead to stock prices that *underreact* in the presence of new information. The example concerning earnings surprises may well illustrate this underreaction. Prices rose slowly following announcements of positive earnings surprises. Announcements of negative surprises had a similar, but opposite, reaction.

The two academic camps have different views of these results. The efficient market believers stress that representativeness and conservatism have opposite implications for stock prices. Which principle, they ask, should dominate in any particular situation? In other words, why should investors overreact to news about Internet stocks but underreact to earnings news? Fama reviewed the academic studies on anomalies, finding that about half of them show overreaction and about half show underreaction.[25] He concludes that this evidence is consistent with the market efficiency hypothesis that anomalies are chance events. In addition, he argues that behavioral finance must do better at specifying which types of information should lead to overreaction and which to underreaction before one rejects market efficiency in favor of behavioral finance.

Adherents of behavioral finance see things a little differently. First, they point out that, as discussed in Section 13.5, the three theoretical foundations of market efficiency appear to be violated in the real world. Second, there are simply too many anomalies, with a number of them being replicated in out-of-sample tests. This argues against anomalies being mere chance events. Finally, though the field has not yet determined why either overreaction and underreaction should dominate in a particular situation, much progress has already been made in a short period of time.[26]

13.8 Implications for Corporate Finance

So far, the chapter has examined both theoretical arguments and empirical evidence concerning efficient markets. We now ask the question: Does market efficiency have any relevance for corporate financial managers? The answer is that it does. Below we consider four implications of efficiency for managers.

---

[25]Fama, Eugene F., "Market Efficiency, Long-Term Returns and Behavioral Finance," *Journal of Financial Economics* 49 (September 1998).

[26]Excellent reviews of this progress can be found in Andrei Shleifer, *Inefficient Markets: An Introduction to Behavioral Finance, op. cit.* and in Nicholas Barberis and Richard Thaler, "A Survey of Behavioral Finance," forthcoming in the *Handbook of the Economics of Finance,* eds. George Constantinides, Milton Harris, and Rene Stulz.

1. Accounting Choices, Financial Choices, and Market Efficiency

The accounting profession provides firms with a significant amount of leeway in their reporting practices. For example, companies may choose between the last-in, first-out (LIFO) or the first-in, first-out (FIFO) method in valuing inventories. They may choose either the percentage-of-completion or the completed-contract method for construction projects. They may depreciate physical assets by either accelerated or straight-line depreciation.

Managers clearly prefer high stock prices to low stock prices. Should managers use the leeway in accounting choices to report the highest possible income? Not necessarily, if markets are efficient. That is, accounting choice should not affect stock price if two conditions hold. First, enough information must be provided in the annual report so that financial analysts can construct earnings under the alternative accounting methods. This appears to be the case for many, though not necessarily all, accounting choices. For example, most skilled analysts can create *pro forma* financial statements under a LIFO assumption if they are provided with actual statements prepared under FIFO. Second, the market must be efficient in the semistrong form. In other words, the market must appropriately use all of this accounting information in determining the market price.

Of course, the issue of whether accounting choice affects stock price is ultimately an empirical matter. A number of academic papers have addressed this issue. Kaplan and Roll found that the switch from accelerated to straight-line depreciation did not affect stock prices.[27] Kaplan and Roll also looked at changes from the deferral method of accounting for the investment tax credit to the flow-through method.[28] They found that a switch would increase accounting earnings but had no effect on stock prices.

Several other accounting procedures have been studied. Hong, Kaplan, and Mandelker found no evidence that the stock market was affected by the artificially higher earnings reported using the pooling method, compared to the purchase method, for reporting mergers and acquisitions.[29] Biddle and Lindahl found that firms switching to the LIFO method of inventory valuation experienced an increase in stock price.[30] This is to be expected in inflationary environments because LIFO valuation can reduce taxes, compared to FIFO. They found that the larger the tax decrease resulting from the use of LIFO, the greater was the increase in stock price. In summary, the above empirical evidence suggests that accounting changes do not fool the market. Therefore, the evidence does not suggest that managers can boost stock price through accounting practices. In other words, the market appears efficient enough to see through different accounting choices.

One caveat is called for here. Our discussion specifically assumed that "financial analysts can construct earnings under the alternative accounting methods." However, companies like Enron, WorldCom, Global Crossing, and Xerox simply reported fraudulent numbers in recent years. There was no way for financial analysts to construct alternative earnings numbers, since these analysts were unaware how the reported numbers were determined. So it was not surprising that the prices of these stocks initially rose well above fair value. Yes, managers can boost prices in this way—as long as they are willing to serve time once they are caught!

Is there anything else that investors can be expected to see through in an efficient market? Consider stock splits and stock dividends. Today Amarillo Corporation has 1 million

---

[27]R. S. Kaplan and R. Roll, "Investor Evaluation of Accounting Information: Some Empirical Evidence," *Journal of Business* 45 (April 1972).

[28]Before 1987, U.S. tax law allowed a 10-percent tax credit on the purchase of most kinds of capital equipment.

[29]H. Hong, R. S. Kaplan, and G. Mandelker, "Pooling vs. Purchase: The Effects of Accounting for Mergers on Stock Prices," *Accounting Review* 53 (1978).

[30]G. C. Biddle and F. W. Lindahl, "Stock Price Reactions to LIFO Adoptions: The Association between Excess Returns and LIFO Tax Savings," *Journal of Accounting Research* (1982).

shares outstanding and reports $10 million of earnings. In the hopes of boosting stock price, the firm's chief financial officer (CFO), Ms. Green, recommends to the board of directors that Amarillo have a 2-for-1 stock split. That is, a shareholder with 100 shares prior to the split would have 200 shares after the split. The CFO contends that each investor would feel richer after the split because he would own more shares.

However, this thinking runs counter to market efficiency. A rational investor knows that he would own the same proportion of the firm after the split as before the split. For example, our investor with 100 shares owns 1/10,000 (100/1 million) of Amarillo's shares prior to the split. His share of the earnings would be $1000 ($10 million/10,000). While he would own 200 shares after the split, there would now be 2 million shares outstanding. Thus, he still would own 1/10,000 of the firm. His share of the earnings would still be $1,000, since the stock split would not affect the earnings of the entire firm.

2. The Timing Decision

Imagine a firm whose managers are contemplating the date to issue equity. This decision is frequently called the *timing* decision. If managers believe that their stock is overpriced, they are likely to issue equity immediately. Here, they are creating value for their current stockholders because they are selling stock for more than it is worth. Conversely, if the managers believe that their stock is underpriced, they are more likely to wait, hoping that the stock price will eventually rise to its true value.

However, if markets are efficient, securities are always correctly priced. Since efficiency implies that stock is sold for its true worth, the timing decision becomes unimportant. Figure 13.12 shows three possible stock price adjustments to the issuance of new stock.

Of course, market efficiency is ultimately an empirical issue. Surprisingly, recent research has called market efficiency into question. Ritter presents evidence that the annual

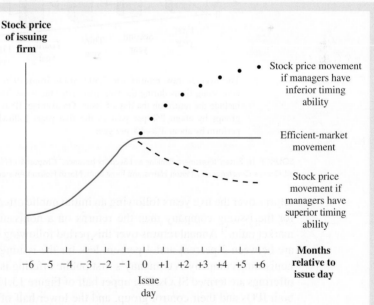

FIGURE 13.12

Three Stock Price Adjustments after Issuing Equity

Studies show that stock is more likely to be issued after stock prices have increased. No inferences on market efficiency can be drawn from this result. Rather, market efficiency implies that the stock price of the issuing firm, on average, neither rises nor falls (relative to stock market indices) *after* issuance of stock.

FIGURE 13.13

Returns on Initial
Public Offerings
(IPOs) and Seasoned
Equity Offerings
(SEOs) in Years
Following Issue

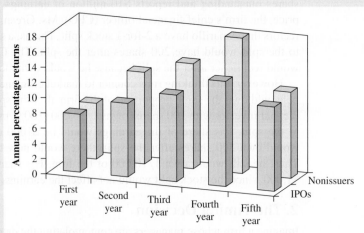

The average raw returns for 7,042 IPOs from 1970–2000 and their matching
nonissuing firms during the five years after the issue. The first-year return does
not include the return on the day of issue.

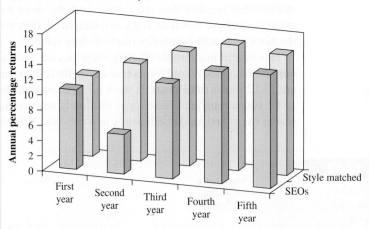

The average raw returns for 7,502 SEOs from 1970–2000 and their matching
nonissuing firms during the five years after the issue. The first-year return does not
include the return on the day of issue. On average, IPOs underperform their control
groups by about 2% per year in the five years following issuance. SEOs underperform by about 3%–4% per year.

SOURCE: Jay Ritter, "Investment Banking and Security Issuance," Chapter 9 of *Handbook of the Economics of Finance,*
ed. George Constantinides, Milton Harris, and Rene Stulz, North Holland: Amsterdam, 2003.

returns over the five years following an initial public offering (IPO) are about 2 percent less
for the issuing company than the returns on a nonissuing company of similar book-to-
market ratio.[31] Annual returns over this period following a seasoned equity offering (SEO)
are between 3 percent and 4 percent less for the issuing company than for a comparable
nonissuing company. A company's first public offering is called an IPO and all subsequent
offerings are termed SEOs. The upper half of Figure 13.13 shows average annual returns of
both IPOs and their control group, and the lower half of the figure shows average annual
returns of both SEOs and their control group.

---

[31]Jay Ritter, "Investment Banking and Security Issuance," Chapter 9 of *Handbook of the Economics of Finance,* ed. George
Constantinides, Milton Harris, and Rene Stulz, North Holland: Amsterdam, 2003.

The evidence in Ritter's paper suggests that corporate managers issue SEOs when the company's stock is overpriced. In other words, managers appear to time the market successfully. The evidence that managers time their IPOs is less compelling, since returns following IPOs are closer to those of their control group.

Does the ability of a corporate official to issue an SEO when the security is overpriced indicate that the market is inefficient in the semistrong form or the strong form? The answer is actually somewhat more complex than it may first appear. On one hand, officials are likely to have special information that the rest of us do not have, suggesting that the market need only be inefficient in the strong form. On the other hand, if the market were truly semistrong efficient, the price would drop immediately and completely upon the announcement of an upcoming SEO. That is, rational investors would realize that stock is being issued, because corporate officials have special information that the stock is overpriced. Indeed, many empirical studies report a price drop on the announcement date. However, Figure 13.13 indicates that there is a further price drop in the subsequent years, suggesting that the market is inefficient in the semistrong form.

If firms can time the issuance of common stock, perhaps they can also time the repurchase of stock. Here, a firm would like to repurchase when its stock is undervalued. Ikenberry, Lakonishok, and Vermaelen find that stock returns of repurchasing firms are abnormally high in the two years following repurchase, suggesting that timing is effective here.[32]

As is always the case, empirical research is never ultimately settled. However, in our opinion, the evidence of the Loughran and Ritter paper and the evidence of the Ikenberry, Lakonishok, and Vermaelen paper, taken together, suggests that managers successfully engage in timing. These papers, if they stand the test of time, constitute evidence against market efficiency.[33]

3. Speculation and Efficient Markets

We normally think of individuals and financial institutions as the primary speculators in financial markets. However, industrial corporations speculate as well. For example, many companies make interest-rate bets. If the managers of a firm believe that interest rates are likely to rise, they have an incentive to borrow, because the present value of the liability will fall with the rate increase. In addition, these managers will have an incentive to borrow long term rather than short term in order to lock in the low rates for a longer period of time. The thinking can get more sophisticated. Suppose that the long-term rate is already higher than the short-term rate. The manager might argue that this differential reflects the market's view that rates will rise. However, perhaps he anticipates a rate increase even greater than what the market anticipates, as implied by the upward-sloping term structure. Again, the manager will want to borrow long term rather than short term.[34]

Firms also speculate in foreign currencies. Suppose that the CFO of a multinational corporation based in the United States believes that the euro will decline relative to the dollar. He would probably issue euro-denominated debt rather than dollar-denominated debt,

---

[32]D. Ikenberry, J. Lakonishok, and T. Vermaelen, "Market Underreaction to Open Market Share Repurchases," *Journal of Financial Economics* (October–November 1995).

[33]There is a vigorous academic debate on Loughran and Ritter's findings. Two papers with contrary conclusions are A. Brav, C. Geczy, and P. A. Gompers, "Is the Abnormal Return Following Equity Issues Anomalous?" *Journal of Financial Economics* 56 (2000), and E. B. Eckbo, R. W. Masulis, and O. Norli, "Seasoned Public Offerings: Resolution of the 'New Issues' Puzzle," *Journal of Financial Economics* 56 (2000). Two papers supporting Loughran and Ritter are D. Ahn and A. Shivdasani, "Long-Term Returns Following Seasoned Equity Issues: Bad Performance or Bad Models," unpublished paper, University of North Carolina (July 1999) and T. Loughran and J. R. Ritter, "Uniformly Least Powerful Tests of Market Efficiency," *Journal of Financial Economics* 5 (March 2000).

[34]Issues such as these concerning the term structure are treated in the appendix to Chapter 5.

Efficient-Market Hypothesis: A Summary

Does Not Say

Prices are uncaused.
Investors are foolish and too stupid to be in the market.
All shares of stock have the same expected returns.
Investors should throw darts to select stocks.
There is no upward trend in stock prices.

Does Say

Prices reflect underlying value.
Financial managers cannot time stock and bond sales.
Managers cannot profitably speculate in foreign currencies.
Managers cannot boost stock prices through creative accounting.

Why Doesn't Everybody Believe It?

There are optical illusions, mirages, and apparent patterns in charts of stock market returns.
The truth is less interesting.
There is evidence against efficiency:

- Two different, but financially identical, classes of stock of same firm selling at different prices.
- Earnings surprises.
- Small versus large stocks.
- Value versus growth stocks.
- Crashes and bubbles.

Three Forms

Weak form (random walk): Current prices reflect past prices; chartism (technical analysis) is useless.
Semistrong form: Prices reflect all public information; most financial analysis is useless.
Strong form: Prices reflect all that is knowable; nobody consistently makes superior profits.

---

since he expects the value of the foreign liability to fall. Conversely, he would issue debt domestically if he believes foreign currencies will appreciate relative to the dollar.[35]

We are perhaps getting a little ahead of our story, since the subtleties of the term structure and foreign debt are treated in other chapters, not this one. However, the big picture question is this: What does market efficiency have to say about the above activity? The answer is quite clear. If financial markets are efficient, managers should not waste their time trying to forecast the movements of interest rates and foreign currencies. Their forecasts will likely be no better than chance. And they will be using up valuable executive time. This is not to say, however, that firms should flippantly pick the maturity or the denomination of their debt in a random fashion. A firm must *choose* these parameters carefully. However, the choice should be based on other rationales, not on an attempt to beat the market. For example, a firm with a project lasting five years might decide to issue five-year debt. A firm might issue yen-denominated debt, because it anticipates expanding into Japan in a big way.

---

[35]Topics such as these are treated in Ch. 31.

The same thinking applies to acquisitions. Many corporations buy up other firms because they think these targets are underpriced. Unfortunately, the empirical evidence suggests that the market is too efficient for this type of speculation to be profitable. And the acquirer never pays just the current market price. The bidding firm must pay a premium above market to induce a majority of shareholders of the target firm to sell their shares. However, this is not to say that firms should never be acquired. Rather, one should consider an acquisition if there are benefits, that is, synergies, from the union. Improved marketing, economies in production, replacement of bad management, and even tax reduction are typical synergies. These synergies are distinct from the perception that the acquired firm is underpriced.

One caveat should be mentioned. We talked earlier about empirical evidence suggesting that SEOs are timed to take advantage of overpriced stock. This makes sense, since managers are likely to know more about their own firm than the market does. However, while managers may very well have special information about their own firm, it is unlikely that they have special information about interest rates, foreign currencies, and other firms. There are simply too many participants in these markets, many of whom are devoting all of their time to forecasting. Managers typically spend most of their time running their own firms, with only a small amount devoted to studying financial markets.

4. Information in Market Prices

The previous section argued that it is quite difficult to forecast future market prices. However, the current and past prices of any asset are known—and of great use. Consider, for example, Becher's study of bank mergers.[36] The author finds that stock prices of acquired banks rise about 23 percent on average upon the first announcement of a merger. This is not surprising, since companies are generally bought out at a premium above current stock price. However, the same study shows that prices of acquiring banks fall almost 5 percent on average upon the same announcement. This is pretty strong evidence that bank mergers do not benefit, and may even hurt, acquiring companies. The reason for this result is unclear, though perhaps acquirers simply overpay for acquisitions. Regardless of the reason, the *implication* is clear. A bank should think deeply before making an acquisition of another bank.

Furthermore, suppose you are the CFO of a company whose stock price drops much more than 5 percent upon announcement of an acquisition. The market is telling you that the merger is quite bad for your firm. Serious consideration should be given to canceling the merger, even if, prior to the announcement, you thought the merger was a good idea.

Of course, mergers are only one type of corporate event. Managers should pay attention to the stock price reaction to any of their announcements, whether it concerns a new venture, a divestiture, a restructuring, or something else.

This is not the only way in which corporations can use the information in market prices. Suppose you are on the board of directors of a company whose stock price has declined precipitously since the current chief executive officer (CEO) was hired. In addition, the prices of competitors have risen over the same time. Though there may be extenuating circumstances, this can be viewed as evidence that the CEO is doing a poor job. Perhaps he should be fired. If this seems harsh, consider that Warner, Watts, and Wruck find a strong negative correlation between managerial turnover and prior stock performance.[37] Figure 13.14 shows that stocks fall on average about 40 percent in price (relative to market movements) in the three years prior to the forced departure of a top manager.

---

[36]David A. Becher, "The Valuation Effects of Bank Mergers," *Journal of Corporate Finance* 6 (2000).

[37]Jerold B. Warner, Ross L. Watts, and Karen H. Wruck, "Stock Prices and Top Management Changes," *Journal of Financial Economics* 20 (1988).

FIGURE 13.14

Stock Performance
Prior to Forced
Departures of
Management

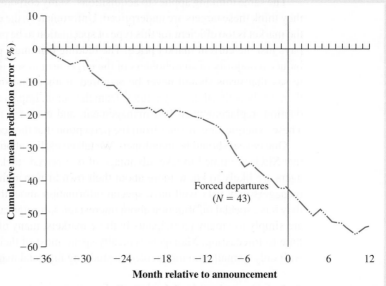

Stock prices decline on average by more than 40% (adjusted for market performance) in
the three years prior to forced departures of management.

SOURCE: Adapted from Figure 1 of Warner, Watts, and Wruck, "Stock Prices and Management Changes," *Journal of Financial Economics* 20 (1988).

If managers are fired for bad stock price performance, perhaps they are rewarded for stock
price appreciation. Hall and Liebman state:

> Our main empirical finding is that CEO wealth often changes by millions of dollars for typical
> changes in firm value. For example, the median total compensation for CEOs is about $1 mil-
> lion if their firm's stock has a 30th percentile annual return (-7.0 percent) and is $5 million if
> the firm's stock has a 70th percentile annual return (20.5 percent). Thus, there is a difference
> of about $4 million in compensation for achieving a moderately above average performance
> relative to a moderately below average performance.[38]

Market efficiency implies that stock prices reflect all available information. We recommend using this information as much as possible in corporate decisions. And at least with
respect to executive firings and executive compensation, it looks as if real world corporations do pay attention to market prices.

Concept
Question

1. **What are four implications of market efficiency for corporate finance?**

13.9 SUMMARY AND CONCLUSIONS

1. An efficient financial market processes the information available to investors and incorporates it
   into the prices of securities. Market efficiency has two general implications. First, in any given time
   period, a stock's abnormal return depends on information or news received by the market in that
   period. Second, an investor who uses the same information as the market cannot expect to earn
   abnormal returns. In other words, systems for playing the market are doomed to fail.

---

[38]Brian J. Hall and Jeffrey B. Liebman, "Are CEOs Really Paid Like Bureaucrats?" *Quarterly Journal of Economics* (August 1998), p. 654.

2. What information does the market use to determine prices? The weak form of the efficient-market hypothesis says that the market uses the past history of prices and is therefore efficient with respect to these past prices. This implies that stock selection based on patterns of past stock-price movements is not better than random stock selection.

3. The semistrong form states that the market uses all publicly available information in setting prices.

4. Strong-form efficiency states that the market uses all of the information that anybody knows about stocks, even inside information.

5. Much evidence from different financial markets supports weak-form and semistrong-form efficiency but not strong-form efficiency.

6. Behavioral finance states that the market is not efficient. Adherents argue that:
   a. Investors are not rational.
   b. Deviations from rationality are similar across investors.
   c. Arbitrage, being costly, will not eliminate inefficiencies.

7. Behaviorists point to many studies, including those showing that small stocks outperform large stocks, value stocks outperform growth stocks, and stock prices adjust slowly to earnings surprises, as empirical confirmation of their beliefs.

8. Four implications of market efficiency for corporate finance are:
   a. Managers cannot fool the market through creative accounting.
   b. Firms cannot successfully time issues of debt and equity.
   c. Managers cannot profitably speculate in foreign currencies and other instruments.
   d. Managers can reap many benefits by paying attention to market prices.

KEY TERMS

bubble theory, *369*

efficient-market hypothesis, *352*

market capitalization, *366*

random walk, *355*

semistrong-form efficiency, *356*

serial correlation, *358*

strong-form efficiency, *356*

weak-form efficiency, *355*

SUGGESTED READINGS

The concept of market efficiency is an important one. Perhaps the classic review articles are

Fama, E. F. "Efficient Capital Markets: A Review of Theory and Empirical Work." *Journal of Finance* (May 1970).

Fama, E. F. "Efficient Capital Markets: II." *Journal of Finance* (December 1991).

Fama, E. F. "Market Efficiency, Long-Term Returns, and Behavioral Finance." *Journal of Financial Economics* (1998).

An entertaining, yet quite informative, book on efficient markets is

Malkiel, B. G. *A Random Walk Down Wall Street.* 7th ed. New York: Norton, 1999.

Two excellent treatments of behavioral finance are:

Shleifer, Andrei. *Inefficient Markets: An Introduction to Behavioral Finance,* Oxford University Press, Oxford, United Kingdom (2000).

Barberis, Nicholas, and Richard Thaler. "A Survey of Behavioral Finance," in the *Handbook of the Economics of Finance,* eds. George Constantinides, Milton Harris, and Rene Stulz. Amsterdam: North Holland, 2003.

QUESTIONS & PROBLEMS

EFFICIENT CAPITAL MARKETS

13.1 a. What rule should a firm follow when making financing decisions?
    b. How can firms create valuable financing opportunities?

13.2 Define the three forms of market efficiency.

13.3 Which of the following statements are true about the efficient-market hypothesis?
    a. It implies perfect forecasting ability.
    b. It implies that prices reflect all available information.
    c. It implies an irrational market.
    d. It implies that prices do not fluctuate.
    e. It results from keen competition among investors.

13.4 Aerotech, an aerospace-technology research firm, announced this morning that it has hired the world's most knowledgeable and prolific space researchers. Before today, Aerotech's stock had been selling for $100. Assume that no other information is received over the next week and the stock market as a whole does not move.

a. What do you expect will happen to Aerotech's stock?

b. Consider the following scenarios:

1. The stock price jumps to $118 on the day of the announcement. In subsequent days it floats up to $123, then falls back to $116.

2. The stock price jumps to $116 and remains at that level.

3. The stock price gradually climbs to $116 over the next week.

Which scenario(s) indicate market efficiency? Which do not? Why?

13.5 When the 56-year-old founder of Gulf & Western, Inc., died of a heart attack, the stock price immediately jumped from $18.00 a share to $20.25, a 12.5 percent increase. This is evidence of market inefficiency, because an efficient stock market would have anticipated his death and adjusted the price beforehand. Assume that no other information is received and the stock market as a whole does not move. Is this statement true or false? Explain.

13.6 On January 10, 1985, the following announcement was made: "Early today the Justice Department reached a decision in the Universal Product Care (UPC) case. UPC has been found guilty of discriminatory practices in hiring. For the next five years, UPC must pay $2 million each year to a fund representing victims of UPC's policies." Should investors not buy UPC stock after the announcement because the litigation will cause an abnormally low rate of return? Assume market efficiency. Explain.

13.7 Newtech Corp. is going to adopt a new chip-testing device that can greatly improve its production efficiency. Do you think the lead engineer can profit from purchasing the firm's stock before the news release on the device? After reading the announcement in *The Wall Street Journal,* should you be able to earn an abnormal return from purchasing the stock? Assume market efficiency.

13.8 Trans Trust Corp. has changed how it accounts for inventory. Taxes are unaffected, although the resulting earnings report released this quarter is 20 percent higher than what it would have been under the old accounting system. There is no other surprise in the earnings report and the change in the accounting treatment was publicly announced. Assume market efficiency. Will the stock price be higher when the market learns that the reported earnings are higher?

13.9 A hypothetical study has documented that firms usually experience a period of price run-up before their public stock offerings. After reading this study, Alex Johnson invests in firms that have just carried out new stock offerings. Based on the study's conclusion that these firms have generally performed very well before the stock offering, can Alex make money using this strategy if market efficiency holds?

13.10 The Durkin Investing Agency has been the best stock picker for the past two years. Before the rise to fame occurred, the Durkin newsletter had 200 subscribers. Those subscribers beat the market consistently, earning substantially higher returns after adjustment for risk and transaction costs. Subscriptions have skyrocketed to 10,000. Now, when the Durkin Investing Agency recommends a stock, the stock price instantly rises several points. The subscribers currently earn only a normal return when they buy recommended stock because the price rises before anybody can act on the information. Briefly explain this phenomenon. Is Durkin's ability to pick stocks consistent with market efficiency?

13.11 Your broker commented that well-managed firms are better investments than poorly managed firms. As evidence, your broker cited a recent study examining 100 small manufacturing firms that, eight years earlier, had been listed in an industry magazine as the best-managed small manufacturers in the country. In the ensuing eight years, the 100 firms have not earned more than the normal market return. Your broker continued to say that if the firms were well managed, they should have produced better-than-average returns. Assume market efficiency. Do you agree with your broker?

13.12 A famous economist just announced in *The Wall Street Journal* his findings that the recession is over and the economy is again entering an expansion. Assume market efficiency. Can you profit from investing in the stock market after you read this announcement?

13.13 Some investors claim to observe patterns in stock market prices. Are such patterns consistent with the efficient markets hypothesis? If so, what form of market efficiency is violated?

13.14 Suppose the market is semistrong-form efficient. Can you expect to earn excess returns if you make trades based on:
   a. Your broker's information about record earnings for a stock?
   b. Rumors about a merger of a firm?
   c. Yesterday's announcement of a successful new product test?

13.15 Imagine that a particular macroeconomic variable that influences your firm's net earnings is positively serially correlated. Assume market efficiency. Would you expect price changes in your stock to be serially correlated? Why or why not?

13.16 The efficient markets hypothesis implies that all mutual funds should obtain the same expected risk-adjusted returns. Therefore, we can simply pick mutual funds at random. Is this statement true or false? Explain.

13.17 Assume that markets are efficient. During a trading day, American Golf Inc. announces that it has lost a contract for a large golfing project, which, prior to the news, was widely believed to have been secured. How should the stock price react to this information if no additional information is released?
   a. The share price will decrease over an extended period of time as investors begin to sell shares of the company.
   b. The share price will decrease below fair value because of the greatly decreased demand for the shares. Eventually, the price would rise back to the correct level.
   c. The share price will decrease immediately to reflect the new information.
   d. More information is needed to determine the movement in the stock price.

13.18 Prospectors, Inc., is a publicly traded gold-prospecting company in Alaska. Although the firm's searches for gold usually fail, the prospectors occasionally find a rich vein of ore. Assume efficient markets. What pattern would you expect to observe for Prospector's cumulative abnormal returns?

THE EVIDENCE

13.19 Some people argue that the efficient markets hypothesis cannot explain the 1987 market crash or the high price-to-earnings ratio of Internet stocks during the late 1990s. What alternative hypothesis is currently used for these two phenomena?

13.20 Delta, United, and American Airlines announced purchases of planes on July 18 (7/18), February 12 (2/12), and October 7 (10/7), respectively. Given the information below, calculate the cumulative abnormal return (CAR) for these stocks as a group. Graph the result and

| | **DELTA** | | | **UNITED** | | | **AMERICAN** | |
Date	Market Return	Company Return	Date	Market Return	Company Return	Date	Market Return	Company Return
7/12	−0.3	−0.5	2/8	−0.9	−1.1	10/1	0.5	0.3
7/13	0.0	0.2	2/9	−1.0	−1.1	10/2	0.4	0.6
7/16	0.5	0.7	2/10	0.4	0.2	10/3	1.1	1.1
7/17	−0.5	−0.3	2/11	0.6	0.8	10/6	0.1	−0.3
7/18	−2.2	1.1	2/12	−0.3	−0.1	10/7	−2.2	−0.3
7/19	−0.9	−0.7	2/15	1.1	1.2	10/8	0.5	0.5
7/20	−1.0	−1.1	2/16	0.5	0.5	10/9	−0.3	−0.2
7/23	0.7	0.5	2/17	−0.3	−0.2	10/10	0.3	0.1
7/24	0.2	0.1	2/18	0.3	0.2	10/13	0.0	−0.1

provide an explanation. All of the stocks have a beta of one and no other announcements are made.

13.21 The following diagram shows the cumulative abnormal returns (CAR) for 386 oil-exploration companies announcing oil discoveries over the period from 1950 to 1980. Month 0 in the diagram is the announcement month. Assume that no other information is received and the stock market as a whole does not move. Is the diagram consistent with market efficiency? Why or why not?

Time in months relative to event month

13.22 The following figures present the results of four cumulative abnormal returns (CAR) studies. Indicate whether the results of each study support, reject, or are inconclusive about the semistrong form of the efficient-market hypothesis. In each figure, time 0 is the date of an event.

a.

b.

c.

d.

13.23 A study analyzed the behavior of the stock prices of firms that had lost antitrust cases. Included in the diagram are all firms that lost the initial court decision, even if the decision was later overturned on appeal. The event at time 0 is the initial, preappeal court decision.

Assume no other information was released, aside from that disclosed in the initial trial. The stock prices all have a beta of one. Is the diagram consistent with market efficiency? Why or why not?

Long-Term Financing: *An Introduction*

EXECUTIVE SUMMARY

This chapter introduces the basic sources of long-term financing: common stock, preferred stock, and long-term debt. Later chapters discuss these topics in more detail. Perhaps no other area of corporate finance is more perplexing to new students of finance than corporate securities such as shares of stock, bonds, and debentures. Whereas the concepts are simple and logical, the language is strange and unfamiliar.

The purpose of this chapter is to describe the basic features of long-term financing. We begin with a look at common stock, preferred stock, and long-term debt and then briefly consider patterns of the different kinds of long-term financing. Discussion of nonbasic forms of long-term finance, such as convertibles and leases, is reserved for later chapters.

14.1 Common Stock

The term **common stock** has no precise meaning. It is usually applied to stock that has no special preference in either dividends or in bankruptcy. A description of the common stock of Anheuser-Busch in 2002 is presented below.

ANHEUSER-BUSCH
Common Stock and Other Shareholder's Equity
December 31, 2002
(in millions)

Common stock, $1 par value, authorized 1.6 billion shares, issued 1,453.4 million shares	$ 1,453.4
Capital in excess of par value	1,024.5
Retained earnings	12,544.0
Treasury stock, at cost	(11,008.6)
Other	
ESOP debt guarantee	(90.3)
Foreign currency translation adjustment	(870.7)
Total equity	**$3,052.3**

Par and No-Par Stock

Owners of common stock in a corporation are referred to as *shareholders* or *stockholders*. They receive stock certificates for the *shares* they own. There is usually a stated value on each stock certificate called the *par value*. However, some stocks have no par value. The par value of each share of the common stock of Anheuser-Busch is $1.

The total par value is the number of shares issued multiplied by the par value of each share and is sometimes referred to as the *dedicated capital* of a corporation. The dedicated capital of Anheuser-Busch is $1 \times 1,453.4$ million shares = $1,453.4 million.

Authorized versus Issued Common Stock

Shares of common stock are the fundamental ownership units of the corporation. The articles of incorporation of a new corporation must state the number of shares of common stock the corporation is authorized to issue.

The board of directors of the corporation, after a vote of the shareholders, can amend the articles of incorporation to increase the number of shares authorized; there is no limit to the number of shares that can be authorized. In 2002 Anheuser-Busch had authorized 1.6 billion shares and had issued 1,453.4 million shares. There is no requirement that all of the authorized shares actually be issued. Although there are no legal limits to authorizing shares of stock, some practical considerations may exist.

1. Some states impose taxes based on the number of authorized shares.
2. Authorizing a large number of shares may create concern on the part of investors, because authorized shares can be issued later *with* the approval of the board of directors but without a vote of the shareholders.

Capital Surplus

Capital surplus usually refers to amounts of directly contributed equity capital in excess of the par value.

EXAMPLE

Suppose 100 shares of common stock have a par value of $2 each and are sold to shareholders for $10 per share. The capital surplus would be ($10 − $2) × 100 = $8 × 100 = $800, and the total par value would be $2 × 100 = $200. What difference does it make if the total capital contribution is reported as par value or capital surplus?

About the only difference is that in most states the par value is locked in and cannot be distributed to stockholders except upon the liquidation of the corporation.

The capital surplus of Anheuser-Busch is $1,024.5 million. This figure indicates that the price of new shares issued by Anheuser-Busch has exceeded the par value and the difference has been entered as *capital in excess of par value*. In most states shares of stock cannot be issued below par value, implying that capital in excess of par value cannot be negative.

Retained Earnings

Anheuser-Busch usually pays out less than one half of its net income as dividends; the rest is retained in the business and is called **retained earnings.** The cumulative amount of retained earnings (since original incorporation) was $12,544 million in 2002.

The sum of the par value, capital surplus, and accumulated retained earnings is the *common equity* of the firm which is usually referred to as the firm's **book value.** The book value represents the amount contributed directly and indirectly to the corporation by equity investors.

EXAMPLE

Suppose Western Redwood Corporation was formed in 1906 with 10,000 shares of stock issued and sold at its $1 par value. Because the stock was sold for $1, the first balance sheet showed a zero amount for capital surplus. By 2002 the company had become very profitable and had retained profits of $100,000. The stockholders' equity of Western Redwood Corporation in 2002 is as follows:

WESTERN REDWOOD CORPORATION
Equity Accounts
January 1, 2002

Common stock, $1 par, 10,000 shares outstanding	$ 10,000
Capital surplus	0
Retained earnings	100,000
Total stockholders' equity	$110,000

$$\text{Book value per share} = \frac{\$110,000}{10,000} = \$11$$

Suppose the company has profitable investment opportunities and decides to sell 10,000 shares of new stock. The current market price is $20 per share. The effect of the sale of stock on the balance sheet at the end of the year will be

WESTERN REDWOOD CORPORATION
Equity Accounts
December 31, 2002

Common stock, $1 par, 20,000 shares outstanding	$ 20,000
Capital surplus ($20 − $1) × 10,000 shares	190,000
Retained earnings	100,000
Total stockholders' equity	$310,000

$$\text{Book value per share} = \frac{\$310,000}{20,000} = \$15.5$$

What happened?

1. Because 10,000 shares of new stock were issued with par value of $1, the par value rose $10,000.
2. The total amount raised by the new issue was $20 × 10,000 = $200,000, and $190,000 was entered into capital surplus.
3. The book value per share increased because the market price of the new stock was higher than the book value of the old stock.

Market Value, Book Value, and Replacement Value

The book value of Anheuser-Busch in 2002 was $3,052.3 million. This figure is based on the number of shares outstanding. The company had issued 1,453.4 million shares and bought back approximately 617.4 million shares, so that the total number of outstanding shares was 1,453.4 million − 617.4 million = 836 million. The shares bought back are called *treasury stock.*

The book value per share was equal to:

$$\frac{\text{Total common shareholders' equity}}{\text{Shares outstanding}} = \frac{\$3052.3 \text{ million}}{836 \text{ million}} = \$3.65$$

Anheuser-Busch is a publicly owned company. Its common stock trades on the New York Stock Exchange (NYSE), and thousands of shares change hands every day. The recent market prices of Anheuser-Busch were between $49 and $52 per share. Thus the market prices were above the book value.

In addition to market and book values, you may hear the term *replacement value*. This refers to the current cost of replacing the assets of the firm. Market, book, and replacement value are equal at the time when a firm purchases an asset. After that time, these values will diverge. The *market-to-book-value* ratio of common stock and *Tobin's Q* (market value of assets/replacement value of assets) introduced in the appendix to Chapter 2 are indicators of the success of the firm. A market-to-book or Tobin's Q ratio greater than 1 indicates the firm has done well with its investment decisions.

Shareholders' Rights

The conceptual structure of the corporation assumes that shareholders elect directors who in turn elect corporate officers—more generally, the management—to carry out their directives. It is the right to elect the directors of the corporation by vote that constitutes the most important control device of shareholders.

Directors are elected each year at an annual meeting by a vote of the holders of a majority of shares who are present and entitled to vote. The exact mechanism for electing directors differs among different companies. The most important difference is whether shares must be voted cumulatively or must be voted straight.

EXAMPLE	Imagine that a corporation has two shareholders: Smith with 25 shares and Marshall with 75 shares. Both want to be on the board of directors. Marshall does not want Smith to be a director. Let us assume that there are four directors to be elected and each shareholder nominates four candidates.

Cumulative Voting   The effect of **cumulative voting** is to permit minority participation. If cumulative voting is permitted, the total number of votes that each shareholder may cast is determined first. That number is usually calculated as the number of shares (owned or controlled) multiplied by the number of directors to be elected. Each shareholder can distribute these votes as he or she wishes over one or more candidates. Smith will get $25 \times 4 = 100$ votes, and Marshall is entitled to $75 \times 4 = 300$ votes. If Smith gives all his votes to himself, he is assured of a directorship. It is not possible for Marshall to divide 300 votes among the four candidates in such a way as to preclude Smith's election to the board.

Straight Voting   If **straight voting** is permitted, Smith may cast 25 votes for each candidate and Marshall may cast 75 votes for each. As a consequence, Marshall will elect all of the candidates.

Straight voting can freeze out minority shareholders; that is the reason many states have mandatory cumulative voting. In states where cumulative voting is mandatory, devices have been worked out to minimize its impact. One such device is to *stagger* the voting for the board of directors. Staggering permits a fraction of the directorships to come to a vote at a particular time. It has two basic effects:

1. Staggering makes it more difficult for a minority to elect a director when there is cumulative voting.

2. Staggering makes successful takeover attempts less likely by making the election of new directors more difficult.

Proxy Voting   A **proxy** is the legal grant of authority by a shareholder to someone else to vote his or her shares. For convenience, the actual voting in large public corporations usually is done by proxy.

Many companies such as Anheuser-Busch have hundreds of thousands of shareholders. Shareholders can come to the annual meeting and vote in person, or they can transfer their right to vote to another party by proxy.

Obviously, management always tries to get as many proxies transferred to it as possible. However, if shareholders are not satisfied with management, an outside group of shareholders can try to obtain as many votes as possible via proxy. They can vote to replace management by adding enough directors. This is called a *proxy fight*.

Other Rights   The value of a share of common stock in a corporation is directly related to the general rights of shareholders. In addition to the right to vote for directors, shareholders usually have the following rights:

1. The right to share proportionally in dividends paid.
2. The right to share proportionally in assets remaining after liabilities have been paid in a liquidation.
3. The right to vote on matters of great importance to stockholders, such as a merger, usually decided at the annual meeting or a special meeting.
4. The right to share proportionally in any new stock sold. This is called the *preemptive right* and will be discussed in detail in later chapters.

Dividends

A distinctive feature of corporations is that they issue shares of stock and are authorized by law to pay dividends to the holders of those shares. **Dividends** paid to shareholders represent a return on the capital directly or indirectly contributed to the corporation by the shareholders. The payment of dividends is at the discretion of the board of directors.

Here are some important characteristics of dividends:

1. Unless a dividend is declared by the board of directors of a corporation, it is not a liability of the corporation. A corporation cannot *default* on an undeclared dividend. As a consequence, corporations cannot become *bankrupt* because of nonpayment of dividends. The amount of the dividend—and even whether or not it is paid—are decisions based on the business judgment of the board of directors.
2. The payment of dividends by the corporation is not a business expense. Dividends are not deductible for corporate tax purposes. In short, dividends are paid out of after-tax profits of the corporation.
3. Dividends received by individual shareholders are for the most part considered ordinary income by the IRS and are fully taxable. However, corporations that own stock in other corporations are permitted to exclude 70 percent of the amounts they receive as dividends. In other words, they are taxed only on the remaining 30 percent.

Classes of Stock

Some firms issue more than one class of common stock. The classes are usually created with unequal voting rights. The Ford Motor Company has Class B common stock, which is not publicly traded (it is held by Ford family interests and trusts). This class has about 40 percent of the voting power, but these shares comprise only about 15 percent of the total outstanding stock.

Many companies issue dual classes of common stock. The reason has to do with control of the firm. Management of a firm can raise equity capital by issuing nonvoting common stock while maintaining voting control. Harry and Linda DeAngelo found that managements' holdings of common stock are usually tilted toward the stock with the superior voting rights.[1] Thus, managerial vote ownership is an important element of corporate control structure.

Lease, McConnell, and Mikkelson found the market prices of stocks with superior voting rights to be about 5 percent higher than the prices of otherwise identical stocks with inferior voting rights.[2] However, DeAngelo and DeAngelo found some evidence that the market value of differences in voting rights may be much higher when control of the firm is involved.

Concept
Questions

1. **What is a company's book value?**
2. **What rights do stockholders have?**
3. **What is a proxy?**

14.2 Corporate Long-Term Debt: The Basics

Securities issued by corporations may be classified roughly as *equity* securities and *debt* securities. The distinction between equity and debt is basic to much of the modern theory and practice of corporate finance.

At its crudest level, debt represents something that must be repaid; it is the result of borrowing money. When corporations borrow, they promise to make regularly scheduled interest payments and to repay the original amount borrowed (that is, the *principal*). The person or firm making the loan is called a *creditor* or *lender.*

Interest versus Dividends

The corporation borrowing the money is called a *debtor* or *borrower.* The amount owed the creditor is a liability of the corporation; however, it is a liability of limited value. The corporation can legally default at any time on its liability.[3] This can be a valuable option. The creditors benefit if the assets have a value greater than the value of the liability, but this would happen only if management were foolish. On the other hand, the corporation and the equity investors benefit if the value of the assets is less than the value of the liabilities, because equity investors are able to walk away from the liabilities and default on their payment.

From a financial point of view, the main differences between debt and equity are the following:

1. Debt is not an ownership interest in the firm. Creditors do not usually have voting power. The device used by creditors to protect themselves is the loan contract (that is, the *indenture*).

2. The corporation's payment of interest on debt is considered a cost of doing business and is fully tax-deductible. Thus interest expense is paid out to creditors before the corporate tax liability is computed. Dividends on common and preferred stock are paid to shareholders after the tax liability has been determined. Dividends are considered a return to shareholders on their contributed capital. Because interest expense can be used

---

[1]H. DeAngelo and L. DeAngelo, "Managerial Ownership of Voting Rights: A Study of Public Corporations with Dual Classes of Common Stock," *Journal of Financial Economics* 14 (1985).

[2]R. C. Lease, J. J. McConnell, and W. H. Mikkelson, "The Market Value of Control in Publicly Traded Corporations," *Journal of Financial Economics* (April 1983).

[3]In practice, creditors can make a claim against the assets of the firm and a court will administer the legal remedy.

to reduce taxes, the government (that is, the IRS) is providing a direct tax subsidy on the use of debt when compared to equity. This point is discussed in detail in the next two chapters.

3. Unpaid debt is a liability of the firm. If it is not paid, the creditors can legally claim the assets of the firm. This action may result in *liquidation* and *bankruptcy.* Thus one of the costs of issuing debt is the possibility of *financial failure,* which does not arise when equity is issued.

Is It Debt or Equity?

Sometimes it is not clear whether a particular security is debt or equity. For example, suppose a 50-year bond is issued with interest payable solely from corporate income if and only if earned, and repayment is subordinate to all other debts of the business. Corporations are very adept at creating hybrid securities that look like equity but are called *debt.* Obviously, the distinction between debt and equity is important for tax purposes. When corporations try to create a debt security that is really equity, they are trying to obtain the tax benefits of debt while eliminating its bankruptcy costs.

Basic Features of Long-Term Debt

Long-term corporate debt usually is denominated in units of $1,000 called the *principal* or *face value.*[4] Long-term debt is a promise by the borrowing firm to repay the principal amount by a certain date, called the *maturity date.* Long-term debt almost always has a par value equal to the face value, and debt price is often expressed as a percentage of the par value. For example, it might be said that General Motors debt is selling at 90, which means that a bond with a par value of $1,000 can be purchased for $900. In this case the debt is selling at a discount because the market price is less than the par value. Debt can also sell at a premium with respect to par value. The borrower using long-term debt generally pays interest at a rate expressed as a fraction of par value. Thus, at $1,000 par value, General Motors' 7-percent debt means that $70 of interest is paid to holders of the debt, usually in semiannual installments (for example, $35 on June 30 and December 31). The payment schedules are in the form of coupons that are detached from the debt certificates and sent to the company for payment.

Different Types of Debt

Typical debt securities are called *notes, debentures,* or *bonds.* A debenture is an unsecured corporate debt, whereas a bond is secured by a mortgage on the corporate property. However, in common usage the word *bond* is used indiscriminately and often refers to both secured and unsecured debt. A note usually refers to an unsecured debt with a maturity shorter than that of a debenture, perhaps under 10 years.

Debentures and bonds are long-term debt. *Long-term debt* is any obligation that is payable more than one year from the date it was originally issued. Sometimes long-term debt—debentures and bonds—is called *funded debt.* Debt that is due in less than one year is unfunded and is accounted for as a current liability. Some debt is perpetual and has no specific maturity. This type of debt is referred to as a *consol.*

---

[4]Many government bonds have larger principal denominations, up to $10,000 or $25,000, and most municipal bonds come in denominations of $5,000.

Repayment

Long-term debt is typically repaid in regular amounts over the life of the debt. The payment of long-term debt by installments is called *amortization.* At the end of the amortization the entire indebtedness is said to be *extinguished.* Amortization is typically arranged by a *sinking fund.* Each year the corporation places money into a sinking fund, and the money is used to buy back the bonds.

Debt may be extinguished before maturity by a call. Historically, almost all publicly issued corporate long-term debt has been *callable.*[5] These are debentures or bonds for which the firm has the right to pay a specific amount, the *call price,* to retire (extinguish) the debt before the stated maturity date. The call price is always higher than the par value of the debt. Debt that is callable at 105 is debt that the firm can buy back from the holder at a price of $1,050 per debenture or bond, regardless of what the market value of the debt might be. Call prices are always specified when the debt is originally issued. However, lenders are given a 5-year to 10-year call-protection period during which the debt cannot be called away. Recently there has been a higher incidence of noncallable offerings.

Seniority

In general terms **seniority** indicates preference in position over other lenders. Some debt is **subordinated.** In the event of default, holders of subordinated debt must give preference to other specified creditors. Usually, this means that the subordinated lenders will be paid off only after the specified creditors have been compensated. However, debt cannot be subordinated to equity.

Security

Security is a form of attachment to property; it provides that the property can be sold in the event of default to satisfy the debt for which security is given. A mortgage is used for security in tangible property; for example, debt can be secured by mortgages on plant and equipment. Holders of such debt have prior claim on the mortgaged assets in case of default. Debentures are not secured by a mortgage. Thus, if mortgaged property is sold in the event of default, debenture holders will obtain something only if the mortgage bondholders have been fully satisfied.

Indenture

The written agreement between the corporate debt issuer and the lender, setting forth maturity date, interest rate, and all other terms, is called an *indenture.* We treat this in detail in later chapters. For now, we note that

1. The indenture completely describes the nature of the indebtedness.
2. It lists all restrictions placed on the firm by the lenders. These restrictions are placed in *restrictive covenants.*

Some typical restrictive covenants are the following:

1. Restrictions on further indebtedness.
2. A maximum on the amount of dividends that can be paid.
3. A minimum level of working capital.

---

[5]When issued, callable industrial corporate debt typically has 10-year protection against being called.

EXAMPLE

The following table shows some of the many long-term debt securities of Anheuser-Busch at the end of 2002 (in millions).

U.S. dollar notes due 2003 to 2013, interest rates from 4.375% to 7.5%	$2,100.0
U.S. dollar debentures due 2009 to 2043, interest rates from 5.95% to 9.0%.	3,150.0
EuroNotes due 2004 to 2006, interest rates from 4.51% to 6.5%	351.0
Medium-term notes due 2010, interest rate 5.625%	200.0
Commercial paper, interest rates of 1.24% and 2.3%, respectively, at year-end	412.9
Industrial revenue bonds, weighted average interest rates of 6.11% and 6.03%, respectively	270.1
ESOP note guarantee due 2004, interest rate 8.25%	90.3
Miscellaneous items	48.0
Unamortized debt discounts	(19.1)
Total debt.	$6,603.2

Anheuser-Busch has many different notes and debentures. As can be seen, there is $412.9 billion of commercial paper. Commercial paper refers to short-term unsecured notes. It is listed as long-term debt because it will be maintained on a long-term basis by "rolling it over." Anheuser-Busch has $5.25 billion in U.S. dollar notes and debentures. There is also a $90.3 million guarantee of employee stock option plan (ESOP) debt.

Concept
Questions

1. **What is corporate debt? Describe its general features.**
2. **Why is it sometimes difficult to tell whether a particular security is debt or equity?**

14.3 Preferred Stock

Preferred stock represents equity of a corporation, but it is different from common stock because it has preference over common stock in the payment of dividends and in the assets of the corporation in the event of bankruptcy. *Preference* means only that the holder of the preferred share must receive a dividend (in the case of an ongoing firm) before holders of common shares are entitled to anything.

Stated Value

Preferred shares have a stated liquidating value, usually $100 per share. The dividend preference is described in terms of dollars per share. For example, General Motors "$5 preferred" translates into a dividend yield of 5 percent of stated value.

Cumulative and Noncumulative Dividends

A preferred dividend is not like interest on a bond. The board of directors may decide not to pay the dividends on preferred shares, and their decision may not have anything to do with current net income of the corporation. Dividends payable on preferred stock are either *cumulative* or *noncumulative*. If preferred dividends are cumulative and are not paid in a particular year, they will be carried forward. Usually both the cumulated (past) preferred dividends plus the current preferred dividends must be paid before the common shareholders can receive anything. Unpaid preferred dividends are *not* debts of the firm. Directors elected by the common shareholders can defer preferred dividends indefinitely. However, if so,

1. Common shareholders must forgo dividends.
2. Though holders of preferred shares do not always have voting rights, they will typically be granted these rights if preferred dividends have not been paid for some time.

Because preferred stockholders receive no interest on the cumulated dividends, some have argued that firms have an incentive to delay paying preferred dividends.

Is Preferred Stock Really Debt?

A good case can be made that preferred stock is really debt in disguise. Preferred shareholders receive a stated dividend only, and if the corporation is liquidated, preferred shareholders get a stated value. In recent years, many new issues of preferred stock have had obligatory sinking funds.

For all these reasons, preferred stock seems like debt, but, unlike debt, preferred stock dividends cannot be deducted as interest expense when determining taxable corporate income. From the individual investor's point of view, preferred dividends are ordinary income for tax purposes. For corporate investors, however, 70 percent of the amounts they receive as dividends from preferred stock are exempt from income taxes.

The yields on preferred stock are typically very low. For example, Citigroup has a Series F preferred stock with a stated $3.18 dividend. This dividend is perpetual, that is, it will be paid each year by Citigroup forever unless called. However, holders of Series F preferred stock have no voting rights. Recently, the market price of the Citigroup preferred stock was $55. The current dividend yield on the Citigroup preferred of 5.8 percent ($3.18/55) was slightly more than U.S. government bond yields on the same date. In fact, it was less than the yield on Citigroup's long-term debt.

Corporate investors have an incentive to hold the preferred stock issued by other corporations over holding their debt because of the 70-percent income tax exemption they receive on preferred stock dividends. Because of this tax exclusion, corporate investors pay a premium for preferred stock; as a consequence, the yields are low. Because individual investors do not receive this tax break, most preferred stock in the United States is owned by corporate investors.

Thus, there are two offsetting tax effects to consider in evaluating preferred stock:

a. Dividends are not deducted from corporate income in computing the tax liability of the issuing corporation. This is the bad news.

b. When a corporation purchases preferred stock, 70 percent of the dividends received are exempt from corporate taxation. This is the good news.

The Preferred-Stock Puzzle

Effect (a) above represents a clear tax disadvantage to the issuance of preferred stock. While (b) represents a tax advantage, both academics and practitioners generally agree that (b) does *not* fully offset (a). In addition, preferred stock requires a regular dividend payment and thus lacks the flexibility of common stock. For these reasons, some have argued that preferred stock should not exist.

Why then do firms issue preferred stock? While the nondeductibility of dividends from taxable corporate income is the most serious obstacle to issuing preferred stock, there are several reasons why preferred stock is issued.

1. Because of the way utility rates are determined in regulatory environments, regulated public utilities can pass the tax disadvantage of issuing preferred stock on to their customers. Consequently, a substantial amount of straight preferred stock is issued by utilities.

2. Companies reporting losses to the IRS may issue preferred stock. Because they have no taxable income from which interest on debt can be deducted, preferred stock imposes no tax penalty relative to debt. In other words, (a) does not apply.

Equity versus Debt

Feature	Equity	Debt
Income	Dividends	Interest
Tax status	Dividends are taxed as personal income. Dividends are not a business expense.	Interest is taxed as personal income. Interest is a business expense, and corporations can deduct interest when computing corporate tax liability.
Control	Common stock and preferred stock usually have voting rights.	Control is exercised with loan agreement.
Default	Firms cannot be forced into bankruptcy for nonpayment of dividends.	Unpaid debt is a liability of the firm. Nonpayment results in bankruptcy.

Bottom line: Tax status favors debt, but default favors equity. Control features of debt and equity are different, but one is not better than the other.

3. Firms issuing preferred stock can avoid the threat of bankruptcy that exists with debt financing. Unpaid preferred dividends are not debts of a corporation, and preferred shareholders cannot force a corporation into bankruptcy because of unpaid dividends.

Concept Questions

1. What is preferred stock?
2. Do you think it is more like debt or equity?
3. What are three reasons why preferred stock is issued?

14.4 Patterns of Financing

Firms use cash flow for capital spending and net working capital. Historically, U.S. firms have spent about 80 percent of cash flow on capital spending and 20 percent on net working capital. Table 14.1 summarizes the patterns of long-term financing for U.S. industrial firms from 1991 to 2002. Here we observe **internal financing**, debt financing, and external equity financing as a percentage of total financing. For example, in 2001 capital spending by U.S. industrial firms was $855.2 billion and increases in net working capital were $127.8 billion. In other words, total business investment spending was $983 billion (855.2 + 127.8 = 983). Capital spending was 855.2/983 = 87% of the total, whereas net working capital was 127.8/983 = 13% of the total.

In 2001, U.S. industrial firms generated $776.6 billion of internal cash flow. Because total business spending exceeded internally generated cash flow (i.e., 983 > 776.6), there was a *financial gap*. This is very typical of U.S. business finance. The financial gap in 2001 was $206.4 billion (i.e., 983 − 776.6 = 206.4). The financial gap is made up by external financing. The financial gap was 21% of total business spending, because internal cash flow was only 79% of total business spending.

One of the challenges of the financial manager is to finance the gap. In 2001, this meant issuing $255.6 billion of new debt because net new equity actually shrank (by $49.3 billion) due to stock buybacks. Figure 14.1 charts these patterns of finance.

Internal financing comes from internally generated cash flow and is defined as net income plus depreciation minus dividends. External financing is net new debt and new shares of equity net of buybacks.

TABLE 14.1	Historical U.S. Financing Patterns (percent), 1991 to 2002											
	1991	1992	1993	1994	1995	1996	1997	1998	1999	2000	2001	2002
Uses of funds (investments)												
Capital spending	96%	77%	74%	72%	66%	80%	71%	83%	81%	89%	87%	98%
Net working capital and other	4%	23%	26%	28%	34%	20%	29%	17%	19%	11%	13%	2%
Total uses %	100%	100%	100%	100%	100%	100%	100%	100%	100%	100%	100%	100%
Total uses (in billions)	$387.40	$499.70	$548.00	$647.40	$789.30	$726.00	$849.60	$909.90	$1,024.40	$1,003.20	$983.00	$815.20
Sources of funds												
Internal financing	109%	88%	88%	85%	77%	87%	79%	79%	74%	74%	79%	97%
External financing	−9%	12%	12%	15%	23%	13%	21%	21%	26%	26%	21%	3%
New debt	−14%	7%	8%	22%	31%	23%	35%	45%	37%	38%	26%	8%
New equity	5%	5%	4%	−7%	−7%	−10%	−13%	−24%	−11%	−12%	−5%	−5%

SOURCE: Board of Governors of the Federal Reserve System, *Flow of Funds Accounts*. www.federalreserve.gov/release/21/current/data.htm

FIGURE 14.1

Financing Decisions
by U.S. Nonfinancial
Corporations

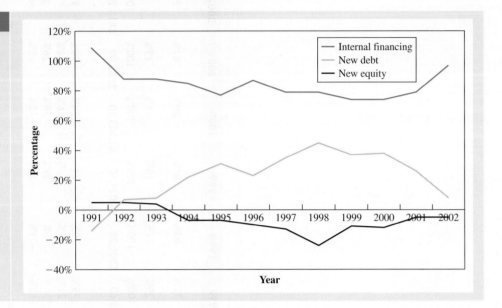

Several features of long-term financing seem clear from Table 14.1.

1. Internally generated cash flow has dominated as a source of financing. Typically, between 70 and 90 percent of long-term financing comes from cash flows that corporations generate internally.

2. Typically, total firm spending is greater than internally generated cash flow. A financial deficit is created by the difference between total firm spending and internally generated cash flow. For example, 79 percent of financing came from internal cash flow in 2001, implying a financial deficit in that year of 21 percent ($100\% - 79\%$). Debt was 26 percent of total financing and -5 percent was financed from new stock issues. This financial deficit has averaged about 20 percent in recent years (Figure 14.2).

3. In general, the financial deficit is covered by (1) borrowing and (2) issuing new equity, the two sources of external financing. However, one of the most prominent aspects of external financing is that new issues of equity (both common stock and preferred stock) in the aggregate seem to be unimportant. Net new issues of equity typically account for a small part of total financing; in the late 1980s and very recently, this figure has been negative.

4. Table 14.2 shows that firms in the United States generate more financing from internally generated cash than firms in other countries. Firms in other countries rely to a greater extent than U.S. firms on external equity.

These data are consistent with the results of a survey conducted by Gordon Donaldson on the way firms establish long-term financing strategies.[6] He found that:

1. The first form of financing used by firms for positive NPV projects is internally generated cash flow: net income plus depreciation minus dividends.

---

[6]G. G. Donaldson, *Corporate Debt Capacity: A Study of Corporate Debt Policy and Determination of Corporate Debt Capacity* (Boston: Harvard Graduate School of Business Administration, 1961). See also S. C. Myers, "The Capital Structure Puzzle," *Journal of Finance* (July 1984).

FIGURE 14.2

The Long-Term
Financial Deficit

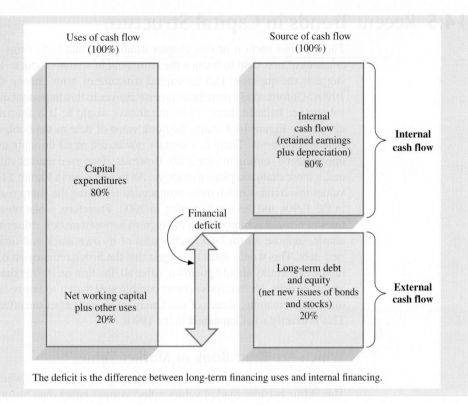

The deficit is the difference between long-term financing uses and internal financing.

TABLE 14.2 | Recent International Financing Patterns: Sources of Funds as a Percentage of Total Sources

	United States	Japan	United Kingdom	Germany	Canada	France
Internally generated funds	82.8	49.3	68.3	65.5	58.3	54.0
Externally generated funds	17.2	50.8	31.7	34.5	41.7	46.0
Increase in long-term debt	17.4	35.9	7.4	31.4	37.5	6.9
Increase in short-term debt	−3.7	9.7	6.1	—	3.8	10.6
Increase in stock	3.5	5.1	16.9	—	10.3	12.4

SOURCE: OECD, *Financial Statements of Nonfinancial Enterprises.*

2. As a last resort a firm will use externally generated cash flow. First, debt is used. Common stock is used last.

These observations, when taken together, suggest a **pecking order** to long-term financing strategy. At the top of the pecking order is using internally generated cash flow, and at the bottom is issuing new equity.

Concept
Questions

1. **What is the difference between internal financing and external financing?**
2. **What are the major sources of corporate financing?**
3. **What factors influence a firm's choices of external versus internal equity financing?**
4. **What pecking order can be observed in the historical patterns of long-term financing?**

14.5 Recent Trends in Capital Structure

The previous section of this chapter established that U.S. firms after 1993 issued large amounts of new debt to finance the retirement of shares of stock. This pattern of financing suggests the question: Did the capital structure of firms change significantly in the mid-1990s? Unfortunately there is no precise answer to this important question. If we used book values (i.e., balance sheet values) the answer would be less dramatic than if we used market values. Figure 14.3 charts the book value of debt to the book value of equity for U.S. nonfinancial firms. There is a slightly downward trend throughout the 1990s and then an upward trend starting in year 2000. However, if we used market values instead of book values, a more dramatic picture emerges. As can be seen in Figure 14.4, when we use market values this trend is much more pronounced reflecting the sharp rise in stock market values in the 1990s and the crash starting in 2000. Therefore, when observing the capital structures of firms, it is important to distinguish between market values and book values. For example, suppose a firm buys back shares of its own stock and finances the purchase with new debt. This would seem to suggest that the firm's reliance on debt should go up and its reliance on equity should go down. After all, the firm has fewer shares of stock outstanding and more debt. The analysis is more complicated than it seems because the market value of the firm's remaining shares of stock may go up and offset the effect of the increased debt. This is exactly what happened in the 1990s.

Which Are Best: Book or Market Values?

In general, financial economists prefer the use of market values when measuring debt ratios. This is true because market values reflect current rather than historical values. Most financial economists believe that current market values better reflect true intrinsic values than do historically based values. However, the use of market values contrasts with the perspective of many corporate practitioners.

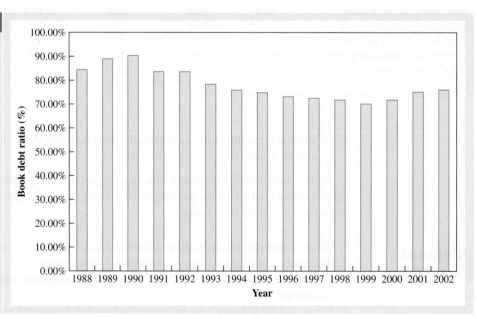

FIGURE 14.3

Book Debt Ratio: Total Debt as a Percentage of Equity for U.S. Nonfarm, Nonfinancial Firms from 1988 to 2002

SOURCE: Board of Governors of the Federal Reserve System, *Flow of Accounts.*

FIGURE 14.4

Market Debt Ratio:
Total Debt as a
Percentage of the
Market Value of
Equity for
U.S. Nonfarm,
Nonfinancial Firms
from 1988 to 2002

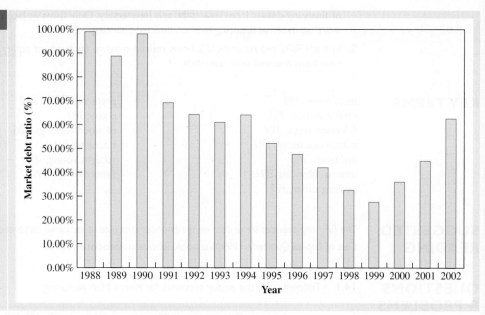

SOURCE: Board of Governors of the Federal Reserve System, *Flow of Funds.*

Our conversations with corporate treasurers suggest to us that the use of book values is popular because of the volatility of the stock market. It is frequently claimed that the inherent volatility of the stock market makes market-based debt ratios move around too much. It is also true that restrictions of debt in bond covenants are usually expressed in book values rather than market values. Moreover, firms such as Standard & Poor's and Moody's use debt ratios expressed in book values to measure credit worthiness.

A key fact is that whether we use book or market values, debt ratios for U.S. nonfinancial firms generally have been below 100 percent of total equity in recent years, that is firms generally use less debt than equity.

14.6 SUMMARY AND CONCLUSIONS

The basic sources of long-term financing are long-term debt, preferred stock, and common stock. This chapter describes the essential features of each.

1. We emphasize that common shareholders have
   a. Residual risk and return in a corporation.
   b. Voting rights.
   c. Limited liability if the corporation elects to default on its debt and must transfer some or all of the assets to the creditors.

2. Long-term debt involves contractual obligations set out in indentures. There are many kinds of debt, but the essential feature is that debt involves a stated amount that must be repaid. Interest payments on debt are considered a business expense and are tax deductible.

3. Preferred stock has some of the features of debt and some of the features of common equity. Holders of preferred stock have preference in liquidation and in dividend payments compared to holders of common equity.

4. Firms need financing for capital expenditures, working capital, and other long-term uses. Most of the financing is provided from internally generated cash flow. In the U.S., only about 25 percent

of financing comes from new debt and new equity. Only firms in Japan have historically relied more on external financing than on internal financing.

5. In the 1980s and recently, U.S. firms retired massive amounts of equity. These share buy-backs have been financed with new debt.

KEY TERMS

book value, 385	preferred stock, 392
capital surplus, 385	proxy, 387
common stock, 384	retained earnings, 385
cumulative voting, 387	seniority, 391
dividends, 388	straight voting, 387
internal financing, 394	subordinated, 391
pecking order, 397	

SUGGESTED READING

The following provides some data on the financial structure of industrial corporations:

Cost of Capital Quarterly. 1999 Yearbook. Ibbotson Associates, 2000.

QUESTIONS & PROBLEMS

COMMON STOCK

14.1   Following are the equity accounts for Kerch Manufacturing.

Common stock, $2 par	$ 135,430
Capital surplus	203,145
Retained earnings	2,370,025
Total	$2,708,600

    a. How many shares are outstanding?
    b. At what average price were the shares sold?
    c. What is the book value of Kerch stock?

14.2   The Eastern Spruce equity accounts for last year are as follows:

Common stock, $1 par, 500 shares outstanding	(1)
Capital surplus	$ 50,000
Retained earnings	100,000
Total	(2)

    a. Fill in the missing numbers.
    b. Eastern decided to issue 1,000 shares of new stock. The current price is $30 per share. Show the effects of the new issue upon the equity accounts.

14.3   Ulrich Inc.'s articles of incorporation authorize the firm to issue 500,000 shares of $5 par-value common stock, of which 325,000 shares have been issued. Those shares were sold at an average of 12 percent over par. In the quarter that ended last week, Ulrich earned $260,000 net income; 4 percent of that income was paid as a dividend. Prior to the close of the books, Ulrich had $3,545,000 in retained earnings. The company owns no treasury stock.
    a. Create the equity statement for Ulrich.
    b. Create a new equity statement that reflects the sale of 25,000 authorized but unissued shares at the price of $4 per share.

14.4   The shareholders of the Unicorn Company need to elect seven new directors. There are 2 million shares outstanding. How many shares do you need to be certain that you can elect at least one director if
    a. Unicorn has straight voting?
    b. Unicorn has cumulative voting?

14.5 Power Inc. is going to elect six board members next month. Betty Brown owns 17.3 percent of the total shares outstanding. How confident can she be to have one of her candidate friends be elected under the cumulative voting rule? And will her friend be elected for certain if the voting procedure is changed to the staggering rule, under which shareholders vote on three board members at a time?

14.6 **a.** An election is being held to fill two seats on the board of directors of a firm in which you hold stock. There is a total of 420 shares outstanding. If the election is conducted under cumulative voting and you own 120 shares, how many more shares must you buy to be assured of earning a seat on the board?

b. The shareholders of Motive Power Corp. need to elect three new directors to the board. There are 2,000,000 shares of common stock outstanding and current share price is $5. If Motive Power uses cumulative voting procedures, how much will it cost to guarantee yourself one seat on the Motive Power's board?

PREFERRED STOCK **14.7** What are the differences between preferred stock and debt?

14.8 Preferred stock doesn't offer corporate tax shield on the dividends paid. Why do we still observe some firms issuing preferred stock?

14.9 The yields on nonconvertible preferred stock are lower than the yields on corporate bonds.
a. Why is there a difference?
b. Which investors are the primary holders of preferred stock? Why?

PATTERNS OF FINANCING **14.10** What are the main differences between corporate debt and equity? Why do some firms try to issue equity in the guise of debt?

RECENT TRENDS IN CAPITAL STRUCTURE **14.11** The Cable Company has $1 million of positive NPV projects it would like to take advantage of. If Cable's managers follow the historical pattern of long-term financing for U.S. industrial firms, what will their financing strategy be?

Capital Structure: *Basic Concepts*

EXECUTIVE SUMMARY

Previous chapters of this book examined the capital-budgeting decision. We pointed out that this decision concerns the left-hand side of the balance sheet. The last two chapters began our discussion of the capital-structure decision,[1] which deals with the right-hand side of the balance sheet.

In general, a firm can choose among many alternative capital structures. It can issue a large amount of debt or it can issue very little debt. It can issue floating-rate preferred stock, warrants, convertible bonds, caps, and callers. It can arrange lease financing, bond swaps, and forward contracts. Because the number of instruments is so large, the variations in capital structures are endless. We simplify the analysis by considering only common stock and straight debt in this chapter. The "bells and whistles," as they are called on Wall Street, must await later chapters of the text. The capital-structure decision we consider is the decision to rely on debt. We examine the factors that are important in the choice of a firm's debt-to-equity ratio.

Our results in this chapter are basic. First we discuss the capital-structure decision in a world with neither taxes nor other capital-market imperfections. Surprisingly, we find that the capital-structure decision is a matter of *indifference* in this world. We next argue that there is a quirk in the U.S. tax code that subsidizes debt financing. Finally, we show that an increase in the firm's value from debt financing leads to an increase in the value of the equity.

---

[1]It is conventional to refer to choices regarding debt and equity as *capital-structure decisions*. However, the term *financial-structure decisions* would be more accurate, and we use the terms interchangeably.

15.1 The Capital-Structure Question and the Pie Theory

How should a firm choose its debt-equity ratio? We call our approach to the capital-structure question the **pie model**. If you are wondering why we chose this name, just take a look at Figure 15.1. The pie in question is the sum of the financial claims of the firm, debt and equity in this case. We *define* the value of the firm to be this sum. Hence, the value of the firm, V, is

$$V \equiv B + S \tag{15.1}$$

where B is the market value of the debt and S is the market value of the equity. Figure 15.1 presents two possible ways of slicing this pie between stock and debt: 40 percent–60 percent and 60 percent–40 percent. If the goal of the management of the firm is to make the firm as valuable as possible, then the firm should pick the debt-equity ratio that makes the pie—the total value—as big as possible.

FIGURE 15.1	
Two Pie Models of Capital Structure	

This discussion begs two important questions:

1. Why should the stockholders in the firm care about maximizing the value of the entire firm? After all, the value of the firm is, by definition, the sum of both the debt and the equity. Instead, why should the stockholders not prefer the strategy that maximizes their interests only?

2. What is the ratio of debt to equity that maximizes the shareholders' interests?

Let us examine each of the two questions in turn.

Concept Question

1. What is the pie model of capital structure?

15.2 Maximizing Firm Value versus Maximizing Stockholder Interests

The following example illustrates that the capital structure that maximizes the value of the firm is the one that financial managers should choose for the shareholders.

EXAMPLE

Suppose the market value of the J. J. Sprint Company is $1,000. The company currently has no debt, and each of J. J. Sprint's 100 shares of stock sells for $10. A company such as J. J. Sprint with no debt is called an *unlevered* company. Further suppose that J. J. Sprint plans to borrow $500 and pay the $500 proceeds to shareholders as an extra cash dividend of $5 per share. After the issuance of debt, the firm becomes *levered*. The investments of the firm will not change as a result of this transaction. What will the value of the firm be after the proposed restructuring?

Management recognizes that, by definition, only one of three outcomes can occur from restructuring. Firm value after restructuring can be either (1) greater than the original firm value of $1,000, (2) equal to $1,000, or (3) less than $1,000. After consulting with investment bankers, management believes that restructuring will not change firm value more than $250 in either direction. Thus, they view firm values of $1,250, $1,000, and $750 as the relevant range. The original capital structure and these three possibilities under the new capital structure are presented next.

	No Debt (original capital structure)	Value of Debt plus Equity after Payment of Dividend (three possibilities)		
		I	**II**	**III**
Debt	$ 0	$ 500	$ 500	$500
Equity	1,000	750	500	250
Firm value	$1,000	$1,250	$1,000	$750

Note that the value of equity is below $1,000 under any of the three possibilities. This can be explained in one of two ways. First, the chart shows the value of the equity *after* the extra cash dividend is paid. Since cash is paid out, a dividend represents a partial liquidation of the firm. Consequently, there is less value in the firm for the equityholders after the dividend payment. Second, in the event of a future liquidation, stockholders will be paid only after bondholders have been paid in full. Thus, the debt is an encumbrance of the firm, reducing the value of the equity.

Of course, management recognizes that there are infinite possible outcomes. The above three are to be viewed as *representative* outcomes only. We can now determine the payoff to stockholders under the three possibilities.

	Payoff to Shareholders after Restructuring		
	I	II	III
Capital gains	−$250	−$500	−$750
Dividends	500	500	500
Net gain or loss to stockholders	$250	$ 0	−$250

No one can be sure ahead of time which of the three outcomes will occur. However, imagine that managers believe that outcome *I* is most likely. They should definitely restructure the firm because the stockholders would gain $250. That is, although the price of the stock declines by $250 to $750, they receive $500 in dividends. Their net gain is $250 = −$250 + $500. Also, notice that the value of the firm would rise by $250 = $1,250 − $1,000.

Alternatively, imagine that managers believe that outcome *III* is most likely. In this case they should not restructure the firm because the stockholders would expect a $250 loss. That is, the stock falls by $750 to $250 and they receive $500 in dividends. Their net loss is −$250 = −$750 + $500. Also, notice that the value of the firm would change by −$250 = $750 − $1,000.

Finally, imagine that the managers believe that outcome *II* is most likely. Restructuring would not affect the stockholders' interest because the net gain to stockholders in this case is zero. Also, notice that the value of the firm is unchanged if outcome *II* occurs.

This example explains why managers should attempt to maximize the value of the firm. In other words, it answers question (1) in Section 15.1. We find in this example that:

Changes in capital structure benefit the stockholders *if and only if* the value of the firm increases.

Conversely, these changes hurt the stockholders if and only if the value of the firm decreases. This result holds true for capital-structure changes of many different types.[2] As a corollary, we can say:

Managers should choose the capital structure that they believe will have the highest firm value, because this capital structure will be most beneficial to the firm's stockholders.

Note however that the example does not tell us which of the three outcomes is most likely to occur. Thus, it does not tell us whether debt should be added to J. J. Sprint's capital structure. In other words, it does not answer question (2) in Section 15.1. This second question is treated in the next section.

Concept
Question

1. **Why should financial managers choose the capital structure that maximizes the value of the firm?**

---

[2]This result may not hold exactly in a more complex case where debt has a significant possibility of default. Issues of default are treated in the next chapter.

15.3 Financial Leverage and Firm Value: An Example

Leverage and Returns to Shareholders

The previous section shows that the capital structure producing the highest firm value is the one that maximizes shareholder wealth. In this section, we wish to determine that optimal capital structure. We begin by illustrating the effect of capital structure on returns to stockholders. We will use a detailed example which we encourage students to study carefully. Once we have this example under our belts, we will be ready to determine the optimal capital structure.

Trans Am Corporation currently has no debt in its capital structure. The firm is considering issuing debt to buy back some of its equity. Both its current and proposed capital structures are presented in Table 15.1. The firm's assets are $8,000. There are 400 shares of the all-equity firm, implying a market value per share of $20. The proposed debt issue is for $4,000, leaving $4,000 in equity. The interest rate is 10 percent.

The effect of economic conditions on earnings per share is shown in Table 15.2 for the current capital structure (all-equity). Consider first the middle column where earnings are *expected* to be $1,200. Since assets are $8,000, the return on assets (ROA) is 15 percent (= $1,200/$8,000). Because assets equal equity for this all-equity firm, return on equity (ROE) is also 15 percent. Earnings per share (EPS) is $3.00 (= $1,200/400). Similar calculations yield EPS of $1.00 and $5.00 in the cases of recession and expansion, respectively.

The case of leverage is presented in Table 15.3. ROA in the three economic states is identical in Tables 15.2 and 15.3, because this ratio is calculated before interest is considered.

TABLE 15.1		Current	Proposed
Financial Structure	Assets	$8,000	$8,000
of Trans Am	Debt	$ 0	$4,000
Corporation	Equity (market and book)	$8,000	$4,000
	Interest rate	10%	10%
	Market value/share	$ 20	$ 20
	Shares outstanding	400	200

The proposed capital structure has leverage, whereas the current structure is all equity.

TABLE 15.2		Recession	Expected	Expansion
Trans Am's Current	Return on assets (ROA)	5%	15%	25%
Capital Structure:	Earnings	$ 400	$1,200	$2,000
No Debt	Return on equity (ROE) = Earnings/Equity	5%	15%	25%
	Earnings per share (EPS)	$1.00	$ 3.00	$ 5.00

TABLE 15.3		Recession	Expected	Expansion
Trans Am's Proposed	Return on assets (ROA)	5%	15%	25%
Capital Structure:				
Debt = $4,000	Earnings before interest (EBI)	$400	$1,200	$2,000
	Interest	−400	−400	−400
	Earnings after interest	$ 0	$ 800	$1,600
	Return on equity (ROE)			
	= Earnings after interest/Equity	0	20%	40%
	Earnings per share (EPS)	0	$4.00	$8.00

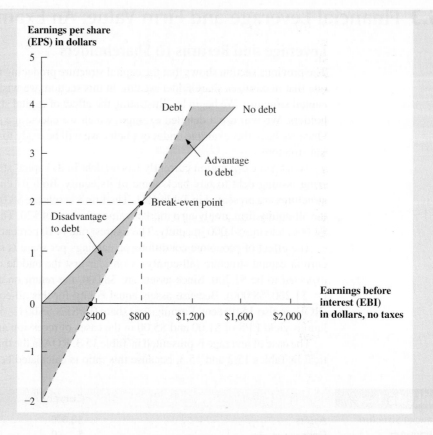

FIGURE 15.2

Financial Leverage:
EPS and EBI for
the Trans Am
Corporation

Since debt is $4,000 here, interest is $400 (= .10 × $4,000). Thus, earnings after interest is $800 (= $1,200 − $400) in the middle (expected) case. Since equity is $4,000, ROE is 20 percent ($800/$4,000). Earnings per share is $4.00 (= $800/200). Similar calculations yield earnings of $0 and $8.00 for recession and expansion, respectively.

Tables 15.2 and 15.3 show that the effect of financial leverage depends on the company's earnings before interest. If earnings before interest is equal to $1,200, the return on equity (ROE) is higher under the proposed structure. If earnings before interest is equal to $400, the ROE is higher under the current structure.

This idea is represented in Figure 15.2. The solid line represents the case of no leverage. The line begins at the origin, indicating that earnings per share (EPS) would be zero if earnings before interest (EBI) were zero. The EPS rises in tandem with a rise in EBI.

The dotted line represents the case of $4,000 of debt. Here, EPS is negative if EBI is zero. This follows because $400 of interest must be paid regardless of the firm's profits.

Now consider the slopes of the two lines. The slope of the dotted line (the line with debt) is higher than the slope of the solid line. This occurs because the levered firm has *fewer* shares of stock outstanding than does the unlevered firm. Therefore, any increase in EBI leads to a greater rise in EPS for the levered firm because the earnings increase is distributed over fewer shares of stock.

Because the dotted line has a lower intercept but a higher slope, the two lines must intersect. The *break-even* point occurs at $800 of EBI. Were earnings before interest to be $800, both firms would produce $2 of earnings per share (EPS). Because $800 is break-even, earnings above $800 lead to greater EPS for the levered firm. Earnings below $800 lead to greater EPS for the unlevered firm.

TABLE 15.4	Payoff and Cost to Shareholders of Trans Am Corporation under the Proposed Structure and under the Current Structure with Homemade Leverage		
	Recession	**Expected**	**Expansion**
Strategy A: Buy 100 Shares of Levered Equity			
EPS of *levered* equity (taken from last line of Table 15.3)	$0	$ 4	$ 8
Earnings per 100 shares	0	400	800
Initial cost = 100 shares @ $20/share = $2,000			
Strategy B: Homemade Leverage			
Earnings per 200 shares in current *unlevered* Trans Am	$1 × 200 = 200	$3 × 200 = 600	$5 × 200 = 1,000
Interest at 10% on $2,000	−200	−200	−200
Net earnings	$ 0	$ 400	$ 800
Initial cost = 200 shares @ $20/share − $2,000 = $2,000			

$$\underbrace{\text{200 shares @ \$20/share}}_{\text{Cost of stock}} - \underbrace{\text{\$2,000}}_{\substack{\text{Amount} \\ \text{borrowed}}} = \text{\$2,000}$$

Investor receives the same payoff whether she (1) buys shares in a levered corporation or (2) buys shares in an unlevered firm and borrows on personal account. Her initial investment is the same in either case. Thus, the firm neither helps nor hurts her by adding debt to capital structure.

The Choice between Debt and Equity

Tables 15.2 and 15.3 and Figure 15.2 are important because they show the effect of leverage on earnings per share. Students should study the tables and figure until they feel comfortable with the calculation of each number in them. However, we have not yet presented the punch line. That is, we have not yet stated which capital structure is better for Trans Am.

At this point, many students believe that leverage is beneficial, because EPS is expected to be $4.00 with leverage and only $3.00 without leverage. However, leverage also creates *risk*. Note that in a recession, EPS is higher ($1.00 versus 0) for the unlevered firm. Thus, a risk-averse investor might prefer the all-equity firm, while a risk-neutral (or less risk-averse) investor might prefer leverage. Given this ambiguity, which capital structure *is* better?

Modigliani and Miller (MM) have a convincing argument that a firm cannot change the total value of its outstanding securities by changing the proportions of its capital structure. In other words, the value of the firm is always the same under different capital structures. In *still* other words, no capital structure is any better or worse than any other capital structure for the firm's stockholders. This rather pessimistic result is the famous **MM Proposition I.**[3]

Their argument compares a simple strategy, which we call Strategy *A*, with a two-part strategy, which we call Strategy *B*. Both of these strategies for shareholders of Trans Am are illuminated in Table 15.4. Let us now examine the first strategy.

Strategy A—Buy 100 shares of the levered equity.

The first line in the top panel of Table 15.4 shows EPS for the proposed levered equity in the three economic states. The second line shows the earnings in the three states for an individual buying 100 shares. The next line shows that the cost of these 100 shares is $2,000.

---

[3]The original paper is F. Modigliani and M. Miller, "The Cost of Capital, Corporation Finance and the Theory of Investment," *American Economic Review* (June 1958).

Let us now consider the second strategy, which has two parts to it.

Strategy B:

1. Borrow $2,000 from either a bank or, more likely, a brokerage house. (If the brokerage house is the lender, we say that this is *going on margin*.)
2. Use the borrowed proceeds plus your own investment of $2,000 (a total of $4,000) to buy 200 shares of the current unlevered equity at $20 per share.

The bottom panel of Table 15.4 shows payoffs under Strategy *B*, which we call the *homemade leverage* strategy. First, observe the middle column, which indicates that 200 shares of the unlevered equity are *expected* to generate $600 of earnings. Assuming that the $2,000 is borrowed at a 10 percent interest rate, the interest expense is $200 (= 0.10 × $2,000). Thus, the net earnings are expected to be $400. A similar calculation generates net earnings of either $0 or $800 in recession or expansion, respectively.

Now, let us compare these two strategies, both in terms of earnings per year and in terms of initial cost. The top panel of the table shows that Strategy *A* generates earnings of $0, $400, and $800 in the three states. The bottom panel of the table shows that Strategy *B* generates the *same* net earnings in the three states.

The top panel of the table shows that Strategy *A* involves an initial cost of $2,000. Similarly, the bottom panel shows an *identical* net cost of $2,000 for Strategy *B*.

This shows a very important result. Both the cost and the payoff from the two strategies are the same. Thus, one must conclude that Trans Am is neither helping nor hurting its stockholders by restructuring. In other words, an investor is not receiving anything from corporate leverage that he or she could not receive on their own.

Note that, as shown in Table 15.1, the equity of the unlevered firm is valued at $8,000. Since the equity of the levered firm is $4,000 and its debt is $4,000, the value of the levered firm is also $8,000. Now suppose that, for whatever reason, the value of the levered firm were actually greater than the value of the unlevered firm. Here, Strategy *A* would cost more than Strategy *B*. In this case, an investor would prefer to borrow on his own account and invest in the stock of the unlevered firm. He would get the same net earnings each year as if he had invested in the stock of the levered firm. However, his cost would be less. The strategy would not be unique to our investor. Given the higher value of the levered firm, no rational investor would invest in the stock of the levered firm. Anyone desiring shares in the levered firm would get the same dollar return more cheaply by borrowing to finance a purchase of the unlevered firm's shares. The equilibrium result would be, of course, that the value of the levered firm would fall, and the value of the unlevered firm would rise until they became equal. At this point, individuals would be indifferent between Strategy *A* and Strategy *B*.

This example illustrates the basic result of Modigliani-Miller (MM) and is commonly called their Proposition I. We state this proposition as:

> MM Proposition I (no taxes): The value of the levered firm is the same as the value of the unlevered firm.

This is perhaps the most important result in all of corporate finance. In fact, it is generally considered the beginning point of modern managerial finance. Before MM, the effect of leverage on the value of the firm was considered complex and convoluted. Modigliani and Miller show a blindingly simple result: If levered firms are priced too high, rational investors will simply borrow on their personal accounts to buy shares in unlevered firms. This substitution is oftentimes called *homemade leverage*. As long as individuals borrow (and lend) on the same terms as the firms, they can duplicate the effects of corporate leverage on their own.

The example of Trans Am Corporation shows that leverage does not affect the value of the firm. Since we showed earlier that stockholders' welfare is directly related to the firm's value, the example indicates that changes in capital structure cannot affect the stockholders' welfare.

A Key Assumption

The MM result hinges on the assumption that individuals can borrow as cheaply as corporations. If, alternatively, individuals can only borrow at a higher rate, one can easily show that corporations can increase firm value by borrowing.

Is this assumption of equal borrowing costs a good one? Individuals who want to buy stock and borrow can do so by establishing a margin account with the broker. Under this arrangement, the broker loans the individual a portion of the purchase price. For example, the individual might buy $10,000 of stock by investing $6,000 of her own funds and borrowing $4,000 from the broker. Should the stock be worth $9,000 on the next day, the individual's net worth or equity in the account would be $5,000 = $9,000 − $4,000.[4]

The broker fears that a sudden price drop will cause the equity in the individual's account to be negative, implying that the broker may not get her loan repaid in full. To guard against this possibility, stock exchange rules require that the individual make additional cash contributions (replenish her margin account) as the stock price falls. Because (1) the procedures for replenishing the account have developed over many years, and (2) the broker holds the stock as collateral, there is little default risk to the broker.[5] In particular, if margin contributions are not made on time, the broker can sell the stock in order to satisfy her loan. Therefore, brokers generally charge low interest, with many rates being only slightly above the risk-free rate.

By contrast, corporations frequently borrow using illiquid assets (e.g., plant and equipment) as collateral. The costs to the lender of initial negotiation and ongoing supervision, as well as of working out arrangements in the event of financial distress, can be quite substantial. Thus, it is difficult to argue that individuals must borrow at higher rates than can corporations.[6]

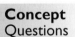

Concept
Questions

1. **Describe financial leverage.**
2. **What is levered equity?**
3. **How can a shareholder of Trans Am undo the company's financial leverage?**

15.4 Modigliani and Miller: Proposition II (No Taxes)

Risk to Equityholders Rises with Leverage

At a Trans Am corporate meeting, a corporate officer said, "Well, maybe it does not matter whether the corporation or the individual levers—as long as some leverage takes place. Leverage benefits investors. After all, an investor's expected return rises with the amount

---

[4]We are ignoring the one-day interest charge on the loan.

[5]Had this text been published before October 19, 1987, when stock prices declined by more than 20 percent, we might have used the phrase "virtually no" risk instead of "little."

[6]One caveat is in order. Initial margin or borrowing is currently limited by law to 50 percent of value. Certain companies, like financial institutions, borrow over 90 percent of their firm's market value. Individuals borrowing against the stock of all-equity corporations cannot duplicate the debt of these highly levered corporations.

of the leverage present." He then pointed out that, as shown in Tables 15.2 and 15.3, the expected return on unlevered equity is 15 percent while the expected return on levered equity is 20 percent.

However, another officer replied, "Not necessarily. Though the expected return rises with leverage, the *risk* rises as well." This point can be seen from an examination of Tables 15.2 and 15.3. With earnings before interest (EBI) varying between $400 and $2,000, earnings per share (EPS) for the stockholders of the unlevered firm vary between $1.00 and $5.00. EPS for the stockholders of the levered firm vary between $0 and $8.00. This greater range for the EPS of the levered firm implies greater risk for the levered firm's stockholders. In other words, levered stockholders have better returns in good times than do unlevered stockholders but have worse returns in bad times. The two tables also show greater range for the ROE of the levered firm's stockholders. The above interpretation concerning risk applies here as well.

The same insight can be taken from Figure 15.2. The slope of the line for the levered firm is greater than the slope of the line for the unlevered firm. This means that the levered stockholders have better returns in good times than do unlevered stockholders but have worse returns in bad times, implying greater risk with leverage. In other words, the slope of the line measures the risk to stockholders, since the slope indicates the responsiveness of ROE to changes in firm performance (earnings before interest).

Proposition II: Required Return to Equityholders Rises with Leverage

Since levered equity has greater risk, it should have a greater expected return as compensation. In our example, the market *requires* only a 15-percent expected return for the unlevered equity, but it requires a 20-percent expected return for the levered equity.

This type of reasoning allows us to develop **MM Proposition II.** Here, MM argue that the expected return on equity is positively related to leverage, because the risk to equityholders increases with leverage.

To develop this position recall from Chapter 12 that the firm's weighted average cost of capital, r_{WACC}, can be written as:[7]

$$\frac{B}{B+S} \times r_B + \frac{S}{B+S} \times r_S \qquad (15.2)$$

where

r_B is the interest rate, also called the cost of debt

r_S is the expected return on equity or stock, also called the *cost of equity* or the *required return on equity*

r_{WACC} is the firm's weighted average cost of capital

B is the value of the firm's debt or bonds

S is the value of the firm's stock or equity

Formula (15.2) is quite intuitive. It simply says that a firm's weighted average cost of capital is a weighted average of its cost of debt and its cost of equity. The weight applied to debt is the proportion of debt in the capital structure, and the weight applied to equity is the proportion of equity in the capital structure. Calculations of r_{WACC} from formula (15.2) for both the unlevered and the levered firm are presented in Table 15.5.

---

[7]Since we do not have taxes here, the cost of debt is r_B, not $r_B(1 - T_C)$ as it was in Chapter 12.

TABLE 15.5		
Cost of Capital Calculations for Trans Am		

$$r_{WACC} = \frac{B}{B+S} \times r_B + \frac{S}{B+S} \times r_S$$

Unlevered firm: $15\% = \dfrac{0}{\$8,000} \times 10\%* + \dfrac{\$8,000}{\$8,000} \times 15\%\dagger$

Levered firm: $15\% = \dfrac{\$4,000}{\$8,000} \times 10\%* + \dfrac{\$4,000}{\$8,000} \times 20\%\ddagger$

*10% is the interest rate.

†From the "Expected" column in Table 15.2, we learn that expected earnings after interest for the unlevered firm are $1,200. From Table 15.1, we learn that equity for the unlevered firm is $8,000. Thus, r_S for the unlevered firm is:

$$\frac{\text{Expected earnings after interest}}{\text{Equity}} = \frac{\$1,200}{\$8,000} = 15\%$$

‡From the "Expected" column in Table 15.3, we learn that expected earnings after interest for the levered firm are $800. From Table 15.1, we learn that equity for the levered firm is $4,000. Thus r_S for the levered firm is:

$$\frac{\text{Expected earnings after interest}}{\text{Equity}} = \frac{\$800}{\$4,000} = 20\%$$

An implication of MM Proposition I is that r_{WACC} is a constant for a given firm, regardless of the capital structure.[8] For example, Table 15.5 shows that r_{WACC} for Trans Am is 15 percent, with or without leverage.

Let us now define r_0 to be the *cost of capital for an all-equity firm*. For the Trans Am Corp., r_0 is calculated as:

$$r_0 = \frac{\text{Expected earnings to unlevered firm}}{\text{Unlevered equity}} = \frac{\$1,200}{\$8,000} = 15\%$$

As can be seen from Table 15.5, r_{WACC} is equal to r_0 for Trans Am. In fact, r_{WACC} must *always* equal r_0 in a world without corporate taxes.

Proposition II states the expected return of equity, r_S, in terms of leverage. The exact relationship, derived by setting $r_{WACC} = r_0$ and then rearranging formula (15.2), is:[9]

MM Proposition II (no taxes)

$$r_S = r_0 + \frac{B}{S}(r_0 - r_B) \tag{15.3}$$

---

[8]This statement holds in a world of no taxes. It does not hold in a world with taxes, a point to be brought out later in this chapter (see Figure 15.6).

[9]This can be derived from formula (15.2) by setting $r_{WACC} = r_0$, yielding:

$$\frac{B}{B+S} r_B + \frac{S}{B+S} r_S = r_0 \tag{15.2}$$

Multiplying both sides by $(B + S)/S$ yields:

$$\frac{B}{S} r_B + r_S = \frac{B+S}{S} r_0$$

We can rewrite the right-hand side as

$$\frac{B}{S} r_B + r_S = \frac{B}{S} r_0 + r_0$$

Moving $(B/S)r_B$ to the right-hand side and rearranging yields:

$$r_S = r_0 + \frac{B}{S}(r_0 - r_B) \tag{15.3}$$

FIGURE 15.3

The Cost of Equity, the Cost of Debt, and the Weighted Average Cost of Capital: MM Proposition II with No Corporate Taxes

$r_S = r_0 + (r_0 - r_B)B/S$

  r_S is the cost of equity

  r_B is the cost of debt

  r_0 is the cost of capital for an all-equity firm

  r_{WACC} is a firm's weighted average cost of capital. In a world with no taxes, r_{WACC} for
    a levered firm is equal to r_0.

  r_0 is a single point while r_S, r_B, and r_{WACC} are all entire lines.

The cost of equity capital, r_S, is positively related to the firm's debt-equity ratio. The firm's weighted average cost of capital, r_{WACC}, is invariant to the firm's debt-equity ratio.

Equation (15.3) implies that the required return on equity is a linear function of the firm's debt-to-equity ratio. Examining equation (15.3), we see that if r_0 exceeds the debt rate, r_B, then the cost of equity rises with increases in the debt-equity ratio, B/S. Normally, r_0 should exceed r_B. That is, because even unleveraged equity is risky, it should have an expected return greater than that of riskless debt. Note that equation (15.3) holds for Trans Am in its levered state:

$$0.20 = 0.15 + \frac{\$4,000}{\$4,000}(0.15 - 0.10)$$

Figure 15.3 graphs equation (15.3). As you can see, we have plotted the relation between the cost of equity, r_S, and the debt-equity ratio, B/S, as a straight line. What we witness in equation (15.3) and illustrate in Figure 15.3 is the effect of leverage on the cost of equity. As the firm raises the debt-equity ratio, each dollar of equity is levered with additional debt. This raises the risk of equity and therefore the required return, r_S, on the equity.

Figure 15.3 also shows that r_{WACC} is unaffected by leverage, a point we made above. (It is important for students to realize that r_0, the cost of capital for an all-equity firm, is represented by a single dot on the graph. By contrast, r_{WACC} is an entire line.)

Example Illustrating Proposition I and Proposition II

EXAMPLE

Luteran Motors, an all-equity firm, has expected earnings of $10 million per year in perpetuity. The firm pays all of its earnings out as dividends, so that the $10 million may also be viewed as the stockholders' expected cash flow. There are 10 million shares outstanding, implying expected annual cash flow of $1 per share. The cost of capital for this unleveraged firm is 10 percent. In addition, the firm will soon build a new plant for $4 million. The plant is expected to generate additional cash flow of

$1 million per year. These figures can be described as:

Current Company	New Plant
Cash flow: $10 million	Initial outlay: $4 million
Number of outstanding shares: 10 million	Additional annual cash flow: $1 million

The project's net present value is:

$$-\$4 \text{ million} + \frac{\$1 \text{ million}}{0.1} = \$6 \text{ million}$$

assuming that the project is discounted at the same rate as the firm as a whole. Before the market knows of the project, the *market-value* balance sheet of the firm is:

LUTERAN MOTORS
Balance Sheet (all equity)

Old assets: $\dfrac{\$10 \text{ million}}{0.1} = \$100$ million	Equity:	$100 million
		(10 million shares of stock)

The value of the firm is $100 million, because the cash flow of $10 million per year is capitalized at 10 percent. A share of stock sells for $10 ($100 million/10 million) because there are 10 million shares outstanding.

The market-value balance sheet is a useful tool of financial analysis. Because students are often thrown off guard by it initially, we recommend extra study here. The key is that the market-value balance sheet has the same form as the balance sheet that accountants use. That is, assets are placed on the left-hand side whereas liabilities and owners' equity are placed on the right-hand side. In addition, the left-hand side and the right-hand side must be equal. The difference between a market-value balance sheet and the accountant's balance sheet is in the numbers. Accountants value items in terms of historical cost (original purchase price less depreciation), whereas financial people value items in terms of market value.

The firm will either issue $4 million of equity or debt. Let us consider the effect of equity and debt financing in turn.

Stock Financing   Imagine that the firm announces that, in the near future, it will raise $4 million in equity in order to build a new plant. The stock price, and therefore the value of the firm, will rise to reflect the positive net present value of the plant. According to efficient markets, the increase occurs immediately. That is, the rise occurs on the day of the announcement, not on the date of either the onset of construction of the power plant or the forthcoming stock offering. The market-value balance sheet becomes:

LUTERAN MOTORS
Balance Sheet
(upon announcement of equity issue to construct plant)

Old assets	$100 million	Equity	$106 million
			(10 million shares of stock)
NPV of plant:			
$-4 \text{ million} + \dfrac{\$1 \text{ million}}{0.1} =$	6 million		
Total assets	$106 million		

Note that the NPV of the plant is included in the market-value balance sheet. Because the new shares have not yet been issued, the number of outstanding shares remains 10 million. The price per share has now risen to $10.60 ($106 million/10 million) to reflect news concerning the plant.

Shortly thereafter, $4 million of stock is issued or *floated*. Because the stock is selling at $10.60 per share, 377,358 ($4 million/$10.60) shares of stock are issued. Imagine that funds are put in the bank *temporarily* before being used to build the plant. The market-value balance sheet becomes:

LUTERAN MOTORS
Balance Sheet
(upon issuance of stock but before construction begins on plant)

Old assets	$100 million	Equity	$110 million
			(10,377,358 shares of stock)
NPV of plant	6 million		
Proceeds from new issue			
of stock (currently			
placed in bank)	4 million		
Total assets	$110 million		

The number of shares outstanding is now 10,377,358 because 377,358 new shares were issued. The price per share is $10.60 ($110,000,000/10,377,358). Note that the price has not changed. This is consistent with efficient capital markets, because the stock price should only move due to new information.

Of course, the funds are placed in the bank only temporarily. Shortly after the new issue, the $4 million is given to a contractor who builds the plant. To avoid problems in discounting, we assume that the plant is built immediately. The balance sheet then becomes:

LUTERAN MOTORS
Balance Sheet
(upon completion of the plant)

Old assets	$100 million	Equity	$110 million
			(10,377,358 shares of stock)
PV of plant: $\dfrac{\$1 \text{ million}}{0.1} =$	10 million		
Total assets	$110 million		

Though total assets do not change, the composition of the assets does change. The bank account has been emptied to pay the contractor. The present value of cash flows of $1 million a year from the plant are reflected as an asset worth $10 million. Because the building expenditures of $4 million have already been paid, they no longer represent a future cost. Hence, they no longer reduce the value of the plant. According to efficient capital markets, the price per share of stock remains $10.60.

Expected yearly cash flow from the firm is $11 million, $10 million of which comes from the old assets and $1 million from the new. The expected return to equityholders is:

$$r_S = \frac{\$11 \text{ million}}{\$110 \text{ million}} = 0.10$$

Because the firm is all equity, $r_S = r_0 = 0.10$.

Debt Financing   Alternatively, imagine that the firm announces that, in the near future, it will borrow $4 million at 6 percent to build a new plant. This implies yearly interest payments of $240,000 ($4,000,000 × 6%). Again the stock price rises immediately to reflect the positive net present value of the plant. Thus, we have:

LUTERAN MOTORS
Balance Sheet
(upon announcement of debt issue to construct plant)

Old assets	$100 million	Equity	$106 million
			(10 million shares of stock)
NPV of plant:			
$-\$4 \text{ million} + \dfrac{\$1 \text{ million}}{0.1} =$ 6 million			
Total assets	$106 million		

The value of the firm is the same as in the equity financing case because (1) the same plant is to be built and (2) MM prove that debt financing is neither better nor worse than equity financing.

At some point, $4 million of debt is issued. As before, the funds are placed in the bank temporarily. The market-value balance sheet becomes:

LUTERAN MOTORS
Balance Sheet
(upon debt issuance but before construction begins on plant)

Old assets	$100 million	Debt	$ 4 million
NPV of plant	6 million	Equity	106 million
			(10 million shares of stock)
Proceeds from debt issue (currently invested in bank)	4 million		
Total assets	$110 million	Debt plus equity	$110 million

Note that debt appears on the right-hand side of the balance sheet. The stock price is still $10.60, in accordance with our discussion of efficient capital markets.

Finally, the contractor receives $4 million and builds the plant. The market-value balance sheet becomes:

LUTERAN MOTORS
Balance Sheet
(upon completion of the plant)

Old assets	$100 million	Debt	$ 4 million
PV of plant	10 million	Equity	106 million
			(10 million shares of stock)
Total assets	$110 million	Debt plus equity	$110 million

The only change here is that the bank account has been depleted to pay the contractor. The equityholders expect yearly cash flow after interest of:

$$\underset{\substack{\text{Cash flow on}\\\text{old assets}}}{\$10,000,000} + \underset{\substack{\text{Cash flow on}\\\text{new assets}}}{\$1,000,000} - \underset{\substack{\text{Interest:}\\\$4 \text{ million} \times 6\%}}{\$240,000} = \$10,760,000$$

The equityholders expect to earn a return of:

$$\frac{\$10,760,000}{\$106,000,000} = 10.15\%$$

This return of 10.15 percent for levered equityholders is higher than the 10 percent return for the unlevered equityholders. This result is sensible because, as we argued earlier, levered equity is riskier. In fact, the return of 10.15 percent should be exactly what MM Proposition II predicts. This prediction can be verified by plugging values into:

$$r_S = r_0 + \frac{B}{S} \times (r_0 - r_B) \tag{15.3}$$

We obtain:

$$10.15\% = 10\% + \frac{\$4,000,000}{\$106,000,000} \times (10\% - 6\%)$$

This example was useful for two reasons. First, we wanted to introduce the concept of market-value balance sheets, a tool that will prove useful elsewhere in the text. Among other things, this technique allows one to calculate the price per share of a new issue of stock. Second, the example illustrates three aspects of Modigliani and Miller:

1. The example is consistent with MM Proposition I because the value of the firm is $110 million after either equity or debt financing.
2. Students are often more interested in stock price than in firm value. We show that the stock price is always $10.60, regardless of whether debt or equity financing is used.
3. The example is consistent with MM Proposition II. The expected return to equityholders rises from 10 to 10.15 percent, just as formula (15.3) states. This rise occurs because the equityholders of a levered firm face more risk than do the equityholders of an unlevered firm.

MM: An Interpretation

The Modigliani-Miller results indicate that managers cannot change the value of a firm by repackaging the firm's securities. Though this idea was considered revolutionary when it was originally proposed in the late 1950s, the MM model and arbitrage proof have since met with wide acclaim.[10]

MM argue that the firm's overall cost of capital cannot be reduced as debt is substituted for equity, even though debt appears to be cheaper than equity. The reason for this is that as the firm adds debt, the remaining equity becomes more risky. As this risk rises, the cost of equity capital rises as a result. The increase in the cost of the remaining equity capital offsets the higher proportion of the firm financed by low-cost debt. In fact, MM prove that the two effects exactly offset each other, so that both the value of the firm and the firm's overall cost of capital are invariant to leverage.

MM use an interesting analogy to food. They consider a dairy farmer with two choices. On the one hand, he can sell whole milk. On the other hand, by skimming he can sell a combination of cream and low-fat milk. Though the farmer can get a high price for the cream, he gets a low price for the low-fat milk, implying no net gain. In fact, imagine that the proceeds from the whole-milk strategy were less than those from the cream–low-fat-milk strategy. Arbitrageurs would buy the whole milk, perform the skimming operation themselves, and resell the cream and low-fat milk separately. Competition between arbitrageurs would tend to boost the price of whole milk until proceeds from the two strategies became equal. Thus, the value of the farmer's milk is invariant to the way in which the milk is packaged.

---

[10]Both Merton Miller and Franco Modigliani were awarded separate Nobel Prizes, in part for their work on capital structure.

In Professor Miller's Words . . .

The Modigliani-Miller results are not easy to understand fully. This point is related in a story told by Merton Miller.[11]

"How difficult it is to summarize briefly the contribution of the [Modigliani-Miller] papers was brought home to me very clearly last October after Franco Modigliani was awarded the Nobel Prize in Economics in part—but, of course, only in part—for the work in finance. The television camera crews from our local stations in Chicago immediately descended upon me. 'We understand,' they said, 'that you worked with Modigliani some years back in developing these M and M theorems and we wonder if you could explain them briefly to our television viewers.'

"'How briefly?' I asked.

"'Oh, take ten seconds,' was the reply.

"Ten seconds to explain the work of a lifetime! Ten seconds to describe two carefully reasoned articles, each running to more than thirty printed pages and each with sixty or so long footnotes! When they saw the look of dismay on my face, they said, 'You don't have to go into details. Just give us the main points in simple, common-sense terms.'

"The main point of the first or cost-of-capital article was, in principle at least, simple enough to make. It said that in an economist's ideal world of complete and perfect capital markets and with full and symmetric information among all market participants, the total market value of all the securities issued by a firm was governed by the earning power and risk of its underlying real assets and was independent of how the mix of securities issued to finance it was divided between debt instruments and equity capital. . . .

"Such a summary, however, uses too many short-handed terms and concepts, like perfect capital markets, that are rich in connotations to economists but hardly so to the general public. So I thought, instead, of an analogy that we ourselves had invoked in the original paper. . . .

"'Think of the firm,' I said, 'as a gigantic tub of whole milk. The farmer can sell the whole milk as is. Or he can separate out the cream and sell it at a considerably higher price than the whole milk would bring. (That's the analogy of a firm selling low-yield and hence high-priced debt securities.) But, of course, what the farmer would have left would be skim milk with low butterfat content and that would sell for much less than whole milk. That corresponds to the levered equity. The M and M proposition says that if there were no costs of separation (and, of course, no government dairy support programs), the cream plus the skim milk would bring the same price as the whole milk.'

"The television people conferred among themselves and came back to inform me that it was too long, too complicated, and too academic.

"'Don't you have anything simpler?' they asked. I thought of another way that the M and M proposition is presented these days, which emphasizes the notion of market completeness and stresses the role of securities as devices for 'partitioning' a firm's payoffs in each possible state of the world among the group of its capital suppliers.

"'Think of the firm,' I said, 'as a gigantic pizza, divided into quarters. If now you cut each quarter in half into eighths, the M and M proposition says that you will have more pieces but not more pizza.'

"Again there was a whispered conference among the camera crew, and the director came back and said:

"'Professor, we understand from the press release that there were two M and M propositions. Can we try the other one?'"

[Professor Miller tried valiantly to explain the second proposition, though this was apparently even more difficult to get across. After his attempt:]

"Once again there was a whispered conversation. They shut the lights off. They folded up their equipment. They thanked me for giving them the time. They said that they'd get back to me. But I knew that I had somehow lost my chance to start a new career as a packager of economic wisdom for TV viewers in convenient ten-second bites. Some have the talent for it . . . and some just don't."

Food found its way into this chapter earlier, when we viewed the firm as a pie. MM argue that the size of the pie does not change, no matter how stockholders and bondholders divide it. MM say that a firm's capital structure is irrelevant; it is what it is by some historical accident. The theory implies that firms' debt-equity ratios could be anything. They are what they are because of whimsical and random managerial decisions about how much to borrow and how much stock to issue.

---

[11]Taken from *GSB Chicago*, University of Chicago (Autumn 1986).

Summary of Modigliani-Miller Propositions without Taxes

Assumptions

- No taxes
- No transaction costs
- Individuals and corporations borrow at same rate

Results

Proposition I: $V_L = V_U$ (Value of levered firm equals value of unlevered firm)

Proposition II: $r_S = r_0 + \dfrac{B}{S}(r_0 - r_B)$

Intuition

Proposition I: Through homemade leverage, individuals can either duplicate or undo the effects of corporate leverage.

Proposition II: The cost of equity rises with leverage, because the risk to equity rises with leverage.

Although scholars are always fascinated with far-reaching theories, students are perhaps more concerned with real-world applications. Do real-world managers follow MM by treating capital-structure decisions with indifference? Unfortunately for the theory, virtually all companies in certain industries, such as banking, choose high debt-to-equity ratios. Conversely, companies in other industries, such as pharmaceuticals, choose low debt-to-equity ratios. In fact, almost any industry has a debt-to-equity ratio to which companies in that industry adhere. Thus, companies do not appear to be selecting their degree of leverage in a frivolous or random manner. Because of this, financial economists (including MM themselves) have argued that real-world factors may have been left out of the theory.

Though many of our students have argued that individuals can only borrow at rates above the corporate borrowing rate, we disagreed with this argument earlier in the chapter. But when we look elsewhere for unrealistic assumptions in the theory, we find two:[12]

1. Taxes were ignored.
2. Bankruptcy costs and other agency costs were not considered.

We turn to taxes in the next section. Bankruptcy costs and other agency costs will be treated in the next chapter. A summary of the main Modigliani-Miller results without taxes is presented in the accompanying boxed section.

Concept Questions

1. **Why does the expected return on equity rise with firm leverage?**
2. **What is the exact relationship between the expected return on equity and firm leverage?**
3. **How are market-value balance sheets set up?**

---

[12]MM were aware of both of these issues, as can be seen in their original paper.

FIGURE 15.4

Two Pie Models of Capital Structure under Corporate Taxes

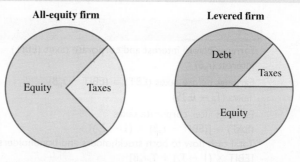

The levered firm pays less in taxes than does the all-equity firm. Thus, the sum of the debt plus the equity of the levered firm is greater than the equity of the unlevered firm.

15.5 Taxes

The Basic Insight

The previous part of this chapter showed that firm value is unrelated to debt in a world without taxes. We now show that, in the presence of corporate taxes, the firm's value is positively related to its debt. The basic intuition can be seen from a pie chart, such as the one in Figure 15.4. Consider the all-equity firm on the left. Here, both equityholders and the IRS have claims on the firm. The value of the all-equity firm is, of course, that part of the pie owned by the equityholders. The proportion going to taxes is simply a cost.

The pie on the right for the levered firm shows three claims: equityholders, debtholders, and taxes. The value of the levered firm is the sum of the value of the debt and the value of the equity. In selecting between the two capital structures in the picture, a financial manager should select the one with the higher value. Assuming that the total area is the same for both pies,[13] value is maximized for that capital structure paying the least in taxes. In other words, the manager should choose the capital structure that the IRS hates the most.

We will show that, due to a quirk in U.S. tax law, the proportion of the pie allocated to taxes is less for the levered firm than it is for the unlevered firm. Thus, managers should select high leverage.

The Quirk in the Tax Code

EXAMPLE

The Water Products Company has a corporate tax rate, T_C, of 35 percent and expected earnings before interest and taxes (EBIT) of $1 million each year. Its entire earnings after taxes are paid out as dividends.

The firm is considering two alternative capital structures. Under plan *I*, Water Products would have no debt in its capital structure. Under plan *II*, the company would have $4,000,000 of debt, B. The cost of debt, r_B, is 10 percent.

---

[13]Under the MM propositions developed earlier, the two pies should be of the same size.

The chief financial officer for Water Products makes the following calculations:

	Plan I	Plan II
Earnings before interest and corporate taxes (EBIT)	$1,000,000	$1,000,000
Interest ($r_B B$)	0	(400,000)
Earnings before taxes (EBT) = (EBIT − $r_B B$)	1,000,000	600,000
Taxes ($T_C = 0.35$)	(350,000)	(210,000)
Earnings after corporate taxes (EAT) = [(EBIT − $r_B B$) × (1 − T_C)]	650,000	390,000
Total cash flow to both stockholders and bondholders [EBIT × (1 − T_C) + $T_C r_B B$]	$ 650,000	$ 790,000

The most relevant numbers for our purposes are the two on the bottom line. Dividends, which are equal to earnings after taxes in this example, are the cash flow to stockholders, and interest is the cash flow to bondholders. Here, we see that more cash flow reaches the owners of the firm (both stockholders and bondholders) under plan *II*. The difference is $140,000 = $790,000 − $650,000. It does not take one long to realize the source of this difference. The IRS receives less taxes under plan *II* ($210,000) than it does under plan *I* ($350,000). The difference here is $140,000 = $350,000 − $210,000.

This difference occurs because the way the IRS treats interest is different from the way it treats earnings going to stockholders.[14] Interest totally escapes corporate taxation, whereas earnings after interest but before corporate taxes (EBT) are taxed at the 35-percent rate.

Present Value of the Tax Shield

The discussion above shows a tax advantage to debt or, equivalently, a tax disadvantage to equity. We now want to value this advantage. The dollar interest is:

$$\text{Interest} = \underbrace{r_B}_{\text{Interest rate}} \times \underbrace{B}_{\text{Amount borrowed}}$$

This interest is $400,000 (10% × $4,000,000) for Water Products. All this interest is tax-deductible. That is, whatever the taxable income of Water Products would have been without the debt, the taxable income is now $400,000 *less* with the debt.

Because the corporate tax rate is 0.35 in our example, the reduction in corporate taxes is $140,000 (0.35 × $400,000). This number is identical to the reduction in corporate taxes calculated previously.

Algebraically, the reduction in corporate taxes is:

$$\underbrace{T_C}_{\text{Corporate tax rate}} \times \underbrace{r_B \times B}_{\text{Dollar amount of interest}} \tag{15.4}$$

That is, whatever the taxes that a firm would pay each year without debt, the firm will pay $T_C r_B B$ less with the debt of B. Expression (15.4) is often called the *tax shield from debt*. Note that it is an *annual* amount.

As long as the firm expects to be in a positive tax bracket, we can assume that the cash flow in expression (15.4) has the same risk as the interest on the debt. Thus, its value can be determined by discounting at the interest rate, r_B. Assuming that the cash flows are

[14]Note that stockholders actually receive more under plan *I* ($650,000) than under plan *II* ($390,000). Students are often bothered by this since it seems to imply that stockholders are better off without leverage. However, remember that there are more shares outstanding in plan *I* than in plan *II*. A full-blown model would show that earnings *per share* are higher with leverage.

perpetual, the present value of the tax shield is:

$$\frac{T_C r_B B}{r_B} = T_C B$$

Value of the Levered Firm

We have just calculated the present value of the tax shield from debt. Our next step is to calculate the value of the levered firm. The annual after-tax cash flow of an unlevered firm is:

$$\text{EBIT} \times (1 - T_C)$$

where EBIT is earnings before interest and taxes. The value of an unlevered firm (that is, a firm with no debt) is the present value of $\text{EBIT} \times (1 - T_C)$:

$$V_U = \frac{\text{EBIT} \times (1 - T_C)}{r_0}$$

where

$$V_U = \text{Present value of an unlevered firm}$$
$$\text{EBIT} \times (1 - T_C) = \text{Firm cash flows after corporate taxes}$$
$$T_C = \text{Corporate tax rate}$$
$$r_0 = \text{The cost of capital to an all-equity firm. As can be seen from}$$
$$\text{the formula, } r_0 \text{ now discounts } after\text{-}tax \text{ cash flows.}$$

As shown previously, leverage increases the value of the firm by the tax shield, which is $T_C B$ for perpetual debt. Thus, we merely add this tax shield to the value of the unlevered firm to get the value of the levered firm.

We can write this algebraically as:[15]

MM Proposition I (corporate taxes)

$$V_L = \frac{\text{EBIT} \times (1 - T_C)}{r_0} + \frac{T_C r_B B}{r_B} = V_U + T_C B \qquad (15.5)$$

Equation (15.5) is MM Proposition I under corporate taxes. The first term in equation (15.5) is the value of the cash flows of the firm with no debt tax shield. In other words, this term is equal to V_U, the value of the all-equity firm. The value of the levered firm is the value of an all-equity firm plus $T_C B$, the tax rate times the value of the debt. $T_C B$ is the present value of the tax shield in the case of perpetual cash flows.[16] Because the tax shield increases with

---

[15]This relationship holds when the debt level is assumed to be constant through time. A different formula would apply if the debt-equity ratio was assumed to be a non-constant over time. For a deeper treatment of this point, see J. A. Miles and J. R. Ezzel, "The Weighted Average Cost of Capital, Perfect Capital Markets and Project Life," *Journal of Financial and Quantitative Analysis* (September 1980).

[16]The following example calculates the present value if we assume the debt has a finite life. Suppose the Maxwell Company has $1 million in debt with an 8-percent coupon rate. If the debt matures in two years and the cost of debt capital, r_B, is 10 percent, what is the present value of the tax shields if the corporate tax rate is 35 percent? The debt is amortized in equal installments over two years.

Year	Loan Balance	Interest	Tax Shield	Present Value of Tax Shield
0	$1,000,000			
1	500,000	$80,000	0.35 × $80,000	$25,454.54
2	0	40,000	0.35 × $40,000	11,570.25
				$37,024.79

The present value of the tax savings is

$$\text{PV} = \frac{0.35 \times \$80,000}{1.10} + \frac{0.35 \times \$40,000}{(1.10)^2} = \$37,024.79$$

The Maxwell Company's value is higher than that of a comparable unlevered firm by $37,024.79.

the amount of debt, the firm can raise its total cash flow and its value by substituting debt for equity.

Divided Airlines is currently an unlevered firm. The company expects to generate $153.85 in earnings before interest and taxes (EBIT), in perpetuity. The corporate tax rate is 35 percent, implying after-tax earnings of $100. All earnings after tax are paid out as dividends.

The firm is considering a capital restructuring to allow $200 of debt. Its cost of debt capital is 10 percent. Unlevered firms in the same industry have a cost of equity capital of 20 percent. What will the new value of Divided Airlines be?

The value of Divided Airlines will be equal to:[17]

$$V_L = \frac{EBIT \times (1 - T_c)}{r_0} + T_c B$$

$$= \frac{\$100}{0.20} + (0.35 \times \$200)$$

$$= \$500 + \$70$$

$$= \$570$$

The value of the levered firm is $570, which is greater than the unlevered value of $500. Because $V_L = B + S$, the value of levered equity, S, is equal to $570 - \$200 = \$370$. The value of Divided Airlines as a function of leverage is illustrated in Figure 15.5.

FIGURE 15.5

The Effect of
Financial Leverage
on Firm Value: MM
with Corporate Taxes
in the Case of
Divided Airlines

Debt reduces Divided's tax burden. As a result, the value of the firm is positively related to debt.

Expected Return and Leverage under Corporate Taxes

MM Proposition II under no taxes posits a positive relationship between the expected return on equity and leverage. This result occurs because the risk of equity increases with leverage. The same intuition also holds in a world of corporate taxes. The exact formula in

---

[17]Note that, in a world with taxes, r_0 is used to discount *after-tax* cash flows.

a world of corporate taxes is:[18]

MM Proposition II (corporate taxes)

$$r_S = r_0 + \frac{B}{S} \times (1 - T_C) \times (r_0 - r_B) \tag{15.6}$$

Applying the formula to Divided Airlines, we get:

$$r_S = 0.2351 = 0.20 + \frac{200}{370} \times (1 - 0.35) \times (0.20 - 0.10)$$

This calculation is illustrated in Figure 15.6.

Whenever $r_0 > r_B$, r_S increases with leverage, a result that we also found in the no-tax case. As stated earlier in this chapter, r_0 should exceed r_B. That is, since equity (even unlevered equity) is risky, it should have an expected return greater than that on the less risky debt.

Let's check our calculations by determining the value of the levered equity in another way. The algebraic formula for the value of levered equity is:

$$S = \frac{(\text{EBIT} - r_B B) \times (1 - T_C)}{r_S}$$

The numerator is the expected cash flow to levered equity after interest and taxes. The denominator is the rate at which the cash flow to equity is discounted.

For Divided Airlines we get:[19]

$$\frac{(\$153.85 - 0.10 \times \$200)(1 - 0.35)}{0.2351} = \$370$$

the same result we obtained earlier.

---

[18]This relationship can be shown as follows: Given MM Proposition I under taxes, a levered firm's market-value balance sheet can be written as

V_U = Value of unlevered firm	B = Debt
$T_C B$ = Tax shield	S = Equity

The value of the unlevered firm is simply the value of the assets without benefit of leverage. The balance sheet indicates that the firm's value increases by $T_C B$ when debt of B is added. The expected cash flow *from* the left-hand side of the balance sheet can be written as

$$V_U r_0 + T_C B r_B \tag{a}$$

Because assets are risky, their expected rate of return is r_0. The tax shield has the same risk as the debt, so its expected rate of return is r_B.

The expected cash *to* bondholders and stockholders together is

$$S r_S + B r_B \tag{b}$$

Expression (b) reflects the fact that stock earns an expected return of r_S and debt earns the interest rate r_B.

Because all cash flows are paid out as dividends in our no-growth perpetuity model, the cash flows going into the firm equal those going to stockholders. Hence (a) and (b) are equal:

$$S r_S + B r_B = V_U r_0 + T_C B r_B \tag{c}$$

Dividing both sides of (c) by S, subtracting $B r_B$ from both sides, and rearranging yields

$$r_S = \frac{V_U}{S} \times r_0 - (1 - T_C) \times \frac{B}{S} r_B \tag{d}$$

Because the value of the levered firm, V_L, equals $V_U + T_C B = B + S$, it follows that $V_U = S + (1 - T_C) \times B$. Thus, (d) can be rewritten as

$$r_S = \frac{S + (1 - T_C) \times B}{S} \times r_0 - (1 - T_C) \times \frac{B}{S} r_B \tag{e}$$

Bringing the terms involving $(1 - T_C) \times (B/S)$ together produces formula (15.6).

[19]The calculation suffers slightly from rounding error because we only carried the discount rate, 0.2351, out to four decimal places.

$$r_S = r_0 + (1 - T_C)(r_0 - r_B)B/S = 0.20 + \left(0.65 \times 0.10 \times \frac{200}{370}\right) = 0.2351$$

Financial leverage adds risk to the firm's equity. As compensation, the cost of equity rises
with the firm's risk. Note that r_0 is a single point, while r_S, r_B, and r_{WACC} are all entire lines.

The Weighted Average Cost of Capital r_{WACC} and Corporate Taxes

In Chapter 12, we defined the weighted average cost of capital (with corporate taxes) as

$$r_{WACC} = \frac{B}{V_L} r_B (1 - T_C) + \frac{S}{V_L} r_S$$

Note that the cost of debt capital, r_B, is multiplied by $(1 - T_C)$ because interest is tax-
deductible at the corporate level. However, the cost of equity, r_S, is not multiplied by this
factor because dividends are not deductible. In the no-tax case, r_{WACC} is not affected by
leverage. This result is reflected in Figure 15.3, which we discussed earlier. However, since
debt is tax-advantaged relative to equity, it can be shown that r_{WACC} declines with leverage
in a world with corporate taxes. This result can be seen in Figure 15.6.

For Divided Airlines, r_{WACC} is equal to

$$r_{WACC} = \left(\frac{200}{570} \times 0.10 \times 0.65\right) + \left(\frac{370}{570} \times 0.2351\right) = .1754$$

Divided Airlines has reduced its r_{WACC} from 0.20 (with no debt) to 0.1754 with reliance on
debt. This result is intuitively pleasing because it suggests that, when a firm lowers its r_{WACC},
the firm's value will increase. Using the r_{WACC} approach, we can confirm that the value of
Divided Airlines is $570.

$$V_L = \frac{EBIT \times (1 - T_C)}{r_{WACC}} = \frac{\$100}{.1754} = \$570$$

Stock Price and Leverage under Corporate Taxes

At this point, students often believe the numbers—or at least are too intimidated to dispute
them. However, they sometimes think we have asked the wrong question. "Why are we
choosing to maximize the value of the firm?" they will say. "If managers are looking out
for the stockholder's interest, why aren't they trying to maximize stock price?" If this question occurred to you, you have come to the right section.

Our response is twofold: First, we showed in the first section of this chapter that the capital structure that maximizes firm value is also the one that most benefits the interests of the
stockholders.[20]

---

[20]At that time, we pointed out that this result may not exactly hold in the more complex case where debt has a significant
possibility of default. Issues of default are treated in the next chapter.

However, that general explanation is not always convincing to students. As a second procedure, we calculate the stock price of Divided Airlines both before and after the exchange of debt for stock. We do this by presenting a set of market-value balance sheets. The market-value balance sheet for the company in its all-equity form can be represented as:

DIVIDED AIRLINES **Balance Sheet** **(all-equity firm)**		
Physical assets: $\dfrac{\$153.85}{0.20} \times (1 - 0.35) = \$500$	Equity	$500 (100 shares)

Assuming that there are 100 shares outstanding, each share is worth $5 = $500/100.

Next imagine that the company announces that, in the near future, it will issue $200 of debt to buy back $200 of stock. We know from our previous discussion that the value of the firm will rise to reflect the tax shield of debt. If we assume that capital markets efficiently price securities, the increase occurs immediately. That is, the rise occurs on the day of the announcement, not on the date of the debt-for-equity exchange. The market-value balance sheet now becomes:

DIVIDED AIRLINES **Balance Sheet** **(upon announcement of debt issue)**			
Physical assets:	$500	Equity	$570 (100 shares)
Present value of tax shield: $T_c B = 35\% \times \$200 =$	70		
Total Assets	$570		

Note that the debt has not yet been issued. Therefore, only equity appears on the right-hand side of the balance sheet. Each share is now worth $570/100 = $5.70, implying that the stockholders have benefited by $70. The equityholders gain because they are the owners of a firm that has improved its financial policy.

The introduction of the tax shield to the balance sheet is perplexing to many students. Although physical assets are tangible, the ethereal nature of the tax shield bothers these students. However, remember that an asset is any item with value. The tax shield has value because it reduces the stream of future taxes. The fact that one cannot touch the shield in the way that one can touch a physical asset is a philosophical, not a financial, consideration.

At some point, the exchange of debt for equity occurs. Debt of $200 is issued, and the proceeds are used to buy back shares. How many shares of stock are repurchased? Because shares are now selling at $5.70 each, the number of shares that the firm acquires is $200/$5.70 = 35.09. This leaves 64.91 (100 − 35.09) shares of stock outstanding. The market-value balance sheet is now:

DIVIDED AIRLINES **Balance Sheet** **(after exchange has taken place)**			
Physical assets:	$500	Equity	$370
		(100 − 35.09 = 64.91 shares)	
Present value of tax shield	70	Debt	200
Total assets	$570	Debt plus equity	$570

Summary of Modigliani-Miller Propositions with Corporate Taxes

Assumptions

- Corporations are taxed at the rate T_C, on earnings after interest.
- No transaction costs.
- Individuals and corporations borrow at same rate.

Results

Proposition I: $V_L = V_U + T_C B$
   (for a firm with perpetual debt)

Proposition II: $r_S = r_0 + \dfrac{B}{S}(1 - T_C)(r_0 - r_B)$

Intuition

Proposition I: Since corporations can deduct interest payments but not dividend payments, corporate leverage lowers tax payments.

Proposition II: The cost of equity rises with leverage, because the risk to equity rises with leverage.

Each share of stock is worth $370/64.91 = $5.70 after the exchange. Notice that the stock price does not change on the exchange date. As we mentioned above, the stock price moves on the date of the announcement only. Because the shareholders participating in the exchange receive a price equal to the market price per share after the exchange, they do not care whether they exchange their stock or not.

This example was provided for two reasons. First, it shows that an increase in the value of the firm from debt financing leads to an increase in the price of the stock. In fact, the stockholders capture the entire $70 tax shield. Second, we wanted to provide more work with market-value balance sheets.

A summary of the main results of Modigliani-Miller with corporate taxes is presented in the accompanying boxed section.

Concept Questions

1. What is the quirk in the tax code making a levered firm more valuable than an otherwise identical unlevered firm?
2. What is MM Proposition I under corporate taxes?
3. What is MM Proposition II under corporate taxes?

15.6 SUMMARY AND CONCLUSIONS

1. We began our discussion of the capital-structure decision by arguing that the particular capital structure that maximizes the value of the firm is also the one that provides the most benefit to the stockholders.

2. In a world of no taxes, the famous Proposition I of Modigliani and Miller proves that the value of the firm is unaffected by the debt-to-equity ratio. In other words, a firm's capital structure is a matter of indifference in that world. The authors obtain their results by showing that either a high or a low corporate ratio of debt to equity can be offset by homemade leverage. The result hinges on the assumption that individuals can borrow at the same rate as corporations, an assumption we believe to be quite plausible.

3. MM's Proposition II in a world without taxes states

$$r_S = r_0 + \frac{B}{S}(r_0 - r_B)$$

This implies that the expected rate of return on equity (also called the *cost of equity* or the *required return on equity*) is positively related to the firm's leverage. This makes intuitive sense, because the risk of equity rises with leverage, a point illustrated by the different sloped lines of Figure 15.2.

4. While the above work of MM is quite elegant, it does not explain the empirical findings on capital structure very well. MM imply that the capital-structure decision is a matter of indifference, while the decision appears to be a weighty one in the real world. To achieve real-world applicability, we next considered corporate taxes.

5. In a world with corporate taxes but no bankruptcy costs, firm value is an increasing function of leverage. The formula for the value of the firm is

$$V_L = V_U + T_C B$$

Expected return on levered equity can be expressed as

$$r_S = r_0 + (1 - T_C) \times (r_0 - r_B) \times \frac{B}{S}$$

Here, value is positively related to leverage. This result implies that firms should have a capital structure almost entirely composed of debt. Because real-world firms select more moderate levels of debt, the next chapter considers modifications to the results of this chapter.

KEY TERMS

MM Proposition I, *407*
MM Proposition II, *410*
MM Proposition I (corporate taxes), *421*

MM Proposition II (corporate taxes), *423*
pie model, *402*

SUGGESTED READINGS

The classic papers by Modigliani and Miller are

Modigliani, F., and M. H. Miller. "The Cost of Capital, Corporation Finance, and the Theory of Investment." *American Economic Review* (June 1958).

Modigliani, F., and M. H. Miller. "Corporate Income Taxes and the Cost of Capital: A Correction." *American Economic Review* (June 1963).

A more recent perspective on the above papers is provided by

Miller, M. "The Modigliani-Miller Propositions after 30 Years" in D. Chew, ed., *The New Corporate Finance: Where Theory Meets Practice* (New York: McGraw-Hill, 1993).

QUESTIONS & PROBLEMS

CAPITAL STRUCTURE WITHOUT TAXES

15.1 Alpha Corporation and Beta Corporation are identical in every way except their capital structures. Alpha Corporation, an all-equity firm, has 5,000 shares of stock outstanding, currently worth $20 per share. Beta Corporation uses leverage in its capital structure. The market value of Beta's debt is $25,000. The cost of this debt is 12 percent per annum. Each firm is expected to have earnings before interest of $350,000 in perpetuity. Neither firm pays taxes. Assume that every investor can borrow at 12 percent per annum.

   a. What is the value of Alpha Corporation?
   b. What is the value of Beta Corporation?
   c. What is the market value of Beta Corporation's equity?
   d. How much will it cost to purchase 20 percent of each firm's equity?
   e. Assuming each firm meets its earnings estimates, what will be the dollar return to each position in part (*d*) over the next year?
   f. Construct an investment strategy in which an investor purchases 20 percent of Alpha's equity and replicates both the cost and dollar return of purchasing 20 percent of Beta's equity.
   g. Is Alpha's equity more or less risky than Beta's equity? Explain.

15.2 Acetate, Inc., has equity with a market value of $20 million and debt with a market value of $10 million. The cost of the debt is 14 percent per annum. Treasury bills that mature in one year yield 8 percent per annum, and the expected return on the market portfolio over the next year is 18 percent. The beta of Acetate's equity is 0.9. The firm pays no taxes.

   a. What is Acetate's debt-equity ratio?

   b. What is the firm's weighted average cost of capital?

   c. What is the cost of capital for an otherwise identical all-equity firm?

15.3 Levered, Inc., and Unlevered, Inc., are identical in every way except their capital structures. Each company expects to earn $96 million before interest per year in perpetuity, with each company distributing all its earnings as dividends. Levered's perpetual debt has a market value of $275 million and costs 8 percent per annum. Levered has 4.5 million shares outstanding, currently worth $100 per share. Unlevered has no debt and 10 million shares outstanding, currently worth $80 per share. Neither firm pays taxes. Is Levered's stock a better buy than Unlevered's stock?

15.4 The Veblen Company and the Knight Company are identical in every respect except that Veblen is not levered. The market value of Knight Company's 6-percent bonds is $1 million. Financial information for the two firms appears below. All earnings streams are perpetuities. Neither firm pays taxes. Both firms distribute all earnings available to common stockholders immediately.

	Veblen	Knight
Projected operating income	$ 300,000	$ 300,000
Year-end interest on debt	—	60,000
Projected earnings available to common stock	$ 300,000	$ 240,000
Required return on equity (r_S)	0.125	0.140
Market value of stock	$2,400,000	$1,714,000
Market value of debt	—	1,000,000
Value of the firm	$2,400,000	$2,714,000
Weighted average cost of capital (r_{WACC})	0.125	0.110
Debt-equity ratio	0	0.584

   a. An investor who is able to borrow at 6 percent per annum wishes to purchase 5 percent of Knight's equity. Can he increase his dollar return by purchasing 5 percent of Veblen's equity if he borrows so that the initial net cost of the two options are the same?

   b. Given the two investment strategies in (a), which will investors choose? When will this process cease?

15.5 Grimsley, Inc., is an all-equity firm with 100,000 shares of common stock outstanding, worth $50 per share. Neither the firm nor its shareholders pay any taxes. Consider three stockholders of Grimsley, Ms. Hannon, Ms. Finney, and Ms. Grace. All three individuals can borrow and lend at 20 percent per annum, the same rate at which the firm lends and borrows. The value of their holdings in Grimsley and of their personal borrowing and lending positions are listed below:

	Value of Grimsley Shares	Total Borrowing	Total Lending
Ms. Hannon	$10,000	$2,000	$ —
Ms. Finney	50,000	—	6,000
Ms. Grace	20,000	—	—

Grimsley's management has recently decided to alter the firm's capital structure so that the debt-to-equity ratio of the firm is 0.25. In order to do this, Grimsley issued $1 million in debt yielding 20 percent per annum and used the funds to repurchase 20,000 shares. None of these shares were repurchased from Ms. Hannon, Ms. Finney, or Ms. Grace.

The three stockholders wish to alter their positions so that their payoffs after the restructuring equal their payoffs prior to the restructuring. Assume that Grimsley immediately distributes all earnings available to stockholders at the end of the year and that the restructuring will have no effect on the firm's earnings before taxes. Show the values of each of the investor's shares in Grimsley, as well as their borrowing and lending positions, after they have adjusted their portfolios.

15.6 Rayburn Manufacturing, Inc., is currently an all-equity firm that pays no taxes. The market value of the firm's equity is $2 million. The cost of this unlevered equity is 18 percent per annum. Rayburn plans to issue $400,000 in debt and use the proceeds to repurchase stock. The cost of debt is 10 percent per annum.

a. After Rayburn repurchases the stock, what will the firm's weighted average cost of capital be?

b. After the repurchase, what will the cost of equity be? Explain.

c. Use your answer to (*b*) to compute Rayburn's weighted average cost of capital after the repurchase. Is this answer consistent with (*a*)?

15.7 Strom, Inc., is an all-equity firm with 250,000 shares of common stock outstanding. Each share is worth $20. The firm pays no taxes. The appropriate discount rate for the firm's unlevered equity is 15 percent. Strom's earnings last year were $750,000, and management expects that the firm's earnings will remain at $750,000 per annum into perpetuity.

Strom is planning to buy a competitor's business for $300,000. Once acquired, the competitor's facilities are expected to increase Strom's earnings by $120,000 per year. The competitor is also an all-equity firm with the same risks as Strom and a required return on its equity of 15 percent.

a. Construct the market-value balance sheet for Strom before the announcement of the buyout is made.

b. Suppose Strom decides to issue equity in order to fund the buyout.

1. According to the efficient-market hypothesis, what will Strom's stock price be immediately after the announcement?

2. Construct Strom's market-value balance sheet immediately after the announcement.

3. How many shares will Strom need to issue in order to fund the buyout?

4. Construct Strom's market-value balance sheet after the equity issue but before the purchase is finalized.

5. Construct Strom's market-value balance sheet after the purchase is finalized.

6. What is the expected return to Strom's equityholders after the buyout?

7. What is Strom's weighted average cost of capital after the buyout?

c. Suppose Strom decides to issue 10 percent debt in order to fund the buyout.

1. Construct Strom's market-value balance sheet immediately after the announcement.

2. Construct Strom's market-value balance sheet after the debt issue but before the purchase is finalized.

3. Construct Strom's market-value balance sheet after the purchase is finalized.

4. What is the expected return to Strom's equityholders after the buyout?

5. What is Strom's weighted average cost of capital after the buyout?

15.8 The Gulf Power Company, an all-equity firm, is planning to build a new power plant. Financial data pertaining to the company and the new power plant are listed below. Assume all earnings are paid out as dividends.

Company Data	
Annual expected earnings (in perpetuity)	$27 million
Number of shares outstanding	10 million
New Power Plant	
Initial outlay	$20 million
Added annual expected earnings (in perpetuity)	$ 3 million

The new power plant has the same risk as existing assets. The current required rate of return on the firm's equity is 10 percent. Assume there are no taxes and no costs of bankruptcy.

a. Construct Gulf's market-value balance sheet before the firm announces that it will build the new power plant. What is the price per share of Gulf's equity?

b. Suppose Gulf decides to issue equity to fund the initial outlay for the power plant.

   1. Construct Gulf's market-value balance sheet immediately after the announcement. What is the new price per share of the firm's equity?

   2. How many shares will Gulf need to issue in order to fund the outlay?

   3. Construct Gulf's market-value balance sheet after the equity issue but before the outlay is made.

   4. Construct Gulf's market-value balance sheet after the outlay has been made.

   5. What will the value of Gulf Power be if common stock is issued to finance the construction of the new power plant?

c. Suppose Gulf decides to issue $20 million of 8-percent bonds in order to fund the initial outlay for the power plant.

   1. Construct Gulf's market-value balance sheet immediately after the announcement. What is the new price per share of the firm's equity?

   2. Construct Gulf's market-value balance sheet after the debt issue but before the outlay is made.

   3. Construct Gulf's market-value balance sheet after the outlay has been made.

   4. What will the value of Gulf Power be if debt is issued to finance the construction of the new power plant?

   5. Calculate the rate of return required by equityholders after both the debt issue and the completion of the new plant.

   6. Calculate the firm's weighted average cost of capital after both the debt issue and the completion of the new plant.

 15.9 In a world with no taxes, no transaction costs, and no costs of financial distress, are the following statements true, false, or uncertain? Explain your answers.

a. If a firm issues equity to repurchase some of its debt, the price per share of the firm's stock will rise because the shares are less risky.

b. Moderate borrowing will not increase the required return on a firm's equity.

15.10 List the three assumptions that lie behind the Modigliani-Miller theory in a world without taxes. Are these assumptions reasonable in the real world? Explain.

15.11 Digital Sound, Inc., is an all-equity firm with 1 million shares of common stock outstanding at $10 per share. Digital is expected to generate $1.5 million of annual earnings in perpetuity. Michael Lefton is interested in acquiring a 1 percent stake in the firm's equity. He will either borrow 20 percent, 40 percent, or 60 percent of the purchase price at an interest rate of 10 percent per annum. Assume that Digital Sound does not pay any taxes and that the firm immediately distributes all of its earnings as dividends.

a. How much will it cost for Michael to purchase 1 percent of Digital's equity, net of debt, given each financing choice?

b. What is the expected return on Michael's investment given each financing choice?

15.12 Locomotive Corporation is planning to repurchase part of its common stock by issuing corporate debt. As a result, the firm's debt-to-equity ratio is expected to rise from 40 percent to 50 percent. The firm currently has $7.5 million worth of debt outstanding. The cost of this debt is 10 percent per annum. Locomotive expects to earn $3.75 million per annum in perpetuity. Locomotive pays no taxes.

a. What is the market value of Locomotive Corporation before and after the repurchase announcement?

b. What is the expected return on the firm's equity (r_S) before the announcement of the stock repurchase plan?

c. What is the expected return on the equity of an otherwise identical all-equity firm (r_0)?

d. What is the expected return on the firm's equity (r_S) after the announcement of the stock repurchase plan?

**CAPITAL
STRUCTURE
WITH
CORPORATE
TAXES**

15.13 The market value of a firm with $500,000 of debt is $1.7 million. The pretax interest rate on debt is 10 percent per annum, and the company is in the 34 percent tax bracket. The company expects $306,000 of earnings before interest and taxes every year in perpetuity.
  a. What would the value of the firm be if it were financed entirely with equity?
  b. What amount of the firm's annual earnings is available to stockholders?

15.14 An all-equity firm has 175,000 shares of common stock outstanding, currently worth $20 per share. Its equity holders require a 20 percent return. The firm decides to issue $1 million of 10 percent debt and use the proceeds to repurchase common stock. According to Modigliani-Miller, what is the market value of the firm's equity after the repurchase? Assume a 30 percent corporate tax rate.

15.15 Strider Publishing Company, an all-equity firm, expects perpetual earnings before interest and taxes (EBIT) of $2.5 million per year. Strider's after-tax, all-equity discount rate is 20 percent. The firm is subject to a 34 percent corporate tax rate.
  a. What is the value of Strider Publishing?
  b. If Strider issues $600,000 of debt and uses the proceeds to repurchase stock, what will the value of the firm be?
  c. Explain any difference in your answers to (a) and (b).
  d. What assumptions are you making when valuing Strider?

15.16 Gibson, Inc., expects perpetual earnings before interest and taxes of $1.2 million per year. The firm's pretax cost of debt is 8 percent per annum, and its annual interest expense is $200,000. Company analysts estimate that the unlevered cost of Gibson's equity is 12 percent. Gibson is subject to a 35 percent corporate tax rate.
  a. What is the value of this firm?
  b. If there are no costs of financial distress or bankruptcy, what percentage of the firm's capital structure would be financed by debt?
  c. Is the conclusion in (b) applicable to the real world?

15.17 Green Manufacturing, Inc., plans to announce that it will issue $2 million of perpetual debt and use the proceeds to repurchase common stock. The bonds will have a 6-percent annual coupon rate. Green is currently an all-equity firm worth $10 million with 500,000 shares of common stock outstanding. After the sale of the bonds, Green will maintain the new capital structure indefinitely. Green currently generates annual pretax earnings of $1.5 million. This level of earnings is expected to remain constant in perpetuity. Green is subject to a corporate tax rate of 40 percent.
  a. What is the expected return on Green's equity before the announcement of the debt issue?
  b. Construct Green's market-value balance sheet before the announcement of the debt issue. What is the price per share of the firm's equity?
  c. Construct Green's market-value balance sheet immediately after the announcement of the debt issue.
  d. What is Green's stock price per share immediately after the repurchase announcement?
  e. How many shares will Green repurchase as a result of the debt issue? How many shares of common stock will remain after the repurchase?
  f. Construct the market-value balance sheet after the restructuring. What is Green's stock price per share after the restructuring?
  g. What is the required return on Green's equity after the restructuring?

15.18 The Holland Company expects perpetual earnings before interest and taxes (EBIT) of $4 million per year. The firm's after-tax, all-equity discount rate (r_0) is 15 percent. Holland is subject to a corporate tax rate of 35 percent. The pretax cost of the firm's debt capital is 10 percent per annum, and the firm has $10 million of debt in its capital structure.
  a. What is Holland's value?
  b. What is Holland's cost of equity (r_S)?
  c. What is Holland's weighted average cost of capital (r_{WACC})?

15.19 Williamson, Inc., has a debt-to-equity ratio of 2.5. The firm's weighted average cost of capital (r_{WACC}) is 15 percent, and its pretax cost of debt is 10 percent. Williamson is subject to a corporate tax rate of 35 percent.

a. What is Williamson's cost of equity capital (r_S)?

b. What is Williamson's unlevered cost of equity capital (r_0)?

c. What would Williamson's weighted average cost of capital (r_{WACC}) be if the firm's debt-to-equity ratio were 0.75? What if it were 1.5?

15.20 General Tools (GT) expects earnings before interest and taxes (EBIT) of $100,000 every year into perpetuity. The firm currently has no debt, but it can borrow at 10 percent per annum. GT's cost of equity (r_0) is 25 percent, and the firm is subject to a corporate tax rate of 40 percent.

a. What is the value of the firm?

b. What will the value of GT be if it borrows $100,000 and uses the proceeds to repurchase equity?

15.21 Stephenson Real Estate Company is an all-equity firm with 15 million shares of common stock outstanding worth $32.50 per share. Stephenson is planning to purchase a huge track of land in southeastern Texas for $100 million. The land will subsequently be leased to tenant farmers, increasing Stephenson's annual expected pretax earnings by $25 million in perpetuity. The firm's unlevered cost of equity capital (r_0) is 12.5 percent. Stephenson is subject to a corporate tax rate of 40 percent. The interest rate on Stephenson's bonds is 8 percent per annum.

a. If Stephenson wishes to maximize its total market value, would you recommend that it issue debt or equity in order to finance the purchase? Explain.

b. Construct Stephenson's market-value balance sheet before it announces the purchase.

c. Suppose Stephenson decides to issue equity in order to finance the purchase.

    1. What is the net present value of the project?

    2. Construct Stephenson's market-value balance sheet after it announces that the firm will finance the purchase using equity. What is the new price per share of the firm's stock? How many shares will Stephenson need to issue in order to finance the purchase?

    3. Construct Stephenson's market-value balance sheet after the equity issue but before the purchase has been made. How many shares of common stock does Stephenson have outstanding? What is the price per share of the firm's stock?

    4. Construct Stephenson's market-value balance sheet after the purchase has been made.

d. Suppose Stephenson decides to issue debt in order to finance the purchase.

    1. What will the market value of Stephenson be if the purchase is financed with debt?

    2. Construct Stephenson's market-value balance sheet after both the debt issue and the land purchase. What is the price per share of the firm's stock?

e. Which method of financing maximizes the per share stock price of Stephenson's equity?

15.22 Locate the annual balance sheets for General Motors (GM), Merck (MRK), and Kellogg (K). For each company calculate the long-term debt-to-equity ratio for the prior two years. Why would these companies use such different capital structures?

15.23 Look up Georgia Pacific (GP) and download the annual income statements. For the most recent year, calculate the marginal tax rate, EBIT, and find the total interest expense. From the annual balance sheets calculate the total long-term debt (including the portion due within one year). Using the interest expense and total long-term debt, calculate the average cost of debt. Next, find the estimated beta for Georgia Pacific on the S&P Stock Report. Use this reported beta and the historical average risk-free rate and market risk premium found in Chapter 9 to calculate the levered cost of equity. Now calculate the unlevered cost of equity, then the unlevered EBIT. What is the unlevered value of Georgia Pacific? What is the value of the interest tax shield and the value of the levered Georgia Pacific?

Capital Structure: *Limits to the Use of Debt*

EXECUTIVE SUMMARY

One question a student might ask is, "Does the MM theory with taxes predict the capital structure of typical firms?" The answer is, unfortunately, "no." The theory states that $V_L = V_U + T_C B$. According to this equation, one can always increase firm value by increasing leverage, implying that firms should issue maximum debt. This is inconsistent with the real world, where firms generally employ only moderate amounts of debt.

However, the MM theory tells us *where to look* when searching for the determinants of capital structure. For example, the theory ignores bankruptcy and its attendant costs. Because these costs are likely to get out of hand for a highly levered firm, the moderate leverage of most firms can now easily be explained. Our discussion leads quite naturally to the idea that a firm's capital structure involves a trade-off between the tax benefits of debt and the costs of financial distress and bankruptcy.

In addition, the MM theory ignores personal taxes. In the real world, the personal tax rate on interest is higher than the personal tax rate on equity distributions. Thus, the personal tax penalties to bondholders tend to offset the tax benefits to debt at the corporate level. Even when bankruptcy costs are ignored, this idea implies that there is an optimal amount of debt for the economy as a whole. The implications of bankruptcy costs and personal taxes are examined in this chapter.

16.1 Costs of Financial Distress

Bankruptcy Risk or Bankruptcy Cost?

As mentioned throughout the previous chapter, debt provides tax benefits to the firm. However, debt puts pressure on the firm, because interest and principal payments are obligations. If these obligations are not met, the firm may risk some sort of financial distress. The ultimate distress is *bankruptcy,* where ownership of the firm's assets is legally transferred from the stockholders to the bondholders. These debt obligations are fundamentally different from stock obligations. While stockholders like and expect dividends, they are not legally entitled to dividends in the way bondholders are legally entitled to interest and principal payments.

We show below that bankruptcy costs, or more generally financial distress costs, tend to offset the advantages to debt. We begin by positing a simple example of bankruptcy. All taxes are ignored to focus only on the costs of debt.

EXAMPLE

The Knight Corporation plans to be in business for one more year. It forecasts a cash flow of either $100 or $50 in the coming year, each occurring with 50-percent probability. The firm has no other assets. Previously issued debt requires payments of $49 of interest and principal. The Day Corporation has identical cash flow prospects but has $60 of interest and principal obligations. The cash flows of these two firms can be represented as:

	Knight Corporation		Day Corporation	
	Boom Times (prob. 50%)	**Recession (prob. 50%)**	**Boom Times (prob. 50%)**	**Recession (prob. 50%)**
Cash flow	$100	$50	$100	$50
Payment of interest and principal on debt	49	49	60	50
Distribution to stockholders	$ 51	$ 1	$ 40	$ 0

For Knight Corporation in both boom times and recession and for Day Corporation in boom times, cash flow exceeds interest and principal payments. In these situations, the bondholders are paid in full and the stockholders receive any residual. However, the most interesting of the four columns involves Day Corporation in a recession. Here, the bondholders are owed $60, but the firm has only $50 in cash. Since we assumed that the firm has no other assets, the bondholders cannot be satisfied in full. If bankruptcy occurs, the bondholders will receive all of the firm's cash, and the stockholders will receive nothing. Importantly, the stockholders do not have to come up with the additional $10 ($60 − $50). Corporations have limited liability in America and most other countries, implying that bondholders cannot sue the stockholders for the extra $10.[1]

We assume that (1) both bondholders and stockholders are risk-neutral and (2) the interest rate is 10 percent. Due to this risk neutrality, cash flows to both stockholders and bondholders are to be discounted at the 10-percent rate.[2] We can evaluate the debt, the equity, and the entire firm for both Knight and Day as follows:

$$S_{\text{KNIGHT}} = \$23.64 = \frac{\$51 \times \frac{1}{2} + \$1 \times \frac{1}{2}}{1.10} \qquad S_{\text{DAY}} = \$18.18 = \frac{\$40 \times \frac{1}{2} + 0 \times \frac{1}{2}}{1.10}$$

$$B_{\text{KNIGHT}} = \$44.54 = \frac{\$49 \times \frac{1}{2} + \$49 \times \frac{1}{2}}{1.10} \qquad B_{\text{DAY}} = \$50 = \frac{\$60 \times \frac{1}{2} + \$50 \times \frac{1}{2}}{1.10}$$

$$V_{\text{KNIGHT}} = \$68.18 \qquad\qquad\qquad V_{\text{DAY}} = \$68.18$$

Note that the two firms have the same value, even though Day runs the risk of bankruptcy. Furthermore, notice that Day's bondholders are valuing the bonds with "their eyes open." Though the promised payment of principal and interest is $60, the bondholders are willing to pay only $50. Hence, their *promised* return or yield is:

$$\frac{\$60}{\$50} - 1 = 20\%$$

---

[1]There are situations where the limited liability of corporation can be "pierced." Typically, fraud or misrepresentation must be present.

[2]Normally, one assumes that investors are *averse* to risk. In that case, the cost of debt capital, r_B, is less than the cost of equity capital, r_S, which rises with leverage as shown in the previous chapter. In addition, r_B may rise when the increase in leverage allows the possibility of default.

For simplicity, we assume *risk neutrality* in this example. This means that investors are indifferent to whether risk is high, low, or even absent. Here, $r_S = r_B$, because risk-neutral investors do not demand compensation for bearing risk. In addition, neither r_S nor r_B rises with leverage. Because the interest rate is 10 percent, our assumption of risk neutrality implies that $r_S = 10\%$ as well.

Though financial economists believe that investors are risk-averse, they frequently develop examples based on risk-neutrality to isolate a point unrelated to risk. This is our approach, because we want to focus on bankruptcy costs—not bankruptcy risk. The same qualitative conclusions from this example can be drawn in a world of risk aversion, albeit with *much* more difficulty for the reader.

Day's debt can be viewed as a *junk bond,* because the probability of default is so high. As with all junk bonds, bondholders demand a high promised yield.

Day's example is not realistic because it ignores an important cash flow to be discussed below. A more realistic set of numbers might be:

Day Corporation			
	Boom Times (prob. 50%)	Recession (prob. 50%)	
Earnings	$100	$50	$S_{DAY} = \$18.18 = \dfrac{\$40 \times \frac{1}{2} + 0 \times \frac{1}{2}}{1.10}$
Debt repayment	60	35	$B_{DAY} = \$43.18 = \dfrac{\$60 \times \frac{1}{2} + \$35 \times \frac{1}{2}}{1.10}$
Distribution to stockholders	$ 40	$ 0	$V_{DAY} = \$61.36$

Why do the bondholders receive only $35 in a recession? If cash flow is only $50, bondholders will be informed that they will not be paid in full. These bondholders are likely to hire lawyers to negotiate or even to sue the company. Similarly, the firm is likely to hire lawyers to defend itself. Further costs will be incurred if the case gets to a bankruptcy court. These fees are always paid before the bondholders get paid. In this example, we are assuming that bankruptcy costs total $15 ($50 − 35).

The value of the firm is now $61.36, an amount below the $68.18 figure calculated earlier. By comparing Day's value in a world with no bankruptcy costs to Day's value in a world with these costs, we conclude

> The possibility of bankruptcy has a negative effect on the value of the firm. However, it is not the *risk* of bankruptcy itself that lowers value. Rather it is the *costs* associated with bankruptcy that lower value.

The explanation follows from our pie example. In a world without bankruptcy costs, the bondholders and the stockholders share the entire pie. However, bankruptcy costs eat up some of the pie in the real world, leaving less for the stockholders and bondholders.

Because the bondholders are aware that they would receive little in a recession, they pay a low price. In this case, their promised return is:

$$\frac{\$60}{\$43.18} - 1 = 39.0\%$$

The bondholders are paying a fair price if they are realistic about both the probability and the cost of bankruptcy. It is the *stockholders* who bear these future bankruptcy costs. To see this, imagine that Day Corporation was originally all equity. The stockholders want the firm to issue debt with a promised payment of $60 and use the proceeds to pay a dividend. If there had been no bankruptcy costs, our results show that bondholders would pay $50 to purchase debt with a promised payment of $60. Hence, a dividend of $50 could be paid to the stockholders. However, if bankruptcy costs exist, bondholders would only pay $43.18 for the debt. In that case, only a dividend of $43.18 could be paid to the stockholders. Because the dividend is smaller when bankruptcy costs exist, the stockholders are hurt by bankruptcy costs.

Concept Questions

1. What does risk neutrality mean?
2. Can one have bankruptcy risk without bankruptcy costs?
3. Why do we say that stockholders bear bankruptcy costs?

16.2 Description of Financial Distress Costs

The preceding example showed that bankruptcy costs can lower the value of the firm. In fact, the same general result holds even if a legal bankruptcy is prevented. Thus, *financial distress costs* may be a better phrase than *bankruptcy costs*. It is worthwhile to describe these costs in more detail.

Direct Costs of Financial Distress: Legal and Administrative Costs of Liquidation or Reorganization

As mentioned earlier, lawyers are involved throughout all the stages before and during bankruptcy. With fees often in the hundreds of dollars an hour, these costs can add up quickly. A wag once remarked that bankruptcies are to lawyers what blood is to sharks. In addition, administrative and accounting fees can substantially add to the total bill. And if a trial takes place, we must not forget expert witnesses. Each side may hire a number of these witnesses to testify about the fairness of a proposed settlement. Their fees can easily rival those of lawyers or accountants. (However, we personally look upon these witnesses more kindly, because they are frequently drawn from the ranks of finance professors.)

Perhaps one of the most well-publicized bankruptcies in recent years concerned a municipality, Orange County, California, not a corporation. This bankruptcy followed large bond-trading losses in the county's financial portfolio. The *Los Angeles Times* stated:

> Orange County taxpayers lost $1.69 billion, and their government, one year ago today, sank into bankruptcy. Now they are spending millions more to get out of it.
>
> Accountants pore over fiscal ledgers at $325 an hour. Lawyers toil into the night—at $385 an hour. Financial advisors from one of the nation's most prominent investment houses labor for the taxpayers at $150,000 a month. Clerks stand by the photocopy machines, running up bills that sometimes exceed $3,000.
>
> Total so far: $29 million. And it's nowhere near over.
>
> The multi-pronged effort to lift Orange County out of the nation's worst municipal bankruptcy has become a money-eating machine, gobbling up taxpayer funds at a rate of $2.4 million a month. That's $115,000 a day.
>
> County administrators are not alarmed.
>
> They say Orange County's bankruptcy was an epic disaster that will require equally dramatic expenditures of taxpayer cash to help it survive. While they have refused to pay several thousand dollars worth of claimed expenses—lavish dinners, big hotel bills—they have rarely questioned the sky-high hourly fees. They predict the costs could climb much higher.
>
> Indeed, participants in the county's investment pool have agreed to create a separate $50 million fund to pay the costs of doing legal battle with Wall Street.[3]

A number of academic studies have measured the direct costs of financial distress. While large in absolute amount, these costs are actually small as a percentage of firm value. White, Altman, and Weiss estimate the direct costs of financial distress to be about 3 percent of the market value of the firm.[4] In a study of direct financial distress costs of 20 railroad bankruptcies, Warner finds that net financial distress costs were, on average, 1 percent of the market value of the firm seven years before bankruptcy and were somewhat larger percentages as bankruptcy approached (for example, 2.5 percent of the market value of the

---

[3]"The High Cost of Going Bankrupt," *Los Angeles Times Orange County Edition,* December 6, 1995. Taken from Lexis/Nexis.

[4]M. J. White, "Bankruptcy Costs and the New Bankruptcy Code," *Journal of Finance* (May 1983); E. I. Altman, " A Further Empirical Investigation of the Bankruptcy Cost Question," *Journal of Finance* (September 1984); and Lawrence A. Weiss, "Bankruptcy Resolution: Direct Costs and Violation of Priority of Claims," *Journal of Financial Economics* 27 (1990).

firm three years before bankruptcy).[5] Lubben estimates the average cost of legal fees alone to be about 1.5 percent of total assets for bankrupt firms.[6]

Of course, few firms end up in bankruptcy. Thus, the preceding cost estimates must be multiplied by the probability of bankruptcy to yield the *expected* cost of bankruptcy. Warner states:

> Suppose, for example, that a given railroad picks a level of debt such that bankruptcy would occur on average once every 20 years (i.e., the probability of going bankrupt is 5 percent in any given year). Assume that when bankruptcy occurs, the firm would pay a lump sum penalty equal to 3 percent of its now current market value. . . .
>
> [Then], the firm's expected cost of bankruptcy is equal to fifteen one-hundredths of one percent of its now current market value.

Indirect Costs of Financial Distress

Impaired Ability to Conduct Business   Bankruptcy hampers conduct with customers and suppliers. Sales are frequently lost because of both fear of impaired service and loss of trust. For example, many loyal Chrysler customers switched to other manufacturers when Chrysler skirted insolvency in the 1970s. These buyers questioned whether parts and servicing would be available were Chrysler to fail. Sometimes the taint of impending bankruptcy is enough to drive customers away. For example, gamblers avoided Atlantis casino in Atlantic City after it became technically insolvent. Gamblers are a superstitious bunch. Many reasoned, "If the casino itself cannot make money, how can I expect to make money there?" A particularly outrageous story concerned two unrelated stores both named Mitchells in New York City. When one Mitchells declared bankruptcy, customers stayed away from both stores. In time, the second store was forced to declare bankruptcy as well.

Though these costs clearly exist, it is quite difficult to measure them. Altman estimates that both direct and indirect costs of financial distress are frequently greater than 20 percent of firm value.[7] Andrade and Kaplan estimate total distress costs to be between 10 percent and 20 percent of firm value.[8] Bar-Or estimates expected future distress costs for firms that are currently healthy to be 8 to 10 percent of operating value, a number below the estimates of either Altman or Andrade and Kaplan.[9] However, unlike Bar-Or, these authors consider distress costs for firms already in distress, not expected distress costs for currently healthy firms.

Cutler and Summers examine the costs of the well-publicized Texaco bankruptcy.[10] In January of 1984, Pennzoil reached what it believed to be a binding agreement to acquire three-sevenths of Getty Oil. However, less than a week later, Texaco acquired all of Getty

[5]J. B. Warner, "Bankruptcy Costs: Some Evidence," *Journal of Finance* (May 1977).

[6]Stephen J. Lubben, "The Direct Costs of Corporate Reorganization: An Empirical Examination of Professional Fees in Large Chapter 11 Cases," *American Bankruptcy Law Journal* (2000).

[7]Altman, *op. cit.* "A Further Empirical Investigation."
   A fascinating and provacative set of articles by Robert Haugen and Lemma Senbet ["The Insignificance of Bankruptcy Costs to the Theory of Optimal Capital Structure." *Journal of Finance* (May 1978); "New Perspectives on Information Asymmetry and Agency Relationships." *Journal of Financial and Quantitative Analysis* (November 1979); "Bankruptcy and Agency Costs: Their Significance to the Theory of Optimal Capital Structure," *Journal of Financial and Quantitative Analysis* (March 1988)] argue that financial distress should, at most, only slightly impair the firm's ability to conduct business. They say that customers, employees, and so on, are concerned with the tenure of the *firm*, which is fundamentally a function of its asset characteristics. This tenure should not be dependent on the way the assets are financed.

[8]Gregor Andrade and Steven N. Kaplan, "How Costly is Financial (Not Economic) Distress? Evidence from Highly Leveraged Transactions that Became Distressed," *Journal of Finance* (October 1998).

[9]Yuval Bar-Or, "An Investigation of Expected Financial Distress Costs," unpublished paper, Wharton School, University of Pennsylvania (March 2000).

[10]David M. Cutler and Lawrence H. Summers, "The Costs of Conflict Resolution and Financial Distress: Evidence from the Texaco-Pennzoil Litigation," *Rand Journal of Economics* (Summer 1988).

at a higher per-share price. Pennzoil then sued Getty for breach of contract. Because Texaco had previously indemnified Getty against litigation, Texaco became liable for damages.

In November 1985, the Texas State Court awarded damages of $12 billion to Pennzoil, although this amount was later reduced. As a result, Texaco filed for bankruptcy. Cutler and Summers identify nine important events over the course of the litigation. They find that Texaco's market value (stock price times number of shares outstanding) fell a cumulative $4.1 billion over these events, whereas Pennzoil rose only $682 million. Thus, Pennzoil gained about one-sixth of what Texaco lost, resulting in a net loss to the two firms of almost $3.5 billion.

What could explain this net loss? Cutler and Summers suggest that it is likely due to costs that Texaco and Pennzoil incurred from the litigation and subsequent bankruptcy. The authors argue that direct bankruptcy fees represent only a small part of these costs, estimating Texaco's after-tax legal expenses to be about $165 million. Legal costs to Pennzoil were more difficult to assess, because Pennzoil's lead lawyer, Joe Jamail, stated publicly that he had no set fee. However, using a clever statistical analysis, the authors estimate his fee to be about $200 million. Thus, one must search elsewhere for the bulk of the costs.

Indirect costs of financial distress may be the culprit here. An affidavit by Texaco stated that, following the lawsuit, some of its suppliers were demanding cash payment. Other suppliers halted or canceled shipments of crude oil. Certain banks restricted Texaco's use of futures contracts on foreign exchange. The affidavit stressed that these constraints were reducing Texaco's ability to run its business, leading to deterioration of its financial condition. Could these sorts of indirect costs explain the $3.5 billion disparity between Texaco's drop and Pennzoil's rise in market value? Unfortunately, although it is quite likely that indirect costs play a role here, there is simply no way to obtain a decent, quantitative estimate for them.

Agency Costs

When a firm has debt, conflicts of interest arise between stockholders and bondholders. Because of this, stockholders are tempted to pursue selfish strategies. These conflicts of interest, which are magnified when financial distress is incurred, impose **agency costs** on the firm. We describe three kinds of selfish strategies that stockholders use to hurt the bondholders and help themselves. These strategies are costly because they will lower the market value of the whole firm.

Selfish Investment Strategy 1: *Incentive to Take Large Risks*   Firms near bankruptcy oftentimes takes great chances, because they believe that they are playing with someone else's money. To see this, imagine a levered firm considering two *mutually exclusive* projects, a low-risk one and a high-risk one. There are two equally likely outcomes, recession and boom. The firm is in such dire straits that should a recession hit, it will come near to bankruptcy with one project and actually fall into bankruptcy with the other. The cash flows for the entire firm if the low-risk project is taken can be described as:

	Value of Entire Firm if Low-Risk Project Is Chosen					
	Probability	**Value of Firm**	**=**	**Stock**	**+**	**Bonds**
Recession	0.5	$100	=	$ 0	+	$100
Boom	0.5	200	=	100	+	100

If recession occurs, the value of the firm will be $100, and if boom obtains, the value of the firm will be $200. The expected value of the firm is $150 (0.5 × $100 + 0.5 × $200).

The firm has promised to pay bondholders $100. Shareholders will obtain the difference between the total payoff and the amount paid to the bondholders. In other words, the bondholders have the prior claim on the payoffs, and the shareholders have the residual claim.

Now suppose that another, riskier project can be substituted for the low-risk project. The payoffs and probabilities are as follows:

		Value of Entire Firm if High-Risk Project Is Chosen				
	Probability	Value of Firm	=	Stock	+	Bonds
Recession	0.5	$ 50	=	$ 0	+	$ 50
Boom	0.5	240	=	140	+	100

The expected value of the *firm* is $145 (0.5 × $50 + 0.5 × $240), which is lower than the expected value of the firm with the low-risk project. Thus, the low-risk project would be accepted if the firm were all equity. However, note that the expected value of the *stock* is $70 (0.5 × 0 + 0.5 × $140) with the high-risk project, but only $50 (0.5 × 0 + 0.5 × $100) with the low-risk project. Given the firm's present levered state, stockholders will select the high-risk project, even though the high-risk project has a *lower* NPV.

The key is that, relative to the low-risk project, the high-risk project increases firm value in a boom and decreases firm value in a recession. The increase in value in a boom is captured by the stockholders, because the bondholders are paid in full (they receive $100) regardless of which project is accepted. Conversely, the drop in value in a recession is lost by the bondholders, because they are paid in full with the low-risk project but receive only $50 with the high-risk one. The stockholders will receive nothing in a recession anyway, whether the high-risk or low-risk project is selected. Thus, financial economists argue that stockholders expropriate value from the bondholders by selecting high-risk projects.

A story, perhaps apocryphal, illustrates this idea. It seems that Federal Express was near financial collapse within a few years of its inception. The founder, Frederick Smith, took $20,000 of corporate funds to Las Vegas in despair. He won at the gaming tables, providing enough capital to allow the firm to survive. Had he lost, the banks would simply have received $20,000 less when the firm reached bankruptcy.

Selfish Investment Strategy 2: Incentive toward Underinvestment   Stockholders of a firm with a significant probability of bankruptcy often find that new investment helps the bondholders at the stockholders' expense. The simplest case might be a real estate owner facing imminent bankruptcy. If he took $100,000 out of his own pocket to refurbish the building, he could increase the building's value by, say, $150,000. Though this investment has a positive net present value, he will turn it down if the increase in value cannot prevent bankruptcy. "Why," he asks, "should I use my own funds to improve the value of a building that the bank will soon repossess?"

This idea is formalized by the following simple example. Consider a firm with $4,000 of principal and interest payments due at the end of the year. It will be pulled into bankruptcy by a recession because its cash flows will be only $2,400 in that state. The firm's cash flows are presented in the left-hand side of Table 16.1. The firm could avoid bankruptcy in a recession by raising new equity to invest in a new project. The project costs $1,000 and brings in $1,700 in either state, implying a positive net present value. Clearly it would be accepted in an all-equity firm.

However, the project hurts the stockholders of the levered firm. To see this, imagine the old stockholders contribute the $1,000 *themselves*.[11] The expected value of the stockholders'

---

[11]The same qualitative results will obtain if the $1,000 is raised from new stockholders. However, the arithmetic becomes much more difficult since we must determine how many new shares are issued.

TABLE 16.1		Firm without Project		Firm with Project	
		Boom	**Recession**	**Boom**	**Recession**
Example Illustrating Incentive to Underinvest	Firm cash flows	$5,000	$2,400	$6,700	$4,100
	Bondholders' claim	4,000	2,400	4,000	4,000
	Stockholders' claim	$1,000	$ 0	$2,700	$ 100

The project has positive NPV. However, much of its value is captured by bondholders. Rational managers, acting in the stockholders' interest, will reject the project.

interest without the project is $500 (0.5 × $1,000 + 0.5 × 0). The expected value with the project is $1,400 (0.5 × $2,700 + 0.5 × $100). The stockholders' interest rises by only $900 ($1,400 − $500) while costing $1,000.

The key is that the stockholders contribute the full $1,000 investment, but the stockholders and bondholders *share* the benefits. The stockholders take the entire gain if boom times occur. Conversely, the bondholders reap most of the cash flow from the project in a recession.

The discussion of selfish strategy 1 is quite similar to the discussion of selfish strategy 2. In both cases, an investment strategy for the levered firm is different from the one for the unlevered firm. Thus, leverage results in distorted investment policy. Whereas the unlevered corporation always chooses projects with positive net present value, the levered firm may deviate from this policy.

Selfish Investment Strategy 3:   *Milking the Property*   Another strategy is to pay out extra dividends or other distributions in times of financial distress, leaving less in the firm for the bondholders. This is known as *milking the property,* a phrase taken from real estate. Strategies 2 and 3 are very similar. In strategy 2, the firm chooses not to raise new equity. Strategy 3 goes one step further, because equity is actually withdrawn through the dividend.

Summary of Selfish Strategies   The above distortions occur only when there is a probability of bankruptcy or financial distress. Thus, these distortions *should not* affect, say, General Electric because bankruptcy is not a realistic possibility for a diversified blue-chip firm such as this. In other words, General Electric's debt will be virtually risk-free, regardless of the projects it accepts. The same argument could be made for regulated companies that are protected by state utility commissions. However, smaller firms in risky industries, such as computers, might be very much affected by these distortions. Firms in the computer industry generally have significant potential future investment opportunities as compared to assets in place and face intense competition and uncertain future revenues. Because the distortions are related to financial distress, we have included them in our discussion of the "Indirect Costs of Financial Distress."

Who pays for the cost of selfish investment strategies? We argue that it is ultimately the stockholders. Rational bondholders know that, when financial distress is imminent, they cannot expect help from stockholders. Rather, stockholders are likely to choose investment strategies that reduce the value of the bonds. Bondholders protect themselves accordingly by raising the interest rate that they require on the bonds. Because the stockholders must pay these high rates, they ultimately bear the costs of selfish strategies. The relationship between stockholders and bondholders is very similar to the relationship between Erroll Flynn and David Niven, good friends and movie stars in the 1930s. Niven reportedly said that the good thing about Flynn was that you knew exactly where you stood with him. When you needed his help, you could always count on him to let you down.

For firms that face these distortions, debt will be difficult and costly to obtain. These firms will have low leverage ratios.

Concept Questions	1. What is the main direct cost of financial distress? 2. What are the indirect costs of financial distress? 3. Who pays the costs of selfish strategies?

16.3 Can Costs of Debt Be Reduced?

As U.S. senators are prone to say, "A billion here, a billion there. Pretty soon it all adds up."[12] Each of the costs of financial distress we mentioned above is substantial in its own right. The sum of them may well affect debt financing severely. Thus, managers have an incentive to reduce these costs. We now turn to some of their methods. However, it should be mentioned at the outset that the methods below can, at most, reduce the costs of debt. They cannot *eliminate* them entirely.

Protective Covenants

Because the stockholders must pay higher interest rates as insurance against their own selfish strategies, they frequently make agreements with bondholders in hopes of lower rates. These agreements, called **protective covenants,** are incorporated as part of the loan document (or *indenture*) between stockholders and bondholders. The covenants must be taken seriously since a broken covenant can lead to default. Protective covenants can be classified into two types: negative covenants and positive covenants.

A **negative covenant** limits or prohibits actions that the company may take. Here are some typical negative covenants:

1. Limitations are placed on the amount of dividends a company may pay.
2. The firm may not pledge any of its assets to other lenders.
3. The firm may not merge with another firm.
4. The firm may not sell or lease its major assets without approval by the lender.
5. The firm may not issue additional long-term debt.

A **positive covenant** specifies an action that the company agrees to take or a condition the company must abide by. Here are some examples:

1. The company agrees to maintain its working capital at a minimum level.
2. The company must furnish periodic financial statements to the lender.

These lists of covenants are not exhaustive. We have seen loan agreements with more than 30 covenants.

Smith and Warner examined public issues of debt and found that 91 percent of the bond indentures included covenants that restricted the issuance of additional debt, 23 percent restricted dividends, 39 percent restricted mergers, and 36 percent limited the sale of assets.[13]

Protective covenants should reduce the costs of bankruptcy, ultimately increasing the value of the firm. Thus, stockholders are likely to favor all reasonable covenants. To see this, consider three choices by stockholders to reduce bankruptcy costs.

1. *Issue No Debt.* Because of the tax advantages to debt, this is a very costly way of avoiding conflicts.
2. *Issue Debt with No Restrictive and Protective Covenants.* In this case, bondholders will demand high interest rates to compensate for the unprotected status of their debt.

---

[12]The original quote is generally attributed to Senator Everett Dirksen. In the 1950s, he reportedly said, "A *million* here, a *million* there. Pretty soon it all adds up." Government spending has increased since that time.

[13]C. W. Smith and J. B. Warner, "On Financial Contracting: An Analysis of Bond Covenants," *Journal of Financial Economics* 7 (1979).

TABLE 16.2	Loan Covenants	
Covenant Type	**Shareholder Action or Firm Circumstances**	**Reason for Covenant**
Financial-statement signals 1. Working capital requirement 2. Interest coverage 3. Minimum net worth	As firm approaches financial distress, shareholders may want firm to make high-risk investments.	Shareholders lose value before bankruptcy; bondholders are hurt much more in bankruptcy than shareholders (limited liability); bondholders are hurt by *distortion of investment that leads to increases in risk.*
Restrictions on asset disposition 1. Limit dividends 2. Limit sale of assets 3. Collateral and mortgages	Shareholders attempt to transfer corporate assets to themselves.	This limits the ability of shareholders to transfer assets to themselves and to *underinvest.*
Restrictions on switching assets	Shareholders attempt to increase risk of firm.	Increased firm risk helps shareholders; bondholders hurt by *distortion of investment that leads to increases in risk.*
Dilution 1. Limit on leasing 2. Limit on further borrowing	Shareholders may attempt to issue new debt of equal or greater priority.	This restricts *dilution of the claim of existing bondholders.*

3. *Write Protective and Restrictive Covenants into the Loan Contracts.* If the covenants are clearly written, the creditors may receive protection without large costs being imposed on the shareholders. The creditors will gladly accept a lower interest rate.

Thus, bond covenants, even if they reduce flexibility, can increase the value of the firm. They can be the lowest-cost solution to the stockholder-bondholder conflict. A list of typical bond covenants and their uses appears in Table 16.2.

Consolidation of Debt

One reason bankruptcy costs are so high is that different creditors (and their lawyers) contend with each other. This problem can be alleviated by proper arrangement of bondholders and stockholders. For example, perhaps one, or at most a few, lenders can shoulder the entire debt. Should financial distress occur, negotiating costs are minimized under this arrangement. In addition, bondholders can purchase stock as well. In this way, stockholders and debtholders are not pitted against each other, because they are not separate entities. This appears to be the approach in Japan where large banks generally take significant stock positions in the firms to which they lend money.[14] Debt-equity ratios in Japan are far higher than those in the United States.

16.4 Integration of Tax Effects and Financial Distress Costs

Modigliani and Miller argue that the firm's value rises with leverage in the presence of corporate taxes. Because this implies that all firms should choose maximum debt, the theory does not predict the behavior of firms in the real world. Other authors have suggested that bankruptcy and related costs reduce the value of the levered firm.

The integration of tax effects and distress costs appears in Figure 16.1. At the top of the figure, the diagonal straight line in the figure represents the value of the firm in a world without bankruptcy costs. The ∩-shaped curve represents the value of the firm with these

---

[14]Legal limitations may prevent this practice in the United States.

FIGURE 16.1

The Optimal Amount
of Debt and the Value
of the Firm

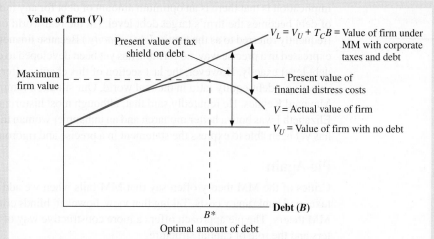

The tax shield increases the value of the levered firm. Financial distress costs lower the value of the levered firm. The two offsetting factors produce an optimal amount of debt at B^*.

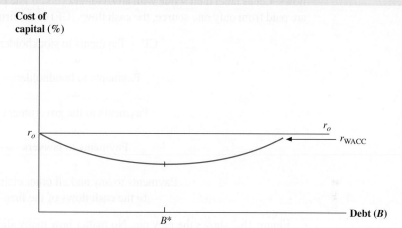

According to the static theory, the r_{WACC} falls initially because of the tax advantage of debt. Beyond point B^*, it begins to rise because of financial distress costs.

costs. This curve rises as the firm moves from all-equity to a small amount of debt. Here, the present value of the distress costs is minimal because the probability of distress is so small. However, as more and more debt is added, the present value of these costs rises at an *increasing* rate. At some point, the increase in the present value of these costs from an additional dollar of debt equals the increase in the present value of the tax shield. This is the debt level maximizing the value of the firm and is represented by B^* in Figure 16.1. In other words, B^* is the optimal amount of debt. Bankruptcy costs increase faster than the tax shield beyond this point, implying a reduction in firm value from further leverage. At the bottom of Figure 16.1, the weighted average cost of capital (r_{WACC}) goes down as debt is added to the capital structure. After reaching B^* the weighted average cost of capital goes up. The optimal amount of debt also produces the lowest weighted average cost of capital.

Our discussion implies that a firm's capital structure decisions involve a trade-off between the tax benefits of debt and the costs of financial distress. In fact, this approach is frequently called the *trade-off* or the *static trade-off* theory of capital structure. The implication is that there is an optimum amount of debt for any individual firm. This amount of debt becomes the firm's target debt level. (In the real world of finance, this optimum is frequently referred to as the firm's *debt capacity*.) Because financial distress costs cannot be expressed in a precise way, no formula has yet been developed to determine a firm's optimal debt level exactly. However, the last section of this chapter offers some rules of thumb for selecting a debt-equity ratio in the real world. Our situation reminds one of a quote of John Maynard Keynes. He reputedly said that, although most historians would agree that Queen Elizabeth I was both a better monarch and an unhappier woman than Queen Victoria, no one has yet been able to express the statement in a precise and rigorous formula.

Pie Again

Critics of the MM theory often say that MM fails when we add such real-world issues as taxes and bankruptcy costs. Taking that view, however, blinds critics to the real value of the MM theory. The pie approach offers a more constructive way of thinking about these matters and the role of capital structure.

Taxes are just another claim on the cash flows of the firm. Let G (for government and taxes) stand for the value of the firm's taxes. Bankruptcy costs are also another claim on the cash flows. Let us label their value with an L (for lawyers?). The pie theory says that these claims are paid from only one source, the cash flows (CF) of the firm. Algebraically, we must have

$$CF = \text{Payments to stockholders}$$
$$+$$
$$\text{Payments to bondholders}$$
$$+$$
$$\text{Payments to the government}$$
$$+$$
$$\text{Payments to lawyers}$$
$$+$$
$$\text{Payments to any and all other claimants}$$
$$\text{to the cash flows of the firm}$$

Figure 16.2 shows the new pie. No matter how many slices we take and no matter who gets them, they must still add up to the total cash flow. The value of the firm, V_T, is unaltered

FIGURE 16.2

The Pie Model with Real-World Factors

by the capital structure. Now, however, we must be broader in our definition of the firm's value

$$V_T = S + B + G + L$$

We previously wrote the firm's value as

$$S + B$$

when we ignored taxes and bankruptcy costs.

Nor have we even begun to exhaust the list of financial claims to the firm's cash flows. To give an unusual example, everyone reading this book has an economic claim to the cash flows of General Motors. After all, if you are injured in an accident, you might sue GM. Win or lose, GM will expend resources dealing with the matter. If you think this is far-fetched and unimportant, ask yourself what GM might be willing to pay every man, woman, and child in the country to have them promise that they would never sue GM, no matter what happened. The law does not permit such payments, but that does not mean that a value to all of those potential claims does not exist. We guess that it would run into the billions of dollars, and, for GM or any other company, there should be a slice of the pie labeled *LS* for "potential lawsuits."

This is the essence of the MM intuition and theory: *V* is V(CF) and depends on the total cash flow of the firm. The capital structure cuts it into slices.

There is, however, an important difference between claims such as those of stockholders and bondholders on the one hand and those of government and potential litigants in lawsuits on the other. The first set of claims are **marketed claims,** and the second set are **nonmarketed claims.** One difference is that the marketed claims can be bought and sold in financial markets, and the nonmarketed claims cannot.

When we speak of the *value of the firm,* we are referring just to the value of the marketed claims, V_M, and not the value of nonmarketed claims, V_N. What we have shown is that the total value,

$$V_T = S + B + G + L$$
$$= V_M + V_N$$

is unaltered. But, as we saw, the value of the marketed claims, V_M, can change with changes in the capital structure.

By the pie theory, any increase in V_M must imply an identical decrease in V_N. Rational financial managers will choose a capital structure to maximize the value of the marketed claims, V_M. Equivalently, rational managers will work to minimize the value of the nonmarketed claims, V_N. These are taxes and bankruptcy costs in the previous example, but they also include all the other nonmarketed claims such as the *LS* claim.

Concept Questions

1. **List all the claims to the firm's assets.**
2. **Describe marketed claims and nonmarketed claims.**
3. **How can a firm maximize the value of its marketed claims?**

16.5 Signaling

The previous section pointed out that the corporate leverage decision involves a trade-off between a tax subsidy and financial distress costs. This idea was graphed in Figure 16.1, where the marginal tax subsidy of debt exceeds the distress costs of debt for low levels of debt. The reverse holds for high levels of debt. The firm's capital structure is optimized where the marginal subsidy to debt equals the marginal cost.

Let's explore this idea a little more. What is the relationship between a company's profitability and its debt level? A firm with low anticipated profits will likely take on a low level of debt. A small interest deduction is all that is needed to offset all of this firm's pretax profits. And, too much debt would raise the firm's expected distress costs. A more successful firm would probably take on more debt. This firm could use the extra interest to reduce the taxes from its greater earnings. And, being more financially secure, this firm would find its extra debt increasing the risk of bankruptcy only slightly. In other words, rational firms raise debt levels (and the concomitant interest payments) when profits are expected to increase.

How do investors react to an increase in debt? Rational investors are likely to infer a higher firm value from a higher debt level. Thus, these investors are likely to bid up a firm's stock price after the firm has, say, issued debt in order to buy back equity. We say that investors view debt as a *signal* of firm value.

Now we get to the incentives of managers to fool the public. Consider a firm whose level of debt is optimal. That is, the marginal tax benefit of debt exactly equals the marginal distress costs of debt. However, imagine that the firm's manager desires to increase the firm's current stock price, perhaps because he knows that many of his stockholders want to sell their stock soon. This manager might want to increase the level of debt just to make investors *think* that the firm is more valuable than it really is. If the strategy works, investors will push up the price of the stock.

The above implies that firms can fool investors by taking on *some* additional leverage. Now let's ask the big question. Are there benefits to extra debt but no costs, implying that all firms will take on as much debt as possible? The answer, fortunately, is that there are costs as well. Imagine that a firm has issued extra debt just to fool the public. At some point the market will learn that the company is not that valuable after all. At this time, the stock price should actually fall *below* what it would have been had the debt never been increased. Why? Because the firm's debt level is now above the optimal level. That is, the marginal tax benefit of debt is below the marginal cost of debt. Thus, if the current stockholders plan to sell, say, half of their shares now and retain the other half, an increase in debt will help them on immediate sales but likely hurt them on later ones.

Now here is the important point: We said earlier that, in a world where managers do not attempt to fool investors, valuable firms issue more debt than less valuable ones. It turns out that, even when managers attempt to fool investors, the more valuable firms will still want to issue more debt than the less valuable firms. That is, while all firms will increase debt levels somewhat to fool investors, the costs of extra debt prevents the less valuable firms from issuing more debt than the more valuable firms issue. Thus, investors can still treat debt level as a signal of firm value. In other words, investors can still view an announcement of debt as a positive sign for the firm.

The above is a simplified example of debt signaling and one can argue that it is too simplified. For example, perhaps the stockholders of some firms want to sell most of their stock immediately while the stockholders of other firms want to sell only a little of theirs now. It is impossible to tell here whether the firms with the most debt are the most valuable or merely the ones with the most impatient stockholders. Since other objections can be brought up as well, signaling theory is best validated by empirical evidence. And, fortunately, the empirical evidence tends to support the theory.

For example, consider the evidence concerning **exchange offers.** Firms often change their debt levels through exchange offers, of which there are two types. The first type of offer allows stockholders to exchange some of their stock for debt, thereby increasing leverage. The second type allows bondholders to exchange some of their debt for stock, decreasing leverage. Figure 16.3 shows the stock price behavior of firms that change their proportions of debt and equity via exchange offers. The solid line in the figure indicates that stock prices rise substantially on the date when an exchange offering increasing leverage is announced.

FIGURE 16.3

Stock Returns at the Time of Announcements of Exchange Offers

Exchange offers change the debt-to-equity ratios of firms. The graph shows that stock prices increase for firms whose exchange offers increase leverage. Conversely, stock prices decrease for firms whose offers decrease leverage.

SOURCE: K. Shah, "The Nature of Information Conveyed by Pure Capital Structure Changes," *Journal of Financial Economics* 36 (August 1994).

(This date is referred to as date 0 in the figure.) Conversely, the dotted line in the figure indicates that stock price falls substantially when an offer decreasing leverage is announced.

The market infers from an increase in debt that the firm is better off, leading to a stock price rise. Conversely, the market infers the reverse from a decrease in debt, implying a stock-price fall. Thus, we say that managers signal information when they change leverage.

Concept Questions

1. **Do managers have an incentive to fool investors by issuing additional debt?**
2. **Is there a cost to issuing additional debt?**
3. **What empirical evidence suggests that managers signal information through debt levels?**

16.6 Shirking, Perquisites, and Bad Investments: A Note on Agency Cost of Equity

The previous section introduced the static trade-off model, where a rise in debt increases both the tax shield and the costs of distress. We now extend the trade-off model by considering an important agency cost of equity. A discussion of this cost of equity is contained in a well-known quote from Adam Smith.[15]

> The directors of such [joint-stock] companies, however, being the managers of other people's money than of their own, it cannot well be expected that they should watch over it with the same anxious vigilance with which the partners in a private copartnery frequently watch over their own. Like the stewards of a rich man, they are apt to consider attention to small matters as not for their master's honor, and very easily give themselves a dispensation from having it. Negligence and profusion, therefore, must always prevail, more or less, in the management of the affairs of such a company.

---

[15] Adam Smith, *The Wealth of Nations* [1776], Cannon edition (New York: Modern Library, 1937), p. 700, as quoted in M. C. Jensen and W. Meckling, "Theory of the Firm: Managerial Behavior, Agency Costs, and Ownership Structure," *Journal of Financial Economics* 3 (1978).

This elegant prose can be restated in modern-day vocabulary. An individual will work harder for a firm if she is one of its owners than if she is just an employee. In addition, the individual will work harder if she owns a large percentage of the company than if she owns a small percentage. This idea has an important implication for capital structure, which we illustrate with the following example.

EXAMPLE

Ms. Pagell is an owner-entrepreneur running a computer-services firm worth $1 million. She currently owns 100 percent of the firm. Because of the need to expand, she must raise another $2 million. She can either issue $2 million of debt at 12-percent interest or issue $2 million in stock. The cash flows under the two alternatives are presented below:

	Debt Issue				Stock Issue			
	Cash Flow	Interest	Cash Flow to Equity	Cash Flow to Ms. Pagell (100% of equity)	Cash Flow	Interest	Cash Flow to Equity	Cash Flow to Ms. Pagell ($33\frac{1}{3}$% of equity)
6-hour days	$300,000	$240,000	$ 60,000	$ 60,000	$300,000	0	$300,000	$100,000
10-hour days	400,000	240,000	160,000	160,000	400,000	0	400,000	133,333

Like any entrepreneur, Ms. Pagell can choose the degree of intensity with which she works. In our example, she can either work a 6- or a 10-hour day. With the debt issue, the extra work brings her $100,000 ($160,000 − $60,000) more income. However, let's assume that with a stock issue she retains only a one-third interest in the equity. Here, the extra work brings her merely $33,333 ($133,333 − $100,000). Being only human, she is likely to work harder if she issues debt. In other words, she has more incentive to *shirk* if she issues equity.

In addition, she is likely to obtain more *perquisites* (a big office, a company car, more expense-account meals) if she issues stock. If she is a one-third stockholder, two-thirds of these costs are paid for by the other stockholders. If she is the sole owner, any additional perquisites reduce her equity stake alone.

Finally, she is more likely to take on capital-budgeting projects with negative net present values. It might seem surprising that a manager with any equity interest at all would take on negative NPV projects, since stock price would clearly fall here. However, managerial salaries generally rise with firm size, indicating that managers have an incentive to accept some unprofitable projects after all the profitable ones have been taken on. That is, when an unprofitable project is accepted, the loss in stock value to a manager with only a small equity interest may be less than the increase in salary. In fact, it is our opinion that losses from accepting bad projects are far greater than losses from either shirking or excessive perquisites. Hugely unprofitable projects have bankrupted whole firms, something that even the largest of expense accounts is unlikely to do.

Thus, as the firm issues more equity, our entrepreneur will likely increase leisure time, work-related perquisites, and unprofitable investments. These three items are called agency costs, because managers of the firm are agents of the stockholders.[16]

This example is quite applicable to a small company considering a large stock offering. Because a manager-owner will greatly dilute his or her share in the total equity in this case, a significant drop in work intensity or a significant increase in fringe benefits is possible.

---

[16]As previously discussed, agency costs are generally defined as the costs from the conflicts of interest among stockholders, bondholders, and managers.

However, the example may be less applicable for a large corporation with many stockholders. For example, consider a large company such as General Motors going public for the umpteenth time. The typical manager there already has such a small percentage stake in the firm that any temptation for negligence has probably been experienced before. An additional offering cannot be expected to increase this temptation.

Who bears the burden of these agency costs? If the new stockholders invest with their eyes open, they do not. Knowing that Ms. Pagell may work shorter hours, they will pay only a low price for the stock. Thus, it is the owner who is hurt by agency costs. However, Ms. Pagell can protect herself to some extent. Just as stockholders reduce bankruptcy costs through protective covenants, an owner may allow monitoring by new stockholders. However, though proper reporting and surveillance may reduce the agency costs of equity, these techniques are unlikely to eliminate them.

It is commonly suggested that leveraged buyouts (LBOs) significantly reduce the above cost of equity. In an LBO, a purchaser (usually a team of existing management) buys out the stockholders at a price above the current market. In other words, the company goes private since the stock is placed in the hands of only a few people. Because the managers now own a substantial chunk of the business, they are likely to work harder than when they were simply hired hands.[17]

Effect of Agency Costs of Equity on Debt-Equity Financing

The preceding discussion on the agency costs of equity should be viewed as an extension of the static trade-off model. That is, we stated in Section 16.4 that the change in the value of the firm when debt is substituted for equity is the difference between (1) the tax shield on debt and (2) the increase in the costs of financial distress (including the agency costs of debt). Now, the change in the value of the firm is (1) the tax shield on debt plus (2) the reduction in the agency costs of equity minus (3) the increase in the costs of financial distress (including the agency costs of debt). The optimal debt-equity ratio would be higher in a world with agency costs of equity than in a world without these costs. However, because costs of financial distress are so significant, the costs of equity do not imply 100-percent debt financing.

Free Cash Flow

Any reader of murder mysteries knows that a criminal must have both motive and opportunity. The above discussion was about motive. Managers with only a small ownership interest have an incentive for wasteful behavior. For example, they bear only a small portion of the costs of, say, excessive expense accounts, and reap all of the benefits.

Now let's talk about opportunity. A manager can only pad his expense account if the firm has the cash flow to cover it. Thus, we might expect to see more wasteful activity in a firm with a capacity to generate large cash flows than in one with a capacity to generate only small flows. This very simple idea, which is formally called the *free cash flow hypothesis,* has recently attracted the attention of the academic community.[18]

---

[17]One professor we know introduces his classes to LBOs by asking the students three questions:

    1. How many of you have ever owned your own car?

    2. How many of you have ever rented a car?

    3. How many of you took better care of the car you owned than the car you rented?

Just as it is human nature to take better care of your own car, it is human nature to work harder when you own more of the company.

[18]The seminal article is Michael C. Jensen, "The Agency Costs of Free Cash Flow: Corporate Finance and Takeovers," *American Economic Review* (May, 1986), pp. 323–39.

A fair amount of academic work supports the hypothesis. For example, a frequently cited paper found that firms with high free cash flow are more likely to make bad acquisitions than firms with low free cash flow.[19]

The hypothesis has important implications for capital structure. Since dividends leave the firm, they reduce free cash flow. Thus, according to the free cash flow hypothesis, an increase in dividends should benefit the stockholders by reducing the ability of managers to pursue wasteful activities. Furthermore, since interest and principal also leave the firm, debt reduces free cash flow as well. In fact, interest and principal should have a greater effect than dividends have on the free-spending ways of managers, because bankruptcy will occur if the firm is unable to make future debt payments. By contrast, a future dividend reduction will cause fewer problems to the managers, since the firm has no legal obligation to pay dividends. Because of this, the free cash flow hypothesis argues that a shift from equity to debt will boost firm value.

In summary, the free cash flow hypothesis provides still another reason for firms to issue debt. We previously discussed the cost of equity; new equity dilutes the holdings of managers with equity interests, increasing their *motive* to waste corporate resources. We now state that debt reduces free cash flow, because the firm must make interest and principal payments. The free cash flow hypothesis implies that debt reduces the *opportunity* for managers to waste resources.

Concept Questions

1. What are agency costs?
2. Why are shirking and perquisites considered an agency cost of equity?
3. How do agency costs of equity affect the firm's debt-equity ratio?
4. What is the free cash flow hypothesis?

16.7 The Pecking-Order Theory

Although the trade-off theory has dominated corporate finance circles for a long time, attention is also being paid to the *pecking-order theory*.[20] To understand this view of the world, let's put ourselves in the position of a corporate financial manager whose firm needs new capital. The manager faces a choice between issuing debt and issuing equity. Previously, we evaluated the choice in terms of tax benefits, distress costs, and agency costs. However, there is one consideration that we have so far neglected: timing.

Imagine the manager saying:

> I want to issue stock in one situation only—when it is overvalued. If the stock of my firm is selling at $50 per share, but I think that it is actually worth $60, I will not issue stock. I would actually be giving new stockholders a gift, because they would receive stock worth $60, but would only have to pay $50 for it. More importantly, my current stockholders would be upset, because the firm would be receiving $50 in cash, but giving away something worth $60. So if I believe that my stock is undervalued, I would issue bonds. Bonds, particularly those with little or no risk of default, are likely to be priced correctly. Their value is primarily determined by the marketwide interest rate, a variable that is publicly known.
>
> But, suppose that our stock is selling at $70. Now I'd like to issue stock. If I can get some fool to buy our stock for $70 while the stock is really only worth $60, I will be making $10 for our current shareholders.

---

[19]L. Lang, R. Stulz, and R. Walkling, "Managerial Performance, Tobin's Q and the Gains in Tender Offers," *Journal of Financial Economics* (1989).

[20]The pecking-order theory is generally attributed to S. C. Myers, "The Capital Structure Puzzle," *Journal of Finance* 39 (July 1984).

Now, although this may strike you as a cynical view, it seems to square well with reality. Before the United States adopted insider trading and disclosure laws, many managers were alleged to have unfairly trumpeted their firm's prospects prior to equity issuance. And, even today, managers seem more willing to issue equity after the price of their stock has risen than after their stock has fallen in price. Thus, timing might be an important motive in equity issuance, perhaps even more important than those motives in the trade-off model. After all, the firm in the preceding example *immediately* makes $10 by properly timing the issuance of equity. Ten dollars worth of agency costs and bankruptcy cost reduction might take many years to realize.

The key that makes the example work is asymmetric information; the manager must know more about his firm's prospects than does the typical investor. If the manager's estimate of the true worth of the company is no better than the estimate of a typical investor, any attempts by the manager to time will fail. This assumption of asymmetry is quite plausible. Managers should know more about their company than do outsiders, because managers work at the company every day. (One caveat is that some managers are perpetually optimistic about their firm, blurring good judgment.)

But we are not done with this example yet; we must consider the investor. Imagine an investor saying:

> I make investments carefully, because it involves my hard-earned money. However, even with all the time I put into studying stocks, I can't possibly know what the managers themselves know. After all, I've got a day job to be concerned with. So, I watch what the managers do. If a firm issues stock, the firm was likely overvalued beforehand. If a firm issues debt, it was likely overvalued.

When we look at both issuers and investors, we see a kind of poker game, with each side trying to outwit the other. There are two prescriptions to the issuer in this poker game. The first one, which is fairly straightforward, is to issue debt instead of equity when the stock is undervalued. The second, which is more subtle, is to issue debt also when the firm is *overvalued*. After all, if a firm issues equity, investors will infer that the stock is overvalued. They will not buy it until the stock has fallen enough to eliminate any advantage from equity issuance. In fact, only the most overvalued firms have any incentive to issue equity. Should even a moderately overpriced firm issue equity, investors will infer that this firm is among the *most* overpriced, causing the stock to fall more than is deserved. Thus, the end result is that virtually no one will issue equity.[21]

This result that essentially all firms should issue debt is clearly an extreme one. It is as extreme as (1) the Modigliani-Miller (MM) result that, in a world without taxes, firms are indifferent to capital structure and (2) the MM result that, in a world of corporate taxes but no financial distress costs, all firms should be 100 percent debt-financed. Perhaps we in finance have a penchant for extreme models!

But, just as one can temper MM's conclusions by combining financial distress costs with corporate taxes, we can temper those of the pure pecking-order theory. This pure version assumes that timing is the financial manager's only consideration. In reality, a manager must consider taxes, financial distress costs, and agency costs as well. Thus, a firm may issue debt only up to a point. If financial distress becomes a real possibility beyond that point, the firm may issue equity instead.

---

[21]In the interest of simplicity, we have not presented our results in the form of a rigorous model. To the extent that a reader wants a deeper explanation, we refer him or her to S. C. Myers. "The Capital Structure Puzzle," *Journal of Finance* (July 1984).

Rules of the Pecking Order

The above discussion presented the basic ideas behind the pecking-order theory. What are the practical implications of the theory for financial managers? The theory provides the following two rules for the real world.

Rule #1 Use Internal Financing   For expository purposes, we have oversimplified by comparing equity to *riskless* debt. Managers cannot use special knowledge of their firm to determine if this type of debt is mispriced, because the price of riskless debt is determined solely by the marketwide interest rate. However, in reality, corporate debt has the possibility of default. Thus, just as managers have a tendency to issue equity when they think it is overvalued, managers also have a tendency to issue debt when they think it is overvalued.

When would managers view their debt as overvalued? Probably in the same situations when they think their equity is overvalued. For example, if the public thinks that the firm's prospects are rosy but the managers see trouble ahead, these managers would view their debt—as well as their equity—as being overvalued. That is, the public might see the debt as nearly risk-free, whereas the managers see a strong possibility of default.

Thus, investors are likely to price a debt issue with the same skepticism that they have when pricing an equity issue. The way managers get out of this box is to finance projects out of retained earnings. You don't have to worry about investor skepticism if you can avoid going to investors in the first place. Thus, the first rule of the pecking order is:

Use Internal Financing.

Rule #2 Issue Safe Securities First   Although investors fear mispricing of both debt and equity, the fear is much greater for equity. Corporate debt still has relatively little risk compared to equity because, if financial distress is avoided, investors receive a fixed return. Thus, the pecking-order theory implies that, if outside financing is required, debt should be issued before equity. Only when the firm's debt capacity is reached should the firm consider equity.

Of course, there are many types of debt. For example, because convertible debt is more risky than straight debt, the pecking-order theory implies that one should issue straight debt before issuing convertibles. Thus, the second rule of pecking-order theory is:

Issue the Safest Securities First.

Implications

There are a number of implications associated with the pecking-order theory that are at odds with the trade-off theory.

1. *There is no target amount of leverage.* According to the trade-off model, each firm balances the benefits of debt, such as the tax shield, with the costs of debt, such as distress costs. The optimal amount of leverage occurs where the marginal benefit of debt equals the marginal cost of debt.

By contrast, the pecking-order theory does not imply a target amount of leverage. Rather, each firm chooses its leverage ratio based on financing needs. Firms first fund projects out of retained earnings. This should lower the percentage of debt in the capital structure, because profitable, internally funded projects raise both the book value and the market value of equity. Additional cash needs are met with debt, clearly raising the debt level. However, at some point the debt capacity of the firm may be exhausted, giving way to equity issuance. Thus, the amount of leverage is determined by the happenstance of available projects. Firms do not pursue a target ratio of debt to equity.

2. *Profitable firms use less debt.* Profitable firms generate cash internally, implying less need for outside financing. Because firms desiring outside capital turn to debt first, profitable firms end up relying on less debt. The trade-off model does not have this implication. The greater cash flow of more profitable firms creates greater debt capacity. These firms will use that debt capacity to capture the tax shield and the other benefits of leverage. Two recent papers find that in the real world, more profitable firms are less levered,[22] a result consistent with the pecking-order theory.

3. *Companies like financial slack.* The pecking-order theory is based on the difficulties of obtaining financing at a reasonable cost. A skeptical investing public thinks a stock is overvalued if the managers try to issue more of it, thereby leading to a stock-price decline. Because this happens with bonds only to a lesser extent, managers rely first on bond financing. However, firms can only issue so much debt before encountering the potential costs of financial distress.

Wouldn't it be easier to have the cash ahead of time? This is the idea behind *financial slack*. Because firms know that they will have to fund profitable projects at various times in the future, they accumulate cash today. They are then not forced to go to the capital markets when a project comes up. However, there is a limit to the amount of cash a firm will want to accumulate. As mentioned earlier in this chapter, too much free cash may tempt managers to pursue wasteful activities.

Concept Questions	**1. What is the pecking-order theory?** **2. What are the problems of issuing equity according to this theory?** **3. What is financial slack?**

16.8 Growth and the Debt-Equity Ratio

While the trade-off between the tax shield and bankruptcy costs (as illustrated in Figure 16.1) is often viewed as the "standard model" of capital structure, it has its critics. For example, some point out that bankruptcy costs in the real world appear to be much smaller than the tax subsidy. Thus, the model implies that the optimal debt/value ratio should be near 100 percent, an implication at odds with reality.[23]

Perhaps the pecking-order theory is more consistent with the real world here. That is, firms are likely to have more equity in their capital structure than implied by the static trade-off theory, because internal financing is preferred to external financing.

In addition, Berens and Cuny argue that growth implies significant equity financing, even in a world with low bankruptcy costs.[24] To explain the idea, we first consider an example of a no-growth firm. Next, we examine the effect of growth on firm leverage.

---

[22]See L. S. Sunder and S. C. Myers, "Testing Static Trade-off Against Pecking Order Models of Capital Structure," *Journal of Financial Economics* (February 1999), and E. F. Fama and K. R. French, "Testing Trade-off and Pecking Order Predictions about Dividends and Debt," *Review of Financial Studies* (Spring 2002). However, Armen Hovakimian, Tim Opler and Sheridan Titman, "The Debt-Equity Choice," *Journal of Financial and Quantitative Analysis* (March 2001) find that while pecking order considerations affect firm debt levels in the short run, firms tend to move to target debt ratios in a manner consistent with the trade-off model.

[23]See Merton Miller's Presidential Address to the American Finance Association, reprinted as "Debt and Taxes," *Journal of Finance* (May 1977).

[24]J. L. Berens and C. L. Cuny, "Inflation, Growth and Capital Structure," *Review of Financial Studies* 8 (Winter 1995).

No-Growth

Imagine a world of perfect certainty[25] where a firm has annual earnings before interest and taxes (EBIT) of $100. In addition, the firm has issued $1,000 of debt at an interest rate of 10 percent, implying interest payments of $100 per year. The cash flows to the firm are:

	Date			
	1	**2**	**3**	**4 . . .**
Earnings before interest and taxes (EBIT)	$100	$100	$100	$100 . . .
Interest	−100	−100	−100	−100 . . .
Taxable income	$ 0	$ 0	$ 0	$ 0

The firm has issued just enough debt so that all EBIT is paid out as interest. Since interest is tax-deductible, the firm pays no taxes. In this example, the equity is worthless because stockholders receive no cash flows. Since debt is worth $1,000, the firm is also valued at $1,000. Therefore, the debt-to-value ratio is 100 percent ($1,000/$1,000).

Had the firm issued less than $1,000 of debt, the corporation would have positive taxable income and, consequently, would have ended up paying some taxes. Had the firm issued more than $1,000 of debt, interest would have exceeded EBIT, causing default. Consequently, the optimal debt-to-value ratio is 100 percent.

Growth

Now imagine another firm where EBIT is also $100 at date 1 but is growing at 5 percent per year.[26] To eliminate taxes, this firm also wants to issue enough debt so that interest equals EBIT. Since EBIT is growing at 5 percent per year, interest must also grow at this rate. This is achieved by increasing debt by 5 percent per year.[27] The debt, EBIT, interest, and taxable income levels are:

	Date				
	0	**1**	**2**	**3**	**4 . . .**
Debt	$1,000	$1,050	$1,102.50	$1,157.63 . . .	
New debt issued		50	52.50	55.13 . . .	
EBIT		$ 100	$ 105	$ 110.25	$115.76 . . .
Interest		−100	−105	−110.25	−115.76 . . .
Taxable income		$ 0	$ 0	$ 0	$ 0

Note that interest on a particular date is always 10 percent of the debt on the previous date. Debt is set so that interest is exactly equal to EBIT. As in the no-growth case, the levered firm has the maximum amount of debt at each date. Default would occur if interest payments were increased.

---

[25]The same qualitative results occur under uncertainty, though the mathematics is more troublesome.

[26]For simplicity, assume that growth is achieved without earnings retention. The same conclusions would be reached with retained earnings, though the arithmetic would become more involved. Of course, growth without earnings retention is less realistic than growth with retention.

[27]Since the firm makes no real investment, the new debt is used to buy back shares of stock.

Because growth is 5 percent per year, the value of the firm is:[28]

$$V_{\text{Firm}} = \frac{\$100}{0.10 - 0.05} = \$2,000$$

The equity at date 0 is the difference between the value of the firm at that time, $2,000, and the debt of $1,000. Hence, equity must be equal to $1,000,[29] implying a debt-to-value ratio of 50 percent (= $1,000/$2,000). Note the important difference between the no-growth and the growth example. The no-growth example has no equity; the value of the firm is simply the value of the debt. With growth, there is equity as well as debt.

We can also value the equity in another way. It may appear at first glance that the stockholders receive nothing, since the EBIT is paid out as interest each year. However, the new debt issued each year can be paid as a dividend to the stockholders. Because the new debt is $50 at date 1 and grows at 5 percent per year, the value of the stockholders' interest is

$$\frac{\$50}{0.10 - 0.05} = \$1,000$$

the same number that we obtained in the previous paragraph.

As we mentioned earlier, any further increase in debt above $1,000 at date 0 would lower the value of the firm in a world with bankruptcy costs. Thus, with growth, the optimal amount of debt is less than 100 percent. Note, however, that bankruptcy costs need not be as large as the tax subsidy. In fact, even with infinitesimally small bankruptcy costs, firm value would decline if promised interest rose above $100 in the first year. The key to this example is that *today's* interest is set equal to *today's* income. While the introduction of future growth opportunities increases firm value, it does not increase the current level of debt needed to shield today's income from today's taxes. Since equity is the difference between firm value and debt, growth increases the value of equity.

The preceding example captures an essential feature of the real world: growth. The same conclusion is reached in a world of inflation but with no growth opportunities. The result of this section, that 100 percent debt financing is suboptimal, holds whether growth opportunities and/or inflation is present. Since most firms have growth opportunities and since inflation has been with us for most of this century, this section's example is based on realistic assumptions.[30] The basic point is this: High-growth firms will have lower debt ratios than low-growth firms.

Concept Question

1. **How do growth opportunities decrease the advantage of debt financing?**

---

[28]The firm can also be valued by a variant of (15.7):

$$V_L = V_U + PVTS$$

$$= \frac{\$100(1 - T_C)}{0.10 - 0.05} + \frac{T_C \times \$100}{0.10 - 0.05} = \$2,000$$

Because of firm growth, both V_U and $PVTS$ are growing perpetuities.

[29]Students are often surprised that equity has value when taxable income is zero. Actually, the equityholders are receiving cash flow each period, since the proceeds from the new debt can be used either to pay dividends or to buy back stock.

[30]Our example assumes a single perpetual bond with level coupon payments. Berens and Cuny (BC) point out (p. 1201) that, with a number of different bonds, a firm might be able to construct an equally optimal capital structure with a greater debt-to-value (D/V) ratio. Because both capital structures are equally optimal, a firm might choose either one.

Although the analysis with many financing instruments is more complex, a firm can still choose a low D/V with no ill effect. Thus, BC's conclusion that firms *can* employ a significant amount of equity in a world with a low level of bankruptcy costs still holds.

16.9 Personal Taxes

So far in the chapter, we have considered corporate taxes only. Unfortunately, the IRS does not let us off that easily. Individuals must pay taxes on interest, dividends, and capital gains in the U.S., as well as in many other countries. To see the effect of personal taxes on capital structure, we have reproduced our Water Products example (from Section 15.5) below.

	Plan I	Plan II
EBIT	$1,000,000	$1,000,000
Interest ($r_B B$)	0	(400,000)
Earnings before taxes	1,000,000	600,000
(EBT = EBIT − $r_B B$)		
Taxes (T_C = 0.35)	(350,000)	(210,000)
Earnings after taxes	650,000	390,000
[EAT = (EBIT − $r_B B$) × (1 − T_C)]		
Add back interest ($r_B B$)	0	400,000
Total cash flow to all investors	$ 650,000	$ 790,000
[EBIT × (1 − T_C) + $T_C r_B B$]		

We now introduce two examples concerning personal taxes, one in which the tax rate on interest equals the tax rate on dividends and one in which the tax rate on interest is higher than the tax rate on dividends.

Equal Tax on Interest and Dividends   To handle personal taxes, we assume that all earnings are paid out as dividends. In addition, we initially assume that dividends and interest are both taxed at a rate of 30 percent. Under this assumption, we have:

	Plan I	Plan II
Dividends	$650,000	$390,000
Personal taxes on dividends		
(Personal rate = 30%)	(195,000)	(117,000)
Dividends after personal taxes	$455,000	$273,000
Interest	0	400,000
Personal taxes on interest	0	(120,000)
Interest after personal taxes	0	280,000
Total cash flow to both bondholders		
and stockholders after personal taxes	$455,000	$553,000

Total taxes paid at both corporate and personal levels are:

Plan *I*:	$350,000	+	$195,000			=	$545,000
	Corporate taxes		Personal taxes on dividends				
Plan *II*:	$210,000	+	$117,000	+	$120,000	=	$447,000
	Corporate taxes		Personal taxes on dividends		Personal taxes on interest		

Total cash flow to all investors after personal taxes is greater under plan *II*. This must be the case because (1) total cash flow was higher when personal taxes were ignored and

(2) all cash flows (both interest and dividends) are taxed at the same personal tax rate. Thus, the conclusion that debt increases the value of the firm still holds. Note that the difference between the two plans in the total cash flow to all investors, $98,000 (553,000 − 455,000), is exactly equal to the difference in taxes of $98,000 (545,000 − 447,000). Thus, the effect of leverage on cash flow is totally explained by taxes.

Higher Tax Rate on Interest Than on Dividends   The previous example used the same tax rate on both interest and dividends. Let's now examine the implications of a higher rate on interest than on dividends. In particular, we now assume that the personal tax rate on dividends is 10 percent and the personal tax rate on interest is 50 percent. The cash flows for the two plans are:

	Plan I	**Plan II**
Dividends	$650,000	$390,000
Personal taxes on dividends (at 10% tax rate)	(65,000)	(39,000)
Dividends after personal taxes	$585,000	$351,000
Interest	0	400,000
Personal taxes on interest (at 50% tax rate)	0	(200,000)
Interest after personal taxes	0	200,000
Total cash flow to both bond-holders and stockholders after personal taxes	$585,000	$551,000

Total taxes paid at both personal and corporate levels are

Plan *I*:	$350,000 Corporate taxes	+	$65,000 Personal taxes on dividends			=	$415,000
Plan *II*:	$210,000 Corporate taxes	+	$39,000 Personal taxes on dividends	+	$200,000 Personal taxes on interest	=	$449,000

In this scenario, the total cash flows are higher under plan *I* than under plan *II*. Though this example is expressed in terms of cash flows, we would expect the value of the firm to be higher under plan *I* than under plan *II*. Which plan does the IRS dislike the most? Clearly, the IRS dislikes plan *I* more because total taxes are lower. The increase in corporate taxes under the all-equity plan is more than offset by the decrease in personal taxes.

Interest receives a tax deduction at the corporate level. Dividends may be taxed at a lower rate than interest at the personal level. The above examples illustrate that total tax at all levels may either increase or decrease with debt, depending on the tax rates in effect.

Current Tax Rates   The maximum personal tax rate on dividends is 15 percent in the U.S. By contrast, the tax rate on interest is equal to the ordinary income tax rate, which can be as high as 35 percent. Thus, the IRS provides a clear personal-tax preference for dividends over interest. In addition, firms can repurchase shares with excess cash instead of paying a dividend. Capital gains are taxed at a maximum of 15 percent as well. However, since the shareholder pays a capital gain tax only on the gain from sale, not the entire proceeds from repurchase, the *effective* tax rate on capital gains is actually lower than 15 percent. Because firms both pay dividends and repurchase shares, the effective personal tax rate on *equity distributions* must be below 15 percent. Thus, the higher personal tax rate on interest offsets to some extent the tax shield to debt at the corporate level.

The Miller Model

Valuation under Personal and Corporate Taxes   The previous example calculated *cash flows* for the two plans under personal and corporate taxes. However, we have made no attempt to determine firm *value* so far. It can be shown that the value of the levered firm can be expressed in terms of an unlevered firm as[31]

$$V_L = V_U + \left[1 - \frac{(1 - T_C) \times (1 - T_S)}{(1 - T_B)} \right] \times B \tag{16.1}$$

T_B is the personal tax rate on ordinary income, such as interest, and T_S is the personal tax rate on equity distributions.

If we set $T_B = T_S$, (16.1) reduces to:

$$V_L = V_U + T_C B \tag{16.2}$$

which is the result we calculated for a world of no personal taxes. Hence, the introduction of personal taxes does not affect our valuation formula as long as equity distributions are taxed identically to interest at the personal level.

However, the gain from leverage is reduced when $T_S < T_B$. Here, more taxes are paid at the personal level for a levered firm than for an unlevered firm. In fact, imagine that $(1 - T_C) \times (1 - T_S) = 1 - T_B$. Formula (16.1) tells us there is no gain from leverage at all! In other words, the value of the levered firm is equal to the value of the unlevered firm. This lack of gain occurs because the lower corporate taxes for a levered firm are *exactly* offset by higher personal taxes. The above results are presented in Figure 16.4. The Miller model is further examined in Appendix B of this chapter.

---

[31]Stockholders receive

$$(\text{EBIT} - r_B B) \times (1 - T_C) \times (1 - T_S)$$

Bondholders receive

$$r_B B \times (1 - T_B)$$

Thus, the total cash flow to all investors is

$$(\text{EBIT} - r_B B) \times (1 - T_C) \times (1 - T_S) + r_B B \times (1 - T_B)$$

which can be rewritten as

$$\text{EBIT} \times (1 - T_C) \times (1 - T_S) + r_B B \times (1 - T_B) \times \left[1 - \frac{(1 - T_C) \times (1 - T_S)}{1 - T_B} \right] \tag{a}$$

The first term in (a) is the cash flow from an unlevered firm after all taxes. The value of this stream must be V_U, the value of an unlevered firm. An individual buying a bond for B receives $r_B B \times (1 - T_B)$ after all taxes. Thus, the value of the second term in (a) must be

$$B \times \left[1 - \frac{(1 - T_C) \times (1 - T_S)}{1 - T_B} \right]$$

Therefore, the value of the stream in (a), which is the value of the levered firm, must be

$$V_U + \left[1 - \frac{(1 - T_C) \times (1 - T_S)}{1 - T_B} \right] \times B$$

FIGURE 16.4

Effect of Financial
Leverage on Firm
Value with Both
Corporate and
Personal Taxes

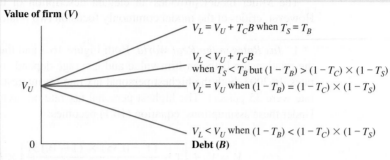

T_C is the corporate tax rate.
T_B is the personal tax rate on interest.
T_S is the personal tax rate on dividends and other equity distributions.
Both personal taxes and corporate taxes are included. Bankruptcy costs and agency costs are ignored.
The effect of debt on firm value depends on T_S, T_C, and T_B.

EXAMPLE

Acme Industries anticipates a perpetual pretax earnings stream of $100,000 and faces a 35-percent corporate tax rate. Investors discount the earnings stream after corporate taxes at 15 percent. The personal tax rate on equity distributions is 12 percent, and the personal tax rate on interest is 28 percent. Acme currently has an all-equity capital structure but is considering borrowing $120,000 at 10 percent.

The value of the all-equity firm is:[32]

$$V_U = \frac{\$100,000 \times (1 - 0.35)}{0.15} = \$433,333$$

The value of the levered firm is:

$$V_L = \$433,333 + \left[1 - \frac{(1 - 0.35) \times (1 - 0.12)}{(1 - 0.28)}\right] \times \$120,000 = \$458,000$$

The advantage to leverage here is $458,000 − $433,333 = $24,667. This is much smaller than $42,000 = 0.35 × $120,000 = $T_C B$, which would have been the gain in a world with no personal taxes.

Acme had previously considered the choice years earlier when $T_B = 50\%$ and $T_S = 18\%$. Here,

$$V_L = \$433,333 + \left[1 - \frac{(1 - 0.35) \times (1 - 0.18)}{(1 - 0.50)}\right] \times \$120,000 = \$425,413$$

In this case, $V_L < V_U$. Hence, Acme was wise not to increase leverage years ago. This inequality occurred because the personal tax rate on interest was much higher than the personal tax rate on equity distributions. In other words, the reduction in corporate taxes from leverage was more than offset by the increase in taxes from leverage at the personal level.

---

[32]Alternatively, we could have said that investors discount the earnings stream after *both* corporate and personal taxes at 13.20 percent [15% × (1 − 0.12)]:

$$V_U = \frac{\$100,000 \times (1 - 0.35) \times (1 - 0.12)}{0.1320} = \$433,333$$

Thus, the same value for the unlevered firm would apply.

The Miller model provides an elegant description of the capital-structure decision. However, critics of the model commonly focus on two related areas:

1. *Tax Rates in the Real World.* Both Figure 16.4 and the previous example show that the relationship between firm value and leverage depends on personal and corporate tax rates. In 2003, both the highest personal tax rate for interest income and the corporate tax rate were 35 percent. The highest personal tax rate on dividend income was 15 percent. Under these assumptions, equation (16.1) becomes:

$$V_L = V_U + \left[1 - \frac{(1 - 0.35) \times (1 - 0.15)}{1 - 0.35} \right] \times B = V_U + 0.15B \qquad (16.3)$$

Since $0.15 > 0$, there is a gain from leverage. Thus, the Miller model predicted all-debt financing in 2003, clearly a result at odds with reality.

One could argue, just as we did earlier, that the *effective* tax rate on equity distributions is below 15 percent, since individuals pay taxes only on the gain from sale, not the entire sales price, when firms repurchase stock. This would reduce the benefit from leverage. However, the typical bond investor is likely to be in a tax bracket well below the maximum of 35 percent, implying *more* gain from leverage. Therefore, even with more accurate estimates of tax brackets, the Miller model is still likely to imply all-debt financing.

2. *Unrealistic Assumptions.* The above discussion casts doubt on an empirical prediction of Miller's work. Perhaps this faulty prediction arises from two assumptions in the Miller model. First, the model ignores costs of financial distress. Second, the model assumes that corporations have unlimited interest deductibility, while in reality, firms can deduct interest only to the extent of their profits before interest. The expected tax benefits of debt financing in the real world are clearly less than under the assumptions of no distress costs and unlimited deductibility.

Two effects are likely to result from the more realistic assumptions.

Corporations should supply less debt, reducing the interest rate. The first unit of debt should increase firm value more than the last unit, because the interest on later units may not be deductible. Because the interest rate is now lower than that in the strict Miller model, firm value should rise when debt is first added to the capital structure. However, as more and more debt is issued, bankruptcy becomes more likely while the full deductibility of interest becomes less likely. Firm value still increases, but at a lower and lower rate. At some point, the probability of tax deductibility is low enough that an incremental dollar of debt is as costly to the firm as an incremental dollar of equity. Firm value then decreases with further leverage.[33]

The results of both financial distress costs and unlimited deductibility of interest are provided in Figure 16.5. This graph looks surprisingly like the curve in Figure 16.1 where the trade-off between the tax shield and financial distress costs is illustrated. Thus, a key change in assumptions may explain why firms are never all-debt financed, even when T_C is high relative to T_B.

---

[33]H. DeAngelo and R. Masulis, "Optimal Capital Structure under Corporate and Personal Taxation," *Journal of Financial Economics* (March 1980), posit a model where interest on debt is not the firm's only tax shield. Investment tax credits, depreciation, and depletion are examples of other tax shields. The authors show results similar to those in this section.

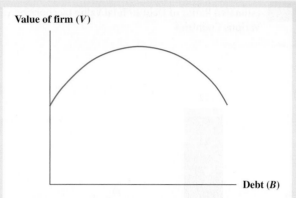

FIGURE 16.5

Value of the Firm under the Miller Model with Both Financial Distress Costs and Limited Deductibility of Interest

The Miller model with both financial distress costs and limited deductibility of interest leads to a ∩-shaped graph similar to the one presented in Figure 16.1. The ∩-shape in Figure 16.1 arose from the trade-off between corporate taxes and financial distress costs.

16.10 How Firms Establish Capital Structure

The theories of capital structure are among the most elegant and sophisticated in the field of finance. Financial economists should (and do!) pat themselves on the back for contributions in this area. However, the practical applications of the theories are less than fully satisfying. Consider that our work on net present value produced an *exact* formula for evaluating projects. Prescriptions for capital structure under either the trade-off model or the pecking-order theory are vague by comparison. No exact formula is available for evaluating the optimal debt-equity ratio. Because of this, we turn to evidence from the real world.

The following empirical regularities are worthwhile to consider when formulating capital-structure policy.

1. *Most corporations have low debt-asset ratios.* How much debt is used in the real world? Figures 14.3 and 14.4 present the debt-to-equity ratios for U.S. industrial firms in both book and market values for the years 1988 to 2002. The debt ratios are usually less than 100 percent. Figure 16.6 shows the debt-to-total-value ratios of firms in different countries in recent years. Differences in accounting procedures make the figures somewhat difficult to interpret. However, the debt ratios of U.S. and Canadian firms are the lowest.

Should we view these ratios as being high or low? As we discussed earlier, academics generally see corporate tax reduction as the chief motivation for debt. Thus, we might wonder if real-world companies issue enough debt to greatly reduce, if not downright eliminate, corporate taxes. The empirical evidence suggests that this is not the case. For example, corporate taxes in the U.S. for 2002 were about $200 billion. Thus, it is clear that corporations do not issue debt up to the point where tax shelters are completely used up.[34] There are clearly limits to the amount of debt corporations can issue, perhaps because of the financial distress costs discussed earlier in this chapter.

2. *A number of firms use no debt.* In a fascinating study, Agrawal and Nagarajan examined approximately 100 firms on the New York Stock Exchange without long-term debt.[35]

---

[34]For further insight, see John Graham, "How Big Are the Tax Benefits of Debt?" *Journal of Finance* (2000).

[35]Anup Agrawal and Nandu Nagarajan, "Corporate Capital Structure, Agency Costs, and Ownership Control: The Case of All-Equity Firms," *Journal of Finance* 45 (September 1990).

| FIGURE 16.6 | Estimated Ratios of Debt to Total Value (accounting value) of Nonfinancial Firms, Various Countries |

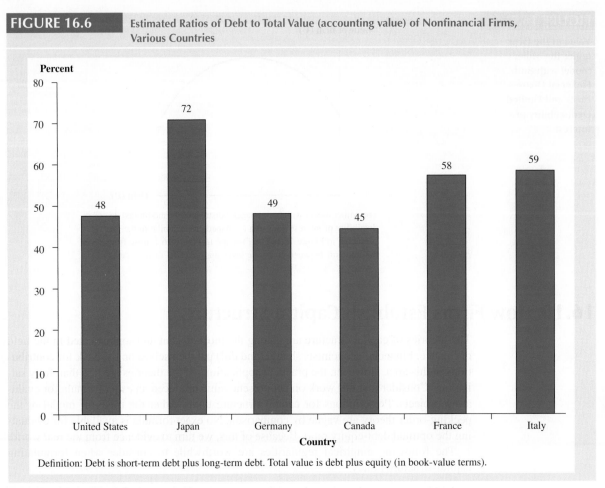

Definition: Debt is short-term debt plus long-term debt. Total value is debt plus equity (in book-value terms).

SOURCE: OECD financial statistics.

They found that these firms are averse to leverage of any kind, with little short-term debt as well. In addition, they have levels of cash and marketable securities well above their levered counterparts. Typically, the managers of these firms have high equity ownership. Furthermore, there is significantly greater family involvement in all-equity firms than in levered firms.

Thus, a story emerges. Managers of all-equity firms are less diversified than the managers of similar, but levered, firms. Because of this, significant leverage represents an added risk that the managers of all-equity firms are loathe to accept.

3. *There are differences in the capital structures of different industries.* There are very significant interindustry differences in debt ratios that persist over time. As can be seen in Table 16.3, debt ratios tend to be very low in high growth industries with ample future investment opportunities such as the drugs and electronics industries. This is true even when the need for external financing is great. Industries such as primary metals and paper, with relatively few investment opportunities and slow growth, tend to use the most debt.

4. *Most corporations employ target debt-equity ratios.* Graham and Harvey asked 392 chief financial officers (CFOs) whether their firms use target debt-equity ratios, with the

TABLE 16.3		Debt as a Percentage of the Market Value of Equity and Debt
Capital Structure Ratios for Selected U.S. Nonfinancial Firms (medians), 5-Year Average	**High leverage**	
	Building construction	52.8
	Hotels and lodging	56.0
	Air transport	47.7
	Gold-Silver mining	42.2
	Paper	51.9
	Low leverage	
	Drugs	4.7
	Electronics	9.8
	Biological products	4.0
	Computers	8.2
	Apparel	5.3

Definition: Debt is the total of short-term debt and long-term debt.

SOURCE: Ibbotson Associates 2003, *Cost of Capital Quarterly*, 2003 Yearbook.

FIGURE 16.7

Survey Results on the Use of Target Debt-Equity Ratios

This figure shows the survey responses of 392 CFOs concerning their use of target debt-equity ratios.

SOURCE: Figure 6 of John Graham and Campbell Harvey, "The Theory and Practice of Corporate Finance," *Journal of Financial Economics* (May/June 2001).

---

results being presented in Figure 16.7.[36] As can be seen, the great majority of the firms use targets, though the strictness of the targets varies across companies. Only 19 percent of the firms avoid target ratios. Results elsewhere in the paper indicate that large firms are more likely than small firms to employ these targets. The CFOs did not specify what they meant by either *flexible* or *strict* targets. However, elsewhere in the study, the respondents indicated that, by and large, they did not rebalance in response to changes in their firm's stock price, suggesting some flexibility in target ratios.

How should companies establish target debt-equity ratios? While there is no mathematical formula for establishing a target ratio, we present three important factors affecting

---

[36]Graham, John and Campbell Harvey, "The Theory and Practice of Corporate Finance," *Journal of Financial Economics* (May/June 2001).

the ratio:

- *Taxes.* As pointed out earlier, firms can only deduct interest for tax purposes to the extent of their profits before interest. Thus, highly profitable firms are more likely to have larger target ratios than less profitable firms.[37]

- *Types of Assets.* Financial distress is costly, with or without formal bankruptcy proceedings. The costs of financial distress depend on the types of assets that the firm has. For example, if a firm has a large investment in land, buildings, and other tangible assets, it will have smaller costs of financial distress than a firm with a large investment in research and development. Research and development typically has less resale value than land; thus, most of its value disappears in financial distress. Therefore, firms with large investments in tangible assets are likely to have higher target debt-equity ratios than firms with large investments in research and development.

- *Uncertainty of Operating Income.* Firms with uncertain operating income have a high probability of experiencing financial distress, even without debt. Thus, these firms must finance mostly with equity. For example, pharmaceutical firms have uncertain operating income because no one can predict whether today's research will generate new drugs. Consequently, these firms issue little debt. By contrast, the operating income of firms in regulated industries, such as utilities, generally has little uncertainty. Relative to other industries, utilities use a great deal of debt.

One final note is in order. Because no formula supports them, the preceding points may seem too nebulous to assist financial decision making. Instead, many real-world firms simply base their capital structure decisions on industry averages. While this may strike some as a cowardly approach, it at least keeps firms from deviating far from accepted practice. After all, the existing firms in any industry are the survivors. Therefore, one should at least pay some attention to their decisions.

Concept Questions

1. List the empirical regularities we observe for corporate capital structure.
2. What are the factors to consider in establishing a debt-equity ratio?

16.11 SUMMARY AND CONCLUSIONS

1. We mentioned in the last chapter that, according to theory, firms should create all-debt capital structures under corporate taxation. Because firms generally assume moderate amounts of debt in the real world, the theory must have been missing something at that point. We state in this chapter that costs of financial distress cause firms to restrain their issuance of debt. These costs are of two types: direct and indirect. Lawyers' and accountants' fees during the bankruptcy process are examples of direct costs. We mention four examples of indirect costs:

    Impaired ability to conduct business.
    Incentive to take on risky projects.
    Incentive toward underinvestment.
    Distribution of funds to stockholders prior to bankruptcy.

---

[37]By contrast, the pecking-order theory argues that profitable firms will employ less debt because they can invest out of retained earnings. However, the pecking-order theory argues against the use of *target* ratios in the first place.

Edison International: A Case for High Debt

Edison International is the parent firm of Southern California Edison (SCE) and five nonutility companies. Southern California Edison is the nation's second largest electric utility in terms of number of customers. SCE currently operates in a highly regulated environment in which it has an obligation to provide electric service to customers in return for a monopoly franchise in Southern California. SCE generated about 90 percent of the total operating revenue for Edison International. Traditionally, long-term debt has been a very prominent part of Edison International's capital structure. Its capital structure in 2002, based on market values, is illustrated next:

2002	$ (in millions)	Percentage
Debt	$14,396	69.9%
Preferred stock	1,358	6.6
Market value of stock	4,847	23.5
Total	$20,601	100.0%

In many ways Edison International is the opposite of Marshall Industries. It has grown slowly over the past several years in a regulated, noncompetitive environment. The company pays out significant dividends. Most of its assets are tangible in the form of transmission, distribution, and generating systems. The following questions were asked of Alan J. Fohrer, executive vice president and chief financial officer of Edison International (as well as Southern California Edison):

RWJ: Traditionally, Edison International has relied on high leverage—why?

AJF: It is a low cost source of funding and we have significant borrowing capacity with a stable revenue stream, high quality assets in place, and for SCE regulatory framework. As you know, the interest on debt is tax-deductible. If we didn't have taxes, it would be much different, but the tax deduction is very important.

RWJ: Does Edison International have a target leverage ratio?

AJF: Not precisely. We want each subsidiary to have ready access to the debt markets. Thus, ratings of BBB and above are important. A rating below BBB would make new borrowing more difficult. The

spreads today are minimal. The biggest issue today is availability.

Edison International is a mature, mostly regulated firm with cash flow that has not been used to keep leverage low. Instead, until recently the company has established a high dividend payout ratio that has given the cash flow back to its investors and kept leverage high. This behavior is consistent with a target debt ratio and the trade-off theory of capital structure. A high percentage of Edison's assets are tangible and state regulatory commissions reduce the possibility that managers can engage in some of the selfish strategies described earlier in this chapter. As a consequence, financial distress costs have been lower for firms like Edison International than for nonregulated firms.

EDISON INTERNATIONAL 2002 (in $ millions except as noted)	
Revenues	$11,488
Net income	$644
Long-term debt	$11,557
Market value of stock	$4,847
Dividend payout ratio	18%
Rate of return on equity	11.9%
Debt to total capital	69.9%
Five-year compound annual growth rate for revenues	11%
Market-to-book value ratio	1.1

Postscript: We had our conversation with Alan Fohrer in 2000. On January 5, 2001, because of skyrocketing wholesale electricity prices, Standard & Poor's lowered its credit rating for Edison International and the company lost its ability to borrow at investment grade interest rates for a short period of time. Furthermore, in 2001 Edison International eliminated its common dividend (and to date it has not been resumed). However, there is direct evidence that financial distress costs for Edison International are lower than for other firms because the state commission granted increased rates to recover some of the wholesale prices from rate payers and this enabled the company to obtain bridge loan financing.

Qualcomm: A Case for Low Debt

Qualcomm is a supplier of digital wireless communications products and services. It is the innovator and implementer of the proprietary code-division multiple access (CDMA), a digital wireless technology. CDMA generates licensing fees, royalties, and chip sales. In addition, Qualcomm has a new high-data-rate (HDR) technology that it expects to transmit data at very high speeds for Internet use and access. Its primary U.S. competitor uses another wireless technology called TDMA. It competes with suppliers of alternative wireless technologies, such as GSM used by Pac Bell and TDMA used by AT&T.

Qualcomm employs about 8,100 people and is headquartered in San Diego. Qualcomm has very little long-term debt. In 2002, its capital structure was:

Long-term debt	$157 million
Market value of stock	$32 billion

Why does Qualcomm rely so little on long-term debt? This question was asked of Anthony S. Thornley, Executive Vice President and Chief Financial Officer of Qualcomm.

RWJ: One thing that stands out from a financial point of view about Qualcomm is that it has almost no long-term debt. Why?

AST: There currently isn't any reason to leverage the company. We can finance our growth from retained earnings and outside equity.

RWJ: Outside equity?

AST: With our high P/E ratio we have a very low cost of equity.

RWJ: Qualcomm is in a very competitive business. Is this a factor in the capital structure?

AST: We are conservative financially and have relied largely on equity to finance the company. However, we have used debt at times when the relative cost was lower than equity.

RWJ: Many of the assets of Qualcomm are intangible, such as the value of its patents and its highly skilled engineers. Does this limit Qualcomm's debt capacity?

AST: Intangible assets have less collateral value than bricks and mortar, but Qualcomm's patents throw off a steady stream of cash flow. Qualcomm has a great deal of debt capacity. We just prefer flexibility at this time.

RWJ: Thanks.

What Can We Learn from Qualcomm?

First, Qualcomm is a firm with very uncertain future outcomes in a very competitive business and with significant intangible assets. This would suggest Qualcomm has a relatively low debt capacity when compared to, say, Edison International. Moreover, the financial management of Qualcomm is conservative by nature. Qualcomm's patents generate a steady stream of cash flow, which enhances debt capacity, but the competitive and fast-paced nature of the telecommunications industry suggests a need for financial slack and flexibility. Second, Qualcomm has experienced a rapid growth in income sales over the past ten years—greater than 25 percent per annum. As a consequence, the tax potential benefits of debt have only recently materialized. Finally, Qualcomm's very high stock price and price-earnings ratio suggest (to its financial management) that this is an opportune time to rely more on equity financing than debt.

A FINANCIAL PROFILE OF QUALCOMM 2002 (in $ millions except as noted)	
Revenues	3,039.6
Net income	618.9
Long-term debt	157
Dividend payout (%)	0
Return on equity (ROE) (%)	11.5
Ten-year compound annual growth in revenues	26%
Recent price-to-earnings ratio	37

2. Because the above costs are substantial and the stockholders ultimately bear them, firms have an incentive for cost reduction. We suggest three cost-reduction techniques:

Protective covenants.
Repurchase of debt prior to bankruptcy.
Consolidation of debt.

3. Because costs of financial distress can be reduced but not eliminated, firms will not finance entirely with debt. Figure 16.1 illustrates the relationship between firm value and debt. In the figure, firms select the debt-to-equity ratio at which firm value is maximized.

4. Signaling theory argues that profitable firms are likely to increase their leverage, since the extra interest payments will offset some of the pretax profits. Rational stockholders will infer higher firm value from a higher debt level. Thus, investors view debt as a signal of firm value.

5. Managers owning a small proportion of a firm's equity can be expected to work less, maintain more lavish expense accounts, and accept more pet projects with negative NPVs than managers owning a large proportion of equity. Since new issues of equity dilute a manager's percentage interest in the firm, the above agency costs are likely to increase when a firm's growth is financed through new equity, rather than through new debt.

6. The pecking-order theory implies that managers prefer internal to external financing. If external financing is required, managers tend to choose the safest securities, such as debt. Firms may accumulate slack to avoid external equity.

7. Berens and Cuny argue that significant equity financing can be explained by real growth and inflation, even in a world of low bankruptcy costs.

8. The results so far have ignored personal taxes. If distributions to equityholders are taxed at a lower effective personal tax rate than are interest payments, the tax advantage to debt at the corporate level is partially offset. In fact, the corporate tax advantage to debt is eliminated if

$$(1 - T_C) \times (1 - T_S) = (1 - T_B)$$

9. Debt-to-equity ratios vary across industries. We present three factors determining the target debt-to-equity ratio:
   a. *Taxes.* Firms with high taxable income should rely more on debt than firms with low taxable income.
   b. *Types of Assets.* Firms with a high percentage of intangible assets such as research and development should have low debt. Firms with primarily tangible assets should have higher debt.
   c. *Uncertainty of Operating Income.* Firms with high uncertainty of operating income should rely mostly on equity.

KEY TERMS

agency costs, *438*
exchange offers, *446*
marketed claims, *445*
negative covenant, *441*

nonmarketed claims, *445*
positive covenant, *441*
protective covenants, *441*

SUGGESTED READINGS

A review of the literature on taxes and capital structure, among other topics, can be found in:
Graham, John R. "Taxes and Corporate Finance: A Review." *Review of Financial Studies* (2003).

Merton Miller's Nobel lecture is reprinted as:
Miller, M. "Leverage." *Journal of Finance* (June 1991).

The pecking-order theory is presented in:
Myers, S. "The Capital Structure Puzzle." *Journal of Finance* (July 1984).

Signaling theory is presented in:
Ross, S. "The Determination of Financial Structure: The Incentive Signal Approach." *Bell Journal of Economics* (1977).

Free cash flow theory is presented in:
Jensen, Michael C. "The Agency Costs of Free Cash Flow: Corporate Finance and Takeovers." *American Economic Review* (May 1986).

Different theories of capital structure are empirically tested in:
Fama, Eugene, and Kenneth R. French. "Testing Tradeoff and Pecking Order Predictions about Dividends and Debt." *Review of Financial Studies* (2002).

Visit us at www.mhhe.com/rwj

An extremely influential set of articles arguing that bankruptcy costs are low are:

Haugen, R. A., and L. Senbet. "The Insignificance of Bankruptcy Costs to the Theory of Optimal Capital Structure." *Journal of Finance* (May 1978).

Haugen, R. A., and L. Senbet. "Bankruptcy and Agency Costs: Their Significance to the Theory of Optimal Capital Structure." *Journal of Financial and Quantitative Analysis* (March 1988).

The following two empirical papers focus on taxes and capital structure:

Graham, John R. "Do Personal Taxes Affect Corporate Financing Decisions?" *Journal of Public Economics* (1999).

Graham, John R. "How Big Are the Tax Benefits of Debt?" *Journal of Finance* (2000).

QUESTIONS & PROBLEMS

COSTS OF FINANCIAL DISTRESS

16.1 Good Time Company is a regional chain department store. It will remain in business for one more year. The probability of a boom year is 60 percent and a recession is 40 percent. It is projected that Good Time will generate a total cash flow of $250 million in a boom year and $100 million in a recession. The firm's required debt payment at the end of the year is $150 million. The market value of Good Time's outstanding debt is $108.93 million. Assume a one-period model, risk neutrality, and an annual discount rate of 12 percent for both the firm's debt and equity. Good Time pays no taxes.

    a. What is the value of the firm's equity?

    b. What is the promised return on Good Time's debt?

    c. What is the value of the firm?

    d. How much would Good Time's debt be worth if there were no bankruptcy costs?

    e. What payoff, after bankruptcy costs, do bondholders expect to receive in the event of a recession?

    f. What cost do bondholders expect Good Time to incur should bankruptcy arise at the end of the year?

16.2 Steinberg Corporation and Dietrich Corporation are identical firms except that Dietrich is more levered. Both companies will remain in business for one more year. The companies' economists agree that the probability of a recession next year is 20 percent and the probability of a continuation of the current expansion is 80 percent. If the expansion continues, each firm will generate earnings before interest and taxes (EBIT) of $2 million. If a recession occurs, each firm will generate earnings before interest and taxes (EBIT) of $0.8 million. Steinberg's debt obligation requires the firm to pay $750,000 at the end of the year. Dietrich's debt obligation requires the firm to pay $1 million at the end of the year. Neither firm pays taxes. Assume a one-period model, risk neutrality, and an annual discount rate of 15 percent.

    a. Assuming there are no costs of bankruptcy, what is the market value of each firm's debt and equity?

    b. What is the value of each firm?

    c. Steinberg's CEO recently stated that Steinberg's value should be higher than Dietrich's since the firm has less debt, and, therefore, less bankruptcy risk. Do you agree or disagree with this statement?

16.3 What are the direct and indirect costs of bankruptcy? Briefly explain each.

16.4 "A firm's stockholders will never want the firm to invest in projects with negative net present values."

    Do you agree or disagree with this statement? Explain your answer.

16.5 Due to large losses incurred in the past several years, a firm has $2 billion in tax-loss carryforwards. This means that the next $2 billion of the firm's income will be free from corporate income taxes. Security analysts estimate that it will take many years for the firm to generate $2 billion in earnings. The firm has a moderate amount of debt in its capital structure. The firm's CEO is deciding whether to issue debt or equity in order to raise the funds needed to finance an upcoming project. Which method of financing would you recommend? Explain.

16.6 Fountain Corporation economists estimate that a good business environment and a bad business environment are equally likely for the coming year. The managers of Fountain must choose between two mutually exclusive projects. Assume that the project Fountain chooses will be the firm's only activity and that the firm will close one year from today. Fountain is obligated to make a $500 payment to bondholders at the end of the year. Assume the firm's stockholders are risk-neutral. Consider the following information pertaining to the two projects:

LOW-RISK PROJECT

Economy	Probability	Project Payoff	Value of Firm		Value of Equity	Value of Debt
Bad	0.5	$500	$500	=	$ 0	$500
Good	0.5	700	700	=	200	500

HIGH-RISK PROJECT

Economy	Probability	Project Payoff	Value of Firm		Value of Equity	Value of Debt
Bad	0.5	$100	$100	=	$ 0	$100
Good	0.5	800	800	=	300	500

    a. What is the expected value of the firm if the low-risk project is undertaken? What if the high-risk project is undertaken? Which of the two strategies maximizes the expected value of the firm?

    b. What is the expected value of the firm's equity if the low-risk project is undertaken? What if the high-risk project is undertaken?

    c. Which project do Fountain's stockholders prefer? Explain.

    d. Suppose bondholders are fully aware that stockholders might choose to maximize equity value rather than total firm value and opt for the high-risk project. To minimize this agency cost, the firm's bondholders decide to use a bond covenant to stipulate that the bondholders can demand a higher payment if Fountainhead chooses to take on the high-risk project. By how much would bondholders need to raise the debt payment so that stockholders would be indifferent between the two projects?

16.7   What measures can stockholders undertake to minimize the costs of debt?

16.8   How do the existence of financial distress costs and agency costs affect Modigliani and Miller's theory in a world where corporations pay taxes?

16.9   What are the sources of the agency costs of equity?

PERSONAL TAXES

16.10   Fortune Enterprises is an all-equity firm that is considering issuing $13.5 million of perpetual 10 percent debt. The firm will use the proceeds of the bond sale to repurchase equity. Fortune distributes all earnings available to stockholders immediately as dividends. The firm will generate $3 million of earnings before interest and taxes (EBIT) every year into perpetuity. Fortune is subject to a corporate tax rate of 40 percent. Financial information for the firm under each of its two possible financial structures is shown below:

	Unlevered	Levered
EBIT	$3,000,000	$3,000,000
Interest	—	1,350,000
EBT	$3,000,000	$1,650,000
Taxes	1,200,000	660,000
Net Income	$1,800,000	$ 990,000

Visit us at www.mhhe.com/rwj

a. Suppose the personal tax rate on interest income (T_B) and equity distributions (T_S) is 30 percent.
  1. Which plan do equityholders prefer?
  2. Which plan does the IRS prefer?
  3. Suppose equityholders demand a 20 percent return after personal taxes on the firm's unlevered equity. What is the value of the firm under each plan?
b. Suppose $T_B = 0.55$ and $T_S = 0.20$.
  1. What is the annual after-tax cash flow to equityholders under each plan?
  2. What is the annual after-tax cash flow to debtholders under each plan?

16.11 When bankruptcy costs are considered, the general expression for the value of a levered firm in a world in which the tax rate on equity distributions (T_S) equals zero is:

$$V_L = V_U + [1 - \{(1 - T_C)/(1 - T_B)\}] \times B - C(B)$$

where V_L = the value of a levered firm
  V_U = the value of an unlevered firm
  B = the market value of the firm's debt
  T_C = the tax rate on corporate income
  T_B = the personal tax rate on interest income
  $C(B)$ = the present value of the costs of financial distress

Assume all investors are risk-neutral.
a. In their no tax model, what do Modigliani and Miller assume about T_C, T_B, and $C(B)$? What do these assumptions imply about a firm's optimal debt-equity ratio?
b. In their model with corporate taxes, what do Modigliani and Miller assume about T_C, T_B, and $C(B)$? What do these assumptions imply about a firm's optimal debt-equity ratio?
c. Consider an all-equity firm that is certain to be able to use interest deductions to reduce its corporate tax bill. If the corporate tax rate is 34 percent, the personal tax rate on interest income is 20 percent, and there are no costs of financial distress, by how much will the value of the firm change if it issues $1 million in debt and used the proceeds to repurchase equity?
d. Consider another all-equity firm that does *not* pay taxes due to large tax-loss carry-forwards from previous years. The personal tax rate on interest income is 20 percent, and there are no costs of financial distress. What would be the change in the value of this firm from adding $1 of perpetual debt rather than $1 of equity?

16.12 Overnight Publishing Company (OPC) has $2 million in excess cash. The firm plans to use this cash either to retire all of its outstanding debt or to repurchase equity. The firm's debt is held by one institution that is willing to sell it back to OPC for $2 million. The institution will not charge OPC any transaction costs. Once OPC becomes an all-equity firm, it will remain unlevered forever. If OPC does not retire the debt, the company will use the $2 million in cash to buy back some of its stock on the open market. Repurchasing stock also has no transaction costs. The company will generate $1,100,000 of annual earnings before interest and taxes in perpetuity regardless of its capital structure. The firm immediately pays out all earnings as dividends at the end of each year. OPC is subject to a corporate tax rate of 35 percent, and the required rate of return on the firm's unlevered equity (r_0) is 20 percent. The personal tax rate on interest income (T_B) is 25 percent and the personal tax rate on equity distributions (T_S) is 10 percent. Ignore bankruptcy costs.
a. What is the value of OPC if it chooses to retire all of its debt and become an unlevered firm?
b. What is the value of OPC if it decides to repurchase stock instead of retire its debt?

16.13 Frodo, Inc., is an all-equity firm with 1,000 shares of common stock outstanding. Investors require a 20 percent return on Frodo's unlevered equity. The company distributes all of its earnings to equityholders as dividends at the end of each year. Frodo estimates that its annual earnings before interest and taxes (EBIT) will be $1,000, $2,000, or $4,200 with probabilities of 0.1, 0.4, and 0.5, respectively. The firm's expectations about earnings will be unchanged in perpetuity. There are no corporate or personal taxes.

a. What is the value of the firm?

b. Suppose Frodo issues $7,500 of debt at an interest rate of 10 percent and uses the proceeds to repurchase 500 shares of common stock.

   1. What is the new value of the firm?

   2. What is the new value of the firm's equity?

   3. What is the required return on the firm's levered equity?

   4. What is the firm's weighted average cost of capital?

c. Suppose that Frodo's earnings are subject to a corporate tax rate of 40 percent.

   1. Will the presence of corporate taxes increase or decrease the value of the firm? Why?

   2. What is the value of the firm?

d. Suppose that, in addition to a tax on corporate income of 40 percent, interest income is taxed at 35 percent and the effective tax rate on equity is 15 percent. Assume that the introduction of the personal tax rate does not affect the required return on the firm's equity. What is the value of Frodo in a world with personal and corporate taxes?

16.14 Mueller Brewing Company is an all-equity firm that has been ordered by the EPA to stop polluting a local river. It must now spend $100 million on pollution-control equipment. The company has three alternatives for obtaining the needed $100 million:

- Sell $100 million of perpetual, corporate bonds with a 20 percent coupon payable at the end of every year. Interest income on these bonds is subject to a personal tax rate of 15 percent.

- Sell $100 million of perpetual pollution-control bonds with a 17 percent coupon payable at the end of every year. The interest on these bonds is not taxable to investors.

- Sell $100 million of common stock with a 9.5 percent current dividend yield.

Mueller Brewing Company is subject to a corporate tax rate of 35 percent. Equity distributions are not taxable to investors. The president of Mueller wants to sell common stock because it carries the lowest rate. Mr. Daniels, the company's treasurer, suggests bond financing because of the tax shield offered by the debt. His analysis shows that the value of the firm would increase by $35 million ($= 0.35 \times$100 million) if Mueller issues debt instead of equity. A newly hired financial analyst, Ms. Henderson, agrees with Mr. Daniels and adds that it does not matter which type of debt is issued since the yields will be bid up to reflect taxes.

a. Comment on the analyses of the president, Mr. Daniels, and Ms. Henderson.

b. Should Mueller be indifferent about which financing plan it chooses? If not, rank the three alternatives and give the benefits and cost of each.

16.15 Sid Whitehead, CEO of the Weinberg Corporation, is evaluating his firm's capital structure. He expects that Weinberg will have perpetual earnings before interest and taxes of $800,000. The after-tax required return on Weinberg's equity if it were an all-equity firm is 10 percent. Currently, the firm has $1.2 million in debt outstanding and is subject to a corporate tax rate of 35 percent. The personal tax rate on interest income is 15 percent, and the personal tax rate on equity distributions is zero. The combined financial distress and agency costs associated with the debt are approximately 5 percent of the total value of the debt.

a. What is the value of the firm?

b. What is the added value of Weinberg's debt?

16.16 New England Textile Corporation (NETC) has decided to relocate to North Carolina in four years. Because of transportation costs and a nonexistent secondary market for used textile machines, all of NETC's machines will be worthless after four years. Mr. Rayon, a plant engineer, recommends that one of the following two machines should be purchased for use in the existing plant over the next four years:

	Heavy-Duty Model	Light-Weight Model
Expected annual cost savings	$640	$616
Economic life	4 years	2 years
Price of machine	$1,000	$500

The machines will be depreciated on a straight-line basis. NETC is subject to a corporate tax rate of 34 percent. NETC obtained the following information for its analysis of various investments and financial proposals:

Asset	Expected Return	Variance	Covariance with Market Return
Risk-free asset	0.1		
Market portfolio	0.2	0.04	
NETC common stock			0.048

NETC, an all-equity firm, has a market value of $10 million.
  a. What is NETC's cost of capital?
  b. Which of the two machines should NETC purchase?
  c. The CFO of NETC is considering the sale of $2 million of 10 percent perpetual bonds and using the proceeds to repurchase NETC stock. If this plan is adopted:
    1. What is the new value of the firm?
    2. What is the value of the firm's equity?
  d. Suppose that, because of the new debt, the firm will face costs associated with possible financial distress. These costs can be expressed as 2 percent of the levered firm value calculated in (c). Do these costs imply that NETC should remain unlevered?

Appendix 16A

Some Useful Formulas of Financial Structure

Definitions

$E(EBIT)$ = A perpetual expectation of cash operating income before interest and taxes

V_U = Value of an unlevered firm

V_L = Value of levered firm

B = Present value of debt

S = Present value of equity

r_S = Cost of equity

r_B = Cost of debt capital

r_0 = Cost of capital to an all-equity firm. In a world of no corporate taxes, the weighted average cost of capital to a levered firm, r_{WACC}, is also equal to r_0. However, with corporate taxes, r_0 is above r_{WACC} for a levered firm.

Model I (No Tax)

$$V_L = V_U = \frac{E(EBIT)}{r_0}$$

$$r_S = r_0 + (r_0 - r_B) \times B/S$$

Model II (Corporate Tax, $T_C > 0$; No Personal Taxes, $T_S = T_B = 0$)

$$V_L = \frac{E[EBIT] \times (1 - T_C)}{r_0} + \frac{T_C r_B B}{r_B} = V_U + T_C B$$

$$r_S = r_0 + (1 - T_C) \times (r_0 - r_B) \times B/S$$

Model III (Corporate Tax, $T_C > 0$; Personal Tax, $T_B > 0$; $T_S > 0$)

$$V_L = V_U + \left[1 - \frac{(1 - T_C) \times (1 - T_S)}{(1 - T_B)} \right] \times B$$

Appendix 16B

The Miller Model and the Graduated Income Tax

In Section 16.9, we assumed a flat personal income tax on interest income. In other words, we assumed that all individuals are subject to the same personal tax rate on interest income. Merton Miller derived the results of this section in a classic paper.[38] However, the genius of his paper was to consider the implications of personal taxes when tax rates differ across individuals.

This *graduated* income tax is consistent with the real world. For example, individuals are currently taxed at rates from 0 to 35 percent in the United States, depending on income. In addition, other entities, such as corporate pension funds, individual retirement accounts (IRAs), and universities, are tax-exempt.

To illustrate Miller's model with graduated taxes, we consider a world where *all* firms initially only issue equity. We assume that $T_C = 35\%$ and $T_S = 0$.[39] The required return on stock, r_S, is 10 percent. In addition, we posit a graduated personal income tax, where tax rates vary between 0 and 50 percent. All individuals are risk-neutral.

Now consider a courageous firm contemplating a \$1,000 issue of debt. What is the interest rate that the firm can pay and still be as well off as if it issued equity? Because debt is tax deductible, the after–corporate tax cost of debt is $(1 - T_C) \times r_B$. However, equity is not deductible at the corporate level, so the after-tax cost of equity is r_S. Thus, the firm is indifferent to whether it issues debt or equity when

$$(1 - T_C) \times r_B = r_S \tag{16.4}$$

Because $T_C = 35\%$ and $r_S = 10\%$, the firm could afford to pay a rate on debt as high as 15.38 percent.

Miller argues that those in the lowest tax brackets (tax-exempt in our example) will buy the debt because they pay the least personal tax on interest. These tax-exempt investors will be indifferent to whether they buy the stock or purchase bonds also yielding 10 percent. Thus, if this firm is the *only* one issuing debt, it can pay an interest rate well below its break-even rate of 15.38 percent.

Noticing the gain to the first firm, many other firms are likely to issue debt. However, if there are only a fixed number of tax-exempt investors, new debt issues must attract people

---

[38]M. Miller, "Debt and Taxes," *Journal of Finance* (May 1977). Yes, this is the same Miller of MM.

[39]The assumption that $T_S = 0$ is perhaps an extreme one. However, it is commonly made in the literature, justified by the investor's ability to defer realization of capital gains indefinitely. Besides, the same qualitative conclusions hold if $T_S > 0$, though the explanation would be more involved.

in higher brackets. Because these individuals are taxed on interest at a higher rate than they are taxed on equity distributions, they will only buy debt if its yield is greater than 10 percent. For example, an individual in the 15-percent bracket has an interest rate after personal tax of $r_B \times (1 - 0.15)$. He will be indifferent to whether he buys bonds or stock if $r_B = 11.765\%$, because $0.11765 \times 0.85 = 10\%$. Because 11.765 percent is less than the 15.38 percent rate of equation (16.4), corporations gain by issuing debt to investors in the 15-percent bracket.

Now consider investors in the 35-percent bracket. A return on bonds of 15.38 percent provides them with a $10\% = 15.38\% \times (1 - 0.35)$ interest rate after personal tax. Thus, they are indifferent to whether they earn a 15.38-percent return on bonds or a 10-percent return on stock. Miller argues that, in equilibrium, corporations will issue enough debt so that investors with personal tax brackets up to and including 35 percent will hold debt.[40] Additional debt will not be issued because the interest rate needed to attract investors in higher tax brackets is above the 15.38-percent rate that corporations can afford to pay.

The beauty of competition is that other companies can so capitalize on someone's innovation that all value to the courageous first entrant is eliminated. According to the Miller model, firms will issue enough debt so that individuals up to and including the 35-percent bracket hold it. In order to induce these investors to hold bonds, the competitive interest rate becomes 15.38 percent. No firm profits from issuing debt in equilibrium. Rather, all firms are indifferent to whether they issue debt or equity in equilibrium.

Miller's work produces three results:

1. In aggregate, the corporate sector will issue just enough debt so that individuals with tax brackets equal to and below the corporate tax rate, T_C, will hold debt, and individuals with higher tax brackets will not hold debt. Thus, individuals in these higher brackets will hold stock.

2. Because people in tax brackets equal to the corporate rate hold debt, there is no gain or loss to corporate leverage. Therefore, the capital-structure decision is a matter of indifference to an individual firm. Though the Miller model is quite sophisticated, this conclusion is identical to that reached by MM in a world without any taxes.

3. As given in equation (16.4), the return on bonds will be higher than the return on stocks of comparable risk. [An adjustment to (16.4) must be made to reflect the greater risk of stocks in the real world.]

EXAMPLE

Consider an economy in which there are four groups of investors and no others:

Group	Marginal Tax Rate (%) on Bonds (T_B)	Personal Wealth (in $ millions)
Finance majors	50%	$1,200
Accounting majors	35	300
Marketing majors	20	150
Management majors	0	50

We assume that investors are risk-neutral and that equity income is untaxed at the personal level for all investors (i.e., $T_S = 0$). All investors can earn a tax-free return of 5.4 percent by investing in foreign real estate; therefore, this is the return on equity. The corporate tax rate is 35 percent.

---

[40]All investors with $T_B < 35$ percent hold bonds. Because investors with $T_B = 35$ percent are indifferent to whether they hold stocks or bonds, only some of them are likely to choose bonds.

Interest payments are tax deductible at the corporate level and taxable at the individual level. Corporations receive a total of $120 million in cash flow before tax and interest. There are no growth opportunities, and every year is the same in perpetuity. What is the range of possible debt-equity ratios?

The return on equity, r_S, will be set equal to the return on foreign real estate, which is 0.054. In a Miller equilibrium, $r_S = (1 - T_C) \times r_B$. Therefore,

$$r_B = \frac{0.054}{1 - 0.35} = 0.0831$$

Given the tax brackets of the different groups of investors, we would expect that finance majors would hold equity and foreign real estate, and accounting majors would be indifferent to whether they held equity or debt. Marketing and management majors would hold bonds because their personal tax rates are below 0.35. Because accounting majors are indifferent to whether they hold bonds or stocks, we must learn what happens if they invest in bonds or equity. If accounting majors use their $300 to buy bonds, $B = \$300 + \$150 + \$50 = \$500$. Then the following calculations can be made.

$$S = \frac{(EBIT - r_B B) \times (1 - T_C)}{r_S}$$

$$= \frac{[\$120 - (0.0831 \times \$500)] \times (1 - 0.35)}{0.054}$$

$$= \$944$$

$$B = \frac{r_B B}{r_B} = \$500$$

$$V_L = S + B = \$944 + \$500 = \$1,444$$

$$\frac{B}{S} = \frac{\$500}{\$944} = 0.530$$

If accounting majors buy stocks and foreign real estate ($B = \$150 + \$50 = \$200$),

$$S = \frac{(EBIT - r_B B) \times (1 - T_C)}{r_S}$$

$$= \frac{[\$120 - (0.0831 \times \$200)] \times (1 - 0.35)}{0.054}$$

$$= \$1,244$$

$$B = \$200$$

$$V_L = S + B = \$1,244 + \$200 = \$1,444$$

$$\frac{B}{S} = \frac{\$200}{\$1,244} = 0.161$$

Thus, depending on the amount of bonds held by accounting majors, the debt-equity ratio in the economy can lie in the range of 0.161 to 0.530.

THE MILLER MODEL AND THE GRADUATED INCOME TAX

16.17 Consider an economy with three investor groups. The personal tax rates on interest income are 10 percent, 20 percent, and 40 percent, respectively, for these three groups. The corporate tax rate is 35 percent, and the effective tax rate on equity distributions is zero. The after-tax required rate of return on all-equity financed projects is 11 percent.

   a. What is the equilibrium interest rate?

   b. For this interest rate, will each of the three groups prefer debt or equity?

c. If Firm A has earnings before interest and taxes (EBIT) of $1 million in perpetuity, what is its value? Does the firm's value vary with different capital structure choices?

16.18 Assume that there are three groups of investors with the following tax rates on interest income:

Group	Investable Funds	T_B (%)
A	$357.1 million	50
B	$220 million	32.5
C	$105 million	10

The after-corporate tax required rate of return on all-equity financed projects is 8.1 percent. The only types of securities available are common stock and corporate bonds. Capital gains and dividends are untaxed at the personal level. Corporate earnings before interest and taxes (EBIT) total $85 million per year in perpetuity. The corporate tax rate is 35 percent. Assume all debt is risk-free.

a. What is the equilibrium interest rate?
b. In equilibrium, will each group invest in debt or equity?
c. What is the market value of all companies?
d. What is the total tax bill?

16.19 Consider an economy in which there are four groups of people:

Group	T_B (%)	Wealth ($ millions)
L	50	500
M	40	300
N	20	200
O	0	500

The after-corporate tax required rate of return on all-equity financed projects is 6 percent. Interest income is taxable at the individual level, but equity income is untaxed at the personal level for all investors. Corporations generate annual earnings before interest and taxes (EBIT) of $150 million in perpetuity. The corporate tax rate is 40 percent.

a. What is the range of possible aggregate debt-equity ratios in the economy?
b. What would your answer to (a) be if the corporate tax rate were 30 percent?

Valuation and Capital Budgeting for the Levered Firm

EXECUTIVE SUMMARY

Instructors often structure the basic course in corporate finance around the two sides of the balance sheet. The left-hand side of the balance sheet contains assets. Chapters 4, 5, 6, 7, and 8 of this textbook treat the capital-budgeting decision, which is a decision concerning the assets of the firm. Chapters 9, 10, 11, and 12 treat the discount rate for a project, so those chapters also concern the left-hand side of the balance sheet. The right-hand side of the balance sheet contains liabilities and owner's equity. Chapters 13, 14, 15, and 16 of this textbook examine the debt-versus-equity decision, which is a decision about the right-hand side of the balance sheet.

While the preceding chapters of this textbook have, for the most part, treated the capital-budgeting decision separately from the capital-structure decision, the two decisions are actually related. As we will see, a project of an all-equity firm might be rejected, while the same project might be accepted for a levered but otherwise identical firm. This occurs because the cost of capital frequently decreases with leverage, thereby turning some negative NPV projects into positive NPV projects.

Chapters 4 through 8 implicitly assumed that the firm is financed with only equity. The goal of this chapter is to value a project, or the firm itself, when leverage is employed. We point out that there are three standard approaches to valuation under leverage: the adjusted-present-value (APV) method, the flow-to-equity (FTE) method, and the weighted-average-cost-of-capital (WACC) method. These three approaches may seem, at first glance, to be quite different. However, we show that, if applied correctly, all three approaches provide the same value estimate.

The three methods discussed next can be used to value either the firm as a whole or a project. The example below discusses project value, though everything we say applies to an entire firm as well.

17.1 Adjusted-Present-Value Approach

The **adjusted-present-value (APV)** method is best described by the following formula:

$$\text{APV} = \text{NPV} + \text{NPVF}$$

In words, the value of a project to a levered firm (APV) is equal to the value of the project to an unlevered firm (NPV) plus the net present value of the financing side effects (NPVF). One can generally think of four side effects:

1. *The Tax Subsidy to Debt.* This was discussed in Chapter 15, where we pointed out that, for perpetual debt, the value of the tax subsidy is $T_C B$. (T_C is the corporate tax rate, and B is the value of the debt.) The material on valuation under corporate taxes in Chapter 15 is actually an application of the APV approach.

2. *The Costs of Issuing New Securities.* As we will discuss in detail in Chapter 20, investment bankers participate in the public issuance of corporate debt. These bankers must be compensated for their time and effort, a cost that lowers the value of the project.

3. *The Costs of Financial Distress.* The possibility of financial distress, and bankruptcy in particular, arises with debt financing. As stated in the previous chapter, financial distress imposes costs, thereby lowering value.

4. *Subsidies to Debt Financing.* The interest on debt issued by state and local governments is not taxable to the investor. Because of this, the yield on tax-exempt debt is generally substantially below the yield on taxable debt. Frequently, corporations are able to obtain financing from a municipality at the tax-exempt rate because the municipality can borrow at that rate as well. As with any subsidy, this subsidy adds value.

While each of the preceding four side effects is important, the tax deduction to debt almost certainly has the highest dollar value in actual situations. For this reason, the following example considers the tax subsidy, but not the other three side effects.[1]

Consider a project of the P. B. Singer Co. with the following characteristics:

Cash inflows: $500,000 per year for the indefinite future

Cash costs: 72% of sales

Initial investment: $475,000

$T_C = 34\%$

$r_0 = 20\%$, where r_0 is the cost of capital for a project of an all-equity firm.

If both the project and the firm are financed with only equity, the project's cash flow is:

Cash inflows	$500,000
Cash costs	−360,000
Operating income	140,000
Corporate tax (.34 tax rate)	−47,600
Unlevered cash flow (UCF)	$ 92,400

The distinction in Chapter 4 between present value and net present value is important for this example. As pointed out in Chapter 4, the *present value* of a project is determined before the initial investment at date 0 is subtracted. The initial investment is subtracted for the calculation of *net* present value.

Given a discount rate of 20 percent, the present value of the project is:

$$\frac{\$92,400}{0.20} = \$462,000$$

The net present value (NPV) of the project, that is, the value of the project to an all-equity firm, is:

$$\$462,000 - \$475,000 = -\$13,000$$

Since the NPV is negative, the project would be rejected by an all-equity firm.

Now imagine that the firm finances the project with exactly $126,229.50 in debt, so that the remaining investment of $348,770.50 ($475,000 − $126,229.50) is financed with equity. The net present value of the project under leverage, which we call the adjusted present value, or the APV, is:

$$APV = NPV + T_C \times B$$
$$\$29,918 = -\$13,000 + 0.34 \times \$126,229.50$$

[1]The Bicksler Enterprises example of Section 17.6 handles both flotation costs and interest subsidies.

That is, the value of the project when financed with some leverage is equal to the value of the project when financed with all equity plus the tax shield from the debt. Since this number is positive, the project should be accepted.[2]

You may be wondering why we chose such a precise amount of debt. Actually, we chose it so that the ratio of debt to the present value of the project under leverage is 0.25.[3]

In this example, debt is a fixed proportion of the present value of the project, not a fixed proportion of the initial investment of \$475,000. This is consistent with the goal of a target debt-to-*market*-value ratio, which we find in the real world. For example, commercial banks typically lend to real estate developers a fixed percentage of the appraised market value of a project, not a fixed percentage of the initial investment.

Concept Questions	1. How is the APV method applied? 2. What additional information beyond NPV does one need to calculate APV?

17.2 Flow-to-Equity Approach

The **flow-to-equity (FTE)** approach is an alternative capital-budgeting approach. The formula simply calls for discounting the cash flow from the project to the equityholders of the levered firm at the cost of equity capital, r_S. For a perpetuity, this becomes:

$$\frac{\text{Cash flow from project to equityholders of the levered firm}}{r_S}$$

There are three steps to the FTE approach.

Step 1: Calculating Levered Cash Flow (LCF)[4]

Assuming an interest rate of 10 percent, the perpetual cash flow to equityholders in our P. B. Singer Co. example is:

Cash inflows	\$500,000.00
Cash costs	−360,000.00
Interest (10% × \$126,229.50)	−12,622.95
Income after interest	127,377.05
Corporate tax (.34 tax rate)	−43,308.20
Levered cash flow (LCF)	\$ 84,068.85

Alternatively, one can calculate levered cash flow (LCF) directly from unlevered cash flow (UCF). The key here is that the difference between the cash flow that equityholders

---

[2]This example is meant to dramatize the potential importance of the tax benefits of debt. In practice, the firm will likely find the value of a project to an all-equity firm to have at least an NPV of zero—such as a financial asset with a discount rate of .20.

[3]That is, the present value of the project after the initial investment has been made is \$504,918 (\$29,918 + \$475,000). Thus, the debt-to-value ratio of the project is 0.25 (\$126,229.50/\$504,918).

This level of debt can be calculated directly. Note that

$$\text{Present value of levered project} = \text{Present value of unlevered project} + T_C \times B$$
$$V_{\text{With debt}} = \$462,000 \qquad\qquad + 0.34 \times .25 \times V_{\text{With debt}}$$

Rearranging the last line, we have

$$V_{\text{With debt}}(1 - 0.34 \times 0.25) = \$462,000$$
$$V_{\text{With debt}} = \$504,918$$

Since debt is 0.25 of value, debt is \$126,229.50 (0.25 × \$504,918).

[4]We use the term *levered cash flow* (LCF) for simplicity. A more complete term would be *cash flow from the project to the equityholders of a levered firm*. Similarly, a more complete term for *unlevered cash flow* (UCF) would be *cash flow from the project to the equityholders of an unlevered firm*.

receive in an unlevered firm and the cash flow that equityholders receive in a levered firm is the after-tax interest payment. (Repayment of principal does not appear in this example, since the debt is perpetual.) One writes this algebraically as:

$$\text{UCF} - \text{LCF} = (1 - T_C)r_B B$$

The term on the right-hand side of this expression is the after-tax interest payment. Thus, since cash flow to the unlevered equityholders (UCF) is $92,400 and the after-tax interest payment is $8,331.15 [(.66).10 × $126,229.50], cash flow to the levered equityholders (LCF) is:

$$\$92,400 - \$8,331.15 = \$84,068.85$$

which is exactly the number we calculated earlier.

Step 2: Calculating r_S

The next step is to calculate the discount rate, r_S. Note that we assumed that the discount rate on unlevered equity, r_0, is .20. As we saw in Chapter 15, the formula for r_S is:

$$r_S = r_0 + \frac{B}{S}(1 - T_C)(r_0 - r_B)$$

Note that our target debt-to-value ratio of 1/4 implies a target debt-to-equity ratio of 1/3. Applying the preceding formula to this example, we have:

$$r_S = .222 = .20 + \frac{1}{3}(.66)(.20 - .10)$$

Step 3: Valuation

The present value of the project's LCF is

$$\frac{\text{LCF}}{r_S} = \frac{\$84,068.85}{.222} = \$378,688.50$$

Since the initial investment is $475,000 and $126,299.50 is borrowed, the firm must advance the project $348,770.50 ($475,000 − $126,229.50) out of its own cash reserves. The *net* present value of the project is simply the difference between the present value of the project's LCF and the investment not borrowed. Thus, the NPV is

$$\$378,688.50 - \$348,770.50 = \$29,918$$

which is identical to the result found with the APV approach.

Concept Questions

1. How is the FTE method applied?
2. What information is needed to calculate FTE?

17.3 Weighted-Average-Cost-of-Capital Method

Finally, one can value a project using the **weighted-average-cost-of-capital** (WACC) method. While this method was discussed in Chapters 12 and 15, it is worthwhile to review it here. The WACC approach begins with the insight that projects of levered firms are simultaneously financed with both debt and equity. The cost of capital is a weighted average of the cost of debt and the cost of equity. As seen in Chapters 12 and 15, the cost of equity is r_S. Ignoring taxes, the cost of debt is simply the borrowing rate, r_B. However, with corporate taxes, the appropriate cost of debt is $(1 - T_C)r_B$, the after-tax cost of debt.

The formula for determining the weighted average cost of capital, r_{WACC}, is:

$$r_{\text{WACC}} = \frac{S}{S + B} r_S + \frac{B}{S + B} r_B (1 - T_C)$$

The weight for equity, $S/(S + B)$, and the weight for debt, $B/(S + B)$, are target ratios. Target ratios are generally expressed in terms of market values, not accounting values. (Recall that another phrase for accounting value is *book value*.)

The formula calls for discounting the *unlevered* cash flow of the project (UCF) at the weighted average cost of capital, r_{WACC}. The net present value of the project can be written algebraically as:

$$\sum_{t=1}^{\infty} \frac{\text{UCF}_t}{(1 + r_{\text{WACC}})^t} - \text{Initial investment}$$

If the project is a perpetuity, the net present value is:

$$\frac{\text{UCF}}{r_{\text{WACC}}} - \text{Initial investment}$$

We previously stated that the target debt-to-value ratio of our project is $1/4$ and the corporate tax rate is .34, implying that the weighted average cost of capital is:

$$r_{\text{WACC}} = \frac{3}{4} \times 0.222 + \frac{1}{4} \times 0.10(0.66) = 0.183$$

Note that r_{WACC}, 0.183, is lower than the cost of equity capital for an all-equity firm, 0.20. This must always be the case, since debt financing provides a tax subsidy that lowers the average cost of capital.

We previously determined the UCF of the project to be $92,400, implying that the present value of the project is:

$$\frac{\$92,400}{0.183} = \$504,918$$

Since this initial investment is $475,000, the NPV of the project is:

$$\$504,918 - \$475,000 = \$29,918$$

In this example, all three approaches yield the same value.

<table>
<tr><td>**Concept**
Question</td><td>**1. How is the WACC method applied?**</td></tr>
</table>

17.4 A Comparison of the APV, FTE, and WACC Approaches

Capital-budgeting techniques in the early chapters of this text applied to all-equity firms. Capital budgeting for the levered firm could not be handled early in the book because the effects of debt on firm value were deferred until the previous two chapters. We learned there that debt increases firm value through tax benefits but decreases value through bankruptcy and related costs.

In this chapter we provide three approaches to capital budgeting for the levered firm. The adjusted-present-value (APV) approach first values the project on an all-equity basis. That is, the project's after-tax cash flows under all-equity financing (called unlevered cash flows, or UCF) are placed in the numerator of the capital-budgeting equation. The discount rate, assuming all-equity financing, appears in the denominator. At this point, the calculation is identical to that performed in the early chapters of this book. We then add the net present value of the debt. We point out that the net present value of the debt is likely to be the sum of four parameters: tax effects, flotation costs, bankruptcy costs, and interest subsidies.

The flow-to-equity (FTE) approach discounts the after-tax cash flow from a project going to the equityholders of a levered firm (LCF). LCF, which stands for levered cash flow, is the residual to equityholders after interest has been deducted. The discount rate is r_S, the cost of capital to the equityholders of a levered firm. For a firm with leverage, r_S must be greater than r_0, the cost of capital for an unlevered firm. This follows from our material in Chapter 15 showing that leverage raises the risk to the equityholders.

The last approach is the weighted-average-cost-of-capital (WACC) method. This technique calculates the project's after-tax cash flows assuming all-equity financing (UCF). The UCF is placed in the numerator of the capital-budgeting equation. The denominator, r_{WACC}, is a weighted average of the cost of equity capital and the cost of debt capital. The tax advantage of debt is reflected in the denominator because the cost of debt capital is determined net of corporate tax. The numerator does not reflect debt at all.

All three approaches perform the same task: valuation in the presence of debt financing. And, as illustrated by the previous example, all three provide the same valuation estimate. However, as we saw before, the approaches are markedly different in technique. Because of this, students often ask questions of the following sort: "How can this be? How can the three approaches look so different and yet give the same answer?" We believe that the best way to handle questions like these is through the following two points.

1. *APV versus WACC.* Of the three approaches, APV and WACC display the greatest similarity. After all, both approaches put the unlevered cash flow (UCF) in the numerator. However, the APV approach discounts these flows at r_0, yielding the value of the unlevered project. Adding the present value of the tax shield gives the value of the project under leverage. The WACC approach discounts UCF at r_{WACC}, which is lower than r_0.

Thus, both approaches adjust the basic NPV formula for unlevered firms in order to reflect the tax benefit of leverage. The APV approach makes this adjustment directly. It simply adds in the present value of the tax shield as a separate term. The WACC approach makes the adjustment in a more subtle way. Here, the discount rate is lowered below r_0. Although we do not provide a proof in the textbook, it can be shown that these two adjustments always have the same quantitative effect.

2. *Entity Being Valued.* The FTE approach appears at first glance to be far different from the other two. For both the APV and the WACC approaches, the initial investment is subtracted out in the final step ($475,000 in our example). However, for the FTE approach, only the firm's contribution to the initial investment ($348,770.50 = $475,000 − $126,229.50) is subtracted out. This occurs because under the FTE approach, only the future cash flows to the levered equityholders (LCF) are valued. By contrast, future cash flows to the unlevered equityholders (UCF) are valued in both the APV and WACC approaches. Thus, since LCFs are net of interest payments, whereas UCFs are not, the initial investment under the FTE approach is correspondingly reduced by debt financing. In this way, the FTE approach produces the same answer that the other two approaches do.

A Suggested Guideline

The net present value of our project is exactly the same under each of the three methods. In theory, this should always be the case.[5] However, one method usually provides an easier

---

[5]See I. Inselbag and H. Kaufold, "Two DCF Approaches for Valuing Companies under Alternative Financial Strategies (and How to Choose Between Them)" *Journal of Applied Corporate Finance* (Spring 1997).

computation than another, and, in many cases, one or more of the methods are virtually impossible computationally. We first consider when it is best to use the WACC and FTE approaches.

If the risk of a project stays constant throughout its life, it is plausible to assume that r_0 remains constant throughout the project's life. This assumption of constant risk appears to be reasonable for most real-world projects. In addition, if the debt-to-value ratio remains constant over the life of the project, both r_S and r_{WACC} will remain constant as well. Under this latter assumption, either the FTE or the WACC approach is easy to apply. However, if the debt-to-value ratio varies from year to year, both r_S and r_{WACC} vary from year to year as well. Using the FTE or the WACC approach when the denominator changes every year is computationally quite complex, and when computations become complex, the error rate rises. Thus, both the FTE and WACC approaches present difficulties when the debt-to-value *ratio* changes over time.

The APV approach is based on the *level* of debt in each future period. Consequently, when the debt level can be specified precisely for future periods, the APV approach is quite easy to use. However, when the debt level is uncertain, the APV approach becomes more problematic. For example, when the debt-to-value ratio is constant, the debt level varies with the value of the project. Since the value of the project in a future year cannot be easily forecast, the level of debt cannot be easily forecast either.

Thus, we suggest the following guideline:

Use WACC or FTE if the firm's target debt-to-value *ratio* applies to the project over its life.

Use APV if the project's *level* of debt is known over the life of the project.

There are a number of situations where the APV approach is preferred. For example, in a leveraged buyout (LBO) the firm begins with a large amount of debt but rapidly pays down the debt over a number of years. Since the schedule of debt reduction in the future is known when the LBO is arranged, tax shields in every future year can be easily forecast. Thus, the APV approach is easy to use here. (An illustration of the APV approach applied to LBOs is provided in the appendix to this chapter.) By contrast, the WACC and FTE approaches are virtually impossible to apply here, since the debt-to-equity value cannot be expected to be constant over time. In addition, situations involving interest subsidies and flotation costs are much easier to handle with the APV approach. (The Bicksler Enterprises example in Section 17.6 applies the APV approach to subsidies and flotation costs.) Finally, the APV approach handles the lease-versus-buy decision much more easily than does either the FTE or the WACC approach. (A full treatment of the lease-versus-buy decision appears in Chapter 24.)

The preceding examples are special cases. Typical capital budgeting situations are more amenable to either the WACC or the FTE approach than to the APV approach. Financial managers generally think in terms of target debt-value *ratios*. If a project does better than expected, both its value and its debt capacity will likely rise. The manager will increase debt correspondingly here. Conversely, the manager would be likely to reduce debt if the value of the project were to decline unexpectedly. Of course, because financing is a time-consuming task, the ratio cannot be adjusted on a day-to-day or a month-to-month basis. Rather, the adjustment can be expected to occur over the long run. As mentioned before, the WACC and FTE approaches are more appropriate than is the APV approach when a firm focuses on a target debt-value ratio.

Because of this, we recommend that the WACC and the FTE approaches, rather than the APV approach, be used in most real-world situations. In addition, frequent discussions

The Three Methods of Capital Budgeting with Leverage

1. Adjusted-present-value (APV) method

$$\sum_{t=1}^{\infty} \frac{\text{UCF}_t}{(1 + r_0)^t} + \text{Additional effects of debt} - \text{Initial investment}$$

     UCF_t = The project's cash flow at date t to the equityholders of an unlevered firm
       r_0 = Cost of capital for project in an unlevered firm

2. Flow-to-equity (FTE) method

$$\sum_{t=1}^{\infty} \frac{\text{LCF}_t}{(1 + r_S)^t} - (\text{Initial investment} - \text{Amount borrowed})$$

     LCF_t = The project's cash flow at date t to the equityholders of a levered firm
       r_S = Cost of equity capital with leverage

3. Weighted-average-cost-of-capital (WACC) method

$$\sum_{t=1}^{\infty} \frac{\text{UCF}_t}{(1 + r_{\text{WACC}})^t} - \text{Initial investment}$$

     r_{WACC} = Weighted average cost of capital

Notes

1. The middle term in the APV formula implies that the value of a project with leverage is greater than the value of the project without leverage. Since $r_{\text{WACC}} < r_0$, the WACC formula implies that the value of a project with leverage is greater than the value of the project without leverage.
2. In the FTE method, cash flow *after interest* (LCF) is used. Initial investment is reduced by *amount borrowed* as well.

Guidelines

1. Use WACC or FTE if the firm's target debt-to-value *ratio* applies to the project over its life.
2. Use APV if the project's *level* of debt is known over the life of the project.

with business executives have convinced us that the WACC is the most widely used method in the real world, by far. Thus, practitioners seem to agree with us that, outside of the special situations mentioned above, the APV approach is a less important method of capital budgeting.

Concept Questions

1. What is the main difference between APV and WACC?
2. What is the main difference between the FTE approach and the other two approaches?
3. When should the APV method be used?
4. When should the FTE and WACC approaches be used?

17.5 Capital Budgeting When the Discount Rate Must Be Estimated

The previous sections of this chapter introduced APV, FTE, and WACC—the three basic approaches to valuing a levered firm. However, one important detail remains. The example in Sections 17.1 through 17.3 *assumed* a discount rate. We now want to show how this rate is determined for real-world firms with leverage, with an application to the three preceding approaches. The example in this section brings together the work in Chapters 9–12 on the discount rate for unlevered firms with that in Chapter 15 on the effect of leverage on the cost of capital.

EXAMPLE

World-Wide Enterprises (WWE) is a large conglomerate thinking of entering the widget business, where it plans to finance projects with a debt-to-value ratio of 25 percent (or, alternatively, a debt-to-equity ratio of 1/3). There is currently one firm in the widget industry, American Widgets (AW). This firm is financed with 40-percent debt and 60-percent equity. The beta of AW's equity is 1.5. AW has a borrowing rate of 12 percent, and WWE expects to borrow for its widget venture at 10 percent. The corporate tax rate for both firms is 0.40, the market-risk premium is 8.5 percent, and the riskless interest rate is 8 percent. What is the appropriate discount rate for WWE to use for its widget venture?

As shown in Sections 17.1–17.3, a corporation may use one of three capital budgeting approaches: APV, FTE, or WACC. The appropriate discount rates for these three approaches are r_0, r_S, and r_{WACC}, respectively. Since AW is WWE's only competitor in widgets, we look at AW's cost of capital to calculate r_0, r_S, and r_{WACC} for WWE's widget venture. The four-step procedure below will allow us to calculate all three discount rates.

1. *Determining AW's Cost of Equity Capital.* First, we determine AW's cost of equity capital, using the security market line (SML) of Chapter 10:

AW's Cost of Equity Capital:

$$r_S = R_F + \beta \times (\bar{R}_M - R_F)$$
$$20.75\% = 8\% + 1.5 \times 8.5\%$$

where $\bar{R}_M$ is the expected return on the market portfolio and R_F is the risk-free rate.

2. *Determining AW's Hypothetical All-Equity Cost of Capital.* We must standardize the preceding number in some way, since AW and WWE's widget venture have different target debt-to-value ratios. The easiest approach is to calculate the hypothetical cost of equity capital for AW, assuming all-equity financing. This can be determined from MM's Proposition II under taxes (see Chapter 15):

AW's Cost of Capital if All-Equity:

$$r_S = r_0 + \frac{B}{S}(1 - T_C)(r_0 - r_B)$$

$$20.75\% = r_0 + \frac{0.4}{0.6}(0.60)(r_0 - 12\%)$$

In the examples of Chapter 15, the unknown in this equation was r_S. However, for this example, the unknown is r_0. By solving the equation, one finds that $r_0 = 0.1825$. Of course, r_0 is less than r_S because the cost of equity capital would be less when the firm employs no leverage.

At this point, firms in the real world generally make the assumption that the business risk of their venture is about equal to the business risk of the firms already in the business. Applying this assumption to our problem, we assert that the hypothetical discount rate of WWE's widget venture if all-equity financed is also 0.1825.[6] This discount rate would be employed if WWE uses the APV approach, since the APV approach calls for r_0, the project's cost of capital in a firm with no leverage.

3. *Determining r_S for WWE's Widget Venture.* Alternatively, WWE might use the FTE approach, where the discount rate for levered equity is determined from:

Cost of Equity Capital for WWE's Widget Venture:

$$r_S = r_0 + \frac{B}{S}(1 - T_C)(r_0 - r_B)$$

$$19.9\% = 18.25\% + \frac{1}{3}(0.60)(18.25\% - 10\%)$$

Note that the cost of equity capital for WWE's widget venture, 0.199, is less than the cost of equity capital for AW, 0.2075. This occurs because AW has a higher debt-to-equity ratio. (As mentioned above, both firms are assumed to have the same business risk.)

4. *Determining r_{WACC} for WWE's Widget Venture.* Finally, WWE might use the WACC approach. The appropriate calculation here is:

r_{WACC} for WWE's Widget Venture:

$$r_{WACC} = \frac{B}{S + B}r_B(1 - T_C) + \frac{S}{S + B}r_S$$

$$16.425\% = \frac{1}{4}10\%(0.60) + \frac{3}{4}19.9\%$$

The preceding example shows how the three discount rates, r_0, r_S, and r_{WACC}, are determined in the real world. These are the appropriate rates for the APV, FTE, and WACC approaches, respectively. Note that r_S for American Widgets is determined first, because the cost of equity capital can be determined from the beta of the firm's stock. As discussed in Chapter 12, beta can easily be estimated for any publicly traded firm, such as AW.

17.6 APV Example

As mentioned earlier in this chapter, firms generally set a target debt-to-equity ratio, allowing the use of WACC and FTE for capital budgeting. APV does not work as well here. However, as we also mentioned earlier, APV is the preferred approach when there are side benefits and side costs to debt. Because the analysis here can be tricky, we now devote an entire section to an example where, in addition to the tax subsidy to debt, both flotation costs and interest subsidies come into play.

---

[6]Alternatively, a firm might assume that its venture would be somewhat riskier since it is a new entrant. Thus, the firm might select a discount rate slightly higher than 0.1825. Of course, no exact formula exists for adjusting the discount rate upwards.

EXAMPLE

Bicksler Enterprises is considering a $10 million project that will last five years, implying straight-line depreciation per year of $2 million. The cash revenues less cash expenses per year are $3,500,000. The corporate tax bracket is 34 percent. The risk-free rate is 10 percent, and the cost of unlevered equity is 20 percent.

The cash flow projections each year are:

	C_0	C_1	C_2	C_3	C_4	C_5
Initial outlay	−$10,000,000					
Depreciation tax shield		$0.34 \times \$2,000,000$ $= \$680,000$	$680,000	$680,000	$680,000	$680,000
Revenue less expenses		$(1-0.34) \times \$3,500,000$ $= \$2,310,000$	$2,310,000	$2,310,000	$2,310,000	$2,310,000

We stated before that the APV of a project is the sum of its all-equity value plus the additional effects of debt. We examine each in turn.

All-Equity Value

Assuming the project is financed with all equity, the value of the project is:

$$-\$10,000,000 + \frac{\$680,000}{0.10} \times \left[1 - \left(\frac{1}{1.10}\right)^5\right] + \frac{\$2,310,000}{0.20} \times \left[1 - \left(\frac{1}{1.20}\right)^5\right] = -\$513,951$$

Initial cost   Depreciation tax shield   Present value of (Cash revenues − Cash expenses)

This calculation uses the techniques presented in the early chapters of this book. Notice that the depreciation tax shield is discounted at the riskless rate of 10 percent. The revenues and expenses are discounted at the higher rate of 20 percent.

An all-equity firm would clearly *reject* this project, because the NPV is −$513,951. And equity-flotation costs (not mentioned in the example) would only make the NPV more negative. However, debt financing may add enough value to the project to justify acceptance. We consider the effects of debt next.

Additional Effects of Debt

Bicksler Enterprises can obtain a five-year, nonamortizing loan for $7,500,000 after flotation costs at the risk-free rate of 10 percent. Flotation costs are fees paid when stock or debt is issued. These fees may go to printers, lawyers, and investment bankers, among others. Bicksler Enterprises is informed that flotation costs will be 1 percent of the gross proceeds of its loan. The previous chapter indicates that debt financing alters the NPV of a typical project. We look at the effects of debt next.

Flotation Costs   Given that flotation costs are 1 percent of the gross proceeds, we have:

$$\$7,500,000 = (1 - 0.01) \times \text{Gross proceeds} = 0.99 \times \text{Gross proceeds}$$

Thus, the gross proceeds are

$$\frac{\$7,500,000}{1 - 0.01} = \frac{\$7,500,000}{0.99} = \$7,575,758$$

This implies flotation costs of $75,758 (1% × $7,575,758). To check the calculation, note that net proceeds are $7,500,000 ($7,575,758 − $75,758). In other words, Bicksler Enterprises receives only $7,500,000. The flotation costs of $75,758 are received by intermediaries, e.g., investment bankers.

Flotation costs are paid immediately but are deducted from taxes by amortizing on a straight-line basis over the life of the loan. The cash flows from flotation costs are:

	Date 0	Date 1	Date 2	Date 3	Date 4	Date 5
Flotation costs	−$75,758					
Deduction		$15,152 = $\dfrac{\$75,758}{5}$	$15,152	$15,152	$15,152	$15,152
Tax shield from flotation costs		$0.34 \times \$15,152$ = **$5,152**	**$5,152**	**$5,152**	**$5,152**	**$5,152**

The relevant cash flows from flotation costs are in boldface. When discounting at 10 percent, the tax shield has a net present value of:

$$\$5,152 \times A_{0.10}^{5} = \$19,530$$

This implies a net cost of flotation of:

$$-\$75,758 + \$19,530 = -\$56,228$$

The net present value of the project after the flotation costs of debt but before the benefits of debt is:

$$-\$513,951 - \$56,228 = -\$570,179$$

Tax Subsidy   Interest must be paid on the gross proceeds of the loan, even though intermediaries receive the flotation costs. Since the gross proceeds of the loan are $7,575,578, annual interest is $757,576 ($7,575,758 × 0.10). The interest cost after taxes is $500,000 [$757,576 × (1 − 0.34)]. Because the loan is nonamortizing, the entire debt of $7,575,758 is repaid at date 5. These terms are indicated below:

	Date 0	Date 1	Date 2	Date 3	Date 4	Date 5
Loan (gross proceeds)	**$7,575,758**					
Interest paid		10% × $7,575,758 = $757,576	$757,576	$757,576	$757,576	$ 757,576
Interest cost after taxes		(1 − 0.34) × $757,576 = **$500,000**	**$500,000**	**$500,000**	**$500,000**	**$ 500,000**
Repayment of debt						**$7,575,758**

The relevant cash flows are listed in boldface in the above table. They are (1) loan received, (2) annual interest cost after taxes, and (3) repayment of debt. Note that we include the *gross* proceeds of the loan as an inflow, since the flotation costs have previously been subtracted.

In Chapter 15 we mentioned that the financing decision can be evaluated in terms of net present value. The net present value of the loan is simply the net present value of each of the three cash flows. This can be represented as:

$$\text{NPV(Loan)} = +\begin{array}{c}\text{Amount}\\\text{borrowed}\end{array} - \begin{array}{c}\text{Present value}\\\text{of after-tax}\\\text{interest payments}\end{array} - \begin{array}{c}\text{Present value}\\\text{of loan}\\\text{repayments}\end{array} \quad (17.1)$$

The calculations for this example are:

$$976,415 = +\$7,575,758 - \frac{\$500,000}{0.10} \times \left[1 - \left(\frac{1}{1.10}\right)^5\right] - \frac{\$7,575,758}{(1.10)^5} \qquad (17.1')$$

The NPV(Loan) is positive, reflecting the interest tax shield.[7]

The adjusted present value of the project with this financing is:

$$\text{APV} = \text{All-equity value} - \text{Flotation costs of debt} + \text{NPV(Loan)} \qquad (17.2)$$

$$\$406,236 = \quad -\$513,951 \quad - \quad \$56,228 \quad + \$976,415 \qquad (17.2')$$

Though we previously saw that an all-equity firm would reject the project, a firm would *accept* the project if a $7,500,000 (net) loan could be obtained.

Because the loan discussed above was at the market rate of 10 percent, we have considered only two of the three additional effects of debt (flotation costs and tax subsidy) so far. We now examine another loan where the third effect arises.

Non–Market-Rate Financing A number of companies are fortunate enough to obtain subsidized financing from a governmental authority. Suppose that the project of Bicksler Enterprises is deemed socially beneficial and the state of New Jersey grants the firm a $7,500,000 loan at 8-percent interest. In addition, all flotation costs are absorbed by the state. Clearly, the company will choose this loan over the one we previously calculated. The cash flows from the loan are:

	Date 0	Date 1	Date 2	Date 3	Date 4	Date 5
Loan received	**$7,500,000**					
Interest paid		8% × $7,500,000 = $600,000	$ 600,000	$ 600,000	$ 600,000	$ 600,000
After-tax interest		(1 − 0.34) × $600,000 = **$396,000**	**$396,000**	**$396,000**	**$396,000**	**$ 396,000**
Repayment of debt						**$ 7,500,000**

The relevant cash flows are listed in boldface in the preceding table. Using equation (17.1), the NPV(Loan) is:

$$\$1,341,939 = +\$7,500,000 - \frac{\$396,000}{0.10} \times \left[1 - \left(\frac{1}{1.10}\right)^5\right] - \frac{\$7,500,000}{(1.10)^5} \qquad (17.1'')$$

Why do we discount the cash flows in equation (17.1″) at 10 percent when the firm is borrowing at 8 percent? We discount at 10 percent because that is the fair or marketwide rate. That is, 10 percent is the rate at which one could borrow *without* benefit of subsidization. The net present value of the subsidized loan is larger than the net present value of the earlier loan because the firm is now borrowing at the below-market rate of 8 percent. Note that the NPV(Loan) calculation in equation (17.1″) captures both the tax effect *and* the non–market-rate effect.

The net present value of the project with subsidized debt financing is:

$$\text{APV} = \text{All-equity value} - \text{Flotation costs of debt} + \text{NPV(Loan)} \qquad (17.2)$$

$$+\$827,988 = \quad -\$513,951 \quad - \quad 0 \quad + \$1,341,939 \qquad (17.2'')$$

---

[7]The NPV (Loan) must be zero in a no-tax world, because interest provides no tax shield there. To check this intuition, we calculate:

$$\text{No-tax case: } 0 = +\$7,575,758 - \frac{\$757,576}{0.10} \times \left[1 - \left(\frac{1}{1.10}\right)^5\right] - \frac{\$7,575,758}{(1.10)^5}$$

The preceding example illustrates the adjusted-present-value (APV) approach. The approach begins with the present value of a project for the all-equity firm. Next, the effects of debt are added in. The approach has much to recommend it. It is intuitively appealing because individual components are calculated separately and added together in a simple way. And, if the debt from the project can be specified precisely, the present value of the debt can be calculated precisely.

17.7 Beta and Leverage

Chapter 12 provides the formula for the relationship between the beta of the common stock and leverage of the firm in a world without taxes. We reproduce this formula here:

The No-Tax Case:

$$\beta_{\text{Equity}} = \beta_{\text{Asset}} \left(1 + \frac{\text{Debt}}{\text{Equity}} \right) \tag{17.3}$$

As pointed out in Chapter 12, this relationship holds under the assumption that the beta of debt is zero.

Since firms must pay corporate taxes in practice, it is worthwhile to provide the relationship in a world with corporate taxes. It can be shown that the relationship between the beta of the unlevered firm and the beta of the levered equity is:[8]

The Corporate-Tax Case:

$$\beta_{\text{Equity}} = \left(1 + \frac{(1 - T_C)\text{Debt}}{\text{Equity}} \right) \beta_{\text{Unlevered firm}} \tag{17.4}$$

when (1) the corporation is taxed at the rate of T_C and (2) the debt has a zero beta.

---

[8]This result holds only if the beta of debt equals zero. To see this, note that

$$V_U + T_C B = V_L = B + S \tag{a}$$

where

V_U = Value of unlevered firm
V_L = Value of levered firm
B = Value of debt in a levered firm
S = Value of equity in a levered firm

As we stated in the text, the beta of the levered firm is a weighted average of the debt beta and the equity beta:

$$\frac{B}{B + S} \times \beta_B + \frac{S}{B + S} \times \beta_S$$

where β_B and β_S are the betas of the debt and the equity of the levered firm, respectively. Because $V_L = B + S$, we have

$$\frac{B}{V_L} \times \beta_B + \frac{S}{V_L} \times \beta_S \tag{b}$$

The beta of the levered firm can *also* be expressed as a weighted average of the beta of the unlevered firm and the beta of the tax shield:

$$\frac{V_U}{V_U + T_C B} \times \beta_U + \frac{T_C B}{V_U + T_C B} \times \beta_B$$

where β_U is the beta of the unlevered firm. This follows from equation (a). Because $V_L = V_U + T_C B$, we have

$$\frac{V_U}{V_L} \times \beta_U + \frac{T_C B}{V_L} \times \beta_B \tag{c}$$

We can equate (b) and (c) because both represent the beta of a levered firm. Equation (a) tells us that $V_U = S + (1 - T_C) \times B$. Under the assumption that $\beta_B = 0$, equating (b) and (c) and using equation (a) yields equation (17.4).

The generalized formula for the levered beta (where β_B is not zero) is:

$$\beta_S = \beta_U + (1 - T_C)(\beta_U - \beta_B)\frac{B}{S}$$

and

$$\beta_U = \frac{S}{B(1 - T_C) + S}\beta_S + \frac{B(1 - T_C)}{B(1 - T_C) + S}\beta_B$$

Because $[1 + (1 - T_C)\text{debt/equity}]$ must be more than 1 for a levered firm, it follows that $\beta_{\text{Unlevered firm}} < \beta_{\text{Equity}}$. The corporate-tax case of equation (17.4) is quite similar to the no-tax case of equation (17.3), because the beta of levered equity must be greater than the beta of the unlevered firm in either case. The intuition that leverage increases the risk of equity applies in both cases.

However, notice that the two equations are not equal. It can be shown that leverage increases the equity beta less rapidly under corporate taxes. This occurs because, under taxes, leverage creates a *riskless* tax shield, thereby lowering the risk of the entire firm.

EXAMPLE

C. F. Lee Incorporated is considering a scale-enhancing project. The market value of the firm's debt is $100 million, and the market value of the firm's equity is $200 million. The debt is considered riskless. The corporate tax rate is 34 percent. Regression analysis indicates that the beta of the firm's equity is 2. The risk-free rate is 10 percent, and the expected market premium is 8.5 percent. What would the project's discount rate be in the hypothetical case that C. F. Lee, Inc., is all-equity?

We can answer this question in two steps.

1. *Determining Beta of Hypothetical All-Equity Firm.* Rearranging equation (17.4), we have:

Unlevered Beta:

$$\frac{\text{Equity}}{\text{Equity} + (1 - T_C) \times \text{Debt}} \times \beta_{\text{Equity}} = \beta_{\text{Unlevered firm}} \qquad (17.5)$$

$$\frac{\$200 \text{ million}}{\$200 \text{ million} + (1 - 0.34) \times \$100 \text{ million}} \times 2 = 1.50$$

2. *Determining Discount Rate.* We calculate the discount rate from the security market line (SML) as:

Discount Rate:

$$r_S = R_F + \beta \times [\overline{R}_M - R_F]$$
$$22.75\% = 10\% + 1.50 \times 8.5\%$$

The Project Is Not Scale-Enhancing

Because the above example assumed that the project is scale-enhancing, we began with the beta of the firm's equity. If the project is not scale-enhancing, one could begin with the equity betas of firms in the industry of the project. For each firm, the hypothetical beta of the unlevered equity could be calculated by equation (17.5). The SML could then be used to determine the project's discount rate from the average of these betas.

EXAMPLE

The J. Lowes Corporation, which currently manufactures staples, is considering a $1 million investment in a project in the aircraft adhesives industry. The corporation estimates unlevered after-tax cash flows (UCF) of $300,000 per year into perpetuity from the project. The firm will finance the project with a debt-to-value ratio of 0.5 (or, equivalently, a debt-to-equity ratio of 1:1).

The three competitors in this new industry are currently unlevered, with betas of 1.2, 1.3, and 1.4. Assuming a risk-free rate of 5 percent, a market-risk premium of 9 percent, and a corporate tax rate of 34 percent, what is the net present value of the project?

We can answer this question in five steps.

1. *Calculating the Average Unlevered Beta in the Industry.* The average unlevered beta across all three existing competitors in the aircraft adhesives industry is:

$$\frac{1.2 + 1.3 + 1.4}{3} = 1.3$$

2. *Calculating the Levered Beta for J. Lowes's New Project.* Assuming the same unlevered beta for this new project as for the existing competitors, we have, from equation (17.4),

Levered Beta:

$$\beta_{Equity} = \left(1 + \frac{(1 - T_C)\,Debt}{Equity}\right)\beta_{Unlevered\ firm}$$

$$2.16 = \left(1 + \frac{0.66 \times 1}{1}\right) \times 1.3$$

3. *Calculating the Cost of Levered Equity for the New Project.* We calculate the discount rate from the security market line (SML) as:

Discount Rate:

$$r_S = R_F + \beta \times [\bar{R}_M - R_F]$$
$$0.244 = 0.05 + 2.16 \times 0.09$$

4. *Calculating the WACC for the New Project.* The formula for determining the weighted average cost of capital, r_{WACC}, is:

$$r_{WACC} = \frac{B}{V}r_B(1 - T_C) + \frac{S}{V}r_S$$

$$0.139 = \frac{1}{2} \times 0.05 \times 0.66 + \frac{1}{2} \times 0.244$$

5. *Determining the Project's Value.* Because the cash flows are perpetual, the NPV of the project is:

$$\frac{Unlevered\ cash\ flows\ (UCF)}{r_{WACC}} - Initial\ investment$$

$$\frac{\$300,000}{0.139} - \$1\ million = \$1.16\ million$$

17.8 SUMMARY AND CONCLUSIONS

Earlier chapters of this text showed how to calculate net present value for projects of all-equity firms. We pointed out in the last two chapters that the introduction of taxes and bankruptcy costs changes a firm's financing decisions. Rational corporations should employ some debt in a world of this type. Because of the benefits and costs associated with debt, the capital-budgeting decision is different for levered firms than for unlevered firms. The present chapter has discussed three methods for capital budgeting by levered firms: the adjusted-present-value (APV), flows-to-equity (FTE), and weighted-average-cost-of-capital (WACC) approaches.

1. The APV formula can be written as:

$$\sum_{t=1}^{\infty} \frac{UCF_t}{(1 + r_0)^t} + Additional\ effects\ of\ debt - Initial\ investment$$

There are four additional effects of debt:
- Tax shield from debt financing
- Flotation costs
- Bankruptcy costs
- Benefit of non–market-rate financing

2. The FTE formula can be written as

$$\sum_{t=1}^{\infty} \frac{LCF_t}{(1 + r_S)^t} - (\text{Initial investment} - \text{Amount borrowed})$$

3. The WACC formula can be written as

$$\sum_{t=1}^{\infty} \frac{UCF_t}{(1 + r_{WACC})^t} - \text{Initial investment}$$

4. Corporations frequently follow the guideline:
   Use WACC or FTE if the firm's target debt-to-value *ratio* applies to the project over its life.
   Use APV if the project's *level* of debt is known over the life of the project.

5. The APV method is used frequently for special situations like interest subsidies, LBOs, and leases. The WACC and FTE methods are commonly used for more typical capital-budgeting situations. The APV approach is a rather unimportant method for typical capital-budgeting situations.

6. The beta of the equity of the firm is positively related to the leverage of the firm.

KEY TERMS   adjusted present value (APV), *477*   weighted average cost of capital, *480*
                 flow to equity (FTE), *479*

SUGGESTED READINGS

The following article contains a superb discussion of some of the subtleties of using WACC for project valuation:

Miles, J., and R. Ezzel. "The Weighted Average Cost of Capital, Perfect Capital Markets and Project Life: A Clarification." *Journal of Financial and Quantitative Analysis* 15 (September 1980).

The following article presents the practical aspects of the APV approach:

T. A. Luehrman. "Using APV: A Better Tool for Valuing Operations." *Harvard Business Review* (May/June 1997).

A fascinating article on the merits of the APV and WACC approaches is:

Inselbag, I., and H. Kaufold. "Two DCF Approaches in Valuing Companies under Alternative Financing Strategies (and How to Choose between Them)." *Journal of Applied Corporate Finance* (Summer 1997).

QUESTIONS & PROBLEMS

ADJUSTED PRESENT VALUE

17.1 Honda and GM are competing to sell a fleet of 25 cars to Hertz. Hertz fully depreciates all of its rental cars over five years using the straight-line method. The firm expects the fleet of 25 cars to generate $100,000 per year in earnings before taxes and depreciation for five years. Hertz is an all-equity firm in the 34-percent tax bracket. The required return on the firm's unlevered equity is 10 percent, and the new fleet will not add to the risk of the firm.
   a. What is the maximum price that Hertz should be willing to pay for the new fleet of cars if it remains an all-equity firm?
   b. Suppose Hertz purchases the fleet from GM for $325,000, and Hertz is able to issue $200,000 of five year, 8 percent debt in order to finance the project. All principal will be repaid in one balloon payment at the end of the fifth year. What is the adjusted present value (APV) of the project?

17.2 Gemini, Inc., an all-equity firm, is considering a $2.1 million investment that will be depreciated according to the straight-line method over its three-year life. The project is expected to generate earnings before taxes and depreciation of $900,000 per year for three years. The investment will not change the risk level of the firm. Gemini can obtain a three-year, 12.5 percent loan to finance the project from a local bank. All principal will be repaid in one balloon payment at the end of the third year. The bank will charge the firm $21,000 in flotation fees, which will be amortized over the three-year life of the loan. If Gemini financed the project entirely with equity, the firm's cost of capital would be 18 percent. The corporate tax rate is 30 percent. Using the adjusted present value (APV) method, determine whether or not Gemini should undertake the project.

17.3   MVP, Inc., has produced rodeo supplies for over 20 years. The company currently has a debt-to-equity ratio of 25 percent and is in the 40 percent tax bracket. The required return on the firm's levered equity is 18 percent. MVP is planning to expand its production capacity. The equipment to be purchased is expected to generate unlevered cash flows according to the following schedule:

Unlevered Cash Flows by Year (in $ millions)				
0	1	2	3	4+
−15	4	8	9	0

(Unlevered cash flows are defined as the after-tax cash flows the equipment would generate under all-equity financing.) MVP has arranged a $6 million debt issue to partially finance the expansion. Under the loan, the company would pay interest of 10 percent at the end of each year on the outstanding balance at the beginning of the year. The firm would also make year-end principal payments of $2 million per year, completely retiring the issue by the end of the third year. Using the adjusted present value (APV) method, determine whether or not MVP should proceed with the expansion.

17.4   Triad Corporation has established a joint venture with Tobacco Road Construction, Inc., to build a toll road in North Carolina. The initial investment in paving equipment is $20 million. The equipment will be fully depreciated using the straight-line method over its economic life of five years. Earnings before interest, taxes, and depreciation collected from the toll road are projected to be $3 million per annum for 20 years starting from the end of the first year. The corporate tax rate is 25 percent. The required rate of return for the project under all-equity financing is 12 percent. The pre-tax cost of debt (r_B) for the joint partnership is 9 percent per annum. In order to encourage investment in the country's infrastructure, the U.S. government will subsidize the project with a $10 million, 15-year loan at an interest rate of 5 percent per year. All principal will be repaid in one balloon payment at the end of year 15. What is the adjusted present value (APV) of this project?

FLOW-TO-EQUITY   **17.5**   Milano Pizza Club owns three identical restaurants popular for their specialty pizzas. Each restaurant has a debt-to-equity ratio of 30 percent and makes interest payments of $25,650 at the end of each year. The cost of the firm's levered equity (r_S) is 21 percent. Each Milano store estimates that annual sales will be $1 million, annual cost of goods sold will be $400,000, and annual general and administrative costs will be $300,000. These cash flows are expected to remain the same forever. The corporate tax rate is 40 percent.
a. Use the flow-to-equity approach to determine the value of Milano Pizza Club's equity.
b. What is the total value of Milano Pizza Club?

WEIGHTED AVERAGE COST OF CAPITAL   **17.6**   If Wild Widgets, Inc., (WWI) were an all-equity firm, it would have a beta of 0.9. WWI has a target debt-to-equity ratio of 0.50. The expected return on the market portfolio is 16 percent, and Treasury bills currently yield 8 percent per annum. WWI one-year, $1,000 par value bonds carry a 7 percent annual coupon and are currently selling for $972.73. The yield on WWI's longer term debt is equal to the yield on its one-year bonds. The corporate tax rate is 34 percent.
a. What is WWI's cost of debt?
b. What is WWI's cost of equity?
c. What is WWI's weighted average cost of capital?

17.7   Bolero, Inc., has compiled the following information on its financing costs:

Type of Financing	Book Value	Market Value	Cost
Long-term debt	$ 5,000,000	$ 2,000,000	10%
Short-term debt	5,000,000	5,000,000	8
Common stock	10,000,000	13,000,000	15
Total	$20,000,000	$20,000,000	

Bolero is in the 34 percent tax bracket and has a target debt-to-equity ratio of 100 percent. Bolero's managers would like to keep the market values of short-term and long-term debt equal.

a.   Calculate the weighted average cost of capital (r_{WACC}) for Bolero using:
  1.   Book-value weights
  2.   Market-value weights
  3.   Target weights
b.   Explain the difference between the WACCs. Which is the correct WACC to use for project evaluation?

17.8   Neon Corporation's stock returns have a covariance with the market portfolio of 0.031. The standard deviation of the returns on the market portfolio is 0.16, and the expected market risk premium is 8.5 percent. Neon's bonds yield 11 percent per annum. The market value of the bonds is $24 million. Neon has 4 million shares of common stock outstanding, each worth $15. Neon's CEO considers the firm's current debt-to-equity ratio optimal. The corporate tax rate is 34 percent, and Treasury bills currently yield 7 percent per annum. Neon is considering the purchase of additional equipment that would cost $27.5 million. The expected unlevered cash flows (UCF) from the equipment are $9 million per year for five years. (Unlevered cash flows are defined as the after-tax cash flows the equipment would generate under all-equity financing.) Purchasing the equipment will not change the risk level of the firm.

a.   Use the weighted-average-cost-of-capital approach to determine whether or not Neon should purchase the equipment.
b.   Suppose Neon decides to fund the purchase of the equipment entirely with debt. By how much will the weighted average cost of capital used in (a) change? Explain your answer.

17.9   National Electric Company (NEC) is considering a $20 million project in its power systems division. Tom Edison, the company's chief financial officer, has evaluated the project and determined that the project's unlevered cash flows will be $8 million per year in perpetuity. Mr. Edison has devised two possibilities for raising the $20 million:

- Issue 10-year, 10 percent debt
- Issue common stock

NEC's pretax cost of debt (r_B) is 10 percent, and its cost of equity is 20 percent. The firm's target debt-to-equity ratio is 200 percent. The project has the same risk as NEC's existing businesses, and it will support the same amount of debt. NEC is in the 34 percent tax bracket. Should NEC accept the project? Use the weighted-average-cost-of-capital method to support your conclusion.

A COMPARISON OF THE APV, FTE, AND WACC APPROACHES

17.10   ABC, Inc., is an unlevered firm with expected annual earnings before taxes of $30 million in perpetuity. The required return on the firm's unlevered equity (r_0) is 18 percent, and the firm distributes all of its earnings as dividends at the end of each year. ABC has 1 million shares of common stock outstanding and is subject to a corporate tax rate of 34 percent. The firm is planning a recapitalization under which it will issue $50 million of perpetual 10 percent debt and use the proceeds to buy back shares.

a.   Calculate the value of ABC before the recapitalization plan is announced. What is the value of ABC's equity before the announcement? What is the price per share?
b.   Use the APV method to calculate the value of ABC after the recapitalization plan is announced. What is the value of ABC's equity after the announcement? What is the price per share?

    c. How many shares will be repurchased? What is ABC's equity value after the repurchase has been completed? What is the price per share?

    d. Use the flow-to-equity method to calculate the value of ABC's equity after the recapitalization.

17.11 Mojito Mint Company has a debt-to-equity ratio of 2/3. The required return on the firm's unlevered equity is 16 percent, and the pretax cost of the firm's debt is 10 percent. Sales revenue for Mojito is expected to remain stable indefinitely at last year's level of $19,740,000. Variable costs amount to 60 percent of sales. Mojito is taxed at the corporate tax rate of 40 percent. The firm distributes all of its earnings as dividends at the end of each year.

    a. If Mojito were financed entirely by equity, how much would it be worth?

    b. What is the required return on the firm's levered equity (r_S)?

    c. Use the weighted-average-cost-of-capital method to calculate the value of Mojito Mint. What is the value of the firm's equity? What is the value of the firm's debt?

    d. Use the flow-to-equity method to calculate the value of Mojito Mint's equity.

17.12 Lone Star Industries just issued $500 of perpetual 10 percent debt and used the proceeds to repurchase stock. The company expects to generate $152 of earnings before interest and taxes in perpetuity. Lone Star distributes all of its earnings as dividends at the end of each year. The firm's unlevered cost of capital is 20 percent, and the corporate tax rate is 40 percent.

    a. What is the value of Lone Star as an unlevered firm?

    b. Use the adjusted-present-value method to calculate the value of Lone Star with leverage. What is the value of the firm's equity?

    c. What is the required return on the firm's levered equity (r_S)?

    d. Use the flow-to-equity method to calculate the value of Lone Star's equity.

CAPITAL BUDGETING FOR PROJECTS THAT ARE NOT SCALE-ENHANCING

17.13 Blue Angel, Inc., a new firm in the holiday gift industry, is considering a project. To better assess the risk of the project, the firm obtained the following information on 10 other firms in the industry:

	Industry Average	Blue Angel
Target D/E	30%	35%
β_{Equity}	1.5	?
r_B	10%	10%

The expected return on the market portfolio is 17 percent, and the risk-free rate is 9 percent. Blue Angel is subject to a corporate tax rate of 40 percent. The project requires an initial outlay of $325,000 and is expected to result in a $55,000 cash inflow at the end of the first year. The project will be financed at Blue Angel's target debt-equity ratio. Annual cash flow from the project will grow at a constant rate of 5 percent until the end of the fifth year and remain constant forever thereafter. Should Blue Angel invest in the project?

THE NPV OF LOANS

17.14 Daniel Kaffe, CFO of Kendrick Enterprises, is evaluating a 10-year, 9 percent loan, with gross proceeds of $4,250,000. Kendrick's pretax cost of debt is 9 percent. Flotation costs are estimated to be 1.25 percent of gross proceeds and will be amortized using a straight-line schedule over the 10-year life of the loan. Kendrick is subject to a corporate tax rate of 40 percent. The loan will not increase the risk of financial distress for the firm.

    a. Calculate the net present value of the loan excluding flotation costs.

    b. Calculate the net present value of the loan including flotation costs.

BETA AND LEVERAGE

17.15 North Pole Fishing Equipment Corporation and South Pole Fishing Equipment Corporation would have identical equity betas of 1.2 if both of them were all-equity financed. The capital structures of the two firms are as follows:

	North Pole	South Pole
Debt	$1,000,000	$1,500,000
Equity	$1,500,000	$1,000,000

The expected return on the market portfolio is 12.75 percent, and the risk-free rate is 4.25 percent. Both firms are subject to a corporate tax rate of 35 percent. Assume the debt beta of each of the two firms equals 0.

a. What is the equity beta of each of the two firms?

b. What is the required rate of return on each of the two firm's equity?

S & P PROBLEMS

17.16 Locate the annual income statements for Walt Disney (DIS) and calculate the marginal tax rate for the company for the last year. Next, find the beta for Disney in the S&P Stock Report. Using the current debt and equity from the most recent annual balance sheet, calculate the unlevered beta for Disney.

Appendix 17A

The Adjusted-Present-Value Approach to Valuing Leveraged Buyouts[9]

Introduction

A leveraged buyout (LBO) is the acquisition by a small group of equity investors of a public or private company financed primarily with debt. The equityholders service the heavy interest and principal payments with cash from operations and/or asset sales. The shareholders generally hope to reverse the LBO within three to seven years by way of a public offering or sale of the company to another firm. A buyout is therefore likely to be successful only if the firm generates enough cash to serve the debt in the early years, and if the company is attractive to other buyers as the buyout matures.

In a leveraged buyout, the equity investors are expected to pay off outstanding principal according to a specific timetable. The owners know that the firm's debt-equity ratio will fall and can forecast the dollar amount of debt needed to finance future operations. Under these circumstances, the adjusted-present-value (APV) approach is more practical than the weighted-average-cost-of-capital (WACC) approach because the capital structure is changing. In this appendix, we illustrate the use of this procedure in valuing the RJR Nabisco transaction, the largest LBO in history.

The RJR Nabisco Buyout   In the summer of 1988, the price of RJR stock was hovering around $55 a share. The firm had $5 billion of debt. The firm's CEO, acting in concert with some other senior managers of the firm, announced a bid of $75 per share to take the firm private in a management buyout. Within days of management's offer, Kohlberg, Kravis and Roberts (KKR) entered the fray with a $90 bid of their own. By the end of November, KKR emerged from the ensuing bidding process with an offer of $109 a share, or $25 billion total. We now use the APV technique to analyze KKR's winning strategy.

The APV method as described in this chapter can be used to value companies as well as projects. Applied in this way, the maximum value of a levered firm (V_L) is its value as an all-equity entity (V_U) plus the discounted value of the interest tax shields from the debt its

---

[9]This appendix has been adapted by Isik Inselbag and Howard Kaufold. The Wharton School, University of Pennsylvania, from their unpublished manuscript entitled "Analyzing the RJR Nabisco Buyout: An Adjusted Present Value Approach."

Visit us at www.mhhe.com/rwj

TABLE 17A.1	1989	1990	1991	1992	1993
RJR Operating Cash Flows (in $ millions)					
Operating income	$2,620	$3,410	$3,645	$3,950	$4,310
Tax on operating income	891	1,142	1,222	1,326	1,448
After-tax operating income	1,729	2,268	2,423	2,624	2,862
Add back depreciation	449	475	475	475	475
Less capital expenditures	522	512	525	538	551
Less change in working capital	(203)	(275)	200	225	250
Add proceeds from asset sales	3,545	1,805			
Unlevered cash flow (UCF)	$5,404	$4,311	$2,173	$2,336	$2,536

TABLE 17A.2	1989	1990	1991	1992	1993
Projected Interest Expenses and Tax Shields (in $ millions)					
Interest expenses	$3,384	$3,004	$3,111	$3,294	$3,483
Interest tax shields ($T_C = 34\%$)	1,151	1,021	1,058	1,120	1,184

assets will support (PVTS).[10] This relation can be stated as

$$V_L = V_U + \text{PVTS}$$

$$= \sum_{t=1}^{\infty} \frac{\text{UCF}_t}{(1 + r_0)^t} + \sum_{t=1}^{\infty} \frac{T_C r_B B_{t-1}}{(1 + r_B)^t}$$

In the second part of this equation, UCF_t is the unlevered cash flow from operations for year t. Discounting these cash flows by the required return on assets, r_0, yields the all-equity value of the company. B_{t-1} represents the debt balance remaining at the end of year $(t - 1)$. Because interest in a given year is based on the debt balance remaining at the end of the previous year, the interest paid in year t is $r_B B_{t-1}$. The numerator of the second term, $T_C r_B B_{t-1}$, is therefore the tax shield for year t. We discount this series of annual tax shields using the rate at which the firm borrows, r_B.[11]

KKR planned to sell several of RJR's food divisions and operate the remaining parts of the firm more efficiently. Table 17A.1 presents KKR's projected unlevered cash flows for RJR under the buyout, adjusting for planned asset sales and operational efficiencies.

With respect to financial strategy, KKR planned a significant increase in leverage with accompanying tax benefits. Specifically, KKR issued almost $24 billion of new debt to complete the buyout, raising annual interest costs to more than $3 billion.[12] Table 17A.2 presents the projected interest expense and tax shields for the transaction.

We now use the data from Tables 17A.1 and 17A.2 to calculate the APV of the RJR buyout. This valuation process is presented in Table 17A.3.

[10]One should also deduct from this value any costs of financial distress. However, we would expect these costs to be small in the case of RJR for two reasons. As a firm in the tobacco and food industries, its cash flows are relatively stable and recession resistant. Furthermore, the firm's assets are divisible and attractive to a number of potential buyers, allowing the firm to receive full value if disposition is required.

[11]The pretax borrowing rate, r_B, represents the appropriate discount rate for the interest tax shields when there is a precommitment to a specific debt repayment schedule under the terms of the LBO. If debt covenants require that the entire free cash flow be dedicated to debt service, the amount of debt outstanding and, therefore, the interest tax shield at any point in time are a direct function of the operating cash flows of the firm. Since the debt balance is then as risky as the cash flows, the required return on assets should be used to discount the interest tax shields.

[12]A significant portion of this debt was of the payment in kind (PIK) variety, which offers lenders additional bonds instead of cash interest. This PIK debt financing provided KKR with significant tax shields while allowing it to postpone the cash burden of debt service to future years. For simplicity of presentation, Table 17A.2 does not separately show cash versus noncash interest charges.

TABLE 17A.3		1989	1990	1991	1992	1993
RJR LBO Valuation (in $ millions except share data)	Unlevered cash flow (UCF)	$ 5,404	$4,311	$2,173	$2,336	$ 2,536
	Terminal value: (3% growth after 1993)					
	Unlevered terminal value (UTV)					23,746
	Terminal value at target debt					26,654
	Tax shield in terminal value					2,908
	Interest tax shields	1,151	1,021	1,058	1,120	1,184
	PV of UCF 1989–93 at 14%	12,224				
	PV of UTV at 14%	12,333				
	Total unlevered value	$24,557				
	PV of tax shields 1989–93 at 13.5%	3,834				
	PV of tax shield in TV at 13.5%	1,544				
	Total value of tax shields	5,421				
	Total value	29,935				
	Less value of assumed debt	5,000				
	Value of equity	$24,935				
	Number of shares	229 million				
	Value per share	$ 108.9				

The valuation presented in Table 17A.3 involves four steps.

Step 1: *Calculating the present value of unlevered cash flows for 1989–93*   The unlevered cash flows for 1989–93 are shown in the last line of Table 17A.1 and the first line of Table 17A.3. These flows are discounted by the required asset return, r_0, which at the time of the buyout was approximately 14 percent. The value as of the end of 1988 of the unlevered cash flows expected from 1989 through 1993 is

$$\frac{5.404}{1.14} + \frac{4.311}{1.14^2} + \frac{2.173}{1.14^3} + \frac{2.336}{1.14^4} + \frac{2.536}{1.14^5} = \$12.224 \text{ billion}$$

Step 2: *Calculating the present value of the unlevered cash flows beyond 1993 (unlevered terminal value)*   We assume the unlevered cash flows grow at the modest annual rate of 3 percent after 1993. The value, as of the end of 1993, of these cash flows is equal to the following discounted value of a growing perpetuity:

$$\frac{2.536(1.03)}{0.14 - 0.03} = \$23.746 \text{ billion}$$

This translates to a 1988 value of

$$\frac{23.746}{1.14^5} = \$12.333 \text{ billion}$$

As in Step 1, the discount rate is the required asset rate of 14 percent.

The total unlevered value of the firm is therefore ($12.224 + $12.333 =) $24.557 billion.

To calculate the total buyout value, we must add the interest tax shields expected to be realized by debt financing.

Step 3: *Calculating the present value of interest tax shields for 1989–93*   Under the prevailing U.S. tax laws in 1989, every dollar of interest reduces taxes by 34 cents. The present value of the interest tax shield for the period from 1989–93 can be calculated by discounting the annual tax savings at the pretax average cost of debt, which was approximately 13.5 percent. Using the tax shields from Table 17A.2, the discounted value of these tax shields is calculated as

$$\frac{1.151}{1.135} + \frac{1.021}{1.135^2} + \frac{1.058}{1.135^3} + \frac{1.120}{1.135^4} + \frac{1.184}{1.135^5} = \$3.834 \text{ billion}$$

Step 4: *Calculating the present value of interest tax shields beyond 1993*   Finally, we must calculate the value of tax shields associated with debt used to finance the operations of the company after 1993. We assume that debt will be reduced and maintained at 25 percent of the value of the firm from that date forward.[13] Under this assumption it is appropriate to use the WACC method to calculate a terminal value for the firm at the target capital structure. This in turn can be decomposed into an all-equity value and a value from tax shields.

If, after 1993, RJR uses 25-percent debt in its capital structure, its WACC at this target capital structure would be approximately 12.8 percent.[14] Then the levered terminal value as of the end of 1993 can be estimated as

$$\frac{2.536(1.03)}{0.128 - 0.03} = \$26.654 \text{ billion}$$

Since the levered value of the company is the sum of the unlevered value plus the value of interest tax shields, it is the case that

$$
\begin{aligned}
\text{Value of tax shields (end 1993)} &= V_L \text{ (end 1993)} - V_U \text{ (end 1993)} \\
&= \$26.654 \text{ billion} - \$23.746 \text{ billion} \\
&= \$2.908 \text{ billion}
\end{aligned}
$$

To calculate the value, as of the end of 1988, of these future tax shields, we again discount by the borrowing rate of 13.5 percent to get[15]

$$\frac{2.908}{1.135^5} = \$1.544 \text{ billion}$$

The total value of interest tax shields therefore equals (\$3.834 + \$1.544) \$5.378 billion.

---

[13]This 25-percent figure is consistent with the debt utilization in industries in which RJR Nabisco is involved. In fact, that was the debt-to-total-market-value ratio for RJR immediately before management's initial buyout proposal. The firm can achieve this target by 1993 if a significant portion of the convertible debt used to finance the buyout is exchanged for equity by that time. Alternatively, KKR could issue new equity (as would occur, for example, if the firm were taken public) and use the proceeds to retire some of the outstanding debt.

[14]To calculate this rate, use the weighted average cost of capital from this chapter:

$$r_{\text{WACC}} = \frac{S}{S + B} r_S + \frac{B}{S + B} r_B (1 - T_C)$$

and substitute the appropriate values for the proportions of debt and equity used, as well as their respective costs. Specifically, at the target debt-value ratio, $B/(S + B) = 25\%$, and $S/(S + B) = (1 - B/(S + B)) = 75\%$. Given this blend,

$$
\begin{aligned}
r_S &= r_0 + \frac{B}{S}(1 - T_C)(r_0 - r_B) \\
&= 0.14 + \frac{0.25}{0.75}(1 - 0.34)(0.14 - 0.135) \\
&= 0.141
\end{aligned}
$$

Using these findings plus the borrowing rate of 13.5 percent in r_{WACC}, we find

$$
\begin{aligned}
r_{\text{WACC}} &= 0.75(0.141) + 0.25(0.135)(1 - 0.34) \\
&= 0.128
\end{aligned}
$$

In fact, this value is an approximation to the true weighted average cost of capital when the market debt-value blend is constant, or when the cash flows are growing. For a detailed discussion of this issue, see Isik Inselbag and Howard Kaufold, "A Comparison of Alternative Discounted Cash Flow Approaches to Firm Valuation." The Wharton School, University of Pennsylvania (June 1990), unpublished paper.

[15]A good argument can be made that since post-1993 debt levels are proportional to firm value, the tax shields are as risky as the firm and should be discounted at the rate r_0.

Adding all of these components together, the total value of RJR under the buyout proposal is $29.935 billion. Deducting the $5 billion market value of assumed debt yields a value for equity of $24.935 billion, or $108.9 per share.

Concluding Comments on LBO Valuation Methods   As mentioned earlier in this chapter, the WACC method is by far the most widely applied approach to capital budgeting. One could analyze an LBO and generate the results of the second section of this appendix using this technique, but it would be a much more difficult process. We have tried to show that the APV approach is the preferred way to analyze a transaction in which the capital structure is not stable over time.

Consider the WACC approach to valuing the KKR bid for RJR. One could discount the operating cash flows of RJR by a set of weighted average costs of capital and arrive at the same $30 billion total value for the company. To do this, one would need to calculate the appropriate rate for each year since the WACC rises as the buyout proceeds. This occurs because the value of the tax subsidy declines as debt principal is repaid. In other words, there is no single return that represents the cost of capital when the firm's capital structure is changing.

There is also a theoretical problem with the WACC approach to valuing a buyout. To calculate the changing WACC, one must know the market value of a firm's debt and equity. But if the debt and equity values are already known, the total market value of the company is also known. That is, one must know the value of the company to calculate the WACC. One must therefore resort to using book-value measures for debt and equity, or make assumptions about the evolution of their market values, in order to implement the WACC method.

Dividends and Other Payouts

EXECUTIVE SUMMARY

In recent years, U.S. corporations have paid out about 40 percent of their net income as cash dividends. However, a significant number of firms pay no cash dividends while many pay dividends in excess of their net income. Corporations view the dividend decision as quite important, because it determines what funds flow to investors and what funds are retained by the firm for reinvestment. Dividend policy can also provide information to the stockholder concerning firm performance.

However, dividends cannot be viewed in isolation. Companies currently devote about 40 percent of net income to share repurchases as well, a percentage much higher than that of only a few decades ago. Thus, dividends and repurchases must be seen as alternative payouts competing for corporate cash flows.

This chapter examines corporate policy concerning dividends and other payouts. The first four sections of the chapter deal with two issues. We discuss the practical aspects of both dividends and share repurchases. We also establish the irrelevance of any payout policy in a world of perfect capital markets. We move on to a world of personal taxes in Section 5, where the advantage of repurchases over dividends is presented. This advantage is perhaps the reason for the rapid growth in repurchases in recent years. However, dividends have hardly vanished, leading us to a search for the benefits of a high-dividend policy in the next two sections.

18.1 Different Types of Dividends

The term *dividend* usually refers to a cash distribution of earnings. If a distribution is made from sources other than current or accumulated retained earnings, the term *distribution* rather than dividend is used. However, it is acceptable to refer to a distribution from earnings as a *dividend* and a distribution from capital as a *liquidating dividend*. More generally, any direct payment by the corporation to the shareholders may be considered part of dividend policy.

The most common type of dividend is in the form of cash. Public companies usually pay **regular cash dividends** four times a year. Sometimes firms will pay a regular cash dividend and an *extra cash dividend*. Paying a cash dividend reduces the corporate cash and retained earnings shown in the balance sheet—except in the case of a liquidating dividend (where paid-in capital may be reduced).

Another type of dividend is paid out in shares of stock. This dividend is referred to as a **stock dividend.** It is not a true dividend, because no cash leaves the firm. Rather, a stock dividend increases the number of shares outstanding, thereby reducing the value of each share. A stock dividend is commonly expressed as a ratio; for example, with a 2-percent stock dividend a shareholder receives one new share for every 50 currently owned.

When a firm declares a **stock split,** it increases the number of shares outstanding. Because each share is now entitled to a smaller percentage of the firm's cash flow, the stock price should fall. For example, if the managers of a firm whose stock is selling at $90 declare a 3:1 stock split, the price of a share of stock should fall to about $30. A stock split strongly resembles a stock dividend except it is usually much larger.

18.2 Standard Method of Cash Dividend Payment

The decision to pay a dividend rests in the hands of the board of directors of the corporation. A dividend is distributable to shareholders of record on a specific date. When a dividend has been declared, it becomes a liability of the firm and cannot be easily rescinded by the corporation. The amount of the dividend is expressed as dollars per share (*dividend per share*), as a percentage of the market price (*dividend yield*), or as a percentage of earnings per share (*dividend payout*).

The mechanics of a dividend payment can be illustrated by the example in Figure 18.1 and the following chronology.

1. **Declaration date.** On January 15 (the declaration date), the board of directors passes a resolution to pay a dividend of $1 per share on February 16 to all holders of record on January 30.

2. **Date of record.** The corporation prepares a list on January 30 of all individuals believed to be stockholders as of this date. The word *believed* is important here, because the dividend will not be paid to those individuals whose notification of purchase is received by the company after January 30.

3. **Ex-dividend date.** The procedure on the date of record would be unfair if efficient brokerage houses could notify the corporation by January 30 of a trade occurring on January 29, whereas the same trade might not reach the corporation until February 2 if executed by a less efficient house. To eliminate this problem, all brokerage firms entitle stockholders to receive the dividend if they purchased the stock three business days before the date of record. The second day before the date of record, which is Wednesday, January 28, in our example, is called the *ex-dividend date.* Before this date the stock is said to trade *cum dividend.*

4. **Date of payment.** The dividend checks are mailed to the stockholders on February 16.

Obviously, the ex-dividend date is important, because an individual purchasing the security before the ex-dividend date will receive the current dividend, whereas another

---

FIGURE 18.1

Example of Procedure for Dividend Payment

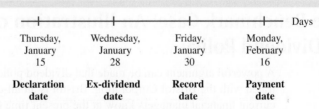

1. *Declaration Date:* The board of directors declares a payment of dividends.
2. *Record Date:* The declared dividends are distributable to shareholders of record on a specific date.
3. *Ex-dividend Date:* A share of stock becomes ex-dividend on the date the seller is entitled to keep the dividend; under NYSE rules, shares are traded ex-dividend on and after the second business day before the record date.
4. *Payment Date:* The dividend checks are mailed to shareholders of record.

FIGURE 18.2

Price Behavior around the Ex-dividend Date for a $1 Cash Dividend

Perfect-world case

Ex-date

$1 is the ex-dividend price drop

The stock price will fall by the amount of the dividend on the ex-date (time 0). If the dividend is $1 per share, the price will be equal to P on the ex-date.

Before ex-date (-1)   Price = $(P + 1)$
Ex-date (0)   Price = P

individual purchasing the security on or after this date will not receive the dividend. The stock price should fall on the ex-dividend date.[1] It is worthwhile to note that this drop is an indication of efficiency, not inefficiency, because the market rationally attaches value to a cash dividend. In a world with neither taxes nor transaction costs, the stock price would be expected to fall by the amount of the dividend:

Before ex-dividend date   Price = $(P + 1)$
On or after ex-dividend date   Price = P

This is illustrated in Figure 18.2.

The amount of the price drop is a matter for empirical investigation. Elton and Gruber have argued that, due to personal taxes, the stock price should fall by less than the dividend.[2] For example, consider the case with no capital gains taxes. On the day before a stock goes ex-dividend, shareholders must decide either (1) to buy the stock immediately and pay tax on the forthcoming dividend, or (2) to buy the stock tomorrow, thereby missing the dividend. If all investors are in the 15-percent bracket and the quarterly dividend is $1, the stock price should fall by $0.85 on the ex-dividend date. That is, if the stock price falls by this amount on the ex-dividend date, purchasers will receive the same return from either strategy.[3]

Concept Questions

1. Describe the procedure of a dividend payment.
2. Why should the price of a stock change when it goes ex-dividend?

18.3 The Benchmark Case: An Illustration of the Irrelevance of Dividend Policy

A powerful argument can be made that dividend policy does not matter. This will be illustrated with the Bristol Corporation. Bristol is an all-equity firm started 10 years ago. The current financial managers know at the present time (date 0) that the firm will dissolve in

---

[1]Empirically, the stock price appears to fall within the first few minutes of the ex-dividend day.

[2]N. Elton and M. Gruber, "Marginal Stockholder Tax Rates and the Clientele Effect," *Review of Economics and Statistics* 52 (February 1970). See also R. Bali and G. L. Hite, "Ex-Dividend Day Stock Price Behavior: Discreteness or Tax-Induced Clienteles?" *Journal of Financial Economics* (February 1998) and M. Frank and R. Jagannathan, "Why Do Stock Prices Drop by Less than the Value of the Dividend? Evidence from a Country without Taxes," *Journal of Financial Economics* (February 1998).

[3]The situation is more complex when taxes on capital gains are considered. Elton and Gruber show that the price drop should be somewhat greater than 85¢ here.

one year (date 1). At date 0 the managers are able to forecast cash flows with perfect certainty. The managers know that the firm will receive a cash flow of $10,000 immediately and another $10,000 next year. Bristol has no additional positive NPV projects.[4]

Current Policy: Dividends Set Equal to Cash Flow

At the present time, dividends (Div) at each date are set equal to the cash flow of $10,000. The value of the firm can be calculated by discounting these dividends. This value is expressed as:

$$V_0 = \text{Div}_0 + \frac{\text{Div}_1}{1 + r_S}$$

where Div_0 and Div_1 are the cash flows paid out in dividends, and r_S is the discount rate. The first dividend is not discounted because it will be paid immediately.

Assuming $r_S = 10\%$, the value of the firm is:

$$\$19,090.91 = \$10,000 + \frac{\$10,000}{1.1}$$

If 1,000 shares are outstanding, the value of each share is

$$\$19.09 = \$10 + \frac{\$10}{1.1} \tag{18.1}$$

To simplify the example, we assume that the ex-dividend date is the same as the date of payment. After the imminent dividend is paid, the stock price will immediately fall to $9.09 ($19.09 − $10). Several members of the board of Bristol have expressed dissatisfaction with the current dividend policy and have asked you to analyze an alternative policy.

Alternative Policy: Initial Dividend Is Greater than Cash Flow

Another policy is for the firm to pay a dividend of $11 per share immediately, which is, of course, a total dividend payout of $11,000. Because the cash runoff is only $10,000, the extra $1,000 must be raised in one of a few ways. Perhaps the simplest would be to issue $1,000 of bonds or stock now (at date 0). Assume that stock is issued and the new stockholders will desire enough cash flow at date 1 to let them earn the required 10-percent return on their date 0 investment.[5] The new stockholders will demand $1,100 of the date 1 cash flow,[6] leaving only $8,900 to the old stockholders. The dividends to the old stockholders will be:

	Date 0	Date I
Aggregate dividends to old stockholders	$11,000	$8,900
Dividends per share	$ 11.00	$ 8.90

The present value of the dividends per share is therefore:

$$\$19.09 = \$11 + \frac{\$8.90}{1.1} \tag{18.2}$$

---

[4]Bristol's investment in physical assets is fixed.

[5]The same results would occur after an issue of bonds, though the argument would be less easily resolved.

[6]Because the new stockholders buy at date 0, their first (and only) dividend is at date 1.

Students often find it instructive to determine the price at which the new stock is issued. Because the new stockholders are not entitled to the immediate dividend, they would pay $8.09 ($8.90/1.1) per share. Thus, 123.61 ($1,000/$8.09) new shares are issued.

The Indifference Proposition

Note that the values in equations (18.1) and (18.2) are equal. This leads to the initially surprising conclusion that the change in dividend policy did not affect the value of a share of stock. However, upon reflection, the result seems quite sensible. The new stockholders are parting with their money at date 0 and receiving it back with the appropriate return at date 1. In other words, they are taking on a zero NPV investment. As illustrated in Figure 18.3, old stockholders are receiving additional funds at date 0 but must pay the new stockholders their money with the appropriate return at date 1. Because the old stockholders must pay back principal plus the appropriate return, the act of issuing new stock at date 0 will not increase or decrease the value of the old stockholders' holdings. That is, they are giving up a

FIGURE 18.3

Current and Alternative Dividend Policies

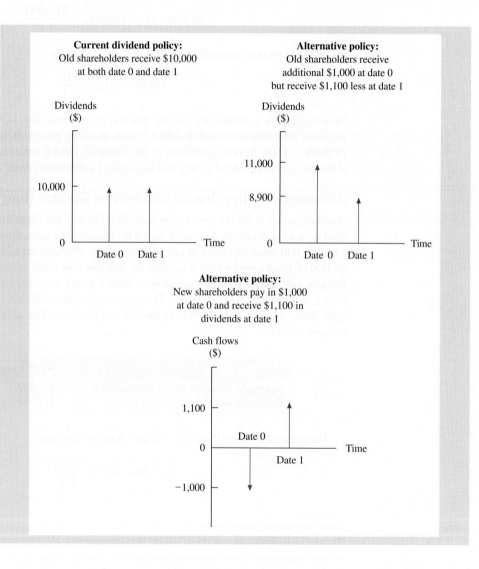

zero NPV investment to the new stockholders. An increase in dividends at date 0 leads to the necessary reduction of dividends at date 1, so the value of the old stockholders' holdings remains unchanged.

This illustration is based on the pioneering work of Miller and Modigliani (MM).[7] Although our presentation is in the form of a numerical example, the MM paper proves that investors are indifferent to dividend policy in the general algebraic case. MM make the following assumptions:

1. There are neither taxes nor brokerage fees, and no single participant can affect the market price of the security through his or her trades. Economists say that perfect markets exist when these conditions are met.

2. All individuals have the same beliefs concerning future investments, profits, and dividends. As mentioned in Chapter 10, these individuals are said to have *homogeneous expectations.*

3. The investment policy of the firm is set ahead of time, and is not altered by changes in dividend policy.

Homemade Dividends

To illustrate the indifference investors have toward dividend policy in our example, we used present-value equations. An alternative and perhaps more intuitively appealing explanation avoids the mathematics of discounted cash flows.

Suppose individual investor *X* prefers dividends per share of $10 at both dates 0 and 1. Would she be disappointed when informed that the firm's management is adopting the alternative dividend policy (dividends of $11 and $8.90 on the two dates, respectively)? Not necessarily, because she could easily reinvest the $1 of unneeded funds received on date 0, yielding an incremental return of $1.10 at date 1. Thus, she would receive her desired net cash flow of $11 − $1 = $10 at date 0 and $8.90 + $1.10 = $10 at date 1.

Conversely, imagine investor *Z* preferring $11 of cash flow at date 0 and $8.90 of cash flow at date 1, who finds that management will pay dividends of $10 at both dates 0 and 1. Here he can sell off shares of stock at date 0 to receive the desired amount of cash flow. That is, if he sells off shares (or fractions of shares) at date 0 totaling $1, his cash flow at date 0 becomes $10 + $1 = $11. Because a $1 sale of stock at date 0 will reduce his dividends by $1.10 at date 1, his net cash flow at date 1 would be $10 − $1.10 = $8.90.

The example illustrates how investors can make **homemade dividends.** In this instance, corporate dividend policy is being undone by a potentially dissatisfied stockholder. This homemade dividend is illustrated by Figure 18.4. Here the firm's cash flows of $10 per share at both dates 0 and 1 are represented by point *A*. This point also represents the initial dividend payout. However, as we just saw, the firm could alternatively pay out $11 per share at date 0 and $8.90 per share at date 1, a strategy represented by point *B*. Similarly, by either issuing new stock or buying back old stock, the firm could achieve a dividend payout represented by any point on the diagonal line.

The previous paragraph describes the choices available to the managers of the firm. The same diagonal line also represents the choices available to the shareholder. For example, if the shareholder receives a per-share dividend distribution of ($11, $8.90), he or she can either reinvest some of the dividends to move down and to the right on the graph or sell off shares of stock and move up and to the left.

---

[7]M. H. Miller and F. Modigliani, "Dividend Policy, Growth and the Valuation of Shares," *Journal of Business* (October 1961). Yes, this is the same MM who gave us a capital-structure theory.

FIGURE 18.4

Homemade
Dividends: A
Trade-Off between
Dividends per Share
at Date 0 and
Dividends per Share
at Date 1

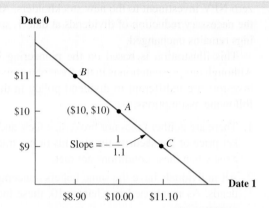

The graph illustrates both (1) how managers can vary dividend policy and (2) how individuals can undo the firm's dividend policy.

Managers varying dividend policy. A firm paying out all cash flows immediately is at point *A* on the graph. The firm could achieve point *B* by issuing stock to pay extra dividends or achieve point *C* by buying back old stock with some of its cash.

Individuals undoing the firm's dividend policy. Suppose the firm adopts the dividend policy represented by point *B:* dividends per share of $11 at date 0 and $8.90 at date 1. An investor can reinvest $1 of the dividends at 10 percent, which will place her at point *A*. Suppose, alternatively, the firm adopts the dividend policy represented by point *A*. An individual can sell off $1 of stock at date 0, placing him at point *B*. No matter what dividend policy the firm establishes, a shareholder can undo it.

The implications of the graph can be summarized in two sentences:

1. By varying dividend policy, the managers can achieve any payout along the diagonal line in Figure 18.4.
2. Either by reinvesting excess dividends at date 0 or by selling off shares of stock at this date, any individual investor can achieve any net cash payout along the diagonal line.

Thus, because both the corporation and the individual investor can move only along the diagonal line, dividend policy in this model is irrelevant. The changes the managers make in dividend policy can be undone by an individual who, by either reinvesting dividends or selling off stock, can move to a desired point on the diagonal line.

A Test

You can test your knowledge of this material by examining these true statements:

1. Dividends are relevant.
2. Dividend policy is irrelevant.

The first statement follows from common sense. Clearly, investors prefer higher dividends to lower dividends at any single date if the dividend level is held constant at every other date. In other words, if the dividend per share at a given date is raised while the dividend per share for each other date is held constant, the stock price will rise. This act can be accomplished by management decisions that improve productivity, increase tax savings, or strengthen product marketing. In fact, you may recall in Chapter 5 we argued that the value of a firm's equity is equal to the discounted present value of all its future dividends.

The second statement is understandable once we realize that dividend policy cannot raise the dividend per share at one date while holding the dividend level per share constant at all other dates. Rather, dividend policy merely establishes the trade-off between dividends at one date and dividends at another date. As we saw in Figure 18.4, an increase in date 0 dividends can be accomplished only by a decrease in date 1 dividends. The extent of the decrease is such that the present value of all dividends is not affected.

Thus, in this simple world, dividend policy does not matter. That is, managers choosing either to raise or to lower the current dividend do not affect the current value of their firm. The above theory is a powerful one, and the work of MM is generally considered a classic in modern finance. With relatively few assumptions, a rather surprising result is shown to be perfectly true.[8] Because we want to examine many real-world factors ignored by MM, their work is only a starting point in this chapter's discussion of dividends. The next part of the chapter investigates these real-world considerations.

Dividends and Investment Policy

The preceding argument shows that an increase in dividends through issuance of new shares neither helps nor hurts the stockholders. Similarly, a reduction in dividends through share repurchase neither helps nor hurts stockholders.

What about reducing capital expenditures to increase dividends? Earlier chapters show that a firm should accept all positive net-present-value projects. To do otherwise would reduce the value of the firm. Thus, we have an important point:

> Firms should never give up a positive NPV project to increase a dividend (or to pay a dividend for the first time).

This idea was implicitly considered by Miller and Modigliani. As we pointed out, one of the assumptions underlying their dividend-irrelevance proposition was, "The investment policy of the firm is set ahead of time and is not altered by changes in dividend policy."

Concept Questions

1. How can an investor make homemade dividends?
2. Are dividends irrelevant?
3. What assumptions are needed to show that dividend policy is irrelevant?

18.4 Repurchase of Stock

Instead of paying dividends, a firm may use cash to repurchase shares of its own stock. Share repurchases have taken on increased importance in recent years. Consider Figure 18.5, which shows the dollar amount of both share repurchases and dividends for U.S. firms for each year between 1972 and 2000. As can be seen, the dollar amount of share repurchases was a small fraction of that of dividends in the early years. However, this fraction has risen over time, with the dollar amount of share repurchases actually exceeding that of dividends in the last two years of the sample period, 1999 and 2000.

Share repurchases are typically accomplished in one of three ways. First, companies may simply purchase their own stock, just as anyone would buy shares of a particular stock. In these *open-market purchases,* the firm does not reveal itself as the buyer. Thus, the seller does not know whether the shares were sold back to the firm or to just another investor.

Second, the firm could institute a *tender offer.* Here, the firm announces to all of its stockholders that it is willing to buy a fixed number of shares at a specific price. For example, suppose Arts and Crafts (A&C), Inc. has 1 million shares of stock outstanding, with a

---

[8]One of the real contributions of MM has been to shift the burden of proof. Before MM, firm value was believed to be influenced by its dividend policy. After MM, it became clear that establishing a correct dividend policy was not obvious at all.

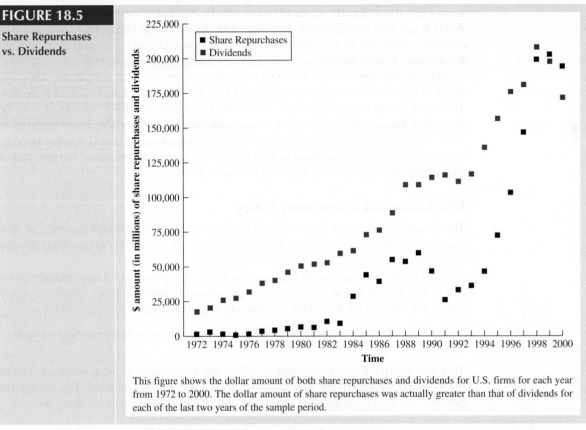

FIGURE 18.5

Share Repurchases
vs. Dividends

This figure shows the dollar amount of both share repurchases and dividends for U.S. firms for each year from 1972 to 2000. The dollar amount of share repurchases was actually greater than that of dividends for each of the last two years of the sample period.

SOURCE: Adapted from Table 1 of Grullon, Gustavo, and Roni Michaely, "Dividends, Share Repurchases, and the Substitution Hypothesis," *Journal of Finance* (August 2002).

stock price of $50 per share. The firm makes a tender offer to buy back 300,000 shares at $60 per share. A&C chooses a price above $50 to induce shareholders to sell, that is, tender, their shares. In fact, if the tender price is set high enough, shareholders may very well want to sell more than the 300,000 shares. In the extreme case where all outstanding shares are tendered, A&C will buy back 3 out of every 10 shares that a shareholder has.

Finally, firms may repurchase shares from specific individual stockholders. This procedure has been called a *targeted repurchase*. For example, suppose the International Biotechnology Corporation purchased approximately 10 percent of the outstanding stock of the Prime Robotics Company (P-R Co.) in April at around $38 per share. At that time, International Biotechnology announced to the Securities and Exchange Commission that it might eventually try to take control of P-R Co. In May, P-R Co. repurchased the International Biotechnology holdings at $48 per share, well above the market price at that time. This offer was not extended to other shareholders.

Companies engage in this type of repurchase for a variety of reasons. In some rare cases a single large stockholder can be bought out at a price lower than that in a tender offer. The legal fees in a targeted repurchase may also be lower than those in a more typical buyback. More frequently, certain stockholders become nuisances to the repurchasing firm. Though targeted repurchases executed for these reasons are in the interest of the remaining shareholders, the shares of large stockholders are often repurchased to avoid a takeover unfavorable to management.

TABLE 18.1	Dividend versus Repurchase Example for Telephonic Industries	
	For Entire Firm	**Per Share**
Extra Dividend		**(100,000 shares outstanding)**
Proposed dividend	$ 300,000	$ 3.00
Forecasted annual earnings after dividend	450,000	4.50
Market value of stock after dividend	2,700,000	27.00
Repurchase		**(90,000 shares outstanding)**
Forecasted annual earnings after repurchase	$ 450,000	$ 5.00
Market value of stock after repurchase	2,700,000	30.00

We now consider an example of a repurchase presented in the theoretical world of a perfect capital market. We next discuss the real-world factors involved in the repurchase decision.

Dividend versus Repurchase: Conceptual Example

Imagine that Telephonic Industries has excess cash of $300,000 (or $3 per share) and is considering an immediate payment of this amount as an extra dividend. The firm forecasts that, after the dividend, earnings will be $450,000 per year, or $4.50 for each of the 100,000 shares outstanding. Because the price-earnings ratio is 6 for comparable companies, the shares of the firm should sell for $27 after the dividend is paid. These figures are presented in the top half of Table 18.1. Since the dividend is $3 per share, the stock would have sold for $30 a share *before* payment of the dividend.

Alternatively, the firm could use the excess cash to repurchase some of its own stock. Imagine that a tender offer of $30 a share is made. Here, 10,000 shares are repurchased so that the total number of shares remaining is 90,000. With fewer shares outstanding, the earnings per share will rise to $5. The price-earnings ratio remains at 6, since both the business and financial risks of the firm are the same in the repurchase case as they were for the dividend case. Thus the price of a share after the repurchase is $30. These results are presented in the bottom half of Table 18.1.

If commissions, taxes, and other imperfections are ignored in our example, the stockholders are indifferent between a dividend and a repurchase. With dividends, each stockholder owns a share worth $27 and receives $3 in dividends, so that the total value is $30. This figure is the same as both the amount received by the selling stockholders and the value of the stock for the remaining stockholders in the repurchase case.

This example illustrates the important point that, in a perfect market, the firm is indifferent between a dividend payment and a share repurchase. This result is quite similar to the indifference propositions established by MM for debt versus equity financing and for dividends versus capital gains.

You may often read in the popular financial press that a repurchase agreement is beneficial because earnings per share increase. Earnings per share do rise for Telephonic Industries if a repurchase is substituted for a cash dividend: The EPS is $4.50 after a dividend and $5 after the repurchase. This result holds because the drop in shares after a repurchase implies a reduction in the denominator of the EPS ratio.

However, the financial press frequently places undue emphasis on EPS figures in a repurchase agreement. Given the irrelevance propositions we have discussed, an increase in EPS need not be beneficial. When a repurchase is financed by excess cash, we showed that, in a perfect capital market, the total value to the stockholder is the same under the dividend payment strategy as under the repurchase strategy.

Dividends versus Repurchases: Real-World Considerations

We previously referred to Figure 18.5, which showed the recent growth in share repurchases. Why do some firms choose repurchases over dividends? Here are perhaps five of the most common reasons.

1. Flexibility   It is well known that firms view dividends as a commitment to their stockholders and are quite hesitant to reduce an existing dividend. Repurchases do not represent a similar commitment. Thus, a firm with a permanent increase in cash flow is likely to increase its dividend. Conversely, a firm whose cash flow increase is only temporary is likely to repurchase shares of stock.[9]

2. Executive Compensation   Executives are frequently given stock options as part of their overall compensation. Let's revisit the Telephonic Industries example of Table 18.1, where the firm's stock was selling at $30 when the firm was considering either a dividend or a repurchase. Further imagine that Telephonic had granted 1,000 stock options to its CEO, Ralph Taylor, two years before the decision was made. At that time the stock price was, say, only $20. This means that Mr. Taylor can buy 1,000 shares for $20 a share at any time between the grant of the options and their expiration, a procedure called *exercising* the options.[10] His gain from exercising is directly proportional to the rise in the stock price above $20. As we saw in the example, the price of the stock would fall to $27 following a dividend but would remain at $30 following a repurchase. The CEO would clearly prefer a repurchase to a dividend because the difference between the stock price and the exercise price of $20 would be $10 ($30 − $20) following the repurchase but only $7 ($27 − $20) following the dividend. Existing stock options will always have greater value when the firm repurchases shares instead of paying a dividend,[11] since the stock price will be greater after a repurchase than after a dividend.

3. Offset to Dilution   In addition, the exercise of stock options increases the number of shares outstanding. In other words, exercise causes dilution of the stock. Firms frequently buy back shares of stock to offset this dilution. However, it is hard to argue that this is a valid reason for repurchase. As we showed in Table 18.1, repurchase is neither better nor worse for the stockholders than a dividend. Our argument holds whether or not stock options have been exercised previously.[12]

4. Repurchase as Investment   Many companies buy back stock because they believe that a repurchase is their best investment. This occurs more frequently when managers believe that the stock price is temporarily depressed. Here, it is likely thought that (1) investment opportunities in nonfinancial assets are few, and (2) the firm's own stock price should rise with the passage of time.

The fact that some companies repurchase their stock when they believe it is undervalued does not imply that the management of the company must be correct; only empirical

---

[9]See Murali Jagannathan, Clifford P. Stephens, and Michael Weisbach, "Financial Flexibility and the Choice between Dividends and Stock Repurchases," *Journal of Financial Economics* 57 (2000) and Wayne Guay and Jarrod Harford, "The Cash-Flow Permanence of Dividend Increases versus Repurchases," *Journal of Financial Economics* 57 (2000) for both an explanation of and empirical support for flexibility.

[10]The exercise price of an executive stock option is generally set equal to the market price at the time of the grant.

[11]See George W. Fenn and Nellie Liang, "Corporate Payout Policy and Managerial Stock Incentives," *Journal of Financial Economics* 60 (2001).

[12]See Kathleen Kahle, "When a Buyback Isn't a Buyback: Open Market Repurchases and Employee Options," *Journal of Financial Economics* 63 (2002).

studies can make this determination. The immediate stock market reaction to the announcement of a stock repurchase is usually quite favorable. In addition, some empirical work has shown that the long-term stock price performance of securities after a buyback is better than the stock price performance of comparable companies that do not repurchase.[13]

5. Taxes   Since taxes for both dividends and share repurchases are treated in depth in the next section, suffice it to say at this point that repurchases provide a tax advantage over dividends.

Concept
Questions

1. In a perfect capital market, are repurchases preferred to dividends?
2. What are five reasons for preferring repurchases to dividends in the real world?

18.5 Personal Taxes, Issuance Costs, and Dividends

The model we used in Section 18.3 to determine the level of dividends assumed that there were no taxes, no transactions costs, and no uncertainty. It concluded that dividend policy is irrelevant. Although this model helps us to grasp some fundamentals of dividend policy, it ignores many real-world factors. It is now time to investigate these practical considerations. We first examine the effect of taxes on the level of a firm's dividends.

In the United States, both cash dividends and capital gains are taxed at a maximum rate of 15 percent. However, since dividends are taxed when distributed while the taxes on capital gains are deferred until the stock is sold, the tax rate on dividends is greater than the *effective* rate on capital gains. A discussion of dividend policy in the presence of personal taxes is facilitated by classifying firms into two types, those without sufficient cash to pay a dividend and those with sufficient cash to do so.

Firms without Sufficient Cash to Pay a Dividend

It is simplest to begin with a firm without cash and owned by a single entrepreneur. If this firm should decide to pay a dividend of $100, it must raise capital. The firm might choose among a number of different stock and bond issues in order to pay the dividend. However, for simplicity, we assume that the entrepreneur contributes cash to the firm by issuing stock to himself. This transaction, diagrammed in the left-hand side of Figure 18.6, would clearly be a *wash* in a world of no taxes. $100 cash goes into the firm when stock is issued and is immediately paid out as a dividend. Thus, the entrepreneur neither benefits nor loses when the dividend is paid, a result consistent with Miller-Modigliani.

Now assume that dividends are taxed at the owner's personal tax rate of 15 percent. The firm still receives $100 upon issuance of stock. However, the entrepreneur does not get to keep the full $100 dividend. Instead, the dividend payment is taxed, implying that the owner receives only $85 net after tax. Thus, the entrepreneur loses $15.

Though the example is clearly contrived and unrealistic, similar results can be reached for more plausible situations. Thus, financial economists generally agree that, in a world of personal taxes, one should not issue stock to pay a dividend.

The direct costs of issuance will add to this effect. Investment bankers must be paid when new capital is raised. Thus, the net receipts due to the firm from a new issue are less than 100 percent of total capital raised. These costs are examined in a later chapter.

---

[13]For example, see David Ikenberry, Joseph Lakonishok, and Theo Vermaelen, "Market Underreaction to Open Market Share Repurchases," *Journal of Financial Economics* 39 (1995).

FIGURE 18.6

Firm Issues Stock in
Order to Pay a
Dividend

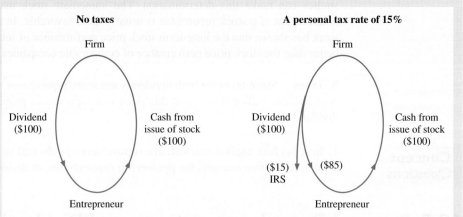

In the no-tax case, the entrepreneur receives the $100 in dividends that he gave to the firm when purchasing stock. The entire operation is called a *wash;* in other words, it has no economic effect. With taxes, the entrepreneur still receives $100 in dividends. However, he must pay $15 in taxes to the IRS. The entrepreneur loses and the IRS wins when a firm issues stock to pay a dividend.

Because the size of new issues can be lowered by a reduction in dividends, we have another argument in favor of a low-dividend policy.

Of course, our advice not to finance dividends through new stock issues might need to be modified somewhat in the real world. A company with a large and steady cash flow for many years in the past might be paying a regular dividend. If the cash flow unexpectedly dried up for a single year, should new stock be issued so that dividends could be continued? While our above discussion would imply that new stock should not be issued, many managers might issue the stock anyway for practical reasons. In particular, stockholders appear to prefer dividend stability. Thus, managers might be forced to issue stock to achieve this stability, knowing full well the adverse tax consequences.

Firms with Sufficient Cash to Pay a Dividend

The previous discussion argues that, in a world with personal taxes, one should not issue stock to pay a dividend. Does the tax disadvantage of dividends imply the stronger policy, "Never pay dividends in a world with personal taxes"?

We argue below that this prescription does not necessarily apply to firms with excess cash. To see this, imagine a firm with $1 million in extra cash after selecting all positive NPV projects and determining the level of prudent cash balances. The firm might consider the following alternatives to a dividend:

1. *Select Additional Capital-Budgeting Projects.* Because the firm has taken all the available positive NPV projects already, it must invest its excess cash in negative NPV projects. This is clearly a policy at variance with the principles of corporate finance.

In spite of our distaste for this policy, researchers have suggested that many managers purposely take on negative NPV projects in lieu of paying dividends.[14] The idea here is that managers would rather keep the funds in the firm, since their prestige, pay, and perquisites are often tied to the firm's size. While managers may help themselves here, they are hurting stockholders. We broached this subject in the section entitled "Free Cash Flow" in Chapter 16, and we will have more to say about it later in this chapter.

---

[14]See, for example, M. C. Jensen, "Agency Costs of Free Cash Flows, Corporate Finance and Takeovers," *American Economic Review* (May 1986).

2. *Acquire Other Companies.* To avoid the payment of dividends, a firm might use excess cash to acquire another company. This strategy has the advantage of acquiring profitable assets. However, a firm often incurs heavy costs when it embarks on an acquisition program. In addition, acquisitions are invariably made above the market price. Premiums of 20 to 80 percent are not uncommon. Because of this, a number of researchers have argued that mergers are not generally profitable to the acquiring company, even when firms are merged for a valid business purpose.[15] Therefore, a company making an acquisition merely to avoid a dividend is unlikely to succeed.

3. *Purchase Financial Assets.* The strategy of purchasing financial assets in lieu of a dividend payment can be illustrated with the following example.

EXAMPLE

The Regional Electric Company has $1,000 of extra cash. It can retain the cash and invest it in Treasury bills yielding 10 percent, or it can pay the cash to shareholders as a dividend. Shareholders can also invest in Treasury bills with the same yield. Suppose the corporate tax rate is 34 percent, and the individual tax rate is 28 percent. However, the maximum tax rate on dividends is 15 percent. How much cash will investors have after five years under each policy?

If dividends are paid now, shareholders will receive:

$$\$1,000 \times (1 - 0.15) = \$850$$

today after taxes. Because their return after personal tax on Treasury bills is 7.2 [.10 × (1 − .28)] percent, shareholders will have

$$\$850 \times (1.072)^5 = \$1,203.35 \tag{18.3}$$

in five years. Note that interest income is taxed at the personal tax rate (28 percent in this example) but dividends are taxed at the lower rate of 15 percent.

If Regional Electric Company retains the cash to invest in Treasury bills, its after-tax interest rate will be .066 [.10 × (1 − .34)]. At the end of five years, the firm will have:

$$\$1,000 \times (1.066)^5 = \$1,376.53$$

If these proceeds are then paid as a dividend, the stockholders will receive

$$\$1,376.53 \times (1 - 0.15) = \$1,170.05 \tag{18.4}$$

after personal taxes at date 5. The result in formula (18.3) is greater than that in (18.4), implying that cash to stockholders will be greater if the firm pays the dividend now.

This example shows that, for a firm with extra cash, the dividend-payout decision will depend on personal and corporate tax rates. If personal tax rates are higher than corporate tax rates, a firm will have an incentive to reduce dividend payouts. However, if personal tax rates are lower than corporate tax rates, a firm will have an incentive to pay out any excess cash as dividends.

In the U.S., both the highest marginal tax rate for individuals and the corporate tax rate were 35 percent in 2003. Since many investors face marginal tax rates well below the maximum, it appears that firms have an incentive not to hoard cash.

However, a quirk in the tax code provides an offsetting incentive. In particular, 70 percent of the dividends that one corporation receives from another corporation are excluded

[15]Richard Roll, "The Hubris Hypothesis of Corporate Takeovers," *Journal of Business* (1986), pp. 197–216, explores this idea in depth.

from corporate tax.[16] Individuals are not granted this exclusion. The quirk increases the likelihood that proceeds will be higher if the firm invests cash in other dividend-paying stocks, rather than paying out cash as a dividend.

The firm's decision to invest in financial assets or to pay a dividend is a complex one, depending on the tax rate of the firm, the marginal tax rates of its investors, and the application of the dividend exclusion. While there are likely many real-world situations where the numbers favor investment in financial assets, few companies actually seem to hoard cash in this manner without limit. The reason is that Section 532 of the Internal Revenue Code penalizes firms exhibiting "improper accumulation of surplus." Thus, in the final analysis, the purchase of financial assets, like selecting negative NPV projects and acquiring other companies, do not obviate the need for companies with excess cash to pay dividends.

4. *Repurchase Shares.* The example we described in the previous section showed that investors are indifferent between share repurchase and dividends in a world without taxes and transaction costs. However, under current tax law, stockholders generally prefer a repurchase to a dividend.

As an example, consider an individual receiving a dividend of $1 on each of 100 shares of a stock. With a 15 percent tax rate, that individual would pay taxes of $15 on the dividend. Selling shareholders would pay lower taxes if the firm repurchased $100 of existing shares. This occurs because taxes are paid only on the *profit* from a sale. The individual's gain on a sale would be only $40 if the shares sold for $100 were originally purchased for, say, $60. The capital gains tax would be $6 (0.15 × $40), a number below the tax on dividends of $15. Note that the tax from a repurchase is less than the tax on a dividend even though the same 15 percent tax rate applies to both the repurchase and the dividend.

Of all the alternatives to dividends mentioned in this section, the strongest case can be made for repurchases. In fact, academics have long wondered why firms *ever* pay a dividend instead of a repurchase. There have been at least two possible reasons for avoiding repurchases. First, Grullon and Michaely point out that, in the past, the Securities and Exchange Commission (SEC) has accused some firms undergoing share repurchase programs of illegal price manipulation.[17] However, these authors indicate that SEC Rule 10b-18, adopted in 1982, provides guidelines for firms to avoid the charge of price manipulation. Since these guidelines are relatively easy to follow, firms should not have to worry about this charge today. In fact, Grullon and Michaely believe that the large increase in buyback programs in recent years is at least partially the result of 10b-18. Second, the IRS can penalize firms repurchasing their own stocks if the only reason is to avoid the taxes that would be levied on dividends. However, this threat has not materialized with the growth in corporate repurchases. Thus, these two reasons do not seem to justify the avoidance of repurchases.

Summary on Personal Taxes

This section suggests that, because of personal taxes, firms have an incentive to reduce dividends. For example, they might increase capital expenditures, acquire other companies, or purchase financial assets. However, due to financial considerations and legal constraints,

---

[16]This exclusion applies if the firm owns less than 20 percent of the stock in the other company. The exclusion rises to 80 percent if the firm owns more than 20 percent of the stock of the other company and is 100 percent if the firm owns more than 80 percent of the stock of the other company. Corporations are not granted an exclusion for interest earned on bonds.

[17]See Gustavo Grullon and Roni Michaely, "Dividends, Share Repurchases, and the Substitution Hypothesis," *Journal of Finance* (August 2002), p. 1677.

rational firms with large cash flows will likely exhaust these activities with plenty of cash left over for dividends.

It is harder to explain why firms pay dividends instead of repurchasing shares. The tax savings from buybacks are significant and fear of either the SEC or the IRS seems overblown. Academics are of two minds here. Some argue that corporations were simply slow to grasp the benefits from repurchases. However, since the idea has firmly caught on, the trend toward replacement of dividends with buybacks will continue. One might even conjecture that dividends will be as unimportant in the future as repurchases were in the past. Conversely, others argue that companies have paid dividends all along for good reason. Perhaps the legal hassles, particularly from the IRS, are significant after all. Or, there may be other, more subtle benefits from dividends. We consider potential benefits of dividends in the next section.

Concept Questions

1. List four alternatives to paying a dividend with excess cash.
2. Indicate a problem with each of these alternatives.

18.6 Real-World Factors Favoring a High-Dividend Policy

In the previous section, we pointed out that taxes must be paid by the recipient of a dividend. Since the tax rate on dividends is above the *effective* tax rate on capital gains, financial managers will seek out ways to reduce dividends. While we discussed the problems with taking on more capital budgeting projects, acquiring other firms, and hoarding cash, we stated that share repurchase has many of the benefits of a dividend with less of a tax disadvantage. In this section, we consider reasons why a firm might pay its shareholders high dividends, even in the presence of personal taxes on these dividends.

Desire for Current Income

It has been argued that many individuals desire current income. The classic example is the group of retired people and others living on a fixed income, proverbially known as "widows and orphans." The argument further states that these individuals would bid up the stock price should dividends rise and bid down the stock price should dividends fall.

Miller and Modigliani point out that this argument does not hold in their theoretical model. An individual preferring high current cash flow but holding low-dividend securities could easily sell off shares to provide the necessary funds. Thus, in a world of no transactions costs, a high–current-dividend policy would be of no value to the stockholder.

However, the current income argument does have relevance in the real world. The sale of stock involves brokerage fees and other transactions costs—direct cash expenses that could be avoided by an investment in high-dividend securities. In addition, the expenditure of one's time when selling securities might further lead many investors to buy high-dividend securities.

However, to put this argument in perspective, it should be remembered that financial intermediaries such as mutual funds can perform repackaging transactions at low cost. Such intermediaries could buy low-dividend stocks and, by a controlled policy of realizing gains, pay their investors at a higher rate.

Behavioral Finance

Suppose it turned out that the transaction costs in selling no-dividend securities could not account for the preference of investors for dividends. Would there still be a reason for high dividends? We introduced the topic of behavioral finance in Chapter 13, pointing out that the ideas of behaviorists represent a strong challenge to the theory of efficient capital markets. It turns out that behavioral finance also has an argument for high dividends.

The basic idea here concerns *self-control,* a concept that, though quite important in psychology, has received virtually no emphasis in finance. While we cannot review all that psychology has to say about self-control, let's focus on one example—losing weight. Suppose Alfred Martin, a college student, just got back from the Christmas break more than a few pounds heavier than he would like. Everyone would probably agree that diet and exercise are the two ways to lose weight. But how should Alfred put this approach into practice? (We'll focus on exercise though the same principle would apply to diet as well.) One way, let's call it the economists' way, would involve trying to make rational decisions. Each day, Al would balance the costs and the benefits of exercising. Perhaps he would choose to exercise on most days, since losing the weight is important to him. However, when he is too busy with exams, he might rationally choose not to exercise because he cannot afford the time. And, he wants to be socially active as well. So he may rationally choose to avoid exercise on days when parties and other social commitments become too time-consuming.

This seems sensible—at first glance. The problem is that he must make a choice every day and there may simply be too many days when his lack of self-control gets the better of him. He may tell himself that he doesn't have the time to exercise on a particular day, simply because he is starting to find exercise boring, not because he really doesn't have the time. Before long, he is avoiding exercise on most days—and overeating in reaction to the guilt from not exercising!

Is there an alternative? One way would be to set rigid rules. Perhaps Alfred decides to exercise five days a week—*no matter what.* While this is not necessarily the best approach for everyone, there is no question that many of us, perhaps most of us, live by a set of rules. For example, Shefrin and Statman[18] suggest some typical rules:

—Jog at least two miles a day

—Do not consume more than 1,200 calories per day

—Bank the wife's salary and only spend from the husband's paycheck

—Save at least 2 percent of every paycheck for children's college education and never withdraw from this fund

—Never touch a drop.

What does this have to do with dividends? Investors must also deal with self-control. Suppose a retiree wants to consume $20,000 a year from savings, in addition to Social Security and her pension. On one hand, she could buy stocks with a dividend yield high enough to generate $20,000 in dividends. On the other hand, she could place her savings in no-dividend stocks, selling off $20,000 each year for consumption. Though these two approaches seem equivalent financially, the second one may allow for too much leeway. If lack of self-control gets the better of her, she might sell off too much, leaving little for her later years. Better, perhaps, to short-circuit this possibility by investing in dividend-paying stocks, with a firm personal rule of *never* "dipping into principal." While behaviorists do not claim that this approach is for everyone, they argue that enough people think this way to explain why firms pay dividends, even though, as we said earlier, dividends are tax-disadvantaged.

Does behavioral finance argue for increased stock repurchases as well as increased dividends? The answer is no, since investors will sell the stock that firms repurchase. As we said above, selling stock involves too much leeway. Investors might sell too many shares

---

[18]Hersh M. Shefrin and Meir Statman, "Explaining Investor Preference for Cash Dividends," *Journal of Financial Economics* 13 (1984).

of stock, leaving little for the later years. Thus, the behaviorist argument may explain why companies pay dividends in a world with personal taxes.

Agency Costs

Although stockholders, bondholders, and management form firms for mutually beneficial reasons, one party may later gain at the other's expense. For example, take the potential conflict between bondholders and stockholders. Bondholders would like stockholders to leave as much cash as possible in the firm so that this cash would be available to pay the bondholders during times of financial distress. Conversely, stockholders would like to keep this extra cash for themselves. That's where dividends come in. Managers, acting on behalf of the stockholders, may pay dividends simply to keep the cash away from the bondholders. In other words, a dividend can be viewed as a wealth transfer from bondholders to stockholders. There is empirical evidence for this view of things. For example, DeAngelo and DeAngelo find that firms in financial distress are reluctant to cut dividends.[19] Of course, bondholders know of the propensity of stockholders to transfer money out of the firm. To protect themselves, bondholders frequently create loan agreements stating that dividends can be paid only if the firm has earnings, cash flow, and working capital above prespecified levels.

Although the managers may be looking out for the stockholders in any conflict with bondholders, the managers may pursue selfish goals at the expense of stockholders in other situations. For example, as discussed in Chapter 16, managers might pad expense accounts, take on pet projects with negative NPVs, or, more simply, not work very hard. Managers find it easier to pursue these selfish goals when the firm has plenty of free cash flow. After all, one cannot squander funds if the funds are not available in the first place. And, that is where dividends come in. Several scholars have suggested that dividends can serve as a way for the board of directors to reduce agency costs.[20] By paying dividends equal to the amount of "surplus" cash flow, a firm can reduce management's ability to squander the firm's resources.

While the above discussion suggests a reason for increased dividends, the same argument applies to share repurchases as well. Managers, acting on behalf of stockholders, can just as easily keep cash from bondholders through repurchases as through dividends. And the board of directors, also acting on behalf of stockholders, can reduce the cash available to spendthrift managers just as easily through repurchases as through dividends. Thus, the presence of agency costs is not an argument for dividends over repurchases. Rather, agency costs imply firms may well increase either dividends or share repurchases rather than hoard large amounts of cash.

Information Content of Dividends and Dividend Signaling

Information Content   While there are many things researchers do not know about dividends, there is one thing that we know for sure: The stock price of a firm will generally rise when the firm announces an increase in the dividend and will generally fall when a dividend reduction is announced. For example, Asquith and Mullins estimate that stock prices rise about 3 percent following announcements of dividend initiations.[21] Healy and

---

[19]H. DeAngelo and L. DeAngelo, "Dividend Policy and Financial Distress: An Empirical Investigation of Troubled NYSE Firms," *Journal of Finance* 45 (1990).

[20]Michael Rozeff, "How Companies Set Their Dividend Payout Ratios," in *The Revolution in Corporate Finance,* edited by Joel M. Stern and Donald H. Chew (New York: Basil Blackwell, 1986). See also Robert S. Hansen, Raman Kumar, and Dilip K. Shome, "Dividend Policy and Corporate Monitoring: Evidence from the Regulated Electric Utility Industry," *Financial Management* (Spring 1994).

[21]P. Asquith and D. Mullins, Jr., "The Impact of Initiating Dividend Payments on Shareholder Wealth," *Journal of Business* (January 1983).

Palepu and Michael, Thaler, and Womack find that stock prices fall about 7 percent following announcements of dividend omissions.[22]

The question is: How should one *interpret* this empirical evidence? Consider the following three positions on dividends:

1. From the homemade-dividend argument of MM, dividend policy is irrelevant, given that future earnings (and cash flows) are held constant.

2. Because of tax effects, a firm's stock price is negatively related to the current dividend when future earnings (or cash flows) are held constant.

3. Because of stockholders' desire for current income, a firm's stock price is positively related to its current dividend, even when future earnings (or cash flows) are held constant.

At first glance, the empirical evidence that stock prices rise when dividend increases are announced may seem consistent with position 3 and inconsistent with positions 1 and 2. In fact, many writers have argued this. However, other authors have countered that the observation itself is consistent with all three positions. They point out that companies do not like to cut a dividend. Thus, firms will raise the dividend only when future earnings, cash flow, and so on are expected to rise enough so that the dividend is not likely to be reduced later to its original level. A dividend increase is management's *signal* to the market that the firm is expected to do well.

It is the expectation of good times, and not only the stockholder's affinity for current income, that raises stock price. The rise in the stock price following the dividend signal is called the **information-content effect** of the dividend. To recapitulate, imagine that the stock price is unaffected or even negatively affected by the level of dividends, given that future earnings (or cash flows) are held constant. Nevertheless, the information-content effect implies that stock price may rise when dividends are raised—if dividends simultaneously cause stockholders to *increase* their expectations of future earnings and cash flows.

Dividend Signaling   We just argued that the market infers a rise in earnings and cash flows from a dividend increase, leading to a higher stock price. Conversely, the market infers a decrease in cash flows from a dividend reduction, leading to a fall in stock price. This raises an interesting corporate strategy: Could management increase dividends just to make the market *think* that cash flows will be higher, even when management knows that cash flows will not rise?

While this strategy may seem dishonest, academics take the position that managers frequently attempt the strategy. Academics begin with the following accounting identity for an all-equity firm:

$$\text{Cash flow}^{23} = \text{Capital expenditures} + \text{Dividends} \qquad (18.5)$$

Equation (18.5) must hold if a firm is neither issuing nor repurchasing stock. That is, the cash flow from the firm must go somewhere. If it is not paid out in dividends, it must be used in some expenditure. Whether the expenditure involves a capital budgeting project or a purchase of Treasury bills, it is still an expenditure.

Imagine that we are in the middle of the year and investors are trying to make some forecast of cash flow over the entire year. These investors may very well use (18.5) to estimate cash flow. For example, suppose that the firm announces current dividends will be

---

[22]P. M. Healy and K. G. Palepu, "Earnings Information Conveyed by Dividend Initiations and Omissions," *Journal of Financial Economics* 21 (1988) and R. Michaely, R. H. Thaler, and K. Womack, "Price Reactions to Dividend Initiations and Omissions: Overreactions or Drift," *Journal of Finance* 50 (1995).

[23]The correct representation of (18.5) involves cash flow, not earnings. However, with little loss of understanding, we could discuss dividend-signaling in terms of earnings, not cash flow.

$50 million and the market believes that capital expenditures are $80 million. The market would then determine cash flow to be $130 million (50 + 80).

Now, suppose that the firm had, alternatively, announced a dividend of $70 million. The market might assume that cash flow remains at $130 million, implying capital expenditures of $60 million (130 − 70). Here, the increase in dividends would hurt stock price, since the market anticipates valuable capital expenditures will be crowded out. Alternatively, the market might assume that capital expenditures remain at $80 million, implying the estimate of cash flow to be $150 million (70 + 80). Stock price would likely rise here, since stock prices usually increase with cash flow. In general, academics believe that models where investors assume capital expenditures remain the same are more realistic. Thus, an increase in dividends improves stock price.

Now we come to the incentives of managers to fool the public. Suppose you are a manager who wants to boost stock price, perhaps because you are planning to sell some of your personal holdings of the company's stock immediately. You might increase dividends so that the market would raise its estimate of cash flow, thereby also boosting the current stock price.

If this strategy is appealing, would anything prevent you from raising dividends without limit? The answer is yes, because there is also a *cost* to raising dividends. That is, the firm will have to forgo some of its profitable projects. Remember that cash flow in (18.5) is a constant, so that an increase in dividends is obtained only by a reduction in capital expenditures. At some point the market will learn that cash flow has not increased but, instead, profitable capital expenditures have been cut. Once the market absorbs this information, stock price should fall below what it would have been had dividends never been raised. Thus, if you plan to sell, say, half of your shares and retain the other half, an increase in dividends should help you on the immediate sale but hurt you when you sell your remaining shares years later. Thus, your decision on the level of dividends will be based, among other things, on the timing of your personal stock sales.

The above is a simplified example of dividend signaling, where the manager sets dividend policy based on maximum benefit for himself.[24] Alternatively, a given manager may have no desire to sell his shares immediately, but knows that, at any one time, plenty of ordinary shareholders will want to do so. Thus, for the benefit of shareholders in general, a manager will always be aware of the trade-off between current and future stock price. And this, then, is the essence of signaling with dividends. It is not enough for a manager to set dividend policy in order to maximize the true (or intrinsic) value of the firm. He must also consider the effect of dividend policy on the current stock price, even if the current stock price does not reflect true value.

Does a motive to signal imply that managers will increase dividends rather than share repurchases? The answer is likely no, since most academic models imply that dividends and share repurchases are perfect substitutes.[25] Rather, these models indicate that managers will consider reducing capital spending (even projects with positive NPVs) in order to increase either dividends or share repurchases.

Concept
Question

1. What are the real-world factors favoring a high-dividend policy?

---

[24]Papers examining fully developed models of signaling include S. Bhattacharya, "Imperfect Information, Dividend Policy, and 'the Bird in the Hand' Fallacy," *Bell Journal of Economics* 10 (1979); S. Bhattacharya, "Nondissipative Signaling Structure and Dividend Policy," *Quarterly Journal of Economics* 95 (1980), p. 1; S. Ross, "The Determination of Financial Structure: The Incentive Signalling Approach," *Bell Journal of Economics* 8 (1977), p. 1; M. Miller and K. Rock, "Dividend Policy under Asymmetric Information," *Journal of Finance* (1985).

[25]Signaling models where dividends and repurchases are not perfect substitutes are contained in Franklin Allen, Antonio Bernardo, and Ivo Welch, "A Theory of Dividends Based on Tax Clienteles," *Journal of Finance* (2002) and John Kose and Joseph Williams, "Dividends, Dilution and Taxes: A Signaling Equilibrium," *Journal of Finance* (1985).

18.7 The Clientele Effect: A Resolution of Real-World Factors?

In the previous two sections, we pointed out that the existence of personal taxes favors a low-dividend policy, whereas other factors favor high dividends. The financial profession had hoped that it would be easy to determine which of these sets of factors dominates. Unfortunately, after years of research, no one has been able to conclude which of the two is more important. This is surprising, since one might be skeptical that the two sets of factors would cancel each other out so perfectly.

However, one particular idea, known as the *clientele effect,* implies that the two sets of factors are likely to cancel each other out after all. To understand this idea, let's separate those investors in high-tax brackets from those in low-tax brackets. Individuals in high-tax brackets likely prefer either no or low dividends. Low–tax-bracket investors generally fall into three categories. First, there are individual investors in low brackets. They are likely to prefer some dividends if they desire current income. Second, pension funds pay no taxes on either dividends or capital gains. Because they face no tax consequences, pension funds will also prefer dividends if they have a preference for current income. Finally, corporations can exclude at least 70 percent of their dividend income but cannot exclude any of their capital gains. Thus, corporations would prefer to invest in high-dividend stocks, even without a preference for current income.

Suppose that 40 percent of all investors prefer high dividends and 60 percent prefer low dividends, yet only 20 percent of firms pay high dividends while 80 percent pay low dividends. Here, the high-dividend firms will be in short supply; thus their stock should be bid up while the stock of low-dividend firms should be bid down.

However, the dividend policies of all firms need not be fixed in the long run. In this example, we would expect enough low-dividend firms to increase their payout so that 40 percent of the firms pay high dividends and 60 percent of the firms pay low dividends. After this has occurred, no type of firm will be better off from changing its dividend policy. Once payouts of corporations conform to the desires of stockholders, no single firm can affect its market value by switching from one dividend strategy to another.

Clienteles are likely to form in the following way:

Group	Stocks
Individuals in high-tax brackets	Zero-to-low-payout stocks
Individuals in low-tax brackets	Low-to-medium-payout stocks
Tax-free institutions	Medium-payout stocks
Corporations	High-payout stocks

To see if you understand the clientele effect, consider the following question: "In spite of the theoretical argument that dividend policy is irrelevant or that firms should not pay dividends, many investors like high dividends. Because of this fact, a firm can boost its share price by having a higher dividend payout ratio." True or false?

The statement is likely to be false. As long as there are already enough high-dividend firms to satisfy dividend-loving investors, a firm will not be able to boost its share price by paying high dividends. A firm can boost its stock price only if an unsatisfied clientele exists. There is no evidence that this is the case.

Our discussion on clienteles followed from the fact that tax brackets vary across investors. If shareholders care about taxes, stock should attract tax clienteles based on dividend yield. This appears to be true. Surveys by Blume, Crockett, and Friend, and by Lewellen,

TABLE 18.2	Decile	Dividend Yield (% per annum)	Marginal Tax* Rate (%)
Relationship between Dividend Yield and Marginal Tax Rate from Direct Observation of Individual Investors' Portfolios	1	7.9%	36%
	2	5.4	35
	3	4.4	38
	4	3.5	39
	5	2.7	38
	6	1.8	41
	7	0.6	40
	8	0.0	41
	9	0.0	42
	10	0.0	41

Stockholders in high marginal tax brackets buy securities with low-dividend yield and vice versa.

*Lewellen et al. use several alternative methods to calculate the marginal tax rate from data on income. The results are broadly similar, and above we give the results for their "Tax-1" definition.

From W. Lewellen, K. L. Stanley, R. C. Lease, and G. C. Schlarbaum, "Some Direct Evidence on the Dividend Clientele Phenomenon," *Journal of Finance* 33 (December 1978), p. 5.

Stanley, Lease, and Schlarbaum in Table 18.2, show that stocks with the highest dividend yields tend to be held by individual investors in low-tax brackets.[26]

An interesting case for the clientele effect on dividend policy is made by John Childs of Kidder Peabody in the following exchange:[27]

> *Joseph T. Willet:* John, you've been around public utilities for a good many years. Why do you think that utilities have such high dividend payout ratios?
>
> *John Childs:* They're raising dividends so they can raise capital. . . . If you take the dividends out of utilities today, you'll never sell another share of stock. That's how important it is. In fact, if a few major utilities (with no special problems) cut their dividends, small investors would lose faith in the utility industry and that would finish the sales of utility stocks.
>
> *John Childs (again):* What you are trying to do with dividend policy is to enhance and strengthen the natural interest of investors in your company. The type of stockholders you attract will depend on the type of company you are. If you're Genentech, you are going to attract the type of stockholders who have absolutely no interest in dividends. In fact, you would hurt the stockholders if you paid dividends. On the other hand, you go over to the other extreme such as utilities' and the yield bank's stocks. There the stockholders are extremely interested in dividends, and these dividends have an effect on market price.

Concept Question

1. What are tax clienteles?

18.8 What We Know and Do Not Know about Dividend Policy

Corporate Dividends Are Substantial

We pointed out earlier in the chapter that dividends are tax-disadvantaged relative to capital gains, because dividends are taxed upon payment while taxes on capital gains are

---

[26]M. Blume, J. Crockett, and I. Friend, "Stockownership in the United States: Characteristics and Trends," *Survey of Current Business* 54 (1974), p. 11. W. Lewellen, K. L. Stanley, R. C. Lease, and G. C. Schlarbaum, "Some Direct Evidence on the Dividend Clientele Phenomenon," *Journal of Finance* 33 (December 1978), p. 5.

[27]Joseph T. Willett, moderator, "A Discussion of Corporate Dividend Policy," in *Six Roundtable Discussions of Corporate Finance with Joel Stern*, ed. by D. H. Chew (New York: Basil Blackwell, 1986). The panelists included Robert Litzenberger, Pat Hess, Bill Kealy, John Childs, and Joel Stern.

FIGURE 18.7   Ratio of Aggregate Dividends to Aggregate Earnings in the United States

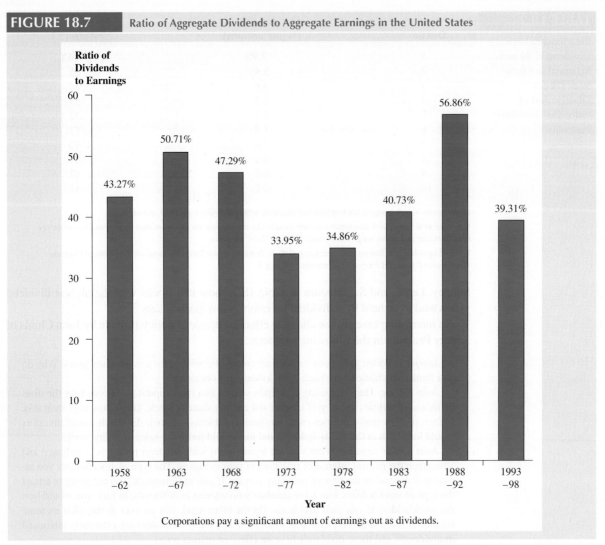

Corporations pay a significant amount of earnings out as dividends.

SOURCE: Table 11 of E. F. Fama and K. R. French, "Disappearing Dividends: Changing Firm Characteristics or Lower Propensity to Pay?" *Journal of Financial Economics* (April 2001).

deferred until sale. Nevertheless, dividends in the U.S. economy are substantial. For example, consider Figure 18.7, which shows the ratio of aggregate dividends to aggregate earnings for firms on the New York Stock Exchange (NYSE), the American Stock Exchange (AMEX), and NASDAQ over various time periods. The ratio is approximately 43 percent for the period from 1963 to 1998. This ratio varies from a low of 33.95 percent in the 1973–77 period to a high of 56.86 percent from 1988 to 1992.

One might argue that the taxation on dividends is actually minimal, perhaps because dividends are paid primarily to individuals in low-tax brackets or because institutions such as pension funds, which pay no taxes, are the primary recipients. However, Peterson, Peterson and Ang conducted an in-depth study of dividends for one representative year, 1979.[28] They found that about two-thirds of dividends went to individuals and that the average marginal

---

[28]P. Peterson, D. Peterson, and J. Ang, "Direct Evidence on the Marginal Rate of Taxation on Dividend Income," *Journal of Financial Economics* 14 (1985).

FIGURE 18.8   Percent of CRSP Firms Paying Dividends

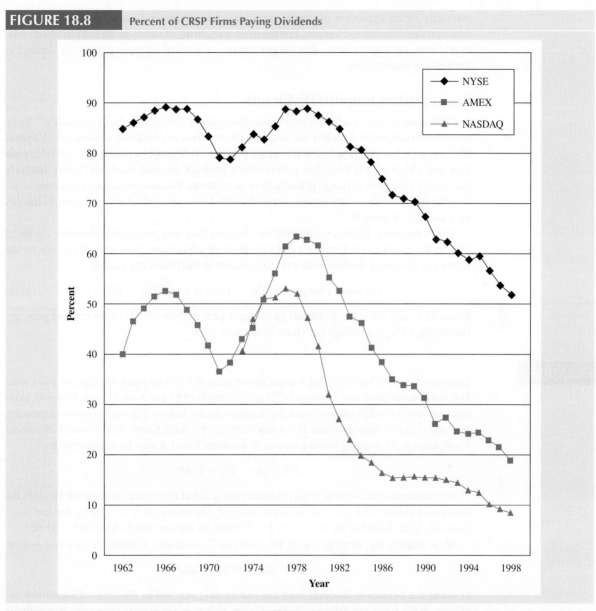

SOURCE: Figure 5 of E. F. Fama and K. R. French, "Disappearing Dividends: Changing Firm Characteristics or Lower Propensity to Pay," *Journal of Financial Economics* (April 2001).

tax bracket for these individuals was about 40 percent. Thus, we must conclude that large amounts of dividends are paid, even in the presence of substantial taxation.

Fewer Companies Pay Dividends

While dividends are substantial, Fama and French (FF) point out that the percentage of companies paying dividends has fallen in recent years.[29] This insight is illustrated in Figure 18.8 for NYSE, AMEX, and NASDAQ firms. FF argue that the decline was caused

---

[29]E. F. Fama and K. R. French, "Disappearing Dividends: Changing Firm Characteristics or Lower Propensity to Pay?" *Journal of Financial Economics* (April 2001).

primarily by an explosion of small, currently unprofitable companies that have recently listed on the different exchanges. For the most part, firms of this type do not pay dividends. In addition, the authors argue that the percentage of firms of all types paying dividends has declined in recent years.

Corporations Smooth Dividends

In 1956, John Lintner made two important observations concerning dividend policy.[30] First, real-world companies typically set long-run target ratios of dividends to earnings. A firm is likely to set a low target ratio if it has many positive NPV projects relative to available cash flow and a high ratio if it has few positive NPV projects. Second, managers know that only part of any change in earnings is likely to be permanent. Because managers need time to assess the permanence of any earnings rise, dividend changes appear to lag earnings changes by a number of periods.

Taken together, Lintner's observations suggest that two parameters describe dividend policy: the target payout ratio (t) and the speed of adjustment of current dividends to the target (s). Dividend changes will tend to conform to the following model:

$$\text{Dividend changes} = \text{Div}_1 - \text{Div}_0 = s \cdot (t\text{EPS}_1 - \text{Div}_1) \tag{18.6}$$

where Div_1 and Div_0 are dividends in the next year and dividends in the current year, respectively. EPS_1 is earnings per share in the next year.

> **EXAMPLE**
>
> Calculator Graphics, Inc. (CGI), has a target payout ratio of 0.30. Last year's earnings per share were $10, and in accordance with the target, CGI paid dividends of $3 per share last year. However, earnings have jumped to $20 this year. Since the managers do not believe that this increase is permanent, they do *not* plan to raise dividends all the way to $6 (0.30 × $20). Rather, their speed of adjustment coefficient, s, is 0.5, implying that the *increase* in dividends from last year to this year will be:
>
> $$0.5 \times (\$6 - \$3) = \$1.50$$
>
> That is, the increase in dividends is the product of the speed of adjustment coefficient, 0.50, times the difference between what dividends would be with full adjustment [$6 (0.30 × $20)] and last year's dividends. Since dividends will increase by $1.50, dividends this year will be $4.50 ($3 + $1.50).
>
> Now, suppose that earnings stay at $20 next year. The increase in dividends next year will be:
>
> $$0.5 \times (\$6 - \$4.50) = \$0.75$$
>
> In words, the increase in dividends from this year to next year will be the speed of adjustment coefficient (0.50) times the difference between what dividends would have been next year with full adjustment ($6) and this year's dividends ($4.50). Since dividends will increase by $0.75, dividends next year will be $5.25 ($4.50 + $0.75). In this way, dividends will slowly rise every year, if earnings in all future years remain at $20. However, dividends will reach $6 only at infinity.

The limiting cases in (18.6) occur when $s = 1$ and $s = 0$. If $s = 1$, the actual change in dividends will be equal to the target change in dividends. Here, full adjustment occurs immediately. If $s = 0$, $\text{Div}_1 = \text{Div}_0$. In other words, there is no change in dividends at all. Real-world companies can be expected to set s between 0 and 1.

---

[30] J. Lintner, "Distribution and Incomes of Corporations among Dividends, Retained Earnings and Taxes," *American Economic Review* (May 1956).

Why William Lyon Homes Pays No Dividend

William Lyon Homes is a $600 million home builder. The company's common stock is listed as WLS on the NYSE. The company has not paid any cash dividends on its common stock. Wilson Lyon Homes has grown in excess of 20 percent in the last several years and in the foreseeable future will follow a policy of retaining earnings in order to help finance its business. In addition, agreements governing senior notes currently prohibit dividend payments.

Why Health Management Associates Pays Dividends

HMA owns and operates about 45 hospitals and generates more than $2.5 billion in net patient service revenue.

On April 29, 2003, HMA's board of directors approved a quarterly cash dividend, and on June 2, 2003, HMA paid shareholders of record as of May 9, 2003, a cash dividend of $0.02 per share. As previously reported, in creating the initial dividend policy, the board of directors cited both HMA's strong operational history over a long period of time, as well as HMA's desire to provide its shareholders with an additional opportunity for a return on their investment. HMA believes that its dividend policy is another indication of its financial strength and prospects, and further differentiates HMA from the rest of the industry.

An implication of Lintner's model is that the dividends-to-earnings ratio rises when a company begins a period of bad times, and the ratio falls when a company reaches a period of good times. Thus, dividends display less variability than do earnings. In other words, firms *"smooth"* dividends.

Payouts Provide Information to the Market

We previously observed that the price of a firm's stock frequently rises when either its current dividend is increased or a stock repurchase is announced. Conversely, the price of a firm's stock can fall significantly when its dividend is cut. In other words, there is information content in payouts. For example, consider what happened to Pacific Enterprises a number of years ago. Faced with poor operating results, Pacific Enterprises omitted its regular quarterly dividend. The next day the common stock dropped from 24⅞ to 18⅛. One reason may be that investors are looking at current dividends for clues concerning the level of future earnings and dividends.

A Sensible Payout Policy

The knowledge of the finance profession varies across topic areas. For example, capital-budgeting techniques are both powerful and precise. A single net-present-value equation can accurately determine whether a multimillion dollar project should be accepted or rejected. The capital asset pricing model and the arbitrage pricing model provide empirically validated relationships between expected return and risk.

Conversely, the field has less knowledge of capital-structure policy. Though a number of elegant theories relate firm value to the level of debt, no formula can be used to calculate the firm's optimum debt-equity ratio. Our profession is forced too frequently to employ rules of thumb, such as treating the industry's average ratio as the optimal one for the firm. The field's knowledge of dividend policy is, perhaps, similar to its knowledge of capital-structure policy. We do know that:

1. The intrinsic value of a firm is reduced when positive NPV projects are rejected in order to pay a dividend.

2. Firms should avoid issuing stock to pay a dividend in a world with personal taxes.

3. Stock repurchases represent a sensible alternative to dividends.

527

The Pros and Cons of Paying Dividends

Pros	Cons
1. Cash dividends can underscore good results and provide support to stock price.	1. Dividends are taxed as ordinary income.
2. Dividends may attract institutional investors who prefer some return in the form of dividends. A mix of institutional and individual investors may allow a firm to raise capital at lower cost because of the ability of the firm to reach a wider market.	2. Dividends can reduce internal sources of financing. Dividends may force the firm to forgo positive NPV projects or to rely on costly external equity financing.
3. Stock price usually increases with the announcement of a new or increased dividend.	3. Once established, dividend cuts are hard to make without adversely affecting a firm's stock price.
4. Dividends absorb excess cash flow and may reduce agency costs that arise from conflicts between management and shareholders.	

The preceding recommendations suggest that firms with many positive NPV projects relative to available cash flow should have low payout ratios. Firms with fewer positive NPV projects relative to available cash flow might want to consider higher payouts. In addition, there is some benefit to dividend stability, and unnecessary changes in dividend payout are avoided by most firms.

However, there is no formula for calculating the optimal dividend-to-earnings ratio. In addition, there is no formula for determining the optimal mix between repurchases and dividends. It can be argued that, for tax reasons, firms should always substitute stock repurchases for dividends. However, while the volume of repurchases has greatly increased over time, dividends do not appear to be on the way out. At the present time, the dollar volume of dividends is only slightly less than that of repurchases.

CASE STUDY

How Firms Make the Decision to Pay Dividends: The Case of Apple Computer

Perhaps the most important dividend decisions a firm must make are when to pay dividends for the first time and when to omit them once they have started. We study the case of Apple Computer for clues to why firms pay dividends and later on omit them.

In 1976 two young friends, Stephen Wozniak and Steven Jobs, built the Apple I Computer in Jobs's garage in the "Silicon Valley" area of Northern California and founded Apple Computer, Inc. The first Apple was built and sold without a monitor, or keyboard. The Apple II was introduced in 1977 and was targeted at the home and educational markets as a personal computer. The Apple II was very successful, and by 1980 over 130,000 units had been sold and Apple's revenues were $117 million. In 1980 Apple "went public" with an initial public offering (IPO) of common stock. Shortly thereafter, Wozniak left Apple and John Scully was hired from Pepsi to become president. Apple did not do well with its Lisa (1983) and Apple III computers, but the Macintosh (1984) was a huge hit—primarily in the home and educational markets. In 1985, after a widely publicized struggle for power with Scully, Jobs left to start another computer company called Next.

In many ways 1986 was a watershed year for Apple. By the end of 1986, Apple had revenues of $1.9 billion and net income of $154 million. From 1980 to 1986 its annual growth rate in net income was 53 percent. In 1986, with Mac Plus, Apple launched an aggressive effort to penetrate the expanding office computer market—the domain of its main rival IBM. However, its future prospects were not necessarily bright. Much depended on Apple's ability to do well in the business market. Competition was very intense in early 1987, and Sun Microsystems slashed the price of its least costly computer workstation to try to stop encroachment by the Apple Mac. However, Apple surprised everyone with large earnings gains in the final quarter of 1987 and by disclosing the fact that the sales on Macintosh models had increased by 41 percent.

To demonstrate its faith in its future, to underscore the recent success of the Mac, and to attract more institutional investors, on April 23, 1987, Apple declared its first ever quarterly dividend of $.12 per share. It also announced a two-for-one stock split. The stock market reacted very positively to the announcement of Apple's initial dividend. On the day of the announcements, its stock increased by $1.75. Over a four-day time span the stock rose by about 8 percent.

The initial dividend turned out to be a positive portent, and the next four years were good years for Apple. At the end of 1990, Apple's revenues, profits, and capital spending had achieved record highs.

	1986	1990	2002
Revenues (in millions)	$1,902	$5,558	$5,742
Net income (in millions)	154	475	−117
Capital spending (in millions)	66	223	144
Stock price	$ 20	$ 48	$ 14
Long-term debt (in millions)	0	0	318
Dividends per share	0	$ .45	0

Why do firms like Apple decide to pay dividends? There is no single answer to this question. In Apple's case, one part of the answer can be traced to Apple's attempt to "signal" the stock market about the potential growth and positive NPV prospects of its attempt to penetrate the office computer market. The payment of dividends can also "ratify" good results. Apple's initial dividend served to convince the market that Apple's success was not temporary.

Why did Apple announce a two-for-one stock split at the same time of its announcement of an initial cash dividend? It is often said that a stock split without a cash dividend is like giving shareholders two five-dollar bills for a $10 bill. Your wallet feels thicker but you are no better off. However, a stock split accompanied by a cash dividend can amplify the positive signal and pack a more powerful message than would be true otherwise. In addition, firms sometimes split their shares, because they believe a low stock price may attract more individual investors and as a consequence increase liquidity. However, the evidence is not clear on this point, and some firms like Berkshire Hathaway disdain stock splits. (Its stock was recently selling at $83,000 a share.)

Was Apple's decision to offer an initial dividend the best decision for the company? This is an impossible question to answer precisely. However, the stock market's positive reaction and Apple's subsequent performance suggest it was a good decision. Unfortunately, the years since 1990 have not been as good for Apple. Its revenue growth has moderated and its profits have declined due to a difficult transition from a high-priced, high-quality producer of personal computers to a more competitively priced producer. It experienced losses in 1996 and 1997. Apple's small market share has become a problem because software developers have been more interested in producing products that could run on Intel-based machines. At the end of 1997, Apple's stock price was at $24 per share—lower than in 1990. In Figure 18.9, we plot Apple's earnings per share and dividends per share from 1980 to 2002. As can be seen, dividend changes have tended to lag earnings changes. In 1992, when earnings per share increased from $3.74 to $4.33 there was no change in dividend payouts.

FIGURE 18.9   Dividend Pattern of Apple Computer from 1983 to 2002

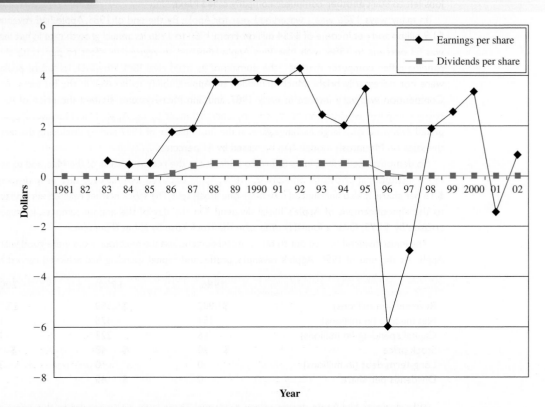

NOTE: These figures adjust for the 2-for-1 stock split in 1987.

And when in 1993, earnings per share declined to $2.45, Apple did not change its dividend payouts. However, Apple's dividend was completely omitted in 1996.

Now we have another question, why did Apple omit its dividend in 1996? The firm had experienced several market setbacks. It was forced to retreat from its much heralded "cloning" strategy. In an important shift in strategic thinking, Apple had started licensing its Mac operating system to other manufacturers. Unfortunately, instead of attracting new buyers, this policy was eroding its own base and sales fell sharply. As a consequence, Apple experienced operating losses of $742 million in 1996 and $379 million in 1997.

Looking back at Figure 18.9, it can be seen that Apple's dividends have been more stable over time than its earnings. This is typical of the dividend policy of most firms. Stability cannot be maintained forever in the face of huge operating losses and most companies ultimately slash dividends if the losses continue.

Apple has not yet resumed its dividend. Its earnings per share climbed to $3.45 in 2000. However, in 2001 Apple experienced negative earnings per share and in 2002 had barely resumed profitability. Current sales appear weak, especially for its iMac consumer product. The market has responded well to its iBook and Power Book portables. A deal with EarthLink could make Apple the exclusive Internet access provider bundled with Macs. Recently the company launched a variety of new software including a new digital video-editing program. Unfortunately Apple's retail distribution still depends heavily on stores and the company will undoubtedly need to invest heavily in new research and development. Now we ask the question: Should Apple resume its dividend payout?

Answer: Not for a while.

18.9 SUMMARY AND CONCLUSIONS

1. The dividend policy of the firm is irrelevant in a perfect capital market because the shareholder can effectively undo the firm's dividend strategy. If a shareholder receives a greater dividend than desired, he or she can reinvest the excess. Conversely, if the shareholder receives a smaller dividend than desired, he or she can sell off extra shares of stock. This argument is due to MM and is similar to their homemade-leverage concept, discussed in Chapter 15.

2. Stockholders will be indifferent between dividends and share repurchases in a perfect capital market.

3. Since dividends in the United States are taxed, companies should not issue stock in order to pay out a dividend.

4. Also because of taxes, firms have an incentive to reduce dividends. For example, they might consider increasing capital expenditures, acquiring other companies, or purchasing financial assets. However, due to financial considerations and legal constraints, rational firms with large cash flows will likely exhaust these activities with plenty of cash left over for dividends.

5. In a world with personal taxes, a strong case can be made for repurchasing shares instead of paying dividends.

6. Nevertheless, there are a number of justifications for dividends even in a world with personal taxes:
   a. Investors in no-dividend stocks incur transaction costs when selling off shares for current consumption.
   b. Behavioral finance argues that investors with limited self-control can meet current consumption needs via high-dividend stocks while adhering to a policy of "never dipping into principal."
   c. Managers, acting on behalf of stockholders, can pay dividends to keep cash from bondholders. The board of directors, also acting on behalf of stockholders, can use dividends to reduce the cash available to spendthrift managers.
   d. Managers may increase dividends to boost current stock price, even at the expense of projects with positive NPVs. This strategy is called *signaling*.

7. The stock market reacts positively to increases in dividends (or an initial payment) and negatively to decreases in dividends. This suggests that there is information content in dividend payments.

8. High (low) dividend firms should arise to meet the demands of dividend-preferring (capital gains-preferring) investors. Because of these clienteles, it is not clear that a firm can create value by changing its dividend policy.

KEY TERMS

clienteles, *522*	homemade dividends, *507*
date of payment, *503*	information-content effect, *520*
date of record, *503*	regular cash dividends, *502*
declaration date, *503*	stock dividend, *502*
ex-dividend date, *503*	stock split, *503*

SUGGESTED READINGS

The breakthrough in the theory of dividend policy is contained in

Miller, M., and F. Modigliani. "Dividend Policy, Growth and the Valuation of Shares." *Journal of Business* (October 1961).

A survey of dividend policy can be found in

Allen, Franklin, and Roni Michaely. "Dividend Policy." In R. A. Jarrow, V. Maksimovic, and W. T. Ziemba (eds.). *Handbooks in Operations Research and Management Science: Finance.* Amsterdam: Elsevier Science (1995), 793–838.

Current trends in dividend policy are examined in

Fama, Eugene F., and Kenneth R. French. "Disappearing Dividends: Changing Firm Characteristics or Lower Propensity to Pay?" *Journal of Financial Economics* (April 2001).

Visit us at www.mhhe.com/rwj

QUESTIONS & PROBLEMS

THE MECHANICS OF DIVIDEND PAYOUTS

18.1   Identify and describe each of the following dates that are associated with a dividend payment on common stock:
February 16
February 24
February 26
March 14

18.2   On April 5, the board of directors of Capital City Golf Club declared a dividend of $.75 per share payable on Tuesday, May 4, to shareholders of record as of Tuesday, April 20. Suppose you bought 350 shares of Capital City stock on April 6 for $8.75 a share. Assume there are no taxes, no transaction costs, and no news between your purchase and sale of the stock. If you were to sell your stocks on April 16, how much would you be able to sell your stock for?

18.3   The Mann Company belongs to a risk class for which the appropriate discount rate is 10 percent. Mann currently has 100,000 outstanding shares selling at $100 each. The firm is contemplating the declaration of a $5 dividend at the end of the fiscal year that just began. Answer the following questions based on the Miller and Modigliani model, which is discussed in the text.
   a. What will be the price of the stock on the ex-dividend date if the dividend is declared?
   b. What will be the price of the stock at the end of the year if the dividend is not declared?
   c. If Mann makes $2 million of new investments at the beginning of the period, earns net income of $1 million, and pays the dividend at the end of the year, how many shares of new stock must the firm issue to meet its funding needs?
   d. Is it realistic to use the MM model in the real world to value stock? Why or why not?

18.4   On February 17, the board of directors of Exertainment Corp. declared a dividend of $1.25 per share payable on March 18 to all holders of record on March 1. All investors are in the 31-percent tax bracket.
   a. What is the ex-dividend date?
   b. Ignoring personal taxes, how much should the stock price drop on the ex-dividend date?

THE BENCHMARK CASE: AN ILLUSTRATION OF THE IRRELEVANCE OF DIVIDEND POLICY

18.5   The growing-perpetuity model expresses the value of a share of stock as the present value of the expected dividends from that stock. How can you conclude that dividend policy is irrelevant when this model is valid?

18.6   Andahl Corporation stock, of which you own 500 shares, will pay a $2-per-share dividend one year from today. Two years from now Andahl will close its doors; stockholders will receive liquidating dividends of $17.5375 per share. The required rate of return on Andahl stock is 15 percent.
   a. What is the current price of Andahl stock?
   b. You prefer to receive equal amounts of money in each of the next two years. How will you accomplish this?

18.7   The net income of Novis Corporation, which has 10,000 outstanding shares and a 100-percent payout policy, is $32,000. The expected value of the firm one year hence is $1,545,600. The appropriate discount rate for Novis is 12 percent.
   a. What is the current value of the firm?
   b. What is the ex-dividend price of Novis's stock if the board follows its current policy?
   c. At the dividend declaration meeting, several board members claimed that the dividend is too meager and is probably depressing Novis's price. They proposed that Novis sell enough new shares to finance a $4.25 dividend.
      1. Comment on the claim that the low dividend is depressing the stock price. Support your argument with calculations.
      2. If the proposal is adopted, at what price will the new shares sell and how many will be sold?

18.8   Gibson Co. has a current period cash flow of $1.2 million and pays no dividends, and the present value of forecasted future cash flows is $15 million. It is an all-equity-financed company with 1 million shares outstanding. Assume the effective personal tax rate is zero.
   a. What is the share price of the Gibson stock?

b. Suppose the board of directors of Gibson Co. announces its plan to pay out 50 percent of its current cash flow as cash dividends to its shareholders. How can Jeff Miller, who owns 1,000 shares of Gibson stock, achieve a zero payout policy on his own?

TAXES, ISSUANCES COSTS, AND DIVIDENDS

18.9 National Business Machine Co. (NBM) has $2 million of extra cash. NBM has two choices to make use of this cash. One alternative is to invest the cash in financial assets. The resulted investment income will be paid out as a special dividend at the end of three years. In this case, the firm can invest in Treasury bills yielding 7 percent, or an 11 percent preferred stock. Only 30 percent of the dividends from investing in preferred stock would be subject to corporate taxes. Another alternative is to pay out the cash as dividends and let the shareholders invest on their own in Treasury bills with the same yield. The corporate tax rate is 35 percent, and the individual tax rate is 31 percent. Should the cash be paid today or in three years? Which of the two options generates the highest after-tax income for the shareholders?

18.10 The University of Pennsylvania pays no taxes on capital gains, dividend income, or interest payments. Would you expect to find low-dividend, high-growth stock in the university's portfolio? Would you expect to find tax-free municipal bonds in the portfolio?

18.11 In their 1970 paper on dividends and taxes, Elton and Gruber reported that the ex-dividend-date drop in a stock's price as a percentage of the dividend should equal the ratio of 1 minus the ordinary income tax rate to 1 minus the capital gains rate; that is,

$$\frac{P_e - P_b}{D} = \frac{1 - T_o}{1 - T_c}$$

where

P_e = The ex-dividend stock price
P_b = The stock price before it trades ex-dividend
D = The amount of the dividend
T_o = The tax rate on ordinary income
T_c = The effective tax rate on capital gains

Note: As we pointed out in the text, effective tax rate of capital gains is less than the actual tax rate, because their realization may be postponed. Indeed, because investors could postpone their realizations indefinitely, the effective rate could be zero.

a. If $T_o = T_c = 0$, how much will the stock's price fall?
b. If $T_o \neq 0$ and $T_c = 0$, how much will it fall?
c. Explain the results you found in (*a*) and (*b*).
d. Do the results of Elton and Gruber's study imply that firms will maximize shareholder wealth by not paying dividends?

18.12 After completing its capital spending for the year, Carlson Manufacturing has $1,000 extra cash. Carlson's managers must choose between investing the cash in Treasury bonds that yield 8 percent or paying the cash out to investors who would invest in the bonds themselves.

a. If the corporate tax rate is 35 percent, what tax rate on ordinary income would make the investors equally willing to receive the dividend and to let Carlson invest the money?
b. Is the answer to (*a*) reasonable? Why or why not?
c. Suppose the only investment choice is stock that yields 12 percent. What personal tax rate will make the stockholders indifferent to the outcome of Carlson's dividend decision?
d. Is this a compelling argument for a low dividend payout ratio? Why or why not?

REAL-WORLD FACTORS FAVORING A HIGH-DIVIDEND POLICY

18.13 The bird-in-the-hand argument, which states that a dividend today is safer than the uncertain prospect of a capital gain tomorrow, is often used to justify high dividend-payout ratios. Explain the fallacy behind the argument.

18.14 The desire for current income is not a valid explanation for preference for high-current-dividend policy, as investors can always create homemade dividends by selling a portion of their stocks. Comment.

18.15 Your aunt is in a high tax bracket and would like to minimize the tax burden of her investment portfolio. She is willing to buy and sell in order to maximize her after-tax returns and she has asked for your advice. What would you suggest she do?

A RESOLUTION OF REAL-WORLD FACTORS?

18.16 In the May 4, 1981, issue of *Fortune*, an article entitled "Fresh Evidence That Dividends Don't Matter" stated, "All told, 115 companies of the 500 [largest industrial corporations] raised their payout every year during the period [1970–1989]. Investors in this . . . group would have fared somewhat better than investors in the 500 as a whole: the median total [annual compound] return of the 115 was 10.7% during the decade versus 9.4% for the 500."

Is this evidence that investors prefer dividends to capital gains? Why or why not?

18.17 Last month Central Virginia Power Company, which had been having trouble with cost overruns on a nuclear plant that it had been building, announced that it was "temporarily suspending dividend payments due to the cash flow crunch associated with its investment program." When the announcement was made, the company's stock price dropped from $28\frac{1}{2}$ to 25. What do you suspect caused the change in the stock price?

18.18 Southern Established Inc. has been paying out regular quarterly dividends ever since 1983. It just slashed the dividend by half in the current fiscal quarter and a more severe cut is to be underway. Southern's stock price dropped from $35.25 to $31.75 when the dividend cut was announced. Explain the possible reasons for this price drop.

18.19 Cap Henderson owns Neotech stock because its price has been steadily rising over the past few years and he expects its performance to continue. Cap is trying to convince Widow Jones to purchase some Neotech stock, but she is reluctant because Neotech has never paid a dividend. She depends on steady dividends to provide her with income.
   a. What preferences are these two investors demonstrating?
   b. What argument should Cap use to convince Widow Jones that Neotech stock is the stock for her?
   c. Why might Cap's argument not convince Widow Jones?

18.20 If the market places the same value on $1 of dividends as on $1 of capital gains, then firms with different payout ratios will appeal to different clienteles of investors. One clientele is as good as another; therefore, a firm cannot increase its value by changing its dividend policy. Yet empirical investigations reveal a strong correlation between dividend payout ratios and other firm characteristics. For example, small, rapidly growing firms that have recently gone public almost always have payout ratios that are zero; all earnings are reinvested in the business. Explain this phenomenon if dividend policy is irrelevant.

18.21 In spite of the theoretical argument that dividend policy should be irrelevant, the fact remains that many investors like high dividends. If this preference exists, a firm can boost its share price by increasing its dividend-payout ratio. Explain the fallacy in this argument.

WHAT WE KNOW AND DO NOT KNOW ABOUT DIVIDEND POLICY

18.22 The Sharpe Co. has a period 0 dividend of $1.25. Its target payout ratio is 40 percent. The period 1 EPS is expected to be $4.5.
   a. If the adjustment rate is 0.3 as defined in the Lintner Model, what will be the Sharpe Co. dividend in period 1?
   b. If the adjustment rate is 0.6 instead, what is the dividend in period 1?

18.23 Empirical research found that there have been significant increases in stock price on the day an initial dividend (i.e., the first time a firm pays a cash dividend) is announced. What does this finding imply about the information content of initial dividends?

S & P PROBLEMS

18.24 Find the annual income statement for U.S. Steel (X), Dow Chemical (DOW), and Micron Technology (MU). What are the dividends for each company over the past five years? Why would these companies have such different dividend policies? Is there anything unusual about the dividends for U.S. Steel? How could the company pay dividends with negative earnings?

STANDARD &POOR'S

Visit us at www.mhhe.com/rwj

Appendix 18A   Stock Dividends and Stock Splits

In addition to the cash dividend, companies may issue stock dividends or split their stock. Since stock dividends and stock splits are quite similar, we treat them together. We begin with examples of these two strategies. Next, their benefits and costs to the firm are discussed.

Example of a Stock Dividend

Imagine a company with 10,000 shares of stock, each selling at $60. With a stock dividend of 10 percent, each stockholder receives one additional share for each 10 that he or she originally owned. Therefore the total number of shares outstanding after the dividend is 11,000. Note that the stockholders receive no cash and that each shareholder's percentage of the total outstanding stock remains the same. Thus a case can be made that a stock dividend is of no value to the firm. More will be said on this later.

Imagine that, before the stock dividend, the equity portion of the firm's balance sheet looks like this:

Common stock (par value set at $12 per share)	$120,000
Capital in excess of par value	200,000
Retained earnings	180,000
Total owner's equity	$500,000

A seemingly arbitrary accounting procedure is used to adjust the balance sheet after the stock dividend. Since 1,000 new shares are issued, $12,000 (1,000 × $12) is transferred to common stock after the dividend. The market price of $60 is $48 above the par value. Thus $48 × 1,000 = $48,000 is shifted to the excess capital account. Because the total value of owner's equity is unchanged by a stock dividend, $60,000 is withdrawn from retained earnings.

After the stock dividend, owner's equity for the firm is represented as:

Common stock (par value set at $12 per share)	$132,000
Capital in excess of par value	248,000
Retained earnings	120,000
Total owner's equity	$500,000

There is actually a good reason behind this procedure. Accountants fear that stock dividends could be used to impress a naive stockholder, even if the firm is doing poorly. This type of accounting treatment limits this possibility, since a stock dividend can never be greater than retained earnings.

Example of a Stock Split

A stock split is similar conceptually to a stock dividend. In a three-for-one split, each shareholder receives two additional shares of stock for each one held originally. Again, no cash is paid out, and the percentage of the entire firm that each shareholder owns is unaffected. However, the accounting of splits differs from the accounting of stock dividends. Imagine in our previous example that a three-for-one-split occurs, raising the number of shares to

30,000. The owner's equity after the split is represented as:

Common stock (30,000 shares with par value set at $4 per share)	$120,000
Capital in excess of par value	200,000
Retained earnings	180,000
Total owner's equity	$500,000

Note that for three of the categories the figures on the right are completely unaffected by the split. Only the par value is changed, being reduced here to $4 per share.

Since stock dividends and stock splits are similar, the dividing point between them is arbitrary.

Value of Stock Splits and Stock Dividends

The laws of logic tell us that stock splits and stock dividends can (1) leave the firm's value unaffected, (2) increase the value of the firm, or (3) decrease its value. Unfortunately, the issues are complex enough that one cannot easily determine which of the three relationships holds.

The Benchmark Case

A strong case can be made that stock dividends and splits do not change either the wealth of any shareholder or the wealth of the firm as a whole. For example, imagine a firm with $100 of earnings and 100 shares outstanding, implying EPS of $1. With a price-earnings ratio of 10, the price per share is $10 and the total market value of the firm is $1,000. Now imagine a 2-for-1 stock split where the number of shares rises to 200 and EPS falls to $0.50. Given the same P/E ratio of 10, the value of each share of stock is now $5. However, with twice the number of shares, the value of the entire firm is still $1,000. The wealth of each stockholder remains the same since the doubling in the number of shares is offset by the halving of the stock price. This result is sensible because (1) total earnings of the firm are held constant, and (2) the percentage of the firm owned by each investor is unchanged.

The same results would hold for a stock dividend. Imagine that the total number of shares is increased by 10 percent to 110. Given that EPS drops to $100/110 = $0.90909, the price per share should fall to $9.0909. Therefore the total value of the firm should remain at $1,000. The wealth of each stockholder should not change because, as with a split, the percentage of the firm that each investor owns remains the same.

Although these results are relatively obvious, they are developed in the idealized world of a perfect capital market. The typical financial manager is aware of many real-world complexities, and for that reason the stock split or stock dividend decision is not treated lightly in practice.

Popular Trading Range

Proponents of stock dividends and stock splits frequently argue that a security has a proper **trading range.** When the security is priced above this level, many investors do not have the funds to buy the common trading unit of 100 shares, called a *round lot.* Although securities can be purchased in *odd-lot* form (fewer than 100 shares), the commissions are more expensive here. Thus firms will split the stock to keep its price in this trading range.

Although this argument is a popular one, its validity has recently been questioned.[31] Mutual funds, pension funds, and other institutions have steadily increased their trading

---

[31]For example, see T. Copeland, "Liquidity Changes Following Stock Splits," *Journal of Finance* (March 1979).

activity since World War II and now handle a sizable percentage of total trading volume. Because these institutions can buy and sell in such huge amounts, they would not regard securities in the popular trading range with any special favor. In fact, whether because of the rise of institutions or some other factor, odd-lot trades comprise a quite small proportion of the market today.

Costs with Stock Splits or Stock Dividends

The reasoning in the previous paragraph minimizes the benefits of a stock split or dividend. In addition, some authors state that there are costs associated with these financial procedures. For example, Copeland argues that two types of transaction costs rise following a stock split. He further reasons that both of these cost increases ultimately reduce the liquidity of the stock, an unexpected result because a rise in liquidity through a broadening of the stockholder base often is given as a reason for a split.[32]

Copeland finds that brokerage fees, measured in percentages, increase after a split. This result is not surprising, since most published price lists of commissions show that brokerage fees for low-priced securities are a larger percentage of sales price than they are for high-priced securities. For example, commissions are generally higher for 400 shares of a security selling at $10 than for 100 shares of a security selling at $40.

The bid-ask spread is the difference between the price at which you sell a security to a dealer and the price at which you buy a security from a dealer. For example, a bid-ask spread of 49½–50 means that an individual can sell a share to the dealer at $49.50 and buy a share at $50, implying a round-trip loss to the investor of $0.50. Copeland finds that the bid-ask spread, expressed as a percentage of sales price, rises after a stock split. This finding is consistent with other work showing that the bid-ask spread is higher in percentage terms for lower-proceed securities.[33] The data suggest that the benefits to the stockholder associated with a stock dividend or stock split are not clearly greater than the costs to him.

Reverse Split

A less frequently encountered financial maneuver is the **reverse split.** In a one-for-three reverse split, each investor exchanges three old shares for one new share. The par value is tripled in the process. As mentioned previously with stock splits and stock dividends, a case can be made that, in a theoretical model, a reverse split changes nothing substantial about the company.

Given real-world imperfections, three related reasons are cited for reverse splits. First, transactions costs to shareholders are often less after the reverse split. This follows the conclusions of Copeland that brokerage commissions per dollar traded rise as the price of the stock falls. Second, the liquidity and marketability of a company's stock are improved when its price is raised to the "popular trading range." Third, stocks selling below a certain level are not considered "respectable," implying that investors bias downward their estimates of these firms' earnings, cash flow, growth, and stability. Some financial analysts argue that a reverse split can achieve instant respectability.

Concept
Questions

1. What is a stock dividend? A stock split?
2. What are the values of a stock dividend and a stock split?

---

[32]Although Copeland's empirical work included only stock splits, the same factors should apply to the stock dividend case.

[33]See H. Demsetz, "The Cost of Transacting," *Quarterly Journal of Economics* 82 (February 1968); and H. Stoll, "The Supply of Dealer Services in Securities Markets," *Journal of Finance* 33 (September 1978).

Visit us at www.mhhe.com/rwj

KEY TERMS   reverse split, *537*   trading range, *536*

SUGGESTED READING   *Evidence on how the market reacts to stock splits and stock dividends is in*

Ranking, G., and Earl Stice. "The Market Reaction to the Choice of Accounting Method for Stock Splits and Large Stock Dividends." *Journal of Financial and Quantitative Analysis* (June 1997).

Visit us at www.mhhe.com/rwj

Part V

Long-Term Financing

Part IV discussed capital structure; we determined the relationship between the firm's debt-equity ratio and the firm's value. The debt we used in Part IV was stylized. In fact, there are many different types of debt. In Part V we discuss how financial managers choose the type of debt that makes the most sense, including straight debt, debt with options, and leasing.

In Chapter 19 we describe the ways firms sell securities to the public. In general, a public issue can be sold as a general cash offer to investors at large, as a privately placed issue with a few institutions, or as a privileged subscription (in the case of equities). We describe the features of these methods and point out some puzzling trends.

In Chapter 20 we describe some basic features of long-term debt. One of the special features of most long-term bonds is that they can be called by the firms before the maturity date. We try to explain why call provisions exist. There are many types of long-term debt, including floating-rate bonds, income bonds, and original-issue discount bonds. We discuss why they exist.

Chapter 21 describes a special form of long-term debt called *leasing*. In general, a rental agreement that lasts for more than one year is a lease. Leases are a source of financing and displace debt in the balance sheet. Many silly reasons are given for leasing, and we present some of them. The major reason for long-term leasing is to lower taxes.

Issuing Securities to the Public

EXECUTIVE SUMMARY

This chapter looks at how corporations issue securities to the investing public. The general procedures for debt and equity are quite similar. This chapter focuses on equity, but the procedures for debt and equity are basically the same.

Before securities can be traded on a securities market, they must be issued to the public. A firm making an issue to the public must satisfy requirements set out in various federal legislation and statutes and enforced by the Securities and Exchange Commission (SEC). In general, investors must be given all material information in the form of a registration statement and prospectus. In the first part of this chapter we discuss what this entails.

A public issue of equity can be sold directly to the public with the help of underwriters. This is called a *general cash offer*. Alternatively, a public equity issue can be sold to the firm's existing stockholders by what is called a *rights offer*. This chapter examines the difference between a general cash offer and a rights offer.

Stock of companies going public for the first time is typically underpriced. We describe this unusual phenomenon and provide a possible explanation.

19.1 The Public Issue

The basic steps in a public offering are depicted in Table 19.1. The Securities Act of 1933 sets forth the federal regulation for all new interstate securities issues. The Securities Exchange Act of 1934 is the basis for regulating securities already outstanding. The SEC administers both acts.

The Basic Procedure for a New Issue

1. Management's first step in any issue of securities to the public is to obtain approval from the board of directors.

2. Next, the firm must prepare and file a **registration statement** with the SEC. This statement contains a great deal of financial information, including a financial history, details of the existing business, proposed financing, and plans for the future. It can easily run to 50 or more pages. The document is required for all public issues of securities with two principal exceptions:

   a. Loans that mature within nine months.

   b. Issues that involve less than $5.0 million.

The second exception is known as the *small-issues exemption.* Issues of less than $5.0 million are governed by **Regulation A,** for which only a brief offering statement—rather than

TABLE 19.1	The Process of Raising Capital	
Steps in Public Offering	**Time**	**Activities**
1. Preunderwriting conferences	Several months	The amount of money to be raised and the type of security to be issued are discussed. The underwriting syndicate and selling group are put together. The underwriting contract is negotiated. Board approval is obtained.
2. Registration statements filed and approved	A 20-day waiting period	The registration statement contains all relevant financial and business information.
3. Pricing the issue	Usually not before the last day of the registration period	For seasoned offerings the price is set close to the prevailing market price. For initial public offerings intensive research and analysis are required.
4. Public offering and sale	Shortly after the last day of the registration period	In a typical firm commitment contract, the underwriter buys a stipulated amount of stock from the firm and sells it at a higher price. The selling group assists in the sale.
5. Market stabilization	Usually 30 days after the offering	The underwriter stands ready to place orders to buy at a specified price on the market.

the above registration statement—is needed. For Regulation A to be operative, no more than $1.5 million may be sold by insiders.

3. The SEC studies the registration statement during a *waiting period*. During this time, the firm may distribute copies of a preliminary **prospectus**. The preliminary prospectus is called a **red herring** because bold red letters are printed on the cover. A prospectus contains much of the information put into the registration statement, and it is given to potential investors by the firm. The company cannot sell the securities during the waiting period. However, oral offers can be made.

A registration statement will become effective on the 20th day after its filing unless the SEC sends a *letter of comment* suggesting changes. After the changes are made, the 20-day waiting period starts anew.

4. The registration statement does not initially contain the price of the new issue. On the effective date of the registration statement, a price is determined and a full-fledged selling effort gets under way. A final prospectus must accompany the delivery of securities or confirmation of sale, whichever comes first.

5. **Tombstone** advertisements are used during and after the waiting period. An example is reproduced in Figure 19.1.

Concept Questions

1. Describe the basic procedures in a new issue.
2. What is a registration statement?

19.2 Alternative Issue Methods

When a company decides to issue a new security, it can sell it as a public issue or a private issue. If it is a public issue, the firm is required to register the issue with the SEC. If the issue is sold to fewer than 35 investors, it can be treated as a private issue. A registration statement is not required in this case.[1]

There are two kinds of public issues: the *general cash offer* and the *rights offer*. Cash offers are sold to all interested investors, and rights offers are sold to existing shareholders.

---

[1]However, regulation significantly restricts the resale of unregistered securities. The purchaser must hold the securities at least two years.

FIGURE 19.1   An Example of a Tombstone Advertisement

58,750,000 Shares

Consolidated Rail Corporation

Common Stock

(per value $1.00 per share)

Price $28 Per Share

The shares are being sold by the United States Government pursuant to the Conrail Privatization Act. The Company will not receive any proceeds from the sale of the shares.

Upon request, a copy of the Prospectus describing these securities and the business of the Company may be obtained within any state from any Underwriter who may legally distribute it within such State. The securities are offered only by means of the Prospectus, and this announcement is neither an offer to sell nor a solicitation of any offer to buy.

52,000,000 Shares

This portion of the offering is being offered in the United States and Canada by the undersigned.

Goldman, Sachs & Co.

The First Boston Corporation

Merrill Lynch Capital Markets

Morgan Stanley & Co.
Incorporated

Salomon Brothers Inc.

Shearson Lehman Brothers Inc.

Alex, Brown & Sons	Dillion, Read & Co. Inc.	Donaldson, Lufkin & Jenrette	Drexel Burnham Lambert	Hambrecht & Quist	E.F. Hutton & Company Inc.

Alex, Brown & Sons   Dillion, Read & Co. Inc.   Donaldson, Lufkin & Jenrette   Drexel Burnham Lambert   Hambrecht & Quist   E.F. Hutton & Company Inc.

Kidder, Peabody & Co.   Lazard Freres & Co.   Montgomery Securities   Prudential-Bache Capital Funding   Robertson, Colman & Stephens

L.F. Rothschild, Unterberg, Towbin, Inc.   Smith Barney, Harris Upham & Co.   Wertheim Schroder & Co.   Dean Witter Reynolds Inc.

William Blair & Company   J.C. Bradford & Co.   Dain Bosworth   A.G. Edwards & Sons, Inc.   McDonald & Co.   Oppenheimer & Co., Inc.

Piper, Jaffray & Hopwood   Prescott, Ball & Turben, Inc.   Thomson McKinnon Securities Inc.   Wheat, First Securities, Inc.

Advest, Inc.   American Securities Corporation   Arnhold and S. Bleichroeder, Inc.   Robert W. Baird & Co.   Bateman Eichler, Hill Richards

Sanford C. Bernstein & Co., Inc.   Blunt Ellis & Loewi   Boettcher & Company, Inc.   Burns Fry and Timmins Inc.   Butcher & Singer Inc.   Cowen & Company

Dominion Securities Corporation   Eberstadt Fleming Inc.   Eppler, Guerin & Tuner, Inc.   First of Michigan Corporation   First Southwest Company

Furman Seiz Mager Dietz & Birney   Gruntal & Co., Incorporated   Howard, Well, Labouisse, Friedrichs   Interstate Securities Corporation

Janney Montgomery Scott Inc.   Johnson, Lane, Space, Smith & Co., Inc.   Jonston, Lemon & Co.   Josephthal & Co.   Ladenburg, Thalman & Co.

Cyrus J. Lawrence   Legg Mason Wood Walker   Morgan Keegan & Company, Inc.   Moseley Securities Corporation   Needham & Company, Inc.

Neuberger & Berman   The Ohio Company   Rauscher Pierce Refsnes, Inc.   The Robinson-Humphrey Company, Inc.   Rothschild Inc.   Stephens Inc.

Stifel, Nicolaus & Company   Sutro & Co.   Tucker, Anthony & R. L. Day, Inc.   Underwood, Neuhaus & Co.   Wood Gundy Corp.

This special bracket of minority-owned and controlled firms assisted the Co-Lead Managers in the United States Offering pursuant to the Conrail Privatization Act.

AIBC Investment Services Corporation   **Daniels & Bell, Inc.**   **Doley Securities, Inc.**

WR Lazard Securities Corporations   **Pryon, Govan, Counts & Co. Inc.**   **Muriel Siebert & Co., Inc.**

6,750,000 Shares

This Portion of the offering is being offered outside the United States and Canada by the undersigned.

Goldman Sachs International Corp.

First Boston International Limited

Merrill Lynch Capital Markets

Morgan Stanley International

Salomon Brothers International Limited

Shearson Lehman Brothers International

Algemene Bank Nederland N.V.   Banque Bruxelles Lambert S.A.   Banque Nationale de Paris   Cazenove & Co.   The Nikko Securities Co., (Europe) Ltd.

Nomura International   N. M. Rothschild & Sons   J. Henry Schroder Wagg & Co.   Société Générate   S. G. Warburg Securities

ABC International Ltd.   Banque Paribas Capital Markets Limited   Caisse Nationale de Credit Agricole   Campagnie de Banque et dinvestissements, CBI

Crédit Lyonnais   Daiwa Europe   IMI Capital Markets (UK) Ltd.   Joh. Berenberg, Gossler & Co.   Leu Securities Limited

Morgan Grenfell & Co.   Peterbroeck, van Campenhout & Cie SCS   Swiss Volksbank   Vereins- und Westbank
Aktiengesellschaft

J. Vontobel & Co. Ltd   M.M. Warburg-Brinckmann, Wirtz & Co.   Westdeutsche Landesbank   Yamaichi International (Europe)
Girozentrale   Limited

March 27, 1987

TABLE 19.2	The Methods of Issuing New Securities	
Method	**Type**	**Definition**
Public		
Traditional negotiated cash offer	Firm-commitment cash offer	Company negotiates an agreement with an investment banker to underwrite and distribute the new stocks or bonds. A specified number of shares is bought by underwriters and sold at a higher price.
	Best-efforts cash offer	Company has investment bankers sell as many of the new shares as possible at the agreed-upon price. There is no guarantee concerning how much cash will be raised.
Privileged subscription	Direct rights offer	Company offers new stock directly to its existing shareholders.
	Standby rights offer	Like the direct rights offer, this contains a privileged subscription arrangement with existing shareholders. The net proceeds are guaranteed by the underwriters.
Nontraditional cash offer	Shelf cash offer	Qualifying companies can authorize all shares they expect to sell over a two-year period and sell them when needed.
	Competitive firm cash offer	Company can elect to award underwriting contract through a public auction instead of negotiation.
Private	Direct placement	Securities are sold directly to purchaser, who cannot resell securities for at least two years.

For information on an IPO try www.ipo.com, or www.ipohome.com

Equity is sold by both the cash offer and the rights offer, though almost all debt is sold by cash offer.

The first public equity issue that is made by a company is referred to as an **initial public offering (IPO)** or an **unseasoned new issue.** All initial public offerings are cash offers because, if the firm's existing shareholders wanted to buy the shares, the firm would not need to sell them publicly. More than $5 billion was raised in 116 IPOs in 1994. A **seasoned new issue** refers to a new issue where the company's securities have been previously issued. A seasoned new issue of common stock may be made by using a cash offer or a rights offer.

These methods of issuing new securities are shown in Table 19.2 and discussed in the next few sections.[2]

19.3 The Cash Offer

As mentioned above, stock is sold to all interested investors in a **cash offer.** If the cash offer is a public one, **investment banks** are usually involved. Investment banks are financial intermediaries who perform a wide variety of services. In addition to aiding in the sale of securities, they may facilitate mergers and other corporate reorganizations, act as brokers to both individual and institutional clients, and trade for their own accounts. You may very well have heard of large Wall Street investment banking houses such as Goldman Sachs, Merrill Lynch, and Salomon Smith Barney. Table 19.3 lists the leading investment bankers for U.S. public security offerings.

---

[2]Table 19.2 describes the main methods for issuing new securities in the U.S. Most initial public offerings in the U.S. use the negotiated cash offer method known as *bookbuilding*. Bookbuilding refers to the way an underwriter builds a book of potential orders and uses the book to set a price. Bookbuilding is the method of equity underwriting choice in most countries (but not all countries). The alternative to bookbuilding is the *auction*. For example, the U.S. Treasury sells Treasury bills and bonds using auctions. With auctions, potential investors submit bids including the number of securities they wish to hold and the price. The securities are sold to the investor with the highest bids.

TABLE 19.3	Top Underwriters of U.S. Debt and Equity
The Leading U.S. Underwriters—1997	**Manager**
	Merrill Lynch
	Salomon Smith Barney
	Morgan Stanley Dean Witter
	Goldman, Sachs
	Lehman Brothers
	JP Morgan
	Credit Suisse First Boston
	Bear, Stearns
	Donaldson, Lufkin & Jenrette
	Chase Manhattan

For corporate issuers, investment bankers perform services such as the following:

Formulating the method used to issue the securities.

Pricing the new securities.

Selling the new securities.

There are two basic methods of issuing securities for cash.

1. **Firm commitment.** Under this method, the investment bank (or a group of investment banks) buys the securities for less than the offering price and accepts the risk of not being able to sell them. Because this function involves risk, we say that the investment banker *underwrites* the securities in a firm commitment. In other words, when participating in a firm-commitment offering, the investment banker acts as an *underwriter.* (Because firm commitments are so prevalent, we will use *investment banker* and *underwriter* interchangeably in this chapter.)

To minimize the risks here, investment bankers combine to form an underwriting group (**syndicate**) to share the risk and to help sell the issue. In such a group, one or more managers arrange or co-manage the deal. The manager is designated as the lead manager or principal manager. The lead manager typically has responsibility for all aspects of the issue. The other investment bankers in the syndicate serve primarily to sell the issue to their clients.

The difference between the underwriter's buying price and the offering price is called the *spread* or *discount.* It is the basic compensation received by the underwriter. Sometimes the underwriter will get noncash compensation in the form of warrants or stock in addition to the spread.

Firm-commitment underwriting is really just a purchase-sale arrangement, and the syndicate's fee is the spread. The issuer receives the full amount of the proceeds less the spread, and all the risk is transferred to the underwriter. If the underwriter cannot sell all of the issue at the agreed-upon offering price, it may need to lower the price on the unsold shares. However, because the offering price usually is not set until the underwriters have investigated how receptive the market is to the issue, this risk is usually minimal. This is particularly true with seasoned new issues because the price of the new issue can be based on prior trades in the security.

2. **Best efforts.** The underwriter bears risk with a firm commitment because it buys the entire issue. Conversely, the syndicate avoids this risk under a best-efforts offering because it does not purchase the shares. Instead, it merely acts as an agent, receiving a commission for each share sold. The syndicate is legally bound to use its best efforts to sell the

TABLE 19.4	Gross Proceeds ($)	All Offerings	Firm Commitment	Best Efforts	Fraction Best Efforts
Initial Public Offerings of Stock Categorized by Gross Proceeds: 1977–1982	100,000–1,999,999	243	68	175	0.720
	2,000,000–3,999,999	311	165	146	0.469
	4,000,000–5,999,999	156	133	23	0.147
	6,000,000–9,999,999	137	122	15	0.109
	10,000,000–120,174,195	180	176	4	0.022
	All offerings	1,027	664	363	0.353

From J. R. Ritter, "The Costs of Going Public," *Journal of Financial Economics* 19 (1987). © Elsevier Science Publishers B.V. (North-Holland).

securities at the agreed-upon offering price. If the issue cannot be sold at the offering price, it is usually withdrawn.

This form is more common for initial public offerings than for seasoned new issues. In addition, a recent study by Jay Ritter shows that best-efforts offerings are generally used for small IPOs and firm-commitment offerings are generally used for large IPOs. His results are reproduced in our Table 19.4. The last column in the table best illustrates his finding.

For either firm-commitment or best-efforts issues, the principal underwriter is permitted to buy shares if the market price falls below the offering price. The purpose is to *support* the market and *stabilize* the price from temporary downward pressure. If the issue remains unsold after a time (for example, 30 days), members may leave the group and sell their shares at whatever price the market will allow.

Many underwriting contracts contain a **Green Shoe provision,** which gives the members of the underwriting group the option to purchase additional shares at the offering price.[3] The stated reason for the Green Shoe option is to cover excess demand and oversubscription. Green Shoe options usually last for about 30 days and involve no more than 15 percent of the newly issued shares. The Green Shoe option is a benefit to the underwriting syndicate and a cost to the issuer. If the market price of the new issue goes above the offering price within 30 days, the underwriters can buy shares from the issuer and immediately resell the shares to the public.

The period after a new issue is initially sold to the public is called the *aftermarket*. During this period, the members of the underwriting syndicate generally do not sell shares of the new issue for less than the offer price.

Almost all underwriting agreements contain *lockups*. Such arrangements specify how long insiders must wait after an IPO before they can sell some of their stock. Typically lockup periods are set at 180 days. Lockups are important because it is not unusual for the number of locked up insider shares to be larger than the number of shares held by the public. Thus there is the possibility that, when the lockup period ends, a large number of shares will be sold by insiders, thereby depressing share prices.

Investment Banks

Investment banks are at the heart of new security issues. They provide advice, market the securities (after investigating the market's receptiveness to the issue), and underwrite the proceeds. They accept the risk that the market price may fall between the date the offering price is set and the time the issue is sold.

In addition, investment banks have the responsibility of pricing fairly. When a firm goes public, particularly for the first time, the buyers know relatively little about the firm's

[3]The Green Shoe Corp. was the first firm to allow this provision.

Robert S. Hansen on the Economic Rationale for the Firm Commitment Offer

Underwriters provide four main functions: certification, monitoring, marketing, and risk bearing.

Certification assures investors that the offer price is fair. Investors have concerns about whether the offer price is unfairly above the stock's intrinsic value. Certification increases issuer value by reducing investor doubt about fairness, making a better offer price possible.

Monitoring of issuing firm management and performance builds value because it adds to shareholders' ordinary monitoring. Underwriters provide collective monitoring on behalf of both capital suppliers and current shareholders. Individual shareholder monitoring is limited because the shareholder bears the entire cost, whereas all owners collectively share the benefit, pro rata. By contrast, in underwriter monitoring all stockholders share both the costs and benefits, pro rata.

Due diligence and legal liability for the proceeds give investors assurance. However, what makes certification and monitoring credible is lead bank reputation in competitive capital markets, where they are disciplined over time. Evidence that irreputable behavior is damaging to a bank's future abounds. Capital market participants punish poorly performing banks by refusing to hire them. The participants pay banks for certification and meaningful monitoring in "quasi-rents" in the spread, which represent the fair cost of "renting" the reputations.

Marketing is finding long-term investors who can be persuaded to buy the securities at the offer price. This would not be needed if demand for new shares were "horizontal." There is much evidence that issuers and syndicates repeatedly invest in costly marketing practices, such as expensive road shows to identify and expand investor interest. Another is organizing members to avoid redundant pursuit of the same customers. Lead banks provide trading support in the issuer's stock for several weeks after the offer.

Underwriting risk is like the risk of selling a put option. The syndicate agrees to buy all new shares at the offer price and resell them at that price or at the market price, whichever is lower. Thus, once the offer begins, the syndicate is exposed to potential losses on unsold inventory should the market price fall below the offer price. The risk is likely to be small, because offerings are typically well prepared for quick sale.

Robert S. Hansen is the Freeman Senior Research Professor of Finance at Tulane University.

operations. After all, it is not rational for a buyer of, say, only 1,000 shares of stock to study the company at length. Instead, the buyer must rely on the judgment of the investment bank, who has presumably examined the firm in detail. Given this asymmetry of information, what prevents the investment banker from pricing the issued securities too high? While the underwriter has a short-run incentive to price high, it has a long-run incentive to make sure that its customers do not pay too much; they might desert the underwriter in future deals if they lose money on this one. Thus, as long as investment banks plan to stay in business over time, it is in their self-interest to price fairly.

In other words, financial economists argue that each investment bank has a reservoir of "reputation capital."[4] Mispricing of new issues, as well as unethical dealings, is likely to reduce this reputation capital.

One measure of this reputation capital is the pecking order among the investment banks. MBA students are aware of this order because they know that accepting a job with a top-tier firm is universally regarded as more prestigious than accepting a job with a lower-tier firm. This pecking order can be seen in Figure 19.1. The investment banks listed diagonally in the figure are considered the most prestigious. These appear alphabetically so that one cannot distinguish the relative status of these firms from the figure. The next set of firms, running from Alex. Brown & Sons to Dean Witter Reynolds, is also in alphabetical order.

---

[4]For example, see R. Carter and S. Manaster, "Initial Public Offerings and Underwriter Reputation," unpublished Iowa State and University of Utah working paper (1988); and R. Beatty and J. Ritter, "Investment Banking, Reputation and the Underpricing of Initial Public Offerings," *Journal of Financial Economics* (1986).

By noting when the alphabetical order begins anew, one can determine the number of firms in each tier.

Investment banks put great importance in their relative rankings and view downward movement in their placement with much distaste. While this jockeying for position may seem as unimportant as the currying of royal favor in the court of Louis XVI, it is explained by the above discussion. In any industry where reputation is so important, the firms in the industry must guard theirs with great vigilance.

There are two basic methods for selecting the syndicate. In a **competitive offer**, the issuing firm can offer its securities to the underwriter bidding highest. In a **negotiated offer**, the issuing firm works with one underwriter. Because the firm generally does not negotiate with many underwriters concurrently, negotiated deals may suffer from lack of competition.

While competitive bidding occurs frequently in other areas of commerce, it may surprise you that negotiated deals in investment banking occur with all but the largest issuing firms. Investment bankers argue that they must expend much time and effort learning about the issuer before setting an issue price and a fee schedule. Except in the case of large issues, these underwriters could not expend the time and effort without the near certainty of receiving the contract.

Studies generally show that issuing costs are higher in negotiated deals than in competitive ones. However, many financial economists argue that issuing firms are not necessarily hurt by negotiated deals. They point out that the underwriter gains much information about the issuing firm through negotiation, information likely to increase the probability of a successful offering.[5]

The Offering Price

Determining the correct offering price is the most difficult thing the lead investment bank must do for an initial public offering. The issuing firm faces a potential cost if the offering price is set too high or too low. If the issue is priced too high, it may be unsuccessful and be withdrawn. If the issue is priced below the true market price, the issuer's existing shareholders will experience an opportunity loss.

Ibbotson has found that unseasoned new equity issues typically have been offered at 11 percent below their true market price.[6] Underpricing helps new shareholders earn a higher return on the shares they buy. However, the existing shareholders of the issuing firm are not necessarily helped by underpricing. To them it is an indirect cost of issuing new securities.

Several studies have confirmed the early research of Ibbotson. For example, Ritter examined approximately 6,974 firms that went public from 1975 through 2000 in the United States. He found that the average IPO rose in price 17.8 percent in the first day of trading following issuance (see Table 19.5). These figures are not annualized!

Another recent dramatic example of underpricing came with the IPO of Shiva Corporation. Shiva makes hardware and software that allow desktop and laptop computers to hook directly into a local area network from outside the office. The initial offering, on November 18, 1994, of 2.76 million shares priced at $15 rose $16½ to $31½ by the end of the first trading day. Goldman Sachs, head of the underwriting syndicate that underwrote

[5]This choice has been studied recently by Robert S. Hansen and Naveen Khanna, "Why Negotiation with a Single Syndicate May Be Preferred to Making Syndicates Compete: The Problem of Trapped Bidders," *Journal of Business* 67 (1994) and S. Bhagat, "The Effect of Management's Choice between Negotiated and Competitive Equity Offerings on Shareholder Wealth," *Journal of Financial and Quantitative Analysis* (1986); and D. Logue and R. Jarrow, "Negotiation vs. Competitive Bidding in the Sales of Securities by Public Utilities," *Financial Management* 7 (1978).

[6]R. Ibbotson, "Price Performance of Common Stock New Issues," *Journal of Financial Economics* 2 (1975).

TABLE 19.5	Year	Number of Offerings*	Average First-Day Return, %[†]	Gross Proceeds ($ in millions)[‡]
Number of Offerings, Average First-Day Return, and Gross Proceeds of Initial Public Offerings: 1975–2000	1975–79	112	5.7	1,124
	1980–89	2,348	6.9	62,596
	1990–99	4,129	20.9	294,070
	2000	385	55.5	66,100
	Total	6,974	17.8	423,890

*The number of offerings excludes IPOs with an offer price of less than $5.00, ADRs, best efforts offers, unit offers, Regulation A offerings (small issues, raising less than $1.5 million during the 1980s), real estate investment trusts (REITs), partnerships, and closed-end funds.

[†]First-day returns are computed as the percentage return from the offering price to the first closing market price.

[‡]Gross proceeds data are from Securities Data Co. and exclude overallotment options but include the international tranche, if any. No adjustments for inflation have been made.

SOURCE: Professor Jay R. Ritter, University of Florida.

TABLE 19.6	Annual Sales of Issuing Firms	Number of Firms	1980–89 First-Day Average Return	Number of Firms	1990–98 First-Day Average Return	Number of Firms	1999–2000 First-Day Average Return
Average First-Day Returns, Categorized by Sales, for IPOs: 1980–2000*	$0≤Sales<$10m	401	10.0%	671	17.6%	333	68.0%
	$10m≤Sales<$20m	264	8.9	373	18.6	128	84.5
	$20m≤Sales<$50m	496	7.8	774	17.5	135	78.5
	$50m≤Sales<$100m	319	6.3	534	13.2	79	57.9
	$100m≤Sales<$200m	215	4.8	414	11.9	51	34.1
	$200m≤Sales	252	3.8	573	8.8	74	23.4

*Data are from Securities Data Co., with corrections by the authors. All sales have been converted into dollars of January 2000 purchasing power, using the Consumer Price Index. Sales are for the last 12 months prior to going public. There are 6,086 IPOs, after excluding IPOs with an offer price of less than $5.00 per share, unit offerings, REITs, ADRs, closed-end funds, and those with missing sales. The average first-day return is 19.0 percent. Sales are measured in millions.

SOURCE: Tim Loughran and Jay R. Ritter "Why Has IPO Underpricing Increased Over Time?" (University of Florida Working Paper, October 2001, as updated by the authors).

the issue, was quoted as saying that pricing an IPO is not just about what the market will bear at the time, but "we are trying to get the company launched for the long term and build a good investor base."[7]

Underpricing: A Possible Explanation

There are several possible explanations for underpricing. But so far there is no agreement among scholars as to which explanation is correct. In our opinion there are two important facts associated with the underpricing puzzle that are key elements to a unifying theory. First, much of the apparent underpricing is concentrated in smaller issues. This point is documented in Table 19.6, which shows that underpricing tends to be attributable to firms with little or no sales in the prior year. These firms tend to be young firms with uncertain future prospects. The increased uncertainty in some way probably attracts risk-averse investors only if underpricing exists. Second, when the price of a new issue is too low, the issue is often *oversubscribed*. This means investors will not be able to buy all of the shares they want, and the underwriters will allocate the shares among investors. The average investor will find it difficult to get shares in an oversubscribed offering because there will not be enough shares

---

[7]*The New York Times,* February 19, 1995, "Anatomy of a High Flying IPO, Problems and All," p. 7.

Jay Ritter on IPO Underpricing around the World

The United States is not the only country in which initial public offerings of common stock (IPOs) are underpriced. The phenomenon exists in every country with a stock market, although the extent of underpricing varies from country to country.

In general, countries with developed capital markets have more moderate underpricing than those with emerging markets. During the Internet bubble of 1999–2000, however, underpricing in the developed capital markets increased dramatically. In the U.S., for example, the average first-day return during 1999–2000 was 65 percent. At the same time that underpricing in the developed capital markets increased, the underpricing of IPOs sold to residents of China moderated. The Chinese average has come down to a mere 257 percent, which is lower than it had been in the early and mid-1990s. After the bursting of the Internet bubble in mid-2000, the level of underpricing in the U.S., Germany, and other developed capital markets has returned to more traditional levels, and the volume of IPOs slowed to a trickle in 2001–2003.

The table below gives a summary of the average first-day returns on IPOs for 38 countries around the world, with the figures collected from a number of studies by various authors. In countries where the first-day price change is limited by regulations, the return is measured until price limits are no longer binding.

Country	Sample Size	Time Period	Average First-Day Return	Country	Sample Size	Time Period	Average First-Day Return
Australia	381	1976–1995	12.1%	Malaysia	401	1980–1998	104.1%
Austria	76	1984–1999	6.5	Mexico	37	1987–1990	33.0
Belgium	86	1984–1999	14.6	Netherlands	143	1982–1999	10.2
Brazil	62	1979–1990	78.5	New Zealand	201	1979–1999	23.0
Canada	500	1971–1999	6.3	Nigeria	63	1989–1993	19.1
Chile	55	1982–1997	8.8	Norway	68	1984–1996	12.5
China	432	1990–2000	256.9	Philippines	104	1987–1997	22.7
Denmark	117	1984–1998	5.4	Poland	149	1991–1998	35.6
Finland	99	1984–1997	10.1	Portugal	21	1992–1998	10.6
France	571	1983–2000	11.6	Singapore	128	1973–1992	31.4
Germany	407	1978–1999	27.7	South Africa	118	1980–1991	32.7
Greece	129	1987–1994	51.7	Spain	99	1986–1998	10.7
Hong Kong	334	1980–1996	15.9	Sweden	251	1980–1994	34.1
India	98	1992–1993	35.3	Switzerland	120	1983–2000	34.9
Indonesia	106	1989–1994	15.1	Taiwan	293	1986–1998	31.1
Israel	285	1990–1994	12.1	Thailand	292	1987–1997	46.7
Italy	164	1985–2000	23.9	Turkey	138	1990–1996	13.6
Japan	1,689	1970–2001	28.4	United Kingdom	3,122	1959–2001	17.4
Korea	477	1980–1996	74.3	United States	14,840	1960–2001	18.4

SOURCE: Jay R. Ritter is Cordell Professor of Finance at the University of Florida. An outstanding scholar, he is well-respected for his insightful analyses of new issues and companies going public.

to go around. While initial public offerings have positive initial returns on average, a significant fraction of them have price drops. An investor submitting an order for all new issues may find that he or she will be allocated more shares in issues that go down in price.

Consider this tale of two investors. Ms. Smarts knows precisely what companies are worth when their shares are offered. Mr. Average knows only that prices usually rise one month after the IPO. Armed with this information, Mr. Average decides to buy 1,000 shares of every IPO. Does Mr. Average actually earn an abnormally high average return across all initial offerings?

The answer is no, and at least one reason is Ms. Smarts. For example, because Ms. Smarts knows that company *XYZ* is underpriced, she invests all her money in its IPO. When the issue is oversubscribed, the underwriters must allocate the shares between Ms. Smarts and Mr. Average. If they do it on a pro rata basis and if Ms. Smarts has bid for twice as many shares as Mr. Average, she will get two shares for each one Mr. Average receives. The net result is that when an issue is underpriced, Mr. Average cannot buy as much of it as he wants.

Ms. Smarts also knows that company *ABC* is overpriced. In this case she avoids its IPO altogether, and Mr. Average ends up with a full 1,000 shares. To summarize, Mr. Average receives fewer shares when more knowledgeable investors swarm to buy an underpriced issue, but he gets all he wants when the smart money avoids the issue.

This is called the *winner's curse,* and it explains much of the reason why IPOs have such a large average return. When the average investor wins and gets his allocation, it is because those who knew better avoided the issue. To counteract the winner's curse and attract the average investor, underwriters underprice issues.[8]

Concept	
Questions	1. **Describe a firm-commitment underwriting and a best-efforts underwriting.**
	2. **Suppose that a stockbroker calls you up out of the blue and offers to sell you some shares of a new issue. Do you think the issue will do better or worse than average?**

19.4 The Announcement of New Equity and the Value of the Firm

It seems reasonable to believe that new long-term financing is arranged by firms after positive net present value projects are put together. As a consequence, when the announcement of external financing is made, the firm's market value should go up. As we mentioned in an earlier chapter, this is precisely the opposite of what actually happens in the case of new equity financing. Asquith and Mullins, Masulis and Korwar, and Mikkelson and Partch have all found that the market value of existing equity drops on the announcement of a new issue of common stock.[9] Plausible reasons for this strange result include:

1. *Managerial Information.* If managers have superior information about the market value of the firm, they may know when the firm is overvalued. If they do, they might attempt to issue new shares of stock when the market value exceeds the correct value. This will benefit existing shareholders. However, the potential new shareholders are not stupid. They will infer overvaluation from the new issue, thereby bidding down the stock price on the announcement date of the issue.

2. *Debt Capacity.* The stereotypical firm chooses a debt-to-equity ratio that balances the tax shield from the debt with the cost of financial distress. When the managers of a firm have special information that the probability of financial distress has risen, the firm is more likely to raise capital through stock than through debt. If the market infers this chain of events, the stock price should fall on the announcement date of an equity issue.

3. *Falling Earnings.*[10] When managers raise capital in amounts that are unexpectedly large (as most unanticipated financings will be) and if investors have a reasonable fix on the

---

[8]This explanation was first suggested in K. Rock, "Why New Issues Are Underpriced," *Journal of Financial Economics* 15 (1986).

[9]P. Asquith and D. Mullins, "Equity Issues and Offering Dilution," *Journal of Financial Economics* 15 (1986); R. Masulis and A. N. Korwar, "Seasoned Equity Offerings: An Empirical Investigation," *Journal of Financial Economics* 15 (1986); and W. H. Mikkelson and M. M. Partch, "The Valuation Effects of Security Offerings and the Issuance Process," *Journal of Financial Economics* 15 (1986).

[10]Robert S. Haugen and Claire Crutchley, "Corporate Earnings and Financings, An Empirical Analysis," *Journal of Business* 20 (1990).

firm's upcoming investments and dividend payouts (as they do because capital expenditure announcements are often well known, as are future dividends), the unanticipated financings are roughly equal to unanticipated shortfalls in earnings (this follows directly from the firm's sources and uses of funds identity). Therefore, an announcement of a new stock issue will also reveal a future earnings shortfall.

Concept
Question

1. **What are some reasons that the price of stock drops on the announcement of a new equity issue?**

19.5 The Cost of New Issues

Issuing securities to the public is not free, and the costs of different issuing methods are important determinants of which will be used. The costs fall into six categories.

1. Spread or underwriting discount

   The spread is the difference between the price the issue receives and the price offered to the public.

2. Other direct expenses

   These are costs incurred by the issuer that are not part of the compensation to underwriters. They include filing fees, legal fees, and taxes—all reported in the prospectus.

3. Indirect expenses

   These costs are not reported in the prospectus and include management time on the new issue.

4. Abnormal returns

   In a seasoned issue of stock, the price drops by 3 percent to 4 percent upon the announcement of the issue. The drop protects new shareholders against the firm's selling overpriced stock to new shareholders.

5. Underpricing

   For initial public offerings, the stock typically rises substantially after the issue date. This is a cost to the firm because the stock is sold for less than its efficient price in the aftermarket.[11]

6. Green Shoe option

   The Green Shoe option gives the underwriters the right to buy additional shares at the offer price to cover overallotments. This is a cost to the firm because the underwriter will only buy additional shares when the offer price is below the price in the aftermarket.

An interesting study by Lee, Lockhead, Ritter, and Zhao reports two of these six costs: underwriting discount and other direct expenses.[12] Their findings for both equity offerings and debt offerings are reproduced in Table 19.7. Three conclusions emerge from the table.

---

[11]Some people have argued that the price in the aftermarket is not efficient after all. However, R. Ibbotson, "Price Performance of Common Stock New Issues," *Journal of Financial Economics* 2 (1975), shows that, on average, new issues exhibit no abnormal price performance over the first five years following issuance. This result is generally viewed as being consistent with market efficiency. That is, the stock obtains an efficient price immediately following issuance and remains at an efficient price.

[12]The notion of economies of scale has been contested by Oya Altinkilic and Robert S. Hansen, "Are There Scale Economies in Underwriting Spreads? Evidence of Rising External Financing Costs," *Review of Financial Studies* 13 (2000). They provide data and analysis that underwriter cost will be U-shaped.

TABLE 19.7 Direct Costs as a Percentage of Gross Proceeds for Equity (IPOs and SEOs) and Straight and Convertible Bonds Offered by Domestic Operating Companies: 1990–94*

	Equity								Bonds							
	IPOs				SEOs				Convertible Bonds				Straight Bonds			
Proceeds ($ in millions)	Number of Issues	Gross Spread	Other Direct Expense	Total Direct Cost	Number of Issues	Gross Spread	Other Direct Expense	Total Direct Cost	Number of Issues	Gross Spread	Other Direct Expense	Total Direct Cost	Number of Issues	Gross Spread	Other Direct Expense	Total Direct Cost
2–9.99	337	9.05%	7.91%	16.96%	167	7.72%	5.56%	13.28%	4	6.07%	2.68%	8.75%	32	2.07%	2.32%	4.39%
10–19.99	389	7.24	4.39	11.63	310	6.23	2.49	8.72	14	5.48	3.18	8.66	78	1.36	1.40	2.76
20–39.99	533	7.01	2.69	9.70	425	5.60	1.33	6.93	18	4.16	1.95	6.11	89	1.54	.88	2.42
40–59.99	215	6.96	1.76	8.72	261	5.05	.82	5.87	28	3.26	1.04	4.30	90	.72	.60	1.32
60–79.99	79	6.74	1.46	8.20	143	4.57	.61	5.18	47	2.64	.59	3.23	92	1.76	.58	2.34
80–99.99	51	6.47	1.44	7.91	71	4.25	.48	4.73	13	2.43	.61	3.04	112	1.55	.61	2.16
100–199.99	106	6.03	1.03	7.06	152	3.85	.37	4.22	57	2.34	.42	2.76	409	1.77	.54	2.31
200–499.99	47	5.67	.86	6.53	55	3.26	.21	3.47	27	1.99	.19	2.18	170	1.79	.40	2.19
500 and up	10	5.21	.51	5.72	9	3.03	.12	3.15	3	2.00	.09	2.09	20	1.39	.25	1.64
Total	1,767	7.31%	3.69%	11.00%	1,593	5.44%	1.67%	7.11%	211	2.92%	.87%	3.79%	1,092	1.62%	.62%	2.24%

*IPO refers to initial public offering and SEO refers to seasoned equity offering.

SOURCE: Inmoo Lee, Scott Lockhead, Jay Ritter, and Quanshui Zhao, "The Costs of Raising Capital," *Journal of Financial Research* 1 (Spring 1996).

TABLE 19.8	Proceeds ($ in millions)	Number of Issues	Gross Spread	Other Direct Expense	Total Direct Cost	Underpricing
Direct and Indirect Costs, in Percentages, of Equity IPOs: 1990–94	2–9.99	337	9.05%	7.91%	16.96%	16.36%
	10–19.99	389	7.24	4.39	11.63	9.65
	20–39.99	533	7.01	2.69	9.70	12.48
	40–59.99	215	6.96	1.76	8.72	13.65
	60–79.99	79	6.74	1.46	8.20	11.31
	80–99.99	51	6.47	1.44	7.91	8.91
	100–199.99	106	6.03	1.03	7.06	7.16
	200–499.99	47	5.67	.86	6.53	5.70
	500 and up	10	5.21	.51	5.72	7.53
	Total	1,767	7.31%	3.69%	11.00%	12.05%

As we have discussed, the underpricing of IPOs is an additional cost to the issuer. To give a better idea of the total cost of going public, Table 19.8 combines the information in Table 19.7 for IPOs with data on the underpricing experience by these firms. Comparing the total direct costs (in the fifth column) to the underpricing (in the sixth column), we see that they are roughly the same size, so the direct costs are only about half of the total. Overall, across all size groups, the total direct costs amount to 11 percent of the amount raised and the underpricing amounts to 12 percent.

SOURCE: Inmoo Lee, Scott Lockhead, Jay Ritter, and Quanshui Zhao, "The Costs of Raising Capital," *Journal of Financial Research* 1 (Spring 1996).

1. The costs in each category, for both equity offerings and debt offerings, decline as the gross proceeds of the offering increase. Thus, it appears that issuance costs are subject to substantial economies of scale.[13]

2. The bottom line of Table 19.7 indicates that, across all offerings, direct expenses are higher for equity offers than for debt offers.

3. Last, and perhaps most important, the costs of issuing securities to the public are quite large. For example, total direct expenses are approximately 17 percent for an initial public offering of less than $10,000,000. In addition, Table 19.8 establishes that underpricing costs are another 16.36 percent. This implies that going public for the first time is a weighty decision. While there are many benefits, such as raising needed capital and spreading ownership, the costs cannot be ignored.

Concept
Questions

1. Describe the costs of a new issue of common stock.
2. What conclusions emerge from analyses of Tables 19.7 and 19.8?

19.6 Rights

When new shares of common stock are offered to the general public, the proportionate ownership of existing shareholders is likely to be reduced. However, if a preemptive right is contained in the firm's articles of incorporation, the firm must first offer any new issue of common stock to existing shareholders. This assures each owner his or her proportionate owner's share.

An issue of common stock to existing stockholders is called a *rights offering*. Here, each shareholder is issued an *option* to buy a specified number of new shares from the firm at a specified price within a specified time, after which the rights expire. For example, a firm

---

[13]Among the most interesting developments in the initial public offering market is that almost all underwriter spreads in recent offerings have been exactly 7 percent. This is documented in H. C. Chen and Jay R. Ritter, "The Seven-Percent Solution," *Journal of Finance* (June 2000); and Robert S. Hansen, "Do Investment Banks Compete in IPO's? The Advent of the 7% Plus Contract," *Journal of Financial Economics* (August 2001).

TABLE 19.9	NATIONAL POWER COMPANY	
Financial Statement before Rights Offering	Balance Sheet and Income Statement	

Balance Sheet

Assets	Shareholder Equity	
	Common stock	$10,000,000
	Retained earnings	10,000,000
Total $20,000,000	Total	$20,000,000

Income Statement

Earnings before taxes	$ 3,030,303
Taxes (34%)	1,030,303
Net income	$ 2,000,000
Earnings per share	2
Shares outstanding	1,000,000
Market price per share	20
Total market value	$20,000,000

whose stock is selling at $30 may let current stockholders buy a fixed number of shares at $10 per share within two months. The terms of the option are evidenced by certificates known as *share warrants* or *rights*. Such rights are often traded on securities exchanges or over the counter.

The Mechanics of a Rights Offering

The various considerations confronting a financial manager in a rights offering are illustrated by the situation of the National Power Company, whose initial financial statements are given in Table 19.9.

National Power earns $2 million after taxes and has 1 million shares outstanding. Earnings per share are $2, and the stock sells at 10 times earnings (that is, its price-earnings ratio is 10). The market price of each share is therefore $20. The company plans to raise $5 million of new equity funds by a rights offering.

The process of issuing rights differs from the process of issuing shares of stock for cash. Existing stockholders are notified that they have been given one right for each share of stock they own. Exercise occurs when a shareholder sends payment to the firm's subscription agent (usually a bank) and turns in the required number of rights. Shareholders of National Power will have several choices: (1) subscribe for the full number of entitled shares, (2) order all the rights sold, or (3) do nothing and let the rights expire.

The financial management of National Power must answer the following questions:

1. What price should the existing shareholders be allowed to pay for a share of new stock?
2. How many rights will be required to purchase one share of stock?
3. What effect will the rights offering have on the existing price of the stock?

Subscription Price

In a rights offering, the **subscription price** is the price that existing shareholders are allowed to pay for a share of stock. A rational shareholder will only subscribe to the rights offering if the subscription price is below the market price of the stock on the offer's expiration date. For example, if the stock price at expiration is $13 and the subscription price is $15, no rational shareholder will subscribe. Why pay $15 for something worth $13? National Power chooses a price of $10, which is well below the current market price of $20.

As long as the market price does not fall by half before expiration, the rights offering will succeed.

Number of Rights Needed to Purchase a Share

National Power wants to raise $5 million in new equity. With a subscription price of $10, it must issue 500,000 new shares. This can be determined by dividing the total amount to be raised by the subscription price:

$$\text{Number of new shares} = \frac{\text{Funds to be raised}}{\text{Subscription price}} = \frac{\$5,000,000}{\$10} = 500,000 \text{ shares}$$

Because stockholders typically get one right for each share of stock they own, 1 million rights will be issued by National Power. To determine how many rights must be exercised to get one share of stock, we can divide the number of existing outstanding shares of stock by the number of new shares:

$$\frac{\text{Number of rights needed}}{\text{to buy a share of stock}} = \frac{\text{"Old" shares}}{\text{"New" shares}} = \frac{1,000,000}{500,000} = 2 \text{ rights}$$

Thus, a shareholder must give up two rights plus $10 to receive a share of new stock. If all the stockholders do this, National Power will raise the required $5 million.

It should be clear that the subscription price, the number of new shares, and the number of rights needed to buy a new share of stock are interrelated. If National Power lowers the subscription price, it must issue more new shares to raise $5 million in new equity. Several alternatives appear here:

Subscription Price	Number of New Shares	Number of Rights Needed to Buy a Share of Stock
$20	250,000	4
10	500,000	2
5	1,000,000	1

Effect of Rights Offering on Price of Stock

Rights clearly have value. In the case of National Power, the right to be able to buy a share of stock worth $20 for $10 is valuable.

Suppose a shareholder of National Power owns two shares of stock just before the rights offering. This situation is depicted in Table 19.10. Initially, the price of National Power is $20 per share, so the shareholder's total holding is worth $2 \times \$20 = \$40$. The stockholder who has two shares will receive two rights. The National Power rights offer gives shareholders with two rights the opportunity to purchase one additional share for $10. The holding of the shareholder who exercises these rights and buys the new share would increase to three shares. The value of the new holding would be $40 + $10 = $50 (the $40 initial value plus the $10 paid to the company). Because the stockholder now holds three shares, the price per share would drop to $50/3 = $16.67 (rounded to two decimal places).

The difference between the old share price of $20 and the new share price of $16.67 reflects the fact that the old shares carried rights to subscribe to the new issue. The difference must be equal to the value of one right, that is, $20 − $16.67 = $3.33.

Just as we learned of an ex-dividend date in the previous chapter, there is an **ex-rights date** here. An individual buying the stock prior to the ex-rights date will receive the rights

TABLE 19.10		The Shareholder
The Value to the Individual Shareholder of National Power's Rights	Initial position	
	Number of shares	2
	Share price	$20
	Value of holding	$40
	Terms of offer	
	Subscription price	$10
	Number of rights issued	2
	Number of rights for a share	2
	After offer	
	Number of shares	3
	Value of holding	$50
	Share price	$16.67
	Value of a right	
	Old price − New price	$20 − $16.67 = $3.33
	$\dfrac{\text{New price} - \text{Subscription price}}{\text{Number of rights for a share}}$	($16.67 − $10)/2 = $3.33

TABLE 19.11		
National Power Company Rights Offering	Initial position	
	Number of shares	1 million
	Share price	$20
	Value of firm	$20 million
	Terms of offer	
	Subscription price	$10
	Number of rights issued	1 million
	Number of rights for a share	2
	After offer	
	Number of shares	1.5 million
	Share price	$16.67
	Value of firm	$25 million
	Value of one right	$20 − $16.67 = $3.33
		or ($16.67 − $10)/2 = $3.33

when distributed. An individual buying the stock on or after the ex-rights date will not receive the rights. In our example, the price of the stock prior to the ex-rights date is $20. An individual buying on or after the ex-rights date is not entitled to the rights. The price on or after the ex-rights date is $16.67.

Table 19.11 shows what happens to National Power. If all shareholders exercise their rights, the number of shares will increase to 1.5 million and the value of the firm will increase to $25 million. After the rights offering the value of each share will drop to $16.67 ($25 million/1.5 million).

An investor holding no shares of National Power stock who wants to subscribe to the new issue can do so by buying rights. An outside investor buying two rights will pay $3.33 × 2 = $6.67 (to account for previous rounding). If the investor exercises the rights at a subscription cost of $10, the total cost would be $10 + $6.67 = $16.67. In return for this expenditure, the investor will receive a share of the new stock, which is worth $16.67.

Of course, outside investors can also buy National Power stock directly at $16.67 per share. In an efficient stock market it will make no difference whether new stock is obtained via rights or via direct purchase.

Effects on Shareholders

Shareholders can exercise their rights or sell them. In either case, the stockholder will neither win nor lose by the rights offering. The hypothetical holder of two shares of National Power has a portfolio worth $40. On the one hand, if the shareholder exercises the rights, he or she ends up with three shares worth a total of $50. In other words, by spending $10, the investor increases the value of the holding by $10, which means that he or she is neither better nor worse off.

On the other hand, a shareholder who sells the two rights for $3.33 each obtains $3.33 × 2 = $6.67 in cash. Because the two shares are each worth $16.67, the holdings are valued at

$$
\begin{array}{llll}
\text{Shares} & = 2 \times \$16.67 & = \$33.33 \\
\text{Sold rights} & = 2 \times \$\ 3.33 & = \$\ 6.67 \\
\text{Total} & & = \$40.00
\end{array}
$$

The new $33.33 market value plus $6.67 in cash is exactly the same as the original holding of $40. Thus, stockholders can neither lose nor gain from exercising or selling rights.

It is obvious that the new market price of the firm's stock will be lower after the rights offering than it was before the rights offering. The lower the subscription price, the greater the price decline of a rights offering. However, our analysis shows that the stockholders have suffered no loss because of the rights offering.

The Underwriting Arrangements

Undersubscription can occur if investors throw away rights or if bad news causes the market price of the stock to fall below the subscription price. To ensure against these possibilities, rights offerings are typically arranged by **standby underwriting.** Here, the underwriter makes a firm commitment to purchase the unsubscribed portion of the issue at the subscription price less a take-up fee. The underwriter usually receives a **standby fee** as compensation for his risk-bearing function.

In practice, the subscription price is usually set well below the current market price, making the probability of a rights failure quite small. Though a small percentage (less than 10 percent) of shareholders fail to exercise valuable rights, shareholders are usually allowed to purchase unsubscribed shares at the subscription price. This **oversubscription privilege** makes it unlikely that the corporate issuer would need to turn to its underwriter for help.

Concept
Questions

1. **Describe the details of a rights offering.**
2. **What are the questions that financial management must answer in a rights offering?**
3. **How is the value of a right determined?**

19.7 The Rights Puzzle

Smith calculated the issuance costs from three alternative methods: an equity issue with underwriting, a rights issue with standby underwriting, and a pure rights issue.[14] The results of his study, which appear in Table 19.12, suggest that a pure rights issue is the cheapest of the three alternatives. The bottom line of the table shows that total costs as a percentage of proceeds is 6.17 percent, 6.05 percent, and 2.45 percent for the three alternatives,

---

[14]C. W. Smith, Jr., "Alternative Methods for Raising Capital: Rights versus Underwritten Offerings," *Journal of Financial Economics* 5 (December 1977).

TABLE 19.12   Costs of Flotation as a Percentage of Proceeds*

Size of Issue (in $ millions)	Underwriting				Rights with Standby Underwriting				Pure Rights	
	Number	Compensation as a Percentage of Proceeds	Other Expenses as a Percentage of Proceeds	Total Cost as a Percentage of Proceeds	Number	Compensation as a Percentage of Proceeds	Other Expenses as a Percentage of Proceeds	Total Cost as a Percentage of Proceeds	Number	Total Cost as a Percentage of Proceeds
Under 0.50	—	—	—	0	—	—	—	8.99	3	—
0.50 to 0.99	6	6.96	6.78	13.74	2	3.43	4.80	8.24	2	4.59
1.00 to 1.99	18	10.40	4.89	15.29	5	6.36	4.15	10.51	5	4.90
2.00 to 4.99	61	6.59	2.87	9.47	9	5.20	2.85	8.06	7	2.85
5.00 to 9.99	66	5.50	1.53	7.03	4	3.92	2.18	6.10	6	1.39
10.00 to 19.99	91	4.84	0.71	5.55	10	4.14	1.21	5.35	3	0.72
20.00 to 49.99	156	4.30	0.37	4.67	12	3.84	0.90	4.74	1	0.52
50.00 to 99.99	70	3.97	0.21	4.18	9	3.96	0.74	4.70	2	0.21
100.00 to 500.00	16	3.81	0.14	3.95	5	3.50	0.50	4.00	9	0.13
Total/average	484	5.02	1.15	6.17	56	4.32	1.73	6.05	38	2.45

*Based on 578 common stock issues registered under the Securities Act of 1933 during 1971–1975. The issues are subdivided by size of issue and method of financing: underwriting, rights with standby underwriting, rights with standby underwriting, and pure rights offering.

Issues are included only if the company's stock was listed on the NYSE, AMEX, or regional exchanges before the offering; any associated secondary distribution represents less than 10 percent of the total proceeds of the issue, and the offering contains no other types of securities. The costs reported are: (1) compensation received by investment bankers for underwriting services rendered, (2) legal fees, (3) accounting fees, (4) engineering fees, (5) trustees' fees, (6) printing and engraving expenses, (7) SEC registration fees, (8) federal revenue stamps, and (9) state taxes.

Modified from C. W. Smith, Jr., "Costs of Underwritten versus Rights Issues," *Journal of Financial Economics* 5 (December 1977), p. 277 (Table 1).

respectively. As the body of the table indicates, this disparity holds when issues of different sizes are separated.

If corporate executives are rational, they will raise equity in the cheapest manner. Thus, the above evidence suggests that issues of pure rights should dominate. Surprisingly, Smith points out that over 90 percent of new issues are underwritten. This is generally viewed as an anomaly in the finance profession, though a few explanations have been advanced.[15]

1. Underwriters increase the stock price. This is supposedly accomplished because of increased public confidence or by the selling effort of the underwriting group. However, Smith could find no evidence of this in an examination of 52 rights offerings and 344 underwritten offerings.

2. Because the underwriter buys the shares at the agreed-upon price, it is providing insurance to the firm. That is, the underwriter loses if it is unable to sell all the shares to the public. This potential loss might mean that the underwriter's effective compensation is less than that measured in Table 19.12. However, the potential economic loss is probably not large. In most cases, the offer price is set within 24 hours of the offering, by which time the underwriter has usually made a careful assessment of the market for the shares.

3. Other arguments include (*a*) the proceeds of underwritten issues are available sooner than are the proceeds from a rights offer, (*b*) underwriters provide a wider distribution of ownership than would be true with a rights offering, (*c*) consulting advice from investment bankers may be beneficial, and (*d*) stockholders find exercising rights a nuisance.

All of the preceding arguments are pieces of the puzzle, but none seems very convincing. Booth and Smith identified a function of the underwriter that had not been taken into account in previous cost studies.[16] They argue that the underwriter *certifies* that the offering price is consistent with the true value of the issue. This certification is implied in the underwriting relationship and is provided when the underwriting firm gets access to inside information and puts its reputation for correct pricing on the line.

Concept Question	I. **Why might a firm prefer a general cash offering to a rights offering?**

19.8 Shelf Registration

To simplify the procedures for issuing securities, the SEC currently allows **shelf registration.** Shelf registration permits a corporation to register an offering that it reasonably expects to sell within the next two years. A master registration statement is filed at the time of registration. The company is permitted to sell the issue whenever it wants over those two years as long as it distributes a short-form statement.

Not all companies are allowed shelf registration. The major qualifications are as follows:

1. The company must be rated *investment* grade.
2. The firm cannot have defaulted on its debt in the past 12 months.
3. The aggregate market value of the firm's outstanding stock must be more than $75 million.
4. The firm must not have violated the Securities Act of 1934 in the past 12 months.

---

[15]It is even more anomalous because rights offerings are used around the world. In fact, they are required by law in many other countries.

[16]Booth and R. Smith, "The Certification Role of the Investment Banker in New Issue Pricing," *Midland Corporate Finance Journal* (Spring 1986).

Hershman reports on the use of the *dribble* method of new equity issuance.[17] With dribbling, a company registers the issue and hires an underwriter to be its selling agent. The company sells shares in small amounts from time to time via a stock exchange. Companies that have had dribble programs include Middle South Utilities, Niagara Mohawk, Pacific Gas and Electric, and the Southern Company. However, the evidence is that shelf registration is almost never used for equity but is used about one-half of the time for debt.[18]

The rule has been very controversial. Several arguments have been made against shelf registration.

1. The timeliness of disclosure is reduced with shelf registration, because the master registration statement may have been prepared up to two years before the actual issue occurs.

2. Some investment bankers have argued that shelf registration will cause a market overhang, because registration informs the market of future issues. It has been suggested that this overhang will depress market prices. However, an empirical analysis by Bhagat, Marr, and Thompson found that shelf registration is less costly than conventional underwriting and found no evidence to suggest a market-overhang effect.[19] Surprisingly, few eligible companies are currently selling equity by using shelf registration.[20]

Concept Questions

1. **Describe shelf registration.**
2. **What are the arguments against shelf registration?**

19.9 The Private Equity Market

The previous sections of this chapter assumed that a company is big enough, successful enough, and old enough to raise capital in the public equity market. Of course, there are many firms that have not reached this stage and cannot use the public equity market. For start-up firms or firms in financial trouble, the public equity market is often not available. The market for **venture capital** is part of the private equity market.[21]

Private Placement

Private placements avoid the costly procedures associated with the registration requirements that are part of public issues. The Securities and Exchange Commission (SEC) restricts private placement issues to no more than a couple of dozen knowledgeable investors including institutions such as insurance companies and pension funds. The biggest drawback of privately placed securities is that the securities cannot be easily resold. Most private placements involve debt securities, but equity securities can also be privately placed.

In 1990, Rule 144A was adopted by the SEC and established a framework for the issuance of private securities to certain qualified institutional investors. The rule has

---

[17]A. Hershman, "New Strategies in Equity Financing," *Dunn's Business Monthly* (June 1983).

[18]D. J. Dennis, "Shelf Registration and the Market in Seasonal Equity Offerings," *Journal of Business* 64 (1991).

[19]S. Bhagat, M. W. Marr, and G. R. Thompson, "The Rule 415 Experiment: Equity Markets," *Journal of Finance* 19 (December 1985).

[20]R. Rogowski and E. Sorenson, "Deregulation in Investment Banking: Shelf Registration, Structure, and Performance," *Financial Management* (Spring 1985).

[21]S. E. Pratt, "Overview and Introduction to the Venture Capital Industry," *Guide to Venture Capital Sources,* 10th ed., 1987 (Venture Economics. Laurel Avenue, Box 348, Wellesley Hills, MA 02181).

FIGURE 19.2

Corporate Equity
Security Offerings

17.7%	← Private Rule 144A placements
16.2%	← Private non-Rule 144A placements
66.1%	← Public equity offering
100%	Total equity offerings

SOURCE: Jennifer E. Bethal and Erik R. Sirri, "Express Lane or Toll Booth in the Desert: The SEC Framework for Securities Issuance," *Journal of Applied Corporate Finance* (Spring 1998).

generated a substantial market for privately underwritten issues. Largely because of Rule 144A, companies raise about one-sixth of the proceeds from all new issues without registration with the SEC. To qualify to buy Rule 144A offerings, investors must have at least $100 million in assets under management. Most private placements are in straight bonds or convertible bonds. However, preferred stock is frequently issued as a private placement. See Figure 19.2.

The Private Equity Firm

A large amount of private equity investment is undertaken by professional private equity managers representing large institutional investors such as mutual funds and pension funds. The limited partnership is the dominant form of intermediation in this market. Typically, the institutional investors act as the limited partners and the professional managers act as general partners. The general partners are firms that specialize in funding and managing equity investments in closely held private firms. The private equity market has been important for both traditional start-up companies and established public firms. Thus, the private equity market can be divided into venture equity and nonventure equity markets. A large part of the nonventure market is made up of firms in financial distress. Firms in financial distress are not likely to be able to issue public equity and typically cannot use traditional forms of debt such as bank loans or public debt. For these firms, the best alternative is to find a private equity market firm.

Suppliers of Venture Capital

As we have pointed out, venture capital is an important part of the private equity market. There are at least four types of suppliers of venture capital. First, a few old-line, wealthy families have traditionally provided start-up capital to promising businesses. For example, over the years, the Rockefeller family has made the initial capital contribution to a number of successful businesses. These families have been involved in venture capital for the better part of this century, if not longer.

Second, a number of private partnerships and corporations have been formed to provide investment funds. The organizer behind the partnership might raise capital from institutional investors, such as insurance companies and pension funds. Alternatively, a group of individuals might provide the funds to be ultimately invested with budding entrepreneurs.

Of the early partnerships, the most well-known is clearly American Research and Development (ARD), which was formed in 1946. Though ARD invested in many companies, its success was largely due to its investment in Digital Equipment Company (DEC). When Textron acquired ARD in 1972, over 85 percent of the shareholders' distribution was due to the investment in DEC.[22] Among the more recent venture capitalists, Arthur Rock & Co. of San Francisco may very well be the best known. Because of its huge success with Apple Computer and other high-tech firms, it has achieved near mythic stature in the venture-capital industry.

Recent estimates put the number of venture-capital firms at about 2,000. Pratt's *Guide to Venture Capital* (Venture Economics) provides a list of the names of many of these firms.[23] The average amount invested per venture has been estimated to be between $1 million and $2 million. However, one should not make too much of this figure, because the amount of financing varies considerably with the venture to be funded.

Stories used to abound about how easily an individual could obtain venture capital. Though that may have been the case in an earlier era, it is certainly not the case today. Venture-capital firms employ various screening procedures to prevent inappropriate funding. For example, because of the large demand for funds, many venture capitalists have at least one employee whose full-time job consists of reading business plans. Only the very best plans can expect to attract funds. Maier and Walker indicate that only about 2 percent of requests actually receive financing.[24]

Third, large industrial or financial corporations have established venture-capital subsidiaries. The Lambda Fund of Drexel Burnham Lambert, Manufacturers Hanover Venture Capital Corp., Citicorp Venture Capital, and Chemical Venture Capital Corporation of Chemical Bank are examples of this type. However, subsidiaries of this type appear to make up only a small portion of the venture-capital market.

Fourth, participants in an informal venture-capital market have recently been identified.[25] Rather than belonging to any venture-capital firm, these investors (often referred to as *angels*) act as individuals when providing financing. However, they should not, by any means, be viewed as isolated. Wetzel and others indicate that there is a rich network of angels, continually relying on each other for advice. A number of researchers have stressed that, in any informal network, there is likely one knowledgeable and trustworthy individual who, when backing a venture, brings a few less experienced investors in with him.

The venture-capital community has unfortunately chosen to refer to these individuals as "dumb dentists." Although a number indeed may be dentists, their intelligence should not be called into question. Wetzel argues that the prototypical angel has income over $100,000,

---

[22]H. Stevenson, D. Muzka, and J. Timmons, "Venture Capital in Transition: A Monte-Carlo Simulation of Changes in Investment Patterns," *Journal of Business Venturing* (Spring 1987).

[23]Pratt, "Overview and Introduction to the Venture Capital Industry."

[24]J. B. Maier and D. Walker, "The Role of Venture Capital in Financing Small Business," *Journal of Business Venturing* (Summer 1987).

[25]See W. E. Wetzel, "The Informal Venture Capital Market: Aspects of Scale and Market Efficiency," *Journal of Business Venturing* (Fall 1987).

net worth over $1,000,000, and substantial business experience and knowledge. As one might expect, the informal venture capitalist is able to tolerate high risks.

Though this informal market may seem small and unimportant, it is perhaps the largest of all sources of venture capital. Wetzel argues that aggregate investments from this source total around $50 billion, about twice the amount invested by more professional venture capitalists. The size of each contribution is smaller here. Perhaps, on average, only $250,000 per venture is raised when the informal market is tapped.

Stages of Financing

A. V. Bruno and T. T. Tyebjee identify six stages in venture-capital financing:[26]

1. *Seed-Money Stage.* A small amount of financing needed to prove a concept or develop a product. Marketing is not included in this stage.
2. *Start-Up.* Financing for firms that started within the past year. Funds are likely to pay for marketing and product development expenditures.
3. *First-Round Financing.* Additional money to begin sales and manufacturing after a firm has spent its start-up funds.
4. *Second-Round Financing.* Funds earmarked for working capital for a firm that is currently selling its product but still losing money.
5. *Third-Round Financing.* Financing for a company that is at least breaking even and is contemplating an expansion. This is also known as mezzanine financing.
6. *Fourth-Round Financing.* Money provided for firms that are likely to go public within half a year. This round is also known as bridge financing.

Although these categories may seem vague to the reader, we have found that the terms are well-accepted within the industry. For example, the venture-capital firms listed in Pratt's *Guide to Venture Capital* indicate which of the above stages they are interested in financing.

The penultimate stage in venture capital finance is the initial public offering.[27] Venture capitalists are very important participants in initial public offerings. Venture capitalists rarely sell all of the shares they own at the time of the initial public offering. Instead, they usually sell out in subsequent public offerings. However, there is considerable evidence that venture capitalists can successfully time IPOs by taking firms public when the market values are at the highest. Figure 19.3 shows the number of IPOs of privately held venture-capital-backed biotechnology companies in each month from 1978 to 1992. The venture-capital-backed IPOs clearly coincide with the ups and downs in the biotech market index in the top panel.

Concept Questions	1. **What are the different sources of venture-capital financing?** 2. **What are the different stages for companies seeking venture-capital financing?** 3. **What is the private equity market?** 4. **What is Rule 144A?**

---

[26]A. V. Bruno and T. T. Tyebjee, "The Entrepreneur's Search for Capital," *Journal of Business Venturing* (Winter 1985).

[27]A very influential paper by Christopher Barry, Chris J. Muscarella, John W. Peavey III, and Michael R. Vetsuypens, "The Role of Venture Capital in the Creation of Public Companies: Evidence from the Going Public Process," *Journal of Financial Economics* 27 (1990), shows that venture capitalists do not usually sell shares at the time of the initial public offering, but they usually have board seats and act as advisors to managers.

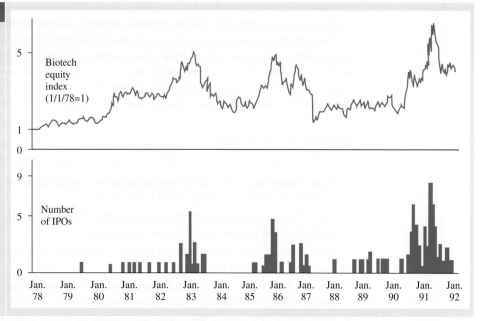

FIGURE 19.3

Initial Public Offerings by Venture-Capital-Backed Biotechnology Firms, January 1978 to January 1992

SOURCE: Joshua Lerner, "Venture Capitalists and the Decision to Go Public," *Journal of Financial Economics* 35 (June 1994).

CASE STUDY

The Decision to Do an Initial Public Offering (IPO): The Case of Medstone International, Inc.

Most firms initially raise equity financing with private placements in the venture-capital market from a small number of investor capitalists. If a firm does well and needs to raise more equity financing, it may decide to sell stock with an initial public offering. We see how this occurs with the case of Medstone International, Inc.

Medstone International, Inc., was created in 1984 to manufacture and sell medical products using the new technology of shockwave lithotripsy. Initially, Medstone raised its cash from contributions from its founders and from banks. From 1984 to 1986 Medstone spent most of its available cash on research and development of the technology of shockwave lithotripsy. Eventually, in 1986, the company developed a product called the Medstone 1050 ST. The purpose of the Medstone 1050 ST was for nonsurgical disintegration of kidney stones and gallstones.

However, it wasn't until 1987 that the company actually generated profits from the Medstone 1050 ST (as follows).

	Summary of Financial Information (in thousands)	
	1986	**1987**
Revenues	$ 25	$ 6,562
Income	(1,698)	680
Assets	865	3,205
Liabilities	6,062	5,517
Equity	(5,197)	(2,312)

By January 1988 Medstone International had obtained an investigative new drug permit from the Food and Drug Administration (FDA) and had entered into an agreement to sell and install the Medstone System in seven U.S. states. In early 1988 the firm's prospects seemed excellent and its founders had reason to be optimistic. But Medstone needed additional cash and its founders wanted the opportunity to cash out, so it hired the Weeden Co., a well-known investment banking firm, to arrange for an initial public offering (IPO) of common stock. In June 1988, Medstone went public with an IPO and sold 1 million shares of stock at $13 per share and raised $11,700,000. Immediately after the IPO there were 4,500,000 shares of Medstone stock outstanding. Insiders owned 3,500,000 shares, and outsiders owned 1,000,000 shares.

	Price to Public	Underwriting Discount	Proceeds to Company
Per share	$13,000,000	$1,300,000	$11,700,000
Total	13,000,000	1,300,000	11,700,000

Although the stock was offered at $13 per share, by the end of the first day, it was selling for $18 (this is a 38.5 percent increase).

As is typical in IPOs, the proceeds from the sale of stock had two purposes: to reduce indebtedness to banks and to cash out insiders, and to finance present and future operations and growth opportunities.

In 1984 when Medstone was formed, it was a "start-up" with no operating history and virtually no manufacturing and marketing experience. Moreover, when Medstone did its IPO, its product had not yet received final FDA approval. The company's potential was great and so were its risks of failure. The company's ultimate success depended upon its ability to form a new business, introduce new products, and successfully compete in the marketplace. However, in the case of medical products, success depends on obtaining FDA approval. Obtaining FDA approval for a new product can be a time-consuming process, and there is no guarantee that final clearance will ever be granted. Unfortunately, Medstone was never able to obtain final FDA approval.

When the company announced that it would no longer try to sell the Medstone 1050 ST, the market for its stock collapsed and the firm was forced to reorganize. Were investors in Medstone too optimistic? If so, they were not alone. The stocks of many IPOs have performed poorly after the offering.

Every IPO is unique but there are some familiar themes.

1. *Underpricing.* Firms going through an IPO usually have their shares underpriced. This means that the initial market price is usually significantly less than their market price prevailing at the end of the first trading day. This is one of the indirect costs of IPOs, and Medstone's underpricing was typical.

2. *Underperformance.* The Medstone IPO did not work out very well for many of the outside investors because the firm ultimately could not sell its Medstone 1050 ST. The Medstone IPO is typical in that the average firm performs very poorly after an IPO. Three years after an IPO, the stock price of firms doing IPOs has typically fallen below the initial price. Interestingly, it is also true for seasoned equity issues. This is a puzzle and several reasons have been put forth to explain it.

3. *Going Public.* Many IPOs such as Medstone are to give inside equity investors an opportunity to exchange their private equity for public equity and cash out their stakes in the firm. Usually only a fraction of the inside equity is sold in the IPO. Later in subsequent common stock sales, the rest of the inside ownership is sold.

19.10 SUMMARY AND CONCLUSIONS

This chapter looks closely at how equity is issued. The main points follow.

1. Large issues have proportionately much lower costs of issuing equity than small ones.

2. Firm-commitment underwriting is far more prevalent for large issues than is best-efforts underwriting. Smaller issues probably primarily use best efforts because of the greater uncertainty of these issues. For an offering of a given size, the direct expenses of best-efforts underwriting and firm-commitment underwriting are of the same magnitude.

3. Rights offerings are cheaper than general cash offers and eliminate the problem of underpricing. Yet, most new equity issues are underwritten general cash offers.

4. Shelf registration is a new method of issuing new debt and equity. The direct costs of shelf issues seem to be substantially lower than those of traditional issues.

5. Venture capitalists are an increasingly important influence in start-up firms and subsequent financing.

KEY TERMS

best efforts, *544*	registration statement, *540*
cash offer, *543*	regulation A, *540*
competitive offer, *547*	seasoned new issue, *543*
ex-rights date, *555*	shelf registration, *559*
firm commitment, *544*	standby fee, *557*
Green Shoe provision, *545*	standby underwriting, *557*
initial public offering (IPO), *543*	subscription price, *554*
investment banks, *543*	syndicate, *544*
negotiated offer, *547*	tombstone, *541*
oversubscription privilege, *557*	unseasoned new issue, *543*
prospectus, *541*	venture capital, *560*
red herring, *541*	

SUGGESTED READINGS

Here are several significant recent articles that have helped shape our understanding of how capital is raised.

Altinkilic, Oya, and Robert S. Hansen. "Are There Economies of Scale in Underwriting Fees? Evidence of Rising External Financing Costs." *Review of Financial Studies* 13 (2000).

Ellis, Katrina, Roni Michaely, and Maureen O'Hara. "When the Underwriter is the Market Maker: An Examination of Trading in the IPO After Market." *Journal of Finance* (June 2000).

Chen, Hsuan-Chi, and Jay R. Ritter. "The Seven Percent Solution," *Journal of Finance* (June 2000).

Aggarwal, Reena. "Stabilization Activities by Underwriters After Initial Public Offerings." *Journal of Finance* (June 2000).

See also

Ritter, Jay, and Ivo Welch. "A Review of IPO Activity, Pricing, and Accounting." *Journal of Finance* (August 2003).

QUESTIONS & PROBLEMS

THE PUBLIC ISSUE

19.1   Define the following terms related to the issuance of public securities.
    a. General cash offer
    b. Rights offer
    c. Registration statement
    d. Prospectus
    e. Initial public offering
    f. Seasoned new issue
    g. Shelf registration

19.2 **a.** What does the Securities Exchange Act of 1933 regulate?
b. What does the Securities Exchange Act of 1934 regulate?

THE CASH OFFER

19.3 What are the comparative advantages of a competitive offer and a negotiated offer, respectively?

19.4 Define the following terms related to underwriting.
a. Firm commitment
b. Syndicate
c. Spread
d. Best efforts

19.5 **a.** Who bears the risk in firm-commitment underwriting? Explain.
b. Who bears the risk in best-efforts underwriting? Explain.

19.6 Suppose the Newton Company has 10,000 shares of stock. Each share is worth $40, and the company's market value of equity is $400,000. Suppose the firm issues 5,000 shares of the new stock at the following prices: $40, $20, and $10. What will be the effect of each of the alternative offering prices on the existing price per share?

19.7 In 1980 a certain assistant professor of finance bought 12 initial public offerings of common stock. He held each of these for approximately one month and then sold them. The investment rule he followed was to submit a purchase order for every firm-commitment initial public offering of oil- and gas-exploration companies. There were 22 such offerings, and he submitted a purchase order for approximately $1,000 of stock for each one. With 10 of these, no shares were allocated to this assistant professor. With five of the 12 offerings that were purchased, fewer than the requested number of shares were allocated.

The year 1980 was very good for oil- and gas-exploration company owners. For the 22 stocks that went public, the stock was selling on average for 80 percent above the offering price within a month. Yet, this assistant professor looked at his performance record and found the $8,400 invested in 12 companies had grown to only $10,100, a return of only about 20 percent. (Commissions were negligible.) Did he have bad luck, or should he have expected to do worse than the average initial-public-offering investor? Explain.

NEW EQUITY & THE VALUE OF THE FIRM

19.8 What are the possible reasons for why the stock price typically drops on the announcement of a seasoned new equity issue?

COST OF NEW ISSUES   **19.9** What are the costs of new issues?

RIGHTS

19.10 Bountiful Beef Processors (BBP) wants to raise equity through a rights offering. BBP has 2,400,000 shares of common stock outstanding, and must raise $12,000,000. The subscription price of the rights will be $15.
a. How many new shares of stock must BBP issue?
b. How many rights will be necessary to purchase one share of stock?
c. What must a shareholder remit to receive one share of stock?

19.11 Jelly Beans, Inc., is proposing a rights offering. There are 100,000 outstanding shares at $25 each. There will be 10,000 new shares issued at a $20 subscription price.
a. What is the value of a right?
b. What is the ex-rights price?
c. What is the new market value of the company?
d. Why might a company have a rights offering rather than a common stock offering?

19.12 Superior, Inc., is a manufacturer of beta-blockers. Management has concluded that additional equity financing is required to increase production capacity, and that these funds are best attained through a rights offering. It has correctly concluded that, as a result of the rights offering, share price will fall from $50 to $45 ($50 is the rights-on price; $45 is the ex-rights price, also known as the *when-issued* price). The company is seeking $5 million in additional funds with a per-share subscription price equal to $25.
a. How many shares were there before the offering?

19.13 A company's stock currently sells for $45 per share. Last week the firm issued rights to raise new equity. To purchase a new share, a stockholder must remit $10 and three rights.
   a. What is the ex-rights stock price?
   b. What is the price of one right?
   c. When will the price drop occur? Why will it occur then?

19.14 Summit Corp.'s stock is currently selling at $13 per share. There are 1 million shares outstanding. The firm is planning to raise $2 million to finance a new project. What is the ex-right stock price, the value of a right, and the appropriate subscription prices, if
   a. Two shares of outstanding stock are entitled to purchase one additional share of the new issue.
   b. Four shares of outstanding stock are entitled to purchase one additional share of the new issue.
   c. How does the stockholders' wealth change from *a* to *b*?

THE NEW ISSUE PUZZLE

19.15 Megabucks Industries is planning to raise fresh equity capital by selling a large new issue of common stock. Megabucks is a publicly traded corporation, and is trying to choose between an underwritten cash offer and a rights offering (not underwritten) to current shareholders. Megabucks' management is interested in maximizing the wealth of current shareholders and has asked you for advice on the choice of issue methods. What is your recommendation? Why?

SHELF REGISTRATION

19.16 Explain why shelf registration has been used by many firms instead of syndication.

VENTURE CAPITAL

19.17 Who are the different suppliers of venture capital?

THE DECISION TO DO AN INITIAL PUBLIC OFFERING (IPO): THE CASE OF MEDSTONE INTERNATIONAL, INC.

19.18 What are the uses for the proceeds from an IPO?

19.19 Every IPO is unique, but what are the basic empirical regularities in IPOs?

S & P PROBLEMS

STANDARD &POOR'S

19.20 Look under the Edgar analytics link for Sara Lee (SLE). Look at the prospectuses and find the most recent securities offered for sale by the company. What were the securities? How much was being offered? You may need to look under the archive link.

Long-Term Debt

EXECUTIVE SUMMARY

The previous chapter introduced the mechanics of new long-term financing, with an emphasis on equity. This chapter takes a closer look at long-term debt instruments.

The chapter begins with a review of the basic features of long-term debt, and a description of some important aspects of publicly issued long-term bonds. We also discuss forms of long-term financing that are not publicly issued: term loans and private-placement bonds. These are directly placed with lending institutions, such as a commercial bank or a life insurance company.

All bond agreements have protective covenants. These are restrictions on the firm that protect the bondholder. We present several types of protective covenants in this chapter.

A large number of publicly issued industrial bonds have call provisions, which enable a company to buy back its bonds at a predetermined call price. This chapter attempts to answer two questions about call provisions.

1. Should firms issue callable bonds?

2. When should such bonds be called?

There are many different kinds of long-term bonds. We discuss three—floating-rate bonds, income bonds, and deep-discount bonds—and analyze what types of bonds are best in different circumstances.

20.1 Long-Term Debt: A Review

Long-term debt securities are promises by the issuing firm to pay interest and principal on the unpaid balance. The *maturity* of a long-term debt instrument refers to the length of time the debt remains outstanding with some unpaid balance. Debt securities can be *short-term* (maturities of one year or less) or *long-term* (maturities of more than one year).[1] Short-term debt is sometimes referred to as *unfunded debt* and long-term debt as *funded debt.*[2]

The two major forms of long-term debt are public issue and privately placed debt. We discuss public-issue bonds first, and most of what we say about them holds true for privately placed long-term debt as well. The main difference between publicly issued and privately placed debt is that private debt is directly placed with a lending institution.

There are many other attributes to long-term debt, including security, call features, sinking funds, ratings, and protective covenants. The boxed material illustrates these attributes.

---

[1]In addition, people often refer to intermediate-term debt, which has a maturity of more than one year and less than three to five years.

[2]The word *funding* generally implies long-term. Thus, a firm planning to *fund* its debt requirements may be replacing short-term debt with long-term debt.

Features of a Hypothetical Bond

	Terms	Explanations
Amount of issue	$100 million	The company issued $100 million of bonds.
Date of issue	10/21/03	The bonds were sold on 10/21/03.
Maturity	12/31/32	The principal will be paid in 30 years.
Denomination	$1,000	Each individual bond will pay $1,000 at maturity.
Annual coupon	10.50	Because the denomination of each bond is $1,000, each bondholder will receive $105 per bond per year.
Offer price	100	The offer price was 100 percent of the denomination, or $1,000 per bond.
Yield to maturity	10.50%	If the bond is held to maturity, bondholders will receive a stated annual rate of return equal to 10.5 percent.
Dates of coupon payments	12/31, 6/30	Coupons of $52.50 will be paid on these dates.
Security	None	The bonds are debentures.
Sinking funds	Annual; begins in 2013	The sinking funds will be sufficient to pay 80 percent of principal, the balance to be paid at maturity.
Call provision	Not callable before 12/31/13 Call price: $1,100	The bonds have a deferred call feature. After 12/31/13 the company can buy back the bonds for $1,100 per bond.
Rating	Moody's Aaa	This is Moody's highest rating. The bonds have the lowest probability of default.

20.2 The Public Issue of Bonds

The general procedures followed for a **public issue** of bonds are the same as those for stocks, as described in the previous chapter. First, the offering must be approved by the board of directors. Sometimes a vote of stockholders is also required. Second, a registration statement is prepared for review by the Securities and Exchange Commission. Third, if accepted, the registration statement becomes *effective* 20 days later, and the securities are sold.

However, the registration statement for a public issue of bonds must include an indenture, a document not relevant for the issue of common stock. An **indenture** is a written agreement between the corporation (the borrower) and a trust company. It is sometimes referred to as the *deed of trust*.[3] The trust company is appointed by the corporation to represent the bondholders. The trust company must (1) be sure the terms of the indenture are obeyed, (2) manage the sinking fund, and (3) represent bondholders if the company defaults on its payments.

The typical bond indenture can be a document of several hundred pages, and it generally includes the following provisions:

1. The basic terms of the bonds.
2. A description of property used as security.

---

[3]The terms *loan agreement* or *loan contract* are usually used for privately placed debt and term loans.

3. Details of the protective covenants.

4. The sinking-fund arrangements.

5. The call provision.

Each of these is discussed next.

The Basic Terms

Bonds usually have a *face value* of $1,000. This is also called the *principal value* or the *denomination* and it is stated on the bond certificate. In addition, the *par value* (i.e., initial accounting value) of a bond is almost always the same as the face value.

Transactions between bond buyers and bond sellers determine the market value of the bond. Actual bond-market values depend on the general level of interest rates, among other factors, and need not equal the face value. The bond price is quoted as a percentage of the denomination. Though interest is paid only twice a year, interest *accrues* continually over the year, and the quoted prices of a bond usually include accrued interest. This is illustrated in the example below.

EXAMPLE

Suppose the Black Corporation has issued 100 bonds. The amount stated on each bond certificate is $1,000. The total face value or principal value of the bonds is $100,000. Further suppose the bonds are currently *priced* at 100, which means 100 percent of $1,000. This means that buyers and sellers are holding bonds at a price per bond of $1,000. If interest rates rise, the price of the bond might fall to, say, 97, which means 97 percent of $1,000, or $970.

Suppose the bonds have a stated interest rate of 12 percent due on January 1, 2050. The bond indenture might read as follows:

> The bond will mature on January 1, 2050, and will be limited in aggregate principal amount to $100,000. Each bond will bear interest at the rate of 12.0% per annum from January 1, 1990, or from the most recent Interest Payment Date to which interest has been paid or provided for. Interest is payable semiannually on July 1 and January 1 of each year.

Suppose an investor buys the bonds on April 1. Since the last interest payment, on January 1, three months of interest at 12 percent per year would have accrued. Because interest of 12 percent a year works out to 1 percent per month, interest over the three months is 3 percent. Therefore, the buyer of the bond must pay a price of 100 percent plus the 3 percent of accrued interest ($30). On July 1 the buyer will receive an interest payment of $60. This can be viewed as the sum of the $30 he or she paid the seller plus the three months of interest, $30, for holding the bond from April 1 to July 1.

As is typical of industrial bonds, the Black bonds are registered. The indenture might read as follows:

> Interest is payable semiannually on July 1 and January 1 of each year to the person in whose name the bond is registered at the close of business on June 15 or December 15, respectively.

This means that the company has a registrar who will record the ownership of each bond. The company will pay the interest and principal by check mailed directly to the address of the owner of record.

When a bond is registered with attached coupons, the bondholder must separate a coupon from the bond certificate and send it to the company registrar (paying agent). Some bonds are in **bearer** form. This means that ownership is not recorded in the company books. As with a registered bond with attached coupons, the holder of the bond certificate separates the coupon and sends it in to the company to receive payment.

There are two drawbacks to bearer bonds. First, they can be easily lost or stolen. Second, because the company does not know who owns its bonds, it cannot notify bondholders of important events. Consider, for example, Mr. and Mrs. Smith, who go to their safe-deposit box and clip the coupon on their 12 percent, $1,000 bond issued by the Black Corporation. They send the coupon to the paying agent and feel richer. A few days later, a notice comes from the paying agent that the bond was retired and its principal paid off one year earlier. In other words, the bond no longer exists. Mr. and Mrs. Smith must forfeit one year of interest. (Of course, they can turn their bond in for $1,000.)

However, bearer bonds have the advantage of secrecy because even the issuing company does not know who the bond's owners are. This secrecy is particularly vexing to taxing authorities because tax collection on interest is difficult if the holder is unknown.

Security

Debt securities are also classified according to the *collateral* protecting the bondholder. Collateral is a general term for the assets that are pledged as a security for payment of debt. For example, *collateral trust bonds* involve a pledge of common stock held by the corporation.

EXAMPLE

Suppose Railroad Holding Company owns all of the common stock of Track, Inc.; that is, Track, Inc., is a wholly owned subsidiary of the Railroad Holding Company. Railroad issues debt securities that pledge the common stock of Track, Inc., as collateral. The debts are collateral trust bonds; U.S. Sur Bank will hold them. If Railroad Holding Company defaults on the debt, U.S. Sur Bank will be able to sell the stock of Track, Inc., to satisfy Railroad's obligation.

Mortgage securities are secured by a mortgage on real estate or other long-term assets of the borrower.[4] The legal document that describes that mortgage is called a *mortgage-trust indenture* or *trust deed.* The mortgage can be *closed-end,* so that there is a limit as to the amount of bonds that can be issued. More frequently it is *open-end,* without limit to the amount of bonds that may be issued.

EXAMPLE

Suppose the Miami Bond Company has buildings and land worth $10 million and a $4 million mortgage on these properties. If the mortgage is closed-end, the Miami Bond Company cannot issue more bonds on this property.

If the bond indenture contains no clause limiting the amount of additional bonds that can be issued, it is an open-end mortgage. In this case the Miami Bond Company can issue additional bonds on its property, making the existing bonds riskier. For example, if additional mortgage bonds of $2 million are issued, the property has been pledged for a total of $6 million of bonds. If Miami Bond Company must liquidate its property for $4 million, the original bondholders will receive ⅔, or 67 percent, of their investment. If the mortgage had been closed-end, they would have received 100 percent of the stated value.

The value of a mortgage depends on the market value of the underlying property. Because of this, mortgage bonds sometimes require that the property be properly maintained and insured. Of course, a building and equipment bought in 1914 for manufacturing slide rules might not have much value no matter how well the company maintains it. The value of any property ultimately depends on its next best economic use. Bond indentures cannot easily insure against losses in economic value.

---

[4]A set of railroad cars is an example of "other long-term assets" used as security.

Sometimes mortgages are on specific property, for example, a single building. More often, blanket mortgages are used. A blanket mortgage pledges many assets owned by the company.

Some bonds represent unsecured obligations of the company. A **debenture** is an unsecured bond, where no specific pledge of property is made. Debenture holders have a claim on property not otherwise pledged: the property that remains after mortgages and collateral trusts are taken into account. At the current time, almost all public bonds issued by industrial and finance companies are debentures. However, most utility and railroad bonds are secured by a pledge of assets.

Protective Covenants

A **protective covenant** is that part of the indenture or loan agreement that limits certain actions of the borrowing company. Protective covenants can be classified into two types: negative covenants and positive covenants. A **negative covenant** limits or prohibits actions that the company may take. Here are some typical examples:

1. Limitations are placed on the amount of dividends a company may pay.
2. The firm cannot pledge any of its assets to other lenders.
3. The firm cannot merge with another firm.
4. The firm may not sell or lease its major assets without approval by the lender.
5. The firm cannot issue additional long-term debt.

A **positive covenant** specifies an action that the company agrees to take or a condition the company must abide by. Here are some examples:

1. The company agrees to maintain its working capital at a minimum level.
2. The company must furnish periodic financial statements to the lender.

The financial implications of protective covenants were treated in detail in the chapters on capital structure. In that discussion, we argued that protective covenants can benefit stockholders because, if bondholders are assured that they will be protected in times of financial stress, they will accept a lower interest rate.

The Sinking Fund

Bonds can be entirely repaid at maturity, at which time the bondholder will receive the stated value of the bond, or they can be repaid before maturity. Early repayment is more typical.

In a direct placement of debt the repayment schedule is specified in the loan contract. For public issues, the repayment takes place through the use of a sinking fund and a call provision.

A *sinking fund* is an account managed by the bond trustee for the purpose of repaying the bonds. Typically, the company makes yearly payments to the trustee. The trustee can purchase bonds in the market or can select bonds randomly using a lottery and purchase them, generally at face value. There are many different kinds of sinking-fund arrangements:

- Most sinking funds start between 5 and 10 years after the initial issuance.
- Some sinking funds establish equal payments over the life of the bond.
- Most high-quality bond issues establish payments to the sinking fund that are not sufficient to redeem the entire issue. As a consequence, there is the possibility of a large *balloon* payment at maturity.

Sinking funds have two opposing effects on bondholders:

1. *Sinking Funds Provide Extra Protection to Bondholders.* A firm experiencing financial difficulties would have trouble making sinking-fund payments. Thus, sinking-fund payments provide an early warning system to bondholders.
2. *Sinking Funds Give the Firm an Attractive Option.* If bond prices fall below the face value, the firm will satisfy the sinking fund by buying bonds at the lower market prices. If bond prices rise above the face value, the firm will buy the bonds back at the lower face value.

The Call Provision

A *call provision* lets the company repurchase or *call* the entire bond issue at a predetermined price over a specified period.

Generally, the call price is above the bond's face value of $1,000. The difference between the call price and the face value is the **call premium.** For example, if the call price is 105, that is, 105 percent of $1,000, the call premium is 50. The amount of the call premium usually becomes smaller over time. One typical arrangement is to set the call premium initially equal to the annual coupon payment and then make it decline to zero over the life of the bond.

Call provisions are not usually operative during the first few years of a bond's life. For example, a company may be prohibited from calling its bonds for the first 10 years. This is referred to as a **deferred call.** During this period the bond is said to be **call-protected.**

Concept Questions

1. Do bearer bonds have any advantage? Why might Mr. "I Like to Keep My Affairs Private" prefer to hold bearer bonds?
2. What advantages and what disadvantages do bondholders derive from provisions of sinking funds?
3. What is a call provision? What is the difference between the call price and the stated price?

20.3 Bond Refunding

Replacing all or part of an issue of outstanding bonds is called bond **refunding.** Usually, the first step in a typical bond refunding is to call the entire issue of bonds at the call price. Bond refunding raises two questions:

1. Should firms issue callable bonds?
2. Given that callable bonds have been issued, when should the bonds be called?

We attempt to answer these questions in this section.

Should Firms Issue Callable Bonds?

Common sense tells us that call provisions have value. First, many publicly issued bonds have call provisions. Second, it is obvious that a call works to the advantage of the issuer. If interest rates fall and bond prices go up, the option to buy back the bonds at the call price is valuable. In bond refunding, firms will typically replace the called bonds with a new bond issue. The new bonds will have a lower coupon rate than the called bonds.

However, bondholders will take the call provision into account when they buy the bond. For this reason, we can expect that bondholders will demand higher interest rates on callable bonds than on noncallable bonds. In fact, financial economists view call provisions as being zero-sum in efficient capital markets.[5] Any expected gains to the issuer from being allowed to refund the bond at lower rates will be offset by higher initial interest rates. We illustrate the zero-sum aspect to callable bonds in the following example.

EXAMPLE

Suppose Kraus Intercable Company intends to issue perpetual bonds of $1,000 face value at a 10-percent interest rate.[6] Annual coupons have been set at $100. There is an equal chance that by the end of the year interest rates will do one of the following:

1. Fall to $6\frac{2}{3}$ percent. If so, the bond price will increase to $1,500.
2. Increase to 20 percent. If so, the bond price will fall to $500.

Noncallable Bond   Suppose the market price of the noncallable bond is the expected price it will have next year plus the coupon, all discounted at the current 10-percent interest rate.[7] The value of the noncallable bond is:

Value of Noncallable Bond:

$$\text{First-year coupon} + \text{Expected price at end of year} \over 1 + r$$

$$= \frac{\$100 + (0.5 \times \$1,500) + (0.5 \times \$500)}{1.10}$$

$$= \$1,000$$

Callable Bond   Now suppose the Kraus Intercable Company decides to issue callable bonds. The call premium is set at $100 over par value and the bonds can be called *only* at the end of the first year.[8] In this case, the call provision will allow the company to buy back its bonds at $1,100 ($1,000 par value plus the $100 call premium). Should interest rates fall, the company will buy a bond for $1,100 that would be worth $1,500 in the absence of a call provision. Of course, if interest rates rise, Kraus would not want to call the bonds for $1,100 because they are worth only $500 on the market.

Suppose rates fall and Kraus calls the bonds by paying $1,100. If the firm simultaneously issues new bonds with a coupon of $100, it will bring in $1,500 ($100/0.0667) at the $6\frac{2}{3}$-percent interest rate. This will allow Kraus to pay an extra dividend to shareholders of $400 ($1,500 − $1,100). In other words, if rates fall from 10 percent to $6\frac{2}{3}$ percent, exercise of the call will transfer $400 of potential bondholder gains to the shareholders.

When investors purchase callable bonds, they realize that they will forfeit their anticipated gains to shareholders if the bonds are called. As a consequence, they will not pay $1,000 for a callable bond with a coupon of $100.

How high must the coupon on the callable bond be so that it can be issued at the par value of $1,000? We can answer this in three steps.

---

[5]See A. Kraus, "An Analysis of Call Provisions and the Corporate Refunding Decision," *Midland Corporate Finance Journal* 1 (Spring 1983), p. 1.

[6]Recall that perpetual bonds have no maturity date.

[7]We are assuming that the current price of the noncallable bonds is the expected value discounted at the risk-free rate of 10 percent. This is equivalent to assuming that the risk is unsystematic and carries no risk premium.

[8]Normally, bonds can be called over a period of many years. Our assumption that the bond can only be called at the end of the first year was introduced for simplicity.

Step 1: Determining End-of-Year Value If Interest Rates Drop   If the interest rate drops to 6⅔ percent by the end of the year, the bond will be called for $1,100. The bondholder will receive both this and the annual coupon payment. If we let C represent the coupon on the callable bond, the bondholder gets the following at the end of the year:

$$\$1,100 + C$$

Step 2: Determining End-of-Year Value If Interest Rates Rise   If interest rates rise to 20 percent, the value of the bondholder's position at the end of the year is:

$$\frac{C}{0.20} + C$$

That is, the perpetuity formula tells us that the bond will sell at $C/0.20$. In addition, the bondholder receives the coupon payment at the end of the year.

Step 3: Solving for C   Because interest rates are equally likely to rise or to fall, the expected value of the bondholder's end-of-year position is:

$$(\$1,100 + C) \times 0.5 + \left(\frac{C}{0.20} + C\right) \times 0.5$$

Using the current interest rate of 10 percent, we set the present value of these payments equal to par:

$$\$1,000 = \frac{(\$1,100 + C) \times 0.5 + \left(\dfrac{C}{0.20} + C\right) \times 0.5}{1.10}$$

C is the unknown in the equation. The equation holds if $C = \$157.14$. In other words, callable bonds can sell at par only if their coupon rate is 15.714 percent.

The Paradox Restated   If Kraus issues a noncallable bond, it will only need to pay a 10-percent interest rate. By contrast, Kraus must pay an interest rate of 15.7 percent on a callable bond. The interest-rate differential makes an investor indifferent whether she buys one of the two bonds in our example or the other. Because the return to the investor is the same with either bond, the cost of debt capital is the same to Kraus with either bond. Thus, our example suggests that there is neither an advantage nor a disadvantage from issuing callable bonds.

Why, therefore, are callable bonds issued in the real world? This question has vexed financial economists for a long time. We now consider four specific reasons why a company might use a call provision:

1. Superior interest-rate predictions.
2. Taxes.
3. Financial flexibility for future investment opportunities.
4. Less interest-rate risk.

Superior Interest-Rate Forecasting   Company insiders may know more about interest-rate changes on its bonds than does the investing public. For example, managers may be better informed about potential changes in the firm's credit rating. Thus, a company may prefer the call provision at a particular time because it believes that the expected fall in interest rates (the probability of a fall multiplied by the amount of the fall) is greater than the bondholders believe.

Although this is possible, there is reason to doubt that inside information is the rationale for call provisions. Suppose firms really had superior ability to predict changes that would affect them. Bondholders would infer that a company expected an improvement in its credit rating whenever it issued callable bonds. Bondholders would require an increase in the coupon rate to protect them against a call if this occurred. As a result, we would expect that there would be no financial advantage to the firm from callable bonds over noncallable bonds.

Of course, there are many non–company-specific reasons why interest rates can fall. For example, the interest-rate level is connected to the anticipated inflation rate. But it is difficult to see how companies could have more information about the general level of interest rates than other participants in the bond markets.

Taxes   Call provisions may have tax advantages if the bondholder is taxed at a lower rate than the company. We have seen that callable bonds have higher coupon rates than noncallable bonds. Because the coupons provide a deductible interest expense to the corporation and are taxable income to the bondholder, the corporation will gain more than a bondholder in a low tax bracket will lose. Presumably, some of the tax saving can be passed on to the bondholders in the form of a high coupon.

Future Investment Opportunities   As we have explained, bond indentures contain protective covenants that restrict a company's investment opportunities. For example, protective covenants may limit the company's ability to acquire another firm or to sell certain assets (for example, a division of the company). If the covenants are sufficiently restrictive, the cost to the shareholders in lost net present value can be large. However, if bonds are callable, the company can buy back the bonds at the call price and take advantage of a superior investment opportunity.[9]

Less Interest-Rate Risk   The call provision will reduce the sensitivity of a bond's value to changes in the level of interest rates. As interest rates increase, the value of a noncallable bond will fall. Because the callable bond has a higher coupon rate, the value of a callable bond will fall less than the value of a noncallable bond. Kraus has argued that, by reducing the sensitivity of a bond's value to changes in interest rates, the call provision may reduce the risk of shareholders as well as bondholders.[10] He argues that, because the bond is a liability of the corporation, the equityholders bear risk as the bond changes value over time. Thus, it can be shown that, under certain conditions, reducing the risk of bonds through a call provision will also reduce the risk of equity.

Calling Bonds: When Does It Make Sense?

The value of the company is the value of the stock plus the value of the bonds. From the Modigliani-Miller theory and the pie model in earlier chapters, we know that firm value is unchanged by how it is divided between these two instruments. Therefore, maximizing

---

[9]This argument is from Z. Bodie and R. A. Taggart, "Future Investment Opportunities and the Value of the Call Provision on a Bond," *Journal of Finance* 33 (1978), p. 4.

[10]A. Kraus, "An Analysis of Call Provisions and the Corporate Refunding Decision," *Midland Corporate Finance Journal* 1 (Spring 1983). Kraus points out that the call provision will not always reduce the equity's interest-rate risk. If the firm as a whole bears interest-rate risk, more of this risk may be shifted from equityholders to bondholders with noncallable debt. In this case, equityholders may actually bear more risk with callable debt.

shareholder wealth means minimizing the value of the callable bond. In a world with no transaction costs, it can be shown that the company should call its bonds whenever the callable-bond value exceeds the call price. This policy minimizes the value of the callable bonds.

The preceding analysis is modified slightly by including the costs from issuing new bonds. These extra costs change the refunding rule to allow bonds to trade at prices above the call price. The objective of the company is to minimize the sum of the value of the callable bonds plus new issue costs. It has been observed that many real-world firms do not call their bonds when the market value of the bonds reaches the call price. Instead, they wait until the market value of the bonds exceeds the call price. Perhaps these issue costs are an explanation. Also, when a bond is called, the holder has about 30 days to surrender the bond and receive the call price in cash. In 30 days the market value of the bonds could fall below the call price. If so, the firm is giving away money. To forestall this possibility, it can be argued that firms should wait until the market value of the bond exceeds the call price before calling bonds.

Concept
Questions

1. **What are the advantages to a firm of having a call provision?**
2. **What are the disadvantages to bondholders of having a call provision?**

20.4 Bond Ratings

Firms frequently pay to have their debt rated. The two leading bond-rating firms are Moody's Investors Service and Standard & Poor's. The debt ratings depend upon (1) the likelihood that the firm will default and (2) the protection afforded by the loan contract in the event of default. The ratings are constructed from information supplied by the corporation, primarily the financial statements of the firm. The rating classes are shown in the accompanying box.

The highest rating debt can have is AAA or Aaa. Debt rated AAA or Aaa is judged to be the best quality and to have the lowest degree of risk. The lowest rating is D, which indicates that the firm is in default. Since the 1980s, a growing part of corporate borrowing has taken the form of *low-grade bonds.* These bonds are also known as either *high-yield bonds* or *junk bonds.* Low-grade bonds are corporate bonds that are rated below *investment grade* by the major rating agencies (that is, below BBB for Standard & Poor's or Baa for Moody's).

Bond ratings are important, because bonds with lower ratings tend to have higher interest costs. However, the most recent evidence is that bond ratings merely reflect bond risk. There is no conclusive evidence that bond ratings affect risk.[11] It is not surprising that the stock prices and bond prices of firms do not show any unusual behavior on the days around a rating change. Because the ratings are based on publicly available information, they probably do not, in themselves, supply new information to the market.[12]

---

[11]M. Weinstein, "The Systematic Risk of Corporate Bonds," *Journal of Financial and Quantitative Analysis* (September 1981); J. P. Ogden, "Determinants of Relative Interest Rate Sensitivity of Corporate Bonds," *Financial Management* (Spring 1987); and F. Reilly and M. Joehnk, "The Association between Market-Based Risk Measures for Bonds and Bond Ratings," *Journal of Finance* (December 1976).

[12]M. Weinstein, "The Effect of a Ratings Change Announcement on Bond Price," *Journal of Financial Economics* 5 (1977). However, Robert W. Holthausen and Richard W. Leftwich, "The Effect of Bond Rating Changes on Common Stock Prices," *Journal of Financial Economics* 17 (September 1986), find that bond rating downgrades are associated with abnormal negative returns of the stock of the issuing firm.

Bond Ratings

	Very High Quality	High Quality	Speculative	Very Poor
Standard & Poor's	AAA AA	A BBB	BB B	CCC CC C D
Moody's	Aaa Aa	A Baa	Ba B	Caa Ca C D

At times both Moody's and Standard & Poor's adjust these ratings. S&P uses plus and minus signs: A+ is the strongest A rating and A− the weakest. Moody's uses a 1, 2, or 3 designation, with 1 indicating the strongest.

Moody's	S&P	
Aaa	AAA	Debt rated Aaa and AAA has the highest rating. Capacity to pay interest and principal is extremely strong.
Aa	AA	Debt rated Aa and AA has a very strong capacity to pay interest and repay principal. Together with the highest rating, this group comprises the high-grade bond class.
A	A	Debt rated A has a strong capacity to pay interest and repay principal. However, it is somewhat more susceptible to adverse changes in circumstances and economic conditions.
Baa	BBB	Debt rated Baa and BBB is regarded as having an adequate capacity to pay interest and repay principal. Whereas it normally exhibits adequate protection parameters, adverse economic conditions or changing circumstances are more likely to lead to a weakened capacity to pay interest and repay principal for debt in this category than in higher-rated categories. These bonds are medium-grade obligations.
Ba	BB	Debt rated in these categories is regarded, on balance, as predominantly speculative. Ba and BB indicate the lowest degree of speculation, and Ca and CC the highest. Although such debt is likely to have some quality and protective characteristics, these are outweighed by large uncertainties or major risk exposure to adverse conditions.
B	B	
Caa	CCC	
Ca	CC	
C	C	This rating is reserved for income bonds on which no interest is being paid.
D	D	Debt rated D is in default, and payment of interest and/or repayment of principal is in arrears.

Data from various editions of *Standard & Poor's Bond Guide* and *Moody's Bond Guide*.

Junk Bonds

The investment community has labeled bonds with a Standard & Poor's rating of BB and below or a Moody's rating of Ba and below as **junk bonds.** These bonds are also called *high-yield* or *low-grade* and we shall use all three terms interchangeably. Issuance of junk bonds has grown greatly in recent years, leading to increased public interest in this form of financing.

TABLE 20.1	Year	Par Value Outstanding (a)	Par Value Defaults	Default Rates
Historical Default Rates—Straight Bonds Only: 1971–June 30, 2003 ($ millions)	June 30, 2003	$750,000	$22,160	2.955%
	2002	$757,000	$96,858	12.795%
	2001	$649,000	$63,609	9.801%
	2000	$597,200	$30,295	5.073%
	1999	$567,400	$23,532	4.147%
	1998	$465,500	$ 7,464	1.603%
	1997	$335,400	$ 4,200	1.252%
	1996	$271,000	$ 3,336	1.231%
	1995	$240,000	$ 4,551	1.896%
	1994	$235,000	$ 3,418	1.454%
	1993	$206,907	$ 2,287	1.105%
	1992	$163,000	$ 5,545	3.402%
	1991	$183,600	$18,862	10.273%
	1990	$181,000	$18,354	10.140%
	1989	$189,258	$ 8,110	4.285%
	1988	$148,187	$ 3,944	2.662%
	1987	$129,557	$ 7,486	5.778%
	1986	$ 90,243	$ 3,156	3.497%
	1985	$ 58,088	$ 992	1.708%
	1984	$ 40,939	$ 344	0.840%
	1983	$ 27,492	$ 301	1.095%
	1982	$ 18,109	$ 577	3.186%
	1981	$ 17,115	$ 27	0.158%
	1980	$ 14,935	$ 224	1.500%
	1979	$ 10,356	$ 20	0.193%
	1978	$ 8,946	$ 119	1.330%
	1977	$ 8,157	$ 381	4.671%
	1976	$ 7,735	$ 30	0.388%
	1975	$ 7,471	$ 204	2.731%
	1974	$ 10,894	$ 123	1.129%
	1973	$ 7,824	$ 49	0.626%
	1972	$ 6,928	$ 193	2.786%
	1971	$ 6,602	$ 82	1.242%
	Arithmetic Average Default Rate	1971 to 2002		3.249%
		1978 to 2002		3.616%
		1985 to 2002		4.561%
	Weighted Average Default Rate (b)	1971 to 2002		5.453%
		1978 to 2002		5.488%
		1985 to 2002		5.597%
	Median Annual Default Rate	1971 to 2002		1.802%

NOTES
(a) As of mid-year.
(b) Weighted by par value of amount outstanding for each year.
SOURCE: Edward I. Altman's compilations and Citigroup estimates.

Table 20.1 presents data on junk-bond financing in the recent past. Column (1) shows the great growth in junk-bond issuance over a 32-year period. Column (3) shows the default rate on junk bonds increased from 1.24 percent in 1971 to 10.27 percent in 1991. In 1999 the default rate was 4.1 percent. Table 20.2 presents data on default rates by Standard & Poor's on cumulative bases for 10 years. It shows that junk bonds can have a 10-year cumulative (if rated CCC) rate of 48.4 percent.

TABLE 20.2	Defaults by Original Rating—All Rated Corporate Bonds*									
		(1971–2002) Years after Issuance									
		1	2	3	4	5	6	7	8	9	10
AAA	Marginal	0.00%	0.00%	0.00%	0.00%	0.03%	0.00%	0.00%	0.00%	0.00%	0.00%
	Cumulative	0.00%	0.00%	0.00%	0.00%	0.03%	0.03%	0.03%	0.03%	0.03%	0.03%
AA	Marginal	0.00%	0.00%	0.33%	0.17%	0.00%	0.00%	0.00%	0.00%	0.03%	0.02%
	Cumulative	0.00%	0.00%	0.33%	0.50%	0.50%	0.50%	0.50%	0.50%	0.53%	0.55%
A	Marginal	0.01%	0.10%	0.02%	0.09%	0.04%	0.10%	0.05%	0.20%	0.11%	0.06%
	Cumulative	0.01%	0.11%	0.13%	0.22%	0.26%	0.36%	0.41%	0.61%	0.72%	0.78%
BBB	Marginal	0.25%	3.42%	1.52%	1.44%	0.92%	0.57%	0.80%	0.26%	0.17%	0.35%
	Cumulative	0.25%	3.66%	5.13%	6.49%	7.35%	7.88%	8.62%	8.85%	9.01%	9.33%
BB	Marginal	1.23%	2.62%	4.53%	2.15%	2.49%	1.14%	1.67%	0.67%	1.76%	3.78%
	Cumulative	1.23%	3.82%	8.17%	10.15%	12.39%	13.39%	14.83%	15.40%	16.89%	20.03%
B	Marginal	3.19%	7.14%	7.85%	8.74%	6.22%	4.28%	3.88%	2.39%	2.07%	0.87%
	Cumulative	3.19%	10.10%	17.16%	24.40%	29.10%	32.14%	34.77%	36.33%	37.65%	38.19%
CCC	Marginal	6.70%	14.57%	16.16%	11.28%	3.36%	10.26%	5.35%	3.25%	0.00%	4.18%
	Cumulative	6.70%	20.29%	33.17%	40.71%	42.70%	48.58%	51.33%	52.92%	52.92%	54.88%

*Rated by S&P at issuance.
Based on 1,513 issues.
SOURCE: Standard & Poor's (New York) and author's compilation.

In our opinion, the growth in junk-bond financing in the 1970s and 1980s can better be explained by the activities of one man than by a number of economic factors. While a graduate student at the Wharton School in the 1970s, Michael Milken observed a large difference between the return on high-yield bonds and the return on safer bonds. Believing that this difference was greater than what the extra default risk would justify, he concluded that institutional investors would benefit from purchases of junk bonds.

His later employment at Drexel Burnham Lambert allowed him to develop the junk-bond market. Milken's salesmanship simultaneously increased the demand for junk bonds among institutional investors and the supply of junk bonds among corporations. Corporations were particularly impressed with Drexel's vast network of institutional clients, allowing capital to be raised quickly. However, with the demise of the junk-bond market and with Michael Milken's conviction of securities fraud, Drexel found it necessary to declare bankruptcy.

The junk-bond market took on increased importance when these bonds were used to finance mergers and other corporate restructurings. Whereas a firm can only issue a small amount of high-grade debt, the same firm can issue much more debt if low-grade financing is allowed as well. Therefore, the use of junk bonds lets acquirers effect takeovers that they could not do with only traditional bond-financing techniques. Drexel was particularly successful with this technique, primarily because their huge base of institutional clients allowed them to raise large sums of money quickly.

At this time, it is not clear how the great growth in junk-bond financing has altered the returns on these instruments. On the one hand, financial theory indicates that the expected returns on an asset should be negatively related to its marketability.[13] Because trading

---

[13]For example, see Y. Amihud and H. Mendelson, "Asset Pricing and the Bid-Ask Spread," *Journal of Financial Economics* (December 1986).

Edward I. Altman[14] on High-Yield "Junk" Bonds

One of the most important developments in corporate finance over the last 25 years has been the reemergence of publicly owned and traded low-rated corporate debt. Originally offered to the public in the early 1900s to help finance some of our emerging growth industries, these high-yield/high-risk bonds virtually disappeared after the rash of bond defaults during the Depression. Recently, however, the junk bond market has been catapulted from an insignificant element in the corporate fixed income market to one of the fastest growing and most controversial types of financing mechanisms.

The term *junk* emanates from the dominant type of low-rated bond issues outstanding prior to 1977 when the "market" consisted almost exclusively of original-issue investment-grade bonds that fell from their lofty status to a higher default risk, speculative-grade level. These so-called fallen angels amounted to about $8.5 billion in 1977. The proportion of these once investment-grade bonds subsequently dropped to as low as 10 percent in the late 1990s, but due to the huge number of rating downgrades in 2001/2002 the proportion jumped to over 20 percent in 2003. The balance of the high-yield market comprises original issue "junk" bonds.

Beginning in 1977, issuers began to go directly to the public to raise capital for growth purposes. Early users of junk bonds were energy-related firms, cable TV companies, airlines, and assorted other industrial companies.

The emerging growth company rationale coupled with relatively high returns to early investors helped legitimize this sector. Most investment banks ignored junk bonds until 1983–1984, when their merits and profit potential became more evident.

Synonymous with the market's growth was the emergence of the investment banking firm Drexel Burnham Lambert and its junk bond wizard, Michael Milken. Drexel established a potent network of issuers and investors and rode the wave of new financing and the consequent surge in secondary trading to become one of the powerful investment banks in the late 1980s. The incredible rise in power of this firm was followed by an equally incredible fall resulting first in government civil and criminal convictions and huge fines for various misdealings and finally the firm's total collapse and bankruptcy in February 1990.

By far, the most controversial aspect of junk bond financing was its role in the corporate restructuring movement from 1985 through 1989. High-leverage transactions, such as leveraged buyouts (LBOs), which occur when a firm is taken private, transformed the face of corporate America, leading to a heated debate as to the economic and social consequences of corporate control changes with debt/equity ratios of at least 6:1. These transactions involved increasingly large companies, and the multibillion dollar takeover became fairly common,

volume in junk bonds has greatly increased in recent years, the marketability has risen as well. This should lower the expected return on junk bonds, thereby benefiting corporate issuers. On the other hand, the increased interest in junk-bond financing by corporations (the increase in the supply schedule of junk bonds) is likely to raise the expected returns on these assets. The net effect of these two forces is unclear.[15]

Junk-bond financing has recently created much controversy. First, because the use of junk bonds increases the firm's interest deduction, Congress and the IRS have registered strong disapproval. Several legislators have suggested denying interest deductibility on junk bonds, particularly when the bonds are used to finance mergers. Second, the media has focused on the effect of junk-bond financing on corporate solvency. Clearly, this form of

---

[14]Dr. Edward I. Altman is Max L. Heine Professor of Finance and Vice Director of the Salomon Center at the Stern School of Business of New York University. He is widely recognized as one of the world's experts on bankruptcy and credit analysis as well as the high-yield bond market.

[15]The actual risk of junk bonds is not known with certainty because it is not easy to measure default rate. Paul Asquith, David W. Mullins, Jr., and Eric D. Wolff, "Original Issue High Yield Bonds: Aging Analysis of Defaults, Exchanges, and Calls," *Journal of Finance* (September 1989), show that the default rate on junk bonds can be greater than 30 percent over the life of the bond. They look at cumulative default rates and find that of all junk bonds issued in 1977 and 1978, 34 percent had defaulted by December 31, 1988. Table 20.1 shows yearly default rates. Edward I. Altman, "Setting the Record Straight on Junk Bonds: A Review of the Research on Default Rates and Returns," *Journal of Applied Corporate Finance* (Summer 1990), shows that yearly default rates of 5 percent are consistent with cumulative default rates of over 30 percent.

capped by the huge $25 billion RJR Nabisco LBO in 1989. LBOs were typically financed with 60 percent senior bank and insurance company debt, about 25 to 30 percent subordinated public debt (junk bonds), and 10 to 15 percent equity. The junk bond segment is sometimes referred to as *mezzanine financing* because it lies between the "balcony" senior debt and the "basement" equity.

These restructurings resulted in large fees to advisors and underwriters and huge premiums to the old shareholders, and they continued as long as the market was willing to buy these new debt offerings at what appeared to be a favorable risk/return trade-off. The bottom fell out of the market in the last six months of 1989 due to a number of factors including a marked increase in defaults, government regulation against S&Ls holding junk bonds, higher interest rates, a recession, and finally, the growing realization of the leverage excesses of certain ill-conceived restructurings.

The default rate rose dramatically to over 4 percent in 1989 and then skyrocketed in 1990 and 1991 to over 10 percent each year, with about $19 billion of defaults in 1991. Throughout 1990, the pendulum of growth in new junk bond issues and returns to investors swung dramatically downward as prices plummeted and the new issue market all but dried up. The following year (1991) was a pivotal period in that despite record defaults, bond prices and new issues rebounded strongly as the prospects for the future brightened.

In the early 1990s, the financial market was questioning the very survival of the junk bond market. The answer was a resounding yes, as the amount of new issuance soared to record annual levels of $38 billion in 1992 and steadily grew to $120 billion in 1997! Coupled with plummeting annual default rates (under 2.0 percent from 1993 to 1997 compared to about 3.5 percent for 1971 through 1997) and returns in these years between 10 and 20 percent, the risk-return characteristics were extremely favorable.

Defaults again erupted, however, in 2001/2002 with the dollar denominated default rate reaching a record 12.8 percent of the market in 2002. This time, however, nobody questioned the survival or legitimacy of the market and most analysts expected default rates to return to their historical mean—estimated to be over 5 percent per year. What did change, however, was a greater emphasis on bringing more creditworthy companies to the market and reliance on prudent credit analysis and hedging techniques. Time will tell if these lessons will persist. Newer dimensions of the junk bond market include the pooling of large numbers of bonds into collateralized bond obligations (CBOs), the establishment of emerging market international issuance, and the now common use of the nonregistered 144a new issuance mechanism.

financing permits the possibility of higher debt-equity ratios. Whether or not this increased leverage will lead to wholesale defaults in an economic downturn, as some commentators have suggested, remains to be seen. Third, the recent wave of mergers has often resulted in dislocations and loss of jobs. Because junk-bond financing has played a role in mergers, it has come under much criticism. The social policy implications of mergers are quite complex, and any final judgment on them is likely to be reserved for the distant future. At any rate, junk-bond financing should not be implicated too strongly in either the social benefits or the social costs of the recent wave of mergers. Perry and Taggart point out that, contrary to popular belief, this form of financing accounts for only a few percent of all mergers.[16]

We discussed the costs of issuing securities in Chapter 19 and established that the costs of issuing debt are substantially less than the costs of issuing equity. Table 20.3 clarifies several questions regarding the costs of issuing debt securities. It contains a breakdown of direct costs for bond issues after the investment and noninvestment grades have been separated.

First, there are substantial economies of scale here as well. Second, investment-grade issues have much lower direct costs, particularly for straight bonds. Finally, there are relatively few noninvestment-grade issues in the smaller size categories, reflecting the fact that

[16]K. Perry and R. Taggart, "The Growing Role of Junk Bonds in Corporate Finance," *Journal of Applied Corporate Finance* (Spring 1988).

TABLE 20.3 Average Gross Spreads and Total Direct Costs for Domestic Debt Issues

| Proceeds ($ in millions) | Convertible Bonds | | | | | | Straight Bonds | | | | | |
| | Investment Grade | | | Noninvestment Grade | | | Investment Grade | | | Noninvestment Grade | | |
	Number of Issues	Gross Spread	Total Direct Cost	Number of Issues	Gross Spread	Total Direct Cost	Number of Issues	Gross Spread	Total Direct Cost	Number of Issues	Gross Spread	Total Direct Cost
2–9.99	0	—	—	0	—	—	14	.58%	2.19%	0	—	—
10–19.99	0	—	—	1	4.00%	5.67%	56	.50	1.19	2	5.13%	7.41%
20–39.99	1	1.75%	2.75%	9	3.29	4.92	64	.86	1.48	9	3.11	4.42
40–59.99	3	1.92	2.43	19	3.37	4.58	78	.47	.94	9	2.48	3.35
60–79.99	4	1.31	1.76	41	2.76	3.37	49	.61	.98	43	3.07	3.84
80–99.99	2	1.07	1.34	10	2.83	3.48	65	.66	.94	47	2.78	3.75
100–199.99	20	2.03	2.33	37	2.51	3.00	181	.57	.81	222	2.75	3.44
200–499.99	17	1.71	1.87	10	2.46	2.70	60	.50	.93	105	2.56	2.96
500 and up	3	2.00	2.09	0	—	—	11	.39	.57	9	2.60	2.90
Total	50	1.81%	2.09%	127	2.81%	3.53%	578	.58%	.94%	446	2.75%	3.42%

SOURCE: Inmoo Lee, Scott Lochhead, Jay Ritter, and Quanshui Zhao, "The Costs of Raising Capital," *Journal of Financial Research* 1 (Spring 1996).

such issues are more commonly handled as private placements, which we discuss in a later section.

1. List and describe the different bond-rating classes.
2. Why don't bond prices change when bond ratings change?
3. Are the costs of bond issues related to their ratings?

20.5 Some Different Types of Bonds

Until now we have considered "plain vanilla" bonds. In this section we look at some more unusual types: floating-rate bonds, deep-discount bonds, and income bonds.

Floating-Rate Bonds

The conventional bonds we have discussed in this chapter have *fixed-dollar obligations.* That is, the coupon rate is set as a fixed percentage of the par value.

With **floating-rate bonds,** the coupon payments are adjustable. The adjustments are tied to an *interest-rate index* such as the Treasury-bill interest rate or the 30-year Treasury-bond rate. For example, in 1974 Citibank issued $850 million of floating-rate notes maturing in 1989. The coupon rate was set at 1 percent above the 90-day Treasury-bill rate and adjusted semiannually.

In most cases the coupon adjusts with a lag to some base rate. For example, suppose a coupon-rate adjustment is made on June 1. The adjustment may be from a simple average of yields on six-month Treasury bills issued during March, April, and May. In addition, the majority of these *floaters* have put provisions and floor-and-ceiling provisions:

1. With a *put provision* the holder has the right to redeem his or her note at par on the coupon payment date. Frequently, the investor is prohibited from redeeming at par during the first few years of the bond's life.

2. With floor-and-ceiling provisions the coupon rate is subject to a minimum and maximum. For example, the minimum coupon rate might be 8 percent and the maximum rate might be 14 percent.

The popularity of floating-rate bonds is connected to *inflation risk.* When inflation is higher than expected, issuers of fixed-rate bonds tend to make gains at the expense of lenders, and when inflation is less than expected, lenders make gains at the expense of borrowers. Because the inflation risk of long-term bonds is borne by both issuers and bondholders, it is in their interests to devise loan agreements that minimize inflation risk.[17]

Floaters reduce inflation risk because the coupon rate is tied to the current interest rate, which, in turn, is influenced by the rate of inflation. This can most clearly be seen by considering the formula for the present value of a bond. As inflation increases the interest rate (the denominator of the formula), inflation increases a floater's coupon rate (the numerator of the formula). Hence, bond value is hardly affected by inflation. Conversely, the coupon rate of fixed-rate bonds cannot change, implying that the prices of these bonds are at the mercy of inflation.

As an alternative, an individual who is concerned with inflation risk can invest in short-term notes, such as Treasury bills, and *roll them over.*[18] The investor can accomplish

---

[17]See B. Cornell, "The Future of Floating Rate Bonds," in *The Revolution in Corporate Finance,* ed. by J. M. Stern and D. H. Chew, Jr. (New York: Basil Blackwell, 1986).

[18]That is, the investor could buy a bill, receive the face value at maturity, use these proceeds to buy a second bill, receive the face value from the second bill at maturity, and so on.

essentially the same objective by buying a floater that is adjusted to the Treasury-bill rate. However, the purchaser of a floater can reduce transactions costs relative to rolling over short-term Treasury bills because floaters are long-term bonds. The same type of reduction in transactions costs makes floaters attractive to some corporations.[19] They benefit from issuing a floater instead of issuing a series of short-term notes.

In an earlier section, we discussed callable bonds. Because the coupon on floaters varies with marketwide interest rates, floaters always sell at or near par. Therefore, it is not surprising that floaters do not generally have call features.

Deep-Discount Bonds

A bond that pays no coupon must be offered at a price that is much lower than its face value. Such bonds are known as **original-issue discount bonds, deep-discount bonds, pure-discount bonds,** or **zero-coupon bonds.** They are frequently called *zeros* for short.

Suppose the DDB Company issues $1,000 of five-year deep-discount bonds when the marketwide interest rate is 10 percent. These bonds do not pay any coupons. The initial price is set at $621 because $621 = \$1,000/(1.10)^5$.

Because these bonds have no intermediate coupon payments, they are quite attractive to certain investors and quite unattractive to others. For example, consider an insurance company forecasting death-benefit payments of $1,000,000 five years from today. The company would like to be sure that it will have the funds to pay off the liability in five years' time. The company could buy five-year zero-coupon bonds with a face value of $1,000,000. The company is matching assets with liabilities here, a procedure that eliminates interest-rate risk. That is, regardless of the movement of interest rates, the firm's set of zeros will always be able to pay off the $1,000,000 liability.

Conversely, the firm would be at risk if it bought coupon bonds instead. For example, if it bought five-year coupon bonds, it would need to reinvest the coupon payments through to the fifth year. Because interest rates in the future are not known with certainty today, one cannot be sure if these bonds will be worth more or less than $1,000,000 by the fifth year.

Now, consider a couple saving for their child's college education in 15 years. They *expect* that, with inflation, four years of college should cost $150,000 in 15 years. Thus, they buy 15-year zero-coupon bonds with a face value of $150,000.[20] If they have forecasted inflation perfectly (and if college costs keep pace with inflation), their child's tuition will be fully funded. However, if inflation rises more than expected, the tuition would be more than $150,000. Because the zero-coupon bonds produce a shortfall, the child might end up working his way through school. As an alternative, the parents might have considered rolling over Treasury bills. Because the yields on Treasury bills rise and fall with the inflation rate, this simple strategy is likely to cause less risk than the strategy with zeros.

The key to these examples concerns the distinction between nominal and real quantities. The insurance company's liability is $1,000,000 in *nominal* dollars. Because the face value of a zero-coupon bond is a nominal quantity, the purchase of zeros eliminates risk. However, it is easier to forecast college costs in real terms than in nominal terms. Thus,

---

[19]Cox, Ingersoll, and Ross developed a framework for pricing floating-rate notes; see J. Cox, J. Ingersoll, and S. A. Ross, "An Analysis of Variable Rate Loan Contracts," *Journal of Finance* 35 (May 1980).

[20]A more precise strategy would be to buy zeros maturing in years 15, 16, 17, and 18, respectively. In this way, the bonds might mature just in time to meet tuition payments.

a zero-coupon bond is a poor choice to reduce the financial risk of a child's college education.

Income Bonds

Income bonds are similar to conventional bonds, except that coupon payments are dependent on company income. Specifically, coupons are paid to bondholders only if the firm's income is sufficient.

Income bonds are a financial puzzle because, from the firm's standpoint, they appear to be a cheaper form of debt than conventional bonds. Income bonds provide the same tax advantage to corporations from interest deductions that conventional bonds do. However, a company that issues income bonds is less likely to experience financial distress. When a coupon payment is omitted because of insufficient corporate income, an income bond is not in default.

Why don't firms issue more income bonds? Two explanations have been offered:

1. *The "Smell of Death" Explanation.* Firms that issue income bonds signal the capital markets of their increased prospect of financial distress.

2. *The "Dead-Weight Costs" Explanation.* The calculation of corporate income is crucial to determining the status of bondholders' income, and stockholders and bondholders will not necessarily agree on how to calculate the income. This creates agency costs associated with the firm's accounting methods.

Although these are possibilities, the work of McConnell and Schlarbaum suggests that no truly satisfactory reason exists for the lack of more investor interest in income bonds.[21]

Concept Question	1. Create an idea of an unusual bond and analyze its features.

20.6 Direct Placement Compared to Public Issues

Earlier in this chapter, we described the mechanics of issuing debt to the public. However, more than 50 percent of all debt is privately placed. There are two basic forms of direct private long-term financing: term loans and private placement.

Term loans are direct business loans with maturities of between 1 year and 15 years. The typical term loan is amortized over the life of the loan. That is, the loan is repaid by equal annual payments of interest and principal. The lenders are commercial banks and insurance companies. A **private placement,** which also involves the sale of a bond or loan directly to a limited number of investors, is very similar to a term loan except that the maturity is longer.

Some important differences between direct long-term financing and public issues are:

1. A direct long-term loan avoids the cost of registration with the Securities and Exchange Commission.

2. Direct placement is likely to have more restrictive covenants.

3. It is easier to renegotiate a term loan and a private placement in the event of a default. It is harder to renegotiate a public issue because hundreds of holders are usually involved.

---

[21]J. McConnell and G. Schlarbaum, "The Income Bond Puzzle," in *The Revolution in Corporate Finance.* ed. by J. M. Stern and D. H. Chew, Jr. (New York: Basil Blackwell, 1986).

4. Life insurance companies and pension funds dominate the private-placement segment of the bond market. Commercial banks are significant participants in the term-loan market.

5. The costs of distributing bonds are lower in the private market.

The interest rates on term loans and private placements are usually higher than those on an equivalent public issue. Hayes, Joehnk, and Melicher found that the yield to maturity on private placements was 0.46 percent higher than on similar public issues.[22] This finding reflects the trade-off between a higher interest rate and more flexible arrangements in the event of financial distress, as well as the lower transaction costs associated with private placements.

Concept **Questions**

1. **What are the differences between private and public bond issues?**
2. **A private placement is more likely to have restrictive covenants than is a public issue. Why?**

20.7 Long-Term Syndicated Bank Loans

Most bank loans are for less than a year. They serve as a short-term "bridge" for the acquisition of inventory and are typically self-liquidating—that is, when the firm sells the inventory, the cash is used to repay the bank loan. We talk about the need for short-term bank loans in the next section of the text. Now we focus on long-term bank loans.

First, we introduce the concept of commitment. Most bank loans are made with a commitment to a firm. That commitment establishes a line of credit and allows the firm to borrow up to a predetermined limit. Most commitments are in the form of a revolving credit commitment (i.e., a revolver) with a fixed term of up to three years or more. Revolving credit commitments are drawn or undrawn depending on whether the firm has a current need for the funds.

Now we turn to the concept of syndication. Very large banks such as Citigroup typically have a larger demand for loans than they can supply, and small regional banks frequently have more funds on hand than they can profitably lend to existing customers. Basically, they cannot generate enough good loans with the funds they have available. As a result, a very large bank may arrange a loan with a firm or country and then sell portions of it to a syndicate of other banks. With a syndicated loan, each bank has a separate loan agreement with the borrowers.

A syndicated loan is a corporate loan made by a group (or syndicate) of banks and other institutional investors. A syndicated loan may be publicly traded. It may be a line of credit and be "undrawn" or it may be drawn and be used by a firm. Syndicated loans are always rated investment grade. However, a *leveraged* syndicated loan is rated speculative grade (i.e., it is "junk"). Every week, *The Wall Street Journal* reports on the number of syndicated loan deals, credit costs, and yields, as seen in Table 20.4. In addition, syndicated loan prices are reported for a group of publicly traded loans. Altman and Suggitt report slightly higher default rates for syndicated loans when compared to comparable corporate bonds.[23]

---

[22]P. A. Hayes, M. D. Joehnk, and R. W. Melicher, "Determinants of Risk Premiums in the Public and Private Bond Market," *Journal of Financial Research* (Fall 1979).

[23]Edward I. Altman and Heather J. Suggitt, "Default Rates in the Syndicated Bank Loan Market: A Longitudinal Analysis," *Journal of Banking and Finance* 24 (2000).

Syndicated Loans / *Trends & Prices*

Syndicated loans are corporate loans made by a group, or syndicate, of banks and institutional investors. 'Undrawn' loans are lines of credit made available to corporations as backing for commercial paper or for general corporate purposes. A basis point is 1/100th of a percentage point.

Deal Flow

A leading indicator of activity, showing new deals mandated or in the market. Deals tallied are transactions priced at or below Libor+150 basis points.

Credit Costs

Average new-issue fees paid by investment-grade issuers on undrawn loans*; in basis points, by credit rating of issuer.

*These loans are assumed to be 100% undrawn. Fees include the facility fee, paid to have a line of credit open and/or the commitment fee, paid to retain the portion of the money that's undrawn.

The Week's Biggest Movers

Biggest gainers and losers among widely-quoted syndicated loans in secondary trading, in the week ended Monday. Listed are the biggest movers among the 105 loans with at least five bids. All loans listed are B-term, or sold to institutional investors.

	LOAN RATING MOODY'S/S&P	COUPON	MATURITY	AVERAGE BID (pct. pts.)	WEEKLY CHANGE (pct. pts.)		LOAN RATING MOODY'S/S&P	COUPON	MATURITY	AVERAGE BID (pct. pts.)	WEEKLY CHANGE (pct. pts.)
Adelphia Commun.	Ba3/N.R.*	L+250	March 21, '09	99.93	+0.07	**Nextlink**	B1/B+	L+350	June 30, '07	99.92	+0.05
Allied Waste	Ba3/BB	L+275	July 1, '06	95.86	+0.16	**Pillowtex**	B3/CCC	L+275	Dec. 31, '04	68.38	+0.13
Casella Waste Sys.	B1/BB–	L+350	Jan. 26, '07	99.05	+1.55	**Safelite Glass**	Caa1/D	L+200	Dec. 29, '04	41.25	+0.25
Federal-Mogul	Ba2/BB	L+225	Dec. 18, '05	92.79	–0.04	**Superior TeleCom**	Ba3/B+	L+375	Nov. 27, '05	98.89	–0.04
Global Crossing	Ba1/BBB–	L+275	July 6, '06	100.38	+0.04	**Tenneco Auto.**	Ba3/BB	L+275	August 5, '07	98.82	–0.17
Huntsman Pkg.	B1/BB–	L+300	April 15, '08	97.34	–0.14	**Thermadyne**	B1/B	L+275	May 22, '05	92.90	–0.2
Integrated Health	N.R.*/N.R.*	L+200	Sept. 30, '04	27.67	–0.17	**Total Renal Care**	B1/B+(a)	L+375	March 31, '08	96.30	+0.20
Kansas City So. Rail	Ba1/BB+	L+350	Dec.17, '06	100.29	+0.05	**U.S. Office Prod.**	Caa1/CCC+	L+250	April 22, '06	58.75	–2
Laidlaw/Safety-Kleen	N.R./CC	L+312.5	May 15, '04	30.57	–0.43	**VenTrust-Ventas**	N.R.*/N.R.*	L+375	Dec. 31, '05	89.00	+1.50
Lincoln Electric	Ba3/BB+	L+300	May 30, '08	100.55	+0.05	**Voicestream Wrlss**	B1/B+	L+350	Jan. 31, '09	99.49	+0.05
Magellan Health	B2/B+	L+250	Feb. 12, '05	85.67	+0.50	**Winstar Commun.**	B2/B+	L+400	Sept. 10, '07	97.05	–0.34
McLeod	Ba2/BB–	L+300	April 12, '08	100.04	+0.05	**Wyndham Intl.**		L+350	June 18, '06	98.49	+0.28
Nextel Finance	Ba2/BB–	L+337.5	April 10, '08	100.44	+0.07						

*Not rated

Advancers	**93**		Total loans with at least one bid: 1,747
Decliners	**97**		Average change in bids: –0.04 percentage point
Unchanged		**1,557**	

Note: These are the averages of indicative bid prices provided by bank-loan traders, excluding the highest bid and expressed as a percentage of the par, or face, value. Coupon, or interest rate, is in 1/100s of a percentage point over Libor, the benchmark London Interbank Offered Rate. All ratings are for specific loans and not for the company itself except as noted with an (a). These prices do not represent actual trades nor are they offers to trade: rather they are estimated values provided by dealers.

20.8 SUMMARY AND CONCLUSIONS

This chapter describes some important aspects of long-term debt financing.

1. The written agreement describing the details of the long-term debt contract is called an *indenture*. Some of the main provisions are security, repayment, protective covenants, and call provisions.

2. There are many ways that shareholders can take advantage of bondholders. Protective covenants are designed to protect bondholders from management decisions that favor stockholders at bondholders' expense.

3. Unsecured bonds are called *debentures* or *notes*. They are general claims on the company's value. Most public industrial bonds are unsecured. In contrast, utility bonds are usually secured. Mortgage bonds are secured by tangible property, and collateral trust bonds are secured by financial securities such as stocks and bonds. If the company defaults on secured bonds, the trustee can repossess the assets. This makes secured bonds more valuable.

4. Long-term bonds usually provide for repayment of principal before maturity. This is accomplished by a sinking fund. With a sinking fund, the company retires a certain number of bonds each year. A sinking fund protects bondholders because it reduces the average maturity of the bond, and its payment signals the financial condition of the company.

5. Most publicly issued bonds are callable. A callable bond is less attractive to bondholders than a noncallable bond. A callable bond can be bought back by the company at a call price that is less than the true value of the bond. As a consequence, callable bonds are priced to obtain higher stated interest rates for bondholders than noncallable bonds.

   Generally, companies should exercise the call provision whenever the bond's value is greater than the call price.

   There is no single reason for call provisions. Some sensible reasons include taxes, greater flexibility, management's ability to predict interest rates, and the fact that callable bonds are less sensitive to interest-rate changes.

6. There are many different types of bonds, including floating-rate bonds, deep-discount bonds, and income bonds. This chapter also compares private placement with public issuance.

KEY TERMS

bearer, *571*	negative covenant, *573*
call premium, *574*	original-issue discount bonds, *586*
call-protected, *574*	positive covenant, *573*
debenture, *573*	private placement, *587*
deep-discount bonds, *586*	protective covenant, *573*
deferred call, *574*	public issue, *570*
floating-rate bonds, *585*	pure-discount bonds, *586*
income bonds, *587*	refunding, *574*
indenture, *570*	zero-coupon bonds, *586*
junk bonds, *579*	

SUGGESTED READING

The following provides a complete coverage of bonds and the bond market:

Fabozzi, F. J., and T. D. Fabozzi, eds. *The Handbook of Fixed Income Securities.* 4th ed. Homewood, Ill.: Irwin Professional Publishing, 1995.

QUESTIONS & PROBLEMS

THE PUBLIC ISSUE OF BONDS

20.1 Raeo Corp. bonds trade at 100 today. The bonds pay semiannual interest that is paid on January 1 and July 1. The coupon on the bonds is 10 percent. How much will you pay for a Raeo bond if today is
   a. March 1.
   b. October 1.
   c. July 1.
   d. August 15.

20.2   Define the following terms:
  a. Protective covenant
  b. Negative covenant
  c. Positive covenant
  d. Sinking fund

20.3   Sinking funds have both positive and negative characteristics to the bondholders. Why?

20.4   Which is riskier to a prospective creditor, an open-end mortgage or closed-end mortgage? Why?

20.5   What is call premium? During what period of time is a bond said to be call-protected?

BOND REFUNDING   **20.6**   KIC, Inc., plans to issue $5 million of perpetual bonds. The face value of each bond is $1,000. The annual coupon on the bonds is 12 percent. Market interest rates on one-year bonds are 11 percent. With equal probability, the long-term market interest rate will be either 14 percent or 7 percent next year. Assume investors are risk-neutral.
  a. If the KIC bonds are noncallable, what is the price of the bonds?
  b. If the bonds are callable one year from today at $1,450, will their price be greater than or less than the price you computed in (*a*)? Why?

20.7   Bowdeen Manufacturing intends to issue callable, perpetual bonds. The bonds are callable at $1,250. One-year interest rates are 12 percent. There is a 60-percent probability that long-term interest rates one year from today will be 15 percent. With a 40-percent probability, long-term interest rates will be 8 percent. To simplify the firm's accounting, Bowdeen would like to issue the bonds at par ($1,000). What must the coupon on the bonds be for Bowdeen to be able to sell them at par?

20.8   Illinois Industries has decided to borrow money by issuing perpetual bonds. The face value of the bonds will be $1,000. The coupon will be 8 percent, payable annually. The one-year interest rate is 8 percent. It is known that next year there is a 65-percent chance that interest rates will decline to 6 percent, and that there is a 35-percent chance that they will rise to 9 percent.
  a. What will the market value of these bonds be if they are noncallable?
  b. If the company instead decides to make the bonds callable, what coupon will be demanded by the bondholders for the bonds to sell at par? Assume that the bonds can be called in one year (i.e., the call date is one year from now) and that the call premium is equal to the annual coupon.
  c. What will be the value of the call provision to Illinois Industries?

20.9   New Business Ventures, Inc., has an outstanding perpetual bond with a face value equal to $1,000 and a 9-percent coupon rate. The bond cannot be called for one year. The call premium is set at $150 over par value. It is forecasted that there is a 40-percent chance that the interest rate will rise to 12 percent, and a 60-percent chance that the interest rate will fall down to 6 percent next year. The current interest rate is 10 percent. What is the current market price of this callable bond?

20.10   Hudson River Electronics has $500 million of 9-percent perpetual bonds outstanding. These bonds can be called at a price of $1,090 for each $1,000 of face value. Under present market conditions, the outstanding bonds can be replaced by $500 million of 7-percent perpetual bonds. The underwriting and legal expenses of this new issue would be $80 million. What would be the net present value of this refunding? Assume that there are no taxes.

20.11   An outstanding issue of Public Express Airlines debentures has a call provision attached. The total principal value of the bonds is $250 million, and the bonds pay an annual coupon of $80 for each $1,000 of face value. The total cost of refunding would be 12 percent of the principal amount raised. The appropriate tax rate for the company is 35 percent. How low does the borrowing cost of Public Express need to drop to justify refunding with a new bond issue?

20.12   Margret Kimberly, CFO of Charles River Associates, is considering whether or not to refinance the two currently outstanding corporate bonds of the firm. The first one is an

8-percent perpetual bond with a $1,000 face value with $75 million outstanding. The second one is a 9-percent perpetual bond with the same face value with $87.5 million outstanding. The call premiums for the two bonds are 8.5 percent and 9.5 percent of the face value, respectively. The transaction costs of the refundings are $10 million and $12 million, respectively. The current interest rates for the two bonds are 7 percent and 7.25 percent, respectively. Which bond should Ms. Kimberly recommend be refinanced? What is the NPV of the refunding?

SOME DIFFERENT TYPES OF BONDS

20.13 What is a "junk bond"? What are some of the controversies created by junk-bond financing?

20.14 Describe the following types of bonds:
a. Floating rate
b. Deep discount
c. Income

DIRECT PLACEMENT COMPARED TO PUBLIC ISSUES

20.15 Which of the following are characteristics of public issues, and which are characteristics of direct financing?
a. SEC registration required
b. Higher interest cost
c. Higher fixed cost
d. Quicker access to funds
e. Active secondary market
f. Easily renegotiated
g. Lower flotation costs
h. Regular amortization required
i. Ease of repurchase at favorable prices
j. High total cost to small borrowers
k. Flexible terms
l. Less intensive investigation required

GENERAL TOPICS

20.16 a. In an efficient market callable and noncallable bonds will be priced in such a way that there will be no advantage or disadvantage to the call provision. Comment.
b. If interest rates fall, will the price of noncallable bonds move up higher than that of callable bonds? Why or why not?

S & P PROBLEMS

STANDARD &POOR'S

20.17 Look under the Edgar link for American Electric Power (AEP) and find the most recent bond issue for the company. What was the amount of bonds issued? What are the coupon rate, maturity date, payment dates, ranking, and restrictive covenants on the bonds? What are the risk factors of the bonds outlined in the prospectus?

Leasing

EXECUTIVE SUMMARY

Almost any asset that can be purchased can be leased, from aircraft to zithers. When we take vacations or business trips, renting a car for a few days frequently seems a convenient thing to do. This is an example of a short-term lease. After all, buying a car and selling it a few days later would be a great nuisance.

Corporations lease both short-term and long-term, but this chapter is primarily concerned with long-term leasing over a term of more than five years. Long-term leasing is a method of financing property, plant, and equipment. More equipment is financed today by long-term leases than by any other method of equipment financing.[1]

Every lease contract has two parties: the lessee and the lessor. The **lessee** is the user of the equipment, and the **lessor** is the owner. Typically, the lessee first decides on the asset needed and then negotiates a lease contract with a lessor. From the lessee's standpoint, long-term leasing is similar to buying the equipment with a secured loan. The terms of the lease contract are compared to what a banker might arrange with a secured loan. Thus, long-term leasing is a form of financing.

Many questionable advantages are claimed for long-term leasing, such as "leasing provides 100-percent financing," or "leasing conserves capital." However, the principal benefit of long-term leasing is tax reduction. Leasing allows the transfer of tax benefits from those who need equipment but cannot take full advantage of the tax benefits associated with ownership to a party who can. If the corporate income tax were repealed, long-term leasing would virtually disappear.

---

[1] P. K. Nevitt and F. J. Fabozzi, *Equipment Leasing,* 2nd ed. (Homewood, Ill.: Dow Jones-Irwin, 1985).

21.1 Types of Leases

The Basics

A *lease* is a contractual agreement between a lessee and lessor. The agreement establishes that the lessee has the right to use an asset and in return must make periodic payments to the lessor, the owner of the asset. The lessor is either the asset's manufacturer or an independent leasing company. If the lessor is an independent leasing company, it must buy the asset from a manufacturer. Then the lessor delivers the asset to the lessee, and the lease goes into effect.

As far as the lessee is concerned, it is the use of the asset that is most important, not who owns the asset. The use of an asset can be obtained by a lease contract. Because the user can also buy the asset, leasing and buying involve alternative financing arrangements for the use of an asset. This is illustrated in Figure 21.1.

FIGURE 21.1 Buying versus Leasing

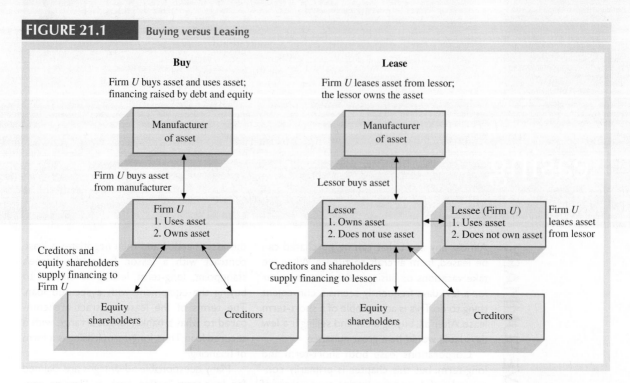

The specific example in Figure 21.1 happens often in the computer industry. Firm *U*, the lessee, might be a hospital, a law firm, or any other firm that uses computers. The lessor is an independent leasing company who purchased the equipment from a manufacturer such as IBM or Apple. Leases of this type are called **direct leases.** In the figure, the lessor issued both debt and equity to finance the purchase.

Of course, a manufacturer like IBM could lease its *own* computers, though we do not show this situation in the example. Leases of this type are called **sales-type leasing.** In this case, IBM would compete with the independent computer-leasing company.

Operating Leases

Years ago, a lease where the lessee received an operator along with the equipment was called an **operating lease.** Though the operating lease defies an exact definition today, this form for leasing has several important characteristics.

1. Operating leases are usually not fully amortized. This means that the payments required under the terms of the lease are not enough to recover the full cost of the asset for the lessor. This occurs because the term or life of the operating lease is usually less than the economic life of the asset. Thus, the lessor must expect to recover the costs of the asset by renewing the lease or by selling the asset for its residual value.

2. Operating leases usually require the lessor to maintain and insure the leased assets.

3. Perhaps the most interesting feature of an operating lease is the cancellation option. This option gives the lessee the right to cancel the lease contract before the expiration date. If the option to cancel is exercised, the lessee must return the equipment to the lessor. The value of a cancellation clause depends on whether future technological and/or economic conditions are likely to make the value of the asset to the lessee less than the value of the future lease payments under the lease.

To leasing practitioners, the above characteristics constitute an operating lease. However, accountants use the term in a slightly different way, as we will see shortly.

Financial Leases

Financial leases are the exact opposite of operating leases, as is seen from their important characteristics:

1. Financial leases do not provide for maintenance or service by the lessor.
2. Financial leases are fully amortized.
3. The lessee usually has a right to renew the lease on expiration.
4. Generally, financial leases cannot be canceled. In other words, the lessee must make all payments or face the risk of bankruptcy.

Because of the above characteristics, particularly (2), this lease provides an alternative method of financing to purchase. Hence, its name is a sensible one. Two special types of financial leases are the sale and lease-back arrangement and the leveraged lease.

Sale and Lease-Back   A **sale and lease-back** occurs when a company sells an asset it owns to another firm and immediately leases it back. In a sale and lease-back, two things happen:

1. The lessee receives cash from the sale of the asset.
2. The lessee makes periodic lease payments, thereby retaining use of the asset.

An example of a sale and lease-back occurred when the city of Oakland, California, used the proceeds of a sale of its city hall and 23 other buildings to help meet the liabilities of the $150 million Police and Retirement System. As part of the same transaction, Oakland leased back the buildings to obtain their continued use.

Leveraged Leases   A **leveraged lease** is a three-sided arrangement among the lessee, the lessor, and the lenders:

1. As in other leases, the lessee uses the assets and makes periodic lease payments.
2. As in other leases, the lessor purchases the assets, delivers them to the lessee, and collects the lease payments. However, the lessor puts up no more than 40 to 50 percent of the purchase price.
3. The lenders supply the remaining financing and receive interest payments from the lessor. Thus, the arrangement on the right-hand side of Figure 24.1 would be a leveraged lease if the bulk of the financing was supplied by creditors.

The lenders in a leveraged lease typically use a nonrecourse loan. This means that the lessor is not obligated to the lender in case of a default. However, the lender is protected in two ways:

1. The lender has a first lien on the asset.
2. In the event of loan default, the lease payments are made directly to the lender.

The lessor puts up only part of the funds but gets the lease payments and all the tax benefits of ownership. These lease payments are used to pay the debt service of the nonrecourse loan. The lessee benefits because, in a competitive market, the lease payment is lowered when the lessor saves taxes.

Concept
Questions

1. **What are some reasons that assets like automobiles would be leased with operating leases, whereas machines or real estate would be leased with financial leases?**
2. **What are the differences between an operating lease and a financial lease?**

21.2 Accounting and Leasing

Before November 1976, a firm could arrange to use an asset through a lease and not disclose the asset or the lease contract on the balance sheet. Lessees needed only to report information on leasing activity in the footnotes of their financial statements. Thus, leasing led to **off–balance-sheet financing.**

In November 1976, the Financial Accounting Standards Board (FASB) issued its *Statement of Financial Accounting Standards No. 13 (FAS 13),* "Accounting for Leases." Under *FAS 13,* certain leases are classified as capital leases. (We present the criteria later in this section.) For a capital lease, the present value of the lease payments appears on the right-hand side of the balance sheet. The identical value appears on the left-hand side of the balance sheet as an asset.

FASB classifies all other leases as operating leases, though FASB's definition differs from that of nonaccountants. (The use of operating leases by nonaccountants was discussed in an earlier section of this chapter.) No mention of the lease appears on the balance sheet for operating leases.

The accounting implications of this distinction are illustrated in Table 21.1. Imagine a firm that, years ago, issued $100,000 of equity in order to purchase land. It now wants to use a $100,000 truck, which it can either purchase or lease. The balance sheet reflecting purchase of the truck is shown at the top of the table. (We assume that the truck is financed entirely with debt.) Alternatively, imagine that the firm leases the truck. If the lease is judged to be an operating one, the middle balance sheet is created. Here, neither the lease liability nor the truck appears on the balance sheet. The bottom balance sheet reflects a capital lease. The truck is shown as an asset and the lease is shown as a liability.

Accountants generally argue that a firm's financial strength is inversely related to the amount of its liabilities. Since the lease liability is hidden with an operating lease, the balance sheet of a firm with an operating lease *looks* stronger than the balance sheet of a firm with an otherwise-identical capital lease. Given the choice, firms would probably classify all their leases as operating ones. Because of this tendency, *FAS 13* states that a lease must

TABLE 21.1	Balance Sheet			
Example of Balance Sheet under FAS 13	Truck is purchased with debt (the company owns a $100,000 truck)			
	Truck	$100,000	Debt	$100,000
	Land	100,000	Equity	100,000
	Total assets	$200,000	Total debt plus equity	$200,000
	Operating lease (the company has an operating lease for the truck)			
	Truck	$ 0	Debt	$ 0
	Land	100,000	Equity	100,000
	Total assets	$100,000	Total debt plus equity	$100,000
	Capital lease (the company has a capital lease for the truck)			
	Assets under capital lease	$100,000	Obligations under capital lease	$100,000
	Land	100,000	Equity	100,000
	Total assets	$200,000	Total debt plus equity	$200,000

be classified as a capital one if at least one of the following four criteria is met:

1. The present value of the lease payments is at least 90 percent of the fair market value of the asset at the start of the lease.
2. The lease transfers ownership of the property to the lessee by the end of the term of the lease.
3. The lease term is 75 percent or more of the estimated economic life of the asset.
4. The lessee can purchase the asset at a price below fair market value when the lease expires. This is frequently called a *bargain-purchase-price option.*

These rules capitalize those leases that are similar to purchases. For example, the first two rules capitalize leases where the asset is likely to be purchased at the end of the lease period. The last two rules capitalize long-term leases.

Some firms have tried to cook the books by exploiting this classification scheme. Suppose a trucking firm wants to lease a $200,000 truck that it expects to use for 15 years. A clever financial manager could try to negotiate a lease contract for 10 years with lease payments having a present value of $178,000. These terms would get around criteria (1) and (3). If criteria (2) and (4) could be circumvented, the arrangement would be an operating lease and would not show up on the balance sheet.

Does this sort of gimmickry pay? The semistrong form of the efficient-capital-markets hypothesis implies that stock prices reflect all publicly available information. As we discussed earlier in this text, the empirical evidence generally supports this form of the hypothesis. Though operating leases do not appear in the firm's balance sheet, information on these leases must be disclosed elsewhere in the annual report. Because of this, attempts to keep leases off the balance sheet will not affect stock price in an efficient capital market.

Concept Questions

1. Define capital lease.
2. Define operating lease.

21.3 Taxes, the IRS, and Leases

The lessee can deduct lease payments for income tax purposes if the lease is qualified by the Internal Revenue Service. Because tax shields are critical to the economic viability of any lease, all interested parties generally obtain an opinion from the IRS before agreeing to a major lease transaction. The opinion of the IRS will reflect the following guidelines:

1. The term of the lease must be less than 30 years. If the term is greater than 30 years, the transaction will be regarded as a conditional sale.
2. The lease should not have an option to acquire the asset at a price below its fair market value. This type of bargain option would give the lessee the asset's residual scrap value, implying an equity interest.
3. The lease should not have a schedule of payments that is very high at the start of the lease term and thereafter very low. Early *balloon* payments would be evidence that the lease was being used to avoid taxes and not for a legitimate business purpose.
4. The lease payments must provide the lessor with a fair market rate of return. The profit potential of the lease to the lessor should be apart from the deal's tax benefits.
5. The lease should not limit the lessee's right to issue debt or pay dividends while the lease is operative.

6. Renewal options must be reasonable and reflect fair market value of the asset. This requirement can be met by granting the lessee the first option to meet a competing outside offer.

The reason the IRS is concerned about lease contracts is that many times they appear to be set up solely to avoid taxes. To see how this could happen, suppose that a firm plans to purchase a $1 million bus that has a five-year class life. Depreciation expense would be $200,000 per year, assuming straight-line depreciation. Now suppose that the firm can lease the bus for $500,000 per year for two years and buy the bus for $1 at the end of the two-year term. The present value of the tax benefits from acquiring the bus would clearly be less than if the bus were leased. The speedup of lease payments would greatly benefit the firm and *de facto* give it a form of accelerated depreciation. If the tax rates of the lessor and lessee are different, leasing can be a form of tax avoidance.

<table>
<tr><td>

**Concept
Question**

</td><td>

1. What are the IRS guidelines for treating a lease contract as a lease for tax purposes?

</td></tr>
</table>

21.4 The Cash Flows of Leasing

In this section we identify the basic cash flows used in evaluating a lease. Consider the decision confronting the Xomox corporation, which manufactures pipe. Business has been expanding, and Xomox currently has a five-year backlog of pipe orders for the Trans-Honduran Pipeline.

The International Boring Machine Corporation (IBMC) makes a pipe-boring machine that can be purchased for $10,000. Xomox has determined that it needs a new machine, and the IBMC model will save Xomox $6,000 per year in reduced electricity bills for the next five years. These savings are known with certainty because Xomox has a long-term electricity purchase agreement with State Electric Utilities, Inc.

Xomox has a corporate tax rate of 34 percent. We assume that five-year straight-line depreciation is used for the pipe-boring machine, and the machine will be worthless after five years.[2]

However, Friendly Leasing Corporation has offered to lease the same pipe-boring machine to Xomox for $2,500 per year for five years. With the lease, Xomox would remain responsible for maintenance, insurance, and operating expenses.[3]

Simon Smart, a recently hired MBA, has been asked to calculate the incremental cash flows from leasing the IBMC machine in lieu of buying it. He has prepared Table 21.2, which shows the direct cash flow consequences of buying the pipe-boring machine and also signing the lease agreement with Friendly Leasing.

To simplify matters, Simon Smart has prepared Table 21.3, which subtracts the direct cash flows of buying the pipe-boring machine from those of leasing it. Noting that only the net advantage of leasing is relevant to Xomox, he concludes the following from his analysis:

1. Operating costs are not directly affected by leasing. Xomox will save $3,960 (after taxes) from use of the IBMC boring machine regardless of whether the machine is owned or leased. Thus, this cash flow stream does not appear in Table 21.3.

2. If the machine is leased, Xomox will save the $10,000 it would have used to purchase the machine. This saving shows up as an initial cash *inflow* of $10,000 in year 0.

---

[2]This is a simplifying assumption because current tax law allows the accelerated method as well. The accelerated method will almost always be the best choice.

[3]For simplicity, we have assumed that lease payments are made at the end of each year. Actually, most leases require lease payments to be made at the beginning of the year.

TABLE 21.2		Year 0	Year 1	Year 2	Year 3	Year 4	Year 5
Cash Flows to Xomox from Using the IBMC Pipe-Boring Machine: Buy versus Lease	**Buy**						
	Cost of machine	−$10,000					
	After-tax operating savings [$3,960 = $6,000 × (1 − 0.34)]		$3,960	$3,960	$3,960	$3,960	$3,960
	Depreciation tax benefit		680	680	680	680	680
		−$10,000	$4,640	$4,640	$4,640	$4,640	$4,640
	Lease						
	Lease payments		−$2,500	−$2,500	−$2,500	−$2,500	−$2,500
	Tax benefits of lease payments ($850 = $2,500 × 0.34)		850	850	850	850	850
	After-tax operating savings		3,960	3,960	3,960	3,960	3,960
	Total		$2,310	$2,310	$2,310	$2,310	$2,310

Depreciation is straight-line. Because the depreciable base is $10,000, depreciation expense per year is $10,000/5 = $2,000. The depreciation tax benefit per year is equal to:

Tax rate × Depreciation expense per year = Depreciation tax benefit
0.34 × $2,000 = $680

TABLE 21.3	**Lease Minus Buy**	Year 0	Year 1	Year 2	Year 3	Year 4	Year 5
Incremental Cash Flow Consequences for Xomox from Leasing Instead of Purchasing	**Lease**						
	Lease payment		−$2,500	−$2,500	−$2,500	−$2,500	−$2,500
	Tax benefit of lease payment		850	850	850	850	850
	Buy (minus)						
	Cost of machine	−(−$10,000)					
	Lost depreciation tax benefit		−680	−680	−680	−680	−680
	Total	$10,000	−$2,330	−$2,330	−$2,330	−$2,330	−$2,330

The bottom line presents the cash flows from leasing relative to the cash flows from purchase. The cash flows would be exactly the *opposite* if we considered the purchase relative to the lease.

3. If Xomox leases the pipe-boring machine, it will no longer own this machine and must give up the depreciation tax benefits. These tax benefits show up as an *outflow*.

4. If Xomox chooses to lease the machine, it must pay $2,500 per year for five years. The first payment is due at the end of the first year. (This is a break, because sometimes the first payment is due immediately.) The lease payments are tax-deductible and, as a consequence, generate tax benefits of $850 (0.34 × $2,500).

The net cash flows have been placed in the bottom line of Table 21.3. These numbers represent the cash flows from *leasing* relative to the cash flows from the purchase. It is arbitrary that we express the flows in this way. We could have expressed the cash flows from the *purchase* relative to the cash flows from leasing. These cash flows would be:

	Year 0	Year 1	Year 2	Year 3	Year 4	Year 5
Net cash flows from purchase alternative relative to lease alternative	−$10,000	$2,330	$2,330	$2,330	$2,330	$2,330

Of course, the cash flows here are the opposite of those in the bottom line of Table 21.3. Depending on our purpose, we may look at either the purchase relative to the lease or vice versa. Thus, the student should become comfortable with either viewpoint.

Now that we have the cash flows, we can make our decision by discounting the flows properly. However, because the discount rate is tricky, we take a detour in the next section before moving back to the Xomox case. In this next section, we show that cash flows in the lease-versus-buy decision should be discounted at the *after-tax* interest rate (i.e., the after-tax cost of debt capital).

21.5 A Detour on Discounting and Debt Capacity with Corporate Taxes

The analysis of leases is difficult, and both financial practitioners and academics have made conceptual errors. These errors revolve around taxes. We hope to avoid their mistakes by beginning with the simplest type of example, a loan for one year. Though this example is unrelated to our lease-versus-buy situation, principles developed here will apply directly to lease-buy analysis.

Present Value of Riskless Cash Flows

Consider a corporation that lends $100 for a year. If the interest rate is 10 percent, the firm will receive $110 at the end of the year. Of this amount, $10 is interest and the remaining $100 is the original principal. A corporate tax rate of 34 percent implies taxes on the interest of $3.40 (0.34 × $10). Thus, the firm ends up with $106.60 ($110 − $3.40) after taxes on a $100 investment.

Now, consider a company that borrows $100 for a year. With a 10-percent interest rate, the firm must pay $110 to the bank at the end of the year. However, the borrowing firm can take the $10 of interest as a tax deduction. The corporation pays $3.40 (0.34 × $10) less in taxes than it would have paid had it not borrowed the money at all. Thus, considering this reduction in taxes, the firm must pay $106.60 ($110 − $3.40) on a $100 loan. The cash flows from both lending and borrowing are displayed in Table 21.4.

TABLE 21.4	Date 0	Date 1
Lending and Borrowing in a World with Corporate Taxes (interest rate is 10 percent and corporate tax rate is 34 percent)	Lending example Lend − $100 6.6% lending rate After-tax lending rate is 6.6%.	Receive + $100.00 of principal Receive + $ 10.00 of interest Pay − $ 3.40 (−0.34 × $10) in taxes + $106.60
	Borrowing example Borrow + $100 6.6% borrowing rate After-tax borrowing rate is 6.6%.	Pay − $100.00 of principal Pay − $ 10.00 of interest Receive + $ 3.40 (0.34 × $10) as a tax rebate − $106.60

General principle: In a world with corporate taxes, riskless cash flows should be discounted at the after-tax interest rate.

The above two paragraphs show a very important result: The firm could not care less whether it received $100 today or $106.60 next year.[4] If it received $100 today, it could lend it out, thereby receiving $106.60 after corporate taxes at the end of the year. Conversely, if it knows today that it will receive $106.60 at the end of the year, it could borrow $100 today. The after-tax interest and principal payments on the loan would be paid with the $106.60 that the firm will receive at the end of the year. Because of the interchangeability illustrated above, we say that a payment of $106.60 next year has a present value of $100. Because $100 = $106.60/1.066, a riskless cash flow should be discounted at the after-tax interest rate of 0.066 $[0.10 \times (1 - 0.34)]$.

Of course, the above discussion considered a specific example. The general principle is:

> In a world with corporate taxes, the firm should discount riskless cash flows at the after-tax riskless rate of interest.

Optimal Debt Level and Riskless Cash Flows (Advanced)

In addition, our simple example can illustrate a related point concerning optimal debt level. Consider a firm that has just determined that the current level of debt in its capital structure is optimal. Immediately following that determination, it is surprised to learn that it will receive a guaranteed payment of $106.60 in one year from, say, a tax-exempt government lottery. This future windfall is an asset that, like any asset, should raise the firm's optimal debt level. How much does this payment raise the firm's optimal level?

Our preceding analysis implies that the firm's optimal debt level must be $100 more than it previously was. That is, the firm could borrow $100 today, perhaps paying the entire amount out as a dividend. It would owe the bank $110 at the end of the year. However, because it receives a tax rebate of $3.40 $(0.34 \times \$10)$, its net repayment will be $106.60. Thus, its borrowing of $100 today is fully offset by next year's government lottery proceeds of $106.60. In other words, the lottery proceeds act as an irrevocable trust that can service the increased debt. Note that we need not know the optimal debt level before the lottery was announced. We are merely saying that, whatever this prelottery optimal level was, the optimal debt level is $100 more after the lottery announcement.

Of course, this is just one example. The general principle is:[5]

> In a world with corporate taxes, one determines the increase in the firm's optimal debt level by discounting a future guaranteed after-tax inflow at the after-tax riskless interest rate.

Conversely, suppose that a second and unrelated firm is surprised to learn that it must pay $106.60 next year to the government for back taxes. Clearly, this additional liability impinges on the second firm's debt capacity. By the above reasoning, it follows that the second firm's optimal debt level must be lowered by exactly $100.

Concept
Question

1. How should one discount a riskless cash flow?

---

[4]For simplicity, assume that the firm received $100 or $106.60 *after* corporate taxes. Since $0.66 = 1 - 0.34$, the pretax inflows would be $151.52 ($100/0.66) and $161.52 ($106.60/0.66), respectively.

[5]This principle holds for riskless or guaranteed cash flows only. Unfortunately, there is no easy formula for determining the increase in optimal debt level from a *risky* cash flow.

21.6 NPV Analysis of the Lease-versus-Buy Decision

The detour leads to a simple method for evaluating leases: discount all cash flows at the after-tax interest rate. From the bottom line of Table 21.3, Xomox's incremental cash flows from leasing versus purchasing are:

	Year 0	Year 1	Year 2	Year 3	Year 4	Year 5
Net cash flows from lease alternative relative to purchase alternative	$10,000	−$2,330	−$2,330	−$2,330	−$2,330	−$2,330

Let us assume that Xomox can either borrow or lend at the interest rate of 7.57575 percent. If the corporate tax rate is 34 percent, the correct discount rate is the after-tax rate of 5 percent [7.57575% × (1 − 0.34)]. When 5 percent is used to compute the NPV of the lease, we have:

$$\text{NPV} = \$10,000 - \$2,330 \times A_{0.05}^5 = -\$87.68 \qquad (21.1)$$

Because the net present value of the incremental cash flows from leasing relative to purchasing is negative, Xomox prefers to purchase.

Equation (21.1) is the correct approach to lease-versus-buy analysis. However, students are often bothered by two things. First, they question whether the cash flows in Table 21.3 are truly riskless. We examine this issue below. Second, they feel that this approach lacks intuition. We address this concern a little later.

The Discount Rate

Because we discounted at the after-tax riskless rate of interest, we have implicitly assumed that the cash flows in the Xomox example are riskless. Is this appropriate?

A lease payment is like the debt service on a secured bond issued by the lessee, and the discount rate should be approximately the same as the interest rate on such debt. In general, this rate will be slightly higher than the riskless rate considered in the previous section. The various tax shields could be somewhat riskier than the lease payments for two reasons. First, the value of the depreciation tax benefits depends on the ability of Xomox to generate enough taxable income to use them. Second, the corporate tax rate may change in the future, just as it fell in 1986 and increased in 1993. For these two reasons, a firm might be justified in discounting the depreciation tax benefits at a rate higher than that used for the lease payments. However, our experience is that real-world companies discount both the depreciation shield and lease payments at the same rate. This implies that financial practitioners view the above two risks as minor. We adopt the real-world convention of discounting the two flows at the same rate. This rate is the after-tax interest rate on secured debt issued by the lessee.

At this point some students still ask the question: Why not use r_{WACC} as the discount rate in lease-versus-buy analysis? Of course, r_{WACC} should not be used for lease analysis because the cash flows are more like debt-service cash flows than operating cash flows and, as such, the risk is much less. The discount rate should reflect the risk of the incremental cash flows.

21.7 Debt Displacement and Lease Valuation

The Basic Concept of Debt Displacement (Advanced)

The previous analysis allows one to calculate the right answer in a simple manner. This clearly must be viewed as an important benefit. However, the analysis has little intuitive

TABLE 21.5	Assets		Liabilities	
Debt Displacement Elsewhere in the Firm When a Lease Is Instituted	*Initial situation*			
	Current	$ 50,000	Debt	$ 60,000
	Fixed	50,000	Equity	40,000
	Total	$100,000	Total	$100,000
	Buy with secured loan			
	Current	$ 50,000	Debt	$ 66,000
	Fixed	50,000	Equity	44,000
	Machine	10,000	Total	$110,000
	Total	$110,000		
	Lease			
	Current	$ 50,000	Lease	$ 10,000
	Fixed	50,000	Debt	56,000
	Machine	10,000	Equity	44,000
	Total	$110,000	Total	$110,000

This example shows that leases reduce the level of debt elsewhere in the firm. Though the example illustrates a point, it is not meant to show a *precise* method for calculating debt displacement.

appeal. To remedy this, we hope to make lease-buy analysis more intuitive by considering the issue of debt displacement.

A firm that purchases equipment will generally issue debt to finance the purchase. The debt becomes a liability of the firm. A lessee incurs a liability equal to the present value of all future lease payments. Because of this, we argue that leases displace debt. The balance sheets in Table 21.5 illustrate how leasing might affect debt.

Suppose a firm initially has $100,000 of assets and a 150-percent optimal debt-equity ratio. The firm's debt is $60,000, and its equity is $40,000. As in the Xomox case, suppose the firm must use a new $10,000 machine. The firm has two alternatives:

1. *The Firm Can Purchase the Machine.* If it does, it will finance the purchase with a secured loan and with equity. The debt capacity of the machine is assumed to be the same as for the firm as a whole.

2. *The Firm Can Lease the Asset and Get 100-Percent Financing.* That is, the present value of the future lease payments will be $10,000.

If the firm finances the machine with both secured debt and new equity, its debt will increase by $6,000 and its equity by $4,000. Its optimal debt-equity ratio of 150 percent will be maintained.

Conversely, consider the lease alternative. Because the lessee views the lease payment as a liability, the lessee thinks in terms of a *liability-to-equity* ratio, not just a debt-to-equity ratio. As mentioned above, the present value of the lease liability is $10,000. If the leasing firm is to maintain a liability-to-equity ratio of 150 percent, debt elsewhere in the firm must fall by $4,000 when the lease is instituted. Because debt must be repurchased, net liabilities only rise by $6,000 ($10,000 − $4,000) when $10,000 of assets are placed under lease.[6]

Debt displacement is a hidden cost of leasing. If a firm leases, it will not use as much regular debt as it would otherwise. The benefits of debt capacity will be lost, particularly the lower taxes associated with interest expense.

---

[6]Growing firms in the real world will not generally repurchase debt when instituting a lease. Rather, they will issue less debt in the future than they would have without the lease.

Optimal Debt Level in the Xomox Example (Advanced)

The previous section showed that leasing displaces debt. Though the section illustrated a point, it was not meant to show the *precise* method for calculating debt displacement. Below, we describe the precise method for calculating the difference in optimal debt levels between purchase and lease in the Xomox example.

From the last line of Table 21.3, we know that the cash flows from the *purchase* alternative relative to the cash flows from the lease alternative are:[7]

	Year 0	Year 1	Year 2	Year 3	Year 4	Year 5
Net cash flows from purchase alternative relative to lease alternative	−$10,000	$2,330	$2,330	$2,330	$2,330	$2,330

An increase in the optimal debt level at year 0 occurs because the firm learns at that time of guaranteed cash flows beginning at year 1. Our detour on discounting and debt capacity told us to calculate this increased debt level by discounting the future riskless cash inflows at the after-tax interest rate.[8] Thus, additional debt level of the purchase alternative relative to the lease alternative is:

Increase in optimal debt level from purchase alternative relative to lease alternative:

$$\$10,087.68 = \frac{\$2,330}{1.05} + \frac{\$2,330}{(1.05)^2} + \frac{\$2,330}{(1.05)^3} + \frac{\$2,330}{(1.05)^4} + \frac{\$2,330}{(1.05)^5}$$

That is, whatever the optimal amount of debt would be under the lease alternative, the optimal amount of debt would be $10,087.68 more under the purchase alternative.

This result can be stated in another way. Imagine there are two identical firms except that one firm purchases the boring machine and the other leases it. From Table 21.3, we know that the purchasing firm generates $2,330 more cash flow after taxes in each of the five years than does the leasing firm. Further imagine that the same bank lends money to both firms. The bank should lend the purchasing firm more money because it has a greater cash flow each period. How much extra money should the bank loan the purchasing firm so that the incremental loan can be paid off by the extra cash flows of $2,330 per year? The answer is exactly $10,087.68, the increase in the optimal debt level we calculated earlier.

To see this, let us work through the example on a year-by-year basis. Because the purchasing firm borrows $10,087.68 more at year 0 than does the leasing firm, the purchasing firm will pay interest of $764.22 ($10,087.68 × 0.0757575) at year 1 on the additional debt. The interest allows the firm to reduce its taxes by $259.83 ($764.22 × 0.34), leaving an after-tax outflow of $504.39 ($764.22 − $259.83) at year 1.

We know from Table 21.3 that the purchasing firm generates $2,330 more cash at year 1 than does the leasing firm. Because the purchasing firm has the extra $2,330 coming in at

---

[7]The last line of Table 21.3 presents the cash flows form the lease alternative relative to the purchase alternative. As pointed out earlier, our cash flows are now reversed because we are now presenting the cash flows from the purchase alternative relative to the lease alternative.

[8]Though our detour considered only riskless cash flows, the cash flows in a leasing example are not necessarily riskless. As we explained earlier, we therefore adopt the real-world convention of discounting at the after-tax interest rate on secured debt issued by the lessee.

TABLE 21.6	Calculation of Increase in Optimal Debt Level If Xomox Purchases Instead of Leases					
	Year 0	**Year 1**	**Year 2**	**Year 3**	**Year 4**	**Year 5**
Outstanding balance of loan	$10,087.68	$8,262.07*	$6,345.17	$4,332.42	$2,219.05	$ 0
Interest		764.22	625.91	480.69	328.22	168.11
Tax deduction on interest		259.83	212.81	163.44	111.59	57.16
After-tax interest expense		$ 504.39	$ 413.10	$ 317.25	$ 216.63	$ 110.95
Extra cash that purchasing firm generates over leasing firm (from Table 24.2)		$2,330.00	$2,330.00	$2,330.00	$2,330.00	$2,330.00
Repayment of loan		$1,825.61†	$1,916.90	$2,012.75	$2,113.37	$2,219.05

Assume that there are two otherwise-identical firms where one leases and the other purchases. The purchasing firm can borrow $10,087.68 more than the leasing firm. The extra cash flow each year of $2,330 from purchasing instead of leasing can be used to pay off the loan in five years.

*$8,262.07 = $10,087.68 − $1,825.61.

†$1,825.61 = $2,330 − $504.39.

year 1 but must pay interest on its loan, how much of the loan can the firm repay at year 1 and still have the same cash flow as the leasing firm has? The purchasing firm can repay $1,825.61 ($2,330 − $504.39) of the loan at year 1 and still have the same net cash flow that the leasing firm has. After the repayment, the purchasing firm will have a remaining balance of $8,262.07 ($10,087.68 − $1,825.61) at year 1. For each of the five years, this sequence of cash flows is displayed in Table 21.6. The outstanding balance goes to zero over the five years. Thus, the annual cash flow of $2,330, which represents the extra cash from purchasing instead of leasing, fully amortizes the loan of $10,087.68.

Our analysis on debt capacity has two purposes. First, we want to show the additional debt capacity from purchasing. We just completed this task. Second, we want to determine whether or not the lease is preferred to the purchase. This decision rule follows easily from the above discussion. By leasing the equipment and having $10,087.68 less debt than under the purchase alternative, the firm has exactly the same cash flow in years 1 to 5 that it would have through a levered purchase. Thus, we can ignore cash flows beginning in year 1 when comparing the lease alternative with the purchase with debt alternative. However, the cash flows differ between the alternatives at year 0. These differences are:

1. *The Purchase Cost at Year 0 of $10,000 Is Avoided by Leasing.* This should be viewed as a cash inflow under the leasing alternative.

2. *The Firm Borrows $10,087.68 Less at Year 0 under the Lease Alternative Than It Can under the Purchase Alternative.* This should be viewed as a cash outflow under the leasing alternative.

Because the firm borrows $10,087.68 less by leasing but saves only $10,000 on the equipment, the lease alternative requires an extra cash outflow at year 0 relative to the purchase alternative of −$87.68 ($10,000 − $10,087.68). Because cash flows in later years from leasing are identical to those from purchasing with debt, the firm should purchase.

This is exactly the same answer we got when, earlier in this chapter, we discounted all cash flows at the after-tax interest rate. Of course, this is no coincidence because the increase in the optimal debt level is also determined by discounting all flows at the after-tax interest rate. The accompanying box presents both methods. (The numbers in the box are in terms of the NPV of the lease relative to the purchase. Thus, a negative NPV indicates that the purchase alternative should be taken.)

Two Methods for Calculating Net Present Value of Lease Relative to Purchase*

Method 1: Discount all cash flows at the after-tax interest rate

$$-\$87.68 = \$10,000 - \$2,330 \times A^5_{0.05}$$

Method 2: Compare purchase price with reduction in optimal debt level under leasing alternative

$$-\$87.68 = \underset{\substack{\text{Purchase} \\ \text{price}}}{\$10,000} - \underset{\substack{\text{Reduction in} \\ \text{optimal debt} \\ \text{level if leasing}}}{\$10,087.68}$$

*Because we are calculating the NPV of the lease relative to the purchase, a negative value indicates that the purchase alternative is preferred.

21.8 Does Leasing Ever Pay: The Base Case

We previously looked at the lease-buy decision from the point of view of the potential lessee, Xomox. Let's now look at the decision from the point of view of the lessor, Friendly Leasing. This firm faces three cash flows, all of which are displayed in Table 21.7. First, Friendly purchases the machine for $10,000 at year 0. Second, because the asset is depreciated straight-line over five year, the depreciation expense at the end of each of the five years is $2,000 ($10,000/5). The yearly depreciation tax shield is $680 ($2,000 × 0.34). Third, because the yearly lease payment is $2,500, the after-tax lease payment is $1,650 [$2,500 × (1 − 0.34)].

Now examine the total cash flows to Friendly Leasing, as displayed in the bottom line of Table 21.7. Those of you with a healthy memory will notice something very interesting. These cash flows are exactly the *opposite* of those of Xomox, as displayed in the bottom line of Table 21.3. Those of you with a healthy sense of skepticism may be thinking something very interesting: "If the cash flows of the lessor are exactly the opposite of those of the lessee, the combined cash flow of the two parties must be zero each year. Thus, there does not seem to be any joint benefit to this lease. Because the net present value to the lessee was −$87.68, the NPV to the lessor must be $87.68. The joint NPV is $0 (−$87.68 + $87.68). There does not appear to be any way for the NPV of both the lessor and the lessee to be positive at the same time. Because one party would inevitably lose money, the leasing deal could never fly."

TABLE 21.7	Cash Flows to Friendly Leasing as Lessor of IBMC Pipe-Boring Machine					
	Year 0	Year 1	Year 2	Year 3	Year 4	Year 5
Cash for machine	−$10,000					
Depreciation tax benefit ($680 = $2,000 × 0.34)		$ 680	$ 680	$ 680	$ 680	$ 680
After-tax lease payment [$1,650 = $2,500 × (1 − 0.34)]		1,650	1,650	1,650	1,650	1,650
Total	−$10,000	$2,330	$2,330	$2,330	$2,330	$2,330

These cash flows are the opposite of the cash flows to Xomox, the lessee (see the bottom line of Table 21.3).

This is one of the most important results of leasing. Though Table 21.7 concerns one particular leasing deal, the principle can be generalized. As long as (1) both parties are subject to the same interest and tax rates and (2) transaction costs are ignored, there can be no leasing deal that benefits both parties. However, there is a lease payment for which both parties would calculate an NPV of zero. Given that fee, Xomox would be indifferent to whether it leased or bought, and Friendly Leasing would be indifferent to whether it leased or not.[9]

A student with an even healthier sense of skepticism might be thinking, "This textbook appears to be arguing that leasing is not beneficial. Yet, we know that leasing occurs frequently in the real world. Maybe, just maybe, the textbook is wrong." Although we will not admit to being wrong (what textbook would?!), we freely admit to being incomplete at this point. The next section considers factors that give benefits to leasing.

21.9 Reasons for Leasing

Proponents of leasing make many claims about why firms should lease assets rather than buy them. Some of the reasons given to support leasing are good, and some are not. We discuss here the reasons for leasing we think are good and some of the ones we think aren't.

Good Reasons for Leasing

If leasing is a good choice, it will be because one or more of the following will be true:

1. Taxes may be reduced by leasing.
2. The lease contract may reduce certain types of uncertainty.
3. Transactions costs can be higher for buying an asset and financing it with debt or equity than for leasing the asset.

Tax Advantages The most important reason for long-term leasing is tax reduction. If the corporate income tax were repealed, long-term leasing would probably disappear. The tax advantages of leasing exist because firms are in different tax brackets.

Should a user in a low tax bracket purchase, he will receive little tax benefit from depreciation and interest deductions. Should the user lease, the lessor will receive the depreciation shield and the interest deductions. In a competitive market, the lessor must charge a low lease payment to reflect these tax shields. Thus, the user is likely to lease rather than purchase.

In our example with Xomox and Friendly Leasing, the value of the lease to Friendly was $87.68. That is:

$$\$87.68 = -\$10,000 + \$2,330 \times A_{0.05}^5$$

However, the value of the lease to Xomox was exactly the opposite ($-\$87.68$). Because the lessor's gains came at the expense of the lessee, no deal could be arranged.

However, if Xomox pays no taxes and the lease payments are reduced to $2,475 from $2,500, both Friendly and Xomox will find there is positive NPV in leasing. Xomox can

---

[9]The break-even lease payment is $2,469.32 in our example. Both the lessor and lessee can solve for this as

$$\$10,000 = \$680 \times A_{0.05}^5 + L \times (1 - 0.34) \times A_{0.05}^5$$

In this case, $L = \$2,469.32$.

rework Table 21.3 with $T_c = 0$, finding that its cash flows from leasing are:

	Year 0	Year 1	Year 2	Year 3	Year 4	Year 5
Cost of machine	$10,000					
Lease payment		−$2,475	−$2,475	−$2,475	−$2,475	−$2,475

The value of the lease to Xomox is:

$$\text{Value of lease} = \$10,000 - \$2,475 \times A_{0.0757575}^{5}$$
$$= \$6.55$$

Notice that the discount rate is the interest rate of 7.57575 percent because tax rates are zero. In addition, the full lease payment of $2,475—and not some lower, after-tax number—is used since there are no taxes. Finally, note that depreciation is ignored, also because no taxes apply.

Given a lease payment of $2,475, the cash flows to Friendly Leasing are:

	Year 0	Year 1	Year 2	Year 3	Year 4	Year 5
Cost of machine	−$10,000					
Depreciation tax shield ($680 = $2,000 × 0.34)		$ 680	$ 680	$ 680	$ 680	$ 680
After-tax lease payment [$1,633.50 = $2,475 × (1 − 0.34)]		$1,633.50	$1,633.50	$1,633.50	$1,633.50	$1,633.50
Total		$2,313.50	$2,313.50	$2,313.50	$2,313.50	$2,313.50

The value of the lease to Friendly is:

$$\text{Value of lease} = -\$10,000 + \$2,313.50 \times A_{0.05}^{5}$$
$$= -\$10,000 + \$10,016.24$$
$$= \$16.24$$

As a consequence of different tax rates, the lessee (Xomox) gains $6.55 and the lessor (Friendly) gains $16.24. Both the lessor and the lessee can gain if their tax rates are different, because the lessor uses the depreciation and interest tax shields that cannot be used by the lessee. The IRS loses tax revenue, and some of the tax gains to the lessor are passed on to the lessee in the form of lower lease payments.

Because both parties can gain when tax rates differ, the lease payment is agreed upon through negotiation. Before negotiation begins, each party needs to know the *reservation* payment of both parties. This is the payment such that one party will be indifferent to whether it entered the lease deal or not. In other words, this is the payment such that the value of the lease is zero. These payments are calculated below.

Reservation Payment of Lessee   We now solve for L_{MAX}, the payment such that the value of the lease to the lessee is zero. When the lessee is in a zero tax bracket, his cash flows, in terms of L_{MAX}, are:

	Year 0	Year 1	Year 2	Year 3	Year 4	Year 5
Cost of machine	$10,000					
Lease payment		$-L_{\text{MAX}}$	$-L_{\text{MAX}}$	$-L_{\text{MAX}}$	$-L_{\text{MAX}}$	$-L_{\text{MAX}}$

This chart implies that:

$$\text{Value of lease} = \$10,000 - L_{\text{MAX}} \times A_{0.0757575}^5$$

The value of the lease equals zero when:

$$L_{\text{MAX}} = \frac{\$10,000}{A_{0.0757575}^5} = \$2,476.62$$

After performing this calculation, the lessor knows that he will never be able to charge a payment above $2,476.62.

Reservation Payment of Lessor   We now solve for L_{MIN}, the payment such that the value of the lease to the lessor is zero. The cash flows to the lessor, in terms of L_{MIN}, are:

	Year 0	Year 1	Year 2	Year 3	Year 4	Year 5
Cost of machine	−$10,000					
Depreciation tax shield ($680 = \$2,000 \times 0.34$)		$680	$680	$680	$680	$680
After-tax lease payment ($T_c = 0.34$)		$L_{\text{MIN}} \times (0.66)$	$L_{\text{MIN}} \times (0.66)$	$L_{\text{MIN}} \times (0.66)$	$L_{\text{MIN}} \times (0.66)$	$L_{\text{MIN}} \times (0.66)$

This chart implies that:

$$\text{Value of lease} = -\$10,000 + \$680 \times A_{0.05}^5 + L_{\text{MIN}} \times (0.66) \times A_{0.05}^5$$

The value of the lease equals zero when

$$L_{\text{MIN}} = \frac{\$10,000}{0.66 \times A_{0.05}^5} - \frac{\$680}{0.066}$$

$$= \$3,499.62 - \$1,030.30$$

$$= \$2,469.32$$

After performing this calculation, the lessee knows that the lessor will never agree to a lease payment below $2,469.32.

A Reduction of Uncertainty   We have noted that the lessee does not own the property when the lease expires. The value of the property at this time is called the *residual value,* and the lessor has a firm claim to it. When the lease contract is signed, there may be substantial uncertainty as to what the residual value of the asset will be. Thus, under a lease contract, this residual risk is borne by the lessor. Conversely, the user bears this risk when purchasing.

It is common sense that the party best able to bear a particular risk should do so. If the user has little risk aversion, he will not suffer by purchasing. However, if the user is highly averse to risk, he should find a third-party lessor more capable of assuming this burden.

This latter situation frequently arises when the user is a small and/or newly formed firm. Because the risk of the entire firm is likely to be quite high and because the principal stockholders are likely to be undiversified, the firm desires to minimize risk wherever possible. A potential lessor, such as a large and publicly held financial institution, is far more capable of bearing the risk. Conversely, this situation is not expected to happen when the user is a blue chip corporation. That potential lessee is more able to bear risk.

Transactions Costs   The costs of changing an asset's ownership are generally greater than the costs of writing a lease agreement. Consider the choice that confronts a person who lives in Los Angeles but must do business in New York for two days. It will clearly be cheaper to rent a hotel room for two nights than it would be to buy an apartment condominium for two days and then to sell it.

Unfortunately, leases generate agency costs as well. For example, the lessee might misuse or overuse the asset, since she has no interest in the asset's residual value. This cost will be implicitly paid by the lessee through a high lease payment. Although the lessor can reduce these agency costs through monitoring, monitoring itself is costly.

Thus, leasing is most beneficial when the transaction costs of purchase and resale outweigh the agency costs and monitoring costs of a lease. Flath argues that this occurs in short-term leases but not in long-term leases.[10]

Bad Reasons for Leasing

Leasing and Accounting Income   In our discussion on "Accounting and Leasing," we pointed out that a firm's balance sheet shows fewer liabilities with an operating lease than with either a capitalized lease or a purchase financed with debt. We indicated that a firm desiring to project a strong balance sheet might select an operating lease. In addition, the firm's return on assets (ROA) is generally higher with an operating lease than with either a capitalized lease or a purchase. To see this, we look at the numerator and denominator of the ROA formula in turn.

With an operating lease, lease payments are treated as an expense. If the asset is purchased, both depreciation and interest charges are expenses. At least in the early part of the asset's life, the yearly lease payment is generally less than the sum of yearly depreciation and yearly interest. Thus, accounting income, the numerator of the ROA formula, is higher with an operating lease than with a purchase. Because accounting expenses with a capitalized lease are analogous to depreciation and interest with a purchase, the increase in accounting income does not occur when a lease is capitalized.

In addition, leased assets do not appear on the balance sheet with an operating lease. Thus, the total asset value of a firm, the denominator of the ROA formula, is less with an operating lease than it is with either a purchase or a capitalized lease. The two preceding effects imply that the firm's ROA should be higher with an operating lease than with either a purchase or a capitalized lease.

Of course, in an efficient capital market, accounting information cannot be used to fool investors. It is unlikely, then, that leasing's impact on accounting numbers should create value for the firm. Savvy investors should be able to see through attempts by management to improve the firm's financial statements.

One Hundred-Percent Financing   It is often claimed that leasing provides 100 percent financing, whereas secured equipment loans require an initial down payment. However, we argued earlier that leases tend to displace debt elsewhere in the firm. Our earlier analysis suggests that leases do not permit a greater level of total liabilities than do purchases with borrowing.

Other Reasons   There are, of course, many special reasons that some companies find advantages in leasing. In one celebrated case, the U.S. Navy leased a fleet of tankers instead of asking Congress for appropriations. Thus, leasing may be used to circumvent capital-expenditure control systems set up by bureaucratic firms.

**Concept
Question**

1. **Summarize the good and bad arguments for leasing.**

---

[10]D. Flath, "The Economics of Short Term Leasing," *Economic Inquiry* 18 (April 1980).

21.10 Some Unanswered Questions

Our analysis suggests that the primary advantage of long-term leasing results from the differential tax rates of the lessor and the lessee. Other valid reasons for leasing are lower contracting costs and risk reduction. There are several questions our analysis has not specifically answered.

Are the Uses of Leases and of Debt Complementary?

Ang and Peterson find that firms with high debt tend to lease frequently as well.[11] This result should not be puzzling. The corporate attributes that provide high debt capacity may also make leasing advantageous. Thus, even though leasing displaces debt (that is, leasing and borrowing are substitutes) for an individual firm, high debt and high leasing can be positively associated when one looks at a number of firms.

Why Are Leases Offered by Both Manufacturers and Third-Party Lessors?

The offsetting effects of taxes can explain why both manufacturers (for example, computer firms) and third-party lessors offer leases.

1. For manufacturer lessors, the basis for determining depreciation is the manufacturer's cost. For third-party lessors, the basis is the sales price that the lessor paid to the manufacturer. Because the sales price is generally greater than the manufacturer's cost, this is an advantage to third-party lessors.
2. However, the manufacturer must recognize a profit for tax purposes when selling the asset to the third-party lessor. The manufacturer's profit for some equipment can be deferred if the manufacturer becomes the lessor. This provides an incentive for manufacturers to lease.

Why Are Some Assets Leased More Than Others?

Certain assets appear to be leased more frequently than others. Smith and Wakeman have looked at nontax incentives affecting leasing.[12] Their analysis suggests many asset and firm characteristics that are important in the lease-or-buy decision. The following are among the things they mention:

1. The more sensitive the value of an asset is to use and maintenance decisions, the more likely it is that the asset will be purchased instead of leased. They argue that ownership provides a better incentive to minimize maintenance costs than does leasing.
2. Price-discrimination opportunities may be important. Leasing may be a way of circumventing laws against charging too *low* a price.

21.11 SUMMARY AND CONCLUSIONS

A large fraction of America's equipment is leased rather than purchased. This chapter both describes the institutional arrangements surrounding leases and shows how to evaluate leases financially.

1. Leases can be separated into two polar types. Though operating leases allow the lessee to use the equipment, ownership remains with the lessor. Although the lessor in a financial lease legally owns the equipment, the lessee maintains effective ownership because financial leases are fully amortized.

---

[11]J. Ang and P. P. Peterson, "The Leasing Puzzle," *Journal of Finance* 39 (September 1984).

[12]C. W. Smith, Jr., and L. M. Wakeman, "Determinants of Corporate Leasing Policy," *Journal of Finance* (July 1985).

Visit us at www.mhhe.com/rwj

2. When a firm purchases an asset with debt, both the asset and the liability appear on the firm's balance sheet. If a lease meets at least one of a number of criteria, it must be capitalized. This means that the present value of the lease appears as both an asset and a liability. A lease escapes capitalization if it does not meet any of these criteria. Leases not meeting the criteria are called *operating leases,* though the accountant's definition differs somewhat from the practitioner's definition. Operating leases do not appear on the balance sheet. For cosmetic reasons, many firms prefer that a lease be called *operating.*

3. Firms generally lease for tax purposes. To protect its interests, the IRS allows financial arrangements to be classified as leases only if a number of criteria are met.

4. We showed that risk-free cash flows should be discounted at the after-tax risk-free rate. Because both lease payments and depreciation tax shields are nearly riskless, all relevant cash flows in the lease-buy decision should be discounted at a rate near this after-tax rate. We use the real-world convention of discounting at the after-tax interest rate on the lessee's secured debt.

5. Though this method is simple, it lacks certain intuitive appeal. In an optional section, we presented an alternative method in the hopes of increasing the reader's intuition. Relative to a lease, a purchase generates debt capacity. This increase in debt capacity can be calculated by discounting the difference between the cash flows of the purchase and the cash flows of the lease by the after-tax interest rate. The increase in debt capacity from a purchase is compared to the extra outflow at year 0 from a purchase.

6. If the lessor is in the same tax bracket as the lessee, the cash flows to the lessor are exactly the opposite of the cash flows to the lessee. Thus, the sum of the value of the lease to the lessee plus the value of the lease to the lessor must be zero. While this suggests that leases can never fly, there are actually at least three good reasons for leasing:
    a. Differences in tax brackets between lessor and lessee.
    b. Shift of risk-bearing to the lessor.
    c. Minimization of transaction costs.
    We also document a number of bad reasons for leasing.

KEY TERMS

debt displacement, *603*	leveraged lease, *595*
direct leases, *594*	off–balance-sheet financing, *596*
financial leases, *595*	operating lease, *594*
lessee, *593*	sale and lease-back, *595*
lessor, *593*	sales-type leases, *594*

SUGGESTED READINGS

Some evidence on the determination of discount rates used in leasing is found in

Schallheim, J. S.; R. E. Johnson; R. C. Lease; and J. J. McConnell. "The Determinants of Yields on Financial Leasing Contracts." *Journal of Financial Economics* (1987).

Other good articles on leasing are

Bowman, R. G. "The Debt Equivalence of Leases: An Empirical Investigation." *Accounting Review* 55 (April 1980).

Crawford, P. J.; C. P. Harper; and J. J. McConnell. "Further Evidence on the Terms of Financial Leases." *Financial Management* 10 (Autumn 1981).

Franks, J. R., and S. D. Hodges. "Valuation of Financial Lease Contracts: A Note." *Journal of Finance* (May 1978).

Myers, S.; D. A. Dill; and A. J. Bautista. "Valuation of Financial Lease Contracts." *Journal of Finance* (June 1976).

Other important readings are

Ang, J., and P. P. Peterson. "The Leasing Puzzle." *Journal of Finance* 39 (September 1984).

McConnell, J. J., and J. S. Schallheim. "Valuation of Asset Leasing Contracts." *Journal of Financial Economics* 12 (August 1983).

Schall, L. D. "The Lease-or-Buy and Asset Acquisition Decisions." *Journal of Finance* 29 (September 1974).

Sivarama, K. V., and R. C. Moyer. "Bankruptcy Costs and Financial Leasing Decisions." *Financial Management* (1994).

Smith, C. W., Jr., and L. M. Wakeman. "Determinations of Corporate Leasing Policy." *Journal of Finance* (July 1985).

Sorenson, I. W., and R. E. Johnson. "Equipment Financial Leasing Practices and Costs: An Empirical Study." *Financial Management* (Spring 1977).

A complete guide to the lease-versus-buy decision is in

Schallheim, James S. *Lease or Buy.* Boston, Mass.: Harvard Business School Press, 1994.

QUESTIONS & PROBLEMS

21.1   Discuss the validity of each of the following statements.
  a. Leasing reduces risk and can reduce a firm's cost of capital.
  b. Leasing provides 100-percent financing.
  c. Firms that do a large amount of leasing will not do much borrowing.
  d. If the tax advantages of leasing were eliminated, leasing would disappear.

21.2   Quartz Corporation is a relatively new firm. Quartz has experienced enough losses during its early years to provide it with at least eight years of tax-loss carryforwards. Thus, Quartz's effective tax rate is zero. Quartz plans to lease equipment from New Leasing Company. The term of the lease is five years. The purchase cost of the equipment is $250,000. New Leasing Company is in the 35-percent tax bracket. There are no transaction costs to the lease. Each firm can borrow at 8 percent.
  a. What is Quartz's reservation price?
  b. What is New Leasing Company's reservation price?
  c. Explain why these reservation prices determine the negotiating range of the lease.

 21.3   Super Sonics Entertainment is considering borrowing money at 11 percent and purchasing a machine that costs $350,000. The machine will be depreciated over five years by the straight-line method and will be worthless in five years. Super Sonics can lease the machine with the year-end payments of $94,200. The corporate tax rate is 35 percent. Should Super Sonics buy or lease?

21.4   Maxwell, Inc., is entering negotiations for the lease of equipment that has a $200,000 purchase price. Maxwell's effective tax rate is zero. Maxwell will be negotiating the lease with Mercer Leasing Corp. The term of the lease is five years. Mercer Leasing Corp. is in the 35-percent tax bracket. There are no transaction costs to the lease. Each firm can borrow at 10 percent. What is the negotiating range of the lease?

21.5   Raymond Rayon Corporation wants to expand its manufacturing facilities. Liberty Leasing Corporation has offered Raymond Rayon the opportunity to lease a machine for $100,000 for five years. The machine will be fully depreciated by the straight-line method. The corporate tax rate for Raymond Rayon is 25 percent, while Liberty Leasing's corporate tax rate is 35 percent. The appropriate before-tax interest rate is 8 percent. Assume lease payments occur at year-end. What is Raymond's reservation price? What is Liberty's reservation price? What is the negotiating range of the lease?

21.6   An asset costs $86.87. Only straight-line depreciation is allowed for this asset. The asset's useful life is two years. It will have no salvage value. The corporate tax rate on ordinary income is 34 percent. The interest rate on risk-free cash flows is 10 percent.
  a. What set of lease payments will make the lessee and the lessor equally well off?
  b. Show the general condition that will make the value of a lease to the lessor the negative of the value to the lessee.
  c. Assume that the lessee pays no taxes and the lessor is in the 34-percent tax bracket. For what range of lease payments does the lease have a positive NPV for both parties?

 21.7   High electricity costs have made Farmer Corporation's chicken-plucking machine economically worthless. There are only two machines available to replace it.

The International Plucking Machine (IPM) model is available only on a lease basis. The annual, end-of-year payments are $2,100 for five years. This machine will save Farmer $6,000 per year through reductions in electricity costs in each of the five years.

As an alternative, Farmer can purchase a more energy-efficient machine from Basic Machine Corporation (BMC) for $15,000. This machine will save $9,000 per year in electricity costs. A local bank has offered to finance the machine with a $15,000 loan. The interest rate on the loan will be 10 percent on the remaining balance and five annual principal payments of $3,000.

Farmer has a target debt-to-asset ratio of 67 percent. Farmer is in the 34-percent tax bracket. After five years, both machines are worthless. Only straight-line depreciation is allowed for chicken-plucking machines. The savings that Farmer will enjoy are known with certainty, because Farmer has a long-term chicken purchase agreement with State Food Products, Inc., and a four-year backlog of orders.

a. Should Farmer lease the IPM machine or purchase the more efficient BMC machine?
b. Does your answer depend on the form of financing for direct purchase?
c. How much debt is displaced by this lease?

21.8 Redwood Timberland Corporation is a furniture manufacturer that is considering installing a milling machine for $420,000. The machine will be straight-line depreciated over seven years and will be worthless after its economic life. Redwood has been financially distressed and thus the company does not appear to get tax shields over the next seven years. American Leasing Company has offered to lease the machine over seven years. The corporate tax rate for Redwood is 35 percent. The appropriate before-tax interest rate is 6 percent for both firms. Lease payments occur at the beginning of the year. What is Redwood's reservation price? What is American's reservation price? What is the negotiating range of the lease?

21.9 Wolfson Corporation has decided to purchase a new machine that costs $3 million. The machine will be worthless after three years. Only straight-line method is allowed by the IRS for this type of machine. Wolfson is in the 35-percent tax bracket.

The Sur Bank has offered Wolfson a three-year loan for $3 million. The repayment schedule is three yearly principal repayments of $1 million and an interest charge of 12 percent on the outstanding balance of the loan at the beginning of each year. Twelve percent is the marketwide rate of interest. Both principal repayments and interest are due at the end of each year.

Cal Leasing Corporation offers to lease the same machine to Wolfson. Lease payments of $1.2 million per year are due at the end of each of the three years of the lease.

a. Should Wolfson lease the machine or buy it with bank financing?
b. What is the annual lease payment that will make Wolfson indifferent to whether it leases the machine or purchases it?

Appendix 21A

APV Approach to Leasing

The box that appeared earlier in this chapter showed two methods for calculating the NPV of the lease relative to the purchase:

1. Discount all cash flows at the after-tax interest rate.
2. Compare the purchase price with reduction in optimal debt level under the leasing alternative.

Surprisingly (and perhaps unfortunately) there is still another method. We feel compelled to present this third method, because it has important links with the adjusted present value (APV) approach discussed earlier in this text. We illustrate this approach using the Xomox example developed in Table 21.3.

In a previous chapter, we learned that the APV of any project can be expressed as:

$$APV = \text{All-equity value} + \text{Additional effects of debt}$$

In other words, the adjusted present value of a project is the sum of the net present value of the project when financed by all equity plus the additional effects from debt financing. In the context of the lease-versus-buy decision, the APV method can be expressed as:

$$
\begin{array}{ccc}
\text{Adjusted present value} & & \text{Net present value of} \\
\text{of the lease relative to} & = & \text{the lease relative to the} \\
\text{the purchase} & & \text{purchase when} \\
& & \text{purchase is financed} \\
& & \text{by all equity}
\end{array}
\quad
\begin{array}{c}
\text{Additional effects when} \\
- \quad \text{purchase is financed} \\
\text{with some debt}
\end{array}
$$

All-Equity Value

From an earlier chapter, we know that the all-equity value is simply the NPV of the cash flows discounted at the *pretax* interest rate. For the Xomox example, we know from Table 21.3 that this value is:

$$\$592.03 = \$10,000 - \$2,330 \times A^5_{0.0757575}$$

This calculation is identical to method 1 in the earlier box except that we are now discounting at the pretax interest rate. The calculation states that the lease is preferred over the purchase by $592.03 if the purchase is financed by all equity. Because debt financing generates a tax subsidy, it is not surprising that the lease alternative would be preferred by almost $600 over the purchase alternative if debt were not allowed.

Additional Effects of Debt

We learned earlier in the text that the interest tax shield in any year is the interest multiplied by the corporate tax rate. Taking the interest in each of the five years from Table 21.6, the present value of the interest tax shield is:

$$\$679.71 = 0.34 \left[\frac{\$764.22}{1.0757575} + \frac{\$625.91}{(1.0757575)^2} + \frac{\$480.69}{(1.0757575)^3} + \frac{\$328.21}{(1.0757575)^4} + \frac{\$168.11}{(1.0757575)^5} \right]$$

This tax shield must be subtracted from the NPV of the lease because it represents interest deductions not available under the lease alternative. The adjusted present value of the lease relative to the purchase is:

$$-\$87.68 = \$592.03 - \$679.71$$

This value is the same as our calculations from the previous two approaches, implying that all three approaches are equivalent. The accompanying box presents the APV approach.

Which approach is easiest to calculate? The first approach is easiest because one need only discount the cash flows at the after-tax interest rate. Though the second and third approaches (in the two boxes) look easy, the extra step of calculating the increased debt capacity is needed for both of them.

Which approach is more intuitive? Our experience is that students generally find the third method the most intuitive. This is probably because they have already learned the APV method from a previous chapter. The second method is generally straightforward to

---

A Third Method for Calculating Net Present Value of Lease Relative to Purchase*†

Method 3: Calculate APV:

$$\text{All-equity value: } \$592.03 = \$10,000 - \$2,330 \times A^5_{0.0757575}$$

Additional effects of debt:‡

$$-\$679.71 = -0.34 \left[\frac{\$764.22}{1.0757575} + \frac{\$625.91}{(1.0757575)^2} + \frac{\$480.69}{(1.0757575)^3} \right.$$
$$\left. + \frac{\$328.21}{(1.0757575)^4} + \frac{\$168.11}{(1.0757575)^5} \right]$$

$$\text{APV} = -\$87.68 = \$592.03 - \$679.71$$

*Because we are calculating the NPV of the lease relative to the purchase, a negative value indicates that the purchase alternative is preferred.

†The first two methods are shown in the earlier box appearing in this chapter.

‡The firm misses the interest deductions if it leases. Because we are calculating the NPV of the lease relative to the purchase, the additional effect of debt is a negative number.

---

those students who have taken the time to understand the increased-debt-level concept. However, the first method seems to have the least intuitive appeal because it is merely a mechanical approach.

Which approach should the practitioner use? The practitioner should use the simplest approach, which is the first. We included the others only for intuitive appeal.

Options, Futures, and Corporate Finance

The public has often viewed options and futures as exotic and risky instruments that individuals enter into at their peril. Although these derivatives can increase risk, they also have important uses to corporations. In Part VI, we discuss these instruments in detail, showing three basic ideas: Recent advances allow options and futures to be easily priced. Options are frequently embedded or hidden in the everyday activities of corporations. Firms can actually use derivatives to reduce risk.

In Chapter 22 we examine options. First we describe the options that trade on organized exchanges. Options are contingent claims on the value of an underlying asset. Every issue of corporate security has option features. Later in the chapter we present a formal model that can be used to value options. The model bears no resemblance to net present value (NPV). Our goal is to present the underlying logic of option valuation. This is important because NPV does not work well for contingent claims.

In Chapter 23, we describe some extensions of option pricing theory. There are option-like features in most investing and financing decisions.

In Chapter 24 we look at bonds with special option features. These bonds are sold as bonds with warrants and as bonds convertible into common stock. A warrant gives the holder a right to buy shares of common stock for cash, and a convertible bond gives the holder the right to exchange it for shares of common stock.

Previous chapters of this text assume that the volatility of the firm is fixed. Chapter 25 shows how firms can use financial instruments to reduce their risk, specifically discussing financial futures.

Options and Corporate Finance:
Basic Concepts

EXECUTIVE SUMMARY

In the summer of 2000, General Mills (GM) made an offer to acquire the Pillsbury division of Diageo PLC. Although the offer was generous, the managers of Diageo were worried about the possibility of a decline in GM's stock price. The deal eventually went through, due to a creative financing technique called a contingent value rights (CVR). Although CVRs may seem arcane, they are really straightforward applications of options, a topic to be examined in this chapter.

Options are special contractual arrangements giving the owner the right to buy or sell an asset at a fixed price anytime on or before a given date. Stock options, the most familiar type, are options to buy and sell shares of common stock. Ever since 1973, stock options have been traded on organized exchanges.

Corporate securities are very similar to the stock options that are traded on organized exchanges. Almost every issue of corporate bonds and stocks has option features. In addition, capital-structure decisions and capital-budgeting decisions can be viewed in terms of options.

We start this chapter with a description of different types of publicly traded options. We identify and discuss the factors that determine their values. Next, we show how common stocks and bonds can be thought of as options on the underlying value of the firm. This leads to several new insights concerning corporate finance. For example, we show how certain corporate decisions can be viewed as options. General Mills' issuance of a CVR is one of these corporate decisions.

22.1 Options

An **option** is a contract giving its owner the right to buy or sell an asset at a fixed price on or before a given date. For example, an option on a building might give the buyer the right to buy the building for $1 million on or anytime before the Saturday prior to the third Wednesday in January 2010. Options are a unique type of financial contract because they give the buyer the right, but not the *obligation,* to do something. The buyer uses the option only if it is advantageous to do so; otherwise the option can be thrown away.

There is a special vocabulary associated with options. Here are some important definitions:

1. **Exercising the option.** The act of buying or selling the underlying asset via the option contract is referred to as *exercising the option.*

2. **Striking or exercise price.** The fixed price in the option contract at which the holder can buy or sell the underlying asset is called the *striking price* or *exercise price.*

3. **Expiration date.** The maturity date of the option is referred to as the *expiration date.* After this date, the option is dead.

4. **American and European options.** An American option may be exercised anytime up to the expiration date. A European option differs from an American option in that it can be exercised only on the expiration date.

22.2 Call Options

The most common type of option is a **call option.** A call option gives the owner the right to buy an asset at a fixed price during a particular time period. There is no restriction on the kind of asset, but the most common ones traded on exchanges are options on stocks and bonds.

For example, call options on IBM stock can be purchased on the Chicago Board Options Exchange. IBM does not issue (that is, sell) call options on its common stock. Instead, individual investors are the original buyers and sellers of call options on IBM common stock. A representative call option on IBM stock enables an investor to buy 100 shares of IBM on or before July 15, at an exercise price of $100. This is a valuable option if there is some probability that the price of IBM common stock will exceed $100 on or before July 15.

The Value of a Call Option at Expiration

What is the value of a call-option contract on common stock at expiration? The answer depends on the value of the underlying stock at expiration.

Let's continue with the IBM example. Suppose the stock price is $130 at expiration. The buyer[1] of the call option has the right to buy the underlying stock at the exercise price of $100. In other words, he has the right to exercise the call. Having the right to buy something for $100 when it is worth $130 is obviously a good thing. The value of this right is $30 ($130 − $100) on the expiration day.[2]

The call would be worth even more if the stock price were higher on expiration day. For example, if IBM were selling for $150 on the date of expiration, the call would be worth $50 ($150 − $100) at that time. In fact, the call's value increases $1 for every $1 rise in the stock price.

If the stock price is greater than the exercise price, we say that the call is *in the money.* Of course, it is also possible that the value of the common stock will turn out to be less than the exercise price. In this case, we say that the call is *out of the money.* The holder will not exercise in this case. For example, if the stock price at the expiration date is $90, no rational investor would exercise. Why pay $100 for stock worth only $90? Because the option holder has no obligation to exercise the call, she can *walk away* from the option. As a consequence, if IBM's stock price is less than $100 on the expiration date, the value of the call option will be 0. In this case the value of the call option is not the difference between IBM's stock price and $100, as it would be if the holder of the call option had the *obligation* to exercise the call.

The payoff of a call option at expiration is:

	Payoff on the Expiration Date	
	If Stock Price Is Less Than $100	**If Stock Price Is Greater Than $100**
Call-option value:	0	Stock price − $100

Figure 22.1 plots the value of the call at expiration against the value of IBM's stock. It is referred to as the *hockey-stick diagram* of call-option values. If the stock price is less

---

[1]We use *buyer, owner,* and *holder* interchangeably.

[2]This example assumes that the call lets the holder purchase one share of stock at $100. In reality, a call lets the holder purchase 100 shares @ $100 per share. The profit would then equal $3000 [($130 − $100) × 100].

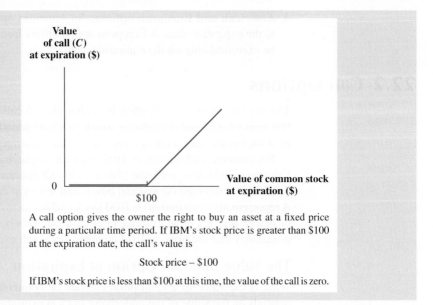

FIGURE 22.1

The Value of a Call Option on the Expiration Date

A call option gives the owner the right to buy an asset at a fixed price during a particular time period. If IBM's stock price is greater than $100 at the expiration date, the call's value is

Stock price − $100

If IBM's stock price is less than $100 at this time, the value of the call is zero.

than $100, the call is out of the money and worthless. If the stock price is greater than $100, the call is in the money and its value rises one-for-one with increases in the stock price. Notice that the call can never have a negative value. It is a *limited-liability instrument,* which means that all the holder can lose is the initial amount she paid for it.

EXAMPLE

Suppose Mr. Optimist holds a one-year call option on TIX common stock. It is a European call option and can be exercised at $150. Assume that the expiration date has arrived. What is the value of the TIX call option on the expiration date? If TIX is selling for $200 per share, Mr. Optimist can exercise the option—purchase TIX at $150—and then immediately sell the share at $200. Mr. Optimist will have made $50 ($200 − $150).

Instead, assume that TIX is selling for $100 per share on the expiration date. If Mr. Optimist still holds the call option, he will throw it out. The value of the TIX call on the expiration date will be zero in this case.

Concept Questions

1. What is a call option?
2. How is a call option's price related to the underlying stock price at the expiration date?

22.3 Put Options

A **put option** can be viewed as the opposite of a call option. Just as a call gives the holder the right to buy the stock at a fixed price, a put gives the holder the right to *sell* the stock for a fixed exercise price.

The Value of a Put Option at Expiration

The circumstances that determine the value of the put are the opposite of those for a call option, because a put option gives the holder the right to sell shares. Let us assume that the exercise price of the put is $50 and the stock price at expiration is $40. The owner of this put option has the right to sell the stock for *more* than it is worth, something that is clearly

FIGURE 22.2

The Value of a Put
Option on the
Expiration Date

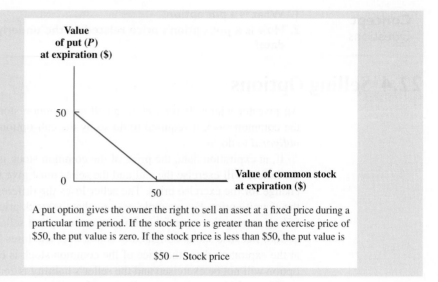

A put option gives the owner the right to sell an asset at a fixed price during a
particular time period. If the stock price is greater than the exercise price of
$50, the put value is zero. If the stock price is less than $50, the put value is

$50 − Stock price

profitable. That is, he can buy the stock at the market price of $40 and immediately sell it
at the exercise price of $50, generating a profit of $10 ($50 − $40). Thus, the value of the
option at expiration must be $10.

The profit would be greater still if the stock price were lower. For example, if the stock
price were only $30, the value of the option would be $20 ($50 − $30). In fact, for every $1
that the stock price declines at expiration, the value of the put rises by $1.

However, suppose that the stock at expiration is trading at $60—or any price above the
exercise price of $50. The owner of the put would not want to exercise here. It is a losing
proposition to sell stock for $50 when it trades in the open market at $60. Instead, the
owner of the put will walk away from the option. That is, he will let the put option expire.

The payoff of this put option is:

	Payoff on the Expiration Date Stock	
	If Stock Price Is Less Than $50	**If Stock Price Is Greater Than $50**
Put-option value	$50 − Stock price	0

Figure 22.2 plots the values of a put option for all possible values of the underlying stock.
It is instructive to compare Figure 22.2 with Figure 22.1 for the call option. The call option
is valuable whenever the stock is above the exercise price, and the put is valuable when the
stock price is below the exercise price.

EXAMPLE

Ms. Pessimist feels quite certain that BMI will fall from its current $160-per-share price. She buys a put.
Her put-option contract gives her the right to sell a share of BMI stock at $150 one year from now. If
the price of BMI is $200 on the expiration date, she will tear up the put option contract because it is
worthless. That is, she will not want to sell stock worth $200 for the exercise price of $150.

On the other hand, if BMI is selling for $100 on the expiration date, she will exercise the option.
In this case, she can buy a share of BMI in the market for $100 per share and turn around and sell
the share at the exercise price of $150. Her profit will be $50 ($150 − $100). The value of the put
option on the expiration date therefore will be $50.

1. **What is a put option?**
2. **How is a put option's price related to the underlying stock price at expiration date?**

22.4 Selling Options

An investor who sells (or *writes*) a call on common stock promises to deliver shares of the common stock if required to do so by the call-option holder. Notice that the seller is *obligated* to do so.

If, at expiration date, the price of the common stock is greater than the exercise price, the holder will exercise the call and the seller must give the holder shares of stock in exchange for the exercise price. The seller loses the difference between the stock price and the exercise price. For example, assume that the stock price is $60 and the exercise price is $50. Knowing that exercise is imminent, the option seller buys stock in the open market at $60. Because she is obligated to sell at $50, she loses $10 ($50 − $60). Conversely, if at the expiration date, the price of the common stock is below the exercise price, the call option will not be exercised and the seller's liability is zero.

Why would the seller of a call place himself in such a precarious position? After all, the seller loses money if the stock price ends up above the exercise price and he merely avoids losing money if the stock price ends up below the exercise price. The answer is that the seller is paid to take this risk. On the day that the option transaction takes place, the seller receives the price that the buyer pays.

Now, let's look at the seller of puts. An investor who sells a put on common stock agrees to purchase shares of common stock if the put holder should so request. The seller loses on this deal if the stock price falls below the exercise price and the holder puts the stock to the seller. For example, assume that the stock price is $40 and the exercise price is $50. The holder of the put will exercise in this case. In other words, he will sell the underlying stock at the exercise price of $50. This means that the seller of the put must buy the underlying stock at the exercise price of $50. Because the stock is only worth $40, the loss here is $10 ($40 − $50).

The values of the "sell-a-call" and "sell-a-put" positions are depicted in Figure 22.3. The graph on the left-hand side of the figure shows that the seller of a call loses nothing

---

FIGURE 22.3   The Payoffs to Sellers of Calls and Puts, and to Buyers of Common Stock

TABLE 22.1			Chicago Board					
Information on the Options of Microsoft Corporation	**Option and NY Close**	**Strike Price**	**Calls—Last**			**Puts—Last**		
			April	**July**	**Oct.**	**April**	**July**	**Oct.**
	Microsoft							
	$90\frac{3}{8}$	85	$6\frac{1}{8}$	$9\frac{3}{4}$	—	$\frac{9}{16}$	$3\frac{1}{2}$	—
	$90\frac{3}{8}$	90	$2\frac{9}{16}$	$7\frac{1}{4}$	$9\frac{7}{8}$	2	5	7
	$90\frac{3}{8}$	95	$\frac{11}{16}$	$4\frac{3}{4}$	—	5	8	—

when the stock price at expiration date is below $50. However, the seller loses a dollar for every dollar that the stock rises above $50. The graph in the center of the figure shows that the seller of a put loses nothing when the stock price at expiration date is above $50. However, the seller loses a dollar for every dollar that the stock falls below $50.

It is worthwhile to spend a few minutes comparing the graphs in Figure 22.3 to those in Figures 22.1 and 22.2. The graph of selling a call (the graph in the left-hand side of Figure 22.3) is the mirror image of the graph of buying a call (Figure 22.1).[3] This occurs because options are a zero-sum game. The seller of a call loses what the buyer makes. Similarly, the graph of selling a put (the middle graph in Figure 22.3) is the mirror image of the graph of buying a put (Figure 22.2). Again, the seller of a put loses what the buyer makes.

Figure 22.3 also shows the value at expiration of simply buying common stock. Notice that buying the stock is the same as buying a call option on the stock with an exercise price of zero. This is not surprising. If the exercise price is 0, the call holder can buy the stock for nothing, which is really the same as owning it.

22.5 Reading *The Wall Street Journal*

Now that we understand the definitions for calls and puts, let's see how these options are quoted. Table 22.1 presents information on the options of Microsoft Corporation from a recent issue of *The Wall Street Journal* (WSJ). The options are traded on the Chicago Board Options Exchange, one of a number of options exchanges. The first column tells us that the stock of Microsoft closed at $90\frac{3}{8}$ per share on the previous day. Now consider the second and third columns. The closing price for an option maturing at the end of April with a strike price of $85 was $6\frac{1}{8}$. Because the option is sold as a 100-share contract, the cost of the contract is $612.5 ($100 \times $6\frac{1}{8}$) before commissions. The call maturing in April with an exercise price of $90 closed at $2\frac{9}{16}$. The call with an exercise price of $85 maturing in October did not trade during the day, as indicated by —.

The last three columns display quotes on puts. For example, a put maturing in April with an exercise price of $95 sells at $5.

22.6 Combinations of Options

Puts and calls can serve as building blocks for more complex option contracts. For example, Figure 22.4 illustrates the payoff from buying a put option on a stock and simultaneously buying the stock.

If the share price is greater than the exercise price, the put option is worthless, and the value of the combined position is equal to the value of the common stock. If instead the

---

[3]Actually, because of differing exercise prices, the two graphs are not quite mirror images of each other. The exercise price in Figure 22.1 is $100 and the exercise price in Figure 22.3 is $50.

FIGURE 22.4   Payoff to the Combination of Buying a Put and Buying the Underlying Stock

FIGURE 22.5   Payoff to the Combination of Buying a Call and Buying a Zero-Coupon Bond

The graph of buying a call and buying a zero-coupon bond is the same as the graph of buying a put and buying the stock in Figure 22.4.

exercise price is greater than the share price, the decline in the value of the shares will be exactly offset by the rise in value of the put.

The strategy of buying a put and buying the underlying stock is called a *protective put*. It is as if one is buying insurance for the stock. The stock can always be sold at the exercise price, regardless of how far the market price of the stock falls.

Note that the combination of buying a put and buying the underlying stock has the same *shape* in Figure 22.4 as the call purchase in Figure 22.1. To pursue this point, let's consider the graph for buying a call, which is shown at the far left of Figure 22.5. This graph is the same as Figure 22.1, except that the exercise price is $50 here. Now, let's try the strategy of:

(Leg A) Buying a call.

(Leg B) Buying a zero-coupon bond with a face value of $50 that matures on the same day that the option expires.

We have drawn the graph of Leg A of this strategy at the far left of Figure 22.5, but what does the graph of Leg B look like? It looks like the middle graph of the figure. That is, anyone buying this zero-coupon bond will be guaranteed to get $50, regardless of the price of the stock at expiration.

What does the graph of *simultaneously* buying both Leg A and Leg B of this strategy look like? It looks like the far-right graph of Figure 22.5. That is, the investor receives a guaranteed $50 from the bond, regardless of what happens to the stock. In addition, the investor receives a payoff from the call of $1 for every $1 that the price of the stock rises above the exercise price of $50.

The far-right graph of Figure 22.5 looks *exactly* like the far-right graph of Figure 22.4. Thus, an investor gets the same payoff from the strategy of Figure 22.4, and the strategy of Figure 22.5, regardless of what happens to the price of the underlying stock. In other words, the investor gets the same payoff from

1. Buying a put and buying the underlying stock.
2. Buying a call and buying a zero-coupon bond.

If investors have the same payoffs from the two strategies, the two strategies must have the *same* cost. Otherwise, all investors will choose the strategy with the lower cost and avoid the strategy with the higher cost. This leads to the interesting result that:

$$\underbrace{\text{Price of underlying stock} + \text{Price of put}}_{\text{Cost of first strategy}} = \underbrace{\text{Price of call} + \text{Present value of exercise price}}_{\text{Cost of second strategy}} \quad (22.1)$$

This relationship is known as **put-call parity** and is one of the most fundamental relationships concerning options. It says that there are two ways of buying a protective put. You can buy a put and buy the underlying stock simultaneously. Here, your total cost is the price of the underlying stock plus the price of the put. Or, you can buy the call and buy a zero-coupon bond. Here, your total cost is the price of the call plus the price of the zero-coupon bond. The price of the zero-coupon bond is equal to the present value of the exercise price, i.e., the present value of $50 in our example.

Equation (22.1) is a very precise relationship. It holds only if the put and the call have both the same exercise price and the same expiration date. In addition, the maturity date of the zero-coupon bond must be the same as the expiration date of the options.

To see how fundamental put-call parity is, let's rearrange the formula, yielding:

$$\text{Price of underlying stock} = \text{Price of call} - \text{Price of put} + \text{Present value of exercise price}$$

This relationship now states that you can replicate the purchase of a share of stock by buying a call, selling a put, and buying a zero-coupon bond. (Note that, because a minus sign comes before "Price of put," the put is sold, not bought.) Investors in this three-legged strategy are said to have purchased a *synthetic* stock.

Let's do one more transformation:

Covered-Call Strategy

$$\text{Price of underlying stock} - \text{Price of call} = -\text{Price of put} + \text{Present value of exercise price}$$

Many investors like to buy a stock and write the call on the stock simultaneously. This is a conservative strategy known as *selling a covered call*. The preceding put-call parity relationship tells us that this strategy is equivalent to selling a put and buying a zero-coupon bond. Figure 22.6 develops the graph for the covered call. You can verify that the covered call can be replicated by selling a put and simultaneously buying a zero-coupon bond.

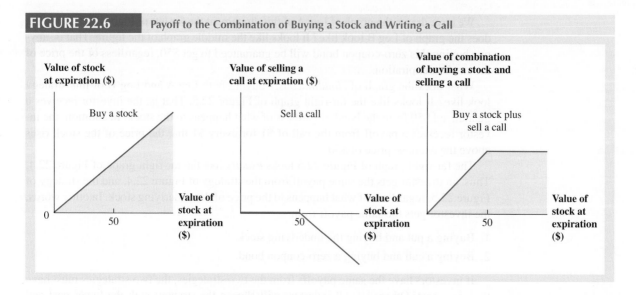

FIGURE 22.6   Payoff to the Combination of Buying a Stock and Writing a Call

Of course, there are other ways of rearranging the basic put-call relationship. For each rearrangement, the strategy on the left-hand side is equivalent to the strategy on the right-hand side. The beauty of put-call parity is that it shows how any strategy in options can be achieved in two different ways.

1. What is put-call parity?

22.7 Valuing Options

In the last section we determined what options are worth on the expiration date. Now we wish to determine the value of options when you buy them well before expiration.[4] We begin by considering the lower and upper bounds on the value of a call.

Bounding the Value of a Call

Lower Bound   Consider an American call that is in the money prior to expiration. For example, assume that the stock price is $60 and the exercise price is $50. In this case, the option cannot sell below $10. To see this, note the simple strategy if the option sells at, say, $9.

Date		Transaction	
Today	(1)	Buy call.	−$ 9
Today	(2)	Exercise call, that is, buy underlying stock at exercise price.	−$50
Today	(3)	Sell stock at current market price.	+$60
Arbitrage profit			+$ 1

---

[4]Our discussion in this section is of American options, because they are traded in the real world. As necessary, we will indicate differences for European options.

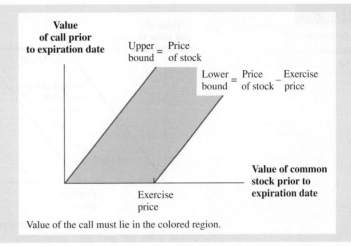

FIGURE 22.7

The Upper and
Lower Boundaries
of Call-Option
Values

Value of the call must lie in the colored region.

The type of profit that is described in this transaction is an *arbitrage* profit. Arbitrage profits come from transactions that have no risk or cost and cannot occur regularly in normal, well-functioning financial markets. The excess demand for these options would quickly force the option price up to at least $10 ($60 − $50).[5]

Of course, the price of the option is likely to sell above $10. Investors will rationally pay more than $10 because of the possibility that the stock will rise above $60 before expiration.

Upper Bound   Is there an upper boundary for the option price as well? It turns out that the upper boundary is the price of the underlying stock. That is, an option to buy common stock cannot have a greater value than the common stock itself. A call option can be used to buy common stock with a payment of an exercise price. It would be foolish to buy stock this way if the stock could be purchased directly at a lower price.

The upper and lower bounds are represented in Figure 22.7. In addition, these bounds are summarized in the bottom half of Table 22.2.

The Factors Determining Call-Option Values

The previous discussion indicated that the price of a call option must fall somewhere in the shaded region of Figure 22.7. We now will determine more precisely where in the shaded region it should be. The factors that determine a call's value can be broken into two sets. The first set contains the features of the option contract. The two basic contractual features are the expiration price and the exercise date. The second set of factors affecting the call price concerns characteristics of the stock and the market.

Exercise Price   An increase in the exercise price reduces the value of the call. For example, imagine that there are two calls on a stock selling at $60. The first call has an exercise price of $50 and the second one has an exercise price of $40. Which call would you rather have? Clearly, you would rather have the call with an exercise price of $40, because that one is $20 ($60 − $40) in the money. In other words, the call with an exercise price of $40 should sell for more than an otherwise-identical call with an exercise price of $50.

---

[5]It should be noted that this lower bound is strictly true for an American option but not for a European option.

FIGURE 22.8

Value of an American
Call as a Function
of Stock Price

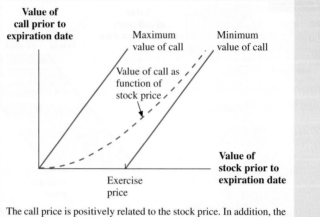

The call price is positively related to the stock price. In addition, the change in the call price for a given change in the stock price is greater when the stock price is high than when it is low.

Expiration Date   The value of an American call option must be at least as great as the value of an otherwise identical option with a shorter term to expiration. Consider two American calls: One has a maturity of nine months and the other expires in six months. Obviously, the nine-month call has the same rights as the six-month call, and also has an additional three months within which these rights can be exercised. It cannot be worth less and will generally be more valuable.[6]

Stock Price   Other things being equal, the higher the stock price, the more valuable the call option will be. For example, if a stock is worth $80, a call with an exercise price of $100 isn't worth very much. If the stock soars to $120, the call becomes much more valuable.

Now consider Figure 22.8, which shows the relationship between the call price and the stock price prior to expiration. The curve indicates that the call price increases as the stock price increases. Furthermore, it can be shown that the relationship is represented, not by a straight line, but by a *convex* curve. That is, the increase in the call price for a given change in the stock price is greater when the stock price is high than when the stock price is low.

There are two special points on the curve in Figure 22.8:

1. *The Stock Is Worthless.* The call must be worthless if the underlying stock is worthless. That is, if the stock has no chance of attaining any value, it is not worthwhile to pay the exercise price in order to obtain the stock.

2. *The Stock Price Is* Very *High Relative to the Exercise Price.* In this situation, the owner of the call knows that he will end up exercising the call. He can view himself as the owner of the stock now, with one difference. He must pay the exercise price at expiration.

Thus, the value of his position, i.e., the value of the call, is:

$$\text{Stock price} - \text{Present value of exercise price}$$

These two points on the curve are summarized in the bottom half of Table 22.2.

---

[6]This relationship need not hold for a European call option. Consider a firm with two otherwise identical European call options, one expiring at the end of May and the other expiring a few months later. Further assume that a *huge* dividend is paid in early June. If the first call is exercised at the end of May, its holder will receive the underlying stock. If he does not sell the stock, he will receive the large dividend shortly thereafter. However, the holder of the second call will receive the stock through exercise after the dividend is paid. Because the market knows that the holder of this option will miss the dividend, the value of the second call option could be less than the value of the first.

FIGURE 22.9

Distribution of
Common-Stock Price
at Expiration for Both
Security *A* and
Security *B*. Options
on the Two Securities
Have the Same
Exercise Price

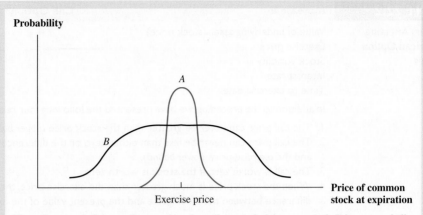

The call on stock *B* is worth more than the call on stock *A* because stock *B* is more volatile. At expiration, a call that deep in the money is more valuable than a call that is only slightly in the money. However, at expiration, a call way out of the money is worth zero, just as is a call only slightly out of the money.

The Key Factor: The Variability of the Underlying Asset   The greater the variability of the underlying asset, the more valuable the call option will be. Consider the following example. Suppose that just before the call expires, the stock price will be either $100 with probability 0.5 or $80 with probability 0.5. What will be the value of a call with an exercise price of $110? Clearly, it will be worthless because no matter what happens to the stock, its price will always be below the exercise price.

Now let us see what happens if the stock is more variable. Suppose that we add $20 to the best case and take $20 away from the worst case. Now the stock has a one-half chance of being worth $60 and a one-half chance of being worth $120. We have spread the stock returns, but, of course, the expected value of the stock has stayed the same:

$$(1/2 \times \$80) + (1/2 \times \$100) = \$90 = (1/2 \times \$60) + (1/2 \times \$120)$$

Notice that the call option has value now because there is a one-half chance that the stock price will be $120, or $10 above the exercise price of $110. This illustrates a very important point. There is a fundamental distinction between holding an option on an underlying asset and holding the underlying asset. If investors in the marketplace are risk-averse, a rise in the variability of the stock will decrease its market value. However, the holder of a call receives payoffs from the positive tail of the probability distribution. As a consequence, a rise in the variability in the underlying stock increases the market value of the call.

This result can also be seen from Figure 22.9. Consider two stocks, *A* and *B*, each of which is normally distributed. For each security, the figure illustrates the probability of different stock prices on the expiration date.[7] As can be seen from the figures, stock *B* has more volatility than does stock *A*. This means that stock *B* has higher probability of both abnormally high returns and abnormally low returns. Let us assume that options on each of the two securities have the same exercise price. To option holders, a return much below average on stock *B* is no worse than a return only moderately below average on stock *A*.

---

[7]This graph assumes that, for each security, the exercise price is equal to the expected stock price. This assumption is employed merely to facilitate the discussion. It is not needed to show the relationship between a call's value and the volatility of the underlying stock.

TABLE 22.2	Increase in	Call Option*	Put Option*
Factors Affecting American Option Values	Value of underlying asset (stock price)	+	−
	Exercise price	−	+
	Stock volatility	+	+
	Interest rate	+	−
	Time to exercise date	+	+

In addition to the preceding, we have presented the following four relationships for American calls:

1. The call price can never be greater than the stock price (*upper bound*).
2. The call price can never be less than either zero or the difference between the stock price and the exercise price (*lower bound*).
3. The call is worth zero if the stock is worth zero.
4. When the stock price is much greater than the exercise price, the call price tends toward the difference between the stock price and the present value of the exercise price.

*The signs (+, −) indicate the effect of the variables on the value of the option. For example, the two +s for stock volatility indicate that an increase in volatility will increase both the value of a call and the value of a put.

In either situation, the option expires out of the money. However, to option holders, a return much above average on stock *B* is better than a return only moderately above average on stock *A*. Because a call's price at the expiration date is the difference between the stock price and the exercise price, the value of the call on *B* at expiration will be higher in this case.

The Interest Rate   Call prices are also a function of the level of interest rates. Buyers of calls do not pay the exercise price until they exercise the option, if they do so at all. The ability to delay payment is more valuable when interest rates are high and less valuable when interest rates are low. Thus, the value of a call is positively related to interest rates.

A Quick Discussion of Factors Determining Put-Option Values

Given our extended discussion of the factors influencing a call's value, we can examine the effect of these factors on puts very easily. Table 22.2 summarizes the five factors influencing the prices of both American calls and American puts. The effect of three factors on puts are the opposite of the effect of these three factors on calls:

1. The put's market value *decreases* as the stock price increases because puts are in the money when the stock sells below the exercise price.
2. The value of a put with a high exercise price is *greater* than the value of an otherwise identical put with a low exercise price for the reason given in (1).
3. A high interest rate *adversely* affects the value of a put. The ability to sell a stock at a fixed exercise price sometime in the future is worth less if the present value of the exercise price is diminished by a high interest rate.

The effect of the other two factors on puts is the same as the effect of these factors on calls:

4. The value of an American put with a distant expiration date is greater than an otherwise identical put with an earlier expiration.[8] The longer time to maturity gives the put holder more flexibility, just as it did in the case of a call.

---

[8]Though this result must hold in the case of an American put, it need not hold for a European put.

5. Volatility of the underlying stock increases the value of the put. The reasoning is analogous to that for a call. At expiration, a put that is way in the money is more valuable than a put only slightly in the money. However, at expiration, a put way out of the money is worth zero, just as is a put only slightly out of the money.

Concept
Questions

1. **List the factors that determine the value of options.**
2. **Why does a stock's variability affect the value of options written on it?**

22.8 An Option-Pricing Formula

We have explained *qualitatively* that the value of a call option is a function of five variables:

1. The current price of the underlying asset, which for stock options is the price of a share of common stock.
2. The exercise price.
3. The time to expiration date.
4. The variance of the underlying asset.
5. The risk-free interest rate.

It is time to replace the qualitative model with a precise option-valuation model. The model we choose is the famous Black-Scholes option-pricing model. You can put numbers into the Black-Scholes model and get values back.

The Black-Scholes model is represented by a rather imposing formula. A derivation of the formula is simply not possible in this textbook, as the students will be happy to learn. However, some appreciation for the achievement as well as some intuitive understanding is in order.

In the early chapters of this book, we showed how to discount capital-budgeting projects using the net-present-value formula. We also used this approach to value stocks and bonds. Why, students sometimes ask, can't the same NPV formula be used to value puts and calls? It is a good question because the earliest attempts at valuing options used NPV. Unfortunately, the attempts were simply not successful because no one could determine the appropriate discount rate. An option is generally riskier than the underlying stock but no one knew exactly how much riskier.

Black and Scholes attacked the problem by pointing out that a strategy of borrowing to finance a stock purchase duplicates the risk of a call. Then, knowing the price of a stock already, one can determine the price of a call such that its return is identical to that of the stock-with-borrowing alternative.

We illustrate the intuition behind the Black-Scholes approach by considering a simple example where a combination of a call and a stock eliminates all risk. This example works because we let the future stock price be one of only *two* values. Hence, the example is called a *two-state option model*. By eliminating the possibility that the stock price can take on other values, we are able to duplicate the call exactly.

A Two-State Option Model

Consider the following example. Suppose the current market price of a stock is $50 and the stock will either be $60 or $40 at the end of the year. Further, imagine a call option on this stock with a one-year expiration date and a $50 exercise price. Investors can borrow at 10 percent. Our goal is to determine the value of the call.

In order to value the call correctly, we need to examine two strategies. The first is to simply buy the call. The second is to:

a. Buy one-half a share of stock.

b. Borrow $18.18, implying a payment of principal and interest at the end of the year of $20 ($18.18 × 1.10).

As you will see shortly, the cash flows from the second strategy exactly match the cash flows from buying a call. (A little later we will show how we came up with the exact fraction of a share of stock to buy and the exact borrowing amount.) Because the cash flows match, we say that we are *duplicating* the call with the second strategy.

At the end of the year, the future payoffs are set out as follows:

Initial Transactions	Future Payoffs	
	If Stock Price Is $60	**If Stock Price Is $40**
1. Buy a call	$60 − $50 = $10	0
2. Buy $\frac{1}{2}$ share of stock	$\frac{1}{2}$ × $60 = $30	$\frac{1}{2}$ × $40 = $20
Borrow $18.18 at 10%	−($18.18 × 1.10) = −$20	−$20
Total from stock and borrowing strategy	$10	0

Note that the future payoff structure of the "buy-a-call" strategy is duplicated by the strategy of "buy stock" and "borrow." That is, under either strategy, an investor would end up with $10 if the stock price rose and $0 if the stock price fell. Thus, these two strategies are equivalent as far as traders are concerned.

Now, if two strategies always have the same cash flows at the end of the year, how must their initial costs be related? The two strategies must have the *same* initial cost. Otherwise, there will be an arbitrage possibility. We can easily calculate this cost for our strategy of buying stock and borrowing. This cost is:

Buy $\frac{1}{2}$ share of stock	$\frac{1}{2}$ × $50 =	$25.00
Borrow $18.18		−$18.18
		$ 6.82

Because the call option provides the same payoffs at expiration as does the strategy of buying stock and borrowing, the call must be priced at $6.82. This is the value of the call option in a market without arbitrage profits.

We left two issues unexplained in the preceding example.

Determining the Delta   How did we know to buy one-half share of stock in the duplicating strategy? Actually, the answer is easier than it might at first appear. The call price at the end of the year will be either $10 or $0, whereas the stock price will be either $60 or $40. Thus, the call price has a potential swing of $10 ($10 − $0) next period, whereas the stock price has a potential swing of $20 ($60 − $40). We can write this in terms of the following ratio:

Delta

$$\frac{\text{Swing of call}}{\text{Swing of stock}} = \frac{\$10 - \$0}{\$60 - \$40} = \frac{1}{2}$$

This ratio is called the *delta* of the call. In words, a $1 swing in the price of the stock gives rise to a $1/2 swing in the price of the call. Because we are trying to duplicate the call with the stock, it seems sensible to buy one-half share of stock instead of buying one call. In other words, the risk of buying one-half share of stock should be the same as the risk of buying one call.

Determining the Amount of Borrowing   How did we know how much to borrow? Buying one-half share of stock brings us either $30 or $20 at expiration, which is exactly $20 more than the payoffs of $10 and $0, respectively, from the call. To duplicate the call through a purchase of stock, we should also borrow enough money so that we have to pay back exactly $20 of interest and principal. This amount of borrowing is merely the present value of $20, which is $18.18 ($20/1.10).

Now that we know how to determine both the delta and the borrowing, we can write the value of the call as:

$$\text{Value of call} = \text{Stock price} \times \text{Delta} - \text{Amount borrowed} \qquad (22.2)$$
$$\$6.82 = \$50 \times \tfrac{1}{2} - \$18.18$$

We will find this intuition very useful in explaining the Black-Scholes model.

Risk-Neutral Valuation   Before leaving this simple example, we should comment on a remarkable feature. We found the exact value of the option without even knowing the probability that the stock would go up or down! If an optimist thought the probability of an up move was very high and a pessimist thought it was very low, they would still agree on the option value. How could that be? The answer is that the current $50 stock price already balances the views of the optimists and the pessimists. The option reflects that balance because its value depends on the stock price.

This insight provides us with another approach to valuing the call. If we don't need the probabilities of the two states to value the call, perhaps we can select *any* probabilities we want and still come up with the right answer. Suppose we selected probabilities such that the return on the stock is equal to the risk-free rate of 10 percent. We know that the stock return given a rise is 20 percent ($60/$50 − 1) and the stock return given a fall is −20 percent ($40/$50 − 1). Thus, we can solve for the probability of a rise necessary to achieve an expected return of 10 percent as:

$$10\% = \text{Probability of a rise} \times 20\% + (1 - \text{Probability of rise}) \times -20\%$$

Solving this formula, we find that the probability of a rise is 3/4 and the probability of a fall is 1/4. If we apply these probabilities to the call, we can value it as:

$$\text{Value of call} = \frac{\tfrac{3}{4} \times \$10 + \tfrac{1}{4} \times \$0}{1.10} = \$6.82$$

the same value that we got from the duplicating approach.

Why did we select probabilities such that the expected return on the stock is 10 percent? We wanted to work with the special case where investors are *risk-neutral*. This case occurs where the expected return on *any* asset (including both the stock and the call) is equal to the risk-free rate. In other words, this case occurs when investors demand no additional compensation beyond the risk-free rate, regardless of the risk of the asset in question.

What would have happened if we had assumed that the expected return on a stock was greater than the risk-free rate? The value of the call would still be $6.82. However, the calculations would be difficult. For example, if we assumed that the expected return on the stock was, say, 11 percent, we would have had to derive the expected return on the call. Although the expected return on the call would be higher than 11 percent, it would take a lot of work to determine it precisely. Why do any more work than you have to? Because we can't think of any good reason, we (and most other financial economists) choose to assume risk-neutrality.

Thus, the preceding material allows us to value a call in the following two ways:

1. Determine the cost of a strategy to duplicate the call. This strategy involves an investment in a fractional share of stock financed by partial borrowing.

2. Calculate the probabilities of a rise and a fall under the assumption of risk-neutrality.

Use those probabilities, in conjunction with the risk-free rate, to discount the payoffs of the call at expiration.

The Black-Scholes Model

The preceding example illustrates the duplicating strategy. Unfortunately, a strategy such as this will not work in the real world over, say, a one-year time frame, because there are many more than two possibilities for next year's stock price. However, the number of possibilities is reduced as the time period is shortened. In fact, the assumption that there are only two possibilities for the stock price over the next infinitesimal instant is quite plausible.[9]

In our opinion, the fundamental insight of Black and Scholes is to shorten the time period. They show that a specific combination of stock and borrowing can indeed duplicate a call over an infinitesimal time horizon. Because the price of the stock will change over the first instant, another combination of stock and borrowing is needed to duplicate the call over the second instant and so on. By adjusting the combination from moment to moment, they can continually duplicate the call. It may boggle the mind that a formula can (1) determine the duplicating combination at any moment and (2) value the option based on this duplicating strategy. Suffice it to say that their dynamic strategy allows them to value a call in the real world just as we showed how to value the call in the two-state model.

This is the basic intuition behind the Black-Scholes (BS) model. Because the actual derivation of their formula is, alas, far beyond the scope of this text, we simply present the formula itself. The formula is

Black-Scholes Model:

$$C = SN(d_1) - Ee^{-rt} N(d_2)$$

where
$$d_1 = [\ln(S/E) + (r + 1/2\sigma^2)t]/\sqrt{\sigma^2 t}$$
$$d_2 = d_1 - \sqrt{\sigma^2 t}$$

This formula for the value of a call, C, is one of the most complex in finance. However, it involves only five parameters:

1. S = Current stock price
2. E = Exercise price of call
3. r = Annual risk-free rate of return, continually compounded
4. σ^2 = Variance (per year) of the continuous return on the stock
5. t = Time (in years) to expiration date

In addition, there is the statistical concept:

$N(d)$ = Probability that a standardized, normally distributed, random variable will be less than or equal to d

---

[9]A full treatment of this assumption can be found in John C. Hull, *Options, Futures and Other Derivatives,* 4th ed. Upper Saddle River, N.J.: Prentice Hall (1999).

Rather than discuss the formula in its algebraic state, we illustrate the formula with an example.

<table>
<tr><td style="background:#000;color:#fff;padding:4px">EXAMPLE</td><td>

Consider Private Equipment Company (PEC). On October 4, of year 0, the PEC April 49 call option had a closing value of $4. The stock itself is selling at $50. On October 4 the option had 199 days to expiration (maturity date = April 21, Year 1). The annual risk-free interest rate, continually compounded, is 7 percent.

This information determines three variables directly:

1. The stock price, S, is $50.

2. The exercise price, E, is $49.

3. The risk-free rate, r, is 0.07.

In addition, the time to maturity, t, can be calculated quickly: The formula calls for t to be expressed in *years*.

4. We express the 199-day interval in years as $t = 199/365$.

In the real world, an option trader would know S and E exactly. Traders generally view U.S. Treasury bills as riskless, so a current quote from *The Wall Street Journal* or a similar newspaper would be obtained for the interest rate. The trader would also know (or could count) the number of days to expiration exactly. Thus, the fraction of a year to expiration, t, could be calculated quickly.

The problem comes in determining the variance of the stock's return. The formula calls for the variance in operation between the purchase date of October 4 and the expiration date. Unfortunately, this represents the future, so the correct value for variance is simply not available. Instead, traders frequently estimate variance from past data, just as we calculated variance in an earlier chapter. In addition, some traders may use intuition to adjust their estimate. For example, if anticipation of an upcoming event is currently increasing the volatility of the stock, the trader might adjust her estimate of variance upward to reflect this. (This problem was most severe right after the October 19, 1987, crash. The stock market was quite risky in the aftermath, so estimates using precrash data were too low.)

The above discussion was intended merely to mention the difficulties in variance estimation, not to present a solution. For our purposes, we assume that a trader has come up with an estimate of variance:

5. The variance of Private Equipment Co. has been estimated to be 0.09 per year.

Using the above five parameters, we calculate the Black-Scholes value of the PEC option in three steps:

Step 1: *Calculate d_1 and d_2.* These values can be determined by a straightforward, albeit tedious, insertion of our parameters into the basic formula. We have

$$d_1 = \left[\ln\left(\frac{S}{E}\right) + (r + 1/2\sigma^2)t \right] \Big/ \sqrt{\sigma^2 t}$$

$$= \left[\ln\left(\frac{50}{49}\right) + (0.07 + 1/2 \times 0.09) \times \frac{199}{365} \right] \Big/ \sqrt{0.09 \times \frac{199}{365}}$$

$$= [0.0202 + 0.0627]/0.2215 = 0.3742$$

$$d_2 = d_1 - \sqrt{\sigma^2 t}$$

$$= 0.1527$$

Step 2: *Calculate $N(d_1)$ and $N(d_2)$.* The values $N(d_1)$ and $N(d_2)$ can best be understood by examining Figure 22.10. The figure shows the normal distribution with an expected value of 0 and a standard

</td></tr>
</table>

FIGURE 22.10

Graph of Cumulative
Probability

Shaded area represents cumulative probability. Because the probability is 0.6459
that a drawing from the standard normal distribution will be below 0.3742, we say
that N(0.3742) = 0.6459. That is, the cumulative probability of 0.3742 is 0.6459.

deviation of 1. This is frequently called the **standardized normal distribution.** We mentioned in
an earlier chapter that the probability that a drawing from this distribution will be between −1 and
+1 (within one standard deviation of its mean, in other words) is 68.26 percent.

Now, let us ask a different question. What is the probability that a drawing from the standardized
normal distribution will be *below* a particular value? For example, the probability that a drawing will
be below 0 is clearly 50 percent because the normal distribution is symmetric. Using statistical terminology, we say that the **cumulative probability** of 0 is 50 percent. Statisticians also say that
N(0) = 50%. It turns out that

$$N(d_1) = N(0.3742) = 0.6459$$
$$N(d_2) = N(0.1527) = 0.5607$$

The first value means that there is a 64.59-percent probability that a drawing from the standardized
normal distribution will be below 0.3742. The second value means that there is a 56.07-percent
probability that a drawing from the standardized normal distribution will be below 0.1527. More
generally, N(d) is the notation that a drawing from the standardized normal distribution will be
below d. In other words, N(d) is the cumulative probability of d. Note that d_1 and d_2 in our example
are slightly above zero, so $N(d_1)$ and $N(d_2)$ are slightly greater than 0.50.

Perhaps the easiest way to determine $N(d_1)$ and $N(d_2)$ is from the EXCEL function NORMSDIST.
In our example, NORMSDIST (0.3742) and NORMSDIST (0.1527) are 0.6459 and 0.5607, respectively.

We can also determine the cumulative probability from Table 22.3. For example, consider d =
0.37. This can be found in the table as 0.3 on the vertical and 0.07 on the horizontal. The value in the
table for d = 0.37 is 0.1443. This value is *not* the cumulative probability of 0.37. One must first make
an adjustment to determine cumulative probability. That is,

$$N(0.37) = 0.50 + 0.1443 = 0.6443$$
$$N(-0.37) = 0.50 - 0.1443 = 0.3557$$

Unfortunately, our table handles only two significant digits, whereas our value of 0.3742 has four
significant digits. Hence, we must interpolate to find N(0.3742). Because N(0.37) = 0.6443 and
N(0.38) = 0.6480, the difference between the two values is 0.0037 (0.6480 − 0.6443). Because
0.3742 is 42 percent of the way between 0.37 and 0.38, we interpolate as:[10]

$$N(0.3742) = 0.6443 + 0.42 \times 0.0037 = 0.6459$$

[10]This method is called *linear interpolation.* It is only one of a number of possible methods of interpolation.

TABLE 22.3		Cumulative Probabilities of the Standard Normal Distribution Function								
d	0.00	0.01	0.02	0.03	0.04	0.05	0.06	0.07	0.08	0.09
0.0	0.0000	0.0040	0.0080	0.0120	0.0160	0.0199	0.0239	0.0279	0.0319	0.0359
0.1	0.0398	0.0438	0.0478	0.0517	0.0557	0.0596	0.0636	0.0675	0.0714	0.0753
0.2	0.0793	0.0832	0.0871	0.0910	0.0948	0.0987	0.1026	0.1064	0.1103	0.1141
0.3	0.1179	0.1217	0.1255	0.1293	0.1331	0.1368	0.1406	0.1443	0.1480	0.1517
0.4	0.1554	0.1591	0.1628	0.1664	0.1700	0.1736	0.1772	0.1808	0.1844	0.1879
0.5	0.1915	0.1950	0.1985	0.2019	0.2054	0.2088	0.2123	0.2157	0.2190	0.2224
0.6	0.2257	0.2291	0.2324	0.2357	0.2389	0.2422	0.2454	0.2486	0.2517	0.2549
0.7	0.2580	0.2611	0.2642	0.2673	0.2704	0.2734	0.2764	0.2794	0.2823	0.2852
0.8	0.2881	0.2910	0.2939	0.2967	0.2995	0.3023	0.3051	0.3078	0.3106	0.3133
0.9	0.3159	0.3186	0.3212	0.3238	0.3264	0.3289	0.3315	0.3340	0.3365	0.3389
1.0	0.3413	0.3438	0.3461	0.3485	0.3508	0.3531	0.3554	0.3577	0.3599	0.3621
1.1	0.3643	0.3665	0.3686	0.3708	0.3729	0.3749	0.3770	0.3790	0.3810	0.3830
1.2	0.3849	0.3869	0.3888	0.3907	0.3925	0.3944	0.3962	0.3980	0.3997	0.4015
1.3	0.4032	0.4049	0.4066	0.4082	0.4099	0.4115	0.4131	0.4147	0.4162	0.4177
1.4	0.4192	0.4207	0.4222	0.4236	0.4251	0.4265	0.4279	0.4292	0.4306	0.4319
1.5	0.4332	0.4345	0.4357	0.4370	0.4382	0.4394	0.4406	0.4418	0.4429	0.4441
1.6	0.4452	0.4463	0.4474	0.4484	0.4495	0.4505	0.4515	0.4525	0.4535	0.4545
1.7	0.4554	0.4564	0.4573	0.4582	0.4591	0.4599	0.4608	0.4616	0.4625	0.4633
1.8	0.4641	0.4649	0.4656	0.4664	0.4671	0.4678	0.4686	0.4693	0.4699	0.4706
1.9	0.4713	0.4719	0.4726	0.4732	0.4738	0.4744	0.4750	0.4756	0.4761	0.4767
2.0	0.4773	0.4778	0.4783	0.4788	0.4793	0.4798	0.4803	0.4808	0.4812	0.4817
2.1	0.4821	0.4826	0.4830	0.4834	0.4838	0.4842	0.4846	0.4850	0.4854	0.4857
2.2	0.4861	0.4866	0.4830	0.4871	0.4875	0.4878	0.4881	0.4884	0.4887	0.4890
2.3	0.4893	0.4896	0.4898	0.4901	0.4904	0.4906	0.4909	0.4911	0.4913	0.4916
2.4	0.4918	0.4920	0.4922	0.4925	0.4927	0.4929	0.4931	0.4932	0.4934	0.4936
2.5	0.4938	0.4940	0.4941	0.4943	0.4945	0.4946	0.4948	0.4949	0.4951	0.4952
2.6	0.4953	0.4955	0.4956	0.4957	0.4959	0.4960	0.4961	0.4962	0.4963	0.4964
2.7	0.4965	0.4966	0.4967	0.4968	0.4969	0.4970	0.4971	0.4972	0.4973	0.4974
2.8	0.4974	0.4975	0.4976	0.4977	0.4977	0.4978	0.4979	0.4979	0.4980	0.4981
2.9	0.4981	0.4982	0.4982	0.4982	0.4984	0.4984	0.4985	0.4985	0.4986	0.4986
3.0	0.4987	0.4987	0.4987	0.4988	0.4988	0.4989	0.4989	0.4989	0.4990	0.4990

$N(d)$ represents areas under the standard normal distribution function. Suppose that $d_1 = 0.24$. This table implies a cumulative probability of $0.5000 + 0.0948 = 0.5948$. If d_1 is equal to 0.2452, we must estimate the probability by interpolating between $N(0.25)$ and $N(0.24)$.

Step 3: *Calculate C.* We have

$$C = S \times [N(d_1)] - Ee^{-rt} \times [N(d_2)]$$
$$= \$50 \times [N(d_1)] - \$49 \times [e^{-0.07 \times (199/365)}] \times N(d_2)$$
$$= (\$50 \times 0.6459) - (\$49 \times 0.9626 \times 0.5607)$$
$$= \$32.295 - \$26.447$$
$$= \$5.85$$

The estimated price of $5.85 is greater than the $4 actual price, implying that the call option is underpriced. A trader believing in the Black-Scholes model would buy a call. Of course, the Black-Scholes model is fallible. Perhaps the disparity between the model's estimate and the market price reflects error in the trader's estimate of variance.

The previous example stressed the calculations involved in using the Black-Scholes formula. Is there any intuition behind the formula? Yes, and that intuition follows from the stock purchase and borrowing strategy in our binomial example. The first line of the

Black-Scholes equation is:

$$C = S \times N(d_1) - Ee^{-rt} N(d_2)$$

which is exactly analogous to equation (22.2):

$$\text{Value of call} = \text{Stock price} \times \text{Delta} - \text{Amount borrowed} \tag{22.2}$$

that we presented in the binomial example. It turns out that $N(d_1)$ is the delta in the Black-Scholes model. $N(d_1)$ is 0.6459 in the previous example. In addition, $Ee^{-rt} N(d_1)$ is the amount that an investor must borrow to duplicate a call. In the previous example, this value is $26.45 ($49 × 0.9626 × 0.5607). Thus, the model tells us that we can duplicate the call of the preceding example by both:

1. Buying 0.6459 share of stock.
2. Borrowing $26.45.

It is no exaggeration to say that the Black-Scholes formula is among the most important contributions in finance. It allows anyone to calculate the value of an option given a few parameters. The attraction of the formula is that four of the parameters are observable: the current price of stock, S, the exercise price, E, the interest rate, r, and the time to expiration date, t. Only one of the parameters must be estimated: the variance of return, σ^2.

To see how truly attractive this formula is, note what parameters are not needed. First, the investor's risk aversion does not affect value. The formula can be used by anyone, regardless of willingness to bear risk. Second, it does not depend on the expected return on the stock! Investors with different assessments of the stock's expected return will nevertheless agree on the call price. As in the two-state example, this is because the call depends on the stock price and that price already balances investors' divergent views.

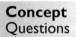

Concept
Questions

1. **How does the two-state option model work?**
2. **What is the formula for the Black-Scholes option-pricing model?**

22.9 Stocks and Bonds as Options

The previous material in this chapter described, explained, and valued publicly traded options. This is important material to any finance student because much trading occurs in these listed options. The study of options has another purpose for the student of corporate finance.

You may have heard the one-liner about the elderly gentleman who was surprised to learn that he had been speaking prose all of his life. The same can be said about the corporate finance student and options. Although options were formally defined for the first time in this chapter, many corporate policies discussed earlier in the text were actually options in disguise. Though it is beyond the scope of this chapter to recast all of corporate finance in terms of options, the rest of the chapter considers the implicit options in three topics:

1. Stocks and bonds as options.
2. Capital-structure decisions as options.
3. Capital-budgeting decisions as options.

We begin by illustrating the implicit options in stocks and bonds through a simple example.

EXAMPLE

The Popov Company has been awarded the concessions at next year's Olympic Games in Antarctica. Because the firm's principals live in Antarctica and because there is no other concession business in that continent, their enterprise will disband after the games. The firm has issued debt to help finance this venture. Interest and principal due on the debt next year will be $800, at which time the debt will be paid off in full. The firm's cash flows next year are forecasted as:

	Popov's Cash-Flow Schedule			
	Very Successful Games	Moderately Successful Games	Moderately Unsuccessful Games	Outright Failure
Cash flow before interest and principal	$1,000	$850	$700	$550
−Interest and principal	−800	−800	−700	−550
Cash flow to stockholders	$ 200	$ 50	$ 0	$ 0

As can be seen, the principals forecasted four equally likely scenarios. If either of the first two scenarios occurs, the bondholders will be paid in full. The extra cash flow goes to the stockholders. However, if either of the last two scenarios occurs, the bondholders will not be paid in full. Instead, they will receive the firm's entire cash flow, leaving the stockholders with nothing.

This example is similar to the bankruptcy examples presented in our chapters on capital structure. Our new insight is that the relationship between the common stock and the firm can be expressed in terms of options. We consider call options first because the intuition is easier. The put-option scenario is treated next.

The Firm Expressed in Terms of Call Options

The Stockholders   We now show that stock can be viewed as a call option on the firm. To illustrate this, Figure 22.11 graphs the cash flow to the stockholders as a function of the

FIGURE 22.11

Cash Flow to Stockholders of Popov Company as a Function of Cash Flow of Firm

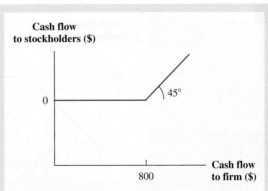

The stockholders can be viewed as having a call option on the firm. If the cash flows of the firm exceed $800, the stockholders pay $800 in order to receive the firm. If the cash flows of the firm are less than $800, the stockholders do not exercise their option. They walk away from the firm, receiving nothing.

cash flow to the firm. The stockholders receive nothing if the firm's cash flows are less than $800; here, all of the cash flows go to the bondholders. However, the stockholders earn a dollar for every dollar that the firm receives above $800. The graph looks exactly like the call-option graphs that we considered earlier in this chapter.

But what is the underlying asset upon which the stock is a call option? The underlying asset is the firm itself. That is, we can view the *bondholders* as owning the firm. However, the stockholders have a call option on the firm with an exercise price of $800.

If the firm's cash flow is above $800, the stockholders would choose to exercise this option. In other words, they would buy the firm from the bondholders for $800. Their net cash flow is the difference between the firm's cash flow and their $800 payment. This would be $200 ($1,000 − $800) if the games are very successful and $50 ($850 − $800) if the games are moderately successful.

Should the value of the firm's cash flows be less than $800, the stockholders would not choose to exercise their option. Instead, they walk away from the firm, as any call-option holder would do. The bondholders then receive the firm's entire cash flow.

This view of the firm is a novel one, and students are frequently bothered by it on first exposure. However, we encourage students to keep looking at the firm in this way until the view becomes second nature to them.

The Bondholders   What about the bondholders? Our earlier cash flow schedule showed that they would get the entire cash flow of the firm if the firm generates less cash than $800. Should the firm earn more than $800, the bondholders would receive only $800. That is, they are entitled only to interest and principal. This schedule is graphed in Figure 22.12.

In keeping with our view that the stockholders have a call option on the firm, what does the bondholders' position consist of? The bondholders' position can be described by two claims:

1. They own the firm.
2. They have written a call against the firm with an exercise price of $800.

As we mentioned before, the stockholders walk away from the firm if cash flows are less than $800. Thus, the bondholders retain ownership in this case. However, if the cash flows

FIGURE 22.12

Cash Flow to Bondholders as a Function of Cash Flow of Firm

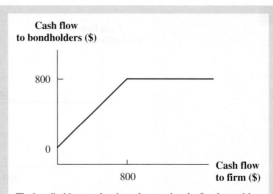

The bondholders can be viewed as owning the firm but writing a call option to the stockholders as well. If the cash flows of the firm exceed $800, the call is exercised against the bondholders. The bondholders give up the firm and receive $800. If the cash flows are less than $800, the call expires. The bondholders receive the cash flows of the firm in this case.

are greater than $800, the stockholders exercise their option. They call the stock away from the bondholders for $800.

The Firm Expressed in Terms of Put Options

The preceding analysis expresses the positions of the stockholders and the bondholders in terms of call options. We can now express the situation in terms of put options.

The Stockholders   The stockholders' position can be expressed by three claims:

1. They own the firm.
2. They owe $800 in interest and principal to the bondholders.

If the debt were risk-free, these two claims would fully describe the stockholders' situation. However, because of the possibility of default, we have a third claim as well.

3. The stockholders own a put option on the firm with an exercise price of $800. The group of bondholders is the seller of the put.

Now consider two possibilities.

Cash Flow Is Less Than $800   Because the put has an exercise price of $800, the put is in the money. The stockholders "put," that is, sell, the firm to the bondholders. Normally, the holder of a put receives the exercise price when the asset is sold. However, the stockholders already owe $800 to the bondholders. Thus, the debt of $800 is simply canceled—and no money changes hands—when the stock is delivered to the bondholders. Because the stockholders give up the stock in exchange for extinguishing the debt, the stockholders end up with nothing if the cash flow is below $800.

Cash Flow Is Greater Than $800   Because the put is out of the money here, the stockholders do not exercise. Thus, the stockholders retain ownership of the firm but pay $800 to the bondholders as interest and principal.

The Bondholders   The bondholders' position can be described by two claims:

1. The bondholders are owed $800.
2. They have sold a put option on the firm to the stockholders with an exercise price of $800.

Cash Flow Is Less Than $800   As mentioned before, the stockholders will exercise the put in this case. This means that the bondholders are obligated to pay $800 for the firm. Because they are owed $800, the two obligations offset each other. Thus, the bondholders simply end up with the firm in this case.

Cash Flow Is Greater Than $800   Here, the stockholders do not exercise the put. Thus, the bondholders merely receive the $800 that is due them.

Expressing the bondholders' position in this way is illuminating. With a riskless default-free bond, the bondholders are owed $800. Thus, we can express the risky bond in terms of a riskless bond and a put:

$$\begin{matrix} \text{Value of} \\ \text{risky bond} \end{matrix} = \begin{matrix} \text{Value of} \\ \text{default-free bond} \end{matrix} - \begin{matrix} \text{Value of} \\ \text{put option} \end{matrix}$$

That is, the value of the risky bond is the value of the default-free bond less the value of the stockholders' option to sell the company for $800.

TABLE 22.4	Stockholders	Bondholders
Positions of Stockholders and Bondholders in Popov Company in Terms of Calls and Puts	**Positions viewed in terms of call options** 1. Stockholders own a call on the firm with exercise price of $800.	1. Bondholders own the firm. 2. Bondholders have sold a call on the firm to the stockholders.
	Positions viewed in terms of put options 1. Stockholders own the firm. 2. Stockholders owe $800 in interest and principal to bondholders. 3. Stockholders own a put option on the firm with exercise price of $800.	1. Bondholders are owed $800 in interest and principal. 2. Bondholders have sold a put on the firm to the stockholders.

A Resolution of the Two Views

We have argued above that the positions of the stockholders and the bondholders can be viewed either in terms of calls or in terms of puts. These two viewpoints are summarized in Table 22.4.

We have found from past experience that it is generally harder for students to think of the firm in terms of puts than in terms of calls. Thus, it would be helpful if there were a way to show that the two viewpoints are equivalent. Fortunately there is *put-call parity*. In an earlier section we presented the put-call parity relationship as equation (22.1), which we now repeat:

$$\text{Price of underlying stock} + \text{Price of put} = \text{Price of call} + \text{Present value of exercise price} \tag{22.1}$$

Using the results of this section, equation (22.1) can be rewritten as:

$$\underbrace{\begin{array}{c} \text{Value of call} \\ \text{on firm} \end{array}}_{\substack{\text{Stockholders'} \\ \text{position in terms} \\ \text{of call options}}} = \underbrace{\begin{array}{c} \text{Value of} \\ \text{firm} \end{array} + \begin{array}{c} \text{Value of put} \\ \text{on firm} \end{array} - \begin{array}{c} \text{Value of} \\ \text{default-free bond} \end{array}}_{\substack{\text{Stockholders' position} \\ \text{in terms of put options}}} \tag{22.3}$$

Going from equation (22.1) to equation (22.3) involves a few steps. First, we treat the firm, not the stock, as the underlying asset in this section. (In keeping with common convention, we refer to the *value* of the firm and the *price* of the stock.) Second, the exercise price is now $800, the principal and interest on the firm's debt. Taking the present value of this amount at the riskless rate yields the value of a default-free bond. Third, the order of the terms in equation (22.1) is rearranged in equation (22.3).

Note that the left-hand side of equation (22.3) is the stockholders' position in terms of call options, as shown in Table 22.4. The right-hand side of equation (22.3) is the stockholders' position in terms of put options, as shown in the table. Thus, put-call parity shows that viewing the stockholders' position in terms of call options is equivalent to viewing the stockholders' position in terms of put options.

Now, let's rearrange terms in equation (22.3) to yield:

$$\underbrace{\begin{array}{c} \text{Value of} \\ \text{firm} \end{array} - \begin{array}{c} \text{Value of call} \\ \text{on firm} \end{array}}_{\substack{\text{Bondholders' position in} \\ \text{terms of call options}}} = \underbrace{\begin{array}{c} \text{Value of} \\ \text{default-free bond} \end{array} - \begin{array}{c} \text{Value of put} \\ \text{on firm} \end{array}}_{\substack{\text{Bondholders' position in} \\ \text{terms of put options}}} \tag{22.4}$$

The left-hand side of equation (22.4) is the bondholders' position in terms of call options, as shown in Table 22.4. The right-hand side of the equation is the bondholders' position in terms of put options, as shown in Table 22.4. Thus, put-call parity shows that viewing the bondholders' position in terms of call options is equivalent to viewing the bondholders' position in terms of put options.

A Note on Loan Guarantees

In the Popov example given earlier, the bondholders bore the risk of default. Of course, bondholders generally ask for an interest rate that is enough to compensate them for bearing risk. When firms experience financial distress, they can no longer attract new debt at moderate interest rates. Thus, firms experiencing distress have frequently sought loan guarantees from the government. Our framework can be used to understand these guarantees.

If the firm defaults on a guaranteed loan, the government must make up the difference. In other words, a government guarantee converts a risky bond into a riskless bond. What is the value of this guarantee?

Recall that, with option pricing,

$$
\begin{array}{ccc}
\text{Value of} & = & \text{Value of} \\
\text{default-free bond} & & \text{risky bond}
\end{array}
\quad + \quad
\begin{array}{c}
\text{Value of} \\
\text{put option}
\end{array}
$$

This equation shows that the government is assuming an obligation that has a cost equal to the value of a put option.

This analysis differs from that of either politicians or company spokespeople. They generally say that the guarantee will cost the taxpayer nothing because the guarantee enables the firm to attract debt, thereby staying solvent. However, it should be pointed out that, although solvency may be a strong possibility, it is never a certainty. Thus, at the time the guarantee is made, the government's obligation has a cost in terms of present value. To say that a government guarantee costs the government nothing is like saying a put on the stock of Microsoft has no value because the stock is *likely* to rise in price.

Actually, the government has had good fortune with loan guarantees. Its two biggest guarantees were to the Lockheed Corporation in 1971 and the Chrysler Corporation in 1980. Both firms nearly ran out of cash and defaulted on loans. In both cases the U.S. government came to the rescue by agreeing to guarantee new loans. Under the guarantees, if Lockheed and Chrysler had defaulted on new loans, the lenders could have obtained the full value of their claims from the U.S. government. From the lender's point of view, the loans became as risk-free as Treasury bonds. These guarantees enabled Lockheed and Chrysler to borrow large amounts of cash and to get through a difficult time. As it turned out, neither firm defaulted.

Who benefits from a typical loan guarantee?

1. If existing risky bonds are guaranteed, all gains accrue to the existing bondholders. The stockholders gain nothing because the limited liability of corporations absolves the stockholders of any obligation in bankruptcy.

2. If new debt is being issued and guaranteed, the new debtholders do not gain. Rather, in a competitive market, they must accept a low interest rate because of the debt's low risk. The stockholders gain here because they are able to issue debt at a low interest rate. In addition, some of the gains accrue to the old bondholders because the firm's value is greater than would otherwise be true. Therefore, if shareholders want all the gains from loan guarantees, they should renegotiate or retire existing bonds before the guarantee is in place. This happened in the Chrysler case.

1. **How can the value of the firm be expressed in terms of call options?**
2. **How can the value of the firm be expressed in terms of put options?**
3. **How does put-call parity relate these two expressions?**

22.10 Capital-Structure Policy and Options

Recall our chapters on capital structure where we showed how managers, acting on behalf of the stockholders, can take advantage of bondholders. A number of these strategies can be explained in terms of options. As an illustration, this section examines one such strategy, the choice between a high-risk project and a low-risk project.

Selecting High-Risk Projects

Imagine a levered firm considering two mutually exclusive projects, a low-risk one and a high-risk one. There are two equally likely outcomes, recession and boom. The firm is in such dire straits that, should a recession hit, it will come near to bankruptcy if the low-risk project is selected and actually fall into bankruptcy if the high-risk project is selected. The cash flows for the firm if the low-risk project is undertaken can be described as:

| | | **Low-Risk Project** | | | | |
	Probability	Value of Firm	=	Stock	+	Bonds
Recession	0.5	$400	=	0	+	$400
Boom	0.5	$800	=	$400	+	$400

If recession occurs, the value of the firm will be $400, and if boom occurs, the value of the firm will be $800. The expected value of the firm is $600 (0.5 × $400 + 0.5 × $800). The firm has promised to pay the bondholders $400. Shareholders will obtain the difference between the total payoff and the amount paid to the bondholders. The bondholders have the prior claim on the payoffs, and the shareholders have the residual claim.

Now suppose that another, riskier project can be substituted for the low-risk project. The payoffs and probabilities are as follows:

| | | **High-Risk Project** | | | | |
	Probability	Value of Firm	=	Stock	+	Bonds
Recession	0.5	$ 200	=	0	+	$200
Boom	0.5	$1,000	=	$600	+	$400

The expected value of the firm is $600 (0.5 × $200 + 0.5 × $1,000), which is identical to the value of the firm with the low-risk project. However, note that the expected value of the stock is $300 (0.5 × 0 + 0.5 × $600) with the high-risk project, but only $200 (0.5 × 0 + 0.5 × $400) with the low-risk project. Given the firm's present levered state, stockholders will select the high-risk project.

The stockholders benefit at the expense of the bondholders when the high-risk project is accepted. The explanation is quite clear: The bondholders suffer dollar for dollar when the firm's value falls short of the $400 bond obligation. However, the bondholders' payments are capped at $400 when the firm does well.

This can be explained in terms of call options. We argued earlier in this chapter that the value of a call rises with an increase in the volatility of the underlying asset. Because the stock is a call option on the firm, a rise in the volatility of the firm increases the value of the stock. In our example, the value of the stock is higher if the high-risk project is accepted.

Table 22.4 showed that the value of a risky bond can be viewed as the difference between the value of the firm and the value of a call on the firm. Because a call's value rises with the risk of the underlying asset, the value of the bond should decline if the firm increases its risk. In our example, the bondholders are hurt when the high-risk project is accepted.

22.11 Mergers and Options

Mergers are structured either as *cash-for-stock* transactions or as *stock-for-stock* transactions. The selling stockholders receive cash from the buyer in the first type of transaction and receive stock in the buying company in the second type of transaction. In the first half of 2000, General Mills (GM) was attempting to acquire the Pillsbury division of Diageo PLC. GM wanted a stock-for-stock transaction and initially offered Diageo 141,000,000 shares of GM's stock. Given that GM was trading at that time at $42.55 per share, the stockholders of Diageo would receive consideration of about $6 billion ($42.55 × 141 million). Although this amount was more than satisfactory to Diageo's management, they were upset with the risk inherent in stock-for-stock transactions. That is, General Mills' shares might be overpriced at $42.55, implying the possibility of a price decline at a later date.

To allay these fears, GM decided to "insure" Diageo's stockholders with a contingent value rights (CVR) plan of up to $642 million or $4.55 ($642 million/141 million) per share. Under this plan, each of the 141 million GM shares issued to Diageo's stockholders would receive in cash the difference between $42.55 and the price of GM's stock one year after the deal's closing date, up to a maximum of $4.55. For example, if GM's stock traded at $40 one year after closing, each newly issued share of GM would receive $2.55 ($42.55 − $40) in cash. Thus, because the cash payment of $2.55 goes with each newly issued share worth $40, the total package is still worth $42.55. However, because the maximum payment is $4.55, no additional insurance is provided for stock price drops below $38 ($42.55 − $4.55). For example, if the stock falls to $36, the total package is worth only $40.55 ($36 + $4.55). In Figure 22.13 the cash payment per share of newly issued GM stock is graphed as a function of GM's stock price one year after the closing date. The total package (price of one share of GM's stock plus the cash payment) is shown in Figure 22.14.

The contingent value rights plan can be viewed in terms of puts. That is, the CVR plan implies that each newly issued share of GM's stock receives a put on GM's stock with an exercise price of $42.55 while selling a put on GM with an exercise price of $38. This idea is illustrated in Figure 22.15. If GM's stock price ends up below $42.55, the cash payoff from each put with an exercise price of $42.55 is equal to the difference between $42.55 and the ending price of GM. However, should the price fall below $38, the put with an exercise price of $38 will also be in the money. Each newly issued share of GM's stock receives a put with an exercise price of $42.55 and writes a put with an exercise price of $38, so each share receives cash of $4.55 ($42.55 − $38) should GM's stock price drop below $38.

Diageo's management liked the contingent value rights plan enough to accept the merger with the CVR agreement attached. This example shows that creative financing techniques, such as the use of puts in this case, can be used to accommodate a buyer who would otherwise be reluctant.

| FIGURE 22.13 | Cash Payment to Each Newly Issued Share of GM Stock in Acquisition of Pillsbury Division of Diageo PLC |

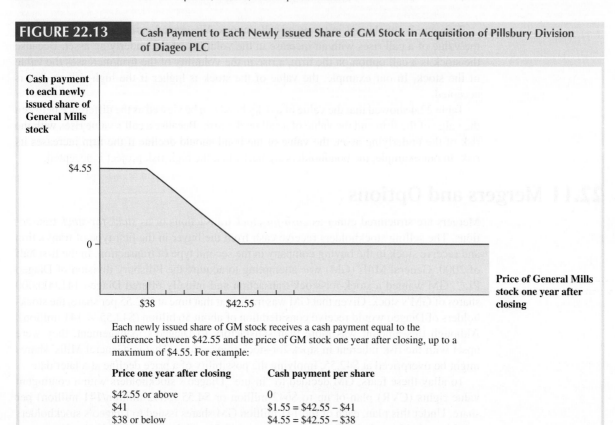

Cash payment to each newly issued share of General Mills stock

$4.55

0

$38 $42.55

Price of General Mills stock one year after closing

Each newly issued share of GM stock receives a cash payment equal to the difference between $42.55 and the price of GM stock one year after closing, up to a maximum of $4.55. For example:

Price one year after closing	Cash payment per share
$42.55 or above	0
$41	$1.55 = $42.55 − $41
$38 or below	$4.55 = $42.55 − $38

| FIGURE 22.14 | |

Total Value of a Newly Issued Share of GM Stock, Including the Cash Payment

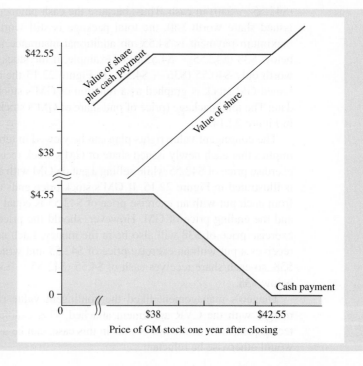

$42.55

Value of share plus cash payment

Value of share

$38

$4.55

Cash payment

0

0    $38 $42.55

Price of GM stock one year after closing

FIGURE 22.15

Payoffs to Implied
Puts in General Mills'
Acquisition of
Pillsbury

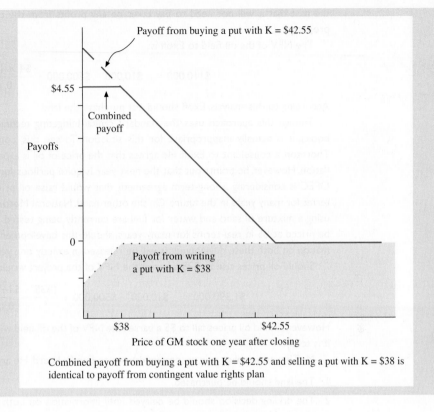

Combined payoff from buying a put with K = $42.55 and selling a put with K = $38 is
identical to payoff from contingent value rights plan

22.12 Investment in Real Projects and Options

Let us quickly review the material on capital budgeting presented earlier in the text. We
first considered projects where forecasts for future cash flows were made at date 0. The
expected cash flow in each future period was discounted at an appropriate risky rate, yielding an NPV calculation. For independent projects, a positive NPV meant acceptance and a
negative NPV meant rejection.

This approach treated risk through the discount rate. We later considered decision-tree
analysis, an approach that handles risk in a more sophisticated way. We pointed out that
the firm will make investment and operating decisions on a project over its entire life. We
value a project today, assuming that future decisions will be optimal. However, we do not
yet know what these decisions will be, because much information remains to be discovered. The firm's ability to delay its investment and operating decisions until the release of
information is an option. We now illustrate this option through an example.

EXAMPLE

Exoff Oil Corporation is considering the purchase of an oil field in a remote part of Alaska. The seller
has listed the property for $10,000 and is eager to sell immediately. Initial drilling costs are $500,000.
The firm anticipates that 10,000 barrels of oil can be extracted each year for many decades. Because
the termination date is so far in the future and so hard to estimate, the firm views the cash flow
stream from the oil as a perpetuity. With oil prices at $20 per barrel and extraction costs at $16 a
barrel, the firm anticipates a net margin of $4 per barrel. Because oil prices are expected to rise
at the inflation rate, the firm assumes that its cash flow per barrel will always be $4 in real terms.
The appropriate real discount rate is 10 percent. The firm has enough tax credits from bad years in

the past that it will not need to pay taxes on any profits from the oil field. Should Exoff buy the property?

The NPV of the oil field to Exoff is:

$$-\$110,000 = -\$10,000 - \$500,000 + \frac{\$4 \times 10,000}{0.10}$$

According to this analysis, Exoff should not purchase the land.

Though this approach uses the standard capital-budgeting techniques of this and other textbooks, it is actually inappropriate for this situation. To see this, consider the analysis of Kirtley Thornton, a consultant to Exoff. He agrees that the price of oil is *expected* to rise at the rate of inflation. However, he points out that the next year is quite perilous for oil prices. On the one hand, OPEC is considering a long-term agreement that would raise oil prices to $35 per barrel in real terms for many years in the future. On the other hand, National Motors recently indicated that cars using a mixture of sand and water for fuel are currently being tested. Thornton argues that oil will be priced at $5 in real terms for many years, should this development prove successful. Full information on both these developments will be released in exactly one year.

Should oil prices rise to $35 a barrel, the NPV of the project would be:

$$\$1,390,000 = -\$10,000 - \$500,000 + \frac{(\$35 - \$16) \times 10,000}{0.10}$$

However, should oil prices fall to $5 a barrel, the NPV of the oil field will be even more negative than it is today.

Mr. Thornton makes two recommendations to Exoff's board. He argues that:

1. The land should be purchased.
2. The drilling decision should be delayed until information on both OPEC's new agreement and National Motors' new automobile is released.

Kirtley explains his recommendations to the board by first assuming that the land has already been purchased. He argues that, under this assumption, the drilling decision should be delayed. Second, he investigates his assumption that the land should have been purchased in the first place. This approach of examining the second decision (whether to drill) after assuming that the first decision (to buy the land) had been made was also used in our earlier presentation on decision trees. Let us now work through Mr. Thornton's analysis.

Assume the land has already been purchased. If the land has already been purchased, should drilling begin immediately? If drilling begins immediately, the NPV is −$110,000. If the drilling decision is delayed until new information is released in a year, the optimal choice can be made at that time. If oil prices drop to $5 a barrel, Exoff should not drill. Instead, the firm should walk away from the project, losing nothing beyond its $10,000 purchase price for the land. If oil prices rise to $35, drilling should begin.

Mr. Thornton points out that, by delaying, the firm will only invest the $500,000 of drilling costs if oil prices rise. Thus, by delaying, the firm saves $500,000 in the case where oil prices drop. Kirtley concludes that, once the land is purchased, the drilling decision should be delayed.[11]

Should the land have been purchased in the first place? We now know that if the land had been purchased, it is optimal to defer the drilling decision until the release of information. Given that we know this optimal decision concerning drilling, should the land be purchased in the first place? Without

---

[11] Actually, there are three separate effects here. First, the firm avoids drilling costs in the case of low oil prices by delaying the decision. This is the effect discussed by Mr. Thornton. Second, the present value of the $500,000 payment is less when the decision is delayed, even if drilling eventually takes place. Third, the firm loses one year of cash inflows through delay.

The first two arguments support delaying the decision. The third argument supports immediate drilling. In this example, the first argument greatly outweighs the other two arguments. Thus, Mr. Thornton avoided the second and third arguments in his presentation.

knowing the exact probability that oil prices will rise, Mr. Thornton is nevertheless confident that the land should be purchased. The NPV of the project at $35 oil prices is $1,390,000 whereas the cost of the land is only $10,000. Kirtley believes that an oil price rise is possible, though by no means probable. Even so, he argues that the high potential return is clearly worth the risk.

This example presents an approach that is similar to our decision-tree analysis of the Solar Equipment Company in a previous chapter. Our purpose in this section is to discuss this type of decision in an option framework. When Exoff purchases the land, it is actually purchasing a call option. That is, once the land has been purchased, the firm has an option to buy an active oil field at an exercise price of $500,000. As it turns out, one should generally not exercise a call option immediately.[12] In this case, the firm should delay exercise until relevant information concerning future oil prices is released.

This section points out a serious deficiency in classical capital budgeting; net-present-value calculations typically ignore the flexibility that real-world firms have. In our example, the standard techniques generated a negative NPV for the land purchase. Yet, by allowing the firm the option to change its investment policy according to new information, the land purchase can easily be justified.

We entreat the reader to look for hidden options in projects. Because options are beneficial, managers are shortchanging their firm's projects if capital-budgeting calculations ignore flexibility.

Concept Question

1. Why are the hidden options in projects valuable?

22.13 SUMMARY AND CONCLUSIONS

This chapter serves as an introduction to options.

1. The most familiar options are puts and calls. These options give the holder the right to sell or buy shares of common stock at a given exercise price. American options can be exercised any time up to and including the expiration date. European options can be exercised only on the expiration date.

2. We showed that a strategy of buying a stock and buying a put is equivalent to a strategy of buying a call and buying a zero-coupon bond. From this, the put-call–parity relationship was established:

$$\begin{matrix} \text{Value of} \\ \text{stock} \end{matrix} + \begin{matrix} \text{Value of} \\ \text{put} \end{matrix} - \begin{matrix} \text{Value of} \\ \text{call} \end{matrix} = \begin{matrix} \text{Present value of} \\ \text{exercise price} \end{matrix}$$

3. The value of an option depends on five factors:
   a. The price of the underlying asset.
   b. The exercise price.
   c. The expiration date.
   d. The variability of the underlying asset.
   e. The interest rate on risk-free bonds.

   The Black-Scholes model can determine the intrinsic price of an option from these five factors.

---

[12]Actually, it can be shown that a call option that pays no dividend should *never* be exercised before expiration. However, for a dividend-paying stock, it may be optimal to exercise prior to the ex-dividend date. The analogy applies to our example of an option in real assets.

The firm would receive cash flows from oil earlier if drilling begins immediately. This is equivalent to the benefit from exercising a call on a stock prematurely in order to capture the dividend. However, in our example, this dividend effect is far outweighed by the benefits from waiting.

4. Much of corporate financial theory can be presented in terms of options. In this chapter we pointed out that
   a. Common stock can be represented as a call option on the firm.
   b. Stockholders enhance the value of their call by increasing the risk of their firm.
   c. Real projects have hidden options that enhance value.

KEY TERMS

American options, *619*

call option, *619*

cumulative probability, *636*

European options, *619*

exercising the option, *618*

expiration date, *618*

option, *618*

put-call parity, *625*

put option, *620*

standardized normal distribution, *636*

striking or exercise price, *618*

SUGGESTED READINGS

The path-breaking article on options is:

Black, Fischer, and Myron Scholes. "The Pricing of Options and Corporate Liabilities." *Journal of Political Economy* 81 (May–June 1973).

For a detailed discussion of options, read:

Hull, John C. *Options, Futures, and Other Derivatives,* 4th Ed. Upper Saddle River, N.J.: Prentice Hall, 1999.

QUESTIONS & PROBLEMS

OPTIONS: GENERAL

22.1   Define the following terms associated with options.
   a. Option
   b. Exercise
   c. Strike price
   d. Expiration date
   e. Call option
   f. Put option

22.2   What is the difference between an American option and a European option?

22.3   Mr. Nash holds an American put option on Delta Triangle, a non-dividend-paying stock. The strike price of the put is $40, and Delta Triangle's stock is currently selling for $35 per share. The current market price of the put is $4.50. Is this option correctly priced? If not, should Mr. Nash buy or sell the option in order to take advantage of the mispricing?

22.4   A call option on Futura Corporation, a non-dividend-paying stock, currently trades for $4. The expiration date of the option is February 25 of next year. The exercise price of the option is $45.
   a. If this is an American option, on what dates can the option be exercised?
   b. If this is a European option, on what dates can the option be exercised?
   c. Suppose the current price of Futura Corporation's stock is $35 per share. Is this option worthless?

22.5   Consider a European call option on Stock A that expires on December 21 and has a strike price of $50.
   a. If Stock A is trading at $55 on December 21, what is the payoff to the owner of the option?
   b. If Stock A is trading at $55 on December 21, what is the payoff to the seller of the option?
   c. If Stock A is trading at $45 on December 21, what is the payoff to the owner of the option?
   d. If Stock A is trading at $45 on December 21, what is the payoff to the seller of the option?
   e. Draw the payoff diagram to the owner of this option with respect to the stock price at expiration.
   f. Draw the payoff diagram to the seller of this option with respect to the stock price at expiration.
   g. If the seller of a call option never receives cash at expiration, why would anyone ever sell a call option?

22.6   Consider a European put option on Stock A that expires on December 21 and has a strike price of $50.

    a. If Stock A is trading at $55 on December 21, what is the payoff to the owner of the option?

    b. If Stock A is trading at $55 on December 21, what is the payoff to the seller of the option?

    c. If Stock A is trading at $45 on December 21, what is the payoff to the owner of the option?

    d. If Stock A is trading at $45 on December 21, what is the payoff to the seller of the option?

    e. Draw the payoff diagram to the owner of this option with respect to the stock price at expiration.

    f. Draw the payoff diagram to the seller of this option with respect to the stock price at expiration.

22.7   Mr. Eisner sold 10 Microsoft put options and bought 5 Microsoft call options. Both options have the same exercise price of $80 and the same expiration date. Draw the payoff diagram with respect to the price of Microsoft stock at expiration.

22.8   Mr. Chang bought two Xerox European call contracts and one Xerox European put contract, both of which expire in three months. Each contract is for 100 options. The exercise price of each call is $70, and the exercise price of each put is $75.

    a. What is the payoff of Mr. Chang's position at expiration if the market price of Xerox stock on the expiration date is $65? What if the market price is $72? What if the market price is $80?

    b. Draw Mr. Chang's payoff diagram with respect to the stock price at expiration.

22.9   Louis holds a six-month European call option contract on Hurricanes, Inc., a non-dividend-paying common stock. Each contract is for 100 options. The exercise price of each call option is $100, and the option will expire in moments. Assume there are no transaction costs or taxes associated with the contract.

    a. What is his cash flow at expiration if the stock is selling for $130?

    b. If the stock is selling for $90, what should Louis do?

22.10   The market price of an American call option written on Stock ABC with a strike price of $50 and 6 months until expiration is $8. ABC's stock is currently trading for $60.

    a. Is there an arbitrage opportunity? If so, describe what you would do to take advantage of the mispricing.

    b. What do arbitrage opportunities such as this imply about the lower bound on the price of American call options?

    c. What is the upper bound on the price of American call options? Explain.

22.11   List the five factors that determine the value of an American call option. State how a change in each factor affects the option's value.

22.12   List the five factors that determine the value of an American put option. State how a change in each factor affects the option's value.

PUT-CALL PARITY   **22.13**   General Eclectics, Inc., has both European call and put options traded on the Chicago Board of Exchange. Both options have the same exercise price of $40 and both expire in one year. General Eclectic's stock does not pay dividends. The call and the put are currently selling for $8 and $2, respectively. The risk-free interest rate is 10 percent per annum. What should the stock price of General Eclectics, Inc., be in order to prevent arbitrage?

22.14   Gimpellian Software, Inc., is a non-dividend-paying common stock that currently trades for $135 per share. Kevin is interested in purchasing a European call option with a strike price of $140 and one year until expiration. Much to his dismay, he discovers that call options are not traded on Gimpellian's stock. In fact, the only options traded on Gimpellian's stock are put options with a strike price of $140 and one year until expiration. These put options are currently trading for $2. The risk-free rate is 25 percent per annum.

a. Compare the market price of the put with the payoff from the immediate exercise of a put option with a strike price of $140. Is this an arbitrage opportunity? Why or why not?

b. Is there a way for Kevin to obtain a synthetic call option with a strike price of $140 and one year until expiration? If there is, what is it? How much would this synthetic call option cost?

c. Draw the payoff diagram at expiration of Kevin's synthetic call position with respect to the stock price.

THE TWO-STATE OPTION-PRICING MODEL

22.15 Ken is interested in buying a European call option written on Northwestern Airlines, Inc., a non-dividend-paying common stock, with a strike price of $110 and one year until expiration. Currently, Northwestern's stock sells for $100 per share. In one year, Ken knows that Northwestern's stock will be trading at either $120 per share or $80 per share. Ken is able to borrow and lend at the risk-free interest rate of 2.5 percent per annum (effective annual yield).

a. How much should Ken expect to pay for his desired call option today?

b. If no options currently trade on Northwestern's stock, is there a way for Ken to create a synthetic call option with identical payoffs to the call option described above? If there is, how would he do it?

c. How much does the synthetic call option cost? Is this greater than, less than, or equal to what the actual call option costs? Does this make sense?

22.16 Rob wishes to buy a European put option on BioLabs, Inc., a non-dividend-paying common stock, with a strike price of $40 and six months until expiration. BioLab's common stock is currently selling for $30 per share, and Rob expects that the stock price will either rise to $60 or fall to $15 in six months. Rob can borrow and lend at the risk-free interest rate of 21 percent per annum (effective annual yield).

a. How much should Rob expect to pay for his desired put option today?

b. If no options currently trade on BioLab's stock, is there a way for Rob to create a synthetic put option with identical payoffs to the put option described above? If there is, how would he do it?

c. How much does the synthetic put option cost? Is this greater than, less than, or equal to what the actual put option costs? Does this make sense?

22.17 Maverick Manufacturing, Inc., must purchase gold in three months to use in its operations. Maverick's management has estimated that if the price of gold were to rise above $375 per ounce, the firm would go bankrupt. The current price of gold is $350 per ounce. The firm's chief financial officer believes that the price of gold will either rise to $400 per ounce or fall to $325 per ounce over the next three months. Management wishes to eliminate any risk of the firm going bankrupt. Maverick can borrow and lend at the risk-free interest rate of 16.99 percent per annum (effective annual yield).

a. Would Maverick be interested in buying a call option or a put option on the price of gold? In order to avoid bankruptcy, what strike price and time to expiration would the firm like this option to have?

b. How much should such an option sell for in the open market?

c. If no options currently trade on gold, is there a way for Maverick to create a synthetic option with identical payoffs to the option described above? If there is, how would the firm do it?

d. How much does the synthetic option cost? Is this greater than, less than, or equal to what the actual option costs? Does this make sense?

22.18 Mark is interested in buying one share of an index fund that tracks the S&P 500. The fund does not pay any dividends. He believes that the fund will either increase by 25 percent or decrease by 20 percent over the next year. Mark is very risk averse and wishes to shield himself from any decrease in the value of the fund below $1,300, without forfeiting any of the fund's upside potential. Mark can borrow and lend at the risk-free interest rate of 7 percent per annum (effective annual yield).

a. Would Mark be interested in buying a call option or a put option on the index fund? What strike price and time to expiration would he like this option to have?

b. How much should such an option sell for in the open market?

c. If no options currently trade on the index fund, is there a way for Mark to create a synthetic option with identical payoffs to the option described above? If there is, how would he do it?

d. How much does the synthetic option cost? Is this greater than, less than, or equal to what the actual option costs? Does this make sense?

THE BLACK-SCHOLES OPTION-PRICING MODEL

22.19 Myron Fisher is interested in purchasing a European call option on Meriwether and Associates, Inc., a non-dividend-paying common stock, with a strike price of $50 and 1 year until expiration. Meriwether's stock is currently trading at $55 per share, and the annual variance of its continuously compounded returns is 0.0625. Treasury bills that mature in one year yield a continuously compounded interest rate of 10 percent per annum. Use the Black-Scholes model to calculate the price of the call option that Myron is interested in buying.

22.20 John Goodfriend is interested in purchasing a European call option on Mozer, Inc., a non-dividend-paying common stock, with a strike price of $25 and six months until expiration. Mozer's stock is currently trading at $15 per share, and the annual variance of its continuously compounded returns is 0.25. Treasury bills that mature in six months yield a continuously compounded interest rate of 8 percent per annum. Use the Black-Scholes model to calculate the price of the call option that John is interested in buying.

22.21 Seth is interested in purchasing a European call option on Brain Enhancers, Inc., a non-dividend-paying common stock, with a strike price of $100 and two years until expiration. Brain Enhancer's stock is currently trading at $100 per share, and the annual variance of its continuously compounded returns is 0.04. Treasury bills that mature in two years yield a continuously compounded interest rate of 5 percent per annum.

a. Use the Black-Scholes model to calculate the price of the call option that Seth is interested in buying.

b. What does put-call parity imply about the price of a put with a strike price of $100 and two years until expiration?

22.22 David is interested in purchasing a European call option on Divine Vines, Inc., a non-dividend-paying common stock, with a strike price of $30 and three months until expiration. Divine's stock is currently trading at $60 per share, and the annual variance of its continuously compounded returns is 0.36. Treasury bills that mature in three months yield a continuously compounded interest rate of 3 percent per annum.

a. Use the Black-Scholes model to calculate the price of the call option that David is interested in buying.

b. What does put-call parity imply about the price of a put with a strike price of $30 and three months until expiration?

22.23 Steve wishes to buy a European call option on Scuba Solutions, Inc., a non-dividend-paying common stock, with a strike price of $35 and one year until expiration. Scuba Solutions is currently selling for $37 per share and Steve's estimate of the annual variance of its continuously compounded returns is 0.0225. Steve can borrow and lend at the continuously compounded risk-free rate of 7 percent per annum.

a. Use the Black-Scholes model to calculate the price of the call option that Steve is interested in buying.

b. Suppose Steve's estimate of the annual variance of the continuously compounded returns on Scuba's stock changes to 0.09. What is the new Black-Scholes price of the call option?

c. Does an increase in the volatility (variance) of the underlying asset increase or decrease the Black-Scholes price of a call option?

d. Scuba's stock price suddenly drops to $20 per share after an announcement that the company will be shutting down its Mediterranean diving operations. Using Steve's new estimate of variance (0.09), calculate the Black-Scholes price of the call option.

22.24 An investor is said to take a position in a "collar" if he buys the asset, buys an out-of-the-money put option on the asset, and sells an out-of-the-money call option on the asset. The two options should have the same time to expiration. Suppose Marie wishes to purchase a collar on Hollywood, Inc., a non-dividend-paying common stock, with six months until expiration. She would like the put to have a strike price of $50 and the call to have a strike price of $120. The current price of Hollywood's stock is $80 per share. Marie can borrow and lend at the continuously compounded risk-free rate of 10 percent per annum, and the annual variance of Hollywood's continuously compounded returns is 0.25. Use the Black-Scholes model to calculate the total cost of the collar that Marie is interested in buying.

APPLICATION OF OPTIONS TO CORPORATE FINANCE

22.25   It is said that the equityholders of a levered firm can be thought of as holding a call option on the firm's assets. Explain what is meant by this statement.

22.26   Strudler Real Estate, Inc., a construction firm financed by both debt and equity, is undertaking a new project. If the project is successful, the value of the firm in one year will be $500 million, but if the project is a failure, the firm will only be worth $320 million. The current value of Strudler is $400 million, a figure that includes the prospects for the new project. Strudler has outstanding zero-coupon bonds due in one year with a face value of $380 million. Treasury bills that mature in one year yield 7 percent per annum (effective annual yield). Strudler pays no dividends.

   a. Use the two-state option-pricing model to find the current value of Strudler's debt and equity.

   b. Suppose Strudler has 500,000 shares of common stock outstanding. What is the price per share of the firm's equity?

   c. Compare the market value of Strudler's debt to the present value of an equal amount of debt that is riskless with one year until maturity. Is the firm's debt worth more than, less than, or the same as the riskless debt's present value? Does this make sense? What factor might cause these two values to be different?

   d. Suppose that in place of the project described above, Strudler's management decides to undertake a project that is even more risky. The value of the firm will either increase to $800 million or decrease to $200 million by the end of the year. Surprisingly, management concludes that the value of the firm today will remain at exactly $400 million, if this risky project is substituted for the less risky one. Use the two-state option-pricing model to determine the value of the firm's debt and equity if the firm plans on undertaking this new project. Which project do bondholders prefer?

22.27   Consider a firm that is financed by both debt and equity. The firm is worth $1 million today and currently has 700 zero-coupon bonds outstanding that mature in six months. Each bond has a face value of $1,000. The firm pays no dividends. The annual variance of the firm's continuously compounded asset returns is 0.16, and Treasury bills that mature in six months yield a continuously compounded interest rate of 8 percent per annum. Use the Black-Scholes model to calculate the individual values of the firm's debt and equity.

Options and Corporate Finance:
Extensions and Applications

EXECUTIVE SUMMARY

This chapter extends the analysis of options contained in Chapter 22. We describe four different types of options found in common corporate finance decisions.

1. Executive stock options and compensation.
2. The embedded option in a start-up company.
3. The option in simple business contracts.
4. The option to shut down and reopen a project.

Option features are pervasive in corporate finance decisions. They are involved in decisions of whether to build, expand, or close a factory, to buy productive assets like trucks or machines, to drill for oil or mine for gold, or to build a building. Sometimes they are involved in decisions about how to pay managers and other employees. In this chapter we do not argue that the NPV approach should be completely jettisoned. In fact, many decisions have few embedded options and, in these cases, optionality can be ignored. However, in many cases, options are an important aspect of the decision and must be separately valued. In practice, there is a decision continuum. At one end of the continuum are decisions with little optionality and at the other are decisions with significant optionality.

In the previous chapter, we presented a few examples of options in corporate finance. We saw that stock is a call option on the firm. We showed that the value of this option could be increased by selecting high-risk rather than low-risk projects. We discussed the embedded option in oil exploration.

However, although the previous chapter presented these options, we made no attempt to *value* them. In this chapter, we will value four embedded options. The first two are handled with the Black-Scholes model. We use the binomial model to value the last two options. Although the Black-Scholes model is more well known, the binomial model is probably used more frequently in the real world. The Black-Scholes model works well on only a narrow set of problems. The flexibility of the binomial model allows it to be applied to a wider range of situations. However, binomial approaches often use complex numerical analyses involving large amounts of computer time. In this regard, binomial approaches are less elegant than the Black-Scholes approach.

23.1 Executive Stock Options

Why Options?

Executive compensation is usually made up of base salary plus some or all of the following elements:

1. Long-term compensation
2. Annual bonuses

TABLE 23.1	2002 Top 10 Option Grants[a]			
Company	CEO	Number of Options Granted (thousands)[b]	Average Stock Price	Grant Value of Options Granted (millions)[c]
Cisco Systems, Inc.	Chambers	6,000	$39.77	$238.6
AOL Time Warner, Inc.	Levin	4,000	$58.15	$232.6
SBC Communications Inc.	Whiacre	3,606	$41.21	$148.6
Qwest Communications International, Inc.	Nacchio	7,250	$16.81	$121.9
Sprint Corporation	Esrey	4,770	$24.82	$118.4
Phillips Petroleum Company (Conoco Phillips)	Mulva	1,739	$57.33	$ 99.7
PepsiCo, Inc.	Reinemund	2,106	$44.92	$ 94.6
Philip Morris Companies, Inc. (Altria)	Bible	1,831	$47.35	$ 86.7
Gillette Company	Kilts	2,650	$32.72	$ 86.7
MBNA Corp.	Lerner	2,250	$31.69	$ 71.3

[a]Based on the 200 largest U.S. industrial and service corporations.

[b]Stock option award includes reload/restoration options as well as other features.

[c]Face value of options granted—the number of options times the stock price.

SOURCE: Pearl Meyer & Partners.

3. Retirement contributions
4. Options

The final component of compensation, options, is by far the biggest part of total compensation for many top executives. Table 23.1 lists the 10 CEOs who received the largest stock option grants during 2002. The rank is in terms of the *face value* of the options granted. This is the number of options times the current stock price.

Knowing the face value of an option does not automatically allow us to determine the market value of the option. We also need to know the exercise price before valuing the option according to either the Black-Scholes model or the binomial model. However, the exercise price is generally set equal to the market price of the stock on the date the executive receives the options. In the next section, we value options under the assumption that the exercise price is equal to the market price.

Options in the stock of the company are increasingly being granted to executives as an alternative to increases in base pay. Some of the reasons given for using options are:

1. Options make executives share the same interests as the stockholders. By aligning their interests, it is argued that executives will make better decisions for the benefit of the stockholders.
2. Using options allows the company to lower the executive's base pay. This removes pressures on morale caused by great disparities between the salaries of executives and those of other employees.
3. Options put an executive's pay at risk, rather than guaranteeing it independent of the performance of the firm.
4. Options are a tax-efficient way to pay employees. Under current tax law, if an executive is given options to purchase company stock and the options are "at the money," they are not considered part of taxable income. The options are taxed only when and if they are eventually exercised.

EXAMPLE

The granting of stock options is not restricted to the highest ranking executives. Starbucks, the coffee chain that started in Seattle, has pushed stock options down to the lowest level employees. To quote its founder, Howard Schultz, "Even though we were a private company, we would grant stock options to every employee companywide, from the top managers to the baristas, in proportion to their level of base pay. They could then, through their efforts, help make Starbucks more successful every year, and if Starbucks someday went public, their options could eventually be worth a good sum of money."

Valuing Executive Compensation

We now attempt to value the options granted to executives. Not surprisingly, the complexity of the total compensation package often makes this a very difficult task. The actual economic value of the options depends on other factors such as the volatility of the underlying stock and the exact terms of the option grant.

Using Table 23.1, we will attempt to estimate the economic value of the options held by the executives listed. To do so we will employ the Black-Scholes option pricing formula from Chapter 22. Of course, we are missing many features of the particular plans and the best we can hope for is a rough estimate. Simple matters such as requiring the executive to hold the option for a fixed period, the freeze-out period, before exercising, can significantly diminish the value of a standard option. Equally important, the Black-Scholes formula has to be modified if the stock pays dividends and is no longer applicable if the volatility of the stock is changing randomly over time. Intuitively, a call option on a dividend-paying stock is worth less than a call on a stock that pays no dividends, since, all other things being equal, the dividends will lower the stock price. Nevertheless, let us see what we can do.

We will assume that all of the options are "at the money," so that their exercise prices are the current stock values. The total exercise prices are thus equal to the reported face value. We will take the risk-free interest rate as 7 percent and assume that the options all have a maturity of five years. Finally, we will ignore the dilution from exercising them as warrants and value them as call options. The last required input, the volatility or standard deviation of the stock, σ, was estimated from the historical returns on each of the stocks. Table 23.2

TABLE 23.2	Value of 2002 Top 10 Option Grants[a]			
Company	CEO	Grant Value of Options Granted (millions)[b]	Annual Stock Standard Deviation (%/year)	Black-Scholes Value (millions)[c]
Cisco Systems, Inc.	Chambers	$238.6	64.68	$140
AOL Time Warner, Inc.	Levin	$232.6	63.13	$135
SBC Communications Inc.	Whiacre	$148.6	43.15	$ 67
Qwest Communications International, Inc.	Nacchio	$121.9	146.65	$111
Sprint Corporation	Esrey	$118.4	70.57	$ 74
Phillips Petroleum Company (Conoco Phillips)	Mulva	$ 99.7	27.98	$ 34
PepsiCo, Inc.	Reinemund	$ 94.6	33.21	$ 36
Philip Morris Companies, Inc. (Altria)	Bible	$ 86.7	36.06	$ 35
Gillette Company	Kilts	$ 86.7	26.97	$ 29
MBNA Corp.	Lerner	$ 71.3	56.68	$ 38

[a]Based on the 200 largest U.S. industrial and service corporations.

[b]Grant value of options granted is the number of options times the stock price.

[c]Stock option award includes reload/restoration options as well as other features that are not being valued here.

SOURCE: Pearl Meyer & Partners.

lists the volatilities for each stock and the estimated value of the stock grants. As can be seen, these values, while large by ordinary standards, are significantly less than the corresponding face values. Notice that the ordering by face value is not the same as that by economic value. For example, the volatility of Qwest raises its Black-Scholes value to $111 million even though its grant value is far less than for Cisco.

EXAMPLE

Consider John Chambers, the chief executive officer (CEO) of Cisco Systems, who was granted six million options. The average stock price at the time of the options grant was $39.77. We will assume that his options are at the money. The risk-free rate is 5 percent and the options expire in five years. The preceding information implies that:

1. The stock price (S) of $39.77 equals the exercise price (E).
2. The risk-free rate $r = 0.05$.
3. The five-year time interval is $t = 5$.

In addition, the variance of Cisco Systems is assumed to be $(0.6468)^2 = 0.4184$.

The above information allows us to estimate the value of John Chambers's options using the Black-Scholes model.

$$C = SN(d_1) - Ee^{-rt}N(d_2)$$
$$d_1 = [(r + 1/2\sigma^2)t]/\sqrt{\sigma^2 t} = 0.896$$
$$d_2 = d_1 - \sqrt{\sigma^2 t} = -.5503$$
$$N(d_1) = 0.8149$$
$$N(d_2) = 0.2911$$
$$e^{-.05 \times 5} = 0.7788$$
$$C = \$39.77 \times 0.8149 - \$39.77 \times (0.7788 \times 0.2911) = \$23.39$$

Thus, the value of a call option on one share of Cisco Systems stock was $23.39. Since Mr. Chambers was granted options on 6 million shares, the market value of his as estimated by the Black-Scholes formula is $140 million (6 million × $23.39).

The values we have computed in Table 23.2 are the economic values of the options if they were to trade in the market. The real question is, whose value are we talking about? Are these the costs of the options to the company? Are they the values of the options to the executives?

Suppose that a company computes the fair market value of the options as we have done in Table 23.2. For purposes of illustration, assume that the options are in the money, and that they are worth $25 each. Suppose, too, that the CEO holds 1 million such options for a total value of $25 million. This is the amount that the options would trade at in the financial markets and that traders and investors would be willing to pay for them.[1] If the company were very large, it would not be unreasonable for it to view this as the cost of granting the options to the CEO. Of course, in return, the company would expect the CEO to improve the value of the company to its shareholders by more than this amount. As we have seen, perhaps the main purpose of options is to align the interests of management with those of the shareholders of the firm. Under no circumstances, though, is the $25 million necessarily a fair measure of what the options are worth to the CEO.

As an illustration, suppose that the CEO of ABC has options on $1 million in shares with an exercise price of $30 per share, and the current price of ABC stock is $50 per share.

---

[1]We ignore warrant dilution in this example. See Chapter 24 for a discussion of warrant dilution.

If the options were exercised today, they would be worth $20 million (an underestimation of their market value). Suppose, in addition, that the CEO owns $5 million in company stock and has $5 million in other assets. The CEO clearly has a very undiversified personal portfolio. By the standards of modern portfolio theory having 25/30 or about 83 percent of your personal wealth in one stock and its options is unnecessarily risky.

While the CEO is wealthy by most standards, significant shifts in the stock value will have dramatic impacts on the CEO's economic well-being. If the value drops from $50 per share to $30 per share, the current exercise value of the options on 1 million shares drops from $20 million down to zero. Ignoring the fact that if the options would have more time to mature they will not lose all of this value, we nevertheless have a rather startling decline in the CEO's net worth from about $30 million to $8 million ($5 million in other assets plus stock that is now worth $3 million). But that is the purpose of giving the options and the stock holdings to the CEO, namely, to make the CEO's fortunes rise and fall with those of the company. It is why the company requires the executive to hold the options, at least for a freeze-out period, rather than letting the executive sell them to realize their value.

The implication is that when options are a large portion of an executive's net worth and the executive is forced by the company to be undiversified, the total value of the position is worth less to the executive than the fair financial market value. As a purely financial matter, an executive might be happier with $5 million in cash rather than $20 million in options. At the least, the executive could then diversify his personal portfolio.

Concept Question

1. Why do companies issue options to executives if they cost the company more than they are worth to the executive? Why not just give cash and split the difference? Wouldn't that make both the company and the executive better off?

23.2 Valuing a Start-Up

Ralph Simmons was not your typical MBA student. Since childhood, he had had one ambition, to open a restaurant that sold alligator meat. He went to business school because he realized that, although he knew 101 ways to cook alligators, he didn't have the business skills necessary to run a restaurant. He was extremely focused, with each course at graduate school being important to him only to the extent that it could further his dream.

While taking his school's course in entrepreneurship, he began to develop a business plan for his restaurant, which he now called Alligator Alley. He thought about marketing, he thought about raising capital, he thought about dealing with future employees. He even devoted a great deal of time to designing the physical layout of the restaurant. Against the advice of his professor in the entrepreneurship class, he decided to design the restaurant in the shape of an alligator, where the front door went through the animal's mouth. Of course, his business plan would not be complete without financial projections. After much thought, he came up with the projections shown in Table 23.3.

The table starts with sales projections, which rise from $300,000 in the first year to a steady state of $1 million a year. Cash flows from operations are shown in the next line, although we leave out the intermediate calculations needed to move from line (1) to line (2). After subtracting Working Capital, the table shows Net Cash Flows in line 4. Net Cash Flows are negative initially, as is quite common in start-ups, but they become positive by Year 3. However, the rest of the table presents the unfortunate truth. The cash flows from the restaurant yield a present value of $582,561, assuming a discount rate of 20 percent. Unfortunately, the cost of the building is greater, at $700,000, implying a negative *net* present value of −$117,439.

TABLE 23.3	Financial Projections for Alligator Alley				
	Year 1	**Year 2**	**Year 3**	**Year 4**	**All Future Years**
(1) Sales	$300,000	$600,000	$900,000	$1,000,000	$1,000,000
(2) Cash flows from operations	−$100,000	−$ 50,000	+$ 75,000	+$ 250,000	+$ 250,000
(3) Increase in working capital	$ 50,000	$ 20,000	$ 10,000	$ 10,000	0
Net cash flows (2) − (3)	−$150,000	−$ 70,000	$ 65,000	$ 240,000	$ 250,000

Present value of net cash flows in years 1–4 (discounted at 20%)   −$20,255

Present value of terminal value $\left[\dfrac{\$250,000}{0.20} \times \dfrac{1}{(1.20)^4} \right] =$ +$602,816

Present value of restaurant $582,561

− Cost of building   −$700,000

Net present value of restaurant   −$117,439

The projections indicate that Ralph's lifelong dream may not come to pass. He cannot expect to raise the capital needed to open his restaurant, and if he did obtain the funding, the restaurant would likely go under anyway. Ralph checked and rechecked the numbers, hoping vainly to discover either a numerical error or a cost-saving omission that would move his venture from the red to the black. In fact, Ralph saw that, if anything, his forecasts are generous, because a 20 percent discount rate and an infinitely lived building are on the optimistic side.

It wasn't until Ralph took a course in corporate strategy that he realized the hidden value in his venture. In that course, his instructor repeatedly stated the importance of positioning a firm to take advantage of new opportunities. Although Ralph didn't see the connection at first, he finally realized the implications for Alligator Alley. His financial projections were based on expectations. There was a 50 percent probability that alligator meat would be more popular than he thought, in which case actual cash flows would exceed projections. And, there was a 50 percent probability that the meat would be less popular, in which case the actual flows would fall short of projections.

If the restaurant did poorly, it would probably fold in a few years, because he would not want to keep losing money forever. However, if the restaurant did well, he would be in a position to expand. If alligator meat proved popular in one locale, it would likely prove popular in other locales as well. Thus, he noticed two options, the option to abandon under bad conditions and the option to expand under good conditions. Although both options can be valued according to the principles of the previous chapter, we focus on the option to expand because it is probably much more valuable.

Ralph reasoned that, as much as he personally liked alligator meat, there were whole regions of the country where consumer resistance would doom Alligator Alley. So he developed a strategy of catering only to those regions where alligator meat is somewhat popular already. He forecast that, although he could expand quickly if the first restaurant proved successful, the market would limit him to 30 additional restaurants.

Ralph believes that this expansion will occur about four years from now. He believes that he will need three years of operating the first restaurant to (1) get the initial restaurant running smoothly and (2) have enough information to place an accurate value on the restaurant. If the first restaurant is successful enough, he will need another year to obtain outside capital. Thus, he will be ready to build the 30 additional units around the fourth year.

Ralph will value his enterprise, including the option to expand, according to the Black-Scholes model. From Table 23.3, we see that each unit cost $700,000, implying a total cost over the 30 additional units of $21,000,000 (30 × $700,000). The present value of the cash inflows from these 30 units is $17,476,830 (30 × $582,561), according to the table. However, because the expansion will occur around the fourth year, this present-value calculation is provided from the point of view of four years in the future. The present value as of today is $8,428,255 [$17,476,830/(1.20)^4], assuming a discount rate of 20 percent per year. Thus, Ralph views his potential restaurant business as an option, where the exercise price is $21,000,000 and the value of the underlying asset is $8,428,255. The option is currently out of the money, a result that follows from the negative value of a typical restaurant, as calculated in Table 23.3. Of course, Ralph is hoping that the option will move into the money within four years.

Ralph needs three additional parameters to use the Black-Scholes model: r, the continuously compounded interest rate; t, the time to maturity; and σ, the standard deviation of the underlying asset. Ralph uses the yield on a four-year zero-coupon bond, which is 3.5 percent, as the estimate of the interest rate. The time to maturity is four years. The estimate of standard deviation is a little trickier, because there is no historical data on alligator restaurants. Ralph finds that the average annual standard deviation of the returns on publicly traded restaurants is 0.35. Because Alligator Alley is a new venture, he reasons that the risk here would be somewhat greater. He finds that the average annual standard deviation for restaurants that have gone public in the last few years is 0.45. Because Ralph's restaurant is newer still, he uses a standard deviation of 0.50.

There is now enough data to value Ralph's venture. The value according to the Black-Scholes model is $1,455,196. The actual calculations are shown in Table 23.4. Of course, Ralph must start his pilot restaurant before he can take advantage of this option. Thus, the net value of the call option less the negative present value of the pilot restaurant is $1,337,757 ($1,455,196 − $117,439). Because this value is large and positive, Ralph decides to stay with his dream of Alligator Alley. He knows that the probability that the restaurant will fail is greater than 50 percent. Nevertheless, the option to expand is important enough that his restaurant business has value. And, if he needs outside capital, he probably can attract the necessary investors.

This finding leads to the appearance of a paradox. If Ralph approaches investors to invest in a single restaurant with no possibility of expansion, he will probably not be able to attract capital. After all, Table 23.3 shows a net present value of −$117,439. However, if Ralph thinks bigger, he will likely be able to attract all the capital that he needs. But this is really not a paradox at all. By thinking bigger, Ralph is offering investors the option, not the obligation, to expand.

The example we have chosen may seem frivolous and, certainly, we added offbeat characteristics for interest. However, if you think that business situations involving options are unusual or unimportant, let us state emphatically that nothing can be further from the truth. The notion of embedded options is at the heart of business. There are two possible outcomes for virtually every business idea. On the one hand, the business may fail, in which case the managers will probably try to shut it down in the most cost-efficient way. On the other hand, the business may prosper, in which case the managers will try to expand. Thus, virtually every business has both the option to abandon and the option to expand. You may have read pundits claiming that the net-present-value approach to capital budgeting is wrong or incomplete. Although criticism of this type frequently irritates the finance establishment, the pundits definitely have a point. If virtually all projects have embedded options, only an approach such as the one we have outlined can be appropriate. Ignoring the options is likely to lead to serious undervaluation.

Concept Questions

1. What are the two options that many businesses have?
2. Why does a strict NPV calculation typically understate the value of a firm or project?

TABLE 23.4	Facts

Valuing a Start-Up Firm (Alligator Alley) as an Option	1. The value of a single restaurant is negative, as indicated by the net-present-value calculation in Table 23.3 of $-$117,439$. Thus, the restaurant would not be funded if there were no possibility of expansion.
	2. If the pilot restaurant is successful, Ralph Simmons plans to create 30 additional restaurants around year 4. This leads to the following observations:
	    a. The total cost of 30 units is $21,000,000 (30 × $700,000).
	    b. The present value of future cash flows as of year 4 is $17,476,830 (30 × $582,561).
	    c. The present value of these cash flows today is $8,428,255 [$17,476,830/(1.20)^4].
	Here, we assume that cash flows from the project are discounted at 20% per annum.
	    Thus, the business is essentially a call option, where the exercise price is $21,000,000 and the underlying asset is worth $8,428,255.
	
	3. Ralph Simmons estimates the standard deviation of the return on Alligator Alley's stock to be 0.50.
	
	Parameters of the Black-Scholes model:
	 S (stock price) = $8,428,255
	E (exercise price) = $21,000,000
	t (time to maturity) = 4 years
	σ (standard deviation) = 0.50
	r (continuously compounded interest rate) = 3.5%
	Calculation from the Black-Scholes model:
	$$C = SN(d_1) - Ee^{-rt}N(d_2)$$
	$$d_1 = [\ln(S/E) + (r + 1/2\sigma^2)t]/\sqrt{\sigma^2 t}$$
	$$d_2 = d_1 - \sqrt{\sigma^2 t}$$
	$$d_1 = \left[\ln\frac{8,428,255}{21,000,000} + \left(0.035 + \frac{1}{2}(0.50)^2\right)4\right]\Big/\sqrt{(0.50)^2 \cdot 4} = -0.27293$$
	$$d_2 = -0.27293 - \sqrt{(0.50)^2 \cdot 4} = -1.27293$$
	$$N(d_1) = N(-0.27293) = 0.3936$$
	$$N(d_2) = N(-1.27293) = 0.1020$$
	$$C = \$8,428,255 \times 0.3936 - \$21,000,000 \times e^{-0.035 \times 4} \times 0.1020$$
	$$= \$1,455,196$$
	
	Value of business including cost of pilot restaurant = $1,455,196 − $117,439
	= $1,337,757

23.3 More on the Binomial Model

Earlier in this chapter, we examined two applications of options, executive compensation and the start-up decision. In both cases we valued an option using the Black-Scholes model. Although this model is justifiably well known, it is not the only approach to option valuation. As mentioned in the previous chapter, the binomial model is an alternative and—in some situations—a superior approach to valuation. The rest of this chapter examines two applications under this binomial model.

Heating Oil

Two-Date Example   Consider Anthony Meyer, a typical heating-oil distributor, whose business consists of buying heating oil at the wholesale level and reselling the oil to

FIGURE 23.1

Movement of
Heating-Oil Prices
from September 1 to
December 1 in a
Two-Date Example

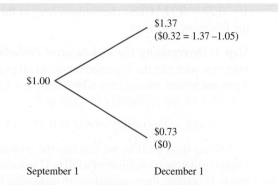

$1.37
($0.32 = 1.37 −1.05)

$1.00

$0.73
($0)

September 1   December 1

The price of heating oil on December 1 will either be $1.37 or $0.73. Because the price on September 1 is $1.00, we say that $u = 1.37$ ($1.37/$1.00) and $d = 0.73$ ($0.73/$1.00). The loss per gallon to Anthony (or, equivalently, the gain per gallon to CECO) of $0.32 in the up-state and $0 in the down-state are shown in parentheses.

homeowners at a slightly higher price. Most of his revenue comes from sales during the winter. Today, September 1, heating oil sells for $1.00 per gallon. Of course, this price is not fixed. Rather, oil prices will vary from September 1 until December 1, the time when his customers will probably be making their big winter purchases of heating oil. Let's simplify the situation by assuming that Anthony believes that oil prices will either be at $1.37 or $0.73 on December 1. Figure 23.1 portrays this possible price movement. This potential price range represents a great deal of uncertainty, because Anthony has no idea which of the two possible prices will actually occur. However, this price variability does not translate into that much risk, because he is able to pass price changes on to his customers. That is, he will charge his customers more if he ends up paying $1.37 per gallon than if he ends up paying $0.73 per gallon.

Of course, Anthony is avoiding risk by passing on that risk to his customers. His customers accept this risk, perhaps because they are each too small to negotiate a better deal with Anthony. This is not the case with CECO, a large electric utility in his area. CECO approaches Anthony with the following proposition. The utility would like to be able to buy *up to* 6 million gallons of oil from him at $1.05 per gallon on December 1.

Although this arrangement represents a lot of oil, both Mr. Meyer and CECO know that Anthony can expect to lose money on it. If prices rise to $1.37 per gallon, the utility will happily buy all 6 million gallons from Anthony at only $1.05 per gallon, clearly creating a loss for the distributor. However, if oil prices decline to $0.73 per gallon, the utility will not buy any oil from Anthony. After all, why should CECO pay $1.05 per gallon to Anthony when the utility can buy all the oil it wants at $0.73 per gallon in the open market? In other words, CECO is asking for a *call option* on heating oil. To compensate Anthony for the risk of loss, the two parties agree that CECO will pay him $500,000 up front for the right to buy up to 6 million gallons of oil at $1.05 per gallon.

Is this a fair deal? Although small distributors may evaluate a deal like this by "gut feel," we can evaluate it more quantitatively using the binomial model described in the previous chapter. In that chapter, we pointed out that option problems can be handled most easily by assuming *risk-neutral pricing*. Under this approach, we first note that oil will either rise 37 percent ($1.37/$1.00 − 1) or fall −27 percent ($0.73/$1.00 − 1) from September 1 to December 1. We can think of these two numbers as the possible returns on heating oil. In addition, we introduce two new terms, u and d. We define u as $1 + 0.37 = 1.37$ and d as

$1 - 0.27 = 0.73$.[2] Using the methodology of the previous chapter, we value the contract in the following two steps.

Step 1: Determining the Risk-Neutral Probabilities   We determine the probability of a price rise such that the expected return on oil exactly equals the risk-free rate. Assuming an 8 percent annual interest rate, which implies a 2 percent rate over the next three months, we can solve for the probability of a rise as:[3]

$$2\% = \text{Probability of rise} \times 0.37 + (1 - \text{Probability of rise}) \times (-0.27)$$

Solving this equation, we find that the probability of a rise is approximately 45 percent, implying that the probability of a fall is 55 percent. In other words, if the probability of a price rise is 45 percent, the expected return on heating oil is 2 percent. In accordance with what we said in the previous chapter, these are the probabilities that are consistent with a world of risk-neutrality. That is, under risk-neutrality, the expected return on any asset would equal the riskless rate of interest. No one would demand an expected return above this riskless rate, because risk-neutral individuals do not need to be compensated for risk-bearing.

Step 2: Valuing the Contract   If the price of oil rises to $1.37 on December 1, CECO will want to buy oil from Anthony at $1.05 per gallon. Anthony will lose $0.32 per gallon, because he buys oil in the open market at $1.37 per gallon, only to resell it to CECO at $1.05 per gallon. This loss of $0.32 is shown in parentheses in Figure 23.1. Conversely, if the market price of heating oil falls to $0.73 per gallon, CECO will not buy any oil from Anthony at all. That is, CECO would not want to pay $1.05 per gallon to Anthony when the utility could buy heating oil in the open market at $0.73 per gallon. Thus, we can say that Anthony neither gains nor loses if the price drops to $0.73. The gain or loss of zero is placed in parentheses under the price of $0.73 in Figure 23.1. In addition, as mentioned earlier, Anthony receives $500,000 up front.

Given these numbers, the value of the contract to Anthony can be calculated as:

$$\underbrace{[0.45 \times (\$1.05 - \$1.37) \times 6 \text{ million} + 0.55 \times 0]/1.02}_{\text{Value of the call option}} + \$500,000 = -\$347,059 \tag{23.1}$$

As in the previous chapter, we are valuing an option using risk-neutral pricing. The cash flows of $-\$0.32$ ($\$1.05 - \$1.37$) and $0 per gallon are multiplied by their risk-neutral probabilities. The entire first term in equation (23.1) is then discounted at $1.02 because the cash flows in that term occur on December 1. The $500,000 is not discounted, because Anthony receives it today, September 1. Because the present value of the contract is negative, Anthony would be wise to reject the contract.

As stated before, the distributor has sold a call option to CECO. The first term in the preceding equation, which equals $-\$847,000$, can be viewed as the value of this call option. It is a negative number because the equation looks at the option from Anthony's point of view. Therefore, the value of the call option would be $+\$847,000$ to CECO. On a per-gallon basis, the value of the option to CECO is:

$$[0.45 (\$1.37 - \$1.05) + 0.55 \times 0]/1.02 = \$0.141 \tag{23.2}$$

Equation (23.2) shows that CECO will gain $0.32 ($1.37 − $1.05) per gallon in the up-state, because CECO can buy heating oil worth $1.37 for only $1.05 under the contract. By contrast, the contract is worth nothing to CECO in the down-state, because the

---

[2]As we will see later, here u and d are consistent with a standard deviation of the annual return on heating oil of 0.63.

[3]For simplicity, we ignore both storage costs and a convenience yield.

FIGURE 23.2

Movement of Heating-Oil Prices in a Three-Date Model

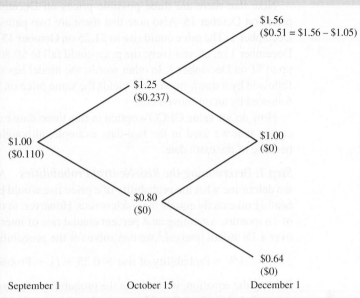

$1.25
($0.237)

$1.00
($0.110)

$0.80
($0)

$1.56
($0.51 = $1.56 − $1.05)

$1.00
($0)

$1.00
($0)

$0.64
($0)

| September 1 | October 15 | December 1 |

The figure shows the prices of a gallon of heating oil on three dates, given $u = 1.25$ and $d = 0.80$. There are three possible prices for heating oil on December 1. For each one of these three prices, we calculate the price on December 1 of a call option on a gallon of heating oil with an exercise price of $1.05. These numbers are in parentheses. Call prices at earlier dates are determined by the binomial model and are also shown in parentheses.

utility will not pay $1.05 for oil selling for only $0.73 in the open market. Using risk-neutral pricing, the formula tells us that the value of the call option on 1 gallon of heating oil is $0.141.

Three-Date Example   Although the preceding example captures a number of aspects of the real world, it has one deficiency. It assumes that the price of heating oil can take on only two values on December 1. This is clearly not plausible, because oil can take on essentially any value in reality. Although this deficiency seems glaring at first glance, it actually is quite correctable; all one has to do is to introduce more intervals over the three-month period of our example.

For example, consider Figure 23.2, which shows the price movement of heating oil over two intervals of 1½ months each.[4] As shown in the figure, the price will be either $1.25 or $0.80 on October 15. We refer to $1.25 as the price in the *up-state* and $0.80 as the price in the *down-state*. Thus, heating oil has returns of 25 percent ($1.25/$1) and −20 percent ($0.80/$1) in the two states.

We assume the same variability as we move forward from October 15 to December 1. That is, given a price of $1.25 on October 15, the price on December 1 will be either $1.56 ($1.25 × 1.25) or $1 ($1.25 × 0.80). Similarly, given a price of $0.80 on October 15, the price on December 1 will be either $1 ($0.80 × 1.25) or $0.64 ($0.80 × 0.80). This assumption of constant variability is quite plausible, because the rate of new information impacting heating oil (or most commodities or assets) is likely to be similar from month to month.

---

[4]Though it is not apparent at first glance, we will see later that the price movement in Figure 23.2 is consistent with the price movement in Figure 23.1.

Note that there are three possible prices on December 1, but there are two possible prices on October 15. Also note that there are two paths, both generating a price of $1 on December 1. The price could rise to $1.25 on October 15 before falling back down to $1 on December 1 or, alternatively, the price could fall to $0.80 on October 15 before going back up to $1 on December 1. In other words, the model has symmetry, where an up-movement followed by a down-movement yields the same price on December 1 as a down-movement followed by an up-movement.

How do we value CECO's option in this three-date example? We employ the same procedure that we used in the two-date example, although we will now need an extra step because of the extra date:

Step 1: Determining the Risk-Neutral Probabilities
As we did in the two-date example, we determine what the probability of a price rise would be such that the expected return on heating oil exactly equals the riskless rate. However, in this case, we work with an interval of 1½ months. Assuming an 8 percent annual rate of interest, which implies a 1 percent rate over a 1½ month interval,[5] we can solve for the probability of a rise as:

$$1\% = \text{Probability of rise} \times 0.25 + (1 - \text{Probability of rise}) \times (-0.20)$$

Solving the equation, we find that the probability of a rise here is 47 percent, implying that the probability of a fall is 53 percent. In other words, if the probability of a rise is 47 percent, the expected return on heating oil is 1 percent per each 1½-month interval. Again, these probabilities are determined under the assumption of risk-neutral pricing.

Note that the probabilities of 47 percent and 53 percent hold for both the interval from September 1 to October 15 and the interval from October 15 to December 1. This is the case because the return in the up-state is 25 percent and the return in the down-state is −20 percent for each of the two intervals. Thus, the preceding equation must apply to each of the intervals separately.

Step 2: Valuing the Option as of October 15
As indicated in Figure 23.2, the option to CECO will be worth $0.51 per gallon on December 1 if the price of heating oil has risen to $1.56 on that date. That is, CECO can buy oil from Anthony at $1.05 when it would otherwise have to pay $1.56 in the open market. However the option will be worthless on December 1 if the price of a gallon of heating oil is either $1 or $0.64 on that date. Here, the option is out of the money because the exercise price of $1.05 is above either $1 or $0.64.

Using these implicit option prices on December 1, we can calculate the value of the call option on October 15. If the price of a gallon of heating oil is $1.25 on October 15, Figure 23.2 shows us that the call option will either be worth $0.51 or $0 on December 1. Thus, if the price of heating oil is $1.25 on October 15, the value of the option on 1 gallon of heating oil at that time is:

$$[0.47 \times 0.51 + 0.53 \times 0]/1.01 = \$0.237$$

Here, we are valuing an option using the same risk-neutral pricing approach that we used in the earlier two-date example. This value of $0.237 is shown in parentheses in Figure 23.2.

We also want to value the option on October 15 if the price at that time is $0.80. However, the value here is clearly zero, as indicated by the calculation:

$$[0.47 \times \$0 + 0.53 \times \$0]/1.01 = 0$$

This is obvious, once one looks at Figure 23.2. We see from the figure that the call must end up out of the money on December 1 if the price of heating oil is $0.80 on October 15.

---

[5]For simplicity, we ignore interest compounding.

Thus, the call must have zero value on October 15 if the price of heating oil is $0.80 on that date.

Step 3: Valuing the Option on September 1   In the previous step, we saw that the price of the call on October 15 would be $0.237 if the price of a gallon of heating oil were $1.25 on that date. Similarly, the price of the option on October 15 would be $0 if oil were selling at $0.80 on that date. From these values, we can calculate the call option value on September 1 as:

$$[0.47 \times \$0.237 + 0.53 \times \$0]/1.01 = \$0.110$$

Notice that this calculation is completely analogous to the calculation of the option value in the previous step, as well as the calculation of the option value in the two-date example that we presented earlier. In other words, the same approach applies regardless of the number of intervals used. As we will see later, we can move to many intervals, which produces greater realism, yet still maintain the same basic methodology.

The previous calculation has given us the value of CECO of its option on 1 gallon of heating oil. Now we are ready to calculate the value of the contract to Anthony. Given the calculations from the previous equation, the contract's value can be written as:

$$-\$0.110 \times 6,000,000 + \$500,000 = -\$160,000$$

That is, Anthony is giving away an option worth $0.110 for each of the 6 million gallons of heating oil. In return, he is receiving only $500,000 up front. On balance, he is losing $160,000. Of course, the value of the contract to CECO is the opposite, so the value to this utility is $160,000.

Extension to Many Dates   We have looked at the contract between CECO and Anthony using both a two-date example and a three-date example. The three-date case is more realistic because more possibilities for price movements are allowed here. However, why stop at just three dates? Moving to 4 dates, 5 dates, 50 dates, 500 dates, and so on, should give us ever more realism. Note that, as we move to more dates, we are merely shortening the interval between dates without increasing the overall time period of three months (September 1 to December 1).

For example, imagine a model with 90 dates over the three months. Here, each interval is approximately one day long, because there are about 90 days in a three-month period. The assumption of two possible outcomes in the binomial model is more plausible over a one-day interval than it is over a 1½-month interval, let alone a three-month interval. Of course, we could probably achieve greater realism still by going to an interval of, say, one hour or one minute.

How does one adjust the binomial model in order to accommodate increases in the number of intervals? It turns out that two simple formulas relate u and d to the standard deviation of the return of the underlying asset:[6]

$$u = e^{\sigma/\sqrt{n}} \quad \text{and} \quad d = 1/u$$

where σ is the standard deviation of the annualized return on the underlying asset (heating oil, in this case) and n is the number of intervals over a year.

When we created the heating oil example, we assumed that the annualized standard deviation of the return on heating oil was 0.63 (or, equivalently, 63 percent). Because there are four quarters in a year, $u = e^{0.63/\sqrt{4}} = 1.37$ and $d = 1/1.37 = 0.73$, as shown in the

---

[6]See John C. Hull, *Options, Futures, and Other Derivatives*, 4th ed. (Upper Saddle River, N.J.: Prentice Hall, 1999) for a derivation of these formulas.

TABLE 23.5	Number of Intervals*	Call Value
Value of a Call on One Gallon of Heating Oil	1	$0.141
	2	0.110
	3	0.122
	4	0.116
	6	0.114
	10	0.114
	20	0.114
	30	0.114
	40	0.114
	50	0.113
	99	0.113
Black-Scholes	Infinity	0.113

In this example, the value of the call according to the binomial model varies as the number of intervals increases. However, the value of the call converges rapidly to the Black-Scholes value. Thus, the binomial model, even with only a few intervals, appears to be a good approximation to Black-Scholes.

*The number of intervals is always one less than the number of dates.

two-date example of Figure 23.1. In the three-date example of Figure 23.2, where each interval is 1½ months long, $u = e^{0.63/\sqrt{8}} = 1.25$ and $d = 1/1.25 = 0.80$. Thus, the binomial model can be applied in practice if the standard deviation of the return of the underlying asset can be estimated.

We stated earlier that the value of the call option on a gallon of heating oil was estimated to be $0.141 in the two-date model and $0.110 in the three-date model. How does the value of the option change as we increase the number of intervals, while keeping the time period constant at three months (from September 1 to December 1)? We have calculated the value of the call for various time intervals in Table 23.5.[7] The realism increases with the number of intervals, because the restriction of only two possible outcomes is more plausible over a short interval than over a long one. Thus, the value of the call when the number of intervals is 99 or infinity is likely more realistic than this value when the number of intervals is, say, 1 or 2. However, a very interesting phenomenon can be observed from the table. Although the value of the call changes as the number of intervals increases, convergence occurs quite rapidly. The call's value when the number of intervals is 6 is almost identical to the value when there are 99 intervals. Thus, a small number of intervals appears serviceable for the binomial model.

What happens when the number of intervals goes to infinity, implying that the length of the interval goes to zero? It can be proved mathematically that one ends up with the value of the Black-Scholes model. This value is also presented in Table 23.5. Thus, one can argue that the Black-Scholes model is the best approach to value the heating-oil option. It is also quite easy to apply. We can use a calculator to value options with Black-Scholes, whereas we must generally use a computer program for the binomial model. However, as shown in Table 23.5, the values from the binomial model, even with relatively few intervals, are quite close to the Black-Scholes value. Thus, although Black-Scholes may save us time, it does not materially affect our estimate of value.

At this point it seems as if the Black-Scholes model is preferable to the binomial model. Who wouldn't want to save time and still get a slightly more accurate value? However,

[7]In this discussion we have used both *intervals* and *dates*. To keep the terminology straight, remember that the number of intervals is always one less than the number of dates. For example, if a model has two dates, it only has one interval.

such is not always the case. There are plenty of situations where the binomial model is preferred to the Black-Scholes model. One such situation is presented in the next section.

23.4 Shutdown and Reopening Decisions

Some of the earliest and most important examples of special options occur in the natural resources and mining industries.

Valuing a Gold Mine

The "Woe Is Me" gold mine was founded in 1878 on one of the richest veins of gold in the West. Thirty years later, by 1908, the mine had been played out, but occasionally, depending on the price of gold, it is reopened. Currently gold is not actively mined at Woe Is Me, but its stock is still traded on the exchange under the ticker symbol, WOE. WOE has no debt and, with about 20 million outstanding shares, it has a market value (stock price times number of shares outstanding) well above $1 billion. WOE owns about 160 acres of land surrounding the mine and has a 100-year government lease to mine gold there. However, land in the desert has a market value of only a few thousand dollars. WOE holds cash and securities and other assets worth about $30 million. What could possibly explain why a company with $30 million in assets and a closed gold mine that is producing no cash flow whatsoever has the market value that WOE has?

The answer lies in the options that WOE implicitly owns in the form of a gold mine. Assume that the current price of gold is about $320 per ounce and the cost of extraction and processing at the mine is about $350 per ounce. It is no wonder that the mine is closed. Every ounce of gold extracted costs $350 and can be sold for only $320 for a loss of $30 per ounce. Presumably, if the price of gold were to rise, the mine could be opened. It costs $2 million to open the mine and when it is opened, production is 50,000 ounces per year. Geologists believe that the amount of gold in the mine is essentially unlimited, and WOE has the right to mine it for the next 100 years. Under the terms of its lease, WOE cannot stockpile gold and must sell each year all the gold it mines that year. Closing the mine requires equipment to be mothballed and some environmental precautions to be put in place and costs $1 million. We will refer to the $2 million required to open the mine as the entry fee or investment and the $1 million to close it as the closing or abandonment cost. (There is no way to avoid the abandonment cost by simply keeping the mine open and not operating.)

From a financial perspective, WOE is really just a package of options on the price of gold disguised as a company and a mine. The basic option is a call on the price of gold where the exercise price is the $350 extraction cost. The option is complicated by having an exercise fee of $2 million—the opening cost—whenever it is exercised and a closing fee of $1 million when it is abandoned. It is also complicated by the fact that it is a perpetual option with no final maturity.

The Abandonment and Opening Decisions

Before trying to figure out the exact value of the option implicit in WOE or, for that matter, in any real option problem, it is useful to see what we can say by just applying common sense. To begin with, the mine should only be opened when the price of gold is sufficiently above the extraction cost of $350 per ounce. Because it costs $2 million to open the mine, the mine should not be opened whenever the price of gold is only slightly above $350. At a gold price of, say, $350.10, the mine wouldn't be opened because the ten-cent profit per ounce translates into $5,000 per year (50,000 ounces × $0.10/ounce). This would not begin to cover the $2 million opening costs. More significantly, though, the mine probably would not be opened if the price rose to $360 per ounce even though a $10 profit per ounce—$500,000 per year—would pay the $2 million opening costs at any reasonable discount rate. The reason is that here, as in all option problems, volatility, in this case the volatility of gold, plays a significant role. Because the gold price is volatile the price has to rise sufficiently above $350 per ounce to make it worth opening the mine. If the price at which the mine is opened is too close to the extraction price of $350 per ounce, say at $360 per ounce, for example, then we would wind up opening the mine every time the price jogged above $360 and finding ourselves operating at a loss or facing a closing decision whenever the gold price jogged down $10 per ounce or only 3 percent down.

The estimated volatility of the return on gold is about 15 percent per year. This means that a single annual standard deviation movement in the gold price is 15 percent of $320 or $48 per year. Surely with this amount of random movement in the gold price, a threshold of $352 is much too low at which to open the mine. A similar logic applies to the closing decision. If the mine is open, then we will clearly keep it open as long as the gold price is above the extraction cost of $350 per ounce since we are profiting on every ounce of gold mined. But, we also won't close the mine down simply because the gold price drops below $350 per ounce. We will tolerate a running loss to keep alive the possibility that the gold price will rise above $350 and to avoid the necessity of having to pay the $1 million abandonment cost only to have to pay another $2 million to reopen the mine.

To summarize, if the mine is currently closed, then it will be opened—at a cost of $2 million—whenever the price of gold rises sufficiently above the extraction cost of $350 per ounce. If the mine is currently operating, then it will be closed down—at a cost of $1 million—whenever the price of gold falls sufficiently below the extraction cost of $350 per ounce. WOE's problem is to find these two threshold prices at which it opens a closed mine and closes an open mine. We call these prices *popen* and *pclose,* respectively, where

$$popen > \$350/ounce > pclose$$

In other words, WOE will open the mine if the gold price option is sufficiently in the money and will close it when the option is sufficiently out of the money.

We know that the more volatile the gold price, the further away popen and pclose will be from $350 per ounce. We also know that the greater the cost of opening the mine the higher popen will be and the greater the cost of abandoning the mine the lower will be pclose. Interestingly, we should also expect that popen will be higher if the abandonment cost is increased. After all, if it costs more to abandon the mine WOE will need to be more assured that the price will stay above the extraction cost when it decides to open the mine. Otherwise, WOE might soon face the costly choice between abandonment and operating at a loss if the price falls below $350 per ounce. Similarly, raising the cost of opening the mine will make WOE more reluctant to close an open mine. As a result, pclose will be lower.

The above arguments have enabled us to reduce the problem of valuing WOE to two stages. First, we have to determine the threshold prices, popen and pclose. Second, given the best choices for these thresholds, we must determine the value of a gold option that is exercised for a cost of $2 million when the gold price rises above popen and is shut down for a cost of $1 million whenever the gold price is below pclose.

When the mine is open, i.e., when the option is exercised, the annual cash flow is equal to the difference between the gold price and the extraction cost of $350 per ounce times 50,000 ounces. When the mine is shut down, it generates no cash flow.

The following diagram describes the decisions available at each point in time.

How do we determine the critical values for popen and pclose and then the value of the mine? It is possible to get a good approximation by using the tools we have currently developed.

Valuing the Simple Gold Mine

Here is what has to be done in order both to determine popen and pclose and to value the mine:

Step 1   Find the risk-free interest rate and the volatility. We will use a semiannual interest rate of 3.4 percent and a volatility of 15 percent per year for gold.

Step 2   Construct a binomial tree and fill it out with gold prices. Suppose, for example, that we set the steps of the tree six months apart. If the annual volatility is 15 percent, u is equal to $e^{0.15/\sqrt{2}}$, which is approximately equal to 1.11. The other parameter, d, is 0.90 (1/1.11). Figure 23.3 illustrates the tree. Starting at the current price of $320, the first 11 percent increase takes the price to $355 in six months. The first 10 percent decrease takes the price to $288. Subsequent steps are up 11 percent or down 10 percent from the previous price. The tree extends for the 100-year life of the lease or 200 six-month steps.

Using our analysis from the previous section, we now compute the risk-adjusted probabilities for each step. Given a semiannual interest rate of 3.4 percent, we have

$$3.4\% = \text{Probability of a rise} \times 0.11 + (1 - \text{Probability of a rise}) \times -0.10.$$

Solving this equation gives us 0.64 for the probability of a rise, implying that the probability of a fall is 0.36. These probabilities are the same for each six-month interval. In other words, if the probability of a rise is 0.64, the expected return on gold is 3.4 percent per each six-month interval. These probabilities are determined under the assumption of risk-neutral pricing. In other words, if investors are risk-neutral, they will be satisfied with an expected return equal to the risk-free rate, because the extra risk of gold will not concern them.

Step 3   Now we turn the computer on and let it simulate, say, 5,000 possible paths through the tree. At each node, the computer has a 0.64 probability of picking an "up" movement in the price and a corresponding 0.36 probability of picking a "down" movement in the price. A typical path might be represented by whether the price rose or fell each six-month period over the next 100 years and it would be a list like

up, up, down, up, down, down, . . . , down

FIGURE 23.3

A Binomial Tree for
Gold Prices

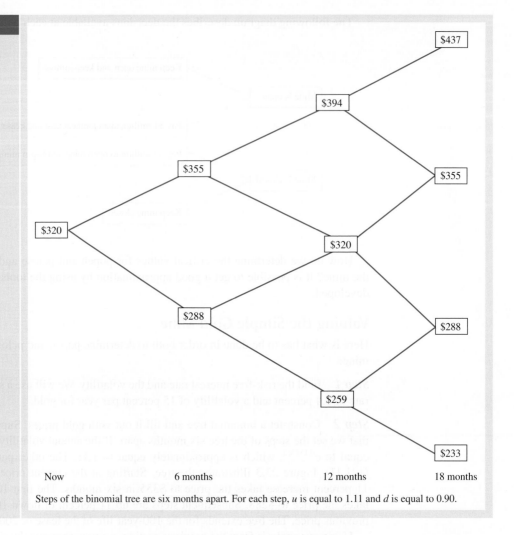

Steps of the binomial tree are six months apart. For each step, u is equal to 1.11 and d is equal to 0.90.

where the first "up" meant the price rose from $320 to $355 in the first six months, the next "up" meant it again went up in the second half of the year from $355 to $394, and so on, ending with a down move in the last half of year 100.

With 5,000 such paths we will have a good sample of all the future possibilities for movement in the gold price.

Step 4   Next we consider possible choices for the threshold prices, popen and pclose. For popen, we let the possibilities be:

$$\text{popen} = \$360 \text{ or } \$370 \text{ or } \dots \text{ or } \$500$$

a total of 15 values. For pclose we let the probabilities be:

$$\text{pclose} = \$340 \text{ or } \$330 \text{ or } \dots \text{ or } \$100$$

a total of 25 values.

We picked these choices because they seemed reasonable and because increments of $10 for each seemed sensible. To be precise, though, we should let the threshold prices change as we move through the tree and get closer to the 100 year-end. Presumably, for

FIGURE 23.4

A Possible Path for the Price of Gold

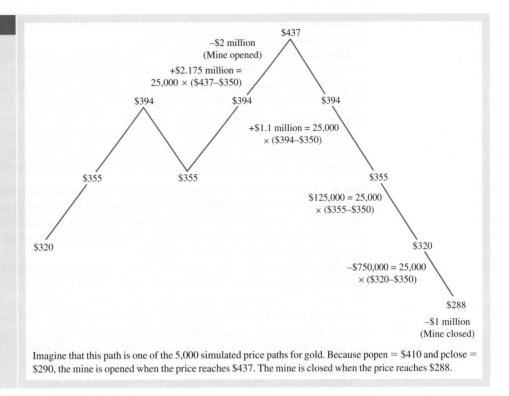

Imagine that this path is one of the 5,000 simulated price paths for gold. Because popen = $410 and pclose = $290, the mine is opened when the price reaches $437. The mine is closed when the price reaches $288.

example, if we decided to open the mine with one year left on the lease, the price of gold should be at least high enough to cover the $2 million-dollar opening costs in the coming year. Since we mine 50,000 ounces per year, in year 99 we will only open the mine if the gold price is at least $40 above the extraction cost, or $390.

While this will become important at the end of the lease, using a constant threshold shouldn't have too big an impact on the value with 100 years to go and we will stick with our approximation of constant threshold prices.

Step 5   We calculate the value of the mines for each pair of choices of popen and pclose. For example, if popen = $410 and pclose = $290, we use the computer to keep track of the cash flows if we opened the mine whenever it was closed and the gold price rose to $410, and closed the mine whenever it was open and the gold price fell to $290. We do this for each of the 5,000 paths we simulated in Step 4.

For example, consider the path illustrated in Figure 23.4 of:

up, up, down, up, up, down, down, down, down

As can be seen from the figure, the price reaches a peak of $437 in 2½ years, only to fall to $288 over the following four six-month intervals. If popen = $410 and pclose = $290, the mine will be opened when the price reaches $437, necessitating a cost of $2 million. However, the firm can sell 25,000 ounces of gold at $437 at that time, producing a cash flow of $2.175 million (25,000 × ($437 − $350)). When the price falls to $394 six months later, the firm sells another 25,000 ounces, yielding a cash flow of $1.1 million (25,000 × ($394 − $350)). The price continues to fall, with the price reaching $320 a year later. Here, the firm realizes a cash outflow, because production costs are $350 per ounce. Next, the price falls to $288. Because this is below pclose of $290, the mine is closed at a cost of

$1 million. Of course, the price of gold will fluctuate in further years, leading to the possibility of future mine openings and closings.

This path is just a possibility. It may or may not occur in any simulation of 5,000 paths. For each of these 5,000 paths that the computer simulated, we have a sequence of semiannual cash flows using a popen of $410 and a pclose of $290. We calculate the present value of each of these cash flows, discounting at the interest rate of 3.4 percent. Summing up across all the cash flows, we have the present value of the gold mine for one path.

We then take the average present value of the gold mine across all the 5,000 simulated paths. This number is the expected value of the mine from following a policy of opening the mine whenever the gold price hits $410 and closing it at a price of $290.

Step 6   The final step is to compare the different expected discounted cash flows from Step 5 for the range of possible choices for popen and pclose and to pick the highest one. This is the best estimate of the expected value of the mine. The value for pclose and popen corresponding to this estimate is our best estimate (within $10) of the points at which to open a closed mine and to shut an open one.

As mentioned in Step 3, there are 15 different values for popen and 25 different values for pclose, implying 375 (15 × 25) different pairs. Consider Table 23.6, which shows the present values associated with the 20 best pairs. The table indicates that the best pair is popen = $400 and pclose = $140, with a present value of $1.467 billion. This number represents the average present value across 5,000 simulations, all assuming the preceding values of popen and pclose. The next best pair is popen = $460 and pclose = $300, with a present value of $1.459 billion. The third best pair has a somewhat lower present value still, and so on.

Of course, our estimate of the value of the mine is $1.467 billion, the present value of the best pair of choices. The market capitalization (price × number of shares outstanding) of WOE should reach this value if the market makes the same assumptions that we did. Note

TABLE 23.6			Estimated Value of
Valuation of Woe Is	popen	pclose	Gold Mine
Me (WOE) Gold	$400	$140	$1,466,720,900
Mine for the 20 Best	460	300	1,459,406,200
Choices of popen and	380	290	1,457,838,700
pclose	370	100	1,455,131,900
	360	190	1,449,708,200
	420	150	1,448,711,400
	430	340	1,448,450,200
	430	110	1,445,396,500
	470	200	1,435,687,400
	500	320	1,427,512,000
	410	290	1,426,483,500
	420	290	1,423,865,300
	400	160	1,423,061,900
	360	320	1,420,748,700
	360	180	1,419,112,000
	380	280	1,417,405,400
	450	310	1,416,238,000
	450	280	1,409,709,800
	440	220	1,408,269,100
	440	240	1,403,398,100

For our simulation, WOE opens the mine whenever the gold price rises above popen and closes the mine whenever the gold price falls below pclose.

that the value of the firm is quite high using an option framework. However, as stated earlier, WOE would appear worthless if a regular discounted cash-flow approach were used. This occurs because the initial price of gold of $320 is below the extraction cost of $350.

This example is not easy, either in terms of concepts or in terms of implementation. However, we believe that the extra work involved in mastering this example is worth it, because it illustrates the type of modeling that actually occurs in corporate finance departments in the real world.

Furthermore, the example illustrates the benefits of the binomial approach. One merely calculates the cash flows associated with each of a number of simulations, discounts the cash flows from each simulation, and averages present values across the simulations. Because the Black-Scholes model is not amenable to simulations, it cannot be used for this type of problem. In addition, there are a number of other situations where the binomial model is more appropriate than is the Black-Scholes model. For example, it is well known that the Black-Scholes model cannot properly handle options with dividend payments prior to the expiration date. This model also does not adequately handle the valuation of an American put. By contrast, the binomial model can easily handle both these situations.

Thus, any student of corporate finance should be well versed with both models. The Black-Scholes model should be used whenever appropriate, because it is simpler to use than is the binomial model. However, for the more complex situations where the Black-Scholes model breaks down, the binomial model becomes a necessary tool.

23.5 SUMMARY AND CONCLUSIONS

This chapter extends the intuitions of one of the most significant concepts in finance: option pricing theory. We describe four different types of special options:

Executive stock options.
The embedded option in a start-up company.
The option in simple business contracts.
The option to shut down and reopen a project.

We try to keep the presentation simple and straightforward from a mathematical point of view. We extend the binomial approach to option pricing in Chapter 22 to many periods. This adjustment brings us closer to the real world, because the assumption of only two prices at the end of an interval is more plausible when the interval is short.

SUGGESTED READINGS

An excellent practical treatment of real options can be found in:

Amran, Martha, and Nalin Kulatilaka. *Real Options.* Cambridge: Harvard Business School Press, 1999.

A more academic treatment can be found in:

Brennan, Michael, and L. Trigeorgis, eds. *Flexibility, Natural Resources, and Strategic Options.* Oxford: Oxford University Press, 1998.

Copeland, Tom, and Vladimir Antikarov. *Real Options: A Practitioner's Guide.* Texere LLC, 2001.

QUESTIONS & PROBLEMS

EXECUTIVE STOCK OPTIONS

23.1   Gary Levin is the chief executive officer of Mountainbrook Trading Company. The board of directors has just granted Mr. Levin 20,000 at-the-money European call options on Mountainbrook's stock, which is currently trading at $50 per share. Mountainbrook's stock pays no dividends. The options will expire in 4 years, and the annual variance of the continuously compounded returns on Mountainbrook's stock is 0.25. Treasury bills that mature in four years currently yield a continuously compounded interest rate of 6 percent per annum.

a. Use the Black-Scholes model to calculate the value of Mr. Levin's stock options.

b. You are Mr. Levin's financial advisor. He must choose between the previously mentioned stock option package and an immediate $450,000 bonus. If he is risk-neutral, which would you recommend?

c. How would your answer to (*b*) change if Mr. Levin were risk-averse and he could not sell the options prior to expiration?

23.2 Jared Lazarus has just been named the new chief executive officer of BluBell Fitness Centers, Inc. In addition to an annual salary of $500,000, his three-year contract states that his compensation will include 10,000 at-the-money European call options on the company's stock that expire in three years. Blubell's current stock price is $30 per share, and the annual variance of the continuously compounded returns on the firm's stock is 0.1225. Blubell pays no dividends. Treasury bills that mature in three years yield a continuously compounded interest rate of 5 percent per annum. Assume that Jared's annual salary payments occur at the end of the year and that these cash flows should be discounted at a rate of 10 percent per annum. Using the Black-Scholes model to calculate the value of the stock options, determine the total value of Jared's compensation package on the date the contract is signed.

REAL OPTIONS

23.3 The Webber Company is an international conglomerate with a real estate division that owns the right to erect an office building on a parcel of land in downtown Sacramento over the next year. This building would cost $10.5 million to construct. Due to low demand for office space in the downtown area, such a building is worth approximately $10 million today. If demand increases, the building would be worth $12.5 million a year from today. If demand decreases, the same office building would only be worth $8 million in a year. The firm can borrow and lend at the risk-free rate of 2.5 percent per annum (effective annual yield). A local competitor in the real estate business has recently offered the Webber Company $750,000 for its right to build an office building on the land. Should Webber accept this offer? Use a two-state model to value the firm's real option.

23.4 Jet Black is an international conglomerate with a petroleum division and is currently competing in an auction to win the right to drill for crude oil on a large piece of land in one year. The current market price of crude oil is $25 per barrel, and the land contains 60,000 barrels of oil. If found, excavating the oil would cost the firm $1.75 million. Treasury bills that mature in one year yield a continuously compounded interest rate of 10 percent per annum, and the annual variance of the continuously compounded returns on the price of crude oil is 0.36. Use the Black-Scholes model to calculate the maximum bid that Jet Black should be willing to make at the auction.

23.5 Sardano and Sons is a large, publicly held company that is considering leasing a warehouse. One of Sardano's divisions specializes in manufacturing steel, and this particular warehouse is the only facility in the area that suits the firm's operations. The current price of steel is $3,000 per ton. If the price of steel falls over the next six months, the firm will purchase 400 tons of steel and produce 5,000 steel rods. Each steel rod will cost Sardano $100 to manufacture, and the firm plans to sell the rods for $300 each. It will take only a matter of days to produce and sell the 5,000 steel rods. If the price of steel rises or remains the same, it will not be profitable for the firm to undertake the project, and Sardano will allow the lease to expire without producing any steel rods. Treasury bills that mature in six months yield a continuously compounded interest rate of 3 percent per annum, and the annual variance of the continuously compounded returns on steel is 0.3025. Use the Black-Scholes model to determine the maximum amount that Sardano and Sons should be willing to pay for the lease.

Warrants and Convertibles

EXECUTIVE SUMMARY

We study two financing instruments in this chapter, warrants and convertibles. A warrant gives the holder the right to buy common stock for cash. In this sense, it is very much like a call. Warrants are generally issued with privately placed bonds, though they are also combined with new issues of common stock and preferred stock. In the case of new issues of common stock, warrants are sometimes given to investment bankers as compensation for underwriting services.

A convertible bond gives the holder the right to exchange the bond for common stock. Therefore, it is a mixed security blurring the traditional line between stocks and bonds. There is also convertible preferred stock.

The chapter describes the basic features of warrants and convertibles. Here are some of the most important questions concerning warrants and convertibles:

1. How can warrants and convertibles be valued?
2. What impact do warrants and convertibles have on the value of the firm?
3. What are the differences between warrants, convertibles, and call options?
4. Why do some companies issue bonds with warrants and convertible bonds?
5. Under what circumstances are warrants and convertibles converted into common stock?

24.1 Warrants

Warrants are securities that give holders the right, but not the obligation, to buy shares of common stock directly from a company at a fixed price for a given period of time. Each warrant specifies the number of shares of stock that the holder can buy, the exercise price, and the expiration date.

From the preceding description of warrants, it is clear that they are similar to call options. The differences in contractual features between warrants and the call options that trade on the Chicago Board Options Exchange are small. For example, warrants have longer maturity periods.[1] Some warrants are actually perpetual, meaning that they never expire at all.

Warrants are referred to as *equity kickers* because they are usually issued in combination with privately placed bonds.[2] In most cases, warrants are attached to the bonds when issued. The loan agreement will state whether the warrants are detachable from the bond, that is, whether they can be sold separately. Usually the warrant can be detached immediately.

---

[1] Warrants are usually protected against stock splits and dividends in the same way that call options are.

[2] Warrants are also issued with publicly distributed bonds and new issues of common stock.

EXAMPLE

Safeway, Inc., is one of the nation's largest supermarket chains. On November 24, 1986, Safeway was acquired in a levered buyout by the private investment firm Kohlberg Kravis Roberts and Co. (KKR). Each share of old common stock was converted into a junior subordinated debenture (i.e., junk bond) and a "merger" warrant. Each warrant gave the holder the right to purchase .279 shares of new common stock for $1.052 per warrant. To purchase one share of common stock, a holder had to give up 3.584 warrants and pay an amount of $3.7691 per warrant. This made the exercise price of the Safeway warrants equal to $13.5085 (3.584 × $3.7691 = $13.5085). The warrants expired on November 24, 1996. They are called *merger warrants* because Safeway issued the warrants in a buyout of old shares.

When Safeway was acquired by KKR, it was a private firm with no publicly traded common stock or warrants. However, KKR took Safeway public on April 26, 1990, by issuing 10 million shares in a new issue of common stock. The stock was listed on the New York Stock Exchange. On that day, several thousand warrants were traded at a closing price of $3\frac{1}{8}$. The price of the Safeway common stock was $12\frac{1}{8}$.

The relationship between the value of Safeway's warrants and its stock price can be viewed like the relationship between a call option and its stock price, described in a previous chapter. Figure 24.1 depicts the relationship for Safeway warrants. The lower limit on the value of the warrants is zero if Safeway's stock price is below $13.5085 per share. If the price of Safeway's common stock rises above $13.5085 per share, the lower limit is the stock price minus $13.5085 divided by 3.584.[3] The upper limit is the price of Safeway's common stock divided by 3.584. A warrant to buy one share of common stock cannot sell at a price above the price of the underlying common stock.

The price of Safeway warrants on April 26, 1990, was higher than the lower limit. The height of the warrant price above the lower limit will depend on the following:

1. The variance of Safeway's stock returns.
2. The time to expiration date.
3. The risk-free rate of interest.
4. The stock price of Safeway.
5. The exercise price.

These are the same factors that determine the value of a call option.

FIGURE 24.1

Safeway Warrants on
April 26, 1990

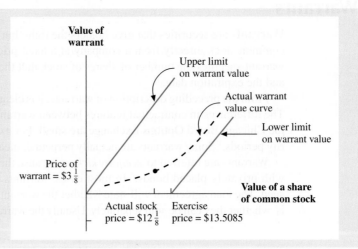

---

[3]We need to divide by 3.584 because it takes 3.584 warrants to purchase one share of stock.

24.2 The Difference between Warrants and Call Options

From the holder's point of view, warrants are similar to call options on common stock. A warrant, like a call option, gives its holder the right to buy common stock at a specified price. Warrants usually have an expiration date, though in most cases they are issued with longer lives than call options. From the firm's point of view, however, a warrant is very different from a call option on the company's common stock.

The most important difference between call options and warrants is that call options are issued by individuals and warrants are issued by firms. When a warrant is exercised, a firm must issue new shares of stock. Each time a warrant is exercised, then, the number of shares outstanding increases.

To illustrate, suppose the Endrun Company issues a warrant giving holders the right to buy one share of common stock at $25. Further suppose the warrant is exercised. Endrun must print one new stock certificate. In exchange for the stock certificate, it receives $25 from the holder.

In contrast, when a call option is exercised, there is no change in the number of shares outstanding. Suppose Ms. Eager holds a call option on the common stock of the Endrun Company. The call option gives Ms. Eager the right to buy one share of the common stock of the Endrun Company for $25. If Ms. Eager chooses to exercise the call option, a seller, say Mr. Swift, is obligated to give her one share of Endrun's common stock in exchange for $25. If Mr. Swift does not already own a share, he must enter the stock market and buy one. The call option is a side bet between buyers and sellers on the value of the Endrun Company's common stock. When a call option is exercised, one investor gains and the other loses. The total number of shares outstanding of the Endrun Company remains constant, and no new funds are made available to the company.

EXAMPLE

To see how warrants affect the value of the firm, imagine that Mr. Gould and Ms. Rockefeller are two investors who have together purchased six ounces of platinum. At the time they bought the platinum, Mr. Gould and Ms. Rockefeller each contributed one-half of the cost, which we will assume was $3,000 for six ounces, or $500 an ounce (they each contributed $1,500). They incorporated, printed two stock certificates, and named the firm the GR Company. Each certificate represents a one-half claim to the platinum. Mr. Gould and Ms. Rockefeller each own one certificate. Mr. Gould and Ms. Rockefeller have formed a company with platinum as its only asset.

A Call Is Issued   Suppose Mr. Gould later decides to sell to Mrs. Fiske a call option issued on Mr. Gould's share. The call option gives Mrs. Fiske the right to buy Mr. Gould's share for $1,800 within the next year. If the price of platinum rises above $600 per ounce, the firm will be worth more than $3,600 and each share will be worth more than $1,800. If Mrs. Fiske decides to exercise her option, Mr. Gould must turn over his stock certificate and receive $1,800.

How would the firm be affected by the exercise? The number of shares will remain the same. There will still be two shares, now owned by Ms. Rockefeller and Mrs. Fiske. If the price of platinum rises to $700 an ounce, each share will be worth $2,100 ($4,200/2). If Mrs. Fiske exercises her option at this price, she will profit by $300.

A Warrant Is Issued Instead   This story changes if a warrant is issued. Suppose that Mr. Gould does not sell a call option to Mrs. Fiske. Instead, Mr. Gould and Ms. Rockefeller have a stockholders' meeting. They vote that GR Company will issue a warrant and sell it to Mrs. Fiske. The warrant will give Mrs. Fiske the right to receive a share of the company at an exercise price of $1,800.[4] If

---

[4]The sale of the warrant brings cash into the firm. We assume that the sale proceeds immediately leave the firm through a cash dividend to Mr. Gould and Ms. Rockefeller. This simplifies the analysis, because the firm with warrants then has the same total value as the firm without warrants.

Mrs. Fiske decides to exercise the warrant, the firm will issue another stock certificate and give it to Mrs. Fiske in exchange for $1,800.

From Mrs. Fiske's perspective, the call option and the warrant *seem* to be the same. The exercise prices of the warrant and the call are the same: $1,800. It is still advantageous for Mrs. Fiske to exercise the option when the price of platinum exceeds $600 per ounce. However, we will show that Mrs. Fiske actually makes less in the warrant situation due to dilution.

The GR Company must also consider dilution. Suppose the price of platinum increases to $700 an ounce and Mrs. Fiske exercises her warrant. Two things will occur:

1. Mrs. Fiske will pay $1,800 to the firm.
2. The firm will print one stock certificate and give it to Mrs. Fiske. The stock certificate will represent a one-third claim on the platinum of the firm.

Because Mrs. Fiske contributes $1,800 to the firm, the value of the firm increases. It is now worth:

$$\text{New value of firm} = \text{Value of platinum} + \text{Contribution to the firm by Mrs. Fiske}$$
$$= \$4,200 + \$1,800$$
$$= \$6,000$$

Because Mrs. Fiske has a one-third claim on the firm's value, her share is worth $2,000 ($6,000/3). By exercising the warrant, Mrs. Fiske gains $2,000 − $1,800 = $200. This is illustrated in Table 24.1.

Dilution   Why does Mrs. Fiske only gain $200 in the warrant case while gaining $300 in the call option case? The key is dilution, that is, the creation of another share. In the call option case, she contributes $1,800 and receives one of the two outstanding shares. That is, she receives a share worth $2,100 ($\frac{1}{2}$ × $4,200). Her gain is $300 ($2,100 − $1,800). We rewrite this gain as:

Gain on Exercise of Call:

$$\frac{\$4,200}{2} - \$1,800 = \$300 \tag{24.1}$$

TABLE 24.1		**Price of Platinum per Share**	
Effect of Call Option and Warrant on the GR Company*	**Value of Firm if:**	**$700**	**$600**
	No Warrant		
	Mr. Gould's share	$2,100	$1,800
	Ms. Rockefeller's share	2,100	1,800
	Firm	$4,200	$3,600
	Call option		
	Mr. Gould's claim	$ 0	$1,800
	Ms. Rockefeller's claim	2,100	1,800
	Mrs. Fiske's claim	2,100	0
	Firm	$4,200	$3,600
	Warrant		
	Mr. Gould's share	$2,000	$1,800
	Ms. Rockefeller's share	2,000	1,800
	Mrs. Fiske's share	2,000	0
	Firm	$6,000	$3,600

*If the price of platinum is $700, the value of the firm is equal to the value of six ounces of platinum plus the excess dollars paid into the firm by Mrs. Fiske. This amount is $4,200 + $1,800 = $6,000.

In the warrant case, she contributes $1,800 and receives a newly created share. She now owns one of the three outstanding shares. Because the $1,800 remains in the firm, her share is worth $2,000 [($4,200 + $1,800)/3]. Her gain is $200 ($2,000 − $1,800). We rewrite this gain as:

Gain on Exercise of Warrant:

$$\frac{\$4,200 + \$1,800}{2 + 1} - \$1,800 = \$200 \tag{24.2}$$

Warrants also affect accounting numbers. Warrants and (as we shall see) convertible bonds cause the number of shares to increase. This causes the firm's net income to be spread over a larger number of shares, thereby decreasing earnings per share. Firms with significant amounts of warrants and convertible issues must report earnings on a *primary* basis and a *fully diluted* basis.

How the Firm Can Hurt Warrant Holders

The platinum firm owned by Mr. Gould and Ms. Rockefeller has issued a warrant to Mrs. Fiske that is *in the money* and about to expire. One way that Mr. Gould and Ms. Rockefeller can hurt Mrs. Fiske is to pay themselves a large dividend. This could be funded by selling a substantial amount of platinum. The value of the firm would fall, and the warrant would be worth much less.

Concept
Questions

1. What is the key difference between a warrant and a traded call option?
2. Why does dilution occur when warrants are exercised?
3. How can the firm hurt warrant holders?

24.3 Warrant Pricing and the Black-Scholes Model (Advanced)

We now wish to express the gains from exercising a call and a warrant in more general terms. The gain on a call can be written as:

Gain from Exercising a Single Call:

$$\underbrace{\frac{\text{Firm's value net of debt}}{\#} - \text{Exercise price}}_{\text{(Value of a share of stock)}} \tag{24.3}$$

Equation (24.3) generalizes equation (24.1). We define the *firm's value net of debt* to be the total firm value less the value of the debt. The total firm value is $4,200 in our example and there is no debt. The # stands for the number of shares outstanding, which is 2 in our example. The ratio on the left is the value of a share of stock. The gain on a warrant can be written as:

Gain from Exercising a Single Warrant:

$$\underbrace{\frac{\text{Firm's value net of debt} + \text{Exercise price} \times \#_w}{\# + \#_w} = \text{Exercise price}}_{\text{(Value of a share of stock after warrant is exercised)}} \tag{24.4}$$

Equation (24.4) generalizes (24.2). The numerator of the left-hand term is the firm's value net of debt *after* the warrant is exercised. It is the sum of the firm's value net of debt *prior* to the warrant's exercise plus the proceeds the firm receives from the exercise. The proceeds equal the product of the exercise price multiplied by the number of warrants. The number of warrants appears as $\#_w$. (Our analysis uses the plausible assumption that all warrants in the money will be exercised.) Note that $\#_w = 1$ in our numerical example. The denominator, $\# + \#_w$, is the number of shares outstanding *after* the exercise of the warrants. The ratio on the left is the value of a share of stock after exercise. By rearranging terms, equation (24.4) can be rewritten as:[5]

Gain from Exercising a Single Warrant:

$$\frac{\#}{\# + \#_w} \times \left(\frac{\text{Firm's value net of debt}}{\#} - \text{Exercise price} \right) \qquad (24.5)$$

(Gain from a call on a firm with no warrants)

Formula (24.5) relates the gain on a warrant to the gain on a call. Note that the term within parentheses is (24.3). Thus, the gain from exercising a warrant is a proportion of the gain from exercising a call in a firm without warrants. The proportion $\#/(\# + \#_w)$ is the ratio of the number of shares in the firm without warrants to the number of shares after all the warrants have been exercised. This ratio must always be less than 1. Thus, the gain on a warrant must be less than the gain on an identical call in a firm without warrants. Note that $\#/(\# + \#_w) = \frac{2}{3}$ in our example, which explains why Mrs. Fiske gains $300 on her call yet gains only $200 on her warrant.

The preceding implies that the Black-Scholes model must be adjusted for warrants. When a call option is issued to Mrs. Fiske, we know that the exercise price is $1,800 and the time to expiration is one year. Though we have posited neither the price of the stock, the variance of the stock, nor the interest rate, we could easily provide these data for a real-world situation. Thus, we could use the Black-Scholes model to value Mrs. Fiske's call.

Suppose that the warrant is to be issued tomorrow to Mrs. Fiske. We know the number of warrants to be issued, the warrant's expiration date, and the exercise price. Using our assumption that the warrant proceeds are immediately paid out as a dividend, we could use the Black-Scholes model to value the warrant. We would first calculate the value of an identical call. The warrant price is the call price multiplied by the ratio $\#/(\# + \#_w)$. As mentioned earlier, this ratio is $\frac{2}{3}$ in our example.

24.4 Convertible Bonds

A **convertible bond** is similar to a bond with warrants. The most important difference is that a bond with warrants can be separated into distinct securities and a convertible bond cannot. A convertible bond gives the holder the right to exchange it for a given number of shares of stock anytime up to and including the maturity date of the bond.

Preferred stock can frequently be converted into common stock. A convertible preferred stock is the same as a convertible bond except that it has an infinite maturity date.

---

[5]To derive formula (24.5), one should separate "Exercise price" in (24.4). This yields

$$\frac{\text{Firm's value net of debt}}{\# + \#_w} - \frac{\#}{\# + \#_w} \times \text{Exercise price}$$

By rearranging terms, one can obtain formula (24.5).

EXAMPLE

Oceandoor Technology is one of the most important manufacturers of rigid magnetic disk drives for computers. Its stock is traded over the counter (OTC).

On November 1, 2003, Oceandoor raised $300 million by issuing 6.75 percent convertible subordinated debentures due in 2022. It planned to use the proceeds to invest in new plant and equipment. Like typical debentures, they had a sinking fund and were callable. Oceandoor's bonds differed from other debentures in their convertible feature: Each bond was convertible into 23.53 shares of common stock of Oceandoor anytime before maturity. The number of shares received for each bond (23.53 in this example) is called the **conversion ratio.**

Bond traders also speak of the **conversion price** of the bond. This is calculated as the ratio of the face value of the bond to the conversion ratio. Because the face value of each Oceandoor bond was $1,000, the conversion price was $42.5 ($1,000/23.53). The bondholders of Oceandoor could give up bonds with a face value of $1,000 and receive 23.53 shares of Oceandoor common stock. This was equivalent to paying $42.5 ($1,000/23.53) for each share of Oceandoor common stock received.

When Oceandoor issued its convertible bonds, its common stock was trading at $22.625 per share. The conversion price of $42.5 was 88 percent higher than the actual common stock price. This 88 percent is referred to as the **conversion premium.** It reflects the fact that the conversion option in Oceandoor convertible bonds was *out of the money.* This conversion premium is typical.

Convertibles are almost always protected against stock splits and stock dividends. If Oceandoor's common stock had been split two for one, the conversion ratio would have been increased from 23.53 to 47.06.

Conversion ratio, conversion price, and conversion premium are well-known terms in the real world. For that reason alone, the student should master the concepts. However, conversion price and conversion premium implicitly assume that the bond is selling at par. If the bond is selling at another price, the terms have little meaning. By contrast, conversion ratio can have a meaningful interpretation regardless of the price of the bond.

EXAMPLE

In January 1999, Amazon.com issued $1.25 billion in convertible bonds. At the time, it was the largest such issue in history. The bonds have a 4.75 percent coupon rate, mature in 2009, and can be converted into Amazon's common stock at a conversion price of $156.05 per share. Each bond has a face value of $1,000, and so the owner can receive 1,000/156.05 = 6.41 shares of Amazon's common stock. This amount of shares is the conversion ratio. When Amazon issued its convertible bonds, its stock was trading at $123 per share. Thus the conversion price of $156.05 was about 27 percent higher than the actual stock price. In 2003, Amazon's stock was trading at only $32—so the conversion feature was not very attractive.

Concept Question

1. What are the conversion ratio, the conversion price, and the conversion premium?

24.5 The Value of Convertible Bonds

The value of a convertible bond can be described in terms of three components: straight bond value, conversion value, and option value. We examine these three components below.

Straight Bond Value

The straight bond value is what the convertible bonds would sell for if they could not be converted into common stock. It will depend on the general level of interest rates and on

As shown, the minimum, or floor, value of a convertible bond is either its
straight bond value or its conversion value, whichever is greater.

the default risk. Suppose that straight debentures issued by Oceandoor had been rated A,
and A-rated bonds were priced to yield 4 percent on November 1, 2003. The straight bond
value of Oceandoor convertible bonds can be determined by discounting the $33.75 semi-
annual coupon payment and principal amount at 4 percent.[6]

$$\text{Straight bond} = \sum_{t=1}^{37} \frac{\$33.75}{1.04^t} + \frac{\$1,000}{(1.04)^{37}}$$

$$= \$33.75 \times A_{0.04}^{37} + \frac{\$1,000}{(1.04)^{37}}$$

$$= \$646.06 + \$234.3$$

$$= \$880.36$$

The straight bond value of a convertible bond is a minimum value. The price of Oceandoor's convertible could not have gone lower than the straight bond value.

Figure 24.2 illustrates the relationship between straight bond value and stock price. In
Figure 24.2 we have been somewhat dramatic and implicitly assumed that the convertible
bond is default free. In this case the straight bond value does not depend on the stock price
and so it is graphed as a straight line.

Conversion Value

The value of convertible bonds depends on conversion value. **Conversion value** is what
the bonds would be worth if they were immediately converted into the common stock at
current prices. Typically, conversion value is computed by multiplying the number of
shares of common stock that will be received when the bond is converted by the current
price of the common stock.

[6]This formula assumes that coupons are paid annually.

FIGURE 24.3

Value of a Convertible Bond versus the Value of the Stock for a Given Interest Rate

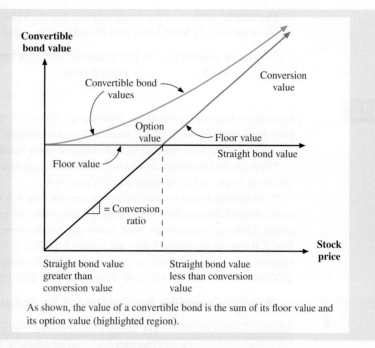

As shown, the value of a convertible bond is the sum of its floor value and its option value (highlighted region).

On November 1, 2003, each Oceandoor convertible bond could have been converted into 23.53 shares of Oceandoor common stock. Oceandoor common was selling for $22.625. Thus, the conversion value was 23.53 × $22.625 = $532.37. A convertible cannot sell for less than its conversion value. Arbitrage prevents this from happening. If Oceandoor's convertible sold for less than $532.37, investors would have bought the bonds and converted them into common stock and sold the stock. The profit would have been the difference between the value of the stock sold and the bond's conversion value.

Thus, convertible bonds have two minimum values: the straight bond value and the conversion value. The conversion value is determined by the value of the firm's underlying common stock. This is illustrated in Figure 24.2. As the value of common stock rises and falls, the conversion price rises and falls with it. When the value of Oceandoor's common stock increased by $1, the conversion value of its convertible bonds increased by $23.53.

Option Value

The value of a convertible bond will generally exceed both the straight bond value and the conversion value.[7] This occurs because holders of convertibles need not convert immediately. Instead, by waiting they can take advantage of whichever is greater in the future, the straight bond value or the conversion value. This option to wait has value, and it raises the value over both the straight bond value and the conversion value.

When the value of the firm is low, the value of convertible bonds is most significantly influenced by their underlying value as straight debt. However, when the value of the firm is very high, the value of convertible bonds is mostly determined by their underlying conversion value. This is illustrated in Figure 24.3.

_____

[7]The most plausible exception is when conversion would provide the investor with a dividend much greater than the interest available prior to conversion. The optimal strategy here could very well be to convert immediately, implying that the market value of the bond would exactly equal the conversion value. Other exceptions occur when the firm is in default or the bondholders are forced to convert.

The bottom portion of the figure implies that the value of a convertible bond is the maximum of its straight bond value and its conversion value, plus its option value:

$$\text{Value of convertible bond} = \text{The greater of (Straight bond value, Conversion value)} + \text{Option value}$$

EXAMPLE

Suppose the Moulton Company has outstanding 1,000 shares of common stock and 100 bonds. Each bond has a face value of $1,000 at maturity. They are discount bonds and pay no coupons. At maturity each bond can be converted into 10 shares of newly issued common stock.

What are the circumstances that will make it advantageous for the holders of Moulton convertible bonds to convert to common stock at maturity?

If the holders of the convertible bonds convert, they will receive $100 \times 10 = 1,000$ shares of common stock. Because there were already 1,000 shares, the total number of shares outstanding becomes 2,000 upon conversion. Thus, converting bondholders own 50 percent of the value of the firm, V. If they do not convert, they will receive $100,000 or V, whichever is less. The choice for the holders of the Moulton bonds is obvious. They should convert if 50 percent of V is greater than $100,000. This will be true whenever V is greater than $200,000. This is illustrated as follows:

Payoff to Convertible Bondholders and Stockholders of the Moulton Company

	(1) $V \le \$100,000$	(2) $\$100,000 < V \le \$200,000$	(3) $V > \$200,000$
Decision:	Bondholders will not convert	Bondholders will not convert	Bondholders will convert
Convertible bondholders	V	$100,000	0.5V
Stockholders	0	$V - \$100,000$	0.5V

Concept Questions

1. What three elements make up the value of a convertible bond?
2. Describe the payoff structure of convertible bonds.

24.6 Reasons for Issuing Warrants and Convertibles

Probably there is no other area of corporate finance where real-world practitioners get as confused as they do on the reasons for issuing convertible debt. In order to separate fact from fantasy, we present a rather structured argument. We first compare convertible debt with straight debt. Then we compare convertible debt with equity. For each comparison, we ask in what situations is the firm better off with convertible debt and in what situations is it worse off.

Convertible Debt versus Straight Debt

Convertible debt pays a lower interest rate than does otherwise identical straight debt. For example, if the interest rate is 10 percent on straight debt, the interest rate on convertible debt might be 9 percent. Investors will accept a lower interest rate on a convertible because of the potential gain from conversion.

Imagine a firm that seriously considers both convertible debt and straight debt, finally deciding to issue convertibles. When would this decision have benefited the firm and when would it have hurt the firm? We consider two situations.

The Stock Price Later Rises So That Conversion Is Indicated   The firm clearly likes to see the stock price rise. However, it would have benefited even more had it previously issued straight debt instead of a convertible. While the firm paid out a lower interest rate than it would have with straight debt, it was obligated to sell the convertible holders a chunk of the equity at a below-market price.

The Stock Price Later Falls or Does Not Rise Enough to Justify Conversion   The firm hates to see the stock price fall. However, as long as the stock price does fall, it is glad that it had previously issued convertible debt instead of straight debt. This is because the interest rate on convertible debt is lower. Because conversion does not take place, our comparison of interest rates is all that is needed.

Summary   Compared to straight debt, the firm is worse off having issued convertible debt if the underlying stock subsequently does well. The firm is better off having issued convertible debt if the underlying stock subsequently does poorly. In an efficient market, one cannot predict future stock price. Thus, we cannot argue that convertibles either dominate or are dominated by straight debt.

Convertible Debt versus Common Stock

Next, imagine a firm that seriously considers both convertible debt and common stock finally decides to issue convertibles. When would this decision benefit the firm and when would it hurt the firm? We consider our two situations.

The Stock Price Later Rises So That Conversion Is Indicated   The firm is better off having previously issued a convertible instead of equity. To see this, consider the Oceandoor case. The firm could have issued stock for $22. Instead, by issuing a convertible, the firm effectively received $42.50 for a share upon conversion.

The Stock Price Later Falls or Does Not Rise Enough to Justify Conversion   No firm wants to see the stock price fall. However, given that the price did fall, the firm would have been better off if it had previously issued stock instead of a convertible. The firm would have benefited by issuing stock above its later market price. That is, the firm would have received more than the subsequent worth of the stock. However, the drop in stock price did not affect the value of the convertible much because the straight bond value serves as a floor.

Summary   Compared with equity, the firm is better off having issued convertible debt if the underlying stock subsequently does well. The firm is worse off having issued convertible debt if the underlying stock subsequently does poorly. One cannot predict future stock price in an efficient market. Thus, we cannot argue that issuing convertibles is better or worse than issuing equity. The above analysis is summarized in Table 24.2.

Modigliani-Miller (MM) pointed out that, abstracting from taxes and bankruptcy costs, the firm is indifferent to whether it issues stock or issues debt. The MM relationship is a quite general one. Their pedagogy could be adjusted to show that the firm is indifferent to whether it issues convertibles or issues other instruments. To save space (and the patience of students), we have omitted a full-blown proof of MM in a world with convertibles. However, the above results are perfectly consistent with MM. Now we turn to the real-world view of convertibles.

The "Free Lunch" Story

The preceding discussion suggests that issuing a convertible bond is no better and no worse than issuing other instruments. Unfortunately, many corporate executives fall into the trap

TABLE 24.2		**If Firm Subsequently Does Poorly**	**If Firm Subsequently Prospers**
The Case for and against Convertible Bonds (CBs)	Convertible bonds (CBs)	No conversion because of low stock price	Conversion because of high stock price
	Compared to:		
	Straight bonds	CBs provide cheap financing because coupon rate is lower.	CBs provide expensive financing because bonds are converted, which dilutes existing equity.
	Common stock	CBs provide expensive financing because firm could have issued common stock at high prices.	CBs provide cheap financing because firm issues stock at high prices when bonds are converted.

of arguing that issuing convertible debt is actually better than issuing alternative instruments. This is a free lunch type of explanation, of which we are quite critical.

EXAMPLE

The stock price of RW Company is $20. Suppose this company can issue subordinated debentures at 10 percent. It can also issue convertible bonds at 6 percent with a conversion value of $800. The conversion value means that the holders can convert a convertible bond into 40 ($800/$20) shares of common stock.

A company treasurer who believes in free lunches might argue that convertible bonds should be issued because they represent a cheaper source of financing than either subordinated bonds or common stock. The treasurer will point out that if the company does poorly and the price does not rise above $20, the convertible bondholders will not convert the bonds into common stock. In this case, the company will have obtained debt financing at below-market rates by attaching worthless equity kickers. On the other hand, if the firm does well and the price of its common stock rises to $25 or above, convertible holders will convert. The company will issue 40 shares. The company will receive a bond with face value of $1,000 in exchange for issuing 40 shares of common stock, implying a conversion price of $25. The company will have issued common stock *de facto* at $25 per share, or 20 percent above the $20 common-stock price prevailing when the convertible bonds were issued. This enables it to lower its cost of equity capital. Thus, the treasurer happily points out, regardless of whether the company does well or poorly, convertible bonds are the cheapest form of financing.

Although this argument may sound quite plausible at first glance, there is a flaw. The treasurer is comparing convertible financing *with straight debt* when the stock subsequently falls. However, the treasurer compares convertible financing *with common stock* when the stock subsequently rises. This is an unfair mixing of comparisons. By contrast, our analysis of Table 24.2 was fair, because we examined both stock increases and decreases when comparing a convertible with each alternative instrument. We found that no single alternative dominated convertible bonds in *both* up and down markets.

The "Expensive Lunch" Story

Suppose we stand the treasurer's argument on its head by comparing (1) convertible financing with straight debt when the stock rises and (2) convertible financing with equity when the stock falls.

From Table 24.2, we see that convertible debt is more expensive than straight debt when the stock subsequently rises. The firm's obligation to sell convertible holders a chunk of the equity at a below-market price more than offsets the lower interest rate on a convertible.

Also from Table 24.2, we see that convertible debt is more expensive than equity when the stock subsequently falls. Had the firm issued stock, it would have received a price higher than its subsequent worth. Therefore, the expensive lunch story implies that convertible debt is an inferior form of financing. Of course, we dismiss both the free lunch and the expensive lunch arguments.

A Reconciliation

In an efficient financial market there is neither a free lunch nor an expensive lunch. Convertible bonds can be neither cheaper nor more expensive than other instruments. A convertible bond is a package of straight debt and an option to buy common stock. The difference between the market value of a convertible bond and the value of a straight bond is the price investors pay for the call-option feature. In an efficient market this is a fair price.

In general, if a company prospers, issuing convertible bonds will turn out to be worse than issuing straight bonds and better than issuing common stock. In contrast, if a company does poorly, convertible bonds will turn out to be better than issuing straight bonds and worse than issuing common stock.

Concept
Questions

1. **What is wrong with the simple view that it is cheaper to issue a bond with a warrant or a convertible feature because the required coupon is lower?**
2. **What is wrong with the Free Lunch story?**
3. **What is wrong with the Expensive Lunch story?**

24.7 Why Are Warrants and Convertibles Issued?

From studies it is known that firms that issue convertible bonds are different from other firms. Here are some of the differences:

1. The bond ratings of firms using convertibles are lower than those of other firms.[8]
2. Convertibles tend to be used by smaller firms with high growth rates and more financial leverage.[9]
3. Convertibles are usually subordinated and unsecured.

The kind of company that uses convertibles provides clues to why they are issued. Here are some explanations that make sense.

Matching Cash Flows

If financing is costly, it makes sense to issue securities whose cash flows match those of the firm. A young, risky, and, it hopes, growing firm might prefer to issue convertibles or bonds with warrants because these will have lower initial interest costs. When the firm is successful, the convertibles (or warrants) will be converted. This causes expensive dilution, but it occurs when the firm can most afford it.

Risk Synergy

Another argument for convertible bonds and bonds with warrants is that they are useful when it is very costly to assess the risk of the issuing company. Suppose you are evaluating a new product by a start-up company. The new product is a biogenetic virus that may increase the yields of corn crops in northern climates. It may also cause cancer. This type of product is difficult to value properly. Thus, the risk of the company is very hard to determine:

---

[8]E. F. Brigham, "An Analysis of Convertible Debentures," *Journal of Finance* 21 (1966).

[9]W. H. Mikkelson, "Convertible Calls and Security Returns," *Journal of Financial Economics* 9 (September 1981), p. 3.

		Firm Risk	
		Low	**High**
TABLE 24.3	Straight bond yield	10%	15%
A Hypothetical Case of the Yields on Convertible Bonds*	Convertible bond yield	6	7

*The yields on straight bonds reflect the risk of default. The yields on convertibles are not sensitive to default risk.

it may be high, or it may be low. If you could be sure the risk of the company was high, you would price the bonds for a high yield, say 15 percent. If it was low, you would price them at a lower yield, say 10 percent.

Convertible bonds and bonds with warrants can protect somewhat against mistakes of risk evaluation. Convertible bonds and bonds with warrants have two components: straight bonds and call options on the company's underlying stock. If the company turns out to be a low-risk company, the straight bond component will have high value and the call option will have low value. However, if the company turns out to be a high-risk company, the straight bond component will have low value and the call option will have high value. This is illustrated in Table 24.3.

However, although risk has effects on value that cancel each other out in convertibles and bonds with warrants, the market and the buyer nevertheless must make an assessment of the firm's potential to value securities, and it is not clear that the effort involved is that much less than is required for a straight bond.

Agency Costs

Convertible bonds can resolve agency problems associated with raising money. In a previous chapter we showed that straight bonds are like risk-free bonds minus a put option on the assets of the firm. This creates an incentive for creditors to force the firm into low-risk activities. In contrast, holders of common stock have incentives to adopt high-risk projects. High-risk projects with negative NPV transfer wealth from bondholders to stockholders. If these conflicts cannot be resolved, the firm may be forced to pass up profitable investment opportunities. However, because convertible bonds have an equity component, less expropriation of wealth can occur when convertible debt is issued instead of straight debt.[10] In other words, convertible bonds mitigate agency costs. One implication is that convertible bonds have less-restrictive debt covenants than do straight bonds in the real world. Casual empirical evidence seems to bear this out.

Backdoor Equity

A popular theory of convertibles views them as backdoor equity.[11] The basic story is that young, small, high-growth firms cannot usually issue debt on reasonable terms due to high financial distress costs. However, the owners may be unwilling to issue equity if current stock prices are too low.

Lewis, Ragolski, and Seward examine the risk shifting and backdoor equity theories of convertible bond debt. They find evidence for both theories.

Concept
Question

1. Why do firms issue convertible bonds and bonds with warrants?

[10]A. Barnea, R. A. Haugen, and L. Senbet, *Agency Problems and Financial Contracting,* Prentice Hall Foundations of Science Series (New York: Prentice Hall, 1985), Chapter VI.

[11]J. Stein, "Convertible Bonds as Backdoor Equity Financing," *Journal of Financial Economics,* 32 (1992). See also Craig M. Lewis, Richard J. Ragolski, and James K. Seward, "Understanding the Design of Convertible Debt," *The Journal of Applied Corporate Finance* (Spring, 1998).

24.8 Conversion Policy

There is one aspect of convertible bonds that we have omitted so far. Firms are frequently granted a call option on the bond. The typical arrangements for calling a convertible bond are simple. When the bond is called, the holder has about 30 days to choose between the following:

1. Converting the bond to common stock at the conversion ratio.
2. Surrendering the bond and receiving the call price in cash.

What should bondholders do? It should be obvious that if the conversion value of the bond is greater than the call price, conversion is better than surrender; and if the conversion value is less than the call price, surrender is better than conversion. If the conversion value is greater than the call price, the call is said to **force conversion.**

What should financial managers do? Calling the bonds does not change the value of the firm as a whole. However, an optimal call policy can benefit the stockholders at the expense of the bondholders. Because we are speaking of dividing a pie of fixed size, the optimal call policy is very simple: Do whatever the bondholders do not want you to do.

Bondholders would love the stockholders to call the bonds when the bond's market value is below the call price. Shareholders would be giving bondholders extra value. Alternatively, should the value of the bonds rise above the call price, the bondholders would love the stockholders not to call the bonds, because bondholders would be allowed to hold onto a valuable asset.

There is only one policy left. This is the policy that maximizes shareholder value and minimizes bondholder value. This policy is:

Call the bond when its value is equal to the call price.

It is a puzzle that firms do not always call convertible bonds when the conversion value reaches the call price. Ingersoll examined the call policies of 124 firms between 1968 and 1975.[12] In most cases he found that the company waited to call the bonds until the conversion value was much higher than the call price. The median company waited until the conversion value of its bonds was 44 percent higher than the call price. This is not even close to the above optimal strategy. Why?

One reason is that if firms attempt to implement the above optimal strategy, it may not be truly optimal. Recall that bondholders have 30 days to decide whether to convert bonds to common stock or to surrender bonds for the call price in cash. In 30 days, the stock price could drop, forcing the conversion value below the call price. If so, the convertible is "out of the money" and the firm is giving away money. The firm would be giving up cash for common stock worth much less. Because of this possibility, firms in the real world usually wait until the conversion value is substantially above the call price before they trigger the call.[13] This is sensible.

Concept Questions	1. **Why will convertible bonds not be voluntarily converted to stock before expiration?**
	2. **When should firms force conversion of convertibles? Why?**

---

[12]J. Ingersoll, "An Examination of Corporate Call Policies on Convertible Bonds," *Journal of Finance* (May 1977). See also M. Harris and A. Raviv, "A Sequential Signalling Model of Convertible Debt Policy," *Journal of Finance* (December 1985). Harris and Raviv describe a signal equilibrium that is consistent with Ingersoll's result. They show that managers with favorable information will delay calls to avoid depressing stock prices.

[13]See Paul Asquith, "Convertible Bonds Are Not Called Late," *Journal of Finance* (September 1995). On the other hand, the stock market usually reacts negatively to the announcement of a call. For example, see A. K. Singh, A. R. Cowan, and N. Nayan, "Underwritten Calls of Convertible Bonds," *Journal of Financial Economics* (March 1991) and M. A. Mazzeo and W. T. Moore, "Liquidity Costs and Stock Price Response to Convertible Security Calls," *Journal of Business* (July 1992).

Ederington, Caton, and Campbell tested various theories on when it is optimal to call convertibles. They found evidence consistent for the preceding 30-day "safety margin" theory. They also found that calls of in-the-money convertibles are highly unlikely if dividends to be received (after conversion) exceed the company's interest payment. See Louis H. Ederington, Gary L. Caton, and Cynthia J. Campbell, "To Call or Not to Call Convertible Debt," *Financial Management* (Spring 1997).

24.9 SUMMARY AND CONCLUSIONS

1. A warrant gives the holder the right to buy shares of common stock at an exercise price for a given period of time. Typically, warrants are issued in a package with privately placed bonds. Afterward they become detached and trade separately.

2. A convertible bond is a combination of a straight bond and a call option. The holder can give up the bond in exchange for shares of stock.

3. Convertible bonds and warrants are like call options. However, there are some important differences:
   a. Warrants and convertible securities are issued by corporations. Call options are traded between individual investors.
      1. Warrants are usually issued privately and are combined with a bond. In most cases the warrants can be detached immediately after the issue. In some cases warrants are issued with preferred stock, with common stock, or in executive compensation programs.
      2. Convertibles are usually bonds that can be converted into common stock.
      3. Call options are sold separately by individual investors (called *writers* of call options).
   b. Warrants and call options are exercised for cash. The holder of a warrant gives the company cash and receives new shares of the company's stock. The holder of a call option gives another individual cash in exchange for shares of stock. When someone converts a bond, it is exchanged for common stock. As a consequence, bonds with warrants and convertible bonds have different effects on corporate cash flow and capital structure.
   c. Warrants and convertibles cause dilution to the existing shareholders. When warrants are exercised and convertible bonds converted, the company must issue new shares of common stock. The percentage ownership of the existing shareholders will decline. New shares are not issued when call options are exercised.

4. Many arguments, both plausible and implausible, are given for issuing convertible bonds and bonds with warrants. One plausible rationale for such bonds has to do with risk. Convertibles and bonds with warrants are associated with risky companies. Lenders can do several things to protect themselves from high-risk companies:
   a. They can require high yields.
   b. They can lend less or not at all to firms whose risk is difficult to assess.
   c. They can impose severe restrictions on such debt.
   Another useful way to protect against risk is to issue bonds with equity kickers. This gives the lenders the chance to benefit from risks and reduces the conflicts between bondholders and stockholders concerning risk.

5. A puzzle particularly vexes financial researchers: Convertible bonds usually have call provisions. Companies appear to delay calling convertibles until the conversion value greatly exceeds the call price. From the shareholders' standpoint, the optimal call policy would be to call the convertibles when the conversion value equals the call price.

KEY TERMS

conversion premium, *683*

conversion price, *683*

conversion ratio, *683*

conversion value, *684*

convertible bond, *682*

force conversion, *691*

warrants, *677*

SUGGESTED READINGS

The following articles analyze when it is optimal to force conversion of convertible bonds:

Asquith, P. "Convertible Bonds Are Not Called Late." *Journal of Finance* (September 1995).

Brennan, M., and E. Schwartz. "Convertible Bonds: Valuation and Optimal Strategies for Call Conversion." *Journal of Finance* (December 1977).

For more on convertibles, see:

Finnerty, John D., and D. R. Emery. *A Practitioner's Guide to Debt Management.* Boston: Harvard Business School Press, 2001.

**QUESTIONS
& PROBLEMS**

WARRANTS

24.1   Define:
    a. Warrant
    b. Convertible bond

24.2   Explain the following limits on the prices of warrants:
    a. If the stock price is below the exercise price of the warrant, the lower bound on the price of a warrant is zero.
    b. If the stock price is above the exercise price of the warrant, the lower bound on the price of a warrant is the difference between the stock price and the exercise price.
    c. An upper bound on the price of any warrant is the current value of the firm's stock.

24.3   **a.** What is the primary difference between warrants and call options?
    b. Why is this difference important? What is dilution?

24.4   Survivor, Inc., an all-equity firm, has two shares of common stock outstanding. Yesterday, the firm's assets consisted of seven ounces of platinum, currently worth $500 per ounce. Today, Survivor issued Tina a warrant for its fair value of $500. The warrant gives Tina the right to buy a single share of the firm's common stock for $1,800 and can be exercised only on its expiration date one year from today. The firm used the proceeds from the issuance to immediately purchase an additional ounce of platinum.
    a. What was the price of a single share of Survivor's stock *before* the warrant was issued?
    b. What is the price of a single share of the Survivor's stock immediately *after* the warrant has been issued?
    c. Suppose platinum is selling for $520 per ounce on the warrant's expiration date in one year. What is the value of a single share of Survivor's common stock on the warrant's expiration date?

24.5   General Modems has five-year warrants that currently trade in the open market. Each warrant gives its owner the right to purchase one share of the firm's common stock for an exercise price of $10.
    a. Suppose General Modem's stock is currently trading for $8 per share. What is the lower limit on the price of the warrant? What is the upper limit?
    b. Suppose General Modem's stock is currently trading for $12 per share. What is the lower limit on the price of the warrant? What is the upper limit?

24.6   The capital structure of Ricketti Enterprises, Inc. consists of 10 million shares of common stock and 1 million warrants. Each warrant gives its owner the right to purchase one share of common stock for an exercise price of $15. Ricketti's current stock price is $17 per share. Each warrant is currently worth $3. What is the firm's new stock price if all warrant holders decide to exercise today? Assume the market does not expect the warrants to be exercised, since the price per warrant is above the exercise value of each warrant ($2 = $17 − $15).

24.7   A warrant with six months until expiration entitles its owner to buy 10 shares of the issuing firm's common stock for an exercise price of $21 per share. If the current market price of the stock is $15 per share, will the market price of the warrant equal zero? Explain.

24.8   Warrant X gives its owner the right to purchase three shares of newly issued common stock of Firm Y for an exercise price of $20 per share. The current market price of Firm Y is $25 per share. What is the minimum value of Warrant X? Explain.

24.9   Superior Clamps, Inc., has a capital structure consisting of 4 million shares of common stock and 500,000 warrants. Each warrant gives its owner the right to purchase one share of newly issued common stock for an exercise price of $20. The warrants are European and will expire one year from today. The market value of Superior's assets is $88 million. The annual variance of the continuously compounded returns on the firm's assets is 0.04. Treasury bills that mature in one year yield a continuously compounded interest rate of 7 percent per annum. Superior pays no dividends. Use the Black–Scholes model to determine the value of a single warrant.

24.10   Omega Airline's capital structure consists of 1.5 million shares of common stock and $10 million (face value) of zero-coupon bonds that mature in six months. The firm just announced that it will issue warrants with an exercise price of $95 and six months until expiration in order to raise the funds to pay off its maturing debt. Each warrant can only be exercised at expiration and gives its owner the right to buy a single newly issued share of Omega's common stock. The firm will place the proceeds from the warrant issue immediately into Treasury bills. Omega's market-value balance sheet shows that the firm will have assets worth $150 million after announcement. Omega pays no dividends. The annual variance of the continuously compounded returns on the firm's assets is 0.5625, and Treasury bills that mature in six months yield a continuously compounded interest rate of 10 percent per annum. Use the Black-Scholes model to determine the number of warrants that Omega must issue today in order to be able to use the proceeds from the sale to pay off the firm's debt obligation in six months.

CONVERTIBLE
BONDS

24.11 An analyst has recently informed you that at the issuance of Firm A's convertible bonds, one of the two following sets of relationships existed:

	Scenario 1	Scenario 2
Face value of each convertible bond	$1,000	$1,000
Straight value of each convertible bond	900	950
Market value of each convertible bond	1,000	900

Assume the bonds are available for immediate conversion. Which of the two scenarios do you believe is more likely? Explain.

24.12 Sportime Fitness Center, Inc., issued convertible bonds, each with a par value of $1,000 and a conversion price of $25 per share. The bonds are available for immediate conversion. The current price of Sportime's common stock is $24 per share. The current market price of each of the firm's convertible bonds is $990. The convertible bond's straight value is not known.
   a. What is the minimum price that each of Sportime's convertible bonds should sell for?
   b. Explain the difference between the current market price of each convertible bond and the value of the common stock into which it can be immediately converted.

24.13 Rob Stevens is the chief executive officer of Isner Construction, Inc., and owns 500,000 shares of the firm's common stock. Isner currently has 4 million shares of common stock and $20 million worth of convertible bonds (face value) outstanding. Each convertible bond has a face value of $1,000 and a conversion price of $20. Each share of common stock is currently selling for $25.
   a. What percentage of the firm's common stock does Rob Stevens own?
   b. If Isner decides to call the convertible bonds and force conversion, what percentage of the firm's common stock will Rob Stevens own? Rob does not own any convertible bonds.

24.14 Hannon Home Products, Inc., recently issued $430,000 worth of 8 percent convertible debentures. Each convertible bond has a face value of $1,000. Each convertible bond can be converted into 28 shares of the firm's common stock anytime before maturity. The current price of Hannon's common stock is $31.25 per share, and the market value of each of Hannon's convertible bonds is $1,180. Answer the following questions related to Hannon's convertible bonds:
   a. What is the conversion ratio?
   b. What is the conversion price?
   c. What is the conversion premium?
   d. What is the conversion value?
   e. If the value of Hannon's common stock increases by $2, what will the conversion value be?

24.15 MGH Medical Supplies, Inc., recently issued a single zero-coupon convertible bond due 10 years from today. The convertible bond, which is currently trading for $400 in the open market, has a face value of $1,000 and can be converted into 25 shares of common stock. Each share of MGH's common stock is currently selling for $12, and otherwise identical non-convertible bonds yield 10 percent per annum (effective annual yield).

a. What is the straight value of the convertible bond?

b. What is its conversion value?

c. What is its option value?

24.16 A $1,000 par convertible debenture has a conversion price for common stock of $180 per share. If the common stock is currently selling for $60 per share, what is the conversion value of the convertible bond?

24.17 Consider a 30-year callable, convertible bond issued by Firm A. The bond has a face value of $1,000, makes 6 percent annual coupon payments, and has a conversion price of $125. Firm A's stock is currently selling for $35 per share. The owner of the bond will be forced to convert if the bond's conversion value is ever greater than or equal to $1,100. The required return on an otherwise identical nonconvertible bond is 12 percent per annum.

a. What is the straight value of the convertible bond?

b. What is its conversion value?

c. If Firm A's stock price were to grow by 15 percent per year forever, how long would it take for the bond's conversion value to exceed $1,100?

Derivatives and Hedging Risk

EXECUTIVE SUMMARY

Hardly a day seems to go by without a story in the popular press about some firm that has taken a major hit to its bottom line from its activities in the derivatives markets. Perhaps the largest losses due to derivative trading involved the U.S. firm MG Refining and Marketing (MGRM) and its German parent Metallgesellschaft (MGAG).[1] In late 1993 and early 1994, the financial press reported more than $1 billion of losses from MGRM's trading in oil futures. MGAG is one of Germany's largest industrial firms, generating more than $17 billion in sales revenue in 1993. It has been a closely held firm with 65 percent of its ownership in the hands of seven large institutional owners including the Deutsche Bank, one of the largest banks in the world.

MGRM's derivatives were a central element in its marketing strategy in which it attempted to offset customers' long-term price guarantees (up to 10 years) on gasoline, heating oil, and diesel fuel purchased from MGRM with futures trading. How did MGRM hedge its resulting exposure to spot price increases? Why did MGRM lose so much money? These are some of the questions that we will address in this chapter.

MGRM is not the only firm with reportedly large losses because of derivatives. Procter & Gamble and Gibson Greeting Cards have allegedly lost hundreds of millions of dollars in trading derivatives. The trading of derivatives by Nicholas Leeson is widely credited with having brought down the venerable international merchant bank of Barings. In addition, we have the Piper Jaffrey funds in which investors in a supposedly secure medium-term government bond fund lost 50 percent of their value, and Orange County (California), whose investments lost so much that there was concern about whether basic public services would be disrupted. Whether all of these really happened because of the use or misuse of derivatives will probably be settled years later in the courts, but in the court of public opinion, the culprit has been named—derivatives—and regulators and politicians are deciding on the sentence.

In this chapter we take a close look at derivatives—what they are, how they work, and the uses to which they can be put. When we are done, you will understand how financial derivatives are designed, and you will be able to decide for yourself in an informed fashion what is happening when the next derivatives scandal erupts.

---

[1]C. Culp and M. Miller, "Metallgesellschaft and the Economics of Synthetic Storage," *Journal of Applied Corporate Finance* (Winter 1995), discuss the MGRM derivative losses.

Derivatives, Hedging, and Risk

The name *derivatives* is self-explanatory. A derivative is a financial instrument whose payoffs and values are derived from, or depend on, something else. Often we speak of the thing that the derivative depends on as the *primitive* or the *underlying*. For example, in Chapter 22 we studied how options work. An option is a derivative. The value of a call option depends on the value of the underlying stock on which it is written. Actually, call options are quite complicated examples of derivatives. The vast majority of derivatives are simpler than call options. Most derivatives are forward or futures agreements or what are called swaps, and we will study each of these in some detail.

Why do firms use derivatives? The answer is that derivatives are tools for changing the firm's risk exposure. Someone once said that derivatives are to finance what scalpels are to surgery. By using derivatives, the firm can cut away unwanted portions of risk exposure and even transform the exposures into quite different forms. A central point in finance is that risk is undesirable. In our chapters on risk and return, we pointed out that individuals would choose risky securities only if the expected return compensated for the risk. Similarly, a firm will accept a project with high risk only if the return on the project compensates for this risk. Not surprisingly, then, firms are usually looking for ways to reduce their risk. When the firm reduces its risk exposure with the use of derivatives, it is said to be **hedging.** Hedging offsets the firm's risk, such as the risk in a project, by one or more transactions in the financial markets.

Derivatives can also be used to merely change or even increase the firm's risk exposure. When this occurs, the firm is **speculating** on the movement of some economic variables— those that underlie the derivative. For example, if a derivative is purchased that will rise in value if interest rates rise, and if the firm has no offsetting exposure to interest rate changes, then the firm is speculating that interest rates will rise and give it a profit on its derivatives position. Using derivatives to translate an opinion about whether interest rates or some other economic variable will rise or fall is the opposite of hedging—it is risk enhancing. Speculating on your views on the economy and using derivatives to profit if that view turns out to be correct is not necessarily wrong, but the speculator should always remember that sharp tools cut deep, and if the opinions on which the derivatives position is based turn out to be incorrect, then the consequences can prove costly. Efficient market theory teaches how difficult it is to predict what markets will do. Most of the sad experiences with derivatives have occurred not from their use as instruments for hedging and offsetting risk, but, rather, from speculation.

25.1 Forward Contracts

We can begin our discussion of hedging by considering forward contracts. One frequently hears the one-liner about the gentleman who was shocked to find he had been speaking prose all his life. Forward contracts are a lot like that; you have probably been dealing in them your whole life without knowing it. Suppose you walk into a bookstore on, say, February 1 to buy the best-seller *Eating Habits of the Rich and Famous*. The cashier tells you that the book is currently sold out, but he takes your phone number, saying that he will reorder it for you. He says the book will cost $10.00. If you agree on February 1 to pick up and pay $10.00 for the book when called, you and the cashier have engaged in a **forward contract.** That is, you have agreed both to pay for the book and to pick it up when the bookstore notifies you. Since you are agreeing to buy the book at a later date, you are *buying* a forward contract on February 1. In commodity parlance, you will be **taking delivery** when you pick up the book. The book is called the **deliverable instrument.**

The cashier, acting on behalf of the bookstore, is selling a forward contract. (Alternatively, we say that he is writing a forward contract.) The bookstore has agreed to turn the book over to you at the predetermined price of $10.00 as soon as the book arrives. The act of turning the book over to you is called **making delivery.** Table 25.1 illustrates the book

TABLE 25.1	February I	Date When Book Arrives
Illustration of Book Purchase as a Forward Contract	**Buyer** Buyer agrees to: 1. Pay the purchase price of $10.00. 2. Receive book when book arrives.	Buyer: 1. Pays purchase price of $10.00. 2. Receives book.
	Seller Seller agrees to: 1. Give up book when book arrives. 2. Accept payment of $10.00 when book arrives.	Seller: 1. Gives up book. 2. Accepts payment of $10.00.

Note that cash does not change hands on February 1. Cash changes hands when the book arrives.

purchase. Note that the agreement takes place on February 1. The price is set and the conditions for sale are set at that time. In this case, the sale will occur when the book arrives. In other cases, an exact date of sale would be given. However, *no* cash changes hands on February 1; cash changes hands only when the book arrives.

Though forward contracts may have seemed exotic to you before you began this chapter, you can see that they are quite commonplace. Dealings in your personal life probably have involved forward contracts. Similarly, forward contracts occur all the time in business. Every time a firm orders an item that cannot be delivered immediately, a forward contract takes place. Sometimes, particularly when the order is small, an oral agreement will suffice. Other times, particularly when the order is larger, a written agreement is necessary.

Note that a forward contract is not an option. Both the buyer and the seller are obligated to perform under the terms of the contract. Conversely, the buyer of an option *chooses* whether or not to exercise the option.

A forward contract should be contrasted with a **cash transaction,** that is, a transaction where exchange is immediate. Had the book been on the bookstore's shelf, your purchase of it would constitute a cash transaction.

Concept Questions

1. What is a forward contract?
2. Give examples of forward contracts in your life.

25.2 Futures Contracts

A variant of the forward contract takes place on financial exchanges. Contracts on exchanges are usually called **futures contracts.** For example, consider Table 25.2, which provides data on trading in wheat for Thursday, September 15, 20X1. Let us focus on the September futures contract, which is illustrated in the first row of the table. The first trade of the day in

TABLE 25.2		Data on Wheat Futures Contracts, Thursday, September 15, 20X1						
						Lifetime		
	Open	High	Low	Settle	Change	High	Open Low	Interest
Sept	411	$416\frac{1}{4}$	407	407	$-6\frac{1}{4}$	421	272	423
Oct	427	$432\frac{1}{4}$	422	$423\frac{1}{4}$	$-5\frac{1}{2}$	$432\frac{1}{4}$	289	47,454
Mar X2	$430\frac{1}{2}$	436	$426\frac{1}{2}$	427	$-4\frac{1}{4}$	436	323	42,823
May	409	$443\frac{1}{2}$	404	405	$-5\frac{1}{2}$	420	330	3,422
July	375	$376\frac{1}{2}$	369	$370\frac{3}{4}$	$-6\frac{3}{4}$	395	327	4,805

the contract was for \$4.11 per bushel. The price reached a high of \$4.16$\frac{1}{4}$ during the day and reached a low of \$4.07. The last trade was also at \$4.07. In other words, the contract *closed* or *settled* at \$4.07. The price dropped 6$\frac{1}{4}$ cents per bushel during the day, indicating that the price closed the previous day at \$4.13$\frac{1}{4}$ (\$4.07 + \$0.0625). The contract had been trading for slightly less than a year. During that time, the price reached a high of \$4.21 per bushel and a low of \$2.72 per bushel. The open interest indicates the number of *contracts outstanding*. The number of contracts outstanding at the close of September 15 was 423.

Though we are discussing a futures contract, let us work with a forward contract first. Suppose you wrote a *forward* contract for September wheat at \$4.07. From our discussion on forward contracts, this would mean that you would agree to turn over an agreed-upon number of wheat bushels for \$4.07 per bushel on some specified date in the remainder of the month of September.

A futures contract differs somewhat from a forward contract. First, the seller can choose to deliver the wheat on any day during the delivery month, that is, the month of September. This gives the seller leeway that he would not have with a forward contract. When the seller decides to deliver, he notifies the exchange clearinghouse that he wants to do so. The clearinghouse then notifies an individual who bought a September wheat contract that she must stand ready to accept delivery within the next few days. Though each exchange selects the buyer in a different way, the buyer is generally chosen in a random fashion. Because there are so many buyers at any one time, the buyer selected by the clearinghouse to take delivery almost certainly did not originally buy the contract from the seller now making delivery.

Second, futures contracts are traded on an exchange whereas forward contracts are generally traded off an exchange. Because of this, there is generally a liquid market in futures contracts. A buyer can net out her futures position with a sale. A seller can net out his futures position with a purchase. This procedure is analogous to the *netting-out* process in the options markets. However, the buyer of an options contract can also walk away from the contract by not exercising it. If a buyer of a futures contract does not subsequently sell her contract, she must take delivery.

Third, and most important, the prices of futures contracts are **marked to the market** on a daily basis. That is, suppose that the price falls to \$4.05 on Friday's close. Because all buyers lost two cents per bushel on that day, they each must turn over the two cents per bushel to their brokers within 24 hours, who subsequently remit the proceeds to the clearinghouse. Because all sellers gained two cents per bushel on that day, they each receive two cents per bushel from their brokers. Their brokers are subsequently compensated by the clearinghouse. Because there is a buyer for every seller, the clearinghouse must break even every day.

Now suppose that the price rises to \$4.12 on the close of the following Monday. Each buyer receives seven cents (\$4.12 − \$4.05) per bushel and each seller must pay seven cents per bushel. Finally, suppose that, on Monday, a seller notifies his broker of his intention to deliver.[2] The delivery price will be \$4.12, which is Monday's close.

There are clearly many cash flows in futures contracts. However, after all the dust settles, the *net price* to the buyer must be the price at which she bought originally. That is, an individual buying at Thursday's closing price of \$4.07 and being called to take delivery on Monday pays two cents per bushel on Friday, receives seven cents per bushel on Monday, and takes delivery at \$4.12. Her net outflow per bushel is −\$4.07 (−\$0.02 + \$0.07 − \$4.12), which is the price at which she contracted on Thursday. (Our analysis ignores the time value of money.) Conversely, an individual selling at Thursday's closing price of \$4.07 and

---

[2]He will deliver on Wednesday, two days later.

Illustration of Example Involving Marking to Market in Futures Contracts

Both buyer and seller originally transact at Thursday's closing price. Delivery takes place at Monday's closing price.*

	Thursday, September 19	Friday, September 20	Monday, September 23	Delivery (notification given by seller on Monday)
Closing price: Buyer	$4.07 Buyer purchases futures contract at closing price of $4.07/bushel.	$4.05 Buyer must pay two cents/bushel to clearinghouse within one business day.	$4.12 Buyer receives seven cents/bushel from clearinghouse within one business day.	Buyer pays $4.12 per bushel and receives grain within one business day.

Buyer's net payment of −$4.07 (−$0.02 + $0.07 − $4.12) is the same as if buyer purchased a forward contract for $4.07/bushel.

Seller	Seller sells futures contract at closing price of $4.07/bushel.	Seller receives two cents/bushel from clearinghouse within one business day.	Seller pays seven cents/bushel to clearinghouse within one business day.	Seller receives $4.12 per bushel and delivers grain within one business day.

Seller's net receipts of $4.07 ($0.02 − $0.07 + $4.12) are the same as if seller sold a forward contract for $4.07/bushel.

*For simplicity, we assume that buyer and seller both (1) initially transact at the same time and (2) meet in delivery process. This is actually very unlikely to occur in the real world because the clearinghouse assigns the buyer to take delivery in a random manner.

notifying his broker concerning delivery the following Monday receives two cents per bushel on Friday, pays seven cents per bushel on Monday, and makes delivery at $4.12. His net inflow per bushel is $4.07 ($0.02 − $0.07 + $4.12), which is the price at which he contracted on Thursday.

These details are presented in the adjacent box. For simplicity, we assumed that the buyer and seller who initially transact on Thursday's close meet in the delivery process.[3] The point in the example is that the buyer's net payment of $4.07 per bushel is the same as if she purchased a forward contract for $4.07. Similarly, the seller's net receipt of $4.07 per bushel is the same as if he sold a forward contract for $4.07 per bushel. The only difference is the timing of the cash flows. The buyer of a forward contract knows that he will make a single payment of $4.07 on the expiration date. He will not need to worry about any other cash flows in the interim. Conversely, though the cash flows to the buyer of a futures contract will net to exactly $4.07 as well, the pattern of cash flows is not known ahead of time.

The mark-to-the-market provision on futures contracts has two related effects. The first concerns differences in net present value. For example, a large price drop immediately

---

[3]As pointed out earlier, this is actually very unlikely to occur in the real world.

following purchase means an immediate outpayment for the buyer of a futures contract. Though the net outflow of $4.07 is still the same as under a forward contract, the present value of the cash outflows is greater to the buyer of a futures contract. Of course, the present value of the cash outflows is less to the buyer of a futures contract if a price rise followed purchase.[4] Though this effect could be substantial in certain theoretical circumstances, it appears to be of quite limited importance in the real world.[5]

Second, the firm must have extra liquidity to handle a sudden outflow prior to expiration. This added risk may make the futures contract less attractive.

Students frequently ask, "Why in the world would managers of the commodity exchanges ruin perfectly good contracts with these bizarre mark-to-the-market provisions?" Actually, the reason is a very good one. Consider the forward contract of Table 25.1 concerning the bookstore. Suppose that the public quickly loses interest in *Eating Habits of the Rich and Famous*. By the time the bookstore calls the buyer, other stores may have dropped the price of the book to $6.00. Because the forward contract was for $10.00, the buyer has an incentive not to take delivery on the forward contract. Conversely, should the book become a hot item selling at $15.00, the bookstore may simply not call the buyer.

As indicated, forward contracts have a very big flaw. Whichever way the price of the deliverable instrument moves, one party has an incentive to default. There are many cases where defaults have occurred in the real world. One famous case concerned Coca-Cola. When the company began in the early 20th century, Coca-Cola made an agreement to supply its bottlers and distributors with cola syrup at a constant price *forever*. Of course, subsequent inflation would have caused Coca-Cola to lose large sums of money had they honored the contract. After much legal effort, Coke and its bottlers put an *inflation-escalator clause* in the contract. Another famous case concerned Westinghouse. It seems the firm had promised to deliver uranium to certain utilities at a fixed price. The price of uranium skyrocketed in the 1970s, making Westinghouse lose money on every shipment. Westinghouse defaulted on its agreement. The utilities took Westinghouse to court but did not recover amounts anything near what Westinghouse owed them.

The mark-to-the-market provisions minimize the chance of default on a futures contract. If the price rises, the seller has an incentive to default on a forward contract. However, after paying the clearinghouse, the seller of a futures contract has little reason to default. If the price falls, the same argument can be made for the buyer. Because changes in the value of the underlying asset are recognized daily, there is no accumulation of loss, and the incentive to default is reduced.

Because of this default issue, forward contracts generally involve individuals and institutions who know and can trust each other. But as W. C. Fields said, "Trust everybody, but cut the cards." Lawyers earn a handsome living writing supposedly air-tight forward contracts, even among friends. The genius of the mark-to-the-market system is that is can prevent default where it is most likely to occur—among investors who do not know each other. Textbooks on futures contracts from one or two decades ago usually include a statement such as "No major default has ever occurred on the commodity exchanges." No textbook published after the Hunt Brothers defaulted on silver contracts in the 1970s can make that claim. Nevertheless, the extremely low default rate in futures contracts is truly awe-inspiring.

Futures contracts are traded in three areas: agricultural commodities, metals and petroleum, and financial assets. The extensive array of futures contracts is listed in Table 25.3.

---

[4]The direction is reversed for the seller of a futures contract. However, the general point that the net present value of cash flows may differ between forward and futures contracts holds for sellers as well.

[5]See John C. Cox, John E. Ingersoll, and Steven A. Ross. "The Relationship between Forward and Future Prices," *Journal of Financial Economics* (1981).

TABLE 25.3	**Contract**	**Contract Size**	**Exchange**
Futures Contracts Listed in *The Wall Street Journal*	**Agricultural (grain and oilseeds)**		
	Corn	5,000 bushels	Chicago Board of Trade (CBT)
	Oats	5,000 bushels	CBT
	Soybeans	5,000 bushels	CBT
	Soybean meal	400 tons	CBT
	Soybean oil	60,000 lbs.	CBT
	Wheat	5,000 bushels	CBT
	Wheat	5,000 bushels	Kansas City (KC)
	Wheat	5,000 bushels	Minneapolis
	Barley	20 metric tons	Winnipeg (WPG)
	Flaxseed	20 metric tons	WPG
	Rapeseed	20 metric tons	WPG
	Wheat	20 metric tons	WPG
	Rye	20 metric tons	WPG
	Agricultural (livestock and meat)		
	Cattle (feeder)	44,000 lbs.	Chicago Mercantile Exchange (CME)
	Cattle (live)	40,000 lbs.	CME
	Hogs	30,000 lbs.	CME
	Pork bellies	40,000 lbs.	CME
	Agricultural (food, fiber, and wood)		
	Cocoa	10 metric tons	Coffee, Sugar and Cocoa Exchange (CSCE)
	Coffee	37,500 lbs.	CSCE
	Cotton	50,000 lbs.	New York Cotton Exchange (CTN)
	Orange juice	15,000 lbs.	CTN
	Sugar (world)	112,000 lbs.	CSCE
	Sugar (domestic)	142,000 lbs.	CSCE
	Lumber	150,000 board feet	CME
	Metals and petroleum		
	Copper (standard)	25,000 lbs.	Commodity Exchange in New York (CMX)
	Gold	100 troy oz.	CMX
	Platinum	50 troy oz.	New York Mercantile (NYM)
	Palladium	100 troy oz.	NYM
	Silver	5,000 troy oz.	CMX
	Silver	1,000 troy oz.	CBT
	Crude oil (light sweet)	1,000 barrels	NYM
	Heating oil no. 2	42,000 gallons	NYM
	Gas oil	100 metric tons	International Petroleum Exchange of London (IPEL)
	Gasoline unleaded	42,000 gallons	NYM
	Financial		
	British pound	62,500 pounds	International Monetary Market in Chicago (IMM)
	Australian dollar	100,000 dollars	IMM
	Canadian dollar	100,000 dollars	IMM
	Japanese yen	12.5 million yen	IMM
	Swiss franc	125,000 francs	IMM
	German mark	125,000 marks	IMM
	Eurodollar	$1 million	London International Financial Futures Exchange (LIFFE)

TABLE 25.3	Contract	Contract Size	Exchange
(concluded)	**Financial**		
	Sterling	500,000 pounds	LIFFE
	Treasury bonds	$1 million	LIFFE
	Long gilt	250,000 pounds	LIFFE
	Eurodollar	$1 million	IMM
	U.S. Dollar Index	500 times Index	Financial Instrument Exchange in New York (FINEX)
	CRB Index	500 times Index	New York Futures Exchange (NYFE)
	Treasury bonds	$100,000	CBT
	Treasury notes	$100,000	CBT
	5-year Treasury notes	$100,000	CBT
	5-year Treasury notes	$100,000	FINEX
	Treasury bonds	$50,000	MCE
	Treasury bonds	$1 million	IMM
	Financial indexes		
	Municipal bonds	1,000 times Bond Buyer Index	CBT
	S&P 500 Index	500 times Index	CME
	NYSE Composite	500 times Index	NYFE
	Kansas City Value Line Index	500 times Index	KC
	Major Market Index	250 times Index	CBT

Concept Questions

1. What is a futures contract?
2. How is a futures contract related to a forward contract?
3. Why do exchanges require futures contracts to be marked to the market?

25.3 Hedging

Now that we have determined how futures contracts work, let us talk about hedging. There are two types of hedges, long and short. We discuss the short hedge first.

EXAMPLE

In June, Bernard Abelman, a Midwestern farmer, anticipates a harvest of 50,000 bushels of wheat at the end of September. He has two alternatives.

1. *Write Futures Contracts against His Anticipated Harvest.* The September wheat contract on the Chicago Board of Trade is trading at $3.75 a bushel on June 1. He executes the following transaction:

Date of Transaction	Transaction	Price per Bushel
June 1	Write 10 September futures contracts	$3.75

He notes that transportation costs to the designated delivery point in Chicago are 30 cents/bushel. Thus, his net price per bushel is $3.45 = $3.75 − $0.30.

2. *Harvest the Wheat without Writing a Futures Contract.* Alternatively, Mr. Abelman could have harvested the wheat without benefit of a futures contract. The risk would be quite great here since no one knows what the cash price in September will be. If prices rise, he will profit. Conversely, he will lose if prices fall.

We say that strategy 2 is an unhedged position because there is no attempt to use the futures markets to reduce risk. Conversely, strategy 1 involves a hedge. That is, a position in the futures market offsets the risk of a position in the physical, that is, in the actual, commodity.

Though hedging may seem quite sensible to you, it should be mentioned that not everyone hedges. Mr. Abelman might reject hedging for at least two reasons.

First, he may simply be uninformed about hedging. We have found that not everyone in business understands the hedging concept. Many executives have told us that they do not want to use futures markets for hedging their inventories because the risks are too great. However, we disagree. While there are large price fluctuations in these markets, hedging actually reduces the risk that an individual holding inventories bears.

Second, Mr. Abelman may have a special insight or some special information that commodity prices will rise. He would not be wise to lock in a price of $3.75 if he expects the cash price in September to be well above this price.

The hedge of strategy 1 is called a **short hedge,** because Mr. Abelman reduces his risk by *selling* a futures contract. The short hedge is very common in business. It occurs whenever someone either anticipates receiving inventory or is holding inventory. Mr. Abelman was anticipating the harvest of grain. A manufacturer of soybean meal and oil may hold large quantities of raw soybeans, which are already paid for. However, the price to be received for meal and oil are not known because no one knows what the market price will be when the meal and oil are produced. The manufacturer may write futures contracts in meal and oil to lock in a sales price. An oil company may hold large inventories of petroleum to be processed into heating oil. The firm could sell futures contracts in heating oil in order to lock in the sales price. A mortgage banker may assemble mortgages slowly before selling them in bulk to a financial institution. Movements of interest rates affect the value of the mortgages during the time they are in inventory. The mortgage banker could sell Treasury-bond futures contracts in order to offset this interest-rate risk. (This last example is treated later in this chapter.)

EXAMPLE

On April 1, Moon Chemical agreed to sell petrochemicals to the U.S. government in the future. The delivery dates and prices have been determined. Because oil is a basic ingredient of the production process, Moon Chemical will need to have large quantities of oil on hand. The firm can get the oil in one of two ways:

1. *Buy the Oil As the Firm Needs It.* This in an unhedged position because, as of April 1, the firm does not know the prices it will later have to pay for the oil. Oil is quite a volatile commodity, so Moon Chemical is bearing a good bit of risk. The key to this risk-bearing is that the sales price to the U.S. government has already been fixed. Thus, Moon Chemical cannot pass on increased costs to the consumer.

2. *Buy Futures Contracts.*[6] The firm can buy futures contracts with expiration months corresponding to the dates the firm needs inventory. The futures contract locks in the purchase price to Moon Chemical. Because there is a crude-oil futures contract for every month, selecting the correct futures contract is not difficult. Many other commodities have only five contracts per year, frequently necessitating buying contracts one month away from the month of production.

As mentioned earlier, Moon Chemical is interested in hedging the risk of fluctuating oil prices because it cannot pass any cost increases on to the consumer. Suppose, alternatively, that Moon Chemical was not selling petrochemicals on fixed contract to the U.S. government. Instead, imagine that the petrochemicals were to be sold to private industry at currently prevailing prices. The price of petrochemicals should move directly with oil prices, because oil is a major component of

---

[6]Alternatively, the firm could buy the oil on April 1 and store it. This would eliminate the risk of price movement, because the firm's oil costs would be fixed upon the immediate purchase. However, this strategy would be inferior to strategy 2 in the common case where the difference between the futures contract quoted on April 1 and the April 1 cash price is less than storage costs.

petrochemicals. Because cost increases are likely to be passed on to the consumer, Moon Chemical would probably not want to hedge in this case. Instead, the firm is likely to choose strategy 1, buying the oil as it is needed. If oil prices increase between April 1 and September 1, Moon Chemical will, of course, find that its inputs have become quite costly. However, in a competitive market, its revenues are likely to rise as well.

Strategy 2 is called a **long hedge** because one *purchases* a futures contract to reduce risk. In other words, one takes a long position in the futures market. In general, a firm institutes a long hedge when it is committed to a fixed sales price. One class of situations involves actual written contracts with customers, such as Moon Chemical had with the U.S. government. Alternatively, a firm may find that it cannot easily pass on costs to consumers or does not want to pass on these costs. For example, a group of students opened a small meat market called *What's Your Beef* near the University of Pennsylvania in the late 1970s.[7] You may recall that this was a time of volatile consumer prices, especially food prices. Knowing that their fellow students were particularly budget-conscious, the owners vowed to keep food prices constant, regardless of price movements in either direction. They accomplished this by purchasing futures contracts in various agricultural commodities.

Making the Decision to Use Derivatives: The Case of Metallgesellschaft

Earlier in the chapter we introduced MG Refining and Marketing (MGRM), a U.S. subsidiary of Metallgesellschaft AG (MGAG).[8] MGRM reportedly lost more than $1 billion from trading derivatives. Essentially, MGRM sold gasoline, heating oil, and diesel fuel at fixed prices for up to 10 years in the future. This is called "selling forward." In 1993 MGRM had sold forward more than 150 million barrels of petroleum products. As in any "selling forward program," MGRM would lose if the prices of petroleum products rose over time. For example, suppose MGRM had agreed to sell 150 million barrels of heating oil 10 years from now at $25 per barrel. In 10 years, if the actual price of heating oil turned out to be $35 per barrel, MGRM would stand to lose $10 for every barrel it must sell. There are several things that MGRM could do to hedge this exposure.

1. MGRM could have attempted to acquire 150 million barrels of oil for forward delivery 10 years from now. If the 10-year forward price had been $25 per barrel, MGRM would have broken even. In theory, this would have been a perfect hedge. Unfortunately, it is almost impossible to find firms who will commit to buying or selling 150 million barrels of oil 10 years in the future. There is no organized 10-year forward market in petroleum products.

2. MGRM could have tried to buy a futures contract that would guarantee delivery of 150 million barrels of oil 10 years from now at $25 per barrel. But, as with forward trading, there is no 10-year futures market for petroleum products.

3. Because no 10-year futures contract existed, MGRM employed a "rolling stack" strategy. That is, they first bought a short-term, say, a one-year, futures contract instead of the 10-year contract. At the end of one year, when the futures contract matured, MGRM wrote another one-year futures contract. The strategy called for a series of 10 one-year futures contracts over the 10 years.

The strategy can be best understood in a two-year example. At date 0, MGRM would sell oil forward 10 years, at, say, $25 a barrel, to its customers. Simultaneously, MGRM would buy a one-year

---

[7]Ordinarily, an unusual firm name in this textbook is a tip-off that it is fictional. This, however, is a true story.

[8]For a spirited debate on what caused the MGRM derivative trading losses, please read: F. R. Edwards and M. S. Canter, "The Collapse of Metallgesellschaft: Unhedgeable Risks, Poor Hedging Strategy or Just Bad Luck," *Journal of Applied Corporate Finance* (Spring 1995); A. S. Mello and J. E. Parsons, "Maturity Structure of a Hedge Matters: Lessons from the Metallgesellschaft Debacle," *Journal of Applied Corporate Finance* (Spring 1995); C. Culp and M. Miller, "Hedging in the Theory of Corporate Finance: A Reply to Our Critics," *Journal of Applied Corporate Finance* (Spring 1995).

futures contract, also at $25 a barrel.[9] Now assume that the spot price of oil, i.e., the price for immediate delivery, rises to $30 a barrel at date 1. Also, at date 2, the price of the one-year futures contract sells at $30 a barrel. Here, MGRM would break even and at date 1, would gain $5 on its first one-year futures contract. That is, its futures contract issued at date 0 requires it to pay $25 for a barrel of oil at date 1. It could immediately sell this oil in the spot market at $30 a barrel. However, at date 2, it would lose $5. That is, its futures contract issued at date 1 requires it to buy oil at $30 a barrel at date 2. This oil must be sold to its customers for only $25 at date 2.

Unfortunately, there are two potential problems with this hedge. First, the entire term structure of oil prices need not move together. For example, if the spot price of oil was only $29 at date 1 while the one-year futures contract was quoted at $30 on that date, the firm would lose $1. That is, the gain on the first contract of $4 ($29 − $25) would be less than the loss of $5 ($30 − $25) on the second contract.

Second, the first contract must be settled before the second contract, necessitating liquidity problems. For example, if oil prices fell at date 1, the loss on the first contract would be settled to that date. The gain on the second contract would occur at date 2.[10] In fact, oil prices did fall over much of the 10-year life of MGRM's hedge, causing large liquidity problems.

The above shows that risks arise even when a position is hedged. However, MGRM created a third risk (and perhaps greater risk) by eliminating their hedge in the middle. Suppose, in our example, that MGRM bought the first futures contract at date 0 but did not buy the second futures contract at date 1. That is, they did not "roll over" their hedge. Since the firm had previously sold oil forward for two years, they would be unhedged over the second year. A rise in oil prices over the second year to pay $35 would mean that MGRM would have to buy oil in the spot market at $35 on date 2 in order to simultaneously sell oil to its customers at $25. While MGRM in the real world had a 10-year contract, the effect was similar. After MGRM failed to roll over its stacked hedge, i.e., failed to buy futures contracts in later years, oil prices rose. MGRM suffered great losses because of this.

Was the decision to terminate the right one? No one can really know the answer to this important question. It may be that the funding requirements from margin calls forced MGRM into liquidating the futures leg of the hedge, precipitating the collapse. It is possible that the rolling stack hedge was not well designed and had more risks than was initially perceived. It is also possible that the program was terminated prematurely and, had MGRM hung on, the hedge would have been operative. Nevertheless, it must be pointed out that MGRM incurred quite a bit of bad luck. Oil prices fell when MGRM was hedged, leading to liquidity problems. Oil prices rose after the hedge was lifted, leading to losses.

Concept
Questions

1. **Define short and long hedges.**
2. **Under what circumstances is each of the two hedges used?**
3. **What is a rolling stack strategy?**

25.4 Interest-Rate Futures Contracts

In this section we consider interest-rate futures contracts. Our examples deal with futures contracts on Treasury bonds because of their high popularity. We first price Treasury bonds and Treasury-bond forward contracts. Differences between futures and forward contracts are explored. Hedging examples are provided next.

---

[9]For simplicity, we assume a level "term structure" of oil prices. A case of nonlevel prices, while more complex, would lead to the same conclusion. We also use the term of one year when rolling stacks are usually in terms of months.

[10]In addition, since futures contracts are marked-to-the-market daily, gains and losses on the first contract must be settled each day over the first year. If oil prices fell, margin calls would have occurred over the first year.

Pricing of Treasury Bonds

As mentioned earlier in the text, a Treasury bond pays semiannual interest over its life. In addition, the face value of the bond is paid at maturity. Consider a 20-year, 8-percent coupon bond that was issued on March 1. The first payment is to occur in six months, that is, on September 1. The value of the bond can be determined as:

Pricing of a Treasury Bond:

$$P_{TB} = \frac{\$40}{1 + r_1} + \frac{\$40}{(1 + r_2)^2} + \frac{\$40}{(1 + r_3)^3} + \cdots + \frac{\$40}{(1 + r_{39})^{39}} + \frac{\$1,040}{(1 + r_{40})^{40}} \quad (25.1)$$

Because an 8-percent coupon bond pays interest of $80 a year, the semiannual coupon is $40. Principal and the semiannual coupons are both paid at maturity. As we mentioned in a previous chapter, the price of the Treasury bond, P_{TB}, is determined by discounting each payment on a bond at the appropriate spot rate. Because the payments are semiannual, each spot rate is expressed in semiannual terms. That is, imagine a horizontal term structure where the effective annual yield is 12 percent for all maturities. Because each spot rate, r, is expressed in semiannual terms, each spot rate is $\sqrt{1.12} - 1 = 5.83\%$. Because coupon payments occur every six months, there are 40 spot rates over the 20-year period.

Pricing of Forward Contracts

Now, imagine a *forward* contract where, on March 1, you agree to buy a new 20-year, 8-percent coupon Treasury bond in six months, that is, on September 1. As with typical forward contracts, you will pay for the bond on September 1, not March 1. The cash flows from both the Treasury bond issued on March 1 and the forward contract that you purchase on March 1 are presented in Figure 25.1. The cash flows on the Treasury bond begin exactly six months earlier than do the cash flows on the forward contract. The Treasury bond is purchased with cash on March 1 (date 0). The first coupon payment occurs on September 1 (date 1). The last coupon payment occurs at date 40, along with the face value of $1,000. The forward contract compels you to pay $P_{\text{FORW.CONT.}}$, the price of the forward contract, on September 1 (date 1). You receive a new Treasury bond at that time. The first coupon payment from the bond you receive occurs on March 1 of the following year (date 2). The last coupon payment occurs at date 41, along with the face value of $1,000.

FIGURE 25.1

Cash Flows for Both a Treasury Bond and a Forward Contract on a Treasury Bond

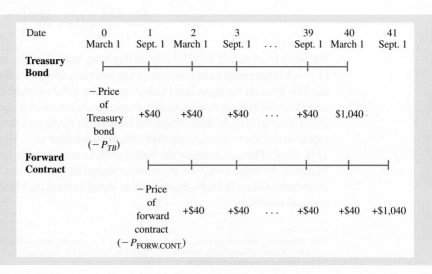

Given the 40 spot rates, equation (25.1) showed how to price a Treasury bond. How does one price the forward contract on a Treasury bond? Just as we saw earlier in the text that net-present-value analysis can be used to price bonds, we will now show that net-present-value analysis can be used to price forward contracts. Given the cash flows for the forward contract in Figure 25.1, the price of the forward contract must satisfy the following equation:

$$\frac{P_{\text{FORW.CONT.}}}{1 + r_1} = \frac{\$40}{(1 + r_2)^2} + \frac{\$40}{(1 + r_3)^3} + \frac{\$40}{(1 + r_4)^4} + \cdots + \frac{\$40}{(1 + r_{40})^{40}} + \frac{\$1{,}040}{(1 + r_{41})^{41}}$$

(25.2)

The right-hand side of equation (25.2) discounts all the cash flows from the delivery instrument (the Treasury bond issued on September 1) back to date 0 (March 1). Because the first cash flow occurs at date 2 (March 1 of the subsequent year), it is discounted by $1/(1 + r_2)^2$. The last cash flow of $1,040 occurs at date 41, so it is discounted by $1/(1 + r_{41})^{41}$. The left-hand side represents the cost of the forward contract as of date 0. Because the actual outpayment occurs at date 1, it is discounted by $1/(1 + r_1)$.

Students often ask, "Why are we discounting everything back to date 0, when we are actually paying for the forward contract on September 1?" The answer is simply that we apply the same techniques to equation (25.2) that we apply to all capital-budgeting problems; we want to put everything in today's (date 0's) dollars. Given that the spot rates are known in the marketplace, traders should have no more trouble pricing a forward contract by equation (25.2) than they would have pricing a Treasury bond by (25.1).

Forward contracts are similar to the underlying bonds themselves. If the entire term structure of interest rates unexpectedly shifts upward on March 2, the Treasury bond issued the previous day should fall in value. This can be seen from equation (25.1). A rise in each of the spot rates lowers the present value of each of the coupon payments. Hence, the value of the bond must fall. Conversely, a fall in the term structure of interest rates increases the value of the bond.

The same relationship holds with forward contracts, as can be seen from rewriting (25.2) as:

$$P_{\text{FORW.CONT.}} = \frac{\$40 \times (1 + r_1)}{(1 + r_2)^2} + \frac{\$40 \times (1 + r_1)}{(1 + r_3)^3} + \frac{\$40 \times (1 + r_1)}{(1 + r_4)^4}$$
$$+ \cdots + \frac{\$40 \times (1 + r_1)}{(1 + r_{40})^{40}} + \frac{\$1{,}040 \times (1 + r_1)}{(1 + r_{41})^{41}}$$

(25.3)

We went from (25.2) to (25.3) by multiplying both the left- and the right-hand sides by $(1 + r_1)$. If the entire term structure of interest rates unexpectedly shifts upward on March 2, the *first* term on the right-hand side of equation (25.3) should fall in value.[11] That is, both r_1 and r_2 will rise an equal amount. However, r_2 enters as a *squared* term, $1/(1 + r_2)^2$, so an increase in r_2 more than offsets the increase in r_1. As we move further to the right, an increase in any spot rate, r_i, more than offsets an increase in r_1. Here r_i enters as the ith power, $1/(1 + r_i)^i$. Thus, as long as the entire term structure shifts upward an equal amount on March 2, the value of a forward contract must fall on that date. Conversely, as long as the entire term structure shifts downward an equal amount on March 2, the value of a forward contract must rise.

---

[11]We are assuming that each spot rate shifts the same amount. For example, suppose that, on March 1, $r_1 = 5\%$, $r_2 = 5.4\%$, and $r_3 = 5.8\%$. Assuming that all rates increase by 1/2 percent on March 2, r_1 becomes 5.5 percent (5% + 1/2%), r_2 becomes 5.9 percent, and r_3 becomes 6.3 percent.

Futures Contracts

The above discussion concerned a forward contract in U.S. Treasury bonds, that is, a forward contract where the deliverable instrument is a U.S. Treasury bond. What about a futures contract on a Treasury bond?[12] We mentioned earlier that futures contracts and forward contracts are quite similar, though there are a few differences between the two. First, futures contracts are generally traded on exchanges, whereas forward contracts are not traded on an exchange. In this case, the Treasury-bond futures contract is traded on the Chicago Board of Trade. Second, futures contracts generally allow the seller a period of time in which to deliver, whereas forward contracts generally call for delivery on a particular day. The seller of a Treasury-bond futures contract can choose to deliver on any business day during the delivery month.[13] Third, futures contracts are subject to the mark-to-the-market convention, whereas forward contracts are not. Traders in Treasury-bill futures contracts must adhere to this convention. Fourth, there is generally a liquid market for futures contracts allowing contracts to be quickly netted out. That is, a buyer can sell his futures contract at any time, and a seller can buy back her futures contract at any time. Conversely, because forward markets are generally quite illiquid, traders cannot easily net out their positions. The popularity of the Treasury-bond futures contract has produced liquidity even higher than that on other futures contracts. Positions in that contract can be netted out quite easily.

The above discussion is not intended to be an exhaustive list of differences between the Treasury-bond forward contract and the Treasury-bond futures contract. Rather, it is intended to show that both contracts share fundamental characteristics. Though there are differences, the two instruments should be viewed as variations of the same species, not different species. Thus, the pricing equation of (25.3), which is exact for the forward contract, should be a decent approximation for the futures contract.

Hedging in Interest-Rate Futures

Now that we have the basic institutional details under our belt, we are ready for examples of hedging using either futures contracts or forward contracts on Treasury bonds. Because the T-bond futures contract is extremely popular whereas the forward contract is traded sporadically, our examples use the futures contract.

EXAMPLE

Ron Cooke owns a mortgage-banking company. On March 1, he made a commitment to loan a total of $1 million to various homeowners on May 1. The loans are 20-year mortgages carrying a 12-percent coupon, the going interest rate on mortgages at the time. Thus, the mortgages are made at par. Though homeowners would not use the term, we could say that he is buying a *forward contract* on a mortgage. That is, he agrees on March 1 to give $1 million to his borrowers on May 1 in exchange for principal and interest from them every month for the next 20 years.

Like many mortgage bankers, he has no intention of paying the $1 million out of his own pocket. Rather, he intends to sell the mortgages to an insurance company. Thus, the insurance company will actually loan the funds and will receive principal and interest over the next 20 years. Mr. Cooke does not currently have an insurance company in mind. He plans to visit the mortgage departments of insurance companies over the next 60 days to sell the mortgages to one or many of them. He sets April 30 as a deadline for making the sale because the borrowers expect the funds on the following day.

---

[12]Futures contracts on bonds are also called *interest-rate futures contracts*.

[13]Delivery occurs two days after the seller notifies the clearinghouse of her intention to deliver.

TABLE 25.4	Mortgage interest rate on April 15	Above 12%	Below 12%
Effects of Changing Interest Rate on Ron Cooke, Mortgage Banker	Sale price to Acme Insurance Company	Below $1 million (We assume $940,000)	Above $1 million (We assume $1.05 million)
	Effect on mortgage banker	He loses because he must loan full $1 million to borrowers.	He gains because he loans only $1 million to borrowers.
	Dollar gain or loss	Loss of $60,000 ($1 million − $940,000)	Gain of $50,000 ($1.05 million − $1 million)

The interest rate on March 1, the date when the loan agreement was made with the borrowers, was 12 percent. April 15 is the date the mortgages were sold to Acme Insurance Company.

Suppose that Mr. Cooke sells the mortgages to the Acme Insurance Co. on April 15. What price will Acme pay for the bonds?

You may think that the insurance company will obviously pay $1 million for the loans. However, suppose interest rates have risen above 12 percent by April 15. The insurance company will buy the mortgage at a discount. For example, suppose the insurance company agrees to pay only $940,000 for the mortgages. Because the mortgage banker agreed to loan a full $1 million to the borrowers, the mortgage banker must come up with the additional $60,000 ($1 million − $940,000) out of his own pocket.

Alternatively, suppose that interest rates fall below 12 percent by April 15. The mortgages can be sold at a premium under this scenario. If the insurance company buys the mortgages at $1.05 million, the mortgage banker will have made an unexpected profit of $50,000 ($1.05 million − $1 million).

Because Ron Cooke is unable to forecast interest rates, this risk is something that he would like to avoid. The risk is summarized in Table 25.4.

Seeing the interest-rate risk, students at this point may ask, "What does the mortgage banker get out of this loan to offset his risk-bearing?" Mr. Cooke wants to sell the mortgages to the insurance company so that he can get two fees. The first is an *origination fee,* which is paid to the mortgage banker from the insurance company on April 15, that is, on the date the loan is sold. An industry standard in certain locales is 1 percent of the value of the loan, that is $10,000 (1% × $1 million). In addition, Mr. Cooke will act as a collection agent for the insurance company. For this service, he will receive a small portion of the outstanding balance of the loan each month. For example, if he is paid 0.03 percent of the loan each month, he will receive $300 (0.03% × $1 million) in the first month. As the outstanding balance of the loan declines, he will receive less.

Though Mr. Cooke will earn profitable fees on the loan, he bears interest-rate risk. He loses money if interest rates rise after March 1, and he profits if interest rates fall after March 1. To hedge this risk, he writes June Treasury-bond futures contracts on March 1. As with mortgages, Treasury-bond futures contracts fall in value if interest rates rise. Because he *writes* the contract, he makes money on these contracts if they fall in value. Therefore, with an interest-rate rise, the loss he endures in the mortgages is offset by the gain he earns in the futures market. Conversely, Treasury-bond futures contracts rise in value if interest rates fall. Because he writes the contracts, he suffers losses on them when rates fall. With an interest-rate fall, the profit he makes on the mortgages is offset by the loss he suffers in the futures markets.

The details of this hedging transaction are presented in Table 25.5. The column on the left is labeled "Cash markets," because the deal in the mortgage market is transacted off an exchange. The column on the right shows the offsetting transactions in the futures market. Consider the first row. The mortgage banker enters into a forward contract on March 1. He simultaneously writes Treasury-bond futures contracts. Ten contracts are written because the deliverable instrument

TABLE 25.5		**Cash Markets**	**Futures Markets**
Illustration of Hedging Strategy for Ron Cooke, Mortgage Banker	March 1	Mortgage banker makes forward contracts to loan $1 million at 12 percent for 20 years. The loans are to be funded on May 1. No cash changes hands on March 1.	Mortgage banker writes 10 June Treasury-bond futures contracts.
	April 15	Loans are sold to Acme Insurance Company. Mortgage banker will receive sale price from Acme on the May 1 funding date.	Mortgage banker buys back all the futures contracts.
	If interest rates rise:	Loans are sold at a price below $1 million. Mortgage banker *loses* because he receives less than the $1 million he must give to borrowers.	Each futures contract is bought back at a price below the sales price, resulting in *profit*. Mortgage banker's profit in futures market offsets loss in cash market.
	If interest rates fall:	Loans are sold at a price above $1 million. Mortgage banker *gains* because he receives more than the $1 million he must give to borrowers.	Each futures contract is bought back at a price above the sales price, resulting in *loss*. Mortgage banker's loss in futures market offsets gain in cash market.

on each contract is $100,000 of Treasury bonds. The total is $1 million (10 × $100,000), which is equal to the value of the mortgages. Mr. Cooke would prefer to write May Treasury-bond futures contracts. Here, Treasury bonds would be delivered on the futures contract during the same month that the loan is funded. Because there is no May T-bond futures contract, Mr. Cooke achieves the closest match through a June contract.

If held to maturity, the June contract would obligate the mortgage banker to deliver Treasury bonds in June. Interest-rate risk ends in the cash market when the loans are sold. Interest-rate risk must be terminated in the futures market at that time. Thus, Mr. Cooke nets out his position in the futures contract as soon as the loan is sold to Acme Insurance.

Risk is clearly reduced via an offsetting transaction in the futures market. However, is risk totally eliminated? Risk would be totally eliminated if losses in the cash markets were *exactly* offset in the futures markets and vice versa. This is unlikely to happen because mortgages and Treasury bonds are not identical instruments. First, mortgages may have different maturities than Treasury bonds. Second, Treasury bonds have a different payment stream than do mortgages. Principal is only paid at maturity on T-bonds, whereas principal is paid every month on mortgages. Because mortgages pay principal continuously, these instruments have a shorter *effective* time to maturity than do Treasury bonds of equal maturity.[14] Third, mortgages have default risk whereas Treasury bonds do not. The term structure applicable to instruments with default risk may change even when the term structure for risk-free assets remains constant. Fourth, mortgages may be paid off early and hence have a shorter *expected maturity* than Treasury bonds of equal maturity.

---

[14]Alternatively, we can say that mortgages have shorter duration than do Treasury bonds of equal maturity. A precise definition of duration is provided later in this chapter.

Because mortgages and Treasury bonds are not identical instruments, they are not identically affected by interest rates. If Treasury bonds are less volatile than mortgages, financial consultants may advise Mr. Cooke to write more than 10 T-bond futures contracts. Conversely, if these bonds are more volatile, the consultant may state that less than 10 futures contracts are indicated. An optimal ratio of futures to mortgages will reduce risk as much as possible. However, because the price movements of mortgages and Treasury bonds are not *perfectly correlated*, Mr. Cooke's hedging strategy cannot eliminate all risk.

The above strategy is called a *short hedge* because Mr. Cooke sells futures contracts in order to reduce risk. Though it involves an interest-rate futures contract, this short hedge is analogous to short hedges in agricultural and metallurgical futures contracts. We argued at the beginning of this chapter that individuals and firms institute short hedges to offset inventory price fluctuation. Once Mr. Cooke makes a contract to loan money to borrowers, the mortgages effectively become his inventory. He writes a futures contract to offset the price fluctuation of his inventory.

We now consider an example where a mortgage banker institutes a long hedge.

EXAMPLE

Margaret Boswell is another mortgage banker. Her firm faces problems similar to those facing Mr. Cooke's firm. However, she tackles the problems through the use of **advance commitments,** a strategy the opposite of Mr. Cooke's. That is, she promises to deliver loans to a financial institution *before* she lines up borrowers. On March 1, her firm agreed to sell mortgages to No-State Insurance Co. The agreement specifies that she must turn over 12-percent coupon mortgages with a face value of $1 million to No-State by May 1. No-State is buying the mortgages at par, implying that they will pay Ms. Boswell $1 million on May 1. As of March 1, Ms. Boswell had not signed up any borrowers. Over the next two months, she will seek out individuals who want mortgages beginning May 1.

As with Mr. Cooke, changing interest rates will affect Ms. Boswell. If interest rates fall before she signs up a borrower, the borrower will demand a premium on a 12-percent coupon loan. That is, the borrower will receive more than par on May 1.[15] Because Ms. Boswell receives par from the insurance company, she must make up the difference.

Conversely, if interest rates rise, a 12-percent coupon loan will be made at a discount. That is, the borrower will receive less than par on May 1. Because Ms. Boswell receives par from the insurance company, the difference is pure profit to her.

The details are provided in the left-hand column of Table 25.6. As did Mr. Cooke, Ms. Boswell finds the risk burdensome. Therefore, she offsets her advance commitment with a transaction in the futures markets. Because she *loses* in the cash market when interest rates fall, she *buys* futures contracts to reduce the risk. When interest rates fall, the value of her futures contracts increases. The gain in the futures market offsets the loss in the cash market. Conversely, she gains in the cash markets when interest rates rise. The value of her futures contracts decreases when interest rates rise, offsetting her gain.

We call this a *long hedge* because Ms. Boswell offsets risk in the cash markets by buying a futures contract. Though it involves an interest-rate futures contract, this long hedge is analogous to long hedges in agricultural and metallurgical futures contracts. We argued at the beginning of this chapter that individuals and firms institute long hedges when their finished goods are to be sold at a fixed price. Once Ms. Boswell makes the advance commitment with No-State Insurance, she has fixed her sales price. She buys a futures contract to offset the price fluctuation of her raw materials, that is, her mortgages.

---

[15]Alternatively, the mortgage would still be at par if a coupon rate below 12 percent were used. However, this is not done since the insurance company only wants to buy 12-percent mortgages.

TABLE 25.6	Illustration of Advance Commitment for Margaret Boswell, Mortgage Banker	
	Cash Markets	**Futures Markets**
March 1	Mortgage banker makes a forward contract (advance commitment) to deliver $1 million of mortgages to No-State Insurance. The insurance company will pay par to Ms. Boswell for the loans on May 1. The borrowers are to receive their funding from mortgage banker on May 1. The mortgages are to be 12-percent coupon loans for 20 years.	Mortgage banker buys 10 June Treasury-bond futures contracts.
April 15	Mortgage banker signs up borrowers to 12-percent coupon, 20-year mortgages. She promises that the borrowers will receive funds on May 1.	Mortgage banker sells all futures contracts.
If interest rates rise:	Mortgage banker issues mortgages to borrowers at a discount. Mortgage banker *gains* because she receives par from insurance company.	Futures contract is sold at a price below purchase price, resulting in *loss*. Mortgage banker's loss in futures market offsets gain in cash market.
If interest rates fall:	Loans to borrowers are issued at a premium. Mortgage banker *loses* because she receives only par from insurance company.	Futures contract is sold at a price above purchase price, resulting in *gain*. Mortgage banker's gain in futures market offsets loss in cash market.

Concept Questions

1. How are forward contracts on bonds priced?
2. What are the differences between forward contracts on bonds and futures contracts on bonds?
3. Give examples of hedging with futures contracts on bonds.

25.5 Duration Hedging

The last section concerned the risk of interest-rate changes. We now want to explore this risk in a more precise manner. In particular, we want to show that the concept of duration is a prime determinant of interest-rate risk. We begin by considering the effect of interest-rate movements on bond prices.

The Case of Zero-Coupon Bonds

Imagine a world where the interest rate is 10 percent across all maturities. A one-year pure discount bond pays $110 at maturity. A five-year pure discount bond pays $161.05 at maturity. Both of these bonds are worth $100, as given by:[16]

Value of One-Year Pure Discount Bond:

$$\$100 = \frac{\$110}{1.10}$$

Value of Five-Year Pure Discount Bond:

$$\$100 = \frac{\$161.05}{(1.10)^5}$$

---

[16]Alternatively, we could have chosen bonds that pay $100 at maturity. Their values would be $90.91 ($100/1.10) and $62.09 [$100/(1.10)^5]. However, our comparisons to come are made easier if both have the same initial price.

TABLE 25.7	Interest Rate	One-Year Pure Discount Bond	Five-Year Pure Discount Bond
Value of a Pure Discount Bond as a Function of Interest Rate	8%	$101.85 = \dfrac{\$110}{1.08}$	$109.61 = \dfrac{\$161.05}{(1.08)^5}$
	10%	$100.00 = \dfrac{\$110}{1.10}$	$100.00 = \dfrac{\$161.05}{(1.10)^5}$
	12%	$98.21 = \dfrac{\$110}{1.12}$	$91.38 = \dfrac{\$161.05}{(1.12)^5}$

For a given interest rate change, a five-year pure discount bond fluctuates more in price than does a one-year pure discount bond.

Which bond will change more when interest rates move? To find out, we calculate the value of these bonds when interest rates are either 8 or 12 percent. The results are presented in Table 25.7. As can be seen, the five-year bond has greater price swings than does the one-year bond. That is, both bonds are worth $100 when interest rates are 10 percent. The five-year bond is worth more than the one-year bond when interest rates are 8 percent and worth less than the one-year bond when interest rates are 12 percent. We state that the five-year bond is subject to more price volatility. This point, which was mentioned in passing in an earlier section of the chapter, is not difficult to understand. The interest-rate term in the denominator, $1 + r$, is taken to the fifth power for a five-year bond and only to the first power for the one-year bond. Thus, the effect of a changing interest rate is magnified for the five-year bond. The general rule is:

> The percentage price changes in long-term pure discount bonds are greater than the percentage price changes in short-term pure discount bonds.

The Case of Two Bonds with the Same Maturity but with Different Coupons

The previous example concerned pure discount bonds of different maturities. We now want to see the effect of different coupons on price volatility. To abstract from the effect of differing maturities, we consider two bonds with the same maturity but with different coupons.

Consider a five-year, 10-percent coupon bond and a five-year, 1-percent coupon bond. When interest rates are 10 percent, the bonds are priced at:

Value of Five-Year, 10-Percent Coupon Bond:

$$\$100 = \frac{\$10}{1.10} + \frac{\$10}{(1.10)^2} + \frac{\$10}{(1.10)^3} + \frac{\$10}{(1.10)^4} + \frac{\$110}{(1.10)^5}$$

Value of Five-Year, 1-Percent Coupon Bond:

$$\$65.88 = \frac{\$1}{1.10} + \frac{\$1}{(1.10)^2} + \frac{\$1}{(1.10)^3} + \frac{\$1}{(1.10)^4} + \frac{\$101}{(1.10)^5}$$

Which bond will change more in *percentage terms* if interest rates change?[17] To find out, we first calculate the value of these bonds when interest rates are either 8 or 12 percent. The results are presented in Table 25.8. As we would expect, the 10-percent coupon bond always sells for more than the 1-percent coupon bond. Also, as we would expect, each bond is worth more when the interest rate is 8 percent than when the interest rate is 12 percent.

---

[17]The bonds are at different prices initially. Thus, we are concerned with percentage price changes, not absolute price changes.

TABLE 25.8	Interest Rate	Five-Year, 10% Coupon Bond
Value of Coupon Bonds at Different Interest Rates	8%	$107.99 = \dfrac{\$10}{1.08} + \dfrac{\$10}{(1.08)^2} + \dfrac{\$10}{(1.08)^3} + \dfrac{\$10}{(\$1.08)^4} + \dfrac{\$110}{(1.08)^5}$
	10%	$100.00 = \dfrac{\$10}{1.10} + \dfrac{\$10}{(1.10)^2} + \dfrac{\$10}{(1.10)^3} + \dfrac{\$10}{(1.10)^4} + \dfrac{\$110}{(1.10)^5}$
	12%	$92.79 = \dfrac{\$10}{1.12} + \dfrac{\$10}{(1.12)^2} + \dfrac{\$10}{(1.12)^3} + \dfrac{\$10}{(1.12)^4} + \dfrac{\$110}{(1.12)^5}$

Interest Rate	Five-Year, 1% Coupon Bond
8%	$72.05 = \dfrac{\$1}{1.08} + \dfrac{\$1}{(1.08)^2} + \dfrac{\$1}{(1.08)^3} + \dfrac{\$1}{(1.08)^4} + \dfrac{\$101}{(1.08)^5}$
10%	$65.88 = \dfrac{\$1}{1.10} + \dfrac{\$1}{(1.10)^2} + \dfrac{\$1}{(1.10)^3} + \dfrac{\$1}{(1.10)^4} + \dfrac{\$101}{(1.10)^5}$
12%	$60.35 = \dfrac{\$1}{1.12} + \dfrac{\$1}{(1.12)^2} + \dfrac{\$1}{(1.12)^3} + \dfrac{\$1}{(1.12)^4} + \dfrac{\$101}{(1.12)^5}$

We calculate percentage price changes for both bonds as the interest rate changes from 10 to 8 percent and from 10 to 12 percent. These percentage price changes are:

	10% Coupon Bond	1% Coupon Bond
Interest rate changes from 10% to 8%:	$7.99\% = \dfrac{\$107.99}{\$100} - 1$	$9.37\% = \dfrac{\$72.05}{\$65.88} - 1$
Interest rate changes from 10% to 12%:	$-7.21\% = \dfrac{\$92.79}{\$100} - 1$	$-8.39\% = \dfrac{\$60.35}{\$65.88} - 1$

As can be seen, the 1-percent coupon bond has a greater percentage price increase than does the 10-percent coupon bond when the interest rate falls. Similarly, the 1-percent coupon bond has a greater percentage price decrease than does the 10-percent coupon bond when the interest rate rises. Thus, we say that the percentage price changes on the 1-percent coupon bond are greater than are the percentage price changes on the 10-percent coupon bond.

Duration

The question, of course, is "Why?" We can answer this question only after we have explored a concept called **duration.** We begin by noticing that any coupon bond is actually a combination of pure discount bonds. For example, the five-year, 10-percent coupon bond is made up of five pure discount bonds:

1. A pure discount bond paying $10 at the end of year 1.
2. A pure discount bond paying $10 at the end of year 2.
3. A pure discount bond paying $10 at the end of year 3.
4. A pure discount bond paying $10 at the end of year 4.
5. A pure discount bond paying $110 at the end of year 5.

Similarly, the five-year, 1-percent coupon bond is made up of five pure discount bonds. Because the price volatility of a pure discount bond is determined by its maturity, we would like to determine the average maturity of the five pure discount bonds that make up a five-year coupon bond. This leads us to the concept of duration.

We calculate average maturity in three steps. For the 10-percent coupon bond, we have these:

1. *Calculate Present Value of Each Payment.* We do this as:

Year	Payment	Present Value of Payment by Discounting at 10%
1	$ 10	$ 9.091
2	10	8.264
3	10	7.513
4	10	6.830
5	110	68.302
		$100.00

2. *Express the Present Value of Each Payment in Relative Terms.* We calculate the relative value of a single payment as the ratio of the present value of the payment to the value of the bond. The value of the bond is $100. We have:

Year	Payment	Present Value of Payment	Relative Value $= \dfrac{\text{Present Value of Payment}}{\text{Value of Bond}}$
1	$ 10	$ 9.091	$9.091/$100 = 0.09091
2	10	8.264	0.08264
3	10	7.513	0.07513
4	10	6.830	0.06830
5	110	68.302	0.68302
		$100.00	1.0

The bulk of the relative value, 68.302 percent, occurs at year 5 because the principal is paid back at that time.

3. *Weight the Maturity of Each Payment by Its Relative Value.* We have:

$$4.1699 \text{ years} = 1 \text{ year} \times 0.09091 + 2 \text{ years} \times 0.08264 + 3 \text{ years} \times 0.07513$$
$$+ 4 \text{ years} \times 0.06830 + 5 \text{ years} \times 0.68302$$

There are many ways to calculate the average maturity of a bond. We have calculated it by weighting the maturity of each payment by the payment's present value. We find that the *effective* maturity of the bond is 4.1699 years. *Duration* is a commonly used word for effective maturity. Thus, the bond's duration is 4.1699 years. Note that duration is expressed in units of time.[18]

Because the five-year, 10-percent coupon bond has a duration of 4.1699 years, its percentage price fluctuations should be the same as those of a zero-coupon bond with a

---

[18]The mathematical formula for duration is

$$\text{Duration} = \frac{PV(C_1)1 + PV(C_2)2 + \cdots + PV(C_T)T}{PV}$$

and

$$PV = PV(C_1) + PV(C_2) + \cdots + PV(C_T)$$

$$PV(C_T) = \frac{C_T}{(1 + r)^T}$$

where C_T is the cash to be received in time T and r is the current discount rate.

Also note that in the above numerical example we discounted each payment by the interest rate of 10 percent. This was done because we wanted to calculate the duration of the bond before a change in the interest rate occurred. After a change in the rate to, say, 8 or 12 percent, all three of our steps would need to reflect the new interest rate. In other words, the duration of a bond is a function of the current interest rate.

duration of 4.1699 years.[19] It turns out that the five-year, 1-percent coupon bond has a duration of 4.8742 years. Because the 1-percent coupon bond has a higher duration than the 10-percent bond, the 1-percent coupon bond should be subject to greater price fluctuations. This is exactly what we found earlier. In general, we say:

> The percentage price changes of a bond with high duration are greater than the percentage price changes of a bond with low duration.

A final question: Why *does* the 1-percent bond have a greater duration than the 10-percent bond, even though they both have the same five-year maturity? As mentioned earlier, duration is an average of the maturity of the bond's cash flows, weighted by the present value of each cash flow. The 1-percent coupon bond receives only $1 in each of the first four years. Thus, the weights applied to years 1 through 4 in the duration formula will be low. Conversely, the 10-percent coupon bond receives $10 in each of the first four years. The weights applied to years 1 through 4 in the duration formula will be higher.

Matching Liabilities with Assets

Earlier in this chapter we argued that firms can hedge risk by trading in futures. Because some firms are subject to interest-rate risk, we showed how they can hedge with interest-rate futures contracts. Firms may also hedge interest-rate risk by matching liabilities with assets. This ability to hedge follows from our discussion of duration.

EXAMPLE

The Physical Bank of New York has the following market-value balance sheet:

PHYSICAL BANK OF NEW YORK
Market-Value Balance Sheet

	Market Value	Duration
Assets		
Overnight money	$ 35 million	0
Accounts-receivable–backed loans	500 million	3 months
Inventory loans	275 million	6 months
Industrial loans	40 million	2 years
Mortgages	150 million	14.8 years
	$1,000 million	
Liabilities and Owners' Equity		
Checking and savings accounts	$ 400 million	0
Certificates of deposit	300 million	1 year
Long-term financing	200 million	10 years
Equity	100 million	
	$1,000 million	

The bank has $1,000 million of assets and $900 million of liabilities. Its equity is the difference between the two: $100 million ($1,000 million − $900 million). Both the market value and the duration of each individual item is provided in the balance sheet. Both overnight money and checking and savings accounts have a duration of zero. This is because the interest paid on these instruments adjusts immediately to changing interest rates in the economy.

The bank's managers think that interest rates are likely to move quickly in the coming months. Because they do not know the direction of the movement, they are worried that their bank is vulnerable to changing rates. They call in a consultant, James Charest, to determine hedging strategy.

---

[19]Actually, this relationship only exactly holds in the case of a one-time shift in a flat yield curve, where the change in the spot rate is identical for all different maturities.

Mr. Charest first calculates the duration of the assets and the duration of the liabilities.[20]

Duration of Assets:

$$2.56 \text{ years} = 0 \text{ years} \times \frac{\$35 \text{ million}}{\$1,000 \text{ million}} + \frac{1}{4} \text{ year} \times \frac{\$500 \text{ million}}{\$1,000 \text{ million}} \tag{25.4}$$

$$+ \frac{1}{2} \text{ year} \times \frac{\$275 \text{ million}}{\$1,000 \text{ million}} + 2 \text{ years} \times \frac{\$40 \text{ million}}{\$1,000 \text{ million}}$$

$$+ 14.8 \text{ years} \times \frac{\$150 \text{ million}}{\$1,000 \text{ million}}$$

Duration of Liabilities:

$$2.56 = 0 \text{ years} \times \frac{\$400 \text{ million}}{\$900 \text{ million}} + 1 \text{ year} \times \frac{\$300 \text{ million}}{\$900 \text{ million}} + 10 \text{ years} \times \frac{\$200 \text{ million}}{\$900 \text{ million}} \tag{25.5}$$

The duration of the assets, 2.56 years, equals the duration of the liabilities. Because of this, Mr. Charest argues that the firm is immune to interest-rate risk.

Just to be on the safe side, the bank calls in a second consultant, Gail Ellert. Ms. Ellert argues that it is incorrect to simply match durations, because assets total $1,000 million and liabilities total only $900 million. If both assets and liabilities have the same duration, the price change on a *dollar* of assets should be equal to the price change on a dollar of liabilities. However, the *total* price change will be greater for assets than for liabilities, because there are more assets than liabilities in this bank. The firm will be immune from interest-rate risk only when the duration of the liabilities is greater than the duration of the assets. Ms. Ellert states that the following relationship must hold if the bank is to be **immunized,** that is, immune to interest-rate risk:

$$\begin{matrix} \text{Duration of} \\ \text{assets} \end{matrix} \times \begin{matrix} \text{Market value of} \\ \text{assets} \end{matrix} = \begin{matrix} \text{Duration of} \\ \text{liabilities} \end{matrix} \times \begin{matrix} \text{Market value} \\ \text{of liabilities} \end{matrix} \tag{25.6}$$

She says that the bank should not *equate* the duration of the liabilities with the duration of the assets. Rather, using equation (25.6), the bank should match the duration of the liabilities to the duration of the assets. She suggests two ways to achieve this match.

1. *Increase the Duration of the Liabilities without Changing the Duration of the Assets.* Ms. Ellert argues that the duration of the liabilities could be increased to

$$\text{Duration of assets} \times \frac{\text{Market value of assets}}{\text{Market value of liabilities}} = 2.56 \text{ years} \times \frac{\$1,000 \text{ million}}{\$900 \text{ million}}$$

$$= 2.84 \text{ years}$$

Equation (25.5) then becomes:

$$2.56 \times \$1 \text{ billion} = 2.84 \times \$900 \text{ million}$$

2. *Decrease the Duration of the Assets without Changing the Duration of the Liabilities.* Alternatively, Ms. Ellert points out that the duration of the assets could be decreased to

$$\text{Duration of liabilities} \times \frac{\text{Market value of liabilities}}{\text{Market value of assets}} = 2.56 \text{ years} \times \frac{\$900 \text{ million}}{\$1,000 \text{ million}}$$

$$= 2.30 \text{ years}$$

Equation (25.6) then becomes:

$$2.30 \times \$1 \text{ billion} = 2.56 \times \$900 \text{ million}$$

---

[20]Note that the duration of a group of items is an average of the duration of the individual items, weighted by the market value of each item. This is a simplifying step that greatly increases duration's practicality.

Though we agree with Ms. Ellert's analysis, the bank's current mismatch was small anyway. Huge mismatches have occurred for real-world financial institutions, particularly savings and loans. S&Ls have frequently invested large portions of their assets in mortgages. The durations of these mortgages would clearly be above 10 years. Much of the funds available for mortgage lending were financed by short-term credit, especially savings accounts. As we mentioned, the duration of such instruments is quite small. A thrift institution in this situation faces a large amount of interest-rate risk, because any increase in interest rates would greatly reduce the value of the mortgages. Because an interest-rate rise would only reduce the value of the liabilities slightly, the equity of the firm would fall. As interest rates rose over much of the 1960s and the 1970s, many S&Ls found that the market value of their equity approached zero.[21]

Duration and the accompanying immunization strategies are useful in other areas of finance. For example, many firms establish pension funds to meet obligations to retirees. If the assets of a pension fund are invested in bonds and other fixed-income securities, the duration of the assets can be computed. Similarly, the firm views the obligations to retirees as analogous to interest payments on debt. The duration of these liabilities can be calculated as well. The manager of a pension fund would commonly choose pension assets so that the duration of the assets is matched with the duration of the liabilities. In this way, changing interest rates would not affect the net worth of the pension fund.

Life insurance companies receiving premiums today are legally obligated to provide death benefits in the future. Actuaries view these future benefits as analogous to interest and principal payments of fixed-income securities. The duration of these expected benefits can be calculated. Insurance firms frequently invest in bonds where the duration of the bonds is matched to the duration of the future death benefits.

The business of a leasing company is quite simple. The firm issues debt to purchase assets, which are then leased. The lease payments have a duration, as does the debt. Leasing companies frequently structure debt financing so that the duration of the debt matches the duration of the lease. If the firm did not do this, the market value of its equity could be eliminated by a quick change in interest rates.

Concept Questions	1. What is duration? 2. How is the concept of duration used to reduce interest-rate risk?

25.6 Swaps Contracts

Swaps are close cousins to forwards and futures contracts. Swaps are arrangements between two counterparts to exchange cash flows over time. There is enormous flexibility in the forms that swaps can take, but the two basic types are **interest-rate swaps** or **currency swaps.** Often these are combined when interest received in one currency is swapped for interest in another currency.

Interest-Rate Swaps

Like other derivatives, swaps are tools that firms can use to easily change their risk exposures and their balance sheets.[22] Consider a firm that has borrowed and carried on its books an

---

[21]Actually, the market value of the equity could easily be negative in this example. However, S&Ls in the real world have an asset not shown on our market-value balance sheet: the ability to generate new, profitable loans. This should increase the market value of a thrift above the market value of its outstanding loans less its existing debt.

[22]Under current accounting rules, most derivatives do not usually show up on firms' balance sheets since they do not have an historical cost (i.e., the amount a dealer would pay on the initial transaction day).

obligation to repay a 10-year loan for $100 million of principal with a 9-percent coupon rate paid annually. Ignoring the possibility of calling the loan, the firm expects to have to pay coupons of $9 million every year for 10 years and a balloon payment of $100 million at the end of the 10 years. Suppose, though, that the firm is uncomfortable with having this large fixed obligation on its books. Perhaps the firm is in a cyclical business where its revenues vary and could, conceivably, fall to a point where it would be difficult to make the debt payment.

Suppose, too, that the firm earns a lot of its revenue from financing the purchase of its products. Typically, for example, a manufacturer might help its customers finance their purchase of its products through a leasing or credit subsidiary. Usually these loans are for relatively short time periods and are financed at some premium over the prevailing short-term rate of interest. This puts the firm in the position of having revenues that move up and down with interest rates while its costs are relatively fixed.

This is a classic situation where a swap can be used to offset the risk. When interest rates rise, the firm would have to pay more on the loan, but it would be making more on its product financing. What the firm would really prefer is to have a floating-rate loan rather than a fixed-rate loan. It can use a swap to accomplish this.

Of course, the firm could also just go into the capital markets and borrow $100 million at a variable interest rate and then use the proceeds to retire its outstanding fixed-rate loan. While this is possible, it is generally quite expensive, requiring underwriting a new loan and the repurchase of the existing loan. The ease of entering into a swap is its inherent advantage.

The particular swap would be one that exchanged its fixed obligation for an agreement to pay a floating rate. Every six months it would agree to pay a coupon based on whatever the prevailing interest rate was at the time in exchange for an agreement from a counter-party to pay the firm's fixed coupon.

A common reference point for floating-rate commitments is called LIBOR. LIBOR stands for the London Interbank Offered Rate, and it is the rate that most international banks charge one another for dollar-denominated loans in the London market. LIBOR is commonly used as the reference rate for a floating-rate commitment, and, depending on the creditworthiness of the borrower, the rate can vary from LIBOR to LIBOR plus one point or more over LIBOR.

If we assume that our firm has a credit rating that requires it to pay LIBOR plus 50 basis points, then in a swap it would be exchanging its fixed 9-percent obligation for the obligation to pay whatever the prevailing LIBOR rate is plus 50 basis points. Figure 25.2 displays how the cash flows on this swap would work. In the figure we have assumed that LIBOR starts at 8 percent and rises for four years to 11 percent and then drops to 7 percent. As the figure illustrates, the firm would owe a coupon of 8.5% × $100 million = $8.5 million in

FIGURE 25.2		Fixed-for-Floating a Swap: Cash Flows ($ million)									
						Coupons					
	Year	1	2	3	4	5	6	7	8	9	10
A. Swap											
Fixed obligation		9	9	9	9	9	9	9	9	9	9
LIBOR floating		−8.5	−9.5	−10.5	−11.5	−7.5	−7.5	−7.5	−7.5	−7.5	−7.5
B. Original Loan											
Fixed obligation		−9	−9	−9	−9	−9	−9	−9	−9	−9	109
Net effect		−8.5	−9.5	10.5	11.5	7.5	7.5	7.5	7.5	7.5	−107.5

year 1, $9.5 million in year 2, $10.5 million in year 3, and $11.5 million in year 4. The precipitous drop to 7 percent lowers the annual payments to $7.5 million thereafter. In return, the firm receives the fixed payment of $9 million each year. Actually, rather than swapping the full payments, the cash flows would be netted. Since the firm is paying variable and receiving fixed—which it uses to pay its lender—in the first year, for example, the firm owes $8.5 million and is owed by its counterparty, who is paying fixed, $9 million. Hence, net, the firm would receive a payment of $.5 million. Since the firm has to pay its lender $9 million, but gets a net payment from the swap of $.5 million, it really only pays out the difference, or $8.5 million. In each year, then, the firm would effectively pay only LIBOR plus 50 basis points.

Notice, too, that the entire transaction can be carried out without any need to change the terms of the original loan. In effect, by swapping, the firm has found a counterparty who is willing to pay its fixed obligation in return for the firm paying a floating obligation.

Currency Swaps

FX stands for foreign exchange, and currency swaps are sometimes called FX swaps. Currency swaps are swaps of obligations to pay cash flows in one currency for obligations to pay in another currency.

Currency swaps arise as a natural vehicle for hedging the risk in international trade. For example, suppose a U.S. firm sells a broad range of its product line in the German market. Every year the firm can count on receiving revenue from Germany in the German currency, deutschemarks, or DM for short. We will study international finance later in this book, but for now we can just observe that, because exchange rates fluctuate, this subjects the firm to considerable risk.

If the firm produces its products in the United States and exports them to Germany, then the firm has to pay its workers and its suppliers in dollars. But, it is receiving some of its revenues in DM. The exchange rate between $ and DM changes over time. As the DM rises in value, the German revenues are worth more $, but as it falls they decline. Suppose that the firm can count on selling 100 million DM of goods each year in Germany. If the exchange rate is 2 DM for each $, then the firm will receive $50 million. But, if the exchange rate were to rise to 3 DM for each $, the firm would only receive $33.333 million for its 100 million DM. Naturally the firm would like to protect itself against these currency swings.

To do so the firm can enter into a currency swap. We will learn more about exactly what the terms of such a swap might be, but for now we can assume that the swap is for five years at a fixed term of 100 million DM for $50 million each year. Now, no matter what happens to the exchange rate between DM and $ over the next five years, as long as the firm makes 100 million DM each year from the sale of its products, it will swap this for $50 million each year.

We have not addressed the question of how the market sets prices for swaps, either interest-rate swaps or currency swaps. In the fixed-for-floating example and in the currency swap, we just quoted some terms. We won't go into great detail on exactly how it is done, but we can stress the most important points.

Swaps, like forwards and futures, are essentially zero-sum transactions, which is to say that in both cases the market sets prices at a fair level, and neither party has any substantial bargain or loss at the moment the deal is struck. For example, in the currency swap, the swap rate is some average of the market expectation of what the exchange rate will be over the life of the swap. In the interest-rate swap, the rates are set as the fair floating and fixed rates for the creditor, taking into account the creditworthiness of the counterparties. We can actually price swaps fairly once we know how to price forward contracts. In our interest-rate swap example, the firm swapped LIBOR plus 50 basis points for a 9-percent fixed rate, all on a principal amount of $100 million. This is equivalent to a series of forward contracts extending out the life of the swap. In year 1, for example, having made the swap, the firm is in the same position that it would be if it had sold a forward contract entitling the buyer to receive LIBOR plus 50 basis points on $100 million in return for a fixed payment of $9 million (9 percent on $100 million). Similarly, the currency swap can also be viewed as a series of forward contracts.

Concept
Question

1. **Show that a currency swap is equivalent to a series of forward contracts.**

Exotics

Up to now we have dealt with the meat and potatoes of the derivatives markets, swaps, options, forwards, and futures. **Exotics** are the complicated blends of these that often produce the surprising results for the buyers.

One of the more interesting types of exotics is called an *inverse floater.* In our fixed-for-floating swap, the floating payments fluctuated with LIBOR. An inverse floater is one that fluctuates inversely with some rate such as LIBOR. For example, the floater might pay an interest rate of 20 percent minus LIBOR. If LIBOR is 9 percent, then the inverse pays 11 percent, and if LIBOR rises to 12 percent, the payments on the inverse would fall to 8 percent. Clearly the purchaser of an inverse profits from the inverse if interest rates fall.

Both floaters and inverse floaters have a supercharged version called *superfloaters* and *superinverses* that fluctuate more than one for one with movements in interest rates. As an example of a superinverse floater, consider a floater that pays an interest rate of 30 percent minus *twice* LIBOR. When LIBOR is 10 percent, the inverse pays:

$$30\% - 2 \times 10\% = 30\% - 20\% = 10\%$$

And if LIBOR falls by 3 percent to 7 percent, then the return on the inverse rises by 6 percent from 10 percent to 16 percent:

$$30\% - 2 \times 7\% = 30\% - 14\% = 16\%$$

Sometimes derivatives are combined with options to bound the impact of interest rates. The most important of these instruments are called *caps* and *floors*. A cap is so named because it puts an upper limit or a cap on the impact of a rise in interest rates. A floor, conversely, provides a floor below which the interest rate impact is insulated.

To illustrate the impact of these, consider a firm that is borrowing short-term and is concerned that interest rates might rise. For example, using LIBOR as the reference interest rate, the firm might purchase a 7 percent cap. The cap pays the firm the difference between LIBOR and 7 percent on some principal amount, provided that LIBOR is greater than 7 percent. As long as LIBOR is below 7 percent, the holder of the cap receives no payments.

By purchasing the cap the firm has assured itself that even if interest rates rise above 7 percent, it will not have to pay more than a 7 percent rate. Suppose that interest rates rise to 9 percent. While the firm is borrowing short-term and paying 9 percent rates, this is offset by the cap, which is paying the firm the difference between 9 percent and the 7 percent limit. For any LIBOR rate above 7 percent, the firm receives the difference between LIBOR and 7 percent, and, as a consequence, it has capped its cost of borrowing at 7 percent.

On the other side, consider a financial firm that is in the business of lending short-term and is concerned that interest rates—and, consequently, its revenues—might fall. The firm could purchase a floor to protect itself from such declines. If the limit on the floor is 7 percent, then the floor pays the difference between 7 percent and LIBOR whenever LIBOR is below 7 percent, and nothing if LIBOR is above 7 percent. Thus, if interest rates were to fall to, say, 5 percent while the firm is only receiving 5 percent from its lending activities, the floor is paying it the difference between 7 percent and 5 percent, or an additional 2 percent.

By purchasing the floor, the firm has assured itself of receiving no less than 7 percent from the combination of the floor and its lending activities.

We have only scratched the surface of what is available in the world of derivatives. Derivatives are designed to meet marketplace needs, and the only binding limitation is the human imagination. Nowhere should the buyer's warning *caveat emptor* be taken more seriously than in the derivatives markets, and this is especially true for the exotics. If swaps are the meat and potatoes of the derivatives markets, then caps and floors are the meat and potatoes of the exotics. As we have seen, they have obvious value as hedging instruments. But, much attention has been focused on truly exotic derivatives, some of which appear to have arisen more as the residuals that were left over from more straightforward deals. We won't examine these in any detail, but suffice it to say that some of these are so volatile and unpredictable that market participants have dubbed them "toxic waste."

25.7 Actual Use of Derivatives

Because derivatives do not usually appear in financial statements, it is much more difficult to observe the use of derivatives by firms when compared to, say, bank debt. Much of our knowledge of corporate derivative use comes from academic surveys. Most surveys report that the use of derivatives appears to vary widespread among large publically traded firms. It appears that about one-half of all publically traded nonfinancial firms use derivatives of some kind.[23] Large firms are far more likely to use derivatives than small firms. Table 25.9 shows that for firms that use derivatives, foreign-currency and interest-rate derivatives are the most frequently used.[24]

The prevailing view is that derivatives can be very helpful in reducing the variability of firm cash flows, which, in turn, reduces the various costs associated with financial distress. Therefore, it is somewhat puzzling that large firms use derivatives more often than small firms—because large firms tend to have less cash flow variability than small firms. Also some surveys report that firms occasionally use derivatives when they want to speculate about future prices and not just to hedge risks.[25]

However, most of the evidence is consistent with the theory that derivatives are most frequently used by firms where financial distress costs are high and access to the capital markets is constrained.[26]

TABLE 25.9		Exposure Managed with Derivatives	Exposure Not Managed with Derivatives
Derivative Usage by Firms Using Derivatives	Foreign exchange	88%	12%
	Interest rate	77%	23%
	Commodity	55%	45%
	Equity	30%	70%

SOURCE: Gordon M. Bodnar, Gregory S. Hayt, and Richard Marston, "1998 Wharton Survey of Financial Risk Management of U.S. Non-Financial Firms," *Financial Management* (Winter 1998). Survey included 400 firms; 50 percent of the firms reported using derivatives.

---

[23]Gordon M. Bodnar, Gregory S. Hayt, and Richard Marston, "1998 Wharton Survey of Finance Risk Management by U.S. Non-Financial Firms," *Financial Management* (Winter 1998).

[24]Howton and Perfect report that interest rate derivatives are the most frequently used derivatives. Shawn D. Howton and Steven B. Perfect, "Currency and Interest-Rate Derivatives Use in U.S. Firms," *Financial Management* (Winter 1998).

[25]Walter Dolde, "The Trajectory of Corporate Financial Risk Management," *Journal of Applied Corporate Finance* (Fall 1993).

[26]Shawn D. Howton and Steven B. Perfect, "Currency and Interest-Rate Derivatives Use in U.S. Firms," *Financial Management* (Winter 1998). See also H. Berkman and M. E. Bradbury, "Empirical Evidence on the Corporate Use of Derivatives," *Financial Management* (Summer 1996).

25.8 SUMMARY AND CONCLUSIONS

1. Firms hedge to reduce risk. This chapter shows a number of hedging strategies.

2. A forward contract is an agreement by two parties to sell an item for cash at a later date. The price is set at the time the agreement is signed. However, cash changes hands on the date of delivery. Forward contracts are generally not traded on organized exchanges.

3. Futures contracts are also agreements for future delivery. They have certain advantages, such as liquidity, that forward contracts do not. An unusual feature of futures contracts is the mark-to-the-market convention. If the price of a futures contract falls on a particular day, every buyer of the contract must pay money to the clearinghouse. Every seller of the contract receives money from the clearinghouse. Everything is reversed if the price rises. The mark-to-the-market convention prevents defaults on futures contracts.

4. We divided hedges into two types: short hedges and long hedges. An individual or firm that sells a futures contract to reduce risk is instituting a short hedge. Short hedges are generally appropriate for holders of inventory. An individual or firm that buys a futures contract to reduce risk is instituting a long hedge. Long hedges are typically used by firms with contracts to sell finished goods at a fixed price.

5. An interest-rate futures contract employs a bond as the deliverable instrument. Because of their popularity, we worked with Treasury-bond futures contracts. We showed that Treasury-bond futures contracts can be priced using the same type of net-present-value analysis that is used to price Treasury bonds themselves.

6. Many firms are faced with interest-rate risk. They can reduce this risk by hedging with interest-rate futures contracts. As with other commodities, a short hedge involves the sale of a futures contract. Firms that are committed to buying mortgages or other bonds are likely to institute short hedges. A long hedge involves the purchase of a futures contract. Firms that have agreed to sell mortgages or other bonds at a fixed price are likely to institute long hedges.

7. Duration measures the average maturity of all the cash flows in a bond. Bonds with high duration have high price variability. Firms frequently try to match the duration of their assets with the duration of their liabilities.

8. Swaps are agreements to exchange cash flows over time. The first major type is an interest-rate swap in which one pattern of coupon payments, say, fixed payments, is exchanged for another, say, coupons that float with LIBOR. The second major type is a currency swap in which an agreement is struck to swap payments denominated in one currency for payments in another currency over time.

KEY TERMS

advance commitments, 712
cash transaction, 698
currency swaps, 719
deliverable instrument, 697
duration, 715
exotics, 722
forward contract, 697
futures contract, 698
hedging, 697

immunized, 718
interest-rate swaps, 719
long hedge, 705
making delivery, 697
marked to the market, 699
short hedge, 704
speculating, 697
swaps, 719
taking delivery, 697

SUGGESTED READINGS

Several cases that illustrate the concepts, tools, and markets for hedging can be found in:

Tufano, Peter. "How Financial Engineering Can Advance Corporate Strategy." *Harvard Business Review* (January–February 1996).

An advanced article on the empirical implications of very recent models for pricing swaps contracts is in:

Minton, Bernadette A. "An Empirical Examination of Basic Valuation Models for Plain Vanilla U.S. Interest Rate Swaps." *Journal of Financial Economics* 44 (Winter 1997).

QUESTIONS & PROBLEMS

FORWARD AND FUTURES CONTRACTS

25.1 Define:
  a. Forward contract
  b. Futures contract

25.2 Explain three ways in which futures contracts differ from forward contracts.

25.3 The following table lists the closing prices for wheat futures contracts (per bushel):

March 15	$5.03
March 16	$5.08
March 17	$5.12
March 18	$5.10
March 19	$4.98

Each contract is for 1 bushel of wheat. Suppose you bought one futures contract for $5.00 as trading began on March 15.

  a. Suppose you receive a notice of delivery from your broker at the end of trading on March 18.
   1. What is the delivery price per bushel?
   2. What price did you pay for the wheat (per bushel)?
   3. What are the daily cash flows associated with this contract?
   4. What is the net amount that you paid for one bushel of wheat?

  b. Suppose you receive a notice of delivery from your broker at the end of trading on March 19.
   1. What is the delivery price per bushel?
   2. What price did you pay for the wheat (per bushel)?
   3. What are the daily cash flows associated with this contract?
   4. What is the net amount that you paid for one bushel of wheat?

25.4 You enter into a forward contract to buy a 10-year, zero-coupon bond that will be issued in one year. The face value of the bond is $1,000, and the 1-year and 11-year spot interest rates are 3 percent per annum and 8 percent per annum, respectively. Both of these interest rates are expressed as effective annual yields (EAYs).
  a. What is the forward price of your contract?
  b. Suppose both the 1-year and 11-year spot rates unexpectedly shift downward by 2 percent. What is the price of a forward contract otherwise identical to yours?

25.5 **a.** How would you create a short position in futures contracts?
  b. In what type of situation does a short position reduce one's overall risk?
  c. How would you create a long position in futures contracts?
  d. In what type of situation does a long position reduce one's overall risk?

25.6 Mark Fisher is a speculator who believes that the futures price of silver will decrease over the next month. What type of futures position should Mark be interested in?

25.7 William Santiago is interested in entering the import/export business. During a recent visit with his financial advisors, he said, "If we play the game right, this is the safest business in the world. By hedging all of our transactions in the foreign-exchange futures market, we can eliminate all of our risk." Do you agree with William's assessment of hedging? Why or why not?

25.8 This morning you agreed to buy a one-year Treasury bond in six months. The bond has a face value of $1,000. Use the semiannual spot interest rates listed below to answer the following questions.

Time Horizon	Annual Spot Interest Rate (EAY)
6 months	9.83%
12 months	10.25%
18 months	10.67%
24 months	11.30%
30 months	11.72%

a. What is the forward price of this contract?

b. Suppose shortly after you purchased the forward contract, all rates increased by 30 basis points. For example, the six-month rate increased from 9.83 percent to 10.13 percent. What is the price of a forward contract otherwise identical to yours given these changes?

25.9 The forward price (f) of a contract on an asset with neither carrying costs nor convenience yield is the current spot price of the asset (S_0) multiplied by 1 plus the appropriate interest rate between the initiation of the contract and the delivery date of the asset. Derive this relationship by comparing the cash flows that result from the following two strategies:

Strategy 1: Buy silver on the spot market today and hold it for one year. (Hint: Do not use any of your own money to purchase the silver.)

Strategy 2: Take on a long position in a silver forward contract for delivery in one year.

Assume that silver is an asset with neither carrying costs nor convenience yield.

25.10 Kevin Ng is a Japanese student who is planning a one-year stay in the United States. He expects to arrive in the U.S. in eight months. He is worried about depreciation in the yen relative to the dollar over the next eight months and wishes to take a position in foreign exchange futures to hedge this risk. What should Kevin's hedging position be? Assume the exchange rate between Japanese and U.S. currencies is quoted as yen/dollar.

25.11 After reading the text's example about Ron Cooke, the mortgage banker, you decide to enter the business. You begin small. You agree to provide $300,000 to an old college roommate to finance the purchase of her home. The loan is a 20-year loan and carries a fixed interest rate of 10 percent, the current market rate of interest. The mortgage payments are made annually. Your former roommate needs the money three months from today. You do not have $300,000, but you intend to sell the mortgage to MAX Insurance Corporation. The president of MAX is an old friend, so you know with certainly he will buy the mortgage. Unfortunately, he is unavailable to meet with you until three months from today. Assume there are Treasury bond futures available for delivery in three months. A single contract is for $100,000 of T-bonds.

a. What is your former roommate's annual mortgage payment?

b. What is the most significant risk you face in this deal?

c. How can you hedge this risk?

d. Suppose that between today and your meeting with the president of MAX, the market rate of interest rises to 12 percent.

1. How much is MAX's president willing to pay you for the mortgage?

2. What will happen to the value of T-bond futures contracts?

3. What will happen to the value of a short position in T-bond futures contracts?

e. Suppose that between today and your meeting with the president of MAX, the market rate of interest falls to 9 percent.

1. How much is MAX's president willing to pay you for the mortgage?

2. What will happen to the value of T-bond futures contracts?

3. What will happen to the value of a short position in T-bond futures contracts?

DURATION

25.12 Consider three zero-coupon, $1,000 face-value bonds. Bond A matures one year from today, Bond B matures five years from today, and Bond C matures ten years from today. The current market interest rate is 11 percent per annum (effective annual yield).

a. What is the current price of each bond?

b. If the market interest rate suddenly rises to 14 percent per annum (effective annual yield), what will be the price of each of these bonds?

c. Which bond experienced the greatest percentage change in price?

25.13 Consider two four-year bonds. Each bond has a face value of $1,000. Bond A pays an annual coupon of 7 percent, and Bond B pays an annual coupon of 11 percent.

a. Calculate the price and duration of each bond if the market interest rate is 10 percent per annum (effective annual yield).

b. Calculate the price of each bond if the market interest rate is 7 percent per annum (effective annual yield).

c. Which bond do you expect experienced the greatest percentage change in price? Explain.

d. What is the percentage change in the price of each bond?

25.14 Calculate the duration of a three-year, $1,000 face-value bond that pays an annual coupon of 9 percent. The bond is selling at par.

25.15 Calculate the duration of a four-year, $1,000 face-value bond that pays an annual coupon of 9 percent. The bond is selling at par.

25.16 Calculate the duration of a four-year, $1,000 face-value bond that pays an annual coupon of 5 percent. The market interest rate is 9 percent per annum (effective annual yield).

25.17 Mr. and Mrs. Hansel have a son who will begin college three years from today. School expenses of $20,000 will need to be paid at the beginning of each of the four years that their son plans to attend college. What is the duration of this liability to the Hansels if the couple can borrow and lend at the market interest rate of 15 percent per annum (effective annual yield)?

25.18 Consider Blue Steel Community Bank's market-value balance sheet:

	Market Value (in millions)	Duration (in years)
Assets		
Federal funds deposits	$ 43	0
Accounts receivable	615	0.33
Short-term loans	345	0.75
Long-term loans	55	5
Mortgages	197	15
Liabilities and Equity		
Checking and savings deposits	$490	0
Certificates of deposit	370	1.5
Long-term financing	250	10
Equity	145	—

a. What is the duration of Blue Steel's assets?

b. What is the duration of Blue Steel's liabilities?

c. Is the bank immune from interest rate risk?

25.19 Consider Magnum Commercial Bank's market-value balance sheet:

	Market Value (in millions)	Duration (in years)
Assets		
Overnight money	$ 100	0
Loans	500	1
Mortgages	1,200	12
Liabilities		
Checking and savings accounts	$ 300	0
Certificates of deposit	400	1.1
Long-term debt	500	19
Equity	600	—

a. What is the duration of Magnum's assets?

b. What is the duration of Magnum's liabilities?

c. Is the bank immune from interest-rate risk?

SWAPS

25.20 The Miller Company and the Edwards Company both need to raise $1 million to fund improvements at their manufacturing plants. Miller has been in business for 40 years and has a very good credit rating. It can borrow at either a fixed rate of 10 percent or at a floating rate based on the LIBOR plus 3 percent. The Edwards Company has experienced some financial distress recently and does not have a strong credit history. It can borrow at either a fixed rate of 15 percent or at a floating rate based on the LIBOR plus 2 percent. Miller believes that the general level of interest rates will fall in upcoming years and therefore would prefer to borrow at a floating rate of interest. Due to its financial difficulties, Edwards would prefer to borrow at a fixed rate of interest so that unexpected increases in the general level of interest rates will not force the firm into bankruptcy.

a. Is there an opportunity for the Miller Company and the Edwards Company to benefit from a swap?

b. Show how you would structure a swap between the two parties.

Short-Term Finance

In Chapter 26 we introduce short-term financial planning, which involves short-lived assets and liabilities. We discuss two aspects of short-term financial planning: (1) the size of the firm's investment in current assets, such as cash, accounts receivable, and inventory, and (2) how to finance short-term assets. We describe the primary tool for short-term financial planning, the cash budget. It incorporates the short-term financial goals of the firm and tells the financial manager the amount of necessary short-term financing.

In Chapter 27 we describe the management of a firm's investment in cash. The chapter divides cash management into three separate areas:

1. Determining the appropriate target cash balance.
2. Collecting and disbursing cash.
3. Investing the excess cash in marketable securities.

Chapter 28 describes what is involved when a firm makes the decision to grant credit to its customers. This decision involves three types of analysis:

1. A firm must decide on the conditions under which it sells its goods and services for credit. These conditions are the terms of the sale.
2. Before granting credit, the firm must analyze the risk that the customer will not pay; this is called *credit analysis*.
3. After credit is extended, the firm must determine how to collect its cash.

Short-Term Finance and Planning

EXECUTIVE SUMMARY

Up to now we have described many of the decisions of long-term finance: capital budgeting, dividend policy, and capital structure. This chapter introduces short-term finance. Short-term finance is an analysis of decisions that affect current assets and current liabilities and will frequently have an impact on the firm within a year.

The term *net working capital* is often associated with short-term financial decision making. Net working capital is the difference between current assets and current liabilities. The focus of short-term finance on net working capital seems to suggest that it is an accounting subject. However, making net working capital decisions still relies on cash flow and net present value.

There is no universally accepted definition of short-term finance. The most important difference between short-term and long-term finance is the timing of cash flows. Short-term financial decisions involve cash inflows and outflows within a year or less. For example, a short-term financial decision is involved when

a firm orders raw materials, pays in cash, and anticipates selling finished goods in one year for cash, as illustrated in Figure 26.1. A long-term financial decision is involved when a firm purchases a special machine that will reduce operating costs over the next five years, as illustrated in Figure 26.2.

Here are some questions of short-term finance:

1. What is a reasonable level of cash to keep on hand (in a bank) to pay bills?

2. How much raw material should be ordered?

3. How much credit should be extended to customers?

This chapter introduces the basic elements of short-term financial decisions. First, we describe the short-term operating activities of the firm, and then we identify alternative short-term financial policies. Finally, we outline the basic elements in a short-term financial plan and describe short-term financing instruments.

26.1 Tracing Cash and Net Working Capital

In this section we trace the components of cash and net working capital as they change from one year to the next. Our goal is to describe the short-term operating activities of the firm and their impact on cash and working capital.

Current assets are cash and other assets that are expected to be converted to cash within the year. Current assets are presented in the balance sheet in order of their accounting **liquidity**—the ease with which they can be converted to cash at a fair price and the time it takes to do so. Table 26.1 gives the balance sheet and income statement of the Tradewinds Manufacturing Corporation for 20X2 and 20X1. The four major items found

FIGURE 26.1	
Short-Term Financial Decision	

FIGURE 26.2	
Long-Term Financial Decision	

TABLE 26.1		

TRADEWINDS MANUFACTURING CORPORATION
December 31, 20X2, and December 31, 20X1
Balance Sheet

	20X2	**20X1**
Assets		
Current assets:		
Cash	$ 500,000	$ 500,000
Marketable securities (at cost)	500,000	450,000
Accounts receivable less allowance for bad debts	2,000,000	1,600,000
Inventories	3,000,000	2,000,000
Total current assets	$ 6,000,000	$4,550,000
Fixed assets (property, plant, and equipment):		
Land	450,000	450,000
Building	4,000,000	4,000,000
Machinery	1,500,000	800,000
Office equipment	50,000	50,000
Less: Accumulated depreciation	2,000,000	1,700,000
Net fixed assets	4,000,000	3,600,000
Prepayments and deferred charges	400,000	300,000
Intangibles	100,000	100,000
Total assets	$10,500,000	$8,550,000
Liabilities		
Current liabilities:		
Accounts payable	$ 1,000,000	$ 750,000
Notes payable	1,500,000	500,000
Accrued expenses payable	250,000	225,000
Taxes payable	250,000	225,000
Total current liabilities	$ 3,000,000	$1,700,000
Long-term liabilities:		
First mortgage bonds, 5% interest, due 2025	3,000,000	3,000,000
Deferred taxes	600,000	600,000
Total liabilities	$ 6,600,000	$5,300,000

Financial Statements

TABLE 26.1	TRADEWINDS MANUFACTURING CORPORATION		
(concluded)	December 31, 20X2, and December 31, 20X1		
	Balance Sheet		
		20X2	**20X1**
	Stockholders' Equity		
	Common stock, $5 par value each; authorized,		
	issued, and outstanding 300,000 shares	$ 1,500,000	$ 1,500,000
	Capital surplus	500,000	500,000
	Accumulated retained earnings	1,900,000	1,250,000
	Total stockholders' equity	3,900,000	3,250,000
	Total liabilities and stockholders' equity	$10,500,000	$ 8,550,000
	Consolidated Income Statement		
	Net sales	$11,500,000	$10,700,000
	Cost of sales and operating expenses:		
	Cost of goods sold	8,200,000	7,684,000
	Depreciation	300,000	275,000
	Selling and administration expenses	1,400,000	1,325,000
	Operating profit	1,600,000	1,416,000
	Other income:		
	Dividends and interest	50,000	50,000
	Total income from operations	1,650,000	1,466,000
	Less: Interest on bonds and other liabilities	300,000	150,000
	Income before provision for income tax	1,350,000	1,316,000
	Provision for income tax	610,000	600,000
	Net profit	$ 740,000	$ 716,000
	Dividends paid out	$ 90,000	$ 132,000
	Retained earnings	$ 650,000	$ 584,000

in the current asset section of the Tradewinds balance sheet are cash, marketable securities, accounts receivable, and inventories.

Analogous to their investment in current assets, firms use several kinds of short-term debt, called current liabilities. Current liabilities are obligations that are expected to require cash payment within one year or within the operating cycle, whichever is shorter.[1] The three major items found as *current liabilities* are accounts payable; accrued wages, taxes, and other expenses payable; and notes payable.

26.2 Defining Cash in Terms of Other Elements

Now we will define cash in terms of the other elements of the balance sheet. The balance sheet equation is:

$$\text{Net working capital} + \text{Fixed assets} = \text{Long-term debt} + \text{Equity} \qquad (26.1)$$

Net working capital is cash plus the other elements of net working capital; that is:

$$\frac{\text{Net working}}{\text{capital}} = \text{Cash} + \frac{\text{Other current}}{\text{assets}} - \frac{\text{Current}}{\text{liabilities}} \qquad (26.2)$$

---

[1] As we will learn in this chapter, the operating cycle begins when inventory is received and ends when cash is collected from the sale of inventory.

Substituting equation (26.2) into (26.1) yields:

$$\text{Cash} + \frac{\text{Other current}}{\text{assets}} - \frac{\text{Current}}{\text{liabilities}} = \frac{\text{Long-term}}{\text{debt}} + \text{Equity} - \frac{\text{Fixed}}{\text{assets}} \qquad (26.3)$$

and rearranging, we find that:

$$\text{Cash} = \frac{\text{Long-term}}{\text{debt}} + \text{Equity} - \frac{\text{Net working capital}}{\text{(excluding cash)}} - \frac{\text{Fixed}}{\text{assets}} \qquad (26.4)$$

The natural interpretation of equation (26.4) is that increasing long-term debt and equity and decreasing fixed assets and net working capital (excluding cash) will increase cash to the firm.

The Sources-and-Uses-of-Cash

We first introduced the statement of cash flows in Chapter 2. This is the accounting statement that describes the sources and uses of cash. In this section we look at where cash comes from and how it is used. From the right-hand side of equation (26.4), we can see an increase in long-term debt and/or equity leads to an increase in cash. Moreover, a decrease in net working capital and/or fixed assets leads to a decrease in cash. In addition, the sum of net income and depreciation increases cash, whereas dividend payments decrease cash. This reasoning allows an accountant to create a statement of cash flows, which shows all the transactions that affect a firm's cash position.

Let us trace the changes in cash for Tradewinds during the year. Notice that Tradewinds' cash balance remained constant during 20X2, even though cash flow from operations was $1.04 million (net income plus depreciation). Why did cash remain the same? The answer is simply that the sources of cash were equal to the uses of cash. From the firm's statement of cash flows (Table 26.2), we find that Tradewinds generated cash as follows:

1. It generated cash flow from operations of $1.04 million.
2. It increased its accounts payable by $250,000. This is the same as increasing borrowing from suppliers.
3. It increased its borrowing from banks by $1 million. This shows up as an increase in notes payable.
4. It increased accrued expenses by $25,000.
5. It increased taxes payable by $25,000, in effect borrowing from the IRS.

Tradewinds used cash for the following reasons:

1. It invested $700,000 in fixed assets.
2. It increased prepayments by $100,000.
3. It paid a $90,000 dividend.
4. It invested in inventory worth $1 million.
5. It lent its customers additional money. Hence, accounts receivable increased by $400,000.
6. It purchased $50,000 worth of marketable securities.

This example illustrates the difference between a firm's cash position on the balance sheet and cash flows from operations.

Concept
Questions

1. What is the difference between net working capital and cash?
2. Will net working capital always increase when cash increases?
3. List the potential uses of cash.
4. List the potential sources of cash.

TABLE 26.2	TRADEWINDS MANUFACTURING CORPORATION	
Sources and Uses of Cash	**Sources and Uses of Cash**	
	(in thousands)	

Sources of Cash:		
Cash flow from operations:		
Net income		$ 740
Depreciation		300
Total cash flow from operations		$1,040
Decrease in net working capital:		
Increase in accounts payable		250
Increase in notes payable		1,000
Increase in accrued expenses		25
Increase in taxes payable		25
Total sources of cash		$2,340
Uses of cash:		
Increase in fixed assets		$ 700
Increase in prepayments		100
Dividends		90
Increase in net working capital:		
Investment in inventory		1,000
Increase in accounts receivable		400
Increase in marketable securities		50
Total uses of cash		$2,340
Change in cash balance		0

26.3 The Operating Cycle and the Cash Cycle

Short-term finance is concerned with the firm's **short-run operating activities.** A typical manufacturing firm's short-run operating activities consist of a sequence of events and decisions:

Events	Decisions
1. Buying raw materials	1. How much inventory to order?
2. Paying cash for purchases	2. To borrow, or draw down cash balance?
3. Manufacturing the product	3. What choice of production technology?
4. Selling the product	4. To offer cash terms or credit terms to customers?
5. Collecting cash	5. How to collect cash?

These activities create patterns of cash inflows and cash outflows that are both unsynchronized and uncertain. They are unsynchronized because the payments of cash for raw materials does not happen at the same time as the receipt of cash from selling the product. They are uncertain because future sales and costs are not known with certainty.

Figure 26.3 depicts the short-term operating activities and cash flows for a typical manufacturing firm along the **cash flow time line.** The **operating cycle** is the time interval between the arrival of inventory stock and the date when cash is collected from receivables. The **cash cycle** begins when cash is paid for materials and ends when cash is collected from receivables. The cash flow time line consists of an operating cycle and a cash cycle. The

FIGURE 26.3

Cash Flow Time Line and the Short-Term Operating Activities of a Typical Manufacturing Firm

The *operating cycle* is the time period from the arrival of stock until the receipt of cash. (Sometimes the operating cycle is defined to include the time from placement of the order until arrival of the stock.) The *cash cycle* begins when cash is paid for materials and ends when cash is collected from receivables.

need for short-term financial decision making is suggested by the gap between the cash inflows and cash outflows. This is related to the lengths of the operating cycle and the accounts payable period. This gap can be filled either by borrowing or by holding a liquidity reserve for marketable securities. The gap can be shortened by changing the inventory, receivable, and payable periods. Now we take a closer look at the operating cycle.

The length of the operating cycle is equal to the sum of the lengths of the inventory and accounts receivable periods. The inventory period is the length of time required to order, produce, and sell a product. The accounts receivable period is the length of time required to collect cash receipts.

The cash cycle is the time between cash disbursement and cash collection. It can be thought of as the operating cycle less the accounts payable period, that is:

$$\text{Cash cycle} = \text{Operating cycle} - \text{Accounts payable period}$$

The accounts payable period is the length of time the firm is able to delay payment on the purchase of various resources, such as wages and raw materials.

In practice, the inventory period, the accounts receivable period, and the accounts payable period are measured by days in inventory, days in receivables, and days in payables, respectively. We illustrate how the operating cycle and the cash cycle can be measured in the following example.

EXAMPLE

Tradewinds Manufacturing is a diversified manufacturing firm with the balance sheet and income statement shown in Table 26.1 for 20X1 and 20X2. The operating cycle and the cash cycle can be determined for Tradewinds after calculating the appropriate ratios for inventory, receivables, and payables. Consider inventory first. The average inventory is:

$$\text{Average inventory} = \frac{\$3 \text{ million} + \$2 \text{ million}}{2} = \$2.5 \text{ million}$$

The terms in the numerator are the ending inventory in the second and first years, respectively.

We next calculate the inventory-turnover ratio:

$$\text{Inventory-turnover ratio} = \frac{\text{Cost of goods sold}}{\text{Average inventory}} = \frac{\$8.2 \text{ million}}{\$2.5 \text{ million}} = 3.3$$

This implies that the inventory cycle occurs 3.3 times a year. Finally, we calculate days in inventory:

$$\text{Days in inventory} = \frac{365 \text{ days}}{3.3} = 110.6 \text{ days}$$

Our calculation implies that the inventory cycle is slightly more than 110 days.

We perform analogous calculations for receivables and payables.[2]

$$\frac{\text{Average}}{\text{accounts receivable}} = \frac{\$2.0 \text{ million} + \$1.6 \text{ million}}{2} = \$1.8 \text{ million}$$

$$\frac{\text{Average}}{\text{receivable turnover}} = \frac{\text{Credit sales}}{\text{Average accounts receivable}} = \frac{\$11.5 \text{ million}}{\$1.8 \text{ million}} = 6.4$$

$$\frac{\text{Days in}}{\text{receivables}} = \frac{365}{6.4} = 57 \text{ days}$$

$$\frac{\text{Average}}{\text{payables}} = \frac{\$1.0 \text{ million} + \$0.75 \text{ million}}{2} = \$0.875 \text{ million}$$

$$\frac{\text{Accounts payable}}{\text{deferral period}} = \frac{\text{Cost of goods sold}}{\text{Average payables}} = \frac{\$8.2 \text{ million}}{\$0.875 \text{ million}} = 9.4$$

$$\frac{\text{Days in}}{\text{payables}} = \frac{365}{9.4} = 38.8 \text{ days}$$

The preceding calculations allow us to determine both the operating cycle and the cash cycle.

$$\frac{\text{Operating}}{\text{cycle}} = \frac{\text{Days in}}{\text{inventory}} + \frac{\text{Days in}}{\text{receivables}}$$

$$= 110.6 \text{ days} + 57 \text{ days} = 167.6 \text{ days}$$

$$\text{Cash cycle} = \text{Operating cycle} - \text{Days in payables}$$

$$= 167.6 \text{ days} - 38.8 \text{ days} = 128.8 \text{ days.}$$

The need for short-term financial decision making is suggested by the gap between the cash inflows and cash outflows. This is related to the lengths of the operating cycles and accounts payable period. This gap can be filled either by borrowing or by holding a liquidity reserve of marketable securities. The gap can be shortened by changing the inventory, receivable, and payable periods. Now we take a closer look at this aspect of short-term financial policy.

Concept Questions

1. **What does it mean to say that a firm has an inventory-turnover ratio of four?**
2. **Describe the operating cycle and the cash cycle. What are the differences between them?**

---

[2]We assume that Tradewinds Manufacturing makes no cash sales.

26.4 Some Aspects of Short-Term Financial Policy

The policy that a firm adopts for short-term finance will be composed of at least two elements:

1. *The Size of the Firm's Investment in Current Assets.* This is usually measured relative to the firm's level of total operating revenues. A flexible or accommodative short-term financial policy would maintain a high ratio of current assets to sales. A restrictive short-term financial policy would entail a low ratio of current assets to sales.

2. *The Financing of Current Assets.* This is measured as the proportion of short-term debt to long-term debt. A restrictive short-term financial policy means a high proportion of short-term debt relative to long-term financing, and a flexible policy means less short-term debt and more long-term debt.

The Size of the Firm's Investment in Current Assets

Flexible short-term financial policies include:

1. Keeping large balances of cash and marketable securities.
2. Making large investments in inventory.
3. Granting liberal credit terms, which results in a high level of accounts receivable.

Restrictive short-term financial policies are:

1. Keeping low cash balances and no investment in marketable securities.
2. Making small investments in inventory.
3. Allowing no credit sales and no accounts receivable.

Determining the optimal investment level in short-term assets requires an identification of the different costs of alternative short-term financing policies. The objective is to trade off the cost of restrictive policies against those of the flexible ones to arrive at the best compromise.

Current asset holdings are highest with a flexible short-term financial policy and lowest with a restrictive policy. Thus, flexible short-term financial policies are costly in that they require higher cash outflows to finance cash and marketable securities, inventory, and accounts receivable. However, future cash inflows are highest with a flexible policy. Sales are stimulated by the use of a credit policy that provides liberal financing to customers. A large amount of inventory on hand ("on the shelf") provides a quick delivery service to customers and increases in sales.[3] In addition, the firm can probably charge higher prices for the quick delivery service and the liberal credit terms of flexible policies. A flexible policy also may result in fewer production stoppages because of inventory shortages.[4]

Managing current assets can be thought of as involving a trade-off between costs that rise with the level of investment and costs that fall with the level of investment. Costs that rise with the level of investment in current assets are called **carrying costs.** Costs that fall with increases in the level of investment in current assets are called **shortage costs.**

Carrying costs are generally of two types. First, because the rate of return on current assets is low compared with that of other assets, there is an opportunity cost. Second, there is the cost of maintaining the economic value of the item. For example, the cost of warehousing inventory belongs here.

---

[3]This is true of some types of finished goods.

[4]This is true of inventory of raw material but not of finished goods.

Determinants of Corporate Liquid Asset Holdings

Firms with High Holdings of Liquid Assets Will Have	Firms with Low Holdings of Liquid Assets Will Have
High-growth opportunities	Low-growth opportunities
High-risk investments	Low-risk investments
Small firms	Large firms
Low-credit firms	High-credit firms

Firms will hold more liquid assets (i.e., cash and marketable securities) to ensure that they can continue investing when cash flow is low relative to positive NPV investment opportunities. Firms that have good access to capital markets will hold less-liquid assets.

SOURCE: Tim Opler, Lee Pinkowitz, René Stulz, and Rohan Williamson, "The Determinants and Implication of Corporate Cash Holdings," *Journal of Financial Economics* 52 (1999).

Shortage costs are incurred when the investment in current assets is low. If a firm runs out of cash, it will be forced to sell marketable securities. If a firm runs out of cash and cannot readily sell marketable securities, it may need to borrow or default on an obligation. (This general situation is called *cash-out*.) If a firm has no inventory (a *stock-out*) or if it cannot extend credit to its customers, it will lose customers.

There are two kinds of shortage costs:

1. *Trading or Order Costs.* Order costs are the costs of placing an order for more cash (*brokerage costs*) or more inventory (*production set-up costs*).

2. *Costs Related to Safety Reserves.* These are costs of lost sales, lost customer goodwill, and disruption of production schedule.

Figure 26.4 illustrates the basic nature of carrying costs. The total costs of investing in current assets are determined by adding the carrying costs and the shortage costs. The minimum point on the total cost curve (CA*) reflects the optimal balance of current assets. The curve is generally quite flat at the optimum, and it is difficult, if not impossible, to find the precise optimal balance of shortage and carrying costs. Usually we are content with a choice near the optimum.

If carrying costs are low and/or shortage costs are high, the optimal policy calls for substantial current assets. In other words, the optimal policy is a flexible one. This is illustrated in the middle graph of Figure 26.4.

If carrying costs are high and/or shortage costs are low, the optimal policy is a restrictive one. That is, the optimal policy calls for modest current assets. This is illustrated in the bottom graph of the figure.

Opler, Pinkowitz, Stulz, and Williamson examine the determinants of holdings of cash and marketable securities by publicly traded firms.[5] They find evidence that firms behave according to the static trade-off model described earlier. Their study focuses only on liquid assets (i.e., cash and market securities), so that carrying costs are the opportunity costs of holding liquid assets and shortage costs are the risks of not having cash when investment opportunities are good.

---

[5]Tim Opler, Lee Pinkowitz, René Stulz, and Rohan Williamson, "The Determinants and Implication of Corporate Cash Holdings," *Journal of Financial Economics* 52 (1999).

FIGURE 26.4

Carrying Costs and Shortage Costs

Flexible policy

Restrictive policy

Carrying costs increase with the level of investment in current assets. They include both opportunity costs and the costs of maintaining the asset's economic value. *Shortage costs* decrease with increases in the level of investment in current assets. They include trading costs and the costs of running out of the current asset (for example, being short of cash).

Alternative Financing Policies for Current Assets

In the previous section we examined the level of investment in current assets. Now we turn to the level of current liabilities, assuming the investment in current assets is optimal.

An Ideal Model   In an ideal economy, short-term assets can always be financed with short-term debt, and long-term assets can be financed with long-term debt and equity. In this economy, net working capital is always zero.

Imagine the simple case of a grain-elevator operator. Grain-elevator operators buy crops after harvest, store them, and sell them during the year. They have high inventories of grain after the harvest and end with low inventories just before the next harvest.

Bank loans with maturities of less than one year are used to finance the purchase of grain. These loans are paid with the proceeds from the sale of grain.

The situation is shown in Figure 26.5. Long-term assets are assumed to grow over time, whereas current assets increase at the end of the harvest and then decline during the year. Short-term assets end at zero just before the next harvest. These assets are financed by short-term debt, and long-term assets are financed with long-term debt and equity. Net working capital—current assets minus current liabilities—is always zero.

Different Strategies in Financing Current Assets   Current assets cannot be expected to drop to zero in the real world, because a long-term rising level of sales will result in some permanent investment in current assets. A growing firm can be thought of as having both a permanent requirement for current assets and one for long-term assets. This total asset requirement will exhibit balances over time reflecting (1) a secular growth trend, (2) a seasonal variation around the trend, and (3) unpredictable day-to-day and month-to-month fluctuations. This is depicted in Figure 26.6. (We have not tried to show the unpredictable day-to-day and month-to-month variations in the total asset requirement.)

Now, let us look at how this asset requirement is financed. First, consider the strategy (strategy *F* in Figure 26.7) where long-term financing covers more than the total asset requirement, even at seasonal peaks. The firm will have excess cash available for investment in marketable securities when the total asset requirement falls from peaks. Because this approach implies chronic short-term cash surpluses and a large investment in net working capital, it is considered a flexible strategy.

FIGURE 26.5

Financing Policy for an Idealized Economy

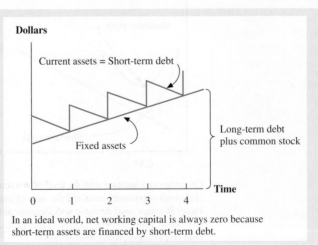

In an ideal world, net working capital is always zero because short-term assets are financed by short-term debt.

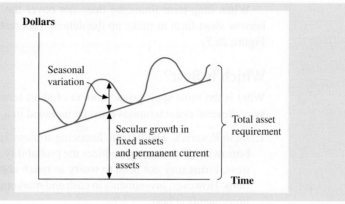

FIGURE 26.6

The Total Asset Requirement over Time

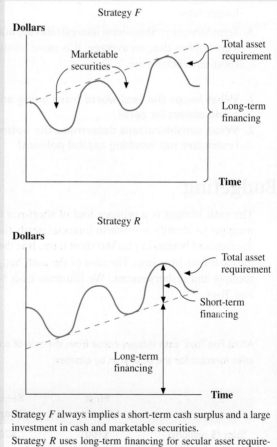

FIGURE 26.7

Alternative Asset-Financing Policies

Strategy *F* always implies a short-term cash surplus and a large investment in cash and marketable securities.

Strategy *R* uses long-term financing for secular asset requirements only, and short-term borrowing for seasonal variations.

When long-term financing does not cover the total asset requirement, the firm must borrow short-term to make up the deficit. This restrictive strategy is labeled strategy *R* in Figure 26.7.

Which Is Best?

What is the most appropriate amount of short-term borrowing? There is no definitive answer. Several considerations must be included in a proper analysis:

1. *Cash Reserves.* The flexible financing strategy implies surplus cash and little short-term borrowing. This strategy reduces the probability that a firm will experience financial distress. Firms may not need to worry as much about meeting recurring, short-run obligations. However, investments in cash and marketable securities are zero net-present-value investments at best.

2. *Maturity Hedging.* Most firms finance inventories with short-term bank loans and fixed assets with long-term financing. Firms tend to avoid financing long-lived assets with short-term borrowing. This type of maturity mismatching would necessitate frequent financing and is inherently risky, because short-term interest rates are more volatile than longer rates.

3. *Term Structure.* Short-term interest rates are normally lower than long-term interest rates. This implies that, on average, it is more costly to rely on long-term borrowing than on short-term borrowing.

Concept
Questions

1. **What keeps the real world from being an ideal one where net working capital could always be zero?**
2. **What considerations determine the optimal compromise between flexible and restrictive net working capital policies?**

26.5 Cash Budgeting

The **cash budget** is a primary tool of short-run financial planning. It allows the financial manager to identify short-term financial needs (and opportunities). It will tell the manager the required borrowing for the short term. It is the way of identifying the cash-flow gap on the cash-flow time line. The idea of the cash budget is simple: It records estimates of cash receipts and disbursements. We illustrate cash budgeting with the following example of Fun Toys.

EXAMPLE

All of Fun Toys' cash inflows come from the sale of toys. Cash budgeting for Fun Toys starts with a sales forecast for the next year, by quarter:

	First Quarter	Second Quarter	Third Quarter	Fourth Quarter
Sales ($ millions)	$100	$200	$150	$100

Fun Toys' fiscal year starts on July 1. Fun Toys' sales are seasonal and are usually very high in the second quarter, due to Christmastime sales. But Fun Toys sells to department stores on credit, and sales do not generate cash immediately. Instead, cash comes later from collections on accounts receivable. Fun Toys has a 90-day collection period, and 100 percent of sales are collected the

TABLE 26.3		First Quarter	Second Quarter	Third Quarter	Fourth Quarter
Sources of Cash (in millions)	Sales	$100	$200	$150	$100
	Cash collections	100	100	200	150
	Starting receivables	100	100	200	150
	Ending receivables	100	200	150	100

following quarter. In other words:

$$\text{Collections} = \text{Last quarter's sales}$$

This relationship implies that:

$$\text{Accounts receivable at end of last quarter} = \text{Last quarter's sales} \qquad (26.5)$$

We assume that sales in the fourth quarter of the previous fiscal year were $100 million. From equation (26.5), we know that accounts receivable at the end of the fourth quarter of the previous fiscal year were $100 million and collections in the first quarter of the current fiscal year are $100 million.

The first quarter sales of the current fiscal year of $100 million are added to the accounts receivable, but $100 million of collections are subtracted. Therefore, Fun Toys ended the first quarter with accounts receivable of $100 million. The basic relation is:

$$\frac{\text{Ending accounts}}{\text{receivable}} = \frac{\text{Starting accounts}}{\text{receivable}} + \text{Sales} - \text{Collections}$$

Table 26.3 shows cash collections for Fun Toys for the next four quarters. Though collections are the only source of cash here, this need not always be the case. Other sources of cash could include sales of assets, investment income, and long-term financing.

Cash Outflow

Next, we consider the cash disbursements. They can be put into four basic categories, as shown in Table 26.4.

1. *Payments of Accounts Payable.* These are payments for goods or services, such as raw materials. These payments will generally be made after purchases. Purchases will depend on the sales forecast. In the case of Fun Toys, assume that:

$$\text{Payments} = \text{Last quarter's purchases}$$
$$\text{Purchases} = 1/2 \text{ next quarter's sales forecast}$$

2. *Wages, Taxes, and Other Expenses.* This category includes all other normal costs of doing business that require actual expenditures. Depreciation, for example, is often thought of as a normal cost of business, but it requires no cash outflow.

3. *Capital Expenditures.* These are payments of cash for long-lived assets. Fun Toys plans a major capital expenditure in the fourth quarter.

4. *Long-Term Financing.* This category includes interest and principal payments on long-term outstanding debt and dividend payments to shareholders.

The total forecasted outflow appears in the last line of Table 26.4.

The Cash Balance

The net cash balance appears in Table 26.5, and a large net cash outflow is forecast in the second quarter. This large outflow is not caused by an inability to earn a profit. Rather, it

TABLE 26.4		First Quarter	Second Quarter	Third Quarter	Fourth Quarter
Disbursement of Cash (in millions)	Sales	$100	$200	$150	$100
	Purchases	100	75	50	50
	Uses of cash				
	Payments of accounts payable	50	100	75	50
	Wages, taxes, and other expenses	20	40	30	20
	Capital expenditures	0	0	0	100
	Long-term financing expenses: interest and dividends	10	10	10	10
	Total uses of cash	$ 80	$150	$115	$180

TABLE 26.5		First Quarter	Second Quarter	Third Quarter	Fourth Quarter
The Cash Balance (in millions)	Total cash receipts	$100	$100	$200	$150
	Total cash disbursements	80	150	115	180
	Net cash flow	20	(50)	85	(30)
	Cumulative excess cash balance	20	(30)	55	25
	Minimum cash balance	5	5	5	5
	Cumulative finance surplus (deficit) requirement	15	(35)	50	20

results from delayed collections on sales. This results in a cumulative cash shortfall of $30 million in the second quarter.

Fun Toys had established a minimum operating cash balance equal to $5 million to facilitate transactions, protect against unexpected contingencies, and maintain compensating balances at its commercial banks. This means that it has a cash shortfall in the second quarter equal to $35 million.

Concept Questions

1. How would you conduct a sensitivity analysis for Fun Toys' net cash balance?
2. What could you learn from such an analysis?

26.6 The Short-Term Financial Plan

Fun Toys has a short-term financing problem. It cannot meet the forecasted cash outflows in the second quarter from internal sources. Its financing options include: (1) unsecured bank borrowing, (2) secured borrowing, and (3) other sources.

Unsecured Loans

The most common way to finance a temporary cash deficit is to arrange a short-term unsecured bank loan. Firms that use short-term bank loans usually ask their bank for either a noncommitted or a committed *line of credit*. A *noncommitted* line is an informal arrangement that allows firms to borrow up to a previously specified limit without going through the normal paperwork. The interest rate on the line of credit is usually set equal to the bank's prime lending rate plus an additional percentage. Most of the time, banks will also require that compensating balances be kept at the bank by the firm. For example, a firm might be required to keep an amount equal to 5 percent on the line of credit.

Committed lines of credit are formal legal arrangements and usually involve a commitment fee paid by the firm to the bank (usually the fee is approximately 0.25 percent of the total committed funds per year). For larger firms the interest rate is often tied to the London Interbank Offered Rate (LIBOR) or to the bank's cost of funds, rather than the prime rate. Midsized and smaller firms often are required to keep compensating balances in the bank.

Compensating balances are deposits the firm keeps with the bank in low-interest or noninterest-bearing accounts. Compensating balances are commonly on the order of 2 to 5 percent of the amount used. By leaving these funds with the bank without receiving interest, the firm increases the effective interest earned by the bank on the line of credit. For example, if a firm borrowing $100,000 must keep $5,000 as a compensating balance, the firm effectively receives only $95,000. A stated interest rate of 10 percent implies yearly interest payments of $10,000 ($100,000 × 0.10). The effective interest rate is 10.53 percent ($10,000/$95,000).

Secured Loans

Banks and other finance companies often require *security* for a loan. Security for short-term loans usually consists of accounts receivable or inventories.

Under **accounts receivable financing,** receivables are either *assigned* or *factored.* Under assignment, the lender not only has a lien on the receivables but also has recourse to the borrower. Factoring involves the sale of accounts receivable. The purchaser, who is called a *factor,* must then collect on the receivables. The factor assumes the full risk of default on bad accounts.

As the name implies, an **inventory loan** uses inventory as collateral. Some common types of inventory loans are

1. *Blanket Inventory Lien.* The blanket inventory lien gives the lender a lien against all the borrower's inventories.
2. *Trust Receipt.* Under this arrangement, the borrower holds the inventory in trust for the lender. The document acknowledging the loan is called the trust receipt. Proceeds from the sale of inventory are remitted immediately to the lender.
3. *Field-Warehouse Financing.* In field-warehouse financing, a public warehouse company supervises the inventory for the lender.

Other Sources

There are a variety of other sources of short-term funds employed by corporations. The most important of these are the issuance of **commercial paper** and financing through **banker's acceptances.** Commercial paper consists of short-term notes issued by large and highly rated firms. Typically these notes are of short maturity, ranging up to 270 days (beyond that limit the firm must file a registration statement with the SEC). Because the firm issues these directly and because it usually backs the issue with a special bank line of credit, the rate the firm obtains is often significantly below the prime rate the bank would charge it for a direct loan.

A banker's acceptance is an agreement by a bank to pay a sum of money. These agreements typically arise when a seller sends a bill or draft to a customer. The customer's bank *accepts* this bill and notes the acceptance on it, which makes it an obligation of the bank.

In this way a firm that is buying something from a supplier can effectively arrange for the bank to pay the outstanding bill. Of course, the bank charges the customer a fee for this service.

Visit us at www.mhhe.com/rwj

Concept Questions

1. What are the two basic forms of short-term financing?
2. Describe two types of secured loans.

26.7 SUMMARY AND CONCLUSIONS

1. This chapter introduces the management of short-term finance. Short-term finance involves short-lived assets and liabilities. We trace and examine the short-term sources and uses of cash as they appear on the firm's financial statements. We see how current assets and current liabilities arise in the short-term operating activities and the cash cycle of the firm. From an accounting perspective, short-term finance involves net working capital.

2. Managing short-term cash flows involves the minimization of costs. The two major costs are carrying costs—the interest and related costs incurred by overinvesting in short-term assets such as cash—and shortage costs, the cost of running out of short-term assets. The objective of managing short-term finance and short-term financial planning is to find the optimal trade-off between these two costs.

3. In an ideal economy the firm could perfectly predict its short-term uses and sources of cash, and net working capital could be kept at zero. In the real world, net working capital provides a buffer that lets the firm meet its ongoing obligations. The financial manager seeks the optimal level of each of the current assets.

4. The financial manager can use the cash budget to identify short-term financial needs. The cash budget tells the manager what borrowing is required or what lending will be possible in the short run. The firm has available to it a number of possible ways of acquiring funds to meet short-term shortfalls, including unsecured and secured loans.

KEY TERMS

accounts receivable financing, 745	compensating balance, 745
banker's acceptances, 745	inventory loan, 745
carrying costs, 737	liquidity, 730
cash budget, 742	operating cycle, 734
cash cycle, 734	shortage costs, 737
cash flow time line, 734	short-run operating activities, 734
commercial paper, 745	

SUGGESTED READINGS

A book that describes working capital management is:

Fabozzi, F., and L. N. Masonson. *Corporate Cash Management Techniques and Analyses.* Homewood, Ill.: Dow Jones–Irwin, 1985.

Kallberg, J. G., and K. Parkinson. *Corporate Liquidity: Management and Measurement.* Burr Ridge, IL: Irwin/McGraw Hill, 1996.

QUESTIONS & PROBLEMS

TRACING CASH AND NET WORKING CAPITAL

26.1 Derive the cash equation from the basic balance sheet equation: assets = liabilities + equity.

26.2 Indicate whether the following corporate actions increase, decrease, or cause no change to cash.
   a. Cash is paid for raw materials purchased for inventory.
   b. A dividend is paid.
   c. Merchandise is sold on credit.
   d. Common stock is issued.
   e. Raw material is purchased for inventory on credit.

    f. A piece of machinery is purchased and paid for with long-term debt.

    g. Payments for previous sales are collected.

    h. Accumulated depreciation is increased.

    i. Merchandise is sold for cash.

    j. Payment is made for a previous purchase.

    k. A short-term bank loan is received.

    l. A dividend is paid with funds received from a sale of common stock.

    m. Allowance for bad debts is decreased.

    n. A piece of office equipment is purchased and paid for with a short-term note.

    o. Marketable securities are purchased with retained earnings.

    p. Last year's taxes are paid.

    q. This year's tax liability is increased.

    r. Interest on long-term debt is paid.

DEFINING CASH IN TERMS OF OTHER ELEMENTS

26.3 Below are the 20X2 balance sheet and income statement for Country Kettles, Inc. Use this information to construct a sources-and-uses-of-cash statement.

COUNTRY KETTLES, INC.
Balance Sheet
December 31, 20X2

	20X2	20X1
Assets		
Cash	$ 42,000	$ 35,000
Accounts receivable	94,250	84,500
Inventory	78,750	75,000
Property, plant, equipment	181,475	168,750
Less: Accumulated depreciation	61,475	56,250
Total assets	$335,000	$307,000
Liabilities and Equity		
Accounts payable	$ 60,500	$ 55,000
Accrued expenses	5,150	8,450
Long-term debt	15,000	30,000
Common stock	28,000	25,000
Retained earnings	226,350	188,550
Total liabilities and equity	$335,000	$307,000

COUNTRY KETTLES, INC.
Income Statement
20X2

Net sales	$765,000
Cost of goods sold...........................	459,000
Sales, general, and administrative costs	91,800
Advertising.................................	26,775
Rent	45,000
Depreciation................................	5,225
Profit before taxes	137,200
Taxes......................................	68,600
Net profit...................................	$ 68,600
Dividends...................................	$ 30,800
Retained earnings............................	$ 37,800

26.4 Following are the 20X2 balance sheet and income statement for the S/B Corporation. Use them to construct a sources-and-uses-of-cash statement.

S/B CORPORATION
Balance Sheet
December 31, 20X2
(in thousands)

	20X2	20X1
Assets		
Cash	$ 388	$ 375
Accounts receivable	1,470	1,219
Inventories	2,663	2,777
Net fixed assets	9,314	9,225
Total assets	$13,835	$13,596
Liabilities and Equity		
Accounts payable	$ 282	$ 259
Bank loan payable	1,300	924
Taxes payable	(33)	99
Accrued expenses payable	95	106
Mortgage	4,000	4,000
Common stock	4,000	4,000
Retained earnings	4,191	4,208
Total liabilities and equity	$13,835	$13,596

S/B CORPORATION
Income Statement
20X2
(in thousands)

Net sales	$1,030
Cost of goods sold:	
Materials	652
Overhead	64
Depreciation	50
Gross profit	264
Selling and administrative costs	98
Profit before taxes	166
Taxes	83
Net profit	$ 83
Dividends paid	$ 100

THE OPERATING CYCLE AND COST CYCLE

26.5 On Eastern Printing Machines Co.'s income statement of 20X1, the cost of goods sold and the credit sales are $200 million and $240 million, respectively. The following data are from its balance sheets.

	($ millions)	
	Dec. 31, 20X1	Dec. 31, 20X2
Inventory	$40	$60
Accounts receivable	30	50
Accounts payable	10	30

a. How many days is Eastern Printing Machines' operating cycle?

b. How many days is Eastern Printing Machines' cash cycle?

26.6 Define:

a. Operating cycle

b. Cash cycle

c. Accounts payable period

26.7 Indicate whether the following company actions increase, decrease, or cause no change to the cash cycle and the operating cycle.
  a. The use of discounts offered by suppliers is decreased.
  b. More finished goods are being produced for orders instead of for inventory.
  c. A greater percentage of raw materials purchases is paid for with cash.
  d. The terms of discounts offered to customers are made more favorable for the customers.
  e. A larger than usual amount of raw materials is purchased as a result of a price decline.
  f. An increased number of customers pays with cash instead of credit.

SOME ASPECTS OF SHORT-TERM FINANCIAL POLICY

26.8 **a.** Define flexible short-term financing.
  b. Define restrictive short-term financing.
  c. When is flexible short-term financing optimal?
  d. When is restrictive short-term financing optimal?

26.9 What are the costs of shortages? Describe them.

26.10 Cleveland Compressor and Pnew York Pneumatic are competing manufacturing firms. Their financial statements are printed below.
  a. How are the current assets of each firm financed?
  b. Which firm has the larger investment in current assets? Why?
  c. Which firm is more likely to incur carrying costs, and which is more likely to incur shortage costs? Why?

CLEVELAND COMPRESSOR
Balance Sheet
December 31, 20X1

	20X2	20X1
Assets		
Cash	$ 13,862	$ 16,339
Net accounts receivable	23,887	25,778
Inventory	54,867	43,287
Total current assets	$ 92,616	$ 85,404
Fixed assets:		
Plant, property, and equipment	101,543	99,615
Less: Accumulated depreciation	34,331	31,957
Net fixed assets	$ 67,212	$ 67,658
Prepaid expenses	1,914	1,791
Other assets	13,052	13,138
Total assets	$174,794	$167,991
Liabilities and Equity		
Current liabilities:		
Accounts payable	$ 6,494	$ 4,893
Notes payable	10,483	11,617
Accrued expenses	7,422	7,227
Other taxes payable	9,924	8,460
Total current liabilities	34,323	32,197
Long-term debt	22,036	22,036
Total liabilities	$ 56,359	$ 54,233
Equity:		
Common stock	38,000	38,000
Paid-in capital	12,000	12,000
Retained earnings	68,435	63,758
Total equity	118,435	113,758
Total liabilities and equity	$174,794	$167,991

Visit us at www.mhhe.com/rwj

CLEVELAND COMPRESSOR
Income Statement
20X2

Income:	
Sales	$162,749
Other income	1,002
Total income	$163,751
Operating expenses:	
Cost of goods sold	103,570
Selling and administrative expenses	28,495
Depreciation	2,274
Total expenses	$134,339
Pretax earnings	29,412
Taxes	14,890
Net earnings	$ 14,522
Dividends	$ 9,845
Retained earnings	$ 4,677

PNEW YORK PNEUMATIC
Balance Sheet
December 31, 20X2

	20X2	20X1
Assets		
Cash	$ 5,794	$ 3,307
Net accounts receivable	26,177	22,133
Inventory	46,463	44,661
Total current assets	78,434	70,101
Fixed assets:		
Plant, property, and equipment	31,842	31,116
Less: Accumulated depreciation	19,297	18,143
Net fixed assets	12,545	12,973
Prepaid expenses	763	688
Other assets	1,601	1,385
Total assets	$93,343	$85,147
Liabilities and Equity		
Current liabilities:		
Accounts payable	$ 6,008	$ 5,019
Bank loans	3,722	645
Accrued expenses	4,254	3,295
Other taxes payable	5,688	4,951
Total current liabilities	19,672	13,910
Equity:		
Common stock	20,576	20,576
Paid-in capital	5,624	5,624
Retained earnings	48,598	46,164
Less: Treasury stock	1,127	1,127
Total equity	73,671	71,237
Total liabilities and equity	$93,343	$85,147

PNEW YORK PNEUMATIC
Income Statement
20X2

Income:	
Sales	$91,374
Other income	1,067
Total income	92,441
Operating expenses:	
Cost of goods sold	59,042
Selling and administrative expenses	18,068
Depreciation	1,154
Total expenses	78,264
Pretax earnings	14,177
Taxes	6,838
Net earnings	$ 7,339
Dividends	$ 4,905
Retained earnings	$ 2,434

26.11 In an ideal economy, net working capital is always zero. Why might net working capital be greater than zero in the real world?

CASH BUDGETING

26.12 The following is the sales budget for the Smithe and Wreston Company for the first quarter of 20X1.

	January	February	March
Sales budget	$90,000	$100,000	$120,000

The aging of credit sales is

30 percent collected in the month of sale

40 percent collected in the month after sale

The accounts receivable balance at the end of the previous quarter is $36,000; $30,000 of that amount is uncollected December sales.

a. Compute the sales for December.

b. Compute the cash collections from sales for each month from January through March.

26.13 The sales budget for your company in the coming year is based on a 20-percent quarterly growth rate with the first quarter projection at $100 million. In addition to this basic trend, the seasonal adjustments for the four quarters are 0, −10, −5, and 15 million dollars, respectively. Generally, 30 percent of the sales can be collected within the month and 50 percent in the following month; the rest of the sales are bad debt. All sales are credit sales. Compute the cash collections from sales for each quarter from the second to the fourth quarter.

26.14 Below are some important figures from the budget of Pine Mulch Company for the second quarter of 20X2.

	April	May	June
Credit sales	$160,000	$140,000	$192,000
Credit purchases	68,000	64,000	80,000
Cash disbursements:			
Wages, taxes, and expenses	8,000	7,000	8,400
Interest	3,000	3,000	3,000
Equipment purchases	50,000		4,000

The company predicts that 10 percent of its sales will never be collected; 50 percent of its sales will be collected in the month of the sale; and the rest of its sales will be collected in the following month. Purchases on trade accounts will be paid in the month following the purchase. In March 20X2 the sales were $180,000.

Use this information to complete the following cash budget:

	April	May	June
Beginning cash balance	$200,000		
Cash receipts:			
Cash collections from credit sales			
Total cash available			
Cash disbursements:			
Pay credit purchases	$ 65,000		
Wages, taxes, and expenses			
Interest			
Equipment purchases			
Total cash disbursed			
Ending cash balance			

26.15 What are the most important considerations in deciding the most appropriate amount of short-term borrowing?

THE SHORT-TERM FINANCIAL PLAN

26.16 List several short-term external financing options.

S & P PROBLEMS

STANDARD &POOR'S

26.17 Locate the annual balance sheets for Hawaiian Electric (HE) and EBay (EBAY). What is the cash amount as the percentage of assets for each company over the past two years? Why would these companies hold such different amounts of cash?

Cash Management

EXECUTIVE SUMMARY

The balance sheet of Singapore Airlines showed total assets of $8.7 billion in March 1994. On this basis, Singapore Airlines was one of the largest transportation firms in the world. In addition, Singapore Airlines held $62.4 million in cash. This cash included currency, demand deposits at commercial banks, and undeposited checks.[1]

Since cash earns no interest, why would Singapore Airlines hold cash? It would seem more sensible for Singapore Airlines to put its cash into marketable securities, such as Treasury bills, and get some investment income. Of course, one reason Singapore Airlines holds cash is to pay for goods and services. Singapore Airlines might prefer to pay its employees in Treasury bills, but the minimum denomination of Treasury bills is $10,000! The firm must use cash because cash is more divisible than Treasury bills.[2]

This chapter is about how firms manage cash. The basic objective in cash management is to keep the investment in cash as low as possible while still operating the firm's activities efficiently and effectively. This chapter separates cash management into three steps:

1. Determining the appropriate target cash balance.
2. Collecting and disbursing cash efficiently.
3. Investing excess cash in marketable securities.

Determining the appropriate target cash balance involves an assessment of the trade-off between the benefit and cost of liquidity. The benefit of holding cash is the convenience in liquidity it gives the firm. The cost of holding cash is the interest income that the firm could have received from investing in Treasury bills and other marketable securities. If the firm has achieved its target cash balance, the value it gets from the liquidity provided by its cash will be exactly equal to the value forgone in interest on an equivalent holding of Treasury bills. In other words, a firm should increase its holding of cash until the net present value from doing so is zero. The incremental liquidity value of cash should decline as more of it is held.

After the optimal amount of cash is determined, the firm must establish procedures so that cash is collected and disbursed as efficiently as possible. This usually reduces to the dictum, "collect early and pay late."

Firms must invest temporarily idle cash in short-term marketable securities. These securities can be bought and sold in the *money market*. Money-market securities have very little risk of default and are highly marketable.

---

[1] It was somewhat unusual for Singapore Airlines to report cash in this way. Usually, a firm's reported cash includes cash equivalents, such as Treasury bills.

[2] Cash is liquid. One property of liquidity is divisibility, that is, how easily an asset can be divided into parts.

27.1 Reasons for Holding Cash

The term cash is a surprisingly imprecise concept. The economic definition of cash includes currency, checking account deposits at commercial banks, and undeposited checks. However, financial managers often use the term cash to include short-term marketable securities. Short-term marketable securities are frequently referred to as "cash equivalents" and include Treasury bills, certificates of deposit, and repurchase agreements. (Several different types of short-term marketable securities are described at the end of this chapter.) The balance sheet item "cash" usually includes cash equivalents.

The previous chapter discussed the management of net working capital. Net working capital includes both cash and cash equivalents. This chapter is concerned with cash, not net working capital, and it focuses on the narrow economic definition of cash.

The basic elements of net working capital management such as carrying costs, shortage costs, and opportunity costs are relevant for cash management. However, cash management is more concerned with how to minimize cash balances by collecting and disbursing cash effectively.

There are two primary reasons for holding cash. First, cash is needed to satisfy the **transactions motive.** Transactions-related needs come from normal disbursement and collection activities of the firm. The disbursement of cash includes the payment of wages and salaries, trade debts, taxes, and dividends. Cash is collected from sales from operations, sales of assets, and new financing. The cash inflows (*collections*) and outflows (*disbursements*) are not perfectly synchronized, and some level of cash holdings is necessary to serve as a buffer. If the firm maintains too small a cash balance, it may run out of cash. If so, it must sell marketable securities or borrow. Selling marketable securities and borrowing involve *trading costs.*

Another reason to hold cash is for **compensating balances.** Cash balances are kept at commercial banks to compensate for banking services rendered to the firm. A minimum required compensating balance at banks providing credit services to the firm may impose a lower limit on the level of cash a firm holds.

The cash balance for most firms can be thought of as consisting of transactions balances and compensating balances. However, it would not be correct for a firm to add the amount of cash required to satisfy its transactions needs to the amount of cash needed to satisfy its compensatory balances to produce a target cash balance. The same cash can be used to satisfy both requirements.

The cost of holding cash is, of course, the opportunity cost of lost interest. To determine the target cash balance, the firm must weigh the benefits of holding cash against the costs. It is generally a good idea for firms to figure out first how much cash to hold to satisfy the transactions needs. Next, the firm must consider compensating-balance requirements, which will impose a lower limit on the level of the firm's cash holdings. Because compensating balances merely provide a lower limit, we shall ignore compensating balances for the following discussion of the target cash balance.

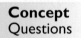

Concept Questions

1. **What is the transactions motive, and how does it lead firms to hold cash?**
2. **What is a compensating balance?**

27.2 Determining the Target Cash Balance

The **target cash balance** involves a trade-off between the opportunity costs of holding too much cash and the trading costs of holding too little. Figure 27.1 presents the problem graphically. If a firm tries to keep its cash holdings too low, it will find itself selling marketable securities (and perhaps later buying marketable securities to replace those sold)

FIGURE 27.1

Costs of Holding Cash

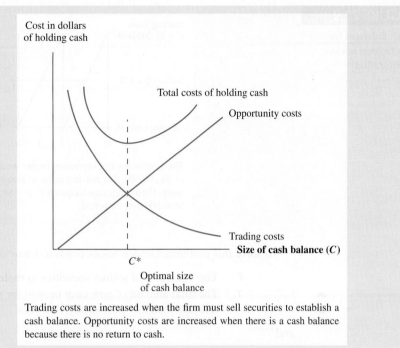

Trading costs are increased when the firm must sell securities to establish a
cash balance. Opportunity costs are increased when there is a cash balance
because there is no return to cash.

more frequently than if the cash balance was higher. Thus, trading costs will tend to fall as
the cash balance becomes larger. In contrast, the opportunity costs of holding cash rise
as the cash holdings rise. At point C^* in Figure 27.1, the sum of both costs, depicted as the
total cost curve, is at a minimum. This is the target or optimal cash balance.

The Baumol Model

William Baumol was the first to provide a formal model of cash management incorporating opportunity costs and trading costs.[3] His model can be used to establish the target cash
balance.

Suppose the Golden Socks Corporation began week 0 with a cash balance of $C = \$1.2$ mil-
lion, and outflows exceed inflows by \$600,000 per week. Its cash balance will drop to zero at
the end of week 2, and its average cash balance will be $C/2 = \$1.2$ million$/2 = \$600,000$
over the two-week period. At the end of week 2, Golden Socks must replace its cash either by
selling marketable securities or by borrowing. Figure 27.2 shows this situation.

If C were set higher, say, at \$2.4 million, cash would last four weeks before the firm
would need to sell marketable securities, but the firm's average cash balance would increase to \$1.2 million (from \$600,000). If C were set at \$600,000, cash would run out in
one week and the firm would need to replenish cash more frequently, but its average cash
balance would fall from \$600,000 to \$300,000.

Because transactions costs must be incurred whenever cash is replenished (for example,
the brokerage costs of selling marketable securities), establishing large initial cash balances
will lower the trading costs connected with cash management. However, the larger the average cash balance, the greater the opportunity cost (the return that could have been earned
on marketable securities).

---

[3]W. S. Baumol, "The Transactions Demand for Cash: An Inventory Theoretic Approach," *Quarterly Journal of Economics* 66
(November 1952).

FIGURE 27.2

Cash Balances for
the Golden Socks
Corporation

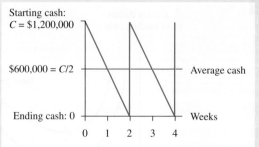

Starting cash:
C = $1,200,000

$600,000 = C/2 .... Average cash

Ending cash: 0

Weeks

0   1   2   3   4

The Golden Socks Corporation begins week 0 with cash
of $1,200,000. The balance drops to zero by the second
week. The average cash balance is $C/2 = \$1,200,000/2 = \$600,000$ over the period.

To solve this problem, Golden Socks needs to know the following three things:

F = The fixed cost of selling securities to replenish cash
T = The total amount of new cash needed for transactions purposes over the relevant planning period, say, one year

and

K = The opportunity cost of holding cash; this is the interest rate on marketable securities

With this information, Golden Socks can determine the total costs of any particular cash-balance policy. It can then determine the optimal cash-balance policy.

The Opportunity Costs   The total opportunity costs of cash balances, in dollars, must be equal to the average cash balance multiplied by the interest rate, or:

$$\text{Opportunity costs (\$)} = (C/2) \times K$$

The opportunity costs of various alternatives are given here:

Initial Cash Balance	Average Cash Balance	Opportunity Costs ($K = 0.10$)
C	$C/2$	$(C/2) \times K$
$4,800,000	$2,400,000	$240,000
2,400,000	1,200,000	120,000
1,200,000	600,000	60,000
600,000	300,000	30,000
300,000	150,000	15,000

The Trading Costs   Total trading costs can be determined by calculating the number of times that Golden Socks must sell marketable securities during the year. The total amount of cash disbursement during the year is $600,000 \times 52$ weeks = $31.2 million. If the initial cash balance is set at $1.2 million, Golden Socks will sell $1.2 million of marketable securities every two weeks. Thus, trading costs are given by:

$$\frac{\$31.2 \text{ million}}{\$1.2 \text{ million}} \times F = 26F$$

The general formula is:

$$\text{Trading costs (\$)} = (T/C) \times F$$

A schedule of alternative trading costs follows:

Total Disbursements during Relevant Period	Initial Cash Balance	Trading Costs ($F = \$1{,}000$)
T	C	$(T/C) \times F$
$31,200,000	$4,800,000	$ 6,500
31,200,000	2,400,000	13,000
31,200,000	1,200,000	26,000
31,200,000	600,000	52,000
31,200,000	300,000	104,000

The Total Cost   The total cost of cash balances consists of the opportunity costs plus the trading costs:

$$\text{Total cost} = \text{Opportunity costs} + \text{Trading costs}$$
$$= (C/2) \times K + (T/C) \times F$$

Cash Balance	Total Cost	$=$	Opportunity Costs	$+$	Trading Costs
$4,800,000	$246,500		$240,000		$ 6,500
2,400,000	133,000		120,000		13,000
1,200,000	86,000		60,000		26,000
600,000	82,000		30,000		52,000
300,000	119,000		15,000		104,000

The Solution   We can see from the preceding schedule that a $600,000 cash balance results in the lowest total cost of the possibilities presented: $82,000. But what about $700,000 or $500,000 or other possibilities? To determine minimum total costs precisely, Golden Socks must equate the marginal reduction in trading costs as balances rise with the marginal increase in opportunity costs associated with cash balance increases. The target cash balance should be the point where the two offset each other. This can be calculated by using either numerical iteration or calculus. We will use calculus, but if you are unfamiliar with such an analysis, you can skip to the solution.

Recall that the total cost equation is:

$$\text{Total cost (TC)} = (C/2) \times K + (T/C) \times F$$

If we differentiate the TC equation with respect to the cash balance and set the derivative equal to zero, we will find that:

$$\frac{d\text{TC}}{dC} = \frac{K}{2} - \frac{TF}{C^2} = 0$$

$$\underset{\text{total cost}}{\text{Marginal}} = \underset{\text{opportunity costs}}{\text{Marginal}} + \underset{\text{trading costs}}{\text{Marginal}^{4}}$$

---

[4]Marginal trading costs are negative because trading costs are *reduced* when C is increased.

The solution for the general cash balance, C^*, is obtained by solving this equation for C:

$$\frac{K}{2} = \frac{TF}{C^2}$$
$$C^* = \sqrt{2TF/K}$$

If $F = \$1,000$, $T = \$31,200,000$, and $K = 0.10$, then $C^* = \$789,936.71$. Given the value of C^*, opportunity costs are:

$$(C^*/2) \times K = \frac{\$789,936.71}{2} \times 0.10 = \$39,496.84$$

Trading costs are:

$$(T/C^*) \times F = \frac{\$31,200,000}{\$789,936.71} \times \$1,000 = \$39,496.84$$

Hence, total costs are:

$$\$39,496.84 + \$39,496.84 = \$78,993.68$$

Limitations   The Baumol model represents an important contribution to cash management. The limitations of the model include the following:

1. *The Model Assumes the Firm Has a Constant Disbursement Rate.* In practice, disbursements can be only partially managed, because due dates differ and costs cannot be predicted with certainty.
2. *The Model Assumes There Are No Cash Receipts during the Projected Period.* In fact, most firms experience both cash inflows and outflows on a daily basis.
3. *No Safety Stock Is Allowed For.* Firms will probably want to hold a safety stock of cash designed to reduce the possibility of a cash shortage or *cash-out*. However, to the extent that firms can sell marketable securities or borrow in a few hours, the need for a safety stock is minimal.

The Baumol model is possibly the simplest and most stripped-down sensible model for determining the optimal cash position. Its chief weakness is that it assumes discrete, certain cash flows. We next discuss a model designed to deal with uncertainty.

The Miller-Orr Model

Merton Miller and Daniel Orr developed a cash-balance model to deal with cash inflows and outflows that fluctuate randomly from day to day.[5] In the Miller-Orr model, both cash inflows and cash outflows are included. The model assumes that the distribution of daily net cash flows (cash inflow minus cash outflow) is normally distributed. On each day the net cash flow could be the expected value or some higher or lower value. We will assume that the expected net cash flow is zero.

Figure 27.3 shows how the Miller-Orr model works. The model operates in terms of upper (H) and lower (L) control limits, and a target cash balance (Z). The firm allows its cash balance to wander randomly within the lower and upper limits. As long as the cash balance is between H and L, the firm makes no transaction. When the cash balance reaches H, such as at point X, then the firm buys $H - Z$ units (or dollars) of marketable securities.

---

[5]M. H. Miller and D. Orr, "A Model of the Demand for Money by Firms," *Quarterly Journal of Economics* (August 1966).

FIGURE 27.3

The Miller-Orr Model

H is the upper control limit. L is the lower control limit. The target cash balance is Z. As long as cash is between L and H, no transaction is made.

This action will decrease the cash balance to Z. In the same way, when cash balances fall to L, such as at point Y (the lower limit), the firm should sell $Z - L$ securities and increase the cash balance to Z. In both situations, cash balances return to Z. Management sets the lower limit, L, depending on how much risk of a cash shortfall the firm is willing to tolerate.

Like the Baumol model, the Miller-Orr model depends on trading costs and opportunity costs. The cost per transaction of buying and selling marketable securities, F, is assumed to be fixed. The percentage opportunity cost per period of holding cash, K, is the daily interest rate on marketable securities. Unlike the Baumol model, the number of transactions per period is a random variable that varies from period to period, depending on the pattern of cash inflows and outflows.

As a consequence, trading costs per period are dependent on the expected number of transactions in marketable securities during the period. Similarly, the opportunity costs of holding cash are a function of the expected cash balance per period.

Given L, which is set by the firm, the Miller-Orr model solves for the target cash balance, Z, and the upper limit, H. Expected total costs of the cash-balance–return policy (Z, H) are equal to the sum of expected transactions costs and expected opportunity costs. The values of Z (the return-cash point) and H (the upper limit) that minimize the expected total cost have been determined by Miller and Orr:

$$Z^* = \sqrt[3]{3F\sigma^2/4K} + L$$

$$H^* = 3Z^* - 2L$$

where * denotes optimal values, and σ^2 is the variance of net daily cash flows.

The average cash balance in the Miller-Orr model is:

$$\text{Average cash balance} = \frac{4Z - L}{3}$$

EXAMPLE

To clarify the Miller-Orr model, suppose $F = \$1,000$, the interest rate is 10 percent annually, and the standard deviation of daily net cash flows is $2,000. The daily opportunity cost, K, is:

$$(1 + K)^{365} - 1.0 = 0.10$$

$$1 + K = \sqrt[365]{1.10} = 1.000261$$

$$K = 0.000261$$

The variance of daily net cash flows is

$$\sigma^2 = (2,000)^2 = 4,000,000$$

Let us assume that $L = 0$:

$$Z^* = \sqrt[3]{(3 \times \$1,000 \times 4,000,000)/(4 \times 0.000261)} + 0$$

$$= \sqrt[3]{(\$11,493,900,000,000)} = \$22,568$$

$$H^* = 3 \times \$22,568 = \$67,704$$

$$\text{Average cash balance} = \frac{4 \times \$22,568}{3} = \$30,091$$

Implications of the Miller-Orr Model   To use the Miller-Orr model, the manager must do four things.

1. Set the lower control limit for the cash balance. This lower limit can be related to a minimum safety margin decided on by management.
2. Estimate the standard deviation of daily cash flows.
3. Determine the interest rate.
4. Estimate the trading costs of buying and selling marketable securities.

These four steps allow the upper limit and return point to be computed. Miller and Orr tested their model using nine months of data for cash balances for a large industrial firm. The model was able to produce average daily cash balances much lower than the averages actually obtained by the firm.[6]

The Miller-Orr model clarifies the issues of cash management. First, the model shows that the best return point, Z^*, is positively related to trading costs, F, and negatively related to K. This finding is consistent with and analogous to the Baumol model. Second, the Miller-Orr model shows that the best return point and the average cash balance are positively related to the variability of cash flows. That is, firms whose cash flows are subject to greater uncertainty should maintain a larger average cash balance.

Other Factors Influencing the Target Cash Balance

Borrowing   In our previous examples, the firm has obtained cash by selling marketable securities. Another alternative is to borrow cash. Borrowing introduces additional considerations to cash management.

1. Borrowing is likely to be more expensive than selling marketable securities because the interest rate is likely to be higher.
2. The need to borrow will depend on management's desire to hold low cash balances. A firm is more likely to need to borrow to cover an unexpected cash outflow the greater its cash flow variability and the lower its investment in marketable securities.

Compensating Balance   The costs of trading securities are well below the lost income from holding cash for large firms. Consider a firm faced with either selling $2 million of Treasury bills to replenish cash or leaving the money idle overnight. The daily opportunity

---

[6]D. Mullins and R. Hamonoff discuss tests of the Miller-Orr model in "Applications of Inventory Cash Management Models," in *Modern Developments in Financial Management,* ed. by S. C. Myers (New York: Praeger, 1976). They show that the model works very well when compared to the actual cash balances of several firms. However, simple rules of thumb do as good a job as the Miller-Orr model.

cost of $2 million at a 10-percent annual interest rate is $0.10/365 = 0.027$ percent per day. The daily return earned on $2 million is $0.00027 \times \$2$ million $= \$540$. The cost of selling $2 million of Treasury bills is much less than $540. As a consequence, a large firm will buy and sell securities many times a day before it will leave substantial amounts idle overnight.

However, most large firms hold more cash than cash-balance models imply. Here are some possible reasons.

1. Firms have cash in the bank as a compensating balance in payment for banking services.
2. Large corporations have thousands of accounts with several dozen banks. Sometimes it makes more sense to leave cash alone than to manage each account on a daily basis.

Concept Questions

1. **What is a target cash balance?**
2. **What are the strengths and weaknesses of the Baumol model and the Miller-Orr model?**

27.3 Managing the Collection and Disbursement of Cash

A firm's cash balance as reported in its financial statements (*book cash* or *ledger cash*) is not the same thing as the balance shown in its bank account (*bank cash* or *collected bank cash*). The difference between bank cash and book cash is called **float** and represents the net effect of checks in the process of collection.

EXAMPLE

Imagine that General Mechanics, Inc., (GMI) currently has $100,000 on deposit with its bank. It purchases some raw materials, paying its vendors with a check written on July 8 for $100,000. The company's books (that is, ledger balances) are changed to show the $100,000 reduction in the cash balance. But the firm's bank will not find out about this check until it has been deposited at the vendor's bank and has been presented to the firm's bank for payment on, say, July 15. Until the check's presentation, the firm's bank cash is greater than its book cash, and it has *positive float*.

Position Prior to July 8:

$$\text{Float} = \text{Firm's bank cash} - \text{Firm's book cash}$$
$$= \quad \$100,000 \quad - \quad \$100,000$$
$$= \quad 0$$

Position from July 8 through July 14:

$$\text{Disbursement float} = \text{Firm's bank cash} - \text{Firm's book cash}$$
$$= \$100,000 \quad - \quad 0$$
$$= \$100,000$$

During the period of time that the check is *clearing*, GMI has a balance with the bank of $100,000. It can obtain the benefit of this cash while the check is clearing. For example, the bank cash could be invested in marketable securities. Checks written by the firm generate *disbursement float*, causing an immediate decrease in book cash but no immediate change in bank cash.

EXAMPLE

Imagine that GMI receives a check from a customer for $100,000. Assume, as before, that the company has $100,000 deposited at its bank and has a *neutral float position*. It deposits the check and increases its book cash by $100,000 on November 8. However, the cash is not available to GMI until its bank has presented the check to the customer's bank and received $100,000 on, say, November 15. In the meantime, the cash position at GMI will reflect a collection float of $100,000.

Position Prior to November 8:

$$\text{Float} = \text{Firm's bank cash} - \text{Firm's book cash}$$
$$= \$100,000 \quad - \quad \$100,000$$
$$= \quad 0$$

Position from November 8 through November 14:

$$\text{Collection float} = \text{Firm's bank cash} - \text{Firm's book cash}$$
$$= \$100,000 \quad - \quad \$200,000$$
$$= -\$100,000$$

Checks received by the firm represent *collection float,* which increases book cash immediately but does not immediately change bank cash. The firm is helped by disbursement float and is hurt by collection float. The sum of disbursement float and collection float is *net float.*

A firm should be more concerned with net float and bank cash than with book cash. If a financial manager knows that a check will not clear for several days, he or she will be able to keep a lower cash balance at the bank than might be true otherwise. Good float management can generate a great deal of money. For example, suppose the average daily sales of Exxon are about $400 million. If Exxon speeds up the collection process or slows down the disbursement process by one day, it frees up $400 million, which can be invested in marketable securities. With an interest rate of 4 percent, this represents overnight interest of approximately $44,000 [($400 million/365) × 0.04].

Float management involves controlling the collection and disbursement of cash. The objective in cash collection is to reduce the lag between the time customers pay their bills and the time the checks are collected. The objective in cash disbursement is to slow down payments, thereby increasing the time between when checks are written and when checks are presented. In other words, collect early and pay late. Of course, to the extent that the firm succeeds in doing this, the customers and suppliers lose money, and the trade-off is the effect on the firm's relationship with them.

Collection float can be broken down into three parts: mail float, in-house processing float, and availability float:

1. *Mail Float* is the part of the collection and disbursement process where checks are trapped in the postal system.
2. *In-House Processing Float* is the time it takes the receiver of a check to process the payment and deposit it in a bank for collection.
3. *Availability Float* refers to the time required to clear a check through the banking system. The clearing process takes place using the Federal Reserve check collection service, using correspondent banks, or using local clearinghouses.

EXAMPLE

A check for $1,000 is mailed from a customer on Monday, September 1. Because of mail, processing, and clearing delays, it is not credited as available cash in the firm's bank until the following Monday, seven days later. The float for this check is:

$$\text{Float} = \$1,000 \times 7 \text{ days} = \$7,000$$

Another check for $7,000 is mailed on September 1. It is available on the next day. The float for this check is:

$$\text{Float} = \$7,000 \times 1 \text{ day} = \$7,000$$

The measurement of float depends on the time lag and the dollars involved. The cost of float is an opportunity cost, because the cash is unavailable for use during the time checks are tied up in the collection process. The cost of float can be determined by (1) estimating the average daily receipts, (2) calculating the average delay in obtaining the receipts, and (3) discounting the average daily receipts by the *delay-adjusted cost of capital.*

EXAMPLE

Suppose that Concepts, Inc., has two receipts each month:

	Amount	Number of Days' Delay	Float
Item 1	$5,000,000	× 3 =	$15,000,000
Item 2	3,000,000	× 5 =	15,000,000
Total	$8,000,000		$30,000,000

The average daily float over the month is equal to:

Average Daily Float:

$$\frac{\text{Total float}}{\text{Total days}} = \frac{\$30,000,000}{30} = \$1,000,000$$

Another procedure that can be used to calculate average daily float is to determine average daily receipts and multiply by the average daily delay.

Average Daily Receipts:

$$\frac{\text{Total receipts}}{\text{Total days}} = \frac{\$8,000,000}{30} = \$266,666.67$$

$$\text{Weighted average delay} = (5/8) \times 3 + (3/8) \times 5$$

$$= 1.875 + 1.875 = 3.75 \text{ days}$$

$$\text{Average daily float} = \text{Average daily receipts} \times \text{Weighted average delay}$$

$$= \$266,666.67 \times 3.75 = \$1,000,000$$

EXAMPLE

Suppose Concepts, Inc., has average daily receipts of $266,667. The float results in this amount being delayed 3.75 days. The present value of the delayed cash flow is:

$$V = \frac{\$266,667}{1 + r_B}$$

where r_B is the cost of debt capital for Concepts, adjusted to the relevant time frame. Suppose the annual cost of debt capital is 10 percent. Then:

$$r_B = 0.1 \times (3.75/365) = 0.00103$$

and:

$$V = \frac{\$266,667}{1 + 0.00103} = \$266,392.62$$

Thus, the net present value of the delay float is $266,392.62 − $266,667 = −$274.38 per day. For a year, this is −$274.38 × 365 = −$100,148.70.

Accelerating Collections

The following is a depiction of the basic parts of the cash collection process.

The total time in this process is made up of mailing time, check-processing time, and check-clearing time. The amount of time cash spends in each part of the cash collection process depends on where the firm's customers and banks are located and how efficient the firm is at collecting cash. Some of the techniques used to accelerate collections and reduce collection time are lockboxes, concentration banking, and wire transfers.

Lockboxes   The **lockbox** is the most widely used device to speed up collections of cash. It is a special post office box set up to intercept accounts receivable payments.

Figure 27.4 illustrates the lockbox system.[7] The collection process is started by customers mailing their checks to a post office box instead of sending them to the firm. The lockbox is maintained by a local bank and is typically located no more than several hundred miles away. Large corporations may maintain more than 20 lockboxes around the country. In the typical lockbox system, the local bank collects the lockbox checks from the post office several times a day. The bank deposits the checks directly to the firm's account. Details of the operation are recorded (in some computer-usable form) and sent to the firm.

A lockbox system reduces mailing time because checks are received at a nearby post office instead of at corporate headquarters. Lockboxes also reduce the firm's processing time because they reduce the time required for a corporation to physically handle receivables and to deposit checks for collection. A bank lockbox should enable a firm to get its receipts processed, deposited, and cleared faster than if it were to receive checks at its headquarters and deliver them itself to the bank for deposit and clearing.

Concentration Banking   Using lockboxes is one way firms can collect checks from customers and get them into deposit banks. Another way to speed up collection is to get the cash from the deposit banks to the firm's main bank more quickly. This is done by a method called **concentration banking.**

With a concentration-banking system, the firm's sales offices are usually responsible for the collection and processing of customer checks. The sales office deposits the checks into a local deposit bank account. Surplus funds are transferred from the deposit bank to the concentration bank. The purpose of concentration banking is to obtain customer checks from nearby receiving locations. Concentration banking reduces mailing time because the firm's sales office is usually nearer than corporate headquarters to the customer. Furthermore, bank clearing time will be reduced because the customer's check is usually drawn on a local

---

[7]Two types of lockboxes are offered by banks. Wholesale lockboxes are used in processing a small number of large-dollar checks. Retail lockboxes are used for processing a large number of smaller checks.

FIGURE 27.4

Overview of Lockbox
Processing

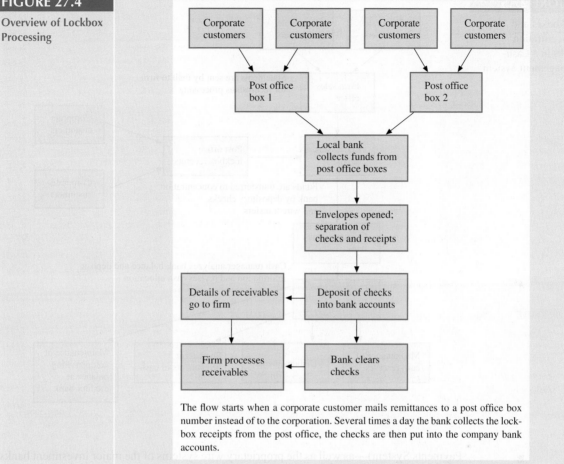

The flow starts when a corporate customer mails remittances to a post office box
number instead of to the corporation. Several times a day the bank collects the lockbox receipts from the post office, the checks are then put into the company bank
accounts.

bank. Figure 27.5 illustrates this process, where concentration banks are combined with
lockboxes in a total cash-management system.

The corporate cash manager uses the pools of cash at the concentration bank for short-
term investing or for some other purpose. The concentration banks usually serve as the
source of short-term investments. They also serve as the focal point for transferring funds
to disbursement banks.

Wire Transfers   After the customers' checks get into the local banking network, the objective is to transfer the surplus funds (funds in excess of required compensating balances)
from the local deposit bank to the concentration bank. The fastest and most expensive way
is by **wire transfer.**[8] Wire transfers take only a few minutes, and the cash becomes available to the firm upon receipt of a wire notice at the concentration bank. Wire transfers take
place electronically, from one computer to another, and eliminate the mailing and check-
clearing times associated with other cash-transfer methods.

Two wire services are available—Fedwire, the Federal Reserve wire service (that is
operated by the Federal Reserve bank system), and CHIPS (Clearing House Interbank

---

[8]A slower and cheaper way is a depository transfer check. This is an unsigned, nonnegotiable check drawn on the local collection
bank and payable to the concentration bank.

FIGURE 27.5

Lockboxes and Concentration Banks in a Cash-Management System

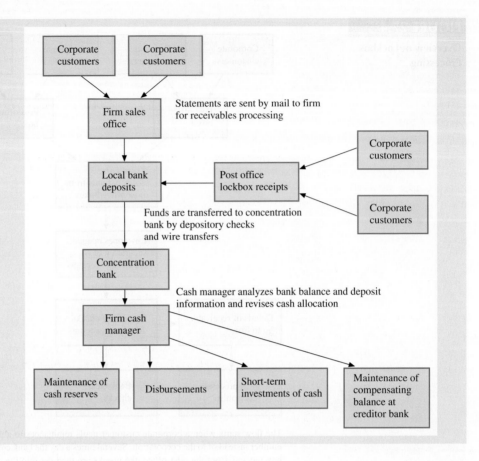

Statements are sent by mail to firm for receivables processing

Funds are transferred to concentration bank by depository checks and wire transfers

Cash manager analyzes bank balance and deposit information and revises cash allocation

Payments System)—as well as the proprietary wire systems of the major investment banks. A typical wire transfer cost is $10, which is split between the originating bank and the receiving bank.

EXAMPLE

The decision to use a bank cash-management service incorporating lockboxes and concentration banks depends on where a firm's customers are located and the speed of the U.S. postal system. Suppose Atlantic Corporation, located in Philadelphia, is considering a lockbox system. Its collection delay is currently eight days. It does business in the southwestern part of the country (New Mexico, Arizona, and California). The proposed lockbox system will be located in Los Angeles and operated by Pacific Bank. Pacific Bank has analyzed Atlantic's cash-gathering system and has concluded it can decrease collection float by two days. Specifically, the bank has come up with the following information on the proposed lockbox system:

Reduction in mailing time	= 1.0 day
Reduction in clearing time	= 0.5 day
Reduction in firm's processing time	= 0.5 day
Total reduction	2.0 days
Daily interest on Treasury bills	= 0.03%
Average number of daily payments to lockboxes	= 200
Average size of payment	= $5,000

The cash flows for the current collection are shown in the following cash flow time chart:

The cash flows for the lockbox collection operation will be as follows:

The average daily collections from the southwestern region are $1 million (200 × $5,000). The Pacific Bank has agreed to operate a lockbox system for an annual fee of $20,000 and $0.30 per check processed.

On this basis the lockbox would increase the collected bank balance by $1 million × 2 = $2 million. The lockbox, in effect, releases $2 million to the firm by reducing processing, mailing, and clearing time by two days.

The Atlantic Corporation can expect to realize a daily return of 0.0003 × $2 million = $600. The yearly savings would be $600 × 365 days = $219,000 under the lockbox system.

The Pacific Bank's charge for this lockbox service would be

Annual variable fee 365 days × 200 checks × $0.30 =	$21,900
Annual fixed fee	$20,000
Total	$41,900

Because the return on released funds exceeds the lockbox system costs, Atlantic should employ Pacific Bank. (We should note, however, that this example has ignored the cost of moving funds into the concentration account.)

Delaying Disbursements

Accelerating collections is one method of cash management; paying more slowly is another. The cash disbursement process is illustrated in Figure 27.6. Techniques to slow down disbursement will attempt to increase mail time and check-clearing time.

Disbursement Float ("Playing the Float Game")

Even though the cash balance at the bank may be $1 million, a firm's books may show only $500,000 because it has written $500,000 in payment checks. The disbursement float of

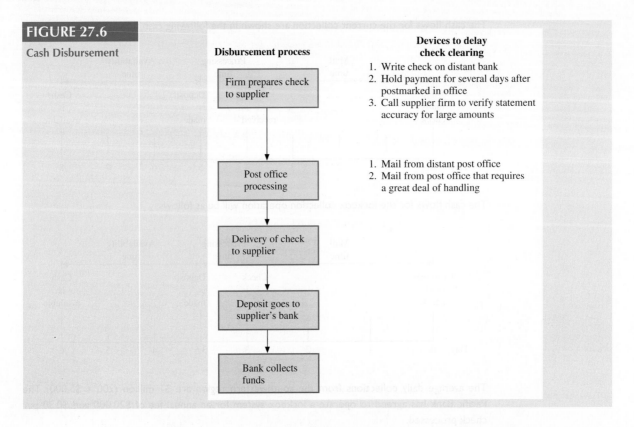

FIGURE 27.6

Cash Disbursement

Disbursement process

Firm prepares check to supplier

Post office processing

Delivery of check to supplier

Deposit goes to supplier's bank

Bank collects funds

Devices to delay check clearing

1. Write check on distant bank
2. Hold payment for several days after postmarked in office
3. Call supplier firm to verify statement accuracy for large amounts

1. Mail from distant post office
2. Mail from post office that requires a great deal of handling

$500,000 is available for the corporation to use until the checks are presented for payment. Float in terms of slowing down payment checks from mail delivery, check-processing time, and collection of funds. This is illustrated in Figure 27.6. Disbursement float can be increased by writing a check on a geographically distant bank. For example, a New York supplier might be paid with checks drawn on a Los Angeles bank. This will increase the time required for the checks to clear through the banking system.

Zero-Balance Accounts

Some firms set up a **zero-balance account (ZBA)** to handle disbursement activity. The account has a zero balance as checks are written. As checks are presented to the zero-balance account for payment (causing a negative balance), funds are automatically transferred in from a central control account. The master account and the ZBA are located in the same bank. Thus, the transfer is automatic and involves only an accounting entry in the bank.

Drafts

Firms sometimes use drafts instead of checks. Drafts differ from checks because they are not drawn on a bank but on the issuer (the firm) and are payable by the issuer. The bank acts only as an agent, presenting the draft to the issuer for payment. When a draft is transmitted to a firm's bank for collection, the bank must present the draft to the issuing firm for acceptance before making payment. After the draft has been accepted, the firm must deposit the necessary cash to cover the payment. The use of drafts rather than checks allows a firm to keep lower cash balances in its disbursement accounts because cash does not need to be deposited until the drafts are presented to it for payment.

Ethical and Legal Questions

The cash manager must work with cash balances collected by the bank and not the firm's book balance, which reflects checks that have been deposited but not collected. If not, a cash manager could be drawing on uncollected cash as a source for making short-term investments. Most banks charge a penalty for use of uncollected funds. However, banks may not have good enough accounting and control procedures to be fully aware of the use of uncollected funds. This raises some ethical and legal questions for the firm.

In May 1985, Robert Fomon, chairman of E. F. Hutton, a large investment bank at the time, pleaded guilty to 2,000 charges of mail and wire fraud in connection with a scheme the firm had operated from 1980 to 1982. E. F. Hutton employees wrote checks totaling hundreds of millions of dollars in uncollected cash, which were invested in short-term money-market assets. E. F. Hutton's systematic overdrafting of accounts is apparently not a widespread practice among corporations, and since the E. F. Hutton affair, firms have been much more careful in managing their cash accounts. Generally, firms are scrupulous in investing only the cash they actually have on hand. E. F. Hutton paid a $2 million fine, reimbursed the government (the U.S. Department of Justice) $750,000, and reserved $8 million for restitution to defrauded banks. We should emphasize that the case against E. F. Hutton was not a case against float management, but rather writing checks with no economic value other than to exploit float.

The Internet: Will It Eliminate Float?

Internet e-commerce is a general term that refers to the possibilities and practice of direct, electronic information exchange between all types of business transactions. One important implication of Internet e-commerce is to electronically transfer financial information and funds between people and firms, thereby eliminating paper invoices, paper checks, and paper mail.

For example, it is now possible for a person to arrange to have her checking account directly debited each month to pay many types of bills. More important, Internet e-commerce allows a seller to send a bill electronically to a buyer—avoiding paper mail. The seller can authorize acceptance of electronic payment with the bank transferring the funds to the seller's account at a different bank. The net effect of all this is that the length of time required to complete a business transaction is significantly shortened.

As the Internet becomes more and more important, float management will evolve to focus on issues surrounding computerized information exchange, most notably security, viruses, hacking, and proprietary systems. We observe an increasing tendency of firms to link important vendors and customers via extranets—which are business networks that extend the firms' intranets.

Concept
Questions

1. Describe collection and disbursement float.
2. What are lockboxes? Concentration banks? Wire transfers?
3. Suppose an overzealous financial manager writes checks on uncollected funds. Aside from legal issues, who is the financial loser in this situation?

27.4 Investing Idle Cash

If a firm has a temporary cash surplus, it can invest in short-term marketable securities. The market for short-term financial assets is called the *money market*. The maturity of short-term financial assets that trade in the money market is one year or less.

Most large firms manage their own short-term financial assets, transacting through banks and dealers. Some large firms and many small firms use money-market funds. These

FIGURE 27.7

Seasonal Cash
Demands

Time 1: A surplus cash flow exists. Seasonal demand for investing is low. The surplus cash flow is invested in short-term marketable securities. Time 2: A deficit cash flow exists. Seasonal demand for investing is high. The financial deficit is financed by selling marketable securities and by bank borrowing.

are funds that invest in short-term financial assets for a management fee. The management fee is compensation for the professional expertise and diversification provided by the fund manager. Among the many money-market mutual funds, some specialize in corporate customers. Banks also offer *sweep accounts,* where the bank takes all excess available funds at the close of each business day and invests them for the firm.

Firms have temporary cash surpluses for these reasons: to help finance seasonal or cyclical activities of the firm, to help finance planned expenditures of the firm, and to provide for unanticipated contingencies.

Seasonal or Cyclical Activities

Some firms have a predictable cash flow pattern. They have surplus cash flows during part of the year and deficit cash flows the rest of the year. For example, Toys "R" Us, a retail toy firm, has a seasonal cash flow pattern influenced by Christmas. Such a firm may buy marketable securities when surplus cash flows occur and sell marketable securities when deficits occur. Of course, bank loans are another short-term financing device. Figure 27.7 illustrates the use of bank loans and marketable securities to meet temporary financing needs.

Planned Expenditures

Firms frequently accumulate temporary investments in marketable securities to provide the cash for a plant-construction program, dividend payment, and other large expenditures. Thus, firms may issue bonds and stocks before the cash is needed, investing the proceeds in short-term marketable securities, and then selling the securities to finance the expenditures.

The important characteristics of short-term marketable securities are their maturity, default risk, marketability, and taxability.

Maturity   *Maturity* refers to the time period over which interest and principal payments are made. For a given change in the level of interest rates, the prices of longer-maturity securities will change more than those for shorter-maturity securities. As a consequence, firms that invest in long-term maturity securities are accepting greater risk than firms that invest in securities with short-term maturities. This type of risk is usually called *interest-rate risk.* Most firms limit their investments in marketable securities to those maturing in less than 90 days. Of course, the expected return on securities with short-term maturities is usually less than the expected return on securities with longer maturities.

Default Risk   *Default risk* refers to the probability that interest or principal will not be paid on the due date and in the promised amount. In previous chapters we observed that various financial reporting agencies, such as Moody's Investors Service and Standard & Poor's, compile and publish ratings of various corporate and public securities. These ratings are connected to default risk. Of course, some securities have negligible default risk, such as U.S. Treasury bills. Given the purposes of investing idle corporate cash, firms typically avoid investing in marketable securities with significant default risk.

Marketability   *Marketability* refers to how easy it is to convert an asset to cash. Sometimes marketability is referred to as *liquidity*. It has two characteristics:

1. *No Price-Pressure Effect.* If an asset can be sold in large amounts without changing the market price, it is marketable. Price-pressure effects are those that come about when the price of an asset must be lowered to facilitate the sale.
2. *Time.* If an asset can be sold quickly at the existing market price, it is marketable. In contrast, a Renoir painting or antique desk appraised at $1 million will likely sell for much less if the owner must sell on short notice.

In general, marketability is the ability to sell an asset for its face market value quickly and in large amounts. Perhaps the most marketable of all securities are U.S. Treasury bills.

Taxability   Several kinds of securities have varying degrees of tax exemption.

1. The interest on the bonds of state and local governments is exempt from federal taxes, and usually from the state and local taxes where the bonds are issued. Pretax expected returns on state and local bonds must be lower than on similar taxable investments and therefore are more attractive to corporations in high marginal tax brackets.
2. Seventy percent of the dividend income on preferred and common stock is exempt from corporate income taxes.

The market price of securities will reflect the total demand and supply of tax influences. The position of the firm may be different from that of the market.

Different Types of Money-Market Securities

Money-market securities are generally highly marketable and short term. They usually have low risk of default. They are issued by the U.S. government (for example, U.S. Treasury bills), domestic and foreign banks (for example, certificates of deposit), and business corporations (commercial paper, for example).

U.S. Treasury bills are obligations of the U.S. government that mature in 90, 180, 270, or 360 days. They are pure discount securities. The 90-day and 180-day bills are sold by auction every week, and 270-day and 360-day bills are sold every month.

U.S. Treasury notes and bonds have original maturities of more than one year. They are interest-bearing securities. The interest is exempt from state and local taxes.

Federal agency securities are securities issued by corporations and agencies created by the U.S. government, such as the Federal Home Loan Bank Board and the Government National Mortgage Association (*Ginnie Mae*). The interest rates on agency issues are higher than those on comparable U.S. Treasury issues. This is true because agency issues are not as marketable as U.S. Treasury issues, and they have more default risk.

Short-term tax exempts are short-term securities issued by states, municipalities, local housing agencies, and urban renewal agencies. They have more default risk than U.S. Treasury issues and are less marketable. The interest is exempt from federal income tax.

As a consequence, the pretax yield on tax exempts is lower than those on comparable securities, such as U.S. Treasury bills.

Commercial paper refers to short-term securities issued by finance companies, banks, and corporations. Commercial paper typically is unsecured notes. Maturities range from a few weeks to 270 days. There is no active secondary market in commercial paper. As a consequence, their marketability is low. (However, firms that issue commercial paper will directly repurchase before maturity.) The default risk of commercial paper depends on the financial strength of the issuer. Moody's and Standard & Poor's publish quality ratings for commercial paper.

Certificates of deposit (CDs) are short-term loans to commercial banks. There are active markets in CDs of 3-month, 6-month, 9-month, and 12-month maturities.

Repurchase agreements are sales of government securities (for example, U.S. Treasury bills) by a bank or securities dealer with an agreement to repurchase. An investor typically buys some Treasury securities from a bond dealer and simultaneously agrees to sell them back at a later date at a specified higher price. Repurchase agreements are usually very short term—overnight to a few days.

Eurodollar CDs are deposits of dollars with foreign banks.

Banker's acceptances are time drafts (orders to pay) issued by a business firm (usually an importer) that have been accepted by a bank that guarantees payment.

Visit us at www.mhhe.com/rwj

Concept Questions

1. **Why do firms find themselves with idle cash?**
2. **What are the types of money-market securities?**

27.5 SUMMARY AND CONCLUSIONS

The chapter discussed how firms manage cash.

1. A firm holds cash to conduct transactions and to compensate banks for the various services they render.

2. The optimal amount of cash for a firm to hold depends on the opportunity cost of holding cash and the uncertainty of future cash inflows and outflows. The Baumol model and the Miller-Orr model are two transactions models that provide rough guidelines for determining the optimal cash position.

3. The firm can make use of a variety of procedures to manage the collection and disbursement of cash in such a way as to speed up the collection of cash and slow down payments. Some methods to speed up collection are lockboxes, concentration banking, and wire transfers. The financial manager must always work with collected company cash balances and not with the company's book balance. To do otherwise is to use the bank's cash without the bank knowing it, raising ethical and legal questions.

4. Because of seasonal and cyclical activities, to help finance planned expenditures, or as a reserve for unanticipated needs, firms temporarily find themselves with cash surpluses. The money market offers a variety of possible vehicles for parking this idle cash.

KEY TERMS

compensating balances, *754*
concentration banking, *764*
float, *761*
lockbox, *764*

target cash balance, *754*
transactions motive, *754*
wire transfer, *765*
zero-balance account (ZBA), *768*

SUGGESTED READING	*For a review of the latest academic research on corporate cash holding, see:*

Opler T., L. Pinkowitz, R. Stulz, and R. Williamson. "Corporate Cash Holdings." *Journal of Applied Corporate Finance,* Spring 2001.

QUESTIONS & PROBLEMS

REASONS FOR HOLDING CASH

DETERMINING THE TARGET CASH BALANCE

27.1   What are the reasons for holding cash?

27.2   Indicate whether the following actions increase, decrease, or cause no change in a company's cash balance.
   a. Interest rates paid on money-market securities rise.
   b. Commissions charged by brokers increase.
   c. The compensating-balance requirement of a bank is lowered.
   d. The cost of borrowing decreases.
   e. The firm's credit rating declines.
   f. Direct fees for banking services are established.

27.3   A company's weekly average cash balances are as follows:

Week 1	$24,000
Week 2	34,000
Week 3	10,000
Week 4	15,000

   If the annual interest rate is 12 percent, what return can be earned on the average cash balances?

27.4   The Casablanca Piano Company is currently holding $800,000 in cash. It projects that over the next year its cash outflows will exceed its cash inflows by $345,000 per month. Each time securities are bought or sold through a broker, the company pays a fee of $500. The annual interest rate on money-market securities is 7 percent.
   a. How much of this cash should be retained and how much should be used to increase the company's holdings of marketable securities?
   b. After the initial investment of excess cash, how many times during the next 12 months will securities be sold?

27.5   Lisa Tylor, CFO of Purple Rain Co., concluded from the Baumol model that the optimal cash balance for the firm is $20 million. The annual interest rate on marketable securities is 7.5 percent. The fixed cost of selling securities to replenish cash is $5,000. Purple Rain's cash flow pattern is well approximated by the Baumol model. What can you infer about Purple Rain's average weekly cash disbursement?

27.6   The variance of the daily net cash flows for the Tseneg Asian Import Company is $1.44 million. The opportunity cost to the firm of holding cash is 8 percent per year. The fixed cost of buying and selling securities is $600 per transaction.
   What should the target cash level and upper limit be, if the tolerable lower limit has been established at $20,000?

27.7   Gold Star Co. and Silver Star Co. both manage their cash flows according to the Miller-Orr model. Gold Star's daily cash flow is controlled between $100,000 and $200,000, whereas Silver Star's daily cash flow is controlled between $150,000 and $300,000. The annual interest rates Gold Star and Silver Star can get are 10 percent and 9 percent, respectively, and the costs per transaction of trading securities are $2,000 and $2,500, respectively.
   a. What are their respective target cash balances?
   b. Which firm's daily cash flow is more volatile?

MANAGING THE COLLECTION AND DISBURSEMENT OF CASH

27.8   Garden Groves, Inc., a Florida-based company, has determined that a majority of its customers are located in the New York City area. Therefore, it is considering using a lockbox system offered by a bank located in New York. The bank has estimated that use of the system will reduce collection float by three days. Based on the following information, should the lockbox system be adopted?

> Average number of payments per day: 150
> Average value of payment: $15,000
> Fixed annual lockbox fee: $80,000
> Variable lockbox fee: $0.50/transaction
> Annual interest rate on money-market securities: 7.5 percent

27.9   A large New England lumber producer, Salisbury Stakes, Inc., is planning to use a lockbox system to speed collections from its customers located in the midwestern United States. A Chicago-area bank will provide this service for an annual fee of $15,000 plus $0.25 per transaction. The estimated reduction in collection and processing time is two days. Treasury bills are currently yielding 6 percent per year.

   If the average customer payment in this region is $4,500, how many customers each day, on average, must use the system to make it profitable?

27.10   Each business day, on average, a company writes checks totaling $12,000 to pay its suppliers. The usual clearing time for these checks is five days. Each day, the company receives payments from its customers in the form of checks totaling $15,000. The cash from the payments is available to the firm after three days.

   Calculate the company's disbursement float, collection float, and net float.

   How would these values change if the collected funds were available in four days instead of three?

27.11   It takes the Herman Company about seven days to receive and deposit checks from customers. The top management of the Herman Company is considering a lockbox system. It is expected that the lockbox system will reduce float time to four days. Average daily collections are $100,000. The marketwide interest rate is 12 percent.

   a. What would the reduction in outstanding cash balances be as a result of implementing the lockbox system?

   b. What is the return that could be earned on these savings?

   c. What is the maximum monthly charge the Herman Company should pay for this lockbox system?

27.12   The Walter Company disburses checks every two weeks that average $200,000 in total and take three days to clear. How much cash can the Walter Company save annually if it delays the transfer of funds from an interest-bearing account that pays 0.04 percent per day for these three days?

27.13   The Miller Company has an agreement with the First National Bank by which the bank handles $4 million in collections each day and requires a $500,000 compensating balance. Miller is contemplating canceling the agreement and dividing its eastern region so that two other banks will handle its business. Banks 1 and 2 will each handle $2 million of collections each day, requiring a compensating balance of $300,000. Miller's financial management expects that collections will be accelerated by one day if the eastern region is divided. The T-bill rate is 7 percent. Should the Miller Company implement the new system? What will the annual net savings be?

27.14   Anthony Marino, CFO of Thousand Years Inc., is evaluating two alternatives of float management: lockbox and concentration banking. The average number of daily payments to lockboxes is 250 with the average size of each payment at $7,500. The lockbox system can reduce the collection float by 1.5 days and concentration banking can reduce the collection float by 1 day. However, the bank charges an annual fee of $30,000 and $0.30 per check processed for the lockbox service. Which method is more economical for Thousand Years, the lockbox system or the concentration-banking system? Assume daily interest on Treasury bills is 0.03 percent.

INVESTING IDLE CASH   **27.15**   What are the important characteristics of short-term marketable securities?

Appendix 27A	# Adjustable-Rate Preferred Stock, Auction-Rate Preferred Stock, and Floating-Rate Certificates of Deposit

Corporate cash managers are continually seeking new ways to improve the return on their surplus cash. Many of the sophisticated investment vehicles developed over the last decade are too illiquid or too risky or have an inappropriate time horizon for use in cash management. However, three instruments—adjustable-rate preferred stock, auction-rate preferred stock, and floating-rate CDs or notes—offer substantial benefits and are currently employed by corporations in their cash-management activities.

Adjustable-Rate Preferred Stock

Adjustable-rate preferred stock (ARPS) is designed to offer rates of return competitive with more traditional money-market instruments while still affording the corporate investor the 80-percent tax exclusion on dividend income—a tax advantage that makes equity investments extremely attractive.

Agencies such as Moody's or Standard & Poor's give issues credit ratings, so the cash manager has a gauge to judge the creditworthiness of the instruments relative to other investments. The dividend rate on these issues is adjusted quarterly at a fixed spread over or under the highest of the 90-day T-bill rate, the 10-year T-note rate, or the 20-year T-bond rate prevailing on the reset date. The spread is specified by each issuer. ARPS issues have *collars*—minimum and maximum dividend-rate levels—that, when hit, result in the issue taking on the characteristics of a fixed-rate preferred instrument.

The floating-rate feature keeps the dividend rate (and thus the overall pretax return) in line with alternative investments and reduces price volatility caused solely by changes in interest rates. The floating rate does not, however, eliminate all of the incremental risk associated with these instruments.

Risk is present in the ARPS market and can be broken down into three categories. Cash managers must continually reevaluate the market in light of changes that might occur in any of the three areas.

The greatest risk in the ARPS market is derived from the limited number of issuers and their clustering in certain industry groups, most notably banking, and the ever-present risk of downgraded ratings. Like any other credit instrument, ARPS is subject to volatility based on the market's perceptions of the strength of the issuer and industry group. The possibility of impaired principal is a real one for ARPS purchasers, because concerns about credit could govern the floating-rate dividend between and on reset dates. The cash manager must be aware that substantial month-to-month volatility (the normal time horizon for corporate evaluation of their cash portfolios) could exist with ARPS investments.

A second risk factor centers around the narrowness of the primary and secondary markets for ARPS. The demand for these issues comes primarily from corporate investors, and the limited nature of this investment base is a factor in evaluating the depth of the market. If a cash manager must liquidate a position quickly, a thin market could exacerbate price pressure. As a result, most corporate investors employ mutual-fund managers who specialize in the ARPS market to run their portfolios. Liquidity is normally next-day with the funds (although principal is by no means guaranteed), and mutual-fund managers represent the most active players in the market.

Finally, changes in the tax code have a great impact on the price of ARPS issues, because their main feature is the tax advantage of the dividend exclusion. The Tax Reform

Visit us at www.mhhe.com/rwj

Act of 1986 reduced this exclusion from 85 to 70 percent. Assuming a 46-percent tax rate, a corporate investor in the ARPS market would have found its dividend income being taxed at 13.8 percent (30 percent taxed at 46 percent) instead of 6.9 percent (15 percent taxed at 46 percent). Such an increase would have undoubtedly resulted in substantial price declines for existing issues. Luckily for both ARPS issuers and purchasers, the top corporate tax rate is now lower than 46 percent, resulting in only a small change for recipients of dividend income. The issue of tax advantage is crucial, because ARPS as an investment is evaluated on an after-tax risk-adjusted basis relative to other instruments. If the added risk inherent in the instrument begins to eclipse the tax advantage, the instrument will become increasingly unattractive.

The adjustable-rate preferred market has not fared as well as early proponents had hoped, primarily because the floating-rate dividend failed to compensate for credit concerns about the issuers. This has resulted in many issues trading below par and has prompted the development of several related instruments. The most successful of these new vehicles is auction-rate preferred stock.

Auction-Rate Preferred Stock

The similarity between ARPS and *auction-rate preferred stock* extends only to the fact that both have a floating dividend rate and afford the corporate investor the same exclusion of taxes on dividends. Auction rates differ from ARPS in the way the dividend is set and in the way these portfolios are managed.

The dividend rate for auction-rate preferred is set not by the issuers but by the market through a process called a *Dutch auction*. The auction permits investors to determine the dividend yield for the 49-day period that is standard between reset dates. The Internal Revenue Service requires that a corporate investor hold dividend-paying stock for at least 45 days to be eligible for the dividend exclusion; 49 days was chosen so the auctions will always occur on the same day of the week for the life of individual issues.

An auction-rate preferred stock is auctioned as follows. Each bidder (someone who already owns shares and wishes to continue to hold them, or a new purchaser) submits to the agent in charge of the auction the number of shares desired and at what dividend level. The lowest rate that sells out the available shares will be the dividend for the 49 days until the next reset/auction. Investors who already own shares going into the auction have the option to take their shares at whatever dividend is set (called *rolling*) or bid the lowest rate they would accept and risk losing some or all of the shares to another bidder who would be willing to take a lower dividend. Of course, shareholders also have the right to simply sell all of their shares at the auction. Although the process is essentially independent, the dividend rate for most issues is usually set at approximately 60 to 80 percent of the 60-day AA commercial paper rate prevailing on auction day.

Auction-rate preferred stock offers the corporate investor several important features:

1. The 49-day reset period is shorter than the 90-day period found in the ARPS market, reducing the potential for price volatility resulting from both interest-rate movement and credit concerns.
2. The auction method of determining the dividend level makes it more likely that the issue will trade at par, minimizing principal impairment. The shorter reset period also offers the cash manager increased liquidity in the event funds are needed for corporate operations between auctions. The auction-rate investor sacrifices some return relative to ARPS because of these features, but still garners a substantial after-tax benefit relative to alternative money-market investments.

3. The auction-rate preferred market is more accessible to the corporate investor, allowing it to invest individually rather than through a mutual fund. Many cash managers prefer the added control this gives them over their portfolios.

The risks associated with auction-rate preferred stock are smaller than those associated with ARPS but must still be considered substantial for the cash manager who may need immediate liquidity or who faces strict return criteria. These risks include the following:

1. *Failed Auctions.* If the agent supervising an auction does not receive enough bids to match offers to sell for existing shares of a particular issue, the auction is considered to have failed. There have been several auction failures, but it is not as catastrophic as it sounds. It means that the dividend rate for the subsequent 49-day period will be set at 110 percent of the 60-day AA commercial paper rate. A seller would therefore be faced with a capital loss if it wished to liquidate.

2. *Issuer Credit Quality.* As with ARPS, all auction-rate preferred issues receive a rating from Moody's or Standard & Poor's. They remain susceptible to perceived or actual changes in that credit quality between reset periods. To facilitate the new market, some large brokers were even guaranteeing to redeem auction-rate preferred at par between reset periods to generate investor participation.

3. *Changes in the Tax Code.* Major changes in the tax code will affect the auction-rate preferred market in much the same manner as they would the APRS market. Once again, it is crucial to remember that these instruments are judged on an after-tax risk-adjusted basis relative to alternative investments.

Auction-rate preferred stock has been extremely well received by the corporate marketplace. The key to its continued success will be diversification of issuers, orderly and successful auctions, and an ongoing after-tax yield advantage relative to other money-market investments.

Floating-Rate Certificates of Deposit

A third investment available to the cash manager looking to increase the return on surplus cash is the *floating-rate certificate of deposit* or note. Our discussion centers on the CD, but the same argument applies to the short-term note, adjusting for time-horizon considerations.

The floating-rate certificate of deposit (FRCD) market presents substantial investment opportunities for the manager of short-term cash. Frequently reset coupons, the hallmark of the FRCD, allow the investor to combine the yield of an intermediate-term instrument with the liquidity of a short-term one. This combination also reduces interest-rate risk and provides for capital maintenance, while continuing to provide attractive returns.

Two issues must be addressed when evaluating the FRCD market:

1. How are the issues priced?
2. Which base rate should be selected?

Floating-rate CDs are priced at a spread above or below a well-known market index such as the London Interbank Offered Rate (LIBOR), T-bills, or commercial paper. The width of the spread reflects the issuer's credit, the maturity of the issue, its liquidity, and the overall level of rates at the time of issuance. In general, this spread is fixed over the life of the security, but some new issues do have a floating spread. When the market perception of credit quality changes significantly from that implied in the spread to the base rate, the price of the security will decline as the market compensates investors for the increased risk.

The actual coupon paid (the index rate plus or minus the predetermined spread) to the investor will be reset periodically, usually monthly, quarterly, or semiannually. It is the floating nature of the coupon that keeps most FRCDs within one to two points of par at all times, as the issue is continually repriced relative to existing market conditions. Price stability will increase with the frequency of reset.

Most FRCDs also feature redemption specifications in the form of call or put options. In the case of a call, the issuer has the option to call the security back from an investor at par, usually within three to five years of issuance. The security can be called on any coupon-payment date, and, as would be expected, the option is usually exercised when the security is trading at a premium. For the put option, the investor has the right to sell the security back to the issuer at par before maturity. The option is usually exercised when the security is trading at a discount. These features must be incorporated into yield calculations, with the call or put dates generally substituted for the maturity date.

The initial price of the FRCD will adapt to reflect market demand for the issue, liquidity, and favorable aspects of the issue's structure. Whether the security trades at a premium or discount to par depends on changes in the market's perception of these and the other factors discussed previously. However, given frequently reset coupons, only drastic changes in issuer quality or quality spreads will prompt significant deterioration of principal.

The price of an FRCD will also be affected if a change occurs in the relationship between index rates, such as a widening of the T-bill/Eurodollar spread. Assume that two FRCDs are priced to identical yields, one at a spread over LIBOR and the other at a spread above T-bills. If the T-bill/Eurodollar spread widens, the FRCDs indexed to LIBOR will experience a price decline. This will occur regardless of the absolute level of interest rates or any shift in market perception of specific credit risk.

In evaluating an FRCD, the selection of an issue based on its index rate can be as important as selection of an issue based on the issuer's credit ratings or maturity. The choice of an index reflects the perception of how the issuer's industry fundamentals will behave relative to that index. For instance, the choice of T-bills as the base implies an analysis of how the issuer will perform relative to a risk-free measure; the choice of commercial paper implies an analysis of the issuer's prospects relative to companies with access to that market.

The base rate will also be important when general quality concerns arise in the market. A LIBOR index will reflect those concerns, and the price of an FRCD indexed to LIBOR should not change drastically, because its coupon is linked directly to a market-determined cost of funds. An FRCD indexed to T-bills, however, might exhibit substantial price volatility over the same time period. The greater the index's sensitivity to market movement, the greater the issue's price stability.

Although the FRCD does not offer the tax advantage of ARPS or auction-rate preferred stock, it gives the cash manager an opportunity to keep returns on excess cash in line with changing interest rates. The secondary market for FRCDs is still developing but is considerably deeper than that for preferred securities.

All of these investments were designed for cash-management activities that allow for investment of cash for longer periods of time. Generally, a cash manager will be using at least a 9-month to 12-month horizon before considering investing in these vehicles. Money should not be committed to these investments unless the manager can be reasonably sure that it will not be needed for corporate operations for at least one year.

Credit Management

EXECUTIVE SUMMARY

When a firm sells goods and services it can (1) be paid in cash immediately or (2) wait for a time to be paid, that is, extend credit to customers. Granting credit is investing in a customer, an investment tied to the sale of a product or service. This chapter examines the firm's decision to grant credit.

An account receivable is created when credit is granted. These receivables include credit granted to other firms, called *trade credit,* and credit granted consumers, called *consumer credit.* About one-sixth of all the assets of industrial firms are in the form of accounts receivable. Trade credit extended by a firm's supplier to the firm appears as an accounts payable. Figure 28.1 illustrates this aspect of trade credit.

The investment in accounts receivable for any firm depends on both the amount of credit sales and the average collection period. For example, if a firm's credit sales per day equal $1,000 and its average collection period is 30 days, its accounts receivable will be equal to $30,000. Thus, a firm's investment in accounts receivable depends on factors influencing credit sales and collection. A firm's credit policy affects these factors.

The following are the components of credit policy:

1. **Terms of the sale.** A firm must decide on certain conditions when selling its goods and services for credit. For example, the terms of sale may specify the credit period, the cash discount, and the type of credit instrument.

2. **Credit analysis.** When granting credit, a firm tries to distinguish between customers that will pay and customers that will not pay. Firms use a number of devices and procedures to determine the probability that customers will pay.

3. **Collection policy.** Firms that grant credit must establish a policy for collecting the cash when it becomes due.

This chapter discusses each of the components of credit policy that makes up the decision to grant credit.

In some ways, the decision to grant credit is connected to the cash collection process described in the previous chapter. This is illustrated in Figure 28.2 with a cash-flow diagram.

The typical sequence of events when a firm grants credit is (1) the credit sale is made, (2) the customer sends a check to the firm, (3) the firm deposits the check, and (4) the firm's account is credited for the amount of the check.

28.1 Terms of the Sale

The terms of sale refer to the period for which credit is granted, the cash discount, and the type of credit instrument. For example, suppose a customer is granted credit with terms of 2/10, net 30. This means that the customer has 30 days from the **invoice** date within which

FIGURE 28.1

Trade Credit

Trade credit extended to a customer by a firm appears as an accounts receivable.
Trade credit extended by the firm's supplier to the firm appears as an accounts payable.

FIGURE 28.2

**The Cash Flows of
Granting Credit**

to pay.[1] In addition, a cash discount of 2 percent from the stated sales price is to be given if payment is made in 10 days. If the stated terms are net 60, the customer has 60 days from the invoice date to pay and no discount is offered for early payment.

When sales are seasonal, a firm might use seasonal dating. O. M. Scott and Sons is a manufacturer of lawn and garden products with a seasonal dating policy that is tied to the growing season. Payments for winter shipments of fertilizer might be due in the spring or summer. A firm offering 3/10, net 60, May 1 dating, is making the effective invoice date May 1. The stated amount must be paid on June 30, regardless of when the sale is made. The cash discount of 3 percent can be taken until May 10.

Credit Period

Credit periods vary among different industries. For example, a jewelry store may sell diamond engagement rings for 5/30, net 4 months. A food wholesaler, selling fresh fruit and produce, might use net 7. Generally a firm must consider three factors in setting a credit period:

1. *The Probability That the Customer Will Not Pay.* A firm whose customers are in high-risk businesses may find itself offering restrictive credit terms.

2. *The Size of the Account.* If the account is small, the credit period will be shorter. Small accounts are more costly to manage, and small customers are less important.

3. *The Extent to Which the Goods Are Perishable.* If the collateral values of the goods are low and cannot be sustained for long periods, less credit will be granted.

Lengthening the credit period effectively reduces the price paid by the customer. Generally this increases sales.

---

[1]An *invoice* is a bill written by a seller of goods or services and submitted to the buyer. The invoice date is usually the same as the shipping date.

Cash Discounts

Cash discounts are often part of the terms of sale. One reason they are offered is to speed up the collection of receivables. The firm must trade this off against the cost of the discount.

Edward Manalt, the chief financial officer of Ruptbank Company, is considering the request of the company's largest customer, who wants to take a 3-percent discount for payment within 20 days on a $10,000 purchase. In other words, he intends to pay $9,700 [$10,000 × (1 − 0.03)]. Normally, this customer pays in 30 days with no discount. The cost of debt capital for Ruptbank is 10 percent. Edward has worked out the cash flow implications illustrated in Figure 28.3. He assumes that the time required to cash the check when the customer receives it is the same under both credit arrangements. He has calculated the present value of the two proposals:

Current Policy:

$$PV = \frac{\$10,000}{1 + (0.1 \times 30/365)} = \$9,918.48$$

Proposed Policy:

$$PV = \frac{\$9,700}{1 + (0.1 \times 20/365)} = \$9,647.14$$

His calculation shows that granting the discount would cost the Ruptbank firm $271.34 ($9,918.48 − $9,647.14) in present value. Consequently, Ruptbank is better off with the current credit arrangement.

FIGURE 28.3

Cash Flows for Different Credit Terms

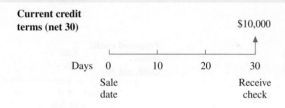

Current credit terms (net 30)

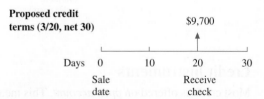

Proposed credit terms (3/20, net 30)

Current situation: Customers usually pay 30 days from the sale date and receive no discount.

Proposed situation: Customer will pay 20 days from the sale date at a 3-percent discount from the $10,000 purchase price.

In the previous example, we implicitly assumed that granting credit had no side effects. However, the decision to grant credit may generate higher sales and involve a different cost structure. The next example illustrates the impact of changes in the level of sales and costs in the credit decision.

EXAMPLE

Suppose that Ruptbank Company has variable costs of $0.50 per $1 of sales. If offered a discount of 3 percent, customers will increase their order size by 10 percent. This new information is shown in Figure 28.4. That is, the customer will increase the order size to $11,000 and, with the 3-percent discount, will remit $10,670 [$11,000 × (1 − 0.03)] to Ruptbank in 20 days. It will cost more to fill the larger order because variable costs are $5,500. The net present values are worked out here:

Current Policy:

$$NPV = -\$5,000 + \frac{\$10,000}{1 + (0.1 \times 30/365)} = \$4,918.48$$

Proposed Policy:

$$NPV = -\$5,500 + \frac{\$10,670}{1 + (0.1 \times 20/365)} = \$5,111.85$$

Now it is clear that the firm is better off with the proposed credit policy. This increase is the net effect of several different factors including the larger initial costs, the earlier receipt of the cash inflows, the increased sales level, and the discount.

FIGURE 28.4

Cash Flows for
Different Credit
Terms: The Impact of
New Sales and Costs

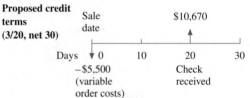

Credit Instruments

Most credit is offered on *open account*. This means that the only formal **credit instrument** is the invoice, which is sent with the shipment of goods, and which the customer signs as evidence that the goods have been received. Afterward, the firm and its customers record the exchange on their accounting books.

At times, the firm may require that the customer sign a *promissory note,* or IOU. This is used when the order is large and when the firm anticipates a problem in collections. Promissory notes can eliminate controversies later about the existence of a credit agreement.

One problem with promissory notes is that they are signed after delivery of the goods. One way to obtain a credit commitment from a customer before the goods are delivered is through the use of a *commercial draft*. The selling firm typically writes a commercial draft calling for the customer to pay a specific amount by a specified date. The draft is then sent to the customer's bank with the shipping invoices. The bank has the buyer sign the draft before turning over the invoices. The goods can then be shipped to the buyer. If immediate payment is required, it is called a *sight draft*. Here, funds must be turned over to the bank before the goods are shipped.

Frequently, even the signed draft is not enough for the seller. In this case, he might demand that the banker pay for the goods and collect the money from the customer. When the banker agrees to do so in writing, the document is called a *banker's acceptance*. That is, the banker *accepts* responsibility for payment. Because banks generally are well-known and well-respected institutions, the banker's acceptance becomes a liquid instrument. In other words, the seller can then sell (*discount*) the banker's acceptance in the secondary market.

A firm can also use a *conditional sales contract* as a credit instrument. This is an arrangement where the firm retains legal ownership of the goods until the customer has completed payment. Conditional sales contracts usually are paid off in installments and have interest costs built into them.

Concept Question

1. **What considerations enter into the determination of the terms of sale?**

28.2 The Decision to Grant Credit: Risk and Information

Locust Industries has been in existence for two years. It is one of several successful firms that develop computer programs. The present financial managers have set out two alternative credit strategies: The firm can offer credit, or the firm can refuse credit.

Suppose Locust has determined that, if it offers no credit to its customers, it can sell its existing computer software for $50 per program. It estimates that the costs to produce a typical computer program are equal to $20 per program.

The alternative is to offer credit. In this case, customers of Locust will pay one period later. With some probability, Locust has determined that if it offers credit, it can charge higher prices and expect higher sales.

Strategy 1: Refuse Credit If Locust refuses to grant credit, cash flows will not be delayed, and period 0 net cash flows, NCF, will be:

$$P_0 Q_0 - C_0 Q_0 = \text{NCF}$$

The subscripts denote the time when the cash flows are incurred, where:

P_0 = Price per unit received at time 0
C_0 = Cost per unit received at time 0
Q_0 = Quantity sold at time 0

The net cash flows at period 1 are zero, and the net present value to Locust of refusing credit will simply be the period 0 net cash flow:

$$\text{NPV} = \text{NCF}$$

For example, if credit is not granted and $Q_0 = 100$, the NPV can be calculated as

$$(\$50 \times 100) - (\$20 \times 100) = \$3,000$$

Strategy 2: Offer Credit Alternatively, let us assume that Locust grants credit to all customers for one period. The factors that influence the decision are listed below.

	Strategy I Refuse Credit	Strategy 2 Offer Credit
Price per unit	$P_0 = \$50$	$P_0' = \$50$
Quantity sold	$Q_0 = 100$	$Q_0' = 200$
Cost per unit	$C_0 = \$20$	$C_0' = \$25$
Probability of payment	$h = 1$	$h = 0.90$
Credit period	0	I period
Discount rate	0	$r_B = 0.01$

The prime ($'$) denotes the variables under the second strategy. If the firm offers credit and the new customers pay, the firm will receive revenues of $P_0'Q_0'$ one period hence, but its costs, $C_0'Q_0'$, are incurred in period 0. If new customers do not pay, the firm incurs costs $C_0'Q_0'$ and receives no revenues. The probability that customers will pay, h, is 0.90 in the example. Quantity sold is higher with credit, because new customers are attracted. The cost per unit is also higher with credit because of the costs of operating a credit policy.

The expected cash flows for each policy are set out as follows:

	Expected Cash Flows	
	Time 0	Time I
Refuse credit	$P_0Q_0 - C_0Q_0$	0
Offer credit	$-C_0'Q_0'$	$h \times P_0'Q_0'$

Note that granting credit produces delayed expected cash inflows equal to $h \times P_0'Q_0'$. The costs are incurred immediately and require no discounting. The net present value if credit is offered is:

$$\text{NPV (offer)} = \frac{h \times P_0'Q_0'}{1 + r_B} - C_0'Q_0'$$

$$= \frac{0.9 \times \$50 \times 200}{1.01} - \$5,000 = \$3,910.89$$

Locust's decision should be to adopt the proposed credit policy. The NPV of granting credit is higher than that of refusing credit. This decision is very sensitive to the probability of payment. If it turns out that the probability of payment is 81 percent, Locust Software is indifferent to whether it grants credit or not. In this case the NPV of granting credit is $3,000, which we previously found to be the NPV of not granting credit:

$$\$3,000 = h \times \frac{\$50 \times 200}{1.01} - \$5,000$$

$$\$8,000 = h \times \frac{\$50 \times 200}{1.01}$$

$$h = 80.8\%$$

The decision to grant credit depends on four factors:

1. The delayed revenues from granting credit, $P_0'Q_0'$.
2. The immediate costs of granting credit, $C_0'Q_0'$.

3. The probability of payment, h.
4. The appropriate required rate of return for delayed cash flows, r_B.

The Value of New Information about Credit Risk

Obtaining a better estimate of the probability that a customer will default can lead to a better decision. How can a firm determine when to acquire new information about the creditworthiness of its customers?

It may be sensible for Locust to determine which of its customers are most likely not to pay. The overall probability of nonpayment is 10 percent. But credit checks by an independent firm show that 90 percent of Locust's customers (computer stores) have been profitable over the last five years and that these customers have never defaulted on payments. The less profitable customers are much more likely to default. In fact, 100 percent of the less profitable customers have defaulted on previous obligations.

Locust would like to avoid offering credit to the deadbeats. Consider its projected number of customers per year of $Q'_0 = 200$ if credit is granted. Of these customers, 180 have been profitable over the last five years and have never defaulted on past obligations. The remaining 20 have not been profitable. Locust Software expects that all of these less profitable customers will default. This information is set out in a table:

Type of Customer	Number	Probability of Nonpayment	Expected Number of Defaults
Profitable	180	0%	0
Less profitable	20	100	20
Total customers	200	10%	20

The NPV of granting credit to the customers who default is:

$$\frac{hP'_0Q'_0}{1 + r_B} - C'_0Q'_0 = \frac{0 \times \$50 \times 20}{1.01} - \$25 \times 20 = -\$500$$

This is the cost of providing them with the software. If Locust can identify these customers without cost, it would certainly deny them credit.

In fact, it actually costs Locust \$3 per customer to figure out whether a customer has been profitable over the last five years. The expected payoff of the credit check on its 200 customers is then:

$$\begin{array}{ccc} \text{Gain from not} & & \text{Cost of} \\ \text{extending credit} & - & \text{credit checks} \\ \$500 & - & \$3 \times 200 = -\$100 \end{array}$$

For Locust, credit is not worth checking. It would need to pay \$600 to avoid a \$500 loss.

Future Sales

Up to this point, Locust has not considered the possibility that offering credit will permanently increase the level of sales in future periods (beyond next month). In addition, payment and nonpayment patterns in the current period will provide credit information that is useful for the next period. These two factors should be analyzed.

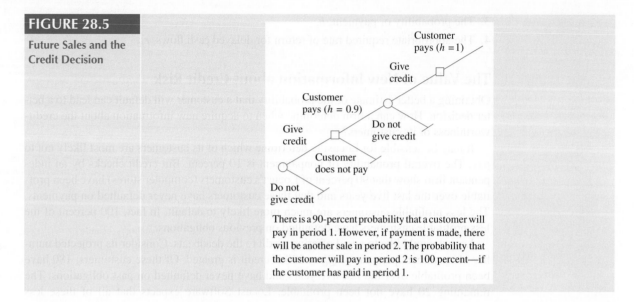

FIGURE 28.5

Future Sales and the
Credit Decision

Customer
pays ($h = 1$)

Give
credit

Customer
pays ($h = 0.9$)

Give
credit

Do not
give credit

Customer
does not pay

Do not
give credit

There is a 90-percent probability that a customer will
pay in period 1. However, if payment is made, there
will be another sale in period 2. The probability that
the customer will pay in period 2 is 100 percent—if
the customer has paid in period 1.

In the case of Locust, there is a 90-percent probability that the customer will pay in
period 1. But, if payment is made, there will be another sale in period 2. The probability
that the customer will pay in period 2, if the customer has paid in period 1, is 100 percent.
Locust can refuse to offer credit in period 2 to customers that have refused to pay in period 1.
This is diagrammed in Figure 28.5.

**Concept
Question**

1. List the factors that influence the decision to grant credit.

28.3 Optimal Credit Policy

So far we have discussed how to compute net present value for two alternative credit policies. However, we have not discussed the optimal amount of credit. At the optimal amount
of credit, the incremental cash flows from increased sales are exactly equal to the carrying
costs from the increase in accounts receivable.

Consider a firm that does not currently grant credit. This firm has no bad debts, no
credit department, and relatively few customers. Now consider another firm that grants
credit. This firm has lots of customers, a credit department, and a bad-debt expense account.

It is useful to think of the decision to grant credit in terms of carrying costs and opportunity costs:

1. *Carrying costs* are the costs associated with granting credit and making an investment
   in receivables. Carrying costs include the delay in receiving cash, the losses from bad
   debts, and the costs of managing credit.

2. *Opportunity costs* are the lost sales from refusing to offer credit. These costs drop as
   credit is granted.

We represent these costs in Figure 28.6.

FIGURE 28.6

The Costs of Granting Credit

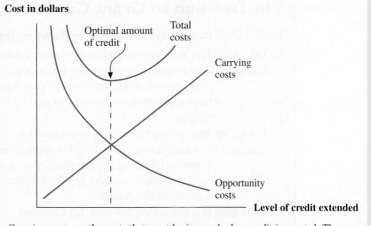

Carrying costs are the costs that must be incurred when credit is granted. They are positively related to the amount of credit extended.

Opportunity costs are the lost sales from refusing credit. These costs drop when credit is granted.

The sum of the carrying costs and the opportunity costs of a particular credit policy is called the *total-credit-cost curve.* A point is identified as the minimum of the total-credit-cost curve. If the firm extends more credit than the minimum, the additional net cash flow from new customers will not cover the carrying costs of this investment in receivables.

The concept of optimal credit policy in the context of modern principles of finance should be somewhat analogous to the concept of the optimal capital structure discussed earlier in the text. In perfect financial markets there should be no optimal credit policy. Alternative amounts of credit for a firm should not affect the value of the firm. Thus, the decision to grant credit would be a matter of indifference to financial managers.

Just as with optimal capital structure, we could expect taxes, monopoly power, bankruptcy costs, and agency costs to be important in determining an optimal credit policy in a world of imperfect financial markets. For example, customers in high tax brackets would be better off borrowing and taking advantage of cash discounts offered by firms than would customers in low tax brackets. Corporations in low tax brackets would be less able to offer credit, because borrowing would be relatively more expensive than for firms in high tax brackets.

In general, a firm will extend trade credit if it has a comparative advantage in doing so. Trade credit is likely to be advantageous if the selling firm has a cost advantage over other potential lenders, if the selling firm has monopoly power it can exploit, if the selling firm can reduce taxes by extending credit, and if the product quality of the selling firm is difficult to determine. Firm size may be important if there are size economies in managing credit.

The optimal credit policy depends on characteristics of particular firms. Assuming that the firm has more flexibility in its credit policy than in the prices it charges, firms with excess capacity, low variable operating costs, high tax brackets, and repeat customers should extend credit more liberally than others.

The Decision to Grant Credit

Trade credit is more likely to be granted by the selling firm if

1. The selling firm has a cost advantage over other lenders.

    Example: The American Manufacturing Co. produces widgets. In a default, it is easier for the American Manufacturing Co. to repossess widgets and resell them than for a finance company to arrange for it with no experience in selling widgets.

2. The selling firm can engage in price discrimination.

    Example: National Motors can offer below-market interest rates to lower income customers that must finance a large portion of the purchase price of cars. Higher income customers pay the list price and do not generally finance a large part of the purchase.

3. The selling firm can obtain favorable tax treatment.

    Example: The A.B. Production Company offers long-term credit to its best customers. This form of financing may qualify as an installment plan and allow the A.B. Production Co. to book profits of the sale over the life of the loan. This may save taxes because the present value of the tax payments will be lower if spread over time.

4. The selling firm has no established reputation for quality products or services.

    Example: Advanced Micro Instruments (AMI) manufactures sophisticated measurement instruments for controlling electrical systems on commercial airplanes. The firm was founded by two engineering graduates from the University of Pennsylvania in 1997. It became a public firm in 1998. To hedge their bets, aircraft manufacturers will ask for credit from AMI. It is very difficult for customers of AMI to assess the quality of its instruments until the instruments have been in place for some time.

5. The selling firm perceives a long-term strategic relationship.

    Example: Food.com is a fast-growing, cash-constrained Internet food distributor. It is currently not profitable. Acme Food will grant Food.com credit for food purchased, because Food.com will generate profits in the future.

SOURCE: Shezad I. Mian and Clifford W. Smith, "Extending Trade Credit and Financing Receivables," *Journal of Applied Corporate Finance* (Spring 1994); Marc Deloof and Marc Jegers, "Trade Credit, Product Quality and Intragroup Trade: Some European Evidence," *Financial Management* (Autumn 1996); Michael Long, I. B. Malitz, and S. A. Ravid, "Trade Credit, Quality Guarantees, and Product Marketability," *Financial Management* (Winter 1993); and Mitchell A. Petersen and Raghuram G. Rajan, "Trade Credit: Theories and Evidence," *The Review of Financial Studies* 10 (1997).

28.4 Credit Analysis

When granting credit, a firm tries to distinguish between customers that will pay and customers that will not pay. There are a number of sources of information for determining creditworthiness.

Credit Information

Information commonly used to assess creditworthiness includes the following:

1. *Financial Statements.* A firm can ask a customer to supply financial statements. Rules of thumb based on financial ratios can be calculated.

2. *Credit Reports on Customer's Payment History with Other Firms.* Many organizations sell information on the credit strength of business firms. The best known and largest firm of this type is Dun & Bradstreet, which provides subscribers with a credit-reference book and credit reports on individual firms. The reference book has credit ratings on many thousands of businesses.

3. *Banks.* Banks will generally provide some assistance to their business customers in acquiring information on the creditworthiness of other firms.

4. *The Customer's Payment History with the Firm.* The most obvious way to obtain an estimate of a customer's probability of nonpayment is whether he or she has paid previous bills.

Credit Scoring

Once information has been gathered, the firm faces the hard choice of either granting or refusing credit. Many firms use the traditional and subjective guidelines referred to as the "five Cs of credit":

1. *Character.* The customer's willingness to meet credit obligations.
2. *Capacity.* The customer's ability to meet credit obligations out of operating cash flows.
3. *Capital.* The customer's financial reserves.
4. *Collateral.* A pledged asset in the case of default.
5. *Conditions.* General economic conditions.

Conversely, firms such as credit-card issuers have developed elaborate statistical models (called **credit-scoring** models) for determining the probability of default. Usually all the relevant and observable characteristics of a large pool of customers are studied to find their historic relation to default. Because these models determine who is and who is not creditworthy, not surprisingly they have been the subject of government regulation. For example, if a model were to find that women default more than men, it might be used to deny women credit. This regulation removes such models from the domain of the statistician and makes them the subject of politicians.

Concept
Questions

1. **What is credit analysis?**
2. **What are the five Cs of credit?**

28.5 Collection Policy

Collection refers to obtaining payment of past-due accounts. The credit manager keeps a record of payment experiences with each customer.

Average Collection Period

Acme Compact Disc Players sells 100,000 compact disc players a year at $300 each. All sales are for credit with terms of 2/20, net 60.

Suppose that 80 percent of Acme's customers take the discounts and pay on day 20; the rest pay on day 60. The **average collection period (ACP)** measures the average amount of time required to collect an account receivable. The ACP for Acme is 28 days:

$$0.8 \times 20 \text{ days} + 0.2 \times 60 \text{ days} = 28 \text{ days}$$

(The average collection period is frequently referred to as *days' sales outstanding* or *days in receivables*.)

Of course, this is an idealized example where customers pay on either one of two dates. In reality, payments arrive in a random fashion, so that the average collection period must be calculated differently.

To determine the ACP in the real world, firms first calculate average daily sales. The **average daily sales (ADS)** equal annual sales divided by 365. The ADS of Acme are:

$$\text{Average daily sales} = \frac{\$300 \times 100,000}{365 \text{ days}} = \$82,192$$

If receivables today are $2,301,376, the average collection period is:

$$\begin{aligned}\text{Average collection period} &= \frac{\text{Accounts receivable}}{\text{Average daily sales}} \\ &= \frac{\$2,301,376}{\$82,192} \\ &= 28 \text{ days}\end{aligned}$$

In practice, firms observe sales and receivables on a daily basis. Consequently, an average collection period can be computed and compared to the stated credit terms. For example, suppose Acme had computed its ACP at 40 days for several weeks, versus its credit terms of 2/20, net 60. With a 40-day ACP, some customers are paying later than usual. It may be that some accounts are overdue.

However, firms with seasonal sales will often find the *calculated* ACP changing during the year, making the ACP a somewhat flawed tool. This occurs because receivables are low before the selling season and high after the season. Thus, firms may keep track of seasonal movement in the ACP over past years. In this way, they can compare the ACP for today's date with the average ACP for that date in previous years. To supplement the information in the ACP, the credit manager may make up an accounts receivable aging schedule.

Aging Schedule

The **aging schedule** tabulates receivables by age of account. In the following schedule, 75 percent of the accounts are on time, but a significant number are more than 60 days past due. This signifies that some customers are in arrears.

Aging Schedule	
Age of Account	**Percentage of Total Value of Accounts Receivable**
0–20 days	50%
21–60 days	25
61–80 days	20
Over 80 days	5
	100%

The aging schedule changes during the year. Comparatively, the ACP is a somewhat flawed tool because it only gives the yearly average. Some firms have refined it so that they can examine how it changes with peaks and valleys in their sales. Similarly, the aging schedule is often augmented by the payments pattern. The *payments pattern* describes the lagged collection pattern of receivables. Like a mortality table that describes the probability that a

23-year-old will live to be 24, the payments pattern describes the probability that a 67-day-old account will still be unpaid when it is 68 days old.

Collection Effort

The firm usually employs the following procedures for customers that are overdue:

1. Sends a delinquency letter informing the customer of the past-due status of the account.
2. Makes a telephone call to the customer.
3. Employs a collection agency.
4. Takes legal action against the customer.

At times, a firm may refuse to grant additional credit to customers until arrearages are paid. This may antagonize a normally good customer and points to a potential conflict of interest between the collections department and the sales department.

Factoring

Factoring refers to the sale of a firm's accounts receivable to a financial institution known as a *factor*. The firm and the factor agree on the basic credit terms for each customer. The customer sends payment directly to the factor, and the factor bears the risk of nonpaying customers. The factor buys the receivables at a discount, which usually ranges from 0.35 to 4 percent of the value of the invoice amount. The average discount throughout the economy is probably about 1 percent.

One point should be stressed. We have presented the elements of credit policy as though they were somewhat independent of each other. In fact, they are closely interrelated. For example, the optimal credit policy is not independent of collection and monitoring policies. A tighter collection policy can reduce the probability of default and this in turn can raise the NPV of a more liberal credit policy.

Concept Question

1. What tools can a manager use to analyze a collection policy?

28.6 How to Finance Trade Credit

In addition to unsecured debt instruments described earlier in this chapter, there are three general ways of financing accounting receivables: secured debt, a captive finance company, and securitization.

Use of secured debt is usually referred to as asset-based receivables financing. This is the predominant form of receivables financing. Many lenders will not lend without security to firms with substantive uncertainty or little equity. With secured debt, if the borrower gets into financial difficulty, the lender can repossess the asset and sell it for its fair market value.

Many large firms with good credit ratings use captive finance companies. The captive finance companies are subsidiaries of the parent firm. This is similar to the use of secured debt because the creditors of the captive finance company have a claim on its assets and, as a consequence, the accounts receivable of the parent firm. A captive finance company is attractive if economies of scale are important and if an independent subsidiary with limited liability is warranted.

Securitization occurs when the selling firm sells its accounts receivable to a financial institution. The financial institution pools the receivables with other receivables and issues securities to finance items.

28.7 SUMMARY AND CONCLUSIONS

1. The components of a firm's credit policy are the terms of sale, the credit analysis, and the collection policy.

2. The terms of sale describe the amount and period of time for which credit is granted and the type of credit instrument.

3. The decision to grant credit is a straightforward NPV decision, and can be improved by additional information about the payment characteristics of the customers. Additional information about the customers' probability of defaulting is valuable, but this value must be traded off against the expense of acquiring the information.

4. The optimal amount of credit the firm offers is a function of the competitive conditions in which it finds itself. These conditions will determine the carrying costs associated with granting credit and the opportunity costs of the lost sales from refusing to offer credit. The optimal credit policy minimizes the sum of these two costs.

5. We have seen that knowledge of the probability that customers will default is valuable. To enhance its ability to assess customers' default probability, a firm can score credit. This relates the default probability to observable characteristics of customers.

6. The collection policy is the method of dealing with past-due accounts. The first step is to analyze the average collection period and to prepare an aging schedule that relates the age of accounts to the proportion of the accounts receivable they represent. The next step is to decide on the collection method and to evaluate the possibility of factoring, that is, selling the overdue accounts.

KEY TERMS

aging schedule, 790	credit instrument, 782
average collection period (ACP), 789	credit periods, 780
average daily sales (ADS), 790	credit scoring, 789
cash discounts, 781	factoring, 791
collection policy, 779	invoice, 779
credit analysis, 779	terms of the sale, 779

SUGGESTED READINGS

Our treatment of the credit decision owes much to:

Bierman, H., Jr., and W. H. Hausman. "The Credit Granting Decision." *Management Science* 16 (April 1970), and Mian, Shezad I., and Clifford W. Smith. "Extending Trade Credit and Financial Receivables." *Journal of Applied Corporate Finance* (Spring 1994).

Three recent articles that establish a theoretical framework and some empirical work on trade credit:

Mian, S. I., and C. Smith. "Extending Trade Credit and Financing Receivables." *Journal of Applied Corporate Finance* (Spring 1994).

Long, M. S.; I. B. Malitz; and S. A. Ravid. "Trade Credit, Quality Guarantees, and Product Marketability." *Financial Management* (Winter 1993).

Lee, Y. W., and J. D. Stowe. "Product Risk, Asymmetric Introduction and Trade Credit." *Journal of Financial and Quantitative Analysis* (June 1993).

An interesting normative article on how to establish trade credit limits is:

Scherr, F. C. "Optimal Trade Credit Limits." *Financial Management* (Spring 1996).

QUESTIONS & PROBLEMS

TERMS OF THE SALE

28.1 The North County Publishing Company has provided the following data:

Annual credit sales = $10 million
Average collection period = 60 days
Terms: Net 30
Interest rate = 10%

North County Publishing proposes to offer a discount policy of 2/10, net 30. It anticipates that 50 percent of its customers will take advantage of this new policy. As a result, the collection period will be reduced to 30 days. Should the North County Publishing Company offer the new credit terms?

28.2   The Webster's Company sells on credit terms of net 45. Its accounts are on average 45 days past due. If annual credit sales are $5 million, what is the company's balance in accounts receivable?

28.3   The Tropeland Company has obtained the following information:

Annual credit sales = $30 million
Collection period = 60 days
Terms: Net 30
Interest rate = 12%

The company is considering offering terms of 4/10, net 30. It anticipates that 50 percent of its customers will take advantage of the discount. The collection period is expected to decrease by one month. Should the new credit policy be adopted?

**THE DECISION TO
GRANT CREDIT:
RISK AND
INFORMATION**

28.4   Berkshire Sports, Inc., operates a mail-order running-shoe business. Management is considering dropping its policy of no credit. The credit policy under consideration by Berkshire follows:

	No Credit	Credit
Price per unit	$35	$40
Cost per unit	$25	$32
Quantity sold	2,000	3,000
Probability of payment	100%	85%
Credit period	0	1
Discount rate	0	3%

a. Should Berkshire offer credit to its customers?
b. What must the probability of payment be before Berkshire would adopt the policy?

28.5   The Theodore Bruin Corporation, a manufacturer of high-quality stuffed animals, does not extend credit to its customers. A study has shown that, by offering credit, the company can increase sales from the current 750 units to 1,000 units. The cost per unit, however, will increase from $43 to $45, reflecting the expense of managing accounts receivable. The current price of a toy is $48. The probability of a customer making a payment on a credit sale is 92 percent, and the appropriate discount rate is 2.7 percent.

By how much should Theodore Bruin increase the price to make offering credit an attractive strategy?

28.6   Fast Typing Co. is in the business of manufacturing and selling Fast-Line Typewriters. It does not offer any credit sales currently. The per unit price and cost of each Fast-Line typewriter are $900 and $600, respectively. Fast Typing Co. is considering the possibility of credit sales. The market price of the typewriter will stay the same with credit sales, but it is expected that the annual sales will increase from 5,000 units to 9,000 units and the per unit cost will go up by $50 due to implementation cost of credit sales. The credit period will be two months and the appropriate discount rate for the credit period is 1.5 percent. What is the minimum probability of repayment that can make Fast Typing Co. indifferent between whether or not to implement the new credit policy?

28.7   The Silver Spokes Bicycle Shop has decided to offer credit to its customers during the spring selling season. Sales are expected to be 300 cycles. The average cost to the shop of a cycle is $240. The owner knows that only 95 percent of the customers will be able to make their payments. To identify the remaining 5 percent, she is considering subscribing to a credit agency. The initial charge for this service is $500, with an additional charge of $4 per individual report. Should she subscribe to the agency?

OPTIMAL CREDIT POLICY

CREDIT ANALYSIS

COLLECTION POLICY

28.8 In principle, how should we decide the optimal credit policy?

28.9 What is the information commonly used to assess creditworthiness of a client?

28.10 Major Electronics sells 85,000 personal stereos each year at a price per unit of $55. All sales are on credit; the terms are 3/15, net 40. The discount is taken by 40 percent of the customers. What is the investment in accounts receivable?

In reaction to a competitor, Major Electronics is considering changing its credit terms to 5/15, net 40, to preserve its sales level. Describe qualitatively how this policy change will affect the company's investment in accounts receivable.

28.11 The Allen Company has monthly credit sales of $600,000. The average collection period is 90 days. The cost of production is 70 percent of the selling price. What is the Allen Company's average investment in accounts receivable?

28.12 The factoring department of Inter American Bank (IAB) is processing 100,000 invoices per year with average invoice value of $1,500. IAB buys the accounts receivable at 4 percent off the invoice value. The average collection period is 30 days. Currently 2 percent of the accounts receivable turns out to be bad debt. The annual interest rate is 10 percent. The annual operating expense of this department is $400,000. What is the gross profit before interest and tax for the factoring department of IAB?

Part VIII

Special Topics

In Part VIII we discuss three special topics: mergers and acquisitions, financial distress, and international corporate finance.

Chapter 29 describes the corporate finance of mergers and acquisitions. The acquisition of one firm by another is a capital-budgeting decision, and the basic principles of NPV apply; that is, a firm should be acquired if it generates positive NPV to the shareholders of the acquiring firm. The purpose of Chapter 29 is to discuss how to value an acquisition candidate. However, the NPV of an acquisition candidate is more difficult to determine than that of a typical investment project because of complex accounting, tax, and legal effects.

Chapter 30 discusses what happens when a firm experiences financial distress. Financial distress is a special circumstance when a firm's cash flow falls below its contractually required payments. Financial restructuring involving private workouts or formal bankruptcy usually follows financial distress.

Our last chapter concerns international corporate finance. Many firms have significant foreign operations and must consider special financial factors that do not directly affect purely domestic firms. These factors include foreign exchange rates, interest rates that vary from country to country, and complex accounting, legal, and tax rules.

Mergers and Acquisitions

EXECUTIVE SUMMARY

There is no more dramatic or controversial activity in corporate finance than the acquisition of one firm by another or the merger of two firms. This chapter addresses two basic questions: Why does a firm choose to merge with or acquire another firm and how does it happen?

The acquisition of one firm by another is, of course, an investment made under uncertainty. The basic principle of valuation applies: A firm should be acquired if it generates a positive net present value to the shareholders of the acquiring firm. However, because the NPV of an acquisition candidate is very difficult to determine, mergers and acquisitions are interesting topics in their own right. Here are some of the special features of this area of finance:

1. The benefits from acquisitions are called *synergies*. It is hard to estimate synergies using discounted cash flow techniques.

2. There are complex accounting, tax, and legal effects when one firm is acquired by another.

3. Acquisitions are an important control device of shareholders. It appears that some acquisitions are a consequence of an underlying conflict between the interests of existing managers and of shareholders. Acquisition by another firm is one way that shareholders can remove managers with whom they are unhappy.

4. Acquisition analysis frequently focuses on the total value of the firms involved. But usually an acquisition will affect the relative values of stocks and bonds, as well as their total value.

5. Mergers and acquisitions sometimes involve unfriendly transactions. Thus, when one firm attempts to acquire another, it does not always involve quiet, gentlemanly negotiations. The sought-after firm may use defensive tactics, including poison pills, greenmail, and white knights.

This chapter starts by introducing the basic legal, accounting, and tax aspects of acquisitions. When one firm acquires another, it must choose the legal framework, the accounting method, and tax status. These choices will be explained throughout the chapter.

The chapter discusses how to determine the NPV of an acquisition candidate. The NPV of an acquisition candidate is the difference between the synergy from the merger and the premium to be paid. We consider the following types of synergy: (1) revenue enhancement, (2) cost reduction, (3) lower taxes, and (4) lower cost of capital. The premium paid for an acquisition is the price paid minus the market value of the acquisition prior to the merger. The premium depends on whether cash or securities are used to finance the offer price.

29.1 The Basic Forms of Acquisitions

There are three basic legal procedures that one firm can use to acquire another firm: (1) merger or consolidation, (2) acquisition of stock, and (3) acquisition of assets.

Merger or Consolidation

A **merger** refers to the absorption of one firm by another. The acquiring firm retains its name and its identity, and it acquires all of the assets and liabilities of the acquired firm. After a merger, the acquired firm ceases to exist as a separate business entity.

A **consolidation** is the same as a merger except that an entirely new firm is created. In a consolidation, both the acquiring firm and the acquired firm terminate their previous legal existence and become part of the new firm. In a consolidation, the distinction between the acquiring and the acquired firm is not important. However, the rules for mergers and consolidations are basically the same. Acquisitions by merger and consolidation result in combinations of the assets and liabilities of acquired and acquiring firms.

EXAMPLE

Suppose firm A acquires firm B in a merger. Further, suppose firm B's shareholders are given one share of firm A's stock in exchange for two shares of firm B's stock. From a legal standpoint, firm A's shareholders are not directly affected by the merger. However, firm B's shares cease to exist. In a consolidation, the shareholders of firm A and firm B would exchange their shares for the share of a new firm (e.g., firm C). Because the differences between mergers and consolidations are not all that important for our purposes, we shall refer to both types of reorganizations as mergers.

There are some advantages and some disadvantages to using a merger to acquire a firm:

1. A merger is legally straightforward and does not cost as much as other forms of acquisition. It avoids the necessity of transferring title of each individual asset of the acquired firm to the acquiring firm.
2. A merger must be approved by a vote of the stockholders of each firm.[1] Typically, votes of the owners of two-thirds of the shares are required for approval. In addition, shareholders of the acquired firm have *appraisal rights*. This means that they can demand that their shares be purchased at a fair value by the acquiring firm. Often the acquiring firm and the dissenting shareholders of the acquired firm cannot agree on a fair value, which results in expensive legal proceedings.

Acquisition of Stock

A second way to acquire another firm is to purchase the firm's voting stock in exchange for cash, shares of stock, or other securities. This may start as a private offer from the management of one firm to another. At some point the offer is taken directly to the selling firm's stockholders. This can be accomplished by use of a tender offer. A **tender offer** is a public offer to buy shares of a target firm. It is made by one firm directly to the shareholders of another firm. The offer is communicated to the target firm's shareholders by public announcements such as newspaper advertisements. Sometimes a general mailing is used in a tender offer. However, a general mailing is very difficult because it requires the names and addresses of the stockholders of record, which are not usually available.

---

[1]Mergers between corporations require compliance with state laws. In virtually all states the shareholders of each corporation must give their assent.

The following are factors involved in choosing between an acquisition of stock and a merger:

1. In an acquisition of stock, no shareholder meetings must be held and no vote is required. If the shareholders of the target firm do not like the offer, they are not required to accept it and they will not tender their shares.

2. In an acquisition of stock, the bidding firm can deal directly with the shareholders of a target firm by using a tender offer. The target firm's management and board of directors can be bypassed.

3. Acquisition of stock is often unfriendly. It is used in an effort to circumvent the target firm's management, which is usually actively resisting acquisition. Resistance by the target firm's management often makes the cost of acquisition by stock higher than the cost by merger.

4. Frequently a minority of shareholders will hold out in a tender offer, and thus the target firm cannot be completely absorbed.

5. Complete absorption of one firm by another requires a merger. Many acquisitions of stock end with a formal merger later.

Acquisition of Assets

One firm can acquire another firm by buying all of its assets. A formal vote of the shareholders of the selling firm is required. This approach to acquisition will avoid the potential problem of having minority shareholders, which can occur in an acquisition of stock. Acquisition of assets involves transferring title to assets. The legal process of transferring assets can be costly.

A Classification Scheme

Financial analysts have typically classified acquisitions into three types:

1. *Horizontal Acquisition.* This is an acquisition of a firm in the same industry as the acquiring firm. The firms compete with each other in their product market.

2. *Vertical Acquisition.* A vertical acquisition involves firms at different steps of the production process. The acquisition by an airline company of a travel agency would be a vertical acquisition.

3. *Conglomerate Acquisition.* The acquiring firm and the acquired firm are not related to each other. The acquisition of a food-products firm by a computer firm would be considered a conglomerate acquisition.

A Note on Takeovers

Takeover is a general and imprecise term referring to the transfer of control of a firm from one group of shareholders to another.[2] A firm that has decided to take over another firm is usually referred to as the **bidder.** The bidder offers to pay cash or securities to obtain the stock or assets of another company. If the offer is accepted, the target firm will give up control over its stock or assets to the bidder in exchange for *consideration* (i.e., its stock, its debt, or cash).

For example, when a bidding firm acquires a target firm, the right to control the operating activities of the target firm is transferred to a newly elected board of directors of the acquiring firm. This is a takeover by acquisition.

---

[2]*Control* can usually be defined as having a majority vote on the board of directors.

FIGURE 29.1

Varieties of Takeovers

Takeovers can occur by acquisition, proxy contests, and going-private transactions. Thus, takeovers encompass a broader set of activities than acquisitions. Figure 29.1 depicts this.

If a takeover is achieved by acquisition, it will be by merger, tender offer for shares of stock, or purchase of assets. In mergers and tender offers, the acquiring firm buys the voting common stock of the acquired firm.

Takeovers can occur with *proxy contests.* Proxy contests occur when a group of shareholders attempts to gain controlling seats on the board of directors by voting in new directors. A *proxy* authorizes the proxy holder to vote on all matters in a shareholders' meeting. In a proxy contest, proxies from the rest of the shareholders are solicited by an insurgent group of shareholders.

In *going-private transactions,* all the equity shares of a public firm are purchased by a small group of investors. The group usually includes members of incumbent management and some outside investors. The shares of the firm are delisted from stock exchanges and can no longer be purchased in the open market.

Concept Questions

1. What is a merger? How does a merger differ from other forms of acquisition?
2. What is a takeover?

29.2 The Tax Forms of Acquisitions

If one firm buys another firm, the transaction may be taxable or tax-free. In a *taxable acquisition,* the shareholders of the acquired firm are considered to have sold their shares, and they have realized capital gains or losses that will be taxed. In a taxable transaction, the *appraised value* of the assets of the selling firm may be revalued, as we explain below.

In a *tax-free acquisition,* the selling shareholders are considered to have exchanged their old shares for new ones of equal value, and they have experienced no capital gains or losses. In a tax-free acquisition, the assets are not revalued.

EXAMPLE

Suppose that 15 years ago Bill Evans started Samurai Machinery (SM) and purchased plant and equipment costing $80,000. These have been the only assets of SM, and the company has no debts. Bill is the sole proprietor of SM and owns all the shares. For tax purposes the assets of SM have been depreciated using the straight-line method over 10 years, and have no salvage value. The annual depreciation expense has been $8,000 ($80,000/10). The machinery has no accounting value today (i.e., it has been written off the books). However, because of inflation, the fair market value of the machinery is $200,000. As a consequence, the S. A. Steel Company has bid $200,000 for all of the outstanding stock of Samurai.

TABLE 29.1	The Incremental Tax Consequences of S. A. Steel Company's Acquisition of Samurai Machinery	
	Type of Acquisition	
Buyer or Seller	**Taxable Acquisition**	**Tax-Free Acquisition**
Bill Evans S. A. Steel	Immediate tax on $120,000 ($200,000 − $80,000) S. A. Steel may elect to write up assets. Here: 1. Assets of Samurai written up to $200,000 (with useful life of 10 years). Annual depreciation expense is $20,000. 2. Immediate tax on $200,000 write-up of assets. Alternatively, S. A. Steel may elect not to write up assets. Here, there is neither additional depreciation nor immediate tax. Typically, acquirer elects *not* to write up assets.	Capital gain tax not paid until Evans sells shares of S. A. Steel No additional depreciation

S. A. Steel acquires Samurai Machinery for $200,000, which is the market value of Samurai's equipment. The book value of the equipment is $0. Bill Evans started Samurai Steel 15 years ago with a contribution of $80,000.

The tax consequences of a tax-free acquisition are better than the tax consequences of a taxable acquisition, because the seller pays no immediate tax on a tax-free acquisition.

Tax-Free Transaction   If Bill Evans receives *shares* of S. A. Steel worth $200,000, the IRS will treat the sale as a tax-free transaction. Thus, Bill will not have to pay taxes on any gain received from the stock. In addition, S. A. Steel will be allowed the same depreciation deduction that Samurai Machinery was allowed. Because the asset has already been fully depreciated, S. A. Steel will receive no depreciation deduction.

Taxable Transaction   If S. A. Steel pays $200,000 in *cash* for Samurai Machinery, it will be a taxable transaction. There will be a number of tax consequences:

1. In the year of the merger, Bill Evans must pay taxes on the difference between the merger price of $200,000 and his initial contribution to the firm of $80,000. Thus, his taxable income is $120,000 ($200,000 − $80,000).

2. S. A. Steel may *elect* to *write up* the value of the machinery. In this case, S. A. Steel will be able to depreciate the machinery from an initial tax basis of $200,000. If S. A. Steel depreciates straight-line over 10 years, depreciation will be $20,000 ($200,000/10) per year.

   If S. A. Steel elects to write up the machinery, S. A. Steel must treat the $200,000 write-up as taxable income immediately.[3]

3. Should S. A. Steel *not* elect the write-up, there is no increase in depreciation. Thus, depreciation remains zero in this example. In addition, because there is no write-up, S. A. Steel does not need to recognize any additional taxable income.

   Because the tax benefits from depreciation occur slowly over time and the taxable income is recognized immediately, the acquirer generally elects *not* to write up the value of the machinery in a taxable transaction.

Because the write-up is not allowed for tax-free transactions and generally not chosen for taxable ones, the only real tax difference between the two types of transactions concerns the taxation of the selling shareholders. Because these individuals can defer taxes under a tax-free situation but must pay taxes immediately under a taxable situation, the tax-free transaction has better tax consequences. The tax implications for both types of transactions are displayed in Table 29.1.

---

[3]Technically, Samurai Machinery pays this tax. However, because Samurai is now a subsidiary of S. A. Steel, S. A. Steel is the effective taxpayer.

29.3 Accounting for Acquisitions

Earlier in this text we mentioned that firms keep two distinct sets of books: the stockholders' books and the tax books. The previous section concerned the effect of acquisitions on the tax books. We now consider the stockholders' books. When one firm acquires another firm, the acquisition is treated using a purchase accounting on the stockholders' books.

The Purchase Method

The **purchase** method of reporting acquisitions requires that the assets of the acquired firm be reported at their fair market value on the books of the acquiring firm. This allows the acquiring firm to establish a new cost basis for the acquired assets.

In a purchase, an accounting term called *goodwill* is created. **Goodwill** is the excess of the purchase price over the sum of the fair market values of the individual assets acquired.

EXAMPLE

Suppose firm A acquires firm B, creating a new firm, AB. Firm A's and firm B's financial positions at the date of the acquisition are shown in Table 29.2. The book value of firm B on the date of the acquisition is $10 million. This is the sum of $8 million in buildings and $2 million in cash. However, an appraiser states that the sum of the fair market values of the individual buildings is $14 million. With $2 million in cash, the sum of the market values of the individual assets in firm B is $16 million. This represents the value to be received if the firm is liquidated by selling off the individual assets separately. However, the whole is often worth more than the sum of the parts in business. Firm A pays $19 million in cash for firm B. This difference of $3 million ($19 million − $16 million) is goodwill. It represents the increase in value by keeping the firm intact as an ongoing business. Firm A issued $19 million in new debt to finance the acquisition. The last balance sheet in Table 29.2 shows what happens under purchase accounting.

1. The total assets of firm AB increase to $39 million. The buildings of firm B appear in the new balance sheet at their current market value. That is, the market value of the assets of the acquired firm becomes part of the book value of the new firm. However, the assets of the acquiring firm (firm A) remain at their old book value. They are not revalued upwards when the new firm is created.

2. The excess of the purchase price over the sum of the fair market values of the individual assets acquired is $3 million. This amount is reported as goodwill. Financial analysts generally ignore goodwill because it has no cash flow consequences. The current accounting practice says that each year firms must assess the value of goodwill on their balance sheets. If the value goes down (this is called *impairment* in accounting speak), the firm must deduct the decrease from earnings otherwise no amortization is required.

TABLE 29.2   Accounting for Acquisitions: Purchase (in $ millions)

Firm A				Firm B				Firm AB			
Cash	$ 4	Equity	$20	Cash	$ 2	Equity	$10	Cash	$ 6	Debt	$19
Land	16			Land	0			Land	16	Equity	20
Buildings	0			Buildings	8			Buildings	14		
Total	$20		$20	Total	$10		$10	Goodwill	3		
								Total	$39		$39

When the purchase method is used, the assets of the acquired firm (firm B) appear in the combined firm's books at their fair market value.

29.4 Determining the Synergy from an Acquisition

Suppose firm A is contemplating acquiring firm B. The value of firm A is V_A and the value of firm B is V_B. (It is reasonable to assume that, for public companies, V_A and V_B can be determined by observing the market price of the outstanding securities.) The difference between the value of the combined firm (V_{AB}) and the sum of the values of the firms as separate entities is the *synergy* from the acquisition:

$$\text{Synergy} = V_{AB} - (V_A + V_B)$$

The acquiring firm must generally pay a premium for the acquired firm. For example, if stock of the target is selling for $50, the acquirer might need to pay $60 a share, implying a premium of $10 or 20 percent. Firm A will want to determine the synergy before entering into negotiations with firm B on the premium.

The synergy of an acquisition can be determined from the usual discounted cash flow model:

$$\text{Synergy} = \sum_{t=1}^{T} \frac{\Delta\text{CF}_t}{(1 + r)^t}$$

where ΔCF_t is the difference between the cash flows at date t of the combined firm and the sum of the cash flows of the two separate firms. In other words, ΔCF_t is the incremental cash flow at date t from the merger. The term, r, is the risk-adjusted discount rate appropriate for the incremental cash flows. This is generally considered to be the required rate of return on the equity of the target.

From the chapters on capital budgeting we know that the incremental cash flows can be separated into four parts:

$$\Delta\text{CF}_t = \Delta\text{Rev}_t - \Delta\text{Costs}_t - \Delta\text{Taxes}_t - \Delta\text{Capital Requirements}_t$$

where ΔRev_t is the incremental revenue of the acquisition, ΔCosts_t is the incremental costs of the acquisition, ΔTaxes_t is the incremental acquisition taxes, and $\Delta\text{Capital Requirements}_t$ is the incremental new investment required in working capital and fixed assets.

29.5 Source of Synergy from Acquisitions

It follows from our classification of incremental cash flows that the possible sources of synergy fall into four basic categories: revenue enhancement, cost reduction, lower taxes, and lower cost of capital.[4]

Revenue Enhancement

One important reason for acquisitions is that a combined firm may generate greater revenues than two separate firms. Increased revenues may come from marketing gains, strategic benefits, and market power.

---

[4]Many reasons are given by firms to justify mergers and acquisitions. When two firms merge, the boards of directors of the two firms adopt an *agreement of merger.* The agreement of merger of U.S. Steel and Marathon Oil is typical. It lists the economic benefits that shareholders can expect from the merger (key words have been italicized):

> U.S. Steel believes that the acquisition of Marathon provides U.S. Steel with an attractive opportunity to *diversify* into the energy business. Reasons for the merger include, but are not limited to, the facts that consummation of the merger will allow U.S. Steel to consolidate Marathon into U.S. Steel's federal *income tax return,* will also contribute to *greater efficiency,* and will enhance the ability to manage capital by permitting the movement of cash between U.S. Steel and Marathon. Additionally, the merger will eliminate the possibility of conflicts of interests between the interests of minority and majority shareholders and will enhance management flexibility. The acquisition will provide Marathon shareholders with a substantial premium over historical market prices for their shares. However, shareholders will no longer continue to share in the future prospects of the company.

Marketing Gains It is frequently claimed that mergers and acquisitions can produce greater operating revenues from improved marketing. Improvements can be made in the following:

1. Previously ineffective media programming and advertising efforts.
2. A weak existing distribution network.
3. An unbalanced product mix.

Strategic Benefits Some acquisitions promise a *strategic* advantage. This is an opportunity to take advantage of the competitive environment if certain situations materialize. In this regard, a strategic benefit is more like an option than it is a standard investment opportunity. For example, imagine that a sewing machine company acquired a computer company. The firm will be well positioned if technological advances allow computer-driven sewing machines in the future. Michael Porter has used the word *beachhead* in his description of the process of entering a new industry to exploit perceived opportunities.[5] The beachhead is used to spawn new opportunities based on *intangible* relationships. He uses the example of Procter & Gamble's initial acquisition of the Charmin Paper Company as a beachhead that allowed Procter & Gamble to develop a highly interrelated cluster of paper products—disposable diapers, paper towels, feminine hygiene products, and bathroom tissue.

Market or Monopoly Power One firm may acquire another to reduce competition. If so, prices can be increased and monopoly profits obtained. Mergers that reduce competition do not benefit society and may be challenged by the U.S. Department of Justice or the Federal Trade Commission.

Cost Reduction

One of the most basic reasons for merger is that a combined firm may operate more efficiently than two separate firms. Thus, when Bank of America agreed to acquire Security Pacific, lower costs were cited as the primary reason. A firm can obtain greater operating efficiency in several different ways through a merger or an acquisition.

Economies of Scale If the average cost of production falls while the level of production increases, there is said to be an economy of scale. Figure 29.2 illustrates that economies of scale result while the firm grows to its optimal size. After this point, diseconomies of scale occur. In other words, average cost increases with further firm growth.

Though the precise nature of economy of scale is not known, it is one obvious benefit of horizontal mergers. The phrase *spreading overhead* is frequently used in connection with economies of scale. This refers to the sharing of central facilities such as corporate headquarters, top management, and a large mainframe computer.

Economies of Vertical Integration Operating economies can be gained from vertical combinations as well as from horizontal combinations. The main purpose of vertical acquisitions is to make coordination of closely related operating activities easier. This is probably the reason why most forest product firms that cut timber also own sawmills and hauling equipment. Economies from vertical integration probably explain why most airline companies own airplanes; it also may explain why some airline companies have purchased hotels and car-rental companies.

Technology transfers are another reason for vertical integration. Consider the merger of General Motors and Hughes Aircraft in 1985. An automobile manufacturer might well

---

[5]M. Porter, *Competitive Advantage* (New York: Free Press, 1985).

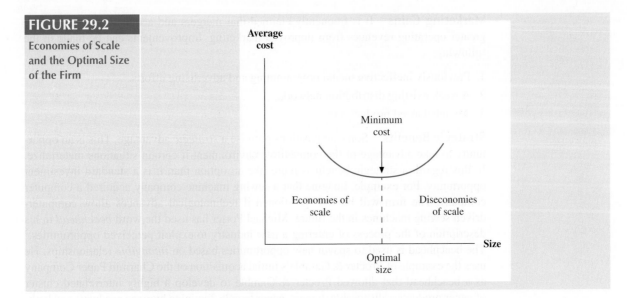

FIGURE 29.2

Economies of Scale and the Optimal Size of the Firm

acquire an advanced electronics firm if the special technology of the electronics firm can improve the quality of the automobile.

Complementary Resources   Some firms acquire others to make better use of existing resources or to provide the missing ingredient for success. Think of a ski-equipment store that could merge with a tennis-equipment store to produce more even sales over both the winter and summer seasons—and better use of store capacity.

Elimination of Inefficient Management   There are firms whose value could be increased with a change in management. For example, Jensen and Ruback argue that acquisitions can occur because of changing technology or market conditions that require a restructuring of the corporation.[6] Incumbent managers in some cases do not understand changing conditions. They have trouble abandoning strategies and styles they have spent years formulating.

The oil industry is an example of managerial inefficiency cited by Jensen. In the late 1970s, changes in the oil industry included reduced expectations of the future price of oil, increased exploration and development costs, and increased real interest rates. As a result of these changes, substantial reductions in exploration and development were called for. However, many oil company managers were unable to downsize their firms. For example, a study by McConnell and Muscarella reports that the stock prices of oil companies tended to decrease with announcements of increases in exploration and development expenditures in the period of 1975–1981.[7]

Acquiring companies sought out oil firms in order to reduce the investment levels of these oil companies.[8] For example, T. Boone Pickens of Mesa Petroleum perceived the changes taking place in the oil industry and attempted to buy several oil companies: Unocal, Phillips, and Getty. The results of these attempted acquisitions have been reduced

---

[6]M. C. Jensen and R. S. Ruback, "The Market for Corporate Control: The Scientific Evidence," *Journal of Financial Economics* 11 (April 1983); and M. C. Jensen, "Agency Costs of Free Cash Flow, Corporate Finance and Takeovers," *American Economic Review* (May 1986).

[7]J. J. McConnell and C. J. Muscarella, "Corporate Capital Expenditure Decisions and the Market Value of the firm," *Journal of Financial Economics* 14 (1985).

[8]More than 26 percent of the total valuation of all takeover transactions involved a selling firm in the oil and gas industry in 1981–1984 [W. T. Grimm, *Mergerstat Review* (1985), p. 41].

TABLE 29.3	**Before Merger**				**After Merger**	
	Firm A		**Firm B**		**Firm AB**	
Tax Effect of Merger of Firms A and B	**If State 1**	**If State 2**	**If State 1**	**If State 2**	**If State 1**	**If State 2**
Taxable income	$200	−$100	−$100	$200	$100	$100
Taxes	68	0	0	68	34	34
Net income	$132	−$100	−$100	$132	$ 66	$ 66

Neither firm will be able to deduct its losses prior to the merger. The merger allows the losses from A to offset the taxable profits from B—and vice versa.

expenditures on exploration and development and huge gains to the shareholders of the affected firms.

Mergers and acquisitions can be viewed as part of the labor market for top management. Jensen and Ruback have used the phrase *market for corporate control,* in which alternative management teams compete for the rights to manage corporate activities.

Tax Gains

Tax gains may be a powerful incentive for some acquisitions. The possible tax gains that can come from an acquisition are the following:

1. The use of tax losses from net operating losses.
2. The use of unused debt capacity.
3. The use of surplus funds.

Net Operating Losses   Sometimes firms have tax losses they cannot take advantage of. These tax losses are referred to as NOL (an acronym for net operating losses). Consider the situation of firm A and firm B.

Table 29.3 shows the pretax income, taxes, and after-tax income for firms A and B. Firm A will earn $200 under state 1 but will lose money under state 2. The firm will pay taxes under state 1 but is not entitled to a tax rebate under state 2. Conversely, firm B will pay taxes of $68 under state 2. Thus, if firms A and B are separate, the IRS will obtain $68 in taxes, regardless of which state occurs. However, if A and B merge, the combined firm will pay $34 in taxes under both state 1 and state 2.

It is obvious that if firms A and B merge, they will pay lower taxes than if they remain separate. Without merger, they do not take advantage of potential tax losses.

The message of the preceding example is that firms need taxable profits to take advantage of potential tax losses. Mergers can sometimes accomplish this. However, there are two qualifications to the previous example:

1. The federal tax laws permit firms that experience alternating periods of profits and losses to equalize their taxes by carryback and carryforward provisions. A firm that has been profitable but has a loss in the current year can get refunds of income taxes paid in *three previous years* and can carry the loss *forward for 15 years.* Thus, a merger to exploit unused tax shields must offer tax savings over and above what can be accomplished by firms via carryovers.[9]
2. The IRS may disallow an acquisition if the principal purpose of the acquisition is to avoid federal tax. This is one of the Catch 22s of the Internal Revenue Code.

---

[9]Under the 1986 Tax Reform Act a corporation's ability to carry forward net operating losses (and other tax credits) is limited when more than 50 percent of the stock changes hands over a three-year period.

Unused Debt Capacity   We argued earlier in the text that the optimal debt-equity ratio is the one where the marginal tax benefit from additional debt is equal to the marginal increase in the financial distress costs from additional debt. Because some diversification occurs when firms merge, the cost of financial distress is likely to be less for the combined firm than is the sum of these present values for the two separate firms. Thus, the acquiring firm might be able to increase its debt-equity ratio after a merger, creating additional tax benefits—and additional value.[10]

Surplus Funds   Another quirk in the tax laws involves surplus funds. Consider a firm that has *free cash flow*. That is, it has cash flow available after payment of all taxes and after all positive net present value projects have been provided for. In this situation, aside from purchasing fixed-income securities, the firm has several ways to spend the free cash flow, including

1. Pay dividends.
2. Buy back its own shares.
3. Acquire shares in another firm.

We have already seen in our previous discussion of dividend policy that an extra dividend will increase the income tax paid by some investors. Investors pay lower taxes in a share repurchase. However, this is not a legal option if the sole purpose is to avoid taxes that would otherwise have been paid by shareholders.

The firm can buy the shares of another firm. This accomplishes two objectives. First, the firm's shareholders avoid taxes from dividends that would have been paid. Second, the firm pays little corporate tax on dividends received from the shares of the firm it has purchased, because 70 percent of the dividend income received from the acquired firm is excluded from the corporate income tax. However, under Section 532 of the tax code the IRS might disallow the tax benefits from a continual strategy of this type.

Instead, the firm might make acquisitions with its excess funds. In a merger no taxes at all are paid on dividends remitted from the acquired firm, and the IRS would not question mergers of this type.

The Cost of Capital

The cost of capital can often be reduced when two firms merge because the costs of issuing securities are subject to economies of scale. As we observed in earlier chapters, the costs of issuing both debt and equity are much lower for larger issues than for smaller issues.

29.6   Calculating the Value of the Firm after an Acquisition

Now that we have listed the possible sources of synergy from a merger, let us see how one would value these sources. Consider two firms. Gamble, Inc., manufactures and markets soaps and cosmetics. The firm has a reputation for its ability to attract, develop, and keep talented people. The firm has successfully introduced several major products in the past two years. It would like to enter the over-the-counter drug market to round out its product line. Shapiro, Inc., is a well-known maker of cold remedies. Al Shapiro, the great-grandson of the founder of Shapiro, Inc., became chairman of the firm last year. Unfortunately, Al

---

[10]Unused debt capacity is cited as a benefit in many mergers. An example was the proposed merger of Hospital Corporation of America and American Hospital Supply Corporation in 1985. Insiders were quoted as saying that the combined companies could borrow as much as an additional $1 billion, 10 times the usual borrowing capacity of Hospital Corporation alone (*The Wall Street Journal,* April 1, 1985). (The merger never took place.)

TABLE 29.4		Net Cash Flow per Year (perpetual)	Discount Rate	Value
Acquisition of Shapiro, Inc., by Gamble, Inc.	Gamble, Inc.	$10.0 million	0.10	$100 million
	Shapiro, Inc.	4.5 million	0.15	30 million*
	Benefits from acquisition:	5.5 million	0.122	45 million
	Strategic fit	3.0 million	0.20	15 million
	Tax shelters	1.0 million	0.05	20 million
	Operating efficiencies	1.5 million	0.15	10 million
	Gamble-Shapiro	20.0 million	0.114	175 million

*The market value of Shapiro's outstanding common stock is $30 million; 1 million shares are outstanding.

knows nothing about cold remedies, and as a consequence, Shapiro, Inc., has had lackluster financial performance. For the most recent year, pretax cash flow fell by 15 percent. The firm's stock price is at an all-time low.

The financial management of Gamble finds Shapiro an attractive acquisition candidate. It believes that the cash flows from the combined firms would be far greater than what each firm would have alone. The cash flows and present values from the acquisition are shown in Table 29.4. The increased cash flows (ΔCF_t) would come from three benefits:

1. *Tax Gains.* If Gamble acquires Shapiro, Gamble will be able to use some tax-loss carry-forwards to reduce its tax liability. The additional cash flows from tax gains should be discounted at the cost of debt capital because they can be determined with very little uncertainty. The financial management of Gamble estimates that the acquisition will reduce taxes by $1 million per year in perpetuity. The relevant discount rate is 5 percent, and the present value of the tax reduction is $20 million.

2. *Operating Efficiencies.* The financial management of Gamble has determined that Gamble can take advantage of some of the unused production capacity of Shapiro. At times Gamble has been operating at full capacity with a large backlog of orders. Shapiro's manufacturing facilities, with a little reconfiguration, can be used to produce Gamble's soaps. Thus, more soaps and cold remedies can be produced without adding to the combined firm's capacity and cost. These operating efficiencies will increase after-tax cash flows by $1.5 million per year. Using Shapiro's discount rate and assuming perpetual gains, the PV of the unused capacity is determined to be $10 million.

3. *Strategic Fit.* The financial management of Gamble has determined that the acquisition of Shapiro will give Gamble a strategic advantage. The management of Gamble believes that the addition of the Shapiro Bac-Rub ointment for sore backs to its existing product mix will give it a better chance to launch successful new skin care cosmetics if these markets develop in the future. Management of Gamble estimates that there is a 50-percent probability that $6 million in after-tax cash flow can be generated with the new skin care products. These opportunities are contingent on factors that cannot be easily quantified. Because of the lack of precision here, the managers decided to use a high discount rate. Gamble chooses a 20-percent rate, and it estimates that the present value of the strategic factors is $15 million (0.50 × $6 million/0.20).

Avoiding Mistakes

The Gamble-Shapiro illustration is very simple and straightforward. It is deceptive because the incremental cash flows have already been determined. In practice an analyst must estimate these cash flows and determine the proper discount rate. Valuing the benefits of a

Michael C. Jensen on Mergers and Acquisitions

Economic analysis and evidence indicate that takeovers, LBOs, and corporate restructurings are playing an important role in helping the economy adjust to major competitive changes in the last two decades. The competition among alternative management teams and organizational structures for control of corporate assets has enabled vast economic resources to move more quickly to their highest-valued use. In the process, substantial benefits for the economy as a whole as well as for shareholders have been created. Overall gains to selling-firm shareholders from mergers, acquisitions, leveraged buyouts, and other corporate restructurings in the 12-year period 1977–1988 total over $500 billion in 1988 dollars. I estimate gains to buying-firm shareholders to be at least $50 billion for the same period. These gains equal 53 percent of the total cash dividends (valued in 1988 dollars) paid to investors by the entire corporate sector in the same period.

Mergers and acquisitions are a response to new technologies or market conditions which require a strategic change in a company's direction or use of resources. Compared to current management, a new owner is often better able to accomplish major change in the existing organizational structure. Alternatively, leveraged buyouts bring about organizational change by creating entrepreneurial incentives for management and by eliminating the centralized bureaucratic obstacles to maneuverability that are inherent in large public corporations.

When managers have a substantial ownership interest in the organization, the conflicts of interest between shareholders and managers over the payout of the company's free cash flow are reduced. Management's incentives are focused on maximizing the value of the enterprise, rather than building empires—often through poorly conceived diversification acquisitions—without regard to shareholder value. Finally, the required repayment of debt replaces management's discretion in paying dividends and the tendency to overretain cash. Substantial increases in efficiency are thereby created.

Michael C. Jensen is Edsel Bryant Ford Professor of Business Administration at Harvard University. An outstanding scholar and researcher, he is famous for his path-breaking analysis of the modern corporation and its relations with its stockholders.

potential acquisition is harder than valuing benefits for standard capital-budgeting projects. Many mistakes can be made. The following are some of the general rules:

1. *Do Not Ignore Market Values.* In many cases it is very difficult to estimate values using discounted cash flows. Because of this, an expert at valuation should know the market prices of comparable opportunities. In an efficient market, prices should reflect value. Because the market value of Shapiro is $30 million, we use this to estimate Shapiro's existing value.

2. *Estimate Only Incremental Cash Flows.* Only incremental cash flows from an acquisition will add value to the acquiring firm. Thus, it is important to estimate the cash flows that are incremental to the acquisition.

3. *Use the Correct Discount Rate.* The discount rate should be the required rate of return for the incremental cash flows associated with the acquisition.[11] It should reflect the risk associated with the *use* of funds, not their *source*. It would be a mistake for Gamble to use its own cost of capital to value the cash flows from Shapiro.

4. *If Gamble and Shapiro Combine, There Will Be Transactions Costs.* These will include fees to investment bankers, legal fees, and disclosure requirements.

29.7 A Cost to Stockholders from Reduction in Risk

The previous section discussed gains to the firm from a merger. In a firm with debt, these gains are likely to be shared by both bondholders and stockholders. We now consider a benefit to the bondholders from a merger, which occurs at the expense of the stockholders.

---

[11]Recall that the required rate of return is sometimes referred to as the *cost of capital,* or the *opportunity cost of capital.*

TABLE 29.5		NPV			
Stock-Swap Mergers		**State 1**	**State 2**	**State 3**	**Market Value**
Base case: two all-equity firms before merger					
Firm A		$ 80	$50	$25	$ 60
Firm B		$ 50	$40	$15	$ 40
Probability		0.5	0.3	0.2	
After merger*					
Firm AB		$130	$90	$40	$100
Firm A, equity and risky debt before merger					
Firm B, all-equity before merger					
Firm A		$ 80	$50	$25	$ 60
Debt		$ 40	$40	$25	$ 37
Equity		$ 40	$10	$ 0	$ 23
Firm B		$ 50	$40	$15	$ 40
After merger†					
Firm AB		$130	$90	$40	$100
Debt		$ 40	$40	$40	$ 40
Equity		$ 90	$50	$ 0	$ 60

Value of debt rises after merger. Value of original stock in acquiring firm falls correspondingly.

*Stockholders in B receive stock value of $40. Therefore, stockholders of A have a value of $100 − $40 = $60 and are *indifferent to merger.*

†Because firm B's stockholders receive stock in firm A worth $40, original stockholders in firm A have stock worth $20 ($60 − $40). Gains and losses from merger are

$20 − $23 = −$3: Therefore, stockholders of A lose $3.

$40 − $37 = $3: Therefore, bondholders of A gain $3.

When two firms merge, the variability of their combined values is usually less than would be true if the firms remained separate entities. A reduction of the variability of firm values can occur if the values of the two firms are less than perfectly correlated. The reduction in variability can reduce the cost of borrowing and make the creditors better off than before. This will occur if the probability of financial distress is reduced by the merger.

Unfortunately, the shareholders are likely to be worse off. The gains to creditors are at the expense of the shareholders if the total value of the firm does not change. The relationship among the value of the merged firm, debt capacity, and risk is very complicated. We now consider two examples.

The Base Case

Consider a base case where two all-equity firms merge. Table 29.5 gives the net present values of firm A and firm B in three possible states of the economy—prosperity, average, and depression. The market value of firm A is $60, and the market value of firm B is $40. The market value of each firm is the weighted average of the values in each of the three states. For example, the value of firm A is:

$$\$60 = \$80 \times 0.5 + \$50 \times 0.3 + \$25 \times 0.2$$

The values in each of the three states for firm A are $80, $50, and $25, respectively. The probabilities of each of the three states occurring are 0.5, 0.3, and 0.2, respectively.

When firm A merges with firm B, the combined firm AB will have a market value of $100. There is no synergy from this merger, and consequently the value of firm AB is the sum of the values of firm A and firm B. Stockholders of B receive stock with a value of $40, and therefore stockholders of A have a value of $100 − $40 = $60. Thus, stockholders of A and B are indifferent to the proposed merger.

One Firm Has Debt

Alternatively, imagine firm *A* has some debt and some equity outstanding before the merger.[12] Firm *B* is an all-equity firm. Firm *A* will default on its debt in state 3 because the net present value of firm *A* in this state is $25, and the value of the debt claim is $40. As a consequence, the full value of the debt claim cannot be paid by firm *A*. The creditors take this into account, and the value of the debt is $37 ($40 × 0.5 + $40 × 0.3 + $25 × 0.2).

Though default occurs without a merger, no default occurs with a merger. To see this, notice that, when the two firms are separate, firm *B* does not guarantee firm *A*'s debt. That is, if firm *A* defaults on its debt, firm *B* does not help the bondholders of firm *A*. However, after the merger the bondholders can draw on the cash flows from both *A* and *B*. When one of the divisions of the combined firm fails, creditors can be paid from the profits of the other division. This mutual guarantee, which is called the *coinsurance effect,* makes the debt less risky and more valuable than before.

The bonds are worth $40 after the merger. Thus, the bondholders of *AB* gain $3 ($40 − $37) from the merger.

The stockholders of firm *A* lose $3 ($20 − $23) from the merger. That is, firm *A*'s stock is worth $23 prior to the merger. The stock is worth $60 after the merger. However, stockholders in firm *B* receive $40 of stock in firm *A*. Hence, those individuals who were stockholders in firm *A* prior to the merger have stock worth only $20 ($60 − $40) after the merger.

There is no net benefit to the firm as a whole. The bondholders gain the coinsurance effect, and the stockholders lose the coinsurance effect. Some general conclusions emerge from the preceding analysis.

1. Bondholders in the aggregate will usually be helped by mergers and acquisitions. The size of the gain to bondholders depends on the reduction of bankruptcy states after the combination. That is, the less risky the combined firm is, the greater are the gains to bondholders.
2. Stockholders of the acquiring firm will be hurt by the amount that bondholders gain.
3. The conclusions apply to mergers and acquisitions where no synergy is present. In the case of synergistic combinations, much depends on the size of the synergy.

How Can Shareholders Reduce Their Losses from the Coinsurance Effect?

The coinsurance effect allows some mergers to increase bondholder values by reducing shareholder values. However, there are at least two ways that shareholders can reduce or eliminate the coinsurance effect. First, the shareholders in firm *A* could retire its debt *before* the merger announcement date and reissue an equal amount of debt after the merger. Because debt is retired at the low, pre-merger price, this type of refinancing transaction can neutralize the coinsurance effect to the bondholders.

Also, note that the debt capacity of the combined firm is likely to increase because the acquisition reduces the probability of financial distress. Thus, the shareholders' second alternative is simply to issue more debt after the merger. An increase in debt following the merger will have two effects, even without the prior action of debt retirement. The interest deduction from new corporate debt raises firm value. In addition, an increase in debt after the merger raises the probability of financial distress, thereby reducing or eliminating the bondholders' gain from the coinsurance effect.

---

[12]This example was provided by David Babbel.

29.8 Two "Bad" Reasons for Mergers

Earnings Growth

An acquisition can create the appearance of earnings growth, which may fool investors into thinking that the firm is worth more than it really is. Suppose Global Resources, Ltd., acquires Regional Enterprises. The financial positions of Global and Regional before the acquisition are shown in Table 29.6. Regional has had very poor earnings growth and sells at a price-earnings ratio much lower than that of Global. The merger creates no additional value. If the market is smart, it will realize that the combined firm is worth the sum of the values of the separate firms. In this case, the market value of the combined firm will be $3,500, which is equal to the sum of the values of the separate firms before the merger.

At these values, Global will acquire Regional by exchanging 40 of its shares for 100 Regional shares,[13] so that Global will have 140 shares outstanding after the merger. Because the stock price of Global after the merger is the same as before the merger, the price-earnings ratio must fall. This is true because the market is smart and recognizes that the total market has not been altered by the merger. This scenario is represented by the third column of Table 29.6.

Let us now consider the possibility that the market is fooled. One can see from Table 29.6 that the acquisition enables Global to increase its earnings per share from $1 to $1.43. If the market is fooled, it might mistake the 43-percent increase in earnings per share for true growth. In this case, the price-earnings ratio of Global may not fall after the merger. Suppose the price-earnings ratio of Global remains equal to 25. The total value of the combined firm will increase to $5,000 (25 × $200), and the stock price per share of Global will increase to $35.71 ($5,000/140). This is reflected in the last column of Table 29.6.

This is earnings-growth magic. Like all good magic, it is an illusion and the shareholders of Global and Regional will receive something for nothing. This may work for a while, but in the long run the efficient market will work its wonders and the value will decline.

Diversification

Diversification often is mentioned as a benefit of one firm acquiring another. Earlier in this chapter, we noted that U.S. Steel included diversification as a benefit in its acquisition of Marathon Oil. In 1982 U.S. Steel was a cash-rich company (over 20 percent of its assets

TABLE 29.6			**Global Resources after Merger**	
Financial Positions of Global Resources, Ltd., and Regional Enterprises	**Global Resources before Merger**	**Regional Enterprises before Merger**	**The Market Is "Smart"**	**The Market Is "Fooled"**
Earnings per share	$ 1.00	$ 1.00	$ 1.43	$ 1.43
Price per share	$ 25.00	$ 10.00	$ 25.00	$ 35.71
Price-earnings ratio	25	10	17.5	25
Number of shares	100	100	140	140
Total earnings	$ 100	$ 100	$ 200	$ 200
Total value	$2,500	$1,000	$3,500	$5,000

Exchange ratio: 1 share in Global for 2.5 shares in Regional.

---

[13]This ratio implies a fair exchange because a share of Regional is selling for 40 percent ($10/$25) of the price of a share of Global.

were in the form of cash and marketable securities). It is not uncommon to see firms with surplus cash articulating a need for diversification.

However, we argue that diversification, by itself, cannot produce increases in value. To see this, recall that a business's variability of return can be separated into two parts: (1) what is specific to the business and called *unsystematic,* and (2) what is *systematic* because it is common to all businesses.

Systematic variability cannot be eliminated by diversification, so mergers will not eliminate this risk at all. By contrast, unsystematic risk can be diversified away through mergers. However, the investor does not need widely diversified companies such as General Electric to eliminate unsystematic risk. Shareholders can diversify more easily than corporations by simply purchasing common stock in different corporations. For example, the shareholders of U.S. Steel could have purchased shares in Marathon if they believed there would be diversification gains in doing so. Thus, diversification through conglomerate merger may not benefit shareholders.[14]

Diversification can produce gains to the acquiring firm only if two things are true:

1. Diversification decreases the unsystematic variability at lower costs than by investors via adjustments to personal portfolios. This seems very unlikely.

2. Diversification reduces risk and thereby increases debt capacity. This possibility was mentioned earlier in the chapter.

<table>
<tr><td>**Concept**
Question</td><td>1. **Why can a merger create the appearance of earnings growth?**</td></tr>
</table>

29.9 The NPV of a Merger

Firms typically use NPV analysis when making acquisitions.[15] The analysis is relatively straightforward when the consideration is cash. The analysis becomes more complex when the consideration is stock.

Cash

Suppose firm *A* and firm *B* have values as separate entities of $500 and $100, respectively. They are both all-equity firms. If firm *A* acquires firm *B*, the merged firm *AB* will have a combined value of $700 due to synergies of $100. The board of firm *B* has indicated that it will sell firm *B* if it is offered $150 in cash.

---

[14]Evidence suggests that diversification can actually hurt shareholders. Randall Mork, Andrei Shleifer, and Robert W. Vishney ["Do Managerial Objectives Drive Bad Acquisitions," *Journal of Finance* 45 (1990), pp. 31–48] show that shareholders did poorly in firms that diversified by acquisition in the 1980s. There is also evidence that diversified firms trade at a discount relative to a portfolio of single-segment firms, most recently from Karl Lins and Henri Servaes, "The International Evidence on the Value of Corporate Diversification," *Journal of Finance* 54 (1999). On the other hand, Matsusaka and Hubbard and Palia find some benefits to diversification in internal capital allocation. See John Matsusaka, "Takeover Motives During the Conglomerate Merge Wave," *Rand Journal of Economics* 24 (1993).

See also R. Glenn Hubbard and Darius Palia, "A Reexamination of the Conglomerate Merger Wave in the 1960s: An Internal Capital Markets View," *Journal of Finance* (June 1999).

One interesting recent study reports a positive relationship between focus and value for diversified firms. See P. G. Berger and E. Ofek, "Diversification's Effect on Firm Value," *Journal of Financial Economics,* 37 (1995). Also see P. G. Berger and E. Ofek, "Causes and Effects of Corporate Refocusing Program," *Review of Financial Studies* 12 (1999).

[15]The NPV framework for evaluating mergers can be found in S. C. Myers, "A Framework for Evaluating Mergers," in *Modern Developments in Financial Management,* ed. by S. C. Myers (New York: Praeger, 1976).

TABLE 29.7	Before Acquisition		After Acquisition: Firm A		
Cost of Acquisition: Cash versus Common Stock	(1)	(2)	(3)	(4) Common Stock† Exchange Ratio (0.75:1)	(5) Common Stock† Exchange Ratio (0.6819:1)
	Firm A	Firm B	Cash*		
Market value (V_A, V_B)	$500	$100	$550	$700	$700
Number of shares	25	10	25	32.5	31.819
Price per share	$ 20	$ 10	$ 22	$ 21.54	$ 22

*Value of firm A after acquisition: cash

$$V_A = V_{AB} - \text{Cash}$$
$$\$550 = \$700 - \$150$$

†Value of firm A after acquisition: common stock

$$V_A = V_{AB}$$
$$\$700 = \$700$$

Should firm A acquire firm B? Assuming that firm A finances the acquisition out of its own retained earnings, its value after the acquisition is:[16]

$$
\begin{aligned}
\text{Value of firm } A \text{ after the acquisition} &= \text{Value of combined firm} - \text{Cash paid} \\
&= \$700 - \$150 \\
&= \$550
\end{aligned}
$$

Because firm A was worth $500 prior to the acquisition, the NPV to firm A's stockholders is:

$$\$50 = \$550 - \$500 \tag{29.1}$$

Assuming that there are 25 shares in firm A, each share of the firm is worth $20 ($500/25) prior to the merger and $22 ($550/25) after the merger. These calculations are displayed in the first and third columns of Table 29.7. Looking at the rise in stock price, we conclude that firm A should make the acquisition.

We spoke earlier of both the synergy and the premium of a merger. We can also value the NPV of a merger to the acquirer as:

$$\text{NPV of a merger to acquirer} = \text{Synergy} - \text{Premium}$$

Because the value of the combined firm is $700 and the premerger values of A and B were $500 and $100, respectively, the synergy is $100 [$700 − ($500 + $100)]. The premium is $50 ($150 − $100). Thus, the NPV of the merger to the acquirer is:

$$\text{NPV of merger to firm } A = \$100 - \$50 = \$50$$

One caveat is in order. This textbook has consistently argued that the market value of a firm is the best estimate of its true value. However, we must adjust our analysis when discussing mergers. If the true price of firm A *without the merger* is $500, the market value of firm A may actually be above $500 when merger negotiations take place. This occurs because the market price reflects the possibility that the merger will occur. For example, if the

---

[16]The analysis will be essentially the same if new stock is issued. However, the analysis will differ if new debt is issued to fund the acquisition because of the tax shield to debt. An adjusted present value (APV) approach would be necessary here.

probability is 60 percent that the merger will take place, the market price of firm *A* will be:

	Market value of firm *A* with merger	×	Probability of merger	+	Market value of firm *A* without merger	×	Probability of no merger
$530 =	$550	×	0.60	+	$500	×	0.40

The managers would underestimate the NPV from merger in equation (29.1) if the market price of firm *A* is used. Thus, managers are faced with the difficult task of valuing their own firm without the acquisition.

Common Stock

Of course, firm *A* could purchase firm *B* with common stock instead of cash. Unfortunately, the analysis is not as straightforward here. In order to handle this scenario, we need to know how many shares are outstanding in firm *B*. We assume that there are 10 shares outstanding, as indicated in column 2 of Table 29.7.

Suppose firm *A* exchanges 7.5 of its shares for the entire 10 shares of firm *B*. We call this an exchange ratio of 0.75:1. The value of each share of firm *A*'s stock before the acquisition is $20. Because $7.5 \times \$20 = \$150$, this exchange *appears* to be the equivalent of purchasing firm *B* in cash for $150.

This is incorrect: The true cost is greater than $150. To see this, note that firm *A* has 32.5 (25 + 7.5) shares outstanding after the merger. Firm *B* shareholders own 23 percent (7.5/32.5) of the combined firm. Their holdings are valued at $161 (23% × $700). Because these stockholders receive stock in firm *A* worth $161, the cost of the merger to firm *A*'s stockholders must be $161, not $150.

This result is shown in column 4 of Table 29.7. The value of each share of firm *A*'s stock after a stock-for-stock transaction is only $21.54 ($700/32.5). We found out earlier that the value of each share is $22 after a cash-for-stock transaction. The difference is that the cost of the stock-for-stock transaction to firm *A* is higher.

This nonintuitive result occurs because the exchange ratio of 7.5 shares of firm *A* for 10 shares of firm *B* was based on the *premerger* prices of the two firms. However, since the stock of firm *A* rises after the merger, firm *B* stockholders receive more than $150 in firm *A* stock.

What should the exchange ratio be so that firm *B* stockholders receive only $150 of firm *A*'s stock? We begin by defining α, the proportion of the shares in the combined firm that firm *B*'s stockholders own. Because the combined firm's value is $700, the value of firm *B* stockholders after the merger is:

Value of Firm *B* Stockholders after Merger:
$$\alpha \times \$700$$

Setting $\alpha \times \$700 = \$150$, we find that $\alpha = 21.43\%$. In other words, firm *B*'s stockholders will receive stock worth $150 if they receive 21.43 percent of the firm after merger.

Now we determine the number of shares issued to firm *B*'s shareholders. The proportion, α, that firm *B*'s shareholders have in the combined firm can be expressed as:

$$\alpha = \frac{\text{New shares issued}}{\text{Old shares} + \text{New shares issued}} = \frac{\text{New shares issued}}{25 + \text{New shares issued}}$$

Plugging our value of α into the equation yields:

$$0.2143 = \frac{\text{New shares issued}}{25 + \text{New shares issued}}$$

Solving for the unknown, we have:

New shares = 6.819 shares

Total shares outstanding after the merger are 31.819 (25 + 6.819). Because 6.819 shares of firm *A* are exchanged for 10 shares of firm *B*, the exchange ratio is 0.6819:1.

Results at the exchange ratio of 0.6819:1 are displayed in column 5 of Table 29.7. Each share of common stock is worth $22, exactly what it is worth in the stock-for-cash transaction. Thus, given that the board of firm *B* will sell its firm for $150, this is the fair exchange ratio, not the ratio of 0.75:1 mentioned earlier.

Cash versus Common Stock

Whether to finance an acquisition by cash or by shares of stock is an important decision. The choice depends on several factors, as follows:

1. *Overvaluation.* If in the opinion of management the acquiring firm's stock is overvalued, using shares of stock can be less costly than using cash.
2. *Taxes.* Acquisition by cash usually results in a taxable transaction. Acquisition by exchanging stock is tax free.
3. *Sharing Gains.* If cash is used to finance an acquisition, the selling firm's shareholders receive a fixed price. In the event of a hugely successful merger, they will not participate in any additional gains. Of course, if the acquisition is not a success, the losses will not be shared and shareholders of the acquiring firm will be worse off than if stock were used.

Concept Question

1. **In an efficient market with no tax effects, should an acquiring firm use cash or stock?**

29.10 Defensive Tactics

Target-firm managers frequently resist takeover attempts. Resistance usually starts with press releases and mailings to shareholders that present management's viewpoint. It can eventually lead to legal action and solicitation of competing bids. Managerial action to defeat a takeover attempt may make target shareholders better off if it elicits a higher offer premium from the bidding firm or another firm. Of course, management resistance may simply reflect pursuit of self-interest at the expense of shareholders. That is, the target managers may resist a takeover in order to preserve their jobs. It is also possible that the target-firm management will take corrective action to increase stock price in order to reduce the takeover benefits. In this section we describe various defensive tactics that have been used by target-firm managements to resist unfriendly takeover attempts.

Divestitures

Target-firm managers considering the prospect of a takeover may decide a narrowing of strategic focus can increase stock price, thereby making a takeover too expensive. If so, they will consider the pros and cons of three kinds of divestitures: a sale of assets, a spin-off, and the issuance of a tracking stock. The basic idea of all three types of divestitures is to reduce the potential diversification discount associated with commingled operations and to increase corporate focus. The sale of a business segment is usually for cash. With a spin-off, the parent company distributes shares of a subsidiary to its shareholders. As a consequence, the shareholders end up with a stake in the parent as well as the subsidiary.

Typically, the stock in the subsidiary is distributed pro rata to the parent-company share-holders. No actual asset sale is involved, and the subsidiary becomes a completely separate company (with its own board of directors, etc.). A variant of the spin-off is called an *equity curveout,* where the stock of the subsidiary is sold to the public in an IPO. Sometimes a spin-off and an equity curveout are combined. A tracking stock is a class of common stock whose value is connected to the performance of a particular segment (division or sub-sidiary) of the parent company's business. The intent of a tracking stock is quite similar to an asset sale or spin-off, which is to give shareholders a pure play on a particular part of the firm. The issue of tracking stock shares can be some form of combination between a pro rata distribution and an IPO. The first tracker was when General Motors issued stock that tracked Electronic Data Systems (EDS). Recently General Motors, AT&T, and Sprint PCS have issued trackers. Tracking stock does not involve a separate, formal entity, as in the case of a spin-off or equity curveout.[17]

The Corporate Charter

The corporate charter refers to the articles of incorporation and corporate bylaws that govern the firm. The corporate charter establishes the conditions that allow a takeover. Firms frequently amend corporate charters to make acquisitions more difficult. For exam-ple, usually two-thirds of the shareholders of record must approve a merger. Firms can make it more difficult to be acquired by requiring 80-percent approval by the shareholders. This is called a *supermajority amendment.* Another device is to *stagger* the election of the board members, which increases the difficulty of electing a new board of directors quickly.

Repurchase Standstill Agreements

Managers may arrange a *targeted repurchase* to forestall a takeover attempt. In a targeted repurchase, a firm buys back its own stock from a potential bidder, usually at a substantial premium. These premiums can be thought of as payments to potential bidders to delay or stop unfriendly takeover attempts. Critics of such payments label them *greenmail.*

In addition, managers of target firms may simultaneously negotiate standstill agree-ments. *Standstill agreements* are contracts where the bidding firm agrees to limit its hold-ings of another firm. These agreements usually lead to cessation of takeover attempts, and announcement of such agreements has had a negative effect on stock prices.

EXAMPLE

On April 2, 1986, Ashland Oil, Inc., the nation's largest independent oil refiner, had 28 million shares outstanding. The company's stock price closed the day before at $49\frac{3}{4}$ per share on the New York Stock Exchange. On April 2, Ashland's board of directors made two decisions:

1. The board approved management's agreement with the Belzberg family of Canada to buy, for $51 a share, the Belzbergs' 2.6 million shares in Ashland. This was part of a standstill agreement that ended a takeover skirmish in which the Belzberg family offered $60 per share for all of the common stock of Ashland.

---

[17]There have been several studies of tracking stocks that seem to suggest returns of about three percent upon the announcement of a tracking stock issue. For example: M. T. Billet and D. C. Mauer, "Diversification and the Value of Internal Capital Market, The Case of Tracking Stock," *Journal of Banking and Finance* (September 2000); J. D. Sousa J. and J. Jacob, "Why Firms Issue Tracking Stock," *Journal of Financial Economics* 56 (2000); D. E. Logue, J. K. Seward, and J. P. Walsh, "Rearranging Residual Claim: A Case for Targeted Stock," *Financial Management* 25 (1996).

On the other hand, Mathew T. Billet and Anand M. Vijh, "Long-Term Returns from Tracking Stocks," University of Iowa, unpublished paper, report negative long-term returns from tracking stocks.

Several recent articles report stock-price gains from asset sales spin-offs and equity curveouts that increase a firm's focus. See, for example: J. Desai and P. Jain, "Firm Performance and Focus: Long Run Stock Market Performance Following Spin-offs," *Journal of Financial Economics* 54 (1999); K. John and E. Ofek, "Asset Sales and Increase in Focus," *Journal of Financial Economics* 37 (1999); and A. Vijh, "Long Term Returns from Equity Curveouts," *Journal of Financial Economics* 51 (1999).

2. The board authorized the company to repurchase 7.5 million shares (27 percent of the out-standing shares) of its stock. The board simultaneously approved a proposal to establish an employee stock-ownership plan to be funded with 5.3 million shares of Ashland stock.

The result of these two actions was to make Ashland invulnerable to unfriendly takeover at-tempts. In effect, the company was selling about 20 percent of its stock to the employee stock-ownership plan. Earlier Ashland had put in place a provision that said 80 percent of the stockhold-ers have to approve a takeover. Ashland's stock price fell by $0.25 over the next two days. Because this move can probably be explained by random error, there is no evidence that Ashland's actions reduced shareholder value.

Exclusionary Self-Tenders

An *exclusionary self-tender* is the opposite of a targeted repurchase. Here, the firm makes a tender offer for a given amount of its own stock while excluding targeted stockholders.

In one of the most celebrated cases in financial history, Unocal, a large integrated oil firm, made a tender offer for 29 percent of its shares while excluding its largest shareholder, Mesa Partners II (led by T. Boone Pickens). Unocal's self-tender was for $72 per share, which was $16 over the prevailing market price. It was designed to defeat Mesa's attempted takeover of Unocal by transferring wealth, in effect, from Mesa to Unocal's other stockholders.

Going Private and Leveraged Buyouts

Going private refers to what happens when the publicly owned stock in a firm is purchased by a private group, usually composed of existing management. As a consequence, the firm's stock is taken off the market (if it is an exchange-traded stock, it is delisted) and is no longer traded. Thus, in going-private transactions, shareholders of publicly held firms are forced to accept cash for their shares.

Going-private transactions are frequently *leveraged buyouts* (LBOs). In a leveraged buyout, the cash-offer price is financed with large amounts of debt. LBOs have recently become quite popular because the arrangement calls for little equity capital. This equity capital is generally supplied by a small group of investors, some of whom are likely to be managers of the firm being purchased.

The selling stockholders are invariably paid a premium above market price in an LBO, just as they are in a merger.[18] As with a merger, the acquirer profits only if the synergy created is greater than the premium. Synergy is quite plausible in a merger of *two* firms, and we delineated a number of types of synergy earlier in the chapter. However, it is much more difficult to explain synergy in an LBO, because only *one* firm is involved.

There are generally two reasons given for the ability of an LBO to create value. First, the extra debt provides a tax deduction, which, as earlier chapters suggested, leads to an increase in firm value. Most LBOs are on firms with stable earnings and with low to mod-erate debt. The LBO may simply increase the firm's debt to its optimum level. In fact, Con-gress has recently taken a skeptical look at LBOs, partly because the increase in debt reduces the U.S. Treasury's tax revenues.

Second, the LBO usually turns the previous managers into owners, thereby increasing their incentive to work hard. The increase in debt is a further incentive because the man-agers must earn more than the debt service to obtain any profit for themselves.

---

[18]H. DeAngelo, L. DeAngelo, and E. M. Rice, "Going Private: Minority Freezeouts and Shareholder Wealth," *Journal of Law and Economics* 27 (1984). They show that the premiums paid to existing shareholders in LBOs and other going-private transactions are about the same as in interfirm acquisitions.

Though it is easy to value the additional tax shields from an LBO, it is quite difficult to value the gains from increased efficiency. Nevertheless, this increased efficiency is considered to be at least as important as the tax shield in explaining the LBO phenomenon.

Of course, one cannot be entirely sure that LBOs create value at all, because the stock price cannot be observed once the company has been taken private. Though one frequently hears of LBO investors achieving great wealth, this is only casual empirical evidence. There may be an equal number of LBO investors who are left with little value after purchasing a company at a premium. The full story on LBOs has certainly not been told at this point.

Other Devices and Jargon of Corporate Takeovers

As corporate takeovers have become more common, a new lexicon has developed. The terms are colorful, and some are listed here:

1. **Golden parachutes.** Some target firms provide compensation to top-level management if a takeover occurs. For example, when the Scoville board endorsed a $523 million tender offer by First City Properties, it arranged for 13 top executives to receive termination payments of about $5 million. This can be viewed as a payment to management to make it less concerned for its own welfare and more interested in stockholders when considering a takeover bid. Alternatively, the payment can be seen as an attempt to enrich management at the stockholders' expense.

2. **Crown jewels.** Firms often sell major assets—crown jewels—when faced with a takeover threat. This is sometimes referred to as the *scorched earth strategy*.

3. **Poison pill.** Poison pill is a term taken from the world of espionage. Agents are supposed to bite a pill of cyanide rather than permit capture. Presumably this prevents enemy interrogators from learning important secrets. In finance, poison pills are used to make a stock repellent to others. A poison pill is generally a right to buy shares in the merged firm at a bargain price. The right is granted to the target firm's shareholders, contingent on another firm acquiring control. The right dilutes the stock so much that the bidding firm loses money on its shares. Thus, wealth is transferred from the bidder to the target.

4. **White knight.** A firm facing an unfriendly merger offer might arrange to be acquired by a different friendly suitor. The firm is thereby rescued by the white knight.

5. **Lockup.** A lockup is an option granted to a friendly suitor (perhaps a white knight) giving the right but not the obligation to purchase stock or a portion of the assets (perhaps the crown jewels) of the target firm at a fixed price in the event of an unfriendly takeover.

6. **Shark repellent.** A shark repellent is any tactic that makes the firm less attractive to a potential unfriendly offerer.

7. **Bear hug.** A bear hug is an unfriendly takeover that is so attractive that the target firm's management has little choice but to accept it.

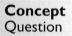

Concept Question

1. What can a firm do to make a takeover less likely?

29.11 Some Evidence on Acquisitions

One of the most controversial issues surrounding our subject is whether mergers and acquisitions benefit shareholders.

TABLE 29.8	Takeover Technique	Target	Bidders
Abnormal Stock-Price Changes Associated with Successful Corporate Takeover Bids	Tender offer	30%	4%
	Merger	20%	0
	Proxy contest	8%	n.a.

n.a. = Not applicable.

Modified from Michael C. Jensen and Richard S. Ruback, "The Market for Corporate Control: The Scientific Evidence," *Journal of Financial Economics* 11 (April 1983), pp. 7, 8. © Elsevier Science Publishers B.V. (North-Holland).

TABLE 29.9	Takeover Technique	Target	Bidders
Abnormal Stock-Price Changes Associated with Unsuccessful Corporate Takeover Bids	Tender offer	−3%	−1%
	Merger	−3%	−5%
	Proxy contest	8%	n.a.

n.a. = Not applicable.

Modified from Michael C. Jensen and Richard S. Ruback, "The Market for Corporate Control: The Scientific Evidence," *Journal of Financial Economics* 11 (April 1983), pp. 7, 8. © Elsevier Science Publishers B.V. (North-Holland).

Do Acquisitions Benefit Shareholders?

Much research has attempted to estimate the effect of mergers and takeovers on stock prices of the bidding and target firms. These studies are called *event studies* because they estimate abnormal stock-price changes on and around the offer-announcement date—the event. Abnormal returns are usually defined as the difference between actual stock returns and a market index or a control group of stocks, to take account of the influence of market-wide effects on the returns of individual securities.

The Short Run

An overview of the short run evidence is reported in Jensen and Ruback. Tables 29.8 and 29.9 summarize the results of numerous studies that look at the effects of mergers and tender offers on stock prices from the announcement date to the completion date. Table 29.8 shows that the shareholders of target companies in successful takeovers achieve large abnormal returns. When the takeover is done by merger the gains are 20 percent, and when the takeover is done by tender offer the gains are 30 percent.

The shareholders of bidding firms do not fare nearly as well. According to the studies summarized in Table 29.8, bidders experience abnormal returns of 4 percent in tender offers, and in mergers the percentage is zero. These numbers are sufficiently small to leave doubt about the effect on bidders. Table 29.9 shows that the shareholders of firms involved in unsuccessful takeover attempts experience small negative returns in both mergers and tender offers. What conclusions can be drawn from Tables 29.8 and 29.9?

1. The results of all event studies suggest that the shareholders of target firms achieve substantial short-term gains as a result of successful takeovers.[19] The gains appear to be larger in tender offers than in mergers. This may reflect the fact that takeovers sometimes start with a friendly merger proposal from the bidder to the management of the target firm. If management rejects the offer, the bidding firm may take the offer directly

---

[19]This has been a consistent finding in all merger studies. G. Mandelker, "Risk and Return: The Case of the Merging Firm," *Journal of Financial Economics* (1974), was one of the first to document the premiums to acquired firms.

to the shareholders with an unfriendly tender offer. The target management may actively oppose the offer with defensive tactics. This often has the result of raising the tender offer from the bidding firm, and, thus, on the average, friendly mergers are arranged at a lower premium than unfriendly tender offers.

2. The shareholders of bidding firms earn comparatively little from takeovers. They earn an average of only 4 percent from tender offers and do not appear to earn anything from mergers. In fact, in an early study by Asquith the shareholders of acquiring firms in successful mergers experienced significantly abnormal losses after the announcement of the merger.[20] These findings are a puzzle.

   a. One possible explanation is that anticipated merger gains were not completely achieved, and thus shareholders experienced losses. Managers of bidding firms may have hubris and tend to overestimate the gains from acquisition.

   b. The bidding firms are usually much larger than the target firms. Thus, the dollar gains to the bidder may be approximately the same as the dollar gains to the shareholders of the target firm at the same time that the *percentage* returns are much lower for the bidding firms.

   c. Management may not be acting in the interests of shareholders when it attempts to acquire other firms. Perhaps it is attempting to increase the size of its firm, even if this reduces its value.

3. The return to the shareholders of targets of unsuccessful merger, measured from the offer date to the cancellation date, is negative. Thus, all the initial gains are lost over the time period during which the merger failure becomes known. The overall average return to shareholders of unsuccessful tender offers is about the same as for unsuccessful merger attempts. However, the story is more complicated. Bradley, Desai, and Kim report that how well shareholders of target firms do in unsuccessful tender offers depends on whether or not future takeover offers are forthcoming. They find that target-firm shareholders realize additional positive gains when a new offer is made but lose everything previously gained if no other offer occurs.[21]

The Long Run

The evidence on long run stock returns following acquisition is provided by Loughran and Vijh. Table 29.10 summarizes the results of their study of nearly 1,000 acquiring (bidding) firms from 1970 to 1989. They compute the average abnormal return to shareholders from the date of the acquisition over a subsequent five-year period. Table 29.10 shows that shareholders of acquiring firms earn negative average abnormal returns. Previously we reported that shareholders of acquiring firms did not fare particularly well in the short run. Now we see that five years after the date of the acquisition, shareholders of acquiring firms continue to do poorly, earning an abnormal average return of −6.5 percent.

Table 29.10 also shows that the method of payment in acquisitions is important in the distribution of long run returns. When the acquirer pays cash for the target, shareholders gain an abnormal average return of 18.5 percent. However, when the acquirer pays with its own stock, shareholders experience a negative abnormal average return of −24.2 percent. Several conclusions can be drawn from Table 29.10.

1. In the long run, the shareholders of acquiring firms experience below average returns. If significant, this finding raises questions about the efficient market hypothesis, since any

---

[20]P. Asquith, "Merger Bids, Uncertainty and Stockholder Returns," *Journal of Financial Economics* 11 (April 1983).

[21]M. Bradley, A. Desai, and E. H. Kim, "The Rationale behind Interfirm Tender Offers: Information or Synergy," *Journal of Financial Economics* 11 (April 1983).

TABLE 29.10		
Abnormal Five-Year Stock Returns of Acquiring Firms from 1970 to 1989	Acquirers using unfriendly cash tender offers	61.7%
	Acquirers who pay cash (both friendly and unfriendly)	18.5%
	All acquirers	−6.5%
	Acquirers using stock	−24.2%

SOURCE: T. Loughran and A. Vijh, "Do Long-Term Shareholders Benefit from Corporate Acquisitions," *Journal of Finance* (December, 1997), Table II. The abnormal returns are measured over a five-year period beginning at the date of the acquisition. For example, the overall sample of 947 acquisitions experienced an average five-year return of 88.2 percent compared to 94.7 percent for a sample of matching firms. The difference equals −6.5 percent (see above).

negative information implicit in an acquisition should be reflected in stock returns by the date of the acquisition.

2. Cash-financed mergers are different than stock-financed mergers. When an acquisition is financed by stock, it is useful to think of the acquisition as a combination of two events: an issue of stock and an acquisition. It is known from Loughran and Ritter (Chapter 18) that the long-term abnormal returns following new equity issues are negative. The poor long run performance of stock-financed mergers could be the result of new stock issues that take place with these mergers.

3. Acquirers can also be divided into friendly and unfriendly cash acquirers. The shares of unfriendly cash acquirers have significantly outperformed those of friendly cash acquirers. One possible interpretation of this is that unfriendly cash bidders are more likely to replace poor management. If so, the removal of poor managers may contribute to the above average long run performance.

Real Productivity

There are many potential synergies from mergers and acquisitions. Unfortunately, it is very hard to precisely measure synergy. In the previous section, we focused on stock-market gains or losses to the shareholders of the acquiring and acquired firms. In very general terms, we found that target-firm shareholders experience stock-market gains and acquiring-firm shareholders experience stock-market losses. There appear to be net gains to stockholders. This would suggest that mergers can increase real productivity. In fact, several recent studies suggest that mergers can increase real productivity. Healey, Palepu, and Ruback report that merged companies' after-tax returns increased substantially after the mergers. They trace this gain to an increase in selling activity (turnover). They find no evidence that merged firms cut back on positive NPV capital expenditures.[22]

Concept
Question

1. What does the evidence say about the benefits of mergers and acquisitions?

29.12 The Japanese Keiretsu

In Japan it has been unusual for firms to grow by large-scale mergers and acquisitions. However, in the late 1980s several Japanese firms acquired large U.S. firms.[23] Most notably, Sony acquired CBS Records in November 1987 and Columbia Pictures in September 1989.

---

[22]P. Healey, K. Palepu, and R. Ruback, "Does Corporate Performance Improve After Mergers," *Journal of Financial Economics* 31 (1997).

[23]W. Carl Kester, *Japanese Takeovers, the Global Contest for Corporate Control,* Cambridge, Mass.: 1991 (Harvard Business School Press). Chapter 5 describes the acquisition experience of several Japanese firms.

Sony's acquisition of Columbia Pictures for $3.45 billion is the largest Japanese acquisition of a U.S. firm. The second largest was Bridgestone Corporation's acquisition of Firestone Tire and Rubber for $2.6 billion in March 1988.

The most interesting Japanese business combinations involve reciprocal shareholding and trading agreements. These networks are called **keiretsu** and involve a group of firms affiliated around a large bank, industrial firm, or trading firm. The Mitsubishi and the Mitsui keiretsu groups are shown in Figure 29.3.

FIGURE 29.3		Mitsubishi	Mitsui
Japanese Keiretsu	Financial Services	Mitsubishi Bank	Mitsui Taiyo Kobe Bank
		Mitsubishi Trust & Banking	Mitsui Trust & Banking
		Meiji Mutual Life	Mitsui Mutual Life
		Tokio Marine & Fire	Taisho Marine & Fire
	Computers, Electronics, and Electrical Equipment	Mitsubishi Electric	Toshiba
	Cars	Mitsubishi Motors	Toyota Motor*
	Trading and Retailing	Mitsubishi	Mitsui
			Mitsukoshi
	Food and Beverage	Kirin Brewery	Nippon Flour Mills
	Construction	Mitsubishi Construction	Mitsui Construction
			Sanki Engineering
	Metals	Mitsubishi Steel Mfg.	Japan Steel Works
		Mitsubishi Materials	Mitsui Mining & Smelting
		Mitsubishi Aluminum	
		Mitsubishi Cable Industries	
	Real Estate	Mitsubishi Estate	Mitsui Real Estate Development
	Oil and Coal	Mitsubishi Oil	
	Rubber and Glass	Asahi Glass	
	Chemicals	Mitsubishi Kasei	Mitsui Toatsu Chemicals
		Mitsubishi Petrochemical	Mitsui Petrochemical Industries
		Mitsubishi Gas Chemical	
		Mitsubishi Plastics Industries	
		Mitsubishi Kasei Polytec	
	Fibers and Textiles	Mitsubishi Rayon	Tory Industries
	Pulp and Paper	Mitsubishi Paper Mills	Oji Paper
	Mining and Forestry		Mitsui Mining
			Hokkaido Colliery & Steamship
	Industrial Equipment	Mitsubishi Heavy Industries	Mitsui Engineering & Shipbuilding
		Mitsubishi Kakoki	
	Cameras and Optics	Nikon	
	Cement		Onoda Cement
	Shipping and Transportation	Nippon Yusen	Mitsui OSK Lines
		Mitsubishi Warehouse & Transportation	Mitsui Warehouse

This table describes the network of firms in the Mitsubishi and Mitsui keiretsu.

*Companies affiliated with more than one group.

SOURCE: *Fortune* (July 15, 1991), p. 81.

Participation in the Mitsubishi or Mitsui keiretsu implies significant reciprocal owner-ship of common stock. It is widely understood that firms within the keiretsu are not to sell these cross-held shares.

Nobody knows for sure what the main benefit of the keiretsu is. However, one of the most important features of the keiretsu is the relationship between the industrial firms and the financial institutions. For example, Mitsubishi Motors may have an extensive relation-ship with Mitsubishi Trust and Banking, Meiji Mutual Life, and Tokio Marine and Fire. This connection between industrial firms and financial institutions within the group may benefit the group by reducing the costs of financial distress that come from getting credi-tors to agree to a restructuring if one of the keiretsu members gets into financial trouble.[24] Reaching an agreement between Mitsubishi Bank and Mitsubishi Motors will be easier if Mitsubishi Motors gets into trouble because both are in the Mitsubishi keiretsu.

Concept
Questions

1. Can you describe a keiretsu?
2. What is a benefit of a keiretsu?

29.13 SUMMARY AND CONCLUSIONS

1. One firm can acquire another in several different ways. The three legal forms of acquisition are merger and consolidation, acquisition of stock, and acquisition of assets. Mergers and consolida-tions are the least costly to arrange from a legal standpoint, but they require a vote of approval by the shareholders. Acquisition by stock does not require a shareholder vote and is usually done via a tender offer. However, it is difficult to obtain 100-percent control with a tender offer. Acquisition of assets is comparatively costly because it requires more difficult transfer of asset ownership.

2. Mergers and acquisitions require an understanding of complicated tax and accounting rules. Mergers and acquisitions can be taxable or tax-free transactions. In a taxable transaction, each selling shareholder must pay taxes on the stock's capital appreciation. Should the acquiring firm elect to write up the assets, additional tax implications arise. However, acquiring firms do not generally elect to write up the assets for tax purposes. The selling stockholders do not pay taxes at the time of a tax-free acquisition.

   Accounting for mergers and acquisitions involves a choice of the purchase method or the pooling-of-interests method. The choice between these two methods does not affect after-tax cash flows of the combined firm. However, most financial managers prefer the pooling-of-interests method, because net income of the combined firm under this method is higher than it is under the purchase method.

3. The synergy from an acquisition is defined as the value of the combined firm (V_{AB}) less the value of the two firms as separate entities (V_A and V_B), or

$$\text{Synergy} = V_{AB} - (V_A + V_B)$$

The shareholders of the acquiring firm will gain if the synergy from the merger is greater than the premium.

4. The possible benefits of an acquisition come from the following:
   a. Revenue enhancement
   b. Cost reduction

[24]This is the argument of Takeo Hoshi, Anil K. Kashyup, and David Scharfstein, "The Role of Banks in Reducing Financial Distress in Japan." A paper in the Finance and Economic Discussion Series, No. 134, Federal Reserve Board, Washington, D. C. (October 1990). See also, W. Carl Kester, "Japanese Corporate Governance and the Conservation of Value in Financial Distress," *Journal of Applied Corporate Finance* (Summer 1991).

c. Lower taxes

d. Lower cost of capital

In addition, the reduction in risk from a merger may actually help bondholders and hurt stockholders.

5. Some of the most colorful language of finance stems from defensive tactics in acquisition battles. *Poison pills, golden parachutes, crown jewels,* and *greenmail* are terms that describe various anti-takeover tactics. These tactics are discussed in this chapter.

6. The empirical research on mergers and acquisitions is extensive. Its basic conclusions are that, on average, the shareholders of acquired firms fare very well, while the shareholders of acquiring firms do not gain much.

7. The keiretsu is a Japanese form of business network. It involves reciprocal shareholding and agreements among member firms.

KEY TERMS

bear hug, *818*	lockup, *818*
bidder, *798*	merger, *797*
consolidation, *797*	poison pill, *818*
crown jewels, *818*	purchase, *801*
golden parachutes, *818*	shark repellent, *818*
goodwill, *801*	tender offer, *797*
keiretsu, *822*	white knight, *818*

SUGGESTED READINGS

Several fun-to-read trade books on mergers and acquisitions have recently been published, including:

Wasserstein, Bruce. *Big Deal: 2000 and Beyond.* Warner Books, 2000. Pitaro, Regina M. *Deals, Deals and More Deals.* Gabelli University Press, 1998.

QUESTIONS & PROBLEMS

THE BASIC FORMS OF ACQUISITIONS

29.1 The Lager Brewing Corporation has acquired the Philadelphia Pretzel Company in a vertical merger. Lager Brewing has issued $300,000 in new long-term debt to pay for its purchase. ($300,000 is the purchase price.) Construct the balance sheet for the new corporation if the merger is treated as a purchase for accounting purposes. The balance sheets shown here represent the assets of both firms at their true market values. Assume these market values are also the book values.

LAGER BREWING CORPORATION
Balance Sheet
(in $ thousands)

Current assets	$ 400	Current liabilities	$ 200
Other assets	100	Long-term debt	100
Net fixed assets	500	Equity	700
Total	$1,000	Total	$1,000

PHILADELPHIA PRETZEL COMPANY
Balance Sheet
(in $ thousands)

Current assets	$ 80	Current liabilities	$ 80
Other assets	40	Equity	120
Net fixed assets	80		
Total	$200	Total	$200

29.2 Suppose the balance sheet for Philadelphia Pretzel in problem 29.1 shows the assets at their book value and not their market value of $240,000. Construct the balance sheet for the new corporation. Again, treat the transaction as a purchase.

29.3 Keep the assumptions of 29.2. Construct the balance sheet for the new corporation. Use the pooling-of-interests method to treat the transaction.

SOURCE OF SYNERGY FROM ACQUISITIONS

29.4 Indicate whether you think the following claims regarding takeovers are true or false. In each case provide a brief explanation for your answer.

a. By merging competitors, takeovers have created monopolies that will raise product prices, reduce production, and harm consumers.

b. Managers act in their own interests at times and, in reality, may not be answerable to shareholders. Takeovers may reflect runaway management.

c. In an efficient market, takeovers would not occur because market price would reflect the true value of corporations. Thus, bidding firms would not be justified in paying premiums above market prices for target firms.

d. Traders and institutional investors, having extremely short time horizons, are influenced by their perceptions of what other market traders will be thinking of stock prospects and do not value takeovers based on fundamental factors. Thus, they will sell shares in target firms despite the true value of the firms.

e. Mergers are a way of avoiding taxes because they allow the acquiring firm to write up the value of the assets of the acquired firm.

f. Acquisitions analysis frequently focuses on the total value of the firms involved. An acquisition, however, will usually affect relative values of stocks and bonds, as well as their total value.

CALCULATING THE VALUE OF THE FIRM AFTER AN ACQUISITION

29.5 The following table shows the projected cash flows and their respective discount rates after the acquisition of Small Fry Co. by Whale Co. Fill in the blanks and calculate the stock price of the new firm if it has $100 million of debt and 5 million shares of stock outstanding.

	Net Cash Flow per Year (Perpetual) (in $ millions)	Discount Rate (%)	Value (in $ millions)
Small Fry Co.	$ 8	16%	?
Whale Co.	20	10	?
Benefits from acquisition	5	?	42.5
Revenue enhancement	2.5	?	12.5
Cost reduction	2	10	?
Tax shelters	0.5	5	?
Whale Co.	33	?	?

A COST TO STOCKHOLDERS FROM REDUCTION IN RISK

29.6 The Chocolate Ice Cream Company and the Vanilla Ice Cream Company have agreed to merge and form Fudge Swirl Consolidated. Both companies are exactly alike except that they are located in different towns. The end-of-period value of each firm is determined by the weather, as shown.

State	Probability	Value
Rainy	0.1	$100,000
Warm	0.4	200,000
Hot	0.5	400,000

The weather conditions in each town are independent of those in the other. Furthermore, each company has an outstanding debt claim of $200,000. Assume that no premiums are paid in the merger.

a. What is the distribution of joint values?

b. What is the distribution of end-of-period debt values and stock values after the merger?

c. Show that the value of the combined firm is the sum of the individual values.

d. Show that the bondholders are better off and the stockholders are worse off in the combined firm than they would have been if the firms remained separate.

29.7 Cholern Electric Company (CEC) is a public utility that provides electricity to the central Colorado area. Recent events at its Mile-High Nuclear Station have been discouraging. Several shareholders have expressed concern over last year's financial statements.

Income Statement Last Year (in $ millions)		Balance Sheet End of Year (in $ millions)	
Revenue	$110	Assets	$400
Fuel	50	Debt	300
Other expenses	30	Equity	100
Interest	30		
Net income	$ 0		

Recently, a wealthy group of individuals has offered to purchase one-half of CEC's assets at fair market price. Management recommends that this offer be accepted because, "We believe our expertise in the energy industry can be better exploited by CEC if we sell our electricity generating and transmission assets and enter the telecommunications business. Although telecommunications is a riskier business than providing electricity as a public utility, it is also potentially very profitable."

Should the management approve this transaction? Why or why not?

TWO "BAD" REASONS FOR MERGERS

29.8 Refer to the Global Resources example in section 29.8 of the text. Suppose that instead of 40 shares, Global exchanges 100 of its shares for the 100 shares of Regional. The new Global Resources will now have 200 shares outstanding and earnings of $200. Assume the market is smart.

a. Calculate Global's value after the merger.
b. Calculate Global's earnings per share.
c. Calculate Global's price per share.
d. Redo your answers to (a), (b), and (c) if the market is fooled.

29.9 Coldran Aviation has voted in favor of being bought out by Arcadia Financial Corporation. Information about each company is presented below.

	Arcadia Financial	Coldran Aviation
Price-earnings ratio	16	10.8
Number of shares	100,000	50,000
Earnings	$225,000	$100,000

Stockholders in Coldran Aviation will receive six-tenths of a share of Arcadia for each share they hold.

a. How will the earnings per share (EPS) for these stockholders be changed?
b. What will be the effect on the original Arcadia stockholders of changes in the EPS?

THE NPV OF A MERGER

29.10 Fly-By-Night Couriers is analyzing the possible acquisition of Flash-in-the-Pan Restaurants. Neither firm has debt. The forecasts of Fly-By-Night show that the purchase would increase its annual after-tax cash flow by $600,000 indefinitely. The current market value of Flash-in-the-Pan is $20 million. The current market value of Fly-By-Night is $35 million. The appropriate discount rate for the incremental cash flows is 8 percent.

a. What is the synergy from the merger?
b. What is the value of Flash-in-the-Pan to Fly-By-Night?
Fly-By-Night is trying to decide whether it should offer 25 percent of its stock or $15 million in cash to Flash-in-the-Pan.

    c. What is the cost to Fly-By-Night of each alternative?

    d. What is the NPV to Fly-By-Night of each alternative?

    e. Which alternative should Fly-By-Night use?

29.11 Freeport Manufacturing is considering making an offer to purchase Portland Industries. The treasurer of Freeport has collected the following information:

	Freeport	**Portland**
Price-earnings ratio	15	12
Number of shares	1,000,000	250,000
Earnings	$1,000,000	$750,000

The treasurer also knows that securities analysts expect the earnings and dividends (currently $1.80 per share) of Portland to grow at a constant rate of 5 percent each year. Her research indicates, however, that the acquisition would provide Portland with some economies of scale that would improve this growth rate to 7 percent per year.

    a. What is the value of Portland to Freeport?

    b. If Freeport offers $40 in cash for each outstanding share of Portland, what would the NPV of the acquisition be?

    c. If instead Freeport were to offer 600,000 of its shares in exchange for the outstanding stock of Portland, what would the NPV of the acquisition be?

    d. Should the acquisition be attempted, and if so, should it be a cash or stock offer?

    e. Freeport's management thinks that 7-percent growth is too optimistic and that 6 percent is more realistic. How does this change your previous answers?

29.12 Harrods PLC has a market value of £600 million and 30 million shares outstanding. Selfridge Department Store has a market value of £200 million and 20 million shares outstanding. Harrods is contemplating acquiring Selfridge Department Store. Harrods' CFO concludes that the combined firm with synergy will be worth £1 billion and Selfridge can be acquired at a premium of £100 million.

    a. If Harrods offers 15 million shares to exchange for the 20 million shares of Selfridge, what will the after-acquisition stock price of Harrods be?

    b. To make the value of a stock offer equivalent to a cash offer of £300 million, what would be the proper exchange ratio of the two stocks?

29.13 Company A is contemplating acquiring company B. Company B's projected revenues, cost, and required investment appear in the table that follows. The table also shows sources for financing company B's investments if B is acquired by A. The table incorporates the following information:

    Company B will immediately increase its leverage with a $110 million loan, which would be followed by a $150 million dividend to company A. (This operation will increase the debt-to-equity ratio of company B from 1/3 to 1/1.)

        Company A will use $50 million of tax-loss carryforwards available from the firm's other operations.

    The terminal, total value of company B is estimated to be $900 million in five years, and the projected level of debt then is $300 million.

    The risk-free rate and the expected rate of return on the market portfolio are 6 percent and 14 percent, respectively. Company A analysts estimate the weighted average cost of capital for their company to be 10 percent. The borrowing rate for both companies is 8 percent. The beta coefficient for the stock of company B (at its current capital structure) is estimated to be 1.25.

    The board of directors of company A is presented with an offer for $68.75 per share of company B, or a total of $550 million for the 8 million shares outstanding.

    Evaluate this proposal. The table that follows may help you.

Visit us at www.mhhe.com/rwj

Projections for Company B
If Acquired by Company A
(in $ millions)

	Year 1	Year 2	Year 3	Year 4	Year 5
Sales	$800	$900	$1,000	$1,125	$1,250
Production costs	562	630	700	790	875
Depreciation	75	80	82	83	83
Other expenses	80	90	100	113	125
EBIT	83	100	118	139	167
Interest	19	22	24	25	27
EBT	64	78	94	114	140
Taxes	32	39	47	57	70
Net income	32	39	47	57	70
Investments:					
Net working capital	20	25	25	30	30
Net fixed assets	15	25	18	12	7
Total	35	50	43	42	37
Sources of financing:					
Net debt financing	35	16	16	15	12
Profit retention	0	34	27	27	25
Total	$ 35	$ 50	$ 43	$ 42	$ 37

Cash Flows—Company A

	Year 0	Year 1	Year 2	Year 3	Year 4	Year 5
Acquisition of B	—					
Dividends from B	150	—		—	—	—
Tax-loss carryforwards			25	25		—
Terminal value		—	—	—	—	—
Total	—	—	—	—	—	—

DEFENSIVE TACTICS

29.14 List the defensive tactics commonly used by target-firm managers to resist unfriendly takeover attempts.

MINICASE U.S. Steel's Acquisition of Marathon Oil

In the summer of 1981, Marathon Oil Company commissioned the First Boston Corporation to prepare an analysis of the underlying asset value of Marathon based solely on publicly available information. Before First Boston could complete the study, Mobil Corporation announced a tender offer for Marathon's common equity, thus launching one of the most eventful takeover stories in American corporate history.

On October 30, 1981, Mobil bid $85 per share for up to 40 million shares of Marathon's common equity. Before the announcement, Marathon stock traded for about $64 per share on the New York Stock Exchange. Before trading on the new information commenced, Marathon management rejected Mobil's offer as grossly inadequate and began seeking a white knight merger candidate. When trading began on Monday, November 2, 1981,

Marathon's shares shot up immediately to the $90-per-share range for a one-day abnormal excess return of more than 30 percent. The market reacted to Mobil's offer by bidding Mobil's common stock down to $25\frac{3}{8}$ for a one-day abnormal return of -4.26 percent. (November 2, 1981, was also the ex-dividend date for a $0.50 per share dividend declared earlier. The share price, however, fell $\frac{5}{8}$.) These data suggest that the market viewed the possible acquisition of Marathon by Mobil at $85 per share as a near-zero net-present-value transaction for Mobil. The dramatic response of Marathon's share price was very likely caused by anticipation of more bidding. These traders were not to be disappointed.

On November 9, the management of U.S. Steel Corporation expressed an interest in acquiring Marathon. The possible takeover price was rumored to be $100 per share in cash and notes. Presumably because the market actually valued this offer as less than Mobil's offer, Marathon's common stock showed an abnormal return for the day of -2.91 percent. The effect of the rumors on U.S. Steel's share price was insignificant, so it may be concluded that the market felt that the transaction at this price would be a zero net-present-value transaction for U.S. Steel as well.

During subsequent negotiations, U.S. Steel raised its price and actually tendered $125 per share for up to 30 million shares of Marathon stock on November 18. On the next trading day Marathon showed a one-day abnormal excess return on its share price of almost 35 percent; again the market roared its approval for the reevaluation of Marathon. U.S. Steel's common, however, showed significantly negative abnormal returns in response to this news. This indicates that the market believed U.S. Steel overbid for Marathon. Mobil's share price showed no significant abnormal return on November 18 and 19.

However, on November 25, Mobil raised its bid to $126 per share, and the market responded by lowering the value of both Mobil and U.S. Steel by significant amounts. Apparently the market believed that at this price the merger was unattractive for both Mobil and U.S. Steel. Marathon's stock fell in price by a significant amount in response to Mobil's offer, perhaps because Mobil's offer and U.S. Steel's offer were valued nearly equally by the market, and this signaled the end of the bidding and the end of speculating in Marathon.

Suppose that a U.S. Steel tender offer is structured in the following way. U.S. Steel will pay $125 (in cash) for 30 million shares of Marathon giving it 50.1 percent of the Marathon shares. After gaining voting control, U.S. Steel intends to merge with Marathon and will pay the remaining shareholders with seven-year notes worth about $85 per share. Further, suppose you own 10 shares of Marathon stock. Should you tender your shares?

Financial Distress

EXECUTIVE SUMMARY

This chapter discusses financial distress, private workouts, and bankruptcy. A firm that does not generate enough cash flow to make a contractually required payment, such as an interest payment, will experience financial distress. A firm that defaults on a required payment may be forced to liquidate its assets. More often, a defaulting firm will reorganize its financial structure. Financial restructuring involves replacing old financial claims with new ones and takes place with private workouts or legal bankruptcy. Private workouts are voluntary arrangements to restructure a company's debt, such as postponing a payment or reducing the size of the payment. Sometimes a private workout is not possible and formal bankruptcy is required. The largest formal bankruptcy in U.S. financial history occurred in December 2, 2002, when Conseco, Inc., filed Chapter 11 bankruptcy. (See Table 30.1 for information on the largest U.S. bankruptcies.)

30.1 What Is Financial Distress?

Financial distress is surprisingly hard to define precisely. This is true partly because of the variety of events befalling firms under financial distress. The list of events is almost endless but here are some examples:

Dividend reductions

Plant closings

Losses

Layoffs

CEO resignations

Plummeting stock prices

Financial distress is a situation where a firm's operating cash flows are not sufficient to satisfy current obligations (such as trade credits or interest expenses) and the firm is forced to take corrective action.[1] Financial distress may lead a firm to default on a contract, and it may involve financial restructuring between the firm, its creditors, and its equity investors. Usually the firm is forced to take actions that it would not have taken if it had sufficient cash flow.

---

[1]This definition is close to the one used by Karen Wruck, "Financial Distress: Reorganization and Organization Efficiency," *Journal of Financial Economics* 27 (1990), p. 425.

TABLE 30.1	Firm	Liabilities (in $ millions)	Bankruptcy Date
The Largest U.S. Bankruptcies	1 Conseco Inc.	$56,639.30	December 2, 2002
	2 WorldCom Inc.	45,984.00	July 2, 2002
	3 Enron Corp.	31,237.00	December 2, 2001
	4 Pacific Gas & Electric Co.	25,717.00	April 6, 2001
	5 UAL Corporation	22,164.00	December 2, 2002
	6 Texaco (including subsidiaries)	21,603.00	April 1, 1987
	7 Conseco Finance Corp.	20,278.50	December 2, 2002
	8 Olympia & York (b)	19,800.00	May 15, 1992
	9 Adelphia Communications Corp.	17,349.10	June 1, 2002
	10 Global Crossing, Ltd.	14,639.00	January 28, 2002
	11 Executive Life Insurance	14,577.00	April 1, 1991
	12 NTL, Inc.	14,134.00	May 2, 2002
	13 Mutual Benefit Life	13,500.00	July 1, 1991
	14 Reliance Group Holdings, Inc.	12,877.47	June 12, 2001
	15 Finova Group, Inc.	11,822.21	March 7, 2001
	16 Swissair	11,704.50	October 1, 2001
	17 NRG Energy, Inc.	11,579.89	May 3, 2003
	18 US Airways Group	10,640.00	August 2, 2002
	19 Kmart Corp.	10,263.00	January 22, 2002
	20 United Pan-Europe Communications NV	10,086.40	December 2, 2002
	21 Campeau (Allied & Federated)	9,947.00	January 1, 1990
	22 First Capital Holdings	9,291.00	May 1, 1991
	23 Home Holdings, Inc.	9,132.00	January 15, 1998
	24 Baldwin United	9,000.00	September 1, 1983
	25 Federal Mogul Corp.	8,232.70	October 1, 2001
	26 Owens Corning	7,375.00	October 5, 2000
	27 Williams Communications Group, Inc.	7,153.80	April 22, 2002
	28 Comdisco, Inc.	6,742.00	July 16, 2001
	29 ANC Rental Corp.	6,252.40	November 13, 2001
	30 Continental Airlines (II)	6,200.00	December 1, 1990

SOURCE: Supplied by Edward I. Altman, NYU Salomon Center, Stern School of Business.

Our definition of financial distress can be expanded somewhat by linking it to insolvency. Insolvency is defined in *Black's Law Dictionary* as:[2]

> Inability to pay one's debts; lack of means of paying one's debts. Such a condition of a woman's (or man's) assets and liability that the former made immediately available would be insufficient to discharge the latter.

This definition has two general themes, stocks and flows.[3] These two ways of thinking about insolvency are depicted in Figure 30.1. The stock-based insolvency occurs when a firm has negative net worth, and so the value of assets is less than the value of its debts. Flow-based insolvency occurs when operating cash flow is insufficient to meet current obligations. Flow-based insolvency refers to the inability to pay one's debts.

Concept Questions

1. Can you describe financial distress?
2. What are stock-based insolvency and flow-based insolvency?

[2] Taken from *Black's Law Dictionary*, 5th ed. (St. Paul, Minn.: West Publishing Company), p. 716.

[3] Edward Altman was one of the first to distinguish between stock-based insolvency and flow-based insolvency. See Edward Altman, *Corporate Financial Distress: A Complete Guide to Predicting, Avoiding and Dealing with Bankruptcy* (New York: John Wiley & Sons, 1993, 2nd edition).

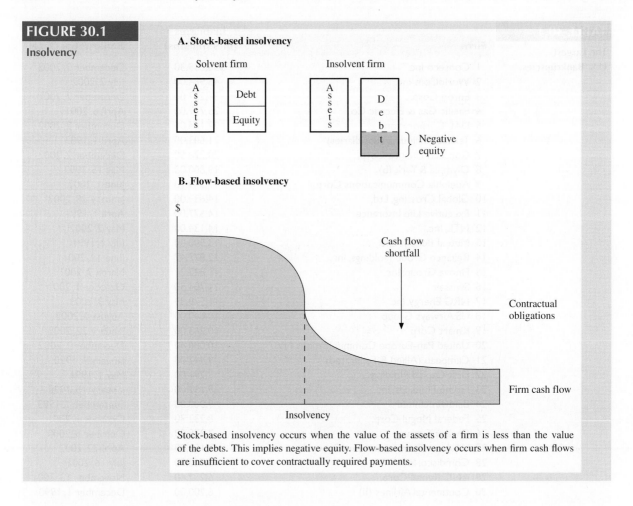

FIGURE 30.1

Insolvency

A. Stock-based insolvency

Solvent firm   Insolvent firm

Assets | Debt

Assets | Equity

Assets | Debt

Negative equity

B. Flow-based insolvency

Cash flow shortfall

Contractual obligations

Firm cash flow

Insolvency

Stock-based insolvency occurs when the value of the assets of a firm is less than the value of the debts. This implies negative equity. Flow-based insolvency occurs when firm cash flows are insufficient to cover contractually required payments.

30.2 What Happens in Financial Distress?

In the early 1990s Trans World Airline, Inc. (TWA) experienced financial distress. It lost money in 1989, 1990, and 1991 and steadily lost its market share to rivals United, American, and Delta. Having seen Eastern and Pan Am disappear, airline travelers had good reason to be nervous about buying tickets from TWA.

In the summer of 1991, TWA General Counsel Mark A. Buckstein bet Carl Icahn, TWA owner and CEO, $1,000 that the airline would be forced to file involuntary bankruptcy by September 1991.[4] Icahn argued that he could arrange a private restructuring and avoid formal bankruptcy. Icahn won the bet, but TWA eventually filed for bankruptcy on January 31, 1992. Icahn was quoted as saying the bankruptcy reorganization would give TWA the time it needed to turn the firm around. The odds favored Icahn because financial distress does not usually result in a firm's death. TWA was reorganized in 1993. Icahn resigned as CEO and gave up all ownership claims. However, TWA continued to struggle and for the second time, on July 3, 1995, filed for bankruptcy. Several months later, it emerged from bankruptcy after exchanging $500 million of debt for equity. Remarkably, on January 9, 2001, the board of TWA again approved a plan to file for bankruptcy. The plan included the

---

[4]The bet was reported in "Carl has 9 lives but he is betting up to $8\frac{1}{2}$," *Business Week,* February 24, 1992.

purchase of TWA by American Airlines for $500 million. (So far, no public firm has ever filed for bankruptcy four times.)

Firms deal with financial distress in several ways, such as:

1. Selling major assets.
2. Merging with another firm.
3. Reducing capital spending and research and development.
4. Issuing new securities.
5. Negotiating with banks and other creditors.
6. Exchanging debt for equity.
7. Filing for bankruptcy.

Items (1), (2), and (3) concern the firm's assets. Items (4), (5), (6), and (7) involve the right-hand side of the firm's balance sheet and are examples of financial restructuring. Financial distress may involve both asset restructuring and financial restructuring (i.e., changes on both sides of the balance sheet).

Some firms may actually benefit from financial distress by restructuring their assets. In an earlier chapter we showed that, in 1986, Goodyear Tire and Rubber's levered recapitalization changed the firm's behavior and forced the firm to dispose of unrelated businesses. Goodyear's cash flow was not sufficient to cover required payments, and it was forced to sell its noncore businesses. For some firms financial distress may bring about new organizational forms and new operating strategies. However, in this chapter we focus on financial restructuring.

Financial restructuring may occur in a private workout or a bankruptcy reorganization under Chapter 11 of the U.S. Bankruptcy Code. Figure 30.2 shows how large public firms move through financial distress. Approximately one-half of the financial restructurings

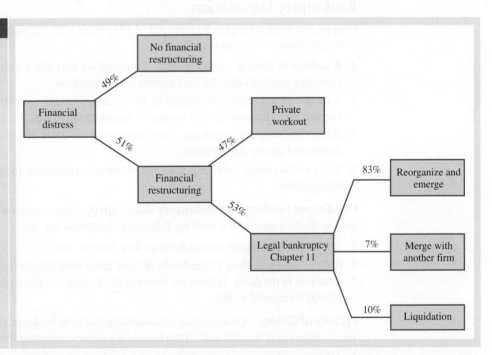

FIGURE 30.2

What Happens in Financial Distress

SOURCE: Karen H. Wruck, "Financial Distress: Reorganization and Organizational Efficiency," *Journal of Financial Economics* 27 (1990), Figure 2. See also Stuart C. Gilson, Kose John, and Larry N. P. Lang, "Troubled Debt Restructurings: An Empirical Study of Private Reorganization of Firms in Defaults," *Journal of Financial Economics* 27 (1990); and Lawrence A. Weiss, "Bankruptcy Resolution: Direct Costs and Violation of Priority of Claims," *Journal of Financial Economics* 27 (1990).

have been done via private workouts. As was true for TWA, most large public firms (83 percent) that file for Chapter 11 bankruptcy are able to reorganize and continue to do business.[5]

Financial distress can serve as a firm's "early warning" system for trouble. Firms with more debt will experience financial distress earlier than firms with less debt. However, firms that experience financial distress earlier will have more time for private workouts and reorganization. Firms with low leverage will experience financial distress later and, in many instances, be forced to liquidate.

<table>
<tr><td>**Concept**
Questions</td><td>1. Why doesn't financial distress always cause firms to die?
2. What is a benefit of financial distress?</td></tr>
</table>

30.3 Bankruptcy Liquidation and Reorganization

Firms that cannot or choose not to make contractually required payments to creditors have two basic options: liquidation or reorganization. This section discusses bankruptcy liquidation and reorganization.

Liquidation means termination of the firm as a going concern; it involves selling the assets of the firm for salvage value. The proceeds, net of transactions costs, are distributed to creditors in order of established priority.

Reorganization is the option of keeping the firm a going concern; it sometimes involves issuing new securities to replace old securities.

Liquidation and formal reorganization may be done by bankruptcy. *Bankruptcy* is a legal proceeding and can be done voluntarily with the corporation filing the petition or involuntarily with the creditors filing the petition.

Bankruptcy Liquidation

Chapter 7 of the Bankruptcy Reform Act of 1978 deals with "straight" liquidation. The following sequence of events is typical:

1. A petition is filed in a federal court. Corporations may file a voluntary petition, or involuntary petitions may be filed against the corporation.
2. A trustee-in-bankruptcy is elected by the creditors to take over the assets of the debtor corporation. The trustees will attempt to liquidate the assets.
3. When the assets are liquidated, after payment of the costs of administration, assets are distributed among the creditors.
4. If any assets remain, after expenses and payments to creditors, they are distributed to the shareholders.

Conditions Leading to Involuntary Bankruptcy   An involuntary bankruptcy petition may be filed by creditors if both the following conditions are met:

1. The corporation is not paying debts as they become due.
2. If there are more than 12 creditors, at least three with claims totaling $5,000 or more must join in the filing. If there are fewer than 12 creditors, then only one with a claim of $5,000 is required to file.

Priority of Claims   Once a corporation is determined to be bankrupt, liquidation takes place. The distribution of the proceeds of the liquidation occurs according to the following priority:

1. *Administration expenses,* associated with liquidating the bankrupt's assets.
2. Unsecured claims arising after the filing of an involuntary bankruptcy petition.

---

[5]However, only about 15 percent of all firms (public or private) going through a Chapter 11 bankruptcy are successfully reorganized.

3. Wages, salaries, and commissions.

4. Contributions to employee benefit plans arising within 180 days before the filing date.

5. Consumer claims.

6. Tax claims.

7. Secured and unsecured creditors' claims.

8. Preferred stockholders' claims.

9. Common stockholders' claims.

The priority rule in liquidation is the **absolute priority rule** (APR).

One qualification to this list concerns secured creditors. Liens on property are outside APR ordering. However, if the secured property is liquidated and provides cash insufficient to cover the amount owed them, the secured creditors join with unsecured creditors in dividing the remaining liquidating value. In contrast, if the secured property is liquidated for proceeds greater than the secured claim, the net proceeds are used to pay unsecured creditors and others.

EXAMPLE

The B. O. Drug Company is to be liquidated. Its liquidating value is $2.7 million. Bonds worth $1.5 million are secured by a mortgage on the B. O. Drug Company corporate headquarters building, which is sold for $1 million; $200,000 is used to cover administrative costs and other claims (including unpaid wages, pension benefits, consumer claims, and taxes). After paying $200,000 to the administrative priority claims, the amount available to pay secured and unsecured creditors is $2.5 million. This is less than the amount of unpaid debt of $4 million.

Under APR all creditors must be paid before shareholders, and the mortgage bondholders have first claim on the $1 million obtained from the sale of the headquarters building.

The trustee has proposed the following distribution:

Type of Claim	Prior Claim	Cash Received under Liquidation
Bonds (secured by mortgage)	$ 1,500,000	$1,500,000
Subordinated debentures	2,500,000	1,000,000
Common stockholders	10,000,000	0
Total	$14,000,000	$2,500,000

Calculation of the Distribution		
Cash received from sale of assets available for distribution		$2,500,000
Cash paid to secured bondholders on sale of mortgaged property		1,000,000
Available to bond- and debenture-holders		$1,500,000
Total claims remaining ($4,000,000 less payment of $1,000,000 on secured bonds)		$3,000,000
Distribution of remaining $1,500,000 to cover total remaining claims of $3,000,000		

Type of Claim Remaining	Claim on Liquidation Proceeds	Cash Received
Bonds	$ 500,000	$ 500,000
Debentures	2,500,000	1,000,000
Total	$3,000,000	$1,500,000

Edward I. Altman* on Corporate Financial Distress and Bankruptcy

As we entered the new millennium, corporate distress and bankruptcy was no longer a niche area of corporate evolution. Indeed, the bankruptcy rate of U.S. corporations reached record proportions in 2001/2002, with as many as 77 *large* corporations filing for protection under Chapter 11 of the Bankruptcy Code with *liabilities* greater than $1 billion—an unprecedented number. While telecommunication firms "lead" the way, airlines, steel companies, retailers, and, in general, a broad cross-section of industrial sectors have succumbed to a combination of excessive debt and poor operating results. The average American company is far riskier today than it was just two decades ago, and the roles of the bankruptcy courts and restructuring specialists have never been more important.

Financial distress of private and public entities throughout the world is a frequent occurrence with important implications to their many stakeholders. While the role of corporate bankruptcy laws is clear—either to provide a legal procedure that permits firms, which have temporary liquidity problems, to restructure and successfully emerge as continuing entities or to provide an orderly process to liquidate assets for the benefit of creditors before asset values are dissipated—bankruptcy laws differ markedly from country to country. It is generally agreed that the U.S. Chapter 11 provisions under the Bankruptcy Reform Act of 1978 provide the most protection for bankrupt firms' assets and result in a greater likelihood of successful reorganization than is found in other countries where liquidation and sale of the assets for the benefit of creditors is more likely the result. But, the U.S. Code's process is usually lengthy (averaging close to two years, except where a sufficient number of creditors agree

in advance via a prepackaged Chapter 11) and expensive and the reorganized entity is not always successful in avoiding subsequent distress. If the reorganization is not successful, then liquidation under Chapter 7 will usually ensue.

Bankruptcy processes in the industrialized world outside the United States strongly favor senior creditors who obtain control of the firm and seek to enforce greater adherence to debt contracts. The U.K. process, for example, is speedy and less costly but the reduced costs can result in undesirable liquidations, unemployment and underinvestment. The new bankruptcy code in Germany attempts to reduce the considerable power of secured creditors but it is still closer to the U.K. system. In the United States, creditors and owners can negotiate "violations" to the "absolute priority rule"—this "rule" holds that more senior creditors must be paid in full, prior to any payments to more junior creditors or to owners. (However, the so-called "violations" to absolute priority have empirically been shown to be relatively small, e.g., under 10 percent of firm value.) Finally, the U.S. system gives the court the right to sanction post-petition debt financing, usually with super-priority status over existing claims, thereby facilitating the continuing operation of the firm. Recently, France has had similar successful experience.

A measure of performance of the U.S. bankruptcy system is the proportion of firms which emerge successfully. The results in the United States of late are somewhat mixed, with close to 70 percent of large firms emerging but probably less than 20 percent of smaller entities. And, a not insignificant number of firms suffer subsequent distress and may file again (Chapter 22).

*Edward I. Altman is Max L. Heine Professor of Finance, NYU Stern School of Business. He is widely recognized as one of the world's experts on bankruptcy and credit analysis as well as the distressed debt and high yield bond markets.

Bankruptcy Reorganization

Corporate reorganization takes place under Chapter 11 of the Federal Bankruptcy Reform Act of 1978. The general objective of a proceeding under Chapter 11 is to plan to restructure the corporation with some provision for repayment of creditors. A typical sequence of events follows:

1. A voluntary petition can be filed by the corporation, or an involuntary petition can be filed by three or more creditors (or one creditor if the total creditors are fewer than 12—see

Regardless of the location, one of the objectives of bankruptcy and other distressed workout arrangements is that creditors and other suppliers of capital clearly know their rights and expected recoveries in the event of a distressed situation. When these are not transparent and/or are based on outdated processes with arbitrary and possibly corrupt outcomes, then the entire economic system suffers and growth is inhibited. Such is the case in several emerging market countries. Revision of these outdated systems should be a priority.

In addition to the comparative benefits of different national restructuring systems, a number of intriguing theoretical and empirical issues are related to the distressed firm. Among these are corporate debt capacity, manager-creditor-owner incentives, ability to predict distress, data and computations for default rate estimation, investment in securities of distressed firms and post-reorganization performance assessment.

Corporate distress has a major impact on creditor/debtor relationships and, combined with business risk and tax considerations, affects the capital structure of companies. One key question is how costly are the *expected* distress costs compared to the *expected* tax benefits of using leverage—the so-called trade-off theory. Most analysts agree that the sum of direct (e.g., legal fees) and indirect costs is in the range of 10–20 percent of firm value.

Whether the taking of excess risk and over-investment are examples of agency conflicts between managers and creditors rests upon one's view as to who are the true residual owners of a distressed firm—the existing equityholders or creditors who will more than likely be the new owners of a reorganized entity. Existing management has the exclusive right to file the first plan of reorganization within 120 days of filing, with exclusivity extensions possible. Their incentives and influence can be biased, however, and not always in accord with other stakeholders, primarily creditors. Limiting this exclusivity would appear to be desirable to speed up the process and restrict managerial abuse.

Distress prediction models have intrigued researchers and practitioners for more than 50 years. Models have evolved from univariate financial statement ratios to multivariate statistical classification models, to contingent claim and market value based approaches and finally to using artificial intelligence techniques. Most large financial institutions have one or more of the above types of models in place as more sophisticated credit-risk management frameworks are being introduced, sometimes combined with aggressive credit asset portfolio strategies. Increasingly, private credit assets are being treated as securities with estimates of default and recovery given default the critical inputs to their valuation.

Perhaps the most intriguing by-product of corporate distress is the development of a relatively new class of investors known as *vultures*. These money managers specialize in securities of distressed and defaulted companies. Defaulted bonds have had a small following ever since the Great Depression of the 1930s, but this has grown to more than 70 institutional "vulture" specialists, actively managing over $60 billion in 2003. The size of the distressed and defaulted market grew dramatically in recent years and by year-end 2002, estimates by this author were over $940 billion (face value) and $510 billion (market value) for the public and private markets combined (mainly public defaulted and distressed bonds and private bank loans). Distressed debt investors have target annual rates of return of 15 to 25 percent. Although these annual returns are sometimes earned, the overall annual rate of return from 1987 through 2002 has been less than 10 percent—similar to the high yield bonds and considerably below returns in the stock market. Yet, the incredible supply of potential investment opportunities has created unprecedented interest in this *alternative asset* class.

the previous section). The involuntary petition must allege that the corporation is not paying its debts.

2. A federal judge either approves or denies the petition. If the petition is approved, a time for filing proofs of claims of creditors and of shareholders is set.

3. In most cases, the corporation (the "debtor in possession") continues to run the business.

4. The corporation is given 120 days to submit a reorganization plan.

5. Creditors and shareholders are divided into classes. A class of creditors accepts the plan if two-thirds of the class (in dollar amount) and one-half of the class (in number) have indicated approval.[6]

6. After acceptance by creditors, the plan is confirmed by the court.

7. Payments in cash, property, and securities are made to creditors and shareholders. The plan may provide for the issuance of new securities.

EXAMPLE

Suppose B. O. Drug Co. decides to reorganize under Chapter 11. Generally, senior claims are honored in full before various other claims receive anything. Assume that the "going concern" value of B. O. Drug Co. is $3 million and that its balance sheet is as shown:

Assets	$3,000,000
Liabilities	
Mortgage bonds	1,500,000
Subordinated debentures	2,500,000
Stockholders' equity	−1,000,000

The firm has proposed the following reorganization plan:

Old Security	Old Claim	New Claim with Reorganization Plan
Mortgage bonds	$1,500,000	$1,500,000
Subordinated debentures	2,500,000	1,000,000

and a distribution of new securities under a new claim with a reorganization plan:

Old Security	Received under Proposed Reorganization Plan
Mortgage bonds	$1,000,000 in 9% senior debentures
	$500,000 in 11% subordinated debentures
Debentures	$1,000,000 in 8% preferred stock
	$500,000 in common stock

However, it will be very difficult for the firm to convince secured creditors (mortgage bonds) to consent to accepting unsecured debentures of equal face value. In addition, the corporation may wish to allow the old stockholders to retain some participation in the firm. Needless to say, this would be a violation of the absolute priority rule and the holders of the debentures would not be happy.

Concept
Questions

1. **What is bankruptcy?**
2. **What is the difference between liquidation and reorganization?**

---

[6]We are describing the standard events in a bankruptcy reorganization. The general rule is that a reorganization plan will be accepted by the court if all of the creditor class accept it and it will be rejected if all of the creditor class reject it. However, if one or more (but not all) of the classes accept it, the plan may be eligible for a "cram down" procedure. A cram down takes place if the bankruptcy court finds a plan fair and equitable and accepts the plan for all creditors.

Absolute Priority Rule

The absolute priority rule states that senior claims are fully satisfied before junior claims receive anything.

Deviation from Rule

Equityholders	Expectation: No payout
	Reality: Payout in 81 percent of cases
Unsecured creditors	Expectation: Full payout after secured creditors
	Reality: Violation in 78 percent of cases
Secured creditors	Expectation: Full payout
	Reality: Full payout in 92 percent of cases

Reasons for Violations

Creditors want to avoid the expense of litigation. Debtors are given a 120-day opportunity to cause delay and harm value.

Managers often own equity and demand to be compensated.

Bankruptcy judges like consensual plans and pressure parties to compromise.

SOURCE: Lawrence A. Weiss, "Bankruptcy Resolution: Direct Costs and Violation of Priority of Claims," *Journal of Financial Economics* 27 (1990).

30.4 Private Workout or Bankruptcy: Which Is Best?

A firm that defaults on its debt payments will need to restructure its financial claims.The firm will have two choices: formal bankruptcy or **private workout.** The previous section described two types of formal bankruptcies: bankruptcy liquidation and bankruptcy reorganization. This section compares private workouts with bankruptcy reorganizations. Both types of financial restructuring involve exchanging new financial claims for old financial claims. Usually senior debt is replaced with junior debt and debt is replaced with equity. Much recent academic research has described what happens in private workouts and formal bankruptcies.[7]

- Historically, one-half of financial restructurings have been private but, recently, formal bankruptcy has dominated.
- Firms that emerge from private workouts experience stock-price increases that are much greater than those for firms emerging from formal bankruptcies.
- The direct costs of private workouts are much less than the costs of formal bankruptcies.
- Top management usually loses pay and sometimes jobs in both private workouts and formal bankruptcies.

These facts, when taken together, seem to suggest that a private workout is much better than a formal bankruptcy. We then ask the question: Why do firms ever use formal bankruptcies to restructure?

---

[7]For example, see Stuart Gilson, "Managing Default: Some Evidence on How Firms Choose between Workouts and Bankruptcy," *Journal of Applied Corporate Finance* (Summer 1991); and Stuart C. Gilson, Kose John, and Larry N. P. Lang, "Troubled Debt Restructuring: An Empirical Study of Private Reorganization of Firms in Defaults," *Journal of Financial Economics* 27 (1990).

The Marginal Firm

For the average firm a formal bankruptcy is more costly than a private workout, but for other firms formal bankruptcy is better. Formal bankruptcy allows firms to issue debt that is senior to all previously incurred debt. This new debt is "debtor in possession" (DIP) debt. For firms that need a temporary injection of cash, DIP debt makes bankruptcy reorganization an attractive alternative to a private workout. There are some tax advantages to bankruptcy. Firms do not lose tax carryforwards in bankruptcy, and the tax treatment of the cancellation of indebtness is better in bankruptcy. Also, interest on prebankruptcy unsecured debt stops accruing in formal bankruptcy.

Holdouts

Bankruptcy is usually better for the equity investors than it is for the creditors. Using DIP debt and stopping prebankruptcy interest on unsecured debt helps the stockholders and hurts the creditors. As a consequence, equity investors can usually hold out for a better deal in bankruptcy. The absolute priority rule, which favors creditors over equity investors, is usually violated in formal bankruptcies. One recent study found that in 81 percent of recent bankruptcies the equity investor obtained some compensation.[8] Under Chapter 11 the creditors are often forced to give up some of their seniority rights to get management and the equity investors to agree to a deal.

Complexity

A firm with a complicated capital structure will have more trouble putting together a private workout. Firms with secured creditors and trade creditors such as Macy's and Carter Hale will usually use formal bankruptcy because it is too hard to reach an agreement with many different types of creditors.

Lack of Information

There is an inherent conflict of interest between equity investors and creditors, and the conflict is accentuated when both have incomplete information about the circumstances of financial distress. When a firm initially experiences a cash flow shortfall, it may not know whether the shortfall is permanent or temporary. If the shortfall is permanent, creditors will push for a formal reorganization or liquidation. However, if the cash flow shortfall is temporary, formal reorganization or liquidation may not be necessary. Equity investors will push for this viewpoint. This conflict of interest cannot easily be resolved.

These last two points are especially important. They suggest that financial distress will be more expensive (cheaper) if complexity is high (low) and information is incomplete (complete). Complexity and lack of information make cheap workouts less likely.

Concept
Questions

1. **What are two ways a firm can restructure its finances?**
2. **Why do firms use formal bankruptcy?**

---

[8]Lawrence A. Weiss, "Bankruptcy Dissolution: Direct Costs and Violation of Priority and Claims," *Journal of Financial Economics* 23 (1990). However, W. Beranek, R. Boehmer, and B. Smith, in "Much Ado about Nothing: Absolute Priority Deviations in Chapter 11," *Financial Management* (Autumn 1996), find 33.8 percent of bankruptcy reorganizations leave the stockholders with nothing. They also point out deviations from the absolute priority rule are to be expected because the bankruptcy code allows creditors to waive their rights if they perceive a waiver to be in their best interests. A rejoinder can be found in Allan C. Eberhart and Lawrence A. Weiss, "The Importance of Deviations from the Absolute Priority Rule in Chapter 11 Bankruptcy Proceedings," *Financial Management* 27 (1998).

TABLE 30.2	Firm	Business	Filing Dates	Approved Date
Recent Prepackaged Bankruptcies of Large U.S. Firms	TWA	Air transport	July 3, 1995	August 23, 1995
	Memorex Telex	Computer equipment	January 6, 1992	February 7, 1992
	Taj Mahal	Casino	August 8, 1991	October 4, 1991
	JPS Textiles	Textiles	February 7, 1991	March 21, 1991
	Southland	7-11 convenience stores	October 24, 1990	March 5, 1991

30.5 Prepackaged Bankruptcy[9]

On October 1, 1986, the Crystal Oil Company filed for protection from its creditors under Chapter 11 of the U.S. Bankruptcy Code. Given the firm's heavy indebtedness, perhaps the outcome was not very surprising. However, less than three months later Crystal Oil came out of bankruptcy with a different capital structure. This surprised many people because, traditionally, bankruptcy has been very costly and often takes many years to emerge from. Crystal Oil avoided a lengthy bankruptcy by negotiating a reorganization plan with its creditors several months before the bankruptcy filing date.

This new reorganization arrangement has been called **prepackaged bankruptcy**. Table 30.2 lists several recent prepackaged bankruptcies of large firms. Prepackaged bankruptcy is a combination of private workout and legal bankruptcy. In prepackaged bankruptcy the firm and most of its creditors agree to private reorganization outside formal bankruptcy. After the private reorganization is put together (i.e., prepackaged), the firm files a formal bankruptcy under Chapter 11.

Prepackaged bankruptcy arrangements require that most creditors reach agreement privately. Prepackaged bankruptcy doesn't seem to work when there are thousands of reluctant trade creditors, such as in the case of a retail trading firm like Macy's and Revco D. S.[10]

The main benefit of prepackaged bankruptcy is that it forces holdouts to accept a bankruptcy reorganization. If a large fraction of a firm's creditors can agree privately to a reorganization plan, the holdout problem may be avoided. It makes a reorganization plan in formal bankruptcy easier to put together.[11]

A study by McConnell, Lease, and Tashjian reports that prepackaged bankruptcies offer many of the advantages of a formal bankruptcy, but they are also more efficient. Their results suggest that the time spent and the direct costs of resolving financial distress are less in a prepackaged bankruptcy than in a formal bankruptcy.[12]

Concept Questions

1. What is prepackaged bankruptcy?
2. What is the main benefit of prepackaged bankruptcy?

---

[9]John McConnell and Henri Servaes "The Economics of Pre-packaged Bankruptcy," *Journal of Applied Corporate Finance* (Summer 1991), describe prepackaged bankruptcy and the Crystal Oil Company.

[10]S. Chattergee, U. S. Dhillon, and G. G. Ramirez, in "Prepackaged Bankruptcies and Workouts," *Financial Management* (Spring 1996), find that firms using prepackaged bankruptcy arrangements are smaller, in better financial shape, and have greater short-term liquidity problems than firms using private workouts or Chapter 11.

[11]The original reorganization plan of Crystal Oil was accepted by the public creditors, but it was not accepted by the secured creditors. During bankruptcy a slightly revised plan was "crammed down" on the secured creditors. A bankruptcy court can force creditors to participate in a reorganization if it can be shown that the plan is "fair and equitable."

[12]John J. McConnell, Ronald Lease, and Elizabeth Tashjian, "Prepacks as a Mechanism for Resolving Financial Distress: The Evidence," *Journal of Applied Corporate Finance* 8 (1996).

The Decision to File for Bankruptcy: The Case of Revco[13]

Revco D. S. has a special place in the history of finance. It was both one of the largest leveraged buyouts and one of the largest bankruptcies in U.S. financial history.

In July 1988, Revco filed for bankruptcy under Chapter 11 of the U.S. Bankruptcy Code. At the time of its bankruptcy it was one of the largest retail drugstore chains in the United States. Revco's bankruptcy came at the end of four very turbulent years.

Up to 1984 the shareholders of Revco had reason to be pleased with its operating results. By 1984 Revco was operating approximately 2,000 stores in 30 states. Its gross profit margins averaged close to 7 percent. From 1971 to 1984 Revco had grown in sales and profits in excess of 20 percent per annum. In January 1984, its stock traded at an all-time high of $37.50. Revco's financial difficulty began in the spring of 1984.[14]

1. In April 1984, E-Ferol, a vitamin product manufactured by a Revco subsidiary, was allegedly linked to 38 infant deaths and was recalled.

2. In May 1984, Revco acquired Odd Lot Trading, Inc., for over $100 million of Revco common stock. The acquisition gave Barnard Marden and Isaac Perlmutter, owners of Odd Lot Trading, 12 percent ownership in Revco. However, Perlmutter and Marden were not passive investors, and they had many new ideas for "improving" Revco. Eventually, hostility broke out between Perlmutter and Marden and Stanley Dworkin, the CEO of Revco.

3. In 1985 Revco's competitors, Rite-Aid and Eckerd, adopted aggressive pricing tactics in an attempt to gain market share.

4. In July 1985, Revco bought out Marden's and Perlmutter's stakes in Revco for $98 million.

5. On December 29, 1986, Revco announced a leveraged buyout (LBO) with a private investor group. Because of the LBO, Revco's long-term debt increased from $44.7 million in 1985 to over $700 million after the LBO in 1986. Eventually, its total debt rose to $1.3 billion, and, in April 1988, Revco announced that it could not make the interest payment on its subordinated notes.

6. In March 1987, Revco decided to change its strategic orientation. Instead of "everyday low prices" on a narrow product line, Revco expanded its product line to include TVs, furniture, and appliances, and used selective promotions.

7. The new strategic orientation did not work, and Revco generated large losses in 1987.

8. In July 1988, Revco filed for bankruptcy under Chapter 11 of the Bankruptcy Code.

9. Four years later, Revco emerged from bankruptcy.

10. On June 2, 1997, Revco was merged into CVS in a $2.9 billion stock swap, making CVS the second largest drugstore chain in the United States. It was reported that CVS would close Revco's headquarters in Twinsburg, Ohio, and reduce costs by eliminating redundant corporate offices and outlets.

Why did Revco file for formal bankruptcy instead of private restructuring? What were the costs of the Revco bankruptcy? There are no easy answers to these questions.

1. *The Direct Costs of Bankruptcy.* Formal bankruptcy can be expensive and time-consuming. Revco was in Chapter 11 bankruptcy for almost four years and paid out over $40.5 million in direct

---

[13]See Karen H. Wruck, "What Really Went Wrong at Revco," *Journal of Applied Corporate Finance* (Summer 1991), pp. 71–92. This article contains an excellent description of the troubles of Revco.

[14]Stephen Phillips, "Revco, Anatomy of an LBO That Failed," *Business Week* (October 3, 1988), describes the troubles of Revco.

bankruptcy costs (2.7 percent of the buyout price).[15] Below are some of the direct bankruptcy fees (in millions).

Law firms	
Baker & Hostetler	$ 7.5
Fried Frank	3.2
Accounting firms	
Arthur Andersen	7.4
Ernst & Young	4.2
Investment bankers	
Lazard Freres	3.5
Other	14.3
	$40.5

2. *The Indirect Costs of Financial Distress.* There are many indirect costs of financial distress, including management distractions, loss of customers, and loss of reputation. The indirect costs of financial distress may occur whether or not formal bankruptcy is declared. In the case of Revco, financial distress caused a costly change in management and strategic direction.

3. *The Costs of a Complicated Financial Structure.* Firms such as Revco that have bank loans, senior subordinated debt, and junior subordinated debt will have a very hard time getting all claimholders to agree to an out-of-court settlement. For a retailer like Revco private agreements are especially difficult because of the large number of trade creditors. It is axiomatic that the more complicated a firm's financial structure, the more difficult it will be to work out private arrangements to avoid bankruptcy. Conflicts between managers, shareholders, and creditors make reaching a private agreement difficult. There is a natural tendency for each group to try to gain value at the expense of the others.

Concept
Questions

1. **Why did it take Revco D. S. so long to emerge from bankruptcy?**
2. **What are some of the costs of the Revco D. S. bankruptcy?**

30.6 SUMMARY AND CONCLUSIONS

This chapter examines what happens when firms experience financial distress.

1. Financial distress is a situation where a firm's operating cash flow is not sufficient to cover contractual obligations. Financially distressed firms are often forced to take corrective action and undergo financial restructuring. Financial restructuring involves exchanging new financial claims for old ones.

2. Financial restructuring can be accomplished with a private workout or formal bankruptcy. Financial restructuring can involve liquidation or reorganization. However, liquidation is not common.

3. Corporate bankruptcy involves Chapter 7 liquidation or Chapter 11 reorganization. An essential feature of the U.S. Bankruptcy Code is the absolute priority rule. The absolute priority rule states that senior creditors are paid in full before junior creditors receive anything. However, in practice the absolute priority rule is often violated.

4. A new form of financial restructuring is prepackaged bankruptcy. It is a hybrid of a private workout and formal bankruptcy.

[15]George Anders, "Revco Saga: On How the Buy Out Bonanza Became a Frenzy of Fees in Chapter 11," *The Wall Street Journal* (May 16, 1991).

5. One of the classic bankruptcies involved Revco D. S. Revco's bankruptcy was long and costly. The main reason was Revco's complicated financial structure, which made agreement among creditors very difficult.

KEY TERMS

absolute priority rule, *835*
financial distress, *830*
liquidation, *834*

prepackaged bankruptcy, *841*
private workout, *839*
reorganization, *834*

SUGGESTED READINGS

An excellent book on financial distress by one of the leading authorities is

Altman, Edward I. *Corporate Financial Distress: A Complete Guide to Predicting, Avoiding and Dealing with Bankruptcy* (New York: John Wiley & Sons, 1993, 2nd edition).

Many recent academic articles on financial distress can be found in

Jenson, Michael, and Richard Rubeck, eds. "Symposium on the Structure and Governance of Enterprise Part II." *Journal of Financial Economics* 27 (1990). Articles by Lawrence Weiss, Stuart G. Gilson, Kose John, Larry N. P. Lang, Steven Kaplan, David Reishus, Frank Easterbrook, and Karen H. Wruck appear.

Senbet, L., and James Seward. "Financial Distress, Bankruptcy and Reorganization." Chapter 28 in *Handbooks in OR and MS,* Vol. 9, R. A. Jarrow, V. Maksimovic, and W. T. Ziembe, eds. (1995).

QUESTIONS & PROBLEMS

FINANCIAL DISTRESS?

BANKRUPTCY LIQUIDATION AND REORGANIZATION

30.1 Define financial distress using the stock-based and flow-based approaches.

30.2 What are some benefits of financial distress?

30.3 When the Beacon Computer Company (BCC) filed for bankruptcy under Chapter 7 of the U.S. Bankruptcy Code, it had the following balance sheet:

Liquidating Value		Claims	
Net realizable assets	$5,000	Trade credit	$1,000
		Secured notes (by a mortgage)	1,000
		Senior debenture	3,000
		Junior debenture	1,000
		Equity	(−1,000)

As trustee, what distribution of liquidating value do you propose?

30.4 When the Master Printing Company filed for bankruptcy, it filed under Chapter 11 of the U.S. Bankruptcy Code. Its balance sheet is shown below:

Assets		Claims	
Going concern value	$15,000	Mortgage bonds	$10,000
		Senior debenture	6,000
		Junior debenture	4,000
		Equity	(−5,000)

As trustee, what reorganization plan would you accept?

PRIVATE WORKOUT OR BANKRUPTCY: WHICH IS BEST?

30.5 Explain the following two terms.
a. APR
b. DIP

30.6 Why do so many firms file for legal bankruptcy when private workouts are so much less expensive?

| Appendix 30A | # Predicting Corporate Bankruptcy: The Z-Score Model[16] |

Many potential lenders use credit scoring models to assess the creditworthiness of prospective borrowers. The general idea is to find factors that enable the lenders to discriminate between good and bad credit risks. To put it more precisely, lenders want to identify attributes of the borrower that can be used to predict default or bankruptcy.

Edward Altman has developed a model using financial statement ratios and multiple discriminant analyses to predict bankruptcy for publicly traded manufacturing firms. The resultant model is of the form:

$$Z = 3.3 \frac{\text{EBIT}}{\text{Total assets}} + 1.2 \frac{\text{Net working capital}}{\text{Total assets}}$$
$$+ 1.0 \frac{\text{Sales}}{\text{Total assets}} + .6 \frac{\text{Market value of equity}}{\text{Book value of debt}}$$
$$+ 1.4 \frac{\text{Accumulated retained earnings}}{\text{Total assets}}$$

where Z is an index of bankruptcy.

A score of Z less than 2.675 indicates that a firm has a 95 percent chance of becoming bankrupt within one year. However, Altman's results show that in practice the area between 1.81 and 2.99 should be thought of as a gray area. In actual use, bankruptcy would be predicted if $Z \le 1.81$ and nonbankruptcy if $Z \ge 2.99$. Altman shows that bankrupt firms and nonbankrupt firms have very different financial profiles one year before bankruptcy. These different financial profits are the key intuition behind the Z-score model and are depicted in Table 30A.1.

Altman's original Z-score model requires a firm to have publicly traded equity and be a manufacturer. He uses a revised model to make it applicable for private firms and

TABLE 30A.1		Average Ratios One Year before Bankruptcy of	
Financial Statement Ratios One Year before Bankruptcy: Manufacturing Firms		**Bankrupt Firms**	**Nonbankrupt Firms**
	$\dfrac{\text{Net working capital}}{\text{Total assets}}$	−6.1%	41.4%
	$\dfrac{\text{Accumulated retained earnings}}{\text{Total assets}}$	−62.6%	35.5%
	$\dfrac{\text{EBIT}}{\text{Total assets}}$	−31.8%	15.4%
	$\dfrac{\text{Market value of equity}}{\text{Total liabilities}}$	40.1%	247.7%
	$\dfrac{\text{Sales}}{\text{Assets}}$	150%	190%

SOURCE: Edward I. Altman, *Corporate Financial Distress and Bankruptcy*, John Wiley & Sons (1993), Table 3.1, p. 109.

---

[16]Edward I. Altman, *Corporate Financial Distress and Bankruptcy*, John Wiley & Sons, N.Y. (1993), Chapter 3.

Visit us at www.mhhe.com/rwj

nonmanufacturers. The resulting model is:

$$Z = 6.56 \frac{\text{Net working capital}}{\text{Total assets}} + 3.26 \frac{\text{Accumulated retained earnings}}{\text{Total assets}}$$

$$+ 1.05 \frac{\text{EBIT}}{\text{Total assets}} + 6.72 \frac{\text{Book value of equity}}{\text{Total liabilities}}$$

where $Z < 1.23$ indicates a bankruptcy prediction,
$1.23 \geq Z \leq 2.90$ indicates a gray area,
and $Z > 2.90$ indicates no bankruptcy.

EXAMPLE

The U.S. Composite Corporation is attempting to increase its line of credit with the First National State Bank. The director of credit management of First National State Bank uses the Z-score model to determine creditworthiness. The U.S. Composite Corporation is not a publicly traded firm so that the revised Z-score model must be used.

The balance sheet and income statement of the U.S. Composite Corporation are in Tables 2.1 and 2.2 (Chapter 2).

The first step is to determine the value of each of the financial statement variables and in the revised Z-score model.

(in millions)

$$\frac{\text{Net working capital}}{\text{Total assets}} = \frac{275}{1,879} = 0.146$$

$$\frac{\text{Accumulated retained earnings}}{\text{Total assets}} = \frac{390}{1,879} = 0.208$$

$$\frac{\text{EBIT}}{\text{Total assets}} = \frac{219}{1,879} = 0.117$$

$$\frac{\text{Book value of equity}}{\text{Total liabilities}} = \frac{805}{588} = 1.369$$

The next step to calculate the revised Z-score is:

$$Z = 6.56 \times 0.146 + 3.26 \times 0.208 + 1.05 \times 0.117 + 6.72 \times 1.369$$

$$= 10.96$$

Finally, we determine that the Z-score is above 2.9, and we conclude that U.S. Composite is a good credit risk.

International Corporate Finance

EXECUTIVE SUMMARY

Corporations that have significant foreign operations are often referred to as *international corporations* or *multinationals*. Table 31.1 lists the largest international corporations using several different measures. There are many familiar names on this list. International corporations must consider many financial factors that do not directly affect purely domestic firms. These include foreign exchange rates, different interest rates from country to country, complex accounting methods for foreign operations, foreign tax rates, and foreign government intervention.

The basic principles of corporate finance still apply to international corporations; like domestic companies, they seek to invest in projects that create more value for the shareholders than they cost and to arrange financing that raises cash at the lowest possible cost. That is, the net present value principle holds for both foreign and domestic operations. However, it is usually more complicated to apply the NPV principle to foreign operations.

Perhaps the most important complication of international finance is foreign exchange. The foreign exchange markets provide information and opportunities for an international corporation when it undertakes capital-budgeting and financing decisions. The relationship among foreign exchange, interest rates, and inflation is defined by the basic theories of exchange rates: purchasing-power parity, interest-rate parity, and the expectations theory.

Typically, international financing decisions involve a choice of three basic approaches:

1. Export domestic cash to the foreign operations.

2. Borrow in the country where the investment is located.

3. Borrow in a third country.

We discuss the merits of each approach.

31.1 Terminology

A common buzzword for the student of finance is **globalization.** The first step in learning about the globalization of financial markets is to conquer the new vocabulary. Here are some of the most common terms used in international finance and in this chapter:

1. An **American Depository Receipt (ADR)** is a security issued in the United States to represent shares of a foreign stock, allowing that stock to be traded in the United States. Foreign companies use ADRs, which are issued in U.S. dollars, to expand the pool of potential U.S. investors. ADRs are available in two forms for about 690 foreign companies: company-sponsored, which are listed on an exchange, and unsponsored, which are usually held by the investment bank that makes a market in the ADR. Both forms are available to individual investors, but only company-sponsored issues are quoted daily in newspapers.

847

TABLE 31.1	Company	Industry	Foreign Assets as % of Total	Foreign Sales as % of Total	Foreign Employment as % of Total
The Top International Corporations	Royal Dutch/Shell	Energy	67.8	73.3	77.9
	Ford	Automotive	29.0	30.6	29.8
	General Electric	Electronics	30.4	24.4	32.4
	Exxon	Energy	73.1	79.6	53.7
	General Motors	Automotive	24.9	29.2	33.9
	Volkswagen	Automotive	84.8	60.8	44.4
	IBM	Computers	51.9	62.7	50.1
	Toyota	Automotive	30.5	45.1	23.0
	Nestlé	Food	86.9	98.2	97.0
	Bayer	Chemicals	89.8	63.3	54.6
	ABB	Electrical equipment	84.7	87.2	93.9
	Nissan	Automotive	42.7	44.2	43.5
	Elf Aquitaine	Energy	54.5	65.4	47.5
	Mobil	Energy	61.8	65.9	52.2
	Daimler-Benz	Automotive	39.2	63.2	22.2

SOURCE: *The Economist,* November 22, 1997, p. 92.

2. The **cross rate** is the exchange rate between two foreign currencies, generally neither of which is the U.S. dollar. The dollar, however, is used as an interim step in determining the cross rate. For example, if an investor wants to sell Japanese yen and buy Swiss francs, he would sell yen against dollars and then buy francs with those dollars. So, although the transaction is designed to be yen for francs, the dollar's exchange rate serves as a benchmark.

3. A **European Currency Unit (ECU)** is a basket of 10 European currencies devised in 1979 and intended to serve as a monetary unit for the *European Monetary System* (EMS). By charter, EMS members reevaluate the composition of the ECU every five years or when there has been a shift of 25 percent or more in the weight of any currency. The German deutschemark is the most heavily weighted currency in the basket, with the French franc, the British pound, and the Dutch guilder each comprising more than 10 percent of the currency. The smallest weights are the Greek drachma, the Luxembourg franc, and the Irish punt.

4. **Eurobonds** are bonds denominated in a particular currency and issued simultaneously in the bond markets of several European countries. For many international companies and governments, they have become an important way to raise capital. Eurobonds are issued outside the restrictions that apply to domestic offerings and are typically syndicated in London. Trading can and does take place anywhere a buyer and a seller are.

5. **Eurocurrency** is money deposited in a financial center outside of the country whose currency is involved. For instance, Eurodollars—the most widely used Eurocurrency— are U.S. dollars deposited in banks outside the United States.

6. **Foreign bonds,** unlike Eurobonds, are issued by foreign borrowers in another nation's capital market and traditionally denominated in that nation's currency. Yankee bonds, for example, are issued in the United States by a foreign country, bank, or company; in recent years, however, some Yankee offerings have been denominated in currencies other than the U.S. dollar. Often the country in which these bonds are issued will draw distinctions between them and bonds issued by domestic issuers, including different tax laws, restrictions on the amount of issues, or tougher disclosure rules.

Foreign bonds often are nicknamed for the country of issuance: Yankee bonds (United States), Samurai bonds (Japan), Rembrandt bonds (the Netherlands), and Bulldog bonds (Britain). Partly because of tougher regulations and disclosure requirements, the foreign-bond market hasn't grown in the past several years with the vigor of the Eurobond market. Nearly half of all foreign bonds are issued in Switzerland.

7. **Gilts,** technically, are British and Irish government securities, although the term also includes issues of local British authorities and some overseas public-sector offerings.

8. The **London Interbank Offered Rate (LIBOR)** is the rate that most international banks charge one another for loans of Eurodollars overnight in the London market. LIBOR is a cornerstone in the pricing of money-market issues and other short-term debt issues by both governments and corporate borrowers. Less creditworthy issuers will often borrow at a rate of more than one point over LIBOR.

9. There are two basic kinds of **swaps:** interest rate and currency. An interest-rate swap occurs when two parties exchange debt with a floating-rate payment for debt with a fixed-rate payment, or vice versa. Currency swaps are agreements to deliver one currency against another currency. Often both types of swaps are used in the same transaction when debt denominated in different currencies is swapped.

Concept
Question

I. **What is the difference between a Eurobond and a foreign bond?**

31.2 Foreign Exchange Markets and Exchange Rates

The **foreign exchange market** is undoubtedly the world's largest financial market. It is the market where one country's currency is traded for another's. Most of the trading takes place in a few currencies: the U.S. dollar ($), German deutschemark (DM), British pound sterling (£), Japanese yen (¥), Swiss franc (SF), and French franc (FF).

The foreign exchange market is an over-the-counter market. There is no single location where traders get together. Instead, traders are located in the major commercial and investment banks around the world. They communicate using computer terminals, telephones, and other telecommunication devices. One element in the communications network for foreign transactions is the *Society for Worldwide Interbank Financial Telecommunications* (SWIFT). It is a Belgian not-for-profit cooperative. A bank in New York can send messages to a bank in London via SWIFT's regional processing centers. The connections are through data-transmission lines.

The many different types of participants in the foreign exchange market include the following:

1. Importers who convert their domestic currency to foreign currency to pay for goods from foreign countries.

2. Exporters who receive foreign currency and may want to convert to the domestic currency.

3. Portfolio managers who buy and sell foreign stocks and bonds.

4. Foreign exchange brokers who match buy and sell orders.

5. Traders who make the market in foreign exchange.

Exchange Rates

An **exchange rate** is the price of one country's currency for another's. In practice, almost all trading of currencies takes place in terms of the U.S. dollar. For example, both the

German deutschemark and the British pound will be traded with their price quoted in U.S. dollars. If the quoted price is the price in dollars of a unit of foreign exchange, the quotation is said to be in *direct* (or American) terms. For example, $1.50 = £1 and $0.40 = DM1 are in direct terms. The financial press frequently quotes the foreign currency price of a U.S. dollar. If the quoted price is the foreign currency price of a U.S. dollar, the quotation is *indirect* (or European). For example, £0.67 = $1 and DM2.5 = $1.

EXAMPLE

In 1984, Japan's economic growth and low inflation began to increase the demand for the yen compared to the dollar. Large U.S. trade deficits in the 1980s and 1990s contributed to this tendency. Figure 31.1 plots the Japanese yen value of a U.S. dollar from 1980 to 2000. The strong U.S. economy in the mid-1990s caused a dollar rebound.

FIGURE 31.1   Japanese Yen Price of a U.S. Dollar from 1980 to 2000

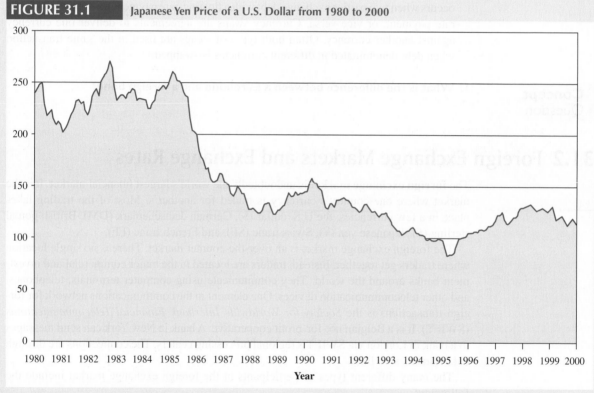

SOURCE: Various issues of the *Los Angeles Times* and *The Wall Street Journal.*

There are two reasons for quoting all foreign currencies in terms of the U.S. dollar. First, it reduces the number of possible cross-currency quotes. For example, with five major currencies, there would potentially be 10 exchange rates. Second, it makes **triangular arbitrage** more difficult. If all currencies were traded against each other, it would make inconsistencies more likely. That is, the exchange rate of the Malaysian ringgit against the United Kingdom pound would be compared to the exchange rate between the U.S. dollar and the United Kingdom pound. This implies a particular rate between the Malaysian ringgit and the U.S. dollar to prevent triangular arbitrage.

EXAMPLE

What if the pound traded for 4 ringgit in Malaysia and $1.60 in London? If the dollar traded for 2 ringgit in Malaysia, the trader would have a triangular opportunity. Starting with $1.60, a trader could purchase £1 in London. This pound could then be used to buy 4 ringgit in Malaysia. With the dollar trading at 2 ringgit, the 4 ringgit could then be traded for $2 in Malaysia as illustrated in Figure 31.2. The net gain from going around this "triangle" would be $2.00 − $1.60 = $0.40. Imagine what the return would be on an initial $1 billion purchase. (Watch out for currency controls in implementing this trade.)

FIGURE 31.2

Triangular Arbitrage

Types of Transactions

Three types of trades take place in the foreign exchange market: spot, forward, and swap. **Spot trades** involve an agreement on the exchange rate today for settlement in two days. The rate is called the **spot-exchange rate.** **Forward trades** involve an agreement on exchange rates today for settlement in the future. The rate is called the **forward-exchange rate.** The maturities for forward trades are usually 1 to 52 weeks. A swap is the sale (purchase) of a foreign currency with a simultaneous agreement to repurchase (resell) it sometime in the future. The difference between the sale price and the repurchase price is called the **swap rate.**

EXAMPLE

On October 11, bank A pays dollars to bank B's account at a New York bank and A receives pounds sterling in its account at a bank in London. On November 11, as agreed to on October 11, the transaction is reversed. A pays the sterling back to B, while B pays back the dollars to A. This is a swap. In effect, A has borrowed pounds sterling while giving up the use of dollars to B.

31.3 The Law of One Price and Purchasing-Power Parity

What determines the level of the spot-exchange rate? One answer is the **law of one price (LOP).** The law of one price says that a commodity will cost the same regardless of the country in which it is purchased. More formally, let $S_£(t)$ be the spot-exchange rate, that is, the number of dollars needed to purchase a British pound at time t.[1] Let $P^{US}(t)$ and $P^{UK}(t)$ be the current U.S. and British prices of a particular commodity, say, apples. The law of one price says that:

$$P^{US}(t) = S_£(t)\, P^{UK}(t)$$

for apples.

The rationale behind LOP is similar to that of triangular arbitrage. If LOP did not hold, arbitrage would be possible by moving apples from one country to another. For example, suppose that apples in New York are selling for $4 per bushel, while in London the price is

[1]Throughout this chapter, we quote foreign exchange in direct or American terms.

£2.50 per bushel. Then the law of one price implies that:

$$\$4 = S_\£(t) \times £2.50$$

and

$$S_\£(t) = \$1.60/£$$

That is, the LOP implied spot-exchange rate is $1.60 per pound.

Suppose instead that the actual exchange rate is $2.00 per pound. Starting with $4, a trader could buy a bushel of apples in New York, ship it to London, and sell it there for £2.50. The pounds sterling could then be converted into dollars at the exchange rate, $2/£, yielding a total of $5 for $1 ($5 − $4) gain.

The rationale of the LOP is that if the exchange rate is not $1.60/£ but is instead, say, $2/£, then forces would be set in motion to change the rate and/or the price of apples. In our example, there would be a whole lot of apples flying from New York to London. Thus, demand for apples in New York would raise the dollar price for apples there, and the supply in London would lower the pound-sterling price. The apple traders converting pounds sterling into dollars, that is, supplying pounds sterling and demanding dollars, would also put pressure on the exchange rate to fall from $2/£.

As you can see, for the LOP to be strictly true, three assumptions are needed:

1. The transactions cost of trading apples—shipping, insurance, wastage, and so on—must be zero.

2. No barriers to trading apples, such as tariffs or taxes, can exist.

3. Finally, an apple in New York must be identical to an apple in London. It won't do for you to send red apples to London if the English eat only green apples.

Given the fact that the transaction costs are not zero and that the other conditions are rarely exactly met, the LOP is really applicable only to traded goods, and then only to very uniform ones. The LOP does not imply that a Mercedes costs the same as a Ford or that a nuclear power plant in France costs the same as one in New York. In the case of the cars, they are not identical. In the case of the power plants, even if they were identical, they are expensive and very difficult to ship.

Because consumers purchase many goods, economists speak of **purchasing-power parity (PPP),** the idea that the exchange rate adjusts so that a *market basket* of goods costs the same, regardless of the country in which it is purchased. In addition, a relative version of purchasing-power parity has evolved. **Relative purchasing-power parity (RPPP)** says that the rate of change in the price level of commodities in one country relative to the rate of change in the price level in another determines the rate of change of the exchange rate between the two countries. Formally,

$$\frac{P^{US}(t+1)}{P^{US}(t)} = \frac{S_\£(t+1)}{S_\£(t)} \times \frac{P^{UK}(t+1)}{P^{UK}(t)}$$

$$\begin{array}{ccc} 1 + \text{U.S.} & = & 1 + \text{Change in} \\ \text{inflation rate} & & \text{foreign exchange rate} \end{array} \times \begin{array}{c} 1 + \text{British} \\ \text{inflation rate} \end{array}$$

This states that the rate of inflation in the United States relative to that in Great Britain determines the rate of change in the value of the dollar relative to that of the pound during the interval t to $t + 1$. It is common to write Π_{US} as the rate of inflation in the United States.

$1 + \Pi_{US}$ is equal to $P^{US}(t + 1)/P^{US}(t)$. Similarly, Π_{UK} is the rate of inflation in Great Britain. $1 + \Pi_{UK}$ is equal to $P^{UK}(t + 1)/P^{UK}(t)$.

Using Π to represent the rate of inflation, the preceding equation can be rearranged as:

$$\frac{1 + \Pi_{US}}{1 + \Pi_{UK}} = \frac{S_£(t + 1)}{S_£(t)} \tag{31.1}$$

We can rewrite this in an appropriate form as:

$$\Pi_{US} \cong \Pi_{UK} + \frac{\dot{S}_£}{S_£}$$

where $\dot{S}_£/S_£$ now stands for the rate of change in the dollars-per-pound exchange rate.

As an example, suppose that inflation in France during the year is equal to 4 percent and inflation in the United States is equal to 10 percent. Then, according to the RPPP, the price of the French franc in terms of the U.S. dollar should rise; that is, the U.S. dollar declines in value in terms of the French franc. Using our approximation, the dollars-per-franc exchange rate should rise by:

$$\frac{\dot{S}_{FF}}{S_{FF}} \approx \Pi_{US} - \Pi_F$$
$$= 10\% - 4\%$$
$$= 6\%$$

where $\dot{S}_{FF}/S_{FF}$ stands for the rate of change in the dollars-per-franc exchange rate. That is, if the French franc is worth \$0.20 at the beginning of the period, it should be worth approximately \$0.212 (\$0.20 × 1.06) at the end of the period.

The RPPP says that the change in the ratio of domestic commodity prices of two countries must be matched in the exchange rate. This version of the law of one price suggests that to estimate changes in the spot rate of exchange, it is necessary to estimate the difference in relative inflation rates. In other words, we can express our formula in expectational terms as:

$$E\left(\frac{\dot{S}_{FF}}{S_{FF}}\right) = E(\Pi_{US}) - E(\Pi_F)$$

If we expect the U.S. inflation rate to exceed the French inflation rate, we should expect the dollar price of French francs to rise, which is the same as saying that the dollar is expected to fall against the franc.

The more exact relationship of equation (31.1) can be expressed in expectational terms as:

$$\frac{E(1 + \Pi_{US})}{E(1 + \Pi_{UK})} = \frac{E[S_£(t + 1)]}{S_£(t)} \tag{31.2}$$

Concept Questions

1. **What is the law of one price? What is purchasing-power parity?**
2. **What is the relationship between inflation and exchange-rate movements?**

31.4 Interest Rates and Exchange Rates: Interest-Rate Parity

The forward-exchange rate and the spot-exchange rate are tied together by the same sort of arbitrage that underlies the law of one price. First, here is some useful terminology. If forward-exchange rates are greater than the spot-exchange rate in a particular currency, the forward foreign currency is said to be at a *premium* (this implies the domestic currency is at a discount). If the values of forward-exchange rates are less than the spot-exchange rate, the forward rate of foreign currency is at a discount.

Suppose we observe that the spot Switzerland franc rate is Switzerland franc 2.50 = $1.00 and the one-month forward Switzerland franc is Switzerland franc 2.40 = $1.00. Because fewer francs are needed to buy a dollar at the forward rate than are needed to buy a dollar at the spot rate, the franc is more valuable in the forward market than in the spot market. This means that the one-month forward Switzerland franc is at a premium. Of course, whatever we say for the franc must be the opposite of what we say for the dollar. In this example, the dollar is at a discount because the forward value is less than the spot value. Forward exchange is quoted in terms of the premium or discount that is to be added onto the spot rate.

Whether forward rates are at a premium or a discount when compared to a domestic currency depends on the relative interest rates in the foreign and domestic currency markets. The **interest-rate–parity theorem** implies that, if interest rates are higher domestically than in a particular foreign country, the foreign country's currency will be selling at a premium in the forward market; and if interest rates are lower domestically, the foreign currency will be selling at a discount in the forward market.

We need some notation to develop the interest-rate–parity theorem. Let $S(0)$ be the current domestic-currency price of spot foreign exchange (current time is denoted by 0). If the domestic currency is the dollar and the foreign exchange is the Switzerland franc (SF), we might observe $S(0) = \$0.40/\text{SF}$. $S(0)$ is in direct or U.S. terms. Let $F(0,1)$ be the current domestic-currency price of forward exchange for a contract that matures in one month. Thus, the contract is for forward exchange one month hence. Let i and i^* be the yearly rates of interest paid on Eurocurrency deposits denominated in the domestic (i) and foreign (i^*) currencies, respectively. Of course, the maturity of the deposits can be chosen to coincide with the maturity of the forward contract. Now consider a trader who has access to the interbank market in foreign exchange and Eurocurrency deposits. Suppose the trader has some dollars to invest for one month. The trader can make a dollar loan or a franc loan. The annual interest rate is 10 percent in francs and 6 percent in dollars. Which is better?

The Dollar Investment

Given an annual interest rate of 6 percent, the one-month rate of interest is 0.5 percent, ignoring compounding. If the trader invests $1 million now, the trader will get $1 million $\times$ 1.005 = $1.005 million at the end of the month. Following is an illustration:

Time 0	Time 1
Lend 1 unit of dollars	Obtain $1 + i \times (1/12)$ units of domestic currency
$1,000,000	$1,000,000 $\times$ (1 + 0.005) = $1,005,000

The Switzerland Franc Investment

The current spot rate is $0.40/SF. This means the trader can currently obtain $1 million/ 0.40 = SF2.5 million. The rate of interest on one-year SF loans is 10 percent. For one month, the interest rate is 0.10/12 = 0.0083. Thus, at the end of one month the trader will obtain SF2.5 million × 1.0083 = SF2,520,750. Of course, if the trader wants dollars at the end of the month, the trader must convert the francs back into dollars. The trader can fix the exchange rate for one-month conversion. Suppose the one-month forward is $0.39869/SF. Then the trader can sell francs forward. This will ensure that the trader gets SF2,520,750 × 0.39869 = $1.005 million at the end of the month. The general relationships are set forth here:

Time 0	Time 1
Purchase 1 unit $[1/S(0)]$ of foreign exchange	Deposit matures and pays $[1/S(0)] \times [1 + i \times (1/12)]$ units of foreign exchange
SF2,500,000	SF2,500,000 × 1.0083 = SF2,520,750
Sell forward $[1/S(0)] \times [1 + i^* \times (1/12)]$ units of forward exchange at the forward rate $F(0,1)$	Deliver foreign exchange in fulfillment of forward contract, receiving $[1/S(0)] \times [1 + i^* \times (1/12)] \times [F(0,1)]$ SF2,500,000 × 1.0083 × 0.39869 = $1,005,000

In our example, the investments earned exactly the same rate of return and $1 + [i \times (1/12)] = [1/S(0)] \times [1 + i^* \times (1/12)] \times [F(0,1)]$. In competitive financial markets, this must be true for risk-free investments. When the trader makes the franc loan, he or she gets a higher interest rate. But the return is the same because the franc must be sold forward at a lower price than it can be exchanged for initially. If the domestic interest rate were different from the covered foreign interest rate, the trader would have arbitrage opportunities.

To summarize, to prevent arbitrage possibilities from existing, we must have equality of the U.S. interest rate and covered foreign interest rates:

$$1 + i = \frac{1}{S(0)} \times (1 + i^*) \times F(0,1)$$

or

$$\frac{1 + i}{1 + i^*} = \frac{F(0,1)}{S(0)} \tag{31.3}$$

The last equation is the famous interest-rate–parity theorem. It relates the forward-exchange rate and the spot-exchange rate to interest-rate differentials. Notice that, if $i > i^*$, the spot rate (expressed as dollars per unit of foreign currency) will be less than the forward rate.

EXAMPLE

Let the spot rate $S(0) = \$0.40/SF$ and the one-year forward rate $F(0,1) = \$0.42/SF$. Let the one-year rates on Eurodollar deposits and Euro-SF deposits be, respectively, $i = 11.3\%$ and $i^* = 6\%$. Then, comparing the return on domestic borrowing with the return on covered foreign lending,

$$\$(1 + i) = \$(1 + 0.113) = \$1.113$$
$$\$[1/S(0)] \times (1 + i^*) \times F(0,1) = \$(1/0.40) \times (1 + 0.06) \times \$0.42 = \$1.113$$

For each dollar borrowed domestically, a trader must repay $1.113. The return from using the $1.00 to buy spot foreign exchange, placing the deposit at the foreign rate of interest, and selling the total return forward would be $1.113. These two amounts are equal, so it would not be worth anyone's time to try to exploit the difference. In this case, interest parity can be said to hold.

The Forward-Discount and Expected Spot Rates

A close connection exists between forward-exchange rates and expected spot rates. A trader's buy and sell decisions in today's forward market are based on the trader's market expectation of the future spot rate. In fact, if traders were completely indifferent to risk, the forward rate of exchange would depend solely on expectations about the future spot rate. For example, suppose the one-year forward rate of Switzerland francs is \$0.40/SF [that is, $F(0,1) = \$0.40/SF$]. This must mean that traders expect the spot rate to be \$0.40/SF in one year [$E(S(1)) = \$0.40/SF$]. If they thought it would be higher, it would create an arbitrage opportunity. Traders would buy francs forward at the low price and sell francs one year later at the expected higher price. This implies that the forward rate of exchange is equal to the expected spot, or (in general terms):

$$F(0,1) = E[S(1)]$$

and

$$\frac{F(0,1)}{S(0)} = \frac{E[S(1)]}{S(0)} \tag{31.4}$$

An equilibrium is achieved only when the forward discount (or premium) equals the expected change in the spot-exchange rate.

Exchange-Rate Risk

Exchange-rate risk is the natural consequence of international operations in a world where foreign currency values move up and down. International firms usually enter into some contracts that require payments in different currencies. For example, suppose that the treasurer of an international firm knows that one month from today the firm must pay £2 million for goods it will receive in England. The current exchange rate is \$1.50/£, and if that rate prevails in one month, the dollar cost of the goods to the firm will be \$1.50/£ × £2 million = \$3 million. The treasurer in this case is obligated to pay pounds in one month. (Alternately, we say that he is *short* in pounds.) A net short or long position of this type can be very risky. If the pound rises in the month to \$2/£, the treasurer must pay \$2/£ × £2 million = \$4 million, an extra \$1 million.

This is the essence of foreign exchange risk. The treasurer may want to hedge his position. When forward markets exist, the most convenient means of hedging is the purchase or sale of forward contracts. In this example, the treasurer may want to consider buying 2 million pounds sterling one month forward. If the one-month forward rate quoted today is also \$1.50/£, the treasurer will fulfill the contract by exchanging \$3 million for £2 million in one month. The £2 million he receives from the contract can then be used to pay for the goods. By hedging today, he fixes the outflow one month from now to exactly \$3 million.

Should the treasurer hedge or speculate? There are usually two reasons why the treasurer should hedge:

1. In an efficient foreign exchange-rate market, speculation is a zero NPV activity. Unless the treasurer has special information, nothing will be gained from foreign exchange speculation.

2. The costs of hedging are not large. The treasurer can use forward contracts to hedge, and if the forward rate is equal to the expected spot, the costs of hedging are negligible. Of course, there are ways to hedge foreign exchange risk other than to use forward contracts. For example, the treasurer can borrow dollars and buy pounds sterling in the spot market today and lend them for one month in London. By the interest-rate–parity theorem, this will be the same as buying the pounds sterling forward.

Richard M. Levich on Forward Exchange Rates

What is the relationship between today's three-month forward exchange rate, which can be observed in the market, and the spot exchange rate of three months from today, which cannot be observed until the future? One popular answer is that there is no relationship. As every bank trader knows, the possibility of covered interest arbitrage between domestic and foreign securities establishes a close link between the forward premium and the interest rate differential. At any moment, a trader can check his screen and observe that the forward premium and the interest rate differentials are nearly identical, especially when Eurocurrency interest rates are used. Thus the trader might say, "The forward rate reflects today's interest differential. It has nothing to do with expectations."

To check the second popular belief, that the forward rate reflects exchange rate expectations, takes a bit more work. Take today's three-month forward rate as of January 15 and compare it to the spot exchange rate that actually exists three months later on April 15. This produces one observation on the forward rate as a forecaster—not enough to accept or reject a theory. The idea that the forward rate might be an unbiased predictor of the future spot rate suggests that, on average and looking at many observations, the prediction error is small. So collect more data using the forward rate of April 15 and match it with the spot rate of July 15, and then the forward rate of July 15 matched to the spot rate of October 15, and so on. Look at the data for 8–10 years to have a large sample of observations.

The data suggest that in the early 1980s when the dollar was very strong, the forward rate significantly *under*estimated the strength of the dollar, and the forward rate was a biased predictor. But from 1985–1987 when the dollar depreciated sharply, the forward rate tended to *over*estimate the strength of the dollar, and the forward rate was again a biased predictor, but with the opposite sign as the earlier period. Looking at all of the 1980s—you guessed it—the forward rate was on average very close to the future spot exchange rate.

There are two messages here. First, even if there were "no relationship" between the forward rate and the future spot rate, the treasurer of General Motors would want to know exactly what that "nonrelationship" was. Because if the forward rate were *consistently* 3 percent higher than, or *consistently* 5 percent lower than, the future spot rate, the treasurer would be facing a tantalizing profit opportunity. A watch that is three minutes fast or five minutes slow is a very useful watch, as long as the bias is known and consistent.

Richard M. Levich is professor of finance and international business at New York University. He has written extensively on exchange rates and other issues in international economics and finance.

Which Firms Hedge Exchange-Rate Risk?

Not all firms with exchange-rate risk exposure hedge. Géczy, Minton, and Schrand report about 41 percent of Fortune 500 firms with foreign currency risk actually attempt to hedge these risks.[2] They find that larger firms with greater growth opportunities are more likely to use currency derivatives to hedge exchange-rate risk than smaller firms with fewer investment opportunities. This suggests that some firms hedge to make sure that they have enough cash on hand to finance their growth. In addition, firms with greater growth opportunities will tend to have higher indirect bankruptcy costs. For these firms, hedging exchange-rate risk will reduce these costs and increase the probability that they will not default on their debt obligations.

The fact that larger firms are more likely to use hedging techniques suggests that the costs of hedging are not insignificant. There may be fixed costs of establishing a hedging operation, in which case, economies of scale may explain why smaller firms hedge less than larger firms.

Concept
Questions

1. **What is the interest-rate–parity theorem?**
2. **Why is the forward rate related to the expected future spot rate?**
3. **How can one offset foreign exchange risk through a transaction in the forward markets?**

---

[2]C. Géczy, B. Minton, and C. Schrand, "Why Firms Use Currency Derivatives," *Journal of Finance* (September 1997). See also D. R. Nance, C. Smith, Jr., and C. W. Smithson, "On the Determinants of Corporate Hedging," *Journal of Finance*, 1993.

31.5 International Capital Budgeting

Kihlstrom Equipment, a U.S.-based international company, is evaluating an investment in China. Kihlstrom's exports of drill bits have increased to such a degree that the company is considering operating a plant in China. The project will cost 20 million yuan, and it is expected to produce cash flows of 8 million yuan a year for the next three years. The current spot-exchange rate for Chinese yuan is $S(0) = \$0.20/\text{yuan}$. How should Kihlstrom calculate the net present value of the projects in U.S. dollars?

Nothing about the fact that the investment is made abroad alters Kihlstrom's NPV criterion. Kihlstrom must identify incremental cash flows and discount them at the appropriate cost of capital. After making the required discounted cash flow calculations, Kihlstrom should undertake projects with a positive NPV. However, two major factors that complicate such international NPV calculations are foreign exchange conversion and repatriation of funds.

Foreign Exchange Conversion

The simplest way for Kihlstrom to calculate the NPV of the investment is to convert all Chinese yuan cash flows to U.S. dollars. This involves a three-step process:

Step 1. Estimate future cash flows in Chinese yuan.

Step 2. Convert to U.S. dollars at the predicted exchange rate.

Step 3. Calculate NPV using the cost of capital in U.S. dollars.

In Table 31.2 we show the application of these three steps to Kihlstrom's China investment. Notice in Table 31.2 that Kihlstrom's Chinese yuan cash flows were converted to dollars by multiplying the foreign cash flows by the predicted foreign exchange rate.

How might Kihlstrom predict future exchange rates? Using the theory of efficient markets, Kihlstrom could calculate NPV using the foreign exchange market's implicit predictions. To figure these out, Kihlstrom can use the basic foreign exchange relationships described in earlier sections of this chapter.

Kihlstrom begins by obtaining publicly available information on exchange rates and interest rates. It finds:

Exchange rate: $S_{FF}(0) = \$0.15/\text{FF}$, i.e., 1 Chinese yuan can be purchased for $0.15.

Interest rate in United States: $i_{US} = 8\%$

Interest rate in China: $i_{China} = 12\%$

TABLE 31.2		End of Year			
		0	**1**	**2**	**3**
Net Present Value of Foreign Cash Flows: Kihlstrom Equipment	Incremental cash flows (CF_{Yuan}) (yuan millions)	−20	8	8	8
	Foreign exchange rate ($/yuan)	0.15	0.145	0.14	0.135
	Foreign exchange-rate conversion	−20 × 0.15	8 × 0.145	8 × 0.14	8 × 0.135
	Incremental cash flows ($ millions)	−3	1.16	1.12	1.08

NPV at 15% = −$0.43 million.

Using equations (31.2), (31.3), and (31.4), Kihlstrom can calculate the following set of relationships:

$$\underbrace{\frac{E(1 + \Pi_{US})}{E(1 + \Pi_{China})}}_{\substack{\text{Relative purchasing-}\\\text{power parity}\\(31.2)}} = \underbrace{\frac{E(S_{yuan}(1))}{S_{yuan}(0)}}_{\substack{\text{Forward rate}\\\text{related to}\\\text{expected spot rate}\\(31.4)}} = \underbrace{\frac{F_{yuan}(0,1)}{S_{yuan}(0)}}_{} = \underbrace{\frac{1 + i_{US}}{1 + i_{China}}}_{\substack{\text{Interest-rate}\\\text{parity}\\(31.3)}} \quad (31.5)$$

From the left, the first equality follows from relative purchasing-power parity. The expected inflation rates in the two countries determine the expected movement in the spot rate, expressed earlier in equation (31.2). The equality between the second and third terms is a consequence of our discussion on forward rates and expected spot rates, expressed earlier in equation (31.4). The last equality is interest-rate parity and appeared earlier in equation (31.3).

We now compare the left-hand term to the right-hand term. We have:

$$\frac{1 + i_{US}}{1 + i_{China}} = \frac{E(1 + \Pi_{US})}{E(1 + \Pi_{China})}$$

$$\frac{1.08}{1.12} = \frac{E(1 + \Pi_{US})}{E(1 + \Pi_{China})}$$

If the expected inflation rate in the United States is 8 percent, it follows that the expected inflation rate in China is 12 percent:

$$\frac{1.08}{1.12} = \frac{1.08}{E(1 + \Pi_{China})}$$

$$E(\Pi_{China}) = 12\%$$

Using relative purchasing-power parity, Kihlstrom can compute the expected spot-exchange rate in one year:

$$\frac{E(1 + \Pi_{US})}{E(1 + \Pi_{China})} = \frac{E[S_{yuan}(1)]}{S_{yuan}(0)}$$

$$\frac{1.08}{1.12} = \frac{E[S_{yuan}(1)]}{0.15}$$

which implies $E[S_{yuan}(1)] = 0.145$. The exchange rate expected at the end of year 2 is obtained from:

$$0.15 \times \left(\frac{1.08}{1.12}\right)^2 = 0.14$$

For year 3, the expected exchange rate is obtained from:

$$0.15 \times \left(\frac{1.08}{1.12}\right)^3 = 0.135$$

Finally, the NPV of the project is computed:

$$NPV = \sum_{t=0}^{3} \frac{CF_{yuan}(t) \times E[S_{yuan}(t)]}{(1 + r^*)^t}$$

where $CF_{yuan}(t)$ refers to the Chinese yuan forecasted to be received in each of the next three years. The discount rate we use is Kihlstrom's U.S. cost of capital. We do not use the U.S. risk-free rate of 8 percent because Kihlstrom's project is risky; a risk-adjusted discount rate must be used. Because the NPV at 15 percent is −$430,000, Kihlstrom should not invest in a subsidiary in China.

In this example we used the foreign exchange market's implicit forecast of future exchange rates. Why not use management's own forecast of foreign exchange rates in the calculations? Suppose that the financial management of Kihlstrom feels optimistic about the Chinese yuan. If its forecasts are sufficiently optimistic and they are used, Kihlstrom's investment in a Chinese subsidiary will generate a positive NPV. But, in general, it is a good idea to separate the economic prospects of an investment and the foreign exchange prospects, and it is unwise to use the latter projections in the NPV calculation. If Kihlstrom wishes to speculate on an increase in the Chinese yuan relative to the U.S. dollar, the best way to do this is to buy Chinese yuan in the forward foreign exchange market. (However, some currencies are more difficult to trade this way than others.) By using the forward-exchange rates implicit in the domestic and foreign interest rates, the firm is using the actual dollar flows that it could, in principle, lock in today by borrowing in the foreign currency. This makes the foreign cash flows equivalent to domestic cash flows.

Unremitted Cash Flows

The previous example assumed that all after-tax cash flows from the foreign investment were remitted to the parent firm. The remittance decision is similar to the dividend for a purely domestic firm. Substantial differences can exist between the cash flows of a project and the amount that is actually remitted to the parent firm. Of course, the net present value of a project will not be changed by deferred remittance if the unremitted cash flows are reinvested at a rate of return equal (as adjusted for exchange rates) to the domestic cost of capital.

A foreign subsidiary can remit funds to a parent in many ways, including the following:

1. Dividends.
2. Management fees for central services.
3. Royalties on the use of trade names and patents.

International firms must pay special attention to remittance for two reasons. First, there may be present and future exchange controls. Many governments are sensitive to the charge of being exploited by foreign firms. Therefore, governments are tempted to limit the ability of international firms to remit cash flows. Another reason is taxes. It is always necessary to determine what taxes must be paid on profits generated in a foreign country. International firms must usually pay foreign taxes on their foreign profits. The total taxes paid by an international firm may be a function of the time of remittance. For example, Kihlstrom's Chinese subsidiary would need to pay taxes in China on the profits it earns in China. Kihlstrom will also pay taxes on dividends it remits to the United States. In most cases Kihlstrom can offset the payment of foreign taxes against the U.S. tax liability. Thus, if the Chinese corporate income tax is 34 percent, Kihlstrom will not be liable for additional U.S. taxes.

The Cost of Capital for International Firms

An important question for firms with international investments is whether the required return for international projects should be different from that of similar domestic projects.

Lower Cost of Capital from International Firm Diversification   In the previous chapter, we expressed some skepticism concerning the benefits of diversification. We can make a stronger case for diversification in international firms than for purely domestic firms. Suppose barriers prevented shareholders in the United States from holding foreign securities; the financial markets of different countries would be segmented. Further suppose that firms in the United States were not subject to the same barriers. In such a case, a firm engaging in international investing could provide indirect diversification for U.S. shareholders that they could not achieve by investing within the United States. This could lead to the lowering of the risk premium on international projects. In general, if the costs of investing abroad are lower for a firm than for its shareholders, there is an advantage to international diversification by firms, and this advantage will be reflected in a lower risk-adjusted discount rate.

Alternatively, if there were no barriers to international investing for shareholders, shareholders could obtain the benefit of international diversification for themselves by buying foreign securities. In this case the project cost of capital for a firm in the United States would not depend on whether the project was in the United States or in a foreign country. In practice, holding foreign securities involves substantial expenses. These expenses include taxes, the costs of obtaining information, and trading costs. This implies that although U.S. investors are free to hold foreign securities, they will not be perfectly internationally diversified.

Lower Cost of Capital from International Shareholder Diversification   Recall our discussion of the CAPM and the market portfolio. Consider the U.S. stock market and a U.S. investor who is not internationally diversified but, instead, is invested only in U.S. stocks. From our previous discussion of diversification, we know this investor would be bearing more risk than if she were able to diversify in the stocks of different countries. Now imagine she can invest in many foreign stocks by diversifying internationally. She should be able to reduce the variance (or standard deviation) of her portfolio significantly.

For this investor, the market-risk premium will be lower than for investors who cannot diversify internationally. In internationally integrated markets, investors with internationally diversified portfolios will measure the risk of an individual stock in terms of a world-market portfolio and global betas. Therefore, the cost of capital of a particular firm will be in terms of a global CAPM, such as:

$$E(R_I) = r_F + B_G \left[E(R_G) - r_F \right]$$

where R_I is the required return on a stock when markets are global, r_F is the risk-free rate, B_G is the global beta, and R_G is the return on the world-market portfolio. A firm with internationally diversified investors will have a cost of capital with a lower market-risk premium [i.e., $E(R_G - r_F)$] and a global beta when compared to a firm with investors that cannot diversify internationally.

Solnik has presented evidence that suggests that international diversification significantly reduces risk for shareholders.[3] He shows that the variance of an internationally diversified portfolio of common stocks is about 33 percent of the variance of individual securities. A diversified portfolio of U.S. stocks will reduce variance by only 50 percent. Table 31.3 shows that a world portfolio has lower risk than a portfolio of stocks within a single country. For example, a citizen of Hong Kong can reduce risk from 12.8 percent to 4.2 percent by investing in a world portfolio. This evidence is consistent with a lower global market-risk premium than is a purely domestic-risk premium. Global betas will be different than purely domestic betas. Stulz has argued that the preceding claim for why

---

[3]B. H. Solnik, "Why Not Diversify Internationally Rather than Domestically?" *Financial Analysts Journal* (July–August 1974). A recent estimate of the benefits of international diversification can be found in Georgio DeSantis and Bruno Gerard, "International Asset Pricing and Portfolio Diversification with Time-Varying Risk, *Journal of Finance* 52 (1997). They estimate that an internationally diversified portfolio will reduce standard deviation by 20 percent when compared to investing in U.S. stocks only.

TABLE 31.3		Beta	Monthly Standard Deviation (%)
Risk Measures for Foreign Market Portfolios	Hong Kong	2.08	12.8%
	Japan	1.42	6.1
	Sweden	.73	6.2
	Norway	.57	5.3
	Belgium	1.06	6.0
	Netherlands	1.01	5.6
	United Kingdom	1.38	7.9
	Denmark	.49	5.5
	France	.69	7.4
	Austria	.19	5.4
	Germany	.70	6.0
	Switzerland	.83	5.7
	Australia	1.39	8.2
	Canada	1.04	5.9
	United States	.97	4.7
	World	1.00	4.2

SOURCE: Campbell R. Harvey, "The World Price of Covariance Risk," *Journal of Finance* (March 1991) from Table I, p. 122 and Table VI, p. 140.

internationalization reduces the cost of capital doesn't capture the complete picture. He agrees that the global market-risk premium is likely to be substantially lower than the risk premium for an isolated country. In addition, he argues that global investing is likely to improve corporate governance and reduce agency costs. The argument goes something like this: Firms in countries with less-developed financial markets will need to improve their governance so that they can raise capital in well-developed capital markets such as the U.S. Foreign firms raising capital in the U.S. must appeal to more sophisticated investors and better market architectures with superior monitoring abilities.[4] Table 31.3 also shows that the systematic risk of foreign stock investment can be very low, as is the case of Austria, or very high, as is the case of Hong Kong.

Foreign Political Risks   Firms may determine that international investments inherently involve more political risk than domestic investments. This extra risk may offset the gains from international diversification. Firms may increase the discount rate to allow for the risk of expropriation and foreign exchange remittance controls.

1. What problems do international projects pose for the use of net-present-value techniques?

31.6 International Financial Decisions

An international firm can finance foreign projects in three basic ways:

1. It can raise cash in the home country and export it to finance the foreign project.
2. It can raise cash by borrowing in the foreign country where the project is located.
3. It can borrow in a third country where the cost of debt is lowest.

---

[4]René M. Stulz, "Globalization, Corporate Finance, and the Cost of Capital," *Journal of Applied Corporate Finance* 12 (1999). See also Ronald M. Schramm and Henry N. Wang, "Measuring the Cost of Capital in an International CAPM Framework," *Journal of Corporate Finance* 12 (1999) and Thomas I. O'Brian, "The Global CAPM and a Firm's Cost of Capital in Different Currencies," *Journal of Corporate Finance* 12 (1999).

If a U.S. firm raises cash for its foreign projects by borrowing in the United States, it has an exchange-rate risk. If the foreign currency depreciates, the U.S. parent firm may experience an exchange-rate loss when the foreign cash flow is remitted to the United States. Of course, the U.S. firm may sell foreign exchange forward to hedge this risk. However, it is difficult to sell forward contracts beyond one year.

Firms in the United States may borrow in the country where the foreign project is located. This is the usual way of hedging long-term foreign exchange risk. Thus, if Kihlstrom Equipment wishes to invest 20 million yuan in China, it may attempt to raise much of the cash in France. Kihlstrom should know that long-term hedging of foreign exchange risk by borrowing in the foreign country is effective only up to the amount borrowed. Any residual (equity) would not be hedged.

Another alternative is to find a country where interest rates are low. However, foreign interest rates may be lower because of lower expected foreign inflation. Thus, financial managers must be careful to look beyond nominal interest rates to real interest rates.

Short-Term and Medium-Term Financing

In raising short-term and medium-term cash, U.S. international firms often have a choice between borrowing from a U.S. bank at the U.S. interest rate or borrowing Eurodollars in the Eurocurrency market.

A **Eurodollar** is a dollar deposited in a bank outside the United States. For example, dollar deposits in Paris, France, are Eurodollars. The Eurocurrency markets are the banks (**Eurobanks**) that make loans and accept deposits in foreign currencies. Most Eurocurrency trading involves the borrowing and lending of time deposits at Eurobanks. For example, a Eurobank receives a Eurodollar deposit from a domestic U.S. bank. Afterward, the Eurobank will make a dollar-denominated loan to a borrowing party. This is the Eurocurrency market. It is not a retail bank market. The customers are corporations and governments.

One important characteristic of the Eurocurrency market is that loans are made on a floating-rate basis. The interest rates are set at a fixed margin above the London Interbank Offered Rate for the given period and currency involved. For example, if the margin is 0.5 percent for dollar loans and the current LIBOR is 8 percent for dollar loans, the dollar borrower will pay an interest rate of 8.5 percent. This rate is usually changed every six months. The dollar loans will have maturities ranging from 3 to 10 years.

It is obvious that in a perfectly competitive financial market the interest rate on a Eurodollar loan in a Eurocurrency market must be the same as the interest rate in the U.S. loan market. If the interest rate on a Eurodollar loan were higher than that on a domestic-dollar loan, arbitrageurs would borrow in the domestic-dollar market and lend in the Eurodollar market. This type of arbitrage trading would force interest rates to be the same in both dollar markets. However, from time to time there are differences between the Eurodollar loan rate and the domestic loan rate. Risk, government regulations, and taxes explain most of the differences.

International Bond Markets

The worldwide public bond market is made up of $21.5 trillion in bonds issued in many currencies. Table 31.4 shows that bonds denominated in dollars make up 44.6 percent of the total. The total worldwide bond market can be divided into domestic bonds and international bonds. Domestic bonds are those issued by a firm in its home country. International bonds are those issued by firms in another currency than the currency of the home country.

TABLE 31.4	Bond Market	Total Publicly Issued (in $ billions)	Percentage of Total
The Top 5 Bond Markets	U.S. dollar	$ 9,683	44.6%
	Japanese yen	3,666	17.1
	British pound	662	3.1
	Canadian dollar	446	2.1
	Danish krone	288	1.3
	Rest of the world	6,855	31.9
	Total world bonds	$21,500	100.00%

Trading in international bonds is over the counter and takes place in loosely connected individual markets. These individual markets are closely tied to the corresponding domestic bond markets. International bonds can be divided into two main types: foreign bonds and Eurobonds.

Foreign Bonds   Foreign bonds are bonds that are issued by foreign borrowers in a particular country's domestic bond market. They are often nicknamed for the country of issuance. They are denominated in the country's domestic currency. For example, suppose a Swiss watch company issues U.S. dollar-denominated bonds in the United States.

These foreign bonds would be called **Yankee bonds.** Like all foreign bonds issued in the United States, Yankee bonds must be registered under the Securities Act of 1933. Yankee bonds are usually rated by a bond-rating agency such as Standard & Poor's Corporation. Many Yankee bonds are listed on the New York Stock Exchange.

Many foreign bonds, such as Yankee bonds, are registered. This makes them less attractive to investors having a disdain for tax authorities. For obvious reasons, these traders like the Eurobond market better than the foreign-bond market. Registered bonds have an ownership name assigned to the bond's serial number. The transfer of ownership of a registered bond can take place only via legal transfer of the registered name. Transfer agents (for example, commercial banks) are required.

Eurobonds   Eurobonds are denominated in a particular currency and are issued simultaneously in the bond markets of several countries. The prefix *Euro* means that the bonds are issued outside the countries in whose currencies they are denominated.

Most Eurobonds are bearer bonds. The ownership of the bonds is established by possession of the bond. In contrast, many foreign bonds are registered.

Most issues of Eurobonds are arranged by underwriting. However, some Eurobonds are privately placed.[5] A public issue with underwriting is similar to the public debt sold in domestic bond markets. The borrower sells its bonds to a group of management banks. Managing banks, in turn, sell the bonds to other banks. The other banks are divided into two groups: underwriters and sellers. The underwriters and sellers sell the bonds to dealers and fund investors. The managing banks also serve as underwriters and sellers. Underwriters usually sell Eurobonds on a firm commitment basis. That is, they are committed to buy the bonds at a prenegotiated price and attempt to sell them at a higher price in the market.

---

[5]In general, the issue costs are lower in private placements, as compared to public issues, and the yields are higher.

Eurobonds appear as straight bonds, floating-rate notes, convertible bonds, zero-coupon bonds, mortgage-backed bonds, and dual-currency bonds.[6]

EXAMPLE

A French automobile firm issues 50,000 bonds with a face value of $1,000 each. When the bonds are issued, they are managed by London merchant bankers and listed on the London Stock Exchange. These are Eurobonds. Each bond has a fixed coupon rate of 6 percent paid annually on August 15.

EXAMPLE

An American firm makes an offering of $500 million of floating-rate notes. The notes are offered in London. The notes mature in 2020 and have semiannual interest of 0.5 percent above the six-month London Interbank Offered Rate. When the bonds are issued, the six-month LIBOR is 10 percent. Thus, in the first six months the American firm will pay interest (at the annual rate) of 10% + 0.5% = 10.5%.

31.7 Reporting Foreign Operations

When a U.S. company prepares consolidated financial statements, the firm translates the local-currency accounts of foreign subsidiaries into the currency that is used for reporting purposes, usually the currency of the home country (that is, dollars). If exchange rates change during the accounting period, accounting gains or losses can occur.

Suppose a U.S. firm acquired a British company in 1982. At that time the exchange rate was £1 = $2. The British firm performed very well during the next few years (according to sterling measurements). During the same period, the value of the pound fell to $1.25. Did the corresponding increase in the value of the dollar make the U.S. company better off? Should the increase be reflected in the measurement of income?

These questions have been among the most controversial accounting questions in recent years. Two issues seem to arise:

1. What is the appropriate exchange rate to use for translating each balance-sheet account?
2. How should unrealized accounting gains and losses from foreign-currency translation be handled?

Currency is currently translated under complicated rules set out in Financial Accounting Standards Boards (FASB) Statement Number 52, which was issued in December 1981. For the most part, FASB Number 52 requires that all assets and liabilities be translated from the subsidiary's currency into the parent's, using the exchange rate that currently prevails. Gains and losses are accumulated in a special account within the shareholders' equity section of the balance sheet. Thus, the impact of translation gains and losses will not be recognized explicitly in net income until the underlying assets and liabilities are sold or liquidated.

---

[6]There is a small but growing international equity market. International equities are stock issues underwritten and distributed to a mix of investors without regard to national borders. Our definition of international equity encompasses two basic types: those issues that have been internationally syndicated and distributed outside all national exchanges (termed *Euroequities*) and those that are issued by underwriters in domestic markets other than their own.

EXAMPLE

To illustrate the accounting problem, suppose we started a small foreign subsidiary in Denmark a year ago. The local currency is the krone, abbreviated Dkr. At the beginning of the year, the exchange rate was Dkr 2 = $1 and the balance in krones looked like this:

Assets	Dkr 8,000	Liabilities	Dkr 4,000
		Equity	Dkr 4,000

At 8 krone to the dollar, the beginning balance sheet in dollar was as follows:

Assets	$1,000	Liabilities	$500
		Equity	$500

Denmark is a quiet place and nothing at all actually happened during the year. As a result, net income was zero before consideration of exchange rate changes. However, the exchange rate did change to 12 krone = $1 because Denmark's inflation was higher than the U. S. inflation rate. (Note this is a hypothetical example.)

Because nothing happened, the accounting ending balance sheet in krone is the same as the beginning. However, if we convert it to dollars at the new exchange rate we obtain:

Assets	$667	Liabilities	$333.5
		Net worth	$333.5

Notice that the equity has decreased by $167.5 ($500 − $333.5) even though net income was zero. Also notice we have not made any adjustments to the income statement.

The exchange rate gains or losses will not be recognized explicitly in net income until the underlying assets and liabilities are sold or otherwise liquidated.

Concept
Question

1. **What issues arise when reporting foreign operations?**

31.8 SUMMARY AND CONCLUSIONS

The international firm has a more complicated life than the purely domestic firm. Management must understand the connection between interest rates, foreign-currency exchange rates, and inflation, and it must become aware of a large number of different financial market regulations and tax systems.

1. This chapter describes some fundamental theories of international finance:
   - The purchasing-power–parity theorem (law of one price).
   - The expectations theory of exchange rates.
   - The interest-rate–parity theorem.

2. The purchasing-power–parity theorem states that $1 should have the same purchasing power in each country. This means that an apple costs the same whether you buy it in New York or in Tokyo. One version of the purchasing-power–parity theorem states that the change in exchange rates between the currencies of two countries is connected to the inflation rates in the countries' commodity prices.

3. The expectations theory of exchange rates states that the forward rate of exchange is equal to the expected spot rate.

4. The interest-rate–parity theorem states that the interest-rate differential between two countries will be equal to the difference between the forward-exchange rate and the spot-exchange rate. This equality must prevail to prevent arbitrageurs from devising get-rich-quick strategies. The

equality requires the rate of return on risk-free investments in the United States to be the same as that in other countries.

Of course, in practice the purchasing-power–parity theorem and the interest-rate-parity theorem cannot work perfectly. Government regulations and taxes prevent this. However, there is much empirical work and intuition that suggests that these theories describe international financial markets in an approximate way.

5. The chapter also describes some of the problems of international capital budgeting. The net-present-value rule is still the appropriate way to choose projects, but the main problem is to choose the correct cost of capital. We argue that it should be equal to the rate that shareholders can expect to earn on a portfolio of domestic and foreign securities. This rate should be about the same as is true for a portfolio of domestic securities. However, two adjustments may be necessary:

a. The cost of capital of an international firm may be *lower* than that of a domestic counterpart because of the benefits of international diversification.

b. The cost of capital of an international firm may be *higher* because of the extra foreign political risks.

6. We briefly describe international financial markets. International firms may want to consider borrowing cash in the local financial market or in Eurocurrency and Eurobond markets. The interest rates are likely to appear different in these markets. Thus, international firms must be careful to consider differences in taxes and government regulations.

KEY TERMS

American Depository Receipt (ADR), *847*
cross rate, *848*
Eurobanks, *863*
Eurobonds, *848*
Eurocurrency, *848*
Eurodollar, *863*
European Currency Unit (ECU), *848*
exchange rate, *849*
foreign bonds, *848*
foreign exchange market, *849*
forward-exchange rate, *851*
forward trades, *851*
gilts, *849*

globalization, *847*
interest-rate–parity theorem, *854*
law of one price (LOP), *851*
London Interbank Offered Rate (LIBOR), *849*
purchasing-power parity (PPP), *852*
relative purchasing-power parity (RPPP), *852*
spot-exchange rate, *851*
spot trades, *851*
swap rate, *851*
swaps, *849*
triangular arbitrage, *850*
Yankee bonds, *864*

SUGGESTED READINGS

Some of the latest academic research in international finance appears in the *Journal of Applied Corporate Finance:* "Global Finance" (Fall 1999); "Emerging Markets and the Asian Crisis" (Fall 1998); "Global Finance and Risk Management" (Fall 1997).

QUESTIONS & PROBLEMS

SOME BASICS

31.1   Use Table 31.5 to answer the following questions:

a. What is the quote in direct terms for the British (i.e., United Kingdom) pound sterling and the U.S. dollar on spot exchange?

b. Is the Japanese yen at a premium or a discount to the U.S. dollar in the forward markets?

c. To which type of foreign exchange participants would the forward prices of the Japanese yen be important? Why? What types of transactions might these participants use to cover their exposed risk in the foreign exchange markets?

d. Suppose you are a Swiss exporter of watches. If you are to be paid in U.S. dollars three months from now for a shipment made to the United States worth $100,000, how many Swiss francs would you receive if you locked in the price today with a forward contract? Would you buy or sell the dollar forward?

e. Calculate the U.K. pound–Indonesian rupiah cross rate for spot exchange in terms of the U.S. dollar. Do the same for the yen–Swiss franc cross rate.

f. In the text a swap transaction is described. Why might both banks profit from the use of such a mutual agreement?

TABLE 31.5	Foreign Currency in Dollars	Dollar in Foreign Currency
Foreign Exchange, Week Ended Thursday, April 16, 200X		
f-Argent (Austral)	0.6515	1.5350
Australia (Dollar)	0.7160	1.3966
Brazil (Cruzado)	0.0419	23.88
Britain (Pound)	1.6317	0.6129
30-day fut	1.6277	0.6144
60-day fut	1.6238	0.6158
90-day fut	1.6204	0.6171
Canada (Dollar)	0.7593	1.3170
30-day fut	0.7591	1.3173
60-day fut	0.7588	1.3179
90-day fut	0.7584	1.3185
y-Chile (Peso)	0.0047	211.34
Colombia (Peso)	0.0043	230.50
Denmark (Krone)	0.1466	6.8220
c-Egypt (Pound)	0.7353	1.3600
f-Ecuador (Sucre)	0.006325	158.10
Finland (Mark)	0.2270	4.4050
Greece (Drachma)	0.0075	132.75
Hong Kong (Dollar)	0.1282	7.8015
y-India (Rupee)	0.0779	12.8400
Indonesia (Rupiah)	0.000611	1635.75
Israel (Shekel)	0.6246	1.6010
Japan (Yen)	0.006993	143.00
30-day fut	0.007009	142.66
60-day fut	0.007027	142.30
90-day fut	0.007042	142.01
Jordan (Dinar)	3.0211	0.33100
Kuwait (Dinar)	3.6740	0.27218
Lebanon (Pound)	0.00813	123.00
z-Mexico (Peso)	0.000860	1163.00
New Zealand (Dollar)	0.5800	1.7241
Norway (Krone)	0.1477	6.7700
Pakistan (Rupee)	0.0578	17.30
y-Peru (Inti)	0.0673	14.85
z-Philippines (Peso)	0.0494	20.2500
Portugal (Escudo)	0.007153	139.80
Saudi Arabia (Rijal)	0.2666	3.7505
Singapore (Dollar)	0.4690	2.1320
S. Korea (Won)	0.001183	845.50
S. Africa (Rand)	0.4975	2.01010
Spain (Peseta)	0.007890	126.75
Sweden (Krona)	0.1586	6.3070
Switzerland (Franc)	0.6691	1.4945
30-day fut	0.6710	1.4904
60-day fut	0.6730	1.4858
90-day fut	0.6743	1.4830
Taiwan (NT $)	0.0294	33.97

TABLE 31.5 *(concluded)*		**Foreign Currency in Dollars**	**Dollar in Foreign Currency**
	Turkey (Lira)	0.001273	785.85
	U.A.E. (Dirham)	0.2723	3.6723
	z-Uruguay (Peso)	0.0050	201.4
	z-Venezuela (Bolivar)	0.0422	23.7000
	Yugoslavia (Dinar)	0.001774	563.71

The Federal Reserve Board's index measuring the value of the dollar against 10 other currencies weighted on the basis of trade was 96.92 Thursday, up 18 points or 0.18 percent from Wednesday's 96.74. A year ago the index was 115.10.

Late prices as of 3:30 P.M. Eastern time as gathered by First American Bank of New York. c, commercial rate; f, financial rate; y, official rate; z, floating rate; r, revised.

Reprinted by permission of *The Wall Street Journal.* © Dow Jones & Company, Inc. All rights reserved.

31.2   Determine whether arbitrage opportunities exist given the following foreign exchange rates.
    a. $1.8/L   SF2/$ SF4/L
    b. ¥100/$ SF2/$ ¥50/SF
    c. HKD7.8/$ ¥100/$ ¥14/HKD

THE LAW OF ONE PRICE AND PURCHASING-POWER PARITY

31.3   Are the following statements true or false? Explain.
    a. If the general price index in Japan rises faster than that in the United States (assuming that there are zero transaction costs, that no barriers to trade exist, and that products are identical in both countries), we would expect the yen to appreciate with respect to the dollar.
    b. Suppose you are a Swiss wine exporter who receives all payments in foreign currency. The French government begins to undertake an expansionary monetary policy. If it is certain that the result will be higher inflation in Switzerland than in other countries, you would be wise to use forward markets to protect yourself against future losses resulting from the deterioration of the value of the Swiss franc.
    c. If you could accurately estimate differences in relative inflation between two countries over a long period of time (and other participants in the market were unable to do so), you could successfully speculate in spot currency markets.

31.4   The inflation rates for Empire White and Empire Black are 5 percent and 10 percent, respectively. At the beginning of the year, the spot rate between the two currencies is 2.5 black dollars per white dollar. What is the approximate spot rate at year-end?

INTEREST RATES AND EXCHANGE RATES: INTEREST-RATE PARITY

31.5   A U.S. corporation, Forever Young, Inc., intends to import $1,000,000 worth of cosmetics from Switzerland and will make payment in SF three months from now. The foreign exchange spot rate of Swiss franc to the U.S. dollar is SF6/$. Annual interest rates for U.S. dollar and Swiss franc are 5 percent and 8 percent, respectively.
    a. What is the three-month forward rate for French franc if interest-rate parity holds?
    b. How can Forever Young, Inc., use currency trading to hedge against the foreign exchange risk associated with the purchase?

INTERNATIONAL CAPITAL BUDGETING

31.6   **a.** The treasurer of a major U.S. firm has $5 million to invest for three months. The annual interest rate in the United States is 12 percent. The interest rate in the United Kingdom is 9 percent. The spot rate of exchange is $2/£ and the three-month forward rate is $2.015/£. Ignoring transaction costs, in which country would the treasurer want to invest the company's capital if he can fix the exchange rate three months hence through a forward contract?
    b. The spot rate of foreign exchange between the United States and the United Kingdom at time t is $1.50/£. If the interest rate in the United States is 13 percent and it is 8 percent in the United Kingdom, what would you expect the one-year forward rate to be if no immediate arbitrage opportunities existed?
    c. If you are an exporter who must make payments in foreign currency three months after receiving each shipment and you predict that the domestic currency will appreciate in value over this period, is there any value in hedging your currency exposure?

31.7   **a.** Suppose it is your task to evaluate two different investments in new subsidiaries for your company, one in your own country and the other in a foreign country. You calculate the cash flows of both projects to be identical after exchange-rate differences. Under what circumstances might you choose to invest in the foreign subsidiary? Give an example of a country where certain factors might influence you to alter this decision and invest at home.

b. Suppose Strom Equipment comes across another investment in Switzerland. The project costs SF10 million and is expected to produce cash flows of SF4 million in year 1 and SF3 million in each of years 2 and 3. The current spot-exchange rate is $0.5/SF1 and the current risk-free rate in the United States is 11.3 percent, compared to that in Switzerland of 6 percent. The appropriate discount rate for the project is estimated to be 15 percent, the U.S. cost of capital for the company. In addition, the subsidiary can be sold at the end of three years for an estimated SF2.1 million. What is the NPV of the project?

c. An investment in a foreign subsidiary is estimated to have a positive NPV, after the discount rate used in the calculations is adjusted for political risk and any advantages from diversification. Does this mean the project is acceptable? Why or why not?

d. If a U.S. firm raises funds for a foreign subsidiary, what are the disadvantages to borrowing in the United States? How would you overcome them?

INTERNATIONAL FINANCIAL DECISIONS

31.8   **a.** What is a Euroyen?

b. If financial markets are perfectly competitive and the Eurodollar rate is above that offered in the U.S. loan market, you would immediately want to borrow money in the United States and invest it in Eurodollars. True or false? Explain.

c. What distinguishes a Eurobond from a foreign bond? Which particular feature makes the Eurobond more popular than the foreign bond?

d. How would you describe a bond issued by a Canadian firm in the United States with payments denominated in U.S. dollars?

S & P PROBLEM

31.9   Nokia stock trades as an American Depository Receipt on the New York Stock Exchange. Assume that one ADR is exchangeable for one share of Nokia stock on the Finnish stock market. Find the monthly closing price of the Nokia ADR for July 2003. Assuming the exchange rate was $1.09/€ and Nokia shares traded for €14.28, explain how you could make an arbitrage profit. What was the profit per share? What exchange rate is necessary to eliminate the arbitrage opportunity?

Appendix A

Mathematical Tables

TABLE A.1   Present Value of $1 to Be Received after T Periods $= 1/(1 + r)^T$

Period	Interest Rate								
	1%	2%	3%	4%	5%	6%	7%	8%	9%
1	0.9901	0.9804	0.9709	0.9615	0.9524	0.9434	0.9346	0.9259	0.9174
2	0.9803	0.9612	0.9426	0.9246	0.9070	0.8900	0.8734	0.8573	0.8417
3	0.9706	0.9423	0.9151	0.8890	0.8638	0.8396	0.8163	0.7938	0.7722
4	0.9610	0.9238	0.8885	0.8548	0.8227	0.7921	0.7629	0.7350	0.7084
5	0.9515	0.9057	0.8626	0.8219	0.7835	0.7473	0.7130	0.6806	0.6499
6	0.9420	0.8880	0.8375	0.7903	0.7462	0.7050	0.6663	0.6302	0.5963
7	0.9327	0.8706	0.8131	0.7599	0.7107	0.6651	0.6227	0.5835	0.5470
8	0.9235	0.8535	0.7894	0.7307	0.6768	0.6274	0.5820	0.5403	0.5019
9	0.9143	0.8368	0.7664	0.7026	0.6446	0.5919	0.5439	0.5002	0.4604
10	0.9053	0.8203	0.7441	0.6756	0.6139	0.5584	0.5083	0.4632	0.4224
11	0.8963	0.8043	0.7224	0.6496	0.5847	0.5268	0.4751	0.4289	0.3875
12	0.8874	0.7885	0.7014	0.6246	0.5568	0.4970	0.4440	0.3971	0.3555
13	0.8787	0.7730	0.6810	0.6006	0.5303	0.4688	0.4150	0.3677	0.3262
14	0.8700	0.7579	0.6611	0.5775	0.5051	0.4423	0.3878	0.3405	0.2992
15	0.8613	0.7430	0.6419	0.5553	0.4810	0.4173	0.3624	0.3152	0.2745
16	0.8528	0.7284	0.6232	0.5339	0.4581	0.3936	0.3387	0.2919	0.2519
17	0.8444	0.7142	0.6050	0.5134	0.4363	0.3714	0.3166	0.2703	0.2311
18	0.8360	0.7002	0.5874	0.4936	0.4155	0.3503	0.2959	0.2502	0.2120
19	0.8277	0.6864	0.5703	0.4746	0.3957	0.3305	0.2765	0.2317	0.1945
20	0.8195	0.6730	0.5537	0.4564	0.3769	0.3118	0.2584	0.2145	0.1784
21	0.8114	0.6598	0.5375	0.4388	0.3589	0.2942	0.2415	0.1987	0.1637
22	0.8034	0.6468	0.5219	0.4220	0.3418	0.2775	0.2257	0.1839	0.1502
23	0.7954	0.6342	0.5067	0.4057	0.3256	0.2618	0.2109	0.1703	0.1378
24	0.7876	0.6217	0.4919	0.3901	0.3101	0.2470	0.1971	0.1577	0.1264
25	0.7798	0.6095	0.4776	0.3751	0.2953	0.2330	0.1842	0.1460	0.1160
30	0.7419	0.5521	0.4120	0.3083	0.2314	0.1741	0.1314	0.0994	0.0754
40	0.6717	0.4529	0.3066	0.2083	0.1420	0.0972	0.0668	0.0460	0.0318
50	0.6080	0.3715	0.2281	0.1407	0.0872	0.0543	0.0339	0.0213	0.0134

*The factor is zero to four decimal places.

TABLE A.1 *(concluded)*

					Interest Rate					
10%	12%	14%	15%	16%	18%	20%	24%	28%	32%	36%
0.9091	0.8929	0.8772	0.8696	0.8621	0.8475	0.8333	0.8065	0.7813	0.7576	0.7353
0.8264	0.7972	0.7695	0.7561	0.7432	0.7182	0.6944	0.6504	0.6104	0.5739	0.5407
0.7513	0.7118	0.6750	0.6575	0.6407	0.6086	0.5787	0.5245	0.4768	0.4348	0.3975
0.6830	0.6355	0.5921	0.5718	0.5523	0.5158	0.4823	0.4230	0.3725	0.3294	0.2923
0.6209	0.5674	0.5194	0.4972	0.4761	0.4371	0.4019	0.3411	0.2910	0.2495	0.2149
0.5645	0.5066	0.4556	0.4323	0.4104	0.3704	0.3349	0.2751	0.2274	0.1890	0.1580
0.5132	0.4523	0.3996	0.3759	0.3538	0.3139	0.2791	0.2218	0.1776	0.1432	0.1162
0.4665	0.4039	0.3506	0.3269	0.3050	0.2660	0.2326	0.1789	0.1388	0.1085	0.0854
0.4241	0.3606	0.3075	0.2843	0.2630	0.2255	0.1938	0.1443	0.1084	0.0822	0.0628
0.3855	0.3220	0.2697	0.2472	0.2267	0.1911	0.1615	0.1164	0.0847	0.0623	0.0462
0.3505	0.2875	0.2366	0.2149	0.1954	0.1619	0.1346	0.0938	0.0662	0.0472	0.0340
0.3186	0.2567	0.2076	0.1869	0.1685	0.1372	0.1122	0.0757	0.0517	0.0357	0.0250
0.2897	0.2292	0.1821	0.1625	0.1452	0.1163	0.0935	0.0610	0.0404	0.0271	0.0184
0.2633	0.2046	0.1597	0.1413	0.1252	0.0985	0.0779	0.0492	0.0316	0.0205	0.0135
0.2394	0.1827	0.1401	0.1229	0.1079	0.0835	0.0649	0.0397	0.0247	0.0155	0.0099
0.2176	0.1631	0.1229	0.1069	0.0930	0.0708	0.0541	0.0320	0.0193	0.0118	0.0073
0.1978	0.1456	0.1078	0.0929	0.0802	0.0600	0.0451	0.0258	0.0150	0.0089	0.0054
0.1799	0.1300	0.0946	0.0808	0.0691	0.0508	0.0376	0.0208	0.0118	0.0068	0.0039
0.1635	0.1161	0.0829	0.0703	0.0596	0.0431	0.0313	0.0168	0.0092	0.0051	0.0029
0.1486	0.1037	0.0728	0.0611	0.0514	0.0365	0.0261	0.0135	0.0072	0.0039	0.0021
0.1351	0.0926	0.0638	0.0531	0.0443	0.0309	0.0217	0.0109	0.0056	0.0029	0.0016
0.1228	0.0826	0.0560	0.0462	0.0382	0.0262	0.0181	0.0088	0.0044	0.0022	0.0012
0.1117	0.0738	0.0491	0.0402	0.0329	0.0222	0.0151	0.0071	0.0034	0.0017	0.0008
0.1015	0.0659	0.0431	0.0349	0.0284	0.0188	0.0126	0.0057	0.0027	0.0013	0.0006
0.0923	0.0588	0.0378	0.0304	0.0245	0.0160	0.0105	0.0046	0.0021	0.0010	0.0005
0.0573	0.0334	0.0196	0.0151	0.0116	0.0070	0.0042	0.0016	0.0006	0.0002	0.0001
0.0221	0.0107	0.0053	0.0037	0.0026	0.0013	0.0007	0.0002	0.0001	*	*
0.0085	0.0035	0.0014	0.0009	0.0006	0.0003	0.0001	*	*	*	*

TABLE A.2   Present Value of an Annuity of $1 per Period for T Periods $= [1 - 1/(1 + r)^T]/r$

Number of Periods	1%	2%	3%	4%	5%	6%	7%	8%	9%
1	0.9901	0.9804	0.9709	0.9615	0.9524	0.9434	0.9346	0.9259	0.9174
2	1.9704	1.9416	1.9135	1.8861	1.8594	1.8334	1.8080	1.7833	1.7591
3	2.9410	2.8839	2.8286	2.7751	2.7232	2.6730	2.6243	2.5771	2.5313
4	3.9020	3.8077	3.7171	3.6299	3.5460	3.4651	3.3872	3.3121	3.2397
5	4.8534	4.7135	4.5797	4.4518	4.3295	4.2124	4.1002	3.9927	3.8897
6	5.7955	5.6014	5.4172	5.2421	5.0757	4.9173	4.7665	4.6229	4.4859
7	6.7282	6.4720	6.2303	6.0021	5.7864	5.5824	5.3893	5.2064	5.0330
8	7.6517	7.3255	7.0197	6.7327	6.4632	6.2098	5.9713	5.7466	5.5348
9	8.5660	8.1622	7.7861	7.4353	7.1078	6.8017	6.5152	6.2469	5.9952
10	9.4713	8.9826	8.5302	8.1109	7.7217	7.3601	7.0236	6.7101	6.4177
11	10.3676	9.7868	9.2526	8.7605	8.3064	7.8869	7.4987	7.1390	6.8052
12	11.2551	10.5753	9.9540	9.3851	8.8633	8.3838	7.9427	7.5361	7.1607
13	12.1337	11.3484	10.6350	9.9856	9.3936	8.8527	8.3577	7.9038	7.4869
14	13.0037	12.1062	11.2961	10.5631	9.8986	9.2950	8.7455	8.2442	7.7862
15	13.8651	12.8493	11.9379	11.1184	10.3797	9.7122	9.1079	8.5595	8.0607
16	14.7179	13.5777	12.5611	11.6523	10.8378	10.1059	9.4466	8.8514	8.3126
17	15.5623	14.2919	13.1661	12.1657	11.2741	10.4773	9.7632	9.1216	8.5436
18	16.3983	14.9920	13.7535	12.6593	11.6896	10.8276	10.0591	9.3719	8.7556
19	17.2260	15.6785	14.3238	13.1339	12.0853	11.1581	10.3356	9.6036	8.9501
20	18.0456	16.3514	14.8775	13.5903	12.4622	11.4699	10.5940	9.8181	9.1285
21	18.8570	17.0112	15.4150	14.0292	12.8212	11.7641	10.8355	10.0168	9.2922
22	19.6604	17.6580	15.9369	14.4511	13.1630	12.0416	11.0612	10.2007	9.4424
23	20.4558	18.2922	16.4436	14.8568	13.4886	12.3034	11.2722	10.3741	9.5802
24	21.2434	18.9139	16.9355	15.2470	13.7986	12.5504	11.4693	10.5288	9.7066
25	22.0232	19.5235	17.4131	15.6221	14.0939	12.7834	11.6536	10.6748	9.8226
30	25.8077	22.3965	19.6004	17.2920	15.3725	13.7648	12.4090	11.2578	10.2737
40	32.8347	27.3555	23.1148	19.7928	17.1591	15.0463	13.3317	11.9246	10.7574
50	39.1961	31.4236	25.7298	21.4822	18.2559	15.7619	13.8007	12.2335	10.9617

TABLE A.2   *(concluded)*

					Interest Rate				
10%	**12%**	**14%**	**15%**	**16%**	**18%**	**20%**	**24%**	**28%**	**32%**
0.9091	0.8929	0.8772	0.8696	0.8621	0.8475	0.8333	0.8065	0.7813	0.7576
1.7355	1.6901	1.6467	1.6257	1.6052	1.5656	1.5278	1.4568	1.3916	1.3315
2.4869	2.4018	2.3216	2.2832	2.2459	2.1743	2.1065	1.9813	1.8684	1.7663
3.1699	3.0373	2.9137	2.8550	2.7982	2.6901	2.5887	2.4043	2.2410	2.0957
3.7908	3.6048	3.4331	3.3522	3.2743	3.1272	2.9906	2.7454	2.5320	2.3452
4.3553	4.1114	3.8887	3.7845	3.6847	3.4976	3.3255	3.0205	2.7594	2.5342
4.8684	4.5638	4.2883	4.1604	4.0386	3.8115	3.6046	3.2423	2.9370	2.6775
5.3349	4.9676	4.6389	4.4873	4.3436	4.0776	3.8372	3.4212	3.0758	2.7860
5.7590	5.3282	4.9464	4.7716	4.6065	4.3030	4.0310	3.5655	3.1842	2.8681
6.1446	5.6502	5.2161	5.0188	4.8332	4.4941	4.1925	3.6819	3.2689	2.9304
6.4951	5.9377	5.4527	5.2337	5.0286	4.6560	4.3271	3.7757	3.3351	2.9776
6.8137	6.1944	5.6603	5.4206	5.1971	4.7932	4.4392	3.8514	3.3868	3.0133
7.1034	6.4235	5.8424	5.5831	5.3423	4.9095	4.5327	3.9124	3.4272	3.0404
7.3667	6.6282	6.0021	5.7245	5.4675	5.0081	4.6106	3.9616	3.4587	3.0609
7.6061	6.8109	6.1422	5.8474	5.5755	5.0916	4.6755	4.0013	3.4834	3.0764
7.8237	6.9740	6.2651	5.9542	5.6685	5.1624	4.7296	4.0333	3.5026	3.0882
8.0216	7.1196	6.3729	6.0472	5.7487	5.2223	4.7746	4.0591	3.5177	3.0971
8.2014	7.2497	6.4674	6.1280	5.8178	5.2732	4.8122	4.0799	3.5294	3.1039
8.3649	7.3658	6.5504	6.1982	5.8775	5.3162	4.8435	4.0967	3.5386	3.1090
8.5136	7.4694	6.6231	6.2593	5.9288	5.3527	4.8696	4.1103	3.5458	3.1129
8.6487	7.5620	6.6870	6.3125	5.9731	5.3837	4.8913	4.1212	3.5514	3.1158
8.7715	7.6446	6.7429	6.3587	6.0113	5.4099	4.9094	4.1300	3.5558	3.1180
8.8832	7.7184	6.7921	6.3988	6.0442	5.4321	4.9245	4.1371	3.5592	3.1197
8.9847	7.7843	6.8351	6.4338	6.0726	5.4509	4.9371	4.1428	3.5619	3.1210
9.0770	7.8431	6.8729	6.4641	6.0971	5.4669	4.9476	4.1474	3.5640	3.1220
9.4269	8.0552	7.0027	6.5660	6.1772	5.5168	4.9789	4.1601	3.5693	3.1242
9.7791	8.2438	7.1050	6.6418	6.2335	5.5482	4.9966	4.1659	3.5712	3.1250
9.9148	8.3045	7.1327	6.6605	6.2463	5.5541	4.9995	4.1666	3.5714	3.1250

TABLE A.3   Future Value of \$1 at the End of T Periods $= (1 + r)^T$

					Interest Rate				
Period	**1%**	**2%**	**3%**	**4%**	**5%**	**6%**	**7%**	**8%**	**9%**
1	1.0100	1.0200	1.0300	1.0400	1.0500	1.0600	1.0700	1.0800	1.0900
2	1.0201	1.0404	1.0609	1.0816	1.1025	1.1236	1.1449	1.1664	1.1881
3	1.0303	1.0612	1.0927	1.1249	1.1576	1.1910	1.2250	1.2597	1.2950
4	1.0406	1.0824	1.1255	1.1699	1.2155	1.2625	1.3108	1.3605	1.4116
5	1.0510	1.1041	1.1593	1.2167	1.2763	1.3382	1.4026	1.4693	1.5386
6	1.0615	1.1262	1.1941	1.2653	1.3401	1.4185	1.5007	1.5869	1.6771
7	1.0721	1.1487	1.2299	1.3159	1.4071	1.5036	1.6058	1.7138	1.8280
8	1.0829	1.1717	1.2668	1.3686	1.4775	1.5938	1.7182	1.8509	1.9926
9	1.0937	1.1951	1.3048	1.4233	1.5513	1.6895	1.8385	1.9990	2.1719
10	1.1046	1.2190	1.3439	1.4802	1.6289	1.7908	1.9672	2.1589	2.3674
11	1.1157	1.2434	1.3842	1.5395	1.7103	1.8983	2.1049	2.3316	2.5804
12	1.1268	1.2682	1.4258	1.6010	1.7959	2.0122	2.2522	2.5182	2.8127
13	1.1381	1.2936	1.4685	1.6651	1.8856	2.1329	2.4098	2.7196	3.0658
14	1.1495	1.3195	1.5126	1.7317	1.9799	2.2609	2.5785	2.9372	3.3417
15	1.1610	1.3459	1.5580	1.8009	2.0789	2.3966	2.7590	3.1722	3.6425
16	1.1726	1.3728	1.6047	1.8730	2.1829	2.5404	2.9522	3.4259	3.9703
17	1.1843	1.4002	1.6528	1.9479	2.2920	2.6928	3.1588	3.7000	4.3276
18	1.1961	1.4282	1.7024	2.0258	2.4066	2.8543	3.3799	3.9960	4.7171
19	1.2081	1.4568	1.7535	2.1068	2.5270	3.0256	3.6165	4.3157	5.1417
20	1.2202	1.4859	1.8061	2.1911	2.6533	3.2071	3.8697	4.6610	5.6044
21	1.2324	1.5157	1.8603	2.2788	2.7860	3.3996	4.1406	5.0338	6.1088
22	1.2447	1.5460	1.9161	2.3699	2.9253	3.6035	4.4304	5.4365	6.6586
23	1.2572	1.5769	1.9736	2.4647	3.0715	3.8197	4.7405	5.8715	7.2579
24	1.2697	1.6084	2.0328	2.5633	3.2251	4.0489	5.0724	6.3412	7.9111
25	1.2824	1.6406	2.0938	2.6658	3.3864	4.2919	5.4274	6.8485	8.6231
30	1.3478	1.8114	2.4273	3.2434	4.3219	5.7435	7.6123	10.063	13.268
40	1.4889	2.2080	3.2620	4.8010	7.0400	10.286	14.974	21.725	31.409
50	1.6446	2.6916	4.3839	7.1067	11.467	18.420	29.457	46.902	74.358
60	1.8167	3.2810	5.8916	10.520	18.679	32.988	57.946	101.26	176.03

*FVIV > 99,999.

TABLE A.3 *(concluded)*

					Interest Rate					
10%	12%	14%	15%	16%	18%	20%	24%	28%	32%	36%
1.1000	1.1200	1.1400	1.1500	1.1600	1.1800	1.2000	1.2400	1.2800	1.3200	1.3600
1.2100	1.2544	1.2996	1.3225	1.3456	1.3924	1.4400	1.5376	1.6384	1.7424	1.8496
1.3310	1.4049	1.4815	1.5209	1.5609	1.6430	1.7280	1.9066	2.0972	2.3000	2.5155
1.4641	1.5735	1.6890	1.7490	1.8106	1.9388	2.0736	2.3642	2.6844	3.0360	3.4210
1.6105	1.7623	1.9254	2.0114	2.1003	2.2878	2.4883	2.9316	3.4360	4.0075	4.6526
1.7716	1.9738	2.1950	2.3131	2.4364	2.6996	2.9860	3.6352	4.3980	5.2899	6.3275
1.9487	2.2107	2.5023	2.6600	2.8262	3.1855	3.5832	4.5077	5.6295	6.9826	8.6054
2.1436	2.4760	2.8526	3.0590	3.2784	3.7589	4.2998	5.5895	7.2058	9.2170	11.703
2.3579	2.7731	3.2519	3.5179	3.8030	4.4355	5.1598	6.9310	9.2234	12.166	15.917
2.5937	3.1058	3.7072	4.0456	4.4114	5.2338	6.1917	8.5944	11.806	16.060	21.647
2.8531	3.4785	4.2262	4.6524	5.1173	6.1759	7.4301	10.657	15.112	21.199	29.439
3.1384	3.8960	4.8179	5.3503	5.9360	7.2876	8.9161	13.215	19.343	27.983	40.037
3.4523	4.3635	5.4924	6.1528	6.8858	8.5994	10.699	16.386	24.759	36.937	54.451
3.7975	4.8871	6.2613	7.0757	7.9875	10.147	12.839	20.319	31.691	48.757	74.053
4.1772	5.4736	7.1379	8.1371	9.2655	11.974	15.407	25.196	40.565	64.359	100.71
4.5950	6.1304	8.1372	9.3576	10.748	14.129	18.488	31.243	51.923	84.954	136.97
5.0545	6.8660	9.2765	10.761	12.468	16.672	22.186	38.741	66.461	112.14	186.28
5.5599	7.6900	10.575	12.375	14.463	19.673	26.623	48.039	86.071	148.02	253.34
6.1159	8.6128	12.056	14.232	16.777	23.214	31.948	59.568	108.89	195.39	344.54
6.7275	9.6463	13.743	16.367	19.461	27.393	38.338	73.864	139.38	257.92	468.57
7.4002	10.804	15.668	18.822	22.574	32.324	46.005	91.592	178.41	340.45	637.26
8.1403	12.100	17.861	21.645	26.186	38.142	55.206	113.57	228.36	449.39	866.67
8.9543	13.552	20.362	24.891	30.376	45.008	66.247	140.83	292.30	593.20	1178.7
9.8497	15.179	23.212	28.625	35.236	53.109	79.497	174.63	374.14	783.02	1603.0
10.835	17.000	26.462	32.919	40.874	62.669	95.396	216.54	478.90	1033.6	2180.1
17.449	29.960	50.950	66.212	85.850	143.37	237.38	634.82	1645.5	4142.1	10143.
45.259	93.051	188.88	267.86	378.72	750.38	1469.8	5455.9	19427.	66521.	*
117.39	289.00	700.23	1083.7	1670.7	3927.4	9100.4	46890.	*	*	*
304.48	897.60	2595.9	4384.0	7370.2	20555.	56348.	*	*	*	*

TABLE A.4	Sum of Annuity of $1 per Period for T Periods $= [(1 + r)^T - 1]/r$

Interest Rate

Number of Periods	1%	2%	3%	4%	5%	6%	7%	8%	9%
1	1.0000	1.0000	1.0000	1.0000	1.0000	1.0000	1.0000	1.0000	1.0000
2	2.0100	2.0200	2.0300	2.0400	2.0500	2.0600	2.0700	2.0800	2.0900
3	3.0301	3.0604	3.0909	3.1216	3.1525	3.1836	3.2149	3.2464	3.2781
4	4.0604	4.1216	4.1836	4.2465	4.3101	4.3746	4.4399	4.5061	4.5731
5	5.1010	5.2040	5.3091	5.4163	5.5256	5.6371	5.7507	5.8666	5.9847
6	6.1520	6.3081	6.4684	6.6330	6.8019	6.9753	7.1533	7.3359	7.5233
7	7.2135	7.4343	7.6625	7.8983	8.1420	8.3938	8.6540	8.9228	9.2004
8	8.2857	8.5830	8.8932	9.2142	9.5491	9.8975	10.260	10.637	11.028
9	9.3685	9.7546	10.159	10.583	11.027	11.491	11.978	12.488	13.021
10	10.462	10.950	11.464	12.006	12.578	13.181	13.816	14.487	15.193
11	11.567	12.169	12.808	13.486	14.207	14.972	15.784	16.645	17.560
12	12.683	13.412	14.192	15.026	15.917	16.870	17.888	18.977	20.141
13	13.809	14.680	15.618	16.627	17.713	18.882	20.141	21.495	22.953
14	14.947	15.974	17.086	18.292	19.599	21.015	22.550	24.215	26.019
15	16.097	17.293	18.599	20.024	21.579	23.276	25.129	27.152	29.361
16	17.258	18.639	20.157	21.825	23.657	25.673	27.888	30.324	33.003
17	18.430	20.012	21.762	23.698	25.840	28.213	30.840	33.750	36.974
18	19.615	21.412	23.414	25.645	28.132	30.906	33.999	37.450	41.301
19	20.811	22.841	25.117	27.671	30.539	33.760	37.379	41.446	46.018
20	22.019	24.297	26.870	29.778	33.066	36.786	40.995	45.762	51.160
21	23.239	25.783	28.676	31.969	35.719	39.993	44.865	50.423	56.765
22	24.472	27.299	30.537	34.248	38.505	43.392	49.006	55.457	62.873
23	25.716	28.845	32.453	36.618	41.430	46.996	53.436	60.893	69.532
24	26.973	30.422	34.426	39.083	44.502	50.816	58.177	66.765	76.790
25	28.243	32.030	36.459	41.646	47.727	54.865	63.249	73.106	84.701
30	34.785	40.568	47.575	56.085	66.439	79.058	94.461	113.28	136.31
40	48.886	60.402	75.401	95.026	120.80	154.76	199.64	259.06	337.88
50	64.463	84.579	112.80	152.67	209.35	290.34	406.53	573.77	815.08
60	81.670	114.05	163.05	237.99	353.58	533.13	813.52	1253.2	1944.8

*FVIFA > 99,999.

TABLE A.4   *(concluded)*

					Interest Rate					
10%	12%	14%	15%	16%	18%	20%	24%	28%	32%	36%
1.0000	1.0000	1.0000	1.0000	1.0000	1.0000	1.0000	1.0000	1.0000	1.0000	1.0000
2.1000	2.1200	2.1400	2.1500	2.1600	2.1800	2.2000	2.2400	2.2800	2.3200	2.3600
3.3100	3.3744	3.4396	3.4725	3.5056	3.5724	3.6400	3.7776	3.9184	4.0624	4.2096
3.6410	4.7793	4.9211	4.9934	5.0665	5.2154	5.3680	5.6842	6.0156	6.3624	6.7251
6.1051	6.3528	6.6101	6.7424	6.8771	7.1542	7.4416	8.0484	8.6999	9.3983	10.146
7.7156	8.1152	8.5355	8.7537	8.9775	9.4420	9.9299	10.980	12.136	13.406	14.799
9.4872	10.089	10.730	11.067	11.414	12.142	12.916	14.615	16.534	18.696	21.126
11.436	12.300	13.233	13.727	14.240	15.327	16.499	19.123	22.163	25.678	29.732
13.579	14.776	16.085	16.786	17.519	19.086	20.799	24.712	29.369	34.895	41.435
15.937	17.549	19.337	20.304	21.321	23.521	25.959	31.643	38.593	47.062	57.352
18.531	20.655	23.045	24.349	25.733	28.755	32.150	40.238	50.398	63.122	78.998
21.384	24.133	27.271	29.002	30.850	34.931	39.581	50.895	65.510	84.320	108.44
24.523	28.029	32.089	34.352	36.786	42.219	48.497	64.110	84.853	112.30	148.47
27.975	32.393	37.581	40.505	43.672	50.818	59.196	80.496	109.61	149.24	202.93
31.772	37.280	43.842	47.580	51.660	60.965	72.035	100.82	141.30	198.00	276.98
35.950	42.753	50.980	55.717	60.925	72.939	87.442	126.01	181.87	262.36	377.69
40.545	48.884	59.118	65.075	71.673	87.068	105.93	157.25	233.79	347.31	514.66
45.599	55.750	68.394	75.836	84.141	103.74	128.12	195.99	300.25	459.45	700.94
51.159	64.440	78.969	88.212	98.603	123.41	154.74	244.03	385.32	607.47	954.28
57.275	72.052	91.025	102.44	115.38	146.63	186.69	303.60	494.21	802.86	1298.8
64.002	81.699	104.77	118.81	134.84	174.02	225.03	377.46	633.59	1060.8	1767.4
71.403	92.503	120.44	137.63	157.41	206.34	271.03	469.06	812.00	1401.2	2404.7
79.543	104.60	138.30	159.28	183.60	244.49	326.24	582.63	1040.4	1850.6	3271.3
88.497	118.16	158.66	184.17	213.98	289.49	392.48	723.46	1332.7	2443.8	4450.0
98.347	133.33	181.87	212.79	249.21	342.60	471.98	898.09	1706.8	3226.8	6053.0
164.49	241.33	356.79	434.75	530.31	790.95	1181.9	2640.9	5873.2	12941.	28172.3
442.59	767.09	1342.0	1779.1	2360.8	4163.2	7343.9	22729.	69377.	*	*
1163.9	2400.0	4994.5	7217.7	10436.	21813.	45497.	*	*	*	*
3034.8	7471.6	18535.	29220.	46058.	*	*	*	*	*	*

TABLE A.5	Future Value of $1 with a Continuously Compounded Rate *r* for *T* Periods: Values of e^{rT}

Period (T)	\multicolumn{10}{c}{Continuously Compounded Rate (r)}
	1%	2%	3%	4%	5%	6%	7%	8%	9%	10%
1	1.0101	1.0202	1.0305	1.0408	1.0513	1.0618	1.0725	1.0833	1.0942	1.1052
2	1.0202	1.0408	1.0618	1.0833	1.1052	1.1275	1.1503	1.1735	1.1972	1.2214
3	1.0305	1.0618	1.0942	1.1275	1.1618	1.1972	1.2337	1.2712	1.3100	1.3499
4	1.0408	1.0833	1.1275	1.1735	1.2214	1.2712	1.3231	1.3771	1.4333	1.4918
5	1.0513	1.1052	1.1618	1.2214	1.2840	1.3499	1.4191	1.4918	1.5683	1.6487
6	1.0618	1.1275	1.1972	1.2712	1.3499	1.4333	1.5220	1.6161	1.7160	1.8221
7	1.0725	1.1503	1.2337	1.3231	1.4191	1.5220	1.6323	1.7507	1.8776	2.0138
8	1.0833	1.1735	1.2712	1.3771	1.4918	1.6161	1.7507	1.8965	2.0544	2.2255
9	1.0942	1.1972	1.3100	1.4333	1.5683	1.7160	1.8776	2.0544	2.2479	2.4596
10	1.1052	1.2214	1.3499	1.4918	1.6487	1.8221	2.0138	2.2255	2.4596	2.7183
11	1.1163	1.2461	1.3910	1.5527	1.7333	1.9348	2.1598	2.4109	2.6912	3.0042
12	1.1275	1.2712	1.4333	1.6161	1.8221	2.0544	2.3164	2.6117	2.9447	3.3201
13	1.1388	1.2969	1.4770	1.6820	1.9155	2.1815	2.4843	2.8292	3.2220	3.6693
14	1.1503	1.3231	1.5220	1.7507	2.0138	2.3164	2.6645	3.0649	3.5254	4.0552
15	1.1618	1.3499	1.5683	1.8221	2.1170	2.4596	2.8577	3.3201	3.8574	4.4817
16	1.1735	1.3771	1.6161	1.8965	2.2255	2.6117	3.0649	3.5966	4.2207	4.9530
17	1.1853	1.4049	1.6653	1.9739	2.3396	2.7732	3.2871	3.8962	4.6182	5.4739
18	1.1972	1.4333	1.7160	2.0544	2.4596	2.9447	3.5254	4.2207	5.0531	6.0496
19	1.2092	1.4623	1.7683	2.1383	2.5857	3.1268	3.7810	4.5722	5.5290	6.6859
20	1.2214	1.4918	1.8221	2.2255	2.7183	3.3201	4.0552	4.9530	6.0496	7.3891
21	1.2337	1.5220	1.8776	2.3164	2.8577	3.5254	4.3492	5.3656	6.6194	8.1662
22	1.2461	1.5527	1.9348	2.4109	3.0042	3.7434	4.6646	5.8124	7.2427	9.0250
23	1.2586	1.5841	1.9937	2.5093	3.1582	3.9749	5.0028	6.2965	7.9248	9.9742
24	1.2712	1.6161	2.0544	2.6117	3.3201	4.2207	5.3656	6.8210	8.6711	11.0232
25	1.2840	1.6487	2.1170	2.7183	3.4903	4.4817	5.7546	7.3891	9.4877	12.1825
30	1.3499	1.8221	2.4596	3.3204	4.4817	6.0496	8.1662	11.0232	14.8797	20.0855
35	1.4191	2.0138	2.8577	4.0552	5.7546	8.1662	11.5883	16.4446	23.3361	33.1155
40	1.4918	2.2255	3.3201	4.9530	7.3891	11.0232	16.4446	24.5235	36.5982	54.5982
45	1.5683	2.4596	3.8574	6.0496	9.4877	14.8797	23.3361	36.5982	57.3975	90.0171
50	1.6487	2.7183	4.4817	7.3891	12.1825	20.0855	33.1155	54.5982	90.0171	148.4132
55	1.7333	3.0042	5.2070	9.0250	15.6426	27.1126	46.9931	81.4509	141.1750	244.6919
60	1.8221	3.3201	6.0496	11.0232	20.0855	36.5982	66.6863	121.5104	221.4064	403.4288

TABLE A.5   *(continued)*

Continuously Compounded Rate (*r*)										
11%	12%	13%	14%	15%	16%	17%	18%	19%	20%	21%
1.1163	1.1275	1.1388	1.1503	1.1618	1.1735	1.1853	1.1972	1.2092	1.2214	1.2337
1.2461	1.2712	1.2969	1.3231	1.3499	1.3771	1.4049	1.4333	1.4623	1.4918	1.5220
1.3910	1.4333	1.4770	1.5220	1.5683	1.6161	1.6653	1.7160	1.7683	1.8221	1.8776
1.5527	1.6161	1.6820	1.7507	1.8221	1.8965	1.9739	2.0544	2.1383	2.2255	2.3164
1.7333	1.8221	1.9155	2.0138	2.1170	2.2255	2.3396	2.4596	2.5857	2.7183	2.8577
1.9348	2.0544	2.1815	2.3164	2.4596	2.6117	2.7732	2.9447	3.1268	3.3201	3.5254
2.1598	2.3164	2.4843	2.6645	2.8577	3.0649	3.2871	3.5254	3.7810	4.0552	4.3492
2.4109	2.6117	2.8292	3.0649	3.3201	3.5966	3.8962	4.2207	4.5722	4.9530	5.3656
2.6912	2.9447	3.2220	3.5254	3.8574	4.2207	4.6182	5.0531	5.5290	6.0496	6.6194
3.0042	3.3201	3.6693	4.0552	4.4817	4.9530	5.4739	6.0496	6.6859	7.3891	8.1662
3.3535	3.7434	4.1787	4.6646	5.2070	5.8124	6.4883	7.2427	8.0849	9.0250	10.0744
3.7434	4.2207	4.7588	5.3656	6.0496	6.8210	7.6906	8.6711	9.7767	11.0232	12.4286
4.1787	4.7588	5.4195	6.1719	7.0287	8.0045	9.1157	10.3812	11.8224	13.4637	15.3329
4.6646	5.3656	6.1719	7.0993	8.1662	9.3933	10.8049	12.4286	14.2963	16.4446	18.9158
5.2070	6.0496	7.0287	8.1662	9.4877	11.0232	12.0871	14.8797	17.2878	20.0855	23.3361
5.8124	6.8210	8.0045	9.3933	11.0232	12.9358	15.1803	17.8143	20.9052	24.5325	28.7892
6.4883	7.6906	9.1157	10.8049	12.8071	15.1803	17.9933	21.3276	25.2797	29.9641	35.5166
7.2427	8.6711	10.3812	12.4286	14.8797	17.8143	21.3276	25.5337	30.5694	36.5982	43.8160
8.0849	9.7767	11.8224	14.2963	17.2878	20.9052	25.2797	30.5694	36.9661	44.7012	54.0549
9.0250	11.0232	13.4637	16.4446	20.0855	24.5325	29.9641	36.5982	44.7012	54.5982	66.6863
10.0744	12.4286	15.3329	18.9158	23.3361	28.7892	35.5166	43.8160	54.0549	66.6863	82.2695
11.2459	14.0132	17.4615	21.7584	27.1126	33.7844	42.0980	52.4573	65.3659	81.4509	101.4940
12.5535	15.7998	19.8857	25.0281	31.5004	39.6464	49.8990	62.8028	79.0436	99.4843	125.2110
14.0132	17.8143	22.6464	28.7892	36.5982	46.5255	59.1455	75.1886	95.5835	121.5104	154.4700
15.6426	20.0855	25.7903	33.1155	42.5211	54.5982	70.1054	90.0171	115.5843	148.4132	190.5663
27.1126	36.5982	49.4024	66.6863	90.0171	121.5104	164.0219	221.4064	298.8674	403.4288	544.5719
46.9931	66.6863	94.6324	134.2898	190.5663	270.4264	383.7533	544.5719	772.7843	1096.633	1556.197
81.4509	121.5104	181.2722	270.4264	403.4288	601.8450	897.8473	1339.431	1998.196	2980.958	4447.067
141.1750	221.4064	347.2344	544.5719	854.0588	1339.431	2100.646	3294.468	5166.754	8103.084	12708.17
244.6919	403.4288	665.1416	1096.633	1808.042	2980.958	4914.769	8103.084	13359.73	22026.47	36315.50
424.1130	735.0952	1274.106	2208.348	3827.626	6634.244	11498.82	19930.37	34544.37	59874.14	103777.0
735.0952	1339.431	2440.602	4447.067	8103.084	14764.78	26903.19	49020.80	89321.72	162754.8	296558.6

TABLE A.5   (concluded)

Period (T)	22%	23%	24%	25%	26%	27%	28%
				Continuously Compounded Rate (r)			
1	1.2461	1.2586	1.2712	1.2840	1.2969	1.3100	1.3231
2	1.5527	1.5841	1.6161	1.6487	1.6820	1.7160	1.7507
3	1.9348	1.9937	2.0544	2.1170	2.1815	2.2479	2.3164
4	2.4109	2.5093	2.6117	2.7183	2.8292	2.9447	3.0649
5	3.0042	3.1582	3.3201	3.4903	3.6693	3.8574	4.0552
6	3.7434	3.9749	4.2207	4.4817	4.7588	5.0351	5.3656
7	4.6646	5.0028	5.3656	5.7546	6.1719	6.6194	7.0993
8	5.8124	6.2965	6.8210	7.3891	8.0045	8.6711	9.3933
9	7.2427	7.9248	8.6711	9.4877	10.3812	11.3589	12.4286
10	9.0250	9.9742	11.0232	12.1825	13.4637	14.8797	16.4446
11	11.2459	12.5535	14.0132	15.6426	17.4615	19.4919	21.7584
12	14.0132	15.7998	17.8143	20.0855	22.6464	25.5337	28.7892
13	17.4615	19.8857	22.6464	25.7903	29.3708	33.4483	38.0918
14	21.7584	25.0281	28.7892	33.1155	38.0918	43.8160	50.4004
15	27.1126	31.5004	36.5982	42.5211	49.4024	57.3975	66.6863
16	33.7844	39.6464	46.5255	54.5982	64.0715	75.1886	88.2347
17	42.0980	49.8990	59.1455	70.1054	83.0963	98.4944	116.7459
18	52.4573	62.8028	75.1886	90.0171	107.7701	129.0242	154.4700
19	65.3659	79.0436	95.5835	115.5843	139.7702	169.0171	204.3839
20	81.4509	99.4843	121.5104	148.4132	181.2722	221.4064	270.4264
21	101.4940	125.2110	154.4700	190.5663	235.0974	290.0345	357.8092
22	126.4694	157.5905	196.3699	244.6919	304.9049	379.9349	473.4281
23	157.5905	198.3434	249.6350	314.1907	395.4404	497.7013	626.4068
24	196.3699	249.6350	317.3483	403.4288	512.8585	651.9709	828.8175
25	244.6919	314.1907	403.4288	518.0128	665.1416	854.0588	1096.633
30	735.0952	992.2747	1339.431	1808.042	2440.602	3294.468	4447.067
35	2208.348	3133.795	4447.067	6310.688	8955.293	12708.17	18033.74
40	6634.244	9897.129	14764.78	22026.47	32859.63	49020.80	73130.44
45	19930.37	31257.04	49020.80	76879.92	120571.7	189094.1	296558.6
50	59874.14	98715.77	162754.8	268337.3	442413.4	729416.4	1202604
55	179871.9	311763.4	540364.9	936589.2	1623346	2813669	4876801
60	540364.9	984609.1	1794075	3269017	5956538	10853520	19776403

| TABLE A.6 | Present Value of $1 with a Continuous Discount Rate r for T Periods: Values of e^{-rT} |

Period	Continuous Discount Rate (r)						
(T)	1%	2%	3%	4%	5%	6%	7%
1	0.9900	0.9802	0.9704	0.9608	0.9512	0.9418	0.9324
2	0.9802	0.9608	0.9418	0.9231	0.9048	0.8869	0.8694
3	0.9704	0.9418	0.9139	0.8869	0.8607	0.8353	0.8106
4	0.9608	0.9231	0.8869	0.8521	0.8187	0.7866	0.7558
5	0.9512	0.9048	0.8607	0.8187	0.7788	0.7408	0.7047
6	0.9418	0.8869	0.8353	0.7866	0.7408	0.6977	0.6570
7	0.9324	0.8694	0.8106	0.7558	0.7047	0.6570	0.6126
8	0.9231	0.8521	0.7866	0.7261	0.6703	0.6188	0.5712
9	0.9139	0.8353	0.7634	0.6977	0.6376	0.5827	0.5326
10	0.9048	0.8187	0.7408	0.6703	0.6065	0.5488	0.4966
11	0.8958	0.8025	0.7189	0.6440	0.5769	0.5169	0.4630
12	0.8869	0.7866	0.6977	0.6188	0.5488	0.4868	0.4317
13	0.8781	0.7711	0.6771	0.5945	0.5220	0.4584	0.4025
14	0.8694	0.7558	0.6570	0.5712	0.4966	0.4317	0.3753
15	0.8607	0.7408	0.6376	0.5488	0.4724	0.4066	0.3499
16	0.8521	0.7261	0.6188	0.5273	0.4493	0.3829	0.3263
17	0.8437	0.7118	0.6005	0.5066	0.4274	0.3606	0.3042
18	0.8353	0.6977	0.5827	0.4868	0.4066	0.3396	0.2837
19	0.8270	0.6839	0.5655	0.4677	0.3867	0.3198	0.2645
20	0.8187	0.6703	0.5488	0.4493	0.3679	0.3012	0.2466
21	0.8106	0.6570	0.5326	0.4317	0.3499	0.2837	0.2299
22	0.8025	0.6440	0.5169	0.4148	0.3329	0.2671	0.2144
23	0.7945	0.6313	0.5016	0.3985	0.3166	0.2516	0.1999
24	0.7866	0.6188	0.4868	0.3829	0.3012	0.2369	0.1864
25	0.7788	0.6065	0.4724	0.3679	0.2865	0.2231	0.1738
30	0.7408	0.5488	0.4066	0.3012	0.2231	0.1653	0.1225
35	0.7047	0.4966	0.3499	0.2466	0.1738	0.1225	0.0863
40	0.6703	0.4493	0.3012	0.2019	0.1353	0.0907	0.0608
45	0.6376	0.4066	0.2592	0.1653	0.1054	0.0672	0.0429
50	0.6065	0.3679	0.2231	0.1353	0.0821	0.0498	0.0302
55	0.5769	0.3329	0.1920	0.1108	0.0639	0.0369	0.0213
60	0.5488	0.3012	0.1653	0.0907	0.0498	0.0273	0.0150

TABLE A.6 *(continued)*

Period (T)	Continuous Discount Rate (r)									
	8%	9%	10%	11%	12%	13%	14%	15%	16%	17%
1	0.9231	0.9139	0.9048	0.8958	0.8869	0.8781	0.8694	0.8607	0.8521	0.8437
2	0.8521	0.8353	0.8187	0.8025	0.7866	0.7711	0.7558	0.7408	0.7261	0.7118
3	0.7866	0.7634	0.7408	0.7189	0.6977	0.6771	0.6570	0.6376	0.6188	0.6005
4	0.7261	0.6977	0.6703	0.6440	0.6188	0.5945	0.5712	0.5488	0.5273	0.5066
5	0.6703	0.6376	0.6065	0.5769	0.5488	0.5220	0.4966	0.4724	0.4493	0.4274
6	0.6188	0.5827	0.5488	0.5169	.04868	0.4584	0.4317	0.4066	0.3829	0.3606
7	0.5712	0.5326	0.4966	0.4630	0.4317	0.4025	0.3753	0.3499	0.3263	0.3042
8	0.5273	0.4868	0.4493	0.4148	0.3829	0.3535	0.3263	0.3012	0.2780	0.2576
9	0.4868	0.4449	0.4066	0.3716	0.3396	0.3104	0.2837	0.2592	0.2369	0.2165
10	0.4493	0.4066	0.3679	0.3329	0.3012	0.2725	0.2466	0.2231	0.2019	0.1827
11	0.4148	0.3716	0.3329	0.2982	0.2671	0.2393	0.2144	0.1920	0.1720	0.1541
12	0.3829	0.3396	0.3012	0.2671	0.2369	0.2101	0.1864	0.1653	0.1466	0.1300
13	0.3535	0.3104	0.2725	0.2393	0.2101	0.1845	0.1620	0.1423	0.1249	0.1097
14	0.3263	0.2837	0.2466	0.2144	0.1864	0.1620	0.1409	0.1225	0.1065	0.0926
15	0.3012	0.2592	0.2231	0.1920	0.1653	0.1423	0.1225	0.1054	0.0907	0.0781
16	0.2780	0.2369	0.2019	0.1720	0.1466	0.1249	0.1065	0.0907	0.0773	0.0659
17	0.2567	0.2165	0.1827	0.1541	0.1300	0.1097	0.0926	0.0781	0.0659	0.0556
18	0.2369	0.1979	0.1653	0.1381	0.1153	0.0963	0.0805	0.0672	0.0561	0.0469
19	0.2187	0.1809	0.1496	0.1237	0.1023	0.0846	0.0699	0.0578	0.0478	0.0396
20	0.2019	0.1653	0.1353	0.1108	0.0907	0.0743	0.0608	0.0498	0.0408	0.0334
21	0.1864	0.1511	0.1225	0.0993	0.0805	0.0652	0.0529	0.0429	0.0347	0.0282
22	0.1720	0.1381	0.1108	0.0889	0.0714	0.0573	0.0460	0.0369	0.0296	0.0238
23	0.1588	0.1262	0.1003	0.0797	0.0633	0.0503	0.0400	0.0317	0.0252	0.0200
24	0.1466	0.1153	0.0907	0.0714	0.0561	0.0442	0.0347	0.0273	0.0215	0.0169
25	0.1353	0.1054	0.0821	0.0639	0.0498	0.0388	0.0302	0.0235	0.0183	0.0143
30	0.0907	0.0672	0.0498	0.0369	0.0273	0.0202	0.0150	0.0111	0.0082	0.0061
35	0.0608	0.0429	0.0302	0.0213	0.0150	0.0106	0.0074	0.0052	0.0037	0.0026
40	0.0408	0.0273	0.0183	0.0123	0.0082	0.0055	0.0037	0.0025	0.0017	0.0011
45	0.0273	0.0174	0.0111	0.0071	0.0045	0.0029	0.0018	0.0012	0.0007	0.0005
50	0.0183	0.0111	0.0067	0.0041	0.0025	0.0015	0.0009	0.0006	0.0003	0.0002
55	0.0123	0.0071	0.0041	0.0024	0.0014	0.0008	0.0005	0.0003	0.0002	0.0001
60	0.0082	0.0045	0.0025	0.0014	0.0007	0.0004	0.0002	0.0001	0.0001	0.0000

TABLE A.6   *(continued)*

					Continuous Discount Rate (*r*)					
18%	**19%**	**20%**	**21%**	**22%**	**23%**	**24%**	**25%**	**26%**	**27%**	**28%**
0.8353	0.8270	0.8187	0.8106	0.8025	0.7945	0.7866	0.7788	0.7711	0.7634	0.7558
0.6977	0.6839	0.6703	0.6570	0.6440	0.6313	0.6188	0.6065	0.5945	0.5827	0.5712
0.5827	0.5655	0.5488	0.5326	0.5169	0.5016	0.4868	0.4724	0.4584	0.4449	0.4317
0.4868	0.4677	0.4493	0.4317	0.4148	0.3985	0.3829	0.3679	0.3535	0.3396	0.3263
0.4066	0.3867	0.3679	0.3499	0.3329	0.3166	0.3012	0.2865	0.2725	0.2592	0.2466
0.3396	0.3198	0.3012	0.2837	0.2671	0.2516	0.2369	0.2231	0.2101	0.1979	0.1864
0.2837	0.2645	0.2466	0.2299	0.2144	0.1999	0.1864	0.1738	0.1620	0.1511	0.1409
0.2369	0.2187	0.2019	0.1864	0.1720	0.1588	0.1466	0.1353	0.1249	0.1153	0.1065
0.1979	0.1809	0.1653	0.1511	0.1381	0.1262	0.1153	0.1054	0.0963	0.0880	0.0805
0.1653	0.1496	0.1353	0.1225	0.1108	0.1003	0.0907	0.0821	0.0743	0.0672	0.0608
0.1381	0.1237	0.1108	0.0993	0.0889	0.0797	0.0714	0.0639	0.0573	0.0513	0.0460
0.1154	0.1023	0.0907	0.0805	0.0714	0.0633	0.0561	0.0498	0.0442	0.0392	0.0347
0.0963	0.0846	0.0743	0.0652	0.0573	0.0503	0.0442	0.0388	0.0340	0.0299	0.0263
0.0805	0.0699	0.0608	0.0529	0.0460	0.0400	0.0347	0.0302	0.0263	0.0228	0.0198
0.0672	0.0578	0.0498	0.0429	0.0369	0.0317	0.0273	0.0235	0.0202	0.0174	0.0150
0.0561	0.0478	0.0408	0.0347	0.0296	0.0252	0.0215	0.0183	0.0156	0.0133	0.0113
0.0469	0.0396	0.0334	0.0282	0.0238	0.0200	0.0169	0.0143	0.0120	0.0102	0.0086
0.0392	0.0327	0.0273	0.0228	0.0191	0.0159	0.0133	0.0111	0.0093	0.0078	0.0065
0.0327	0.0271	0.0224	0.0185	0.0153	0.0127	0.0105	0.0087	0.0072	0.0059	0.0049
0.0273	0.0224	0.0183	0.0150	0.0123	0.0101	0.0082	0.0067	0.0055	0.0045	0.0037
0.0228	0.0185	0.0150	0.0122	0.0099	0.0080	0.0065	0.0052	0.0043	0.0034	0.0028
0.0191	0.0153	0.0123	0.0099	0.0079	0.0063	0.0051	0.0041	0.0033	0.0026	0.0021
0.0159	0.0127	0.0101	0.0080	0.0063	0.0050	0.0040	0.0032	0.0025	0.0020	0.0016
0.0133	0.0105	0.0082	0.0065	0.0051	0.0040	0.0032	0.0025	0.0019	0.0015	0.0012
0.0111	0.0087	0.0067	0.0052	0.0041	0.0032	0.0025	0.0019	0.0015	0.0012	0.0009
0.0045	0.0033	0.0025	0.0018	0.0014	0.0010	0.0007	0.0006	0.0004	0.0003	0.0002
0.0018	0.0013	0.0009	0.0006	0.0005	0.0003	0.0002	0.0002	0.0001	0.0001	0.0001
0.0007	0.0005	0.0003	0.0002	0.0002	0.0001	0.0001	0.0000	0.0000	0.0000	0.0000
0.0003	0.0002	0.0001	0.0001	0.0001	0.0000	0.0000	0.0000	0.0000	0.0000	0.0000
0.0001	0.0001	0.0000	0.0000	0.0000	0.0000	0.0000	0.0000	0.0000	0.0000	0.0000
0.0001	0.0000	0.0000	0.0000	0.0000	0.0000	0.0000	0.0000	0.0000	0.0000	0.0000
0.0000	0.0000	0.0000	0.0000	0.0000	0.0000	0.0000	0.0000	0.0000	0.0000	0.0000

TABLE A.6   (concluded)

Period (T)	Continuous Discount Rate (r)						
	29%	30%	31%	32%	33%	34%	35%
1	0.7483	0.7408	0.7334	0.7261	0.7189	0.7118	0.7047
2	0.5599	0.5488	0.5379	0.5273	0.5169	0.5066	0.4966
3	0.4190	0.4066	0.3946	0.3829	0.3716	0.3606	0.3499
4	0.3135	0.3012	0.2894	0.2780	0.2671	0.2567	0.2466
5	0.2346	0.2231	0.2122	0.2019	0.1920	0.1827	0.1738
6	0.1755	0.1653	0.1557	0.1466	0.1381	0.1300	0.1225
7	0.1313	0.1225	0.1142	0.1065	0.0993	0.0926	0.0863
8	0.0983	0.0907	0.0837	0.0773	0.0714	0.0659	0.0608
9	0.0735	0.0672	0.0614	0.0561	0.0513	0.0469	0.0429
10	0.0550	0.0498	0.0450	0.0408	0.0369	0.0334	0.0302
11	0.0412	0.0369	0.0330	0.0296	0.0265	0.0238	0.0213
12	0.0308	0.0273	0.0242	0.0215	0.0191	0.0169	0.0150
13	0.0231	0.0202	0.0178	0.0156	0.0137	0.0120	0.0106
14	0.0172	0.0150	0.0130	0.0113	0.0099	0.0086	0.0074
15	0.0129	0.0111	0.0096	0.0082	0.0071	0.0061	0.0052
16	0.0097	0.0082	0.0070	0.0060	0.0051	0.0043	0.0037
17	0.0072	0.0061	0.0051	0.0043	0.0037	0.0031	0.0026
18	0.0054	0.0045	0.0038	0.0032	0.0026	0.0022	0.0018
19	0.0040	0.0033	0.0028	0.0023	0.0019	0.0016	0.0013
20	0.0030	0.0025	0.0020	0.0017	0.0014	0.0011	0.0009
21	0.0023	0.0018	0.0015	0.0012	0.0010	0.0008	0.0006
22	0.0017	0.0014	0.0011	0.0009	0.0007	0.0006	0.0005
23	0.0013	0.0010	0.0008	0.0006	0.0005	0.0004	0.0003
24	0.0009	0.0007	0.0006	0.0005	0.0004	0.0003	0.0002
25	0.0007	0.0006	0.0004	0.0003	0.0003	0.0002	0.0002
30	0.0002	0.0001	0.0001	0.0001	0.0001	0.0000	0.0000
35	0.0000	0.0000	0.0000	0.0000	0.0000	0.0000	0.0000
40	0.0000	0.0000	0.0000	0.0000	0.0000	0.0000	0.0000
45	0.0000	0.0000	0.0000	0.0000	0.0000	0.0000	0.0000
50	0.0000	0.0000	0.0000	0.0000	0.0000	0.0000	0.0000
55	0.0000	0.0000	0.0000	0.0000	0.0000	0.0000	0.0000
60	0.0000	0.0000	0.0000	0.0000	0.0000	0.0000	0.0000

Solutions to Selected End-of-Chapter Problems

CHAPTER 2

2.1 Total assets = $128,000
    Common stock = $88,000

2.2 Common stock = $110,000,000
    RE = $22,000,000

2.7 Total cash flow to investors = ($5,000)

2.8 **a.** The difference in cash flow is the sum of the differences in cash flows from operations investing activities, and financing activities.
    b. $25
    c. −$25

CHAPTER 3

3.2 **a.** $3.24 million
    b. Total liabilities = $525 million
    c. Total liabilities = 574.26

CHAPTER 4

4.1 **a.** $1,628.89
    b. $1,967.15
    c. $2,653.30
    d. $628.89

4.4 $92.30

4.5 $187,780.23

4.6 **a.** PV_1 = $10,000 PV_2 = $20,000
    b. PV_1 = $ 9,090.91 PV_2 = $12,418.43
    c. PV_1 = $ 8,333.33 PV_2 = $ 8,037.55
    d. r = 18.921%

4.9 $1,609,866.18

4.15 $6,714.61

4.19 Choose Bank America

4.22 $901.58

4.28 $13.25

4.29 Yes, since it has a positive NPV, $201.91

4.31 $1,658.98

4.32 9.0626%

4.38 No

4.39 $440,011.02

4.42 $415,783.60

4.43 NPV = $3,041.91, revise the textbook.

CHAPTER 5

5.2 **a.** $1,000.00
    b. $828.41
    c. $1,231.15

5.6 **a.** 0.1236%
    b. $748.49
    c. $906.15

5.16 2,754 Shares

5.19 $23.75

5.21 $29.40

CHAPTER 6

6.1 **a.** Project A
    b. Project B

6.3 **a.** 56.25%

6.5 44%

6.7 For Project A: IRR_1 = 0%;
                 IRR_2 = 100%
    For Project B: IRR = 36.1944%

6.9 **a.** 13.99%
    d. −$359.95

CHAPTER 7

7.4 PV = $13,348,256

7.6 NPV = $129,870

7.8 NPV = $84,709

7.13 $NPV_A = \$1,446$
$NPV_B = \$120$
Choose Project A

7.15 $NPV = -\$20,576$

CHAPTER 8

8.1 $12,500,000

8.3 Option 2

CHAPTER 9

9.1 **a.** $500
b. $1,500
c. 8.11%

9.4 5.29%

9.6 $E(R) = 10.4\%$

9.11 **a.** 15.9%, **b.** 0.02916

9.13 **a.** $E(R) = 8.8\%$
b. Standard deviation = 0.03311

9.14 **a.** $\overline{R}_M = 15.3\%$
b. $\overline{R}_T = 6.28\%$

CHAPTER 10

10.1 **a.** $\overline{R} = 10.57\%$
b. $\sigma = 7.20\%$

10.4 Weight of Atlas stock $= \frac{2}{3}$
Weight of Babcock stock $= \frac{1}{3}$

10.5 $\overline{R}_p = 16.2\%$
$\sigma_p = 18.23\%$

10.14 **b.** 13.5%

10.19 **a.** 9.9%
b. 21.43%

10.27 3%, 18.71%

CHAPTER 11

11.4 **a.** $R_A = 10.5 + 1.2 \times (R_M - 14.2) + \epsilon_A$
$R_B = 13.0 + 0.98 \times (R_M - 14.2) + \epsilon_B$
$R_C = 15.7 + 1.37 \times (R_M - 14.2) + \epsilon_C$
b. $R_p = 12.925 + 1.1435 \times (R_M - 14.2) + 0.30\epsilon_A$
$+ 0.45\epsilon_B + 0.25\epsilon_C$
c. $R_p = 13.8398\%$

11.6 **a.** $Var(R_{1p}) = .0225$
$Var(R_{2p}) = .00225$
A risk-averse investor will prefer to invest in the second market.
b. $Var(R_{1p}) = .0585$
$Var(R_{2p}) = .0025$
A risk-averse investor will prefer to invest in the second market.

c. $Var(R_{1p}) = .0225$
$Var(R_{2p}) = .0225$
Indifferent between investing in the two markets.

d. Indifference implies that the variances of the portfolios in the two markets are equal.
$Corr\ (\epsilon_{2i}, \epsilon_{2j}) = Corr\ (\epsilon_{1i}, \epsilon_{1j}) + .5$

CHAPTER 12

12.1 No, since NPV is negative

12.12 **a.** 14.74%
b. 9.645%

CHAPTER 14

14.1 **a.** 67,715 shares
b. Average price = $5 per share
c. Book value = $40 per share

14.2 **a.** Common stock = $500
Total = $150,500

CHAPTER 15

15.3 Levered

15.9 **a.** False
b. False

15.15 **a.** $8,250,000
b. $8,454,000

15.16 **a.** $7,375,000

CHAPTER 16

16.10 **a.** Total cash flow to stakeholders:
Equity plan = $1,260,000
Debt plan = $1,638,000
b. Taxes (Debt) = $1,362,000
Taxes (Equity) = $1,740,000
c. $V_U = \$6,300,000$
$V_L = \$11,700,000$
d. Total cash flow to stakeholders:
Equity plan = $1,440,000
Debt plan = $1,399,500

16.12 **a.** $3,217,500
b. $3,657,500

CHAPTER 17

17.1 **a.** $I = \$350,625.29$
b. B/C NPV = $18,285.17
APV = $40,005.51

17.6 **a.** $r_B = 10\%$, pre-tax
b. $r_s = 17.576\%$
After-tax cost of debt = 6.6%
c. 13.917%

17.7 **a.** *i.* WACC = 0.1047

    ii. WACC = 0.1173

    iii. WACC = 0.1047

17.8 **a.** Neon should make the purchase (14.42%)

CHAPTER 18

18.4 **a.** February 27

    b. $1.25

18.6 **a.** $15

18.22 **a.** 1.415

    b. 1.58

CHAPTER 19

19.6 At $40, P = $40.00

    At $20, P = $33.33

    At $10, P = $30.00

19.10 **a.** 800,000 shares

    b. 3

    c. $15 and three rights

19.11 **a.** Ex-rights price = $24.55

    b. Value of a right = $0.45

    c. Value = $2,700,500

19.13 **a.** $36.25

    b. $ 8.75

CHAPTER 20

20.6 **a.** P = $1,266.41

20.8 **a.** V_{NC} = $1,164.61

    b. C = $77.63

    c. $130.12

20.10 NPV = $17,857,143

CHAPTER 21

21.7 **a.** Lease vs. buy NPV = $3,177.78

    c. $18,177.78

CHAPTER 22

22.6 **a.** $0

    b. $0

    c. $5

    d. $5

22.13 $42.36

22.19 $11.30

22.21 **a.** $16.13

    b. $ 6.61

CHAPTER 23

23.3 Webber should not accept the offer.

23.4 Max. bid = $370,237

CHAPTER 24

24.4 **a.** $1,750

    b. $1,750

    c. $1,986.67

24.5 **a.** Lower limit = $0

       Upper limit = $8

    b. Lower limit = $2

       Upper limit = $12

24.14 **a.** 28

    b. $35.71

    c. 14.27%

    d. $875

    e. $931

24.16 $333.33

CHAPTER 25

25.3 **a.** *i.* $5.10

       ii. $5.10 per barrel

    b. *i.* $4.98 per bushel

       ii. $4.98 per barrel

25.11 **a.** C = $35,237.89

25.13 **a.** A = $904.90; B = $1,031.70

    b. A = $1000; B = $1

25.17 4.3262 years

25.20 **a.** Yes

CHAPTER 27

27.3 $2,298.72

27.4 **a.** $243,193; $556,807

    b. 17 times

27.12 $6,240

CHAPTER 28

28.3 Tropeland should not adopt the policy.

28.4 **a.** No

    b. Greater than 99.57%

28.6 If greater than 92.10%

28.12 $1,400,000

CHAPTER 29

29.8 **a.** $3,500
    b. $1
    c. $17.50

29.10 **a.** $7,500,000
    b. $27,500,000
    c. $15,625,000
    d. $11,875,000
    e. Cash alternative

CHAPTER 31

31.3 **a.** False
    b. False
    c. True

31.4 BD 2.625/WD

31.5 **a.** FF 6.04/$

Glossary

AAR Average accounting return.

ACRS Accelerated cost recovery system.

APT Arbitrage pricing theory.

Absolute priority rule (APR) Establishes priority of claims under liquidation.

Accelerated cost recovery system (ACRS) A system used to depreciate assets for tax purposes. The current system, enacted by the 1986 Tax Reform Act, is very similar to the ACRS established in 1981. The current system specifies the depreciable lives (recovery periods) and rates for each of several classes of property.

Accounting insolvency Total accounting liabilities exceed total accounting assets. A firm with negative net worth is insolvent on the books.

Accounting liquidity The ease and quickness with which assets can be converted to cash.

Accounts payable Money the firm owes to suppliers.

Accounts receivable Money owed to the firm by customers.

Accounts receivable financing A secured short-term loan that involves either the assigning of receivables or the factoring of receivables. Under assignment, the lender has a lien on the receivables and recourse to the borrower. Factoring involves the sale of accounts receivable. Then the purchaser, called the factor, must collect on the receivables.

Accounts receivable turnover Credit sales divided by average accounts receivable.

Additions to net working capital Component of cash flow of firm, along with operating cash flow and capital spending.

Adjusted present value Net present value adjusted for taxes, financial distress costs and other financial side-effects.

Advance commitment A promise to sell an asset before the seller has lined up purchase of the asset. This seller can offset risk by purchasing a futures contract to fix the sales price.

Agency costs Costs of conflicts of interest among stockholders, bondholders, and managers. Agency costs are the costs of resolving these conflicts. They include the costs of providing managers with an incentive to maximize shareholder wealth and then monitoring their behavior, and the cost of protecting bondholders from shareholders. Agency costs are borne by stockholders.

Agency theory The theory of the relationship between principals and agents. It involves the nature of the costs of resolving conflicts of interest between principals and agents.

Aggregation Process in corporate financial planning whereby the smaller investment proposals of each of the firm's operational units are added up and in effect treated as a big picture.

Aging schedule A compilation of accounts receivable by the age of account.

American Depository Receipt (ADR) A security issued in the United States to represent shares of a foreign stock, enabling that stock to be traded in the United States.

American option An option contract that may be exercised anytime up to the expiration date. A European option may be exercised only on the expiration date.

Amortization Repayment of a loan in installments.

Angels Individuals providing venture capital.

Annual percentage rate The interest rate in annual terms.

Annualized holding-period return The annual rate of return that when compounded T times, would have given the same T-period holding return as actually occurred from period 1 to period T.

Annuity A level stream of equal dollar payments that lasts for a fixed time. An example of an annuity is the coupon part of a bond with level annual payments.

Annuity factor The term used to calculate the present value of the stream of level payments for a fixed period.

Annuity in advance An annuity with an immediate initial payment.

Annuity in arrears An annuity with a first payment one full period hence, rather than immediately. That is, the first payment occurs on date 1 rather than on date 0.

Appraisal rights Rights of shareholders of an acquired firm that allow them to demand that their shares be purchased at a fair value by the acquiring firm.

Appropriate discount rate The discount rate used in valuation that properly reflects risk.

Arbitrage Buying an asset in one market at a lower price and simultaneously selling an identical asset in another market at a higher price. This is done with no risk and after all costs are properly accounted for.

Arbitrage pricing theory (APT) An equilibrium asset pricing theory that is derived from a factor model by using diversification and arbitrage. It shows that the expected return on any risky asset is a linear combination of various factors.

Arithmetic average The sum of the values observed divided by the total number of observations—sometimes referred to as the mean.

Asset beta The sensitivity of a firm's asset value to that of the overall economy.

Assets Anything that the firm owns that generates future benefits.

891

Asset requirements A common element of a financial plan that describes projected capital spending and the proposed uses of net working capital.

Auction market A market where all traders in a certain good meet (usually at one place) to buy or sell an asset. The NYSE is an example.

Autocorrelation The correlation of a variable with itself over successive time intervals.

Availability float Refers to the time required to clear a check through the banking system.

Average (mean) Usually refers to the arithmetic mean (see also the **geometric mean**).

Average accounting return (AAR) The average project earnings after taxes and depreciation divided by the average book value of the investment during its life.

Average collection period Average amount of time required to collect an account receivable. Also referred to as days sales outstanding.

Average cost of capital A firm's required payout to the bondholders and the stockholders expressed as a percentage of capital contributed to the firm. Average cost of capital is computed by dividing the total required cost of capital by the total amount of contributed capital.

Average daily sales Annual sales divided by 365 days.

Balance sheet A statement showing a firm's accounting value on a particular date. It reflects the equation, Assets = Liabilities + Stockholders' equity.

Balloon payment Large final payment, as when a loan is repaid in installments.

Banker's acceptance Agreement by a bank to pay a given sum of money at a future date.

Bankruptcy State of being unable to pay debts. Thus the ownership of the firm's assets is transferred from the stockholders to the bondholders.

Bankruptcy costs See **Financial distress costs.**

Bargain-purchase-price option Gives lessee the option to purchase the asset at a price below fair market value when the lease expires.

Basic IRR rule Accept the project if IRR is greater than the discount rate; reject the project if IRR is less than the discount rate.

Bearer bond A bond issued without record of the owner's name. Whoever holds the bond (the bearer) is the owner.

Benchmark An index or average whose movement is considered a general indicator of the direction of the overall market.

Best-efforts underwriting An offering in which an underwriter agrees to distribute as much of the offering as possible and to return any unsold shares to the issuer.

Beta coefficient A measure of the sensitivity of a security's return to movements in an underlying factor. It is a measured systematic risk.

Bidder A firm or person that has made an offer to take over another firm.

Black-Scholes call pricing equation An exact formula for the price of a call option. The formula requires five variables: the risk-free interest rate, the variance of the underlying stock, the exercise price, the price of the underlying stock, and the time to expiration.

Blanket inventory lien A secured loan that gives the lender a lien against all the borrower's inventories.

Bond A long-term debt of a firm. In common usage, the term *bond* often refers to both secured and unsecured debt.

Book cash A firm's cash balance as reported in its financial statements. Also called ledger cash.

Book value The firm's total assets minus the total liabilities (i.e., net worth).

Book value per share Per-share accounting equity value of a firm. Total accounting equity divided by the number of outstanding shares.

Borrow To obtain or receive money on loan with the promise or understanding of returning it or its equivalent.

Break-even analysis Analysis of the level of sales at which a project would make zero profit.

Bubble theory (of speculative markets) Security prices sometimes move wildly above their fundamental values.

Business failure The risk that the firm's stockholders bear if the firm is financed only with equity.

Buying the index Purchasing the stocks in the Standard & Poor's 500 in the same proportion as the index to achieve the same return.

CAPM Capital asset pricing model.

CAR Cumulative abnormal return.

Call option The right—but not the obligation—to buy a fixed number of shares of stock at a stated price within a specified time.

Call premium The price of a call option on common stock.

Call price of a bond Amount at which a firm has the right to repurchase its bonds or debentures before the stated maturity date. The call price is always set at equal to or more than the par value.

Call protected Describes a bond that is not allowed to be called, usually for a certain early period in the life of the bond.

Call provision A written agreement between an issuing corporation and its bondholders that gives the corporation the option to redeem the bond at a specified price before the maturity date.

Callable Refers to a bond that is subject to be repurchased at a stated call price before maturity.

Capital-asset-pricing model (CAPM) An equilibrium asset pricing theory that shows that equilibrium rates of expected return on all risky assets are a function of their covariance with the market portfolio.

Capital budgeting Planning and managing expenditures for long-lived assets.

Capital gains The positive change in the value of an asset. A negative capital gain is a capital loss.

Capital market line The efficient set of all assets, both risky and riskless, which provides the investor with the best possible opportunities.

Capital markets Financial markets for long-term debt and for equity shares.

Capital rationing The case where funds are limited to a fixed dollar amount and must be allocated among competing projects.

Capital structure The mix of the various debt and equity capital maintained by a firm. Also called financial structure. The composition of a corporation's securities used to finance its investment activities; the relative proportions of short-term debt, long-term debt, and owners' equity.

Capital surplus Amounts of directly contributed equity capital in excess of the par value.

Carrying costs Costs that increase with increases in the level of investment in assets (usually refers to current assets).

Carrying value Book value.

Cash budget A forecast of cash receipts and disbursements expected by a firm in the coming year. It is a short-term financial planning tool.

Cash cow A company that pays out a substantial proportion of earnings to stockholders as dividends.

Cash cycle In general, the time between cash disbursement and cash collection. In net working capital management, it can be thought of as the operating cycle less the accounts payable payment period.

Cash discount A discount given for a cash purchase. One reason a cash discount may be offered is to speed up the collection of receivables.

Cash flow Cash generated by the firm and paid to creditors and shareholders. It can be classified as (1) cash flow from operations, (2) cash flow from changes in fixed assets, and (3) cash flow from changes in net working capital.

Cash flow after interest and taxes Net income plus depreciation.

Cash-flow time line Line depicting the operating activities and cash flows for a firm over a particular period.

Cash offer A public equity issue that is sold to all interested investors.

Cash transaction A transaction where exchange is immediate, as contrasted to a forward contract, which calls for future delivery of an asset at an agreed-upon price.

Cashout Refers to situation where a firm runs out of cash.

Certificates of deposit Short-term loans to commercial banks.

Change in net working capital Difference between net working capital from one period to another.

Changes in fixed assets Component of cash flow that equals sales of fixed assets minus the acquisition of fixed assets.

Characteristic line The line relating the expected return on a security to different returns on the market.

Clearing The exchanging of checks and balancing of accounts between banks.

Clientele effect Argument that stocks attract clienteles based on dividend yield or taxes. For example, a tax clientele effect is induced by the difference in tax treatment of dividend income and capital gains income; high tax-bracket individuals tend to prefer low-dividend yields.

Coinsurance effect Refers to the fact that the merger of two firms decreases the probability of default on either's debt.

Collateral Assets that are pledged as security for payment of debt.

Collateral trust bond A bond secured by a pledge of common stock held by the corporation.

Collection float An increase in book cash with no immediate change in bank cash, generated by checks deposited by the firm that have not cleared.

Collection policy Procedures followed by a firm in attempting to collect accounts receivable.

Commercial draft Demand for payment.

Commercial paper Short-term, unsecured promissory notes issued by corporations with a high credit standing. Their maturity ranges up to 270 days.

Common equity Book value.

Common stock Equity claims held by the "residual owners" of the firm, who are the last to receive any distribution of earnings or assets.

Compensating balance Deposit that the firm keeps with the bank in a low-interest or non-interest-bearing account to compensate banks for bank loans or services.

Competitive offer Method of selecting an investment banker for a new issue by offering the securities to the underwriter bidding highest.

Composition Voluntary arrangement to restructure a firm's debt, under which payment is reduced.

Compound interest Interest that is earned both on the initial principal and on interest earned on the initial principal in previous periods. The interest earned in one period becomes in effect part of the principal in a following period.

Compound value Value of a sum after investing it over one or more periods. Also called future value.

Compounding Process of reinvesting each interest payment to earn more interest. Compounding is based on the idea that interest itself becomes principal and therefore also earns interest in subsequent periods.

Concentration banking The use of geographically dispersed collection centers to speed up the collection of accounts receivable.

Conditional sales contract An arrangement whereby the firm retains legal ownership of the goods until the customer has completed payment.

Conflict between bondholders and stockholders These two groups may have interests in the corporation that conflict. Sources of conflict include dividends, dilution, overinvestment, and underinvestment. Protective covenants work to resolve these conflicts.

Conglomerate acquisition Acquisition in which the acquired firm and the acquiring firm are not related, unlike a horizontal or a vertical acquisition.

Consol A bond that carries a promise to pay a coupon forever; it has no final maturity date and therefore never matures.

Consolidation A merger in which an entirely new firm is created.

Consumer credit Credit granted to consumers. Trade credit is credit granted to other firms.

Contingent claim Claim whose value is directly dependent on, or is contingent on, the value of its underlying assets. For example, the debt and equity securities issued by a firm derive their value from the total value of the firm.

Contingent pension liability Under ERISA, the firm is liable to the plan participants for up to 30 percent of the net worth of the firm.

Continuous compounding Interest compounded continuously, every instant, rather than at fixed intervals.

Contribution margin Amount that each additional product, such as a jet engine, contributes to after-tax profit of the whole project: (Sales price − Variable cost) × $(1 - T_c)$, where T_c is the corporate tax rate.

Conversion premium Difference between the conversion price and the current stock price divided by the current stock price.

Conversion price The amount of par value exchangeable for one share of common stock. This term really refers to the stock price and means the dollar amount of the bond's par value that is exchangeable for one share of stock.

Conversion ratio The number of shares per $1,000 bond (or debenture) that a bondholder would receive if the bond were converted into shares of stock.

Conversion value What a convertible bond would be worth if it were immediately converted into the common stock at the current price.

Convertible bond A bond that may be converted into another form of security, typically common stock, at the option of the holder at a specified price for a specified period of time.

Corporation Form of business organization that is created as a distinct "legal person" composed of one or more actual individuals or legal entities. Primary advantages of a corporation include limited liability, ease of ownership, transfer, and perpetual succession.

Correlation A standardized statistical measure of the dependence of two random variables. It is defined as the covariance divided by the standard deviations of two variables.

Cost of equity capital The required return on the company's common stock in capital markets. It is also called the equityholders' required rate of return because it is what equityholders can expect to obtain in the capital market. It is a cost from the firm's perspective.

Coupon The stated interest on a debt instrument.

Covariance A statistical measure of the degree to which random variables move together.

Credit analysis The process of determining whether a credit applicant meets the firm's standards and what amount of credit the applicant should receive.

Credit instrument Device by which a firm offers credit, such as an invoice, a promissory note, or a conditional sales contract.

Credit period Time allowed a credit purchaser to remit the full payment for credit purchases.

Credit scoring Determining the probability of default when granting customers credit.

Creditor Person or institution that holds the debt issued by a firm or individual.

Cross rate The exchange rate between two foreign currencies, neither of which is generally the U.S. dollar.

Crown jewels An antitakeover tactic in which major assets—the crown jewels—are sold by a firm when faced with a takeover threat.

Cum dividend With dividend.

Cumulative abnormal return (CAR) Sum of differences between the expected return on a stock and the actual return that comes from the release of news to the market.

Cumulative dividend Dividend on preferred stock that takes priority over dividend payments on common stock. Dividends may not be paid on the common stock until all past dividends on the preferred stock have been paid.

Cumulative probability The probability that a drawing from the standardized normal distribution will be below a particular value.

Cumulative voting A procedure whereby a shareholder may cast all of his or her votes for one member of the board of directors.

Current asset Asset that is in the form of cash or that is expected to be converted into cash in the next 12 months, such as inventory.

Current liabilities Obligations that are expected to require cash payment within one year or the operating period.

Current ratio Total current assets divided by total current liabilities. Used to measure short-term solvency of a firm.

Date of payment Date that dividend checks are mailed.

Date of record Date on which holders of record in a firm's stock ledger are designated as the recipients of either dividends or stock rights.

Dates convention Treating cash flows as being received on exact dates—date 0, date 1, and so forth—as opposed to the end-of-year convention.

Days in receivables Average collection period.

Days sales outstanding Average collection period.

De facto Existing in actual fact although not by official recognition.

Dealer market A market where traders specializing in particular commodities buy and sell assets for their own account. The OTC market is an example.

Debenture An unsecured bond, usually with maturity of 15 years or more. A debt obligation backed by the general credit of the issuing corporation.

Debt Loan agreement that is a liability of the firm. An obligation to repay a specified amount at a particular time.

Debt capacity Ability to borrow. The amount a firm can borrow up to the point where the firm value no longer increases.

Debt displacement The amount of borrowing that leasing displaces. Firms that do a lot of leasing will be forced to cut back on borrowing.

Debt ratio Total debt divided by total assets.

Debt service Interest payments plus repayments of principal to creditors, that is, retirement of debt.

Decision trees A graphical representation of alternative sequential decisions and the possible outcomes of those decisions.

Declaration date Date on which the board of directors passes a resolution to pay a dividend of a specified amount to all qualified holders of record on a specified date.

Dedicated capital Total par value (number of shares issued multiplied by the par value of each share). Also called dedicated value.

Deed of trust Indenture.

Deep-discount bond A bond issued with a very low coupon or no coupon and selling at a price far below par

value. When the bond has no coupon, it is also called a pure-discount or original-issue-discount bond.

Default risk The chance that interest or principal will not be paid on the due date and in the promised amount.

Defeasance A debt-restructuring tool that enables a firm to remove debt from its balance sheet by establishing an irrevocable trust that will generate future cash flows sufficient to service the decreased debt.

Deferred call A provision that prohibits the company from calling the bond before a certain date. During this period the bond is said to be call protected.

Deferred nominal life annuity A monthly fixed-dollar payment beginning at retirement age. It is nominal because the payment is fixed in dollar amount at any particular time, up to and including retirement.

Deferred taxes Noncash expense.

Deficit The amount by which a sum of money is less than the required amount; an excess of liabilities over assets, of losses over profits, or of expenditure over income.

Deliverable instrument The asset in a forward contract that will be delivered in the future at an agreed-upon price.

Denomination Face value or principal of a bond.

Depreciation A noncash expense, such as the cost of plant or equipment, charged against earnings to write off the cost of an asset during its estimated useful life.

Depreciation tax shield Portion of an investment that can be deducted from taxable income.

Dilution Loss in existing shareholders' value. There are several kinds of dilution: (1) dilution of ownership, (2) dilution of market value, and (3) dilution of book value and earnings, as with warrants and convertible issues. Firms with significant amounts of warrants or convertible issues outstanding are required to report earnings on a "fully diluted" basis.

Direct lease A lease under which a lessor buys equipment from a manufacturer and leases it to a lessee.

Disbursement float A decrease in book cash but no immediate change in bank cash, generated by checks written by the firm.

Discount If a bond is selling below its face value, it is said to sell at a discount.

Discount rate Rate used to calculate the present value of future cash flows.

Discounted payback period method An investment decision rule in which the cash flows are discounted at an interest rate and the payback rule is applied on these discounted cash flows.

Discounting Calculating the present value of a future amount. The process is the opposite of compounding.

Distribution A type of dividend paid by a firm to its owners from sources other than current or accumulated retained earnings.

Diversifiable risk A risk that specifically affects a single asset or a small group of assets. Also called unique or unsystematic risk.

Dividend Payment made by a firm to its owners, either in cash or in stock. Also called the *income component* of the return on an investment in stock.

Dividend growth model A model wherein dividends are assumed to be at a constant rate in perpetuity.

Dividend payout ratio Amount of cash paid to shareholders expressed as a percentage of earnings per share.

Dividend yield Dividends per share of common stock divided by market price per share.

Dividends per share Amount of cash paid to shareholders expressed as dollars per share.

Double-declining balance depreciation Method of accelerated depreciation.

DuPont system of financial control Highlights the fact that return on assets (ROA) can be expressed in terms of the profit margin and asset turnover.

Duration The weighted average time of an asset's cash flows. The weights are determined by present value factors.

EAC Equivalent annual cost.

EBIT Earnings before interest and taxes.

EMH Efficient market hypothesis.

ERISA Employee Retirement Income Security Act of 1974.

Economic assumptions Economic environment in which the firm expects to reside over the life of the financial plan.

Effective annual interest rate The interest rate as if it were compounded once per time period rather than several times per period.

Efficient market hypothesis (EMH) The prices of securities fully reflect available information. Investors buying bonds and stocks in an efficient market should expect to obtain an equilibrium rate of return. Firms should expect to receive the "fair" value (present value) for the securities they sell.

Efficient set Graph representing a set of portfolios that maximize expected return at each level of portfolio risk.

End-of-year convention Treating cash flows as if they occur at the end of a year (or, alternatively, at the end of a period), as opposed to the date convention. Under the end-of-year convention, the end of year 0 is the present, end of year 1 occurs one period hence, and so on.

Equilibrium rate of interest The interest rate that clears the market. Also called market-clearing interest rate.

Equity Ownership interest of common and preferred stockholders in a corporation. Also, total assets minus total liabilities, or net worth.

Equity beta The asset beta adjusted for leverage.

Equity kicker Used to refer to warrants because they usually are issued in combination with privately placed bonds.

Equity share Ownership interest.

Equivalent annual cost (EAC) The net present value of cost divided by an annuity factor that has the same life as the investment.

Equivalent loan The amount of the loan that makes leasing equivalent to buying with debt financing in terms of debt capacity reduction.

Erosion Cash-flow amount transferred to a new project from customers and sales of other products of the firm.

Eurobanks Banks that make loans and accept deposits in foreign currencies.

Eurobond An international bond sold primarily in countries other than the country in whose currency the issue is denominated.

Eurocurrency Money deposited in a financial center outside of the country whose currency is involved.

Eurodollar A dollar deposited in a bank outside the United States.

Eurodollar CD Deposit of dollars with foreign banks.

European Currency Unit (ECU) An index of foreign exchange consisting of about 10 European currencies, originally devised in 1979.

European option An option contract that may be exercised only on the expiration date. An American option may be exercised any time up to the expiration date.

Event study A statistical study that examines how the release of information affects prices at a particular time.

Ex rights or ex dividend Phrases used to indicate that a stock is selling without a recently declared right or dividend. The ex-rights or ex-dividend date is generally four business days before the date of record.

Exchange rate Price of one country's currency for another's.

Exclusionary self-tender The firm makes a tender offer for a given amount of its own stock while excluding targeted stockholders.

Ex-dividend date Date four business days before the date of record for a security. An individual purchasing stock before its ex-dividend date will receive the current dividend.

Exercise price Price at which the holder of an option can buy (in the case of a call option) or sell (in the case of a put option) the underlying stock. Also called the striking price.

Exercising the option The act of buying or selling the underlying asset via the option contract.

Exotics Very complicated contingent claims for derivatives.

Expectations hypothesis (of interest rates) Theory that forward interest rates are unbiased estimates of expected future interest rates.

Expected return Average of possible returns weighted by their probability.

Expiration date Maturity date of an option.

Extension Voluntary arrangements to restructure a firm's debt, under which the payment date is postponed.

Extinguish Retire or pay off debt.

Face value The value of a bond that appears on its face. Also referred to as par value or principal.

Factor A financial institution that buys a firm's accounts receivables and collects the debt.

Factor model A model in which each stock's return is generated by common factors, called the systematic sources of risk.

Factoring Sale of a firm's accounts receivable to a financial institution known as a factor.

Fair market value Amount at which common stock would change hands between a willing buyer and a willing seller, both having knowledge of the relevant facts. Also called market price.

Feasible set Opportunity set.

Federal agency securities Securities issued by corporations and agencies created by the U.S. government, such as the Federal Home Loan Bank Board and Government National Mortgage Association (Ginnie Mae).

Field warehouse financing A form of inventory loan in which a public warehouse company acts as a control agent to supervise the inventory for the lender.

Financial Accounting Standards Board (FASB) The governing body in accounting.

Financial distress Events preceding and including bankruptcy, such as violation of loan contracts.

Financial distress costs Legal and administrative costs of liquidation or reorganization (direct costs); an impaired ability to do business and an incentive toward selfish strategies such as taking large risks, underinvesting, and milking the property (indirect costs).

Financial intermediaries Institutions that provide the market function of matching borrowers and lenders or traders. Financial institutions may be categorized as depository, contractual savings, and investment-type.

Financial lease A long-term noncancelable lease, generally requiring the lessee to pay all maintenance fees.

Financial leverage Extent to which a firm relies on debt. Financial leverage is commonly measured by the ratio of long-term debt to long-term debt plus equity.

Financial markets Markets that deal with cash flows over time, where the savings of lenders are allocated to the financing needs of borrowers.

Financial requirements In the financial plan, financing arrangements that are necessary to meet the overall corporate objective.

Financial risk The additional risk that the firm's stockholders bear when the firm is financed with debt as well as equity.

Firm commitment underwriting An underwriting in which an investment banking firm commits to buy the entire issue and assumes all financial responsibility for any unsold shares.

Firm's net value after debt Total firm value minus value of debt.

First principle of investment decision making An investment project is worth undertaking only if it increases the range of choices in the financial markets. To do this, it must be at least as desirable as what is available to shareholders in the financial markets.

Fixed asset Long-lived property owned by a firm that is used by a firm in the production of its income. Tangible fixed assets include real estate, plant, and equipment. Intangible fixed assets include patents, trademarks, and customer recognition.

Fixed cost A cost that is fixed in total for a given period of time and for given volume levels. It is not dependent on the amount of goods or services produced during the period.

Fixed-dollar obligations Conventional bonds for which the coupon rate is set as a fixed percentage of the par value.

Float The difference between bank cash and book cash. Float represents the net effect of checks in the process of collection, or clearing. *Positive float* means the firm's bank cash is greater than its book cash until the check's presentation. Checks written by the firm generate *disbursement float,* causing an immediate decrease in book cash but no change in bank cash. In *neutral float position,* bank cash equals book cash. Checks written by the firm represent *collection float,* which increases book cash immediately but does not immediately change bank cash. The sum of disbursement float and collection float is *net float.*

Floater Floating-rate bond.

Floating-rate bond A debt obligation with an adjustable coupon payment.

Flow to equity (FTE) A valuation approach that emphasizes cash flows to equity.

Forced conversion If the conversion value of a convertible is greater than the call price, the call can be used to force conversion.

Foreign bonds An international bond issued by foreign borrowers in another nation's capital market and traditionally denominated in that nation's currency.

Foreign exchange market Market in which arrangements are made today for future exchange of major currencies; used to hedge against major swings in foreign exchange rates.

Forward contract An arrangement calling for future delivery of an asset at an agreed-upon price.

Forward-exchange rate A future day's exchange rate between two major currencies.

Forward trade An agreement to buy or sell based on exchange rates established today for settlement in the future.

Free cash flow Cash flow after taxes, interest and all positive NPV opportunities.

Frequency distribution The organization of data to show how often certain values or ranges of values occur.

Fully diluted See **Dilution.**

Funded debt Long-term debt.

Future value Value of a sum after investing it over one or more periods. Also called compound value.

Futures contract Obliges traders to purchase or sell an asset at an agreed-upon price on a specified future date. The long position is held by the trader who commits to purchase. The short position is held by the trader who commits to sell. Futures differ from forward contracts in their standardization, exchange trading, margin requirements, and daily settling (market to market).

GAAP Generally Accepted Accounting Principles.

General cash offer A public issue of a security that is sold to all interested investors, rather than only to existing shareholders.

General partnership Form of business organization in which all partners agree to provide some portion of the work and cash and to share profits and losses. Each partner is liable for the debts of the partnership.

Generally accepted accounting principles (GAAP) A common set of accounting concepts, standards, and procedures by which financial statements are prepared.

Geometric mean Annualized holding-period return.

Gilts British and Irish government securities.

Going-private transactions Publicly owned stock in a firm is replaced with complete equity ownership by a private group. The shares are delisted from stock exchanges and can no longer be purchased in the open market.

Golden parachute Compensation paid to top-level management by a target firm if a takeover occurs.

Goodwill The excess of the purchase price over the sum of the fair market values of the individual assets acquired.

Greenmail Payments to potential bidders to cease unfriendly takeover attempts.

Green-Shoe provision A contract provision that gives the underwriter the option to purchase additional shares at the offering price to cover overallotments.

Growing perpetuity A constant stream of cash flows without end that is expected to rise indefinitely. For example, cash flows to the landlord of an apartment building might be expected to rise a certain percentage each year.

Growth opportunity Opportunity to invest in profitable projects.

Growth stock portfolio A portfolio of stocks perceived to have high growth prospects (in cash flows, etc.).

Hedging Taking a position in two or more securities that are negatively correlated (taking opposite trading positions) to reduce risk.

High-yield bond Junk bond.

Holder-of-record date The date on which holders of record in a firm's stock ledger are designated as the recipients of either dividends or stock rights. Also called date of record.

Holding period Length of time that an individual holds a security.

Holding-period return The rate of return over a given period.

Homemade dividends An individual investor can undo corporate dividend policy by reinvesting excess dividends or selling off shares of stock to receive a desired cash flow.

Homemade leverage Idea that as long as individuals borrow (and lend) on the same terms as the firm, they can duplicate the effects of corporate leverage on their own. Thus, if levered firms are priced too high, rational investors will simply borrow on personal accounts to buy shares in unlevered firms.

Homogeneous expectations Idea that all individuals have the same beliefs concerning future investments, profits, and dividends.

Horizontal acquisition Merger between two companies producing similar goods or services.

IPO Initial public offering.

IRR Internal rate of return.

Idiosyncratic risk An unsystematic risk.

Immunized Immune to interest-rate risk.

In the money Describes an option whose exercise would produce profits. Out of the money describes an option whose exercise would not be profitable.

Income bond A bond on which the payment of income is contingent on sufficient earnings. Income bonds are commonly used during the reorganization of a failed or failing business.

Income statement Financial report that summarizes a firm's performance over a specified time period.

Incremental cash flows Difference between the firm's cash flows with and without a project.

Incremental IRR IRR on the incremental investment from choosing a large project instead of a smaller project.

Indenture Written agreement between the corporate debt issuer and the lender, setting forth maturity date, interest rate, and other terms.

Independent project A project whose acceptance or rejection is independent of the acceptance or rejection of other projects.

Inflation An increase in the amount of money in circulation, resulting in a fall in its value and rise in prices.

Inflation-escalator clause A clause in a contract providing for increases or decreases in inflation based on fluctuations in the cost of living, production costs, and so forth.

Information-content effect The rise in the stock price following the dividend signal.

In-house processing float Refers to the time it takes the receiver of a check to process the payment and deposit it in a bank for collection.

Initial public offering (IPO) The original sale of a company's securities to the public. Also called an unseasoned new issue.

Inside information Nonpublic knowledge about a corporation possessed by people in special positions inside a firm.

Instruments Financial securities, such as money market instruments or capital market instruments.

Interest coverage ratio Earnings before interest and taxes divided by interest expense. Used to measure a firm's ability to pay interest.

Interest on interest Interest earned on reinvestment of each interest payment on money invested.

Interest rate The price paid for borrowing money. It is the rate of exchange of present consumption for future consumption, or the price of current dollars in terms of future dollars.

Interest rate on debt The firm's cost of debt capital. Also called return on the debt.

Interest-rate–parity theorem The interest rate differential between two countries will be equal to the difference between the forward-exchange rate and the spot-exchange rate.

Interest-rate risk The chance that a change in the interest rate will result in a change in the value of a security.

Interest subsidy A firm's deduction of the interest payments on its debt from its earnings before it calculates its tax bill under current tax law.

Internal financing Net income plus depreciation minus dividends. Internal financing comes from internally generated cash flow.

Internal rate of return (IRR) A discount rate at which the net present value of an investment is zero. The IRR is a method of evaluating capital expenditure proposals.

Inventory A current asset, composed of raw materials to be used in production, work in process, and finished goods.

Inventory loan A secured short-term loan to purchase inventory. The three basic forms are a blanket inventory lien, a trust receipt, and field warehouse financing.

Inventory turnover ratio Ratio of annual sales to average inventory that measures how quickly inventory is produced and sold.

Investment banks Financial intermediaries who perform a variety of services, including aiding in the sale of securities, facilitating mergers and other corporate reorganizations, acting as brokers to both individual and institutional clients, and trading for their own accounts.

Investment grade bond Debt that is rated BBB and above by Standard & Poor's or Baa and above by Moody's.

Invoice Bill written by a seller of goods or services and submitted to the purchaser.

Irrelevance result The MM theorem that a firm's capital structure is irrelevant to the firm's value.

Junk bond A speculative grade bond, rated Ba or lower by Moody's, or BB or lower by Standard & Poor's, or an unrated bond. Also called a high-yield or low-grade bond.

Keiretsu A confederation of Japanese firms connected with cross holders of equity investments and a banking firm.

LBO Leveraged buyout.

LIBOR London Interbank Offered Rate.

Law of one price (LOP) A commodity will cost the same regardless of what currency is used to purchase it.

Lease A contractual arrangement to grant the use of specific fixed assets for a specified time in exchange for payment, usually in the form of rent. An operating lease is generally a short-term cancelable arrangement, whereas a financial, or capital, lease is a long-term noncancelable agreement.

Ledger cash A firm's cash balance as reported in its financial statements. Also called book cash.

Legal bankruptcy A legal proceeding for liquidating or reorganizing a business.

Lend To provide money temporarily on the condition that it or its equivalent will be returned, often with an interest fee.

Lessee One that receives the use of assets under a lease.

Lessor One that conveys the use of assets under a lease.

Letter of comment A communication to the firm from the Securities and Exchange Commission that suggests changes to a registration statement.

Level-coupon bond Bond with a stream of coupon payments that are the same throughout the life of the bond.

Leveraged buyout Takeover of a company by using borrowed funds, usually by a group including some member of existing management.

Leveraged equity Stock in a firm that relies on financial leverage. Holders of leveraged equity face the benefits and costs of using debt.

Leveraged lease Tax-oriented leasing arrangement that involves one or more third-party lenders.

Liabilities Debts of the firm in the form of financial claims on a firm's assets.

Limited partnership Form of business organization that permits the liability of some partners to be limited by the amount of cash contributed to the partnership.

Limited-liability instrument A security, such as a call option, in which all the holder can lose is the initial amount put into it.

Line of credit A *noncommitted* line of credit is an informal agreement that allows firms to borrow up to a previously specified limit without going through the normal paperwork. A *committed* line of credit is a formal legal arrangement and usually involves a commitment fee paid by the firm to the bank.

Lintner's dividend observations John Lintner's work (1956) suggested that dividend policy is related to a target level of dividends and the speed of adjustment of change in dividends.

Liquidating dividend Payment by a firm to its owners from capital rather than from earnings.

Liquidation Termination of the firm as a going concern. Liquidation involves selling the assets of the firm for salvage value. The proceeds, net of transaction costs, are distributed to creditors in order of established priority.

Liquidity Refers to the ease and quickness of converting assets to cash. Also called marketability.

Liquidity-preference hypothesis Theory that the forward rate exceeds expected future interest rates.

Lockbox Post office box set up to intercept accounts receivable payments. Lockboxes are the most widely used device to speed up collection of cash.

London Interbank Offered Rate (LIBOR) Rate the most creditworthy banks charge one another for large loans of Eurodollars overnight in the London market.

Long hedge Protecting the future cost of a purchase by purchasing a futures contract to protect against changes in the price of an asset.

Long run A period of time in which all costs are variable.

Long-term debt An obligation having a maturity of more than one year from the date it was issued. Also called funded debt.

Low-grade bond Junk bond. A bond with a value below investment grade.

MM Proposition I A proposition of Modigliani and Miller (MM) which states that a firm cannot change the total value of its outstanding securities by changing its capital structure proportions. Also called an irrelevance result.

MM Proposition II A proposition by Modigliani and Miller (MM) which states that the cost of equity is a linear function of the firm's debt-equity ratio.

Mail float Refers to the part of the collection and disbursement process where checks are trapped in the postal system.

Make a market The obligation of a specialist to offer to buy and sell shares of assigned stocks. It is assumed that this makes the market liquid because the specialist assumes the role of a buyer for investors if they wish to sell and a seller if they wish to buy.

Making delivery Refers to the seller's actually turning over to the buyer the asset agreed upon in a forward contract.

Marked to market Describes the daily settlement of obligations on futures positions.

Market capitalization Price per share of stock multiplied by the number of shares outstanding.

Market clearing Total demand for loans by borrowers equals total supply of loans from lenders. The market clears at the equilibrium rate of interest.

Market model A one-factor model for returns where the index that is used for the factor is an index of the returns on the whole market.

Market portfolio In concept, a value-weighted index of all securities. In practice, it is an index, such as the S&P 500, that describes the return of the entire value of the stock market, or at least the stocks that make up the index. A market portfolio represents the average investor's return.

Market price The current amount at which a security is trading in a market.

Market risk Systematic risk. This term emphasizes the fact that systematic risk influences to some extent all assets in the market.

Market value The price at which willing buyers and sellers trade a firm's assets.

Marketability Refers to the ease and quickness of converting an asset to cash. Also called liquidity.

Marketed claims Claims that can be bought and sold in financial markets, such as those of stockholders and bondholders.

Market-to-book (M/B) ratio Market price per share of common stock divided by book value per share.

Maturity date The date on which the last payment on a bond is due.

Merger Combination of two or more companies.

Minimum variance portfolio The portfolio of risky assets with the lowest possible variance. By definition, this portfolio must also have the lowest possible standard deviation.

Money markets Financial markets for debt securities that pay off in the short term (usually less than one year).

Money purchase plan A defined benefit contribution plan in which the participant contributes some part and the firm contributes at the same or a different rate. Also called an individual account plan.

Monte Carlo simulation An exercise that identifies outcomes and probabilities and generates possible scenarios.

Mortgage securities A debt obligation secured by a mortgage on the real property of the borrower.

Multiple rates of return More than one rate of return from the same project that make the net present value of the project equal to zero. This situation arises when the IRR method is used for a project in which negative cash flows follow positive ones.

Multiples Another name for price/earnings ratios.

Mutually exclusive investment decisions Investment decisions in which the acceptance of a project precludes the acceptance of one or more alternative projects.

NPV Net present value.

NPV rule Invest in all positive NPV opportunities.

NPVGO model A model valuing the firm in which net present value of new investment opportunities is explicitly examined. NPVGO stands for net present value of growth opportunities.

Negative covenant Part of the indenture or loan agreement that limits or prohibits actions that the company may take.

Negotiated offer The issuing firm negotiates a deal with one underwriter to offer a new issue rather than taking competitive bidding.

Net cash balance Beginning cash balance plus cash receipts minus cash disbursements.

Net float Sum of disbursement float and collection float.

Net investment Gross, or total, investment minus depreciation.

Net operating losses (NOL) Losses that a firm can take advantage of to reduce taxes.

Net present value (NPV) The present value of future cash returns, discounted at the appropriate market interest rate, minus the present value of the cost of the investment.

Net present value rule An investment is worth making if it has a positive NPV. If an investment's NPV is negative, it should be rejected.

Net working capital Current assets minus current liabilities.

Netting out To get or bring in as a net; to clear as profit.

Neutral flat position See **Float.**

Nominal cash flow A cash flow expressed in nominal terms if the actual dollars to be received (or paid out) are given.

Nominal interest rate Interest rate unadjusted for inflation.

Noncash item Expense against revenue that does not directly affect cash flow, such as depreciation and deferred taxes.

Nonmarketed claims Claims that cannot be easily bought and sold in the financial markets, such as those of the government and litigants in lawsuits.

Normal annuity form The manner in which retirement benefits are paid out.

Normal distribution Symmetric bell-shaped frequency distribution that can be defined by its mean and standard deviation.

Note Unsecured debt, usually with maturity of less than 15 years.

Odd lot Stock trading unit of less than 100 shares.

Off-balance-sheet financing Financing that is not shown as a liability on a company's balance sheet.

One-factor APT A special case of the arbitrage pricing theory that is derived from the one-factor model by using diversification and arbitrage. It shows the expected return on any risky asset is a linear function of a single factor. The CAPM can be expressed as one-factor APT in which a single factor is the market portfolio.

Open account A credit account for which the only formal instrument of credit is the invoice.

Operating activities Sequence of events and decisions that create the firm's cash inflows and cash outflows. These activities include buying and paying for raw materials, manufacturing and selling a product, and collecting cash.

Operating cash flow Earnings before interest and depreciation minus taxes. It measures the cash generated from operations, not counting capital spending or working capital requirements.

Operating cycle The time interval between the arrival of inventory stock and the date when cash is collected from receivables.

Operating lease Type of lease in which the period of contract is less than the life of the equipment and the lessor pays all maintenance and servicing costs.

Operating leverage The degree to which a company's costs of operation are fixed as opposed to variable. A firm with high operating costs compared to a firm with a low operating leverage, and hence relatively larger changes in EBIT with respect to a change in the sales revenue.

Opportunity cost Most valuable alternative that is given up. The rate of return used in NPV computation is an opportunity interest rate.

Opportunity set The possible expected return—standard deviation pairs of all portfolios that can be constructed from a set of assets. Also called a feasible set.

Option A right—but not an obligation—to buy or sell underlying assets at a fixed price during a specified time period.

Original-issue-discount bond A bond issued with a discount from par value. Also called a deep-discount or pure-discount bond.

Out of the money Describes an option whose exercise would not be profitable. In the money describes an option whose exercise would produce profits.

Oversubscribed issue Investors are not able to buy all the shares they want, so underwriters must allocate the shares among investors. This occurs when a new issue is underpriced.

Oversubscription privilege Allows shareholders to purchase unsubscribed shares in a rights offering at the subscription price.

Over-the-counter (OTC) market An informal network of brokers and dealers who negotiate sales of securities (not a formal exchange).

Par value The nominal or face value of stocks or bonds. For stock, it is a relatively unimportant value except for bookkeeping purposes.

Partnership Form of business organization in which two or more co-owners form a business. In a general partnership each partner is liable for the debts of the partnership. Limited partnership permits some partners to have limited liability.

Payback period rule An investment decision rule which states that all investment projects that have payback periods equal to or less than a particular cutoff period are accepted, and all of those that pay off in more than the particular cutoff period are rejected. The payback period is the number of years required for a firm to recover its initial investment required by a project from the cash flow it generates.

Payments pattern Describes the lagged collection pattern of receivables, for instance the probability that a 72-day-old account will still be unpaid when it is 73 days old.

Payout ratio Proportion of net income paid out in cash dividends.

Pecking order in long-term financing Hierarchy of long-term financing strategies, in which using internally generated cash is at the top and issuing new equity is at the bottom.

Percentage of sales approach A financial planning protocol that specifies balance sheet and income statement items as a proportion of sales.

Perfect markets Perfectly competitive financial markets.

Perfectly competitive financial markets Markets in which no trader has power to change the price of goods or services. Perfect markets are characterized by the following conditions: (1) Trading is costless, and access to the financial markets is free. (2) Information about borrowing and lending opportunities is freely available. (3) There are many traders, and no single trader can have a significant impact on market prices.

Performance shares Shares of stock given to managers on the basis of performance as measured by earnings per share

and similar criteria—a control device used by shareholders to tie management to the self-interest of shareholders.

Perpetuity A constant stream of cash flows without end. A British consol is an example.

Perquisites Management amenities such as a big office, a company car, or expense-account meals. "Perks" are agency costs of equity, because managers of the firm are agents of the stockholders.

Pie model of capital structure A model of the debt-equity ratio of the firm, graphically depicted in slices of a pie that represents the value of the firm in the capital markets.

Plug A variable that handles financial slack in the financial plan.

Poison pill Strategy by a takeover target company to make a stock less appealing to a company that wishes to acquire it.

Portfolio Combined holding of more than one stock, bond, real estate asset, or other asset by an investor.

Portfolio variance Weighted sum of the covariances and variances of the assets in a portfolio.

Positive covenant Part of the indenture or loan agreement that specifies an action that the company must abide by.

Positive float See **Float.**

Post Particular place on the floor of an exchange where transactions in stocks listed on the exchange occur.

Preemptive right The right to share proportionally in any new stock sold.

Preferred stock A type of stock whose holders are given certain priority over common stockholders in the payment of dividends. Usually the dividend rate is fixed at the time of issue. Preferred stockholders normally do not receive voting rights.

Premium If a bond is selling above its face value, it is said to sell at a premium.

Prepackaged bankruptcy Bankruptcy arrangements are worked out before the formal filing.

Present value The value of a future cash stream discounted at the appropriate market interest rate.

Present value factor Factor used to calculate an estimate of the present value of an amount to be received in a future period.

Price takers Individuals who respond to rates and prices by acting as though they have no influence on them.

Priced out Means the market has already incorporated information, such as a low dividend, into the price of a stock.

Price-to-earnings (P/E) ratio Current market price of common stock divided by current annual earnings per share.

Primary market Where new issues of securities are offered to the public.

Principal The value of a bond that must be repaid at maturity. Also called the face value or par value.

Principle of diversification Highly diversified portfolios will have negligible unsystematic risk. In other words, unsystematic risks disappear in portfolios, and only systematic risks survive.

Private placement The sale of a bond or other security directly to a limited number of investors.

Private workout Financial restructuring takes place in lieu of formal bankruptcy.

Pro forma statements Projected income statements, balance sheets, and sources and uses statements for future years.

Profit margin Profits divided by total operating revenue. The net profit margin (net income divided by total operating revenue) and the gross profit margin (earnings before interest and taxes divided by the total operating revenue) reflect the firm's ability to produce a good or service at a high or low cost.

Profitability index A method used to evaluate projects. It is the ratio of the present value of the future expected cash flows after initial investment divided by the amount of the initial investment.

Promissory note Written promise to pay.

Prospectus The legal document that must be given to every investor who contemplates purchasing registered securities in an offering. It describes the details of the company and the particular offering.

Protective covenant A part of the indenture or loan agreement that limits certain actions a company takes during the term of the loan to protect the lender's interest.

Proxy A grant of authority by the shareholder to transfer his or her voting rights to someone else.

Proxy contest Attempt to gain control of a firm by soliciting a sufficient number of stockholder votes to replace the existing management.

Public issue Sales of securities to the public.

Purchase accounting Method of reporting acquisitions requiring that the assets of the acquired firm be reported at their fair market value on the books of the acquiring firm.

Purchasing power parity (PPP) Idea that the exchange rate adjusts to keep purchasing power constant among currencies.

Pure discount bond Bonds that pay no coupons and only pay back face value at maturity. Also referred to as "bullets" and "zeros."

Put option The right to sell a specified number of shares of stock at a stated price on or before a specified time.

Put provision Gives holder of a floating-rate bond the right to redeem his or her note at par on the coupon payment date.

Put-call parity The value of a call equals the value of buying the stock plus buying the put plus borrowing at the risk-free rate.

Q ratio or Tobin's Q ratio Market value of firm's assets divided by replacement value of firm's assets.

Quick assets Current assets minus inventories.

Quick ratio Quick assets (current assets minus inventories) divided by total current liabilities. Used to measure short-term solvency of a firm.

R squared (R^2) Square of the correlation coefficient proportion of the variability explained by the linear model.

Random walk Theory that stock price changes from day to day are at random; the changes are independent of each other and have the same probability distribution.

Real cash flow A cash flow is expressed in real terms if the current, or date 0, purchasing power of the cash flow is given.

Real interest rate Interest rate expressed in terms of real goods; that is, the nominal interest rate minus the expected inflation rate.

Receivables turnover ratio Total operating revenues divided by average receivables. Used to measure how effectively a firm is managing its accounts receivable.

Red herring First document released by an underwriter of a new issue to prospective investors.

Refunding The process of replacing outstanding bonds, typically to issue new securities at a lower interest rate than those replaced.

Registration statement The registration that discloses all the pertinent information concerning the corporation that wants to make the offering. The statement is filed with the Securities and Exchange Commission.

Regular cash dividend Cash payment by firm to its shareholders, usually four times a year.

Regulation A The securities regulation that exempts small public offerings (those valued at less than $1.5 million) from most registration requirements.

Relative purchasing power parity (RPPP) Idea that the rate of change in the price level of commodities in one country relative to the price level in another determines the rate of the exchange rate between the two countries' currencies.

Reorganization Financial restructuring of a failed firm. Both the firm's asset structure and its financial structure are changed to reflect their true value, and claims are settled.

Replacement value Current cost of replacing the firm's assets.

Replacement-chain problem Idea that future replacement decisions must be taken into account in selecting among projects.

Repurchase agreement (repos) Short-term, often overnight, sales of government securities with an agreement to repurchase the securities at a slightly higher price.

Repurchase of stock Device to pay cash to firm's shareholders that provides more preferable tax treatment for shareholders than dividends. Treasury stock is the name given to previously issued stock that has been repurchased by the firm.

Residual dividend approach An approach that suggests that a firm pay dividends if and only if acceptable investment opportunities for those funds are currently unavailable.

Residual losses Lost wealth of the shareholders due to divergent behavior of the managers.

Residual value Usually refers to the value of a lessor's property at the time the lease expires.

Restrictive covenants Provisions that place constraints on the operations of borrowers, such as restrictions on working capital, fixed assets, future borrowing, and payment of dividend.

Retained earnings Earnings not paid out as dividends.

Retention ratio Retained earnings divided by net income. Also called the plowback ratio.

Return Profit on capital investment or securities.

Return on assets (ROA) Income divided by average total assets.

Return on equity (ROE) Net income after interest and taxes divided by average common stockholders' equity.

Reverse split The procedure whereby the number of outstanding stock shares is reduced; for example, two outstanding shares are combined to create only one.

Rights offer An offer that gives a current shareholder the opportunity to maintain a proportionate interest in the company before the shares are offered to the public.

Risk averse A risk-averse investor will consider risky portfolios only if they provide compensation for risk via a risk premium.

Risk class A partition of the universal set of risk measure so that projects that are in the same risk class can be comparable.

Risk premium The excess return on the risky asset that is the difference between expected return on risky assets and the return on risk-free assets.

Round lot Common stock trading unit of 100 shares or multiples of 100 shares.

S&P 500 Standard & Poor's Composite Index.

SEC Securities and Exchange Commission.

SML Security market line.

SMP Security market plane.

Safe harbor lease A lease to transfer tax benefits of ownership (depreciation and debt tax shield) from the lessee, if the lessee could not use them, to a lessor that could.

Sale and lease-back An arrangement whereby a firm sells its existing assets to a financial company which then leases them back to the firm. This is often done to generate cash.

Sales forecast A key input to the firm's financial planning process. External sales forecasts are based on historical experience, statistical analysis, and consideration of various macroeconomic factors; internal sales forecasts are obtained from internal sources.

Sales-type lease An arrangement whereby a firm leases its own equipment, such as IBM leasing its own computers, thereby competing with an independent leasing company.

Scale enhancing Describes a project that is in the same risk class as the whole firm.

Scenario analysis Analysis of the effect on the project of different scenarios, each scenario involving a confluence of factors.

Seasoned new issue A new issue of stock after the company's securities have previously been issued. A seasoned new issue of common stock can be made by using a cash offer or a rights offer.

Secondary markets Already-existing securities are bought and sold on the exchanges or in the over-the-counter market.

Security market line (SML) A straight line that shows the equilibrium relationship between systematic risk and expected rates of return for individual securities. According to the SML, the excess return on a risky asset is equal to the excess return on the market portfolio multiplied by the beta coefficient.

Security market plane (SMP) A plane that shows the equilibrium relationship between expected return and the beta coefficient of more than one factor.

Semistrong-form efficiency Theory that the market is efficient with respect to all publicly available information.

Seniority The order of repayment. In the event of bankruptcy, senior debt must be repaid before subordinated debt receives any payment.

Sensitivity analysis Analysis of the effect on the project when there is some change in critical variables such as sales and costs.

Separation principle The principle that portfolio choice can be separated into two independent tasks: (1) determination of the optimal risky portfolio, which is a purely technical problem, and (2) the personal choice of the best mix of the risky portfolio and the risk-free asset.

Separation theorem The value of an investment to an individual is not dependent on consumption preferences. All investors will want to accept or reject the same investment projects by using the NPV rule, regardless of personal preference.

Serial covariance The covariance between a variable and the lagged value of the variable; the same as autocovariance.

Set of contracts perspective View of corporation as a set of contracting relationships among individuals who have conflicting objectives, such as shareholders or managers. The corporation is a legal contrivance that serves as the nexus for the contracting relationships.

Shareholder Holder of equity shares. The terms *shareholders* and *stockholders* usually refer to owners of common stock in a corporation.

Shark repellent Action taken by firm to make firm less attractive to potential bidders.

Shelf life Number of days it takes to get goods purchased and sold, or days in inventory.

Shelf registration An SEC procedure that allows a firm to file a master registration statement summarizing planned financing for a two-year period, and then file short statements when the firm wishes to sell any of the approved master statement securities during that period.

Shirking The tendency to do less work when the return is smaller. Owners may have more incentive to shirk if they issue equity as opposed to debt, because they retain less ownership interest in the company and therefore may receive a smaller return. Thus, shirking is considered an agency cost of equity.

Short hedge Protecting the value of an asset held by selling a futures contract.

Short run That period of time in which certain equipment, resources, and commitments of them are fixed.

Short sale Sale of a security that an investor doesn't own but has instead borrowed.

Shortage costs Costs that fall with increases in the level of investment in current assets.

Short-run operating activities Events and decisions concerning the short-term finance of a firm, such as how much inventory to order and whether to offer cash terms or credit terms to customers.

Short-term debt An obligation having a maturity of one year or less from the date it was issued. Also called unfunded debt.

Short-term tax exempts Short-term securities issued by states, municipalities, local housing agencies, and urban renewal agencies.

Side effects Effects of a proposed project on other parts of the firm.

Sight draft A commercial draft demanding immediate payment.

Signaling approach Approach to the determination of optimal capital structure asserting that insiders in a firm have information that the market does not; therefore the choice of capital structure by insiders can signal information to outsiders and change the value of the firm. This theory is also called the asymmetric information approach.

Simple interest Interest calculated by considering only the original principal amount.

Sinking fund An account managed by the bond trustee for the purpose of repaying the bonds.

Small issues exemption Securities issues that involve less than $1.5 million are not required to file a registration statement with the Securities and Exchange Commission. Instead they are governed by Regulation A, for which only a brief offering statement is needed.

Sole proprietorship A business owned by a single individual. The sole proprietorship pays no corporate income tax but has unlimited liability for business debts and obligations.

Speculating Extremely high-risk investing.

Spot-exchange rate Exchange rate between two currencies for immediate delivery.

Spot-interest rate Interest rate fixed today on a loan that is made today.

Spot trade An agreement on the exchange rate today for settlement in two days.

Spread underwriting Difference between the underwriter's buying price and the offering price. The spread is a fee for the service of the underwriting syndicate.

Spreadsheet A computer program that organizes numerical data into rows and columns on a terminal screen, for calculating and making adjustments based on new data.

Stakeholders Both stockholders and bondholders.

Stand-alone principle Investment principle that states a firm should accept or reject a project by comparing it with securities in the same risk class.

Standard deviation The positive square root of the variance. This is the standard statistical measure of the spread of a sample.

Standardized normal distribution A normal distribution with an expected value of 0 and a standard deviation of 1.

Standby fee Amount paid to an underwriter who agrees to purchase any stock that is not subscribed to the public investor in a rights offering.

Standby underwriting An agreement whereby an underwriter agrees to purchase any stock that is not purchased by the public investor.

Standstill agreements Contracts where the bidding firm in a takeover attempt agrees to limit its holdings of another firm.

Stated annual interest rate The interest rate expressed as a percentage per annum, by which interest payment is determined.

Static theory of capital structure Theory that the firm's capital structure is determined by a trade-off of the value of tax shields against the costs of bankruptcy.

Stock dividend Payment of a dividend in the form of stock rather than cash. A stock dividend comes from treasury stock, increasing the number of shares outstanding, and reduces the value of each share.

Stock split The increase in the number of outstanding shares of stock while making no change in shareholders' equity.

Stockholder Holder of equity shares in a firm. The terms *stockholder* and *shareholders* usually refer to owners of common stock.

Stockholders' books Set of books kept by firm management for its annual report that follows Financial Accounting Standards Board rules. The tax books follow the IRS rules.

Stockholders' equity The residual claims that stockholders have against a firm's assets, calculated by subtracting total liabilities from total assets; also net worth.

Stockout Running out of inventory.

Straight voting A shareholder may cast all of his or her votes for each candidate for the board of directors.

Straight-line depreciation A method of depreciation whereby each year the firm depreciates a constant proportion of the initial investment less salvage value.

Striking price Price at which the put option or call option can be exercised. Also called the exercise price.

Strong-form efficiency Theory that the market is efficient with respect to all available information, public or private.

Subordinate debt Debt whose holders have a claim on the firm's assets only after senior debtholders' claims have been satisfied.

Subscription price Price that existing shareholders are allowed to pay for a share of stock in a rights offering.

Sum-of-the-year's-digits depreciation Method of accelerated depreciation.

Sunk cost A cost that has already occurred and cannot be removed. Because sunk costs are in the past, such costs should be ignored when deciding whether to accept or reject a project.

Super-majority amendment A defensive tactic that requires 80 percent of shareholders to approve a merger.

Surplus funds Cash flow available after payment of taxes in the project.

Sustainable growth rate The only growth rate possible with preset values for four variables: profit margin, payout ratio, debt-equity ratio, and asset utilization ratio, if the firm issues no new equity.

Swap Exchange between two securities or currencies. One type of swap involves the sale (or purchase) of a foreign currency with a simultaneous agreement to repurchase (or sell) it.

Swap rate The difference between the sale (purchase) price and the price to repurchase (resell) it in a swap.

Sweep account Account in which the bank takes all excess available funds at the close of each business day and invests them for the firm.

Syndicate A group of investment banking companies that agree to cooperate in a joint venture to underwrite an offering of securities for resale to the public.

Systematic Common to all businesses.

Systematic risk Any risk that affects a large number of assets, each to a greater or lesser degree. Also called market risk or common risk.

Systematic risk principle Only the systematic portion of risk matters in large, well-diversified portfolios. Thus, the expected returns must be related only to systematic risk.

T-bill Treasury bill.

T-period holding-period return The percentage return over the T-year period an investment lasts.

Takeover General term referring to transfer of control of a firm from one group of shareholders to another.

Taking delivery Refers to the buyer's actually assuming possession from the seller of the asset agreed upon in a forward contract.

Target cash balance Optimal amount of cash for a firm to hold, considering the trade-off between the opportunity costs of holding too much cash and the trading costs of holding too little.

Target firm A firm that is the object of a takeover by another firm.

Target payout ratio A firm's long-run dividend-to-earnings ratio. The firm's policy is to attempt to pay out a certain percentage of earnings, but it pays a stated dollar dividend and adjusts it to the target as increases in earnings occur.

Targeted repurchase The firm buys back its own stock from a potential bidder, usually at a substantial premium, to forestall a takeover attempt.

Tax books Set of books kept by firm management for the IRS that follows IRS rules. The stockholders' books follow Financial Accounting Standards Board rules.

Taxable acquisition An acquisition in which shareholders of the acquired firm will realize capital gains or losses that will be taxed.

Taxable income Gross income less a set of deductions.

Tax-free acquisition An acquisition in which the selling shareholders are considered to have exchanged their old shares for new ones of equal value, and in which they have experienced no capital gains or losses.

Technical insolvency Default on a legal obligation of the firm. For example, technical inventory occurs when a firm doesn't pay a bill.

Tender offer Public offer to buy shares of a target firm.

Term structure Relationship between spot-interest rates and maturities.

Terms of sale Conditions on which firm proposes to sell its goods and services for cash or credit.

Time value of money Price or value put on time. Time value of money reflects the opportunity cost of investing at a risk-free rate. The certainty of having a given sum of money today is worth more than the certainty of having an equal sum at a later date because money can be put to profitable use during the intervening time.

Tobin's Q Market value of assets divided by replacement value of assets. A Tobin's Q ratio greater than 1 indicates the firm has done well with its investment decisions.

Tombstone An advertisement that announces a public offering of securities. It identifies the issuer, the type of security, the underwriters, and where additional information is available.

Total asset-turnover ratio Total operating revenue divided by average total assets. Used to measure how effectively a firm is managing its assets.

Total cash flow of the firm Total cash inflow minus total cash outflow.

Trade acceptance Written demand that has been accepted by a firm to pay a given sum of money at a future date.

Trade credit Credit granted to other firms.

Trading costs Costs of selling marketable securities and borrowing.

Trading range Price range between highest and lowest prices at which a security is traded.

Transactions motive A reason for holding cash that arises from normal disbursement and collection activities of the firm.

Treasury bill Short-term discount debt maturing in less than one year. T-bills are issued weekly by the federal government and are virtually risk free.

Treasury bond or note Debt obligations of the federal government that make semiannual coupon payments and are sold at or near par value in denominations of $1,000 or more. They have original maturities of more than one year.

Treasury stock Shares of stock that have been issued and then repurchased by a firm.

Triangular arbitrage Striking offsetting deals among three markets simultaneously to obtain an arbitrage profit.

Trust receipt A device by which the borrower holds the inventory in "trust" for the lender.

Underpricing Issuing of securities below the fair market value.

Underwriter An investment firm that buys an issue of security from the firm and resells it to the investors.

Unfunded debt Short-term debt.

Unit benefit formula Method used to determine a participant's benefits in a defined benefit plan by multiplying years of service by the percentage of salary.

Unseasoned new issue Initial public offering (IPO).

Unsystematic What is specific to a firm.

Unsystematic risk See **Diversifiable risk.**

VA principle Value additivity principle.

Value additivity (VA) principle In an efficient market the value of the sum of two cash flows is the sum of the values of the individual cash flows.

Value portfolios Portfolios of common-share stocks that emphasize short-run pay-outs and earnings.

Variable cost A cost that varies directly with volume and is zero when production is zero.

Variance of the probability distribution The expected value of squared deviation from the expected return.

Venture capital Early-stage financing of young companies seeking to grow rapidly.

Vertical acquisition Acquisition in which the acquired firm and the acquiring firm are at different steps in the production process.

WACC Weighted average cost of capital.

Waiting period Time during which the Securities and Exchange Commission studies a firm's registration statement. During this time the firm may distribute a preliminary prospectus.

Warrant A security that gives the holder the right—but not the obligation—to buy shares of common stock directly from a company at a fixed price for a given time period.

Wash Gains equal losses.

Weak-form efficiency Theory that the market is efficient with respect to historical price information.

Weighted average cost of capital (WACC) The average cost of capital on the firm's existing projects and activities. The weighted average cost of capital for the firm is calculated by weighting the cost of each source of funds by its proportion of the total market value of the firm. It is calculated on a before- and after-tax basis.

Weighted average maturity A measure of the level of interest-rate risk calculated by weighting cash flows by the time to receipt and multiplying by the fraction of total present value represented by the cash flow at that time.

White knight A friendly new bidder in a hostile takeover contest.

Winner's curse The average investor wins—that is, gets the desired allocation of a new issue—because those who knew better avoided the issue.

Wire transfer An electronic transfer of funds from one bank to another that eliminates the mailing and check-clearing times associated with other cash-transfer methods.

Yankee bonds Foreign bonds issued in the United States by foreign banks and corporations.

Yield to maturity The discount rate that equates the present value of interest payments and redemption value with the present price of the bond.

Zero-balance account (ZBA) A checking account in which a zero balance is maintained by transfer of funds from a master account in an amount only large enough to cover checks presented.

Zero-coupon bonds Bonds with no coupons.

Name Index

Subject Index

Study Tools Available with This Book!

Prepare for Exams with the *NEW* Ross/Westerfield/Jaffe Student CD-ROM!

Included with every new book purchased is a CD-ROM created especially to help you master corporate finance concepts. This CD-ROM contains electronic chapter-specific, self-grading quizzes that can help you assess your topic knowledge for each chapter. Excel Templates are included for specified end-of-chapter problems to help with problem-solving skills. You will also find links to video clips and additional online study material.

Online Learning Center (OLC) with NEW Ethics in Finance PowerWeb Available at www.mhhe.com/rwj

Find Additional Study Resources Here!

This website follows the text chapter-by-chapter with digital supplementary content specific to this book. The *Instructor's Edition* contains the password-protected Instructor's Manual and PowerPoints, and the *Student Edition* includes free online study materials developed specifically for this edition.

Purchasers of new books will find an access code card included with this text for FREE access to *Ethics in Finance* PowerWeb. This online resource provides recent articles from both academic and popular press resources that pertain to ethics in finance. A news feed continually updates the site, providing an easy way to bring the most current real-world information into the classroom. The Instructor's Edition is password-protected and includes the teaching resources for this text.

Standard & Poor's Educational Version of Market Insight Available at www.mhhe.com/edumarketinsight

Use the Same Real Data Professionals Use!

McGraw-Hill/Irwin is proud to partner with Standard & Poor's to offer access to the Educational Version of Market Insight FREE with this text. A passcode card is bound into new books, which gives you access to six years of financial data, along with industry trends, stock reports, and much more, for over 600 top companies. Relevant chapters contain end-of-chapter problems that use this data to gain a better understanding of practical business situations.

Some Useful Formulas

1 Present Value (Chapter 4)

The discounted value of T future cash flows

$$PV = \frac{C_1}{1 + r} + \frac{C_2}{(1 + r)^2} + \cdots + \frac{C_T}{(1 + r)^T} = \sum_{t=1}^{T} \frac{C_t}{(1 + r)^t}$$

2 Net Present Value (Chapter 4)

Present value minus initial costs

$NPV = PV - Cost$

$C_0 = -Cost$

$$NPV = C_0 + \sum_{t=1}^{T} \frac{C_t}{(1 + r)^t}$$

3 Perpetuity (Chapter 4)

The value of C received each year, forever

$$PV = \frac{C}{r}$$

4 Annuity (Chapter 4)

The value of C received each year for T years

$$PV = \frac{C}{r}[1 - 1/(1 + r)^T]$$

5 Growing Perpetuity (Chapter 4)

The value of a perpetuity that grows at rate g, where the first payment is C

$$PV = \frac{C}{r - g}$$

6 Growing Annuity (Chapter 4)

The value of a T-period annuity that grows at the rate g, where the first payment is C

$$PV = C\left[\frac{1}{r - g} - \frac{1}{r - g} \times \left(\frac{1 + g}{1 + r}\right)^T\right]$$

7 Measures of Risk for Individual Assets (Chapter 10)

$$Var(R_A) = \sigma_A^2 = \text{Expected value of } (R_A - \bar{R}_A)^2$$

$$SD(R_A) = \sigma_A = \sqrt{Var(R_A)}$$

$$Cov(R_A, R_B) = \sigma_{AB} = \text{Expected value of } [(R_A - \bar{R}_A)(R_B - \bar{R}_B)]$$

$$Corr(R_A, R_B) = \rho_{AB} = Cov(R_A R_B)/\sigma_A \sigma_B$$

8 Expected Return on a Portfolio of Two Assets (Chapter 10)

$$\bar{R}_p = X_A\bar{R}_A + X_B\bar{R}_B$$

9 Variance of a Portfolio of Two Assets (Chapter 10)

$$\sigma_p^2 = X_A^2 \times \sigma_A^2 + 2X_A X_B \times \sigma_{AB} + X_B^2 \times \sigma_B^2$$

6/81

ALSO BY LEONARD LEWIN

A VIEW FROM THE BENCH

A VIEW FROM THE BENCH

BY RED HOLZMAN

WITH LEONARD LEWIN

W·W·NORTON & COMPANY·NEW YORK·LONDON

Copyright © 1980 by Red Holzman and Leonard Lewin
Published simultaneously in Canada by George J. McLeod Limited,
Toronto. Printed in the United States of America.

First Edition

All Rights Reserved

Library of Congress Cataloging in Publication Data
Holzman, Red.
A view from the bench.

1. Basketball players—United States—Biography.
2. Basketball—Psychological aspects. 3. National
Basketball Association. I. Lewin, Leonard. II. Title.
GV884.A1H63 1980   796.32′3′0922 [B]   80–18855
ISBN 0–393–01351–0

W. W. Norton & Company, Inc. 500 Fith Avenue, New York, N.Y.
10110
W. W. Norton & Company Ltd. 25 New Street Square, London
EC4A

1 2 3 4 5 6 7 8 9 0

I respectfully dedicate this book to David (Sonny) Werblin to whom I am grateful for taking me off the tennis courts and out of the supermarkets.

CONTENTS

2   THE MATCHUPS

INTRODUCTION

When a man has spent many unbroken years with the same venture, he gains some distinction as an authority in that field. Red Holzman is just such a man. He has been involved with the National Basketball Association as player, scout, coach, and general manager for over thirty years and, thereby, has acquired a keen professional insight into the sport.

It is because of that tenure and the significant years of service that this book has been written. When it came down one day to considering just what kind of book it would be, it was decided to just let Red Holzman run his fingers through the Yellow Pages of the NBA and discuss some of the things that have influenced his thinking.

He would discuss some of the players and incidents that have had an impact on a sport that has become one of the country's major industries. He would choose players more for the opportunity to deal with their unique qualities than their All-Star standings. In other words, there is no intention to set this book up as the means by which Red Holzman picks his all-time, All-Star team. He leaves that for others so inclined.

Those players with whom he deals are not necessarily the

best. However, by the very nature of their accomplishments, those included in the book would have to be considered for an all-time team. In fact, the basic idea was to work with a cross section of the finest players the NBA has ever seen since it went into business in 1946 as the Basketball Association of America and then merged with the old National League to become what it is today.

It was in 1948 that the Rochester Royals came into the league and brought with them a former CCNY player named Red Holzman. So, in effect, he has been associated with just about every important player who has ever performed in the league. And it's that knowledge and experience that informs this book's evaluation of the people who have played the game, and how they played it.

Holzman takes the fans behind the scenes and invites them to sit on the bench with him. They get to see what he has seen from his spot on the sidelines. They get a peek at some of the strategy and they learn why things happen that might slip past the average viewer. They might even learn how to look at a game a little differently after seeing things through the eyes of such a distinguished coach.

A View from the Bench is not a routine trip down memory lane. Otherwise, Holzman would have included chapters on Bob Pettit, whom he coached with Milwaukee and with the St. Louis Hawks; certainly George Mikan, the Bill Russell of his time; Joe Fulks, the first pure shooting genius of the league; and other Hall-of-Famers. Actually, Holzman decided to reach back only as far as when Bob Cousy and Bill Sharman were joined on the Celtics by Russell. That moment represents the perfect demarcation line between the "old" and the "new" players and provides a better perspective on those who have excelled in the modern pro game.

Therefore, many "great names" have been excluded from Holzman's lineup for the book. He purposely has avoided dealing with the Knicks in the Players section because he preferred to consider them strictly as a team. Also, they are well represented among the five key matchups he has chosen to illustrate the little wars within the wars that have gone on in the NBA: Dave DeBusschere vs. Gus Johnson, Bill Bradley vs.

John Havlicek, Walt Frazier vs. Earl Monroe, and Willis Reed vs. Kareem Abdul-Jabbar. And, of course, the daddy of all the matchups: Russell vs. Wilt Chamberlain.

Each matchup had its own quality and style, and Holzman reviews them, studies them, and deals with the whys and wherefores of the confrontations. Each representative in the section on individual players had his own personality and his own impact on the game. Somewhere along the way, Holzman, during a coaching career that spanned over six hundred victories, was involved with them.

Think of them. Russell, Chamberlain, Jerry West, Oscar Robertson, Rick Barry, Julius Erving, Elvin Hayes, to name a few. Some things humorous. Some things exciting. Some things dramatic. But all things an insight into the playing of the game by the best of those who have played it.

Holzman, of course, deals heavily with the 1970s and the championship years for the Knicks that led to his being voted Coach of the Decade by the professional basketball writers of America. It's all here, through the eyes of a man who was player, scout, general manager, and coach; a man who helped fashion the game as it's played today.

Leonard Lewin

1 THE PLAYERS

BOB COUSY

Question: Name one thing Bob Cousy and Oscar Robertson have in common. Hint: it's something no other backcourt player ever accomplished in the NBA.

Answer: They're the only small men to be voted MVP by their fellow players. Jerry West never made it. Walt Frazier never made it. I say this to emphasize the impact Cousy had on a pro sport that grew into a big man's game and has permitted the small man only an occasional triumph.

Our paths first crossed in 1950 when Cousy came into the league. I was with the Rochester Royals and we won the NBA championship that year by beating the Knicks in seven games. I don't remember much detail about Cousy the rookie other than that he was flashy from the start.

He was hard to play because he'd come down the floor with the ball and hook a pass to a teammate before you could blink. He was quick, not really fast. He was what we called in those days "loosey-goosey," which meant he played loose and you'd never know when he would fling one of his fancy passes or fire a long one-hander.

I had heard a lot about him, of course. He had gone to Andrew Jackson High School in New York and, as a New Yorker out of Brooklyn's Franklin K. Lane High, I'd gotten the word about the flashy kid from Queens. In those days, high school basketball in the Garden was a big thing, so it was hard to keep a secret if you had an unusual player.

Cousy made himself an unusual player by learning to use his left hand after fracturing his right wrist as a youngster. He went to the schoolyards with a cast on the wrist and played lefthanded, otherwise he couldn't have played at all.

Basketball was nothing in New England until Cousy led Holy Cross to the NCAA championship in 1950. That was Red Auerbach's first season as coach of the Celtics and, when the draft came up, he had to make his first big decision about Cousy.

Walter Brown owned the Boston Garden and the Boston Bruins, and had put himself into hock after deciding to put together a pro basketball franchise in the league that was formed in 1946. The story has been told many times but it's worth repeating. Brown, looking for anything to sell tickets and stimulate interest in his team, wanted to draft Cousy and cash in on the new basketball excitement he had generated in the area. But Auerbach refused.

Those were the shaky, pioneer years of the league when it had not yet managed to overcome the huge lead owned by college basketball. Brown and all the owners needed the box-office receipts to stay alive, while the coaches were concerned with winning to keep their jobs.

It was understandable, therefore, when Auerbach told his boss, after the suggested drafting of Cousy: "Am I supposed to win or worry about local yokels?" Auerbach needed a center, not a flashy college kid who just happened to play his college ball in the Boston area but was too small for the Celtics' most urgent need.

Brown allowed Auerbach to make the decision. "Just win," the owner told his coach, which, I must say, the coach managed to do quite often through the years. At that time, though, Auerbach picked seven-foot Charlie Share of Bowling Green and, boy, did the wolves howl.

I remember going into Boston and reading the papers in those days, when the coverage was not that extensive for the

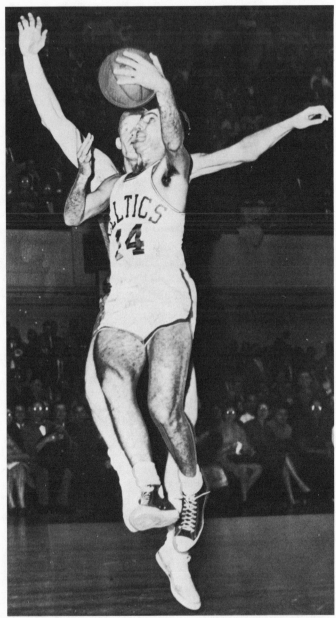

Cousy driving around John Kerr of the Syracuse Nations, 1961

Celtics but was unanimous about Auerbach. He didn't make many friends when he turned down Cousy, who had become a greater local hero than Paul Revere.

Luck was with the Celtics, though, just as it has to be with all teams and coaches engaged in the process of trying to be the absolute best among so many qualified to be champions. Five of the seventeen teams that had participated in the 1950 draft folded before the season started. At that point, the league signed all the players and dealt them around to the surviving teams in a dispersal draft.

Cousy wound up in Chicago with Max Zaslofsky, one of the league's best shooters, and Andy Phillip, one of the league's best playmakers. Then the Stags folded before the season began, so a special meeting was called to distribute those three players among the Knicks, Celtics and Philadelphia Warriors.

They all wanted Zaslofsky, the shooter. Maurice Podoloff, the man who had helped set up the league as its first commissioner, decided to put the names in a hat to break the deadlock. The Celtics were to pick first because they had finished last in the standings, but Brown, one of the finest gentlemen the league has ever known, turned to Ned Irish of the Knicks and said: "No. I'd be ashamed to take another first pick. You go first, Ned."

Irish picked Zaslofsky. Brown wound up with Cousy. It wasn't until 1957 that the Celtics were to get Bill Russell and win their first championship, but Cousy was to become a Boston landmark. For a long time, I always assumed that when Auerbach stepped down as coach Cousy would replace him, but it didn't work that way. Russell was still playing when Auerbach decided to quit, and Red felt it would be better to have a coach who could motivate Russell—which Russell did for himself for two more championships until he retired as player-coach after the 1968–69 playoffs.

Cousy, for a long while, was the highest-paid player in the NBA except for Chamberlain. I think the following wire story, which moved throughout the country on December 20, 1956, tells you something about the salaries in those days:

" . . . All-American Bill Russell has signed a one-year contract for a reported $17,000 with the Boston Celtics, but the incomparable Bob Cousy still reigns as the highest-paid player on the club.

"You don't think I'd give anybody as much as I'm giving Cousy, do you?" Walter Brown, Celtics owner, asked. "I'd be crazy to do such a thing after the way Cousy has killed himself around here for seven years playing the style of ball he has."

"Cousy is believed to be drawing about $22,000 a year—the highest in the NBA. Russell is believed to have signed for a $3,000 bonus and $14,000 for the remaining two-thirds of the season."

That was before Chamberlain entered the league as an astronomical $30,000 rookie and improved salary conditions for Cousy and everyone else. Cousy's $22,000 would be the equivalent of $500,000 by today's standards. I sometimes wonder what they would pay him these days, because he is one old-time player I know could perform just as well in today's game.

I think Cousy would be a star in the world of Walton, Erving, Hayes, Unseld, Barry, Dave Cowens, David Thompson, and Larry Bird, though he stopped playing in 1963. He was, in effect, the trigger for the Celtics' fast break that pioneered the run-and-shoot game. He could shoot and make the play and would start in any backcourt these days.

I say that for good reason and from experience. I remember the night Cousy stepped in against the Knicks and played at the age of forty. We had just won our seventeenth in a row at the start of the 1969–70 season. We had tied the league record held by Boston (1959) and Washington (1946), both of whom, ironically, had been coached by Auerbach. We also were 22–1 and had passed the old NBA record of 16–1 for the fastest start by the 1948 Washington Caps.

And we were in Cleveland to see if we could make it a record eighteen straight on a neutral floor against a Cincinnati team coached by Cousy. He had placed himself on the active roster a few games prior to that but we felt it was just a formality. We never expected to see him in the game that night. Certainly not when he took off his warmup jacket and went to the scorer's table with the Royals leading us 101–98 and only 1:49 left to our streak.

I couldn't believe it. He had been out of the game for over

six years while coaching at Boston College and now he was putting himself in at such a critical stage? Oscar Robertson had just fouled out and Cousy figured he was the only one on the bench who could handle the pressure of the situation. I admired him but was confused. Once a pro, always a pro, I told myself as I advised my players to pressure him when he got the ball and let him shoot because he had been away too long to make any shot under those conditions.

Was I in for a surprise. The first time he got the ball, he fired a crisp, crosscourt pass to Norm Van Lier for a jumper that matched a basket by Frazier, and we were still behind by three with less time to play. Then Cousy, forgetting the game was played with a twenty-four-second, not a grandfather clock, turned it back with a drive that drew two shots. He'd never make them. He'd been away too long. Would he? Could he?

He did. He made them both. The elastic might've gone from his legs but the nerves were still ice cold. He didn't stop fighting us, trying to out-think us, until we somehow stole the ball three times and won, 106–105, in one of the wildest finishes I've ever experienced.

Cousy was responsible for it. I don't know of anyone else capable of being out of the game for so long, performing for those few minutes like he'd never been away, except for Chamberlain. I always felt Wilt could step right in and play long after he quit playing. Until he was 60, at least.

Cousy made the Celtics tick long before Russell joined him to trigger the fast break of championships. Bob was the heart of the team, Russell added the soul. Cousy suffered intensely through the years the Celtics couldn't beat the Knicks, then became one of the main reasons why the Knicks couldn't beat the Celtics.

He was from New York and seemed to save his most dramatic and exciting moments for the Knicks or the Garden. Once, way back in 1954, the Knicks were leading the Celtics by four in the Garden with thirty-eight seconds to go, when Cousy stole the ball twice to tie it in regulation and help the Celtics win in double overtime. In the All-Star game of the same year, same place, George Mikan tied the game for the West with two foul shots at the buzzer and Cousy won it with ten of the East's fourteen points in overtime.

I always understood that Bob Davies, one of my teammates at Rochester, invented the behind-the-back dribble when he played for Seton Hall, but Cousy certainly made it what it is today. He turned it into an offensive weapon that Frazier, Monroe, Tiny Archibald, and most guards copied and used as a routine move.

Cousy could do more with a basketball than anyone I know. Pete Maravich had a similar flair and came closest to Bob with one big difference: Cousy learned to control the ball and play within himself, while Maravich sometimes still seems to play a little too fast for himself and his teammates.

"I never worked on the trick stuff," Cousy explained. "The behind-the-back dribble just happened. The first time I ever used it I was a junior in college. The score was tied. We were trying to hold the ball for one shot. There were ten seconds left and the fellow playing me took a step to my right side.

"I was driving right all the time, so he overplayed me to my right and I had no place to go. I couldn't stop the dribble I had started and I needed a step, so I put the ball behind my back and went left. I got my step and made a left-handed shot. I had never practiced. It just happened."

He had a knack of making things just happen. Some considered him a showboat because he threw the fanciest passes in the league. There were many times when I was fooled by his now-you-see-it-now-you-don't ballhandling But I never considered him a hotdog. For one thing, he never gave me that much time to notice when I played him.

"If I thought anything would add a few thousand dollars to my salary and not hurt the team, I'd try it," was his response. "I don't do things to make fools out of anyone." He was so good, it just came out that way when he had the ball.

He had the longest arms I've ever seen on what we consider a small man in pro basketball. His fingertips almost touched his knees. He also had tremendous hands that wrapped around a basketball like it was a baseball, which is why he controlled a ball so well. He was the best playmaker in the league and, with Oscar Robertson, the best all-time, in my opinion.

Yet, Cousy didn't think so in his early pro years. "I don't go in much for idols," he said, while becoming the idol of Boston and basketball fans wherever there was an NBA franchise. "But if I had to name an idol, I'd pick Dick McGuire. He's the best playmaker in the league. He's a good shooter, too, but he won't shoot."

That's the same Dick McGuire I replaced as coach of the Knicks in 1967 who helped me as an assistant and a scout. I knew just what Cousy was talking about. McGuire was on the 1950–51 Knick team the Royals beat for the championship; I played against him at times but I played him to pass, not shoot.

The Knicks paid him to pass but there came a time when Ned Irish offered to pay him a bonus to shoot. I think it was ten dollars for every shot but Dick still refused and insisted on making the play. Money wasn't everything in those days because, I guess, none of it was around.

Today they've got nothing but money so now they can use playmakers like McGuire and Cousy. They looked to make the play first, and I don't think basketball can afford to lose that no matter how much progress brings change. I believe the sport prospers more when it comes up with new faces such as Phil Ford of Kansas City, who knows how to make the play and, more importantly, looks to make it.

Cousy, of course, became the super playmaker, and Dick McGuire had the distinction of having to play him when the Knicks and Celtics met. One night, McGuire had his usual difficult time with Cousy up in the Boston Garden as the Celtics came from way back to win.

There was no question that Cousy had been the difference with twenty-three points and thirteen assists, and Dick wasn't too happy in the dressing room. "You don't play him right," shouted Dick's effervescent brother Al, who was a substitute guard with the Knicks. "I told you. You've got to give him more room. You play him too tight."

Dick was the older brother and the better player. In fact, one reason why he went to St. John's was because Joe Lapchick, later to be his coach on the Knicks, promised to bring in Allie on a package deal when he got out of high school. Dick was not happy the way his kid brother had yelled at him that night in Boston.

"You tell me how to play a guy I've played maybe a hundred times," snapped Dick, who had an extremely high boiling point. "There's only one way to play him, You pray, Al. You pray and even that works only sometimes."

That didn't stop Allie. He hopped onto the training table when he spotted a new audience of Boston writers, who idolized Cousy, and shouted: "I own Cousy!" The Boston papers blew it up and it became the war cry every time Al McGuire came to town with the Knicks to face Cousy.

"Nobody was going to stop Cousy, but I had a gimmick," said Allie after he became a national spokesman with his coaching success at Marquette some ten years later. "They used to put me on Cousy and every time they'd set a block for him to shoot, I'd knock the guy setting the block into him. I'd foul the guy, they'd blow the whistle, Cousy wouldn't get the basket, and it looked in the box score as though he couldn't score on me.

"Of course, I fouled out in about six minutes every time we played the Celtics, so it wasn't perfect. But it kept me with the Knicks for at least a year after I was really through." Allie was not only sharp, he was fearless, and that helped.

One night, Bob Brannum, who was the Celtics' cop at the time, informed Cousy he would block for him on Allie. Nothing would happen then. Sure. As soon as Brannum put his big body in front of Cousy, he was shoved almost into the seats. They didn't call the younger McGuire "Allie-Cat" for nothing in his college days.

Cousy was a legend—the greatest player of all time, some insisted—when he came to New York shortly before Christmas in 1956. There was a game with the Knicks that night and Cousy was lounging in the hotel lobby when someone brought over a tall young man who had to be a basketball player.

"How do you do, Mr. Cousy," said the tall young man, who turned out to be Bill Russell.

Cousy was startled by the formality. It made him feel like an old man. Besides, he reminded Russell, they had met at the White House when President Eisenhower had invited a group of athletes to lunch. They talked small talk and Russell excused himself because his wife was waiting upstairs. Russell was in New York for the Holiday Festival at the time, and little did he and Cousy know how their paths would cross the next time and affect pro basketball history.

Cousy was considered the greatest then but it wasn't long before he was calling Russell the greatest. "Russ would make a contender out of any team," said Cousy after the Celtics won the title for the first time in 1957, lost to the Hawks when Russell was hurt in 1958, and then kept on winning in the ensuing years. "He's meant a championship for us for five years now and this season [1961–62], the way he's playing, and the pride with which he plays has given us all the pickup to carry on our streak as long as we can."

That was a big part of Cousy, the player. He was all team. "For someone like myself who gets such a bang out of feeding and setting up plays," he said, "it's a pleasure to play with Russ. He simplifies everything for me and, at my age, I could use the assistance."

Cousy was thirty-three, and a year away from quitting but no one realized it at the time. I don't think he realized it. No player looks forward to quitting and few can afford the luxury of setting a deadline. Yet, he knew he was nearing the end and must have had that in mind when he was induced into talking about an all-star team.

He had been around long enough to bridge the gap between the early greats and the new ones. "I'd want," he said, "Oscar Robertson, Jerry West, Elgin Baylor, and Bob Pettit with Bill Russell, of course. With Russell you couldn't have Wilt Chamberlain if you're limited to five by position."

Not a bad team once you added Cousy. They were all his contemporaries. "West," he said, "is great now. He has some room for improvement in scoring and taking more initiative. He will get better on his offensive moves but Jerry and Oz will dominate the league as backcourt men for a long time to come.

"I'd say Russell is the most valuable player in the league. He keeps improving. He dribbles better than any big man. He moves better. He has no equal as a rebounder. He hustles more. He's the best defensive player in the league. He doesn't have that good shooting touch but he's learned so much that he's even becoming a scoring threat." Russell did a lot for Cousy and Cousy did a lot for Russell.

Russell's rebounding got Cousy the ball and his defense allowed Cousy to use his quick hands to gamble and play the ball. It was much the same with Frazier on the Knicks. Our team defense enabled Clyde to cheat and attempt to steal the ball.

Cousy and Sharman never won a championship until Russell came along and then Cousy got better, if that was possible. Bob and the Celtics played the game at an all-out pace but Cousy never seemed to tire.

He got trickier and younger as the years went by. "After playing with a guy for so many years," said Sharman, "you think you know every one of his tricks and moves, but every game he shows you something else. I've never seen anybody who could respond to the situations that crop up in a game faster than Bob."

Cousy kept going and going, and they kept asking him the same question as the years piled on: How long are you going to play? "Let's put it this way," he said. "I'll keep going as long as Auerbach's around. I don't think I want to break in a new coach."

Long forgotten were the painful early days, when an unwanted Cousy went to Boston on a freak bounce and suddenly began getting blamed when the Celtics didn't win because he had become so important. One day, way back in 1953, Cousy decided he wanted to be traded. By then he had established himself as a performing hero, not just another college star the Boston crowd idolized because he had done so much for Holy Cross's image.

First Walter Brown said he wasn't shooting enough, then Auerbach said he wasn't passing enough. Boston had gotten off to a 15–16 start and trailed the Knicks and the Syracuse Nats in the standings. Those were the days when Auerbach was trying to get Cousy to control his dribbling and playmaking.

"When Brown criticized me for not shooting enough, I let it go because he's footing the bills," said Cousy. "But now Auerbach says I'm not passing enough. Both charges are uncalled for. I like playing in Boston and want to stay here, but not if I'm caught in the middle."

Cousy was first in assists and third in NBA scoring at the time and couldn't understand the crossfire. Auerbach wanted him to hit the cornermen more often and forget about the fancy dribbling and behind-the-back passes. It really wasn't serious. None of us in the league paid any attention to it. It only proved that even an outstanding player such as Cousy can have problems at times.

There was no divorce. Not even a separation. Championship team pictures continued year after year. Boston became the most explosive force basketball had ever seen and Cousy was the man with his finger on the trigger. With Cousy running the fast break, the Celtics introduced the big inning to basketball.

Cousy ran a wide-open offense, so it was difficult to stay with him. The little I played him when I was nearing the end of my playing days, and he was just about starting, I'd pick him up quickly and try to force him to give up the ball if I could. I can't remember being too successful at it.

I wandered off to play awhile with the Milwaukee Hawks and then coach the team and was quite happy someone else had the pleasure of playing Cousy. He never did much to help my career as a player or coach. One time, however, he did strike a blow for the small man in basketball, of which I was one of the species.

Everyone listened to him in those days. He'd been in the NBA ten years and made the All-Star team ten years. He was only six-one, but he stood taller than anyone the way he handled a ball and ran the Boston offense.

"It's a shame the way the big men have taken over the game," he told a listening pro basketball world that hung on his every word. "In my dealings with the younger kids at camp, the little fellows ask me the same question: 'Do we have a chance?' What answer can I give them? I'm convinced that in another decade there won't be a player in pro ball who is under six-five. If a coach has a chance to choose between two players, he has to gamble on the six-five man instead of the six-footer."

At thirty-four, Cousy finally decided it might be wise to hang up his sneakers. He had done all he could for the Celtics, pro basketball, and himself. He had helped keep the game alive at a time when it was bouncing on angry waves and many franchises and investors drowned. He was the greatest six-one box-office attraction the game has ever seen.

It was hard to believe that Cousy wasn't good enough to break into the Holy Cross starting lineup when the Crusaders were playing freshmen, and then went on to six NBA championships with the Celtics. He led the league in assists the first four years and never dropped below the top three in his thirteen years as the unparalleled playmaker.

At one time, after Chamberlain entered the league at $30,-000, the Celtics gave Cousy a raise that once again made him the highest-paid player in the NBA. Brown considered him the greatest and wanted him to be paid like the greatest. "If we do any business at all, no one who has ever played the game will be anywhere near him," promised the Celtics owner, who gave his star attraction a base salary and a percentage of the growing gate.

That was in 1959, when Cousy was thirty. Four years later, Cousy announced it would be his last season. He was honored all around the league as he made his way to a final appearance in each of the nine franchise cities.

He came to New York on March 4, 1963 for his farewell in the Garden, where it had all started when he was a schoolboy. It was the end of an era for pro basketball. I watched him pass, run, and shoot as he led the Celtics to a victory over the Knicks that clinched first place in the East. I wondered why he was quitting.

Richie Guerin, Gene Shue, Tom Gola, and the other Knicks still couldn't handle him. They made him stand in the middle of the floor as thousands cheered. The Knicks said things about him. The Celtics said things about him.

"It's hard to put into words what he meant to me from the start," Russell told New York. "I liked him right away, which was important. But then, he always had a pride, a dignity, and a winning attitude. We try, all the time, to make the word Celtics synonymous with 'class' and Cousy was always there to lead us. It may sound corny but I consider the years I've played with him the golden years."

By then, Cousy had adjusted to the idea it would all be over soon. Yet I got the feeling that he felt a little sad when it came time to say goodbye to the Garden. "This was always like a second home to me," he acknowledged. "The biggest thrill, I guess, was that 1953 All-Star game we won in overtime. The biggest change in basketball since I'm in it is the jump shot. Kids are so good with it now, they don't bother to learn other phases of the game and that's bad.

"There's a great shortage in the pros of what I consider real playmakers—men who move the defense and create openings, rather then just deliver the ball where openings already exist. I've been a very fortunate man and now one more championship would have a real special meaning for me."

There were no tears. He was to cry himself dry on Bob Cousy Night in the Boston Garden two weeks later. The Johnstown Flood never produced more water than when Cousy cried, his wife, Missy, cried, his daughters, Marie Collette and Mary Patricia cried, his mother and father cried, his teammates cried, the fans cried.

"I knew we were in trouble," one of the Syracuse players said after Cousy finally led the Celtics to a 125–116 win that night, "when I saw the referees crying, too." The Boston Irish had picked the perfect time to honor Cousy the Frenchman—St. Patrick's Day, March 17, 1963.

"It was the greatest day of Bob's life," said Mrs. Cousy. "How do you describe the kindness of people? You can't put it into words. It's something you feel and will remain with you always."

Cousy stood there in uniform, a towel draped around his neck, and listened as Russell and friends paid tribute. He put the towel to his eyes to dry away one last tear when a voice in the gallery yelled: "We love you, Cooz!" More tears.

Cousy gurgled his speech that night, I guess. I wasn't there but I've been told that it was one of the most emotional scenes they've ever had in Boston, where they've had a few with so many championships. There was a standing ovation that lasted forever when Cousy finally finished his speech; his wife could recall only one other occasion that came close to matching it.

"It was during the days when the Knicks and Celtics were great rivals," she said, referring to the early 1950s when her husband first heated it up. "It was during the semifinals of a playoff. The game went into double overtime when Bob fouled out. He had played his heart out and the Boston fans gave him a standing ovation that lasted a full two minutes. I thought I'd never experience that again but Bob Cousy Night surpassed it. It was the greatest."

There was only one more thing left for Cousy. A last championship as a fitting climax to a playing career that had spanned some twenty years of exhausting competition. He got it when Jerry West, Elgin Baylor, Dick Barnett, and the other Lakers submitted in the sixth game of the championship series out in Los Angeles.

When it was over, Cousy sat on the trainer's table pulling the tape off his left foot. He was sweaty, tired, and in pain from a twisted ankle that forced him out with about eleven minutes to go. It appeared as though he'd finish his final game on the bench but some ice enabled him to come back limping.

Boston was leading by only a point at the time and there were only four minutes left in Cousy's brilliant NBA career, but he made it. He went out like he came in—a winner. "I think God has been very good to me. He's granted me my last wish," said Cousy as he prepared to sip championship wine for the last time.

A few days after the Boston team came back for a ticker-tape ride through the city (for a change), Cousy was on his way to New York for a speaking engagement. He drove his car with the license plates "Celtics 14" up to a toll booth along the turnpike and flipped two dimes and a nickel at the basket.

He missed. A guard picked up the coins, handed them to Cousy, and said: "You're retiring, aren't you? Just as well."

Cousy smiled and drove away.

BILL RUSSELL

On December 22, 1956, Bill Russell, star of the Olympic-winning United States basketball team, played his first game as a Boston Celtic. This was the headline in a Boston paper after the Celtics, playing at home, had beaten the St. Louis Hawks 95–93: "Russell Defensive Star in Pro Debut."

Three games later, after the Celtics had beaten the Philadelphia Warriors at home, 120–97, this was the headline: "Russell Puts Defense Back in NBA." That tells it all. The Bill Russell Story. He did more for defense than Dr. James Naismith, who invented defense and offense in the game of basketball.

You must understand what was going on in pro basketball at the time Russell appeared on the scene, with the 1956–57 season in progress, to appreciate his impact on the sport. The big name centers were Larry Foust of the Pistons, Harry Gallatin of the Knicks, Neil Johnston of the Warriors, Charley Share of the Hawks, Johnny Kerr of the Syracuse Nats, and Clyde Lovellette of the Minneapolis Lakers. All were offense-oriented, some exceptionally big, such as Foust, Share, and Lovellette, but rather slow. Boston had the only quick center in Easy Ed Macauley and he, also, was offense-oriented.

It is no wonder that there weren't too many NBA people who

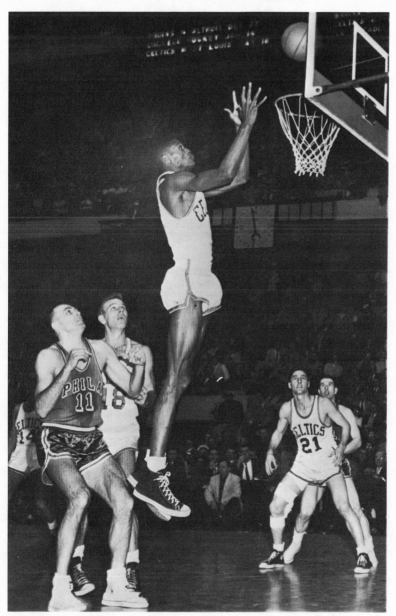

Bill Russell rebounding in 1956

fully appreciated Russell and his defensive style of play. Big men in those days were supposed to get the ball and score enough points to neutralize each other. Speed wasn't a priority, either. Neither was shot blocking, a unique and freakish art twenty-five years ago.

Centers were big, slow, and built for the battle of the boards. They were built more for power than grace and style, a pattern set by George Mikan's success as the top center of his generation as the Lakers won four titles in five years: 1949, 1950, 1952, 1953. Those were the days when every coach, scout, and owner looked for another Mikan.

Then along came Russell to change the pattern overnight—much to the surprise of some people who took a little time to recognize that the defensive specialist from San Francisco University was going to revolutionize the game, and much to the surprise of some who saw him perform very well in Madison Square Garden but did not fully appreciate what he was and might be in the league. Actually, there were a few other players involved in that 1955 Holiday Festival in whom some of the NBA teams were more interested—for their own good reasons, which is how teams normally draft.

The Knicks, for example, were impressed by the way Russell's defense and scoring had made an unbeaten team of the Dons, but they had their eyes on Sihugo Green, a local player. Green had played ball at Boys High in Brooklyn and developed into an All-America shooting guard at Duquesne.

Green was quick, strongly built, could shoot and make the play. Since the Knicks had three centers in Gallatin, Ray Felix, and Walter Dukes, they looked beyond Russell though he had an outstanding tournament. They needed scoring and ball handling in the backcourt more than a center, so Green, who had been a high school teammate of Tommy Davis (later to become an outstanding hitter with the Dodgers), was the player they wanted most.

Besides, Russell wasn't considered that exceptional in the East, which didn't see him play often enough to appreciate his defense and basketball instincts. He sneaked into New York, though San Francisco was the NCAA champion and had won thirty-four in a row. It so happened that Holy Cross, another

Festival team, had an exciting group of players led by a big forward named Tommy Heinsohn. They were the excitement in the East.

Heinsohn and Holy Cross got most of the media attention, naturally. Everyone wrote about Heinsohn, the young man from Union City, New Jersey, who grew up dreaming about playing with the Knicks someday and then wound up with you know who. Russell, an All-America and mostly responsible for the best record in the country and the best team in the country, was an afterthought and a freak.

Russell and San Francisco were playing Heinsohn and Holy Cross, not the other way around. It bothered Russell. It was, in his mind, an extension of the media's lack of respect for him when everyone made a big deal about Tom Gola of LaSalle and, especially, Kenny Sears of Santa Clara, but practically ignored him. Sears was named Player of the West Coast and Russell just couldn't believe that or accept it.

He was openly bothered when he picked up the New York papers and saw the treatment given him. "Don't you think I read the papers?" he said. "Don't you think I know they've been cutting me up since I've been here? I was cut to pieces real good. It's like knives. It hurts."

Strangely, it was Heinsohn, later to be his teammate in Boston, who got on his nerves. Russell had nothing against Tommy, just the writers who seemed to think Heinsohn was the only good player in the tournament. Heinsohn was a forward but Russell was hoping coach Phil Woolpert would let him play Tommy to give the eastern writers a little spot education.

New Yorkers know their basketball because it is their schoolyard game. Everyone grows up with it. In Russell's case, they simply had never seen a tall defensive specialist blocking shots in their playgrounds, so Russell was a new species, in effect. Somewhat similar to Hank Luisetti of Stanford, when he first came to Madison Square Garden and revolutionized the eastern style of shooting with his one-handers.

Russell's defensive style was something new but Heinsohn's style was familiar and exciting. So the media dwelt on Tommy and the people went wild over him while Russell and his exceptional record was ignored. And Russell, who hardly needed motivation, was motivated.

He couldn't hide it. I now know why I never heard Russell sing "I Love New York" whenever he came to the Garden to play the Knicks. "At the hotel, he felt pretty bad," said K. C. Jones, who was to help Russell beat the Crusaders that night, just as he helped beat the Knicks when they became Celtics teammates. "Everybody building up Tommy Heinsohn in the papers and knocking Bill down. He's just a big fellow. He's no freak. He didn't like that kind of reading. When the coach said for him to play Heinsohn, he didn't say anything. He just smiled. He was hoping for it, I guess."

Heinsohn paid the price. Russell, who started basketball late in high school and was only four years into the game, fed a lot of important data into Tommy's mental computer as the Dons won, 67–51. Heinsohn, the big scorer, got ten points in the first half, two in the second, and never got to shoot a foul. Russell, the big defender, got twenty-four points, grabbed twenty-two rebounds, and blocked a few shots.

It was not easy for Heinsohn to forget and it helped when they became teammates and the Celtics had to sell Russell, the defensive freak, to a Boston area that was just wild about Bob Cousy. "I became the number one Russell salesman whenever Auerbach needed someone to talk about Russell," Tommy has explained. "I was even at Russell's first press conference and had to answer a lot of questions about him."

Tommy also had to answer a lot of questions about Russell that night in the Garden. "I didn't get my thirty, did I?" was Heinsohn's first answer. "Usually, I pick up fourteen or fifteen points outside and get the rest inside. Against San Francisco, I got just one basket in close."

Russell, of course, had proved himself once more. He was to enter the NBA needing to prove himself more before everyone finally believed him. Russell mentioned how he had hoped his coach would let him play Heinsohn in the festival semifinal because of the challenge.

"What else does a fellow play ball for but a competitive challenge," he said. "What did I have to prove? Heinsohn's a great ballplayer. Everybody wrote that in the papers. I wanted to prove I'm as good as he is. Can you blame me for wanting to prove that?" His coach came over and told Russell he had been just great. "I wanted to be," said Russell.

That's why the Celtics won so many championships after they got him. He had the talent and he wanted to be great. There was no challenge too big for him. A lot of people in the NBA saw that just a little too late.

Rochester, having finished with the worst record the year before, had the first crack at Russell but had no chance. Les Harrison, my old coach and owner of the team, needed money and wound up negotiating with the Garden for his pick. I'll say this for Les: he took the time to talk to Russell, who priced Rochester out by suggesting he'd like $25,000 a year to sign.

Russell has said he deliberately made it so high because he had no desire to play in Rochester. Meanwhile, the Knicks were interested in the first pick because they wanted Green. They were ready to give up Dukes, who was from Rochester, and Harrison needed to help attendance. But, as I understand it, Les also wanted $100,000 and that killed the deal. So Rochester picked first, took Green and kept him; Boston picked second in St. Louis' place and got Russell and also wound up with Heinsohn as a territorial pick. This, of course, after the Celtics had arranged to acquire the Hawks' early draft position by giving them Easy Ed Macauley and Cliff Hagan, two outstanding players.

Russell went away to Melbourne, Australia for the Olympics and returned with the NBA season in progress. He entered his first game for the Celtics as a sub. Arnie Risen started against Bob Pettit and the Hawks, the power team in the West at the time. A sellout crowd turned out in Boston for the debut of the lanky, much-publicized rookie center with the strange playing style. Nurtured on Cousy, Bill Sharman, and other fast-breaking scorers, the Boston fans couldn't understand why the Celtics would give up a good shooter such as Macauley for a defensive-minded player like Russell.

They soon found out why, as did everyone around the league. Russell came off the bench to play against Pettit and Share, a huge but slow seven-footer, and left his imprint. He blocked three or four shots on Pettit, a couple on difficult twisting jumpers, and got Share a few times. He broke up passes and intimidated some Hawks driving to the basket.

Russell played twenty-one minutes and scored only six points but he let the Hawks know he was on the floor. "I have to admit I was very nervous," he said after the game. "I was very tight all the way. My shooting was way off and I was just plain lousy at the foul line. This pro game is wonderful. I learned a lot even when I was just sitting on the bench."

A few days later, he played his first pro game in Madison Square Garden and it was fairly obvious that the NBA was going to learn a lot from him. He was beginning to find his niche and it was only his third game. He had learned quickly that the Celtics didn't need his scoring. They had enough of that through the years but never could win a championship with it. His biggest contribution would be on defense, harassing the shooters and giving up the ball to Cousy, Sharman, Heinsohn, Frank Ramsey, and the good Boston shooters.

His assignment the night of his Garden debut in the opening game of a doubleheader was to play Philadelphia's Neil Johnston, one of the league's all-time scoring greats, and Russell almost shut him out. Russell played twenty-three minutes and chased Johnston to the bench three times. Neil got fourteen of his seventeen points in the final period and only a few when Russell was on the floor.

"I just had a bad night," Johnston insisted. "I don't think Russell did anything special to bother me." They still didn't believe him. Of course, it was early, and Russell's approach to the game was new to the stars in the league, too. They didn't know his strength.

Neither did Russell at the beginning. He kept talking about offense while destroying teams on defense. I guess it was a hangover from his college days, when his quickness and size enabled him to score easy baskets in close and on rebounds. Heinsohn even mentioned something about Russell's scoring potential the night they met in the Holiday Festival.

"Russell is a great pivot man," Tommy had said. "He could score fifty points a game." Fortunately for the NBA, that never happened. Can you imagine what the teams would have had to put up with if Russell could score like Chamberlain and played defense like Russell?

Russell was still talking about his shots the night he came close to the league rebound record by grabbing thirty-four against the Warriors in Boston. That was the night they began talking about him putting defense back into the NBA. Philadelphia had a tall team at the time and was considered unbeatable off the boards but Russell and the other Celts outrebounded them, 95–56, while beating them by twenty-three points.

This is an excerpt from a newspaper report on Russell's performance that night. I remind you it was only his fourth game and he was playing before home fans who really didn't understand his style of play. "Perhaps the biggest revolution Russell may be starting is a renewed interest in defense in the professional game, whose rules have helped push scoring duels to dizzy heights," the story said. "The capacity crowd of 13,909 at the Boston Garden greeted Russell's defensive efforts with wild cheering.

"Russell already has proved his ability to block the twisting jump shots of Bob Pettit and the hook shots of Neil Johnston —league scoring aces. Not long ago, both were considered to possess unstoppable shots. Undoubtedly, Russell would have smashed Johnston's rebounding record [39] had he not fouled out with eight minutes left. Russell is playing with men his own height but his tremendous jumping ability launched by a slender frame is unmatched."

Quite an endorsement for a rookie who had to spend so much time proving himself to others. But Russell wanted to talk about his poor shooting the night before in the losing game with the Warriors in New York. "I missed my first fifteen shots but my teammates kept yelling encouragement. 'Keep throwing 'em up, Bill,' they yelled. I guess I'm getting over my stage fright."

Russell was a star from the start but there were many who still wondered and questioned. There was one Boston columnist, a Cousy man, I guess, who kept asking if Russell was really worth the $20,000 the Celtics were paying him just to rebound and play defense.

Was he worth it? Well, everywhere he went, there were sell-

outs as the people turned out to see this new NBA phenomenon. In his first five games, he played before over 64,000 people
at a time when the arenas were not huge. He drew 12,000 on
a Saturday afternoon for his debut in Boston, despite the lifting of the local blackout for the nationally televised event.
Then came capacities of 9000 in Fort Wayne, over 18,000 in
New York, 13,909 back in Boston, and 11,439 for his first appearance at Philadelphia's Convention Hall.

Nobody in the history of the NBA had drawn like that—not
even George Mikan, the biggest draw of his time. Russell was
in Philadelphia for the opening game of the doubleheaders
they played in those days, but they broke down the doors to see
him against Rochester. They know their basketball in Philadelphia and they noisily cheered his every move, a friendly,
objective treatment that was to disappear when Wilt Chamberlain arrived and Russell became the mortal enemy.

That night, Russell scored fifteen points, grabbed twenty-
one rebounds, and harassed enough Rochester shooters for the
Celtics to win, 97–92. He was coming on and he knew it. He
was more comfortable. "I feel a little better," he said. "But I'm
not in real good shape, yet. The layoff after the Olympics soft-
ened me up. There's plenty of time to get in shape, though,
isn't there? Another forty or fifty games?"

His teammates weren't worried. They already realized he
was the missing link. He was the rebounder, defensive genius
and intelligent team player they needed to finally win the
championship that always had evaded them. "I may have had
a few reservations the first couple of games," said Cousy, "but
he's convinced me now. The way he covers that defensive
board is really something. Not to mention the blocked shots.
And his offense will pick up. Remember, he's not in shape and
he's only playing twenty-nine minutes or so. When he starts
leaping like that for long periods, wow!"

It wasn't long before they began to complain about Russell,
the first real sign of greatness. They don't complain about
players who can't beat you. Eddie Gottlieb said what was on
a lot of losing teams' minds as Russell knocked shots away and
drove terror into the minds of those who dared drive on him.
Gottlieb charged that Russell was playing an illegal one-man

zone defense and many of his blocks were illegal goaltending.

Gottlieb, the owner of the Philadelphia team at the time, cited an example. "Paul Arizin went underneath for a simple backboard layup and, as the ball headed for the basket, Russell batted it away," complained Gottlieb, whose team was the defending champion. "If this isn't goaltending, I want somebody to tell me what it is."

It was pure Bill Russell, of course. He was the master of timing. He was so agile and had such body control, he'd not only block the shot but he'd grab it. To this day, few players have been able to develop that knack. Most swat the ball into the seats and the other team gets it back. Russell would play volleyball with it and then fire it out for a fast break and two points the other way. A four-point play, in reality.

Jocko Collins, the supervisor of officials, vindicated Russell on both charges. "As far as I'm concerned, Russell is playing legitimate," he said. "He blocks shots legally and I've seen him come out and pick up players, so how can you say he's playing a one-man zone?"

I think Gottlieb would've been safer if he had accused Russell of playing a five-man zone. It sure looked like it the way he covered the court. I saw him block shots underneath and the next minute he was blocking a shot outside.

The players struck back at Russell the only way they knew how. Contact. Under the boards. They roughed him up at the beginning. They had to find out how tough he was. Joe Lapchick, the old Knicks coach, used to say: "In this league, they ask you the question right away." There was just such a night in New York where Gallatin, known as Harry-the-Horse for his rugged build and rough gait, gave Russell an early lesson on NBA etiquette.

I guess Russell never forgot it because Gallatin never was one of Bill's favorite players or even coaches when Harry moved into that job in St. Louis for a while. Gallatin first went outside and shot over Russell, who refused to come out and glued himself underneath for the defensive rebound. At the other end, Harry planted himself underneath and used his body, hands, and elbows to box or shove him out.

Russell took it calmly and said: "I'm learning. My education will go on for some time—until I die, I guess. When I stop learning, I'll quit."

His teammates were more upset. It was against the Celtics' pride for any of them to be pushed around—especially by the Knicks, then and now a team to be beaten, not liked. "He's got to learn to get mad under there," suggested Cousy. "He's got to expect them to play him this way more and more," said Sharman. "They're gonna keep trying to take him outside and they're gonna rough him up."

Russell showed he learned fast. He heard his teammates talking and assured them: "I think I'll be a little more ready the next time. I'll know a little better what to expect. This was the way I heard it would be. This was the roughest I've seen it yet but it wasn't that way until tonight."

The Knicks beat the Celtics that night but Russell learned and they found it much more difficult in the years to follow. He was a sharp student of the game and had a mind like a sponge.

"There's a lot for me to learn," he said only a month into his new career. "They play much better defense than I ever thought I'd see. I used to watch pro basketball on TV and I'd see them knocking in ninety, one hundred points and I'd say to myself: 'That's no defense at all.' Then I got here and saw that they do defend against you and the fellows still score. Truthfully, I didn't think the caliber of the players would be so good but everybody's good. There's not a guy in this league who can't kill you.

"In my first game against St. Louis, Pettit feinted a shot and I jumped eight miles in the air. I went against Johnston and never knew a man could be so strong. Against Charley Share one game, I tried to get position. I braced myself and leaned back against him and I don't even think I made an impression on him. He was so strong, he scared me. I dug in my heels and I'll be darned if they didn't start sliding out from under me. I played against Earl Lloyd and he took me outside. I know he likes to drive and could take a two-hand set and I said to myself: 'Let him shoot over me.' So he did and didn't miss."

That was Bill Russell. Always learning and looking to improve. Always searching for ways to win. Constantly driven by an inner force that he described as "a fear of losing." Boston won its first championship in his first year when it beat St. Louis in double overtime in the seventh game. And it might have had ten titles in a row if Russell hadn't twisted an ankle and played hurt in the 1957–58 playoff final that the Hawks won, 4–2.

The Celtics then won eight in a row before Chamberlain and the 76ers ended that streak in 1967. Players came and went but Boston kept winning as long as Russell was there. Each year, he had to prove he could win without some fading Celtic star. Sharman was the first to go, then Cousy, then Ramsey, then Heinsohn. By the time 1965 rolled around, Russell was the only one left from the team that had won Boston's first championship.

Still, the Celtics kept on winning, though Russell took on the added burden of player-coach. They won two more championships in the next three years before Russell decided to retire after beating Chamberlain and the Lakers in seven games in the 1968–69 season. He had proved himself, finally.

Let me tell you what kind of competitor he was if you don't know by now. The 1965–66 Celtics went off on a sixteen-game winning streak. They were riding comfortably in first place on their way to another championship for a change. But they lost in Syracuse and the streak was over.

Russell approached Auerbach in the dressing room. "Can I speak to you a minute?" he asked, yanking Red into a corner where no one could hear them.

"How about calling a meeting before tomorrow's game?" said Russell. "I figured we'd have a meeting but not so soon—maybe after tomorrow's game," said Red. "We've been bad the last two," said Russell. "We haven't been playing well. I figure it's time to go over the mistakes we've been making, including mine."

He played like it was his birthright to win every game. He settled for nothing less. "Guys told me," said Auerbach, "when I appointed him captain that he'd be a tough man because—well, that thing about him not giving autographs, for instance. But he has so much pride in himself and in this team that nothing is more important to him than making it the best he's ever played on. He has K. C. and Satch feeling the same way, so that one loss, even after a winning streak, becomes something to worry about."

One of the things that fascinated me about Russell was the way he played defense without concentrating on his man or the ball. He'd watch the entire court to see what everyone was doing. I sometimes thought he knew when someone was taking a drink in the stands. He'd watch for things to develop and then make his move.

He was especially rough on the Knicks because we never had a big man to match him until we got Reed. But then it took a few years for us to get the players surrounding Willis to make us a championship team. By then Russell was gone. It would've been interesting to see what the Knicks' championship teams could've done against him.

I know this much, the other Knicks teams didn't do too well. The Celtics had a modest winning streak of nineteen games against the Knicks before it came to an end one day in Boston. That was sometime before I replaced Dick McGuire as coach in the 1967–68 season.

Russell teams were particularly rough on the Knicks, which is what made us Russell experts. From his first season in 1956–57 to his last in 1968–69, the Knicks took only one regular season series from the Celtics. That was in his final season but he almost killed himself in an effort to prevent it. We inspired him that way, it seemed.

It happened on February 2, 1969, and don't think Russell gave in easily. That's the game where he flew through the air in a last-second fling at a three-point play that would tie it, slammed the ball through, and wound up in the hospital after crashing to the floor. We won, 95–94, we were ahead in the series, 4–1, with only two games left between us, and Russell had almost made his point, for a change.

They say he went to the hospital because he banged his knee badly but it was really from exhaustion. First place in the East was involved and Russell wasn't about to yield that without a fight. We had beaten them 109–82 the night before in New York and Russell had seen a few things about the new Knicks he wanted to discourage right away, if possible.

We were becoming a team and a threat. We were making the jokes after the game, instead of being the victim of them. Bill Bradley had a hot night in the Garden with 11-for-15 and Willis Reed, our captain, yelled over to Cazzie Russell: "Hey, Caz. Dollar Bill is playing your game. Look, twenty-eight points, thirty-five minutes, and one rebound."

Then Reed, remembering we had hit twenty-three of twenty-four foul shots, turned to Dave DeBusschere and said: "You get the game ball. You missed the only foul shot." The next night, Dick Barnett shot us ahead in the closing minutes and we wound up telling the jokes again, but not until after Russell had given us and everyone a scare.

We were leading by three when Russell called time with twelve seconds to play. We knew what was coming. The ball would be lobbed toward the basket and Russell would try and jam it in while hoping to get fouled for a three-point play. I told my players to forget about the basket. Let the Celtics score it, "But no foul," I repeated over and over in the huddle.

I was still yelling "No foul!" when the ball was lobbed toward Russell near the basket on the old alley-oop play. The pass was a little away from the hoop, so Russell had to extend himself in midair and, thereby, lost his balance after slam-dunking. Reed instinctively backed away, as Russell came tumbling down like a collapsing skyscraper, in order to avoid having a foul called on him.

Russell hit the floor with a sickening crash. The game was over, we had won, but Russell looked seriously hurt. They got him to the dressing room and took him to the hospital in an ambulance. There were stories he might miss the playoffs but they didn't know Russell.

They certainly didn't know that he hated hospitals more than losing. One day, he just took his clothes and walked out. But I'll never forget that last-second play and the sight of Russell hitting the floor and laying there right in front of our bench. We learned something that day. It took a lot to put Russell out of action for long and, also, the alley-oop was such a good play to beat the final buzzer, we used it a few times to beat some other teams.

Russell was always good for some excitement or a laugh. He

had a way of being noticed. I remember the night when he was player-coach of the Celtics and he came to the opening of the new Garden on October 29, 1968. Boston was in the first game against Chicago and the Knicks played and beat the Warriors.

They were still building the place, so it was a rush opening and easy to get lost because there were no directional signs posted. Sure enough, Russell led the Celtics through the labyrinths and they got lost. They finally found their way to the main arena on the fifth floor of the eight-floor structure and got on the court almost too late to practice.

Then Russell took a look at the basket supports and noticed they had forgotten to wrap them with padding so no one would get hurt banging into them. That held up the game. So did a little matter of part of the ceiling dropping onto the floor while Sanders was about to shoot two foul shots. By then, the Celtics were in the process of answering the annual claims they were too old to win.

It was only the fifth game of the season, but the Celtics were hearing the same old story. Sanders standing on the foul line, with 4:43 left in the game and the Bulls leading by four, was one of the old men the critics had in mind. I must say he aged a lot before he got off the line.

Other Celtics, such as Havlicek, then twenty-eight, simply made room for another championship ring in their vaults. "I know we're getting old," said Havlicek, "but how long have we been hearing that? Besides, who cares how old you are as long as you can play the game. They said that when I was a rookie. I've been on five championship teams in the six years I've been here and hopefully I'll be on another this year." He must've known something.

Russell, the old man of the team at thirty-four, told a story about his eighty-nine-year-old grandfather, his fifty-six-year-old father, and an uncle, who had been visiting his home outside Boston. "You realize, four generations in my house at the same time," said Russell. "The trouble was, my grandfather couldn't stay but a week, though. He said he had to get back home to Monroe, Louisiana, to take care of the old people."

So much for old men and the Celtics. Back to Sanders, standing on the line and getting set to shoot. His concentration was broken by a strange buzz from the crowd and then a crash. He turned towards the Celtics' bench and discovered why. A four-inch by two-inch piece of sheet metal had fallen from the unfinished walkway below the roof and just missed the Boston bench.

No one was hurt but a lot of nerves were shattered. Sam Jones streaked toward the dressing room, assuming the roof was caving in. "It's hard to concentrate with that stuff going on," suggested Russell. Sanders missed both fouls and the Celtics went on to lose the game to the Bulls by six points.

Too bad we couldn't think of a few more distractions before Russell finally announced he was through winning championships. We thought we had a good shot at him in 1968–69, his last season when we finished ahead of the Celtics in the standings and earned the home court advantage in the playoffs. We lost that advantage in the first game at the Garden and the series, 4–2.

Russell was thirty-five and had the most mileage on his odometer but he played younger than anyone. He hadn't yet announced it was to be his last season and no one would have believed him after the way he played in those final six games against us. He just wouldn't give up and his indomitable spirit was best reflected when we won the fifth game and went back to Boston trailing, 3–2, but with a chance to still win it.

"I got to blame myself considerably for this one tonight," he said, though he had twenty-five points, sixteen rebounds, six assists, and who knows how many of our shots he harrassed and spoiled. "I didn't play too well in the first half at all. I started slow. I got only six points and six rebounds in the first half. After all, Reed had his third personal in the first quarter and he still was in there at the end. I should have worked on him sooner."

Russell and the Celtics closed us out by only a point in the final game and there was a strange sense of exhilaration for a losing dressing room when it was over. Our players vowed they'd be back the next year. It was a warning for Russell to be ready. But Russell announced he was through in a magazine article that summer after beating the Lakers for his eleventh championship ring in thirteen years.

"I've lost my competitive edge," he explained. "If I went out to play now, the other guys would know I didn't really care. That's no way to play." He had earned the right to quit at the top.

He had inflicted so much anguish and frustration on the players and teams in his thirteen seasons, yet the NBA was sorry to see him go. No one, not even Mikan, the player of his time, had influenced pro basketball as much. Russell was just about everyone's all-time pro center and, to many, the one who had the most impact on the game. As that early headline had said, he put defense back into the game.

I think Jerry West said it best. West had felt the rejecting force of Russell through the years. The Lakers and Celtics met in more finals than any other teams and West never won a championship until his 1971–72 team beat the Knicks. So West had earned the undisputed role of resident expert on Russell and the losers who had failed to beat the Celtics throughout the years.

"Their whole team plays well," West said after losing another title to the Celtics. "But give the credit to one guy—that's Bill Russell. He is the best basketball player I've ever seen. They talk about Wilt Chamberlain but, for me, Russell always rises to the occasion. He is the all-time MVP."

What more can I say?

JERRY WEST

I'm not one to fantasize. Life is full of too many stark realities to indulge in that luxury, although once in a while my mind will wander to something that might have been. That's when I think back to Jerry West, who played, it seems, a long time ago.

It was right after West and the West Virginia Mountaineers team had been eliminated in the NCAA tournament by New York University in March of 1960. An NBA draft was coming up and West was going to be the second-best prize in the bag of college seniors. Oscar Robertson, the acknowledged number one player at the time, was sure to be taken by the Cincinnati Royals as a territorial designation.

The Minneapolis Lakers would be next and Bob Short, the man who owned the team, had made it clear West was his pick. Jim Pollard, the Laker coach at the time, was supposed to be leaning toward Darrall Imhoff, a solid center from the University of California, who had distinguished himself in both Pacific Coast and National competition. Those were the days when every team felt it was the top priority to find a center, and Pollard felt Imhoff fit the Lakers' needs better than West. But not Short. He had been unusually successful with

Elgin Baylor as his number one pick in 1958 and had seen the forward from Seattle University develop into an important star. West, he hoped, would be equally successful. He was hoping to revive basketball in Minneapolis, where George Mikan had once created a dynasty, and he felt that West could attract the fans. Of course, this was before Short had the idea of moving the Lakers to Los Angeles for the beginning of the 1960–61 season.

There was one problem. West didn't want to play for the Lakers. He wanted the Knicks and made sure Short and everyone concerned with pro basketball knew it. "I don't want to play for Minneapolis," he announced shortly after his last game for West Virginia. "Minneapolis just isn't a good team. It just isn't a good situation. I prefer the Knicks. I'd certainly like to get with them."

If West remained adamant and Short could be convinced the Lakers would be better off taking someone like Imhoff, who wanted to play for them, then West would get his wish. As it was, the Knicks wanted him so badly, Ned Irish was afraid to breathe. He had lost Baylor in the '58 draft, and he dreaded the same thing happening with West. At the time Elgin still had a year's playing eligibility in Seattle if he wanted it, and he did everything he could to decoy Short and the Lakers, because he too wanted to play his pro ball in Madison Square Garden. Baylor insisted he had no intention of turning pro and stuck to it stubbornly as the draft approached. But then Short paid him a visit at his home in Washington, D.C., to have a little chat and sweeten the offer, and soon thereafter the Lakers announced that Baylor would be their number one choice when the draft started.

Fuzzy Levane was the Knicks' coach when they lost out on Baylor and I knew how badly he and Ned felt about it. Fuzzy and I were old friends and teammates in Rochester and, I imagine, his coaching job with the Knicks might have lasted more than a season and a third if Short had not influenced Baylor to play for the Lakers.

The same might be said of Carl Braun, who replaced Fuzzy with the 1959–60 season in progress and was coaching the Knicks when they failed to get West. Who knows what chain

JERRY WEST

COACH

reaction would have taken place if Short had allowed West to be drafted by the Knicks. It's possible the team's destiny might have changed to the point where I wouldn't have been asked to replace Dick McGuire in 1967.

Now there's a fantasy for you, which is the reason why I prefer not to indulge. West, of course, never got to play for New York, nor did he ever play in Minneapolis. The Lakers immediately moved to Los Angeles and West played all his games out there for Short until he unloaded the franchise on Jack Kent Cooke for $5 million.

West was a big reason why a franchise that threatened to fold in Minneapolis, where so many championships were won, became such a bonanza on the west coast. West, with the help of Baylor, turned it into a going concern and a status hangout for the Hollywood sports crowd. Although the Knicks needed a big man badly at the time, they would have made an exception for West. Ironically, picking third, they settled for Imhoff, the big man the Lakers left.

In the world of strange bounces, Freddie Schaus, who coached West at West Virginia, became his first coach with the Lakers. Everyone knew how Schaus felt about West even before they joined forces to introduce pro basketball to Los Angeles, previously an exclusive football area that had added major league baseball to its interests only a few years earlier when the Dodgers skipped there from Brooklyn.

Schaus once told the world that he wouldn't trade West for Robertson and he meant it. That's when both were closing out their college days and heading for the 1960 Olympics on one of the finest teams the United States ever put together. I had seen enough of West in the games he had played in the Garden to know that he didn't need any help from his coach to convince people he could play the game better than most.

Still, Schaus did tell those who were interested why West was such a unique and rare talent. "He's as good as I've seen at his height and experience," said Freddie, who, by the way, also played a little pro ball with the Knicks in 1953–54, when I was still playing in Rochester. "We list him at six-three but he's a shade off. He jumps center for us and controls the tap in 80 percent of our games. The other night against Satch

Sanders of NYU, who's six-six, Sanders controlled the second
half but Jerry had it in the first half."

That's a part of West few people ever knew. I confess, I
didn't realize West had jumped center at times in college. I
always wondered why he got up so high on jump shots and
rebounds against us.

West was a forward in his college days and led his team in
scoring, rebounds, assists, field goal percentage, and making
West Virginia a household name. "Most people assume Jerry
would have to be a backcourt man," explained Schaus, "but a
former coach in the NBA told me he'd give him at least a shot
at a corner position. Jerry could do it offensively. He could
rebound enough and probably do a job defensively on the man
he'd be covering. As short as he is, he could handle the third-
biggest man in the pros. He has the defensive quickness to
handle the man and, at the offensive end, he'd do more than
his share."

Schaus had the privilege of wrestling with that problem
when West picked the Lakers. As I remember it, Freddie had
to sit West for a game or two during the transition period most
college players go through, no matter how good. Somewhere
along the way, Schaus decided the backcourt was West's best
position and the front court's loss became pro history's gain.

I don't think many pro basketball fans would argue if you
lumped West, Robertson, and Cousy as the best backcourt men
to play the game. I wouldn't want to separate them, though in
some ways they were different. West had the better shooting
touch and played the better defense with an instinct and intellect that was a coach's dream.

I know it was this coach's dream at one time to see him play
for the Knicks. He never stopped talking about it through the
years. Every time there was a lull or disappointment in his
career, he'd say: "I'd like to play for the Knicks." Unfortunately, there never was a serious development in that direction and he wound up playing all his years with the Lakers,
the team he didn't want to play for in the first place.

West had all the elements of a super pro when he entered
the league. Strangely, he developed late in college. In his junior year, he was only good enough to be voted to the third

All-America team. But by the end of his senior year, they spoke of him in the same sentence, or at least the same paragraph, as the Big O.

West had to walk in Oscar's shadow before he made his own. Every college game he played, they compared him with Oscar. Everywhere he went, he had to compare himself with Oscar.

One night in New York, after West Virginia had been upset by a St. John's team coached by Joe Lapchick, someone actually asked Jerry: "If you were a coach and you had your pick of two players, Jerry West or Oscar Robertson, who would you take?"

Tough? Not for West. "Oscar Robertson," he said, flicking it off like one of his clever passes. "Oscar Robertson's a different type of ballplayer than I am," he added. There are those who say West caught up with the Big O and might've even passed him in the pros. I won't touch that other than to say both made an impact that time and future players will find hard to match or erase.

I remember that night in the Garden against St. John's very well. West was by far the best player on the floor though his team lost. He scored thirty-two points and picked off thirteen rebounds. Even then, he showed the poise and leadership that would make the Lakers the best team in the NBA along with the Celtics and Bill Russell.

West had the Garden and all of New York talking about him and the Big O. "Oscar's got everything and is stronger as well as a few inches bigger but West is a true All-America and a sure-shot pro," said Lapchick, a Robertson man all the way. "This is the way I'd put it," said Lou Carnesecca, a Lapchick assistant at the time who would succeed Joe in the big job when the latter retired. "Robertson is devastating, West is very, very good."

There was more. Charley Eckman, the basketball official who had become coach of the Detroit Pistons, said: "West plays defense. I've seen the Big O for five years and I'll take this kid over him." It was an ongoing argument that continued into the pros and then some.

West came from a little town called Cabin Creek and was the biggest thing the state of West Virginia turned out at the time. He taught himself to play basketball by bouncing a ball for hours while sitting on the floor and shooting baskets until it got dark outside his home. Sometimes he'd knock on the neighbor's door and ask her to turn on the porch lights so he could shoot a little longer in the enveloping darkness. It was there he learned the moves that were to lead the Los Angeles Lakers out of the darkness and into so many playoffs against the Celtics before West finally won his one and only championship in 1972 after Wilt Chamberlain had joined him.

No one in the history of the NBA won so many division titles without winning a championship. Year after year, it seemed, he would lead the Lakers into the finals only to run into that Boston frustration named Russell.

It started in West's second year when the Lakers took the Celtics to a seventh game in overtime before losing. Then it was six games in the 1963 championship series, five in 1965, seven in '66, six in '68, and seven in 1969, which was Russell's last season. West had to wait all those years for Russell to leave Boston before he won a championship. And when he finally did win, it was against us, the Knicks.

By then, he had become the pro player supreme. He was a long way from his early experiences with the Lakers, when he was a rather shaky rookie being asked to help sell big league basketball to the West Coast. I sometimes use West as an example for those rookies who come out of college as All-America players not accustomed to losing but run into problems and surprises.

Most college players think they can step right into the pros and turn it on. They soon learn, as West had to learn. In his second pro game, for example, the Lakers were playing the St. Louis Hawks in Los Angeles and West brought the ball up the floor. There was a play set up and West started it by passing to Hot Rod Hundley, who flipped to Baylor.

Then a strange thing happened to West. His man, Johnny McCarthy, dropped off and double teamed Baylor. Nobody dropped off West in college. Nobody left him open. No doubt there was a moment of apprehension. "What am I supposed to do now?" he must've thought.

It wasn't easy. West scored twenty in his first game against

Oscar Robertson and Cincinnati, fifteen against the Hawks, and then was held to only nine by the Knicks. His scoring was shrinking. They were taking advantage of him.

Once, a player gave him a routine fake and West instinctively went with it and backed off. The player had an easy open shot that he hit. "I retreated too much," West acknowledged. "I crossed my feet so I couldn't recover right away. In college, I could've gotten away with things like that. There, you always played away from your weakness. Here, they force you to play it. Here, there are so many things like that. They get you into a bad position and get the shot on you. If you leave an open man, he'll always hit the shot on you. College kids will miss lots of times."

All they ever talked about was the Big O. Few mentioned Russell to West until West ran into him for the first time in an exhibition game. Jerry experienced a shock that he never forgot, although Russell kept recharging him through the years. West saw an early opening and drove for the hoop with a quick first step that made him just about unstoppable.

That quick first step was West's trademark. He'd get it on you and, if you recovered and dropped back, he'd pull up for the jump shot. If not, he'd go all the way. I used to tell my players to make sure they didn't give him that first step but no one, not even a textbook, could stop West from doing that.

Anyway, West got his quick first step on the Celtic playing him and went right for the hoop. Suddenly a big hand swooshed from out of nowhere and jammed the ball into West's open mouth as he gasped in awe and surprise.

It was West's first experience with Mr. Russell but not his last. "Russell makes you think," explained West, the rookie. "You just can't drive on him. He blocks everything you shoot. You go in for the layup and think you're open and he comes out of nowhere. It gives you an eerie feeling. If you can't drive and your jump shot's not falling, you've got to start learning something new real fast."

Such as taking up another trade or hobby, for example. West eventually got the Celtics and Russell talking about him. They kept beating his team but not him. He'd make them nervous by always demanding the ball for the last shot and many times hitting it. No game was safe with him on the floor. I think he became Mr. Clutch primarily because of the things he did against the Celtics in all their championship games.

I guess the 1969 playoffs said it all. West poured shots through a funnel in all seven games. He had a thirty-nine-point average that just failed to prevent Russell's eleventh championship in thirteen years. He scored fifty-eight in the second game and forty-two in the last one in which he added twelve assists and thirteen rebounds.

The Celtics won despite West and were lucky or just talented enough to do so. "I have never seen a better clutch player than Jerry West," conceded Russell after Jerry had donated his fifty-eight points to the Lakers' 120–118 second game win. "We played well enough to win easily but we lost."

It was a playoff high for West but he refused to dwell on it. He was that way. Instead, he talked about how Chamberlain had helped freeze Russell so he could get off forty-one shots, of which he hit twenty-one. "Russell doesn't contest me that much on drives because of Wilt," explained West. "He can't afford to leave him to come to me. What I try to do is look for him first on a drive. If I don't see him, I just forget about him."

Havlicek had the honor of playing West once in a while and had a perfect view. "Jerry was fantastic and he really killed us," said Hondo, who also had the nasty habit of calling for the last shot and making it in many games with the Lakers as well as the Knicks.

It ended the usual way for West, with Boston taking the seventh game, a wild one, in Los Angeles. West had lost, again, but only another championship. He had gained in the eyes of the Celtics and everyone in the league. West had played the final three games with a hamstring pull heavily taped and the Celtics still squeezed in by only two points.

"I don't know how he did it," said Larry Siegfried, who, with Sam Jones, shared most of the backcourt responsibilities against West. "He's tremendous. I'm in the winner's dressing room. He's in the loser's room. But he's a winner. He'll always be a winner. He gets my vote for everything."

West was in New York a few days later to accept a car, his award as MVP of the playoffs. He must have felt somewhat compensated for having failed to win the championship against the Celtics for the fifth time in seven years until he actually saw the Dodge Charger.

"The color was Celtic green and I expected to see eleven Boston numbers on it," said West, who promised to exchange it for another color. I wouldn't have blamed him if he had driven it over Bill Russell on the test drive. How else could West have gotten even for so much frustration?

The afternoon before the final game of the '69 championship he had taken a drive down to Marina Del Rey to watch the boats float by and think about the championship he'd finally win in the Forum that night. "I felt sure we were going to win," said West, who always felt sure he was going to win, which is why he was so difficult to beat. "I kept thinking about all the happy faces I'd see after the game. That's how sure I was we were going to win. I said to myself it was going to be some night and it was some nightmare.

"The toughest thing was the Celtic dressing room was right next door to us and we could hear all the noise they were making. It killed me to hear them so happy and see our dressing room looking like a graveyard."

It's sad to say but the Knicks were equally responsible for turning the Lakers' dressing room into a graveyard for West the next season. Of course, he hadn't won a championship in nine years, while the Knicks hadn't won one in twenty-four, or since the league started in 1946. So someone had to break a streak when the Knicks team of 1969–70 took on the Lakers team of West, Chamberlain, and Baylor for the title.

We were to open in the Garden because we had gained the home court advantage with 60–22, the best record in the league. The Lakers were hot, though, having swept the Phoenix Suns in three and made it seven in a row by taking four straight from the Atlanta Hawks. And Chamberlain had just returned from a miracle recovery after surgery on his knee that the doctors had predicted would keep him out for the season.

With Chamberlain back from his knee operation, the Lakers were a new and different team than the one we had beaten four out of six during the season. "We've played well," acknowledged West, recognizing what the return of Wilt had meant. "But the Knicks played better. We're conscious of their defense, which makes their offense more effective. They get their easy baskets from their defense, which makes us aware that we must be careful passing the ball and only take good shots.

"When the Celtics had their good teams, they didn't just have one great defensive man, they had three. Bill Russell, of course, Tom Sanders, and K. C. Jones were the best at their positions. People think it's an offensive game but the Knicks' defense, like the Celtics', helps their offense. Reed, DeBusschere, and Frazier made All-League, the best at their positions. The Knicks are one of the smartest teams I've ever seen. They're very intelligent. They do things with the ball. Red Holzman has done a fantastic job."

I was ready to accept everything West had said on face value if the Lakers would have allowed us to win by default. We still had to play the games and find a way to keep West from destroying us. He was capable of that in any game.

I had no secret formulas. I had only two ways to go against West: Dick Barnett or Walt Frazier. I guess some people wondered why I chose to give Barnett the West assignment. One small reason was they were once teammates with the Lakers, so Barnett was more familiar with his moves.

Actually, it was a matter of defensive styles. Clyde's strength was in stealing the ball and doubling up on a man, which meant he had to cheat on defense. No one could cheat on West and get away with it. Barnett played a man more honestly and, therefore, would make West work harder to get his shot.

Besides, Barnett, in my opinion, was one of the smartest defensive players who was ever underrated. He'd pick West up as soon as possible and bump him with his stomach all the way down the floor. Those were the days when they allowed that type of contact against the ballhandler and Barnett took advantage of it.

West was quicker with his moves but Barnett made up for it with anticipation and a determination to stay between West and the basket under all conditions. It wasn't perfect but it was the best I could devise against one of the quickest and most effective shooters the game has ever seen.

West got more than forty three times on us during the regular season, so you can imagine what might've been if Barnett, the Knick who played him best, in the coach's opinion, hadn't been on him. One night, the Lakers decided to isolate Barnett one-on-one on West to see what happened. It was one of the strangest things I've ever seen on a basketball court.

It was in the Garden and West brought the ball down slowly along the sideline. While Barnett backtracked and kept position between Jerry and the basket, the other four Lakers swung to the opposite side of the floor—just about in front of the Los Angeles bench. The four other Knicks positioned themselves off their men near the foul area to help Barnett if West attempted to drive around him.

Some of our men dropped off far enough for the Laker bench to scream "Zone! Zone!". They probably were right but there was too much confusion over the surprise strategy for the officials to notice. Someone finally came out to help Barnett and force West to pass the ball, which was fine with us. We never saw that play again, also fine with us.

West had enough ways of beating us, anyway. In the clutch, all he needed was the ball. I'll never forget the shot he made to send the third game of the 1970 championship into overtime. He had already scored thirty-three points in the first game, thirty-four in the second game in New York to send the series to Los Angeles tied, and was to score thirty-four more in the third.

I don't know how many baskets he scored in that series but I remember only one. I can still see him taking a few strides after grabbing the out-of-bounds pass-in from under our basket by Chamberlain and flinging a two-hander a good step or two from midcourt. I don't know if it sailed fifty-five or sixty or a thousand feet. It went straight in like it had eyes to beat the buzzer and tie the score at 102.

West made 9016 baskets in his fourteen NBA years, once scoring fifty-three in a playoff against Russell and the Celtics, but I'm sure he never made another shot like that one. It was enough to make you faint if you were wearing a Knicks uniform. It was enough to make DeBusschere, who had just put us ahead by two with three seconds to go, collapse to the floor as he stood under the Laker basket and saw the shot come through.

We were all shocked. I had never seen anything like it—not under the pressure of a championship series. Here we had the game won and now we had to play an extra five minutes to "win" it, again, which we did by pulling ourselves off the floor and outscoring the Lakers, 9–6, in overtime under exhausting emotional conditions.

"I was dumfounded," said DeBusschere. "My heart [sank]. It's the longest clutch shot I've ever seen. I was directly under the basket and my heart dropped into my stomach. It just defeated me and that's why I collapsed on the floor. My mind went blank. I couldn't believe it. Clyde and I just stared at each other."

Clyde just stood there and stared into space. He was trying to figure out how West did it. We had underestimated Mr. Clutch, obviously. Frazier and all our players were frozen on the court and I had to call them to the bench to remind them we still had an overtime, otherwise they'd still be out there.

"It was depressing," said Frazier. "A shot like that at a time like that. I was looking at Jerry and then I watched the ball and then I said to myself: 'That damn ball is going in.' I'm standing there like a bird dog pointing to the locker room. I was telling myself things like that just didn't happen. It was a nightmare."

Why us? Why the Knicks, who had never won a championship? I'm sure West was in his dressing room after the shot was wasted and asked the same things to himself. They told me later that he had tears in his eyes as he sat alone in a side room with icepacks on his knees.

All that mattered to West was that the Knicks were ahead, 2–1, instead of being down, 2–1. It was just another shot in another losing game. "I knew the game wasn't over and we had to go into overtime," he explained. "If the shot had ended the game, it would have felt great."

We won but felt numb. We weren't exactly overwhelmed by winning a game we easily could have lost. West just scared us. He had won the second game with two clutch foul shots two seconds from the end and now this. He never gave you much room to maneuver, which reminds me of a funny experience West and Mel Counts had in New York during the series.

They went strolling through Times Square, where the little swindles in the area had not yet grown into the epidemic of big ones. They wanted to see M-A-S-H and they paid two dollars each to get into the theater. Once inside, they found themselves looking at a sex movie.

"How'd we get in here?" West asked Counts.

"Don't ask me," said the seven-foot forward. "You're the leader. I'm just following you."

"Let's get out of here," said West. "Man," he added, when he noticed there was a double entrance to the theater and they'd gone through the wrong door, "we sure got caught in a switch. They sure don't give you much of a chance to maneuver."

There were times I wished I could have maneuvered West through a wrong door in the Garden and loaded him on a train leaving Penn Station. He had the relentless knack of hurting his opponents. I didn't need him, for example, pointing out after that amazing shot of his that it had been illegal.

West saw the replay before I did and said that Chamberlain had taken a step onto the court when he had passed the ball. "Nobody saw it at the time and nobody called it," said Jerry. "I wish the hell they had called it," said Wilt, "Then we would have lost in regulation and there would have been five minutes less of disappointment."

West's disappointment ended when the Lakers beat us, 4–1, for the 1972 championship. We won the first game in Los Angeles and the Lakers swept the next four. It had taken eleven years but West finally had the championship that had so painfully eluded him. Baylor was gone without ever winning the title but now West had his.

"Right now," he said after it was in the bank, "I feel about eight feet tall. . . . What I'm thinking about are all those summers when people said derogatory things and kept asking what happened to us. Now I won't have to face that any more. They'll be asking the Knicks."

It had been an exhilarating season for West. The Lakers had set a league record of thirty-three wins in a row and it had ended the only way it really matters. You can win all the games you want during the regular season but, if you don't win the championship, all the work and effort of training camp and eighty-two games mean nothing.

West had to agonize through 835 regular season games and 135 playoff games before he got a championship ring. He stayed around for one more crack at the Knicks and retired at thirty-five after we beat the Lakers in 1973 for our second title. He left a legacy that included a regular season scoring average of 27 and 29.1 for the playoffs.

Once, in 1964–65, he actually averaged over forty for eleven playoff games. He left a lot of players who had played him talking to themselves—and talking about him. I know the Knicks said a lot about him.

"Nobody can stop him one-on-one," said Frazier, who took over the assignment of guarding West when Barnett retired. "You know he's going to get his shot off and, when he gets it off, it's going in. When they clear out one side for him, you know it's going to be rough."

Now Mike Riordan, who got to play West more after leaving our 1970 championship team to join the Bullets. "I don't know who said it first," said Mike, "I think maybe it was K. C. Jones, about the only one who could stop Jerry is West himself. All you can do is play him as tight as you can without fouling him. He amazes me every time I see him. Once I picked him up full court and he still comes down and scores. Once he used up his dribble, I got on him tighter and it didn't even matter. Two points. You feel it's all for nothing. Nobody's going to stop him, but the harder he works, the more tired he gets faster."

Barnett, our resident expert on West, had this to say: "I know when I'm playing him, all I try to do is play the percentage, make him take his shot from maybe a step further out than he wants to."

Sure. Great in theory and most times in practice. But remember the night West was forced to take a shot against the Knicks a lot further out than he wanted? That says it all about Jerry West.

WILT CHAMBERLAIN

What Bill Russell did for defense in the NBA, Wilt Chamberlain did for offense. Maybe even more because the record book is full of Wilt's scoring records but there are few mentions of Russell.

From the time that Chamberlain was a tall, skinny kid playing for Overbrook High in Philadelphia, he was destined to make a big impact in the pros. Even before he decided to play his college ball at Kansas University, he inspired a rule change that enabled Eddie Gottlieb, the owner of the Philadelphia Warriors, to get a guarantee Chamberlain would play for him when he became eligible for the 1959 draft.

Gottlieb electioneered for a Territorial High School rule that permitted teams to draft high school players who played within seventy-five miles of their franchise. That terminated a recruiting panic among many pro teams that had desperately tried to get the guaranteed young superstar to attend college in their area.

In fact, when Wilt finally quit Kansas after his junior year and spent another year with the Harlem Globetrotters waiting to become eligible for the NBA draft, a group of enterprising Kansas City people thought they had come up with a great

Chamberlain *vs.* New York in the 1973 playoffs

idea. Put a team in Kansas City and get Chamberlain, a guaranteed franchise by himself. There were two problems with that: (1) the promoters couldn't raise the money, and (2) even if they had, they couldn't have gotten Wilt because he had been labeled for shipment to Philadelphia by the high school rule.

It was under that same Territorial High School rule that the Cincinnati Royals were able to tab Jerry Lucas before he went to Ohio State. Lucas, who was to come to the Knicks eventually and help us win a championship, had been an All-America high school player in Middletown, Ohio. He gained so much fame and notoriety as a high school player, they hung up a sign at the city limits that read: "Home of Jerry Lucas."

The Royals almost lost Lucas after he had helped Ohio State become NCAA champions. A rival pro league was being formed and Luke signed a personal services contract to play ball for a Cleveland shipbuilder and sports enthusiast named George Steinbrenner. The league never got going and Lucas sat out a year, getting paid to do nothing by Steinbrenner, before joining Cincinnati. That's why Lucas is listed as being drafted by the Royals in 1962 but didn't start playing until 1963.

Chamberlain wasn't in the league long when they began talking of another rule change because of him. Wilt's immediate success as a pro put the Territorial Rule under the microscope and resulted, eventually, in its being abandoned. The league had put the rule in to help the franchises acquire some instant gate attractions by being able to guarantee "local" high school and college stars coming home.

It was just one of the many ways Chamberlain left his huge imprint on the game. He came roaring into the league as a high school and college sensation and went out like a lion, ending a career that never had a dull moment. He was like a huge ship in the ocean—he sure knew how to make waves. Sometimes without even trying.

By nature of his overwhelming talent, Wilt was the center of attention wherever he walked and played. As soon as he signed to play his first season in the NBA, there were shock waves among some players. The higher-priced players, to be exact.

They didn't like the seven-foot rookie coming into the league and making more money than anyone. Wilt's deal was reportedly a basic $30,000 salary plus attendance bonuses that would enable him to earn well over $50,000. Now, mind you, that was long before the NBA's average salary reached the $100,000 level. Actually, at that time, Bob Cousy was supposed to be the highest-priced player at $22,000, so Chamberlain became the target of the very players he was about to help by raising the salary standards.

Chamberlain was to become the first $100,000 player in the NBA, inspiring Bill Russell to ask for "one dollar more" from the Celtics. Russell got it because Boston had benefited most from his rivalry with Chamberlain through the years. Their paths crossed, twisted, and wound around each other in so many ways that to this day, it's hard to mention one without the other. It began the day Chamberlain agreed to play for the Philadelphia Warriors and ended only when Russell went into retirement.

I saw Wilt's first game against the Knicks in the Garden and it was awesome. He was more agile then. He was quicker. He was leaner. A sapling who was to grow into a redwood as the years went on. He was a shooter that night, not the scorer he became by using his strength going to the basket. He hit twenty-foot jumpers facing the basket.

When his New York debut was over, Wilt, the twenty-three-year-old kid, had played all but fifteen seconds of the game, grabbed twenty-eight rebounds, and scored forty-three points. Fuzzy Levane was the Knick coach and I was a scout and we agreed what Chamberlain had done was not fair. Not human.

"You mean we have to face him twelve more times?" Fuzzy said to me.

"I've never been in a game with a greater performance or even watched one," said Richie Guerin, who later that season was to score fifty-seven points that became the Knicks' all-time high for a game.

"I guess he lived up to the advance notices," said Gottlieb, whose franchise depended on what Wilt would do for him. Those were the days when teams were struggling to stay alive from what they made at the gate. Big television money wasn't available. "No rookie ever broke in like that," added Gotty, who, as a league pioneer, had seen them all since 1946. "Not Bill Russell, not George Mikan, not anybody. I've never seen anything like it."

Chamberlain had hit the NBA like a tornado. "He's tremendous, there's no doubt about it," said Carl Braun after Wilt's contributions had beaten the Knicks, 118–109. "But it's not something we haven't seen before—like Russell, I mean. He disorganizes you under the basket the same way. With Wilt, of course, there's that offense on top of it, which is better than Russell's. He hit on all those jumpers."

Yes, Wilt hit on all those jumpers. That may be hard to believe by those who remember the trouble Chamberlain had with fadeaways and foul shots. Wilt did come into the league with a good touch from the outside, which made his early scoring that much more significant. He wasn't just dunking the ball then.

By the time Wilt got through just about one quarter of his first seventy-five-game season, the printers were working on changes in the record book. In seventeen games, he was on the bench for only twenty-seven minutes of a possible 816, going the full forty-eight in nine. He hadn't scored less than twenty-four points, his high was fifty, he hit over forty six times and in the thirties six times. He averaged 30.2 rebounds a game, against a 22.4 league record, once pulled forty-three and fell under twenty with seventeen in one game. And his 35.6 scoring pace was well ahead of Pettit's 29.2 league record.

"He's getting the ball for Philadelphia and that's what they needed," said Jungle Jim Loscutoff, whose job with the Celtics was to prevent players from doing just that.

"He's scoring a lot of points for them," said Frank Ramsey, who did a good job of doing that for the Celtics, himself.

"Thank goodness," said Gottlieb. "I'm paying him enough money to score for us. I signed him without even knowing if he could shoot!"

"You think maybe I'll be able to get some more money out

of him if I prove it?" said Chamberlain.

"Who needs him in the league, especially with Russell around?" said little Al Bianchi to Larry Costello, his Syracuse backcourt teammate. "What's gonna happen to us little guys? With Wilt in there goaltending, we'll never be able to get a layup."

First Russell and then Chamberlain. They revolutionized the game under the ten-foot-high rims and inspired suggestions about raising the baskets or lowering the floor to help the little man. As a little man who played on a championship team in Rochester, I sympathized but was thankful I didn't have to drive on Chamberlain or bump into him.

It wasn't long before NBA minds figured out a way to contain Wilt. At least, the Minneapolis Lakers thought they had discovered something by holding the ball until the twenty-four-second clock ran down before taking a shot. The Lakers didn't win but they limited Wilt to twenty-eight and twenty-six points, practically a shutout the way he was scoring at the time.

"The greatest single force to come into pro basketball" is what coach Ed Macauley called Wilt after the Hawks and Warriors had played nine exhibition games against each other. "We plan to play him straight and see what happens. If we're not successful, then we'll do anything. We may try pressing him in the dressing room or deflating the ball."

Everyone was excited about what Wilt was doing—except Wilt. He just went on pulling down rebounds, scoring points in bunches, and interrupting people who had the audacity to drive on him as he planted himself near the hoop. As someone pointed out, "For a rookie, he has the guts of a burglar."

Nothing bothered Wilt in those days. Not even Russell. Wilt was what they might call today a big, cool cat for a youngster walking among so many big names in the world of pro basketball. One day, for example, a card game started in the Dallas airport while the Hawks and Warriors were traveling together on their exhibition tour.

Wilt, always ready for a game, was deeply involved playing when he asked one of the watching players to do him a favor. "Get me a Coke and get one for yourself," Wilt said. "Get me a sandwich and get one for yourself."

The player, another rookie, rebelled at the order. "Where do you come off with that stuff?" the player said to Wilt. "You're just a rookie like me." Wilt never blinked. "Rookie my foot," he said. "I've been a pro for six years." He was that good, he might've been a pro since high school.

Wilt became a target from many different directions. He invited some things with his self-expressed candor that prompted him to say exactly what he had in his mind. He was sensitive and bothered by the way the pro teams roughed him up. He even announced he was quitting after his first year in the NBA. He had left Kansas University, he said, because it no longer was basketball. Four guys would gang up on him and the other would play a one-man floating zone.

He said that was no fun. He said pro basketball no longer was any fun because the roughness put him in the position of fighting rather than playing. On March 25, 1960, after the Celtics and Russell had just beaten him and the Warriors 4–2 in the playoff semi-finals, he told the world: "I'll never play basketball in the NBA again. This is my last game. This is it."

Wilt had led the league in scoring with 37.6 and rebounding with 28.9. He had taken a Philadelphia team that had finished fourth and last in the Eastern Division with a 32–40 record and improved it with a 49–26 second-place finish behind the 59–16 championship Celtics. He had sold a lot of tickets and whipped up great interest in the NBA at a time when it was desperately needed.

Yet, he was leaving. Why? "If I continue, I feel it may be bad for me and my race," he said. "If I come back next year and score less than I have, I may have to punch eight or nine guys in the face. I may lose my poise. I don't want to."

Wilt had been pushed and shoved, and he had pushed and shoved, throughout his first season as opponents tried everything to compensate for his physical advantages. Never a fight but a few near misses until the second game of his first playoffs against the Celtics when Wilt took a swing at Tommy Heinsohn.

Heinsohn's job was to step in front of Wilt on a fast break and pick him off to spring Russell. In the process, Tommy took a lot of hammering and threats as Chamberlain kept running into him. "Hey, you, if you get in my way one more time, I'm gonna kill you," Wilt finally warned Heinsohn.

Wilt was mild-mannered and not an angry man for all the abuse he took but his patience was fading fast. Chamberlain was so big and strong, he often said he was afraid to swing at someone because of the damage he might do. This time he couldn't take it anymore so he threw his right in Heinoshn's direction. Tommy made one of his better defensive moves and ducked. The punch sailed over his head and cracked Wilt's teammate Tom Gola on the back of the head.

Despite great pain, Wilt took another swing at Heinsohn and fell to the floor. Chamberlain had to play the rest of the series with a bandage over his badly swollen hand. I guess that's when the bad blood between Wilt and the Celtics began boiling.

Wilt didn't retire, though. He had a few more fights and skirmishes but only one that was serious. Clyde Lovellette, a big, rugged guy who used to travel with two six-guns just for laughs, broke Wilt's jaw with a flying elbow in a game. Chamberlain waited a couple of years and finally got even by decking Lovellette.

Otherwise, Chamberlain was a gentle giant. Some considered him a freak. He surely couldn't hide in a crowd. His staggering hulk and prominence in the NBA world made him a target many times. "Any team going against him is under pressure," explained Frank McGuire, who was Wilt's second coach in Philadelphia. "But not until you're with Chamberlain every day do you begin to appreciate how much strain there is on him constantly. Then you realize how long he's been under it."

One day, Wilt was sitting in the Warriors' office, reading a newspaper, when a woman and her husband dropped in to buy tickets. "Can we get his autograph?" the woman asked Gottlieb after spotting Wilt. She got it.

"Tell him to stand up," the man then said.

"Why should he do that?" asked Gottlieb.

"Because I want to see how tall he is," was the reply.

"What is he, a freak or something that he has to stand up so you can look him over?" said Gottlieb, annoyed.

"Sure he's a freak," the woman said testily.

"Lady," said Gottlieb, getting in his parting shot, "did it ever occur to you that maybe your husband is the freak?"

Wilt listened but didn't react. He had heard it before so many times. Looking down on everyone else was one of the things he learned to live with because he had such an early start. They began staring at him when he was fourteen and towered at six-seven over all the other kids in the neighborhood.

One of the things that helped establish a strong relationship beyond player-coach was McGuire's constant defense and explaining of Chamberlain. "He's a human being," McGuire would remind those who looked on Wilt as a monster. "We've been hearing about him and watching him and the papers have been writing about him for so long, we're inclined to forget he's only twenty-four and has had to learn to live in a fish bowl before most normal-sized people learn to live a normal life where they can hide their own fears in a crowd. Wilt can't hide. Everything he thinks has got to stay inside him and sometimes must come out. The world's shooting at him and there's no armor he can wear to protect himself."

Wilt contributed to his own unique problems by being so big and good. It was easy to blame him for everything because he was so conspicuous. I remember a game in the Garden in his second season when he didn't play so well. The Knicks beat the Warriors and Chamberlain was held responsible for it.

McGuire had to go out of his way to explain that Wilt hadn't loafed and wasn't disinterested as some charged. Frank disclosed how the Knicks had called a time-out with a few seconds to play and he had discussed matchups with his team. "I told Chamberlain to take Darrall Imhoff," said McGuire, "but he said to me: 'Johnny Green might be tougher to handle underneath.' I asked, 'You want him?' and he said: 'Yeah, let me take Green.' He was looking for the toughest. He wasn't looking to duck the pressure."

Pressure swirled around Chamberlain from the minute he came into the NBA and began tearing the record book to shreds. I guess his hundred-point game against the Knicks in

1962 will stand as his biggest monument, though he might be able to think of a few others. He was in the league three years at the time and people had been predicting he'd hit a hundred some night.

He had reached the fifties so many times, they had stopped counting. Earlier in the 1961–62 season, he had scored seventy-eight in triple overtime against the Lakers and McGuire had wondered how far away was a hundred. He found out on March 3, 1962, in Hershey, Pennsylvania, where the Knicks and Warriors set a single-game record by scoring 316 points.

The Knicks scored 147 and lost because the Warriors got twenty-two more. They had to hold up the game when Wilt slammed a dunk for his one hundredth point and the fans rushed onto the floor to congratulate him with forty-six seconds to go. He had made thirty-six baskets on sixty-three shots but what he'll never forget was making twenty-eight of his thirty-two foul shots.

Remember, Wilt was to become one of the poorest foul shooters the game has ever known—especially for someone who owns all the scoring records. Somewhere along the way he lost his confidence and touch. That night, he was out of the textbook as the Warriors kept feeding him and the Knicks kept fouling him to keep him from reaching a hundred.

"I wasn't even thinking of hitting one hundred," he said, though he had fifty-nine by halftime. "After putting in nine straight free throws, I was thinking about a foul shooting record." That was Wilt's fantasy—making foul shots.

Three Knicks scored over thirty in that game but no one will ever remember it. Guerin had thirty-nine, Willie Naulls had thirty-one, and Cleveland Buckner had thirty-three. The fans kept screaming "Give it to Wilt!" as he neared one hundred and that's what Guy Rodgers, Al Attles, and Paul Arizin did. Wilt scored thirty-one points in the final quarter alone. It was one night's work to Wilt.

The more he scored and rebounded, the more he became a target. The more he played and lost against the Celtics and Russell, the more they taunted him. Especially in Boston, where Chamberlain became the biggest personal challenge of all. One night, Wilt missed a series of three taps and the Boston Garden public address announcer proclaimed: "Chamberlain just broke a Garden record for having missed the most shots in a quarter."

McGuire was furious. Wilt just stored it in his memory book that became loaded with entries before he was through. There were times he struck back, though. He once authored a magazine article in which he cited a few bush tactics by the league and the people in it. He got his teammates upset by criticizing Adolph Schayes' coaching just as the 76ers were starting another playoff series with the Celtics.

He was driven by a great desire to win and, as it developed, to beat Russell and the Celtics. Before it became an obsession, Wilt, in one of his candid moments, took the time to analyze things as they existed early in 1962. It provided a look into the deepest recesses of Wilt's thinking before losing in the playoffs and frustration brought down a protective shield. This is what Chamberlain had to say:

"It's my honest belief that I could do as well as Russell defensively and he could almost match me offensively if we switched teams. What it comes down to is a matter of concentration. You can't concentrate on both defense and offense without losing a piece of each. It's physically impossible under the grind of an eighty-game schedule in the NBA. So each of us emphasizes that part of the game that best serves his club.

"There's no doubt in my mind that if Russell directed his efforts toward that end, he could raise his scoring average from nineteen to thirty without any difficulty. But he realizes that defense is more important to the structure of the Celtics. That gives them the one phase of the game they would lack if Bill concentrated on shooting. On the other hand, our short suit is scoring and that's what I've got to do to show the Warriors to their best advantage.

"Getting back to Russell and his value to the Celtics and the way they use him. We beat Boston in a game he didn't play. They were so accustomed to relying on him for defensive balance, they couldn't adjust in his absence. It's been so long since they had to pick up a man going through that they forgot how to do it.

"To anaylyze it further—and I don't want this to sound like a knock at Russell—many times you'll see him walking back on offense and often, by the time he gets there, Cousy or Heinsohn already have taken a shot off their fast break. But he's not worried because he's thinking more of covering up on defense than scoring. Playing that way, Bill conserves his energy. Under the same circumstances with the Warriors, I have to run up the court and get into position to score. In other words, if he had to play the same type of ball that I do, he wouldn't have enough stamina left to get up and block shots consistently in the closing minutes when it's most important.

"Does the challenge manifest itself more in head-to-head competition? I'd have to say I play harder against Boston because they're number one rather than because of Russell. Maybe there's a subconscious awareness of a personal duel. I guess I think more of defense playing against him. Obviously he thinks more of offense playing against me. The proof is that he takes more shots against us than any other team in the league. Sometimes he'll go as high as thirty-five shots with us, whereas twenty is closer to his par.

"I don't get any special exhilaration out of scoring in the fifties and sixties. People don't realize the pressure of being expected to do it every night. Ask Roger Maris. If the Yankees lose, it's because he didn't hit a home run and how can you expect him to hit one every day? I'd rather score thirty a night and play more defense. I know I can do it and next year I hope to do it if we're lucky to come up with a backcourt man who can hit consistently. After all, we don't have any Cousys or Sam Joneses on our team to take a lot of the load off me.

"I've been accused of selfishness at team expense. I've matured now and don't let things bother me that did the first two years. But this I'm sensitive to because it's a bum rap. I even went so far as to discuss it with Eddie Gottlieb, the owner, Frank McGuire, the coach, and Tom Gola, our captain. They all told me to concentrate on scoring. There was a game in Syracuse where the Nats were converging on me and I was passing off. Gola finally said: 'Look, you've got to shoot because we depend on you to put the ball in the basket. And if that's your job, you've got to accept it as such.' I'm not trying to be vain but when a situation comes up and you need a home run to win a game, you don't let the pitcher bat with the best hitter on the bench."

Wilt was the best hitter the NBA has ever seen, no doubt about that. He was a great basketball machine and I always said he probably could still be playing if he wanted. He was a wonderful physical specimen who never got out of shape. My own personal experiences with him didn't occur until I became coach of the Knicks in December, 1967, and I always found him a tough competitor.

One-on-one he would've murdered Russell and everyone. But playing five-on-five, Wilt was consigned to a specific role because of his ability to score so easily, whereas the Celtics fit Russell into their team concept better. I know there was one night when Wilt scored fifty-two points against Russell and other nights when he got mad enough to tear a telephone book apart—with one hand.

There was one particular game in the 1965–66 playoffs that Boston won, 4–1. Wilt started out playing team ball—looking to hit the open man all the time. No one hit for the 76ers, so by the third game, he got mad and took the offense into his own hands. He powered Russell and everyone into the seats in a one-man fury that won the game and showed the Celtics once more what he was capable of doing under certain conditions.

I'm not saying Wilt was the perfect player. I'm just saying he had awesome talent and maybe was right when he claimed Boston might've won as much with him as with Russell. We'll never know, though, will we?

I do know that as time went on, and Wilt's teams kept losing in the playoffs, he became more sensitive to the criticism. He quit again in 1965, shortly after the San Francisco Warriors traded him back to Philadelphia. It happened during the All-Star break when Franklin Mieuli, the owner, and Alex Hannum, the coach, decided they preferred to keep a young Nate Thurmond and get rid of an older Chamberlain.

"I've had it," Wilt said in announcing he would retire at the end of the season after the trade. "I'm not a selfish player about points and I've never been one. I'm tired of hearing all that blame rests on me. I'm sick of the criticism and people saying I've never played with a winning team. Everything I've done since I started playing basketball I've done under orders. Nobody can get the ball in the hole better than I and that's what every coach I've played for has wanted me to do. This is getting to be a damned joke. Year after year, depending upon how my team is going, that's the amount of abuse I get. Last season, when we won the Western Division in San Francisco, people started saying I'd become a team player. This year, because the team's in last place, I've been selfish. How do you figure it?"

That didn't change until the 1966–67 season, when Chamberlain won his first championship. Strangely, the 76ers beat San Francisco, 4–2, in the final after taking care of the Celtics, 4–1, in the Eastern final. He couldn't have planned it better: one team had just given up on him, and the other had been responsible for so many bitter moments and memories.

There were times that Wilt dreamed of playing in New York. He thought it might happen when Gottlieb first sold his Philadelphia Warriors' franchise to San Francisco for a reported $850,000—a good price in those days (1962). Gottlieb indicated he'd take $450,000 for Wilt.

Wilt's name kept popping up with the Knicks every so often. He was hoping to come to New York at the time San Francisco decided it had to split up Chamberlain and Thurmond. Wilt became optimistic when he heard the Knicks were talking to the Warriors. Then he learned the Knicks were interested in getting Thurmond.

There was more talk when Willis Reed retired because of his bad knees and Jerry Lucas went with him, leaving us slightly short at center. I was coaching the Knicks at the time and there were discussions about Chamberlain coming out of retirement but that never worked out.

I guess I'll best remember him for the championship games the Knicks played against Wilt once he joined the Lakers. How could I forget! We beat him, Jerry West, and Elgin Baylor in that unforgettable seven-game series in 1969–70 that brought the NBA championship to New York for the first time.

That's the series where Reed got hurt in the fifth game but we came from behind to win it. Then Willis missed the sixth game and had to take injections in his hip just before the seventh and final game. Will anyone ever forget how Reed came out of the darkness just before the start of that last game, joined the starting lineup late and proceeded to hit his first three shots though he could hardly move without pain?

That had to be a heartbreaking loss for Chamberlain, West, and Baylor, who got the worst of it. Baylor, never on a championship team, though he was one of the game's all-time great players, and wasn't around when West finally won his first title. The Lakers beat us in five games in the 1971–72 final to give Chamberlain a second championship.

We were back at the Lakers the following season to win our second championship but Chamberlain had proved his point. He wasn't a loser. He had won one championship with the 76ers and another with the Lakers. If not for Russell, he might've won many more.

Wilt was so proud after he had beaten us out of the 1972 title. He had played forty-six minutes and twenty-three seconds and had blocked at least ten of our shots in the final game. He had twenty-nine rebounds, twenty-four points, and was MVP of the series. His size and basketball intelligence had been too much for us. He got a tremendous ovation from the Forum fans when Bill Sharman finally took Wilt out.

"For a long time, me and friends of mine, we'd hear: 'Wilt can't win the big ones,' " he said. "I couldn't feel any greater winning this one. This one should ease the pain for West. After you lose the big one, it takes a whole lot out of you."

It was just Chamberlain's destiny to be identified with trouble, I guess. For example, the time he and the Lakers were delayed flying out of Chicago's O'Hare Airport. They had to wait three hours because of mechanical difficulties and a federal customs agent examined the players' equipment bags during the long delay.

"I know you guys are okay but I have to do this," the agent apologized. Wilt was a little ticked off and let off some steam by saying to West: "The way I feel right now, if I had a gun in my bag, I might shoot somebody." Innocent enough.

However, during a ten-minute wait on the plane before takeoff, they asked Chamberlain to get off. An agent wanted to talk to him. The plane left without Wilt, who had to explain his crack about the gun. Those were the nervous days of many hijackings.

"If I had been a hijacker, I wouldn't have left the plane with the man," explained Wilt, after an FBI man had accused him of talking about hijacking.

Someone asked why they would suspect him, Wilt Chamberlain of the Lakers, and ask him to get off the plane in the first place. "I guess, having a beard, being seven-feet tall and black might have something to do with it," he answered. "I wonder what would have happened if Bob Hope had made the same remark."

I don't know myself. But I do know that Bob Hope couldn't play basketball anything like Wilt Chamberlain. Few could.

OSCAR ROBERTSON

Bill Russell was sitting in a Syracuse restaurant before the 1961 All-Star game when a stranger came to his table. A menu was handed to the Celtics star and, in one of those rare moments of history, Russell signed an autograph.

The autograph hound looked at the signature, said something, and walked away from Russell, who watched with a smile on his face. "Did he think you were Wilt Chamberlain?" Russell was asked. "No, he thought I was Oscar Robertson," the great Boston center answered.

Later that night, Robertson, the rookie, led the West to a one-sided victory over the East and was named MVP in his first All-Star showing. "Now you understand why that man was so annoyed," Russell offered after the game. "That Number 18 is quite a rookie."

That Number 18 became one of the all-time players in pro history, just as he was one of the all-time players in college history. Oscar was only about one-third into his rookie season when he represented the Cincinnati Royals on a western squad that included Bob Pettit, Elgin Baylor, Jerry West, Wayne Embry, and Hot Rod Hundley.

The East was highly favored with a stacked deck of aces

Robertson tries to find a way around Jerry West.

such as Russell, Chamberlain, Adolph Schayes, Paul Arizin, Tommy Heinsohn, Bob Cousy, Richie Guerin, and Tom Gola. I was between jobs in basketball at the time but, like most people close to the sport, I felt there was no way the East could lose with that lineup. Besides, Red Auerbach, the hottest hand in the game, was coaching the East, adding another important dimension to the impossible job facing the West.

Yet the West won, 153–131, and Robertson was the reason. He played thirty-four minutes, scored twenty-three points, fed to thirteen more baskets, and grabbed nine rebounds. For years Bob Cousy had dominated the backcourt as its best ball-handler and playmaker. Now the players had seen Oscar come into the league and pick right up against the pros where he had left off against the colleges. Only the likes of Russell and Chamberlain had shown such adaptability, but no so-called small man had ever walked in as a rookie and had such an immediate impact on the league. Robertson, only six-five, had beaten Russell and Chamberlain together and they were two of the greatest individual forces ever to wear NBA uniforms.

As I have said, Cousy was the brilliant small man who had stood so tall in the big world of the NBA and few ever expected to see another like him—until Oscar showed up. "He's proved everything," said Guerin, who had just gone head-to-head with Robertson in the game, "and he's getting better all the time. The only weakness Oscar has is in his temperament. He has a tendency to complain but you can't blame him for that. He just does everything out there and everything so well."

Remember, Oscar was only about twenty-five games into his first season and already was moving the best players in the league around like pawns on a chessboard. He was one of the few players in my memory who actually controlled the pace of the game on both sides. He handled the ball all the time and his teammates reacted to what he did—and so did the defense.

To really appreciate what Oscar accomplished right away, consider Jerry West, who came into the league at the same time as a highly touted All-America. While Robertson took charge of things right away, West struggled at the beginning and actually spent a few of his rookie days on the bench despite the fact that Freddie Schaus, who had been his coach at West Virginia, was his coach with the Lakers.

I don't have to remind you how West wound up his career as one of the all-time great players. But it is significant that Oscar started and finished as a star. He was an instant and total success in that All-Star game in Syracuse, and the excitement he generated then followed him throughout his career.

"He has fantastic body control and extremely quick reflexes," said Russell, who had heard all about Robertson the college star but knew much more after playing against him. "Everything he does is done without obvious exertion. He's also stronger than he seems to be from the outside and has a grasp of the right move that is almost instinctive."

Robertson was the Cadillac of ballplayers. A luxurious machine built along rich lines that stood out in a crowd. He played with the magnificent ease and smoothness of Joe DiMaggio and the physical strength of a Larry Czonka. On offense, to get his shot, he maneuvered you closer and closer to the basket with his powerful body or dissected the defense with his fine passing.

It was always that way with him. He was born with a basketball in his mouth, I guess. He came into the league as the complete player and simply scared everyone who thought about how much better he might get. "What's the point in trying to figure out how good he can become," said Carl Braun, who coached the Knicks in Oscar's first season. "Isn't it enough that he scares you now? What he could be at the end of this year or the year after is enough to give you the shakes."

I used to look at Oscar in a different way. Every time I saw him playing the backcourt, I'd sort of laugh and think back to my playing days. When I played small guard for Nat Holman at City College, our center was a little over six feet, and here was Oscar, six-five and 220, playing the backcourt. Times had really changed.

Oscar had been a forward at the University of Cincinnati but had made the transition to the backcourt in the pros without skipping a beat. No one was surprised, though. Few, if any, really thought he would have any problems. Though Robertson entered the NBA eighteen years ago, when there were different folks and strokes, he could step right into today's game and perform better than the best of them. Oscar's kind of talent could fit forever.

He was smoother than a billiard ball. There never was any wasted motion. Cousy was an exciting passer. So is Pistol Pete Maravich. They did things with a flair. Oscar was quietly effective. He never made a fancy pass. He could throw a perfect bounce pass on the break with such timing and finesse, they were never stolen or missed. I never saw anyone who could do so much with a ball with such little effort.

Oscar made his loudest noises as a college player in Madison Square Garden. New York went wild over him the first time he showed up in 1958 as a sophomore. He was nineteen and a wide-eyed, young man with a friendly smile. His first reaction to the big city was to marvel at all the movie theaters and the seven TV channels on the set in his hotel room.

"My, my," he said, smiling. "We've only got three channels back home." He came to New York with a Cincinnati team that owned an 8–2 record and left an adopted son after scoring a record fifty-six points against Seton Hall. The sophisticated basketball minds of New York had discovered a new college hero to stand alongside others such as Hank Luisetti, who had introduced the one-hand shot to the Big Apple, and George Mikan, the first super center of the sport.

No one raved more about Oscar than Joe Lapchick, who, as coach of the Knicks before returning to St. John's, saw Robertson make his first New York appearance. Anytime I talked to Joe about basketball, the subject invariably would turn to Oscar. "He has to be the greatest college player ever," Joe would say. "He has the greatest reflexes. His hands, his feet, his body move so tremendously fast. Those hands are a beauty to watch."

Oscar had the slick, fast hands of a Las Vegas dealer. He became the biggest thing to hit New York since the Empire State Building. The New York writers voted him the outstanding visiting college player three years in a row. He was better known on the streets of New York than in his own hometown. They followed his every move and accomplishment as he scored forty-five, forty-three, thirty-six, forty-eight, forty-two,

thirty-seven, and forty-seven points in one stretch while passing and rebounding in his idle moments.

He couldn't walk the streets without being recognized. One
time, Oscar took a cab from the East Side Air Terminal to the
hotel on the West Side where he was staying with his college
teammates. The cab driver, who recognized him, turned to
someone when Robertson got out of the cab, and said: "Gee,
that kid's going to make a million bucks before he grows up."

He swept New York and the country off their feet. In his
college days, his shooting touch sort of overshadowed his passing. "I got my shooting touch by practicing, I guess, and these,"
he said, spreading huge hands. Oscar talked about how he
learned by watching game films of Sihugo Green, a solid
shooter with fine techniques who had played for the Royals
from 1957–59.

"Si would be up in the air," the young college player explained, "and you see his guard coming up to meet him, and
like he was walking up there off the ground, Si'd move the ball
left or right according to the defender's position. That's the
way to get the shot off right. That way it doesn't matter if a
man's on you."

That's the way Oscar did it and that's the way Dick Barnett,
Walt Frazier, and others would hang in the air and get shots
off on players all over them. Even in those days as a college
sophomore, the talk was about Oscar and the pros. "You
know," he said, "I couldn't go in the pros now. I got a lot to
learn in the next two years. I'm only nineteen. I got time."

He always was "old" for his age on a basketball court. I
remember a game in the 1959 Holiday Festival when Providence figured it had done a tremendous job by holding him to
twenty-five points. The Friars' entire aggressive defense was
aimed at stopping Oscar from scoring. "It's all right," he said
after Cincinnati had won. "I expect that. It's nothing unusual.
They were going to hold the score down, but they let a man
free and we won."

Oscar managed nineteen rebounds, five assists, deflected a
lot of passes, guarded the middle on defense, boxed out, and
triggered the fast break. That's all. Once he was surrounded
by three players but spun open for his jump shot. Another time

he flicked a pass by a Providence player into the air, grabbed it, and shot it through the hoop before hitting the floor.

He was a most unusual college basketball player who went on to become an even more unusual pro basketball player. He knew so much about the game, he adjusted quickly to anything and everything. For example, he was quick to determine the professional technique for rebounding. "You come from high school to college," he said even before he got into the pro game, "and right soon you start to learn that rebounding's more than jumping for that ball. We had a game down in Houston and they worked me over real good. I got more elbows in my face than I'd seen in my life. I made up my mind then I'd have to learn to use my elbows. From then on I started swinging them."

That amused me. I always thought Dr. Naismith learned the game from Oscar, who played intellectually and earned his nickname the same way. At the time Robertson was tearing up college basketball, James Thurber wrote "The Wonderful O." So Oscar Robertson immediately became "the Wonderful O" and eventually "the Big O."

Oscar came out of the Indianapolis Dust Bowl, a playground where the young and the hopeful gathered to play basketball. Life had been a dusty trail for the Big O, whose older athletic brothers Henry and Bailey accomplished things in basketball that inspired their younger brother to do them one better. It all began in a sharecroppers' cabin in Tennessee, where the grandfather struggled to feed his family off a small piece of land. Later, Oscar's mother, Mazell Robertson, moved her family to a tarpaper shack in Indianapolis, where she worked in a beauty parlor and provided a good home atmosphere for her sons.

Somewhere along the way, Oscar acquired a competitive spirit that always made him fight to be the best. Once, he was thrown off the junior high school basketball squad for getting out of hand because of his consuming desire to make the team. Another time, he forced a friend he knew could beat him in ping-pong to play almost all night until he couldn't beat Oscar anymore. Once he came home and found his mother ill and promised her: "Someday I'm going to make enough money to pay all your bills and make you sit down and rest and never work again."

He was a young man with a mission. Basketball was to be the way out for him, his mother, and his family. No one was going to take that away without a fight. He carried a basketball winter and summer, day and night. Always dribbling. Always getting the feel of the ball. One day, someone came along while Oscar was wandering around the Cincinnati campus with his basketball, took it out of his hands, and bounced it on the concrete pavement.

The Big O was furious. "Don't ever do that again!" Oscar screamed, yanking the basketball back. "What did I do to the ball but bounce it?" he was asked. "You bounced it on the concrete," said Oscar. "You spoil the feel of the ball that way."

I never carried basketball and the fundamentals that far but I appreciated what it meant because that's what made Oscar what he was. He was determined to be the best and he played the game that way. One night in a Holiday Festival game at Madison Square Garden, an Iowa University team was leading Cincinnati by eleven points and nothing was going right.

So Oscar decided to keep the ball and take charge. He wound up with fifty points as his team came from behind to win. "We were behind and I had to start sometime," he explained. "I guess what I did was all right because we had to catch up, but I missed a few easy ones."

I always felt he played like someone desperately trying to prove something, though he never admitted it. He always seemed to be responding to some inner challenge, and everyone was a threat to whatever he was seeking. He accepted the role of leadership because he felt that was part of his destiny. He made up his mind to be the best player when he was young and quietly and confidently did everything to accomplish that.

His span of concentration was remarkable. Nothing distracted him. He broke the most important individual college scoring records with a 33.8 average for one season and 2941 for eighty-eight career games before turning pro. He was the first pick by the Cincinnati Royals in the 1960 draft.

I was back home in Cedarhurst, Long Island, those days, selling insurance, but I still went to some of the Knicks games.

I remember the first game Oscar played against the Knicks as a rookie. He had scored forty-nine points in helping the Royals win their first two games, which was quite encouraging for a team that had finished last the year before and was depending on Oscar to change that.

He was a little nervous and unsure of himself in the first half, though he had played enough in the Garden to feel at home. He made only two of his first twelve shots but, before it was over, he added twenty-one points to the seven he had scored in the first half and maneuvered his teammates to a 113–105 win.

His touch was off in the first half. You could see that. His timing was uncertain and Guerin, playing him smartly, never gave him an inch. Richie pressured him, staying on top of Oscar so that he couldn't relax and think things over. It took Oscar over eight minutes to get his first basket and he didn't get another until about three minutes before the half.

One time, Guerin reached in and relieved Oscar of a dribble. Another time, he had a shot blocked, he was pressed into forcing another, and someone dribbled around him to score. I don't think anyone in the Garden that night was worried. Not even Oscar.

Sure enough, the real Oscar Robertson showed up in the second half. He stole the ball to make it a two-point game with about five minutes to go, and then blocked two shots and fed Wayne Embry to put the Royals ahead to stay. That triggered more talk comparing him to Cousy.

"He's a great pro already," suggested Jack Twyman, who had finished second to Wilt Chamberlain the season before in scoring but now was stepping aside for a rookie. "He does for us what Cousy did for Boston. He'll be an all-time great in this league, no doubt about that."

Oscar got all the attention that night and that was the way it was to be while he was playing basketball. I had an emotional interest in the Royals because I played for them when they were in Rochester. That's when Lester Harrison owned and coached the team.

Rochester beat the Knicks in seven games for the 1950–51 NBA championship and, in one of those strange bounces of life, the Knicks didn't win their first title until I was coaching them in 1969–70. So Oscar's first game against the Knicks had some special significance to me.

I was interested when Twyman said: "The mistake a lot of people make about Oscar is that they underestimate him as a defensive player. They keep watching for his shots and all the time he's killing off the other team's passes, picking up the loose ball and hitting the loose man. What he's done is [get] everybody on our team conscious of working without the ball. You don't move without it if you don't think you're going to get it, but Oscar's got everybody thinking they'll get it and so they're moving. He gives us the shot we need. He's made a great difference on our team and he'll make a great difference in the league."

As expected, Oscar was an instant success. He kept scoring thirty a game, ran the Cincinnati offense with intelligent passing that put him high on the list of real assists, not some of the "free" ones that were handed out, and convinced everyone he was a Picasso painting, a Hope Diamond or some other rare and precious commodity.

"I've been the leading backcourt scorer in the league over the last nine years and the best average I ever got was 22.3 in 1958," said Bill Sharman of the Celtics, who later was to move to the Lakers as coach and then general manager. "Last year, Detroit's Gene Shue beat that with a 22.8 average. Now along comes Robertson as a rookie averaging more than thirty."

The thing that impressed me was that no one was ever jealous of Oscar or resented his individual success. There was always a feeling of respect for a great and unusual talent. And it came from everyone who appreciated how basketball should be played because that's the way Oscar played it.

Dick McGuire, one of the outstanding ballhandlers of his time and coach of the Pistons when Oscar entered the league, said this: "Oscar is better than Cousy in every way." McGuire knew because he had played against Cousy and also played with him in a few All-Star games where they had dazzled everyone with their ballhandling.

"He knows all phases of the game," said Tommy Heinsohn, another member of the Boston team that was winning all the championships in those days. "If he couldn't pass, you could play him differently but, if you double teamed him for a second, you gambled. That calls for a pass and he'll pass it."

Cousy even joined in. "Robertson is the best of his kind ever to come into this game," he said. There was a strange parallel in their respective careers. Cousy was the greatest until Oscar came along to replace him; and ironically, Cousy was the first leader of the Players Association, whereas Robertson was the leader through the turbulent years that led to the ground rules for the NBA-ABA merger and the free agent market. Each man's tenure reflected his stature as a player as well as his willingness to take the heat of leadership.

Oscar never was afraid to put himself out in front. He played the game that way. The Big O never turned the Royals into a championship team but it wasn't his fault. He made them respectable and competitive so that they made the playoffs during one six-year stretch when Philadelphia and Boston were the powers in the East.

Players came and went but the one thing I think Oscar really never got in Cincinnati was a big center to work with him. Embry was outstanding in his own way but there was no Russell, Chamberlain, Thurmond, or Abdul-Jabbar to dominate a game. Oscar mentioned that when those who just didn't understand basketball blamed him because the Royals never won a title.

I think the point was proved when Oscar moved on to Milwaukee and, with Abdul-Jabbar at center, got his one and only championship. To me, Oscar didn't have to prove how great he was by winning a title. That never entered my mind when I thought of him.

I always judged him on what I saw him do. I couldn't forget, for example, that in his first ten All-Star games, his side won nine. He won his first two when Cincinnati was in the Western Division and lost the only one when the Royals switched to the East before he shifted back to the West with Milwaukee in his closing years.

I don't think any athlete in any sport ever influenced the All-Star Game and its outcome more consistently than Oscar. I generally don't deal in statistics, because sometimes they can be misleading, but just look at these: twenty-three points, nine rebounds, fourteen assists, West wins 153–131; twenty-six points, seven rebounds, thirteen assists, West wins 150–130; twenty-one points, three rebounds, six assists, East wins 115–108; twenty-six points, fourteen rebounds, eight assists, East wins 111–107; twenty-eight points, six rebounds, eight assists, East wins 124–123; seventeen points, ten rebounds, eight assists, East wins 137–94; twenty-six points, two rebounds, five assists, East loses 135–120; eighteen points, one rebound, five assists, East wins 144–124; twenty-four points, six rebounds, five assists, East wins 123–112; twenty-one points, six rebounds, four assists, East wins 142–135.

That's the Oscar Robertson I knew. He was the first "small man" to crack the $100,000 salary barrier after Chamberlain and Russell opened the way. He was always tough on the Knicks. I remember 1969, when we were beginning to make serious waves after too many years of looking up at everyone. I had replaced Dick McGuire as coach around Christmas in 1967 and soon after the 1968–69 season started, we made the trade for Dave DeBusschere that was to be the making of the Knicks, so to speak.

We were winning by the time we went to Cincinnati for a February game in 1969, but we hadn't played against Robertson and the Royals since we'd signed DeBusschere two months before. We were anxious to see how our new team would do against an old foe, and sure enough, we found out.

Oscar got only nineteen points that night but it was the same old story. He controlled the game and made us do what he wanted us to do. Cincinnati won by ten and Ed Jucker, the coach then, said: "The Knicks look the same to me. They're the talk of the NBA but we have beaten them four out of five now. In all fairness, I didn't see them play the way I've been reading about."

In all fairness, Oscar was just too much, as usual. He was one of the few players we pursued year after year in an effort to get him. Eddie Donovan and I always agreed that Oscar would solve a lot of our problems, so Eddie never failed to bring up his name when he talked to Cincinnati.

We never got close because the Royals never wanted to part

with Robertson when we wanted him. Once, in a rare moment of yielding or testing, Cincinnati said something about swapping Willis Reed for Robertson when the subject came up but nothing ever happened. For one thing, Ned Irish, who ran the Knicks at the time as team president, made Reed an untouchable. For another, I don't really think the Royals were really serious about it at the time.

The time did, however, come when Oscar really was available, but the Knicks weren't ready. That was when Cousy, then coach of the Royals, was in the process of rebuilding his team. He had traded Jerry Lucas to San Francisco and then sent Oscar to Baltimore for Gus Johnson early in 1970, only to have Robertson cancel the deal.

Oscar, at the time, was the only player in the league who had the right in his contract to refuse a trade. That's how valuable he was. The Royals had traded him to the Bullets without his permission and he refused to go. He wanted to play where there was a dominating center or in a situation where he could get a championship ring before he was through. Baltimore was in the throes of growing pains and indecision.

I know our new situation in New York would have interested Oscar, but the timing was wrong. Six years earlier, we might've given the franchise for him. Donovan had just moved out of coaching into the general manager's job. I was chief scout and traveling salesman in charge of new merchandise, and Oscar would have been a dream for us then.

We made no secret of it. We had a young Walt Frazier coming on in 1970 and it made no sense to rip out any part of our growing organization to get Oscar, still talented but with little time left. He was getting older, so the Knicks had to pass. The deal for DeBusschere shut the door on Oscar because it gave us the missing link in our scheme.

Oscar would have looked just great in a Knicks uniform. We might've won a championship with him but I don't know if we would've won without DeBusschere. Anyway, Oscar got his championship in Milwaukee, where he chose to go after Cincinnati tried to send him to Baltimore.

"I don't have to go anyplace I don't want to go," he said. "There is a clause in my contract which gives me final approval on any trade and evidently somebody didn't read the fine print very well. They can't ship me here, ship me there. I'm in trouble here in Cincinnati and I'm being told to go to more trouble in Baltimore."

Cousy had to do more shopping. He had approached the Knicks early in the season but we were in the process of winning eighteen straight, a league record then, and in no mood to disrupt things. I heard that Cousy intended to come back to us if Cincinnati hadn't finally made a new deal with the Bucks that was acceptable to Oscar. The Royals took Flynn Robinson, a 21.8 shooting guard, and Charley Paulk, a six-foot-eight forward who had been in the Army for two years.

I understand Cousy had shopped Robertson around with a few other teams before trying to deal him to the Bullets. Cousy said so. "We mentioned Oscar in passing to the Lakers but they obviously weren't going to give up Wilt Chamberlain," said Bob. "Then the Phoenix Suns offered us Gail Goodrich and Jim Fox, as well as Greg Howard, a six-nine kid from New Mexico who had played in Italy, but Oscar's people nixed Phoenix."

That's when the Milwaukee deal crystallized and Oscar agreed to move there because of Abdul-Jabbar, a young, talented center who might mean a championship. Cousy wasn't certain that Oscar and Kareem would constitute an automatic title. He was quite candid, as always.

"It could go either way," he explained. "It could project them to the championship because Oscar surely will have a great incentive to show up Cincinnati for trading him, as well as to be on a championship team for the first time. But there's the other side of the coin. Two superstars don't always mesh. The onus is on Oscar. If he decides to adjust to Alcindor, he could be terrific. But he's going to have to be aware that there's a big man in that hole."

Oscar and his wife Yvonne were in the Garden the night the Bullets beat us by a point in the seventh game and qualified to play Milwaukee for the 1970–71 championship. It had taken the Big O and Abdul–Jabbar only one season to show they could work together.

"It's going to be tougher than we think," said Mrs. Robertson, who'd shared her husband's anguish over not winning a title. "It's going to be tough but I think we'll win," said Mr. Robertson. "Don't be so confident," said Mrs. Robertson. "I won't be and I don't want to go overboard," said Mr. Robertson. "I want to believe Baltimore will be formidable, but if we don't win, it would be very disappointing."

I was disappointed because the Bullets had just knocked the Knicks out of a chance to win a second straight title so I knew what Oscar was talking about. He had never won one and, to someone with his brilliant talent, it had to be devastating. If the Knicks had to lose, I could think of no one at the time I'd rather see get a crack at the championship than Oscar. He had earned it.

I realized how it must have gnawed at him to hear some people suggest he'd never won the big one as though it had been his fault. "If we do it now, they can't say that anymore," he said as he faced his first opportunity to win the big one after eleven years in the NBA.

There was a noticeable touch of anxiety as Oscar discussed the Bullets and what was to come. "We'll do what we've been doing all season," he told those who were interested in how he finally would win the big one. "We'll work inside with Lew. We'll run. We'll keep the ball moving. I don't think Unseld will try to stop Lew in tight. He'll try to keep him away from the boards. He'll muscle him. He'll move around a lot to front him and make us lob the ball to him while he tries to get help from the back.

"I don't think Unseld will be able to stop him at all. The guy's just too big and he's become a terrific ballplayer. It's not going to be an easy thing with Monroe but I try to keep the ball away from him as much as possible. When he gets it, I try to make him go into spots he doesn't want to go. I heard he's passing off more, and when he's doing that, he's not shooting."

Oscar didn't have to worry. The Bullets had nothing left emotionally or otherwise after they had upset the Knicks by taking the final game on our floor. Milwaukee swept them in four, Abdul-Jabbar had his first title in his second season, and Oscar Robertson had finally gotten his.

Two years later, Oscar sat in the Boston Garden after the

Bucks had tied the NBA championship series 3–3 and was a tired, old man of thirty-six. He had just played all fifty-eight minutes of a grueling overtime game that sent the playoff back to Milwaukee, where the Celtics won and deprived the Big O of another title.

Abdul-Jabbar was in one corner of the dressing room as Oscar sat exhausted in another. "I personally don't think he has anything to prove," Kareem said of the Big O. "I remember they once gave me an NCAA booklet. I looked in it and the records didn't belong to me, Bill Walton, or Elvin Hayes. They belong to Oscar. He's still Oscar."

JOHN HAVLICEK

It was about an hour after the Knicks had eliminated the Celtics in the 1973 playoffs. Everyone was loose and happy as we climbed on the bus that was waiting inside the Boston Garden.

That bus was a moment to remember by itself. In order to get it into the Garden that day, it had to be backed up a steep wooden ramp that was just a little wider than the bus itself. It had to be backed up because the area inside the Garden was jammed with hockey nets and other paraphernalia and there was no room to turn the bus around if it had been driven in head first.

Did you ever zip up the Coney Island Steeplechase backwards? That's the sensation we got driving up that wooden ramp at a forty-five-degree angle, with the driver peeking through his side window to make sure his tires didn't hit the sides, and the Knicks in the back shouting seeing-eye-dog instructions.

We survived that and the seven-game series with the Celtics, so the talk was light and the laughter was heavy as we waited for Walt Frazier, generally the last Knick to get aboard. Suddenly, John Havlicek and his wife Beth came along. There

Havlicek scrambles for a loose ball.

was no reason for him to be there because the exit from the Garden was in another area.

Havlicek climbed into the bus and announced: "Good luck, fellows." That was Havlicek. Always the gentleman. Always the human being. Always a good winner but never a sore loser. In all the years I knew him when I scouted and then coached the Knicks, I never heard anyone whisper a bad word about him. I hardly ever saw him play a bad game. I never heard him say anything to embarrass himself, his teammates, or the sport.

Here, the Celtics had just lost an aggravating seven-game series to us. Havlicek had hurt his shoulder in the third game. He missed the fourth game but came back to struggle through the next three before we finally beat them. It was significant that only Havlicek of all the Celtics went out of his way to wish the Knicks luck as they headed for the championship series against the Lakers.

I wouldn't have expected less. Just as I didn't expect anything less from Havlicek after he suffered a painful injury running into a blind pick by Dave DeBusschere in the third game, and was back playing with one useful arm two games later.

The fourth game was played in Madison Square Garden and I don't think Havlicek will ever forget what happened when he walked across the floor toward the Boston bench. He was in street clothes as he trailed coach Tommy Heinsohn and assistant coach John Killela. I was chatting with someone near our bench when I heard the crowd noise—soft at first but getting louder. Then the applause that grew and grew into a standing ovation, one of the warmest spontaneous tributes I've seen for a visiting player.

New York fans were repaying Havlicek, unable to play that night, for eleven exciting years of outstanding performance and entertainment. It was a touching moment, especially when you consider that Havlicek wore the uniform of the Celtics, who were to the Knicks what the Red Sox were to the Yankees. "Something I'll always remember about New York," said Havlicek, moved by the sincerity of the fans. "They

showed they respected me as a player. The most knowledgeable crowd in the whole league. They appreciated my style
and what I had done."

Why not? So had I, despite the games he cost the Knicks
through the years. So had the league. So had the entire world
of basketball. It isn't often that a Havlicek comes along and
touches the lives of sports people. He was the prototype of the
perfect player and attitude. He was twenty-two when he entered the NBA and thirty-five when he left and I never heard
one harsh word about him or the way he played.

Under other circumstances, I might've felt sorry he wasn't
able to play that night but c'est la guerre, which means when
you are in a war, every little bit helps. I'm sure Havlicek
squirmed on the bench as he watched the Knicks overcome a
seventeen-point deficit and go on to beat the Celtics in double
overtime without him. We put on a full-court press that might
not have been effective if Havlicek had been on the floor to
handle it.

We woke up a little late but just in time to salvage a game
we couldn't afford to lose on our court. Not in the playoffs,
when a small edge like that could provide the difference in a
series. It didn't suprise me to see the Celtics do so well without
Havlicek, the type of player no team can afford to lose. I had
seen it happen so often. Coaches call it a letdown. It works
both ways. It did that night. Without Havlicek, the Celtics
knew they had to play harder and better. On our side, we
subconscously figured it would be a lot easier, so we became
a bit too casual. You've seen it. A team plays like it feels it can
win the game anytime it pleases.

We put the ball on the floor too much, early in the game. We
let the Celtics take charge and make us react. All a coach can
do under those conditions is to keep making changes on the
floor, hoping to find the right combination and change the
pace of the game.

Dave Cowens and the other Celtics busted their passes and
hustled more to compensate for Havlicek, while I used every
combination I could think of to get our adrenalin flowing. We
finally got the help we needed from our bench. Henry Bibby,

John Gianelli, and Phil Jackson, some of the best ball-pressuring players the half-court and full-court press has ever seen, did it for us.

They helped to finally break down the Celtics' concentration and stranglehold on the game. They forced turnovers and the kind of fouls a team commits when it's losing its poise and a big lead. We won the game and took a 3–1 lead back to Boston instead of being in the more disastrous position of being tied 2–2.

That was the strength of that Knicks team. I had complete faith in everyone on the bench. It was a team of twelve players who knew their roles. The bench got us back into the game and the starters won it. It wasn't an artistic success but the score was.

"The only credit we deserve is that we woke up and came back," said Dave DeBusschere, concerned as I was how we had to struggle against a Celtic team without Havlicek. "For most of the game, we just stood around, dribbled too much, and weren't looking for each other as we should have been."

We had to win that game or go back to Boston tied at two, putting us in a dangerous position of falling behind and losing the playoffs. "The Knicks probably felt they had the advantage with me not playing," said Havlicek. "Our guys were fantastic. They deserved to win. It's incredible they wound up losing after leading by seventeen."

He had seen sixteen of those points disappear in the fourth quarter alone but he said something after it was over that reflected his depth of understanding. He had walked into the Celtics' dressing room with his teammates and was there when they dropped onto their seats completely exhausted from fifty-eight minutes of inspired effort. No coach could have asked for more.

"I got a big lump looking at the expressions of wear and tear," said Havlicek, "the exhaustion on their faces. The pride of losing." Yes, the pride of losing. Havlicek knew. He had lost but never without pride. Never without giving all he had.

That's why I wasn't surprised when he was back in uniform for the fifth game of the 1973 playoff series, or when we were beaten by a point in Boston. He couldn't start but he played and that was enough to pick up the Celtics. He had spent forty-five minutes taking treatment in the trainer's room and came out with an icebag that was tied to his right shoulder with an ace bandage.

Tommy Heinsohn played it safe by not using him until the second quarter, and then sent him in for Don Chaney in the backcourt. Heinsohn didn't want Havlicek exposing his bad shoulder to the contact that goes on underneath with the big men. A sensible move. Hondo came off the bench firing, though. He hit his first shot, a short one-hander, then the next with a flying one-hander off the board.

He soon started to shoot and pass left-handed because the shoulder was bothering him, but he kept playing. He shortened his range and shot only while going to the basket. I think our players deliberately avoided contact with him. They treated him with too much kindness and respect because he was hurt.

I had to remind Bill Bradley, Walt Frazier, DeBusschere, and the others that we couldn't afford to be nice to anybody in the playoffs. We were now going into the sixth game and we still needed one to clinch. We tightened up on Havlicek after losing that one and finally made it in the seventh game only when we treated him with total disrespect.

By the time the seventh and final game started, I had convinced all the Knicks that this was no time for sympathy. Havlicek's popularity had to end in the dressing room. It did.

Hondo came trotting onto the floor for Chaney, who had drawn his third personal with about three minutes left to intermission. The Boston fans erupted. This was Havlicek time. The deciding game, the dramatic moment, and the Celtic noise that always seemed to work when it was needed.

This one time it didn't. Frazier immediately stole the ball from Havlicek and went in for a layup that put us ahead by three. A few seconds later, Hondo, ignoring his bad shoulder, raised the ball over his head and fired a two-handed pass towards the basket that went out of bounds. We turned that into a Phil Jackson basket at the other end.

Havlicek tried driving the hoop but Frazier blocked the shot that Dean Meminger scooped up and turned into another basket when he flipped ahead to DeBusschere, who shoveled it to Jerry Lucas for the score. Three Havlicek plays, three Knick baskets. When it was over, we felt a little sorry for Havlicek but our respect for him was even greater.

Don Nelson said it best about his teammate. "I said the best team was going to win and the best team won," said the forward who helped win a few championships in Boston himself. "But we were without John. We needed his offense. We really missed him. He did all right in one game but the last two games, the Knicks played him as though he had two arms."

Why not? He had been playing us for years as though he had a dozen legs. There was no way he could've run so much and for so long on the regular human issue of two legs. On stamina alone he'd be among the top players who ever played the game. It would've been fair to those who had to play him or those who had to coach against him if he had been blessed only with his inhuman endurance. God had to compound it by making him a good scorer, smart ballhandler, and intelligent defensive player with quickness of mind, hands, and feet.

I'll say this much for Havlicek: he made coaching strategy easy. I didn't have to tell Bradley how he had to play Hondo, just as I'm sure other coaches had no secrets. It was run, run, run, and stay between him and the basket if you could. It was estimated at one time that Havlicek ran from three to five miles a game but it had to seem like the Boston Marathon for those who played him.

"Maybe I've run around the world," he once said. What made him such an unusual athlete, other than his running, was that he could hit from anywhere and invariably was involved with the decisive shot or play.

Those are the great players. The ones who always play as though they are proving their worth. Every game is a new test for their talent and nerves. "It's my responsibility on this team," Havlicek always would say. "I've always liked to test myself. I have a lot of self-discipline."

When he was around six, he'd run between the milestones on the highway near his home to prove he could run a mile. Once he went a whole season in college without drinking a Coke just to build discipline. He just kept going, that's all. He discovered it was worth something for him not to stop. It became his style.

"I created a situation for myself," he explained. "I got to where I am by running. I have to keep running. To maintain that standard is very hard but it's what I have to do. It's a simple philosophy—nothing complicated about it. Run as hard as you can for as long as you can. If you're going to do it, do it right."

Havlicek sure did it right. No one ever did it better. He could've made it big in any sport. Woody Hayes used to introduce him as the best quarterback in the Big Ten though he never played football at Ohio State. He didn't play baseball either, after hitting over .400 as a freshman. He wasn't interested in tennis but was the class champion, and the swimming coach drooled when he saw Havlicek swimming for fun in the Ohio State pool. One time he stood on the twenty and threw a football eighty yards into the end zone.

He was a natural athlete in love with basketball. Several NFL teams sent him questionaires though he only played basketball at Ohio State. He was drafted by Paul Brown for the Cleveland Browns, a powerhouse at the time, and he went to training camp with them before joining the Celtics.

"I figured if I couldn't make it in football, I could always come back and play basketball," he explained. "The football idea fascinated me. I was an all-state quarterback in high school and most of the eighty or so college scholarship offers were for football, but my favorite sport was basketball."

Havlicek's pro football career didn't last too long. Brown saw the quickness that made Hondo the fastest in the forty-yard sprints, and figured he had a fine pass-catching end. Hondo made it to one exhibition game and that's all.

On his first play, he flanked to the outside and blocked a defensive back to spring Jimmy Brown for forty-eight yards to the two. Havlicek was the tight end on the next play and found himself staring into the face of Big Daddy Lipscomb, the 310-pound monster. The next thing Hondo knew, he was buried under a pile of humanity, his helmet was gone, and he was the last man up on his feet.

"We ran two more plays, we got the touchdown, and that was

the end of me," said Havlicek. He heard the haunting call of the Celtics and the rest was basketball history. He came to the team as the last pick on the first round of the 1962 draft and was on eight Boston championship teams—six with Russell, two without him.

I first saw him on the Ohio State championship team when I was scouting for the Knicks. It was an interesting Buckeye squad with Jerry Lucas, Bobby Knight, Larry Siegfried, and Havlicek. A lot of poise and intelligence. Ohio State came to the Garden to play St. John's when Havlicek was a junior and what impressed me was his defense.

Havlicek was not the scorer on that team. You could see then that he was quick and he could run all night. Actually, Ohio State came from thirteen back in the second half when Havlicek led a zone press that rattled St. John's.

Lucas got most of the attention that night. Some noticed Havlicek's defense. "Our defense is what did it," Havlicek said after the game. "As soon as we went into the rat game, St. John's seemed to lose its poise."

I don't think the Celtics really appreciated what they had when the other teams passed on Havlicek on the first round and he landed in Boston. He got there when the Celtics were loaded in the backcourt, which was really Havlicek's position at the time. Bob Cousy, Sam Jones, and K. C. Jones were ahead of him. Besides, Frank Ramsey was the Sixth Man supreme at the time.

It was no accident that part of the Celtics' championship run coincided with the Sixth Man theme. First Ramsey, then Havlicek, and finally Paul Silas. "There probably will be a temptation to start Havlicek," said Red Auerbach one day. That time came when Russell was coaching and the Celtics suffered an injury to starting forward Satch Sanders in the 1968 playoffs.

Havlicek would come in for a forward in trouble or a guard in trouble and lift the Celtics right up. Someone once asked Russell what happened if no one was in trouble. "Then John can sit," Russell cackled.

Sanders got hurt in the playoffs with the Pistons, who were leading the Celtics 2–1, and Russell made Havlicek an emergency starter. The Celtics swept the next three, beat Wilt

Chamberlain and the 76ers with Havlicek still starting, and then whipped the Lakers for the title.

The move won the championship that season for the Celtics. It was made by Russell in his usual humorous manner. "Russell came to me and said he wished he had two of me, one for the backcourt and one for the front," recalled Havlicek. "I told him he'd have to be Houdini and cut me in half."

So Havlicek ran in the backcourt and ran in the front court, sometimes for over forty minutes. He apologized for not being able to play more as a starter. He had prepared himself to run but not for forty-eight minutes in the grueling pro game that was accelerating more with every year.

That's the only break Havlicek gave the other teams. He sat once in a while. "I ran everywhere when I was young," he explained. "I ran to the store, to school, everywhere. That way I had more time to play ball. If I had to run an errand, I'd get it done quicker. I'd run home from school for my lunch and I'd run back after lunch. I knew just how long it would take me: forty-five seconds. With about thirteen minutes for lunch, I'd be back on the playground in fifteen minutes, which gave me forty-five minutes to play before class. I was always wrapped up in some kind of ball."

They should name the twenty-four-second clock after him as a memorial. Havlicek went back to being the Sixth Man for a while but Heinsohn finally let him finish his last years as a starter. Tommy made the move in the middle of his first season as coach, which was 1969–70. Havlicek became a full-time player the year Dave Cowens joined the Celtics and Heinsohn was searching for some stability.

Russell and Sam Jones had retired together and left Heinsohn with some gaping holes. I remember playing the Celtics an exhibition game and was puzzled by some of the strange names on the team. So were the referees. "Are these the Celtics?" one of the refs asked Havlicek.

Havlicek had to wonder at times. He still ran and ran but sometimes found himself running into his new bewildered teammates. Heinsohn soon discovered he couldn't afford the luxury any longer of bringing Havlicek in off the bench. "It's been a tradition to come off the bench on this team," explained

Hondo. "But since my first season, I always started in the playoffs."

He moved into the natural leadership of the Celtics as each season took its toll on another player. First Ramsey, which made him the Sixth Man. Then K. C. Jones, Sam Jones, and Russell. "I inherited the leadership then," said Havlicek. "I'll be the leader until someone comes along and does the job better than me."

No one did, so he finally had to quit after the 1978 season. He scored his first basket on a dunk against the Knicks on October 20, 1962 in Boston. He scored the first basket in the new Garden on a jumper on February 14, 1968. And he scored a lot of baskets that helped beat the Knicks, the Lakers, and many other teams in the championship games of the playoffs.

I guess one of his greatest moments was the night in 1974 when he stood in the jammed dressing room in Milwaukee after the Celtics had won their first title without Russell. They bathed him in champagne as he strolled around the room hugging and kissing his teammates. The Celtics had won one under his leadership and he was grateful. He was that kind of totally dedicated individual.

"You've got to make exceptions," said Chaney after Havlicek gave him a wet kiss. "He's the leader. I don't mind. He can kiss me." It was Hondo's seventh championship ring and he was to earn one more two years later before he retired to open a jewelry store, I guess.

Jerry West once said: "His body is meant to go on forever." I remember a 1972 playoff game in the Garden, when we beat the Celtics for a 3–1 lead and Havlicek got twenty-seven but was hurt a few times at the other end when he wound up on DeBusschere. "I'd rather have Bradley guard him," DeBusschere told me, candidly.

John Havlicek, a player never to be forgotten.

RICK BARRY

Keith Wilkes, first in the winners' dressing room, was screaming: "We're the world champions!" as Al Attles, coach of the Golden State Warriors, began dancing with the 1975 Rookie of the Year. Derrek Dickey, George Johnson, Cliff Ray, and the other players were hugging, yelling, and going just plain crazy.

Off on the side, practically unnoticed, sat Rick Barry. His head was buried in his hands and he was crying. His tears and the victory champagne were flowing together. The emotional dam had burst within him after ten years of fun, pain, legal fights, and team switching.

He had finally won a championship with the team that had brought him into the NBA in the first place. He had left the Warriors to help build the ABA, the new league just getting off the ground. He had come back a few years later and here he was, sitting in the winner's dressing room after the Washington Bullets were beaten, 4–0, for the 1975 title.

Barry, an emotional player and captain of the team, couldn't control his feelings. Ray walked over, patted him on his head and back, but Rick never looked up. His eyes were wet and red. Dickey dropped by and dumped champagne on his head.

"I'll take it, I'll take it," said a revived Barry, leaping off the bench, finally, to join the wild celebration. "This has been a fantasy year," he said as someone flipped him a towel to dry his face. "One of the most unique teams in basketball history. A team that cares for each other. The most beautiful individuals I've ever been associated with."

Yes, Barry was a most emotional player. And a very good one, besides. Maybe one of the best forwards who ever played the game. When you think about it, it's hard to think of many better all-around players. "He is the best all-around player in the game today," announced Tommy Heinsohn whose defending champion Celtics had been surprised by the Bullets in the eastern final.

Barry played on lots of emotion and talent. He would wind himself up in the dressing room and go out and shoot, pass, and scream at you. He played with an intensity that boiled over whenever anyone or anything got in his way. Such as the night in Baltimore back in 1967, when the Knicks were playing the Warriors in the first game of a doubleheader. They played NBA doubleheaders in the eastern cities in those days. They were a holdover from the college doubleheaders that had become popular in Madison Square Garden and spread to Buffalo, Boston, Philadelphia, and other parts until the NBA outgrew them.

Dick Van Arsdale was playing Barry, as usual, and was roughing him up, as usual. Van discovered the best way to play Rick was in his socks and never give him an inch of breathing room. Barry had a short fuse and irritated easily, which was part of Van's defensive purpose in the first place.

The closer Van stuck to Barry, the more irritated Rick became. Suddenly, with 2:46 to go in the first period, Barry exploded. Not at Van Arsdale at first, but at the refs for not calling a foul on him.

"Take me out!" Rick yelled to Bill Sharman, the coach. Sharman sympathized because he had learned all about the pushing and shoving that sometimes led Barry to fight when he was with the Celtics, but he ignored the demand. He knew Rick's low boiling-point and how it would simmer down quickly. This time, it didn't.

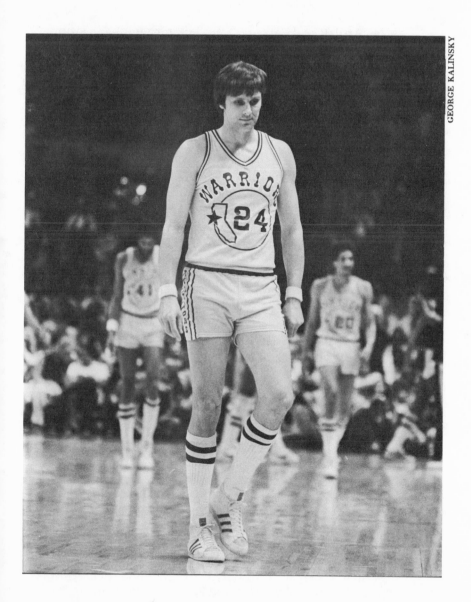

Van Arsdale and Barry resumed bumping until Van swung an elbow. Rick swung a fist. It was a short, shoving sort of punch that landed on Van Arsdale as he was heading for the floor off-balance. The next thing Rick knew, he was on the floor with a front capped tooth missing from a sneak punch.

Who threw the sneak punch? "I don't think you can say I knocked him down," said Van Arsdale, smiling. "Walt Bellamy did it," said Barry. "Ask Nate Thurmond. I'm almost positive Nate saw him do it."

Thurmond confirmed that Bellamy had been the culprit. "That's why I chewed him out," said Nate, who got into a shoving match with the Knick center over the incident. There was one thing wrong with the whole affair. Barry found it out later—much later.

The Knick who had sneaked the punch that put Barry on the floor was caught with evidence in hand. Willis Reed had to have Rick's capped tooth extracted from a knuckle on his left hand. The Knicks laughed but Barry didn't.

It was his own fault. Who told him to be so good that he became a target for every team that played against him? "They're all playing Rick tight," said Sharman, who had to also shake himself loose in order to get off his shots as a player. "It's definitely inciting. That Tom Hawkins (Lakers) is a nice kid but he got instructions to play Barry tight and he was thrown out of a game for roughing him up. Rick can't turn in any direction without running into an arm."

I first ran across Rick when I was scouting. He had played his high school ball in Roselle Park, New Jersey and went to Miami University, where I dropped by to see him about a half-dozen times before he became eligible for the 1965 draft. He was a skinny kid and most scouting reports mentioned that while saying he was an outstanding shooter, a good ballhandler for a six-seven forward, and an intense competitor with a flair for making the winning plays.

So how come the Knicks didn't draft him? Rick always blamed Ned Irish for that. "That is what made me mad," said Barry, who grew up close to the Garden and always wanted to play there. "Ned Irish said the Knicks weren't interested in me because I was too skinny and flaky. He never met me but passed judgment on me and I never could understand why."

There was a game in the Garden when Barry was a sopho-more at Miami and he got so mad over a fifth personal that fouled him out, he heaved the ball at the basket in a temper tantrum. And then there was the time he threw a punch at a player during another college game in the Garden when he was a junior. "I was only a kid then," he said, when he dis-cussed the punching incident. "This guy was giving me a tough time and, on one jump ball, he hit me in the jaw as we were going up. I came down, hit him in the jaw, hit him good, and if the same thing came up again, I'd do it again. I did a lot of stupid things but between my junior and senior years I changed a lot. If I was going to play pro ball, I had to act like a grownup."

There are those who say that what made Barry so distinctive and outstanding for so long was the boyish enthusiasm for the game that he never lost. I don't think Ned Irish had much against him, either. I know this: if Barry had come out of college any other year, the Knicks would've taken him.

However, in the 1965 draft, Bill Bradley was eligible and Irish was determined to get him. Bradley had been so exciting in the Holiday Festival tournament against Cazzie Russell and Michigan that Ned made up his mind Dollar Bill would be a Knick. It took two years while Bradley attended Oxford but he finally made it.

That was a strange draft. If you look at the official records of the NBA, you will see the Warriors are listed as making Fred Hetzel the first pick. That's a technicality.

Actually, the league had voted to give the Warriors and the Knicks two first-round draft picks that year as special com-pensation for having finished last in their divisions. Since the Knicks were designating Bradley as a territorial choice, thus making him our automatic first pick, the Warriors were al-lowed two picks in a row before we chose again.

San Francisco announced Fred Hetzel and Rick Barry in that order. Since Hetzel's name was mentioned first, he is listed as the number one pick that year, not Barry. The Knicks took Dave Stallworth as their second pick on the first round. As things turned out we did very well; it was a wise choice.

Barry never forgot, though. "Every team was looking for six-eight forwards who weighed 240 when I came out but I had the quickness and speed," explained Barry, who was a lanky 210-pounder when he was drafted. "I can get up and get out before the big guys get to the ball. You got to time yourself and get to the ball before the guys with the size and the weight."

Some didn't agree at first. Some felt the rough pros might break the skinny college kid in half. One owner told me he actually sent three scouts to look at Barry for divergent opinions. "They decided he couldn't make it," the owner said. "We figured he couldn't take the belting."

Barry not only took it, he dished it out. I remember a night when he actually outrebounded Wilt Chamberlain, 25–22. They didn't play against each other; Rick just got more rebounds than one of the best rebounders the game has ever seen. "I just jumped over him," said Rick. "In this game, you've got to be aggressive. Guys are pushing and shoving and you've got to hold your own. You can't let them get away with anything or else they'll try to do whatever they want to you. Me? I'm a perfectionist. If anybody is going to do what they want, I want it to be me."

He was immediately called "Super Rook" by his teammates. He came into the NBA with a college crewcut and soon set his own style by having his hair razor-cut and shaped for $6.50 a crack—unheard of in those days. It added to his flake image in the eyes of those who thought of him that way.

"Is that any reason for anybody to think I'm a flake?" he asked. "I used to wear it crewcut but my ears stuck out and my wife got me to change. Wearing it styled this way does something for a person. It makes you feel like somebody. It makes you look like somebody."

That was Rick Barry. He always had to look like something and feel like somebody. That's the way he played basketball —like all eyes were on him, so he had better be as near-perfect as possible. He never settled for less, which is why he argued with opponents, the refs, his teammates, and himself at times.

He was tough to play because he was smart and could do so much with the ball. He could hit ten in a row from far outside when he was hot, make the play on the move, and drive his man out of his mind trying to stay with him. Van Arsdale and DeBusschere played him best for the Knicks because they had the size, strength, and perseverance, plus the knowledge that contact would irritate Rick and spoil his fine-tuning.

Barry was a streak shooter and our approach was to break up his rhythm and keep him from getting too hot. He became the NBA scoring leader in 1967, ending a seven-year run by Wilt Chamberlain, which indicates why we thought in terms of slowing him down and not stopping him.

There was a night against the Knicks when Dick McGuire, then the coach, discovered another Barry dimension. Rick set a Garden pro record on December 14, 1965 with fifty-seven points that included twenty-one free throws. "He moves exceptionally well without the ball," observed McGuire, neglecting the free throws because by then Barry was accepted as the greatest NBA foul shooter of all time.

Barry was a 90 percent foul shooter, which put him on top of an all-time list that had Sharman second, little Cal Murphy third, Mike Newlin fourth, and Larry Siegfried of the championship Celtics fifth. On November 16, 1976, Rick set the NBA record with a run of sixty straight. "I had hoped to make eighty or ninety in a row but I didn't concentrate," he said after cracking Murphy's record of fifty-eight in a row by hitting eight straight against Seattle before missing.

His success at the foul line was even more remarkable to basketball technicians because he was the only one using the obsolete underhand shot. In my playing days, that was an accepted way of shooting. In fact, Nat Holman, my college coach, was an expert at it when he was a star with the Original Celtics and taught it to all his college players.

Barry taught it to George Johnson when he joined the Warriors at center and they were the only modern pros to use it to my knowledge. Underhand foul shooting was just something else that made Rick distinctive. He was determined to be an exciting player and he had the style and personality for it. No game could be played without the fans noticing him. I don't know if it was intentional on his part but it sure came out that way.

He didn't mind expressing his views, either, especially on

the vanishing art of fundamental basketball as the one-on-one game grew in the pros. "Most of the guys have great talent to begin with but in high school and college, coaches took advantage of them," he analyzed. "They just put them on the floor and let them do their thing. They didn't teach them what the game was all about.

"So many guys are weak on fundamentals and don't work on things like shooting free throws. They don't know what to do if the man who's guarding them turns his head away, or how to handle a hundred given situations that come up in basketball. If you'd give a written test to pro players about the basics of the game and the rules and so forth, I'd bet they'd get about 60 percent of the answers right. If you got five smart players on the floor at the same time, they'd make a mockery out of any team."

No pro coach would argue with Barry. Something did happen in recent years that started a trend of college players not equipped enough in fundamentals to handle the team concept NBA coaches desire. It's become increasingly more difficult to teach team ball because the players have not been basically prepared and come to the pros as specialists.

Barry knew from experience that the smarter teams win championships. Physical attributes can get you just so far. More than that is required to go all the way and become the best team. Examine the teams that have won championships through the years and you will see what separates the good ones from the better ones.

I think Rick knew the formula all the time because he has been the prototype of the smart, fundamentally prepared player since he learned how to play. I think he appreciated it even more when his 1975 teammates played and acted like a team.

There was a game in the Garden in December of the 1974–75 season when Barry scored forty-four points and was getting all the attention in the Warriors' dressing room. He had scored sixteen in the first period without missing. I used three different players on him but it didn't make a difference. Rick was more than hot—he was sizzling.

We were never in the game because of Barry, fundamentally, but also because the Warriors were molding together fast after failing to make the playoffs the previous season. "I like the way we're playing," said Rick after we had lost by eighteen on our court. "We're running and that's my style. We have no problems."

There was no inner turmoil, no tension between players. They were looking for each other on the floor and moving the ball to the open man. They were helping out on defense. Every game seemed to be more than a basketball game to Rick and his teammates.

Al Attles, the coach, had thrown together a team of no-names and they accepted Barry as their leader. "I really didn't know him except as a basketball player," said Cliff Ray, the center who had just come over to the Warriors from the Chicago Bulls, "but I've found him a real warm person."

Winning always helps create a smoother interaction but his teammates seemed surprised by Barry, the person. He was accommodating in many ways. Ray recalled a small problem he had when he shipped to San Francisco from Chicago without furniture.

"I didn't have a TV set or anything, and Rick offered me his stereo," said Cliff. "If Rick or Jeff Mullens are going out, they always ask the other guys to come along. I've never experienced anything like this."

It wasn't always that smooth with Barry. He was in the NBA only two seasons when the ABA was formed and influenced him to sign with the Oakland franchise owned by singer Pat Boone. By then, Rick was a rising shooting star the new league needed to establish instant credibility and attention.

Barry had just won the NBA scoring title with an amazing 35.6 average that was ten points better than Robertson's second-place finish and 11½ points better than Chamberlain's third place finish. Besides, the young Warriors had staged an exciting finish of their own by sweeping into the playoff final only to lose to a highly talented and favored Philadelphia team.

There was no loss of heart in San Francisco because Chamberlain, Billy Cunningham, Luke Jackson, Chet Walker, and Hal Greer had taken the title, 4–2. A great future was predicted for the Warriors. Some even said Barry and Thurmond were the foundation of a guaranteed dynasty. They were inseparable and Franklin Mieuli, the owner of the Warriors, once said their salary packages were closely related—if Barry got more money, Thurmond would get more money.

Then came the news that Barry was moving across the Bay Bridge to play for the Oakland Oaks. No one was more stunned than Thurmond, who had figured he and Barry would bring a championship to San Francisco. The tall center got on the phone and called Rick.

"I realize that maybe it's useless trying," said Nate, "but I want to try to make you change your mind and stay and play with us."

It was useless. Barry was gone and it is interesting to point out why.

In effect, Barry's move was basketball history because he was the first big-name NBA player to jump to the other league. Rick gave an insight into the details and influences of the deal Boone offered to bring his gate-appeal to the newborn ABA.

"Mieuli offered to give me $40,000 and five percent of the gate," said Barry. "I don't think he really considered the ABA a threat because last season I was paid $30,000 plus five percent of the gate, which came to an additional $13,000. In actuality, I was being offered a $10,000 raise."

So Rick went off and accepted some of Boone's extensive music money. He signed a three-year personal services contract for $75,000 a year, plus a 15 percent interest in the Oaks, plus 5 percent of the regular season home gate in excess of $600,000 but couldn't exceed $10,000 a season plus the opportunity to get into the movies.

It was a fascinating deal for Rick, only twenty-three and facing a rich future. But not right away because Mieuli took the case to court and Barry had to wait a year to join the Oaks when it was ruled he owed the Warriors an option year on his contract with them. "I can wait one year," said Boone, "but what I hope to do is reason with Mr. Mieuli and the Warriors. I would like to purchase Rick's contract. Right now, the season will start and Barry won't be playing for us."

What Pat got was a $4½-million lawsuit from Mieuli, but no

Barry. There was talk at the time that Rick would resolve the stalemate by playing the season with the Warriors. "He called me and said it would be awkward to do that and he decided to sit it out," said Boone. "He said it would do no one any good, so he said it would be better for him to sit out the whole season."

I'll say this for Franklin Mieuli: he's one persistent man. The chase was on and Mieuli never stopped using the full-court press until he got Barry back after a playing season with Oakland, a year with Washington, and two years with the New York Nets. It was simply a case of Mieuli not forgetting what young Rick Barry had done in the 1967 season that promised a San Francisco championship someday.

I don't think Mieuli will ever forget the fifth game of the playoff series in Philadelphia, a game that his team won only to delay the eventual agony of defeat. Barry's performance was unforgettable because it happened despite a hostile, wild crowd that threw eggs at him and called him Superbaby.

Barry responded by shutting everything out. He hit ten-for-twenty in the first half, then dropped off four-for-seventeen. He got cold but never stopped shooting, moving the ball, and doing the things that pros do or should do in periods of adversity.

"It's a funny game," Rick explained for those who don't realize it's a funny game. "I was getting open shots and missing them. I was hot and turned cold. I had to try to do other things to help. When I was missing, if I let myself get disgusted, I'd be defeating my own purpose. You can't let the game beat you. You've got to beat the game."

He beat the game that night and Mieuli loved it. Rick tied it with four minutes to play and hit a technical two minutes later to put the Warriors ahead by two. He made the biggest play when the Warriors were leading by a point with ninety seconds left.

Rick took the ball right to the hoop, with Chamberlain waiting to jam it down his throat. Barry not only made the basket by somehow twisting away from Wilt's long reach but drew a foul that resulted in a clinching three-pointer. "I had to do something," he said. "I was more of a liability until then.

Frankly, I stunk. I was miserable."

Sharman, his coach, didn't think so. He wasn't surprised that Barry had found a way to beat the goaltending Chamberlain or even had had the courage to challenge him in a critical situation where a blocked shot might have meant the ballgame.

"Ordinarily, we try not to take it to Chamberlain, especially in a situation like that," said Sharman. "I tell the other players to keep it away from Wilt but with Barry I leave it to his judgment. Going to the basket, he's got the best moves in basketball. He's got reflexes and body balance like Baylor had. He saw he could go and went."

The Warriors lost to the 76ers in the next game but Mieuli was a happy man. He saw something big in the future. He detected the making of a championship basketball team so he sent all the players and their wives off to Hawaii as a reward and down payment on what Mieuli was sure to come.

It didn't come because Barry went. "I doubt sincerely if Mieuli will take me back," said Rick one day while suggesting the worst that could happen in his ABA adventure was his becoming a free agent available to the NBA. "But," he added, "do you think Ned Irish and the Knicks would take me after the things they said about me?"

The answer would have been yes if the Knicks had a chance to get Barry the second time around. But the closest he got to New York was with the Nets. Oakland folded after one season and he was sold to Washington, creating another strange bounce in the saga of Rick Barry.

He immediately signed a five-year contract with Mieuli only to have the court tell him he first had to fulfill the remaining two years of his ABA contract. They couldn't make it in Washington so the franchise moved to Virginia with the idea of floating many home dates around the South in order to cash in on the Rick Barry interest.

That didn't work because Rick talked himself off the Squires and onto the Nets before the 1970–71 season started. He told Virginia fans he'd be fat and indifferent. He said that he didn't want his children to grow up with Southern accents. "I said those things without malice," he explained. "Maybe it wasn't a nice thing to do but it was the only thing I could think of. They were up in arms and I couldn't blame them. If it didn't work, I would have publicly apologized. I think the people would have understood. The important thing, anyway, is what you do on the floor."

Barry performed on the floor very well for the Nets and then returned to the Warriors. His wandering days were over. Or were they? He did indicate he was glad to be home again and was tired of the restless days of the past. "This sort of thing creates chaos," he said, referring to player disorders. "It's not good for the league and it's not good for basketball. I realize that now. I learned it the hard way."

He returned to a Warriors team that had changed its name from San Francisco to Golden State since he left, as well as to a lot of new faces. Thurmond was still there; so was Jeff Mullins and Joe Ellis, a sub, but Al Attles, a teammate in 1966–67, was now the coach.

Barry was in a new situation but he treated the Knicks like he had never left. We went to Oakland to face him the first time after his return and had an eight-game winning streak going. He took care of that with twelve-for-twenty and twenty-six points, sixteen rebounds, and four assists.

"No, I don't think the league has changed that much in the five years I've been away," he said after he had helped beat a Knicks team that was to become the champion by twenty-three points. He had picked up against us where he had left off and, therefore, assumed nothing in the league had changed.

DeBusschere played him that night and played him well, as usual, but Barry was too much. He began firing those long jumpers for which there is no defense, especially when they go in. It was a performance that made him almost as happy as Cazzie Russell, whom we had traded to the Warriors the season before in order to get Jerry Lucas.

"This game's fun for me now," said Barry. "Yes, fun. It's the first time I think I've really felt that way as a pro. I never thought I'd ever have the chance to be a complete player until now. Everywhere I played, the pressure was on me to score. Here, with Cazzie, Mullins, and Nate when he has to, I don't have to do all the scoring. Look, I only took twenty shots to-night."

I always got the impression that Rick had an extra incentive against the Knicks that dated back to the 1965 draft. I say that because Rick never hid his feelings about playing for New York and never making it. "New York is the best town of all for an ambitious sports star," said Rick, an ambitious sports star. Then, in his book *Confessions of a Basketball Gypsy,* he made this reference to the Knicks' taking Bradley: "New York picked Bill Bradley, who had won 'Player of the Year' honors. Bradley had been a great star at Princeton, even though his style of play was not suited for pro stardom, and he had won a Rhodes scholarship to Oxford and was bound for England."

I don't think Bradley ever made the Knicks sorry they drafted him. Two championships and a championship series with the Lakers in a four-year span speak for Dollar Bill and what he contributed to the team concept. Yet, Rick never let the Knicks forget and I, for one, wouldn't have minded if he hadn't been such an outstanding player and helped beat us so often.

Bradley, the shrewd politician, never responded to Barry's inuendos. Once Dollar did made an oblique reference, though. Barry had paid DeBusschere the compliment of saying Dave was the best defensive forward in the game. DeBusschere returned the compliment by saying Barry was the best offensive forward in the game. Bradley broke the tie by saying DeBusschere was the better of the two at both ends of the court.

I just don't know how Barry missed getting his career high of sixty-four points against the Knicks. I figured he'd save that for us instead of wasting it in Oakland against the Trail Blazers on March 27, 1974. Only Chamberlain and Baylor had scored more in a single game, which not only put Barry in exceptional company, but also explained what kind of shooter the Knicks and the league had to contend with through the years.

We on the Knicks always expected problems when we went to Oakland and, especially, when Barry came to the Garden. A home team is supposed to have an edge on its court but Rick seemed to think the Garden was his court. At least, he played that way.

One night he had a bad night—scored only forty-four, stuck his quick hands into our offense to steal a few passes, played a lot of forward and a little guard, and was just an awful pain in the game. He was tougher on us than he ever was and I found out why from Attles, another old friend of the Knicks since the days he grew up across the Hudson River in Newark, New Jersey. Attles explained that instead of designating a team captain as was his custom, he engaged in the more democratic process of allowing the players to choose their own leader.

They chose Barry by unanimous vote and it worked miracles on him and the Warriors. "You know how team captains are," explained Attles. "You generally designate the oldest guy, which is why, in one sense, Thurmond was our captain for so many years."

A team captain can be important if, like Willis Reed was for the Knicks, he is a leader and inspires a collective effort from everyone. Otherwise, a captain shakes hands with the officials and the other team captain, and also is the only one permitted to officially complain to the referees during times-out.

"You look at our team," said Attles, "and we have what you might say is a mish-mash. But Barry's held it together. I can't believe that anyone's playing better basketball or doing more for the team. Since he was elected captain, he's gone out of his way to help the younger players. He's been a third coach. In the past, everyone considered him a prima donna. Maybe he was self-conscious about asserting himself."

He got the Warriors off to a fast start in 1974 and they never stopped. He led the league in steals and free throws, finished second to Bob McAdoo's 34.5 scoring average with 30.6, was sixth in assists and the only one in the top ten who wasn't a guard and led his team to the championship.

He was murder against the Knicks as the Warriors beat us 3–1 in the season series. If he didn't get forty points on us, it was an off night for him. "He's the spark, he's the life of the team," said Walt Frazier after Rick got forty-four on one of his routine nights playing us. "He's a forward who's the quarter-back of the team and that's never been done before."

Nobody had to remind me what a good passing forward can mean to a team. Rick was an exceptional passer. That's why Attles slipped him into the backcourt at times when a situation demanded it. Al didn't keep Rick there too long because he knew Barry's ballhandling hurt the defensive team more up front, where forwards who can make the play are precious commodities. Attles liked to use Barry at guard in order to take advantage of his size and shooting ability, creating a mismatch where Rick could take a smaller man inside and go over him.

I liked to play Jackson on Rick because Phil had lanky arms and defensive intelligence. I couldn't do that too often because Jackson really represented the Knicks' reserve strength. However, when DeBusschere needed a rest or was in foul trouble or was gone when the 1974–75 season rolled around, Phil got the assignment. As the years went by, Phil learned to have even more respect for Barry and what he could do. There was a night when Rick hit every shot in the book—and a few that weren't. He made spinning left-hand hooks, two-hand scoops, left-handed and right-handed drives, and twenty-five-footers.

In between, Barry ran a few backdoor plays for his team-mates and, in the course of events, fouled out Jackson. "It takes great timing to run plays down to perfection like he does," Phil said of Rick, admiringly. "A ballplayer like Bob McAdoo, eventually he comes right at you. But Barry has a sixth sense or something.

"He has the ability to communicate with teammates just with his eyes. He has the ability to see how his man is playing him and when to make the right break. I overplay him to make it difficult for him to get the ball but sometimes he'll catch it and shoot in mid-air with one motion. It's pretty difficult to stop him because he can get the ball just about anytime he wants."

By now, you realize Barry was a very smart player. He knew how to set his man up and then break free for the ball. And when he got the ball, he always knew what to do with it. I can understand why some of the players who played him wanted to rap him once in a while and slow him down.

When Rick first came into the league, he'd hurt a team in spurts. He learned to hurt you throughout the game and there was no better evidence than his final championship victory in the NBA after so many years of jumping around. He had found his home, at last.

"The most rewarding thing," he said about that eventful day with the Warriors in Landover, Maryland, after wiping away the tears and victory champagne, "The happiest thing that's ever happened to me. It's everything. I only wish I was in a position to retire right now."

Four seasons later he was starting a new career in Houston with the Rockets. He had found a new home, again, at the age of thirty-four. Rick Barry, it seemed, would never get old.

ELVIN HAYES

Elvin Hayes sat in the Washington Bullets' dressing room with a prayer book at his side. His team was in the process of eliminating the defending champion Boston Celtics from the 1975 playoffs and he was telling everyone how he had become a better person and player by discovering God.

"This is the closest I've been," said Hayes as the Bullets were about to nail down a championship confrontation with the Golden State Warriors. "This is the closest I've been to maybe being even the Eastern Conference champion."

Hayes, usually a nonstop talker once started, turned himself off briefly to gather his thoughts. So much data had been fed into his computer throughout the years, he was groping for the right keys to hit. Elvin's seven turbulent years in the NBA had led many to wonder if he had gotten the nickname Big E for Effort or for Enigma.

"The struggles, the hardships," he said, thinking back to the high of being drafted number one in 1968 by the San Diego Rockets and to the many lows that followed. "The mountains, the rocks. The agony through the years."

Hayes, a sensitive young man, was destined, for some reason, to be plagued by troubles from the minute he became a

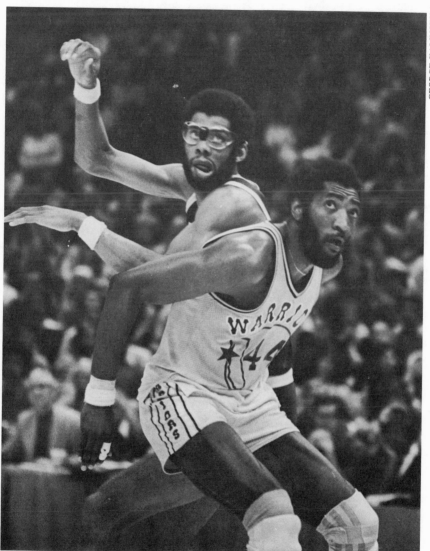

Hayes on defense against Jabbar

pro basketball player. He arrived with outstanding credentials, but the first problem, in my mind, was that he was expected to turn a San Diego franchise that was only a year old into an artistic and financial success immediately.

I guess he had only himself to blame because of what he had done against Lew Alcindor in a super UCLA-Houston game in the Astrodome that drew a record 52,693. Alcindor, of course, came into the league a year after Hayes and transformed the Milwaukee Bucks, also one year old at the time, into a playoff team right way.

That didn't happen in San Diego and Elvin was blamed for it. People said if he was such a good center, how come the Rockets struggled while the Bucks fast broke past a lot of teams on the way to the top. There was one glaring difference between Alcindor and Hayes: Lew was seven-two and a natural pro center who could turn a team into a winner by himself, whereas the Big E, at six-nine and one-half, was a natural college center but, actually, a big forward in the towering world of Russell, Chamberlain, Thurmond, Bob Lanier, and the other giants who inhabited the NBA.

It is significant that when Elvin's journey from San Diego to Houston with the Rockets finally wound up with the Bullets in Landover, Maryland, he operated as a big forward. Unseld, two inches shorter but much wider, handled the bigger and stronger specimens. That big game against Alcindor in January 1968 created the great expectation that took many years to overcome before Hayes found his niche by leading the Bullets to a championship.

You have to understand the nature of that Astrodome college spectacle and the matchup with Alcindor to appreciate the impact it had on Elvin's future. I had watched Elvin grow up in college ball. I was scouting for the Knicks when I began hearing about him. I first saw him play in 1966 and quickly realized he had one important quality every scout looks for: the ability to be the most conspicuous and productive player on the floor in almost every game.

He was a winner. Of course, there are a lot of winners in college ball who come to the pros and fail to make the transition. Sometimes they are too small. Sometimes not quick enough. Sometimes they are just over their heads when they get to the competitive level of a league that has All-America players it hasn't used up yet.

Elvin was so obviously head and shoulders above the crowd, he was no secret when he came to the Garden to play his first game in New York as a sophomore. We were in the old building on Eighth Avenue between Forty-ninth and Fiftieth streets at the time. The occasion was a regular season game between Houston and Dayton, two teams already picked to play in the 1966 NCAA tournament coming up.

Dayton was a solid team built around Donnie May, a fine-shooting small forward the Knicks were to draft two years later, and seven-foot Henry Finkel, who wound up with the Boston Celtics and a championship ring. Houston lost but Elvin was the most conspicuous and productive player on the floor. He scored twenty-two points, grabbed seventeen rebounds, and provided the strength and quickness that made him so distinctive and won so many games for Houston University, the Rockets, and the Bullets.

Finkel, a tough shooter muscling around the pivot, finished far back in all the footraces and wound up with seven points. Elvin, meanwhile, ran the Cougars from sixteen back at halftime to a near victory. He was an exceptional talent and no one appreciated it more than the New York fans, who grow up playing basketball on the streets and in the schoolyard and treat it like a second religion.

It was easy to see that Elvin had the early jitters from his first exposure to New York as well as the tradition and pressures the Garden represented. "It's a big place and we were kind of nervous," acknowledged the Big E, then twenty-one. I understood because the Garden has been kind of a second home to me as a college and pro player, scout, coach, and general manager. I think I've spent more time there than at my home in Cedarhurst, Long Island, and it still seems large and imposing to me.

On the Knicks, we're experts on Hayes because of Willis Reed, a quiet recruiter for Grambling, his old college. There were twenty-five schools chasing the Big E, a kid from Rayville, Louisiana, who had grown up idolizing Reed, a kid from

Bernice, Louisiana, who had made it big at Grambling.

"We wanted him to go to Grambling," explained Willis. "He wanted to go to Grambling and we had him over to the school a few times. But his sisters wanted him to go to Southern University in Baton Rouge. He didn't want to go there and his sisters didn't want him to go to Grambling because Southern was one of our big rivals."

Actually, two of Elvin's sisters had worked their way through Southern, which explained their loyalty to that college. The tie was broken by the coach at Texas Southern. He went to Grady Lewis, the coach at Houston, and tipped him off to a high-school kid who could be as good as Bill Russell.

Lewis wondered why the favor, and the coach told him that Texas Southern had to play both Grambling and Southern and didn't want either to get the kid. I don't know how Houston influenced him but Elvin Hayes went there and helped break the color line in what was a non-integrated sports program at the time.

By his senior year, the Alcindor-Hayes, UCLA-Houston matchup had become the Muhammad Ali-Joe Frazier series of its time. UCLA ripped Houston in the semifinals of the 1967 NCAA tournament and went on to win the title over the bodies of the dead Cougars.

Houston didn't like it. Elvin didn't like it. He had outscored Alcindor 25–19 and outrebounded him 24–20 in their personal duel but UCLA had won by fifteen, so Hayes wasn't ready to concede anything to the man he had just played. He said something about Alcindor standing around on defense and suggested that he might not be the superplayer everyone seemed to be making him.

Hayes didn't think he was doing any harm and Alcindor, apparently, didn't know about the statements or didn't care when he invited the Big E to see Louisville at night with him after the game. Alcindor had helped UCLA break open the game early by conceding Elvin his fifteen-foot jumpers while dropping back on defense to shut off the inside. I assume that's why the Big E accused Alcindor of standing around on defense and thought nothing of it when he accepted Lew's friendly gesture after the game.

"He came over and said, 'Let's go out somewhere,' so I went," said Elvin when the subject came up before their Astrodome rematch a year later. "We just walked around and looked at Louisville. We both had to be in early because we had games the next night."

They shopped the next day and toured the city again at night. They talked basketball. They were conspicuous strangers in a strange city who found a way to feel comfortable by isolating themselves one-on-one. "We talked about a lot of things and I got to know him well," explained Elvin. "One thing I learned was that whatever publicity he got didn't affect him personally because kids stopped him on the street and he'd start a conversation with them."

If publicity ever affected him, personally, Abdul-Jabbar never let anyone know it. He had a way of keeping it all inside until the accumulation became uncontrollable. Then he'd blow up, which accounts for some of the explosive incidents in which Kareem has been involved through the years. He has been known to throw a punch once in a while.

Hayes, on the other hand, never got that angry but did have a more sensitive antenna than Kareem when it came to the pressures that exist for those expected to win all the time. "I came from a small town in Louisiana and never got any publicity in high school," explained Elvin. "Lew was learning in New York and he got all the experience and publicity. When you hear about a guy but don't know him, you don't care too much if you bump him or not. But we talked and now I look at him and I'm thinking his future in basketball can be at stake on any play."

Elvin didn't say a word about how his own future was involved. There was this new respect for Alcindor the man and, therefore, the player. "Even though I scored more points than him last year, he's still the number one ballplayer in my mind," Elvin said before the matchup in the Astrodome. "Maybe thinking that way hurts me going into a game like this; I don't know. Maybe knowing him the way I do now hurts."

And so they met, again, and this time Elvin won. This time Houston, 16–0, beat UCLA, 46–0, by two points and there was euphoria in Texas. The Astrodome almost became another Unidentified Flying Object. There had been nothing personal between Hayes and Alcindor other than the personal desire to be the best and win.

They both had downplayed the individual aspects of their matchup but it was there, just as it is in every game of basketball despite the team aspects of the sport. There are battles within battles and the two best college centers in the country had just waged one and Hayes had been spectacular at both ends.

He hit seventeen baskets on thirty-two shots and twice had challenged Alcindor at the hoop and gone over him. The Big E blocked five shots, two on Lew, and grabbed fifteen rebounds. He played the closing 12:18 with four personals but never fouled out while Alcindor wound up with fifteen points in a losing game.

Later, it was revealed that Alcindor had played with a damaged eye but that didn't damage Elvin's performance. "I played him like Russell plays Chamberlain," said Hayes when it was over. "I just gave him room. When you're playing someone five and a half inches taller than you are, you just work yourself out on every jump. You go just as hard as you can."

Abdul-Jabbar wasn't very happy with the developments that night. "Elvin's hoping you and he can get together tonight, take in some parties," someone told him. "Elvin's not a real friend of mine, just an acquaintance," was the response.

It was a great night for Elvin and established him as the College Player of the Year, despite Alcindor. He had come a long way from the time the Houston coach sent an assistant to Eula Britton High in Rayville, Louisiana, to get a picture of the athlete who couldn't make his high school team as a freshman and sophomore, so he joined the band as a drum major.

Coach Lewis wanted to see what the young man whom Houston was about to use to break the color line looked like. The assistant coach asked Elvin for a picture of himself and was told: "I don't have any. I never had a picture taken in a basketball uniform."

The picture was to change, of course. Elvin's picture was to be plastered everywhere so that his chiseled features became quite familiar and recognizable. He was to eventually buy a home in the lovely San Diego suburb of La Jolla but never forgot where he came from and the struggle to overcome all the hardships in his life.

"You know," he'd tell people, "I never had shoes until I was a freshman in high school. I'd always go barefooted. I remember once I was going somewhere, to a football game, I think, and I had to borrow a pair of shoes from another boy. I was always borrowing some shoes but this kid wore 11 and I wore a 13 then. They cramped me so much, I had to walk with my heels out of them. That was the most miserable day of my life."

Once he was a stammerer, which explains, in part, why the words just pour from his mouth when he starts talking. Three times he was expelled from elementary school. He ran around with kids who also thought the world was against them, so why worry? Why go to school when the only way was down, anyway?

"My mother really pushed us," he explained, speaking of Mrs. Savannah Hayes, mother of six, whose husband had died when Elvin was in junior high. "She made fifty-seven dollars a week running boilers to keep the steam and pressure up, reading the gauges, watching them so they wouldn't get hot. She was determined that everyone of us get an education. When I was in tenth grade, my sister Christine was my teacher. She used to embarrass me making me work. I didn't want to be embarrassed, so I had to work."

He learned to appreciate those days and laugh when he recalled them. He was to become the target of a bidding war between the ABA and NBA that made him a rich man and, also, made insignificant things he had done as a youngster more significant. For example, the time he had to scrape up four dollars to buy his mother a new galvanized washbucket after ruining the old one practicing basketball.

"I took this old washbucket and hung it up against the back of our house," he explained. "I had this big, soft rubber ball. We couldn't afford a real basketball. And I'd spend all my time practicing my jump shots. The bucket had sprung a leak and my mother was going to plug it but it was too late. I had taken a hammer and a chisel and knocked out the bottom. I had to get her a new one, so I went to work cutting grass for someone. He gave me a dollar a day and it took me four days to get the money. My mother always taught me one lesson or another and none of it was bad."

There were funny things said and done once Elvin's NBA status was determined by a coin flip between San Diego and the Baltimore Bullets. The Rockets won and took Elvin, the Bullets lost and got Unseld. Not a bad losing flip when you consider that Abe Pollin, one of the nice-guy owners in the league, wound up with both of them, eventually.

It was the second year in a row that Abe's team had lost a flip and come up a winner, anyway. The year before, Detroit won and took Jimmy Walker, so the Bullets had to settle for Earl Monroe. Now there's a way to lose and enjoy it.

The ABA announced an all-out war to get Elvin for the new league, which is when things got funny as I look back at them now. There were claims by the Houston Mavericks that the NBA and the San Diego Rockets gave Hayes illegal up-front money to commit to their league. All I know is that the NBA didn't want to lose Elvin or anyone of his stature to the ABA in those days, and that was a major consideration in the Rockets' agreeing to pay him some $100,000 a year for four years.

That was a lot of money for a 1968 rookie, though Abdul-Jabbar got $1 million when he joined the NBA-ABA war the next season. The Houston Mavericks cried loud and long when they lost Elvin. "Our first offer of $500,000 for three years was just a start," they insisted. "We were prepared to pay as much as $750,000. We will pay Hayes $750,000 now, tomorrow, or next week. There is more money in the ABA than there is in the NBA."

Next, Slater Martin, the coach and general manager, had his opinion too. Slater followed me as coach of the St. Louis Hawks and was the Cal Murphy of his day on the George Mikan championship teams in Minneapolis. "Hayes made a hurried and costly decision that he may regret for some time to come," said Slater, the quickest guard in the league in his time.

I wonder if Elvin thought of that when things got rough for

him soon after the honeymoon in San Diego ended. The first time I brought the Knicks out there that season, the papers were full of stories about him. There were problems. All was not as smooth as it had looked when the Big E prepared for his first game against Seattle.

A lot was expected from him and he, apparently, expected a lot more than he found as he entered the pros as a savior for the San Diego franchise. By the time the Knicks got out there, he wasn't talking. He'd play, dress fast without showering, and rush out of the Sports Arena while his teammates still were undressing and unwinding.

There were problems with his teammates. I learned from the papers that he felt some were shutting him out from the ball and some felt he never passed when he got it. As a coach, I really didn't care what was happening with San Diego and Elvin, as long as it helped us win. I had a tough enough job figuring out how to stop Elvin from beating us with his shooting, rebounding, and shotblocking.

He was too quick and agile for anyone we had, so we had to do other things to compensate for those disadvantages. We had to deny him the ball first, force him out of his range before he got it, and then try to break up his concentration and rhythm as he shot.

Willis Reed, of course, had the strength and intelligence to do all those things with a relative degree of success. No one had total success with Elvin. Despite all his rookie problems and distractions, the Big E became the first NBA player to score one thousand points that season. There were some fine shooters and scorers around like Wilt Chamberlain and Oscar Robertson, whose nickname—the Big O—led to Hayes being called the Big E. Yet, by the time Elvin had played thirty-five games, he had 1,037 points on a 30.5 average, and was leading the league in scoring and problems.

He scored twenty-five, blocked seven shots, and hauled in fourteen rebounds in his first game against the Sonics, and San Diego figured it was on its way. I remember the first time he got his big hands on the ball against the Knicks. He grabbed it and, in almost the same motion, shot a turnaround jumper over Reed that went through without touching the net. How many hundreds or thousands of times he did that, I don't know, but no pivotman ever shot better against us. I said shot, not scored, because Elvin was an outstanding shooter no matter how much pressure we put on him.

Strangely, John Gianelli, when he was with the Knicks, was able to do a good defensive job on him. Gianelli was a natural defensive player and had the size, agility, and instinct to harass Elvin's shots. Phil Jackson also bothered the Big E at times with his long reach and general intelligence.

Elvin came into the league as a shooter and scored a lot of points but his team didn't win. People got upset at him and vice versa. He was in a revolving door in those days. So were his coaches, teammates, and everyone touched by the ongoing saga.

Jack McMahon, his first pro coach, went. Alex Hannum came and went when the Rockets pulled out of San Diego and went to Houston. Teammates came and went, as Rudy Tomjanovich and Murphy arrived in the draft. Elvin's life remained in turmoil.

He was at home in San Diego with his wife and daughter when the phone rang and a friend asked if he had heard the news. "I'm being traded," said the Big E, who had expected anything at any time. He had improved the Rockets somewhat, with 37–45, 27–55, and 40–42 seasons after they'd gone 15–67 before he joined them, but hadn't made them a winner.

He was informed that the Rockets were moving to Houston, where Elvin had created all his basketball excitement in the first place. Was he happy to be coming home again? "I'm mad, really mad," he said at the time. "I made a lot of friends out here. Things had started to open up. I bought a home. I thought I was here to stay. San Diego had become such a beautiful place. I'm going to miss it."

He went to Houston and encountered more problems. They changed coaches and the Rockets still didn't win enough, let alone a championship. You heard stories once more that he was a bad actor. He wouldn't do this, couldn't do that. And then he went to the Bullets and found a home at last.

The Bullets decided to break up an aging team that had made so many playoffs but never had gone all the way. They sent Jack Marin, the forward I remembered for all his furious battles in the playoffs with Bill Bradley of the Knicks, to Houston for the Big E.

We had beaten the Bullets in the 1972 playoffs and a few weeks later they announced the deal. They needed someone bigger, stronger, and more productive than Marin to help Unseld, and the Big E was the one.

There were no dramatic developments with the Bullets right away. They didn't win the title the next season or the next or the next. We eliminated Elvin and his new team, 4–1, on our way to the 1973 championship and did it again, in 1974, but the new Washington Bullets were on their way. The Big E was fitting in and it was just a matter of time before he'd turn the team into the big winner.

He knew it. Everyone knew it. He was happy and relaxed. I remember him coming into the Garden for the first time with the Bullets back in 1973 and noticing the difference in his attitude. There was less tension in his face and game.

"I don't have to defend myself anymore," he explained. "This is a team atmosphere here. No one is blaming me if we lose. They used to tell me to shoot the ball and, if we lost, when I came into the dressing room, they would say: 'Elvin Hayes is shooting too much.' "

He mentioned a game the Bullets had just lost in Philadelphia. He had scored only nine points but no one indicated he hadn't scored enough. No one hinted he hadn't done the job that was expected of him. Those are the things that are more likely to happen in a losing situation. For one thing, the Bullets were not losers and, for another, I guess they understood how sensitive Elvin was about anything that even suggested he was to blame for losing.

"He doesn't like criticism," said Gene Shue, who was coaching the Bullets then, "but I don't think there's any individual who likes to be blamed if he thinks he's done well. Elvin, since he's been with us, would rather come to the bench and say he did something wrong. I never knew that about him because of his reported problems and after talking to some people about him."

I really believe that Unseld had a significant influence on

Elvin. Wes was one of the most stable individuals I've ever seen in pro ball. He provided a quiet leadership money couldn't buy. It rubbed off on you if you were on the same team and that's what I think happened to Elvin.

I really believe the Big E found peace and tranquility with the Bullets because Unseld created the mood and atmosphere. Wes himself noticed the change but was too modest to mention his own influence. "As far as his being a baby and always crying, he's apparently changed," said Unseld, who, when he retires, should have a monument erected to him in Washington—or, at least, in the Hall of Fame at Springfield. "He's not losing here and that helps. There are no signs of a bad attitude. Everybody snaps once in a while but that's nothing."

Elvin noticed the change, himself, but offered different reasons for it. "When I came into this league as a rookie," he explained, "what did I know about pro basketball? If I scored thirty and we won, it would be fine and good. If we lost, they would say I couldn't do nothing but shoot the ball.

"They used to say no one could coach me. No one can win with me. When you're losing, everyone takes shots at you. It was the same for me as with Chamberlain. But now, here with the Bullets, if I have a bad game, the coach doesn't get on me and curse me out. All I'm asked to do is go out and break my back, which is what I've always done."

Basketball can be awfully tedious and demanding because there is so much money and other things at stake, but it also should be enjoyable. Winning is the best way to make it enjoyable but there are times when some people can even take the fun out of winning.

Elvin, obviously, was one athlete who spent a great portion of his career proving and finding himself. People still talk of him as a center when, in considering his impact on the game, he is a big forward. He never really belonged in the same company with Russell, Chamberlain, Abdul-Jabbar, and Bill Walton, though he played them at times and, therefore, is considered one of them by many.

Elvin changed when he went to the Bullets. He got a nice $1-million package and the opportunity to make a sharp change of direction in his life. I remember the Knicks' first playoff against him in his newest uniform. It had to be something special to him because we had our best teams in those days, but never had come up against Elvin in the playoffs when he was with San Diego or Houston.

There was one particular night—the fourth game, to be exact—when he wrecked us just about by himself. He hit ten of his first eleven shots and wound up with thirty-five points. Besides, he switched to play DeBusschere on defense because Unseld was having a difficult time and Shue decided it was time to try something else for a change.

The Big E had just beaten us to send that 1973 series back to New York but he wasn't talking about what he had done when it was over. He brushed off mention of his defense that had allowed DeBusschere two shots in the first twenty minutes. He was concerned only with a story he didn't like.

It was about Unseld, who, supposedly, was chewed out by the coach and blamed for the Bullets' having lost the first three games to the Knicks. Elvin was furious. "That's a lot of BS," said the Big E, fuming that Unseld, of all people, could be blamed for losing any game.

Things surely had changed. Now the blame was on someone else's head but Elvin still didn't like it. I found it interesting reading but nothing else. I was more interested in the "stat" sheet that night, especially the one at halftime that showed Frazier, our high scorer, with eight points, Bradley next with six, Monroe five, Reed three, and DeBusschere with two. Some offense.

We eliminated Hayes and the Bullets in the next game and he had to wait five more years before the Great Expectation of 1968 was fulfilled. Before that, there was one more important series with the Knicks. It was in 1974 and Hayes came awfully close. A seventh game in New York, that we won because Elvin played tired, shot only five for fifteen and let Gianelli grab eleven offensive rebounds.

"I'm only human," he told those who pushed around him to hear if he had anything new to offer about losing in the playoffs. "I played eighty-two games this season and seven playoff games. If you base what I did on one game, then you're a hypocrite."

He played almost the entire game and series without taking a rest. I know. I kept looking for substitutions to tire him. I used everyone on the bench but me and Danny Whalen, our trainer, but Elvin still averaged 28.2 points, 16.3 rebounds, intimidated our shooters on defense, and only sat for seven minutes in the first six games.

He had earned the right to be tired in the seventh game. Let's put it another way: thank goodness he *got* tired. I know the Knicks were grateful; otherwise they wouldn't have had the opportunity to go on to the next round, where we lost to the Celtics on their way to their first championship without Bill Russell.

"He was tired the whole game," Gianelli said in our dressing room. "He didn't have his jumping ability and his quickness wasn't there. He wasn't as offensive-minded tonight."

Elvin always played on momentum and he just ran out of it that night. We started every game with the idea of not letting him get off well. The more he missed early, the more he kept missing. He was so finely tuned and wound up, it didn't take much to throw off his timing. At least, that's what we thought, though it didn't always work that way.

"He had to be tired because he played almost every minute in every game," said Frazier. "It's funny. You don't think you're tired, yet you just don't do the things you normally do. The mind is willing but the body isn't. Too many minutes caught up with him. Also the pressure. He hasn't been through a seventh playoff game before. That gets you tired. We've been through it before."

But there was to be another seventh game in the playoffs for the Big E. It came in the 1978 championship series with Seattle, and Elvin was to play only thirty minutes in the deciding game because he fouled out. But he won. Elvin finally won, and Unseld finally won. It was the first championship ring for both.

They did it the hard way, too. They spotted the Sonics a 3–2 lead going back home to Seattle. The Bullets wiped out the homecourt advantage with a thirty-five-point win that was the widest gap in playoff history, then went home to clinch it. No longer did Hayes need to worry about being considered a loser.

In his own quiet, or unquiet way, Elvin Hayes made his impact on the sport as a dominating big forward who played like a very tall center when necessary.

DAVE COWENS

Whenever Dave Cowens is mentioned, the same picture of him comes to mind. I see Cowens, a rookie for the Celtics in 1970, playing his first game against the Knicks. He is chasing after one of our players on a breakaway and getting him from behind to spoil a basket. With the Celtics down by twelve points with about a minute to go, Walt Frazier has flipped a breaking pass to one of our guys who was way out ahead of the field. But Cowens, never giving up despite the game being long gone, chases and manages to get there in time to block the layup.

I hadn't known too much about Cowens when he was playing his college ball at Florida State because I was the coach and general manager of the Knicks at the time. Dick McGuire was our scout and he had come back and said Cowens was a very intense ballplayer who was exceptionally quick for his size. He could run and jump and had remarkable basketball intelligence on defense because he was so quick and alert against the ball.

"If there is one thing missing," McGuire had said at the time, "it was outside shooting. If he is going to play as a power-forward in the NBA, he has to learn to shoot better from out-

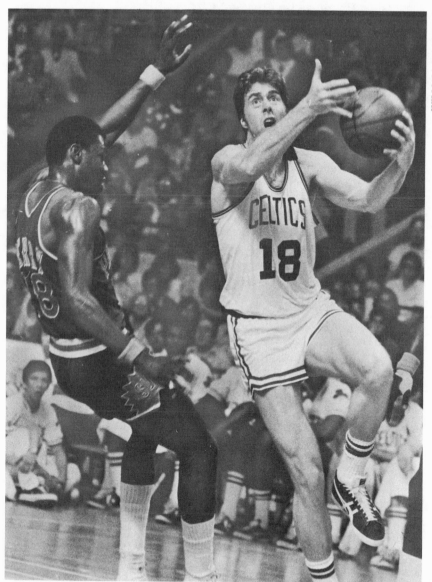

Cowens goes to the basket past Curtis Perry of Phoenix.

side. His range isn't that good."

On the other hand, the Celtics' scout, Mal Graham, raved about Cowens, and told Heinsohn, the coach of the Celtics, that Cowens could probably play center in the NBA. Although Heinsohn wasn't entirely convinced, he still felt that Cowens was the man he wanted no matter what.

It proved to be a nervous draft for Heinsohn, because the Celtics were picking fourth. In the first round, Detroit took Lanier, then San Diego chose Rudy Tomjanovich. Remarkably, the Celtics were home because Atlanta, picking next, had switched spots with San Francisco by giving the Warriors the NBA rights to Zelmo Beaty, who had gone to play in the ABA. They had done this in order to be in a position to get Pete Maravich.

Most people aren't aware of the luck inherent in the draft system that can make or break a team. The Celtics probably never would have gotten Cowens if not for some strange bounces, especially where San Diego was concerned. Bob Lanier, of course, was going to be the number one pick no matter what, despite the fact that he had to have a knee operation for torn cartilage soon after he played his final game for St. Bonaventure.

The critical thing that eventually landed Cowens in Boston, where he helped the Celtics win two titles in three seasons ('74 and '76), was the decision on Maravich. The Rockets, who would eventually move to Houston, had to turn him down because they felt Pistol Pete's money demands would be too hard on their bank account. At the time there was no major pro basketball excitement in San Diego, as it was the first time around for the city. So the Rockets decided to make Tomjanovich the number two pick of the draft. That clinched Cowens for Boston because Atlanta already had made the deal with the Warriors sending Maravich to the Hawks. So the Celtics had a man they imagined playing as a big forward opposite Havlicek. But they soon changed their minds.

Cowens, of course, had been a center in college but was considered too small to compete in the pros against Wilt Chamberlain, Nate Thurmond, Walt Bellamy, Kareem Abdul-Jabbar, and all the other towering centers of the time. In his first game against the Knicks, an exhibition in Utica in 1979, Heinsohn was still playing him at forward. The Celtics didn't think he was tall enough to play center, but that first night, he climbed all over us for twenty-three rebounds, while Dave DeBusschere played him, which told us something about Cowens' future in the NBA. DeBusschere, one of the better defensive rebounders, was certainly tops at boxing his man out. Yet Cowens had beaten him twenty-three times. Four seasons later, the league would see young Dave Cowens help make the Celtics a championship team.

"He is big, strong, and runs well," said DeBusschere after the game. "He really hits the boards. He's quick too." In fact, it had been noticeable right from the start, when Heinsohn brought Cowens to Boston after the draft of 1970. Although Mal Graham, the scout, had raved about Cowens' speed and endurance, Heinsohn was not entirely convinced he was tall enough to play center in the NBA.

Heinsohn tested Cowens for the first time in some three-on-three Summer scrimmages with the help of Don Nelson and Satch Sanders, both of whom were still playing. "We've got a horse," said Satch, who, incidentally, was later succeeded as coach of the Celtics by Cowens himself.

It is interesting to note that the Celtics started the 1970–71 season with Garfield Smith at center and seven-foot Henry Finkel as backup. What seemed to convince Heinsohn that Cowens was big enough to compete in the battle of the boards against the giants in the league was what happened on his own team. Cowens was strong enough to yank the ball away from Smith off the boards, so it was only about two or three games into the regular season that the critical switch was made.

Cowens left power-forward to play center. He gave away a lot of height at the position but compensated for it with his intensity, strength, jumping ability, and overall basketball intelligence. He was to make it big as a small center, surprising a lot of people. But the Knicks knew better. We had established a pretty good record with small centers. Willis Reed, in effect, was the first small center to have a major impact on the game. We won two championships with the six-nine Reed and it might've been more if not for the games he missed with bad knees that eventually forced him to retire long before his time.

Jerry Lucas was another relatively small man who was a great center for the Knicks. Lucas was six-eight and always played the big forward in Cincinnati and San Francisco after being traded there. But to me, his best position was as a small center. He was an outstanding defensive rebounder against any bigger man; he could make the play, which is rare from the center position; he was smart enough to compensate for his lack of size on defense against the Chamberlains and Abdul-Jabbars, and he had the great outside shot that brought the big goaltenders away from the boards and opened it up for the other players.

The Knicks actually traded Cazzie Russell to the Warriors because I felt Lucas was the perfect insurance at center for Reed's knee problems. We had to have someone who fit into our style of play because Reed's injuries often made him unavailable. We were lucky to have Lucas in 1971–72 because Willis played only eleven games that season. We still went to the final and lost to the Lakers, but even so, few appreciated what Lucas, the small center, meant to the Knicks in those days. It was Cowens, however, who came on to further establish a place for the small center in the NBA. Along with Reed and Lucas, he made it clear that size is not the only requirement for the man in the middle.

It was a case of almost instant success for Cowens, if not for the Celtics. His intensity and desire to win made an immediate impact on the game. There were times I thought Boston had five players named Cowens on defense as I watched him jump at our guards, zip to the corners, and then get back to the middle in time to protect that area.

Cowens became the new Bill Russell in Boston. He had only that one serious shooting problem McGuire had mentioned in his scouting report: he was hesitant about taking the outside shot. He was perpetual motion like Havlicek, he was a defensive dynamo, he was a strong leaper under the boards, but he had this shooting weakness. Teams spotted it and soon dropped off and gave him the outside.

That didn't last long. Heinsohn finally got the message home one day. He told Cowens what everyone was doing and how it was hurting the team. "You've got to take them," Heinsohn said, referring to the outside shots. Cowens was apprehensive about taking them because he was afraid he'd miss. "But I can't hit 'em," Cowens replied. "Take 'em and miss 'em," said Heinsohn. "The more you miss now, the more you'll make later."

Cowens listened and performed. He developed good range. Not as deep as Lucas or as accurate as Reed, who was outstanding with jumpers inside twenty feet, but good enough to take advantage when the defense gave him room. Cowens became a shooter and a scorer, not only turning the Celtics into a championship team, but also rounding out his own dimensions as one of the game's finest small centers.

"I was very conscious of the sizes of other centers when I first played against them in this league," he said. "But it seems to me that now they've become very conscious of my speed." Again, I think of that speed and the night he actually spotted Frazier a half-dozen steps in a playoff game and caught Clyde before he reached the basket.

Cowens really began to throw his strength around in the 1973 playoffs against the Knicks. That was the series when Havlicek hurt his shoulder during our fourth-game double-overtime victory, although we still had to go seven games to win the final one in Boston. I have an extremely vivid recollection of Cowens' fifth-game performance at a time when the Celtics had to win to keep their hopes alive.

We had just taken a 3–1 lead in the Garden before we lost the fifth game by a point in Boston, primarily because of Cowens' intense desire to win. We might have ended it that night if Cowens hadn't caught Frazier from behind on that one sure basket. In addition to his defensive feats, Cowens scored thirty-two points and sixteen rebounds, although we used Reed, Lucas, and John Gianelli against him. He jumped all over our forwards and guards; he fired the outlet passes that triggered Boston's fast break; and he worked out of the pivot and moved outside to open things up when we tried to jam the middle. Finally, when it came down to our last attempt to win, he had his hand waving furiously in Reed's face to harass the final jump shot that missed. There was no denying how much Cowens had grown with the Celtics. The statistics proved he had become even more valuable to the Celtics than Havlicek.

By the end of that fifth game, Cowens had played more minutes than any man on either team, grabbed the most rebounds, hit the most baskets, scored more points than anyone other than Frazier, and was the single most dominating force in the series. "Right now, he's relentless," said DeBusschere after the game. "He was good his first two years. He was great this year. What will he be like in two more years? I wouldn't want to be on the floor with him whenever it is he reaches his peak."

There was one time when Cowens drove through the middle and Phil Jackson stepped in his way in an attempt to draw a charging foul. Jackson not only got a blocking foul but almost wound up impaled on Cowens' knee. "I thought I was hit by a runaway freight train," said Jackson. Cowens was fast and relentless that night, and although we tried everything possible, he was too much. Generally we gave him the outside shot to keep him from muscling inside, but that night he was hitting them. We talked constantly of boxing Cowens off the boards, but that didn't work either. He played every minute, of every game as if it were the championship, and he would have no consolation other than victory.

Such determination is what made him Dave Cowens. One night, he played forty minutes against the Knicks, got only eleven rebounds and brooded about it after the game. "That's not good enough to win," he observed. "I just wasn't rebounding effectively tonight. I was okay on the defensive end but I didn't do enough on the offensive end."

He was the type who got wound up over every game and could hardly talk about it when it was over. He would sit in the trainer's room in Boston or find a quiet place in the visitors' dressing room on the road to sip Nutrament and calm his nervous stomach. Since he no doubt upset his opponents' stomachs, it was only fair that he feel the heartburn himself.

He came to the Celtics when they desperately needed something to reestablish their glory. Havlicek was the only true remnant of the Russell era that had produced all those championships, and Hondo soon recognized that Cowens might be the answer to the decadence that had set in. Havlicek was the dean and Cowens respected him for what he represented and what he still was capable of doing.

One night, referee Richie Powers hit Cowens with a fifty-dollar technical for "an overt gesture." Cowens was upset. "You have to live with such things. You got to bite your tongue," Havlicek advised his young teammate. "It's not that easy," said Cowens. "Dave, you've got many years ahead of you. Wait till you get to be an old geezer and then you'll understand," said Havlicek. "What's a geezer?" asked Cowens. "When you're a geezer, you'll value fifty dollars more and you won't get technicals," said Havlicek, who finally revealed why he never got technicals.

I used to get tired just watching Havlicek run so much. Now I was getting twice as tired watching Cowens run with him. If I felt that way, how about the players who had to play Cowens? Lucas, for example. They were just about the same size but Lucas needed a rest once in a while. Cowens could run through daylight into darkness and then back to daylight again.

Lucas had just gone through one of those nights with Cowens, when he had run faster and longer than he was used to. This time, Cowens had caught Dean Meminger and Frazier from behind with his uncanny speed and determination, jumped at the forwards in the corner, and then came out once to force Frazier to pump a hurried twenty-footer over him.

Now, although Lucas was always in good playing shape, Cowens sent him to the bench a few times a little tired. "I can't recall anyone his size that active," said Lucas. "Not at the pace he goes. Russell would rest but Cowens is running on every play. He's all over the place."

Sometimes in the early stages of his playing days with the Celtics, he would forget he was a center and wander outside. I remember our playoff series with the Celtics in 1972 when it happened in the first two games and Cowens had to be reminded he no longer was a power forward. Of course, we didn't mind, and the Celtics forgave him, too, because the Knicks were in championship form at the time and Cowens, still young in the league, was in his first playoffs. Naturally we were much happier to see Cowens roaming around outside rather than forcing inside, where we would have had to contend with his offensive rebounding. Besides, when he worked inside, he opened things up and that we didn't want. But Heinsohn was excited. "I want him to play like a center," he said. "I don't want him to play like a forward."

So Cowens went inside and outside and helped beat us in the third game of that series. He hit ten of his eighteen shots and I really couldn't tell if he shot as a forward or center. It was the only game the Celtics took from us in the series but we knew Cowens, co-Rookie of the Year with Portland's Geoff Petrie the previous season, had to be undisputed Sophomore of the Year for 1971–72.

By the end of his second year, Cowens had more than lived up to Boston's expectations. He had rekindled the fans' interest in the Celtics because he was playing just like Heinsohn had said he would right after he was drafted: "He's a big mobile kid who showed well on the boards in college. He's got Irish red hair and I hope he plays that way."

That was the perfect description of Cowens' game—fiery red. He had the built-in attitude a coach would love to be able to teach. He became a threat to the Knicks and, therefore, was booed sometimes by New York fans who didn't like the idea of him beating us. Yet, it never affected his intensity, no matter the score or the attitude of the crowd.

One time in the Garden, we were actually ahead of the Celtics, 94–61, and he was out there still diving for loose balls and chasing breakaways. He actually picked up a fifth personal trying to stop a fast-break basket though the Celtics were over thirty points behind.

Nothing changed by the time Cowens began his third NBA season and was on his way to being named MVP. His intense desire to win was matched only by his dread of losing. You could feel the heat that burned just below the surface of his skin. "He's an animal," Frazier said. "If he goes wild, look out."

Fortunately, Cowens took it out on a basketball most of the time. It was the perfect release for the hostility and anger that motivated much of his game. He had one of those frustrating nights against us one time when we ended a Celtics eight-game winning streak. They were leading the Eastern Division at that time, which was late in the 1972–73 season.

Cowens was angry most of the game and our players knew it. "He was so bugged, you could see the heat rising in him and his neck getting redder than his hair," said DeBusschere. Of course, there were times when it all boiled over and Cowens got into a few heavyweight matches. But such times were rare when you consider his intensity and the nature of the game he played.

As time went on, the Celtic way became the Cowens way. Reed had been the first to open the eyes of the pro world to the fact that small centers could do it. After Reed first called attention to the issue, Cowens helped change the thinking and then added the exclamation point.

"What he can do is so evident and yet everybody was laughing at us for playing him at center," Heinsohn said in Boston. "He's a dynamic player and he's added a new dimension to the position. People have never seen the position played that way. He takes a rebound on one end and then takes a pass at the other end for a basket after a fast break."

It was that speed that made the difference. Cowens was exceptionally fast for a man his size, or any size, for that matter, which explained why he was able to catch so many players on breakaways. "I can run a hundred yards with anyone in this league, so I use my speed," he explained.

One night in Boston, we had to play a tired Reed forty-four minutes against Cowens because Lucas was home with the flu. Willis was worn out, having just come off a season of tendinitis in one knee. It was back in December 1972 when the Celtics were in championship form and getting stronger. In fact, they won for the twenty-eighth time in thirty-three games that night and went from there to a 68–14 season finish, Boston's best season record. Cowens hit seventeen of his twenty-seven shots and played with the kind of sustained fury that was to become his trademark. Under the circumstances, it was an outstanding contribution by Reed, who never once asked to be taken out despite the pressure on him.

I couldn't afford to remove Reed for any long stretch because the game was close until the final minutes. Willis always wanted to be on the floor in all the important minutes of a game, and what coach wouldn't have it that way? Reed gave out as much as he took but he never worked harder than he did that night and he never got more weary.

Cowens was capable of doing that to anyone on any night. "Sure I got tired," said Willis. "Cowens was just brilliant. He's the perfect center for the running Boston offense. He's not a dominant center like Wilt Chamberlain, Kareem Abdul-Jabbar, or Nate Thurmond but he fits this particular Boston team better than Bill Russell did. He does everything, including score."

One of Cowens' most admirable traits was that he wasn't concerned how the Celtics won as long as they won. That explained why, after a playoff game with Buffalo, he said: "I was glad Bob McAdoo scored fifty-two points as long as we won."

Enthusiasm was something he never had to work at. He was born with it and it showed in every game. He was hard to discourage and, most times, all you could do was keep the pressure on and just hope you could knock his fine-tuning off. One night I used four different centers against him: Reed, Lucas, Gianelli, and Jackson. Result of game: Boston 113, New York 88.

So much for strategy, especially when a Cowens is involved. It's hard to devise a plan to defeat someone who won't stand still long enough to let it work. Cowens' game was motion and speed and his motivation was basic: "You see," he once said, "the only thing that really matters to me is to play on a winning team and the only way to play on a winning team is to play for a team that wins a championship."

He got his first championship when the Celtics beat the Bucks in seven games in 1974. His shooting had become so proficient that in 1973, Boston swept all four games from the Lakers during the regular season because Wilt Chamberlain stayed in close on defense to protect the middle and let Cowens shoot from outside. "I spent a whole summer shooting baskets, until my arm ached," explained Cowens, just in case some didn't know he had improved his shooting. He practiced ten-foot hooks from the pivot, swinging to the baseline for under-hand layups, and twenty-footers from the outside.

That was Cowens. He was good but had to be better. Not for himself but to help the Celtics win. He never appeared to be someone who cared to analyze his game. He just played as hard as he could and with intense desire. "All I know is, the enthusiasm is something that I never had to work at," he explained.

He only lost it once, and that was after the Celtics had beaten the Bucks for the 1974 title and the Suns for the 1976 championship. On November 10, 1976, Cowens, then twenty-eight and eight games into his seventh season, suddenly decided he didn't want to play anymore. He just walked out on a $250,000 salary not long after he had been delighted with his second championship ring.

It came as a shock to me because Cowens was the last player I figured would walk away from the sport unless he was sure he no longer had it. Winning is fun and I assumed he had been having fun as the Celtics won, primarily because of him. It was a strange development. I figured Cowens had to be un-happy about a few things to leave a championship team at the start of a season, but I had no idea what those things were.

All kinds of explanations were offered. He was simply ex-hausted from basketball, having gone from the sixth and de-ciding championship game with the Suns right to a summer full of basketball camps. Some of his best Celtic friends were gone: Finkel, Nelson, Paul Westphal, Don Chaney, and Paul Silas. The eternal flame had finally burned down.

"He's just tired of basketball; it's as simple as that," ex-plained Nelson, one of Cowens' closest friends, who was to become coach in Milwaukee. "I don't feel like a superstar; I just feel like a normal person who quit his job, that's all," said Cowens.

While the pro basketball world waited and wondered, Cow-ens took a job around the horses he loved. He was hired as assistant general manager for the New England harness track in Foxboro, Massachusetts, and settled down into what he in-dicated would be a new career. It was hard for me to believe that a young man of his playing talent had decided to end it all with so much still ahead for him in the sport.

His retirement came at a time when the Celtics had made some moves to get new parts. They didn't want the team falling apart again, as it had when Russell and Sam Jones departed in the same season. Cowens left with Boston at 4–4 and two months later returned to Boston Garden.

It was Homecoming Night and 15,040 were on hand to see Cowens' comeback against Bill Walton and Portland. The fire was there but not the miracle. "Intensity, it's what my game's all about," he said after twenty-one minutes of playing time had satisfied Celtics fans that the raging fire was back. But there were no miracles. Cowens didn't turn things around. The Celtics were in one of those deteriorating stages that often creeps up on teams in the NBA.

It wasn't easy to regain the playing touch. Nor was he the panacea for all the team's problems. "This is like pre-season all over again for me," he said. "Even if you stay in shape like I did, you still have to get into game condition. I was ready to play the game with my usual intensity but the situation became too heavy."

With Cowens back, the Celtics went on to finish second in the Atlantic Division with 44–38 but were beaten by the 76ers in the opening round of the playoffs, 4–3. Things got worse the next season when Boston dropped to 32–50, its worst record ever, and didn't make the playoffs. What's more, Havlicek, the old dependable who had bridged the gap between two championship periods in Boston, decided not to run again.

Havlicek's departure came at the wrong time for Cowens and the Celtics. It put additional stress on the ability of Cowens to motivate himself night in and night out for a team that was on the verge of disaster once more. He had helped bring back the glory days of Bill Russell and now Cowens faced the problem of doing it once more.

It had to be exhausting for Cowens to even think about turning on the intensity every night under the circumstances, a demand which had contributed to his early retirement in the first place. His game was obviously suffering as the Celtics lost their winning touch and winning players.

Cowens had been the Celtics' heart and Havlicek the soul. Now Cowens was alone and so were the Celtics. They couldn't motivate him and he couldn't motivate himself. I think the critical moment came when Boston played the Knicks in the Garden early in the 1978–79 season and Cowens got only one rebound.

"We need his intensity all the time," said Auerbach, so he named Cowens player-coach. Now, in my mind, that's an impossible job for anyone. It worked for Russell because he had players still good enough to win championships. The Celtics felt they had nothing to lose trying it again, because Cowens was losing his motivation and they weren't going to win without him.

Russell had won two titles as player-coach. The Celtics figured lightning might strike again and Cowens was enthusiastic about the move. "If they're gonna change coaches," said Cowens, who replaced Sanders after a 2–12 start, "I'd rather be playing for Cowens because I know Cowens."

Boston got the old Celtic pride back from Cowens but that wasn't the solution to the problem. Cowens was able to motivate himself; he came back jumping, running, and driving to win. But it didn't work out. He was indeed the motivator but he didn't have the players to win.

It wasn't long before Cowens probably began thinking about going back to the cab he once drove to ease his tensions. He spent seventeen dollars for a three-year hack license, thirty-five dollars to rent the cab, and eight dollars for gasoline, and surprised a few passengers around Boston. "I've ridden in a lot of cabs and I wanted to see what it would be like to drive one," he explained. "I made a few bucks."

One of Cowens' early games as player-coach was against the Knicks and he did a terrible thing; he beat us. I had just returned to coaching the team and we had won our first five games when we went to Boston.

I can't tell you much about Cowens the coach, but Cowens the player looked better than ever. He kept himself in the game for forty-six minutes, which, come to think of it, was pretty smart coaching. He seemed highly motivated to me, although I couldn't ever remember seeing him otherwise against the Knicks.

"Look, Dave isn't really doing a lot of coaching," said Jo-Jo White, revealing a team secret. "The move was made to give him something to work himself up for every night. It's no fun going out there and losing every night after all these years. Now he has more incentive. And now we can relax and play ball."

The wild look had returned to Cowens' eyes. He was motivated once more but a coach needs more than just himself to win. The Celtics finished the season last, with a 29–53 record. Russell had been able to succeed as player-coach because he had had Havlicek, Sam Jones, Larry Siegfried, Don Nelson, Tom Sanders, Bailey Howell, and Wayne Embry to help him win the NBA title in 1968 and in 1969.

So Cowens' tenure as a coach lasted only one season but his tenure as a player was long and distinguished. I used to enjoy his physical combats with Reed because they were two of the finest competitors I've ever seen, and perfect examples of winning players. The greater the heat, the more they wanted to be in the kitchen.

Cowens, like Willis, taught me how Abdul-Jabbar should be played. They both played him the same way. Since they didn't have the size, they had to use their strength and their brains. They worked on not letting Kareem take any shot he wanted. On the skyhook, for example, all Cowens could do once Kareem got the ball was to force him a foot or two beyond the shooting range he wanted. Anything to break up Kareem's rhythm and get him out of the groove.

It was always a pleasure to see Cowens play Bill Walton. A matchup in intelligence if not in size, Cowens used the main weapon available to him to compensate for the height advantage Walton had on him: speed. If you watched Cowens closely when he played Walton, he'd run Bill all over the place. Up the court, down the court. On the move constantly because it seemed to be the only way to keep Walton from controlling the game himself.

Other than size, there are five ways I judge a center: defense, rebounding, passing, scoring, and running. Cowens had them all, which is what they'll always remember about him when they talk about the outstanding centers in the game. That and his intensity will get Dave Cowens his rightful place in the Hall of Fame.

JULIUS ERVING

Someone once said that there were three pro basketball leagues operating at the same time: the National Basketball Association, the American Basketball Association, and Julius Erving.

Dr. J was a league unto himself as he performed first for the Virginia Squires and then the New York Nets. His brand of magic had its roots at Roosevelt High out in Long Island, grew in Harlem's Rucker League and the University of Massachusetts, and travelled throughout the land once he decided to turn pro.

He created the attention that the ABA needed to survive in its struggle to gain equal footing with the NBA. I wouldn't go so far as to say the ABA wouldn't have made it without Erving, but he very nearly pumped enough air into it to keep it afloat.

He was a happening in the ABA. Where teams were averaging 1,500 people, 5,000 would show up to see him play. Where the average was 5,000, there would be 8,000. Where there might be 12,000, such as in Denver, one of the solid franchises, there would be 15,000 when he brought his magic show to town.

I could relate to what the ABA was going through in those

arry Bird of the Celtics tries to contain Dr. J.

days. It was the same when I first became a pro player in the National Basketball League. That was a struggle in small gyms, in front of small crowds, for small money. Then the BAA came along and the National League merged with it. We still played in small places, except for New York, Boston, and Philadelphia, in front of small crowds, for small money.

We, in the NBA, had our Julius Erving in Elgin Baylor, eventually. Baylor was the first to come along with that uncanny body and hand control that enabled him to twist through the defense and put the ball in the basket from crazy angles. Baylor was marvelous, the best of his time, and considered by many who played against him and watched him maybe the best of all time.

Erving, I must say, has a chance to be better. Dr. J is quicker than Baylor and jumps higher. All that remains is for Erving to perform as well and as long as Baylor did, which was from 1958–72, when he had to quit after playing only nine games and wasn't in uniform when the Lakers finally won the 1972 championship.

Baylor never did play on a championship team. Dr. J did it twice in the ABA and came close soon after the Nets traded him to the Philadelphia 76ers. But no one would ever consider Dr. J or Baylor losers just because they failed to win a championship right away. One doesn't measure the talent of an Erving in that way. Instead, let me recall that first exhibition game we played against the Nets in October of 1973.

We had just won our second championship. Erving had just signed an eight-year contract calling for an estimated $2.5-million with the Nets, and was coming home from Virginia and a brief stay with the Atlanta Hawks of the NBA after a court battle for his services. More about that later.

It was the ideal setting for the first meeting between the two New York teams from different leagues. Merger was nowhere in sight at the time but the two managements got together and concluded it would be good business to give New York fans a chance to see Dr. J, the returning hero from the Long Island neighborhood, against the champions of the other league.

They were right. There were 17,226 for the first game in the Garden and a 15,800 sellout the next night in the Nassau Coliseum. Generally speaking, I'm so involved with my players and watching the flow of our defense and offense, I rarely recall the specifics of any one play by the other team. That's why I always used game films a few hours before we played a team to get a fresh reminder as to who did what to whom.

But on this first night of the Nets and Dr. J against the Knicks, I do remember one particular play. There were about thirty seconds to go and the Nets had the game locked up when Walt Frazier bobbled the ball near midcourt. Dr. J scooped it up and there was a roar, though the Nets were safely in front by eight.

I had seen Dr. J's routine, as he slammed in twenty-five points with an assortment of drives and slam-dunks. The crowd roar got louder as he broke for the hoop and one more basket. Everyone in the Garden knew what was coming but Erving can be full of surprises. He streaked for the front of the hoop, turned slightly to his left as he started his leap and flipped the ball through with a reverse dunk.

It was as though Picasso had just inscribed his name on a finished painting. Pure Julius Erving. A team and a coach trailing hopelessly with no time left might resent the little flourish under other circumstances. We knew Erving hadn't meant to rub it in. It was simply instinct on his part, so we didn't mind.

"Nothing is premeditated," explained Erving. "Ninety percent of the things I do, I've done before, either in a regular game or in some playground. The other one percent . . . well, I even surprise myself. That last shot, even if it was the beginning of the game, I'd have done it."

Our defense for Erving wasn't bad at all as long as Dave DeBusschere was available to play him. DeBusschere was our troubleshooter against all power forwards. He was so good, no one had to tell him how to play a man. He knew when to stay close or give up the outside and how to use his strong body and good hands.

The trouble was DeBusschere got kicked in the thigh when we were ahead, 35–28, and never returned to the game. DeBusschere may have been the finest defensive forward of all time. The Knicks used him to harass and slow down forwards sometimes four inches taller and once in a while on some centers in an emergency. He meant so much to our team style, we just weren't as efficient when he wasn't playing.

Dave had watched Erving play for the Nets on television a few times and it took him only a few minutes to adjust when they met. "You don't want him to get the ball off the break," explained DeBusschere. "His speed, jumping ability, body control in the air, and ball control make him nearly impossible to stop. If he gets the ball on the run in an open field, you're in trouble."

We geared our defense for Erving because we knew the Nets went to him most of the time. He was their offense. That changed when he got to the 76ers, where they had George McGinnis and Doug Collins, who were pretty good scorers, so he had to share the ball more.

We had an advantage over Erving and the Nets because we were a championship team that had played defense together for so long. DeBusschere knew he would get help on Dr. J if he needed it—and against a one-on-one artist such as Dr. J, there were times he needed it. But, in the long run, our team defense always followed the same basic concepts and made the Knicks more prepared for all the Ervings they met.

We worked on defense all the time and everyone understood what had to be done whenever we faced someone of Erving's unique ability. "The rule the Knicks follow on defense is: 'See the ball' and we hear it from the bench as a constant reminder," said DeBusschere when asked how to play Dr. J. "The trick is to sort of split your vision between the man you're guarding, no matter where he is on the floor, and the ball. That way you can see the ball all the time and deprive him of it better because you know when it's coming. I try to screen off my man, block off the pass routes to him. Like against Dr. J and the Nets, you want to cut off the outlet pass to him."

That's the way DeBusschere played Erving until Dave left the Knicks to become general manager of the Nets for the 1974–75 season. Dave's philisophical approach to Dr. J was the same the Knicks had for all the super scorers: "I went into a game against Erving or any star forward who averaged twenty-five points a game thinking he probably is going to get his twenty-five on me, no matter what. What I wanted to do by using my body, my hands, and my arms was to make sure that, if my man makes his twenty-five most nights by taking eighteen shots from the floor, against me he was going to have to take thirty. I'd make him work harder and create as many forced shots as I could."

From the beginning, Erving had two claims to fame. He was the man the Nets went to at the end of a close game when they needed a three-point basket; and he was the man with the contract entanglements in two different leagues.

It all started when Erving, a junior, decided he wanted to see more of life than playing ball in the solitary confinement of New England. He wanted to play pro ball but there was a rule in both the ABA and NBA against it at the time. Neither league was permitted to draft a player whose class had not been graduated.

Erving's agent first approached the Nets, who were coached by Lou Carnesecca at the time. Dr. J wanted to play near his Long Island home but Carnesecca turned him down because of the league rule. However, Erving found a new home and a sympathetic ear when Earl Foreman, owner of the Virginia Squires of the ABA, decided to risk signing him.

Foreman won, the Nets lost by playing the game within the rules, and the ABA gained the one player who was to mean so much to the new league. The NBA was well aware of Erving, though I don't believe anyone really knew he was such an exceptional pro talent. No one had considered drafting him because of the rule.

The Erving experience led to the installation of the hardship draft in the NBA and enabled it to compete with the ABA for undergrad players. Erving was an instant sensation in Virginia but regretted not having landed in New York. That changed once he was in the league. The Nets became interested in Erving and eventually got him after some rather wild bidding and strange bounces.

Milwaukee had gained the NBA rights to Erving but the Atlanta Hawks decided to sign him while a legal hassle was going on over his Virginia contract. The Hawks actually used Dr. J in two exhibition games for which the late Commissioner Walter Kennedy fined them $50,000 for defying league rules.

Money was flying around as though it were going out of style. It made me dizzy to read about it. Erving was contesting a Virginia contract that had three more years to run at $150,-000 per season, the Hawks gave him a $250,000 non-returnable bonus to sign a five-year contract worth $1.3 million, and the Nets finally got him with a $1.9 million deal: over seven years.

Roy Boe, who ran the Nets for a syndicate, insisted the deal was the richest contract in sports history. I don't know about that but the details sure sounded rich to me. "The contract calls for salaries which escalate from a base of $185,000 in the first year to $275,000 in the last year, plus the right to receive incentive bonuses which could reach $60,000," explained Boe. "Julius also was given a $300,000 cash bonus on signing, $200,-000 in deferred payment and substantial throw-ins, such as a ten-year, $100,000 interest-free loan, payment toward his living quarters, and a new car every two years."

And to think I signed my first pro contract with the Rochester Royals for the stunning sum of $400 a month in 1945. Erving's 1973 deal with the Nets was a lot of money for its time but then in 1979 along came a young basketball demon named David Thompson to get, so they say, $800,000 a year from Denver. And then there was Pete Maravich and his $650,000 from Atlanta and so on ad infinitum.

Erving had accomplished exactly what he had in mind when he decided to leave the University of Massachusetts and college ball. "I've done everything I can do playing where I am," he had said. "I can always go back to college but now what I want to do is make money." He made money like he made baskets—by the basketful.

He came to the Nets when that franchise had a new building and needed his gate appeal and excitement. The Nets had to pay Atlanta and Virginia a combined $1.5 million to obtain Erving with all legal releases. Yet, they considered it money well spent when Dr. J's name began popping up in conversations about the country's top players.

Dr. J became synonymous with the best in pro basketball at a time when most people were more aware of NBA players and, according to greater attendance, much more interested in them than in ABA players. Dr. J was a name every basketball fan got to know soon. It was a nickname picked up in high school that was was to become as identifiable as the Big O.

"A friend in high school kept telling me he was going to be a professor, so I told him I was going to be a doctor and we started calling each other that," Erving explained one August day in 1972 while playing summer ball in the Rucker League. "Everybody had a nickname for me here in the Rucker League. They called me Houdini and Black Moses. I told them if they were going to call me anything, call me Doctor. That was my nickname."

A nickname helps if you can play and Dr. J certainly could play. He became the Nets franchise as soon as they signed him for the 1973–74 season. He was a legend in the neighborhoods that reached out beyond the Nassau Coliseum. He had grown up as one of the schoolyard kids and still was one of them when he returned as a star to play in his backyard.

He still wandered over to the playground near his Roosevelt, Long Island, home where he had grown up to scrimmage with youngsters. "I played one-on-one, two-on-two, three-on-three," recalled the young, new millionaire. "Sometimes on Sunday, kids from other towns would come over and we played five-on-five all day. The years I was in college, I ran the league in the park. I had the keys then. I turned the lights off when I left, sometimes around midnight. I worked on shooting and dribbling. If somebody else was around, I'd play one-on-one, a hundred points win. We didn't play for money. We just played for ego, for pride."

The Nets cashed in on that pride and effort right away. Erving became the dominating force of the team that went on to win the title in his first year. Every game seemed to produce more Ervingisms than the last one. People came to see what surgery Dr. J would perform on his next patient.

For example, Dan Issel of the Kentucky Colonels came to the Nassau Coliseum for an early meeting with Erving, the new Net. They were the two best-scoring forwards in the league and the Nets and Colonels were the two best teams. The Nets won the game by one point in an exciting finish but all they remembered was what Erving had done.

Dr. J got thirty points in all, sixteen in the final "magic show" period, when he owned the ball because it was a close game. In the first period, a Kentucky player drove for a sure layup only to have Erving come from out of nowhere to deflect the shot, control it in mid-air and bang it out of bounds off the shooter's leg. Dr. J then broke downcourt on the pass-in by the Nets and converted a pass into a slam-dunk.

Dr. J became notorious for such things. The Knicks once owned New York all by themselves but Erving soon claimed a large following for himself and the Nets. He played the game for love and money. "I love the game," he said when someone inquired about all the money involvements. "I love to play. I'd play for nothing if everybody else did. But when in Rome, live as the Romans do."

He learned to live well. He bought a big home. He got married and drove fancy cars. He kept winning for the Nets and doing exceptional things that had NBA fans, true to the more established league in their own fashion, wondering if Erving really was as good as or better than Baylor, Bob Pettit, Tommy Heinsohn, Rick Barry, and other power forwards.

One night as a rookie in Norfolk, he tossed in fifty-three points for Virginia against the Nets, leaving him fourteen short of the league record with 1:14 to go. Al Bianchi, coach of the Squires, was asked if he was going to let Julius go for the record. "That's eleven more points in seventy-four seconds," said Bianchi, a former playmaking and shooting guard for Syracuse and Philadelphia in the NBA. "Who do you think he is. . . . Superman?"

There were people in the ABA in those days who thought Erving was more Superman than Clark Kent. And for good reason. He was the ABA's leading scorer, near the top in steals and blocked shots, and not far from the lead in rebounds and assists. I wasn't there to see him because I was busy trying to get the Knicks into the playoffs but I never stopped hearing Julius Erving stories.

One night in Lexington, he scored forty-one against the Colonels as the Nets won, 114–112, getting eleven of his team's thirteen points in overtime. The next night he got forty-one again, against the Indiana Pacers. In the Lexington game, the Nets called time thirteen seconds from the end of overtime with the score tied.

Kevin Loughery, the coach, set up the final play for Erving, naturally. "Everybody clear out and let Doc go one-on-one," Loughery told his players. "Just let Doc go one-on-one." That was money in the bank.

Erving worked the clock and then maneuvered for a fifteen-foot jumper that went in at the buzzer. "That's the part of the game I really loved as a kid," he explained. "That challenge of daring to be great. If you rise to the challenge and are successful, it gives your confidence a definite reinforcement. As a pro, most of my moves are impulsive, instinctive. I can do the things I do because I put in time experimenting with them. I know what I should do in certain situations and that's what I do. It doesn't require thinking about them. It's a court awareness of knowing what the situation is and what it calls for. But you can't be inhibited. I'd hate to be in a position where I had to play like that."

In another game against the Colonels, the good Doctor had a statistic line that looked like this: forty-five minutes, twelve-for-twenty-four field goals, eighteen-for-eighteen from the foul line, eighteen rebounds, ten assists, and forty-two points. "That's one of the best lines you'll ever see," said Rod Thorn, then Loughery's assistant with the Nets who later became general manager of the Chicago Bulls.

Erving did consistently better against the teams in the ABA because he had more freedom there. He was the super scorer in the new league and the Nets went to him whether they needed the points or not. "I don't know if he'll ever have an average game," said Hubie Brown, who coached the Colonels before moving over to the Atlanta Hawks in the NBA just before the merger. "He's just a great player. I mention that every time he plays us."

They still talk about Erving's worst night. It came against the Colonels in Louisville just before the 1976 playoffs that were to be the ABA's last. He went forty-six minutes without a field goal. He got only two baskets on eleven shots but made them both in the final two minutes when the Nets rallied to within two after being down by twenty-three. "I guess," said Artis Gilmore, the Kentucky center, "it shows that he's human just like the rest of us."

There are nights like that. I remember a time when DeBusschere, a good shooter, took nine shots and missed them all. On the other hand, there was the time DeBusschere stayed out all night before the 1967 All-Star game in San Francisco, when he was playing for Detroit, and he hit his first ten shots. Go figure that out.

Although Loughery used Erving principally as his power forward he also played him at center and in the backcourt because he could jump and handle the ball so well. He was the perfect example of how much the game had changed since I played. Erving, David Thompson, Elvin Hayes, Larry Bird, Magic Johnson, and the leapers of the past ten years or so play the game above the hoop. When I played, we were smaller and slam-dunking was for the privileged tall centers like George Mikan, Clyde Lovellette, and Charlie Share. We were lucky to reach the hoop.

That's what made Erving's flying moves to the basket so distinctive. He always played the game over the hoop. He'd take off and stay up so long, sailing to the basket, there were times they could've called a three-seconds-in-the-air violation on him.

To watch him was not to believe. He'd wrap his unusually large hands around the ball and slam it through like a baseball. As I've said, pro basketball people had seen the slam-dunk before, but not the way Erving did it. Besides, he won games because he was such a fine player and not just some freak out of a neighborhood schoolyard.

People with hard-line positions on outstanding players of our time began changing their minds. Adolph Rupp was one. Rupp's college teams at Kentucky University were legendary. He had developed many of the best players and had seen the best through all the years that led up to his joining the Board of Directors of the Kentucky Colonels, who played some home games on the University campus.

Rupp always considered Jerry West and Oscar Robertson one-two until he saw Erving play. He saw Dr. J do a few things in a couple of games against the Colonels that changed his mind. In the final game of the 1974 regular season, with first place on the line, Erving hit a three-pointer at the buzzer to send the game into overtime. Then he scored eleven of the Nets' thirteen points to win it and finish with forty-one.

Then there was a playoff game between the two teams a few weeks later. This time the score was tied when the Nets passed the ball in to Erving in front court. There were seventeen seconds on the clock and Dr. J dribbled for thirteen, then made his move for the winning basket.

"I think right now that Julius Erving is the best," said Rupp. "West proved over a long period of time that he was the best as far as I'm concerned and I want to see what this guy does over the next seven or eight years."

Rupp, seventy-two at the time, didn't live long enough to see it all but what he did see convinced him that Erving was ranked right at the top of the backboard with the best of them. "He's a young man with supreme confidence," said the man they called the Baron. "Some of the best players I've ever had didn't want to take the last shot. He's a Babe Ruth. Ruth pointed out to the stands where he was going to hit a home run and he hit it there. Julius is the same way. Everyone in the house knows he's going to take the last shot and he still makes them. He wants to do it because he knows how to do it."

I can't explain why but there are players who want the last shot and get upset when they don't get the ball, and others who never want it. West, of course, thrived on clutch shooting. Tommy Heinsohn was good at it, so were John Havlicek and Sam Jones of the Celtics. Earl Monroe, too.

I think one of the things that made our championship teams of 1970 and 1973 so good was that everyone on the floor was not afraid to take the last shot. That was what made our offense so effective in tight games. We'd move the ball to the open man without fear that he couldn't make the pressure shot. We'd set up a last-second play but Willis Reed, Bill Bradley, Walt Frazier, Dick Barnett, DeBusschere, or Monroe were all capable of hitting the winner. It's tougher for an Erving, of course, when he is the one taking the last shot all the time and everyone knows it. It's easier to adjust a defense under those conditions, which is what made Erving, West, et al clutch-shooters in the first place.

In those days, the Colonels-Nets rivalry was just about the most heated in the ABA. Erving did all the things to Kentucky that he did to the other teams but the stature of the rivalry made the Colonels experts on the subject.

"When you think about Julius Erving, you're thinking of a third-year pro who never played his senior year in college," said Kentucky coach Babe McCarthy at the time of his team's 1974 playoff defeat by the Nets. "To me, he's got more ability than any player I've ever seen. He does everything with the least effort. When he makes those fantastic shots, it's not a showboat thing. That's just part of him and part of his greatness."

Erving was only twenty-four when he began to look for more playing room. Although it never affected his attitude it had to bother him playing before smaller crowds in the ABA while the NBA players were getting all the attention from the public and network television.

He never made it a secret that he liked the bigger and better money that was being distributed in the NBA. He became a valuable piece of merchandise in the total market and, eventually, that and a series of circumstances led to his leaving the Nets for Philadelphia and the 76ers. His last hurrah before the ABA merged with the NBA for the 1976–77 season was to stage one of his finest Magic Shows in the final championship game with the Denver Nuggets.

I think that game really told us in the NBA what Julius Erving was all about because we hadn't seen him play that much. It was game six before a 15,934 sellout madhouse in the Nassau Coliseum and the Nets came from twenty-two behind in the third period to win by six and take the title, 4–2.

Julius scored thirty-one, grabbed nineteen rebounds, and had five assists. But he showed what kind of total player he was by by working at forward, guard, and center. Every time Loughery was in manpower trouble, he'd move Dr. J around. Denver was a tough team with David Thompson, Dan Issel (who had come over from Kentucky), Bobby Jones, and a young seven-foot center named Marvin Webster, who wound up with the Knicks a few years later.

It was Erving who triggered the comeback with thirteen points in the final five minutes of the third period. Julius earned the car as MVP of the playoffs and it gave Loughery the opportunity to expand on what had, by then, become his favorite subject: Julius Erving.

"There are very few guys who can play all three positions," said Loughery, who developed into one of the finest coaches in the game. "DeBusschere has done it. He played center a few times with the Knicks and, when he was with the Pistons early in his career, he played guard. Havlicek would be too small for center and Spencer Haywood would have trouble at guard.

"Not many players are equipped to play all three positions but Erving is. If we used him at guard, he'd be an All-Star. At center, his size hurts him but he's a leaper." By the time the merger came around, Erving had done enough on a basketball court to convince the older heads in the NBA he was a most unusual piece of merchandise.

The Knicks had played him enough to have a good, experienced viewpoint. The only player we had who did a respectable job on Erving was DeBusschere, and we had some respectable team defensive players in those days. John Gianelli, for instance. He learned only after Julius had swooshed around him a few times with that effective head and body feint, followed by that long, quick first step.

"I played him wrong," admitted Gianelli after a bad experience. "He beat me a few times because I played him too close. That's not the way DeBusschere does it. Dave keeps him from getting the ball. He's more physical than I am. He knows all the tricks. Dave puts the strong arm of the law on him."

Erving became the highest-priced art treasure in the history of basketball when he was traded by the Nets to the 76ers for $6.5 million. That took place after the merger, when Julius asked the Nets to renegotiate his contract and pay him by NBA superstar standards.

Roy Boe apparently decided he couldn't afford that on top of the estimated $4 million his franchise had to pay in merger indemnities. So Erving went to Philadelphia for $3 million and Eugene Dixon, who had just purchased the 76ers from Irv

Kosloff, agreed to pay Julius another $3.5 million for five years.

I remember when you could buy an entire NBA franchise for a lot less than $6.5 million, which is why, I assume, some people referred to Erving as a franchise. I know the Knicks wanted him when the Nets decided to offer him to a waiting market. The Knicks were on line but the Nets, apparently, wanted more money from New York than from any other city.

"Other teams were offering $3 million but we were told the Knicks would have to pay $4 million," said Mike Burke, president of the Knicks. We dropped out, which was too bad. As a coach, I would prefer to have had Erving playing for the Knicks than against us.

Erving would have answered a lot of our problems at power forward but I learned long ago not to worry about things you can't control. So on October 22, 1976, Dr. J strolled into his new dressing room at the Spectrum in Philadelphia to walk across water in an NBA game for the first time.

"I feel like a stranger," he said as reporters and television crews crowded around him. "I was asking people where to go when I walked in tonight."

He walked into a new situation. He no longer had to do it all by himself. There was more support because of George McGinnis, Doug Collins, Fred Carter, and Caldwell Jones, a big center who had played in the ABA against Erving. It was an unforgettable evening that became forgettable when the 76ers, now expected to be a championship force, lost the game to San Antonio.

Julius got a standing ovation when he entered six minutes before the end of the first half. He was a little shaky. He threw a crosscourt pass that was stolen, missed a driving hook, committed a backcourt foul, and missed four straight free throws.

It wasn't exactly the expected contribution to this night in history but Erving promised he wouldn't miss eight of thirteen free throws again. "Things fell out and that never happened before," he said, "but we accomplished something. You could see moments when the team looked super. The potential is there."

The NBA was excited. The whole city of Philadelphia was

excited. Erving had to stand a full two minutes when first introduced and then waved a doctor's bag he had just been given to acknowledge the fans' greeting. "That ovation was probably the greatest ovation I've ever received," he said. "I figured I should wave the bag until they quieted down."

Erving played nineteen minutes and got seventeen of his nineteen points in the second half. "Well, I guess we won't go undefeated now," said Shue, his response to the assumption that Erving or any one player can make a team unbeatable. "That was really a touching thing—a really touching thing," said McGinnis, referring to Erving's reception. McGinnis had been the big man with the 76ers after he left Indiana of the ABA before the merger. But now he was moving over for Dr. J as gracefully as possible.

Everyone seemed to concede the 76ers the title now that they had both Erving and McGinnis. That's why we play all eighty-two games, I guess. I haven't seen anyone, from the best to the worst team, ever concede anything in all the years I've been associated with pro ball. You had to play to win it.

Erving was thirty games into his first season with the 76ers when he returned to the Nassau Coliseum in his new uniform. Only half the place was filled and there was a mixed reaction from the people who felt deprived when their main interest in the world of pro basketball left. Dr. J seemed to take all the excitement with him.

There were banners: "We Still Love You Julius" and "Julius Erving is Okay Even Though He Went Away" and "Come Back Doc" but basketball no longer was the same out in Long Island after Erving departed for Philadelphia.

The Nets, of course, left for a new home in New Jersey, while the 76ers went in search of the Holy Grail, the NBA title. "You're never going to see Dr. J again, that's over," predicted McGinnis, suggesting the 76ers were too strong to rely on Erving alone. "Julius is a very good basketball player and he just might be playing for an NBA title team this year."

Portland beat the 76ers in six games for the title in the 1976–77 season. The 76ers shipped McGinnis to Denver for Bobby Jones to get more defense and team balance after the champion Washington Bullets eliminated them in the Eastern final of the 1978 playoffs.

No reflection on Erving and his unusual ability. A truly unusual talent. I can't remember any other time that network television cancelled a game because one player couldn't make it. Erving was holding out when the Nets were supposed to open the 1976–77 TV season against the Oakland Warriors.

"We had scheduled the game to show the national audience Julius Erving in action," said Barry Frank of CBS. "Without Julius, we felt the game did not have quite the same interest."

That just about says it best where Julius Erving, basketball player unusual, is concerned.

KAREEM ABDUL-JABBAR

Early in 1965, the NBA owners gathered in Boston for some secret business. The results of the meeting leaked out early in June and had a major influence on the destiny of the Knicks and, no doubt, many other teams.

Coming out of Michigan University in one more year would be Cazzie Russell, an exciting player the Detroit Pistons felt could provide immediate stimulus to their interests. Heading for UCLA as a freshman was Lew Alcindor, a player from the streets of New York who the Knicks were certain would help them and the league most by wearing their uniform.

So they gathered in the Celtics' territory to determine if there should be some emergency changes in the draft rules to accommodate Detroit and New York. And the arguments started. Fred Zollner, owner of the Pistons, put his best foot forward this way while trying for special dispensation to make the popular Cazzie Russell a Detroit property: "If we get Cazzie, and we get stronger, we will draw more money when we come to play on your court."

Ned Irish, speaking for the Knicks, had a more basic reason for acquiring the rights to Alcindor, who hadn't yet played a college game. Irish suggested that the young center from

Power Memorial Academy in Manhattan would fit best in the city where he had grown up to be seven-one or better.

Actually, they were arguing on the same side but there was a small difference in methods. Zollner was in favor of reapplying the college territorial rule that had just been terminated in the 1965 draft when Bill Bradley of the Knicks and Gail Goodrich of the Lakers had become the last picks under the rule. Irish wanted to resurrect the High School Territorial Rule that had enabled Wilt Chamberlain to return to Philadelphia as a pro after his college days at Kansas University.

And so they argued. And, as things often happen when so many divergent viewpoints and interests get together in one room, there were some strange developments. Detroit and New York tried and failed to get the owners to consider a package vote on Alcindor and Russell and the issue was taken up on specifics.

Amid the infighting, a bit of comical confusion developed. First, the East was against helping the Knicks, and the West, following similar partisan lines, didn't want to help the Pistons at its own expense. Thus, two owners who voted yes for Detroit to get Russell, voted no for the Knicks to get Alcindor.

In the final vote, it was 5–3 against both teams and both ideas. And one of those voting against Detroit was New York. Yes, the Knicks. Why? Well, for some reason, the Pistons had finally decided to vote against the entire idea of territorial picks and rely on an attempt to get Russell under special dispensation. So Irish decided that if the Pistons were not on the Knicks' side, the Knicks weren't on the Pistons' side.

Very serious business at the time but humorous when you look back at it. Just think what might've been if New York and Detroit had succeeded. The face of the league would have been changed. Kareem Abdul-Jabbar would have become a Knick for 1969–70, the season we won our first NBA title. And Cazzie Russell would have been in a Detroit uniform for the 1966–67 season, which is when the Knicks got him after beating the Pistons in a coin toss for the right to pick first in that draft.

I don't know what might've, could've, or would've been if the Knicks had Abdul-Jabbar through the years. I do know he was

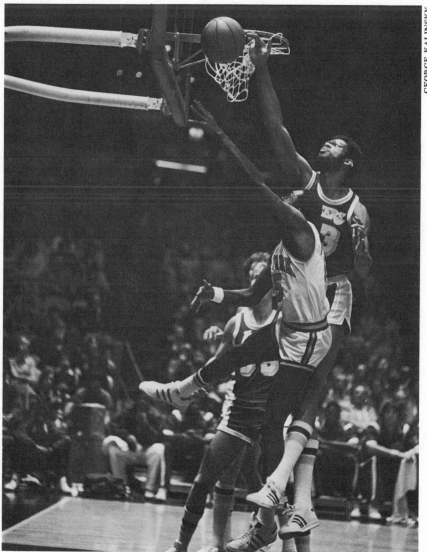

Jabbar blocks a shot by Earl Monroe of the Knicks.

destined from the start to move alongside Bill Russell, Wilt Chamberlain, Willis Reed, George Mikan, and Bill Walton as the NBA centers who have had the greatest impact on the game. From the first moment I heard about him and saw him as a high-school player, I knew Kareem was going to have a major influence on the league someday.

There were others who shared that opinion and a few who suggested it might be wise to wait and see if Kareem, a tall, skinny kid, would be physically strong enough to handle the contact in the pros. He had become a landmark in New York City by the time he reached eighteen. He was called Lew or Lewie in those days and attracted so much attention, that his coach, Jack Donohue, who later went on to coach at Holy Cross, built a wall around him.

Donohue figured Kareem needed protection from all the coaches, scouts, and people wanting to talk to him. It's not easy for a teenager to handle the pressure and the telephone calls coming in, sometimes very late at night, from hundreds of college people interested in him. Kareem was known from coast to coast and it was difficult for a seven-footer to hide, anyway.

"People stop me on the street. They yell out of cabs and mail trucks and they ask me which college I'm picking," Kareem explained one day. "One guy jumped out of a bar to ask me on my way to school this morning. I tell them all that I just don't know."

At first the attention pleased Kareem. He felt like something special. That was when he first started playing basketball with the kids in the neighborhood, grammar school, and finally high school. People kept telling him to play because he was so tall, so he did. "I was about eight, and I was in the fourth grade at grammar school and was about five feet tall, when they began telling me," he recalled. "It really began paying off for me when I was thirteen. I was six-seven then."

He was, also, at thirteen on his way to Power Memorial on a scholarship. He didn't realize what was on the way. He never expected the radical change in his life—when at fifteen, he became a seven-footer. "It changed," he said. "I never could be me. I lost my privacy."

Kareem always seemed to be a very private person to me. In all the years he has been in the league, few words have been exchanged between us. But he had my respect. He had a certain quiet dignity that I liked. Not once in all the years of losing important games to the Knicks and listening to his hometown New York fans boo him, did I know him to complain. Not once did I hear him alibi.

I wasn't surprised because of some of the things I had heard about him before he came into the league. Some of the things that his mother and his high-school coach said about him provided an insight into the kind of player and person he would become in the pros.

Kareem's mother and father, Lewis Alcindor, Sr., didn't want their son to go so far away as UCLA but yielded because of his special qualities. "Lew won his first trophy in baseball," explained Mrs. Alcindor. "He was twelve and playing center field and pitching in the little league.

"He was a quiet boy. Good, studious, considerate. He used to rollerskate a lot, he liked to swim and he was a good marble shooter as a boy. He liked steak but not potatoes and was a big milk drinker."

Then there was Donohue, the high-school coach. "There are none better to coach," he told people. "Not only as a player but as a person. I have a rule on my team. A player who scores a basket has to thank the man who threw him the pass.

"Lewie picked that up right away. He scored so much, playing in the middle and us looking for him all the time, but he never failed to let the feeder know he was appreciated. More importantly, when a play didn't work, he took the blame even though it wasn't his fault. If the pass was bad or got away, he'd say: 'My fault.' He knew it wasn't but it made him feel better. It was important to him."

Kareem's emergence as a teenage basketball celebrity reminded me of Wilt Chamberlain. The same thing had happened to Wilt ten years before, when Wilt was a seven-foot phenom at Overbrook High School in Philadelphia. Chamberlain was moved to compare himself with Kareem since he, too, had to fight off all the colleges who wanted him to pursue his education with them.

Chamberlain was in the best position to make comparisons. "Lew chose the peaceful way," he pointed out. "He was sheltered. The pressures were kept away. I went more for the hard knocks. I got around more, did more, and saw more of life. No one shielded me. It's impossible to say which way is better. What works for one won't necessarily work for another. End results count. If Lew Alcindor is a success, at whatever he does, his way was obviously right for him. The same with me."

They hounded Wilt in his junior year and never stopped. He said: "Seventy-seven major colleges contacted me by my count and about 125 minor ones. They wrote and called and came to my house. For two years, they gave me no rest. There was pressure and confusion. They scarcely gave me a chance to make a choice."

Kareem went to Wilt in his own high-school days to get some first-hand impressions of what it was all about. "I never tried to persuade him about a college or anything else," Wilt explained. "I just told him what it had been like for me and let him take it from there. As for playing comparisons, I utilized physical attributes more . . . height, speed, strength. Lew has physical advantages, too. But he also uses his head more. The game has advanced in the last ten years, so he has, too."

Chamberlain and Abdul-Jabbar were on a collision course and they knew it. By the time Kareem entered the NBA, he found Russell gone, so Wilt was considered the supreme test for the young Wonder Man from UCLA, out of New York. In the early days, when Kareem was in high school and stargazing, Wilt would take him to the Maurice Stokes Game at Kutsher's Country Club in Monticello, New York, and even play one-on-one with him.

It was at a time when Kareem was in awe of Wilt. I assume Kareem was well aware of Chamberlain's all-around athletic gifts and respected him more because of them. I know this: everywhere Kareem went as a member of the UCLA team, and with every championship they won, people talked about the days when he would be a pro.

I remember the time he came to New York with UCLA when he was a senior to play in the 1968 Holiday Festival. It was a rare opportunity for Garden fans to see him since he had left to play college ball in the Far West. The Garden was filled with scouts, former players, and many others anxious to appraise Kareem as a future pro.

I wasn't there because I was on the road with the Knicks but Eddie Donovan gave me a report. Providence, Princeton, and St. John's weren't exactly the Celtics, Lakers, or Knicks, of course. "I want to see him tested," suggested Adolph Schayes, one of the all-time great forwards who then was supervisor of NBA officials. "Right now, he's playing against the boys. I want to see him against the men."

Schayes was speaking from experience. He had come into the league a mild, rather passive All-America at New York University and soon felt the physical force of the pros. He soon learned the hard facts of life under Al Cervi, a coach who believed that the shortest distance between two points was through someone's body, Pro basketball was a contact sport and no place, especially for the mastodons, to exist strictly on finesse.

It wasn't long before Schayes became one of the most respected power forwards in the league. He thrived where others of ability failed because the heart wasn't there to handle the punishment. I went through it as a player, though I must say, thankfully, that smaller players such as myself took a little less punishment than the bigger ones.

Kareem had to live in the world of heavyweights, where they really don't accept how good you are until they see how you react to a good shot on the jaw. In the push and shove of the high school and college world, Kareem had done well. Exceptionally well. No one questioned his supremacy at those levels. The pros simply ask for just a little more.

What Donovan told me wasn't critical but sort of an X-ray of Kareem's situation at the time. "He won't be able to overpower the Chamberlains, Russells, Thurmonds, Bellamys, or Reeds," said Donovan, who was to leave his job as Knicks' general manager soon after Kareem joined the league and then return to New York after establishing a franchise in Buffalo. "Here, he's doing only what coach John Wooden wants him to do. In the league, he'll have to contend with the physical matchups. Lew's stronger now than he was a year ago and more active but, with us, there's a war going on underneath when the shot goes up. He's never been in that kind of war."

Pro people talk that way about college players all the time. It makes no difference how good the player is and how effective he was in college. The yardstick is the pros. That's how you tell if they can stand the contact and the punishment. That's one of the things I always looked for in a player when I was scouting. I knew the NBA could be responsible for cruel and unusual punishment and players had to be equipped to handle it.

"It's one thing to be pushed but it's another thing not to be able to push back," Kareem would say, suggesting he'd pick up a foul when he shoved. "That shackles me. I get annoyed sometimes. I try not to get mad. You get mad, it can affect your game."

Donohue used to mention how Kareem once came to him during a time-out and complained that the other team was deliberately stepping on his toes. Kareem, a kid then, learned how to deal with that his own way. War teaches you how to defend yourself and the real war began for Kareem the first time he played against Chamberlain.

It was at the Stokes Game the summer of 1969—a game that didn't mean a thing other than for those interested in seeing how Chamberlain reacted to Abdul-Jabbar and vice versa. Before then, there had been quite a skirmish between the ABA and the NBA for Kareem's services. Kareem had given each league the opportunity to make one offer to him. He'd go to the highest bidder between the New York franchise of the ABA and the Milwaukee franchise of the NBA.

The ABA had steered Abdul-Jabbar to New York, figuring that's where he would prefer to play in that league. In our league, the Bucks had won a coin toss with Phoenix and made Kareem the first pick in the 1969 draft. I was in Phoenix with the Knicks at the time the Suns lost the toss and a chance to win the championship sooner.

It had been done in a three-way telephone hookup with Commissioner Walter Kennedy flipping a half-dollar in his New York office. Phoenix called heads and it came up tails. "It was very, very quiet in our office but you could hear the Milwaukee guys going crazy over the phone," said coach John Kerr, who was in the Phoenix office with general manager Jerry Colangelo. "It was so quiet in our office, I could hear Jerry's heart stop. It was very depressing. It was the closest I've ever been to the loser of a million dollars."

Bad enough. But when Kerr got home, his eight-year-old son, Matt, playing basketball in the driveway, greeted him with: "Hey, Dad. You blew the flip, didn't ya?" There was joy in Milwaukee, though, and the Bucks were prepared to spend plenty. The franchise was only a year old and here was a chance for instant success. Kareem, as I understand it, was ready to come home and play for the Nets, though they were playing out in Commack, Long Island, and didn't have their new home at the Nassau Coliseum until a few years later.

Arthur Brown, owner of the Nets, offered Kareem $1,000,000 in the presence of ABA Commissioner George Mikan. Wes Pavalon, on the other hand, representing the stockholders of the Bucks, came in with a bid estimated between $1,400,000 and $1,700,000, depending on how an option to buy shares in the public corporation was evaluated.

The ABA tried for a second shot by boosting its bid but was turned down. "If they had made it on Tuesday, they would have won and Lew would've played for the Nets," said Sam Gilbert, a real-estate man from Los Angeles who represented Kareem and many other UCLA players. "Lew didn't want to be demeaned for flesh-peddling, that's why he came up with one bid and will honor it. He is a boy of tremendous integrity. His stature is much taller than any building we have."

Then came the night in the Sports Academy gym at Kutsher's when Kareem and Wilt came face to face at the start of the Stokes Game. Kareem gave Wilt a head fake to the right, broke past him to the left, and slam-dunked his first basket. That had followed a Wilt move in which he had whirled around Kareem in the pivot and powered in for a stuff-shot of his own.

They each had six baskets that night but Kareem blocked three shots and the pros were satisfied he would answer back. He hadn't played a real game yet but the tough critics of the

NBA were impressed. "It's tough enough that he's seven feet," observed Ray Scott, a physical forward with the Bullets at the time, "but to get beaten by his quickness, that's something else."

Chamberlain was MVP of the game but Abdul-Jabbar was the conversation piece. "The man is good, that's all there is to it," said Wilt. "Wilt's hundred-point scoring record may go this season," suggested Walt Frazier, not knowing that Kareem was too team-oriented and unpretentious to consider anything like that. "Lew's a good foul shooter and that will help him. He looked great. He followed up good off the boards. He's nonchalant and cool. He doesn't get excited. He seemed like a real pro."

He sure was. He didn't know everything but you could see Kareem was more than capable of playing with the big boys. "He's got a few things to learn but he's great," said Red Auerbach, who coached the winning East team that included Kareem and Willis Reed. "Once he let Zelmo Beaty lock his arms on a rebound and that could cost a game but he's quick and he knows what he's doing out there."

Kareem was satisfied, in his own quiet way. He realized it was only an exhibition game that didn't really count but he had played against Wilt and proved himself, especially when he drove around him for his slam-dunk. "I kind of surprised myself on that one," said Kareem. "It seems Wilt always was doing that when I was a boy and you don't expect to play him like that. He told me it was a nice shot."

The thing that always impressed me about Kareem was his low-key reaction to life. He handled everything with exceptional poise. I remember the time the Knicks went to Milwaukee for a game and how he played despite a threat to his life. That's when some members of his Hanafi Muslim cult were murdered in his Washington home. He didn't go into hiding. He played, though it was strange to see all those security people hanging around the Milwaukee bench and following him everywhere.

Then there was the 1971 night in the Garden, soon after he had announced that he was now Kareem Abdul-Jabbar and no longer Lew Alcindor. During the course of the game, John

Condon, who handles the microphone for Knick games in the Garden, announced: "Basket by Jabbar." A little later, after Kareem had left the game and was coming back, he softly said to Condon: "Would you please refer to me as Abdul-Jabbar and not just Jabbar from now on?"

Kareem was an unusual young man and player. Milwaukee fans realized it right away. There were 10,482 jammed into Milwaukee Arena on June 24, 1969 just to watch the rookie scrimmage shortly after he'd signed. He scored thirty-five points and got a standing ovation from the newest fans in the league.

"Lew's a smart ballplayer," said coach Larry Costello, a smart player from a different era when he was firing two-hand set shots for Syracuse and Philadelphia. "He knows when to conserve himself. He gets the ball out there for the fast break, then he watches how it develops. If the guards hold up, he comes up to join the attack. If the fast break goes, what's the use of him rushing up just in time to run back to the other end?"

Bill Russell did that and was a master at pacing himself. Wilt did it. Kareem had to do it because he was another forty-eight-minute player and had to save his strength and stamina in some way. That was his style and the young Milwaukee Bucks were happy to have it on their side.

"One of our problems was that when we got the ball, everyone would rush up the court and no one would be back on defense," said assistant coach Tom Nissalke, who was to leave the Bucks in 1971 and go on to bigger and better things in the ABA and NBA. "You've got to like the way he plays safety, too —the way he just waits there when they come in on him and makes them make the first move."

Kareem finally met up with Wilt in a real game out in Los Angeles on October 24, 1969 and it was a California Mexican standoff. Wilt got twenty-five points and twenty-five rebounds, Kareem managed twenty-three points and twenty rebounds. Most importantly, Kareem wasn't muscled out of the Forum.

In fact, Wilt was the one who mentioned the contact between them. "I thought he was more physical against me than I was against him," said Wilt. "He's very strong, very quick, and moves very well without the ball. I don't really think he surprised me at all."

Chamberlain, Jerry West, and Elgin Baylor won the game, 123–112, but the Los Angeles fans, who watched Kareem in his college days and predicted the pros would never stop him, were convinced they were right. I wasn't surprised the way Kareem reacted, either. I knew he was a basketball intellect and would adjust to anything he hadn't experienced before.

Wilt had a tough time blocking shots at first because Kareem was just as tall but soon he stopped a couple. So Kareem began faking the hook shot. He showed it to Wilt, then spun the other way for a layup. Kareem was on his way and Milwaukee was to finally accomplish what a lot of NBA teams haven't done yet—it won a championship before Abdul-Jabbar left to return to Los Angeles.

Kareem had come a long way in such a short time in the pros. I often thought of some things that had been said about him as he moved through college ball with the greatest of ease. He was so far above the crowd when he was playing at UCLA, it really was difficult to get an exact reading on him.

For example, Rudy LaRusso, who had played his college ball at Dartmouth—not exactly a basketball factory—knew all about NBA muscle. He had fought his way through the pros with Los Angeles and San Francisco for years and knew what it took. "Nate, Wilt, and Russ," said Rudy, referring to Thurmond, Chamberlain, and Russell, the dominating centers of the time, "might not eat him up, but they'd certainly have good nights against him."

Partly true. Russell never got the chance, of course, but Chamberlain and Thurmond had their good nights against Abdul-Jabbar, just as he had his good nights against them. "I haven't seen anyone in college ball who can play one-on-one with him at all," said Wooden, his coach at UCLA. "For pro ball, he can be the best potentially. I don't say he is. Right now, he's not mature enough and strong enough physically to come into the league and play on an even basis. He could play and help a lot of teams but not on the basis of a Chamberlain, Russell, or Thurmond."

But Kareem did, on the basis of Kareem Abdul-Jabbar. He

adjusted to the pro game quicker than anyone I've ever seen other than Russell and Chamberlain. I guess something Bob Cousy once said should've tipped everyone as to Kareem's aptitude and unique qualities.

"He'll have to get used to being belted and bruised by the pros," said Cousy after his Boston College team lost to UCLA in the Garden. "I'll have to learn to cope with it, not get used to it," said Kareem, who was to respond violently in his own way when things got too rough for him. He didn't get used to the violence and found it difficult to cope.

I never knew him as someone wanting to be treated as a special person. His high-school coach remembers him the same way. A special kind of basketball player never seeking special privileges. "He was just another kid on the floor when I first saw him," Donohue has recalled. "It was in our gym at Power. I had gone to watch some other kid in a CYO game when one of the Brothers said there was a boy playing who was six-seven. You don't see many six-seven kids in grammar school. Well, when he matured and got so good, the toughest job was to treat him the same as the other kids. So, when I got tickets to the Garden games, Lewie never got one until he was a senior and captain of the team. Then he knew he was getting them because he was a senior, not because he was a special kid."

But Kareem was something special as a player. He was the first seven-footer with such speed and quick coordination. He came into the league when it was losing the Russell magic and established immediate attention and excitement throughout the league—especially in New York, where the Knicks had grown and he represented a threat to a championship team that had taken so long to create.

Boston fans got to know him and respect him though they lamented: "Oh, it would be great to see him against Russell." They never got to see the matchup because Russell retired before the 1969 season started. Kareem got forty-eight in his first game against the Celtics in Milwaukee and twenty-eight more on his first visit to the Boston Garden two weeks later plus the inevitable comparison to Russell.

Milwaukee beat the Celtics that night—October 28, 1969—

but Kareem, an astute young man, didn't gloat. He never did. Even when he led the Bucks to a four-game sweep of the Bullets for the 1970–71 championship, he didn't abuse the losers. "I wish it had been the Knicks," he told everyone.

Kareem somehow managed to say the right things at the right time. The night he helped beat the Celtics in Boston without Russell, he said: "Yeah, but number 6 isn't here now. That makes a difference."

What a difference Kareem made. He transformed the worst team in the league into a serious contender. Then with the addition of Oscar Robertson, he led the Bucks to the title. But after the Big O retired and the Bucks made some bad trades, things weren't the same for Kareem and the team began its plunge. The snow, the cold, and the isolation began to take its toll, especially after the Bucks traded Lucius Allen, Kareem's closest friend on the team and a former UCLA teammate.

"Here's a guy who out of eighty-two games is going to play seventy-nine great ones," Allen said of his friend. "Great ones in his stats, in the things he does. Yet, he's going to lose half of those games, maybe more. It has to be a great psychological thing for him. He has to feel something when he doesn't win enough after playing like that. I can't put it in words, but it's got to be depressing."

Kareem is one of the finest players to ever play the game and the Knicks always appreciated that, though we beat him and Milwaukee four straight in 1970, our only playoff series with the Bucks. We didn't spare the checkbook or the roster when we heard he wanted to leave Milwaukee in 1975 and preferred to play in New York or Los Angeles. We called the Bucks right away to see what it would take to get him.

I was in Seattle with the Knicks when I heard that Kareem had informed the Bucks he would not play for them the following season. I was told he insisted that either he be traded or he would sit out the remaining year of his contract. I talked it over with Mike Burke and Eddie Donovan and it was decided to go all out. Spare no expense or players.

I can say this: we didn't get Kareem but no one ever made a more serious effort to get a player than the Knicks did. We offered Wayne Embry, the Bucks' general manager, all assortments of players, some not even on our roster, that we promised to try to get if Milwaukee was interested. We lost.

Los Angeles won by sending David Meyers, Elmore Smith, Brian Winters, Junior Bridgeman, and $1-million of Jack Kent Cooke's money to Milwaukee for Abdul-Jabbar and Walt Wesley. The Knicks would have topped that if given the chance but we never got it.

That's why I was surprised when I heard what Kareem had to say when he held his first press conference in Los Angeles. In answer to a question about not going to New York, he said: "I don't care to go where I'm not wanted." I couldn't believe it, not after the full-court press we put on in trying to get him.

I can only assume it was a lack of communication. The Knicks were not allowed to talk to Kareem because of the tampering rule but someone failed to 'i form him of our serious negotiations. Anyway, we lost him to Los Angeles, where he renewed his California rivalry with Bill Walton, another UCLA center who has had quite an impact on the NBA during the time his health has permitted him to play.

They first met on October 4, 1974. It was a Milwaukee home game at Dayton University and Walton, the number-one pick in the draft by Portland, was nervous and outclassed. "Everybody goes through it," said Kareem after outscoring Walton 28–8 in the time they played against each other. "You just have to learn the game. I lost my first regular-season game. I went against Nate Thurmond. I had five points and five rebounds. We got beat, beaten to death."

Funny thing. Thurmond always was one of Kareem's toughest opponents through the years. Nate had the size and quickness to harass Kareem's shots and block a lot of them. Walton moved in on Kareem after a while and there are some who insist Bill passed the man who had preceded him at UCLA.

However, on that first night against each other, Walton was the typical rookie breaking into the NBA. "I was anxious," admitted the young man who was to carry the Trail Blazers to the 1977 championship only two seasons later. "It's memorable because I had such a bad night. Like I've been saying all along, he's the best player I've ever seen."

Kareem never talked too much about himself. In the right company, he displayed a quick sense of humor. Once in Detroit on a bus, someone said: "Porters will handle our luggage" to which Kareem replied: "Which one, Howard or Kevin," both of whom were with the Pistons at the time.

One time he really opened up about his younger days in upper Manhattan, when he followed the Brooklyn Dodgers, the football Giants, and the Knicks. I guess he always dreamed of playing for the Knicks but we weren't lucky enough to get him.

"My year was 1955," he said, recalling the year the Dodgers won their first World Series by beating the Yankees. "I was in third grade and everybody in my school was a Yankee fan. They had an endless winter with me. I was a diehard football Giants' fan in the seventh and eighth grades. I went to all their games and sat in the bleachers. I used to buy two cups of coffee and just hold them to keep my hands warm. I spent about a dollar on coffee. That's why my number has been 33—it was Mel Triplett's number.

"I still don't like the Baltimore Colts because they beat the Giants, and I didn't like Wisconsin then because it was so cold whenever the Giants played the Packers there. And the Knicks in those days, very sad. Charlie Tyra, Donnis Butcher, Cleveland Buckner. In the summer, I liked to swim at Rockaway where my father was a lifeguard. I like being alive on the planet Earth."

As I have said, Kareem is an unusual person and player. He was named Most Valuable Player five times in his first seven years, whereas it took Bill Russell 10 years to accomplish that feat. Abdul-Jabbar then became the first player to win it by being voted MVP in 1980.

Kareem Abdul-Jabbar now is in his thirties. He says he is older and wiser, if that's possible. "Kareem is the best," Jerry West once said when asked to compare him with Walton and the other active NBA centers. "He is the most dominating player in the game. And he has a tremendous burden because he is expected to do more than anybody in the league—score, rebound, block shots."

The league will remember Kareem as a strong force in the days he played. I will remember him as a player from New York who got away, never to return despite so many efforts by the Knicks to bring him back to his roots.

BILL WALTON

One day, Willis Reed and Bill Bradley, the Knicks' resident philosophers, were sitting in our dressing room and gabbing. The subject: Bill Walton, who, reportedly, had rejected a $2-million offer from the Philadelphia 76ers to pass up his senior year at UCLA and turn pro. They wanted him to apply to the NBA as a hardship case, which would qualify him for the 1973 draft. The 76ers had just finished an embarrassing season in which they had won only nine of their eighty-two games. They were desperately in need of rebuilding, and winning the coin toss with Portland, which gave them first pick in the draft, was the first step on the road to recovery.

Ironically, the same two teams finished last in their Conferences the next season, when Walton actually became eligible for the draft. That time, the Trail Blazers won the toss of the coin and thereby inherited Walton and eventually won a championship before he moved on.

Rejected by Walton, the 76ers made Doug Collins their first draft pick in 1973 and the Trail Blazers chose Barry Parkhill, who did not last too long. The next season, when Portland picked first and took Walton, the 76ers took Marvin Barnes, who elected to play in the ABA. Fortunately for the 76ers,

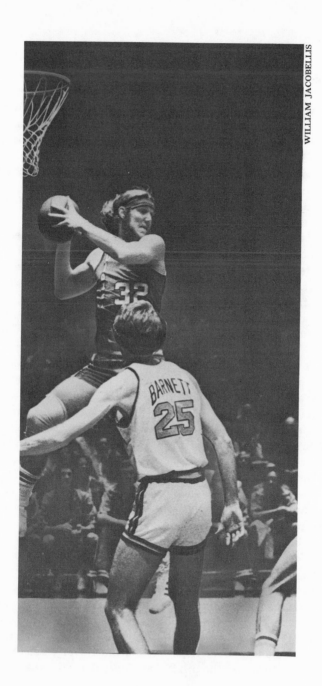

Collins developed into a fine player although, strangely, he, like Walton, ran into a succession of foot problems that cost him many games.

Anyway, Reed said he didn't understand how Walton could turn down all that money and risk the chance of getting nothing if he was hurt in college and never made pro ball. But Bradley had been through a similar barrage of publicity and generous salary offers, and he had chosen to go to Oxford as a Rhodes Scholar. So he was speaking from experience when he told Willis: "I know about as much about Bill Walton as I do about the Aga Kahn. But from what I understand, he dislikes the disproportionate amount of publicity he's received. People regard him as a star player, not as a person, and I can understand him not liking that."

Bradley had faced a similiar situation when the Knicks drafted him fresh out of Princeton for the 1965–66 season. Everyone knew Bradley the player but few knew Bradley the person. And Bradley the person decided two years at Oxford was worth the wait.

"I never had that problem," said Reed, who had played in the privacy of Grambling, where the basketball spotlight was not as bright as at Princeton or UCLA. "I never was College Player of the Year," added Willis, who came up from the mines and became one of pro basketball's priceless gems.

Bradley shrugged off this reference to the haves and have-nots. "From what I've read," said Bradley, picking up on Walton, "his father is a social worker in San Diego. I don't know if he would qualify as a hardship case, anyway. But that's a technicality. If he decided he wanted to play next season, the league would let him."

"He's got bad knees," pointed out Reed, an expert on the subject. "Suppose he got hurt? He might never get an opportunity like that again. I think he made a mistake."

It was just idle dressing-room talk, but Reed and Bradley were creating the prologue to the Bill Walton Story. It was to become a drama of painful injuries, big money, and a constant struggle by Walton against over-publicity. Considering the size of the talent and the stature of the player, I can't remember anything like the Bill Walton Story in all my years around the NBA.

Walton came into the league already a distinctive individual. He was a three-time All-America at UCLA, where he had helped run the championship streak to seven before failing in his senior year. He was given a $2-million deal to pump life into the relatively new Portland franchise, which he did rejuvenate. He was an intellectual free spirit with ideas of his own about basketball and how he wanted to live.

"All my life I've played basketball for myself and for my teammates and now I'm in a position where other people expect me to play for them," he said soon after making the transition from college to pro basketball. "I'm not used to that. It's been a period of adjustment. There are certain requirements you must fulfill to play. Basically, you are required to live and act a certain way. In effect, you're being told what to do when you're not playing. But I'm trying my best to work it out."

At first there was a conflict between his personal life and the image he was expected to maintain as a professional. He entered the NBA as the "second coming" of Kareem Abdul-Jabbar, who had helped UCLA to some of its seven straight titles. There were many fanatical Los Angeles fans who even claimed Walton was a better all-around center than Kareem and would show it in the pros.

They had watched Walton block shots like Bill Russell, play both ends like Abdul-Jabbar, and make the play better than either. They had seen Walton play with acumen, agility, speed, intensity, and enthusiasm, so they were puzzled when he said: "Let's face it. On a world scale, basketball doesn't mean much."

He was a young man with the turmoil of the world on his mind at the time. He was a young man who passed up the chance to represent his country in the 1972 Olympics to go backpacking with his sister in the California Sierras and Canadian Rockies. He was a young man trying to send out social and political messages while attempting to blend quietly into the student crowd on the campus.

He soon found out that being inconspicuous was rather difficult for a six-eleven, freckle-faced, redheaded basketball star. He wanted to be considered the average human being but he was just too conspicuous to hide in a crowd. He should've known he was unique when he shot from six-one to six-seven during one summer between the ages of fourteen and fifteen. He certainly should have known when his Helix High team won forty-four in a row and two District titles. And when he went to UCLA, where the Uclans won eighty-eight in a row and two NCAA titles, there should have been no doubt that he was destined to stand out in a crowd.

I remember reading that he demonstrated with a number of UCLA students, got arrested, and was fined, but I don't remember the names of the others arrested with him. Walton had to learn to live with that. He had to go through many inner struggles and attitude changes. For example, there was a time when pro ball and big money did not appeal to him, but playing for fun in college did.

"I imagine I'll have to go on with the game if I'm going to make the most of myself," Walton said during the period when the ABA and the NBA were trying to talk him into quitting UCLA after his junior year. "But I want to do more with my life than win a few games. I can make a lot of money but money doesn't mean that much to me. It can't buy happiness and I want to be happy.

"I'm built for basketball and I like it and have the potential to be a top player but I'm not sure that I want it for a profession. It's just a game. I play because it's fun. If other people want to take it too seriously, that's their hangup."

I guess that's why Walton had some early problems adjusting to the pros and his teammates when he first came into the league. They didn't understand him and he didn't understand them. He almost quit soon after he started. I can't tell you exactly why. All I know is that Walton, in his first game against us, wasn't the Walton I knew from watching him play for UCLA.

He worked only eighteen minutes in his first appearance against the Knicks and was no factor in our losing the game to Portland. He played like a lost soul and showed no signs of the great talent I knew he had.

Not long after that, the Trail Blazers came to New York without Walton. He was left home after missing seven games because of bone spurs on his foot. That's when stories began appearing that he was thinking of quitting pro basketball.

His teammates sensed his uneasiness. "I've probably talked with him more than anybody on the team," said Princeton's Geoff Petrie, who had been the Trail Blazers' first draft choice when they entered the NBA as an expansion team in 1970. "The last couple of weeks he became pretty remote. His locker was next to mine. He'd usually come in and say something. He just began shrugging his shoulders and didn't want to talk about it."

It was a season to forget. Few things worked out for the young star, especially his first confrontation with Abdul-Jabbar. The meeting had all the earmarks of a Russell-Chamberlain matchup but the drama never developed. Kareem got fifty points and Walton seven on national television in a game in Milwaukee that the Bucks completely dominated.

Walton, of course, had just returned after missing eighteen games and had been back only three games when asked to face the man who had made UCLA history before him. Walton played only twenty-one minutes, so he wasn't fully responsible for what Kareem did. But Abdul-Jabbar did get twenty-two points while Walton was on the court.

It was an almost reluctant Walton who played that night. He seldom looked to shoot, hitting two-for-five, and preferred to give up the ball, earning seven assists. "It was fun playing against Kareem," Walton said. It was probably more fun for Kareem, who saw a lot in that first meeting, despite Walton's brief moments of action. "He is a very sound defensive player," said the Milwaukee center. "He's very quick, rebounds well, and can block a lot of shots."

Kareem was describing the real Walton the NBA had to wait a while to see. I had heard and read many stories about Walton when he was at UCLA and had seen him play a few times and knew what he was capable of doing. He was equipped with the finest all-around playing talent for a big man that I'd ever seen. His basic knowledge of the game, his ballhandling, and his ability to make the play were all outstanding. Like a guard, he could bounce-pass the ball through a crowd in the the the middle and hit his man underneath. In that respect, he was a tall Oscar Robertson. He couldn't do it all by himself, but he certainly could help, and he was smart enough to recognize it himself. "I can't win for a team, but I can help a team win" is the way Walton put it.

It was late in January 1975 when Walton finally paid a small dividend to the Trail Blazers. They went to Detroit and lost, but Walton got twenty-five points, eleven rebounds, and in that game played as an integrated part of the team. "That's the best he's played and the longest he's played since he's been back," said Wilkens.

Those were turbulent times for Walton. Personal conflicts and injuries had combined to put his obvious talent in storage. But those who knew him, such as Keith Wilkes, a UCLA teammate, kept the faith.

Wilkes had come into the NBA with Walton and landed with Golden State as a first-round pick. Keith understood Walton, both as a man and a player, better than anyone in the league. After all, they had been teammates for four years in college, and in that time had played only four losing games for the Bruins.

"Bill has never played for a losing team," explained Wilkes. "I'm sure that's a tough adjustment for him to make. Playing the older guys is different, too. Some guys with families think of pro ball as a job rather than just fun. Accepting that is an adjustment. We talk pretty frankly when we see each other and I'm sure he wants to play."

I, too, came to that conclusion despite the little I saw of him in his early NBA days. I was intrigued by the smooth way he triggered a fast break, among other things. He'd get the ball off the board and have it upcourt in no time. The move was a John Wooden trademark for all his centers at UCLA, and Walton was exceptionally smooth at it. He had acquired the knack of sweeping up the rebound and making the outlet pass while in mid-air, a move that Bill Russell had also excelled at.

It often seemed as if Walton had been born with these skills, but he explained it otherwise. He said it all began after he twisted a knee and needed surgery during his sophomore year in high school. "I couldn't run very well, even after the operation," explained Walton. "So there was no way I could stay with everybody in our fast break. So, all I did was get the rebound, make the quick pass, and watch everyone go. I couldn't help but get good at it because I did it so much."

That's what I keep telling my players. Repetition is the best prescription for improvement. That's why I drill them in fundamentals until they react instinctively without having to think of what they must do. In Walton's case, he learned out of adversity, although I'm inclined to think he would have perfected the outlet pass anyway. But he showed his fighting side again when he overcame his early injuries in Portland and put a few fine games together. Soon after he visited New York early in 1975, he had one five-game stretch where he was able to average thirty-eight minutes per game, and in that time averaged sixteen points, fourteen rebounds, eight assists, and four blocked shots.

It was obvious what a whole Walton could do. Although Wilkens knew what his rookie center was going through, it wasn't easy for the coach to see such talent deprived of playing time because of injuries, especially when the Trail Blazers were losing. Yet Wilkens continued to support his controversial star. "Walton is an individual," he said. "He has his own personality. When he's on the floor and does the job I want, that's all he owes. He's beginning to do that now and I think that's going to shut up all the critics.

"It's like some people asking me how Bill is adjusting to the league. Hell, he hasn't even played a year. Give the man a chance to play, to reflect. Give me a chance to reflect on what improvements he has made all year long."

Unfortunately for Wilkens, he wasn't given too much opportunity to see Walton produce for Portland. In his rookie season, Walton gave Wilkens only thirty-five games and the Blazers finished 36–46. Next season when Walton played fifty-one games and the Blazers wound up 37–45, Wilkens was gone. Jack Ramsay came over from Buffalo for the 1976–77 season; Walton healed enough to play sixty-five games—the most he ever played before moving to San Diego—and the Blazers won the championship.

Significantly, Portland was a serious contender for a second straight championship the next season when a hairline fracture was discovered in Walton's foot. He was finished after fifty-eight games and only got back in time for token appearances in two playoff games as Seattle eliminated the Blazers 4–2 in the Western semifinal.

To really appreciate what Walton's string of injuries meant to him and, therefore, the Trail Blazers, you only have to recall his own candid evaluation after his first two years as a pro. "I still enjoy my privacy," he said. "But I like winning, too. I really enjoy playing basketball. I'm a basketball player and intend to keep playing for a while.

"It's never much fun when you're playing with a serious injury or even when you're recovering. And that's the way it always seems to be with me. Hurt or recovering. I'll play three minutes and then I'll get winded. But even with that, I don't think about not playing basketball."

I think the thing that appealed to me about Walton was his intensity. In a coach's vernacular, he came to win every game and I never saw him let up just because he was facing an easy team. All teams seemed the same to him and he played just as hard no matter what name they wore across their shirts. Yet, as far as I know, he was not a sore loser, though he obviously didn't like to lose. He was accustomed to winning but apparently he had prepared himself. "It's a little nicer to win," he said, "but it's not reality to win all the time. You know more about yourself and your friends when you lose."

Walton could afford to talk that way because he was an unusual talent who could create a winning situation, as could Russell, Abdul-Jabbar, Chamberlain, and Willis Reed. No one hated to lose more than Reed and no one was more competitive. But he, too, could accept losing as a part of reality. The problem with losing, of course arises when it becomes a habit.

I remember Portland's first visit to the Garden in Walton's second season, when Wilkens was still coach. Walton had broken a toe during the summer and then, in his first exhibition game of the 1975–76 season, John Havlicek caused a three-stitch cut in his eyelid with a flying elbow. By the time the regular season rolled around and the Blazers came to New York for their first game, Walton already had twisted an ankle and had lost more games than he cared to count. He was able to play twenty-four minutes against us but when Portland really needed him, he couldn't get off the bench, which was lucky for us. There were eight minutes left and we were struggling to maintain an eight-point lead that had dwindled from eighteen.

Neal Walk and John Gianelli were our two centers at the time. Both were pretty good outside shooters for big men, so I told them to make Walton move outside whenever they could so he wouldn't be around the boards to rebound. It helped, as things turned out.

"Walk and Gianelli were out on the perimeter," explained Walton after telling his coach the ankle was too sore for him to come back into the game. "Walk was playing twenty feet from the basket and setting picks. I couldn't help the team if I couldn't chase people."

Although Walton limped through only twenty-four minutes of the game, he managed to prove himself to the satisfaction of the demanding New York fans. He grabbed twelve rebounds by laying back and also whipped off some fine passes while scoring twelve points. I had seen enough to want to have Walton playing for the Knicks if we ever had a chance of getting him.

We never did. We tried but Walton preferred playing ball on the West Coast, where he had grown up and played in college. As soon as Portland agreed to trade him before the 1978–79 season, the Knicks sent team president Mike Burke, general manager Eddie Donovan, and Reed out there to talk to him.

By then, though damaged, Walton had become one of the most valuable pieces of NBA merchandise. He had proven what most people knew all along: that with him healthy, a team could win a championship. He proved it for Ramsay, who said it on the day he replaced Wilkens as coach, June 1, 1976.

"It's going to take a healthy Bill Walton," said Ramsay, who had coached Buffalo for four years, when asked what it would take for the Blazers to win. Wilkens also knew it, just as he also knew that a coach is judged by his won-and-lost record and nothing more.

Wilkens wasn't the first coach to say: "When you're winning, everyone thinks you're a genius." He then added, quite prophetically, I must say: "Next year, what if Walton stays healthy? Everyone will consider the coach a genius. Ironically, it could happen." And ironically, it did. Walton got hurt again, but managed to stay healthy for sixty-five games, giving Ramsay his first NBA title in his first season in Portland. Walton led the league in rebounding with a 14.4 average, blocked shots with a 3.25 average, hit for 18.6 points a game, and averaged almost four assists a game, high for a center when you consider that most of the top ten that year were guards who ranged from five a game to Indiana's Don Busse, who averaged 8.3.

Wilkens knew what a healthy Walton could do because he had seen it during the 1975–76 season, when the Blazers won seven straight before a stress fracture of his ankle put the towering center on the sidelines for another month. The Blazers had put together a 10–3 record and were making a serious move towards their first playoff berth as Walton averaged 20.8 points, 17.8 rebounds, and 5.2 assists.

They were in third place in the Pacific Division when Walton got hurt again. The time he took to tape himself up became a league joke. There was one game when it actually took forty minutes to tape and bandage Walton's assorted problems, inspiring trainer Ron Culp to say: "He'll be the first man in the history of the National Basketball Association to play without any exposed skin."

It was in again, out again with Walton so often that everyone was surprised Blue Cross didn't withdraw his coverage. Then, for one season, it all stopped. Walton became healthy enough to play. We should have known when he showed up for his third attempt to play a full season with fewer bandages and a new look: he had gotten a haircut that eliminated the ponytail he used to wear.

This was a new Walton, as night after night he appeared in the Blazers' starting lineup. He was now twenty-four and stronger than ever, having added some thirty pounds of muscle through a weight-lifting program designed to keep him in some sort of shape during all that time lost through injuries.

"I heard he was a scrawny guy but he looks as big as Jabbar to me," observed Sonny Parker, then a Warriors rookie. "He must weigh 250 pounds." Walton was listed at 235, and he certainly looked bigger and stronger than he had as a rookie. He played that way, too. He was a lot tougher to move around and he never shied away from contact now that his new strength allowed him to prevail in the pivot and in the battle for rebounds.

The Blazers finished second in their division the season they won the championship, but I assume that's because Walton missed eighteen regular season games. What I saw indicated that Portland wasn't the same without him. Ramsay felt the same way. In fact, Jack wound up saying some startling things about his center, even suggesting that he might be the greatest all-around center ever.

"Walton is more skilled in all facets of the game," said Ramsay, who had seen the best of the modern centers since first coaching the 1968–69 Philadelphia 76ers team. "Wilt was a great rebounder, a great shotblocker and, he became a better shooter but he had no range and he was a terrible foul shooter. Russell was the best defensively, a fierce competitor. Kareem is the best offensive player of the three. But to me, Bill does all of those things well. Reed and Cowens were different types. Bill is a great, great player."

What Walton did for Portland was provide the kind of team-unselfishness that made the Knicks so distinctive when they won championships in 1970 and 1973. Walton was the catalyst for Maurice Lucas, Lionel Hollins, Bob Gross, and Dave Twardzik as the Blazers won the title in only their seventh season in the league.

The Blazers (49–33) finished second in the division to the Lakers (53–29) but gained the final by eliminating Denver, 4–2, and Los Angeles, 4–0. Walton had an exceptional team series in his first playoff meeting with Abdul-Jabbar, as the two old grads shook the nerves of all those UCLA fans who had seen them both play at different times for the same alma mater. Kareem was named Most Valuable Player for the fifth straight time but everyone was impressed by what Walton had accomplished. In 19 playoff games he averaged 18.2 points, 15 rebounds, 5.5 assists, 3.4 blocked shots, and about a steal a game.

It was ironic for both Walton and Ramsay that the final test would pit them against the 76ers.

Ramsay, because he once coached the 76ers, and Walton because he once turned down the 76ers when they tried to coax him into leaving UCLA. Walton often recalls the time Gene Shue, then the 76ers' coach, and the late Irv Kosloff, then owner of the 76ers, walked into his hotel room in St. Louis after the Uclans had beaten Memphis State for the 1973 NCAA championship.

Walton had switched to the lavish Presidential suite where a victory party was to be staged after he had hit twenty-one of his twenty-two shots and scored forty-four points. In walked Shue and Kosloff with their offer of big money they assumed he couldn't refuse. They didn't realize Walton had been shifted to the suite because he was too big for the routine smaller rooms in the hotel, so he played a game with them when they saw his layout with its telephones, television sets, and a bed big enough to sleep four or five. Shue told Walton the 76ers would like him to come and play for the 76ers and they'd give him a lot of money. "I told them: 'You've got to be kidding. How can you folks do any better than this?' " said Walton, waving to his luxurious suite. He told them that's the way UCLA treats him, so he was going to stay.

It took some time but Walton eventually learned what NBA excitement really meant. He found out when the Blazers turned away a favored Philadelphia team that had so much firepower in Julius Erving, George McGinnis, and Doug Collins, it was considered inconceivable that anyone could beat them.

But the Blazers did it and I was one of those who suspected they might because of Walton. I saw much of the Knicks in the way the Blazers played team defense and looked for the open man on offense. Of course, I never suspected McGinnis would run into trouble with his shooting, but things like that happen, and it helped the Blazers win.

Walton dominated the series though the Blazers played an outstanding team game. They ran the fast-break with pin-point finesse, moved the ball with intelligence when forced to slow down, and put the pressure on the 76ers' offense with a smart, helping-out defense. There was no doubt they were the best as Walton made up for lost time.

It was a season in which Walton didn't lose a thing until he went home to Portland and led the team in a wild victory parade through the streets of the Northwest city. Then, he lost a ten-speed bicycle he used to lead the triumphant Blazers past some 50,000 screaming citizens. Someone swiped his bike in the midst of the frenzy.

"It was maybe the stupidest thing I've ever done," said Walton after deciding to do something different for the fans by letting them see a six-eleven center lead a parade on a bike. Despite the loss of his wheels Walton had a tremendous time that day.

He couldn't remember having so much fun though he had been involved in high school and college championships. "This is as much fun as I've ever had in any sport since I started playing when I was eight years old," he told a mob in Portland's Federal Plaza as he poured cold beer over the head of Mayor Neil Goldschmidt.

Walton had found a home but as it turned out not for long. The season after the championship he was again plagued with injuries. "It's very, very nice to win a championship," he said as the 1977–78 season began, "but I'm sure it's nicer to win it twice in a row."

I would say the Blazers might have won it twice in a row if Walton hadn't come up with one of his stress fractures late in the season. Walton began the season laughing and having fun because of his new championship ring and then it ended. He was hurt, again, and the Blazers were without him, again.

No team can lose the services of a Walton and not be affected. I knew what it meant when we lost Reed for the 1971–72 season; he played only eleven games, and we were beaten, 4–1, by the Lakers in the championship series. "He means a great deal to us," said Ramsay of Walton. "I wouldn't say everything but as close to everything as he can come."

I remember a healthy Walton coming to New York early in the 1977–78 season and being asked what had pleased him most so far. "That we're 35–6," he said, explaining that each game was a new excitement. "Every game starts at zero-zero," he added. "We have very dedicated athletes on our team, guys who enjoy keeping mentally and physically ready for each game. We keep pushing, we don't let up. It's fun."

Winning was fun at the time but losing began setting in when Walton went out of the lineup. The Blazers skidded to a 23–18 finish and were knocked out of the playoffs by Seattle in the first round, 4–2. Walton never played another game for the Blazers. He was out all of 1978–79 with a foot injury, and finally influenced Portland to offer him around for a trade.

A break in Walton's left foot was discovered after the Blazers had tied the series with Seattle by taking the second game. Walton had missed the final twenty-two games of the regular season, with the Blazers losing fourteen of them. He had returned for the opening playoff game and contributed seventeen points and sixteen rebounds to the 104–95 loss. But in the second game, he played only fifteen minutes, scoring ten points before injuring his foot.

The Knicks made a sincere, serious effort to get him to play in New York once permission was given by Portland to talk to him. I still think he was determined to play for San Diego, where he grew up, or Los Angeles, where he had played his college ball. When he finally decided to sign with San Diego, he indicated he would be more comfortable in sunny, relaxed California than in busy old New York.

I don't think the Knicks ever really had a shot at Walton though Dr. Ernie Vandeweghe, who once played for the Knicks, tried to influence him. "I explained all the advantages of playing in New York and helping to create a winner," said Vandeweghe, who was with the Knicks in 1951 when I played for the Rochester Royals and we beat them for the championship in seven games.

Vandy, whose son Kiki also was a UCLA basketball star, was Walton's advisor by that time but he couldn't influence him to play for the Knicks.

"I told him: 'They'll love you in San Diego but they'll appreciate you more in New York because they know good basketball,'" explained Vandeweghe. "I told him the best places to play were New York and Los Angeles and he agreed with that.

"I felt the New York market was the best if he was mainly

interested in money. I told him New York has the media, the press coverage, Madison Avenue, and all that extra money to be made."

I think it boiled down to Walton and his wife preferring that he not play in New York. San Diego finally won the sweepstakes. Walton's last official game with Portland was on May 7, 1978 and he didn't play again in a regular season game until he put on a Clippers' uniform on January 29, 1980.

"Call it what you want but I'm rejuventated," he told the people in San Diego when he signed with the Clippers. "I'm home again. My feet are better and I'll be ready when the season starts."

He wasn't. They discovered another stress fracture in his foot after he had pushed himself hard in training camp. He never made the season opener. His foot went back into a cast and there was talk that his bones were too fragile and he might never play again.

He missed 160 consecutive games but he came back. He entered a game against Phoenix in San Diego with 1:44 left in the opening period, played fourteen minutes, scored eight points, grabbed four rebounds, had one assist, and committed five turnovers. He was as rusty as his hair.

Once, he was fouled in the backcourt and, on his first opportunity to score after his long layoff, he fired two shots that were too short. "That was definitely the worst I felt all night," he said. "I felt excitement and anxiety and even some apprehension. There wasn't one twinge of pain all night. I'm going to have to regain my mental confidence but the more I get whacked around out there, the faster I'll adapt."

Bill Walton had made it back again. At twenty-seven, he led the league in comebacks. Yet, in his relatively short career, he had established himself as an irresistible force in the world of the NBA. That is, until he hurt his foot again and missed the last 68 games of the 1980 season.

2 THE MATCHUPS

CHAMBERLAIN – RUSSELL

They met for the first time in a regular season game on November 8, 1959 in the Boston Garden. In the center's circle just before the opening jump, Wilt Chamberlain and Bill Russell shook hands and wished each other good luck.

The greatest war in the history of the league was on. Russell gave away three inches and forty pounds to the seven-one, 260-pound rookie from Philadelphia. When the game ended, they smiled wearily at each other and shook hands again at the edge of the court.

Chamberlain outscored Russell 30–22, Russell outrebounded Wilt 35–30, and the Celtics won, 115–106. It was considered a statistical standoff and for ten years, until Russell retired after the 1968–69 season, they would engage in their war within a war. Always with some respect for each other and the Herculean job they had to face whenever they met but, eventually, to generate into a personal feud.

That first night, though, Chamberlain and Russell were competitive, respectful, and civil toward each other. Time was to take care of that. Many things were to disrupt the relationship that started out with great curiosity, awe, and mutual respect. Russell already had helped the Celtics win two titles in three years, while Chamberlain was becoming a household word as a high-school player at Overbrook in Philadelphia and then Kansas University.

Chamberlain and Russell were kind to each other when their historic meeting was over. "I only wish I could have been that good as a rookie," said Russell, who merely led the Celts to their first NBA title in his rookie year. "Russell is the toughest I've played or expect to play," said Chamberlain, not knowing at the time what an influence Russell would have on his life.

The Celtics agreed with Chamberlain to a man. Bob Cousy and Bill Sharman said Wilt ranked with the best but they preferred Russell. "Wilt is really remarkable," said Frank Ramsey, the super sub. "But I think the Celtics can handle him better than any other club because we have Russell to do it. I can't see any other team that can control Chamberlain."

Chamberlain actually said he thought Russell had a slight edge that night. Those were the days when Wilt's objectivity was relatively pure. The feud hadn't heated up yet. Chamberlain against Russell had not reached the championship proportions that sometimes influence many attitudes and turn things into bitterness.

Basketball is only a game but there is so much at stake. Boston, for example, hadn't won a championship until Russell came along and then won eleven in thirteen years. Every team and player became a personal threat to that supremacy and was treated accordingly. When Chamberlain came along, he represented the biggest threat, so he got all the heat throughout the years.

I know. I saw Chamberlain against the world developing even before Wilt entered the NBA. He was such a dominating force, there were those who felt any team he played for would win the championship. That's really not the way it works. It certainly didn't work that way when Wilt came into the league and found the Celtics an immovable object.

There were those in the league who knew Chamberlain wasn't going to beat the Celtics all by himself. I was scouting at the time but Wilt was the favorite topic of discussion. I remember some of the things Easy Ed Macauley said. He had

gone to St. Louis in the trade that enabled the Celtics to get Russell, so Macauley was quite familiar with Boston and the dynasty it was building.

"The one thing that might hurt him," Macauley said of Wilt, "is that he's playing so much—forty-five, forty-six, forty-eight minutes a game. Chamberlain's extremely strong but nobody's that strong that he can play our kind of scedule and keep up that kind of pace.

"There are times when he seems to poop out a bit and has to coast. Now Russell can do that because he's got Cousy, Sharman, Heinsohn, and the others with him. Chamberlain can't. But Chamberlain's going to get stronger and, as he gets stronger and goes full speed, he's going to be really something. He's got a lot of confidence in himself and he looks like he wants to get better. He wants to improve. He wants to learn.

"I don't think Philadelphia will beat the Celtics out of the Eastern Division title. Philadelphia doesn't have the Celtics' team balance. Boston has a whole bench full of guys who can come in and kill you but Philadelphia falls off too sharply after the first five or six players. What happens if one of Philadelphia's first five gets hurt? They'd be in bad shape in Philly."

Macauley was right and I think that Chamberlain always remembered what Easy Ed had said. I know through the years, Wilt contended that the Celtics always had the better players surrounding Russell; otherwise the results might have been different. Maybe. That's hard to say, though I sure would have liked to see what would have happened had Chamberlain played for the Celtics and Russell been with Philadelphia, San Francisco, and the Lakers.

As things turned out, Wilt and Russell met in nine NBA playoffs with Chamberlain winning only with Philadelphia, 4–1, in the 1966–67 season. In games played, Russell and the Celtics were far ahead, 29–18. And every year that Chamberlain's team was eliminated, the heat got hotter and everything Wilt did during the season was forgotten.

In Wilt's first year, he averaged 37.6 a game but the Celtics beat the Philadelphia Warriors in the semifinals, 4–2. Two years later, Wilt had his 50.4 season and carried the Celtics to seven games but Philadelphia lost, 109–107, in Boston. The next time, Wilt was wearing a San Francisco uniform in 1963–64 and the Celtics won, 4–1.

The following season, Wilt was back in Philadelphia for the final thirty-five games and pushed Boston to seven games in the playoffs, with the Celtics winning the last one, 110–109. In 1965–66, the Celtics routed the 76ers, 4–1, but Wilt came back the following season to end Boston's dominance over him in a 4–1 series.

I guess the 1967–68 playoff series with the Celtics will go down as the most frustrating of all for Wilt. The 76ers were leading, 3–1, and Boston came on to take the next three games, the final 100–96, in Philadelphia. By then many things had happened to build a tall barrier between Chamberlain and Russell that finally reached the breaking point when Boston's playing coach made his last playoff appearance a winning one against Wilt in the 1968–69 season.

But I'm way ahead of myself. Let's go back to the Maurice Stokes Game in 1959 at Kutsher's Country Club. This was Wilt's actual first appearance against some of the NBA players he'd be playing against when the season started. The seeds of the Chamberlain-Russell rivalry were growing even then. "Chamberlain is everything that Russell is and more," said Neil Johnston, who was to become Wilt's first pro coach.

Chamberlain had played for the all-star team coached by Fuzzy Levane, then coach of the Knicks, and had been mainly responsible for beating an all-star team coached by Red Auerbach, 85–61. I know the game was played on an outdoor asphalt court and really meant nothing but Cousy, Ramsey, and Heinsohn were on Auerbach's team and their pride in the Celtics and Russell had to be affected.

Wilt had played only about a half but scored twenty points, grabbed fourteen rebounds, and blocked ten shots. On one play, they came at Wilt on a three-on-one. Cousy faked to Guy Sparrow of the Warriors, passed to Ramsey, whose jumper was blocked by Chamberlain. The ball sailed to Sparrow, who went up for another jumper but Wilt got that one, too.

"Now I know how the other teams had to feel when they found Russell batting the ball down their throats," said Ramsey. "Potentially, I'd have to say Chamberlain's got the nod over Russell," suggested Cousy. "He's never played against the pros and he does so much, already. He shoots so much better than Bill but this is a challenge for Russell and he's always been able to meet all challenges."

Auerbach was more conservative and careful. "It's not fair to compare these two as incoming pros," he said. "Wilt's been kicking around for a couple of years and Russell came right to us right from college without ever having seen a pro game, much less playing in one."

With a start like that, it was inevitable that Russell and Chamberlain would go under the microscope. Everything that was said or done would be magnified. The weight of players, coaches, owners, fans, writers, and cities were thrown into this heralded matchup from the start and had an influence on it.

For example, I'm sure Wilt never forgot something Boston owner Walter Brown said when Chamberlain was only a sophomore at Kansas. Wilt was over two years away from entering the NBA but the league had consigned him to Philadelphia by voting in a High School Territorial Rule. The vote was 7–1, with only the Knicks voting against it because they wanted a shot at Chamberlain in the regular draft, but Brown issued a blast, anyway.

It happened in February 1957, a few months after Russell had joined the Celtics. "No NBA team can pay Chamberlain what he gets to go to college," Brown claimed. "He shouldn't be allowed to play in the NBA. He has proselytized himself to stay in college. The colleges don't have the guts to disqualify him. I have no definite proof what might be the figure he's getting but it is a matter of fact no one in the NBA can afford to pay Chamberlain what he gets at Kansas."

Walter Brown was such a nice guy and everyone was surprised when he let off all that steam about Chamberlain. I'm sure Wilt would say it added to the Boston animosity when he finally got around to challenging Russell and the Celtics' superiority. Brown was mad at the time. The Celtics were on a losing streak and he had assumed Boston was finally to win a world championship after getting Russell.

"We have the manpower to win this year and we expect to

win it," he said in a few words after his comments on Chamberlain, the sophomore. "If we don't win it all, you won't recognize the team next year. And it won't be the coach that will be fired."

Now you understand what Chamberlain faced when he came into the league as a threat to Boston's position on top of the pro basketball world. Right from the start, Wilt was a marked man. When Chamberlain blocked so many shots in his first Stokes game, Ramsey turned to Cousy and said: "We'd better start yelling about goaltending now or we'll have trouble getting them to do anything about it when the season starts."

Chamberlain came into the league and rewrote the record book but each year the championship evaded his team. It was a friendly rivalry with Russell at the start. They even socialized. Russell, married, would invite Chamberlain, a bachelor, to drop around and have dinner with him and his wife when he got to Boston.

They were the focal points on their teams and had much in common. They were outstanding basketball players and personalities but both were struggling in their own ways for certain goals. As seven-foot black athletes, they had to break down the areas of prejudice that prevented them from getting equal treatment as human beings.

When their relationship deteriorated, nothing could stop it. So much was at stake in the games they played against each other. Besides, the more the Celtics won, the more Russell was termed a winner and Chamberlain a loser. I didn't think that right or fair but I had nothing to do with it.

After all, there were times when the Celtics beat Chamberlain's team in the final seconds of the seventh game in a playoff series. Certainly, no one could blame Wilt when Sam Jones or John Havlicek or Tommy Heinsohn hit a last-second basket, but they did. From Russell's viewpoint, he looked at it as a physical challenge from the start. He had to find a way to compensate for Wilt's size, weight, and skills. As their rivalry got more intense, Heinsohn, for one, claimed that Russell actually found ways to psych Chamberlain. It was Tommy's contention that Russell sometimes would allow Wilt to do anything he desired once the game was out of reach.

Russell didn't reserve that strategy for Wilt. He used it against all the scorers in the NBA. I saw him do it against the Knicks many times. Dick Barnett was one of the few little men who challenged him successfully at times but Russell would lay back against him and wait for a crucial spot to block his shot.

Heinsohn insists he never heard Russell say an unkind word about Chamberlain in all the years he played with Bill. Heinsohn also says the greatest game Chamberlain ever played against the Celtics was his first game with the Philadelphia Warriors during a Madison Square Garden double header in 1959.

"It may sound absurd but I saw the real Wilt Chamberlain play only once—that night in New York," said Heinsohn in his book, *Heinsohn, Don't You Ever Smile?*. "Wilt was just awesome grabbing rebounds, blocking shots, and knocking Russell out of his way. I think Russell made up his mind that night that the best way to handle Wilt was with kindness. Never bring out the animal in him. I could usually guess what Russell was thinking but he was smart enough to keep his thoughts to himself so that they wouldn't get into the papers."

I remember a game in Philadelphia where Russell had one of his greatest games against Chamberlain. It was early in the 1961–62 season and the Celtics won, 112–98, with Wilt and Russell battling each other for forty-eight minutes. Wilt wound up with twenty-eight points and thirty-three rebounds, while Russell had twenty-one points, twenty-five rebounds, and four assists.

But Russell was overwhelming. He got his hands on about a dozen shots by Wilt and many more by the other Warriors. He controlled the defensive board all by himself and he triggered the fast breaks. He had the Warriors so bewildered, Wilt only scored twice in the first twenty-two minutes and had nine points by the half.

"Have you ever seen anything like him?" asked Cousy when Russell had finished.

"He was tremendous," said Frank McGuire, the Philadelphia coach. "I thought he might weaken in the second half but he kept it up for forty-eight minutes."

"It was incredible tonight," said Normie Drucker, the referee. "It's unbelievable some of the blocks he made without touching the man."

Chamberlain had the size and power, Russell had the finesse. Together, they gave NBA fans years and years of competitive enjoyment and arguments. Wilt came into the league firing jump shots from the top of the key but weight lifting turned the upper half of his body into a powerhouse, so he perfected his short game. He proved the shortest distance between two points was the slam-dunk.

In the early stages of their rivally, Russell suggested that Wilt was the better player. He had more weapons. "But I'm as valuable to Boston as he is to Philadelphia," Russell added. "Sometimes, I do a lot of daydreaming. I live a lot subconsciously, perhaps as much as I do consciously, and in these daydreams I think how it would be if I could once have a game where I'd score fifty or sixty points and get fifty rebounds against a real, good center."

He was thinking of Chamberlain. "I'm too much of an egotist to envy anybody," he said when asked about it. "I certainly don't envy Chamberlain, although I admire him." He then broke it down in a comparison of Wilt and himself.

It was early in Wilt's first season and Russell didn't like the comparisons even then. "In a way, they're unfair to me," he said. "I won't mention our difference in size, although it's there. Obviously, I'm not a scorer and primarily he is. He's the best thing that's happened to the league. He's making the ballplayers better players. I know I'm trying harder. Perhaps too hard.

"He's a better rebounder than I am, that's apparent. He's a high scorer and there's not much more to basketball from the fans' point of view. But for our club, there are a lot of things I do that don't show up in the statistics, things he doesn't do."

Russell itemized and therein revealed why he and his Celtic teammates managed to beat Chamberlain and his teammates in the playoffs. "Like our offense," Russell explained. "It's fast break. The sooner Cooz or Sharman gets the ball, the sooner we're in business. They know I'll get them the ball. I use myself as a decoy a lot. I get the ball in the pivot, make a move to the middle to draw somebody else in, and hit the free man, maybe Heinsohn. Tommy's man comes at me, but he's got to go back to Tommy. He's coming back, Heinsohn can drive on him or if he doesn't come back, Tommy's got the shot. In the books that doesn't show as an assist for me, but the last two years I still have been second in assists on our team. I could score only ten points but still help the team win."

I guess that's what Wilt meant through the years when he kept insisting that Russell played with better players—a better team. While Wilt had to score, rebound, play defense, and handle the ball, Russell, he felt, was just one part of a stronger machine. Besides, Wilt would always point out, the Celtics were lucky because they never suffered a serious injury during the playoffs except when Russell twisted an ankle in his second year and the St. Louis Hawks won the NBA title.

When a rivally such as this one develops, every little development becomes ammunition for either side. The comparisons were made and then Russell and Chamberlain had to live out their challenge.

"Chamberlain has more physical equipment than I have although I'm quicker," said Russell. "I mean not only his tremendous size, but strength, brute strength. I found it out the hard way in our first game. We both got our hands on a rebound. I know I have good hands, strong hands. I tried to take the ball away from him. So he picked up the ball and me, too. I was hoping he wouldn't decide to dunk or I'd be in real trouble going through that basket.

"I work harder on defense than Wilt does. He plays defense differently. Once, we went into two overtimes and I played fifty-five minutes, taking only nine shots. I got the ball a lot in the pivot but if I saw a man with a better shot, I passed off. I could get a lot of points but I don't think it will help our team. I figure Chamberlain has to get a lot of points to help his team. If he's got to get thirty-five points for his team to win, and he gets them, then he's doing his job. I only think about winning."

Different players, different teams, different approaches. At first, Boston won and Chamberlain went home satisfied that he and his teammates had done their best under the circumstances. Then, as the years went by, the tension got greater and the outside forces became more noticeable. There were frayed tempers, angry words, taunting statements, and even threatened fights.

Russell kept quiet but many others talked for and about him. They answered all the questions about Russell's head-to-head competition with Chamberlain and added a little fuel to the fire along the way. There was an argument between Russell and Chamberlain during the 1965–66 playoffs that finally brought simmering bad feelings to the surface.

Larry Siegfried of Boston and Billy Cunningham of Philadelphia got into a swinging match and Russell stepped in as a peacemaker. Out of it came two versions. The Philly version: "Russell got too rough and Wilt told him he'd meet him outside. Russell said nothing until he got near the protection of his bench and then said 'Why not now?' The Boston version: "There was an incident earlier this season in which Chamberlain grabbed Siegfried. Russell told Wilt that if it happened again, he would have to help Siegfried. So when the fight with Cunningham broke out and Chamberlain went for Siegfried, Russell thought Wilt was being a bit too rough on Larry and told him so."

There was another playoff incident with Sam Jones grabbing a stool to defend himself against Chamberlain. That was blown up to king-sized proportions, especially when the Celtics beat Wilt's team in the playoffs once more. Auerbach had said many things about Chamberlain that had gotten under his skin, so during one playoff game Wilt went after Red. That prompted Russell to step between them and warn Wilt: "You'll have to go through me to get to him."

By then, Russell had withdrawn all invitations for Chamberlain to dine at his home. Their confrontations had grown to the proportions of Patton vs. Rommel. Every insignificant happening became significant. Chamberlain got the worst of it because Boston kept winning.

Wilt finally made it in 1967. He sat in the dressing room after the 76ers had eliminated Russell and the Celtics, 4–1, by coming from sixteen points back to win the final game, 140–116, and told his teammates: "This beating Boston was the thing we have been trying to do. It was a great accomplishment. We have been chasing them for nine years, yet I'm not as happy now as I will be in July and August when I walk down the street and won't have all those people saying: 'How come you guys didn't beat Boston?.' It will feel good then."

Wilt had pulled down a record forty-one rebounds in one game while ending the Celtics' run of eight straight titles. "Wilt played real, fine team ball," said Adolph Schayes, who had been replaced as coach of the 76ers by Alex Hannum that season. "He's thrown away that fadeaway shot completely. He's closer to the basket for rebounds, to pass out, to pick. For years Boston used that quick thrust that breaks a team's back. One team works twenty seconds and misses. The other team gets the ball and in two seconds makes a basket and it has a demoralizing effect."

Wilt had finally beaten Russell and the Celtics in the playoffs but it was to be the only time. Philadelphia became the champion by beating San Francisco in the final series, and Wilt got another title when he was with the Lakers and they beat the Knicks in the 1971–72 final. He had one more crack at Russell and the Celtics when he was with the Lakers, with the usual result.

When the Lakers signed Wilt, the stories started that they would need three basketballs because of Jerry West, Elgin Baylor, and Wilt. Someone asked Auerbach what he thought of the Los Angeles situation and Wilt got upset over what Red said.

"It wasn't a story in the first place," explained Auerbach. "It was just some remarks I made at a clinic when everybody was conceding the championship to L.A. What I said was that I never saw a championship won in July."

Wilt didn't interpret it that way. Actually, Auerbach wasn't one of his favorite spokesmen. They had drifted far apart since they first met when Chamberlain had been a bellhop at Kutsher's during the summer months and Auerbach got him on the court to help him with his basketball. "For twenty-five years I've known this man," Wilt said on a hot summer day in 1968. "And for ten years, I've taken his bull. I don't have to take it anymore. He should take half his money and give it to Bill

Russell. That's what it comes down to."

Auerbach, Boston, and Russell had gotten on Chamberlain's nerves. What bothered Wilt was that Auerbach reportedly had suggested that his arrival in Los Angeles meant trouble for West and Baylor. "In effect," said Chamberlain, "he was saying that I would make Baylor and West so subservient, they would be willing to be caddies on my team."

It must be said that for a man of his ability and contributions to the game, Chamberlain was the object of an unusual amount of abuse and ridicule. Some said he brought it on himself with his candid criticism of others. Some said his losing experiences against the Celtics and Russell turned him inside out with frustration and self-righteousness that annoyed people.

He was an unusually talented player who just happened to come along at the wrong time to win NBA championships. He was called a loser by those who never really appreciated what it took to beat Russell and the Celtics. It was like calling Ted Williams a loser because Joe DiMaggio and the Yankees used to beat the Red Sox so often. Pure nonsense.

Unfortunately for Wilt, his crusade against Russell was to wind up as it had started. Never mind all the close, seven-game series that Boston managed to win from Chamberlain teams somehow. Now it came down to the final playoff game against Russell in 1969. Each team won every game on its court and they went back to Los Angeles for the seventh one. L.A. had the home court advantage by finishing first in the West with 55–27 while the Celtics had finished fourth in the East with 48–34.

Wilt hurt his knee and went to the bench with about five minutes left and the Lakers trailing. Mel Counts came in and the Lakers closed in. But Chamberlain never got back into the game, the Lakers lost by two, and a few days after it was over, Russell made some uncomplimentary public remarks about Wilt for the first time.

Russell criticized Wilt for removing himself in such a critical spot and said he wouldn't have put Chamberlain back into the game if he had been coach. Russell not only supported Lakers coach Butch van Breda Kolff but also dug deeply into

Wilt for not playing in whatever pain he had at that decisive stage.

Wilt was forced to rehash the game and his pain. "The thing that kills me," Chamberlain said at the time, "was we had a chance to win and he [Van Breda Kolff] wouldn't put me back in. I don't see how he could have left me on the bench. I asked him about ten times. The first time he said: 'Wait. Wait.' The next few times he didn't even answer. He could have left Counts in and put me in. We had the ball three times when we were one down and I had a chance to rebound and go against Russell."

Russell had five personals at the time. Wilt also had had five since the third quarter and still had blocked a couple of spinning shots by Russell before he left to ice his injured knee. "I thought we were going to win," said Wilt when it was over. "They didn't beat us, we beat ourselves. You don't mind being beaten by a superior team but to go out and beat yourself is a shame."

And to lose to Russell and the Celtics was more than a shame to Chamberlain at that point. That was the last game against each other, and they haven't spoken since. One time, Russell, in his days as ABC-TV color man on the NBA's Game of the Week, actually impersonated Wilt Chamberlain, with whom he hadn't talked in years.

A woman, mistaking Russell for Chamberlain on a flight to Los Angeles, said: "I'm from Bel-Air. You have a magnificent house." She was referring to the $1,500,000 dreamhouse Chamberlain had built. Russell thanked her and then called over the stewardess. His impish mind couldn't resist the opportunity, so he had the stewardess inform the woman that she and her husband were invited by Mr. Chamberlain to attend a big party that night at his home.

Russell never found out whether they showed because Chamberlain never told him. Wilt never forgave Russell for blasting him. "He made the statement and it was disgraceful," said Wilt. "He never came to me to discuss it, either." Too bad.

It was such an unhappy ending to so many fine years of entertainment and enjoyment. Chamberlain vs. Russell? Will we ever see anything like it, again, in our lifetime? I doubt it.

DEBUSSCHERE-JOHNSON

*G*us Johnson's face was twisted with fierce intensity. His mouth was open like a blowfish gasping for air and his left arm was dug into the chest of the man guarding him as they struggled for position in the pivot.

Dave DeBusschere, the other man, was braced with all his strength against the body of the man trying to overpower him. The sweat glistened on Johnson's face and there was a look of fierce determination in the eyes of DeBusschere.

Johnson was on offense, DeBusschere on defense. The Classic Confrontation, they called it. Man against man. Will against will. Body against body. Mind against mind. It was etched on their faces as they jockeyed and shoved and refused to give an inch.

And the thing about this Johnson vs. DeBusschere confrontation was that it was only a posed picture. The two classic power forwards were posing for a magazine cover. Out of pure habit, they challenged each other in the studio on camera as though the NBA championship depended on it. I always recall that incident whenever someone brings up the subject of DeBusschere and Johnson, which is often.

I found out about that picture from DeBusschere. He told me

how he and Gus began throwing elbows as soon as the photographer advised them to assume their positions. It was instinct and I guess that would be the way they'd greet each other to this day.

DeBusschere vs. Johnson. The dream matchup to most pro basketball fans who watched the Knicks and Bullets play throughout the years. They were born for each other. They seemed destined to meet under the searching lights of the NBA and in the glare of television cameras that spread their battles throughout the pro basketball world.

Johnson went to high school in Akron, DeBusschere in Detroit. Johnson went to college in Idaho, DeBusschere in Detroit. Johnson came to the pros in Baltimore, DeBusschere in Detroit. Johnson was firmly entrenched with the Bullets from the start, DeBusschere was in a rut in Detroit until the Knicks got him during the 1968–69 season and then went on to win their first title the next season.

DeBusschere was no mystery to the pros. Everyone knew he was an outstanding talent in college and a guaranteed first-round status in the draft. I was scouting for the Knicks in Dave's college days and came back with enough evidence to convince us to draft him if we had the chance. You couldn't help being impressed. He was a winner. He was a big, strong kid, he could shoot, and he played smart defense. It only took the Knicks six years to get him.

By then, DeBusschere had gone through a couple of careers. He was a $65,000 Bonus Baby and pitched four years for the White Sox, played for the Pistons, and then became the youngest coach in the history of the NBA when owner Fred Zollner made him player-coach at the age of twenty-four. That was in 1964 and it appeared as though DeBusschere would be rooted forever in Detroit and the Knicks would never get him.

We would have grabbed DeBusschere in the 1962 draft but only the Pistons got a shot at him because of the territorial rule that existed then. The rule was put in by the original NBA owners in 1946, the first season, in order to enable each franchise to protect the college stars playing in their territory. That way, the teams could cash in on the natural gate appeal that college basketball players monopolized at the time.

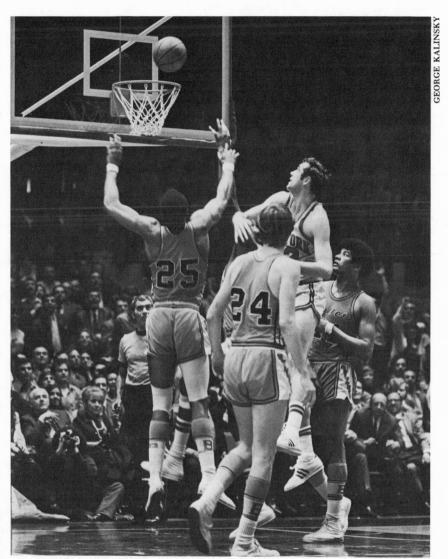

Johnson (25) and DeBusschere waiting for a rebound.

So the Pistons named DeBusschere as their territorial pick on the first round. Billy McGill, an outstanding six-nine center from Utah, was the first actual pick in the draft by Chicago. Then the Knicks took Paul Hogue, a six-nine center from the University of Cincinnati; St. Louis chose Zelmo Beaty, a six-nine center from Prairie View; Syracuse picked Len Chappell, a six-eight center from Wake Forest; Cincinnati got Jerry Lucas, a six-eight Ohio State center who went to the Royals as a territorial high school pick; Philadelphia landed another center, six-eight and one half Wayne Hightower, who had succeeded Wilt Chamberlain at the University of Kansas, and Los Angeles took still another center, six-ten LeRoy Ellis of St. John's. That left the poor Boston Celtics picking last as the champions, and all that remained for them was a young man named John Havlicek from Ohio State.

There was a reason why Havlicek lasted so long. At least, that's the story you heard after Havlicek became a pro basketball legend and those who passed on him had to justify why. He was drafted by the Cleveland Browns and everyone figured he'd be playing pro football when he went to camp with them.

How wrong we were. How wrong we were the next year, when the teams gathered for the 1963 draft. The Knicks picked first and took Art Heyman, a six-five guard from Duke; Baltimore chose Rod Thorn, a six-four guard from the University of West Virginia and, hopefully, another Jerry West; San Francisco got Nate Thurmond, the six-eleven center from Bowling Green; Detroit went for Eddie Miles, a six-four shooting guard from Seattle; Cincinnati stayed at home by taking Tom Thacker, a six-two guard from the University of Cincinnati; St. Louis picked a sleeper in Gerry Ward, a six-four guard from Boston College; Syracuse chose Tom Hoover, a six-ten center from Villanova; Los Angeles wound up with Roger Strickland, a six-five small forward from Jacksonville U., and the champion Celtics took Bill Green, a Colorado State player who never played for them and was so undistinguished, they never bothered to record his height.

I tell you all of this for a reason. It involves the second round of the 1963 draft. We were up first, again, and this time we decided to take Jerry Harkness, a New York boy who had played high school ball at DeWitt Clinton and had become a good shooting guard for Loyola of Chicago. Next up was Baltimore for its second crack and that's when it got Gus Johnson. It's hard to believe that Johnson lasted until the second round, just like it's hard to believe that everyone passed on Willis Reed in the first round of the 1964 draft and the Knicks got him on the second. Johnson was one of those late bloomers, that's all. He flew through the air for little Idaho in the Northwest but the pro scouts weren't tuned into his speed and agility at the time.

The flying slam-dunk hadn't become what Julius Erving, George McGinnis, and David Thompson have made it today. Johnson was way ahead of the times. He could leap to the moon but few knew about it. Few even knew Gus had jumped center on the Akron High School team on which Thurmond played forward.

Johnson was a fantastic athlete. One day, for example, he was sitting in the stands at an Idaho College track meet when the coach decided he could use a few points in the high jump. So the coach called on Johnson, who soared six-five for third place while wearing sneakers and khaki pants.

Few knew that when Johnson first came into the NBA. They soon began noticing a lot of things about him. There was more to him than the star-shaped diamond inlay that twinkled from an upper front tooth. They soon learned the man with the magnificent body could run, jump, shoot, and play defense. He did everything with a flair. He took off from the foul line for slam-dunks and smashed hoops and backboards with the ferocity of his game.

He played big forwards, small forwards, centers, and guards. He was brittle, sometimes erratic, sometimes showboat but always a player the Knicks had to stop to win. He was only six-five but no one played taller.

"Nobody appreciates what I have to do," he would say. "Maybe I would be more consistent if I wasn't asked to do so much. I'm fighting guards or centers on one end of the court and forwards on the other. I've never had the chance to concentrate on my offense. Just once, I'd like to play on a team with a big man and a good forward so I could see how really tough I am. I believe I'm the best. I mean that. I can do so many things others can't do. Maybe too many things. I've been asked to do too much as long as I've been playing ball."

DeBusschere was less erratic but a lot like Johnson in some ways. Dave was six-six and also had the body and intelligence to play guards, big and small forwards, and sometimes centers. Actually, when DeBusschere broke in with the Pistons, his first coach, Dick McGuire, had him play in the backcourt at times because he handled the ball so well.

Today, a six-six guard is not unique in the NBA. But when DeBusschere broke in, he was considered a monster in the backcourt. Of course, he didn't play there too often. Just often enough to perfect his ballhandling and help the Knicks with it when we finally won a championship. Ballhandling was to be one of the trademarks of our team that went so far because of its ability to hit the open man.

Four of the five starters on the 1969–70 team played backcourt at one time or another: DeBusschere, Walt Frazier, Dick Barnett, and Bill Bradley. Only Willis Reed had not spent time at guard, but for a big man he made up for it with a ballhandling instinct that got the ball to the right man at the right time.

I saw all those things in DeBusschere while watching him play in college and then with the Detroit Pistons. So did everyone else. I guess many other teams also chased him but we finally succeeded because we never gave up. Every coaching or front office change by the Pistons brought us back to Detroit. No good, though.

Still, the Knicks kept trying. We became so tuned into the situation that the slightest tremor was picked up by our sensitive seismograph. Thus, Eddie Donovan, then our general manager, was able to acquire some critical information that led to the trade for DeBusschere more than a year later.

Donovan was standing with Detroit scout Paul Seymour in a runway at the Garden one night watching a game. They were chatting about this and that when the subject turned to DeBusschere, as usual. Seymour said something about Dave that made Donovan's ears perk up but he didn't press it. Eddie stored it away as valuable knowledge if he ever got a chance to use it.

The Knicks got the chance when Seymour was promoted to head coach and the man in charge of player personnel. Donovan and I discussed it when the Knicks had some early problems in the 1968–69 season. We decided it was time to go back to our DeBusschere program. It was now or never, based on the clue Seymour gave Donovan that night in the Garden that DeBusschere might not be an untouchable in Paul's book.

It still turned out to be difficult. No matter what Seymour thought, DeBusschere was a hero to owner Fred Zollner and an untouchable to Ed Coil, the general manager. There were many discouraging moments and at times Donovan was on the verge of giving it all up as hopeless. But Eddie and I talked and decided DeBusschere was a rare commodity that was worth pursuing. DeBusschere was our Holy Grail.

We finally found it on December 19, 1968. The Knicks were on a road trip and Donovan was in constant touch with me on the DeBusschere developments. Seymour, in charge of the Pistons, needed a center and we were in a good position to offer one—Walt Bellamy. Things heated up for a while, then seemed to cool off as we moved to Boston. We won there on December 18, bringing our record to 18–17 after a 6–13 start.

Coil didn't seem interested in a deal for DeBusschere but Donovan, with me pushing, kept going back. Every mention of DeBusschere met with resistance from Coil until the Knicks left for Boston and I got a call there from Donovan. He informed me the Pistons had suddenly said there was no way they could justify an even-up swap of DeBusschere for Bellamy.

The logjam had been broken. We agreed to give the Pistons Butch Komives and Bellamy for DeBusschere and the deal was finally made though it was held up by Garden management on a technicality. That technicality finally was resolved but Donovan and I held our breath until we almost turned blue in our anxiety that the deal might be lost.

Finally, in Detroit, of all places, the Knicks announced they had acquired the services of DeBusschere and he would be facing his old team the very next night. We had gone there from Boston for a game with the Pistons. DeBusschere made the transition in Cobo Arena on December 20, 1968. He strolled into our dressing room and shook hands all around. He was nervous and the Detroit fans made him feel even more self-conscious when they gave him a long standing ovation when he was introduced in a Knick uniform. He played thirty-seven minutes, grabbed a game-high fifteen rebounds, and was game high scorer with twenty-one points.

He had fit in smoothly and some seemed suprised. I wasn't and neither was DeBusschere. "I didn't think it was hard at all," DeBusschere said. "I did get a little tired out there. I had only four hours sleep last night. Everyone in the country was calling me up to seven in the morning."

I remember the most important thing he said. "I'll try like hell to make New York a winner," he promised the night he played his first game with the Knicks. That's why Donovan and I wanted him. That's why we were ready to give up even more than Bellamy and Komives to get DeBusschere if it had been necessary.

He turned out to be even a better rebounder and defensive player than we had realized. That's the way it is. Sometimes it's the player and the situation. DeBusschere had to carry a heavier load with the Pistons. With the Knicks, he was the missing valve in a team machine.

DeBusschere immediately solved a major problem. He played the power and scoring forwards who were hurting the Knicks. He was also smart enough to play the quick smaller forwards when they were the major threats. DeBusschere was our troubleshooter when we had to keep a forward from killing us.

On his first night with us, we beat the Pistons by forty-eight points (135–87), the widest Knick victory margin until then— a matter of twenty-two years. We never stopped rolling. We made playoffs after playoffs. We won two championships before DeBusschere retired in 1974 and every year, it seemed, the Knicks had to get past Baltimore and Gus Johnson.

I can't help but wonder what might have been if our persistence had not shaken DeBusschere free from Detroit's stranglehold on him.

I can't help but be grateful for the success of the negotiations, so carefully handled in order not to frighten the Pistons by exposing our interest in DeBusschere prematurely.

All deals are not handled that way. This one had to be because we had learned how obstinate the Pistons were about discussing DeBusschere. I guess these words by Ed Coil best explain our strategy and its success: "We were talking about giving another player for Bellamy but then Eddie Donovan asked me if DeBusschere was available. I said it's a possibility but I told him not in a straight deal. We would have to have somebody else."

The DeBusschere-Johnson matchup wouldn't have been the same without the Baltimore-New York playoff showcase. Both were too professional to consider their meetings as more than just another tough night's work in a tough game. Johnson played all the top forwards and so did DeBusschere, and it was hard for them to separate one from another. A night playing against Bill Bridges, Elgin Baylor, Rick Barry, Tommy Heinsohn, Billy Cunningham, Spencer Haywood, Connie Hawkins, or Jerry Lucas was just as exhilarating and exhausting as playing against each other.

Yet, there was something special when DeBusschere and Johnson met, though I, as a coach, usually don't notice such things. I hardly ever remember the specifics of a game because when I'm on the bench, I'm watching the flow of the teams. I look for breakdowns in our defense that enable the other team to score on us. In DeBusschere's case, I'd look to see if he was tired and that's about all. I never concerned myself about the technical parts of his game. He knew how to play basketball as well as anyone.

That's why when the writers would come to me after a game and ask what I thought about a slam-dunk or a blocked shot or the great pick DeBusschere set to free Bill Bradley for a shot, I drew a blank most times. I was more concerned that Johnson wasn't overpowering DeBusschere because Dave needed a rest.

There are some things you can't forget though you are a coach and don't enjoy the luxury of isolating situations during a game. Johnson always fascinated me because he was such an incredible physical specimen and played for a team the Knicks had to keep beating every year to advance in the playoffs. It was my job as the coach to notice Johnson and see to it that he didn't beat the Knicks—too often.

It started, I guess, in the 1968–69 season when the Knicks swept the Bullets, 4–0, in the opening round of the playoffs. Baltimore had finished with the best record in the NBA and the Knicks had finished third but we beat the Bullets in four straight games. Johnson didn't play, though, because of knee surgery.

Gus was to be bothered by bad knees through the remaining years of his career but that only made his performances against DeBusschere all the more magnificent. Anyone who saw them go at it in the 1969–70 playoffs would appreciate it. The series went seven games, including a double overtime in the first one, and I had to admire Johnson, the way he played in pain—but not until we won the final game in the Garden by thirteen points.

People came to see the Knicks play the Bullets and left talking about the mini-war between DeBusschere and Johnson. It built from the start of the series until Gus erupted in the sixth game to help the Bullets tie and send it back to New York for the clincher. When Johnson and DeBusschere got together under the boards, it was like rubbing two huge trees together and setting a fire. This one set off a blaze.

DeBusschere's pride was hurt when Johnson erupted for fifteen in the third period alone and wound up with thirty-one for the sixth game. DeBusschere got into foul trouble early. He picked up three quick ones and I had to put Phil Jackson on Johnson. Now Jackson was a good defensive player but Johnson was quick and jumped over Phil a lot easier than against DeBusschere, who sometimes couldn't stop Gus from playing volleyball under the boards.

"One of the important things when playing Johnson," DeBusschere would say, "is not to let him get off a flying dunk and score early. I'd make sure I stayed between him and the basket. I'd take a blow if I had to and a lot of times I had to. He'd get discouraged after a while. When he found out he couldn't do that to me, he went bananas. He'd go wild and force crazy shots."

Well, that night in Baltimore, the confrontation saw Johnson go wild and make his shots, and he couldn't resist reminding DeBusschere about it. "Usually I didn't like talking to anybody," DeBusschere said. "I was very quiet and didn't believe in players mouthing off to other players."

This time, as they were leaving the court after the sixth game, Johnson reminded DeBusschere of the big game he'd just had. "If I was there you wouldn't have had such an easy time," replied DeBusschere, meaning foul trouble had limited him. Then DeBusschere reminded Johnson of some of his own good games and they left smiling at each other.

The next night in New York, they were lining up for the opening tap and DeBusschere said to Johnson: "Here we go for the finish. Good luck, I mean it." Johnson said: "Good luck to you, too, and I mean it." Then DeBusschere said: "Let's battle."

They battled and the Knicks won but Johnson didn't lose in our eyes. DeBusschere hit for twelve baskets and twenty-eight points as we took another step toward the championship we finally won by beating Wilt Chamberlain and the Lakers. But DeBusschere and Johnson had fought their usual atomic war and earned more respect for each other. They led the league in black and blue when they got through hammering each other.

"They won, so you can say I got burned," said Johnson, who finally helped the Bullets beat the Knicks and DeBusschere in the 1970–71 playoffs. That was to be his best playoff shot at us and I'll never forget it. I'll never forget the way Johnson pushed himself against DeBusschere despite the pain in both knees.

Gus came to the Garden for the first game of the 1969–70 opening series that we won by a point but he couldn't play. He was a cripple with fluid on his left knee, which needed injections, and a damaged right knee that needed surgery. "Goddam," he said as the Bullets left the dressing room to play without him. "If I'm hurt, I'm done. Who takes care of my kids? I'm not just living for today. There's tomorrow. There's the rest of my life. I'm not a youngster anymore."

He was thirty-two and suffering. A few days earlier, he took injections and then went out and helped the Bullets qualify to play the Knicks by scoring nineteen points, grabbing seventeen rebounds, and getting eight assists against the 76ers. An outstanding performance for a crippled player, but that's what was expected from Johnson. The thing he remembered was the needle. "Here I am, a big six-five cat, 235 pounds, and there's a little nurse seeing you crying," he said before coming out to play against us in the second game of the series.

Gus went on to play the second game and every game after that despite his bad knees. DeBusschere had his back full trying to keep Johnson from climbing over him for tap-ins. The shock absorbers in Johnson's damaged knees still had plenty of spring in them and the contact that went on between them under the boards was something right out of the Pittsburgh Steelers' defensive line.

DeBusschere played him perfectly in every game but Johnson did enough damage. Dave would give him the outside shot to make sure Gus didn't get a step on him to set up his flying slam-dunk. Yet, Johnson wound up the Bullets' top scorer with an 18.4 average and pulled down over ten rebounds a game despite DeBusschere and his own painful knees.

It was the sixth game of that series, though, that really put the spotlight on the DeBusschere-Johnson matchup. The Bullets had to win or they were finished. Johnson opened the second half by hitting three baskets. Then Gus and Earl Monroe proceeded to get twenty-eight of Baltimore's thirty third-quarter points. Somewhere along the way, DeBusschere tried to stop the deluge and yelled: "Call time, Red. Goddam it, we're all screwed up out here."

The Knicks gathered around me at the bench. Everyone had a suggestion. "Shut up, let DeBusschere talk," I said. Dave was annoyed because we weren't playing aggressive defense and helping out against Monroe and Johnson. It was the right analysis but it didn't stop Johnson.

DeBusschere was bothered by that game. "I felt lousy," he said. "I was frustrated. I knew I couldn't play that badly." He had shot two-for-eleven and Johnson's performance had made him feel that much more responsible for the series going seven games.

But then it was over and the Knicks had won and DeBusschere was talking about Johnson. Who else? "Hell, Gus is the difference between the Bullets this year and last year, when we beat them four straight," said Dave. "He wasn't inferior tonight. There were just a couple of shots he made yesterday he didn't make today."

Johnson made it the following season, when DeBusschere was on the losing side as the Bullets upset us in seven games. They won the final game in the Garden when Wes Unseld jumped out and blocked a corner shot by Bill Bradley that could've tied it. Johnson was as young as anyone as the Bullets raced to the dressing room as winners.

It was to be Johnson's last crack at the Knicks in the playoffs. It was to be DeBusschere's last crack at Johnson in the playoffs. Gus was traded to Phoenix soon after the 1971–72 playoffs ended. Yet, it will be a long time before they forget his confrontations with DeBusschere and the Knicks.

In three playoff series, Johnson wound up with a 9–10 won and lost record against DeBusschere by discounting the 1969–70 first game he missed. Like Muhammad Ali against Joe Frazier or Willie Mays against Sandy Koufax, DeBusschere against Johnson was one of the finest matchups of all time.

"Man, it's war," was the way Johnson once put it, and that just about said it all.

MONROE-FRAZIER

*I*t is hard for me to think of Earl Monroe as being anything but a Knick. All those games the Pearl played against the Knicks for Baltimore are just distant memories. I know if you ask him, he'll say: "We lost the playoffs in four games to the Knicks in 1969, in seven the next year, and then won in seven the next year but the seven-game series we lost was the best series I've ever seen."

He wasn't much of a spectator in it. Walt Frazier might've appreciated it, though, because Monroe was always his responsibility when we played the Bullets. The Pearl and Clyde were one of the game's superior matchups and then they teamed up to win a championship for the Knicks.

"He came into a difficult, difficult position," explained Dave DeBusschere in evaluating Monroe's move to the Knicks. "He was a man with immense pride and intelligence who had to swallow his pride to adjust. I remember Earl saying to me: 'This is Clyde's town, Clyde's basketball. I just want to play on a winner.' Until Earl learned the system, a lot of us questioned whether he and Frazier were compatible. One of them had to make the entire adjustment and Earl did it completely."

I knew when we made the trade for Monroe he could do it.

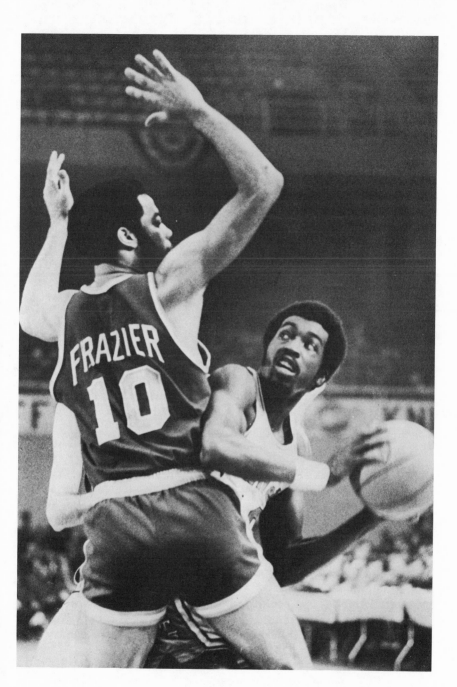

I knew that Earl would have to make the adjustment because we already were a championship team and it would be easier for him to change than the rest of us. Clyde was our ballhandler so Monroe had to do things differently. He couldn't have the ball all the time as he had with Baltimore.

I couldn't understand why anyone thought there'd be trouble after watching Monroe play. Sure, he shot a lot with the Bullets and dribbled a lot but I had seen him make some outstanding plays, so I knew he could pass the ball if necessary. And on the Knicks, it was necessary.

Monroe was a money-player. Anything could happen with him on the floor. We never hesitated when we heard Baltimore had finally decided to trade him. I know he went out to see the Indiana Pacers at one time but I never really believed he wanted to play in the ABA. He wanted to play in New York and we wanted him, no matter what they said about Monroe and Frazier being incompatible in the same backcourt.

Still, they said Monroe and Frazier never could play together. They were playalikes to some extent. They both wanted the ball, but the way Dr. James Naismith invented the game of basketball, it was played with only one ball. The NBA, with all its progressive changes, had not devised a way to use two basketballs.

Monroe, at times, was accused of playing without a basketball. His magic made it disappear. Many a night, Frazier and all the Knicks chased around looking for it, only to find Earl had hidden it in the basket. It was ironic that Frazier and Monroe should arrive in the NBA at the same time and then go on to establish such an individual rivalry until they became teammates.

I had scouted Frazier at Southern Illinois, a small basketball school, and figured I might have a secret. Clyde had been ineligible in his sophomore season but came to the Garden in 1967 and was named the Most Valuable Player in the National Invitation Tournament. He had another year of college eligibility but was qualified for the 1967 draft because his class had been graduated. He was well known by then.

The Knicks did their homework and determined that Frazier would turn pro if we drafted him, otherwise he might go back to college for another year of basketball. We were picking fifth. Detroit had the first pick plus the fourth because of a deal with the Lakers. The Pistons made Jimmy Walker, the Providence guard, the first pick; Baltimore then took Monroe; Chicago chose Clem Haskins, a guard from Western Kentucky; Detroit took forward Sonny Dove of St. John's as its second pick, and that's how we got Frazier. I'd say that was a pretty good draft year for the Knicks the way things turned out.

Frazier and Monroe were by far the best players drafted and we eventually wound up with both of them. Both were flamboyant in their own ways. Frazier off the court with his expensive fur coats and matching lifestyle, The Pearl on the court with his expansive Magic Show that became his patented lifestyle in the NBA.

Monroe was no surprise pick, though; like Frazier, he also came from a small school—Winston-Salem, North Carolina. Earl had gained national attention by leading his team to the small college championship while averaging forty-two points. "We were a jovial team," explained the Pearl, dropping the first hint of a fun-and-games personality.

"All I can tell you is that he has color," said Gene Shue, the Bullets' coach at the time. "It's everything he does. The way he passes. The way he walks and runs. You know he has it as soon as you see him, like a Ted Williams. We're going to be fun to watch the next season. I guarantee you that."

And the next season, and the next season, and the next season until Monroe decided he didn't want to play in Baltimore anymore, so we traded two players from our 1969–70 championship team, Mike Riordan and Dave Stallworth, to get him. Basketball was fun-and-winning with Earl. One time, his college team played Akron on its court for the regional championship. "Their star was Something Smith," recalled Monroe. "They had a big sign across the top of their fieldhouse: 'Earl Monroe Just a Myth, Can't Compare with Something Smith.' We won. I scored forty-nine. When the game was over, we had three guys standing on each other to get the sign down."

Monroe had watched the Harlem Globetrotters and worked

on an act of his own. He'd put a ball on the floor and kick it to a teammate. He'd cradle the ball in his left arm and then whip his right hand behind him and punch the ball to a cutting teammate. Once in a while he'd center the ball the length of the court through his legs. Pure magic.

He explained that he had to learn extra tricks because he was a small guy playing against big guys in the Philadelphia schoolyards and had to find some way to beat them. "I had to develop flukey-duke shots, what we call la-la, hesitating in the air as long as possible before shooting," he told those who wondered about his magic.

Earl had a strange introduction to the NBA the day he was drafted. The Pistons had announced that Walker was going to be their first choice, so the Bullets knew they were getting Monroe and went to his home in Philadelphia to bring him to New York.

"They came down to get me at four o'clock in the morning but I wasn't expecting them," said Earl. He wasn't home, either. He was hiding from the American Basketball Association, which was trying to sign him.

He got home near dawn but his best clothes were not exactly the luxurious type he wears today. So Buddy Jeanette, then the Baltimore general manager, loaned Monroe his jacket, the publicity man gave Earl a clean shirt, and they were on their way. Earl rejected their offer of underwear, though.

It was Ray Scott, a teammate in Baltimore, who once said this: "God couldn't go one-on-one with Earl." Monroe had arthritic knees, aching feet, and other problems that made him look as though he was playing his last game but the show went on and on.

I wasn't up to date on Earl when he first came into the league. I no longer was scouting for the Knicks. I had become coach with 1967–68 in progress so I never got to see Monroe play in his last college season. I had seen enough of him in earlier college games to know he was an exciting offensive player.

I was to learn a lot more about him. So was Frazier, who didn't get the Monroe assignment from me right away. It took Clyde time to get the rhythm of the NBA game. He was used to controlling the ball and the pace in the college game but the pros fast-broke more and played quicker defense.

I discovered Clyde's fast hands and alert defense when he was at Southern Illinois and we concentrated on that at the beginning. Clyde, Bill Bradley, and Phil Jackson had joined the Knicks in the same season, and I used them at first to run and to harass the offense. For some reason, Frazier was apprehensive about shooting, though he had taken charge of the offense in the second half of the NIT championship game with Marquette to win it for the Salukis.

One reason for Clyde's early shooting shyness probably was related to our having five guards on the team. We had Frazier, Bradley (who broke in playing the backcourt but eventually was switched to small forward), Butch Komives, Emmette Bryant, and Dick Barnett. That was a difficult playing-time situation for any rookie and it led to Clyde's moments of uncertainty until he learned to relax.

"I was afraid to shoot early in the season," said Clyde after I made a few moves that established him firmly in the backcourt and helped him loosen up. "I'd take a shot and, if I made it, I'd take another. If I didn't, I'd look too much to pass. Every time I missed, I could just hear the fans saying: 'Why the hell is he shooting?' It was rough."

I think he became the real Walt Frazier in a game against the Celtics and Bill Russell. It was sometime in late January or early February 1968 when Clyde hit seven of eight shots. In another stretch of two games against Boston, he scored forty-eight points and got nineteen assists. What really convinced Clyde he had arrived as a pro were twenty-nine foul shots driving the middle on Russell in those two games.

A fresh rookie doing that to the greatest defensive center to play the game. Clyde was proud of his new muscles. "I never drove this much in college," he said. "Can you imagine driving against the likes of Russell? I did it on one move: drive left, spin right, and I was under the basket. I missed some easy shots because I didn't realize I could get that far. I went too fast. I don't know how to shoot up close, going right to the basket. I didn't practice it because I didn't expect to get many of them."

Frazier's defense was ahead of his offense at the start but eventually his scoring caught up once he got the rhythm of our team game and recognized when and where his points helped. It wasn't long before the league got to know about his fast hands and the wise remarks about them. Bill Hosket, a teammate, observed: "Clyde could strip a car while it's going forty miles an hour."

Our first look at Monroe was during a national TV game in Baltimore. He put on his Magic Show right away, twisting and shooting with such unorthodox finesse, I knew right away we'd have to find someone to contain him. All we did was lose by twenty-three, which made it that much more difficult for me to forget.

Monroe was brash for a rookie. He showed no respect for anyone once the game started. He challenged the big and the small and it was easy to interpret his Magic Show as showboating. There were some who claimed his head was just a bit too big.

We didn't think so on the Knicks. We admired his talent. We recognized what it took for Earl to slither through the big men and twist his body out of the way to get off his shots. "That's bull," was Cazzie Russell's response to the showboating charges. "A guy has to have some cockiness or he wouldn't be so good. That's confidence. It's a positive thing."

Earl sure was a positive thing. He fascinated everyone. The fans, the opponents, and his teammates. Kevin Loughery, who played alongside Monroe from the moment he broke in, never ceased marvelling at the Pearl's contortionist skills. Loughery said a long time ago what others got to recognize much later.

"If you think about entertainment," was the way Loughery put it, "Earl puts on the best show in the game. As an individual, I'd prefer to see him play over Lew Alcindor, Oscar Robertson, and Jerry West. I think he's the most unique player I've ever seen."

That was quite a mouthful because Loughery said that about Monroe ten years ago. Kevin said other things. "He's not fast or quick," explained Kevin, who was to become one of the game's leading coaches with the New York and New Jersey Nets. "He can't jump this far off the floor. He's always in traffic. He likes contact on his shot. He makes two or three changes off his original move but is always on the hoop with his shots. When you ask him what he did, he honestly doesn't know. He might be as good an offensive player as we have in the game and his style has contributed towards changing it, the way he dribbles, backs into his man, gets into his area, and gets off his spin move. I see it but I can't believe it."

If Loughery couldn't believe it, how do you think I felt as a coach who had to do something about Monroe. That something turned out to be Frazier. Not really by himself, because we always played a team defense that helped out. On offense, it was hit the open man. On defense, it was get the open man. I decided to put Frazier on Monroe for a few reasons. First, Clyde was stronger and had the body to keep Earl from moving him around. Clyde also was a smart defensive player with quick hands. And, of great importance, Clyde was such a scoring threat at the other end, Earl had to play him tough and figured to get a little tired, which might hurt his shooting.

Clyde ran most of our plays and had the ball most of the time, which would force Monroe to work harder. "Give the ball to Clyde!" I would yell whenever the Knicks forgot who owned the ball on our team. There were times I switched Dick Barnett onto Monroe in order to change things, but not for long.

Monroe belonged to Frazier and vice versa. No Baltimore-New York playoff game would have been the same without them playing each other and there were plenty of those opportunities. They had a lot of time to get acquainted as the Knicks got better and we played the Bullets in 1968–69, 1969–70, 1970–71, 1971–72, and 1972–73.

Earl wore a Baltimore uniform the first three times and a New York uniform the last two. In the first three, he played against Frazier; in the next two, he played alongside him. Never a dull moment as the Bullets won only in 1970–71.

Actually, the Knicks won six straight games before Monroe was able to enjoy a winning one. We won four straight in the 1968–69 playoffs and the first two of the 1969–70 playoffs, but the Pearl let us know he was trouble right from the start. He was going to be the focal point of every game, win or lose, in the continuing series that stretched out over five years.

I remember the third game of our 1968–69 sweep, for example. The Pearl had scored thirty-two in the opener and added twenty-nine in the second game. Now he was on his way to twenty-seven more, which gave him eighty-eight for three games or seven more than Frazier got over the same span, which sort of took the sting out of Monroe's scoring, as I had hoped when the matchup was created.

There were only two points separating us when Frazier fouled Monroe with thirty-five seconds to go. "I thought I'd blown the whole thing," said Clyde as the Pearl stepped to the line with a shot at knotting the game at 116. Frazier had meant to grab Monroe for a non-shooting foul because we weren't as yet over the limit but the Pearl squirmed away and got two in the act of shooting.

Earl missed them both and we won by three points. The Knicks knew they had gotten away luckily. Monroe had shown us a thing or two again, despite the missed foul shots that had something to do with Frazier tiring him.

"That's what's wrong with this game," said our scout, Dick McGuire, after watching Monroe's dazzling magic. "You play the guy perfectly, like Frazier plays him, but he still gets his shot off and scores. He'll twist around you or force you into committing yourself before he takes his shot."

McGuire was a purist from the old two-hand set school, and expected solid defense to stop shooters as it had in his playing days with the Knicks. It no longer worked that way and Monroe was making sure everyone recognized it.

Then there was Dave DeBusschere, our resident defensive expert. "Nobody, really, can play him one-on-one," said Dave, failing to include God as Ray Scott once did. "I know I don't know what way he's going. He fakes you out and comes back into you again. There's no secret what we try to do with him. We force him down the side and attempt to keep the ball out of the middle, where he's got the room to maneuver to go the other way."

Frazier also had a Monroe secret. "I try to move him on defense," said Clyde. "I try to make him work on offense, taking him one-on-one. I'm trying to wear him down." The only things that were worn down were the sneakers Frazier and Monroe burned up playing each other.

I'm not one to take anything away from players such as Monroe and his Baltimore teammates who played alongside him in the backcourt, but Frazier and Barnett had an edge over them, in my opinion. Clyde and Dick were finely tuned into each other and won many games for the Knicks the way they teamed on defense.

We had one distinct advantage over the Bullets whenever a game came down to the last shot. We knew Monroe would take it. On the Knicks, anyone on the floor who had the open shot would take it. True, we'd set up a final shot when the game was on the line but there never was any panic or desperate passes because we had faith in Frazier, Barnett, DeBusschere, Bradley, or Reed if they wound up with the ball.

Baltimore always gave the ball to Earl and let him go one-on-one—not a bad percentage play if Monroe is on your side. How many times the Knicks did that after the Pearl joined us . . . as many times as the Bullets did it, with one major difference: we were in the better position to defend against the whirling, swirling moves of Monroe.

There were a few critical times in the regular season and in our many playoff games; while Earl worked on Frazier, Barnett came off the blind side to steal the ball. Tricky Dick Barnett was smart and had a fine sense of anticipation, while Clyde had the strong body and quick hands to maneuver Monroe into the traps we set.

In the opening game of the 1969–70 playoffs, Earl had avoided most of the traps as the Bullets battled the Knicks to a tie at the end of regulation time. This wasn't supposed to happen because we were playing in the Garden, and losing the opening game on our floor would be dangerous.

We threw the book at the Pearl but couldn't stop him. We steered him into certain lanes, double-teamed, Frazier pressed him while Barnett tried sneaking over from the blind side, and Monroe still wound up with thirty-nine. However, Clyde made the defensive plays when it really counted. He took advantage of the Pearl's deep sense of concentration. He'd almost go into a trance while maneuvering Frazier.

Monroe had the uncanny ability of shutting everything out but the man he was trying to trap in his one-on-one web. The Pearl would get so involved in what he was doing, he sometimes didn't know what time it was. He actually thought the buzzer that sent the game into overtime was the end of the third period. "What's that five minutes doing up there?" he asked Frazier when the five extra minutes for overtime was posted on the scoreboard.

It was only a moment's lapse. Monroe soon had the Bullets leading, 110–108, with something over thirty seconds left in overtime. What was worse, they had the ball. A basket now and we were dead. Monroe brought the ball across midcourt slowly and Frazier picked him up right away.

Earl went into his act. Spinning, twisting, dribbling. He was killing as much time as possible while maneuvering Frazier closer and closer to the shooting zone. Barnett was off on the side, trying to sneak in off the blind side, but the Pearl was wise to him.

Suddenly, Clyde's hand flicked out like the tongue of a snake and the ball was knocked out of Monroe's hands. Barnett scooped it up and was fouled driving for the basket. He got two foul shots and tied it. A small miracle. Then another. On the very next play, Clyde did it again to Monroe. The ball was knocked loose and Barnett was on his way once more to the basket.

I glanced at the clock and there were only five seconds left as Barnett, chased by Fred Carter, dribbled for the winning basket. What a way to win. But we didn't on that play. Carter, only six-three, somehow managed to leap as Barnett went up to lay the shot against the backboard and blocked it. Uncanny. Unbelievable.

We screamed that Carter had pinned the shot against the backboard, which would be goaltending and an automatic two winning points for the Knicks. "I caught the ball with my hand before the ball hit the backboard," Carter insisted. "My hand hit it up. I knew Barnett had a step on me but I'm quicker than he is and I caught up with him."

Referee Mendy Rudolph agreed with Carter's version but we went on to win anyway, 120–117. We went on to win the series in seven interesting, exciting games. Monroe and Frazier never gave each other an inch. Earl's knee acted up in the sixth game and Gene Shue decided it might be easier to take him off Clyde on defense.

So the Pearl played Barnett in the final game and Tricky Dick got thirteen baskets on him. "I was waiting for Barnett to get old," mused Carter when it was over. But who could forget Monroe in a losing cause. Not Frazier, who bore the scars of battle on his weary face.

Monroe and Frazier had fought, scratched, and used all their ingenuity to contain each other. Each was capable of breaking open a ballgame and that's why they were matched. What Monroe might get, Frazier might get back. That's what matchups are all about in pro basketball.

No coach should allow one player or position to create an imbalance. That's why I matched Monroe with Frazier. Ace against ace. Power against power. If Monroe got thirty-four, Frazier might get thirty-four. The idea was not to allow the Bullets to get a big edge at that one position.

Frazier enjoyed the assignment. It was not easy but it was fun for Clyde because playing the Monroes is what pro basketball is all about when you have Frazier's talent. They saw so much of each other, Clyde could've played the Pearl in his sleep.

Matter of fact, Clyde thought of that. "I'm tired of dreaming of that cat," he said after the winning series sent us against Milwaukee and Lew Alcindor. "He's like a horror movie. It's a lot of sweat chasing him. He's such a great shooter. I say to myself: 'How can I stop him?' "

Someone once suggested a gun was the best way. The Knicks sure could've used one on the Pearl when we got together with the Bullets for our annual playoff at the end of the 1970–71 season. We had won the championship the year before by beating the Lakers in that seventh game when Willis Reed dramatically hobbled from the dressing room to hit his first three shots against Wilt Chamberlain. Now we were back defending it.

The Pearl was too much. We were fundamentally the same teams but the Bullets outlasted us in seven games this time.

They were the same old exciting, interesting, slashing battles, with Frazier and Monroe continuing their mini-war, and it went down to the last shot in the final game that ended in the Garden, 93–91.

Let me give you an example of how much Monroe contributed in just one game. The lead changed hands six times on six baskets coming down the stretch and the Pearl, scoring seven points, did this: drove past Frazier, through Reed and DeBusschere, for a three-pointer; fouled by Frazier, made two; drove across key, just missed incredible left-handed hook, but made two when fouled.

Another time: Blocks Frazier shot from behind, feeds for two off fast break; hits in the corner over Frazier; drives past Reed for two from underneath; dribbles the clock and makes two when fouled by Barnett. All that, besides twenty-nine points on eleven-for-twenty-four shooting. And in a losing game, no less.

We won the first one but Monroe and the Bullets won the last one. We solved the Monroe problem by the next playoffs. We traded Mike Riordan and Dave Stallworth to Baltimore for him on November 10, 1971. Now Frazier had Monroe alongside him as we beat the Bullets in the playoffs, 4–2. Our Rolls-Royce backcourt. "Can you envision two better guards than Earl and Clyde?" asked DeBusschere.

They were something to watch when they played each other. Then Monroe deserted the Bullets by joining Frazier and the enemy. When the Pearl went back to Baltimore the first time, he saw this banner: "Benedict Monroe." How soon they forgot.

BRADLEY – HAVLICEK

When Bill Bradley first came to the Knicks, I assumed he'd stop in New York just long enough to pick up a uniform and then head straight to the Hall of Fame in Springfield, Massachusetts.

No NBA rookie ever created more media demand than Bradley when he finally joined the Knicks with the 1967 season in progress. Wilt Chamberlain's introduction was quite feverish but he was far enough from the media capital of the world to miss the dimension of excitement and attention that playing in New York seems to provide. I remember Abe Saperstein holding a press conference at the old Toots Shor's to announce Chamberlain was joining the Harlem Globetrotters but it was nothing like Bradley's first press conference at Leone's.

Wilt was leaving Kansas University after his junior year and Saperstein was signing him for the year he had to sit out before Chamberlain became eligible for the draft. Bradley went away to Oxford for two years and the excitement he had generated at Princeton was nurtured all that time. It was like a two-year buildup to the day Bradley finally announced he would play pro ball.

I was a scout for the Knicks at the time but I was there and saw the turnout for his first press conference. Muhammad Ali couldn't have packed the place any better. It was standing room only among the newspapers, radio, and television people when Ned Irish made it official that the Knicks' territorial pick of 1965 was ready to play.

Cazzie Russell's $400,000 contract had been a major breakthrough for an NBA rookie, excluding Chamberlain's historic first deal that had made him the highest-paid player in the league. Bradley's $500,000 contract was better than Cazzie's, so they immediately called the young man from Crystal City, Missouri, "Dollar Bill."

From that moment on, every city Bradley visited for the first time smothered Dollar Bill for interviews. And for the first time in NBA history, the Knicks had to arrange for a special press conference at every franchise stop in order to accommodate the demands for interviews. They always said that Bradley was destined to make it big in politics when his basketball-playing days were through and I got the feeling that every new press conference was just another step in "The Making of a President."

Havlicek was firmly established in the league by the time Bradley walked on the scene. They had little contact at the start because it took a while for Bill to develop, whereas Hondo was a super Sixth Man for championship teams five of his first six years in Boston. Actually, I can't remember the exact moment when I decided to play Bradley on Havlicek. Like a lot of things that occur in the NBA, it just happened.

Dave DeBusschere always got the power forward and Bradley played the smaller one. So when we played the Celtics after DeBusschere joined us in the 1968–69 season, the Havlicek-Bradley matchup was created. I think basketball benefited from it. They were meant for each other. Wind them up and they never stopped running.

Playing without the ball. Trying to run and hide from each other. Weaving in and out of traffic like New York cab drivers. Playing in each other's shorts and sometimes grabbing them in order to stay close.

Bradley didn't always play Havlicek. Sometimes I'd switch DeBusschere onto him, or Phil Jackson. It all depended on the

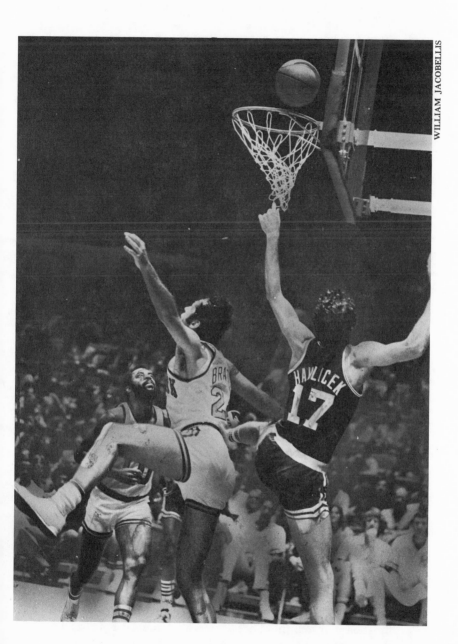

situations because sometimes Bradley would get into early foul trouble and I had to nurse him so he would be available for the more critical late stages of a game. I made it a strategy when I took over coaching the Knicks that I wouldn't let any starter pick up more than three personals in the first half.

As soon as Bradley or any starter got three, he was out and I'd start him in the second half. That way Havlicek got to see a lot of our defensive forwards. Also many of our guards, because Hondo also played the backcourt when the Celtics got into trouble back there. Then it became the responsibility of Walt Frazier, Dick Barnett, or Earl Monroe to keep up with Mr. Perpetual Motion.

Ironically, Bradley, like Havlicek, broke into the NBA in the backcourt. Bill was six-five and, in those days, the league was in a big forward cycle. Besides, the Knicks already had two small forwards in Cazzie and Dick Van Arsdale, so there just wasn't any room up front for Dollar Bill.

I changed that for two reasons. One, Bradley's ballhandling and shooting were good from the backcourt but he wasn't quick enough on defense. Also, we lost Van Arsdale to Phoenix in the 1968 expansion draft, so there was room up front for Bradley. That eventually created another problem—the kind a coach likes.

Cazzie and Dollar Bill found themselves fighting for the same job. Cazzie was the starter when Bradley became a Knick but Cazzie was to lose his job in a turn of events that made us a better team. That's because Cazzie had the gift of being able to come off the bench with guns blazing like John Wayne.

Bradley, on the other hand, was not the same coming off the bench. The Knicks were far more effective with Dollar Bill starting and Cazzie performing as our Sixth Man and giving us a huge lift when substitutes generally provide a small letdown. Bradley wasn't just given the job. He had to earn it.

He was out of sync when he played his first game for the Knicks against the Pistons in the Garden. It was December 9, 1967 and Dick McGuire was the coach. Bradley had just finished four months of active duty with the Air Force and his lieutenant's uniform was hanging in his locker as he put on a Knicks uniform for the first time.

I was in the dressing room as a scout. Eddie Donovan and Ned Irish were there to see their precious commodity. McGuire had briefed Bradley in the few minutes they had to get ready for the game.

"We've got only seven plays, each with options," explained McGuire. "There's nothing hard about them and I've gone over all of them with Bill. The only other thing we've talked about is defense. I explained to him that he can use his hands more in the pros."

Bradley had a rough time that night. A sellout crowd gave him a standing reception and made so much noise whenever he hit a practice shot, the Pistons turned around to watch him. He didn't come off the bench until the second period and then had to consult with Butch Komives during foul shots to determine what he should do on offense against a Detroit pressing defense.

He scored only eight points but I liked what I saw in the second half. Here he was, only a rookie under the added tension of a nervous debut, and he started taking charge of our offense, directing his teammates where to go on the floor.

Eddie Miles, who played Bradley, was impressed. Miles, later to have a fling with the Knicks when I became coach, put his finger on a Dollar Bill resource that was to help us win two championships. It also explained why, when the time came, I put him on Havlicek.

"I didn't see any basic weakness in his defense," said Miles, a man with a strong body and shooting moves. "He didn't turn his head when the ball was passed over him, which a lot of rookies do. Offensively, he looked for the open man and showed poise. He had trouble with his dribble because he dribbles high and he's gonna lose the ball that way."

That's another reason why I switched Bradley to forward when I got the chance. He wasn't a good dribbler for the fast hands in the pros. His passing was intelligent and would be more useful up front because forwards who can handle the ball well and make a play are rare.

Bradley had to survive a lot to get there but he finally made it once he recovered from injuries when a car knocked him down. He was only a few games into his career with the Knicks when a young lady driving an MG along Eighth Avenue set a pick on him. Bradley was walking across the street toward a restaurant from his apartment house a few blocks from the old Garden when the accident took place.

He hurt his hip, wrist, and dignity. It was embarrassing, like his second game with the Knicks, when we blew a twenty-one-point lead to the St. Louis Hawks and lost in double overtime. We would have won in regulation if Bradley hadn't made a rookie mistake. He wound up with twenty-seven points before fouling out two minutes from the end.

Bradley missed his first shot after coming off the bench and then hit eight in a row. He was that kind of streak shooter throughout his career. Bradley was on his way to becoming a hero in only his second game when disaster struck.

Dick Barnett hit a shot that put the Knicks ahead 124–122, with thirty-seven seconds to go. Then Lennie Wilkens missed for the Hawks and Walt Bellamy rebounded with twenty-four seconds left. All the Knicks had to do was run the clock or get fouled and extend their lead to more than a basket, which would be sufficient at that time.

With fifteen seconds left on the regulation clock, Bradley forced an off-balance shot that Bill Bridges smothered. The Hawks picked it up and Wilkens sent it into overtime, with the Hawks eventually winning. I liked the way Bradley handled it. He wasn't angry or upset. He never lost the poise that was to contribute so much in the following games and years. "I don't enjoy any game you lose, unless it's for fun, like tennis," he told the media crush that pinned him against a wall in the dressing room. "Too bad I took that bad shot when I did. It occurred to me on the way up that I shouldn't have shot it. After it didn't go in, I appreciated that I should have used up the clock."

McGuire the coach was satisfied, just as Holzman the coach was to be satisfied when he soon took over Bradley and the Knicks. "A lot of guys got passes off changes," observed McGuire. "Bradley hit quite a few guys. It seemed like there was a lot more movement."

The seeds of Hit the Open Man were being planted. "One

guy starts to pass, everybody starts moving and you start looking for the open man," said Cazzie Russell, now a teammate
of the man who beat him out of a Holiday Festival MVP during
a Michigan-Princeton final that was one of the most exciting
games ever.

There was one improvisation that convinced me Bradley
was an exceptional player who would have a major role in the
sport. Russell called to Bradley: "Set up." Dollar Bill faked to
the middle, with Cazzie picking off Joe Caldwell, who was
Bradley's man. Bradley shouted "Two," cut around Cazzie,
took a pass from him and hit a jumper.

Bradley the rookie looked like he'd been a pro for a dozen
years. He picked up the flow so easily, but it took time to put
it all together. I know. I had to sit him about a month after I
took over from McGuire. I told the press: "He has been going
bad lately. I want him to get himself together. The kid's had
a lot of pressure. I want him to sit and watch a game even if
it means blowing it."

He sat near me as we beat the Royals in Cincinnati by two
points in overtime. Once in a while I talked to him. Once in
a while he talked to me. At the end, we both got the job done.
Bradley always had a lot of class. He was eager to learn. There
were people who were jealous of the publicity he had gotten
and claimed he wasn't that good. I used to tell him that the
roof will cave in on those guys—that he'd kill them some
night.

The day after I benched him in Cincinnati, we were in
Evansville, Ohio and he drove to a gym and actually practiced
all by himself for two hours. That's another reason I put him
on Havlicek. There was no way Hondo would discourage
Bradley no matter how much running and scoring he did.

There was just one more turning point before the matchup
occurred. Bradley had to become a starter. He got his chance
by accident and never gave it back. Cazzie broke an ankle in
a game against Seattle shortly after the 1968–69 All-Star
break. It happened four games after Bradley, filling in with
Cazzie on National Guard assignment, played thirty-seven
minutes in San Diego despite an upset stomach, contributing
eleven assists and nine rebounds.

I considered that game the making of Bradley. It convinced me he was ready to start but I couldn't make a change because Cazzie was shooting sensationally and we were winning. Then with two seconds to go in our game with the Sonics in the Garden, one of those cruel twists of fate took place. Cazzie sneaked downcourt and DeBusschere fired a long pass that center Bob Rule managed to deflect. Joe Kennedy, a big, rugged forward, dove for the free ball, fell on Cazzie's leg, and there was a break.

That's when Bradley stepped in as a starter. We went up and up with Bradley and DeBusschere at the forwards and soon were able to compete on an equal level with the Celtics. Our rivalry got hotter as we won more, but we never did beat Boston in the playoffs until Bill Russell retired with eleven championships in thirteen years following the 1968–69 season.

Once the Knicks replaced the Celtics as champions in 1969–70, Bradley against Havlicek took on more meaning. More people noticed. Bradley even noticed.

"I guard John Havlicek—by far the most difficult job I have in a season," Bradley wrote in *Life on the Run*. "Havlicek's every movement has a purpose and his teammates look for him constantly. If I am a split second behind him, or respond to his fakes away from the ball, he receives a pass and gets a basket. He never lets down and his stamina seems endless.

"I've played him for six years. If he gets twenty-five points, and I get fifteen, and we win, I think I have done a great job. Testing my ability against his superior skills gives me great satisfaction. Both of us know instinctively how far we can challenge each other without destroying our mutual respect. If he makes a cut to the basket without the ball, I might try to stop him with a stiff-arm to the hip. He might respond by grabbing my arm for leverage and hurtling past me . . . each doing some holding and pushing but never turning the natural aggressiveness of the game into hostility."

In all the years of individual and team intensity, I never saw Bradley and Havlicek come even close to fighting. That's what made their matchup a thing of beauty. They played their own little game of hide-and-seek at both ends of the court. Bradley would duck behind Reed or DeBusschere to block out Havlicek, and John would use Russell or Cowens to screen himself from Dollar Bill.

Bradley was the better shooter but Havlicek was the better scorer. Havlicek was quicker and could jump higher but Bradley had an innate intelligence that compensated for his physical deficiencies. In the long run, Havlicek did more offensive damage but Bradley made it all worthwhile because the Knicks beat the Celtics a lot after Russell was gone.

At the beginning, when I took over, I yelled at Bradley and that shocked him a little. Later, when the Knicks matured and created a team rhythm, I changed my approach and Dollar Bill must have wound up thinking I was Mr. Nice Guy. How could I continue to yell at Bradley when he sacrificed himself and his body so often in confrontations with Havlicek and helped us finally pay the Celtics back just a little for so many years of abuse?

Russell was still around for the 1968–69 season when the Celtics beat us, 4–2. That was a disappointing finish for the Knicks because we had wound up six games ahead of them in the regular season. Boston ended up fourth but went on to beat the Lakers for player-coach Russell's final championship before he retired.

That's the year we swept the Eastern Division champion Bullets and were shooting high. Havlicek and his teammates scattered us like so many pieces of Skylab by beating us in the Boston Garden in the second for a 2–0 lead we couldn't do a thing about. That second game taught Bradley and the rest of us a lot, especially since we had to win because we had lost the opening game of the series on our court.

It was a game that would take us a long time to forget. We lost, 112–97, in a rout. At one time, the Celtics led by twenty-nine and when Russell took himself out with 8:23 to go, they were ahead 95–69. It was most frustrating for the Knicks, who were just growing. I yanked all the starters but Dick Barnett and put in Nate Bowman, Donnie May, Mike Riordan, and Bill Hosket to finish it out.

There was one dry spell of almost six and one half minutes where we didn't get a basket. Russell was intimidating around the hoop but our shooting was awful. We were jittery. It was a game where we invented new ways of giving up the ball. DeBusschere was zero-for-nine, the Knicks were thirty-three-for-ninety-six. Bradley was called for double-dribbling, Barnett passed the ball to Havlicek. "They started to press after our defense caused them to make mistakes," said Hondo, who gave Bradley a rough night. "It wasn't one of our better games," said Bradley. "I don't know why things like this happen but I hope it discourages them," said Russell.

It didn't. We were much better the next game in Madison Square Garden. In the first game, I had to ease Bradley out of there as our forwards were outscored by thirty-five points. In the second game, the Celtics' forwards outscored ours by forty. "Every time I thought about it I got sick," said Bradley, who wouldn't have minded what Havlicek had done if we were winning.

Bradley played Havlicek like an angry man in the third game. They were nose to nose, shove to shove, bump for bump for thirty-two minutes as they both played forty-eight. It would've taken surgery to separate them. And when it was over, Havlicek had eight points, getting only two while Bradley was playing him.

At the other end, where Russell was goaltending, Bradley fired eighteen points. It was something of a surprise at the time because Dollar Bill always seemed to have trouble just keeping up with Havlicek. "You find forwards with more physical ability," Havlicek said of the man with whom he'd engage in a tag-team match for many years, "but there are none smarter."

We had beaten the Celtics six out of seven in the regular season and this was to be our first playoff win over them in three games. I knew we had them (that night, anyway) when Havlicek began complaining to the officials about Bradley. Hondo thought some of the pushing, shoving, and bumping were fouls by Bill. That indicated the kind of job Bradley did on him.

It was unlike Havlicek to complain, so it was obvious that Bradley's nagging defense had gotten to him. "One of the influences on me," said Bill, "from my father and high school coach, was to play hard within the rules. Keep your mouth shut and play the game."

That's the way he always played Havlicek and vice versa. There were very few words between them. Just an admiring glance or a lift of the eyebrow in appreciation of an outstanding move, play, or shot.

Bradley was coming along. I liked the way he played Havlicek and got maximum mileage out of his own talent. Bill wasn't the superstar he had been in college but he was becoming a force in the Knicks' concept. If we were going to beat the Celtics in the future, Bradley would have to do all he could to keep Havlicek from running all over us.

"Part of playing basketball is to adjust to the way the game is played that night," said Bradley after he adjusted his game to slow down Havlicek for the first time in the playoffs. "Physical contact is just part of it. You can't separate the physical part from the rest. It's always there."

That was another thing about Bradley. We could always depend on him to say something profound whether or not the situation called for something profound. He didn't get to say too much the rest of that series because it ended in Boston after six games.

I heard the players promise to be back the next year in the Boston Garden dressing room after it was over. They were. But not in Boston. That's because Russell was gone and the Celtics finished next to last in the Eastern Division in 1969–70, when we went all the way to the championship. They missed the playoffs.

Next season, the same old story without Russell. For the second year in a row there was no Bradley-Havlicek playoff matchup though they had a few interesting ones during the season. I remember one night in December when Russell showed up at our place in the Garden to see what was going on with his old team.

Havlicek, thirty-one at the time, still was running longer than anyone, and the Celtics managed to beat us. Russell sat and watched Bradley chase Havlicek, who scored nineteen of his twenty-five points in the second half and never stopped running.

"He's crazy," said Russell, cackling. "One of these days he's going to find out that he can't do that anymore."

Anyway, it's hard to believe, but despite what Havlicek did to us and Bradley, in particular, I didn't want to ever see him quit. He was the type of man you just hope would go on playing forever. He was remarkable that night and many other nights against us.

It was rare that anyone stopped Havlicek from scoring and running. While Bradley concentrated on him, Havlicek played every man in sight as a part of Boston's switching defense. He got ten points in the third period that put the Celtics ahead of us by sixteen. Russell's prediction that Havlicek would find out some night he couldn't do it anymore would have to wait many years.

"It'll happen but I don't know when," Havlicek said that night in 1971. "I still go forty-eight minutes. I still play back and front court. I still guard everybody but the center. I know I'm going to be playing everybody, front and back. I had Bradley, DeBusschere, Jackson, Frazier, Barnett, Monroe, and even Meminger."

I remember talking to Tommy Heinsohn that night after Havlicek ran a lot younger than Bradley. "The older he gets, the more he runs," said the Celtics coach. In the dressing room after the game, Havlicek reached into his bag and took out two chocolate bars. "For energy?" he was asked. "Energy I've got," he said. "I'm just hungry."

In the 1971–72 playoffs, Havlicek and Bradley chased each other for only five games and we won, 4–1. In 1972–73, they chased each other for seven games and we won, 4–3, as Havlicek played the last three with an injured right shoulder after running into a DeBusschere pick. In 1973–74, Bradley chased Havlicek in vain as the Celtics won, 4–1, and went on to win their first NBA title without Russell.

I remember the fourth game of that last important playoff series with the Celtics. They now had an experienced Dave Cowens and we had Willis Reed and Dave DeBusschere injured and on their way out. I admired Bradley for the way he pursued Havlicek on a night that Hondo did nothing wrong. It was like Alydar chasing Affirmed during their horseracing classics but never giving up.

Havlicek scored thirty-six points, including eight of ten down the stretch as we lost, 98–91, and fell hopelessly behind in the series, 3–1. We made one good move late in the game by slicing a seven-point deficit to one with twenty-six seconds left. There was a time-out and I told the players to play an honest defense. Up on everybody. Give no one room.

In the other huddle, I found out later, Havlicek was calling a play for himself. We more or less guessed it. That's the type of player he was—the type who never flinched when it came down to taking the last shot. The play called for Havlicek to fake a move around the key and take a pass for a layup.

Though we knew what was coming, it worked because Bradley got caught in traffic and Havlicek was gone before anyone could cover. That's basketball. Even if you know what's coming, it doesn't guarantee that you can stop it. It's execution that counts and Havlicek executed and we didn't.

On the other hand, there was another game in the same series when the Celtics were losing by two and Havlicek also called his own play. That time he missed. You win some, you lose some.

Bradley versus Havlicek proved it. They were the perfect example of winning some and losing some. Sometimes Havlicek won. Sometimes Bradley won. I can't remember any game where either went away embarrassed or feeling that he had given away even an inch on the floor.

Anytime the Celtics and Knicks played, I knew Bradley and Havlicek were this close to being this close. I sure wish I had had more time to watch them.

REED-JABBAR

Willis Reed sat on his stool in front of his dressing stall and the sweat rolled off his round face. I walked over and said: "Nice game." He looked at me through tired eyes and smiled.

He deserved to be tired. He had just played against the world's tallest basketball player. If not the world's tallest, certainly the world's best tallest basketball player. A young man named Lew Alcindor, fresh out of UCLA, where he had helped John Wooden win a few NCAA championships.

It wasn't Reed's first look at Alcindor. The Knicks had played the Milwaukee Bucks an exhibition game in the Garden and Lew was in that game for only twenty minutes because of a bad ankle and the fact that he fouled out with 7:26 to go. "I can beat him," said Reed after we lost that game, "but it's a hard night's work."

I knew that. Reed didn't have to tell me. I saw Lew take a rebound over Willis' head and stick it right back in. Few players were able to do that to Reed. He was too big, strong, and physical for that. I guess Reed never forgot it.

At that moment, Willis realized he would have to move a mountain when he played the young man who had grown so

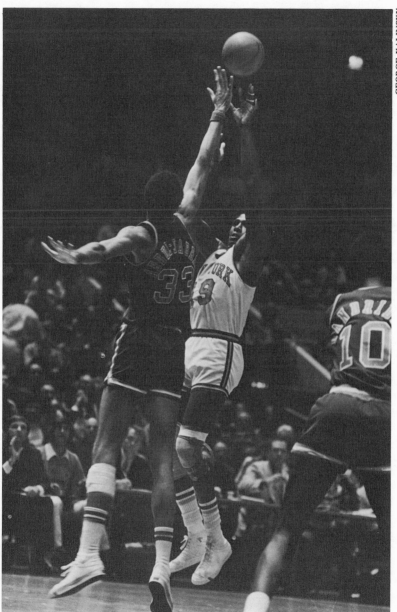

tall on the streets of New York. There wouldn't be a second's rest. The only break Reed got in the few years he played Alcindor before retiring was that Lew didn't grow any taller after changing his name to Kareem Abdul-Jabbar.

Reed always insisted Kareem was taller than his listed seven-two. I wasn't going to dispute that because Willis had to play him and should know. "I really think he's seven-four," said Reed after testing the new Milwaukee center, who had come into the league for the 1968–69 season. "He towers over me. He looks down on me."

I noticed that. I swear that the top of Reed's head fit nicely under Kareem's chin when they lined up for the center jump. Willis, of course, generally was listed at six-ten but he would tell people "I'm really a small six-nine" when they asked.

"Willis can measure me if he wants," said Alcindor in those days before he became Abdul-Jabbar.

"He's a head taller than Willis," said Dave DeBusschere. "A lot bigger. At least seven-four, seven-five."

"The last time I was measured, I was a shade under seven-two," insisted Alcindor. "He's just jealous that he's not taller." He meant Reed.

Maybe. I never talked to Reed about that. It seemed to me Willis was satisfied the way he was, anyway. Alcindor was just another challenge to him. A fresh, new face that Willis would have to contend with—just as he had to contend with Wilt Chamberlain and Bill Russell when he first came into the league.

Alcindor, or Kareem, got his message across in the first regular season meeting with Reed. We had discussed how to play him in the dressing room before the game and it was agreed we'd give Willis as much help as possible. Kareem was not only tall but extremely quick for a man his size. Besides, he was well-coordinated and tricky.

It was a pretty good strategy meeting but Kareem still went out and got three Knicks into foul trouble, including Willis. In the process, he blocked about six of our shots, scored thirty-six points, and got twenty-seven rebounds. He made us alter a lot of our shots and we won only because we were a better team and he was new to his teammates.

There was one graphic moment when Kareem learned what Reed was all about, that Willis was going to be a physical problem as long as they played against each other. Some time in the third quarter, Reed felt pressure or an elbow on his back. I don't know if he knew who was back there but Willis suddenly whirled with his right hand cocked. He never threw it.

I'm sure that when Reed saw it was Alcindor, the rookie, he pulled the punch. Anyway, Lew froze on the floor. I don't think he was frightened. He was just shocked but I'm sure he never forgot it. He knew every evening with Reed was going to be a rough one from then on.

Kareem Abdul-Jabbar, as I'll refer to him from now on, had come into the league expecting to be muscled. The NBA always was a muscle league for the big men. "I've been muscling back," said Kareem, who had a near-fight with Darrall Imhoff in Philadelphia before coming to the Garden for his first game against the Knicks.

A few things stick in my mind about that first encounter with Kareem. Once, he forced Walt Frazier to change a shot in the last second and miss. Another time, he came off the side and blocked a shot on Dick Barnett, driving the middle. "He must have been ten feet away," said Reed, who added: "Good thing I don't have to play him every night. One day, the guy is going to wake up and find out how really good he is. I just hope he doesn't. He's got all that equipment. It's great to have that much height and all those skills."

And only twenty-two, besides. Reed was only twenty-seven but beginning to show the wear and tear of a powerful body that had been through so much playing punishment throughout the years. He was such a competitor, though. I didn't have to discuss what Kareem had just done to him in their first meaningful matchup.

Reed knew what he had to do. He knew he would have to adjust to Kareem's size and skills. He didn't need Guy Rodgers of Milwaukee to tell him how good his new teammate was and how much potential he had but Willis was interested, anyway.

Rodgers was the only one in the league whose career had touched those of Abdul-Jabbar, Chamberlain, and Nate Thurmond, then a top center in the league. "The best way to be honest and fair," said Rodgers, "is to compare the guys at the same stage. Wilt and Nate were a lot stronger, but not as versatile as Lew. Wilt broke all scoring records, the hundred point game, for instance, and I was convinced they wouldn't be touched. I'm now convinced that one day if Lew gets hot, he can do it, although he's not the type to hog the ball."

What impressed me was not Kareem's strength but his quickness, quick hands and movement. That first night, he had Reed and our defense spinning. He moved all over the place, with all kinds of shots—the right hand hook, the roll-in, the fake-one-way-and-bank-the-other, and the soft jumper.

Reed sure knew what he was talking about when he said it had been a hard night's work. "You don't see big men do all the things he did," said Dave DeBusschere, who spent a lot of time trying to help Willis. "He has to learn to hold the ball higher and it's only a matter of time. Wilt never brings the ball down. Lew showed it to me a few times."

I was happy to get away with winning the game. Someone came into my little office off the dressing room and asked what I thought of Milwaukee now. The previous season, as an expansion team, the Bucks had finished last in the East with a 27–55 record. Abdul-Jabbar, in his first season, was to lead them to a second-place finish behind us with a 56–26 record. That was a twenty-nine–game flip-flop, mainly because of Kareem.

"You know when I want to play Milwaukee again?" I told the reporter. "Never, that's when." Milwaukee wasn't my favorite city, anyway.

I had coached there in the days of the Milwaukee Hawks when the NBA was only eight years old. I had Bob Pettit and an interesting team but we couldn't draw. I remember the night Ben Kerner was convinced he had to move the franchise to St. Louis and better times.

Kerner had a sharp business mind and would work late into the night on promotional ideas that might sell tickets. One night, Ben decided to give a $1.05 pound of coffee and a ticket to the game to every customer for the price of $1. "The worst they could do was make a nickel and they still didn't come," said Kerner after we played to our usual empty seats.

But I was back in Milwaukee with the Knicks a few days after our introduction to Kareem in New York. This time, we won a little easier. This time we played Kareem like we were going to play him all the time. This time Reed forced Kareem out of position as much as he could.

From that moment on, Reed knew what he had to do against Kareem. At the defensive end, Willis would plant himself solidly behind Kareem in the pivot and body him as far away from the basket as he could to make his skyhooks more difficult. At the offensive end, Willis took Kareem outside and made sure he always moved to tire him.

That was the secret. We had to make Kareem work hard every minute and tire him or we didn't stand a chance. It was a hard night's work for Reed but he loved it. I don't know whether it was circumstantial or not, but the Knicks managed to win a lot of games from Milwaukee in the closing minutes and I always felt Reed was greatly responsible. He had the hardest job and sometimes Kareem did play as though he was just a little tired at the end.

Reed's great physical qualities and basketball intelligence enabled us to create a strategy for Kareem and the Bucks that eventually proved we were doing something right. We let Willis play Kareem with the hope of limiting him to whatever he was capable of getting while we concentrated on stopping Bobby Dandridge, Jon McGlocklin, Greg Smith, and the other players. We didn't cheat as much on defense against Milwaukee because we didn't want anyone adding a big game to the one Kareem was certain to have on his own.

There was no stopping him. Reed's job was to limit the damage. Let me give you an idea. There was one stretch where Kareem scored thirty-six, twenty-seven, twenty-six, twenty-five, forty-two, and twenty-six against us but we won four of the six games. Reed only outscored him once during that stretch and never did outrebound him. Willis just didn't allow Kareem to beat us all by himself, which he was quite capable of doing to anyone.

Kareem, all by himself, made the Knicks-Bucks rivalry a heated one. Coming from New York, and with his tremendous size and skills, he represented a towering challenge to us and the Garden fans. He became Public Enemy Number one overnight.

People in New York came to the Garden to root for Reed against Abdul-Jabbar, just as they jammed the smaller Milwaukee arena to root for Kareem against Willis. We never had to face Kareem without Reed until we opened the 1972–73 season. By then, Willis and the rest of the Knicks had done their job well against him.

Of the first six games of Kareem's opening season, the Knicks had taken four. We went on to win twelve of sixteen and four of the five playoff games we had with Reed playing. It got to the point, every time the Knicks played the Bucks, it was Reed against Abdul-Jabbar in the minds of the fans but not the players and coaches. We knew better.

Yet, the fans persisted. It became a crusade between two cities. New York, at the start, was more fortunate because the Knicks kept winning. But Milwaukee got its night. The Bucks finally beat us in Milwaukee after losing ten in a row. You never heard so much noise as on that night of January 2, 1970 when 10,746 fans sounded like 100,000.

We were lucky the roof didn't cave in. We had been out there a month earlier and Bill Bradley, with eleven seconds left, had hit a shot from the corner that had beaten the Bucks, who hadn't won a game from us since coming into the league the previous season. "That one was like a smack in the face," Kareem had said.

There wasn't anything Reed could do about it that night. Larry Costello's game plan was to go to Kareem and let us worry about it. "Costello really tries to get him up for me," said Willis, suggesting that Larry's frustration at losing to the Knicks so often was putting a greater load on Kareem. "They go to him more against us. There's nothing I can do. He has such a height advantage on me."

Kareem had sixteen in the first quarter, twenty-four at the half, thirty-one at the third quarter, and forty-one overall. The Bucks cleared it out for Kareem and let him work on Reed. They opened the floor and spread out so that we couldn't drop anyone off to help. They took advantage of all the shots and moves Kareem had, and he had plenty. That night, they set the pace of the game. The fans went wild as the Bucks played our pressing defense and controlled the game.

When it was over, I walked across the floor to our dressing room. I was delayed for a few minutes. Then I saw Kareem come out of his dressing room. Thousands of fans cheered him, again, as he went on the post-game television show. "It's come, I think so," he said. "There are things I know I can do now. I've stopped rushing my shots. We learned a lot the other times we played New York. The last few games, we felt it inside. It was directly after losing to the Knicks by one point." He meant the Bradley shot.

We were a marked team in the eyes of Kareem and Milwaukee in general. Kareem, at twenty-four, had become the single greatest force in the game by his second season. We depended on Reed's strong body, keen mind, and outside shooting to control him enough to give us a shot at winning. We depended on a lot of other things, such as DeBusschere, Frazier, Bradley, Barnett, and our bench, but in the eyes of the public it seemed to come down to Reed vs. Abdul-Jabbar.

"They try to make a big thing about me and him," said Willis. "But that's not the game we play. I don't think I'll be doing anything like stopping him. We play team basketball. You just don't come out and say: 'Stop that one man.' It doesn't work that way with us."

There was no one who could tell Reed how to play Kareem. He found out for himself and no one did it better considering the difference in size. Willis was not a weakling or someone who needed to be pitied but he did look like the ballboy alongside Kareem. Or like a Piper Cub alongside a 747.

Reed worked hard to establish a defensive position. He couldn't let Kareem get too deep or it would be all over. Kareem had the mobility and wingspread. "With a guy like that," Willis would say, "movement is important on offense so he doesn't stand in the middle and clog it. When he gets the ball, he's always trying to move closer to the basket, so you got to establish your position. I don't know how much that helps but that's what you've got to do."

Even I had to laugh when I heard Reed say he didn't muscle

Kareem. Kareem had to laugh when Reed, as coach of the Knicks years later, complained to the refs about Abdul-Jabbar's shoving and pushing. "Willis should go back and look at the films of when he played me," was Kareem's reminder. "He pushed me all over the court. That's the only way he could play me."

The thing that helped Reed and the Knicks was that he only conceded Kareem his size. "I know he has all the advantages," Willis would tell anyone who asked. "But I don't consider myself an underdog. There's such a difference in size, I really can't tell you what I'm going to do until the game starts. But if it comes down to him getting fifty and we win, I'll take it."

Kareem never talked much and the few things he said about himself and Willis were brief and succinct. He was a quiet young man who treated Willis with silent respect. He talked less and less as the games went on between the Knicks and Bucks. He wanted so badly to beat the Knicks because he came from New York yet was the prime target of the Garden fans. I must say he took an inordinate amount of abuse that sometimes embarrassed me, though I understood the fanaticism of people who pay to root for their team and players.

I guess the best example I can think of was the night we eliminated the Bucks from the 1969–70 playoffs. Kareem had been awesome knocking out the 76ers in their series, 4–1. He was runaway Rookie of the Year and a definite threat to our existence, though we had set a record of eighteen straight that year, finished with a 60–22 record that was the best in the NBA, and had beaten the Bullets 4–3 in our playoff.

Kareem issued a type of warning that I guess was meant for the Knicks but might have been for Reed. "I'm more fluid and I'm not worrying," he said. "I know how Willis plays now. I try my best to hold him down. I'm not going to hold him out. Nobody does."

That was shortly before the playoffs. Milwaukee had beaten us two straight at the end of the regular season and was feeling its muscles. I rested DeBusschere in the last one, playing him only six minutes, and Frazier took the night off because he had a slight injury. I didn't like the idea of losing to the Bucks in the Garden because it can give a team big ideas but there was nothing I could do about it. My playing days had ended long ago.

"It was a good game for us," acknowledged Costello, the Milwaukee coach. "Everyone was up for it. You could feel the spirit before the game. You get yourself up more for New York."

Nobody got up higher than Kareem. He had a head start, of course. He kept talking about that game Bradley had stolen from the Bucks and felt that was the turning point against us. He and his teammates now were ready to show Reed and the Knicks they could beat them.

A wonderful attitude. That's what made Kareem what he was. A winner. He had always won. In high school, college, and now in the pros, except for the Knicks. We were the only team that gave Milwaukee so much trouble and it bothered him. "We should've won that one," he said, referring to the Bradley game. "No reason why we should've lost it. We felt we could beat the best after that one. I know we can win it all."

There was one problem with Kareem's theory. We also thought we could win it all. Milwaukee wound up winning only the third game. We won the first two at home and the second was the one that really hurt because we beat the Bucks by a point as Kareem missed two foul shots near the buzzer. I thought Reed played one of his finest games against Kareem and I guess the Milwaukee players did, also.

Greg Smith, the six-five forward who played Bradley, thought the game turned at center. Kareem got twenty-three rebounds but Reed matched that with nineteen. Kareem scored thirty-eight points and Reed matched that with thirty-six. "I think Willis was out to prove something," suggested Smith. "It was a battle between the two best centers in the league. Willis was in a real mean mood tonight."

Players around the league had learned to be careful when Reed got that intense. Smith, a fearless rebounder and fighter under the boards, was well aware of it. "I hit Reed in the mouth with my elbow as I came down with a rebound one time," he explained, "and I apologized fast. As quickly as I could get it out of my mouth."

Kareem wasn't talking after the game though he had been

outstanding, as usual. He'd played almost a perfect team game. Even his ballhandling was sharp as he picked up eight assists. But he had lost in New York, again, and had nothing to say because he had failed at the end.

"He's really depressed," Smith explained for him. "He really loves to play in New York. Missing those two foul shots at the end spoiled the whole thing. I'd feel awful if I missed those shots. Wouldn't anyone?"

There were only fifty-two seconds to go when Kareem missed the shots that would've won the game. We won because we concentrated on limiting the damage Kareem's teammates did. That's the way we always managed to compensate for what Kareem did to us. We knew when it came down to the wire, they'd go to him and we'd apply all our pressure on him then.

Kareem's misses wiped out all the things he had done to us. Once he went high in the air for a McGlocklin pass, palmed it at the top of his jump, and guided it before coming down to Smith cutting past Bradley. Frazier fell off one time to help Reed, and Kareem whipped a pass to Flynn Robinson for a basket. Another time he threaded a sea of arms to hit Bobby Dandridge, the open man.

"They wanted to win and he was out there to do it for them," said Reed, whose real strength was being at his best in our toughest games. "I didn't expect Reed to score that many points," said Costello, forgetting that's why Willis was Willis. Height alone wouldn't beat Reed or the Knicks.

Kareem had played a superb game but no one could get him to discuss it. I couldn't blame him, in a way. It had been one aggravating loss to the Knicks after another and what could he say. He did say something before leaving. "I'm just doing a job. I have a job to do," he muttered when congratulated for a super performance.

He was asked what was in his mind when he missed the foul shots. "I missed them," he said as he grabbed his bag and left. I was a bit sorry for him because I know from experience what it meant to lose a game like that.

I was happy for us, of course, and especially for Reed. I could tell by the big smile on his face how he felt about the job he had just done. "My most satisfying game," said Willis, who was to play a lot more satisfying games before he was through.

He had played against Russell and Chamberlain but this one meant more to him. He had matched Abdul-Jabbar's great skills at a time when it put us two wins away from the championship round in the playoffs. "I can't remember a game I and the other guy played so well," said Willis. "Right now, he's got to be the toughest center in the league to guard, with Chamberlain out with a bad knee. He goes this way. He goes that way and back to the middle. He makes you work. I look like his little brother."

It was clearly Reed's night, under the circumstances, and we all appreciated it. We didn't think Kareem and the Bucks could play any better and we had beaten them. Reed had hit outside when Kareem didn't come out and also when he did while waving a long telephone-pole arm in Willis' face.

By the time the final playoff game came around in the Garden, the Knicks really appreciated Kareem's talent. So did the New York fans, I guess, though they had a strange way of showing it. Well, not really strange when you think about it. Fans generally boo the athlete who represents the greatest threat to their team and Kareem was all of that and more.

Reed had only kind words for Kareem; yet, as popular as Willis was, he couldn't influence the fans. They enjoyed every bitter moment Kareem suffered and let him know it. The coup de grace came when we were leading Milwaukee by about forty at the start of the fourth quarter of the final game and Costello removed him.

It started slowly in the balcony and picked up force like a wave heading for the beach. Thousands of Garden voices began singing: "Goodbye Looie / Goodbye Looie / Goodbye Looie / We hate to see you go." I looked over at the Milwaukee bench and Kareem was sitting there with a blank look on his face, hands folded and staring into nowhere.

It was pure fanomania and Kareem took it better than we did. He understood though he didn't like it. "Whenever I've played in New York, the majority of the fans have rooted against me," he pointed out. "I can't feel too badly. It's their problem. If they want to act that way, it's their business.

Maybe they do it because they're scared. We've got nothing to be ashamed of. We're a very young team and we probably shouldn't even have been playing for the Eastern Division championship."

I don't like to hear fans boo a man like Jabbar, but it's all part of sports. I know some of our players were bothered by it. "I don't think he deserved it," said DeBusschere. "He gave his all in the series. He did everything he could but he didn't get help from his supporting cast. He has to play a lot under pressure, which he'll have to live with, but he took his club a long, long way."

Something always seemed to happen to Kareem and the Bucks when they were playing Reed and the Knicks. In one game, they were leading by eighteen and we scored the last nineteen to beat them. They fortified themselves by getting Oscar Robertson to help Kareem for the 1970–71 season and it continued to happen.

The Bucks got off on a hot streak that season, but we beat them three out of four. "The three times we've beaten them has got to hurt them psychologically," suggested DeBusschere. "We're the only team they don't handle, the only team they don't manhandle. They've got to be asking themselves if we've got their number."

I don't deal in things like that, unless DeBusschere meant nineteen, which was Reed's number. The only game we had lost to the Bucks in that stretch was in Milwaukee when Willis had just come out of the hospital after a stomach problem. In one win, we were eight points behind in the final quarter and in another we came from fourteen back in the closing eight minutes.

By the time the season had ended, Kareem had proved the Garden fans were right for isolating him as a threat to their team. We lost to the Bullets in the playoffs and the Bucks swept Baltimore, 4–0, for the championship. Kareem was sitting on top of the world but not New York, evidently.

"I would've preferred beating the Knicks," he said after winning the title in only his second year.

He never got the chance. Kareem and Milwaukee were knocked out of the playoffs by Golden State the next season while we lost in the final to the Lakers without Reed, who played only eleven games that season because of a bad knee.

Golden State eliminated the Bucks once more in the 1972–73 season and the Knicks, with Reed back, won a second championship by beating the Lakers, 4–1. Reed's last playoff was in 1973–74. The Knicks were beaten by the Celtics, who then went on to whip Kareem and the Bucks in the championship series.

But Kareem vs. Reed was good while it lasted. Too bad it couldn't have gone on forever. Or at least a few more years.

"It's people against people," was the way Kareem viewed it.

"It's not me against Kareem," was the way Reed viewed it.

It sure looked like it at times, is all I can say.

APPENDIX

KAREEM ABDUL-JABBAR

Born April 16, 1947. Height 7:02. Weight 232.

Alma Mater—UCLA '69.

Drafted by Milwaukee on first round, 1969.

Traded by Milwaukee with Walt Wesley to Los Angeles for Elmore Smith, Brian Winters, Dave Meyers, and Junior Bridgeman, June 16, 1975.

NBA REGULAR SEASON RECORD

	G.	FGA	FGM	Pct	FTA	FTM	Pct.	Reb.	Ast.	PF	Pts.	Avg.
69–70—Milwaukee	82	1810	938	.518	743	485	.653	1190	337	283	2361	28.8
70–71—Milwaukee	81	1843	1063	.577	681	470	.690	1311	272	264	2596	31.7
71–72—Milwaukee	81	2019	1159	.574	732	504	.689	1346	370	235	2822	34.8
72–73—Milwaukee	76	1772	982	.554	460	328	.713	1224	379	208	2292	30.2
73–74—Milwaukee	81	1759	948	.539	420	295	.702	1178	386	238	2191	27.0
74–75—Milwaukee	65	1584	812	.513	426	325	.763	912	264	205	1949	30.0
75–76—L.A.	82	1728	914	.529	636	447	.703	1383	413	292	2275	27.7
76–77—L.A.	82	1533	888	.579	536	376	.701	1090	319	262	2152	26.2
77–78—L.A.	62	1205	663	.550	350	274	.783	801	269	182	1600	25.8
78–79—L.A.	80	1347	777	.577	474	349	.736	1025	431	230	1903	23.8
Totals	773	16600	9144	.551	5458	3853	.706	11460	3440	2399	22141	28.6

NBA PLAYOFF RECORD

	G.	FGA.	FGM.	Pct.	FTA.	FTM.	Pct.	Reb.	Ast.	PF.	Pts.	Avg.
69–70—Milwaukee	10	245	139	.567	101	74	.733	168	41	25	352	35.2
70–71—Milwaukee	14	295	152	.515	101	68	.673	238	35	45	372	26.6
71–72—Milwaukee	11	318	139	.437	54	38	.704	200	56	35	316	28.7
72–73—Milwaukee	6	138	59	.428	35	19	.543	97	17	26	137	22.8
73–74—Milwaukee	16	402	224	.557	91	67	.736	253	78	41	515	32.2
76–77—L.A.	11	242	147	.607	120	87	.725	195	45	42	381	34.6
77–78—L.A.	3	73	38	.521	9	5	.556	41	11	14	81	27.0
78–79—L.A.	8	152	88	.579	62	52	.839	101	38	26	228	28.5
Totals	79	1865	986	.529	573	410	.716	1293	321	254	2382	30.2

RICK BARRY

Born March 28, 1944. Height 6:07. Weight 220.

Alma Mater—Miami '65.

Drafted by San Francisco on first round, 1965.

Completed contract with Golden State; signed by Houston as Veteran Free Agent, June 17, 1978. Golden State received John Lucas and cash as compensation.

ABA REGULAR SEASON RECORD

		2-Point			3-Point										
	G.	FGM	FGA	Pct.	FGM	FGA	Pct.	FTM	FTA	Pct.	Reb.	Ast.	Pts.	Avg.
68–69—Oak.	35	389	757	.514	3	10	.300	403	454	.888	329	136	1190	34.0
69–70—Wash.	52	509	907	.511	8	39	.205	400	463	.864	363	178	1442	27.7
70–71—New York	59	613	1262	.486	19	86	.221	451	507	.890	401	294	1734	29.4
71–72—New York	80	829	1732	.479	73	237	.308	241	730	.330	602	327	2518	31.5
Totals	226	2340	4748	.493	103	374	.275	1895	2154	.880	1695	935	6884	30.5

NBA REGULAR SEASON RECORD

	G.	FGA	FGM	Pct.	FTA	FTM	Pct.	Reb.	Ast.	PF	Pts.	Avg.
65–66—San Fran.	80	1698	745	.439	660	569	.862	850	173	297	2059	25.7
66–67—San Fran.	78	2240	1011	.451	852	753	.884	714	282	258	2775	35.6
72–73—Golden State	82	1630	737	.452	397	358	.902	728	399	245	1832	22.3
73–74—Golden State	80	1746	796	.456	464	417	.899	540	484	265	2009	25.1
74–75—Golden State	80	2217	1028	.464	436	394	.904	456	492	225	2450	30.6
75–76—Golden State	81	1624	707	.435	311	287	.923	496	496	215	1701	21.0
76–77—Golden State	79	1551	682	.440	392	359	.916	422	475	194	1723	21.8
77–78—Golden State	82	1686	760	.451	409	378	.924	449	446	188	1898	23.1
78–79—Hous.	80	1000	461	.461	169	160	.947	277	502	195	1082	13.5
Totals	722	15392	6927	.450	4090	3675	.899	4932	3749	2082	17529	24.3

NBA PLAYOFF RECORD

	G.	FGA.	FGM.	Pct.	FTA.	FTM.	Pct.	Reb.	Ast.	PF.	Pts.	Avg.
66–67—San Fran.	15	489	197	.403	157	127	809	113	58	49	521	34.7
72–73—Golden Stolden State	11	164	65	.396	55	50	.909	54	24	41	180	16.4
74–75—Golden State	17	426	189	.444	110	101	.918	94	103	51	479	28.2
75–76—Golden State	13	289	126	.436	68	60	.882	84	84	40	312	24.0
76–77—Golden State	10	262	122	.466	44	40	.909	59	47	32	284	28.4
78–79—Hous.	2	25	8	.320	8	8	1.000	8	9	8	24	12.0
Totals	68	1655	707	.427	442	386	.873	412	325	221	1800	26.5

Bill Bradley

Born July 28, 1943. Height 6:05. Weight 210.

Alma Mater—Princeton '65.

Drafted by New York on first round (territorial choice), 1965.

NBA REGULAR SEASON RECORD

	G.	FGA	FGM	Pct.	FTA	FTM	Pct.	Reb.	Ast.	PF	Pts.	Avg.
67–68—New York	45	341	142	.416	104	76	731	113	137	138	360	8.0
68–69—New York	82	948	407	.429	253	206	.814	350	302	295	1020	12.4
69–70—New York	67	897	413	.460	176	145	.824	239	268	219	971	14.5
70–71—New York	78	912	413	.453	175	144	.823	260	280	245	970	12.4
71–72—New York	78	1085	504	.465	199	169	.849	250	315	254	1177	15.1
72–73—New York	82	1252	575	.459	194	169	.871	301	367	273	1319	16.1
73–74—New York	82	1112	502	.451	167	146	.874	253	242	278	1150	14.0
74–75—New York	79	1036	452	.436	165	144	.873	251	247	283	1048	13.3
75–76—New York	82	906	392	.433	148	130	.878	234	247	256	914	11.1
76–77—New York	67	274	127	.464	42	34	.810	103	128	122	288	4.3
Totals	742	8763	3927	.448	1623	1363	.840	2354	2533	2363	9217	12.4

NBA PLAYOFF RECORD

	G.	FGA.	FGM.	Pct.	FTA.	FTM.	Pct.	Reb.	Ast.	PF.	Pts.	Avg.
67–68—New York	6	28	12	429	13	9	.692	6	2	7	33	5.5
68–69—New York	10	141	65	.461	39	30	.769	73	40	38	160	16.0
69–70—New York	19	233	100	.429	43	35	.814	72	60	59	235	12.4
70–71—New York	12	132	56	.424	19	14	.737	41	43	40	126	10.5
71–72—New York	16	227	106	.467	56	47	.839	47	54	66	259	16.2
72–73—New York	17	221	99	.448	50	40	.800	57	45	59	238	14.0
73–74—New York	12	159	63	.396	29	25	.862	28	13	39	151	12.6
74–75—New York	3	24	9	.375	2	2	1.000	9	6	5	20	6.7
Totals	95	1165	510	.438	251	202	.805	333	263	313	1222	12.9

Wilt Chamberlain

Born August 21, 1936. Height 7:01. Weight 275.

Alma Mater—Kansas '59.

Drafted by Philadelphia on first round (territorial choice), 1959.

Traded by San Francisco to Philadelphia for Paul Neumann, Connie Dierking, Lee Shaffer and cash, January 15, 1965.

Traded by Philadelphia to Los Angeles for Jerry Chambers, Archie Clark and Darrall Imhoff, July 9, 1968.

NBA REGULAR SEASON RECORD

	G.	FGA.	FGM.	Pct.	FTA.	FTM.	Pct.	Reb.	Ast.	PF.	Pts.	Avg.
59–60—Phila.	72	2311	1065	461	991	577	.582	1941	168	150	2707	37.6
60–61—Phila.	79	2457	1251	.509	1054	531	.504	2149	148	130	3033	38.4
61–62—Phila.	80	3159	1597	.505	1363	835	.613	2052	192	123	4029	50.4
62–63—San Fran.	80	2770	1463	.528	1113	660	.593	1946	275	136	3586	44.8
63–64—San Fran.	80	2298	1204	.524	1016	540	.531	1787	403	182	2948	36.9
64–65—S.F.-Phil.	73	2083	1063	.510	880	408	.464	1673	250	146	2534	34.7
65–66—Phila.	79	1990	1074	.540	976	501	.513	1943	414	171	2649	33.5
66–67—Phila.	81	1150	785	.683	875	386	.441	1957	630	143	1956	24.1
67–68—Phila.	82	1377	819	.595	932	354	.380	1952	702	160	1992	24.3
68–69—Los Ang.	81	1099	641	.583	857	382	.446	1712	366	142	1664	20.5
69–70—Los Ang.	12	227	129	.568	157	70	.446	221	49	31	328	27.3
70–71—Los Ang.	82	1226	668	.545	669	360	.538	1493	352	174	1696	20.7
71–72—Los Ang.	82	764	496	.649	524	221	.422	1572	329	196	1213	14.8
72–73—Los Ang.	82	586	426	.727	455	232	.510	1526	365	191	1084	13.2
Totals	1045	23497	12681	.540	11862	6057	.511	23924	4643	2075	31419	30.1

NBA PLAYOFF RECORD

	G.	FGA.	FGM.	Pct.	FTA.	FTM.	Pct.	Reb.	Ast.	PF.	Pts.	Avg.
59–60—Phila.	9	252	125	.496	110	49	.445	232	19	17	299	33.2
60–61—Phila.	3	96	45	.469	38	21	553	69	6	10	111	37.0
61–62—Phila.	12	347	162	.467	151	96	.636	319	37	27	420	35.0
63–64—San Fran.	12	322	175	.543	139	66	.475	302	39	27	416	34.7
64–65—Phila.	11	232	123	.530	136	76	.559	299	48	29	322	29.3
65–66—Phila.	5	110	56	.509	68	28	.412	151	15	10	140	28.0
66–67—Phila.	15	228	132	.579	160	62	.388	437	135	37	326	21.7
67–68—Phila.	13	232	124	.534	158	60	.380	321	85	29	308	23.7
68–69—Los Ang.	18	176	96	.545	148	58	.392	444	46	56	250	13.9
69–70—Los Ang.	18	288	158	.549	202	82	.406	399	81	42	398	22.1
70–71—Los Ang.	12	187	85	.455	97	50	.515	242	53	33	220	18.3
71–72—Los Ang.	15	142	80	.563	122	60	.492	315	49	47	220	14.7
72–73—Los Ang.	17	116	64	.552	98	49	.500	383	60	48	177	10.4
Totals	160	2728	1425	.522	1627	757	.465	3913	673	412	3607	27.5

Bob Cousy

Born August 9, 1928. Height 6:01. Weight 175.

Alma Mater—Holy Cross '50.

NBA REGULAR SEASON RECORD

	G.	FGA.	FGM.	Pct.	FTA.	FTM.	Pct.	Reb.	Ast.	PF.	Pts.	Avg.
50–51—Boston	69	1138	401	.352	365	276	.756	474	341	185	1078	15.6
51–52—Boston	66	1388	512	.369	506	409	.808	421	441	190	1433	21.7
52–53—Boston	71	1320	464	.352	587	479	.816	449	547	227	1407	19.8
53–54—Boston	72	1262	486	.385	522	411	.787	394	518	201	1383	19.2
54–55—Boston	71	1316	522	.397	570	460	.807	424	557	165	1504	21.2
55–56—Boston	72	1223	440	.360	564	476	.844	492	642	206	1356	18.8
56–57—Boston	64	1264	478	.378	442	363	.821	309	478	134	1319	20.6
57–58—Boston	65	1262	445	.353	326	277	.850	322	463	136	1167	18.0
58–59—Boston	65	1260	484	.384	385	329	.855	359	557	135	1297	20.0
59–60—Boston	75	1481	568	.383	403	319	.791	352	715	146	1455	19.4
60–61—Boston	76	1382	513	.371	452	352	.779	331	591	196	1378	18.1
61–62—Boston	75	1181	462	.391	333	251	.754	261	584	135	1175	15.7
62–63—Boston	76	988	392	.397	298	219	.735	201	515	175	1003	13.2
63–69						Voluntarily Retired						
69–70—Cincinnati	7	3	1	.333	3	3	1.000	5	10	11	5	0.7
Totals	924	16468	6168	.375	5756	4624	.803	4794	6959	2242	16960	18.4

NBA PLAYOFF RECORD

	G.	FGA.	FGM.	Pct.	FTA.	FTM.	Pct.	Reb.	Ast.	PF.	Pts.	Avg.
50–51—Boston	2	42	9	.214	12	10	.833	15	12	8	28	14.0
51–52—Boston	3	65	26	.400	44	41	.932	12	19	13	93	31.0
52–53—Boston	6	120	46	.383	73	61	.836	25	37	21	153	25.5
53–54—Boston	6	116	33	.284	75	60	.800	32	38	20	126	21.0
54–55—Boston	7	139	53	.381	48	46	.958	43	65	26	152	21.7
55–56—Boston	3	56	28	.500	25	23	.920	24	26	4	79	26.3
56–57—Boston	10	207	67	.324	91	68	.747	61	93	27	202	20.2
57–58—Boston	11	196	67	.342	75	64	.853	71	82	20	198	18.0
58–59—Boston	11	221	72	.326	94	70	.745	76	119	28	214	19.5
59–60—Boston	13	262	80	.305	51	39	.765	48	116	27	199	15.3
60–61—Boston	10	147	50	.340	88	67	.761	43	91	33	167	16.7
61–62—Boston	14	241	86	.357	76	52	.684	64	123	43	224	16.0
62–63—Boston	13	204	72	.353	47	39	.830	32	116	44	183	14.1
Totals	109	2116	689	.326	799	640	.801	546	937	314	2018	18.5

Dave Cowens

Born October 25, 1948. Height 6:09. Weight 230.

Alma Mater—Florida State '70.

Drafted by Boston on first round, 1970.

NBA REGULAR SEASON RECORD

	G.	FGA	FGM	Pct.	FTA	FTM	Pct.	Reb.	Ast.	PF	Pts.	Avg.
70–71—Boston	81	1302	550	.422	373	273	.732	1216	228	350	1373	17.0
71–72—Boston	79	1357	657	.484	243	175	.720	1203	245	314	1489	18.8
72–73—Boston	82	1637	740	.452	262	204	.779	1329	333	311	1684	20.5
73–74—Boston	80	1475	645	.437	274	228	.832	1257	354	294	1518	19.0
74–75—Boston	65	1199	569	.475	244	191	.783	958	296	243	1329	20.4
75–76—Boston	78	1305	611	.468	340	257	.756	1246	325	314	1479	19.0
76–77—Boston	50	756	328	.434	198	162	.818	697	248	181	818	16.4
77–78—Boston	77	1220	598	.490	284	239	.842	1078	351	297	1435	18.6
78–79—Boston	68	1010	488	.483	187	151	.807	652	242	263	1127	16.6
Totals	660	11261	5186	.461	2405	1880	.782	9636	2622	2567	12252	18.6

NBA PLAYOFF RECORD

	G.	FGA.	FGM.	Pct.	FTA.	FTM.	Pct.	Reb.	Ast.	PF.	Pts.	Avg.
71–72—Boston	11	156	71	.455	47	28	.596	152	33	50	170	15.5
72–73—Boston	13	273	129	.473	41	27	.659	216	48	54	285	21.9
73–74—Boston	18	370	161	.435	59	47	.797	240	66	85	269	20.5
74–75—Boston	11	236	101	.428	26	23	.885	181	46	50	225	20.5
75–76—Boston	18	341	156	.457	87	66	.759	296	83	85	378	21.0
76–77—Boston	9	148	66	.446	22	17	.773	134	36	37	149	16.6
Totals	80	1524	684	.449	282	208	.738	1219	312	361	1576	19.7

Dave DeBusschere

Born October 16, 1940. Height 6:06. Weight 235.

Alma Mater—Detroit '62.

Drafted by Detroit on first round (territorial choice), 1962.

Traded by Detroit to New York for Walt Bellamy and Howard Komives December 19, 1968.

NBA REGULAR SEASON RECORD

	G.	FGA.	FGM.	Pct.	FTA.	FTM.	Pct.	Reb.	Ast.	PF.	Pts.	Avg.
62–63—Detroit	80	944	406	.430	287	206	.718	694	207	247	1018	12.7
63–64—Detroit	15	133	52	.391	43	25	.581	105	23	32	128	8.6
64–65—Detroit	79	1196	508	.425	437	306	.700	874	253	242	1322	16.7
65–66—Detroit	79	1284	524	.408	378	249	.659	916	209	252	1297	16.4

	G	FGA	FGM	Pct.	FTA	FTM	Pct.	Reb.	Ast.	PF	Pts.	Avg.
66–67—Detroit	78	1278	531	.415	512	361	.705	924	216	297	1423	18.2
67–68—Detroit	80	1295	573	.442	435	289	.664	1081	181	304	1435	17.9
68–69—Det.-New York	76	1140	506	.444	328	229	.698	888	191	290	1241	16.3
69–70—New York	79	1082	488	.451	256	176	.688	790	194	244	1152	14.6
70–71—New York	81	1243	523	.421	312	217	.696	901	220	237	1263	15.6
71–72—New York	80	1218	520	.427	265	193	.728	901	291	219	1233	15.4
72–73—New York	77	1224	532	.435	260	194	.746	787	259	215	1258	16.3
73–74—New York	71	1212	559	.461	217	164	.756	757	253	222	1282	18.1
Totals	875	13249	5722	.432	3730	2609	.699	9618	2497	2801	14053	16.1

NBA PLAYOFF RECORD

	G.	FGA.	FGM.	Pct.	FTA.	FTM.	Pct.	Reb.	Ast.	PF.	Pts.	Avg.
62–63—Detroit	4	59	25	.424	44	30	.682	63	6	14	80	20.0
67–68—Detroit	6	106	45	.425	45	26	.578	97	13	23	116	19.3
68–69—New York	10	174	61	.351	50	41	.820	148	33	43	163	16.3
69–70—New York	19	309	130	.421	68	45	.662	220	46	63	305	16.1
70–71—New York	12	202	84	.416	44	29	.659	156	22	40	197	16.4
71–72—New York	16	242	109	.450	64	48	.750	193	37	51	266	16.6
72–73—New York	17	265	117	.442	40	31	.775	179	58	57	265	15.6
73–74—New York	12	166	63	.380	29	18	.621	99	38	36	144	12.0
Totals	96	1523	634	.416	384	268	.698	1155	253	327	1536	16.0

Julius Erving

Born February 22, 1950. Height 6:07. Weight 200

Alma Mater—Massachusetts '72.

Entered NBA with Nets, 1976.

Sold by Nets to Philadelphia, October 20, 1976.

ABA REGULAR SEASON RECORD

		2-Point				3-Point								
	G.	FGA	FGM	Pct.	FGA	FGM	Pct.	FTM	FTA	Pct.	Reb.	Ast.	Pts.	Avg.
71–72—Virginia	84	907	1810	.501	3	16	.188	467	627	.745	1319	335	2290	27.3
72–73—Virginia	71	889	1780	.499	5	24	.208	475	612	.776	867	298	2268	31.9
73–74—New York	84	897	1742	.515	17	43	.395	454	593	.766	899	434	2299	27.4
74–75—New York	84	885	1719	.515	29	87	.333	486	608	.799	914	462	2343	27.9
75–76—New York	84	915	1770	.517	34	103	.330	530	662	.801	925	423	2462	29.3
Totals	407	4493	8821	.509	88	273	.322	2412	3102	.778	4924	1952	11662	28.7

NBA REGULAR SEASON RECORD

	G.	FGA	FGM	Pct.	FTA	FTM	Pct.	Reb.	Ast.	PF	Pts.	Avg.
76–77—Phila.	82	1373	685	.499	515	400	.777	695	306	251	1770	21.6
77–78—Phila.	74	1217	611	.502	362	306	.845	481	279	207	1528	20.6
78–79—Phila.	78	1455	715	.491	501	373	.745	564	357	207	1803	23.1
Totals	234	4045	2011	.497	1378	1079	.783	1740	942	665	5101	21.8

NBA PLAYOFF RECORD

	G	FGA	FGM	Pct.	FTA	FTM	Pct.	Reb.	Ast.	PF	Pts.	Avg.
76–77—Phila.	19	390	204	.523	134	110	.821	122	85	45	518	27.3
77–78—Phila.	10	180	88	.489	56	42	.750	97	40	30	218	21.8
78–79—Phila.	9	172	89	.517	67	51	.761	70	53	22	229	25.4
Totals	38	742	381	.513	257	203	.790	289	178	97	965	25.4

Walt Frazier

Born March 29, 1945. Height 6:04. Weight 205.

Alma Mater—Southern Illinois '67.

Drafted by New York on first round, 1967.

Acquired from New York by Cleveland as compensation for anticipated signing of Veteran Free Agent Jim Cleamons, October 7, 1977.

NBA REGULAR SEASON RECORD

	G.	FGA	FGM	Pct.	FTA	FTM	Pct.	Reb.	Ast.	PF	Pts.	Avg.
67–68—New York	74	568	256	.451	235	154	.655	313	305	199	666	9.0
68–69—New York	80	1052	531	.505	457	341	.746	499	635	245	1403	17.5
69–70—New York	77	1158	600	.518	547	409	.748	465	629	203	1609	20.9
70–71—New York	80	1317	651	.494	557	434	.779	544	536	240	1736	21.7
71–72—New York	77	1307	669	.512	557	450	.808	513	446	185	1788	23.2
72–73—New York	78	1389	681	.490	350	286	.817	570	461	186	1648	21.1
73–74—New York	80	1429	674	.472	352	295	.838	536	551	212	1643	20.5
74–75—New York	78	1391	672	.483	400	331	.828	465	474	205	1675	21.5
75–76—New York	59	969	470	.485	226	186	.823	400	351	163	1126	19.1
76–77—New York	76	1089	532	.489	336	259	.771	293	403	194	1323	17.4
77–78—Cleve.	51	714	336	.471	180	153	.850	209	209	124	825	16.2
78–79—Cleve.	12	122	54	.443	27	21	.778	20	32	22	129	10.8
Totals	822	12505	6126	.490	4224	3319	.786	4827	5032	2178	15571	18.9

NBA PLAYOFF RECORD

	G.	FGA.	FGM.	Pct.	FTA.	FTM.	Pct.	Reb.	Ast.	PF	Pts.	Avg.
67–68—New York	4	33	12	.364	18	14	.778	22	25	12	38	9.5
68–69—New York	10	177	89	.503	57	34	.596	74	91	30	212	21.2
69–70—New York	19	247	118	.478	89	68	.764	149	156	53	304	16.0
70–71—New York	12	204	108	.529	75	55	.733	70	54	45	271	22.6
71–72—New York	16	276	148	.536	125	92	.736	112	98	48	388	24.3
72–73—New York	17	292	150	.514	94	73	.777	124	106	52	373	21.9
73–74—New York	12	225	113	.502	49	44	.898	95	48	41	270	22.5
74–75—New York	3	46	29	630	16	13	.813	20	21	4	71	23.7
Totals	93	1500	767	.511	523	393	.751	666	599	285	1927	20.7

John Havlicek

Born April 8, 1940. Height 6:05. Weight 205.

Alma Mater—Ohio State '62.

Drafted by Boston on first round, 1962.

NBA REGULAR SEASON RECORD

	G.	FGA	FGM	Pct.	FTA	FTM	Pct.	Reb.	Ast.	PF	Pts.	Avg.
62–63—Boston	80	1085	483	.445	239	174	.728	534	179	189	1140	14.3
63–64—Boston	80	1535	640	.417	422	315	.746	428	238	227	1595	19.9
64–65—Boston	75	1420	570	.401	316	235	.744	371	199	200	1375	18.3
65–66—Boston	71	1328	530	.399	349	274	.785	423	210	158	1334	18.8
66–67—Boston	81	1540	684	.444	441	365	.828	532	278	210	1733	21.4
67–68—Boston	82	1551	666	.429	453	368	.812	546	384	237	1700	20.7
68–69—Boston	82	1709	692	.405	496	387	.780	570	441	247	1771	21.6
69–70—Boston	81	1585	736	.464	578	488	.844	635	550	211	1960	24.2
70–71—Boston	81	1982	892	.450	677	554	.818	730	607	200	2338	28.9
71–72—Boston	82	1957	897	.458	549	458	.834	672	614	183	2252	27.5
72–73—Boston	80	1704	766	.450	431	370	.858	567	529	195	1902	23.8
73–74—Boston	76	1502	685	.456	416	346	.832	487	447	196	1716	22.6
74–75—Boston	82	1411	642	.455	332	289	.870	484	432	231	1573	19.2
75–76—Boston	76	1121	504	.450	333	281	.844	314	278	204	1289	17.0
76–77—Boston	79	1283	580	.452	288	235	.816	382	400	208	1395	17.7
77–78—Boston	82	1217	546	.449	269	230	.855	332	328	185	1322	16.1
Totals	1270	23930	10513	.439	6589	5369	.815	8007	6114	3281	26395	20.8

NBA PLAYOFF RECORD

	G.	FGA.	FGM.	Pct.	FTA.	FTM.	Pct.	Reb.	Ast.	PF	Pts.	Avg.
62–63—Boston	11	125	56	.448	27	18	.667	53	17	28	130	11.8
63–64—Boston	10	159	61	.384	44	35	.795	43	32	26	157	15.7
64–65—Boston	12	250	88	.352	55	46	.836	88	29	44	222	18.5
65–66—Boston	17	374	153	.409	113	95	.841	154	70	69	401	23.6
66–67—Boston	9	212	95	.448	71	57	.803	73	28	30	247	27.4
67–68—Boston	19	407	184	.452	151	125	.828	164	142	67	493	25.9
68–69—Boston	18	382	170	.445	138	118	.855	179	100	58	458	25.4
71–72—Boston	11	235	108	.460	99	85	.859	92	70	35	301	27.4
72–73—Boston	12	235	112	.477	74	61	.824	62	65	24	285	23.8
73–74—Boston	18	411	199	.484	101	89	.881	116	108	43	487	27.1
74–75—Boston	11	192	83	.432	76	66	.868	57	51	38	232	21.1
75–76—Boston	15	180	80	.444	47	38	.809	56	51	22	198	13.2
76–77—Boston	9	167	62	.371	50	41	.820	49	62	33	165	18.3
Totals	172	3329	1451	.436	1046	874	.836	1186	825	517	3776	22.0

Elvin Hayes

Born November 17, 1945. Height 6:09½. Weight 235.

Alma Mater—Houston '68.

Drafted by San Diego on first round, 1968.

Traded by Houston to Baltimore for Jack Marin and future considerations, June 23, 1972.

NBA REGULAR SEASON RECORD

	G.	FGA	FGM	Pct.	FTA	FTM	Pct.	Reb.	Ast.	PF	Pts.	Avg.
68–69—San Diego	82	2082	930	.447	746	467	.626	1406	113	266	2327	28.4
69–70—San Diego	82	2020	914	.452	622	428	.688	1386	162	270	2256	27.5
70–71—San Diego	82	2215	948	.428	676	454	.672	1362	186	225	2350	28.7
71–72—Houston	82	1918	832	.434	615	399	.649	1197	270	233	2063	25.2
72–73—Baltimore	81	1607	713	.444	434	291	.671	1177	127	232	1717	21.2
73–74—Washington	81	1627	689	.423	495	357	.721	1463	163	252	1735	21.4
74–75—Washington	82	1668	739	.443	534	409	.766	1004	206	238	1887	23.0
75–76—Washington	80	1381	649	.470	457	287	.628	878	121	293	1585	19.8
76–77—Washington	82	1516	760	.501	614	422	.687	1029	158	312	1942	23.7
77–78—Washington	81	1409	636	.451	514	326	.634	1075	149	313	1598	19.7
Totals	815	17443	7810	.448	5707	3840	.673	11977	1655	2634	19460	23.9

NBA PLAYOFF RECORD

Sea.—Team	G.	FGA.	FGM.	Pct.	FTA.	FTM.	Pct.	Reb.	Ast.	PF.	Pts.	Avg.
68–69—San Diego	6	114	60	526	53	35	.660	83	5	21	155	25.8
72–73—Baltimore	5	105	53	505	33	23	.697	57	5	16	129	25.8
73–74—Washington	7	143	76	.531	41	29	.707	111	21	23	181	25.9
74–75—Washington	17	372	174	.468	127	86	.677	186	37	70	434	25.5
75–76—Washington	7	122	54	.443	55	32	.582	88	10	24	140	20.0
76–77—Washington	9	173	74	.428	59	41	.695	122	17	39	189	21.0
77–78—Washington	21	385	189	.491	133	79	.594	279	43	86	457	21.8
Totals	72	1414	680	.481	501	325	.649	926	138	279	1685	23.4

Gus Johnson

Born December 13, 1938. Height 6:06. Weight 235.

Alma Mater—Idaho '63.

Drafted by Baltimore on second round, 1963.

Traded by Baltimore to Phoenix for a future draft choice, April 10, 1972.

NBA REGULAR SEASON RECORD

	G.	FGA.	FGM.	Pct.	FTA.	FTM.	Pct.	Reb.	Ast.	PF.	Pts.	Avg.
63–64—Baltimore	78	1329	571	.430	319	210	.658	954	169	321	1352	17.3
64–65—Baltimore	76	1379	577	.418	386	261	.676	988	270	258	1415	18.6
65–66—Baltimore	42	661	273	.413	178	131	.736	546	114	136	677	16.1
66–67—Baltimore	73	1377	620	.450	383	271	.708	855	194	281	1511	20.7
67–68—Baltimore	60	1033	482	.467	270	180	.667	782	159	223	1144	19.1
68–69—Baltimore	49	782	359	.459	223	160	.717	568	97	176	878	17.9
69–70—Baltimore	78	1282	578	.451	272	197	.724	1086	264	269	1353	17.3
70–71—Baltimore	66	1090	494	.453	290	214	.738	1128	192	227	1202	18.2
71–72—Baltimore	39	269	103	.383	63	43	.683	226	51	91	249	6.4
Totals	561	9202	4057	.441	2384	1667	.699	7133	1510	1982	9781	17.4

NBA PLAYOFF RECORD

	G.	FGA.	FGM.	Pct.	FTA.	FTM.	Pct.	Reb.	Ast.	PF.	Pts.	Avg.
64–65—Baltimore	10	173	62	.358	46	34	.739	111	34	38	158	15.8
65–66—Baltimore	1	4	1	.250	0	0	.000	0	0	1	2	2.0
69–70—Baltimore	7	111	51	.459	34	27	.794	80	9	20	129	18.4
70–71—Baltimore	11	128	54	.422	47	35	.745	114	30	34	143	13.0
71–72—Baltimore	5	30	9	.300	2	2	1.000	25	3	17	20	4.0
Totals	34	446	177	.397	129	98	.760	330	76	110	452	13.3

Earl Monroe

Born November 21, 1944. Height 6:03½. Weight 190.

Alma Mater—Winston-Salem State College '67.

Drafted by Baltimore on first round, 1967.

Traded by Baltimore to New York for Dave Stallworth, Mike Riordan and cash, November 10, 1971.

NBA REGULAR SEASON RECORD

	G.	FGA	FGM	Pct.	FTA	FTM	Pct.	Reb.	Ast.	PF	Pts.	Avg.
67–68—Baltimore	82	1637	742	.453	649	507	.781	465	349	282	1991	24.3
68–69—Baltimore	80	1837	809	.440	582	447	.768	280	392	261	2065	25.8
69–70—Baltimore	82	1557	695	.446	641	532	.830	257	402	258	1922	23.4
70–71—Baltimore	81	1501	663	.442	506	406	.802	213	354	220	1732	21.4
71–72—Balt.-N.Y.	63	662	287	.434	224	175	.781	100	142	139	749	11.9
72–73—New York	75	1016	496	.488	208	171	.822	245	288	195	1163	15.5
73–74—New York	41	513	240	.468	113	93	.823	121	110	97	573	14.0
74–75—New York	78	1462	668	.457	359	297	.827	327	270	200	1633	20.9
75–76—New York	76	1354	647	.478	356	280	.787	173	304	209	1574	20.7
76–77—New York	77	1185	613	.517	366	307	.839	223	366	197	1533	19.9
77–78—New York	76	1123	556	.495	291	242	.832	182	361	189	1354	17.8
78–79—New York	64	699	329	.471	154	129	.838	74	189	123	787	12.3
Totals	875	14546	6745	.464	4449	3586	.806	2760	3527	2370	17076	19.5

NBA PLAYOFF RECORD

	G.	FGA.	FGM.	Pct.	FTA.	FTM.	Pct.	Reb.	Ast.	PF.	Pts.	Avg.
68–69—Baltimore	4	114	44	.386	31	25	.806	21	16	10	113	28.3
69–70—Baltimore	7	154	74	.481	60	48	.800	23	28	23	196	28.0
70–71—Baltimore	18	356	145	.407	135	107	.793	64	74	56	397	22.1
71–72—New York	16	185	76	.411	57	45	.789	45	47	41	197	12.3
72–73—New York	16	211	111	.526	48	36	.750	51	51	39	258	16.1
73–74—New York	12	165	81	.491	55	47	.855	48	25	26	209	17.4
74–75—New York	3	45	12	.267	22	18	.818	9	6	6	42	14.0
77–78—New York	6	62	24	.389	18	11	.611	5	17	15	59	9.8
Totals	82	1292	567	.439	426	337	.791	266	264	216	1471	17.9

Willis Reed

Born June 25, 1942. Height 6:10. Weight 240.

Alma Mater—Grambling '64.

Drafted by New York on second round, 1964.

NBA REGULAR SEASON RECORD

	G.	FGA.	FGM.	Pct.	FTA.	FTM.	Pct.	Reb.	Ast.	PF.	Pts.	Avg.
64–65—New York	80	1457	629	.432	407	302	.742	1175	133	339	1560	19.5
65–66—New York	76	1009	438	.434	399	302	.757	883	91	323	1178	15.5
66–67—New York	78	1298	635	.489	487	358	.735	1136	126	293	1628	20.9
67–68—New York	81	1346	659	.490	509	367	.721	1073	159	343	1685	20.8
68–69—New York	82	1351	704	.521	435	325	.747	1191	190	314	1733	21.1
69–70—New York	81	1385	702	.507	464	351	.756	1126	161	287	1755	21.7
70–71—New York	73	1330	614	.462	381	299	.785	1003	148	228	1527	20.9
71–72—New York	11	137	60	.438	39	27	.692	96	22	30	147	13.4
72–73—New York	69	705	334	.474	124	92	.742	590	126	205	760	11.0
73–74—New York	19	184	84	.457	53	42	.792	141	30	49	210	11.1
Totals	650	10202	4859	.476	3298	2465	.747	8414	1186	2411	12183	18.7

NBA PLAYOFF RECORD

	G.	FGA.	FGM.	Pct.	FTA.	FTM.	Pct.	Reb.	Ast.	PF.	Pts.	Avg.
66–67—New York	4	80	43	.538	25	24	.960	55	7	19	110	27.5
67–68—New York	6	98	53	.541	30	22	.733	62	11	24	128	21.3
68–69—New York	10	198	101	.510	70	55	.786	141	19	40	257	25.7
69–70—New York	18	378	178	.471	95	70	.737	248	51	60	426	23.7
70–71—New York	12	196	81	.413	39	26	.667	144	27	41	188	15.7
72–73—New York	17	208	97	.466	21	18	.857	129	30	65	212	12.5
73–74—New York	11	45	17	.378	5	3	.600	22	4	26	37	3.4
Totals	78	1203	570	.474	285	218	.765	801	149	275	1358	17.4

Oscar Robertson

Born November 24, 1938. Height 6:05. Weight 220.

Alma Mater—Cincinnati '60.

Drafted by Cincinnati on first round (territorial choice), 1960.

Traded by Cincinnati to Milwaukee for Flynn Robinson and Charlie Paul, April 21, 1970.

NBA REGULAR SEASON RECORD

	G.	FGA.	FGM.	Pct.	FTA.	FTM.	Pct.	Reb.	Ast.	PF.	Pts.	Avg.
60–61—Cincinnati	71	1600	756	473	794	653	822	716	690	219	2165	30.5
61–62—Cincinnati	79	1810	866	.478	872	700	.803	985	899	258	2432	30.8
62–63—Cincinnati	80	1593	825	.518	738	614	.810	835	758	293	2264	28.3
63–64—Cincinnati	79	1740	840	.483	938	800	.853	783	868	280	2480	31.4
64–65—Cincinnati	75	1681	807	.480	793	665	.839	674	861	205	2279	30.4
65–66—Cincinnati	76	1723	818	.475	881	742	.842	586	847	227	2378	31.3
66–67—Cincinnati	79	1699	838	.493	843	736	.873	486	845	226	2412	30.5
67–68—Cincinnati	65	1321	660	.500	660	576	.873	391	633	199	1896	29.2
68–69—Cincinnati	79	1351	656	.486	767	643	.838	502	772	231	1955	24.7
69–70—Cincinnati	69	1267	647	.511	561	454	.809	422	558	175	1748	25.3
70–71—Milwaukee	81	1193	592	.496	453	385	.850	462	668	203	1569	19.4
71–72—Milwaukee	64	887	419	.472	330	276	.836	323	491	116	1114	17.4
72–73—Milwaukee	73	983	446	.454	281	238	.847	360	551	167	1130	15.5
73–74—Milwaukee	70	772	338	.438	254	212	.835	279	446	132	888	12.7
Totals	1040	19620	9508	.485	9185	7694	.838	7804	9887	2931	26710	25.7

PLAYOFF RECORD

	G.	FGA.	FGM.	Pct.	FTA.	FTM.	Pct.	Reb.	Ast.	PF.	Pts.	Avg.
61–62—Cincinnati	4	81	42	.519	39	31	.795	44	44	18	115	28.8
62–63—Cincinnati	12	264	124	.470	154	133	.864	156	108	41	381	31.8
63–64—Cincinnati	10	202	92	.455	127	109	.858	89	84	30	293	29.3
64–65—Cincinnati	4	89	38	.427	39	36	.923	19	48	14	112	28.0
65–66—Cincinnati	5	120	49	.408	68	61	.897	38	39	20	159	31.8
66–67—Cincinnati	4	64	33	.516	37	33	.892	16	45	9	99	24.8
70–71—Milwaukee	14	210	102	.486	69	52	.754	70	124	39	256	18.3

	G.	FGA	FGM	Pct.	FTA	FTM	Pct.	Reb.	Ast.	PF	Pts.	Avg.
71–72—Milwaukee	11	140	57	.407	36	30	.833	64	83	29	144	13.1
72–73—Milwaukee	6	96	48	.500	34	31	.912	28	45	21	127	21.2
73–74—Milwaukee	16	200	90	.450	52	44	.846	54	149	46	224	14.0
Totals	86	1466	675	.460	655	560	.855	578	769	267	1910	22.2

Bill Russell

Born February 12, 1934. Height 6:10. Weight 220.

Alma Mater—San Francisco '56.

Drafted by Boston, which traded Cliff Hagan and Ed Macauley to St. Louis, April 30, 1956, for No. 1 draft choice.

NBA REGULAR SEASON RECORD

	G.	FGA.	FGM.	Pct.	FTA.	FTM.	Pct.	Reb.	Ast.	PF.	Pts.	Avg.
56–57—Boston	48	649	277	.427	309	152	.492	943	88	143	706	14.7
57–58—Boston	69	1032	456	.442	443	230	.519	1564	202	181	1142	16.6
58–59—Boston	70	997	456	.457	428	256	.598	1612	222	161	1168	16.7
59–60—Boston	74	1189	555	.467	392	240	.612	1778	277	210	1350	18.2
60–61—Boston	78	1250	532	.426	469	258	.550	1868	264	164	1322	16.9
61–62—Boston	76	1258	575	.457	481	286	.594	1891	341	207	1436	18.9
62–63—Boston	78	1182	511	.432	517	287	.555	1843	348	189	1309	16.8
63–64—Boston	78	1077	466	.433	429	236	.550	1930	370	190	1168	15.0
64–65—Boston	78	980	429	.438	426	244	.573	1878	410	204	1102	14.1
65–66—Boston	78	943	391	.415	405	223	.551	1779	371	221	1005	12.9
66–67—Boston	81	870	395	.454	467	285	.610	1700	472	258	1075	13.4
67–68—Boston	78	858	365	.425	460	247	.537	1451	357	242	977	12.5
68–69—Boston	77	645	279	.433	388	204	.526	1484	374	231	762	9.9
Totals	963	12930	5687	.440	5614	3148	.561	21721	4096	2601	14522	15.1

NBA PLAYOFF RECORD

	G.	FGA.	FGM.	Pct.	FTA.	FTM.	Pct.	Reb.	Ast.	PF.	Pts.	Avg.
56–57—Boston	10	148	54	.365	61	31	.508	244	32	41	139	13.9
57–58—Boston	9	133	48	.361	66	40	.606	221	24	24	136	15.1
58–59—Boston	11	159	65	.409	67	41	.612	305	40	28	171	15.5
59–60—Boston	13									38	241	18.5
60–61—Boston	10	171	73	.427	86	45	.523	299	48	24	191	19.1
61–62—Boston	14	253	116	.458	113	82	.726	370	70	49	314	22.4
62–63—Boston	13	212	96	.453	109	72	.661	326	66	36	264	20.3
63–64—Boston	10	132	47	.356	67	37	.552	272	44	23	131	13.1
64–65—Boston	12	150	79	.527	76	40	.526	302	76	43	198	16.5
65–66—Boston	17	261	124	.475	123	76	.618	428	85	60	324	19.1
66–67—Boston	9	86	31	.360	52	33	.635	198	50	32	95	10.6
67–68—Boston	19	242	99	.409	130	76	.585	434	99	73	274	14.4
68–69—Boston	18	182	77	.423	81	41	.506	369	98	65	195	10.8
Totals	165	2335	1003	.430	1106	667	.603	4104	770	536	2673	16.2

Bill Walton

Born November 5, 1952. Height 6:11. Weight 225.

Alma Mater—UCLA '74.

Drafted by Portland on first round, 1974.

Completed contract with Portland; signed by San Diego as Veteran Free Agent, May 13, 1979.

NBA REGULAR SEASON RECORD

	G.	FGA.	FGM.	Pct.	FTA	FTM	Pct.	Tot.	Ast.	PF	Pts.	Avg.
74–75—Port.	35	345	177	513	137	94	.686	441	167	115	448	12.8
75–76—Port.	51	732	345	.471	228	133	.583	681	220	144	823	16.1
76–77—Port.	65	930	491	.528	327	228	.697	934	245	174	1210	18.6
77–78—Port.	58	882	460	.522	246	177	.720	766	291	145	1097	18.9
78–79—Port.						Injured						
Totals	209	2889	1473	.510	938	632	.674	2822	923	578	3578	17.1

NBA PLAYOFF RECORD

	G	FGA	FGM	Pct.	FTA	FTM	Pct.	Tot.	Ast.	PF	Pts.	Avg.
76–77—Port.	19	302	153	507	57	39	.684	288	104	80	345	18.2
77–78—Port.	2	18	11	.611	7	5	.714	22	4	1	27	13.5
Totals	21	320	164	.513	64	44	.688	310	108	81	372	17.7

Jerry West

Born May 28, 1938. Height 6:03. Weight 185.

Alma Mater—West Virginia '60.

Drafted by Los Angeles on first round, 1960.

NBA REGULAR SEASON RECORD

	G.	FGA.	FGM.	Pct.	FTA.	FTM.	Pct.	Reb.	Ast.	PF	Pts.	Avg.
60–61—Los Ang.	79	1264	529	.419	497	331	.666	611	333	213	1389	17.6
61–62—Los Ang.	75	1795	799	.445	926	712	.769	591	402	173	2310	30.8
62–63—Los Ang.	55	1213	559	.461	477	371	.778	384	307	150	1489	27.1
63–64—Los Ang.	72	1529	740	.484	702	584	.832	443	403	200	2064	28.7
64–65—Los Ang.	74	1655	822	.497	789	648	.821	447	364	221	2292	31.0
65–66—Los Ang.	79	1731	818	.473	977	840	.860	562	480	243	2476	31.3
66–67—Los Ang.	66	1389	645	.464	686	602	.878	392	447	160	1892	28.7
67–68—Los Ang.	51	926	476	.514	482	391	.811	294	310	152	1343	26.3
68–69—Los Ang.	61	1156	545	.471	597	490	.821	262	423	156	1580	25.9
69–70—Los Ang.	74	1673	831	.497	785	647	.824	338	554	160	2309	31.2
70–71—Los Ang.	69	1351	667	.494	631	525	.832	320	655	180	1859	26.9
71–72—Los Ang.	77	1540	735	.477	633	515	.814	327	747	209	1985	25.8
72–73—Los Ang.	69	1291	618	.479	421	339	.805	289	607	138	1575	22.8
73–74—Los Ang.	31	519	232	.447	198	165	.833	116	206	80	629	20.3
Totals	932	19032	9016	.474	8801	7160	.814	5376	6238	2435	25192	27.0

NBA PLAYOFF RECORD

Sea.—Team	G.	FGA.	FGM.	Pct.	FTA.	FTM.	Pct.	Reb.	Ast.	PF.	Pts.	Avg.
60–61—Los Ang.	12	202	99	.490	166	77	.726	104	63	39	275	22.9
61–62—Los Ang.	13	310	144	.465	150	121	.807	88	57	38	409	31.5
62–63—Los Ang.	13	286	144	.503	100	74	.740	106	61	34	362	27.8
63–64—Los Ang.	5	115	57	.496	53	42	.792	36	17	20	156	31.2
64–65—Los Ang.	11	351	155	.442	155	137	.884	63	58	37	447	40.6
65–66—Los Ang.	14	357	185	.518	125	109	.872	88	79	40	479	34.2
66–67—Los Ang.	1	0	0	.000	0	0	.000	1	0	0	0	0.0
67–68—Los Ang.	15	313	165	.527	169	132	.781	81	82	47	462	30.8
68–69—Los Ang.	18	423	196	.463	204	164	.804	71	135	52	556	30.9
69–70—Los Ang.	18	418	196	.469	212	170	.802	66	151	55	562	31.2
71–72—Los Ang.	15	340	128	.376	106	88	.830	73	134	39	344	22.9
72–73—Los Ang.	17	336	151	.449	127	99	.780	76	132	49	401	23.6
73–74—Los Ang.	1	9	2	.222	0	0	.000	2	1	1	4	4.0
Totals	153	3460	1622	.469	1507	1213	805	855	970	451	4457	29.1